NATIONAL PARTY PLATFORMS
1840–1972

compiled by DONALD BRUCE JOHNSON and KIRK H. PORTER

University of Illinois Press, Urbana, Chicago, London

© 1956, 1966, 1970, 1973, by The Board of Trustees of the University of Illinois
Manufactured in the United States of America. Library of Congress
Catalog Card No. 73-81566

ISBN 0-252-00414-0

PREFACE

It is not possible for anyone to be certain that he has collected all of the national party platforms. There are two very good reasons for this: it has not always been possible to determine exactly what a political party is, and at times it has been difficult to determine just what constitutes the platform of an organization claiming to be a national party. Individuals form groups which they call national parties though they offer candidates in only one or two states, and then go out of existence after the next election. Other minor parties persist year after year with very small organizations and few supporters at the polls. Thus, the criteria for determining which parties or organizations shall have their platforms included in what might purport to be a complete collection, of necessity, must be somewhat arbitrary. We have taken some account of the size of the group which professed to be a national party, the relative permanence of the organization, and its historical significance. We have included the platforms of those parties which have seemed to be of consequence by these standards.

Occasionally, as in the period before 1860, in 1912, and again in 1948, a segment of a major party has withdrawn from a party convention, assembled in a convention of its own, nominated candidates, and adopted a platform. Where these defections have proved to be of real importance, the platforms have been included. The most recent example is that of the States' Rights Party, popularly known as the "Dixiecrats," leaders of which left the Democratic Convention of 1948 over the issue of civil rights. Such factional parties, historically, have in some years had a great influence upon party development and in other years have had virtually no effect at all. Similarly, ideological or primarily single issue parties (such as the American Independent Party in recent elections) have had varying impacts on American political history.

This collection does not pretend to be a history of political parties, and does not pretend to contain the platform of every group that has chosen to call itself a political party. Nevertheless, we have assembled here authenticated copies of all the platforms of the major parties, and of the principal minor parties.

In the platforms of the parties in the nineteenth century, it was often difficult to know what comprised the actual platform. Decisions had to be made concerning the inclusion or exclusion of resolutions added after conventions had adjourned, resolutions thanking committee members, and other statements of appreciation. This problem was not as great in compiling the more recent platforms, and the material included in these documents contains few belated resolutions or dubious apparent revisions.

The sources from which these platforms have been obtained have varied. Political party platforms are not government documents, and no public official is responsible for collecting or preserving them. Indeed, in reference to many of the minor parties, party officers themselves have assumed no responsibility for preserving official copies of the platforms. Occasionally, they cannot be had even from party headquarters, if in fact headquarters still exist. In the case of the major parties, official proceedings of the conventions have been published and utilized in some years; more recently, the platforms have been published in the *Congressional Record*. But even these may have been surreptitiously edited in minor ways. With reference to the less prominent parties, the platforms have been obtained through correspondence with party leaders during the campaigns and from campaign literature issued by party headquarters. It should be noted that sometimes there is variation in copies of a platform obtained from the same party headquarters. Platforms in some instances obviously have been altered, edited, or corrected before being published in party literature or pamphlets, and official records may be literally non-existent. In the platforms presented here, no revisions whatever have been attempted. We have followed literally the punctuation and capitalization found in the official proceedings, or, in the case of the minor parties, in the campaign literature. No endeavor has been made to edit, correct, or reparagraph the material in this volume, and the platforms are unabridged. Where headings appear to have been part of the official proceedings, they have been retained; where they seem to have been inserted by those who prepared the literature, they usually have been omitted. The use of newspapers, almanacs, and contemporaneous secondary sources has been avoided as much as possible to preserve the authenticity of original sources, but in a few instances such media have seemed to be the most reliable.

Perhaps a word should be said about the significance of American party platforms. It has been asserted that the platforms of our major parties are unnecessarily long, repetitious, evasive, equivocal, and couched in phrases that mean many things to various publics. They are often silent on matters of vital concern to the nation, not binding on the candidates, and forgotten by the party leaders. It has been charged that there is little significant difference between the platforms of the Republican and Democratic parties, and that the resolutions included are mere "catch-alls" to obtain the widest possible support. From time to time, certain presidential candidates have repudiated specific planks in the party platforms, and nearly all candidates have been forced to ignore some portions of the platforms which were made before the nominees were chosen.

All of these statements have been true at one time or another in our history. In some years, portions of the platforms have been meaningless tirades designed to create temporary enthusiasm among already partisan delegates at the national conventions. In reality, party platforms are much more than this, and anyone who has observed meetings of the resolutions committee at a national nominating convention can attest the fact that many individuals representing diverse ideas and interests become greatly concerned indeed over what does or does not go into a party platform. If this is true, then what functions does the party platform fulfill on the American political scene in any particular year?

In the first place, unsatisfactory as they may be, party platforms are the principal official statements that exist of party principles and policies. To be sure, there are other important statements, but the platforms are evidence of what those party leaders who draft the declarations believe to be the important issues of the year. Furthermore, the platforms, in a sense, pay homage to those who have been able to incorporate their ideas into certain planks. In this way, platforms often reflect political trends. Developments of new economic, social, and political movements may be observed, particularly when declarations contained in previous minor party platforms are adopted by the major parties after sufficient public opinion has been generated to support the change. Secondly, platforms invariably cite weaknesses in the program of the opposition parties, and thus foreshadow issues that become significant in the campaigns or on the social or economic scene during a particular era.

Platforms also serve as a criterion by which to judge party success or failure during an administration, and provide the voters with information with which to evaluate the organization. This function points to the fact that there is usually a distinction between the platform of the party in power and the platforms of other parties attempting to gain control of the government. The platform of the president's party invariably will illustrate the desires, achievements, and thoughts of the chief executive in office. Recent presidents have demanded that platform drafts be cleared with them before submission to the conventions. The planks will reflect the interests important within the administration and the ambitions of the incumbent. On the other hand, the platforms of the major out-party, or parties, will usually be formulated as a result of a more turbulent struggle of interest groups, and the product may be a greater conglomeration of invective and promise. All parties utilize the platforms as propaganda by which to attract attention to party activities. Moreover, this function is emphasized for the major parties by the testimony of those group representatives appearing before resolutions committees, and the relative effects of such testimony which are reflected in the planks of the final document.

Most importantly, the platforms usually assert certain party principles and objectives which, stated generally, serve as a catalyst for the factions within the party and the voters represented by these factions. This is the overriding purpose of the platforms which has been implicit in all of these criticisms and explanations. The platforms are instruments of parties attempting to gain control of the government. In a democracy where majority votes are necessary to achieve this control, a degree of consensus is demanded. The platforms represent an endeavor to unite the party and amalgamate as many interest groups as possible to obtain a workable consensus. Given the confederate nature of our parties, the economic,

social, sectional, racial, and other interests abroad in the nation, the platforms represent an accommodation of these interests in any one election year and an illustration of the emphasis these forces place upon particular issues. Of necessity, some platform pronouncements often must be vague to encompass the party regulars and to attract new adherents. They must be designed to offend as few people as possible, but at the same time, they are significant reflections of interest group strengths within the party organization. The very equivocations used are meaningful because they emphasize the issues on which the party factions must hedge to maintain or obtain support. In short, platforms are one indication of the predominant forces in operation during any election year and a statement of the issues which individuals representing these forces believe to have the greatest popular appeal. In this sense, they are one barometer of opinion in American political history.

Finally, recent research has revealed that very significant numbers of party pledges have achieved reality in legislation and public administration, and that promises made frequently *are* carried out. (See Paul T. David, "Party Platforms as National Plans," *Public Administration Review,* XXXI, May/June, 1971, 305–315, and Gerald M. Pomper, *Elections in America,* New York: Dodd, Mead, 1968, chs. 7 and 8, and other sources cited by these authors.) In a way, this is a refutation of those who cite the most conspicuous examples of candidates and party leaders who have ignored platform declarations, and lends credence to the belief that those who possess the power to forge winning combinations do endeavor to carry out the platforms that were formulated by the same coalescing process.

I should like to thank the many party officials and other persons who have cooperated in the compilation, typing, and correspondence involved in the assembly of this volume.

D.B.J.
Department of Political Science
University of Iowa

Kirk H. Porter, who assembled the first book of National Party Platforms, 1840–1924 (*New York: Macmillan, 1924) which is included in this volume, died in May of 1972. His lifelong interest in political parties and politics made this collection possible. We are all indebted to him for his political research.*

CONTENTS

☒ CAMPAIGN OF 1840

Most students of politics agree that the Anti-Masonic Party held the first national convention in Philadelphia in 1830. At the gathering, a statement of eight resolutions declaring against free masonry, proposed by William Seward, was approved by the delegates. In September, 1831, the members of the party held another national convention in Baltimore at which William Wirt was nominated for president. Shortly thereafter, in December of 1831, the National Republican Party also held a convention in Baltimore and nominated candidates for president and vice-president. This convention did not, however, draw up a platform. In May of 1832, a gathering of "young men" of the party met in Washington, D.C. They went through various ceremonies, conducted a "solemn procession," and adopted a list of resolutions that have been called the platform of the National Republican Party. A contemporary account of this meeting is to be found in Niles' National Register.

Aside from these documents, which are not exactly true platforms, no platforms, in the proper sense of the term, were adopted in 1832 or in 1836. In the latter year, the National Republicans made no national nominations. The remnants of the Anti-Masonic Party during this period were gradually absorbed by other parties.

Under the circumstances it is fair to assert that the serious business of platform making did not begin until 1840. And in that year the Democrats alone drew up and adopted a platform in their national nominating convention. It is presented in this volume as the first national party platform.

Democratic Platform of 1840

1. *Resolved,* That the federal government is one of limited powers, derived solely from the constitution, and the grants of power shown therein, ought to be strictly construed by all the departments and agents of the government, and that it is inexpedient and dangerous to exercise doubtful constitutional powers.

2. *Resolved,* That the constitution does not confer upon the general government the power to commence and carry on, a general system of internal improvements.

3. *Resolved,* That the constitution does not confer authority upon the federal government, directly or indirectly, to assume the debts of the several states, contracted for local internal improvements, or other state purposes; nor would such assumption be just or expedient.

4. *Resolved,* That justice and sound policy forbid the federal government to foster one branch of industry to the detriment of another, or to cherish the interests of one portion to the injury of another portion of our common country —that every citizen and every section of the country, has a right to demand and insist upon an equality of rights and privileges, and to complete and ample protection of person and property from domestic violence, or foreign aggression.

5. *Resolved,* That it is the duty of every branch of the government, to enforce and practice the most rigid economy, in conducting our public affairs, and that no more revenue ought to be raised, than is required to defray the necessary expenses of the government.

6. *Resolved,* That congress has no power to charter a national bank; that we believe such an institution one of deadly hostility to the best interests of the country, dangerous to our republican institutions and the liberties of the people, and calculated to place the business of the country within the control of a concentrated money power, and above the laws and the will of the people.

7. *Resolved,* That congress has no power, under the constitution, to interfere with or control the domestic institutions of the several states, and that such states are the sole and proper judges of everything appertaining to their own affairs, not prohibited by the constitution; that all efforts by abolitionists or others, made to induce congress to interfere with questions of slavery, or to take incipient steps in relation thereto, are calculated to lead to the most alarming and dangerous consequences, and that all such efforts have an inevitable tendency to diminish the happiness of the people, and endanger the stability and permanency of the union, and ought not to be countenanced by any friend to our political institutions.

8. *Resolved,* That the separation of the moneys of the government from banking institutions, is indispensable for the safety of the funds of the government, and the rights of the people.

9. *Resolved,* That the liberal principles embodied by Jefferson in the Declaration of Independence, and sanctioned in the constitution, which makes ours the land of liberty, and the asylum of the oppressed of every nation, have ever been cardinal principles in the democratic faith; and every attempt to abridge the present privilege of becoming citizens, and the owners of soil among us, ought to be resisted with the same spirit which swept the alien and sedition laws from our statute-book.

The two major parties of this year were the Whig Party and the Democratic Party. The Liberty Party was composed chiefly of abolitionists, some of whom had met in 1840 and nominated candidates but did not issue a platform. The Liberty Party is sometimes called the Liberty-Abolitionist Party, and sometimes simply the Abolitionist Party.

Democratic Platform of 1844

1. *Resolved,* That the American Democracy place their trust, not in factitious symbols, not in displays and appeals insulting to the judgment and subversive of the intellect of the people, but in a clear reliance upon the intelligence, patriotism, and the discriminating justice of the American masses.

Resolved, That we regard this as a distinctive feature of our political creed, which we are proud to maintain before the world, as the great moral element in a form of government springing from and upheld by the popular will; and we contrast it with the creed and practice of Federalism, under whatever name or form, which seeks to palsy the will of the constituent, and which conceives no imposture too monstrous for the popular credulity.

Resolved, therefore, That, entertaining these views, the Democratic party of this Union, through their delegates assembled in general convention of the States, coming together in a spirit of concord, of devotion to the doctrines and faith of a free representative government, and appealing to their fellow-citizens for the rectitude of their intentions, renew and reassert before the American people the declaration of principles avowed by them on a former occasion, when, in general convention, they presented their candidates for the popular suffrages.

1. That the Federal Government is one of limited powers, derived solely from the Constitution, and the grants of power shown therein ought to be strictly construed by all the departments and agents of the government, and that it is inexpedient and dangerous to exercise doubtful constitutional powers.

2. That the Constitution does not confer upon the General Government the power to commence or carry on a general system of internal improvements.

3. That the Constitution does not confer authority upon the Federal Government, directly or indirectly, to assume the debts of the several States, contracted for local internal improvements or other State purposes; nor would such assumption be just or expedient.

4. That justice and sound policy forbid the Federal Government to foster one branch of industry to the detriment of another, or to cherish the interests of one portion to the injury of another portion of our common country—that every citizen and every section of the country has a right to demand and insist upon an equality of rights and privileges, and to complete and ample

protection of person and property from domestic violence or foreign aggression.

5. That it is the duty of every branch of the government to enforce and practice the most rigid economy in conducting our public affairs, and that no more revenue ought to be raised than is required to defray the necessary expenses of the government.

6. That Congress has no power to charter a United States Bank, that we believe such an institution one of deadly hostility to the best interests of the country, dangerous to our republican institutions and the liberties of the people, and calculated to place the business of the country within the control of a concentrated money power, and above the laws and the will of the people.

7. That Congress has no power, under the Constitution, to interfere with or control the domestic institutions of the several States; and that such States are the sole and proper judges of everything pertaining to their own affairs, not prohibited by the Constitution; that all efforts, by abolitionists or others, made to induce Congress to interfere with questions of slavery, or to take incipient steps in relation thereto, are calculated to lead to the most alarming and dangerous consequences, and that all such efforts have an inevitable tendency to diminish the happiness of the people and endanger the stability and permanency of the Union, and ought not to be countenanced by any friend to our Political Institutions.

8. That the separation of the money of the government from banking institutions is indispensable for the safety of the funds of the government and the rights of the people.

9. That the liberal principles embodied by Jefferson in the Declaration of Independence, and sanctioned in the Constitution, which makes ours the land of liberty and the asylum of the oppressed of every nation, have ever been cardinal principles in the Democratic faith; and every attempt to abridge the present privilege of becoming citizens, and the owners of soil among us, ought to be resisted with the same spirit which swept the alien and sedition laws from our statute-book.

Resolved, That the proceeds of the Public Lands ought to be sacredly applied to the national objects specified in the Constitution, and that we are opposed to the laws lately adopted, and to any law for the Distribution of such proceeds among the States, as alike inexpedient in policy and repugnant to the Constitution.

Resolved, That we are decidedly opposed to taking from the President the qualified veto power by which he is enabled, under restrictions and responsibilities amply sufficient to guard the public interest, to suspend the passage of a bill, whose merits cannot secure the approval of two-thirds of the Senate and House of Representatives, until the judgment of the people can be obtained thereon, and which has thrice saved the American People from the corrupt and tyrannical domination of the Bank of the United States.

Resolved, That our title to the whole of the Territory of Oregon is clear and unquestionable; that no portion of the same ought to be ceded to England or any other power, and that the re-occupation of Oregon and the re-annexation of Texas at the earliest practicable period are great American measures, which this Convention recommends to the cordial support of the Democracy of the Union.

Liberty Platform of 1844

PREAMBLE

Being assembled in general Convention, as the representatives of the Liberty party in the United States, and feeling it incumbent on us to set forth, clearly and fully, the principles which govern us, and the purposes which we seek to accomplish, and this, the rather because these principles and purposes have been much misunderstood, and either ignorantly or maliciously much misrepresented: be it therefore

1. *Resolved,* That human brotherhood is a cardinal doctrine of true Democracy, as well as of pure Christianity, which spurns all inconsistent limitations; and neither the political party which repudiates it, nor the political system which is not based upon it, nor controlled in its practical workings, by it, can be truly Democratic or permanent.

2. *Resolved,* That the Liberty party, placing itself upon this broad principle, will demand the absolute and unqualified divorce of the General Government from Slavery, and also the restoration of equality of rights, among men, in every State where the party exists, or may exist.

3. *Resolved,* That the Liberty party has not

been organized for any temporary purpose, by interested politicians, but has arisen from among the people, in consequence of a conviction, hourly gaining ground, that no other party in the country represents the true principles of American Liberty, or the true spirit of the Constitution of the United States.

4. *Resolved,* That the Liberty party has not been organized merely for the overthrow of Slavery. Its first decided effort must indeed be directed against slaveholding, as the grossest form and most revolting manifestation of Despotism; but it will also carry out the principles of Equal Rights, into all their practical consequences and applications, and support every just measure conducive to individual and social freedom.

5. *Resolved,* That the Liberty party is not a Sectional party, but a National party—has not originated in a desire to accomplish a single object, but in a comprehensive regard to the great interests of the whole country—is not a new party, or a third party, but is the party of 1776, reviving the principles of that memorable era, and striving to carry them into practical application.

6. *Resolved,* That it was understood in the time of the Declaration and the Constitution, that the existence of slavery in some of the States, was in derogation of the principles of American Liberty, and a deep stain upon the character of the country, and the implied faith of the States and the Nation was pledged, that slavery should never be extended beyond its then existing limits; but should be gradually, and, yet, at no distant day, wholly abolished by State authority.

7. *Resolved,* That the faith of the States, and the nation they pledged, was most nobly redeemed by the voluntary abolition of slavery in several of the States, and by the adoption of the ordinance of 1787, for the government of the Territory North West of the river Ohio, then the only Territory in the United States, and consequently the only Territory subject in this respect to the control of Congress, by which ordinance slavery was forever excluded from the vast regions which now compose the States of Ohio, Indiana, Illinois, Michigan, and the Territory of Wiskonsan, and an incapacity to bear up any other than freemen, was impressed on the soil itself.

8. *Resolved,* That the faith of the States and Nation thus pledged, has been shamefully violated by the omission, on the part of many of the States, to take any measures whatever for the abolition of slavery within their respective limits; by the continuance of slavery in the District of Columbia, and in the Territories of Louisiana and Florida; by the legislation of Congress; by the protection afforded by national legislation and negotiation to slaveholding in American vessels, on the high seas, employed in the coastwise slave traffic; and by the extension of slavery far beyond its original limits, by acts of Congress, admitting new slave States into the Union.

9. *Resolved,* That the fundamental truths of the Declaration of Independence, that all men are endowed by their Creator with certain inalienable rights, among which are life, liberty, and the pursuit of happiness, was made the fundamental law of our National Government, by that amendment of the constitution which declares that no person shall be deprived of life, liberty or property, without due process of law.

10. *Resolved,* That we recognize as sound, the doctrine maintained by slaveholding Jurists, that slavery is against natural rights, and strictly local, and that its existence and continuance rest on no other support than State legislation, and not on any Authority of Congress.

11. *Resolved,* That the General Government has, under the Constitution, no power to establish or continue slavery any where, and therefore that all treaties and acts of Congress establishing, continuing or favoring slavery in the District of Columbia, in the Territory of Florida, or on the high seas, are unconstitutional, and all attempts to hold men as property within the limits of exclusive national jurisdiction, ought to be prohibited by law.

12. *Resolved,* That the plea sometimes urged, in behalf of the constitutionality of slaveholding under the sanction of national legislation, that the continuance of slavery was secured in the District of Columbia, by stipulations in the Deeds of cession by Virginia and Maryland, and in Florida by the provisions of the Treaty with Spain is false in fact; and the other plea, sometimes urged to the same purpose, that Congress might constitutionally authorize slaveholding in the District, under the power to legislate for the same in all cases whatsoever, and in Florida under the power to make needful rules and regulations for the government of national territories, and in American vessels on the seas under the power to regulate

commerce, cannot be sound in law, so long as the great Interdict of the People against depriving *any person* of life, liberty, or property, without due process of law, remains unaltered.

13. *Resolved,* That the provision of the Constitution of the United States, which confers extraordinary political powers on the owners of slaves, and thereby constituting the two hundred and fifty thousand slaveholders in the slave States a privileged aristocracy; and the provision for the reclamation of fugitive slaves from service, are anti-republican in their character, dangerous to the liberties of the people, and ought to be abrogated.

14. *Resolved,* That the operation of the first of these provisions is seen in the growth of a power in the country, hostile to free institutions, to free labor, and to freedom itself, which is appropriately denominated the slave power; this power has maintained slavery in the original States, has secured its continuance in the District and in the Territories, has created seven new slave States, has caused disastrous fluctuations in our national policy, foreign and domestic, has gradually usurped the control of our home legislation, has waged unrelenting war against the most sacred rights of freedom, has violated and set at naught the right of petition, has dictated the action of political parties, has filled almost all the offices of the National Government with slaveholders, and the abettors of slaveholders, and threatens, if not arrested in its career, the total overthrow of popular freedom.

15. *Resolved,* That the practical operation of the second of these provisions, is seen in the enactment of the act of Congress respecting persons escaped from their masters, which act, if the construction given to it by the Supreme Court of the United States in the case of Prigg *vs.* Pennsylvania be correct, nullifies the habeas corpus acts of all the States, takes away the whole legal security of personal freedom, and ought therefore to be immediately repealed.

16. *Resolved,* That the peculiar patronage and support hitherto extended to slavery and slaveholding, by the General Government, ought to be immediately withdrawn, and the example and influence of national authority ought to be arrayed on the side of Liberty and free labor.

17. *Resolved,* That we cherish no harsh or unkind feelings towards any of our brethren of the slave States, while we express unmitigated abhorrence of that system of slaveholding which has stripped a large portion of their population of every right, and which has established an aristocracy worse than feudal in the midst of Republican States, and which denies to the poor non-slaveholder and his children the benefits of education, and crushes them in the dust, or drives them out as exiles from the land of their birth.

18. *Resolved,* That the impoverished and embarrassed condition of the slave States, so much deplored by their own statesmen, may be clearly traced to the fact that the coerced, reluctant, and ill-directed labor of slaves will not supply their own scanty subsistence, and also support their masters in the habits of wasteful extravagance which slavery generates.

19. *Resolved,* That the withering and impoverishing effect of slavery on the free States, is seen in the fact, among many others, that these States are taxed to the amount of about half a million of dollars a year, to pay the deficits of the slave States, and that the slave States have received, for years past, to the amount, as it is estimated, of more than ten millions of dollars a year, for which no payment has ever been, or ever will be made.

20. *Resolved,* That we behold with sorrow and shame, and indignation, the dishonor brought upon the name of the country by the influence of the slave power upon our National Government —corrupting its administration at home—paralyzing all generous action and utterance in behalf of right and freedom abroad, and exhibiting the American people to the world in the ridiculous and contemptible character of patrons of the slave trade.

21. *Resolved,* That we are inflexibly opposed to that policy of the General Government, which plies every art, and strains every effort of negotiation, to secure the markets of the world for the products of slave labor, while the products of free labor are to a great extent, confined to the non-paying market of the slave States; and we insist that it is the duty of the Government, in its intercourse with foreign nations, to employ all its influence, and to exert its utmost energies to extend the markets for the products of free labor, and we do not doubt that if this duty be performed in good faith, the result will be most auspicious to the general and permanent prosperity of the country.

22. *Resolved,* That we are fully persuaded that it is indispensably necessary to the salvation of the union of the States, to the preservation of the liberties of the people, and to the permanent restoration of prosperity in every department of business, that the National Government be rescued from the grasp of the slave power; that the spirit and practice of slaveholding be expelled from our National Legislature, and that the administration of the Government be conducted henceforth in conformity with the principles of the Constitution, and for the benefit of the whole population.

23. *Resolved,* That the practice of the General Government, which prevails in the slave States, of employing slaves upon the public works, instead of free laborers, and paying aristocratic masters, with a view to secure or reward political services, is utterly indefensible, and ought to be abandoned.

24. *Resolved,* That we believe intelligence, religion, and morality, to be the indispensable supports of good government, and are therefore in favor of general education; we believe, also, that good government itself is necessary to the welfare of society, and are therefore in favor of rigid public economy, and strict adherence to the principles of justice in every department of its administration.

25. *Resolved,* That freedom of speech and of the press, and the right of petition, and the right of trial by jury, are sacred and inviolable; and that all rules, regulations and laws, in derogation of either are oppressive, unconstitutional, and not to be endured by a free people.

26. *Resolved,* That we regard voting in an eminent degree, as a moral and religious duty, which when exercised, should be by voting for those who will do all in their power for immediate emancipation.

27. *Resolved,* That we can never lose our vote, although in ever so small a minority, when cast for the slave's redemption; as each vote for the slave, whether in minority or majority, is a part of that great mass of means which will work out his final deliverance.

28. *Resolved,* That the Whig and Democratic parties always throw away their votes, whether in a majority or minority, and do worse than throw them away, as long as they cast them for binding the slave with fetters, and loading him with chains, and for depriving him of himself, his wife and his children, which these parties always have done, in bowing down to the slaveholding portions of said parties.

29. *Resolved,* That we especially entreat the friends of Liberty in the slave States to reflect on the vast importance of voting openly for Liberty, and Liberty men; and to remember and adopt the words of the illustrious Washington, who said, "There is but one proper and effectual mode by which the abolition of slavery can be accomplished, and that is by legislative authority; and this, as far as my suffrage will go, shall not be wanting."

30. *Resolved,* That we earnestly exhort the Liberty men everywhere, to organize for efficient action in their respective States, counties, cities, towns, and districts, and not to turn to the right side or to the left, until despotism shall have been driven from its last entrenchment, and thanksgivings for victory in the second great struggle for Liberty and Independence shall be heard throughout the land.

31. *Resolved,* That we most earnestly recommend that the Liberty party make efforts to secure the control of the town power, so that every officer shall be a Liberty party man; and that our friends should not fail to nominate a Liberty ticket annually in their towns, and sustain the same, never yielding to a compromise with the other parties.

32. *Resolved,* That a county and State organization of the Liberty party should be faithfully maintained; and we also recommend that our friends employ some proper person to lecture, organize, and distribute tracts in each Congressional district, in the several States, for the space of at least three months in a year.

33. *Resolved,* That the friends of Liberty in each town form tract organizations, of men and women, to distribute tracts in every family in such towns, by directing the labors of said tract distribution, so that no neighborhood or family be overlooked or unsupplied.

34. *Resolved,* That it be recommended that said tract distributors circulate petitions through the several towns, praying Congress to abolish the abominable act of Congress, of the 12th of February, 1793, so that we may be delivered from the unconstitutional obligation to become kidnappers on our own soil.

35. *Resolved,* That this Convention recommend to the friends of Liberty in all those free States where any inequality of rights and privi-

leges exists on account of color, to employ their utmost energies to remove all such remnants and effects of the slave system.

36. *Resolved,* That we cordially welcome our colored fellow citizens to fraternity with us in the *Liberty party,* in its great contest to secure the rights of mankind, and the religion of our common country.

37. *Whereas,* The Constitution of these United States is a series of agreements, covenants, or contracts between the people of the United States, each with all, and all with each; and

Whereas, It is a principle of universal morality, that the moral laws of the Creator are paramount to all human laws; or, in the language of an apostle, that "we ought to obey God, rather than men;"—and

Whereas, The principle of Common Law—that any contract, covenant, or agreement, to do an act derogatory to natural right, is vitiated and annulled by its inherent immorality—has been recognized by one of the Justices of the Supreme Court of the United States, who, in a recent case, expressly holds that "*any* contract that rests upon such a basis, is *void*";—and

Whereas, The third clause of the second section of the fourth article of the Constitution of the United States—when construed as providing for the surrender of a fugitive slave—*does* "rest upon such a basis," in that it is a contract to rob a man of a natural right—namely, his natural right to his own liberty; and is, therefore, absolutely *void.*

Therefore, Resolved, That we hereby give it to be distinctly understood, by this nation and the world, that, as abolitionists, considering that the strength of our cause lies in its righteousness —and our hope for it in our conformity to the LAWS OF GOD, and our respect for the RIGHTS OF MAN, we owe it to the Sovereign Ruler of the Universe, as a proof of our allegiance to Him, in all our civil relations and offices, whether as private citizens, or as public functionaries sworn to support the Constitution of the United States, to regard and to treat the third clause of the second section of the fourth article of that instrument, whenever applied to the case of a fugitive slave, as utterly null and void, and consequently as forming no part of the Constitution of the United States, whenever we are called upon, or sworn, to support it.

38. *Resolved,* That the power given to Con-

gress by the Constitution, to provide for calling out the militia to suppress insurrection, does not make it the duty of the Government to maintain slavery, by military force, much less does it make it the duty of the citizens to form a part of such military force. When freemen unsheath the sword it should be to strike for *Liberty,* not for Despotism.

39. *Resolved,* That to preserve the peace of the citizens, and secure the blessings of freedom, the Legislature of each of the free States, ought to keep in force suitable statutes rendering it penal for any of its inhabitants to transport, or aid in transporting from such State, any person sought, to be thus transported, merely because subject to the slave laws of any other States; this remnant of independence being accorded to the free States, by the decision of the Supreme Court, in the case of Prigg, *vs.* the State of Pennsylvania.

40. *Resolved,* That we recognize in Daniel O'Connell, a true Patriot of the Liberty school, and admire his consistent devotion to freedom throughout the world. We thank him and the Irish people whom he represents, for their sympathy with us in our great struggle.

41. *Resolved,* That the thanks of this Convention are hereby tendered to Professor Taylor, for his kindness in furnishing the spacious tent, belonging to the Oberlin Collegiate Institute, which has been occupied by the Convention during its sittings.

42. *Resolved,* That the doings of the Convention be published, under the direction of the Secretaries.

43. *Resolved,* That the thanks of this Convention be tendered to the authorities of the County of Erie, and of the city of Buffalo, for the use of the Court House and the Park for its sittings.

44. *Resolved,* That the thanks of this Convention be presented to the President, Vice-Presidents, and Secretaries, for their services during its session.

Whig Platform of 1844

Resolved, That, in presenting to the country the names of Henry Clay for president, and of Theodore Frelinghuysen for vice-president of the United States, this Convention is actuated by the conviction that all the great principles of the

Whig party—principles inseparable from the public honor and prosperity—will be maintained and advanced by these candidates.

Resolved, That these principles may be summed as comprising, a well-regulated currency; a tariff for revenue to defray the necessary expenses of the government, and discriminating with special reference to the protection of the domestic labor of the country; the distribution of the proceeds of the sales of the public lands; a single term for the presidency; a reform of executive usurpations; —and, generally—such an administration of the affairs of the country as shall impart to every branch of the public service the greatest practicable efficiency, controlled by a well regulated and wise economy.

Resolved, That the name of Henry Clay needs no eulogy; the history of the country since his first appearance in public life is his history; its brightest pages of prosperity and success are identified with the principles which he has upheld, as its darkest and more disastrous pages are with

every material departure in our public policy from those principles.

Resolved, That in Theodore Frelinghuysen we present a man pledged alike by his revolutionary ancestry and his own public course to every measure calculated to sustain the honor and interest of the country. Inheriting the principles as well as the name of a father who, with Washington, on the fields of Trenton and of Monmouth, perilled life in the contest for liberty, and afterwards, as a senator of the United States, acted with Washington in establishing and perpetuating that liberty, Theodore Frelinghuysen, by his course as Attorney-General of the State of New Jersey for twelve years, and subsequently as a senator of the United States for several years, was always strenuous on the side of law, order, and the constitution, while as a private man, his head, his hand, and his heart have been given without stint to the cause of morals, education, philanthropy, and religion.

☒ CAMPAIGN OF 1848

The two major parties in 1848 were the Democratic Party and the Whig Party. The Free Soil Party of this campaign was the outgrowth of the Liberty Party of 1844. The Liberty Party had absorbed some abolitionists from both of the major parties and the new name was adopted. The Democrats who withdrew from their party to join the new one were sometimes called "Barnburners." In some isolated cases the Barnburners held independent conventions. Whigs who left their party were sometimes called "Conscience" Whigs.

Democratic Platform of 1848

Resolved, That the American Democracy place their trust in the intelligence, the patriotism, and the discriminating justice of the American people.

Resolved, That we regard this as a distinctive feature of our political creed, which we are proud to maintain before the world as the great moral element in a form of government springing from and upheld by the popular will; and we contrast it with the creed and practice of Federalism, under whatever name or form, which seeks to palsy the will of the constituent, and which conceives no imposture too monstrous for the popular credulity.

Resolved, therefore, That, entertaining these views, the Democratic party of this Union, through their Delegates assembled in general convention of the States, coming together in a spirit of concord, of devotion to the doctrines and faith of a free representative government, and appealing to their fellow-citizens for the rectitude of their intentions, renew and reassert before the American people the declaration of principles avowed by them when, on a former occasion, in general convention, they presented their candidates for the popular suffrage.

1. That the Federal Government is one of limited powers, derived solely from the Constitution; and the grants of power shown therein ought to be strictly construed by all the departments and agents of the Government; and that it is inexpedient and dangerous to exercise doubtful constitutional powers.

2. That the Constitution does not confer upon the General Government the power to commence and carry on a general system of internal improvements.

3. That the Constitution does not confer authority upon the Federal Government, directly or indirectly, to assume the debts of the several States, contracted for local internal improvements, or other State purposes; nor would such assumption be just and expedient.

4. That justice and sound policy forbid the Federal Government to foster one branch of industry to the detriment of another, or to cherish the interests of one portion to the injury of another

portion of our common country; that every citizen, and every section of the country, has a right to demand and insist upon an equality of rights and privileges, and to complete and ample protection of persons and property from domestic violence or foreign aggression.

5. That it is the duty of every branch of the Government to enforce and practice the most rigid economy in conducting our public affairs, and that no more revenue ought to be raised than is required to defray the necessary expenses of the Government, and for the gradual but certain extinction of the debt created by the prosecution of a just and necessary war, after peaceful relations shall have been restored.

6. That Congress has no power to charter a national bank; that we believe such an institution one of deadly hostility to the best interests of the country, dangerous to our republican institutions and the liberties of the people, and calculated to place the business of the country within the control of a concentrated money power, and above the laws and the will of the people; and that the results of Democratic legislation, in this and all other financial measures upon which issues have been made between the two political parties of the country, have demonstrated to candid and practical men of all parties, their soundness, safety, and utility in all business pursuits.

7. That Congress has no power under the Constitution to interfere with or control the domestic institutions of the several States, and that such States are the sole and proper judges of everything appertaining to their own affairs, not prohibited by the Constitution; that all efforts of the Abolitionists or others made to induce Congress to interfere with questions of slavery, or to take incipient steps in relation thereto, are calculated to lead to the most alarming and dangerous consequences; and that all such efforts have an inevitable tendency to diminish the happiness of the people, and endanger the stability and permanence of the Union, and ought not to be countenanced by any friend to our political institutions.

8. That the separation of the moneys of the Government from banking institutions is indispensable for the safety of the funds of the Government and the rights of the people.

9. That the liberal principles embodied by Jefferson in the Declaration of Independence, and

sanctioned in the Constitution, which makes ours the land of liberty, and the asylum of the oppressed of every nation, have ever been cardinal principles in the Democratic faith, and every attempt to abridge the present privilege of becoming citizens and the owners of soil among us, ought to be resisted with the same spirit which swept the alien and sedition laws from our statute-book.

Resolved, That the proceeds of the public lands ought to be sacredly applied to the national object specified in the Constitution; and that we are opposed to any law for the distribution of such proceeds among the States, as alike inexpedient in policy and repugnant to the Constitution.

Resolved, That we are decidedly opposed to taking from the President the qualified veto power, by which he is enabled, under restrictions and responsibilities amply sufficient to guard the public interests, to suspend the passage of a bill whose merits cannot secure the approval of two-thirds of the Senate and House of Representatives, until the judgment of the people can be obtained thereon, and which has saved the American people from the corrupt and tyrannical domination of the Bank of the United States, and from a corrupting system of general internal improvements.

Resolved, That the war with Mexico, provoked on her part by years of insult and injury, was commenced by her army crossing the Rio Grande, attacking the American troops, and invading our sister State of Texas; and that, upon all the principles of patriotism and laws of nations, it is a just and necessary war on our part, in which every American citizen should have shown himself on the side of his country, and neither morally nor physically, by word or by deed, have given "aid and comfort to the enemy."

Resolved, That we would be rejoiced at the assurance of peace with Mexico founded on the just principles of indemnity for the past and security for the future; but that, while the ratification of the liberal treaty offered to Mexico remains in doubt, it is the duty of the country to sustain the administration in every measure necessary to provide for the vigorous prosecution of the war, should that treaty be rejected.

Resolved, That the officers and soldiers who have carried the arms of their country into Mexico, have crowned it with imperishable glory. Their unconquerable courage, their daring enterprise, their unfaltering perseverance and fortitude when assailed on all sides by innumerable foes, and that more formidable enemy, the diseases of the climate, exalt their devoted patriotism into the highest heroism, and give them a right to the profound gratitude of their country, and the admiration of the world.

Resolved, That the Democratic National Convention of the thirty States composing the American Republic, tender their fraternal congratulations to the National Convention of the Republic of France, now assembled as the free-suffrage representatives of the sovereignty of thirty-five millions of republicans, to establish government on those eternal principles of equal rights for which *their* Lafayette and *our* Washington fought side by side in the struggle for our own national independence; and we would especially convey to them, and to the whole people of France, our earnest wishes for the consolidation of their liberties, through the wisdom that shall guide their counsels, on the basis of a democratic constitution, not derived from grants or concessions of kings or parliaments, but originating from the only true source of political power recognized in the States of this Union—the inherent and inalienable right of the people, in their sovereign capacity, to make and to amend their forms of government in such manner as the welfare of the community may require.

Resolved, That in view of the recent development of the grand political truth, of the sovereignty of the people, and their capacity and power for self-government, which is prostrating thrones and erecting republics on the ruins of despotism in the Old World, we feel that a high and sacred duty is devolved, with increased responsibility, upon the Democratic party of this country, as the party of the *people,* to sustain and advance among us constitutional "liberty, equality, and fraternity," by continuing to resist all monopolies and exclusive legislation for the benefit of the few at the expense of the many, and by a vigilant and constant adherence to those principles and compromises of the Constitution which are broad enough and strong enough to embrace and uphold the Union as it was, the Union as it is, and the Union as it shall be, in the full expansion of the energies and capacity of this great and progressive people.

Voted, That a copy of these resolutions be forwarded, through the American Minister at Paris, to the National Convention of the Republic of France.

Resolved, That the fruits of the great political triumph of 1844, which elected James K. Polk and George M. Dallas President and Vice-President of the United States, have fulfilled the hopes of the Democracy of the Union—in defeating the declared purposes of their opponents to create a national bank; in preventing the corrupt and unconstitutional distribution of the land proceeds, from the common treasury of the Union, for local purposes; in protecting the currency and the labor of the country from ruinous fluctuations, and guarding the money of the people for the use of the people, by the establishment of the constitutional treasury; in the noble impulse given to the cause of free trade, by the repeal of the tariff in 1842 and the creation of the more equal, honest, and productive tariff of 1846; and that, in our opinion, it would be a fatal error to weaken the bands of political organization by which these great reforms have been achieved, and risk them in the hands of their known adversaries, with whatever delusive appeals they may solicit our surrender of that vigilance, which is the only safeguard of liberty.

Resolved, That the confidence of the Democracy of the Union in the principles, capacity, firmness, and integrity of James K. Polk, manifested by his nomination and election in 1844, has been signally justified by the strictness of his adherence to sound Democratic doctrines, by the purity of purpose, the energy and ability which have characterized his administration in all our affairs at home and abroad; that we tender to him our cordial congratulations upon the brilliant success which has hitherto crowned his patriotic efforts, and assure him, that at the expiration of his Presidential term, he will carry with him to his retirement the esteem, respect, and admiration of a grateful country.

Resolved, That this Convention hereby present to the people of the United States, Lewis Cass, of Michigan, as the candidate of the Democratic party for the office of President, and William O. Butler, of Kentucky, as the candidate of the Democratic party for the office of Vice-President of the United States.

Free Soil Platform of 1848

Whereas, We have assembled in Convention, as a union of *Freemen,* for the sake of Freedom, forgetting all past political differences in a common resolve to maintain the rights of Free Labor against the aggressions of the Slave Power, and to secure Free Soil for a Free People:

And whereas, The political Conventions recently assembled at Baltimore and Philadelphia, the one stifling the voice of a great constituency entitled to be heard in its deliberations, and the other abandoning its distinctive principles for mere availability, have dissolved the national party organizations heretofore existing, by nominating for the Chief Magistracy of the United States, under Slaveholding dictation, candidates, *neither of whom* can be supported by the opponents of Slavery-extension, without a *sacrifice of consistency, duty,* and *self-respect.*

And whereas, These nominations, so made, furnish the occasion and demonstrate the necessity of the union of the People under the banners of Free Democracy, in a solemn and formal *declaration* of their *independence* of the *Slave Power,* and of their fixed determination to rescue the Federal Government from its control:

Resolved, therefore, that we, the people here assembled, remembering the example of our *fathers* in the days of the first Declaration of Independence, putting our trust in God for the triumph of our cause, and invoking his guidance in our endeavors to advance it, do now plant ourselves upon the NATIONAL PLATFORM OF FREEDOM, in opposition to the Sectional Platform of Slavery.

Resolved, That Slavery in the several States of this Union which recognize its existence, depends upon the State laws alone, which cannot be repealed or modified by the Federal Government, and for which laws that Government is not responsible. We therefore propose no interference by Congress with Slavery within the limits of any State.

Resolved, That the PROVISO of Jefferson, to prohibit the existence of Slavery, after 1800 in all the Territories of the United States, Southern and Northern; the votes of six States, and sixteen delegates, in the Congress of 1784, for the Proviso, to three States and seven delegates against it; the actual exclusion of Slavery from the North-western Territory by the ORDINANCE OF 1787, *unanimously* adopted by the States in Congress, and the entire history of that period, clearly show that it was the settled policy of the nation, *not* to *extend, nationalize,* or *encourage,* but to limit, localize, and discourage, Slavery; and to *this policy* which should never have been departed from, the Government ought to *return.*

Resolved, That our fathers ordained the Constitution of the United States, in order, among other great national objects, to establish justice, promote the general welfare, and secure the blessings of Liberty; but expressly *denied* to the Federal Government, which they created, all constitutional power to *deprive any person* of life, *liberty,* or property, without due legal process.

Resolved, That in the judgment of this Convention, Congress has no more power to make a SLAVE than to make a KING; no more power to institute or establish SLAVERY, than to institute or establish a MONARCHY. No such power can be found among those specifically conferred by the Constitution, or derived by just implication from them.

Resolved, THAT IT IS THE DUTY OF THE FEDERAL GOVERNMENT TO RELIEVE ITSELF FROM ALL RESPONSIBILITY FOR THE EXISTENCE OR CONTINUANCE OF SLAVERY WHEREVER THAT GOVERNMENT POSSESS CONSTITUTIONAL POWER TO LEGISLATE ON THAT SUBJECT, AND IS THUS RESPONSIBLE FOR ITS EXISTENCE.

Resolved, That the true, and, in the judgment of this Convention, the *only* safe means of preventing the extension of Slavery into territory now free, is to prohibit its existence in all such territory by *an act of Congress.*

Resolved, That we accept the issue which the Slave Power has forced upon us, and to their demand for more Slave States and more Slave Territory, our calm but final answer is: No more Slave States and no more Slave Territory. Let the soil of our extensive domains be kept free, for the hardy pioneers of our own land, and the oppressed and banished of other lands seeking homes of comfort and fields of enterprise in the New World.

Resolved, That the bill lately reported by the Committee of Eight in the Senate of the United States, was no compromise, but an absolute surrender of the rights of the non-slaveholders of the States; and while we rejoice to know that a measure which, while opening the door for the introduction of Slavery into Territories now free, would also have opened the door to litigation and strife among the future inhabitants thereof, to the ruin of their peace and prosperity, was defeated in the House of Representatives,—its passage, in hot haste, by a majority, embracing several Senators who voted in open violation of the known will of their constituents, should warn the People to see to it, that their representatives be not suffered to betray them. There must be no more compromises with Slavery: if made, they must be repealed.

Resolved, That we demand Freedom and established institutions for our brethren in Oregon, now exposed to hardships, peril, and massacre, by the reckless hostility of the Slave Power to the establishment of Free Government for Free Territories—and not only for them, but for our new brethren in California and New Mexico.

And whereas, It is due not only to this occasion, but to the whole people of the United States, that we should also declare ourselves on certain other questions of national policy, therefore,

Resolved, That we demand CHEAP POSTAGE for the people; a retrenchment of the expenses and patronage of the Federal Government; the *abolition* of all *unnecessary* offices and salaries; and the election by the People of all civil officers in the service of the Government, so far as the same may be practicable.

Resolved, That *river* and *harbor improvements,* when demanded by the safety and convenience of commerce with foreign nations, or among the several States, are objects of *national concern;* and that it is the duty of Congress, in the exercise of its constitutional powers, to provide therefor.

Resolved, That the FREE GRANT TO ACTUAL SETTLERS, in consideration of the expenses they incur in making settlements in the wilderness, which are usually fully equal to their actual cost, and of the public benefits resulting therefrom, of reasonable portions of the public lands, under suitable limitations, is a wise and just measure of public policy, which will promote, in various ways, the interest of all the States of this Union; and we therefore recommend it to the favorable consideration of the American People.

Resolved, That the obligations of honor and patriotism require the earliest practical payment of the national debt, and we are therefore in favor of such a tariff of duties as will raise revenue adequate to defray the necessary expenses of the Federal Government, and to pay annual instalments of our debt and the interest thereon.

Resolved, That we inscribe on our banner, "FREE SOIL, FREE SPEECH, FREE LABOR, and FREE MEN," and under it we will fight on, and fight ever, until a triumphant victory shall reward our exertions.

Whig Platform of 1848

1. *Resolved,* That the Whigs of the United States, here assembled by their Representatives, heartily ratify the nominations of General Zachary Taylor as President and Millard Fillmore as Vice-President of the United States, and pledge themselves to their support.

2. *Resolved,* That the choice of General Taylor as the Whig candidate for President we are glad to discover sympathy with a great popular sentiment throughout the nation—a sentiment which, having its origin in admiration of great military success, has been strengthened by the development, in every action and every word, of sound conservative opinions, and of true fidelity to the great example of former days, and to the principles of the Constitution as administered by its founders.

3. *Resolved,* That General Taylor, in saying that, had he voted in 1844, he would have voted the Whig ticket, gives us the assurance—and no better is needed from a consistent and truth-speaking man—that his heart was with us at the crisis of our political destiny, when Henry Clay was our candidate and when not only Whig principles were well defined and clearly asserted, but Whig measures depended on success. The heart that was with us then is with us now, and we have a soldier's word of honor, and a life of public and private virtue, as the security.

4. *Resolved,* That we look on General Taylor's administration of the Government as one conducive of Peace, Prosperity, and Union. Of Peace —because no one better knows, or has greater reason to deplore, what he has seen sadly on the field of victory, the horrors of war, and especially of a foreign and aggressive war. Of Prosperity— now more than ever needed to relieve the nation from a burden of debt, and restore industry— agricultural, manufacturing and commercial—to

its accustomed and peaceful functions and influences. Of Union—because we have a candidate whose very position as a Southwestern man, reared on the banks of the great stream whose tributaries, natural and artificial, embrace the whole Union, renders the protection of the interests of the whole country his first trust, and whose various duties in past life have been rendered, not on the soil or under the flag of any State or section, but over the wide frontier, and under the broad banner of the Nation.

5. *Resolved*, That standing, as the Whig Party does, on the broad and firm platform of the Constitution, braced up by all its inviolable and sacred guarantees and compromises, and cherished in the affections because protective of the interests of the people, we are proud to have, as the exponent of our opinions, one who is pledged to construe it by the wise and generous rules which Washington applied to it, and who has said, (and no Whig desires any other assurance) that he will make Washington's Administration the model of his own.

6. *Resolved*, That as Whigs and Americans, we are proud to acknowledge our gratitude for the great military services which, beginning at Palo Alto, and ending at Buena Vista, first awakened the American people to a just estimate of him who is now our Whig Candidate. In the discharge of a painful duty—for his march into the enemy's country was a reluctant one; in the

command of regulars at one time and volunteers at another, and of both combined; in the decisive though punctual discipline of his camp, where all respected and beloved him; in the negotiations of terms for a dejected and desperate enemy; in the exigency of actual conflict, when the balance was perilously doubtful—we have found him the same —brave, distinguished and considerate, no heartless spectator of bloodshed, no trifler with human life or human happiness, and we do not know which to admire most, his heroism in withstanding the assaults of the enemy in the most hopeless fields of Buena Vista—mourning in generous sorrow over the graves of Ringgold, of Clay, or of Hardin—or in giving in the heat of battle, terms of merciful capitulation to a vanquished foe at Monterey, and not being ashamed to avow that he did it to spare women and children, helpless infancy, and more helpless age, against whom no American soldier ever wars. Such a military man, whose triumphs are neither remote nor doubtful, whose virtues these trials have tested, we are proud to make our Candidate.

7. *Resolved*, That in support of this nomination we ask our Whig friends throughout the nation to unite, to co-operate zealously, resolutely, with earnestness in behalf of our candidate, whom calumny cannot reach, and with respectful demeanor to our adversaries, whose Candidates have yet to prove their claims on the gratitude of the nation.

NOTE:

A Whig National Convention, at which General Zachary Taylor was nominated for the presidency, was assembled for three days beginning June 7, 1848, in Philadelphia, Pennsylvania. The Convention adopted no Platform of Principles at that time. On the evening of the final day of the sessions, however, a ratification meeting was held in Philadelphia, at which Governor William F. Johnston of Pennsylvania presided. Speeches were given by Governor John Morehead of North Carolina, who had presided over the nominating convention, by General Leslie Coombs of Kentucky, and by several other persons. Participants in this meeting adopted the platform printed here. It evidently was

drawn up by the Pennsylvania Whig State Ratifying Convention, but it is noteworthy that the first resolution is made in the name of "the Whigs of the United States, here assembled by their Representatives. . . ."

We insert this cautionary footnote because the platform, to our knowledge, was neither adopted nationally nor regarded as the official party platform by all of the ideologically divided Whigs that year. See *A Political Text-book for 1860: Comprising a Brief View of Presidential Nominations and Elections Including All the National Platforms Ever Yet Adopted*: . . . , compiled by Horace Greeley and John F. Cleveland and published by the Tribune Association in New York (1860) pages 15 and 16; also *Niles Register*, vol. 74, pages 349, 354-358.

The two major parties in 1852 were the Democratic Party and the Whig Party. The Free Democratic Party was the Party that had appeared in 1848 as the Free Soil Party and in 1844 as the Liberty Party. By 1852 it had enlarged considerably due to the advent of many who deserted the old parties.

The Free Democratic Party is referred to by several different names. It is called the Free Soil Party, the Free Soil Democratic Party, the Independent Party and the Independent Democratic Party. But in article XX of its own platform **it** refers to itself as the Free Democratic Party.

Democratic Platform of 1852

Resolved, That the American democracy place their trust in the intelligence, the patriotism, and the discriminating justice of the American people.

Resolved, That we regard this as a distinctive feature of our political creed, which we are proud to maintain before the world as the great moral element in a form of government springing from and upheld by the popular will; and we contrast it with the creed and practice of federalism, under whatever name or form, which seeks to palsy the will of the constituent, and which conceives no imposture too mónstrous for the popular credulity.

Resolved, therefore, That, entertaining these views, the democratic party of this Union, through their delegates assembled in a general convention, coming together in a spirit of concord, of devotion to the doctrines and faith of a free representative government, and appealing to their fellow-citizens for the rectitude of their intentions, renew and reassert before the American people the declaration of principles avowed by them when on for-

mer occasions, in general convention, they have presented their candidates for the popular suffrages.

1. That the federal government is one of limited powers, derived solely from the constitution, and the grants of power made therein ought to be strictly construed by all the departments and agents of the government; and that it is inexpedient and dangerous to exercise doubtful constitutional powers.

2. That the constitution does not confer upon the general government the power to commence and carry on a general system of internal improvements.

3. That the constitution does not confer authority upon the federal government, directly or indirectly, to assume the debts of the several States, contracted for local and internal improvements or other State purposes; nor would such assumption be just or expedient.

4. That justice and sound policy forbid the federal government to foster one branch of industry to the detriment of any other, or to cherish the

interests of one portion to the injury of another portion of our common country; that every citizen, and every section of the country, has a right to demand and insist upon an equality of rights and privileges, and to complete an ample protection of person and property from domestic violence or foreign aggression.

5. That it is the duty of every branch of the government to enforce and practice the most rigid economy in conducting our public affairs, and that no more revenue ought to be raised than is required to defray the necessary expenses of the government, and for the gradual but certain extinction of the public debt.

6. That Congress has no power to charter a national bank; that we believe such an institution one of deadly hostility to the best interests of the country, dangerous to our republican institutions and the liberties of the people, and calculated to place the business of the country within the control of a concentrated money power, and above the laws and the will of the people; and that the results of democratic legislation in this and all other financial measures upon which issues have been made between the two political parties of the country, have demonstrated, to candid and practical men of all parties, their soundness, safety, and utility in all business pursuits.

7. That the separation of the moneys of the government from banking institutions is indispensable for the safety of the funds of the government and the rights of the people.

8. That the liberal principles embodied by Jefferson in the Declaration of Independence, and sanctioned in the constitution, which make ours the land of liberty and the asylum of the oppressed of every nation, have ever been cardinal principles in the democratic faith; and every attempt to abridge the privilege of becoming citizens and the owners of the soil among us ought to be resisted with the same spirit that swept the alien and sedition laws from our statute-books.

9. That Congress has no power under the constitution to interfere with or control the domestic institutions of the several States, and that such States are the sole and proper judges of everything appertaining to their own affairs not prohibited by the constitution; that all efforts of the abolitionists or others made to induce Congress to interfere with questions of slavery, or to take incipient steps in relation thereto, are calculated to lead to the most alarming and dangerous consequences; and that all such efforts have an inevitable tendency to diminish the happiness of the people and endanger the stability and permanency of the Union, and ought not to be countenanced by any friend of our political institutions.

Resolved, That the foregoing proposition covers, and was intended to embrace, the whole subject of slavery agitation in Congress; and therefore the democratic party of the Union, standing on this national platform, will abide by and adhere to a faithful execution of the acts known as the compromise measures settled by the last Congress—"the act for reclaiming fugitives from service or labor" included; which act, being designed to carry out an express provision of the constitution, cannot, with fidelity thereto be repealed nor so changed as to destroy or impair its efficiency.

Resolved, That the democratic party will resist all attempts at renewing, in congress or out of it, the agitation of the slavery question, under whatever shape or color the attempt may be made.

Resolved, That the proceeds of the public lands ought to be sacredly applied to the national object specified in the Constitution; and that we are opposed to any law for the distribution of such proceeds among the states as, alike inexpedient in policy and repugnant to the constitution.

Resolved, That we are decidedly opposed to taking from the President the qualified veto power, by which he is enabled, under restrictions and responsibilities amply sufficient to guard the public interests, to suspend the passage of a bill whose merits cannot secure the approval of two-thirds of the Senate and House of Representatives, until the judgment of the people can be obtained thereon, and which has saved the American people from the corrupt and tyrannical domination of the Bank of the United States, and from a corrupting system of general internal improvements.

Resolved, That the democratic party will faithfully abide by and uphold the principles laid down in the Kentucky and Virginia resolutions of 1798, and in the report of Mr. Madison to the Virginia legislature in 1799; that it adopts those principles as constituting one of the main foundations of its political creed, and is resolved to carry them out in their obvious meaning and import.

Resolved, That the war with Mexico, upon all the principles of patriotism and the laws of nations, was a just and necessary war on our part, in which every American citizen should have shown himself on the side of his country, and neither morally nor physically, by word or deed, have given "aid and comfort to the enemy."

Resolved, That we rejoice at the restoration of friendly relations with our sister republic of Mexico, and earnestly desire for her all the blessings and prosperity which we enjoy under republican institutions; and we congratulate the American people on the results of that war, which have so manifestly justified the policy and conduct of the democratic party, and insured to the United States, "indemnity for the past and security for the future."

Resolved, That, in view of the condition of popular institutions in the Old World, a high and sacred duty is devolved, with increased responsibility upon the democratic party of this country, as the party of the people, to uphold and maintain the rights of every State, and thereby the Union of the States, and to sustain and advance among us constitutional liberty, by continuing to resist all monopolies and exclusive legislation for the benefit of the few at the expense of the many, and by a vigilant and constant adherence to those principles and compromises of the constitution, which are broad enough and strong enough to embrace and uphold the Union as it was, the Union as it is, and the Union as it shall be, in the full expansion of the energies and capacity of this great and progressive people.

Free Democratic Platform of 1852

Having assembled in National Convention as the delegates of the Free Democracy of the United States, united by a common resolve to maintain right against wrongs, and freedom against slavery; confiding in the intelligence, patriotism, and the discriminating justice of the American people, putting our trust in God for the triumph of our cause, and invoking his guidance in our endeavors to advance it, we now submit to the candid judgment of all men the following declaration of principles and measures:

I. That Governments, deriving their just powers from the consent of the governed, are instituted among men to secure to all, those inalienable rights of life, liberty, and the pursuit of happiness, with which they are endowed by their Creator, and of which none can be deprived by valid legislation, except for crime.

II. That the true mission of American Democracy is to maintain the liberties of the people the sovereignty of the States, and the perpetuity of the Union, by the impartial application to public affairs, without sectional discriminations, of the fundamental principles of equal rights, strict justice, and economical administration.

III. That the Federal Government is one of limited powers, derived solely from the Constitution, and the grants of power therein ought to be strictly construed by all the departments and agents of the Government, and it is inexpedient and dangerous to exercise doubtful constitutional powers.

IV. That the Constitution of the United States, ordained to form a more perfect union, to establish justice, and secure the blessings of liberty, expressly denies to the General Government all power to deprive any person of life, liberty, or property, without due process of law; and therefore the Government, having no more power to make a slave than to make a king, and no more power to establish slavery than to establish monarchy, should at once proceed to relieve itself from all responsibility for the existence of slavery wherever it possesses constitutional power to legislate for its extinction.

V. That, to the persevering and importunate demands of the slave power for more slave States, new slave Territories, and the nationalization of slavery, our distinct and final answer is—no more slave States, no slave Territory, no nationalized slavery, and no national legislation for the extradition of slaves.

VI. That slavery is a sin against God and a crime against man, which no human enactment nor usage can make right; and that Christianity, humanity, and patriotism, alike demand its abolition.

VII. That the Fugitive Slave Act of 1850 is repugnant to the Constitution, to the principles of the common law, to the spirit of Christianity, and to the sentiments of the civilized world. We therefore deny its binding force upon the American People, and demand its immediate and total repeal.

VIII. That the doctrine that any human law is a finality, and not subject to modification or repeal, is not in accordance with the creed of the founders of our Government, and is dangerous to the liberties of the people.

IX. That the acts of Congress known as the Compromise measures of 1850, by making the admission of a sovereign State contingent upon the adoption of other measures demanded by the special interest of slavery; by their omission to guarantee freedom in free Territories; by their attempt to impose unconstitutional limitations on the power of Congress and the people to admit new States; by their provisions for the assumption of five millions of the State debt of Texas, and for the payment of five millions more and the cession of a large territory to the same State under menace, as an inducement to the relinquishment of a groundless claim, and by their invasion of the sovereignty of the States and the liberties of the people through the enactment of an unjust, oppressive, and unconstitutional Fugitive Slave Law, are proved to be inconsistent with all the principles and maxims of Democracy, and wholly inadequate to the settlement of the questions of which they are claimed to be an adjustment.

X. That no permanent settlement of the slavery question can be looked for, except in the practical recognition of the truth, that slavery is sectional, and freedom national; by the total separation of the General Government from slavery, and the exercise of its legitimate and constitutional influence on the side of freedom; and by leaving to the States the whole subject of slavery and the extradition of fugitives from service.

XI. That all men have a natural right to a portion of the soil; and that, as the use of the soil is indispensable to life, the right of all men to the soil is as sacred as their right to life itself.

XII. That the public lands of the United States belong to the people, and should not be sold to individuals nor granted to corporations, but should be held as a sacred trust for the benefit of the people, and should be granted in limited quantities, free of cost, to landless settlers.

XIII. That a due regard for the Federal Constitution, and sound administrative policy, demand that the funds of the General Government be kept separate from banking institutions; that inland and ocean postage should be reduced to the lowest possible point; that no more revenue should be raised than is required to defray the strictly necessary expenses of the public service,

and to pay off the public debt; and that the power and patronage of the Government should be diminished by the abolition of all unnecessary offices, salaries, and privileges, and by the election by the people of all civil officers in the service of the United States, so far as may be consistent with the prompt and efficient transaction of the public business.

XIV. That river and harbor improvements, when necessary to the safety and convenience of commerce with foreign nations or among the several States, are objects of national concern, and it is the duty of Congress in the exercise of its constitutional powers to provide for the same.

XV. That emigrants and exiles from the Old World should find a cordial welcome to homes of comfort and fields of enterprise in the New; and every attempt to abridge their privilege of becoming citizens and owners of the soil among us ought to be resisted with inflexible determination.

XVI. That every nation has a clear right to alter or change its own Government, and to administer its own concerns in such manner as may best secure the rights and promote the happiness of the people; and foreign interference with that right is a dangerous violation of the law of nations, against which all independent Governments should protest, and endeavor by all proper means to prevent; and especially is it the duty of the American Government, representing the chief republic of the world, to protest against and by all proper means to prevent the intervention of Kings and Emperors against nations seeking to establish for themselves republican or constitutional Governments.

XVII. That the independence of Hayti ought to be recognised by our Government, and our commercial relations with it placed on the footing of the most favored nations.

XVIII. That as, by the Constitution, "the citizens of each State shall be entitled to all privileges and immunities of citizens of the several States," the practice of imprisoning colored seamen of other States, while the vessels to which they belong lie in port, and refusing to exercise the right to bring such cases before the Supreme Court of the United States, to test the legality of such proceedings, is a flagrant violation of the Constitution, and an invasion of the rights of the citizens of other States, utterly inconsistent with the professions made by the slaveholders, that they wish the provisions of the Constitution faithfully observed by every State in the Union.

XIX. That we recommend the introduction into all treaties, hereafter to be negotiated between the United States and foreign nations, of some provision for the amicable settlement of difficulties by a resort to decisive arbitration.

XX. That the Free Democratic party is not organized to aid either the Whig or Democratic wing of the great Slave Compromise party of the nation, but to defeat them both; and that repudiating and renouncing both, as hopelessly corrupt, and utterly unworthy of confidence, the purpose of the Free Democracy is to take possession of the Federal Government, and administer it for the better protection of the rights and interests of the whole people.

XXI. That we inscribe on our banner, FREE SOIL, FREE SPEECH, FREE LABOR, and FREE MEN, and under it will fight on and fight ever, until a triumphant victory shall reward our exertions.

XXII. That upon this Platform the Convention presents to the American People, as a candidate for the office of President of the United States, JOHN P. HALE, of New Hampshire, and as a candidate for the office of Vice-President of the United States, George W. Julian, of Indiana, and earnestly commends them to the support of all freemen and parties.

Whig Platform of 1852

The Whigs of the United States, in Convention assembled, firmly adhering to the great conservative principles by which they are controlled and governed, and now as ever relying upon the intelligence of the American people, with an abiding confidence in their capacity for self-government, and their devotion to the Constitution and the Union, do proclaim the following as the political sentiments and determination for the establishment and maintenance of which their national organization as a party was effected:

First: The Government of the United States is of a limited character, and it is confined to the exercise of powers expressly granted by the Constitution, and such as may be necessary and proper for carrying the granted powers into full execution, and that all powers not granted or neces-

sarily implied are expressly reserved to the States respectively and to the people.

Second: The State Governments should be held secure in their reserved rights, and the General Government sustained on its constitutional powers, and that the Union should be revered and watched over as the palladium of our liberties.

Third: That while struggling freedom everywhere enlists the warmest sympathy of the Whig party, we still adhere to the doctrines of the Father of his Country, as announced in his Farewell Address, of keeping ourselves free from all entangling alliances with foreign countries, and of never quitting our own to stand upon foreign ground, that our mission as a republic is not to propagate our opinions, or impose on other countries our form of government by artifice or force; but to teach, by example, and show by our success, moderation and justice, the blessings of self-government, and the advantages of free institutions.

Fourth: That, as the people make and control the Government, they should obey its constitution, laws and treaties, as they would retain their self-respect, and the respect which they claim and will enforce from foreign powers.

Fifth: Revenue sufficient for the expenses of an economical administration of the Government in time of peace ought to be derived from a duty on imports, and not from direct taxation; and in laying such duties, sound policy requires a just discrimination, whereby suitable encouragement may be afforded to American industry, equally to all classes, and to all parts of the country.

Sixth: The Constitution vests in Congress the power to open and repair harbors, and remove obstructions from navigable rivers, whenever such improvements are necessary for the common defence, and for the protection and facility of commerce with foreign nations, or among the States, said improvements being, in every instance, national and general in their character.

Seventh: The Federal and State Governments are parts of one system, alike necessary for the common prosperity, peace and security, and ought to be regarded alike with a cordial, habitual and immovable attachment. Respect for the authority of each and acquiescence in the just constitutional measures of each, are duties required by the plainest considerations of national, state, and individual welfare.

Eighth: That the series of acts of the Thirty-first Congress,—the act known as the Fugitive Slave Law, included—are received and acquiesced in by the Whig Party of the United States as a settlement in principle and substance, of the dangerous and exciting question which they embrace; and, so far as they are concerned, we will maintain them, and insist upon their strict enforcement, until time and experience shall demonstrate the necessity of further legislation to guard against the evasion of the law on one hand, and the abuse of their powers on the other, not impairing their present efficiency; and we deprecate all further agitation of the question thus settled, as dangerous to our peace; and will discountenance all efforts to continue or renew such agitation whenever, wherever, or however the attempt may be made; and we will maintain this system as essential to the nationality of the Whig party and of the Union.

The two major parties in 1856 were the Republican Party and the Democratic Party. The Whig Party had very nearly disappeared; those that were left were sometimes called the "Silver Grays." The new Republican Party had absorbed most of the Free Soil Party of previous years.

The American Party was an entirely new organization. It is popularly known as the "Know-Nothing Party" because its members were supposed to say "I know nothing," when asked about the new party. The party is frequently called the Native American Party, but they call themselves simply the American Party in their own platform. The Whigs nominated the same candidate for president as the American Party, but repudiated the American Platform and adopted one of their own.

American (Know Nothing) Platform of 1856

I. An humble acknowledgment to the Supreme Being who rules one universe, for His protecting care vouchsafed to our fathers in their revolutionary struggle, and hitherto manifested to us, their descendants, in the preservation of the liberties, the independence and the union of these states.

II. The perpetuation of the Federal Union, as the palladium of our civil and religious liberties, and the only sure bulwark of American independence.

III. *Americans must rule America;* and to this end, *native*-born citizens should be selected for all state, federal, or municipal offices of government employment, in preference to naturalized citizens—*nevertheless,*

IV. Persons born of American parents residing temporarily abroad, shall be entitled to all the rights of native-born citizens; but

V. No person should be selected for political station (whether of native or foreign birth), who recognizes any alliance or obligation of any description to any foreign prince, potentate or power, who refuses to recognize the federal and state constitutions (each within its own sphere), as paramount to all other laws, as rules of particular [political] action.

VI. The unequalled recognition and maintenance of the reserved rights of the several states, and the cultivation of harmony and fraternal goodwill between the citizens of the several states, and to this end, non-interference by Congress with questions appertaining solely to the individual states, and non-intervention by each state with the affairs of any other state.

VII. The recognition of the right of the native-born and naturalized citizens of the United States, permanently residing in any territory thereof, to frame their constitutions and laws, and to regulate their domestic and social affairs in their own mode, subject only to the provisions of the federal Constitution, with the right of admission into the Union whenever they have the requisite population for one representative in Congress. *Provided, always,* That none but those who are citizens of the United States, under the Constitution and laws thereof, and who have a fixed residence in any such territory, are to participate in the formation of the constitution, or in the enactment of laws for said territory or state.

VIII. An enforcement of the principles that no state or territory can admit other than native-born citizens to the right of suffrage, or of holding political office unless such persons shall have been naturalized according to the laws of the United States.

IX. A change in the laws of naturalization, making a continued residence of twenty-one years, of all not heretofore provided for, an indispensable requisite for citizenship hereafter, and excluding all paupers or persons convicted of crime from landing upon our shores; but no interference with the vested rights of foreigners.

X. Opposition to any union between Church and State; no interference with religious faith or worship, and no test oaths for office, except those indicated in the 5th section of this platform.

XI. Free and thorough investigation into any and all alleged abuses of public functionaries, and a strict economy in public expenditures.

XII. The maintenance and enforcement of all laws until said laws shall be repealed, or shall be declared null and void by competent judicial authority.

XIII. Opposition to the reckless and unwise policy of the present administration in the general management of our national affairs, and more especially as shown in removing "Americans" (by designation) and conservatives in principle, from office, and placing foreigners and ultraists in their places, as shown in a truckling subserviency to the stronger, and an insolent and cowardly bravado toward the weaker powers; as shown in reopening sectional agitation, by the repeal of the Missouri Compromise; as shown in granting to unnaturalized foreigners the right of suffrage in Kansas and Nebraska, as shown in its vacillating

course on the Kansas and Nebraska question; as shown in the removal of Judge Bronson from the collectorship of New York upon false and untenable grounds; as shown in the corruptions which pervade some of the departments of the government; as shown in disgracing meritorious naval officers through prejudice or caprice; as shown in the blundering mismanagement of our foreign relations.

XIV. Therefore, to remedy existing evils, and prevent the disastrous consequences otherwise resulting therefrom, we would build up the "American Party" upon the principles hereinbefore stated eschewing all sectional questions, and uniting upon those purely national, and admitting into said party all American citizens (referred to in the 3rd, 4th, and 5th sections) who openly avow the principles and opinions heretofore expressed, and who will subscribe their names to this platform.—*Provided nevertheless,* that a majority of those members present at any meeting of a local council where an applicant applies for membership in the American party, may, for any reason by them deemed sufficient, deny admission to such applicant.

XV. A free and open discussion of all political principles embraced in our platform.

Democratic Platform of 1856

Resolved, That the American Democracy place their trust in the intelligence, the patriotism, and the discriminating justice of the American people.

Resolved, That we regard this as a distinctive feature of our political creed, which we are proud to maintain before the world, as the great moral element in a form of government springing from and upheld by the popular will; and we contrast it with the creed and practice of Federalism, under whatever name or form, which seeks to palsy the will of the constituent, and which conceives no imposture too monstrous for the popular credulity.

Resolved, therefore, That, entertaining these views, the Democratic party of this Union, through their Delegates assembled in a general Convention, coming together in a spirit of concord, of devotion to the doctrines and faith of a free representative government, and appealing to their fellow-citizens for the rectitude of their intentions, renew and re-assert before the American people, the declarations of principles avowed by them when, on former occasions in general Convention, they have presented their candidates for the popular suffrage.

1. That the Federal Government is one of limited power, derived solely from the Constitution; and the grants of power made therein ought to be strictly construed by all the departments and agents of the government; and that it is inexpedient and dangerous to exercise doubtful constitutional powers.

2. That the Constitution does not confer upon the General Government the power to commence and carry on a general system of internal improvements.

3. That the Constitution does not confer authority upon the Federal Government, directly or indirectly, to assume the debts of the several States, contracted for local and internal improvements, or other State purposes; nor would such assumption be just or expedient.

4. That justice and sound policy forbid the Federal Government to foster one branch of industry to the detriment of any other, or to cherish the interests of one portion to the injury of another portion of our common country; that every citizen and every section of the country has a right to demand and insist upon an equality of rights and privileges, and to complete and ample protection of persons and property from domestic violence or foreign aggression.

5. That it is the duty of every branch of the Government to enforce and practice the most rigid economy in conducting our public affairs, and that no more revenue ought to be raised than is required to defray the necessary expenses of the Government, and for the gradual but certain extinction of the public debt.

6. That the proceeds of the public lands ought to be sacredly applied to the national objects specified in the Constitution; and that we are opposed to any law for the distribution of such proceeds among the States, as alike inexpedient in policy and repugnant to the Constitution.

7. That Congress has no power to charter a national bank; that we believe such an institution one of deadly hostility to the best interests of the country, dangerous to our republican institutions and the liberties of the people, and calcu-

lated to place the business of the country within the control of a concentrated money power, and above the laws and the will of the people; and that the results of Democratic legislation in this and all other financial measures upon which issues have been made between the two political parties of the country, have demonstrated to candid and practical men of all parties, their soundness, safety, and utility, in all business pursuits.

8. That the separation of the moneys of the Government from banking institutions is indispensable for the safety of the funds of the Government and the rights of the people.

9. That we are decidedly opposed to taking from the President the qualified veto power, by which he is enabled, under restrictions and responsibilities amply sufficient to guard the public interests, to suspend the passage of a bill whose merits cannot secure the approval of two-thirds of the Senate and House of Representatives, until the judgment of the people can be obtained thereon, and which has saved the American people from the corrupt and tyrannical domination of the Bank of the United States, and from a corrupting system of general internal improvements.

10. That the liberal principles embodied' by Jefferson in the Declaration of Independence, and sanctioned by the Constitution, which makes ours the land of liberty and the asylum of the oppressed of every nation, have ever been cardinal principles in the Democratic faith, and every attempt to abridge the privilege of becoming citizens and the owners of soil among us, ought to be resisted with the same spirit which swept the alien and sedition laws from our statute-books.

And Whereas, Since the foregoing declaration was uniformly adopted by our predecessors in National Conventions, an adverse political and religious test has been secretly organized by a party claiming to be exclusively American, it is proper that the American Democracy should clearly define its relation thereto, and declare its determined opposition to all secret political societies, by whatever name they may be called.

Resolved, That the foundation of this union of States having been laid in, and its prosperity, expansion, and pre-eminent example in free government, built upon entire freedom in matters of religious concernment, and no respect of person in regard to rank or place of birth; no party can justly be deemed national, constitutional, or in accordance with American principles, which bases its exclusive organization upon religious opinions and accidental birth-place. And hence a political crusade in the nineteenth century, and in the United States of America, against Catholic and foreign-born is neither justified by the past history or the future prospects of the country, nor in unison with the spirit of toleration and enlarged freedom which peculiarly distinguishes the American system of popular government.

Resolved, That we reiterate with renewed energy of purpose the well considered declarations of former Conventions upon the sectional issue of Domestic slavery, and concerning the reserved rights of the States.

1. That Congress has no power under the Constitution, to interfere with or control the domestic institutions of the several States, and that such States are the sole and proper judges of everything appertaining to their own affairs, not prohibited by the Constitution; that all efforts of the abolitionists, or others, made to induce Congress to interfere with questions of slavery, or to take incipient steps in relation thereto, are calculated to lead to the most alarming and dangerous consequences; and that all such efforts have an inevitable tendency to diminish the happiness of the people and endanger the stability and permanency of the Union, and ought not to be countenanced by any friend of our political institutions.

2. That the foregoing proposition covers, and was intended to embrace the whole subject of slavery agitation in Congress; and therefore, the Democratic party of the Union, standing on this national platform, will abide by and adhere to a faithful execution of the acts known as the compromise measures, settled by the Congress of 1850; "the act for reclaiming fugitives from service or labor," included; which act being designed to carry out an express provision of the Constitution, cannot, with fidelity thereto, be repealed, or so changed as to destroy or impair its efficiency.

3. That the Democratic party will resist all attempts at renewing, in Congress or out of it, the agitation of the slavery question under whatever shape or color the attempt may be made.

4. That the Democratic party will faithfully abide by and uphold, the principles laid down in the Kentucky and Virginia resolutions of 1798, and in the report of Mr. Madison to the Virginia Legislature in 1799; that it adopts those principles as constituting one of the main foundations of its political creed, and is resolved to carry them out in their obvious meaning and import.

And that we may more distinctly meet the issue on which a sectional party, subsisting exclusively on slavery agitation, now relies to test the fidelity of the people, North and South, to the Constitution and the Union—

1. *Resolved,* That claiming fellowship with, and desiring the co-operation of all who regard the preservation of the Union under the Constitution as the paramount issue—and repudiating all sectional parties and platforms concerning domestic slavery, which seek to embroil the States and incite to treason and armed resistance to law in the Territories; and whose avowed purposes, if consummated, must end in civil war and disunion, the American Democracy recognize and adopt the principles contained in the organic laws establishing the Territories of Kansas and Nebraska as embodying the only sound and safe solution of the "slavery question" upon which the great national idea of the people of this whole country can repose in its determined conservatism of the Union—NON-INTERFERENCE BY CONGRESS WITH SLAVERY IN STATE AND TERRITORY, OR IN THE DISTRICT OF COLUMBIA.

2. That this was the basis of the compromises of 1850—confirmed by both the Democratic and Whig parties in national Conventions—ratified by the people in the election of 1852, and rightly applied to the organization of Territories in 1854.

3. That by the uniform application of this Democratic principle to the organization of territories, and to the admission of new States, with or without domestic slavery, as they may elect—the equal rights, of all the States will be preserved intact—the original compacts of the Constitution maintained inviolate—and the perpetuity and expansion of this Union insured to its utmost capacity of embracing, in peace and harmony, every future American State that may be constituted or annexed, with a republican form of government.

Resolved, That we recognize the right of the people of all the Territories, including Kansas and Nebraska, acting through the legally and fairly expressed will of a majority of actual residents, and whenever the number of their inhabitants justifies it, to form a Constitution, with or without domestic slavery, and be admitted into the Union upon terms of perfect equality with the other States.

Resolved, Finally, That in view of the condition of popular institutions in the Old World (and the dangerous tendencies of sectional agitation, combined with the attempt to enforce civil and religious disabilities against the rights of acquiring and enjoying citizenship, in our own land)—a high and sacred duty is devolved with increased responsibility upon the Democratic party of this country, as the party of the Union, to uphold and maintain the rights of every State, and thereby the Union of the States; and to sustain and advance among us constitutional liberty, by continuing to resist all monopolies and exclusive legislation for the benefit of the few, at the expense of the many, and by a vigilant and constant adherence to those principles and compromises of the Constitution, which are broad enough and strong enough to embrace and uphold the Union as it was, the Union as it is, and the Union as it shall be, in the full expansion of the energies and capacity of this great and progressive people.

1. *Resolved,* That there are questions connected with the foreign policy of this country, which are inferior to no domestic question whatever. The time has come for the people of the United States to declare themselves in favor of free seas and progressive free trade throughout the world, and, by solemn manifestations, to place their moral influence at the side of their successful example.

2. *Resolved,* That our geographical and political position with reference to the other States of this continent, no less than the interest of our commerce and the development of our growing power, requires that we should hold as sacred the principles involved in the Monroe Doctrine: their bearing and import admit of no misconstruction; they should be applied with unbending rigidity.

3. *Resolved,* That the great highway which nature, as well as the assent of the States most immediately interested in its maintenance, has marked out for a free communication between the Atlantic and the Pacific oceans, constitutes one of the most important achievements realized by the spirit of modern times and the unconquer-

able energy of our people. That result should be secured by a timely and efficient exertion of the control which we have the right to claim over it, and no power on earth should be suffered to impede or clog its progress by any interference with the relations it may suit our policy to establish between our government and the Governments of the States within whose dominions it lies. We can, under no circumstances, surrender our preponderance in the adjustment of all questions arising out of it.

4. *Resolved,* That, in view of so commanding an interest, the people of the United States cannot but sympathize with the efforts which are being made by the people of Central America to regenerate that portion of the continent which covers the passage across the Interoceanic Isthmus.

5. *Resolved,* That the Democratic party will expect of the next Administration that every proper effort be made to insure our ascendency in the Gulf of Mexico, and to maintain a permanent protection to the great outlets through which are emptied into its waters the products raised out of the soil and the commodities created by the industry of the people of our Western valleys and the Union at large.

Resolved, That the Democratic party recognizes the great importance, in a political and commercial point of view, of a safe and speedy communication, by military and postal roads, through our own territory, between the Atlantic and Pacific coasts of this Union, and that it is the duty of the Federal Government to exercise promptly all its constitutional power to the attainment of that object, thereby binding the Union of these States in indissoluble bonds, and opening to the rich commerce of Asia an overland transit from the Pacific to the Mississippi River, and the great lakes of the North.

Resolved, That the administration of Franklin Pierce has been true to the great interests of the country. In the face of the most determined opposition it has maintained the laws, enforced economy, fostered progress, and infused integrity and vigor into every department of the government at home. It has signally improved our treaty relations, extended the field of commercial enterprise, and vindicated the rights of American citizens abroad. It has asserted with eminent impartiality the just claims of every section, and has at all times been faithful to the Constitution. We therefore proclaim our unqualified approbation of its measures and its policy.

Republican Platform of 1856

This Convention of Delegates, assembled in pursuance of a call addressed to the people of the United States, without regard to past political differences or divisions, who are opposed to the repeal of the Missouri Compromise; to the policy of the present Administration; to the extension of Slavery into Free Territory; in favor of the admission of Kansas as a Free State; of restoring the action of the Federal Government to the principles of Washington and Jefferson; and for the purpose of presenting candidates for the offices of President and Vice-President, do

Resolved: That the maintenance of the principles promulgated in the Declaration of Independence, and embodied in the Federal Constitution are essential to the preservation of our Republican institutions, and that the Federal Constitution, the rights of the States, and the union of the States, must and shall be preserved.

Resolved: That, with our Republican fathers, we hold it to be a self-evident truth, that all men are endowed with the inalienable right to life, liberty, and the pursuit of happiness, and that the primary object and ulterior design of our Federal Government were to secure these rights to all persons under its exclusive jurisdiction; that, as our Republican fathers, when they had abolished Slavery in all our National Territory, ordained that no person shall be deprived of life, liberty, or property, without due process of law, it becomes our duty to maintain this provision of the Constitution against all attempts to violate it for the purpose of establishing Slavery in the Territories of the United States by positive legislation, prohibiting its existence or extension therein. That we deny the authority of Congress, of a Territorial Legislation, of any individual, or association of individuals, to give legal existence to Slavery in any Territory of the United States, while the present Constitution shall be maintained.

Resolved: That the Constitution confers upon Congress sovereign powers over the Territories of the United States for their government; and that in the exercise of this power, it is both the

right and the imperative duty of Congress to prohibit in the Territories those twin relics of barbarism—Polygamy, and Slavery.

Resolved: That while the Constitution of the United States was ordained and established by the people, in order to "form a more perfect union, establish justice, insure domestic tranquility, provide for the common defense, promote the general welfare, and secure the blessings of liberty," and contain ample provision for the protection of the life, liberty, and property of every citizen, the dearest Constitutional rights of the people of Kansas have been fraudulently and violently taken from them.

Their Territory has been invaded by an armed force;

Spurious and pretended legislative, judicial, and executive officers have been set over them, by whose usurped authority, sustained by the military power of the government, tyrannical and unconstitutional laws have been enacted and enforced;

The right of the people to keep and bear arms has been infringed.

Test oaths of an extraordinary and entangling nature have been imposed as a condition of exercising the right of suffrage and holding office.

The right of an accused person to a speedy and public trial by an impartial jury has been denied;

The right of the people to be secure in their persons, houses, papers, and effects, against unreasonable searches and seizures, has been violated;

They have been deprived of life, liberty, and property without due process of law;

That the freedom of speech and of the press has been abridged;

The right to choose their representatives has been made of no effect;

Murders, robberies, and arsons have been instigated and encouraged, and the offenders have been allowed to go unpunished;

That all these things have been done with the knowledge, sanction, and procurement of the present National Administration; and that for this high crime against the Constitution, the Union, and humanity, we arraign that Administration, the President, his advisers, agents, supporters, apologists, and accessories, either *before* or *after* the fact, before the country and before the world; and that it is our fixed purpose to bring the actual perpetrators of these atrocious outrages and their accomplices to a sure and condign punishment thereafter.

Resolved, That Kansas should be immediately admitted as a state of this Union, with her present Free Constitution, as at once the most effectual way of securing to her citizens the enjoyment of the rights and privileges to which they are entitled, and of ending the civil strife now raging in her territory.

Resolved, That the highwayman's plea, that "might makes right," embodied in the Ostend Circular, was in every respect unworthy of American diplomacy, and would bring shame and dishonor upon any Government or people that gave it their sanction.

Resolved, That a railroad to the Pacific Ocean by the most central and practicable route is imperatively demanded by the interests of the whole country, and that the Federal Government ought to render immediate and efficient aid in its construction, and as an auxiliary thereto, to the immediate construction of an emigrant road on the line of the railroad.

Resolved, That appropriations by Congress for the improvement of rivers and harbors, of a national character, required for the accommodation and security of our existing commerce, are authorized by the Constitution, and justified by the obligation of the Government to protect the lives and property of its citizens.

Resolved, That we invite the affiliation and cooperation of the men of all parties, however differing from us in other respects, in support of the principles herein declared; and believing that the spirit of our institutions as well as the Constitution of our country, guarantees liberty of conscience and equality of rights among citizens, we oppose all legislation impairing their security.

Whig Platform of 1856

Resolved, That the Whigs of the United States are assembled here by reverence for the Constitution, and unalterable attachment to the National Union, and a fixed determination to do all in their power to preserve it for themselves and posterity. They have no new principles to announce—no new platform to establish, but are content broadly to rest where their fathers have rested upon the Constitution of the United States, wishing no safer guide, no higher law.

Resolved, That we regard with the deepest anxiety the present disordered condition of our national affairs. A portion of the country being ravaged by civil war and large sections of our population embittered by mutual recriminations, and we distinctly trace these calamities to the culpable neglect of duty by the present National Administration.

Resolved, That the Government of these United States was formed by the conjunction in political unity of widespread geographical sections, materially differing not only in climate and products, but in their social and domestic institutions, and that any cause that shall permanently array these sections in political hostility and organized parties, founded only on geographical distinctions must inevitably prove fatal to the continuance of the National Union.

Resolved, That the Whigs of the United States have declared as a fundamental article of their political faith, the absolute necessity for avoiding geographical parties; that the danger so clearly discerned by the "Father of his Country," founded on geographical distinction, has now become fearfully apparent in the agitation convulsing the nation, which must be arrested at once if we would preserve our Constitutional Union from dismemberment, and the name of America from being blotted out from the family of civilized nations.

Resolved, That all who revere the Constitution and Union, must look with alarm at the parties in the field in the present Presidential campaign— one claiming only to represent sixteen Northern States, and the other appealing to the passions and prejudices of the Southern States—that the success of either faction must add fuel to the flame which now threatens to wrap our dearest interest in a common ruin.

Resolved, That the only remedy for an evil so appalling is to support the candidate pledged to neither geographical section nor arrayed in political antagonism, but holding both in just and equal regard; that we congratulate the friends of the Union that such a candidate exists in Millard Fillmore.

Resolved, That, without adopting or referring

to the peculiar principles of the party which has already selected Millard Fillmore as their candidate, we look to him as a well-tried and faithful friend of the Constitution and the Union, eminent alike for his wisdom and firmness, for his justice and moderation in foreign relations, for his calm and pacific temperament, well becoming a great and enlightened Government. For his devotion to the Constitution in its true spirit, and his inflexibility in executing the laws; but, beyond all these attributes, of being representative of neither of the two sectional parties now struggling for political supremacy.

Resolved, That in the present exigency of political affairs, we are not called upon to discuss subordinate questions of administration in exercising the Constitutional powers of government. It is enough to know that civil war is raging, and the Union is in peril; and proclaim a conviction that the restoration of the Fillmore Presidency will furnish the best if not the only means of restoring peace.

The two major parties in 1860 were the Democratic Party and the Republican Party. A faction of the Democrats broke away from the regular convention, called themselves the Democratic Party and nominated candidates. To differentiate them from the regular party they are usually referred to as the Breckenridge Democrats, since John C. Breckenridge was their nominee.

The Constitutional Union Party was composed largely of those who had been members of the American Party in 1856.

Constitutional Union Platform of 1860

Whereas, Experience has demonstrated that Platforms adopted by the partisan Conventions of the country have had the effect to mislead and deceive the people, and at the same time to widen the political divisions of the country, by the creation and encouragement of geographical and sectional parties; therefore

Resolved, that it is both the part of patriotism and of duty to *recognize* no political principle other than THE CONSTITUTION OF THE COUNTRY, THE UNION OF THE STATES, AND THE ENFORCEMENT OF THE LAWS, and that, as representatives of the Constitutional Union men of the country, in National Convention assembled, we hereby pledge ourselves to maintain, protect, and defend, separately and unitedly, these great principles of public liberty and national safety, against all enemies, at home and abroad; believing that thereby peace may once more be restored to the country; the rights of the People and of the States re-established, and the Government again placed in that condition of justice, fraternity and equality,

which, under the example and Constitution of our fathers, has solemnly bound every citizen of the United States to maintain a more perfect union, establish justice, insure domestic tranquillity, provide for the common defense, promote the general welfare, and secure the blessings of liberty to ourselves and our posterity.

Democratic Platform of 1860

1. *Resolved,* That we, the Democracy of the Union in Convention assembled, hereby declare our affirmance of the resolutions unanimously adopted and declared as a platform of principles by the Democratic Convention at Cincinnati, in the year 1856, believing that Democratic principles are unchangeable in their nature, when applied to the same subject matters; and we recommend, as the only further resolutions, the following:

2. Inasmuch as difference of opinion exists in the Democratic party as to the nature and extent of the powers of a Territorial Legislature, and as

to the powers and duties of Congress, under the Constitution of the United States, over the institution of slavery within the Territories,

Resolved, That the Democratic party will abide by the decision of the Supreme Court of the United States upon these questions of Constitutional law.

3. *Resolved,* That it is the duty of the United States to afford ample and complete protection to all its citizens, whether at home or abroad, and whether native or foreign born.

4. *Resolved,* That one of the necessities of the age, in a military, commercial, and postal point of view, is speedy communication between the Atlantic and Pacific States; and the Democratic party pledge such Constitutional Government aid as will insure the construction of a Railroad to the Pacific coast, at the earliest practicable period.

5. *Resolved,* That the Democratic party are in favor of the acquisition of the Island of Cuba on such terms as shall be honorable to ourselves and just to Spain.

6. *Resolved,* That the enactments of the State Legislatures to defeat the faithful execution of the Fugitive Slave Law, are hostile in character, subversive of the Constitution, and revolutionary in their effect.

7. *Resolved,* That it is in accordance with the interpretation of the Cincinnati platform, that during the existence of the Territorial Governments the measure of restriction, whatever it may be, imposed by the Federal Constitution on the power of the Territorial Legislature over the subject of the domestic relations, as the same has been, or shall hereafter be finally determined by the Supreme Court of the United States, should be respected by all good citizens, and enforced with promptness and fidelity by every branch of the general government.

Democratic (Breckenridge Faction) Platform of 1860

Resolved, That the platform adopted by the Democratic party at Cincinnati be affirmed, with the following explanatory resolutions:

1. That the Government of a Territory organized by an act of Congress is provisional and temporary, and during its existence all citizens of the United States have an equal right to settle with their property in the Territory, without their rights, either of person or property, being destroyed or impaired by Congressional or Territorial legislation.

2. That it is the duty of the Federal Government, in all its departments, to protect, when necessary, the rights of persons and property in the Territories, and wherever else its constitutional authority extends.

3. That when the settlers in a Territory, having an adequate population, form a State Constitution, the right of sovereignty commences, and being consummated by admission into the Union, they stand on an equal footing with the people of other States, and the State thus organized ought to be admitted into the Federal Union, whether its Constitution prohibits or recognizes the institution of slavery.

Resolved, That the Democratic party are in favor of the acquisition of the Island of Cuba, on such terms as shall be honorable to ourselves and just to Spain, at the earliest practicable moment.

Resolved, That the enactments of State Legislatures to defeat the faithful execution of the Fugitive Slave Law are hostile in character, subversive of the Constitution, and revolutionary in their effect.

Resolved, That the Democracy of the United States recognize it as the imperative duty of this Government to protect the naturalized citizen in all his rights, whether at home or in foreign lands, to the same extent as its native-born citizens.

WHEREAS, One of the greatest necessities of the age, in a political, commercial, postal and military point of view, is a speedy communication between the Pacific and Atlantic coasts. Therefore be it

Resolved, That the National Democratic party do hereby pledge themselves to use every means in their power to secure the passage of some bill, to the extent of the constitutional authority of Congress, for the construction of a Pacific Railroad from the Mississippi River to the Pacific Ocean, at the earliest practicable moment.

Republican Platform of 1860

Resolved, That we, the delegated representatives of the Republican electors of the United States, in Convention assembled, in discharge of the duty we owe to our constituents and our country, unite in the following declarations:

1. That the history of the nation during the last four years, has fully established the propriety and necessity of the organization and perpetuation of the Republican party, and that the causes which called it into existence are permanent in their nature, and now, more than ever before, demand its peaceful and constitutional triumph.

2. That the maintenance of the principles promulgated in the Declaration of Independence and embodied in the Federal Constitution, "That all men are created equal; that they are endowed by their Creator with certain inalienable rights; that among these are life, liberty and the pursuit of happiness; that to secure these rights, governments are instituted among men, deriving their just powers from the consent of the governed," is essential to the preservation of our Republican institutions; and that the Federal Constitution, the Rights of the States, and the Union of the States must and shall be preserved.

3. That to the Union of the States this nation owes its unprecedented increase in population, its surprising development of material resources, its rapid augmentation of wealth, its happiness at home and its honor abroad; and we hold in abhorrence all schemes for disunion, come from whatever source they may. And we congratulate the country that no Republican member of Congress has uttered or countenanced the threats of disunion so often made by Democratic members, without rebuke and with applause from their political associates; and we denounce those threats of disunion, in case of a popular overthrow of their ascendency as denying the vital principles of a free government, and as an avowal of contemplated treason, which it is the imperative duty of an indignant people sternly to rebuke and forever silence.

4. That the maintenance inviolate of the rights of the states, and especially the right of each state to order and control its own domestic institutions according to its own judgment exclusively, is essential to that balance of powers on which the perfection and endurance of our political fabric depends; and we denounce the lawless invasion by armed force of the soil of any state or territory, no matter under what pretext, as among the gravest of crimes.

5. That the present Democratic Administration has far exceeded our worst apprehensions, in its measureless subserviency to the exactions of a sectional interest, as especially evinced in its desperate exertions to force the infamous Lecompton Constitution upon the protesting people of Kansas; in construing the personal relations between master and servant to involve an unqualified property in persons; in its attempted enforcement everywhere, on land and sea, through the intervention of Congress and of the Federal Courts of the extreme pretensions of a purely local interest; and in its general and unvarying abuse of the power intrusted to it by a confiding people.

6. That the people justly view with alarm the reckless extravagance which pervades every department of the Federal Government; that a return to rigid economy and accountability is indispensable to arrest the systematic plunder of the public treasury by favored partisans; while the recent startling developments of frauds and corruptions at the Federal metropolis, show that an entire change of administration is imperatively demanded.

7. That the new dogma that the Constitution, of its own force, carries slavery into any or all of the territories of the United States, is a dangerous political heresy, at variance with the explicit provisions of that instrument itself, with contemporaneous exposition, and with legislative and judicial precedent; is revolutionary in its tendency, and subversive of the peace and harmony of the country.

8. That the normal condition of all the territory of the United States is that of freedom: That, as our Republican fathers, when they had abolished slavery in all our national territory, ordained that "no persons should be deprived of life, liberty or property without due process of law," it becomes our duty, by legislation, whenever such legislation is necessary, to maintain this provision of the Constitution against all attempts to violate it; and we deny the authority of Congress, of a territorial legislature, or of any individuals, to give legal existence to slavery in any territory of the United States.

9. That we brand the recent reopening of the African slave trade, under the cover of our national flag, aided by perversions of judicial power, as a crime against humanity and a burning shame to our country and age; and we call upon Congress to take prompt and efficient measures for

the total and final suppression of that execrable traffic.

10. That in the recent vetoes, by their Federal Governors, of the acts of the legislatures of Kansas and Nebraska, prohibiting slavery in those territories, we find a practical illustration of the boasted Democratic principle of Non-Intervention and Popular Sovereignty, embodied in the Kansas-Nebraska Bill, and a demonstration of the deception and fraud involved therein.

11. That Kansas should, of right, be immediately admitted as a state under the Constitution recently formed and adopted by her people, and accepted by the House of Representatives.

12. That, while providing revenue for the support of the general government by duties upon imports, sound policy requires such an adjustment of these imports as to encourage the development of the industrial interests of the whole country; and we commend that policy of national exchanges, which secures to the workingmen liberal wages, to agriculture remunerative prices, to mechanics and manufacturers an adequate reward for their skill, labor, and enterprise, and to the nation commercial prosperity and independence.

13. That we protest against any sale or alienation to others of the public lands held by actual settlers, and against any view of the free-homestead policy which regards the settlers as paupers or suppliants for public bounty; and we demand the passage by Congress of the complete and satisfactory homestead measure which has already passed the House.

14. That the Republican party is opposed to any change in our naturalization laws or any state legislation by which the rights of citizens hitherto accorded to immigrants from foreign lands shall be abridged or impaired; and in favor of giving a full and efficient protection to the rights of all classes of citizens, whether native or naturalized, both at home and abroad.

15. That appropriations by Congress for river and harbor improvements of a national character, required for the accommodation and security of an existing commerce, are authorized by the Constitution, and justified by the obligation of Government to protect the lives and property of its citizens.

16. That a railroad to the Pacific Ocean is imperatively demanded by the interests of the whole country; that the federal government ought to render immediate and efficient aid in its construction; and that, as preliminary thereto, a daily overland mail should be promptly established.

17. Finally, having thus set forth our distinctive principles and views, we invite the co-operation of all citizens, however differing on other questions, who substantially agree with us in their affirmance and support.

In this year there were only the Democratic and the Republican Parties. A group known as the Radical Republicans broke away from the regular organization, nominated candidates and issued a platform. This so-called party, however, disappeared before the election.

Democratic Platform of 1864

Resolved, That in the future, as in the past, we will adhere with unswerving fidelity to the Union under the Constitution as the only solid foundation of our strength, security, and happiness as a people, and as a framework of government equally conducive to the welfare and prosperity of all the States, both Northern and Southern.

Resolved, That this convention does explicitly declare, as the sense of the American people, that after four years of failure to restore the Union by the experiment of war, during which, under the pretense of a military necessity of war-power higher than the Constitution, the Constitution itself has been disregarded in every part, and public liberty and private right alike trodden down, and the material prosperity of the country essentially impaired, justice, humanity, liberty, and the public welfare demand that immediate efforts be made for a cessation of hostilities, with a view of an ultimate convention of the States, or other peaceable means, to the end that, at the earliest practicable moment, peace may be restored on the basis of the Federal Union of the States.

Resolved, That the direct interference of the military authorities of the United States in the recent elections held in Kentucky, Maryland, Missouri, and Delaware was a shameful violation of the Constitution, and a repetition of such acts

in the approaching election will be held as revolutionary, and resisted with all the means and power under our control.

Resolved, That the aim and object of the Democratic party is to preserve the Federal Union and the rights of the States unimpaired, and they hereby declare that they consider that the administrative usurpation of extraordinary and dangerous powers not granted by the Constitution—the subversion of the civil by military law in States not in insurrection; the arbitrary military arrest, imprisonment, trial, and sentence of American citizens in States where civil law exists in full force; the suppression of freedom of speech and of the press; the denial of the right of asylum; the open and avowed disregard of State rights; the employment of unusual test-oaths; and the interference with and denial of the right of the people to bear arms in their defense is calculated to prevent a restoration of the Union and the perpetuation of a Government deriving its just powers from the consent of the governed.

Resolved, That the shameful disregard of the Administration to its duty in respect to our fellow-citizens who now are and long have been prisoners of war and in a suffering condition, deserves the severest reprobation on the score alike of public policy and common humanity.

Resolved, That the sympathy of the Democratic party is heartily and earnestly extended to the soldiery of our army and sailors of our navy, who are and have been in the field and on the sea under the flag of our country, and, in the events of its attaining power, they will receive all the care, protection, and regard that the brave soldiers and sailors of the republic have so nobly earned.

Republican Platform of 1864

1. *Resolved,* That it is the highest duty of every American citizen to maintain against all their enemies the integrity of the Union and the paramount authority of the Constitution and laws of the United States; and that, laying aside all differences of political opinion, we pledge our-selves, as Union men, animated by a common sentiment and aiming at a common object, to do everything in our power to aid the Government in quelling by force of arms the Rebellion now raging against its authority, and in bringing to the punishment due to their crimes the Rebels and traitors arrayed against it.

2. *Resolved,* That we approve the determina-tion of the Government of the United States not to compromise with Rebels, or to offer them any terms of peace, except such as may be based upon an unconditional surrender of their hostility and a return to their just allegiance to the Con-stitution and laws of the United States, and that we call upon the Government to maintain this position and to prosecute the war with the ut-most possible vigor to the complete suppression of the Rebellion, in full reliance upon the self-sacrificing patriotism, the heroic valor and the undying devotion of the American people to the country and its free institutions.

3. *Resolved,* That as slavery was the cause, and now constitutes the strength of this Rebellion, and as it must be, always and everywhere, hostile to the principles of Republican Government, jus-tice and the National safety demand its utter and complete extirpation from the soil of the Republic; and that, while we uphold and maintain the acts and proclamations by which the Government, in its own defense, has aimed a deathblow at this gigantic evil, we are in favor, furthermore, of such an amendment to the Constitution, to be made by the people in conformity with its provisions, as shall terminate and forever prohibit the existence of Slavery within the limits of the jurisdiction of the United States.

4. *Resolved,* That the thanks of the American people are due to the soldiers and sailors of the Army and Navy, who have periled their lives in defense of the country and in vindication of the honor of its flag; that the nation owes to them some permanent recognition of their patriotism and their valor, and ample and permanent pro-vision for those of their survivors who have re-ceived disabling and honorable wounds in the service of the country; and that the memories of those who have fallen in its defense shall be held in grateful and everlasting remembrance.

5. *Resolved,* That we approve and applaud the practical wisdom, the unselfish patriotism and the unswerving fidelity to the Constitution and the principles of American liberty, with which Abraham Lincoln has discharged, under circum-stances of unparalleled difficulty, the great duties and responsibilities of the Presidential office; that we approve and indorse, as demanded by the emergency and essential to the preservation of the nation and as within the provisions of the Con-stitution, the measures and acts which he has adopted to defend the nation against its open and secret foes; that we approve, especially, the Proc-lamation of Emancipation, and the employment as Union soldiers of men heretofore held in slavery; and that we have full confidence in his determina-tion to carry these and all other Constitutional measures essential to the salvation of the country into full and complete effect.

6. *Resolved,* That we deem it essential to the general welfare that harmony should prevail in the National Councils, and we regard as worthy of public confidence and official trust those only who cordially indorse the principles proclaimed in these resolutions, and which should character-ize the administration of the government.

7. *Resolved,* That the Government owes to all men employed in its armies, without regard to distinction of color, the full protection of the laws of war—and that any violation of these laws, or of the usages of civilized nations in time of war, by the Rebels now in arms, should be made the sub-ject of prompt and full redress.

8. *Resolved,* That foreign immigration, which in the past has added so much to the wealth, de-velopment of resources and increase of power to the nation, the asylum of the oppressed of all na-

tions, should be fostered and encouraged by a liberal and just policy.

9. *Resolved,* That we are in favor of the speedy construction of the railroad to the Pacific coast.

10. *Resolved,* That the National faith, pledged for the redemption of the public debt, must be kept inviolate, and that for this purpose we recommend economy and rigid responsibility in the public expenditures, and a vigorous and just system of taxation; and that it is the duty of every loyal state to sustain the credit and promote the use of the National currency.

11. *Resolved,* That we approve the position taken by the Government that the people of the United States can never regard with indifference the attempt of any European Power to overthrow by force or to supplant by fraud the institutions of any Republican Government on the Western Continent and that they will view with extreme jealousy, as menacing to the peace and independence of their own country, the efforts of any such power to obtain new footholds for Monarchical Government, sustained by foreign military force, in near proximity to the United States.

In this year there were only the Democratic and Republican Parties. It is to be observed that the first sentence of the Republican Platform refers to the Party as the National Union Republican Party. There is nothing to indicate however that the party had intended to adopt a new name.

Democratic Platform of 1868

The Democratic party in National Convention assembled, reposing its trust in the intelligence, patriotism, and discriminating justice of the people; standing upon the Constitution as the foundation and limitation of the powers of the government, and the guarantee of the liberties of the citizen; and recognizing the questions of slavery and secession as having been settled for all time to come by the war, or the voluntary action of the Southern States in Constitutional Conventions assembled, and never to be renewed or reagitated; does, with the return of peace, demand,

First. Immediate restoration of all the States to their rights in the Union, under the Constitution, and of civil government to the American people.

Second. Amnesty for all past political offenses, and the regulation of the elective franchise in the States, by their citizens.

Third. Payment of the public debt of the United States as rapidly as practicable. All moneys drawn from the people by taxation, except so much as is requisite for the necessities of the government, economically administered, being honestly applied to such payment, and where the obligations of the government do not expressly state upon their face, or the law under which they were issued does not provide, that they shall be paid in coin, they ought, in right and in justice, to be paid in the lawful money of the United States.

Fourth. Equal taxation of every species of property, according to its real value, including government bonds and other public securities.

Fifth. One currency for the government and the people, the laborer and the office-holder, the pensioner and the soldier, the producer and the bond-holder.

Sixth. Economy in the administration of the government, the reduction of the standing army and navy; the abolition of the Freedmen's Bureau; and all political instrumentalities designed to secure negro supremacy; simplification of the system and discontinuance of inquisitorial modes of assessing and collecting internal revenue, so that the burden of taxation may be equalized and lessened, the credit of the government and the currency made good; the repeal of all enactments for enrolling the State militia into national forces in time of peace; and a tariff for revenue upon foreign imports, such as will afford incidental protection to domestic manufactures, and as will, without impairing the revenue, impose the least burden upon, and best promote and encourage the great industrial interests of the country.

Seventh. Reform of abuses in the administration; the expulsion of corrupt men from office; the abrogation of useless offices; the restoration of rightful authority to, and the independence of the executive and judicial departments of the government; the subordination of the military to the civil power, to the end that the usurpations of Congress and the despotism of the sword may cease.

Eighth. Equal rights and protection for naturalized and native-born citizens at home and abroad; the assertion of American nationality, which shall command the respect of foreign powers, and furnish an example and encouragement to people struggling for national integrity, constitutional liberty, and individual rights, and the maintenance of the rights of naturalized citizens against the absolute doctrine of immutable allegiance and the claims of foreign powers to punish them for alleged crimes committed beyond their jurisdiction.

In demanding these measures and reforms we arraign the Radical party for its disregard of right, and the unparalleled oppression and tyranny which have marked its career.

After the most solemn and unanimous pledge of both Houses of Congress to prosecute the war exclusively for the maintenance of the government and the preservation of the Union under the Constitution, it has repeatedly violated that most sacred pledge, under which alone was rallied that noble volunteer army which carried our flag to victory.

Instead of restoring the Union, it has, so far as in its power, dissolved it, and subjected ten States, in time of profound peace, to military despotism and negro supremacy.

It has nullified there the right of trial by jury; it has abolished the *habeas corpus,* that most sacred writ of liberty; it has overthrown the freedom of speech and of the press; it has substituted arbitrary seizures and arrests, and military trials and secret star-chamber inquisitions, for the constitutional tribunals; it has disregarded in time of peace the right of the people to be free from searches and seizures; it has entered the post and telegraph offices, and even the private rooms of individuals, and seized their private papers and letters without any specific charge or notice of affidavit, as required by the organic law; it has converted the American capitol into a Bastile; it has established a system of spies and official espionage to which no constitutional monarchy of Europe would now dare to resort; it has abolished the right of appeal, on important constitutional

questions, to the Supreme Judicial tribunal, and threatens to curtail, or destroy, its original jurisdiction, which is irrevocably vested by the Constitution; while the learned Chief Justice has been subjected to the most atrocious calumnies, merely because he would not prostitute his high office to the support of the false and partisan charges preferred against the President. Its corruption and extravagance have exceeded anything known in history, and by its frauds and monopolies it has nearly doubled the burden of the debt created by the war; it has stripped the President of his constitutional power of appointment, even of his own Cabinet. Under its repeated assaults the pillars of the government are rocking on their base, and should it succeed in November next and inaugurate its President, we will meet, as a subjected and conquered people, amid the ruins of liberty and the scattered fragments of the Constitution.

And we do declare and resolve, That ever since the people of the United States threw off all subjection to the British crown, the privilege and trust of suffrage have belonged to the several States, and have been granted, regulated, and controlled exclusively by the political power of each State respectively, and that any attempt by congress, on any pretext whatever, to deprive any State of this right, or interfere with its exercise, is a flagrant usurpation of power, which can find no warrant in the Constitution; and if sanctioned by the people will subvert our form of government, and can only end in a single centralized and consolidated government, in which the separate existence of the States will be entirely absorbed, and an unqualified despotism be established in place of a federal union of co-equal States; and that we regard the reconstruction acts so-called, of Congress, as such an usurpation, and unconstitutional, revolutionary, and void.

That our soldiers and sailors, who carried the flag of our country to victory against a most gallant and determined foe, must ever be gratefully remembered, and all the guarantees given in their favor must be faithfully carried into execution.

That the public lands should be distributed as widely as possible among the people, and should be disposed of either under the pre-emption or homestead laws, or sold in reasonable quantities, and to none but actual occupants, at the minimum price established by the government. When grants of the public lands may be deemed necessary for the encouragement of important public improvements, the proceeds of the sale of such lands, and not the lands themselves, should be so applied.

That the President of the United States, Andrew Johnson, in exercising the power of his high office in resisting the aggressions of Congress upon the Constitutional rights of the States and the people, is entitled to the gratitude of the whole American people; and in behalf of the Democratic party, we tender him our thanks for his patriotic efforts in that regard.

Upon this platform the Democratic party appeals to every patriot, including all the Conservative element, and all who desire to support the Constitution and restore the Union, forgetting all past differences of opinion, to unite with us in the present great struggle for the liberties of the people; and that to all such, to whatever party they may have heretofore belonged, we extend the right hand of fellowship, and hail all such co-operating with us as friends and brethren.

Resolved, That this convention sympathize cordially with the workingmen of the United States in their efforts to protect the rights and interests of the laboring classes of the country.

Resolved, That the thanks of the convention are tendered to Chief Justice Salmon P. Chase for the justice, dignity, and impartiality with which he presided over the court of impeachment on the trial of President Andrew Johnson.

Republican Platform of 1868

The National Union Republican Party of the United States, assembled in National Convention, in the city of Chicago, on the 20th day of May, 1868, make the following declaration of principles:

First—We congratulate the country on the assured success of the reconstruction policy of Congress, as evinced by the adoption, in the majority of the States lately in rebellion, of constitutions securing equal civil and political rights to all, and regard it as the duty of the Government to sustain those constitutions, and to prevent the people of such States from being remitted to a state of anarchy or military rule.

Second—The guaranty by Congress of equal suffrage to all loyal men at the South was demanded by every consideration of public safety, of gratitude, and of justice, and must be maintained; while the question of suffrage in all the loyal States properly belongs to the people of those States.

Third—We denounce all forms of repudiation as a national crime; and national honor requires the payment of the public indebtedness in the utmost good faith to all creditors at home and abroad, not only according to the letter, but the spirit of the laws under which it was contracted.

Fourth—It is due to the labor of the nation, that taxation should be equalized and reduced as rapidly as the national faith will permit.

Fifth—The National Debt, contracted as it has been for the preservation of the Union for all time to come, should be extended over a fair period of redemption, and it is the duty of Congress to reduce the rate of interest thereon whenever it can be done honestly.

Sixth—That the best policy to diminish our burden of debt, is to so improve our credit that capitalists will seek to loan us money at lower rates of interest than we now pay and must continue to pay so long as repudiation, partial or total, open or covert, is threatened or suspected.

Seventh—The Government of the United States should be administered with the strictest economy; and the corruptions which have been so shamefully nursed and fostered by Andrew Johnson call loudly for radical reform.

Eighth—We profoundly deplore the untimely and tragic death of Abraham Lincoln, and regret the accession of Andrew Johnson to the Presidency, who has acted treacherously to the people who elected him and the cause he was pledged to support; has usurped high legislative and judicial functions; has refused to execute the laws; has used his high office to induce other officers to ignore and violate the laws; has employed his executive powers to render insecure the property, the peace, the liberty, and life of the citizen; has abused the pardoning power; has denounced the National Legislature as unconstitutional; has persistently and corruptly resisted, by every means in his power, every proper attempt at the reconstruction of the States lately in rebellion; has perverted the public patronage into an engine of wholesale corruption; and has been justly impeached for high crimes and misdemeanors, and properly pronounced guilty thereof by the vote of thirty-five senators.

Ninth—The doctrine of Great Britain and other European powers, that because a man is once a subject, he is always so, must be resisted, at every hazard, by the United States, as a relic of the feudal times, not authorized by the law of nations, and at war with our national honor and independence. Naturalized citizens are entitled to be protected in all their rights of citizenship, as though they were native-born; and no citizen of the United States, native or naturalized, must be liable to arrest and imprisonment by any foreign power, for acts done or words spoken in this country; and, if so arrested and imprisoned, it is the duty of the Government to interfere in his behalf.

Tenth—Of all who were faithful in the trials of the late war, there were none entitled to more especial honor than the brave soldiers and seamen who endured the hardships of campaign and cruise, and imperilled their lives in the service of the country. The bounties and pensions provided by law for these brave defenders of the nation, are obligations never to be forgotten. The widows and orphans of the gallant dead are the wards of the people—a sacred legacy bequeathed to the nation's protecting care.

Eleventh—Foreign immigration, which in the past, has added so much to the wealth, development of resources, and increase of power to this nation—the asylum of the oppressed of all nations—should be fostered and encouraged by a liberal and just policy.

Twelfth—This Convention declares its sympathy with all the oppressed people which are struggling for their rights.

Thirteenth—We highly commend the spirit of magnanimity and forgiveness with which men who have served in the rebellion, but now frankly and honestly co-operate with us in restoring the peace of the country, and reconstructing the Southern State Governments upon the basis of impartial justice and equal rights, are received back into the communion of the loyal people; and we favor the removal of the disqualifications and restrictions imposed upon the late rebels, in the same measure as the spirit of disloyalty will die out, and as may be consistent with the safety of the loyal people.

Fourteenth—We recognize the great principles laid down in the immortal Declaration of Independence as the true foundation of Democratic Government; and we hail with gladness every effort toward making these principles a living reality on every inch of American soil.

⊠ CAMPAIGN OF 1872

Six different parties issued platforms in 1872. This happened because factions broke away from both of the major parties, and two entirely new parties appeared. A faction headed by Horace Greeley called itself the Liberal Republican Party. The Democratic Party nominated the same candidates and adopted the same platform as the Liberal Republicans. This greatly displeased certain of the Democrats who broke away from their party and came to be known as the Straight-Out Democrats. This made four parties in the field, though two of them had the same candidates and platform.

The Labor Reform Party appeared for the first time, as did the Prohibition Party. The Labor Reform Party was a forerunner of the Greenback Party which appeared later.

Democratic Platform of 1872

We, the Democratic Electors of the United States in Convention assembled, do present the following principles, already adopted at Cincinnati, as essential to just government.

1. We recognize the equality of all men before the law, and hold that it is the duty of the Government in its dealings with the people to mete out equal and exact justice to all, of whatever nativity, race, color or persuasion, religion or politics.

2. We pledge ourselves to maintain the union of these States, emancipation and enfranchisement; and to oppose any reopening of the questions settled by the thirteenth, fourteenth and fifteenth amendments of the Constitution.

3. We demand the immediate and absolute removal of all disabilities imposed on account of the rebellion which was finally subdued seven years ago, believing that universal amnesty will result in complete pacification in all sections of the country.

4. Local self-government, with impartial suffrage, will guard the rights of all citizens more securely than any centralized power. The public welfare requires the supremacy of the civil over the military authority, and the freedom of person under the protection of the *habeas corpus*. We demand for the individual the largest liberty consistent with public order; for the State, self-government, and for the Nation a return to the methods of peace and the constitutional limitations of power.

5. The Civil Service of the Government has become a mere instrument of partisan tyranny and personal ambition, and an object of selfish greed. It is a scandal and reproach upon free

institutions, and it breeds a demoralization dangerous to the perpetuity of Republican Government.

6. We therefore regard a thorough reform of the Civil Service as one of the most pressing necessities of the hour; that honesty, capacity, and fidelity constitute the only valid claim to public employment; that the offices of the Government cease to be a matter of arbitrary favoritism and patronage, and that public station shall become again a place of honor. To this end it is imperatively required that no President shall be a candidate for re-election.

7. We demand a system of Federal taxation which shall not unnecessarily interfere with the industry of the people and which shall provide the means necessary to pay the expenses of the Government, economically administered, the pensions, the interest on the public debt, and a moderate annual reduction of the principal thereof; and recognizing that there are in our midst honest but irreconcilable differences of opinion with regard to the respective systems of protection and free trade, we remit the discussion of the subject to the people in their Congressional Districts, and the decision of the Congress thereon, wholly free from Executive interference or dictation.

8. The public credit must be sacredly maintained, and we denounce repudiation in every form and guise.

9. A speedy return to specie payment is demanded alike by the highest considerations of commercial morality and honest government.

10. We remember with gratitude the heroism and sacrifices of the soldiers and sailors of the Republic, and no act of ours shall ever detract from their justly earned fame for the full reward of their patriotism.

11. We are opposed to all further grants of lands to railroads or other corporations. The public domain should be held sacred to actual settlers.

12. We hold that it is the duty of the Government, in its intercourse with foreign nations, to cultivate the friendships of peace by treating with all on fair and equal terms, regarding it alike dishonorable either to demand what is not right or to submit to what is wrong.

13. For the promotion and success of these vital principles, and the support of the candidates nominated by this Convention, we invite and cordially welcome the co-operation of all patriotic citizens without regard to previous political affiliations.

Democratic (Straight-Out) Platform of 1872

Whereas, A frequent recurrence to first principles and eternal vigilance against abuses are the wisest provisions for liberty, which is the source of progress, and fidelity to our constitutional system is the only protection for either; therefore

Resolved, That the original basis of our whole political structure is consent in every part thereof. The people of each State voluntarily created their State, and the States voluntarily formed the Union; and each State provided by its written Constitution for everything a State could do for the protection of life, liberty, and property within it, and each State, jointly with the others, provided a Federal Union for foreign and interstate relations.

Resolved, That all Governmental powers, whether State or Federal, are trust powers coming from the people of each State, and that they are limited to the written letter of the Constitution and the laws passed in pursuance of it; which powers must be exercised in the utmost good faith, the Constitution itself proving in what manner they may be altered and amended.

Resolved, That the interests of labor and capital should not be permitted to conflict, but should be harmonized by judicious legislation. While such a conflict continues, labor, which is the parent of wealth, is entitled to paramount consideration.

Resolved, That we proclaim to the world that principle is to be preferred to power; that the Democratic party is held together by the cohesion of time-honored principles, which they will never surrender in exchange for all the offices which Presidents can confer. The pangs of the minorities are doubtless excruciating; but we welcome an eternal minority under the banner inscribed with our principles, rather than an almighty and everlasting majority purchased by their abandonment.

Resolved, That having been betrayed at Baltimore into a false creed and a false leadership by the Convention, we repudiate both, and appeal to the people to approve our platform and to rally to the polls and support the true platform and the candidates who embody it.

Labor Reform Platform of 1872

1. We hold that all political power is inherent in the people, and free government founded on their authority and established for their benefit; that all citizens are equal in political rights, entitled to the largest religious and political liberty compatible with the good order of society, as also the use and enjoyment of the fruits of their labor and talents; and no man, or set of men, is entitled to exclusive separate emoluments and privileges from the Government, but in consideration of public services; and any laws destructive of these fundamental principles are without moral binding force, and should be repealed; and believing that all evils resulting from unjust legislation now affecting the industrial classes can be removed by the adoption of the principles contained in the following declaration: Therefore,

2. *Resolved,* That it is the duty of the Government to establish a just standard of distribution of capital and labor by providing a purely national circulating medium based on the faith and resources of the nation, issued directly to the people without the intervention of any system of banking corporations, which money shall be a legal tender in the payment of all debts, public and private, and interchangeable, at the option of the holder, for Government bonds bearing a rate of interest not to exceed 3.75 per cent, subject to future legislation by Congress.

3. *Resolved,* That the national debt should be paid in good faith, according to the original contract, at the earliest option of the Government, without mortgaging the property of the people and the future earnings of labor, to enrich a few capitalists at home and abroad.

4. *Resolved,* That justice demands that the burdens of government should be so adjusted as to bear equally on all classes and interests; and that the exemption from taxation of Government bonds bearing extortionate rates of interest is a violation of all just principles of revenue laws.

5. *Resolved,* That the public lands of the United States belong to the people, and should not be sold to individuals nor granted to corporations, but should be held as a sacred trust for the benefit of the people, and should be granted free of cost to landless settlers only, in amounts not exceeding 160 acres of land.

6. *Resolved,* That Congress should modify the tariff so as to admit free such articles of common use as we can neither produce nor grow, and lay duties for revenue mainly upon articles of luxury, and upon such articles of manufacture as we, having the raw materials in abundance, will assist in further developing the resources of the country.

7. *Resolved,* That the presence in our country of Chinese laborers imported by capitalists in large numbers for servile use, is an evil entailing want and its consequent train of misery and crime on all classes of the American people, and should be prohibited by legislation.

8. *Resolved,* That we ask for the enactment of a law by which all mechanics and day laborers employed by or on behalf of the Government, whether directly or indirectly, through persons, firms, or corporations, contracting with the State, shall conform to the reduced standard of eight hours a day recently adopted by Congress for the national employes, and also for an amendment to the act of incorporation for cities and towns, by which all laborers and mechanics employed at their expense shall conform to the same number of hours.

9. *Resolved,* That the enlightened spirit of the age demands the abolition of the system of contract labor in our prisons and other reformatory institutions.

10. *Resolved,* That the protection of life, liberty, and property are the three cardinal principles of government, and the first two more sacred than the latter; therefore, money for prosecuting wars should, as it is required, be assessed and collected from the wealth of the country, and not entailed as a burden on posterity.

11. *Resolved,* That it is the duty of the government to so exercise its power over railroads and telegraph corporations that they shall not in any case be privileged to exact such rates of freight, transportation or charges by whatever name, as may bear unduly or inequitably upon either producer or consumer.

12. *Resolved,* That there should be such a reform in the Civil Service of the National Government as will remove it beyond all partisan influ-

ence, and place it in the charge and under the direction of intelligent and competent business men.

13. *Resolved,* That as both history and experience teach us that power ever seeks to perpetuate itself by any and all means at its command, and that its prolonged possession in the hands of one person is always dangerous to the liberty of free people, and believing, too, that the spirit of our organic laws and the stability and safety of our free institutions are best obeyed on the one hand and secured on the other, by a regular constitutional change in the chief of the country at each quadrennial election, therefore, we are in favor of limiting the occupancy of the Presidential chair to one term.

14. *Resolved,* That we are in favor of granting general amnesty and restoring the Union at once on the basis of equality of rights and privileges to all; the impartial administration of justice being the only true bond of the union to bind the States together and restore the Government of the people.

Liberal Republican Platform of 1872

We, the Liberal Republicans of the United States in National Convention assembled at Cincinnati, proclaim the following principles as essential to just government.

First: We recognize the equality of all men before the law, and hold that it is the duty of Government in its dealings with the people to mete out equal and exact justice to all of whatever nativity, race, color, or persuasion, religious or political.

Second: We pledge ourselves to maintain the union of these States, emancipation, and enfranchisement, and to oppose any re-opening of the questions settled by the Thirteenth, Fourteenth, and Fifteenth Amendments to the Constitution.

Third: We demand the immediate and absolute removal of all disabilities imposed on account of the Rebellion, which was finally subdued seven years ago, believing that universal amnesty will result in complete pacification in all sections of the country.

Fourth: Local self-government, with impartial suffrage, will guard the rights of all citizens more securely than any centralized power. The public welfare requires the supremacy of the civil over the military authority, and freedom of person under the protection of the *habeas corpus.* We demand for the individual the largest liberty consistent with public order; for the State, self-government, and for the nation a return to the methods of peace and the constitutional limitations of power.

Fifth: The Civil Service of the Government has become a mere instrument of partisan tyranny and personal ambition and an object of selfish greed. It is a scandal and reproach upon free institutions and breeds a demoralization dangerous to the perpetuity of republican government. We therefore regard such thorough reforms of the Civil Service as one of the most pressing necessities of the hour; that honesty, capacity, and fidelity constitute the only valid claim to public employment; that the offices of the Government cease to be a matter of arbitrary favoritism and patronage, and that public station become again a post of honor. To this end it is imperatively required that no President shall be a candidate for re-election.

Sixth: We demand a system of Federal taxation which shall not unnecessarily interfere with the industry of the people, and which shall provide the means necessary to pay the expenses of the Government economically administered, the pensions, the interest on the public debt, and a moderate reduction annually of the principal thereof; and, recognizing that there are in our midst honest but irreconcilable differences of opinion with regard to the respective systems of Protection and Free Trade, we remit the discussion of the subject to the people in their Congress Districts, and to the decision of Congress thereon, wholly free of Executive interference or dictation.

Seventh: The public credit must be sacredly maintained, and we denounce repudiation in every form and guise.

Eighth: A speedy return to specie payment is demanded alike by the highest considerations of commercial morality and honest government.

Ninth: We remember with gratitude the heroism and sacrifices of the soldiers and sailors of the Republic, and no act of ours shall ever detract from their justly-earned fame or the full reward of their patriotism.

Tenth: We are opposed to all further grants

of lands to railroads or other corporations. The public domain should be held sacred to actual settlers.

Eleventh: We hold that it is the duty of the Government, in its intercourse with foreign nations to cultivate the friendship of peace, by treating with all on fair and equal terms, regarding it alike dishonorable either to demand what is not right, or to submit to what is wrong.

Twelfth: For the promotion and success of these vital principles and the support of the candidates nominated by this Convention, we invite and cordially welcome the co-operation of all patriotic citizens, without regard to previous affiliations.

Prohibition Platform of 1872

Resolved, That we reaffirm the following resolutions adopted by the National Prohibition Convention, held at Chicago, Sept. 2, 1869:

"*Whereas,* Protection and allegiance are reciprocal duties, and every citizen who yields obedience to the just demands of the Government is entitled to the full, free and perfect protection of that Government in the enjoyment of personal security, personal liberty and private property; and

"*Whereas,* The traffic in intoxicating drinks greatly impairs the personal security and personal liberty of a large mass of citizens, and renders private property insecure; and

"*Whereas,* All other political parties are hopelessly unwilling to adopt an adequate policy on this question; therefore

"We, in National Convention assembled, as citizens of this free Republic, sharing the duties and responsibilities of its Government, in discharge of a solemn duty we owe to our country and our race, unite in the following declaration of principles:

"1. That while we acknowledge the pure patriotism and profound statesmanship of those patriots who laid the foundations of this Government, securing at once the rights of the States severally, and their inseparable union by the Federal Constitution, we would not merely garnish the sepulchers of our republican fathers, but we do hereby renew our solemn pledges of fealty to the imperishable principles of civil and re-

ligious liberty embodied in the Declaration of American Independence and our Federal Constitution.

"2. That the traffic in intoxicating beverages is a dishonor to Christian civilization, inimical to the best interests of society, a political wrong of unequalled enormity, subversive of the ordinary objects of government, not capable of being regulated or restrained by any system of license whatever, but imperatively demanding for its suppression effective legal Prohibition by both State and National legislation."

3. That while we recognize the good providence of Almighty God in supervising the interests of this nation from its establishment to the present time, having organized our party for the legal Prohibition of the liquor traffic, our reliance for success is upon the same omnipotent arm.

4. That there can be no greater peril to the nation than the existing party competition for the liquor vote; that any party not openly opposed to the traffic, experience shows, will engage in this competition, will court the favor of the criminal classes, will barter away the public morals, the purity of the ballot, and every object of good government, for party success.

5. That while adopting national political measures for the Prohibition of the liquor traffic, we will continue the use of all moral means in our power to persuade men away from the injurious practice of using intoxicating beverages.

6. That we invite all persons, whether total abstainers or not, who recognize the terrible injuries inflicted by the liquor traffic, to unite with us for its overthrow, and to secure thereby peace, order and the protection of persons and property.

7. That competency, honesty and sobriety are indispensable qualifications for holding public office.

8. That removals from public service for mere difference of political opinion is a practice opposed to sound policy and just principles.

9. That fixed and moderate salaries should take the place of official fees and perquisites; the franking privilege, sinecures, and all unnecessary offices and expenses should be abolished, and every possible means be employed to prevent corruption and venality in office; and by a rigid system of accountability from all its officers, and guards over the public treasury, the utmost econ-

omy should be practiced and enforced in every department of the Government.

10. That we favor the election of President, Vice-President and United States Senators by direct vote of the people.

11. That we are in favor of a sound national currency, adequate to the demands of business and convertible into gold and silver at the will of the holder, and the adoption of every measure compatible with justice and the public safety, to appreciate our present currency to the gold standard.

12. That the rates of inland and ocean postage, of telegraphic communication, of railroad and water transportation and travel, should be reduced to the lowest practicable point, by force of laws wisely and justly framed, with reference not only to the interest of capital employed but to the higher claim of the general good.

13. That an adequate public revenue being necessary, it may properly be raised by impost duties and by an equitable assessment upon the property and legitimate business of the country; nevertheless we are opposed to any discrimination of capital against labor, as well as to all monopoly and class legislation.

14. That the removal of the burdens, moral, physical, pecuniary and social, imposed by the traffic in intoxicating drinks will, in our judgment, emancipate labor and practically thus promote labor reform.

15. That the fostering and extension of common schools under the care and support of the State, to supply the want of a general and liberal education, is a primary duty of a good government.

16. That the right of suffrage rests on no mere circumstance of color, race, former social condition, sex or nationality, but inheres in the nature of man; and when from any cause it has been withheld from citizens of our country who are of suitable age and mentally and morally qualified for the discharge of its duties, it should be speedily restored by the people in their sovereign capacity.

17. That a liberal and just policy should be pursued to promote foreign immigration to our shores, always allowing to the naturalized citizens equal rights, privileges and protection under the Constitution with those who are native-born.

Republican Platform of 1872

The Republican party of the United States, assembled in National Convention in the city of Philadelphia, on the 5th and 6th days of June, 1872, again declares its faith, appeals to its history, and announces its position upon the questions before the country.

First. During eleven years of supremacy it has accepted with grand courage the solemn duties of the time. It suppressed a gigantic rebellion, emancipated four millions of slaves, decreed the equal citizenship of all, and established universal suffrage. Exhibiting unparalleled magnanimity, it criminally punished no man for political offenses, and warmly welcomed all who proved loyalty by obeying the laws and dealing justly with their neighbors. It has steadily decreased with firm hand the resultant disorders of a great war, and initiated a wise and humane policy toward the Indians. The Pacific railroad and similar vast enterprises have been generously aided and successfully conducted, the public lands freely given to actual settlers, immigration protected and encouraged, and a full acknowledgment of the naturalized citizens' rights secured from European Powers. A uniform national currency has been provided, repudiation frowned down, the national credit sustained under the most extraordinary burdens, and new bonds negotiated at lower rates. The revenues have been carefully collected and honestly applied. Despite large annual reductions of the rates of taxation, the public debt has been reduced during General Grant's Presidency at the rate of a hundred millions a year, great financial crises have been avoided, and peace and plenty prevail throughout the land. Menacing foreign difficulties have been peacefully and honorably composed, and the honor and power of the nation kept in high respect throughout the world. This glorious record of the past is the party's best pledge for the future. We believe the people will not intrust the Government to any party or combination of men composed chiefly of those who have resisted every step of this beneficent progress.

Second. The recent amendments to the national Constitution should be cordially sustained because they are right, not merely tolerated because they are law, and should be carried out according to their spirit by appropriate legislation, the enforcement of which can safely be entrusted only to the party that secured those amendments.

Third. Complete liberty and exact equality in the enjoyment of all civil, political, and public rights should be established and effectually maintained throughout the Union, by efficient and appropriate State and Federal legislation. Neither the law nor its administration should admit any discrimination in respect of citizens by reason of race, creed, color, or previous condition of servitude.

Fourth. The National Government should seek to maintain honorable peace with all nations, protecting its citizens everywhere, and sympathizing with all people who strive for greater liberty.

Fifth. Any system of the civil service under which the subordinate positions of the government are considered rewards for mere party zeal is fatally demoralizing, and we therefore favor a reform of the system by laws which shall abolish the evils of patronage, and make honesty, efficiency, and fidelity the essential qualifications for public positions, without practically creating a life-tenure of office.

Sixth. We are opposed to further grants of the public lands to corporations and monopolies, and demand that the national domain be set apart for free homes for the people.

Seventh. The annual revenue, after paying current expenditures, pensions, and the interest on the public debt, should furnish a moderate balance for the reduction of the principal and that revenue, except so much as may be derived from a tax upon tobacco and liquors, should be raised by duties upon importations, the details of which should be so adjusted as to aid in securing remunerative wages to labor, and to promote the industries, prosperity, and growth of the whole country.

Eighth. We hold in undying honor the soldiers and sailors whose valor saved the Union. Their pensions are a sacred debt of the nation, and the widows and orphans of those who died for their country are entitled to the care of a generous and grateful people. We favor such additional legislation as will extend the bounty of the Government to all our soldiers and sailors who were honorably discharged, and who, in the line of duty, became disabled, without regard to the length of service or the cause of such discharge.

Ninth. The doctrine of Great Britain and other European powers concerning allegiance—"Once a subject always a subject"—having at last, through the efforts of the Republican party, been abandoned, and the American idea of the individual's right to transfer allegiance having been accepted by European nations, it is the duty of our Government to guard with jealous care the rights of adopted citizens against the assumption of unauthorized claims by their former governments; and we urge continued careful encouragement and protection of voluntary immigration.

Tenth. The franking privilege ought to be abolished, and the way prepared for a speedy reduction in the rates of postage.

Eleventh. Among the questions which press for attention is that which concerns the relations of capital and labor, and the Republican party recognizes the duty of so shaping legislation as to secure full protection and the amplest field for capital, and for labor—the creator of capital—the largest opportunities and a just share of the mutual profits of these two great servants of civilization.

Twelfth. We hold that Congress and the President have only fulfilled an imperative duty in their measures for the suppression of violent and treasonable organizations in certain lately rebellious regions, and for the protection of the ballot-box, and therefore they are entitled to the thanks of the nation.

Thirteenth. We denounce repudiation of the public debt, in any form or disguise, as a national crime. We witness with pride the reduction of the principal of the debt, and of the rates of interest upon the balance, and confidently expect that our excellent national currency will be perfected by a speedy resumption of specie payment.

Fourteenth. The Republican party is mindful of its obligations to the loyal women of America for their noble devotion to the cause of freedom. Their admission to wider fields of usefulness is viewed with satisfaction, and the honest demand of any class of citizens for additional rights should be treated with respectful consideration.

Fifteenth. We heartily approve the action of Congress in extending amnesty to those lately in rebellion, and rejoice in the growth of peace and fraternal feeling throughout the land.

Sixteenth. The Republican party proposes to respect the rights reserved by the people to themselves as carefully as the powers delegated by them to the State and to the Federal Government. It disapproves of the resort to unconstitutional laws for the purpose of removing evils, by interference with rights not surrendered by the people to either the State or National Government.

Seventeenth. It is the duty of the general Government to adopt such measures as may tend to encourage and restore American commerce and ship-building.

Eighteenth. We believe that the modest patriotism, the earnest purpose, the sound judgment, the practical wisdom, the incorruptible integrity, and the illustrious services of Ulysses S. Grant have commended him to the heart of the American people, and with him at our head we start to-day upon a new march to victory.

Nineteenth. Henry Wilson, nominated for the Vice-Presidency, known to the whole land from the early days of the great struggle for liberty as an indefatigable laborer in all campaigns, an incorruptible legislator and representative man of American institutions, is worthy to associate with our great leader and share the honors which we pledge our best efforts to bestow upon them.

In this campaign there were the two major parties and two distinct minor parties. The Prohibitionists appeared for the second time but called themselves the Prohibition Reform Party in their platform. The Independent Party of this campaign, sometimes called the Independent National Party, is more generally known as the Greenback Party. It later adopted that name.

Democratic Platform of 1876

We, the delegates of the Democratic party of the United States, in National Convention assembled, do hereby declare the administration of the Federal Government to be in great need of immediate reform; do hereby enjoin upon the nominees of this Convention, and of the Democratic party in each State, a zealous effort and co-operation to this end, and do here appeal to our fellow-citizens of every former political connection to undertake with us this first and most pressing patriotic duty for the Democracy of the whole country. We do here reaffirm our faith in the permanence of the Federal Union, our devotion to the Constitution of the United States, with its amendments universally accepted as a final settlement of the controversies that engendered civil war, and do here record our steadfast confidence in the perpetuity of republican self-government; in absolute acquiescence in the will of the majority, the vital principle of republics; in the supremacy of the civil over the military; in the two-fold separation of church and state, for the sake alike of civil and religious freedom; in the equality of all citizens before just laws of their own enactment; in the liberty of individual conduct unvexed by sumptuary laws; in the faith-

ful education of the rising generation, that they may preserve, enjoy and transmit these best conditions of human happiness and hope. We behold the noblest products of a hundred years of changeful history. But while upholding the bond of our Union and great charter of these our rights, it behooves a free people to practice also that eternal vigilance which is the price of liberty.

Reform is necessary to rebuild and establish in the hearts of the whole people the Union eleven years ago happily rescued from the danger of the secession of States, but now to be saved from a corrupt centralism which, after inflicting upon ten States the rapacity of carpet-bag tyrannies, has honeycombed the offices of the Federal Government itself with incapacity, waste and fraud; infected States and municipalities with the contagion of misrule, and locked fast the prosperity of an industrious people in the paralysis of hard times. Reform is necessary to establish a sound currency, restore the public credit and maintain the national honor.

We denounce the failure for all these eleven years to make good the promise of the legal tender notes, which are a changing standard of value in the hands of the people, and the non-payment of which is a disregard of the plighted faith of the nation.

We denounce the improvidence which, in eleven years of peace, has taken from the people in Federal taxes thirteen times the whole amount of the legal-tender notes and squandered four times their sum in useless expense, without accumulating any reserve for their redemption. We denounce the financial imbecility and immorality of that party, which, during eleven years of peace, has made no advance toward resumption, no preparation for resumption, but instead has obstructed resumption by wasting our resources and exhausting all our surplus income, and while annually professing to intend a speedy return to specie payments, has annually enacted fresh hindrances thereto. As such hindrance we denounce the resumption clause of the act of 1875 and we here demand its repeal. We demand a judicious system of preparation by public economies, by official retrenchments, and by wise finance, which shall enable the nation soon to assure the whole world of its perfect ability and its perfect readiness to meet any of its promises at the call of the creditor entitled to payment.

We believe such a system, well-advised, and, above all, intrusted to competent hands for execution, creating at no time an artificial scarcity of currency, and at no time alarming the public mind into a withdrawal of that vast machinery of credit by which ninety-five per cent of our business transactions are performed—a system open and public and inspiring general confidence—would from the day of its adoption bring healing on its wings to all our harassed industries, set in motion the wheels of commerce, manufactures and the mechanic arts, restore employment to labor, and renew in all its natural sources the prosperity of the people.

Reform is necessary in the sum and mould of Federal taxation, to the end that capital may be set free from distrust, and labor lightly burdened. We denounce the present tariff levied upon nearly four thousand articles as a masterpiece of injustice, inequality and false pretense, which yields a dwindling and not a yearly rising revenue, has impoverished many industries to subsidize a few. It prohibits imports that might purchase the products of American labor; it has degraded American commerce from the first to an inferior rank upon the high seas; it has cut down the values of American manufactures at home and abroad; it has depleted the returns of American agriculture, an industry followed by half our people; it costs the people five times more than it produces to the treasury, obstructs the process of production and wastes the fruits of labor; it promotes fraud, fosters smuggling, enriches dishonest officials, and bankrupts honest merchants. We demand that all custom-house taxation shall be only for revenue. Reform is necessary in the scale of public expense, Federal, State and municipal. Our Federal taxation has swollen from sixty millions gold in 1860 to four hundred and fifty millions currency in 1870; our aggregate taxation from one hundred and fifty-four millions gold in 1860 to seven hundred and thirty millions currency, in 1870, all in one decade; from less than five dollars per head to more than eighteen dollars per head. Since the peace the people have paid to their tax-gatherers more than thrice the sum of the national debt, and more than twice the sum for the Federal Government alone. We demand a rigorous frugality in every department and from every officer of the Government.

Reform is necessary to put a stop to the profligate waste of public lands and their diversion from actual settlers by the party in power, which has squandered two hundred millions of acres upon railroads alone, and out of more than thrice that aggregate has disposed of less than a sixth directly to the tillers of the soil.

Reform is necessary to correct the omissions of a Republican Congress and the errors of our treaties and our diplomacy, which has stripped our fellow-citizens of foreign birth and kindred race, re-erasing [re-crossing] the Atlantic from the shield of American citizenship, and has exposed our brethren of the Pacific coast to the incursions of a race not sprung from the same great parent stock, and in fact now by law denied citizenship through naturalization as being unaccustomed to the traditions of a progressive civilization, one exercised in liberty under equal laws; and we denounce the policy which thus discards the liberty-loving German and tolerates the revival of the coolie-trade in Mongolian women for immoral purposes, and Mongolian men held to perform servile labor contracts, and demand such modification of the treaty with the Chinese Empire, or such legislation within constitutional limitations, as shall prevent further importation or immigration of the Mongolian race.

Reform is necessary and can never be effected

but by making it the controlling issue of the election and lifting it above the two issues with which the office-holding classes and the party in power seek to smother it:—

First—The false issue with which they would enkindle sectarian strife in respect to the public schools, of which the establishment and support belong exclusively to the several States, and which the Democratic party has cherished from their foundation, and is resolved to maintain without partiality or preference for any class, sect or creed, and without contributions from the treasury to any.

Second—The false issue by which they seek to light anew the dying embers of sectional hate between kindred peoples once unnaturally estranged but now reunited in one indivisible republic, and a common destiny.

Reform is necessary in the civil service. Experience proves that efficient economical conduct of the government is not possible if its civil service be subject to change at every election, be a prize fought for at the ballot-box, be an approved reward of party zeal instead of posts of honor assigned for proved competency and held for fidelity in the public employ; that the dispensing of patronage should neither be a tax upon the time of our public men nor an instrument of their ambition. Here again, profession falsified in the performance attest that the party in power can work out no practical or salutary reform. Reform is necessary even more in the higher grades of the public service. President, Vice-President, judges, senators, representatives, cabinet officers —these and all others in authority are the people's servants. Their offices are not a private perquisite; they are a public trust. When the annals of this Republic show disgrace and censure of a Vice-President; a late Speaker of the House of Representatives marketing his rulings as a presiding officer; three Senators profiting secretly by their votes as law-makers; five chairmen of the leading committees of the late House of Representatives exposed in jobbery; a late Secretary of the Treasury forcing balances in the public accounts; a late Attorney-General misappropriating public funds; a Secretary of the Navy enriched and enriching friends by a percentage levied off the profits of contractors with his department; an Ambassador to England censured in a dishonorable speculation; the President's Private Secretary barely es-

caping conviction upon trial for guilty complicity in frauds upon the revenue; a Secretary of War impeached for high crimes and misdemeanors— the demonstration is complete, that the first step in reform must be the people's choice of honest men from another party, lest the disease of one political organization infect the body politic, and lest by making no change of men or parties, we get no change of measures and no real reform.

All these abuses, wrongs, and crimes, the product of sixteen years' ascendency of the Republican party, create a necessity for reform, confessed by Republicans themselves; but their reformers are voted down in Convention and displaced from the cabinet. The party's mass of honest voters is powerless to resist the eighty thousand office-holders, its leaders and guides. Reform can only be had by a peaceful civic revolution. We demand a change of system, a change of administration, a change of parties, that we may have a change of measures and of men.

Resolved, That this Convention, representing the Democratic party of the States, do cordially indorse the action of the present House of Representatives in reducing and curtailing the expenses of the Federal Government, in cutting down enormous salaries, extravagant appropriations, and in abolishing useless offices and places not required by the public necessities, and we shall trust to the firmness of the Democratic members of the House that no committee of conference and no misinterpretation of rules will be allowed to defeat these wholesome measures of economy demanded by the country.

Resolved, That the soldiers and sailors of the Republic, and the widows and orphans of those who have fallen in battle, have a just claim upon the care, protection and gratitude of their fellow-citizens.

Independent (Greenback) Platform of 1876

The Independent party is called into existence by the necessities of the people whose industries are prostrated, whose labor is deprived of its just reward by a ruinous policy which the Republican and Democratic parties refuse to change, and in view of the failure of these parties to furnish relief to the depressed industries of the country, thereby disappointing just hopes and expectations of the suffering people, we declare our principles and invite all independent and patriotic men to join our ranks in this movement for financial reform and industrial emancipation:

First. We demand the immediate and unconditional repeal of the Specie-Resumption act of January 14, 1875, and the rescue of our industries from ruin and disaster resulting from its enforcement; and we call upon all patriotic men to organize in every Congressional district of the country with a view of electing representatives to Congress who will carry out the wishes of the people in this regard, and stop the present suicidal and destructive policy of contraction.

Second. We believe that a United States note, issued directly by the Government, and convertible on demand into United States obligations bearing a rate of interest not exceeding one cent a day on each $100, and exchangeable for United States notes at par, will afford the best circulating medium ever devised; such United States notes should be full legal-tender for all purposes except for payment of such obligations as are by existing contracts expressly made payable in coin; and we hold that it is the duty of the Government to provide such circulating medium, and insist in the language of Thomas Jefferson, that "bank paper must be suppressed and the circulation restored to the nation, to whom it belongs."

Third. It is the paramount duty of the Government in all its legislation to keep in view the full development of all legitimate business,— agricultural, mining, manufacturing and commercial.

Fourth. We most earnestly protest against any further issue of gold bonds for sale in foreign markets, by which we would be made for a long period "hewers of wood and drawers of water" to foreigners, especially as the American people would gladly and promptly take at par all bonds the Government may need to sell, provided they are made payable at the option of the holder, and bearing interest at 3.65 per cent per annum, or even a lower rate.

Fifth. We further protest against the sale of Government bonds for the purpose of purchasing silver to be used as a substitute for our more convenient and less fluctuating fractional currency, which, although well calculated to enrich owners of silver mines, yet in operation it will still further

oppress in taxation an already overburdened people.

Prohibition Reform Platform of 1876

The Prohibition Reform party of the United States, organized in the name of the people to revive, enforce and perpetuate in the Government the doctrines of the Declaration of Independence, submit in this Centennial year of the Republic for the suffrages of all good citizens the following platform of national reforms and measures:

1. The legal Prohibition in the District of Columbia, the Territories and in every other place subject to the laws of Congress, of the importation, exportation, manufacture and traffic of all alcoholic beverages, as high crimes against society; an Amendment of the National Constitution to render these Prohibitory measures universal and permanent, and the adoption of treaty stipulations with foreign Powers to prevent the importation and exportation of all alcoholic beverages.

2. The abolition of class legislation and of special privileges in the Government, and the adoption of equal suffrage and eligibility to office without distinction of race, religious creed, property or sex.

3. The appropriation of the public lands in limited quantities to actual settlers only; the reduction of the rates of inland and ocean postage, of telegraphic communication, of railroad and water transportation and travel to the lowest practical point by force of laws, wisely and justly framed, with reference not only to the interests of capital employed but to the higher claims of the general good.

4. The suppression, by law, of lotteries and gambling in gold, stocks, produce and every form of money and property, and the penal inhibition of the use of the public mails for advertising schemes of gambling and lotteries.

5. The abolition of those foul enormities, polygamy and the social evil, and the protection of purity, peace and happiness of homes by ample and efficient legislation.

6. The national observance of the Christian Sabbath, established by laws prohibiting ordinary labor and business in all departments of public service and private employments (works of neces-

sity, charity and religion excepted) on that day.

7. The establishment by mandatory provisions in National and State Constitutions, and by all necessary legislation, of a system of free public schools for the universal and forced education of all the youth of the land.

8. The free use of the Bible, not as a ground of religious creeds, but as a text-book of purest morality, the best liberty and the noblest literature, in our public schools, that our children may grow up in its light and that its spirit and principles may pervade our nation.

9. The separation of the Government in all its departments and institutions, including the public schools and all funds for their maintenance, from the control of every religious sect or other association, and the protection alike of all sects by equal laws, with entire freedom of religious faith and worship.

10. The introduction into all treaties, hereafter negotiated with foreign Governments, of a provision for the amicable settlement of international difficulties by arbitration.

11. The abolition of all barbarous modes and instruments of punishment; the recognition of the laws of God and the claims of humanity in the discipline of jails and prisons, and of that higher and wiser civilization worthy of our age and nation, which regards the reform of criminals as a means for the prevention of crime.

12. The abolition of executive and legislative patronage, and the election of President, Vice-President, United States Senators, and of civil officers, so far as practicable, by the direct vote of the people.

13. The practice of a friendly and liberal policy to immigrants from all nations, the guaranty to them of ample protection and of equal rights and privileges.

14. The separation of the money of Government from all banking institutions. The National Government only should exercise the high prerogative of issuing paper money, and that should be subject to prompt redemption on demand, in gold and silver, the only equal standards of value recognized by the civilized world.

15. The reduction of the salaries of public officers in a just ratio with the decline of wages and market prices, the abolition of sinecures, unnecessary offices and official fees and perquisites;

the practice of strict economy in Government expenses, and a free and thorough investigation into any and all alleged abuses of public trusts.

Republican Platform of 1876

When, in the economy of Providence, this land was to be purged of human slavery, and when the strength of government of the people by the people and for the people was to be demonstrated, the Republican party came into power. Its deeds have passed into history, and we look back to them with pride. Incited by their memories, and with high aims for the good of our country and mankind, and looking to the future with unfaltering courage, hope, and purpose, we, the representatives of the party, in national convention assembled, make the following declaration of principles:—

1. The United States of America is a nation, not a league. By the combined workings of the national and state governments, under their respective constitutions, the rights of every citizen are secured at home and abroad, and the common welfare promoted.

2. The Republican party has preserved these governments to the hundredth anniversary of the nation's birth, and they are now embodiments of the great truth spoken at its cradle, that all men are created equal; that they are endowed by their Creator with certain inalienable rights, among which are life, liberty, and the pursuit of happiness; that for the attainment of these ends governments have been instituted among men, deriving their just powers from the consent of the governed. Until these truths are cheerfully obeyed, and if need be, vigorously enforced, the work of the Republican party is unfinished.

3. The permanent pacification of the Southern section of the Union and the complete protection of all its citizens in the free enjoyment of all their rights, are duties to which the Republican party is sacredly pledged. The power to provide for the enforcement of the principles embodied in the recent constitutional amendments is vested by those amendments in the Congress of the United States; and we declare it to be the solemn obligation of the legislative and executive departments of the government to put into immediate

and vigorous exercise all their constitutional powers for removing any just causes of discontent on the part of any class, and securing to every American citizen complete liberty and exact equality in the exercise of all civil, political, and public rights. To this end we imperatively demand a congress and a chief executive whose courage and fidelity to these duties shall not falter until these results are placed beyond dispute or recall.

4. In the first act of congress, signed by President Grant, the national government assumed to remove any doubt of its purpose to discharge all just obligations to the public creditors, and solemnly pledged its faith "to make provisions at the earliest practicable period, for the redemption of the United States notes in coin." Commercial prosperity, public morals, and the national credit demand that this promise be fulfilled by a continuous and steady progress to specie payment.

5. Under the constitution, the President and heads of departments are to make nominations for office, the senate is to advise and consent to appointments, and the house of representatives is to accuse and prosecute faithless officers. The best interest of the public service demands that these distinctions be respected; that senators and representatives who may be judges and accusers should not dictate appointments to office. The invariable rule for appointments should have reference to the honesty, fidelity, and capacity of the appointees, giving to the party in power those places where harmony and vigor of administration require its policy to be represented, but permitting all others to be filled by persons selected with sole reference to the efficiency of the public service and the right of citizens to share in the honor of rendering faithful service to their country.

6. We rejoice in the quickened conscience of the people concerning political affairs. We will hold all public officers to a rigid responsibility, and engage that the prosecution and punishment of all who betray official trusts shall be speedy, thorough, and unsparing.

7. The public school system of the several states is the bulwark of the American republic; and, with a view to its security and permanence, we recommend an amendment to the constitution of the United States, forbidding the application of any public funds or property for the benefit of any school or institution under sectarian control.

8. The revenue necessary for current expenditures and the obligations of the public debt must be largely derived from duties upon importations, which, so far as possible, should be so adjusted as to promote the interests of American labor and advance the prosperity of the whole country.

9. We reaffirm our opposition to further grants of the public lands to corporations and monopolies, and demand that the national domain be devoted to free homes for the people.

10. It is the imperative duty of the government so to modify existing treaties with European governments, that the same protection shall be afforded to the adopted American citizen that is given to native-born, and all necessary laws be passed to protect emigrants, in the absence of power in the states for that purpose.

11. It is the immediate duty of congress fully to investigate the effects of the immigration and importation of Mongolians on the moral and material interests of the country.

12. The Republican party recognizes with approval the substantial advances recently made toward the establishment of equal rights for women, by the many important amendments effected by Republican legislatures in the laws which concern the personal and property relations of wives, mothers, and widows, and by the appointment and election of women to the superintendence of education, charities, and other public trusts. The honest demands of this class of citizens for additional rights, privileges, and immunities should be treated with respectful consideration.

13. The constitution confers upon congress sovereign power over the territories of the United States for their government. And in the exercise of this power it is the right and duty of congress to prohibit and extirpate in the territories that relic of barbarism, polygamy; and we demand such legislation as will secure this end and the supremacy of American institutions in all the territories.

14. The pledges which our nation has given to our soldiers and sailors must be fulfilled. The grateful people will always hold those who imperilled their lives for the country's preservation in the kindest remembrance.

15. We sincerely deprecate all sectional feel-

ing and tendencies. We therefore note with deep solicitude that the Democratic party counts, as its chief hope of success, upon the electoral vote of a united South, secured through the efforts of those who were recently arrayed against the nation; and we invoke the earnest attention of the country to the grave truth, that a success thus achieved would reopen sectional strife and imperil national honor and human rights.

16. We charge the Democratic party with being the same in character and spirit as when it sympathized with treason; with making its control of the house of representatives the triumph and opportunity of the nation's recent foes; with reasserting and applauding in the national capitol the sentiments of unrepentant rebellion; with sending Union soldiers to the rear, and promoting Confederate soldiers to the front; with deliberately proposing to repudiate the plighted faith of the government; with being equally false and imbecile upon the over-shadowing financial question; with thwarting the ends of justice, by its partisan mismanagements and obstruction of investigation; with proving itself, through the period of its ascendency in the lower house of congress, utterly incompetent to administer the government;—and we warn the country against trusting a party thus alike unworthy, recreant, and incapable.

17. The national administration merits commendation for its honorable work in the management of domestic and foreign affairs, and President Grant deserves the continued hearty gratitude of the American people, for his patriotism and his eminent services in war and in peace.

18. We present as our candidates for President and Vice-President of the United States two distinguished statesmen, of eminent ability and character, and conspicuously fitted for those high offices, and we confidently appeal to the American people to intrust the administration of their public affairs to Rutherford B. Hayes and William A. Wheeler.

In 1880 there were the same four parties that existed in 1876. In addition to the two major parties there was the Independent Party of 1876, now appearing as the Greenback Party. The Prohibitionists retained the title Prohibition Reform Party.

Democratic Platform of 1880

The Democrats of the United States, in Convention assembled, declare:

1. We pledge ourselves anew to the constitutional doctrines and traditions of the Democratic party as illustrated by the teachings and example of a long line of Democratic statesmen and patriots, and embodied in the platform of the last National Convention of the party.

2. Opposition to centralization and to that dangerous spirit of encroachment which tends to consolidate the powers of all the departments in one, and thus to create whatever be the form of government, a real despotism. No sumptuary laws; separation of Church and State, for the good of each; common schools fostered and protected.

3. Home rule; honest money, consisting of gold and silver, and paper convertible into coin on demand; the strict maintenance of the public faith, State and National, and a tariff for revenue only.

4. The subordination of the military to the civil power, and a general and thorough reform of the civil service.

5. The right to a free ballot is the right preservative of all rights, and must and shall be maintained in every part of the United States.

6. The existing administration is the representative of conspiracy only, and its claim of right to surround the ballot-boxes with troops and deputy marshals, to intimidate and obstruct the election, and the unprecedented use of the veto to maintain its corrupt and despotic powers, insult the people and imperil their institutions.

7. We execrate the course of this administration in making places in the civil service a reward for political crime, and demand a reform by statute which shall make it forever impossible for a defeated candidate to bribe his way to the seat of the usurper by billeting villains upon the people.

8. The great fraud of 1876-77, by which, upon a false count of the electoral votes of two States, the candidate defeated at the polls was declared to be President, and for the first time in American history, the will of the people was set aside under a threat of military violence, struck a deadly blow at our system of representative government. The Democratic party, to preserve the country from the horrors of a civil war, submitted for the time in firm and patriotic faith that the people would punish this crime in 1880. This issue precedes and dwarfs every other. It imposes a more sacred duty upon the people of the Union than ever addressed the conscience of a nation of free men.

9. The resolution of Samuel J. Tilden not again to be a candidate for the exalted place to which he was elected by a majority of his countrymen, and from which he was excluded by the

leaders of the Republican party, is received by the Democrats of the United States with deep sensibility, and they declare their confidence in his wisdom, patriotism, and integrity, unshaken by the assaults of a common enemy, and they further assure him that he is followed into the retirement he has chosen for himself by the sympathy and respect of his fellow-citizens, who regard him as one who, by elevating the standards of public morality, merits the lasting gratitude of his country and his party.

10. Free ships and a living chance for American commerce on the seas, and on the land no discrimination in favor of transportation lines, corporations, or monopolies.

11. Amendment of the Burlingame Treaty. No more Chinese immigration, except for travel, education, and foreign commerce, and that even carefully guarded.

12. Public money and public credit for public purposes solely, and public land for actual settlers.

13. The Democratic party is the friend of labor and the laboring man, and pledges itself to protect him alike against the cormorant and the commune.

14. We congratulate the country upon the honesty and thrift of a Democratic Congress which has reduced the public expenditure $40,-000,000 a year; upon the continuation of prosperity at home, and the national honor abroad, and, above all, upon the promise of such a change in the administration of the government as shall insure us genuine and lasting reform in every department of the public service.

Greenback Platform of 1880

Civil government should guarantee the divine right of every laborer to the results of his toil, thus enabling the producers of wealth to provide themselves with the means for physical comfort, and the facilities for mental, social and moral culture; and we condemn as unworthy of our civilization the barbarism which imposes upon the wealth-producers a state of perpetual drudgery as the price of bare animal existence. Notwithstanding the enormous increase of productive power, and the universal introduction of labor-saving machinery, and the discovery of new agents for the increase of wealth, the task of the laborer is scarcely lightened, the hours of toil are but little shortened; and few producers are lifted from poverty into comfort and pecuniary independence. The associated monopolies, the international syndicate and other income classes demand dear money and cheap labor: a "strong government," and hence a weak people.

Corporate control of the volume of money has been the means of dividing society into hostile classes, of the unjust distribution of the products of labor, and of building up monopolies of associated capital endowed with power to confiscate private property. It has kept money scarce, and scarcity of money enforces debt, trade and public and corporate loans. Debt engenders usury, and usury ends in the bankruptcy of the borrower. Other results are deranged markets, uncertainty in manufacturing enterprise and agriculture, precarious and intermittent employment for the laborers, industrial war, increasing pauperism and crime, and the consequent intimidation and disfranchisement of the producer and a rapid declension into corporate feudalism; therefore, we declare:

First—That the right to make and issue money is a sovereign power to be maintained by the people for the common benefit. The delegation of this right to corporations is a surrender of the central attribute of sovereignty, (void) of constitutional sanction, conferring upon a subordinate and irresponsible power absolute dominion over industry and commerce. All money, whether metallic or paper, should be issued and its volume controlled by the Government, and not by or through banking corporations, and when so issued should be a full legal-tender for all debts, public and private.

Second—That the bonds of the United States should not be refunded, but paid as rapidly as practicable, according to contract. To enable the Government to meet these obligations, legal-tender currency should be substituted for the notes of the National banks, the National banking system abolished, and the unlimited coinage of silver, as well as gold, established by law.

Third—That labor should be so protected by National and State authority as to equalize the burdens and insure a just distribution of its results; the eight-hour law of Congress should be enforced, the sanitary condition of industrial establishments placed under rigid control; the competition of contract labor abolished, a bureau of labor statistics established, factories, mines, and workshops inspected, the employment of children under fourteen years of age forbidden, and wages paid in cash.

Fourth—Slavery being simply cheap labor, and cheap labor being simple slavery, the importation and presence of Chinese serfs necessarily tends to brutalize and degrade American labor, therefore immediate steps should be taken to abrogate the Burlingame Treaty.

Fifth—Railroad land grants forfeited by reason of non-fulfillment of contract should be immediately reclaimed by the Government, and henceforth the public domain reserved exclusively as homes for actual settlers.

Sixth—It is the duty of Congress to regulate inter-State commerce. All lines of communication and transportation should be brought under such legislative control as shall secure moderate, fair and uniform rates for passenger and freight traffic.

Seventh—We denounce as destructive to prosperity and dangerous to liberty, the action of the old parties in fostering and sustaining gigantic land, railroad, and money corporations and monopolies, invested with, and exercising powers belonging to the Government, and yet not responsible to it for the manner of their exercise.

Eighth—That the Constitution, in giving Congress the power to borrow money, to declare war, to raise and support armies, to provide and maintain a navy, never intended that the men who loaned their money for an interest consideration should be preferred to the soldier and sailor who perilled their lives and shed their blood on land and sea in defense of their country, and we condemn the cruel class legislation of the Republican party, which, while professing great gratitude to the soldier, has most unjustly discriminated against him and in favor of the bondholder.

Ninth—All property should bear its just proportion of taxation, and we demand a graduated income tax.

Tenth—We denounce as most dangerous the efforts everywhere manifested to restrict the right of suffrage.

Eleventh—We are opposed to an increase of the standing army in times of peace, and the insidious scheme to establish an enormous military power under the guise of militia laws.

Twelfth—We demand absolute democratic rules for the government of Congress, placing all representatives of the people upon an equal footing, and taking away from committees a veto power greater than that of the President.

Thirteenth—We demand a government of the people, by the people, and for the people, instead of a government of the bondholder, by the bondholder, and for the bondholder; and we denounce every attempt to stir up sectional strife as an effort to conceal monstrous crimes against the people.

Fourteenth—In the furtherance of these ends we ask the co-operation of all fair-minded people. We have no quarrel with individuals, wage no war upon classes, but only against vicious institutions. We are not content to endure further discipline from our present actual rulers, who, having dominion over money, over transportation, over land and labor, and largely over the press and machinery of Government, wield unwarrantable power over our institutions, and over our life and property.

Resolved: That every citizen of due age, sound mind, and not a felon, be fully enfranchised, and that this resolution be referred to the States, with recommendation for their favorable consideration.

Prohibition Reform Platform of 1880

The Prohibition Reform party of the United States, organized in the name of the people to revive, enforce and perpetuate in the Government the doctrines of the Declaration of Independence, submit for the suffrages of all good citizens the following platform of national reforms and measures:

1. In the examination and discussion of the temperance question it has been proven, and is an accepted truth, that alcoholic drinks, whether fermented, brewed or distilled, are poisonous to the healthy human body, the drinking of which is not only needless but hurtful, necessarily tending to form intemperate habits, increasing greatly the number, severity and fatal termination of diseases, weakening and deranging the intellect, polluting the affections, hardening the heart and corrupting the morals, depriving many of reason and still more of its healthful exercise, and annually bringing down large numbers to untimely

graves, producing in the children of many who drink a predisposition to intemperance, insanity and various bodily and mental diseases, causing a diminution of strength, feebleness of vision, fickleness of purpose and premature old age, and producing to all future generations a deterioration of moral and physical character. The legalized importation, manufacture and sale of intoxicating drinks minister to their uses and teach the erroneous and destructive sentiment that such use is right, thus tending to produce and perpetuate the above-mentioned evils. Alcoholic drinks are thus the implacable enemy of man as an individual.

2. That the liquor traffic is to the home equally an enemy, proving a disturber and a destroyer of its peace, prosperity and happiness, taking from it the earnings of the husband, depriving the dependent wife and children of essential food, clothing and education, bringing into it profanity and abuse, setting at naught the vows of the marriage altar, breaking up the family and sundering children from parents, and thus destroying one of the most beneficent institutions of our Creator, and removing the sure foundation for good government, national prosperity and welfare.

3. That to the community it is equally an enemy, producing demoralization, vice and wickedness; its places of sale being often resorts for gambling, lewdness and debauchery, and the hiding places of those who prey upon society, counteracting the efficacy of religious effort and of all means for the intellectual elevation, moral purity, social happiness and the eternal good of mankind, without rendering any counteracting or compensating benefits, being in its influence and effect evil and only evil, and that continually.

4. That to the State it is equally an enemy, legislative inquiry, judicial investigation and the official reports of all penal, reformatory and dependent institutions showing that the manufacture and sale of such beverages is the promoting cause of intemperance, crime and pauperism, of demands upon public and private charity; imposing the larger part of taxation, thus paralyzing thrift, industry, manufacture and commercial life, which but for it would be unnecessary; disturbing the peace of the streets and highways; filling prisons and poorhouses; corrupting politics, legislation and the execution of the laws; shortening

lives, diminishing health, industry and productive power in manufacture and art; and is manifestly unjust as well as injurious to the community upon which it is imposed, and contrary to all just views of civil liberty, as well as a violation of a fundamental maxim of our common law to use your own property or liberty so as not to injure others.

5. That it is neither right nor politic for the State to afford legal protection to any traffic or system which tends to waste the resources, to corrupt the social habits and to destroy the health and lives of the people; that the importation, manufacture and sale of intoxicating beverages is proven to be inimical to the true interests of the individual, the home, the community, the State, and destructive to the order and welfare of society, and ought, therefore, to be classed among crimes to be prohibited.

6. That in this time of profound peace at home and abroad the entire separation of the general Government from the drink traffic, and its Prohibition in the District of Columbia, the Territories and in all places and ways over which (under the Constitution) Congress has control or power, is a political issue of first importance to the peace and prosperity of the nation. There can be no stable peace and protection to personal liberty, life or property until secured by National and State Constitutional Prohibition enforced by adequate laws.

7. That all legitimate industries require deliverance from taxation and loss which the liquor traffic imposes upon them, and financial or other legislation cannot accomplish so much to increase production and cause demand for labor, and as a result, for the comfort of living, as the suppression of this traffic would bring to thousands of homes as one of its blessings.

8. That the administration of Government and the execution of the laws being by and through political parties, we arraign the Republican party, which has been in continuous power in the nation for 20 years, as being false to its duty, as false to its loudly-proclaimed principles of "equal justice to all and special favors to none," and of protection to the weak and dependent; and that through moral cowardice it has been and is unable to correct the mischief which the trade in liquor has constantly inflicted upon the industrial interests, commerce and social happiness of the people. On the contrary, its subjection to and

complicity with the liquor interest appears: (1) By the facts that 5,652 distilleries, 2,830 breweries, and 175,266 places of sale of the poisonous liquors, involving an annual waste, direct and indirect, to the nation of $1,500,000,000, and a sacrifice of 100,000 lives, have under its legislation grown up and been fostered as a legitimate source of revenue; (2) That during its history six Territories have been organized and five States admitted into the Union with Constitutions provided and approved by Congress, but the Prohibition of this debasing and destructive traffic has not been provided for, nor even the people given at the time of admission the power to forbid it in any one of them; (3) That its history further shows that not in a single instance has an original Prohibitory law been enacted in any State controlled by it, while in four States so governed the laws found on its advent to power have been repealed; (4) That at its National Convention of 1872 it declared as a part of its party faith that "it disapproves of a resort to unconstitutional laws for the purpose of removing evils by interference with the right not surrendered by the people to either State or National Government," which the author of this plank says "was adopted by the Platform Committee with the full and explicit understanding that its purpose was the discountenancing of all so-called temperance (Prohibitory) and Sunday laws"; (5) That notwithstanding the deep interest felt by the people during the last quadrennium in the legal suppression of the drink curse, shown by many forms of public expression, this party at its last National Convention, held in Chicago during the present month, in making new promises by its platform, says not one word on this question, nor holds out any hope of relief.

9. That we arraign also the Democratic party as unfaithful and unworthy of reliance on this question; for although not clothed with power, but occupying the relation of the opposition party during 20 years past, strong in number and organization, it has allied itself with the liquor-traffickers and has become in all the States of the Union their special political defenders. In its National Convention of 1876, as an article of its political faith, it declared against Prohibition and just laws in restraint of the trade in drink by saying it was opposed to what it was pleased to call "all sumptuary laws." The National party has been dumb on the question.

10. That the drink-traffickers, realizing that history and experience, in all ages, climes and conditions of men declare their business destructive to all good, and finding no support from the Bible, morals or reason, appeal to misapplied law for their justification, and entrench themselves behind the evil elements of political party for defense, party tactics and party inertia having become the battling forces protecting this evil.

11. That in view of the foregoing facts and history, we cordially invite all voters, without regard to former party affiliation, to unite with us in the use of the ballot for the abolition of the drink system now existing under the authority of our National and State Governments. We also demand as a right that women, having in other respects the privileges of citizens, shall be clothed with the ballot for their protection, and as a rightful means for a proper settlement of the liquor question.

12. That to remove the apprehensions of some who allege that loss of public revenue would follow the suppression of the drink trade, we confidently point to the experience of government abroad and at home, which shows that thrift and revenue from consumption of legitimate manufactures and commerce have so largely followed the abolition of the drink as to fully supply all loss of liquor taxes.

13. That we recognize the good providence of Almighty God, who has preserved and prospered us as a nation, and, asking for his spirit to guide us to ultimate success, we will look for it, relying upon his omnipotent arm.

Republican Platform of 1880

The Republican party, in National Convention assembled, at the end of twenty years since the Federal Government was first committed to its charge, submits to the people of the United States this brief report of its administration:

It suppressed a rebellion which had armed nearly a million of men to subvert the national authority. It reconstructed the Union of the States, with freedom instead of slavery as its corner-stone. It transformed 4,000,000 human beings from the likeness of things to the rank of citizens. It relieved Congress from the infamous work of hunting fugitive slaves, and charged it to see that slavery does not exist. It has raised the value of our paper currency from 38 per cent to the par of gold. It has restored upon a solid basis payment in coin of all national obligations, and has given us a currency absolutely good and equal in every part of our extended country. It has lifted the credit of the Nation from the point where six per cent bonds sold at eighty-six to that where four per cent bonds are eagerly sought at a premium.

Under its administration, railways have increased from 31,000 miles in 1860, to more than 82,000 miles in 1879.

Our foreign trade increased from $700,000,000 to $1,115,000,000 in the same time, and our exports, which were $20,000,000 less than our imports in 1860, were $265,000,000 more than our imports in 1879.

Without resorting to loans, it has, since the war closed, defrayed the ordinary expenses of Government besides the accruing interest of the public debt, and has disbursed annually more than $30,000,000 for soldiers' and sailors' pensions. It has paid $880,000,000 of the public debt, and, by refunding the balance at lower rates, has reduced the annual interest-charge from nearly $150,000,000 to less than $89,000,000. All the industries of the country have revived; labor is in demand; wages have increased, and throughout the entire country there is evidence of a coming prosperity greater than we have ever enjoyed.

Upon this record the Republican party asks for the continued confidence and support of the people, and this Convention submits for their approval the following statement of the principles and purposes which will continue to guide and inspire its efforts.

1. We affirm that the work of the Republican party for the last twenty-one years has been such as to commend it to the favor of the Nation; that the fruits of the costly victories which we have achieved through immense difficulties should be preserved; that the peace regained should be cherished; that the Union should be perpetuated, and that the liberty secured to this generation should be transmitted undiminished to other generations; that the order established and the

credit acquired should never be impaired; that the pensions promised should be paid; that the debt so much reduced should be extinguished by the full payment of every dollar thereof; that the reviving industries should be further promoted, and that the commerce already increasing should be steadily encouraged.

2. The Constitution of the United States is a supreme law, and not a mere contract. Out of confederated States it made a sovereign nation. Some powers are denied to the Nation, while others are denied to the States; but the boundary between the powers delegated and those reserved is to be determined by the National and not by the State tribunal.

3. The work of popular education is one left to the care of the several States, but it is the duty of the National Government to aid that work to the extent of its constitutional power. The intelligence of the Nation is but the aggregate of the intelligence in the several States, and the destiny of the Nation must be guided, not by the genius of any one State, but by the aggregate genius of all.

4. The Constitution wisely forbids Congress to make any law respecting the establishment of religion, but it is idle to hope that the Nation can be protected against the influence of secret sectarianism while each State is exposed to its domination. We, therefore, recommend that the Constitution be so amended as to lay the same prohibition upon the Legislature of each State, and to forbid the appropriation of public funds to the support of sectarian schools.

5. We affirm the belief, avowed in 1876, that the duties levied for the purpose of revenue should so discriminate as to favor American labor; that no further grants of the public domain should be made to any railway or other corporation; that slavery having perished in the States, its twin barbarity, polygamy, must die in the Territories; that everywhere the protection accorded to a citizen of American birth must be secured to citizens by American adoption; that we deem it the duty of Congress to develop and improve our sea-coast and harbors, but insist that further subsidies to private persons or corporations must cease; that the obligations of the Republic to the men who preserved its integrity in the day of battle are undiminished by the lapse of fifteen years since

their final victory. To do them honor is, and shall forever be, the grateful privilege and sacred duty of the American people.

6. Since the authority to regulate immigration and intercourse between the United States and foreign nations rests with the Congress of the United States and the treaty-making power, the Republican party, regarding the unrestricted immigration of the Chinese as a matter of grave concernment under the exercise of both these powers, would limit and restrict that immigration by the enactment of such just, humane and reasonable laws and treaties as will produce that result.

7. That the purity and patriotism which characterized the earlier career of Rutherford B. Hayes in peace and war, and which guided the thoughts of our immediate predecessors to him for a presidential candidate, have continued to inspire him in his career as Chief Executive; and that history will accord to his administration the honors which are due to an efficient, just and courteous discharge of the public business, and will honor his vetoes interposed between the people and attempted partisan laws.

8. We charge upon the Democratic party the habitual sacrifice of patriotism and justice to a supreme and insatiable lust for office and patronage; that to obtain possession of the National Government, and control of the place, they have obstructed all efforts to promote the purity and to conserve the freedom of the suffrage, and have devised fraudulent ballots and invented fraudulent certification of returns; have labored to unseat lawfully elected members of Congress, to secure at all hazards the vote of a majority of the States in the House of Representatives; have endeavored to occupy by force and fraud the places of trust given to others by the people of Maine, rescued by the courage and action of Maine's patriotic sons; have, by methods vicious in principle and tyrannical in practice, attached partisan legislation to appropriation bills, upon whose passage the very movement of the Government depended; have crushed the rights of the individual; have advocated the principles and sought the favor of the Rebellion against the Nation, and

have endeavored to obliterate the sacred memories of the war, and to overcome its inestimably valuable results of nationality, personal freedom and individual equality.

The equal, steady and complete enforcement of the law, and the protection of all our citizens in the enjoyment of all privileges and immunities guaranteed by the Constitution, are the first duties of the Nation. The dangers of a solid south can only be averted by a faithful performance of every promise which the Nation has made to the citizen. The execution of the laws, and the punishment of all those who violate them, are the only safe methods by which an enduring peace can be secured and genuine prosperity established through the South. Whatever promises the Nation makes the Nation must perform. A Nation cannot safely relegate this duty to the States. The solid south must be divided by the peaceful agencies of the ballot, and all honest opinions must there find free expression. To this end honest voters must be protected against terrorism, violence or fraud. And we affirm it to be the duty and the purpose of the Republican party to use all legitimate means to restore all the States of this Union to the most perfect harmony that may be possible, and we submit to the practical, sensible people of these United States to say whether it would not be dangerous to the dearest interests of our country at this time to surrender the administration of the National Government to a party which seeks to overthrow the existing policy, under which we are so prosperous, and thus bring distrust and confusion where there is now order, confidence and hope.

9. The Republican party, adhering to the principle affirmed by its last National Convention, of respect for the constitutional rules governing appointments to office, adopts the declaration of President Hayes that the reform of the civil service should be thorough, radical and complete. To this end it demands the co-operation of the Legislative with the Executive Departments of the Government, and that Congress shall so legislate that fitness, ascertained by proper practical tests, shall admit to the public service.

There were six parties in the campaign of 1884. In addition to the two major parties there were two minor parties, and what might be called off-shoots from each of the two minor parties, making six in all. The Prohibition Party of this year drops the word "Reform" from its name. It is often referred to, however, as the Prohibition Reform Party or the National Prohibition Home Protection Party, although it repudiates the latter title in its platform of 1884. Another, very small group of Prohibitionists appeared as the American Prohibition National Party.

The Anti-Monopoly Party of this year nominated the same candidates as the Greenbackers. And this latter group now appears as the Greenback National Party. It is sometimes referred to as the National Party or the Greenback-Labor Party.

American Prohibition National Platform of 1884

We hold: 1. That ours is a Christian and not a heathen Nation, and that the God of the Christian Scriptures is the author of civil government.

2. That the Bible should be associated with books of science and literature in all our educational institutions.

3. That God requires and man needs a Sabbath.

4. That we demand the prohibition of the importation, manufacture, and sale of intoxicating drinks.

5. That the charters of all secret lodges granted by our Federal and State Legislatures should be withdrawn and their oaths prohibited by law.

6. We are opposed to putting prison labor or depreciated contract labor from foreign countries in competition with free labor to benefit manufacturers, corporations, and speculators.

7. We are in favor of a thorough revision and enforcement of the law concerning patents and inventions for the prevention and punishment of frauds either upon inventors or the general public.

8. We hold to and will vote for woman suffrage.

9. We hold that the civil equality secured to all American citizens by Arts. 13, 14, and 15 of our amended National Constitution should be preserved inviolate, and the same equality should be extended to Indians and Chinamen.

10. That international differences should be settled by arbitration.

11. That land and other monopolies should be discouraged.

12. That the General Government should furnish the people with an ample and sound currency.

13. That it should be the settled policy of the Government to reduce the tariffs and taxes as rapidly as the necessities of revenue and vested business interest will allow.

14. That polygamy should be immediately suppressed by law and that the Republican party is censurable for its long neglect of its duty in respect to this evil.

15. And, finally, we demand for the American people the abolition of Electoral Colleges and a direct vote for President and Vice-President of the United States.

Anti-Monopoly Platform of 1884

The Anti-Monopoly organization of the United States in convention assembled, declares:

1. That labor and capital should be allies and we demand justice for both by protecting the rights of all against privileges for the few.

2. That corporations, the creatures of law, should be controlled by law.

3. That we propose the greatest reduction practicable in public expenses.

4. That in the enactment and vigorous execution of just laws, equality of rights, equality of burdens, equality of privileges, and equality of powers in all citizens will be secured.

To this end, we further declare:

5. That it is the duty of the Government to immediately exercise its constitutional prerogative to regulate commerce among the States. The great instruments by which this commerce is carried on are transportation, money, and the transmission of intelligence. They are now mercilessly controlled by giant monopolies, to the impoverishment of labor, and the crushing out of healthful competition, and the destruction of business security. We hold it, therefore, to be the imperative and immediate duty of Congress to pass all needful laws for the control and regulation of those great agents of commerce in accordance with the oft-repeated decisions of the Supreme Court of the United States.

6. That these monopolies, which have exacted from enterprise such heavy tribute, have also inflicted countless wrongs upon the toiling millions of the United States, and no system of reform should commend itself to the support of the people which does not protect the man who earns his bread by the sweat of his face. Bureaus of labor statistics must be established, both State and National; arbitration take the place of brute force in the settlement of disputes between employer and employed; the National eight-hour law be honestly enforced; the importation of foreign labor *under contract* be made illegal; and whatever practical reforms may be necessary for the protection of united labor must be granted, to the end that unto the toiler shall be given that proportion of the profits of the thing or value created which his labor bears to the cost of production.

7. That we approve and favor the passage of an Inter-State Commerce bill. Navigable waters should be improved by the Government and be free.

8. We demand the payment of the bonded debt as it falls due; the election of the United States Senators by the direct vote of the people of their respective States; a graduated income tax; and a tariff, which is a tax upon the people, that shall be so levied as to bear as lightly as possible upon necessaries. We denounce the present tariff as being largely in the interest of monopoly, and demand that it be speedily and radically reformed in the interest of labor instead of capital.

9. That no further grants of public lands shall be made to corporations. All enactments granting land to corporations should be strictly construed; and all land-grants should be forfeited where the terms upon which the grants were made have not been strictly complied with. The public lands must be held for homes for actual settlers, and must not be subject to purchase or control by non-resident foreigners or other speculators.

10. That we deprecate the discrimination of American legislation against the greatest of American industries—agriculture, by which it has been deprived of nearly all beneficial legislation while forced to bear the brunt of taxation. And we demand for it the fostering care of Government and the just recognition of its importance in the development and advancement of our land. And we appeal to the American farmer to co-operate with us in our endeavors to advance the National interests of the country, and the over-

throw of monopoly in every shape when and wherever found.

Democratic Platform of 1884

The Democratic party of the Union, through its representatives in National Convention assembled, recognizes that, as the nation grows older, new issues are born of time and progress, and old issues perish. But the fundamental principles of the Democracy, approved by the united voice of the people, remain, and will ever remain, as the best and only security for the continuance of free government. The preservation of personal rights; the equality of all citizens before the law; the reserved rights of the States; and the supremacy of the Federal Government within the limits of the Constitution, will ever form the true basis of our liberties, and can never be surrendered without destroying that balance of rights and powers which enables a continent to be developed in peace, and social order to be maintained by means of local self-government.

But it is indispensable for the practical application and enforcement of these fundamental principles, that the Government should not always be controlled by one political party. Frequent change of administration is as necessary as constant recurrence to the popular will. Otherwise abuses grow, and the Government, instead of being carried on for the general welfare, becomes an instrumentality for imposing heavy burdens on the many who are governed, for the benefit of the few who govern. Public servants thus become arbitrary rulers.

This is now the condition of the country. Hence a change is demanded. The Republican party, so far as principle is concerned, is a reminiscence; in practice, it is an organization for enriching those who control its machinery. The frauds and jobbery which have been brought to light in every department of the Government, are sufficient to have called for reform within the Republican party; yet those in authority, made reckless by the long possession of power, have succumbed to its corrupting influence, and have placed in nomination a ticket against which the independent portion of the party are in open revolt.

Therefore a change is demanded. Such a change was alike necessary in 1876, but the will of the people was then defeated by a fraud which can never be forgotten, nor condoned. Again, in 1880, the change demanded by the people was defeated by the lavish use of money contributed by unscrupulous contractors and shameless jobbers who had bargained for unlawful profits, or for high office.

The Republican party during its legal, its stolen, and its bought tenure of power, has steadily decayed in moral character and political capacity.

Its platform promises are now a list of its past failures.

It demands the restoration of our Navy. It has squandered hundreds of millions to create a navy that does not exist.

It calls upon Congress to remove the burdens under which American shipping has been depressed. It imposed and has continued those burdens.

It professes a policy of reserving the public lands for small holdings by actual settlers. It has given away the people's heritage till now a few railroads, and non-resident aliens, individual and corporate, possess a larger area than that of all our farms between the two seas.

It professes a preference for free institutions. It organized and tried to legalize a control of State elections by Federal troops.

It professes a desire to elevate labor. It has subjected American workingmen to the competition of convict and imported contract labor.

It professes gratitude to all who were disabled, or died in the war, leaving widows and orphans. It left to a Democratic House of Representatives the first effort to equalize both bounties and pensions.

It proffers a pledge to correct the irregularities of our tariff. It created and has continued them. Its own Tariff Commission confessed the need of more than twenty per cent reduction. Its Congress gave a reduction of less than four per cent.

It professes the protection of American manufactures. It has subjected them to an increasing flood of manufactured goods, and a hopeless competition with manufacturing nations, not one of which taxes raw materials.

It professes to protect all American industries. It has impoverished many to subsidize a few.

It professes the protection of American labor. It has depleted the returns of American agriculture—an industry followed by half of our people.

It professes the equality of all men before the law. Attempting to fix the status of colored citizens, the acts of its Congress were overset by the decision of its Courts.

It "accepts anew the duty of leading in the work of progress and reform." Its caught criminals are permitted to escape through contrived delays or actual connivance in the prosecution. Honeycombed with corruption, outbreaking exposures no longer shock its moral sense. Its honest members, its independent journals, no longer maintain a successful contest for authority in its councils or a veto upon bad nominations.

That change is necessary is proved by an existing surplus of more than $100,000,000, which has yearly been collected from a suffering people. Unnecessary taxation is unjust taxation. We denounce the Republican party for having failed to relieve the people from crushing war taxes which have paralyzed business, crippled industry, and deprived labor of employment and of just reward.

The Democracy pledges itself to purify the Administration from corruption, to restore economy, to revive respect for law, and to reduce taxation to the lowest limit consistent with due regard to the preservation of the faith of the Nation to its creditors and pensioners.

Knowing full well, however, that legislation affecting the operations of the people should be cautious and conservative in method, not in advance of public opinion, but responsive to its demands, the Democratic party is pledged to revise the tariff in a spirit of fairness to all interests.

But in making reduction in taxes, it is not proposed to injure any domestic industries, but rather to promote their healthy growth. From the foundation of this Government, taxes collected at the Custom House have been the chief source of Federal Revenue. Such they must continue to be. Moreover, many industries have come to rely upon legislation for successful continuance, so that any change of law must be at every step regardful of the labor and capital thus involved. The process of reform must be subject in the execution to this plain dictate of justice.

All taxation shall be limited to the requirements of economical government. The necessary reduction and taxation can and must be effected without depriving American labor of the ability to compete successfully with foreign labor, and without imposing lower rates of duty than will be ample to cover any increased cost of production which may exist in consequence of the higher rate of wages prevailing in this country.

Sufficient revenue to pay all the expenses of the Federal Government, economically administered, including pensions, interest, and principal on the public debt, can be got, under our present system of taxation, from the custom house taxes on fewer imported articles, bearing heaviest on articles of luxury, and bearing lightest on articles of necessity.

We, therefore, denounce the abuses of the existing tariff; and, subject to the preceding limitations, we demand that Federal taxation shall be exclusively for public purposes and shall not exceed the needs of the Government economically administered.

The system of direct taxation known as the "Internal Revenue," is a war tax, and so long as the law continues, the money derived therefrom should be sacredly devoted to the relief of the people from the remaining burdens of the war, and be made a fund to defray the expenses of the care and comfort of worthy soldiers disabled in line of duty in the wars of the Republic and for the payment of such pensions as Congress may from time to time grant to such soldiers, a like fund for the sailors having been already provided; and any surplus should be paid into the Treasury.

We favor an American continental policy based upon more intimate commercial and political relations with the fifteen sister Republics of North, Central, and South America, but entangling alliances with none.

We believe in honest money, the gold and silver coinage of the Constitution, and a circulating medium convertible into such money without loss.

Asserting the equality of all men before the law, we hold that it is the duty of the Government, in its dealings with the people, to mete out equal and exact justice to all citizens of whatever nativity, race, color, or persuasion—religious or political.

We believe in a free ballot and a fair count; and we recall to the memory of the people the noble struggle of the Democrats in the Forty-fifth and Forty-sixth Congresses, by which a reluctant Republican opposition was compelled to assent to legislation making everywhere illegal the presence of troops at the polls, as the conclusive proof that a Democratic administration will preserve liberty with order.

The selection of Federal officers for the Territories should be restricted to citizens previously resident therein.

We oppose sumptuary laws which vex the citizen and interfere with individual liberty; we favor honest Civil Service Reform, and the compensation of all United States officers by fixed salaries; the separation of Church and State; and the diffusion of free education by common schools, so that every child in the land may be taught the rights and duties of citizenship.

While we favor all legislation which will tend to the equitable distribution of property, to the prevention of monopoly, and to the strict enforcement of individual rights against corporate abuses, we hold that the welfare of society depends upon a scrupulous regard for the rights of property as defined by law.

We believe that labor is best rewarded where it is freest and most enlightened. It should therefore be fostered and cherished. We favor the repeal of all laws restricting the free action of labor, and the enactment of laws by which labor organizations may be incorporated, and of all such legislation as will tend to enlighten the people as to the true relations of capital and labor.

We believe that the public lands ought, as far as possible, to be kept as homesteads for actual settlers; that all unearned lands heretofore improvidently granted to railroad corporations by the action of the Republican party should be restored to the public domain; and that no more grants of land shall be made to corporations, or be allowed to fall into the ownership of alien absentees.

We are opposed to all propositions which upon any pretext would convert the General Government into a machine for collecting taxes to be distributed among the States, or the citizens thereof.

In reaffirming the declaration of the Democratic platform of 1856, that, "the liberal principles embodied by Jefferson in the Declaration of Independence, and sanctioned in the Constitution, which make ours the land of liberty and the asylum of the oppressed of every Nation, have ever been cardinal principles in the Democratic faith," we nevertheless do not sanction the importation of foreign labor, or the admission of servile races, unfitted by habits, training, religion, or kindred, for absorption into the great body of our people, or for the citizenship which our laws confer. American civilization demands that against the immigration or importation of Mongolians to these shores our gates be closed.

The Democratic party insists that it is the duty of the Government to protect, with equal fidelity and vigilance, the rights of its citizens, native and naturalized, at home and abroad, and to the end that this protection may be assured, United States papers of naturalization, issued by courts of competent jurisdiction, must be respected by the Executive and Legislative departments of our own Government, and by all foreign powers.

It is an imperative duty of this Government to efficiently protect all the rights of persons and property of every American citizen in foreign lands, and demand and enforce full reparation for any invasion thereof.

An American citizen is only responsible to his own Government for any act done in his own country, or under her flag, and can only be tried therefor on her own soil and according to her laws; and no power exists in this Government to expatriate an American citizen to be tried in any foreign land for any such act.

This country has never had a well-defined and executed foreign policy save under Democratic administration; that policy has ever been, in regard to foreign nations, so long as they do not act detrimental to the interests of the country or hurtful to our citizens, to let them alone; that as a result of this policy we call the acquisition of Louisiana, Florida, California, and of the adjacent Mexican territory by purchase alone, and contrast these grand acquisitions of Democratic statesmanship with the purchase of Alaska, the sole fruit of a Republican administration of nearly a quarter of a century.

The Federal Government should care for and improve the Mississippi River and other great waterways of the Republic, so as to secure for the interior States easy and cheap transportation to tide water.

Under a long period of Democratic rule and policy, our merchant marine was fast overtaking and on the point of outstripping that of Great Britain.

Under twenty years of Republican rule and policy, our commerce has been left to British bottoms, and almost has the American flag been swept off the high seas.

Instead of the Republican party's British policy, we demand for the people of the United States an American policy.

Under Democratic rule and policy our merchants and sailors, flying the stars and stripes in every port, successfully searched out a market for the varied products of American industry.

Under a quarter of a century of Republican rule and policy, despite our manifest advantage of all other nations in high-paid labor, favorable climate and teeming soils; despite freedom of trade among all these United States; despite their population by the foremost races of men and an annual immigration of the young, thrifty and adventurous of all nations; despite our freedom here from the inherited burdens of life and industry in the old-world monarchies—their costly war navies, their vast tax-consuming, non-producing standing armies; despite twenty years of peace—that Republican rule and policy have managed to surrender to Great Britain, along with our commerce, the control of the markets of the world.

Instead of the Republican party's British policy, we demand on behalf of the American Democracy, an American policy.

Instead of the Republican party's discredited scheme and false pretense of friendship for American labor, expressed by imposing taxes, we demand in behalf of the Democracy, freedom for American labor by reducing taxes, to the end that these United States may compete with unhindered powers for the primacy among nations in all the arts of peace and fruits of liberty.

With profound regret we have been apprised by the venerable statesman through whose person was struck that blow at the vital principle of republics (acquiescence in the will of the majority), that he cannot permit us again to place in his hands the leadership of the Democratic hosts, for the reason that the achievement of reform in the administration of the Federal Government is an undertaking now too heavy for his age and failing strength.

Rejoicing that his life has been prolonged until the general judgment of our fellow-countrymen is united in the wish that that wrong were righted in his person, for the Democracy of the United States we offer to him in his withdrawal from public cares not only our respectful sympathy and esteem, but also that best homage of freemen, the pledge of our devotion to the principles and the cause now inseparable in the history of this Republic from the labors and the name of Samuel J. Tilden.

With this statement of the hopes, principles and purposes of the Democratic party, the great issue of Reform and change in Administration is submitted to the people in calm confidence that the popular voice will pronounce in favor of new men, and new and more favorable conditions for the growth of industry, the extension of trade, the employment and the due reward of labor and of capital, and the general welfare of the whole country.

Greenback National Platform of 1884

Eight years ago our young party met in this city for the first time, and proclaimed to the world its immortal principles, and placed before the American people as a presidential candidate that great philanthropist and spotless statesman, Peter Cooper. Since that convention our party has organized all over the Union, and through discussion and agitation has been educating the people to a sense of their rights and duties to themselves and their country. These labors have accomplished wonders. We now have a great, harmonious party, and thousands who believe in our principles in the ranks of other parties.

"We point with pride to our history." We forced the remonetization of the silver dollar; prevented the refunding of the public debt into long-time bonds; secured the payment of the bonds, until the "best banking system the world ever saw" for robbing the producer now totters because of its contracting foundation; we have stopped the squandering of our public domain upon corporations; we have stopped the wholesale destruction of the greenback currency, and secured a decision of the Supreme Court of the United States establishing forever the right of the people to issue their own money.

Notwithstanding all this, never in our history have the banks, land-grant railroads, and other monopolies, been more insolent in their demands for further privileges—still more class legislation.

In this emergency the dominant parties are arrayed against the people, and are the abject tools of the corporate monopolies.

In the last Congress they repealed over $12,-000,000 of annual taxes for the banks, throwing the burden upon the people to pay or pay interest thereon.

Both old parties in the present Congress vie with each other in their efforts to further repeal taxes in order to stop the payment of the public debt, and save the banks whose charters they have renewed for twenty years. Notwithstanding the distress of business, the shrinkage of wages and panic, they persist in locking up, on various pretexts, $400,000,000 of money, every dollar of which the people pay interest upon, and need, and most of which should be promptly applied to pay bonds now payable.

The old parties are united—as they cannot agree what taxes to repeal—in efforts to squander the income of the Government upon every pretext rather than pay the debt.

A bill has already passed the United States Senate making the banks a present of over $50,-000,000 more of the people's money in order to enable them to levy a still greater burden of interest-taxes.

A joint effort is being made by the old party leaders to overthrow the sovereign constitutional power of the people to control their own financial affairs and issue their own money, in order to forever enslave the masses to bankers and other business. The House of Representatives has passed bills reclaiming nearly 100,000,000 acres of lands granted to and forfeited by railroad companies. These bills have gone to the Senate, a body composed largely of aristocratic millionaires, who, according to their own party papers, generally purchased their elections in order to protect great monopolies which they represent. This body has thus far defied the people and the House, and refused to act upon these bills in the interest of the people.

Therefore, we, the National party of the United States, in national convention assembled, this 29th day of May A. D. 1884, declare:

1. That we hold the late decision of the Supreme Court on the legal-tender question to be a full vindication of the theory which our party has always advocated on the right and authority of Congress over the issue of legal-tender notes, and we hereby pledge ourselves to uphold said decision, and to defend the Constitution against alterations or amendments intended to deprive the people of any rights or privileges conferred by that instrument. We demand the issue of such money in sufficient quantities to supply the actual demand of trade and commerce, in accordance with the increase of population and the development of our industries. We demand the substitution of greenbacks for national bank notes and the prompt payment of the public debt. We want that money which saved our country in time of war and which has given it prosperity and happiness in peace. We condemn the retirement of the fractional currency and the small denominations of greenbacks, and demand their restoration. We demand the issue of the hoards of money now locked up in the United States Treasury, by applying them to the payment of the public debt now due.

2. We denounce, as dangerous to our republican institutions, those methods and policies of the Democratic and Republican parties which have sanctioned or permitted the establishment of land, railroad, money and other gigantic corporate monopolies; and we demand such governmental action as may be necessary to take from such monopolies the powers they have so corruptly and unjustly usurped, and restore them to the people, to whom they belong.

3. The public lands, being the natural inheritance of the people, we denounce that policy which has granted to corporations vast tracts of land, and we demand that immediate and vigorous measures be taken to reclaim from such corporations, for the people's use and benefit, all such land grants as have been forfeited by reason of non-fulfillment of contract, or that may have been wrongfully acquired by corrupt legislation, and that such reclaimed lands and other public domain be henceforth held as a sacred trust, to be granted only to actual settlers in limited quantities; and we also demand that the alien ownership of land, individual or corporate, shall be prohibited.

4. We demand Congressional regulation of inter-State commerce. We denounce "pooling," stock watering and discrimination in rates and charges, and demand that Congress shall correct these abuses, even, if necessary, by the construction of national railroads. We also demand the

establishment of a government postal telegraph system.

5. All private property, all forms of money and obligations to pay money, should bear their just proportion of the public taxes. We demand a graduated income tax.

6. We demand the amelioration of the condition of labor by enforcing the sanitary laws in industrial establishments, by the abolition of the convict labor system, by a rigid inspection of mines and factories, by a reduction of the hours of labor in industrial establishments, by fostering educational institutions, and by abolishing child labor.

7. We condemn all importations of contract labor, made with a view of reducing to starvation wages the workingmen of this country, and demand laws for its prevention.

8. We insist upon a constitutional amendment reducing the terms of United States Senators.

9. We demand such rules for the government of Congress as shall place all Representatives of the people upon an equal footing, and take away from committees a veto power greater than that of the President.

10. The question as to the amount of duties to be levied upon various articles of import has been agitated and quarreled over and has divided communities for nearly a hundred years. It is not now and never will be settled unless by the abolition of indirect taxation. It is a convenient issue—always raised when the people are excited over abuses in their midst. While we favor a wise revision of the tariff laws, with a view to raising a revenue from luxuries rather than necessaries, we insist that as an economic question its importance is insignificant as compared with financial issues; for whereas we have suffered our worst panics under low and also under high tariff, we have never suffered from a panic nor seen our factories and workshops closed while the volume of money in circulation was adequate to the needs of commerce. Give our farmers and manufacturers money as cheap as you now give it to our bankers, and they can pay high wages to labor, and compete with all the world.

11. For the purpose of testing the sense of the people upon the subject, we are in favor of submitting to a vote of the people an amendment to the Constitution in favor of suffrage regardless of sex, and also on the subject of the liquor traffic.

12. All disabled soldiers of the late war should be equitably pensioned, and we denounce the policy of keeping a small army of office-holders whose only business is to prevent, on technical grounds, deserving soldiers from obtaining justice from the government they helped to save.

13. As our name indicates, we are a National party, knowing no East, no West, no North, no South. Having no sectional prejudices, we can properly place in nomination for the high offices of State as candidates, men from any section of the Union.

14. We appeal to all people who believe in our principles to aid us by voice, pen and votes.

Prohibition Platform of 1884

1. The Prohibition party, in National Convention assembled, acknowledge Almighty God as the rightful sovereign of all men, from whom the just powers of government are derived and to whose laws human enactments should conform as an absolute condition of peace, prosperity and happiness.

2. That the importation, manufacture, supply and sale of alcoholic beverages, created and maintained by the laws of the National and State Governments during the entire history of such laws, are everywhere shown to be the promoting cause of intemperance, with resulting crime and pauperism, making large demands upon public and private charity; imposing large and unjust taxation for the support of penal and sheltering institutions, upon thrift, industry, manufactures and commerce; endangering the public peace; desecrating the Sabbath; corrupting our politics, legislation and administration of the laws; shortening lives, impairing health and diminishing productive industry; causing education to be neglected and despised; nullifying the teachings of the Bible, the church and the school, the standards and guides of our fathers and their children in the founding and growth of our widely-extended country; and which, imperilling the perpetuity of our civil and religious liberties, are baleful fruits by which we know that these laws are contrary to God's laws and contravene our happiness. We therefore call upon our fellow-citizens to aid in the repeal of these laws and in the legal suppression of this baneful liquor traffic.

3. During the 24 years in which the Republican party has controlled the general Government and many of the States, no effort has been made to change this policy. Territories have been created, Governments for them established, States admitted to the Union, and in no instance in either case has this traffic been forbidden or the people been permitted to prohibit it. That there are now over 200,000 distilleries, breweries, wholesale and retail dealers in their products, holding certificates and claiming the authority of Government for the continuation of the business so destructive to the moral and material welfare of the people, together with the fact that they have turned a deaf ear to remonstrance and petition for the correction of this abuse of civil government, is conclusive that the Republican party is insensible to or impotent for the redress of these wrongs, and should no longer be entrusted with the powers and responsibilities of Government. Although this party in its late National Convention was silent on the liquor question, not so its candidates, Messrs. Blaine and Logan. Within the year past Mr. Blaine has recommended that the revenue derived from the liquor traffic be distributed among the States; and Senator Logan has, by bill, proposed to devote these revenues to the support of the public schools. Thus both virtually recommend the perpetuation of the traffic, and that the States and their citizens become partners in the liquor crime.

4. That the Democratic party has in its national deliverances of party policy arrayed itself on the side of the drink-makers and sellers by declaring against the policy of Prohibition under the false name of "sumptuary laws"; that when in power in many of the States it has refused remedial legislation, and that in Congress it has obstructed the creation of a Commission of Inquiry into the effects of this traffic, proving that it should not be entrusted with power and place.

5. That there can be no greater peril to the nation than the existing competition of the Republican and Democratic parties for the liquor vote. Experience shows that any party not openly opposed to the traffic will engage in this competition, will court the favor of the criminal classes, will barter the public morals, the purity of the ballot and every trust and object of good government for party success. Patriots and good citizens should therefore, immediately withdraw from all connection with these parties.

6. That we favor reforms in the abolition of all sinecures with useless offices and officers, and in elections by the people instead of appointments by the President; that as competency, honesty and sobriety are essential qualifications for office, we oppose removals except when absolutely necessary to secure effectiveness in vital issues; that the collection of revenues from alcoholic liquors and tobacco should be abolished, since the vices of men are not proper subjects of taxation; that revenue from customs duties should be levied for the support of the Government economically administered, and in such manner as will foster American industries and labor; that the public lands should be held for homes for the people, and not bestowed as gifts to corporations, or sold in large tracts for speculation upon the needs of actual settlers; that grateful care and support should be given to our soldiers and sailors disabled in the service of their country, and to their dependent widows and orphans; that we repudiate as un-American and contrary to and subversive to the principles of the Declaration of Independence, that any person or people should be excluded from residence or citizenship who may desire the benefits which our institutions confer upon the oppressed of all nations; that while these are important reforms, and are demanded for purity of administration and the welfare of the people, their importance sinks into insignificance when compared with the drink traffic, which now annually wastes $800,000,000 of the wealth created by toil and thrift, dragging down thousands of families from comfort to poverty, filling jails, penitentiaries, insane asylums, hospitals and institutions for dependency, impairing the health and destroying the lives of thousands, lowering intellectual vigor and dulling the cunning hand of the artisan, causing bankruptcy, insolvency and loss in trade, and by its corrupting power endangering the perpetuity of free institutions; that Congress should exercise its undoubted power by prohibiting the manufacture and sale of intoxicating beverages in the District of Columbia, the Territories of the United States and all places over which the Government has exclusive jurisdiction; that hereafter no State should be admitted to the Union until its Constitution shall expressly and forever prohibit polygamy and the manufacture and sale of intoxicating beverages, and that Congress shall submit to

the States an Amendment to the Constitution forever prohibiting the importation, exportation, manufacture and sale of alcoholic drinks.

7. We earnestly call the attention of the mechanic, the miner and manufacturer to the investigation of the baneful effects upon labor and industry of the needless liquor business. It will be found the robber who lessens wages and profits, foments discontent and strikes, and the destroyer of family welfare. Labor and all legitimate industries demand deliverance from the taxation and loss which this traffic imposes; and no tariff or other legislation can so healthily stimulate production, or increase the demand for capital and labor, or insure so much of comfort and content to the laborer, mechanic and capitalist as would the suppression of this traffic.

8. That the activity and co-operation of the women of America for the promotion of temperance has in all the history of the past been a strength and encouragement which we gratefully acknowledge and record. In the later and present phase of the movement for the Prohibition of the traffic, the purity of purpose and method, the earnestness, zeal, intelligence and devotion of the mothers and daughters of the Woman's Christian Temperance Union have been eminently blessed of God. Kansas and Iowa have been given them as "sheaves" of rejoicing, and the education and arousing of the public mind, and the now prevailing demand for the Constitutional Amendment, are largely the fruit of their prayers and labors. Sharing in the efforts that shall bring the question of the abolition of this traffic to the polls, they shall join in the grand "Praise God, from whom all blessings flow," when by law victory shall be achieved.

9. That, believing in the civil and the political equality of the sexes, and that the ballot in the hands of woman is her right for protection and would prove a powerful ally for the abolition of the liquor traffic, the execution of the law, the promotion of reform in civil affairs, the removal of corruption in public life, we enunciate the principle and relegate the practical outworking of this reform to the discretion of the Prohibition party in the several States according to the condition of public sentiment in those States.

10. That we gratefully acknowledge the presence of the divine spirit guiding the counsels and granting the success which has been vouchsafed

in the progress of the temperance reform; and we earnestly ask the voters of these United States to make the principles of the above declaration dominant in the Government of the nation.

Republican Platform of 1884

The Republicans of the United States in National Convention assembled renew their allegiance to the principles upon which they have triumphed in six successive Presidential elections; and congratulate the American people on the attainment of so many results in legislation and administration, by which the Republican party has, after saving the Union, done so much to render its institutions just, equal and beneficent, the safeguard of liberty and the embodiment of the best thought and highest purpose of our citizens.

The Republican party has gained its strength by quick and faithful response to the demands of the people for the freedom and equality of all men; for a united nation, assuring the rights of all citizens; for the elevation of labor; for an honest currency; for purity in legislation, and for integrity and accountability in all departments of the government, and it accepts anew the duty of leading in the work of progress and reform.

We lament the death of President Garfield, whose sound statesmanship, long conspicuous in Congress, gave promise of a strong and successful administration; a promise fully realized during the short period of his office as President of the United States. His distinguished services in war and peace have endeared him to the hearts of the American people.

In the administration of President Arthur, we recognize a wise, conservative and patriotic policy, under which the country has been blessed with remarkable prosperity; and we believe his eminent services are entitled to and will receive the hearty approval of every citizen.

It is the first duty of a good government to protect the rights and promote the interests of its own people.

The largest diversity of industry is most productive of general prosperity, and of the comfort and independence of the people.

We, therefore, demand that the imposition of duties on foreign imports shall be made, not "for revenue only," but that in raising the requisite revenues for the government, such duties shall be so levied as to afford security to our diversified industries and protection to the rights and wages of the laborer; to the end that active and intelligent labor, as well as capital, may have its just reward, and the laboring man his full share in the national prosperity.

Against the so-called economic system of the Democratic party, which would degrade our labor to the foreign standard, we enter our earnest protest.

The Democratic party has failed completely to relieve the people of the burden of unnecessary taxation by a wise reduction of the surplus.

The Republican party pledges itself to correct the inequalities of the tariff, and to reduce the surplus, not by the vicious and indiscriminate process of horizontal reduction, but by such methods as will relieve the tax-payer without injuring the laborer or the great productive interests of the country.

We recognize the importance of sheep husbandry in the United States, the serious depression which it is now experiencing, and the danger threatening its future prosperity; and we, therefore, respect the demands of the representatives of this important agricultural interest for a readjustment of duties upon foreign wool, in order that such industry shall have full and adequate protection.

We have always recommended the best money known to the civilized world; and we urge that efforts should be made to unite all commercial nations in the establishment of an international standard which shall fix for all the relative value of gold and silver coinage.

The regulation of commerce with foreign nations and between the States, is one of the most important prerogatives of the general government; and the Republican party distinctly announces its purpose to support such legislation as will fully and efficiently carry out the constitutional power of Congress over inter-State commerce.

The principle of public regulation of railway corporations is a wise and salutary one for the protection of all classes of the people; and we favor legislation that shall prevent unjust discrimination and excessive charges for transportation, and that shall secure to the people, and the railways alike, the fair and equal protection of the laws.

We favor the establishment of a national bureau of labor; the enforcement of the eight hour law, a wise and judicious system of general education by adequate appropriation from the national revenues, wherever the same is needed. We believe that everywhere the protection to a citizen of American birth must be secured to citizens by American adoption; and we favor the settlement of national differences by international arbitration.

The Republican party, having its birth in a hatred of slave labor and a desire that all men may be truly free and equal, is unalterably opposed to placing our workingmen in competition with any form of servile labor, whether at home or abroad. In this spirit, we denounce the importation of contract labor, whether from Europe or Asia, as an offense against the spirit of American institutions; and we pledge ourselves to sustain the present law restricting Chinese immigration, and to provide such further legislation as is necessary to carry out its purposes.

Reform of the civil service, auspiciously begun under Republican administration, should be completed by the further extension of the reform system already established by law, to all the grades of the service to which it is applicable. The spirit and purpose of the reform should be observed in all executive appointments; and all laws at variance with the objects of existing reform legislation should be repealed, to the end that the dangers to free institutions, which lurk in the power of official patronage, may be wisely and effectively avoided.

The public lands are a heritage of the people of the United States, and should be reserved as far as possible for small holdings by actual settlers. We are opposed to the acquisition of large tracts of these lands by corporations or individuals, especially where such holdings are in the hands of non-resident or aliens. And we will endeavor to obtain such legislation as will tend to correct this evil. We demand of Congress the speedy forfeiture of all land grants which have lapsed by reason of non-compliance with acts of incorporation, in all cases where there has been no attempt in good faith to perform the conditions of such grants.

The grateful thanks of the American people are due to the Union soldiers and sailors of the late war; and the Republican party stands pledged to suitable pensions for all who were disabled, and for the widows and orphans of those who died in the war. The Republican party also pledges itself to the repeal of the limitations contained in the arrears act of 1879. So that all invalid soldiers shall share alike, and their pensions begin with the date of disability or discharge, and not with the date of application.

The Republican party favors a policy which shall keep us from entangling alliances with foreign nations, and which gives us the right to expect that foreign nations shall refrain from meddling in American affairs; a policy which seeks peace and trade with all powers, but especially with those of the Western Hemisphere.

We demand the restoration of our navy to its old-time strength and efficiency, that it may in any sea protect the rights of American citizens and the interests of American commerce; and we call upon Congress to remove the burdens under which American shipping has been depressed, so that it may again be true that we have a commerce which leaves no sea unexplored, and a navy which takes no law from superior force.

Resolved, That appointments by the President to offices in the Territories should be made from the *bona-fide* citizens and residents of the Territories wherein they are to serve.

Resolved, That it is the duty of Congress to enact such laws as shall promptly and effectually suppress the system of polygamy within our Territories; and divorce the political from the ecclesiastical power of the so-called Mormon church; and that the laws so enacted should be rigidly enforced by the civil authorities, if possible, and by the military, if need be.

The people of the United States, in their organized capacity, constitute a Nation and not a mere confederacy of States; the National Government is supreme within the sphere of its national duties; but the States have reserved rights which should be faithfully maintained. Each should be guarded with jealous care, so that the harmony of our system of government may be preserved and the Union kept inviolate.

The perpetuity of our institutions rests upon the maintenance of a free ballot, an honest count, and correct returns. We denounce the fraud and violence practised by the Democracy in Southern States, by which the will of a voter is defeated, as dangerous to the preservation of free institutions; and we solemnly arraign the Democratic party as being the guilty recipient of fruits of such fraud and violence.

We extend to the Republicans of the South, regardless of their former party affiliations, our cordial sympathy; and we pledge to them our most earnest efforts to promote the passage of such legislation as will secure to every citizen, of whatever race and color, the full and complete recognition, possession and exercise of all civil and political rights.

☒ CAMPAIGN OF 1888

In 1888 in addition to the two major parties and the Prohibitionists three new groups appear. The American Party issued a platform that is suggestive of the Know-Nothing Party of 1856. And two new labor groups appear. There was the Union Labor Party, and a much smaller group, which may be considered a rival faction, known as the United Labor Party.

American Platform of 1888

Believing that the time has arrived when a due regard for the present and future prosperity of our country makes it imperative that the people of the United States of America should take full and entire control of their government, to the exclusion of revolutionary and incendiary foreigners, now seeking our shores from every quarter of the globe, and recognizing that the first and most important duty of an American citizen is to maintain the Government in all attainable purity and strength, we make the following declaration of principles:

Resolved, That all law-abiding citizens of the United States of America, whether native or foreign born, are political equals (except as provided by the Constitution), and all are entitled to and should receive the full protection of the laws.

Whereas, There are seventeen states in this Union wherein persons are allowed to vote at all elections without being citizens of the United States; and,

Whereas, Such a system tends to place the management of the Government in the hands of those who owe no allegiance to our political institutions; therefore,

Resolved, That the Constitution of the United States should be so amended as to prohibit the Federal and State governments from conferring upon any person the right to vote unless such person be a citizen of the United States.

Resolved, That we are in favor of fostering and encouraging American industries of every class and kind, and declare that the assumed issue "Protection" *vs.* "Free Trade" is a fraud and a snare. The best "protection" is that which protects the labor and life blood of the republic from the degrading competition with and contaminations by imported foreigners; and the most dangerous "free trade" is that in paupers, criminals, communists, and anarchists, in which the balance has always been against the United States.

Whereas, One of the greatest evils of unrestricted foreign immigration is the reduction of the wages of the American workingman and workingwoman to the level of the underfed and underpaid labor of foreign countries: therefore,

Resolved, That we demand that no immigrant shall be admitted into the United States without a passport obtained from the American Consul at the port from which he sails; that no passport shall be issued to any pauper, criminal, or insane person, or to any person who, in the judgment of the consul, is not likely to become a desirable citizen of the United States; and that for each immigrant passport there shall be collected by the Consul issuing the same the sum of one hundred dollars ($100), to be by him paid into the Treasury of the United States.

Resolved, That the present naturalization laws of the United States should be unconditionally repealed.

Resolved, That the soil of America should belong to Americans; That no alien non-resident should be permitted to own real estate in the United States, and that the realty possessions of the resident alien should be limited in value and area.

Resolved, That we favor educating the boys and girls of American citizens as mechanics and artisans, thus fitting them for the places now filled by foreigners, who supply the greater part of our skilled labor, and thereby almost entirely control the great industries of our country, save, perhaps, that of agriculture alone; and that our boys and girls may be taught trades, we demand the establishment and maintenance of free technical schools.

Resolved, That universal education is a necessity of our Government, and that our American free school system should be preserved and maintained as the safeguard of American liberty.

Resolved, That no language except the English shall be taught in the common schools supported at the public expense.

Whereas, an unemployed population is the greatest evil that can befall any nation, and in this country it cannot be eliminated by European methods, such as extra police and standing armies, therefore,

Resolved, That the surplus in the Treasury should be devoted to the material improvement of our coast and frontier defences, and the construction of an American navy in American workshops, by American labor.

Resolved, That we demand the enactment of a law which shall require all persons having charge in any way of any department, bureau, or division of the Government to forthwith dismiss from the public service all persons employed in or about any such department, bureau, or division in any way or manner who are not citizens of the United States; that no person shall be appointed to or hold office or place in the service of the United

States who is not a citizen of the United States either by nativity or by full naturalization, according to law.

Resolved, That after the year 1898 it shall be required of every voter before he exercises the right of suffrage to be able to read the written or printed Constitution of the United States, in the English language, and to write his own name upon the register, to show that he is fitted to share in the administration of the government of the republic.

Resolved, That we recognize the right of labor to organize for its protection, by all lawful and peaceful means to secure to itself the greatest reward for its thrift and industry; and we believe in governmental arbitration in the settlement of industrial differences.

Resolved, That we are in favor of such legislation by Congress as will re-establish the American marine.

Resolved, That no flag shall float on any public buildings, municipal, State, or National, in the United States, except the Municipal, State, or National flag of the United States—the flag of the Stars and Stripes.

Resolved, That we reassert the American principles of absolute freedom of religious worship and belief, the permanent separation of Church and State; and we oppose the appropriation of public money or property to any church or institution administered by a church.

We maintain that all church property should be subject to taxation.

Resolved, That the Presidential term shall be extended to six years, and the President shall be ineligible to re-election.

Resolved, That the American Party declares that it recognizes no North, no South, no East, no West in these United States, but one people, pledged to the general welfare and to liberty and independence.

Democratic Platform of 1888

The Democratic party of the United States, in National Convention assembled, renews the pledge of its fidelity to Democratic faith and reaffirms the platform adopted by its representatives in the Convention of 1884, and indorses the views expressed by President Cleveland in his last annual message to Congress as the correct interpretation of that platform upon the question of Tariff reduction; and also indorses the efforts of our Democratic Representatives in Congress to secure a reduction of excessive taxation.

Chief among its principles of party faith are the maintenance of an indissoluble Union of free and indestructible States, now about to enter upon its second century of unexampled progress and renown; devotion to a plan of government regulated by a written Constitution, strictly specifying every granted power and expressly reserving to the States or people the entire ungranted residue of power; the encouragement of a jealous popular vigilance directed to all who have been chosen for brief terms to enact and execute the laws, and are charged with the duty of preserving peace, insuring equality and establishing justice.

The Democratic party welcomes an exacting scrutiny of the administration of the Executive power which four years ago was committed to its trust in the selection of Grover Cleveland as President of the United States; and it challenges the most searching inquiry concerning its fidelity and devotion to the pledges which then invited the suffrages of the people.

During a most critical period of our financial affairs, resulting from over taxation, the anomalous condition of our currency, and a public debt unmatured, it has by the adoption of a wise and conservative course, not only averted disaster, but greatly promoted the prosperity of the people.

It has reversed the improvident and unwise policy of the Republican party touching the public domain, and has reclaimed from corporations and syndicates, alien and domestic, and restored to the people, nearly one hundred millions of acres of valuable land to be sacredly held as homesteads for our citizens.

While carefully guarding the interests of the taxpayers and conforming strictly to the principles of justice and equity, it has paid out more for pensions and bounties to the soldiers and sailors of the Republic than was ever paid before during an equal period.

By intelligent management and a judicious and economical expenditure of the public money it has set on foot the reconstruction of the American Navy upon a system which forbids the recurrence of scandal and insures successful results.

It has adopted and consistently pursued a firm and prudent foreign policy, preserving peace with all nations while scrupulously maintaining all the rights and interests of our Government and people at home and abroad.

The exclusion from our shores of Chinese laborers has been effectually secured under the provisions of a treaty, the operation of which has been postponed by the action of a Republican majority in the Senate.

Honest reform in the Civil Service has been inaugurated and maintained by President Cleveland, and he has brought the public service to the highest standard of efficiency, not only by rule and precept, but by the example of his own untiring and unselfish administration of public affairs.

In every branch and department of the Government under Democratic control, the rights and welfare of all the people have been guarded and defended; every public interest has been protected, and the equality of all our citizens before the law, without regard to race or section, has been steadfastly maintained.

Upon its record, thus exhibited, and upon the pledge of a continuance to the people of these benefits of good government, the National Democracy invokes a renewal of popular trust by the re-election of a Chief Magistrate who has been faithful, able and prudent.

They invoke in addition to that trust, the transfer also to the Democracy of the entire legislative power.

The Republican party, controlling the Senate and resisting in both Houses of Congress a reformation of unjust and unequal tax laws, which have outlasted the necessities of war and are now undermining the abundance of a long peace, deny to the people equality before the law and the fairness and the justice which are their right.

Thus the cry of American labor for a better share in the rewards of industry is stifled with false pretenses, enterprise is fettered and bound down to home markets; capital is discouraged with doubt, and unequal, unjust laws can neither be properly amended nor repealed.

The Democratic party will continue, with all the power confided to it, the struggle to reform these laws in accordance with the pledges of its last platform indorsed at the ballot-box by the suffrages of the people.

Of all the industrious freemen of our land, an immense majority, including every tiller of the soil, gain no advantage from excessive tax laws; but the price of nearly everything they buy is increased by the favoritism of an unequal system of tax legislation.

All unnecessary taxation is unjust taxation.

It is repugnant to the creed of Democracy, that by such taxation the costs of the necessaries of life should be unjustifiably increased to all our people.

Judged by Democratic principles, the interests of the people are betrayed, when, by unnecessary taxation, trusts and combinations are permitted and fostered, which, while unduly enriching the few that combine, rob the body of our citizens by depriving them of the benefits of natural competition. Every Democratic rule of governmental action is violated when through unnecessary taxation a vast sum of money, far beyond the needs of an economical administration, is drawn from the people and the channels of trade, and accumulated as a demoralizing surplus in the National Treasury.

The money now lying idle in the Federal Treasury, resulting from superfluous taxation amounts to more than $125,000,000, and the surplus collected is reaching the sum of more than $60,000,000 annually.

Debauched by this immense temptation the remedy of the Republican party is to meet and exhaust by extravagant appropriations and expenses, whether constitutional or not, the accumulation of extravagant taxation.

The Democratic remedy is to enforce frugality in public expense and abolish needless taxation.

Our established domestic industries and enterprises should not, and need not, be endangered by a reduction and correction of the burdens of taxation. On the contrary, a fair and careful revision of our tax laws, with due allowance for the difference between the wages of American and foreign labor, must promote and encourage every branch of such industries and enterprises by giving them assurance of an extended market and steady and continuous operations.

In the interest of American labor, which should in no event be neglected, the revision of our tax laws contemplated by the Democratic party would promote the advantage of such labor by cheapening the cost of necessaries of life in the home of every workingman and at the same time securing to him steady and remunerative employment.

Upon this great issue of tariff reform, so closely concerning every phase of our national life, and upon every question involved in the problem of good government, the Democratic party submits its principles and professions to the intelligent suffrages of the American people.

Resolution Presented by Mr. Scott, of Pennsylvania:

Resolved, That this convention hereby indorses and recommends the early passage of the bill for the reduction of the revenue now pending in the House of Representatives.

Resolution Presented by Mr. Lehmann, of Iowa:

Resolved, That a just and liberal policy should be pursued in reference to the Territories; that the right of self-government is inherent in the people and guaranteed under the Constitution; that the Territories of Washington, Dakota, Montana and New Mexico are, by virtue of population and development, entitled to admission into the Union as States, and we unqualifiedly condemn the course of the Republican party in refusing Statehood and self-government to their people.

Resolution Presented by ex-Governor Leon Abbett, of New Jersey:

Resolved, That we express our cordial sympathy with the struggling people of all nations in their effort to secure for themselves the inestimable blessings of self-government and civil and religious liberty. And we especially declare our sympathy with the efforts of those noble patriots who, led by Gladstone and Parnell, have conducted their grand and peaceful contest for home rule in Ireland.

Prohibition Platform of 1888

The Prohibition party, in National Convention assembled, acknowledging Almighty God as the source of all power in government, do hereby declare:

1. That the manufacture, importation, exportation, transportation and sale of alcoholic beverages should be made public crimes, and prohibited as such.

2. That such Prohibition must be secured through Amendments to our National and State

Constitutions, enforced by adequate laws adequately supported by administrative authority; and to this end the organization of the Prohibition party is imperatively demanded in State and Nation.

3. That any form of license, taxation or regulation of the liquor traffic is contrary to good government; that any party which supports regulation, license or taxation enters into alliance with such traffic and becomes the actual foe of the State's welfare, and that we arraign the Republican and Democratic parties for their persistent attitude in favor of the license iniquity, whereby they oppose the demand of the people for Prohibition, and, through open complicity with the liquor crime, defeat the enforcement of law.

4. For the immediate abolition of the Internal Revenue system, whereby our National Government is deriving support from our greatest national vice.

5. That an adequate public revenue being necessary, it may properly be raised by import duties; but import duties should be so reduced that no surplus shall be accumulated in the Treasury, and that the burdens of taxation shall be removed from foods, clothing and other comforts and necessaries of life, and imposed on such articles of import as will give protection both to the manufacturing employer and producing laborer against the competition of the world.

6. That the right of suffrage rests on no mere circumstances of race, color, sex or nationality, and that where, from any cause, it has been withheld from citizens who are of suitable age, and mentally and morally qualified for the exercise of an intelligent ballot, it should be restored by the people through the Legislatures of the several States, on such educational basis as they may deem wise.

7. That civil service appointments for all civil offices, chiefly clerical in their duties, should be based upon moral, intellectual and physical qualifications, and not upon party service or party necessity.

8. For the abolition of polygamy and the establishment of uniform laws governing marriage and divorce.

9. For prohibiting all combinations of capital to control and to increase the cost of products for popular consumption.

10. For the preservation and defense of the Sabbath as a civil institution, without oppressing any who religiously observe the same on any other than the first day of the week.

11. That arbitration is the Christian, wise and economical method of settling national differences, and the same method should, by judicious legislation, be applied to the settlement of disputes between large bodies of employes and their employers; that the abolition of the saloon would remove the burdens, moral, physical, pecuniary and social, which now oppress labor and rob it of its earnings, and would prove to be a wise and successful way of promoting labor reform, and we invite labor and capital to unite with us for the accomplishment thereof; that monopoly in land is a wrong to the people, and the public lands should be reserved to the actual settlers; and that men and women should receive equal wages for equal work.

12. That our immigration laws should be so enforced as to prevent the introduction into our country of all convicts, inmates of other dependent institutions, and others physically incapacitated for self-support, and that no person should have the ballot in any State who is not a citizen of the United States.

13. Recognizing and declaring that Prohibition of the liquor traffic has become the dominant issue in national politics, we invite to full party fellowship all those who, on this one dominant issue, are with us agreed, in the full belief that this party can and will remove sectional differences, promote national unity, and insure the best welfare of our entire land.

Resolved, That we hold that men are born free and equal, and should be made secure in all their civil and political rights.

Resolved, That we condemn the Democratic and Republican parties for persistently denying the right of self-government to the 600,000 people of Dakota.

Republican Platform of 1888

The Republicans of the United States assembled by their delegates in National Convention, pause on the threshold of their proceedings to honor the memory of their first great leader—the immortal champion of liberty and the rights of the people—Abraham Lincoln; and to cover also with wreaths of imperishable remembrance and gratitude the heroic names of our later leaders who have been more recently called away from our councils—Grant, Garfield, Arthur, Logan, Conkling. May their memories be faithfully cherished!

We also recall with our greetings, and with prayer for his recovery, the name of one of our living heroes, whose memory will be treasured in the history of both Republicans and of the Republic—the name of that noble soldier and favorite child of victory, Philip H. Sheridan. In the spirit of those great leaders and of our own devotion to human liberty, and with that hostility to all forms of despotism and oppression which is the fundamental idea of the Republican party, we send fraternal congratulations to our fellow Americans of Brazil upon their great act of emancipation, which completed the abolition of slavery throughout the two American continents. We earnestly hope that we may soon congratulate our fellow-citizens of Irish birth upon the peaceful recovery of home rule for Ireland.

We reaffirm our unswerving devotion to the National Constitution and the indissoluble Union of the States; to the autonomy reserved to the States under the Constitution; to the personal rights and liberties of citizens in all the States and Territories of the Union, and especially to the supreme and sovereign right of every lawful citizen, rich or poor, native or foreign born, white or black, to cast one free ballot in public elections, and to have that ballot duly counted. We hold the free and honest popular ballot and the just and equal representation of all the people to be the foundation of our Republican government and demand effective legislation to secure the integrity and purity of elections, which are the fountains of all public authority. We charge that the present Administration and the Democratic majority in Congress owe their existence to the suppression of the ballot by a criminal nullification of the Constitution and laws of the United States.

We are uncompromisingly in favor of the American system of protection; we protest against its destruction as proposed by the President and his party. They serve the interests of Europe; we will support the interests of America. We accept the issue, and confidently appeal to the people for their judgment. The protective system must be maintained. Its abandonment has always been followed by general disaster to all interests, except those of the usurer and the sheriff. We denounce the Mills bill as destructive to the general business, the labor and the farming interests of the country, and we heartily indorse the consistent and patriotic action of the Republican Representatives in Congress in opposing its passage.

We condemn the proposition of the Democratic party to place wool on the free list, and we insist that the duties thereon shall be adjusted and maintained so as to furnish full and adequate protection to that industry throughout the United States.

The Republican party would effect all needed reduction of the National revenue by repealing the taxes upon tobacco, which are an annoyance and burden to agriculture, and the tax upon spirits used in the arts, and for mechanical purposes, and by such revision of the tariff laws as will tend to check imports of such articles as are produced by our people, the production of which gives employment to our labor, and releases from import duties those articles of foreign production (except luxuries), the like of which cannot be produced at home. If there shall remain a larger revenue than is requisite for the wants of the government we favor the entire repeal of internal taxes rather than the surrender of any part of our protective system at the joint behests of the whiskey trusts and the agents of foreign manufacturers.

We declare our hostility to the introduction into this country of foreign contract labor and of Chinese labor, alien to our civilization and constitution; and we demand the rigid enforcement of the existing laws against it, and favor such immediate legislation as will exclude such labor from our shores.

We declare our opposition to all combinations of capital organized in trusts or otherwise to control arbitrarily the condition of trade among our citizens; and we recommend to Congress and the State Legislatures in their respective jurisdictions such legislation as will prevent the execution of all schemes to oppress the people by undue charges on their supplies, or by unjust rates for the transportation of their products to market. We approve the legislation by Congress to prevent alike unjust burdens and unfair discriminations between the States.

We reaffirm the policy of appropriating the public lands of the United States to be homesteads for American citizens and settlers—not aliens—which the Republican party established in 1862 against the persistent opposition of the Democrats in Congress, and which has brought our great Western domain into such magnificent development. The restoration of unearned railroad land grants to the public domain for the use of actual settlers, which was begun under the Administration of President Arthur, should be continued. We deny that the Democratic party has ever restored one acre to the people, but declare that by the joint action of the Republicans and Democrats in Congress about 60,000,000 acres of unearned lands originally granted for the construction of railroads have been restored to the public domain, in pursuance of the conditions inserted by the Republican party in the original grants. We charge the Democratic Administration with failure to execute the laws securing to settlers the title to their homesteads, and with using appropriations made for that purpose to harass innocent settlers with spies and prosecutions under the false pretense of exposing frauds and vindicating the law.

The government by Congress of the Territories is based upon necessity only to the end that they may become States in the Union; therefore, whenever the conditions of population, material resources, public intelligence and morality are such as to insure a stable local government therein, the people of such Territories should be permitted as a right inherent in them to form for themselves constitutions and State government, and be admitted into the Union. Pending the preparation for Statehood, all officers thereof should be selected from the *bona-fide* residents and citizens of the Territory wherein they are to serve. South Dakota should of right be immediately admitted as a State in the Union under the constitution framed and adopted by her people, and we heartily indorse the action of the Republican Senate in twice passing bills for her admission. The refusal of the Democratic House of Representatives, for partisan purposes, to favorably consider these bills is a willful violation of the sacred American principle of local self-government, and merits the condemnation of all just men. The pending bills in the Senate to enable the people of Washington, North Dakota and Montana Territories to form constitutions and establish State governments, should be passed without unnecessary delay. The Republican party pledges itself to do all in its

power to facilitate the admission of the Territories of New Mexico, Wyoming, Idaho and Arizona to the enjoyment of self-government as States, such of them as are now qualified, as soon as possible, and the others as soon as they may become so.

The political power of the Mormon Church in the Territories as exercised in the past is a menace to free institutions too dangerous to be longer suffered. Therefore we pledge the Republican party to appropriate legislation asserting the sovereignty of the Nation in all Territories where the same is questioned, and in furtherance of that end to place upon the statute books legislation stringent enough to divorce the political from the ecclesiastical power, and thus stamp out the attendant wickedness of polygamy.

The Republican party is in favor of the use of both gold and silver as money, and condemns the policy of the Democratic Administration in its efforts to demonetize silver.

We demand the reduction of letter postage to one cent per ounce.

In a Republic like ours, where the citizen is the sovereign, and the official the servant, where no power is exercised except by the will of the people, it is important that the sovereign—the people—should possess intelligence. The free school is the promoter of that intelligence which is to preserve us a free Nation; therefore, the State or Nation, or both combined, should support free institutions of learning sufficient to afford every child growing up in the land the opportunity of a good common school education.

We earnestly recommend that prompt action be taken by Congress in the enactment of such legislation as will best secure the rehabilitation of our American merchant marine, and we protest against the passage by Congress of a free ship bill as calculated to work injustice to labor by lessening the wages of those engaged in preparing materials as well as those directly employed in our shipyards. We demand appropriations for the early rebuilding of our navy; for the construction of coast fortifications and modern ordnance and other approved modern means of defense for the protection of our defenseless harbors and cities; for the payment of just pensions to our soldiers; for necessary works of National importance in the improvement of harbors and the channels of internal, coastwise, and foreign commerce; for the encouragement of the shipping interests of the Atlantic, Gulf and Pacific States, as well as for the payment of the maturing public debt. This policy will give employment to our labor, activity to our various industries, increase the security of our country, promote trade, open new and direct markets for our produce, and cheapen the cost of transportation. We affirm this to be far better for our country than the Democratic policy of loaning the government's money, without interest, to "pet banks."

The conduct of foreign affairs by the present Administration has been distinguished by its inefficiency and its cowardice. Having withdrawn from the Senate all pending treaties effected by Republican Administrations for the removal of foreign burdens and restrictions upon our commerce, and for its extension into better markets, it has neither effected nor proposed any others in their stead. Professing adherence to the Monroe doctrine it has seen with idle complacency the extension of foreign influence in Central America and of foreign trade everywhere among our neighbors. It has refused to charter, sanction or encourage any American organization for construction of the Nicaragua Canal, a work of vital importance to the maintenance of the Monroe doctrine and of our National influence in Central and South America, and necessary for the development of trade with our Pacific territory, with South America, and with the islands and further coasts of the Pacific Ocean.

We arraign the present Democratic Administration for its weak and unpatriotic treatment of the fisheries question, and its pusillanimous surrender of the essential privileges to which our fishing vessels are entitled in Canadian ports under the treaty of 1818, the reciprocal maritime legislation of 1830, and the comity of nations, and which Canadian fishing vessels receive in the ports of the United States. We condemn the policy of the present Administration and the Democratic majority in Congress toward our fisheries as unfriendly and conspicuously unpatriotic, and as tending to destroy a valuable National industry, and an indispensable resource of defense against a foreign enemy. "The name American applies alike to all citizens of the Republic and imposes upon all alike the same obligation of obedience to the laws. At the same time that citizenship is and must be the panoply and safeguard of him

who wears it, and protect him, whether high or low, rich or poor, in all his civil rights. It should and must afford him protection at home and follow and protect him abroad in whatever land he may be on a lawful errand."

The men who abandoned the Republican party in 1884 and continue to adhere to the Democratic party have deserted not only the cause of honest government, of sound finance, of freedom and purity of the ballot, but especially have deserted the cause of reform in the civil service. We will not fail to keep our pledges because they have broken theirs, or because their candidate has broken his. We therefore repeat our declaration of 1884, to wit: "The reform of the civil service, auspiciously begun under the Republican Administration, should be completed by the further extension of the reform system already established by law, to all the grades of the service to which it is applicable. The spirit and purpose of the reform should be observed in all executive appointments, and all laws at variance with the object of existing reform legislation should be repealed, to the end that the dangers to free institutions which lurk in the power of official patronage may be wisely and effectively avoided."

The gratitude of the Nation to the defenders of the Union cannot be measured by laws. The legislation of Congress should conform to the pledges made by a loyal people and be so enlarged and extended as to provide against the possibility that any man who honorably wore the Federal uniform shall become the inmate of an almshouse, or dependent upon private charity. In the presence of an overflowing treasury it would be a public scandal to do less for those whose valorous service preserved the government. We denounce the hostile spirit shown by President Cleveland in his numerous vetoes of measures for pension relief, and the action of the Democratic House of Representatives in refusing even a consideration of general pension legislation.

In support of the principles herewith enunciated we invite the co-operation of patriotic men of all parties, and especially of all workingmen, whose prosperity is seriously threatened by the free-trade policy of the present Administration.

Resolution Relating to Prohibition

Offered by Mr. Boutelle, of Maine:

The first concern of all good government is the

virtue and sobriety of the people and the purity of their homes. The Republican party cordially sympathizes with all wise and well-directed efforts for the promotion of temperance and morality.

Union Labor Platform of 1888

PREAMBLE

General discontent prevails on the part of the wealth-producer. Farmers are suffering from a poverty which has forced most of them to mortgage their estates, and the prices of products are so low as to offer no relief except through bankruptcy. Laborers are sinking into greater dependence. Strikes are resorted to without bringing relief, because of the inability of employers in many cases to pay living wages, while more and more are driven into the street. Business men find collections almost impossible, and meantime hundreds of millions of idle public money which is needed for relief is locked up in the United States Treasury or placed without interest in favored banks, in grim mockery of distress. Land monopoly flourishes as never before, and more owners of the soil are daily becoming tenants. Great transportation corporations still succeed in extorting their profits on watered stock through unjust charges. The United States Senate has become an open scandal, its membership being purchased by the rich in open defiance of the popular will. Various efforts are made to squander the public money, which are designed to empty the Treasury without paying the public debt. Under these and other alarming conditions, we appeal to the people of our country to come out of old party organizations, whose indifference to the public welfare is responsible for this distress, and aid the Union Labor Party to repeal existing class legislation and relieve the distress of our industries by establishing the following:

PLATFORM

While we believe that the proper solution of the financial distress will greatly relieve those now in danger of losing their homes by mortgage foreclosures, and enable all industrious persons to secure a home as the highest result of civilization, we oppose land monopoly in every form, demand the forfeiture of unearned grants, the limitation of land ownership, and such other legislation as

will stop speculation in lands and holding it unused from those whose necessities require it. We believe the earth was made for the people and not to make an idle aristocracy to subsist through rents upon the toils of the industrious, and that corners in land are as bad as corners in food, and that those who are not residents or citizens should not be allowed to own lands in the United States. A homestead should be exempt to a limited extent from execution or taxation.

The means of communication and transportation shall be owned by the people, as is the United States postal system.

The establishment of a national monetary system in the interest of the producer, instead of the speculator and usurer, by which the circulating medium, in necessary quantity and full legal tender, shall be issued directly to the people without the intervention of banks and loaned to citizens upon land security at a low rate of interest so as to relieve them from the extortion of usury and enable them to control the money supply. Postal savings banks should be established, and while we have free coinage of gold we should have free coinage of silver. We demand the immediate application of all the money in the United States Treasury to the payment of the bonded debt, and condemn the further issue of interest-bearing bonds, either by the National Government or by States, Territories or municipalities.

Arbitration should take the place of strikes and other injurious methods of settling labor disputes. The letting of convict labor to contractors should be prohibited, the contract system be abolished on public works, the hours of labor in industrial establishments be reduced commensurate with the increased production by labor-saving machinery, employees protected from bodily injury, equal pay for equal work for both sexes, and labor, agricultural, and co-operative associations be fostered and encouraged by law. The foundation of a republic is in the intelligence of its citizens, and children who are driven into workshops, mines, and factories are deprived of the education which should be secured to all by proper legislation.

We demand the passage of a service pension bill to every honorably discharged soldier and sailor of the United States.

A graduated income tax is the most equitable system of taxation, placing the burden of government on those who can best afford to pay, instead of laying it on the farmers and producers, and exempting millionaires, bond-holders and corporations.

We demand a constitutional amendment making United States senators elective by a direct vote of the people.

We demand the strict enforcement of laws prohibiting the importation of subjects of foreign countries under contract.

We demand the passage and enforcement of such legislation as will absolutely exclude the Chinese from the United States.

The right to vote is inherent in citizenship irrespective of sex, and is properly within the province of state legislation.

The paramount issues to be solved in the interests of humanity are the abolition of usury, monopoly, and trusts, and we denounce the Democratic and Republican parties for creating and perpetuating these monstrous evils.

United Labor Platform of 1888

We, the delegates of the United Labor Party of the United States, in National Convention assembled, hold that the corruptions of government and the impoverishment of the masses result from neglect of the self-evident truths proclaimed by the founders of this republic, that all men are created equal and are endowed with inalienable rights. We aim at the abolition of the system which compels men to pay their fellow-creatures for the use of the common bounties of nature, and permits monopolizers to deprive labor of natural opportunities for employment.

We see access to farming land denied to labor, except on payment of exorbitant rent or the acceptance of mortgage burdens, and labor, thus forbidden to employ itself, driven into the cities. We see the wage-workers of the cities subjected to this unnatural competition, and forced to pay an exorbitant share of their scanty earnings for cramped and unhealthful lodgings. We see the same intense competition condemning the great majority of business and professional men to a bitter and often unavailing struggle to avoid bankruptcy, and that while the price of all that labor produces ever falls, the price of land ever rises.

We trace these evils to a fundamental wrong—the making of the land on which all must live the exclusive property of but a portion of the community. To this denial of natural rights are due want of employment, low wages, business depressions, that intense competition which makes it so difficult for the majority of men to get a comfortable living, and that wrongful distribution of wealth which is producing the millionaire on one side and the tramp on the other.

To give all men an interest in the land of their country; to enable all to share in the benefits of social growth and improvement; to prevent the shutting out of labor from employment by the monopolization of natural opportunities; to do away with the one-sided competition which cuts down wages to starvation rates; to restore life to business and prevent periodical depressions; to do away with that monstrous injustice which deprives producers of the fruits of their toil, while idlers grow rich; to prevent the conflicts which are arraying class against class, and which are fraught with menacing dangers to society—we propose so to change the existing system of taxation that no one shall be taxed on the wealth he produces, nor any one suffered to appropriate wealth he does not produce by taking to himself the increasing values which the growth of society adds to land.

What we propose is not the disturbing of any man in his holding or title, but, by taxation of land according to its value and not according to its area, to devote to common use and benefit those values which arise not from the exertion of the individual, but from the growth of society, and to abolish all taxes on industry and its products. This increased taxation of land values must, while relieving the working farmer and small homestead owner of the undue burdens now imposed upon them, make it unprofitable to hold land for speculation, and thus throw open abundant opportunities for the employment of labor and the building up of homes.

We would do away with the present unjust and wasteful system of finance, which piles up hundreds of millions of dollars in treasury vaults while we are paying interest on an enormous debt; and we would establish in its stead a monetary system in which a legal-tender circulating medium should be issued by the Government without the intervention of banks.

We wish to abolish the present unjust and wasteful system of ownership of railroads and telegraphs by private corporations—a system which, while failing to supply adequately public needs, impoverishes the farmer, oppresses the manufacturer, hampers the merchant, impedes travel and communication, and builds up enormous fortunes and corrupting monopolies that are becoming more powerful than the Government itself. For this system we would substitute Government ownership and control for the benefit of the whole people instead of private profit.

While declaring the foregoing to be the fundamental principles and aims of the United Labor Party, and while conscious that no reform can give effectual and permanent relief to labor that does not involve the legal recognition of equal rights to natural opportunities, we, nevertheless, as measures of relief from some of the evil effects of ignoring those rights, favor such legislation as may tend to reduce the hours of labor, to prevent the employment of children of tender years, to avoid the competition of convict labor with honest industry, to secure the sanitary inspection of tenements, factories, and mines, and to put an end to the abuse of conspiracy laws.

We desire also to so simplify the procedure of our courts, and diminish the expense of legal proceedings, that the poor may therein be placed on an equality with the rich, and the long delays which now result in scandalous miscarriages of justice may be prevented.

Since the ballot is the only means by which, in our republic the redress of political and social grievances is to be sought, we especially and emphatically declare for the adoption of what is known as the Australian system of voting, in order that the effectual secrecy of the ballot, and the relief of candidates for public office from the heavy expenses now imposed upon them, may prevent bribery and intimidation, do away with practical discriminations in favor of the rich and unscrupulous, and lessen the pernicious influence of money in politics.

We denounce the Democratic and Republican parties as hopelessly and shamelessly corrupt, and, by reason of their affiliation with monopolies, equally unworthy of the suffrages of those who do not live upon public plunder; we therefore require of those who would act with us that they sever all connection with both.

In support of these aims, we solicit the co-operation of all patriotic citizens who, sick of the degradation of politics, desire by constitutional methods to establish justice, to preserve liberty, to extend the spirit of fraternity, and to elevate humanity.

In 1892 there were the two major parties and the Prohibition Party. The two labor parties of 1888 disappeared and in their place appears the Socialist Labor Party.

Another party, known as the People's Party, also appeared. This party is quite generally known as the Populist Party. It grew out of an organization known as the Farmer's Alliance. It is sometimes called the National People's Party, but the word "National" does not appear to be a true part of its name.

Democratic Platform of 1892

The representatives of the Democratic party of the United States, in National Convention assembled, do reaffirm their allegiance to the principles of the party, as formulated by Jefferson and exemplified by the long and illustrious line of his successors in Democratic leadership, from Madison to Cleveland; we believe the public welfare demands that these principles be applied to the conduct of the Federal Government, through the accession to power of the party that advocates them; and we solemnly declare that the need of a return to these fundamental principles of free popular government, based on home rule and individual liberty, was never more urgent than now, when the tendency to centralize all power at the Federal capital has become a menace to the reserved rights of the States that strikes at the very roots of our Government under the Constitution as framed by the fathers of the Republic.

We warn the people of our common country, jealous for the preservation of their free institutions, that the policy of Federal control of elections, to which the Republican party has committed itself, is fraught with the gravest dangers, scarcely less momentous than would result from a revolution practically establishing monarchy on the ruins of the Republic. It strikes at the North as well as at the South, and injures the colored citizen even more than the white; it means a horde of deputy marshals at every polling place, armed with Federal power; returning boards appointed and controlled by Federal authority, the outrage of the electoral rights of the people in the several States, the subjugation of the colored people to the control of the party in power, and the reviving of race antagonisms, now happily abated, of the utmost peril to the safety and happiness of all; a measure deliberately and justly described by a leading Republican Senator as "the most infamous bill that ever crossed the threshold of the Senate." Such a policy, if sanctioned by law, would mean the dominance of a self-perpetuating oligarchy of office-holders, and the party first intrusted with its machinery could be dislodged from power only by an appeal to the reserved right of the people to resist oppression, which is inherent in all self-governing communities. Two years ago this revolutionary policy was emphatically condemned by the people at the polls, but in contempt of that verdict the Republican party has defiantly declared in its latest authoritative utterance that its success in the coming elections will mean the enactment of the Force Bill and the usurpation of despotic control over elections in all the States.

Believing that the preservation of Republican government in the United States is dependent upon the defeat of this policy of legalized force and fraud, we invite the support of all citizens who desire to see the Constitution maintained in its integrity with the laws pursuant thereto, which have given our country a hundred years of unexampled prosperity; and we pledge the Democratic party, if it be intrusted with power, not only to the defeat of the Force Bill, but also to relentless opposition to the Republican policy of profligate expenditure, which, in the short space of two years, has squandered an enormous surplus and emptied an overflowing Treasury, after piling new burdens of taxation upon the already overtaxed labor of the country.

We denounce Republican protection as a fraud, a robbery of the great majority of the American people for the benefit of the few. We declare it to be a fundamental principle of the Democratic party that the Federal Government has no constitutional power to impose and collect tariff duties, except for the purpose of revenue only, and we demand that the collection of such taxes shall be limited to the necessities of the Government when honestly and economically administered.

We denounce the McKinley tariff law enacted by the Fifty-first Congress as the culminating atrocity of class legislation; we indorse the efforts made by the Democrats of the present Congress to modify its most oppressive features in the direction of free raw materials and cheaper manufactured goods that enter into general consumption; and we promise its repeal as one of the beneficent results that will follow the action of the people in intrusting power to the Democratic party. Since the McKinley tariff went into operation there have been ten reductions of the wages of the laboring man to one increase. We deny that there has been any increase of prosperity to the country since that tariff went into operation, and we point to the fullness and distress, the wage reductions and strikes in the iron trade, as the best possible evidence that no such prosperity has resulted from the McKinley Act.

We call the attention of thoughtful Americans to the fact that after thirty years of restrictive taxes against the importation of foreign wealth, in exchange for our agricultural surplus, the homes and farms of the country have become burdened with a real estate mortgage debt of over $2,500,-000,000, exclusive of all other forms of indebtedness; that in one of the chief agricultural States of the West there appears a real estate mortgage debt averaging $165 per capita of the total population, and that similar conditions and tendencies are shown to exist in other agricultural-exporting States. We denounce a policy which fosters no industry so much as it does that of the Sheriff.

Trade interchange, on the basis of reciprocal advantages to the countries participating, is a time-honored doctrine of the Democratic faith, but we denounce the sham reciprocity which juggles with the people's desire for enlarged foreign markets and freer exchanges by pretending to establish closer trade relations for a country whose articles of export are almost exclusively agricultural products with other countries that are also agricultural, while erecting a custom-house barrier of prohibitive tariff taxes against the richest countries of the world, that stand ready to take our entire surplus of products, and to exchange therefor commodities which are necessaries and comforts of life among our own people.

We recognize in the Trusts and Combinations, which are designed to enable capital to secure more than its just share of the joint product of Capital and Labor, a natural consequence of the prohibitive taxes, which prevent the free competition, which is the life of honest trade, but believe their worst evils can be abated by law, and we demand the rigid enforcement of the laws made to prevent and control them, together with such further legislation in restraint of their abuses as experience may show to be necessary.

The Republican party, while professing a policy of reserving the public land for small holdings by actual settlers, has given away the people's heritage, till now a few railroads and non-resident aliens, individual and corporate, possess a larger area than that of all our farms between the two seas. The last Democratic administration reversed the improvident and unwise policy of the Republican party touching the public domain, and reclaimed from corporations and syndicates, alien and domestic, and restored to the people nearly one hundred million (100,000,000) acres of valuable land, to be sacredly held as homesteads for our citizens, and we pledge ourselves to continue this policy until every acre of land so unlawfully held shall be reclaimed and restored to the people.

We denounce the Republican legislation known as the Sherman Act of 1890 as a cowardly makeshift, fraught with possibilities of danger in the future, which should make all of its supporters, as well as its author, anxious for its speedy repeal. We hold to the use of both gold and silver as the standard money of the country, and to the coinage of both gold and silver without discriminating against either metal or charge for mintage, but the dollar unit of coinage of both metals must be of equal intrinsic and exchangeable value, or be adjusted through international agreement or by such safeguards of legislation as shall insure the maintenance of the parity of the two metals and the equal power of every dollar at all times in the markets and in the payment of debts; and we demand that all paper currency shall be kept at par with and redeemable in such coin. We insist upon this policy as especially necessary for the protection of the farmers and laboring classes, the first and most defenseless victims of unstable money and a fluctuating currency.

We recommend that the prohibitory 10 per cent tax on State bank issues be repealed.

Public office is a public trust. We reaffirm the declaration of the Democratic National Convention of 1876 for the reform of the civil service, and we call for the honest enforcement of all laws regulating the same. The nomination of a President, as in the recent Republican Convention, by delegations composed largely of his appointees, holding office at his pleasure, is a scandalous satire upon free popular institutions and a startling illustration of the methods by which a President may gratify his ambition. We denounce a policy under which the Federal office-holders usurp control of party conventions in the States, and we pledge the Democratic party to reform these and all other abuses which threaten individual liberty and local self-government.

The Democratic party is the only party that has ever given the country a foreign policy consistent and vigorous, compelling respect abroad and inspiring confidence at home. While avoiding entangling alliances, it has aimed to cultivate friendly relations with other nations, and especially with our neighbors on the American Continent, whose destiny is closely linked with our own, and we view with alarm the tendency to a policy of irritation and bluster which is liable at any time to confront us with the alternative of humiliation or war. We favor the maintenance of a navy strong enough for all purposes of national defense, and to properly maintain the honor and dignity of the country abroad.

This country has always been the refuge of the oppressed from every land—exiles for conscience sake—and in the spirit of the founders of our Government we condemn the oppression practised by the Russian Government upon its Lutheran and Jewish subjects, and we call upon our National Government, in the interest of justice and humanity, by all just and proper means, to use its prompt and best efforts to bring about a cessation of these cruel persecutions in the dominions of the Czar and to secure to the oppressed equal rights.

We tender our profound and earnest sympathy to those lovers of freedom who are struggling for home rule and the great cause of local self-government in Ireland.

We heartily approve all legitimate efforts to prevent the United States from being used as the dumping ground for the known criminals and professional paupers of Europe; and we demand the rigid enforcement of the laws against Chinese immigration and the importation of foreign workmen under contract, to degrade American labor and lessen its wages; but we condemn and denounce any and all attempts to restrict the immigration of the industrious and worthy of foreign lands.

This Convention hereby renews the expression of appreciation of the patriotism of the soldiers and sailors of the Union in the war for its preservation, and we favor just and liberal pensions for all disabled Union soldiers, their widows and dependents, but we demand that the work of the Pension Office shall be done industriously, impartially and honestly. We denounce the present administration of that office as incompetent, corrupt, disgraceful and dishonest.

The Federal Government should care for and improve the Mississippi River and other great waterways of the Republic, so as to secure for the interior States easy and cheap transportation to tide water. When any waterway of the Republic is of sufficient importance to demand the aid of the Government, such aid should be extended upon a definite plan of continuous work, until permanent improvement is secured.

For purposes of national defense and the promotion of commerce between the States, we recognize the early construction of the Nicaragua Canal and its protection against foreign control as of great importance to the United States.

Recognizing the World's Columbian Exposition as a national undertaking of vast importance, in which the General Government has invited the co-operation of all the powers of the world, and appreciating the acceptance by many of such powers of the invitation so extended, and the broad and liberal efforts being made by them to contribute to the grandeur of the undertaking, we are of opinion that Congress should make such necessary financial provision as shall be requisite to the maintenance of the national honor and public faith.

Popular education being the only safe basis of popular suffrage, we recommend to the several States most liberal appropriations for the public schools. Free common schools are the nursery of good government, and they have always received the fostering care of the Democratic party, which favors every means of increasing intelligence. Freedom of education, being an essential of civil and religious liberty, as well as a necessity for the development of intelligence, must not be interfered with under any pretext whatever. We are opposed to State interference with parental rights and rights of conscience in the education of children as an infringement of the fundamental Democratic doctrine that the largest individual liberty consistent with the rights of others insures the highest type of American citizenship and the best government.

We approve the action of the present House of Representatives in passing bills for admitting into the Union as States of the Territories of New Mexico and Arizona, and we favor the early admission of all the Territories having the necessary population and resources to entitle them to Statehood, and while they remain Territories we hold that the officials appointed to administer the government of any Territory, together with the Districts of Columbia and Alaska, should be *bona-fide* residents of the Territory or district in which their duties are to be performed. The Democratic party believes in home rule and the control of their own affairs by the people of the vicinage.

We favor legislation by Congress and State Legislatures to protect the lives and limbs of railway employees and those of other hazardous transportation companies, and denounce the inactivity of the Republican party, and particularly the Republican Senate, for causing the defeat of measures beneficial and protective to this class of wage workers.

We are in favor of the enactment by the States of laws for abolishing the notorious sweating system, for abolishing contract convict labor, and for prohibiting the employment in factories of children under 15 years of age.

We are opposed to all sumptuary laws, as an interference with the individual rights of the citizen.

Upon this statement of principles and policies, the Democratic party asks the intelligent judgment of the American people. It asks a change of administration and a change of party, in order that there may be a change of system and a change of methods, thus assuring the maintenance unimpaired of institutions under which the Republic has grown great and powerful.

People's Platform of 1892

Assembled upon the 116th anniversary of the Declaration of Independence, the People's Party of America in their first national convention, invoking upon their action the blessing of Almighty God, put forth in the name and on behalf of the people of this country, the following preamble and declaration of principles:

PREAMBLE

The conditions which surround us best justify our co-operation; we meet in the midst of a nation brought to the verge of moral, political, and material ruin. Corruption dominates the ballot-box, the Legislatures, the Congress, and touches even the ermine of the bench. The people are demoralized; most of the States have been compelled to isolate the voters at the polling places to prevent universal intimidation and bribery. The newspapers are largely subsidized or muzzled, public opinion silenced, business prostrated, homes covered with mortgages, labor impoverished, and the land concentrating in the hands of capitalists. The urban workmen are denied the right to organize for self-protection; imported pauperized labor beats down their wages, a hireling standing army, unrecognized by our laws, is established to shoot them down, and they are rapidly degenerating into European conditions. The fruits of the toil of millions are boldly stolen to build up colossal fortunes for a few, unprecedented in the history of mankind; and the possessors of these, in turn despise the Republic and endanger liberty. From the same prolific womb of governmental injustice we breed the two great classes—tramps and millionaires.

The national power to create money is appropriated to enrich bond-holders; a vast public debt payable in legal tender currency has been funded into gold-bearing bonds, thereby adding millions to the burdens of the people.

Silver, which has been accepted as coin since the dawn of history, has been demonetized to add to the purchasing power of gold by decreasing the value of all forms of property as well as human labor, and the supply of currency is purposely abridged to fatten usurers, bankrupt enterprise, and enslave industry. A vast conspiracy against mankind has been organized on two continents, and it is rapidly taking possession of the world. If not met and overthrown at once, it forebodes terrible social convulsions, the destruction of civilization, or the establishment of an absolute despotism.

We have witnessed for more than a quarter of a century the struggles of the two great political parties for power and plunder, while grievous wrongs have been inflicted upon the suffering people. We charge that the controlling influence dominating both these parties have permitted the existing dreadful conditions to develop without serious effort to prevent or restrain them. Neither do they now promise us any substantial reform. They have agreed together to ignore, in the coming campaign, every issue but one. They propose to drown the outcries of a plundered people with the uproar of a sham battle over the tariff, so that capitalists, corporations, national banks, rings, trusts, watered stock, the demonetization of silver and the oppressions of the usurers may all be lost sight of. They propose to sacrifice our homes, lives, and children on the altar of mammon; to destroy the multitude in order to secure corruption funds from the millionaires.

Assembled on the anniversary of the birthday of the nation, and filled with the spirit of the grand general and chief who established our independence, we seek to restore the government of the Republic to the hands of "the plain people," with which class it originated. We assert our purposes to be identical with the purposes of the National Constitution, to form a more perfect union and establish justice, insure domestic tranquillity, provide for the common defense, promote the general welfare, and secure the blessings of liberty for ourselves and our posterity.

We declare that this Republic can only endure as a free government while built upon the love of the whole people for each other and for the nation; that it cannot be pinned together by bayonets; that the civil war is over and that every passion and resentment which grew out of it must die with it, and that we must be in fact, as we are in name, one united brotherhood of freemen.

Our country finds itself confronted by conditions for which there is no precedent in the history of the world; our annual agricultural productions amount to billions of dollars in value, which must, within a few weeks or months be exchanged for billions of dollars' worth of commodities consumed in their production; the existing currency supply is wholly inadequate to make this exchange; the results are falling prices, the formation of combines and rings, the impoverishment of the producing class. We pledge ourselves that, if given power, we will labor to correct these evils by wise and reasonable legislation, in accordance with the terms of our platform.

We believe that the power of government—in other words, of the people—should be expanded (as in the case of the postal service) as rapidly and as far as the good sense of an intelligent people and the teachings of experience shall justify, to the end that oppression, injustice and poverty, shall eventually cease in the land.

While our sympathies as a party of reform are naturally upon the side of every proposition which will tend to make men intelligent, virtuous and temperate, we nevertheless regard these questions, important as they are, as secondary to the great issues now pressing for solution, and upon which not only our individual prosperity, but the very existence of free institutions depend; and we ask all men to first help us to determine whether we are to have a republic to administer, before we differ as to the conditions upon which it is to be administered, believing that the forces of reform this day organized will never cease to move forward, until every wrong is remedied, and equal rights and equal privileges securely established for all the men and women of this country.

PLATFORM

We declare, therefore,

First—That the union of the labor forces of the United States this day consummated shall be permanent and perpetual; may its spirit enter into all hearts for the salvation of the Republic and the uplifting of mankind.

Second—Wealth belongs to him who creates it, and every dollar taken from industry without an equivalent is robbery. "If any will not work, neither shall he eat." The interests of rural and civic labor are the same; their enemies are identical.

Third—We believe that the time has come when the railroad corporations will either own the people or the people must own the railroads, and should the government enter upon the work of owning and managing all railroads, we should favor an amendment to the Constitution by which all persons engaged in the government service shall be placed under a civil service regulation of the most rigid character, so as to prevent the increase of the power of the national administration by the use of such additional government employees.

Finance—We demand a national currency, safe, sound, and flexible, issued by the general government only, a full legal tender for all debts, public and private, and that without the use of banking corporations, a just, equitable and efficient means of distribution direct to the people, at a tax not to exceed 2 per cent per annum, to be provided as set forth by the sub-treasury plan of the Farmers' Alliance, or a better system; also by payments in discharge of its obligations for public improvements.

1. We demand free and unlimited coinage of silver and gold at the present legal ratio of 16 to 1.

2. We demand that the amount of circulating medium be speedily increased to not less than $50 per capita.

3. We demand a graduated income tax.

4. We believe that the money of the country should be kept as much as possible in the hands of the people, and hence we demand that all State and national revenues shall be limited to the necessary expenses of the government, economically and honestly administered.

5. We demand that postal savings banks be established by the government for the safe deposit of the earnings of the people and to facilitate exchange.

Transportation—Transportation being a means of exchange and a public necessity, the government should own and operate the railroads in the interest of the people. The telegraph and telephone, like the post office system, being a necessity for the transmission of news, should be owned and operated by the government in the interest of the people.

Land—The land, including all the natural sources of wealth, is the heritage of the people, and should not be monopolized for speculative purposes, and alien ownership of land should be prohibited. All land now held by railroads and other corporations in excess of their actual needs, and all lands now owned by aliens, should be reclaimed by the government and held for actual settlers only.

Prohibition Platform of 1892

The Prohibition Party, in National Convention assembled, acknowledging Almighty God as the source of all true government, and His law as the standard to which human enactments must conform to secure the blessings of peace and prosperity, presents the following declaration of principles:

The liquor traffic is a foe to civilization, the arch enemy of popular government, and a public nuisance. It is the citadel of the forces that corrupt politics, promote poverty and crime, degrade the nation's home life, thwart the will of the people, and deliver our country into the hands of rapacious class interests. All laws that under the guise of regulation legalize and protect this traffic or make the Government share its ill-gotten gains, are "vicious in principle and powerless as a remedy." We declare anew for the entire suppression of the manufacture, sale, importation, exportation and transportation of alcoholic liquors as a beverage by Federal and State legislation, and the full powers of Government should be exerted to secure this result. Any party that fails to recognize the dominant nature of this issue in American politics is undeserving of the support of the people.

No citizen should be denied the right to vote on account of sex, and equal labor should receive equal wages, without regard to sex.

The money of the country should consist of gold, silver, and paper, and be issued by the General Government only, and in sufficient quantity to meet the demands of business and give full opportunity for the employment of labor. To this end an increase in the volume of money is demanded, and no individual or corporation should be allowed to make any profit through its issue. It should be made a legal tender for the payment of all debts, public and private. Its volume should be fixed at a definite sum per capita and made to increase with our increase in population.

Tariff should be levied only as a defense against foreign governments which levy tariff upon or bar out our products from their markets, revenue being incidental. The residue of means necessary to an economical administration of the Government should be raised by levying a burden on what the people possess, instead of upon what they consume.

Railroad, telegraph, and other public corporations should be controlled by the Government in the interest of the people, and no higher charges allowed than necessary to give fair interest on the capital actually invested.

Foreign immigration has become a burden upon industry, one of the factors in depressing wages and causing discontent; therefore our immigration laws should be revised and strictly enforced. The time of residence for naturalization should be extended, and no naturalized person should be allowed to vote until one year after he becomes a citizen.

Non-resident aliens should not be allowed to acquire land in this country, and we favor the limitation of individual and corporate ownership of land. All unearned grants of land to railroad companies or other corporations should be reclaimed.

Years of inaction and treachery on the part of the Republican and Democratic parties have resulted in the present reign of mob law, and we demand that every citizen be protected in the right of trial by constitutional tribunals.

All men should be protected by law in their right to one day's rest in seven.

Arbitration is the wisest and most economical and humane method of settling national differences.

Speculations in margins, the cornering of grain, money and products, and the formation of pools, trusts, and combinations for the arbitrary advancement of prices should be suppressed.

We pledge that the Prohibition Party, if elected to power, will ever grant just pensions to disabled veterans of the Union army and navy, their widows and orphans.

We stand unequivocally for the American Public School, and opposed to any appropriation of any public moneys for sectarian schools. We declare that only by united support of such common schools, taught in the English language, can we hope to become and remain a homogeneous and harmonious people.

We arraign the Republican and Democratic Parties as false to the standards reared by their founders; as faithless to the principles of the illustrious leaders of the past to whom they do homage with the lips; as recreant to the "higher law," which is as inflexible in political affairs as in personal life; and as no longer embodying the aspirations of the American people, or inviting the confidence of enlightened, progressive patriotism. Their protest against the admission of "moral issues" into politics is a confession of their own moral degeneracy. The declaration of an eminent authority that municipal misrule is "the one conspicuous failure of American politics" follows as a natural consequence of such degeneracy, and it is true alike of cities under Republican and Democratic control. Each accuses the other of extravagance in congressional appropriations, and both are alike guilty; each protests when out of power against the infraction of the civil-service laws, and each when in power violates those laws in letter and spirit; each professes fealty to the interests of the toiling masses, but both covertly truckle to the money power in their administration of public affairs. Even the tariff issue, as represented in the Democratic Mills bill and the Republican McKinley bill, is no longer treated by them as an issue upon great and divergent principles of government, but is a mere catering to different sectional and class interests. The attempt in many States to wrest the Australian ballot system from its true purpose, and to so de-form it as to render it extremely difficult for new parties to exercise the right of suffrage, is an outrage upon popular government. The competition of both the parties for the vote of the slums, and their assiduous courting of the liquor power and subserviency to the money power, has resulted in placing those powers in the position of practical arbiters of the destinies of the nation. We renew our protest against these perilous tendencies, and invite all citizens to join us in the upbuilding of a party that has shown in five national campaigns that it prefers temporary defeat to an abandonment of the claims of justice, sobriety, personal rights and the protection of American homes.

Recognizing and declaring that prohibition of the liquor traffic has become the dominant issue in national politics, we invite to full party fellowship all those who on this one dominant issue are with us agreed, in the full belief that this party can and will remove sectional differences, promote national unity, and insure the best welfare of our entire land.

Resolved, That we favor a liberal appropriation by the Federal Government for the World's Columbian Exposition, but only on the condition that the sale of intoxicating drinks upon the Exposition grounds is prohibited, and that the Exposition be kept closed on Sunday.

Republican Platform of 1892

The representatives of the Republicans of the United States, assembled in general convention on the shores of the Mississippi River, the everlasting bond of an indestructible Republic, whose most glorious chapter of history is the record of the Republican party, congratulate their countrymen on the majestic march of the nation under the banners inscribed with the principles of our platform of 1888, vindicated by victory at the polls and prosperity in our fields, workshops and mines, and make the following declaration of principles:

We reaffirm the American doctrine of protection. We call attention to its growth abroad. We maintain that the prosperous condition of our country is largely due to the wise revenue legislation of the Republican congress.

We believe that all articles which cannot be produced in the United States, except luxuries, should be admitted free of duty, and that on all

imports coming into competition with the products of American labor, there should be levied duties equal to the difference between wages abroad and at home. We assert that the prices of manufactured articles of general consumption have been reduced under the operations of the tariff act of 1890.

We denounce the efforts of the Democratic majority of the House of Representatives to destroy our tariff laws by piecemeal, as manifested by their attacks upon wool, lead and lead ores, the chief products of a number of States, and we ask the people for their judgment thereon.

We point to the success of the Republican policy of reciprocity, under which our export trade has vastly increased and new and enlarged markets have been opened for the products of our farms and workshops. We remind the people of the bitter opposition of the Democratic party to this practical business measure, and claim that, executed by a Republican administration, our present laws will eventually give us control of the trade of the world.

The American people, from tradition and interest, favor bi-metallism, and the Republican party demands the use of both gold and silver as standard money, with such restrictions and under such provisions, to be determined by legislation, as will secure the maintenance of the parity of values of the two metals so that the purchasing and debt-paying power of the dollar, whether of silver, gold, or paper, shall be at all times equal. The interests of the producers of the country, its farmers and its workingmen, demand that every dollar, paper or coin, issued by the government, shall be as good as any other.

We commend the wise and patriotic steps already taken by our government to secure an international conference, to adopt such measures as will insure a parity of value between gold and silver for use as money throughout the world.

We demand that every citizen of the United States shall be allowed to cast one free and unrestricted ballot in all public elections, and that such ballot shall be counted and returned as cast; that such laws shall be enacted and enforced as will secure to every citizen, be he rich or poor, native or foreign-born, white or black, this sovereign right, guaranteed by the Constitution. The free and honest popular ballot, the just and equal representation of all the people, as well as their just and equal protection under the laws, are the foundation of our Republican institutions, and the party will never relax its efforts until the integrity of the ballot and the purity of elections shall be fully guaranteed and protected in every State.

SOUTHERN OUTRAGES

We denounce the continued inhuman outrages perpetrated upon American citizens for political reasons in certain Southern States of the Union.

FOREIGN RELATIONS

We favor the extension of our foreign commerce, the restoration of our mercantile marine by home-built ships, and the creation of a navy for the protection of our National interests and the honor of our flag; the maintenance of the most friendly relations with all foreign powers; entangling alliances with none; and the protection of the rights of our fishermen.

We reaffirm our approval of the Monroe doctrine and believe in the achievement of the manifest destiny of the Republic in its broadest sense.

We favor the enactment of more stringent laws and regulations for the restriction of criminal, pauper and contract immigration.

MISCELLANEOUS

We favor efficient legislation by Congress to protect the life and limbs of employees of transportation companies engaged in carrying on interState commerce, and recommend legislation by the respective States that will protect employees engaged in State commerce, in mining and manufacturing.

The Republican party has always been the champion of the oppressed and recognizes the dignity of manhood, irrespective of faith, color, or nationality; it sympathizes with the cause of home rule in Ireland, and protests against the persecution of the Jews in Russia.

The ultimate reliance of free popular government is the intelligence of the people, and the maintenance of freedom among men. We therefore declare anew our devotion to liberty of thought and conscience, of speech and press, and approve all agencies and instrumentalities which contribute to the education of the children of the land, but while insisting upon the fullest measure of religious liberty, we are opposed to any union of Church and State.

We reaffirm our opposition, declared in the Republican platform of 1888, to all combinations of capital organized in trusts or otherwise, to control arbitrarily the condition of trade among our citizens.

We heartily indorse the action already taken upon this subject, and ask for such further legislation as may be required to remedy any defects in existing laws, and to render their enforcement more complete and effective.

We approve the policy of extending to towns, villages and rural communities the advantages of the free delivery service, now enjoyed by the larger cities of the country, and reaffirm the declaration contained in the Republican platform of 1888, pledging the reduction of letter postage to 1 cent at the earliest possible moment consistent with the maintenance of the Post Office Department and the highest class of postal service.

We commend the spirit and evidence of reform in the civil service, and the wise and consistent enforcement by the Republican party of the laws regulating the same.

NICARAGUA CANAL

The construction of the Nicaragua Canal is of the highest importance to the American people, both as a measure of National defense and to build up and maintain American commerce, and it should be controlled by the United States Government.

TERRITORIES

We favor the admission of the remaining Territories at the earliest practicable date, having due regard to the interests of the people of the Territories and of the United States. All the Federal officers appointed for the Territories should be selected from *bona-fide* residents thereof, and the right of self-government should be accorded as far as practicable.

ARID LANDS

We favor the cession, subject to the homestead laws, of the arid public lands, to the States and Territories in which they lie, under such Congressional restrictions as to disposition, reclamation and occupancy by settlers as will secure the maximum benefits to the people.

THE COLUMBIAN EXPOSITION

The World's Columbian Exposition is a great national undertaking, and Congress should promptly enact such reasonable legislation in aid thereof as will insure a discharge of the expenses and obligations incident thereto, and the attainment of results commensurate with the dignity and progress of the Nation.

INTEMPERANCE

We sympathize with all wise and legitimate efforts to lessen and prevent the evils of intemperance and promote morality.

PENSIONS

Ever mindful of the services and sacrifices of the men who saved the life of the Nation, we pledge anew to the veteran soldiers of the Republic a watchful care and recognition of their just claims upon a grateful people.

HARRISON'S ADMINISTRATION

We commend the able, patriotic and thoroughly American administration of President Harrison. Under it the country has enjoyed remarkable prosperity and the dignity and honor of the Nation, at home and abroad, have been faithfully maintained, and we offer the record of pledges kept as a guarantee of faithful performance in the future.

Socialist Labor Platform of 1892

The Socialist Labor Party of the United States, in convention assembled, reasserts the inalienable right of all men to life, liberty, and the pursuit of happiness.

With the founders of the American republic we hold that the purpose of government is to secure every citizen in the enjoyment of this right; but in the light of our social conditions we hold, furthermore, that no such right can be exercised under a system of economic inequality, essentially destructive of life, of liberty, and of happiness.

With the founders of this republic we hold that the true theory of politics is that the machinery of government must be owned and controlled by the whole people; but in the light of our industrial development we hold, furthermore, that the true theory of economics is that the machinery of production must likewise belong to the people in common.

To the obvious fact that our despotic system of economics is the direct opposite of our democratic system of politics, can plainly be traced the existence of a privileged class, the corruption of government by that class, the alienation of public property, public franchises and public functions to that class, and the abject dependence of the mightiest of nations upon that class. Again, through the perversion of democracy to the ends of plutocracy, labor is robbed of the wealth which it alone produces, is denied the means of self-employment, and, by compulsory idleness in wage-slavery, is even deprived of the necessaries of life. Human power and natural forces are thus wasted, that the plutocracy may rule. Ignorance and misery, with all their concomitant evils, are perpetuated, that the people may be kept in bondage. Science and invention are diverted from their humane purpose to the enslavement of women and children.

Against such a system the Socialistic Labor Party once more enters its protest. Once more it reiterates its fundamental declaration, that private property in the natural sources of production and in the instruments of labor is the obvious cause of all economic servitude and political dependence; and

WHEREAS, the time is fast coming when, in the natural course of social evolution, this system, through the destructive action of its failures and crises, on the one hand, and the constructive tendencies of its trusts and other capitalistic combinations, on the other hand, shall have worked out its own downfall; therefore, be it

RESOLVED, That we call upon the people to organize with a view to the substitution of the co-operative commonwealth for the present state of planless production, industrial war, and social disorder—a commonwealth in which every worker shall have the free exercise and full benefit of his faculties, multiplied by all the modern factors of civilization. We call upon them to unite with us in a mighty effort to gain by all practicable means the political power.

In the meantime, and with a view to immediate improvement in the condition of labor, we present the following "Demands":

SOCIAL DEMANDS

1. Reduction of the hours of labor in proportion to the progress of production.

2. The United States shall obtain possession of the railroads, canals, telegraphs, telephones,

and all other means of public transportation and communication.

3. The municipalities to obtain possession of the local railroads, ferries, water-works, gas-works, electric plants, and all industries requiring municipal franchises.

4. The public lands to be declared inalienable. Revocation of all land grants to corporations or individuals, the conditions of which have not been complied with.

5. Legal incorporation by the States of local Trade Unions which have no national organization.

6. The United States to have the exclusive right to issue money.

7. Congressional legislation providing for the scientific management of forests and waterways, and prohibiting the waste of the natural resources of the country.

8. Inventions to be free to all; the inventors to be remunerated by the nation.

9. Progressive income tax and tax on inheritances; the smaller incomes to be exempt.

10. School education of all children under fourteen years of age to be compulsory, gratuitous, and accessible to all by public assistance in meals, clothing, books, etc., where necessary.

11. Repeal of all pauper, tramp, conspiracy, and sumptuary laws. Unabridged right of combination.

12. Official statistics concerning the condition of labor. Prohibition of the employment of children of school age and of the employment of female labor in occupations detrimental to health or morality. Abolition of the convict labor contract system.

13. All wages to be paid in lawful money of the United States. Equalization of women's wages with those of men where equal service is performed.

14. Laws for the protection of life and limb in all occupations, and an efficient employer's liability law.

POLITICAL DEMANDS

1. The people to have the right to propose laws and to vote upon all measures of importance, according to the Referendum principle.

2. Abolition of the Presidency, Vice-Presidency, and Senate of the United States. An Executive Board to be established, whose members are to be elected, and may at any time be recalled by the House of Representatives as the only legislative body. The States and Municipalities to adopt corresponding amendment to their constitutions and statutes.

3. Municipal self-government.

4. Direct vote and secret ballots in all elections. Universal and equal right of suffrage, without regard to color, creed, or sex. Election days to be legal holidays. The principle of minority representation to be introduced.

5. All public officers to be subject to recall by their respective constituencies.

6. Uniform civil and criminal law throughout the United States. Administration of justice to be free of charge. Abolition of capital punishment.

In this year, as in 1872, factions broke away from both of the major parties. This made four parties in addition to the Prohibition Party, and the Socialist Labor Party, which from this time on is regularly found as a minor party. The People's Party, or Populists, also appeared, but nominated the same candidate for President as the Democratic Party. The National Party was a group of Prohibitionists who did not wish to ally themselves with the Prohibition Party.

The split in the major parties came over the issue of free silver. Hence appears the National Democratic Party, approving the gold standard and opposing the regular Democrats, and the National Silver Party, largely composed of Republicans who approved free silver. They nominated the same candidates as the Democrats.

Democratic Platform of 1896

We, the Democrats of the United States in National Convention assembled, do reaffirm our allegiance to those great essential principles of justice and liberty, upon which our institutions are founded, and which the Democratic Party has advocated from Jefferson's time to our own— freedom of speech, freedom of the press, freedom of conscience, the preservation of personal rights, the equality of all citizens before the law, and the faithful observance of constitutional limitations.

During all these years the Democratic Party has resisted the tendency of selfish interests to the centralization of governmental power, and steadfastly maintained the integrity of the dual scheme of government established by the founders of this Republic of republics. Under its guidance and teachings the great principle of local self-government has found its best expression in the maintenance of the rights of the States and in its assertion of the necessity of confining the general government to the exercise of the powers granted by the Constitution of the United States.

The Constitution of the United States guarantees to every citizen the rights of civil and religious liberty. The Democratic Party has always been the exponent of political liberty and religious freedom, and it renews its obligations and reaffirms its devotion to these fundamental principles of the Constitution.

THE MONEY PLANK

Recognizing that the money question is paramount to all others at this time, we invite at-

97

tention to the fact that the Federal Constitution named silver and gold together as the money metals of the United States, and that the first coinage law passed by Congress under the Constitution made the silver dollar the monetary unit and admitted gold to free coinage at a ratio based upon the silver-dollar unit.

We declare that the act of 1873 demonetizing silver without the knowledge or approval of the American people has resulted in the appreciation of gold and a corresponding fall in the prices of commodities produced by the people; a heavy increase in the burdens of taxation and of all debts, public and private; the enrichment of the money-lending class at home and abroad; the prostration of industry and impoverishment of the people.

We are unalterably opposed to monometallism which has locked fast the prosperity of an industrial people in the paralysis of hard times. Gold monometallism is a British policy, and its adoption has brought other nations into financial servitude to London. It is not only un-American but anti-American, and it can be fastened on the United States only by the stifling of that spirit and love of liberty which proclaimed our political independence in 1776 and won it in the War of the Revolution.

We demand the free and unlimited coinage of both silver and gold at the present legal ratio of 16 to 1 without waiting for the aid or consent of any other nation. We demand that the standard silver dollar shall be a full legal tender, equally with gold, for all debts, public and private, and we favor such legislation as will prevent for the future the demonetization of any kind of legal-tender money by private contract.

We are opposed to the policy and practice of surrendering to the holders of the obligations of the United States the option reserved by law to the Government of redeeming such obligations in either silver coin or gold coin.

INTEREST-BEARING BONDS

We are opposed to the issuing of interest-bearing bonds of the United States in time of peace and condemn the trafficking with banking syndicates, which, in exchange for bonds and at an enormous profit to themselves, supply the Federal Treasury with gold to maintain the policy of gold monometallism.

AGAINST NATIONAL BANKS

Congress alone has the power to coin and issue money, and President Jackson declared that this power could not be delegated to corporations or individuals. We therefore denounce the issuance of notes intended to circulate as money by National banks as in derogation of the Constitution, and we demand that all paper which is made a legal tender for public and private debts, or which is receivable for dues to the United States, shall be issued by the Government of the United States and shall be redeemable in coin.

TARIFF RESOLUTION

We hold that tariff duties should be levied for purposes of revenue, such duties to be so adjusted as to operate equally throughout the country, and not discriminate between class or section, and that taxation should be limited by the needs of the Government, honestly and economically administered. We denounce as disturbing to business the Republican threat to restore the McKinley law, which has twice been condemned by the people in National elections and which, enacted under the false plea of protection to home industry, proved a prolific breeder of trusts and monopolies, enriched the few at the expense of the many, restricted trade and deprived the producers of the great American staples of access to their natural markets.

Until the money question is settled we are opposed to any agitation for further changes in our tariff laws, except such as are necessary to meet the deficit in revenue caused by the adverse decision of the Supreme Court on the income tax. But for this decision by the Supreme Court, there would be no deficit in the revenue under the law passed by the Democratic Congress in strict pursuance of the uniform decisions of that court for nearly 100 years, that court having in that decision sustained Constitutional objections to its enactment which had previously been over-ruled by the ablest Judges who have ever sat on that bench. We declare that it is the duty of Congress to use all the Constitutional power which remains after that decision, or which may come from its reversal by the court as it may hereafter be constituted, so that the burdens of taxation may be equally and impartially laid, to the end that wealth may bear its due proportion of the expense of the Government.

IMMIGRATION AND ARBITRATION

We hold that the most efficient way of protecting American labor is to prevent the importation of foreign pauper labor to compete with it in the home market, and that the value of the home market to our American farmers and artisans is greatly reduced by a vicious monetary system which depresses the prices of their products below the cost of production, and thus deprives them of the means of purchasing the products of our home manufactories; and as labor creates the wealth of the country, we demand the passage of such laws as may be necessary to protect it in all its rights.

We are in favor of the arbitration of differences between employers engaged in interstate commerce and their employees, and recommend such legislation as is necessary to carry out this principle.

TRUSTS AND POOLS

The absorption of wealth by the few, the consolidation of our leading railroad systems, and the formation of trusts and pools require a stricter control by the Federal Government of those arteries of commerce. We demand the enlargement of the powers of the Interstate Commerce Commission and such restriction and guarantees in the control of railroads as will protect the people from robbery and oppression.

DECLARE FOR ECONOMY

We denounce the profligate waste of the money wrung from the people by oppressive taxation and the lavish appropriations of recent Republican Congresses, which have kept taxes high, while the labor that pays them is unemployed and the products of the people's toil are depressed in price till they no longer repay the cost of production. We demand a return to that simplicity and economy which befits a Democratic Government, and a reduction in the number of useless offices, the salaries of which drain the substance of the people.

FEDERAL INTERFERENCE IN LOCAL AFFAIRS

We denounce arbitrary interference by Federal authorities in local affairs as a violation of the Constitution of the United States, and a crime against free institutions, and we especially object to government by injunction as a new and highly dangerous form of oppression by which Federal Judges, in contempt of the laws of the States and rights of citizens, become at once legislators, judges and executioners; and we approve the bill passed at the last session of the United States Senate, and now pending in the House of Representatives, relative to contempts in Federal courts and providing for trials by jury in certain cases of contempt.

PACIFIC RAILROAD

No discrimination should be indulged in by the Government of the United States in favor of any of its debtors. We approve of the refusal of the Fifty-third Congress to pass the Pacific Railroad Funding bill and denounce the effort of the present Republican Congress to enact a similar measure.

PENSIONS

Recognizing the just claims of deserving Union soldiers, we heartily indorse the rule of the present Commissioner of Pensions, that no names shall be arbitrarily dropped from the pension roll; and the fact of enlistment and service should be deemed conclusive evidence against disease and disability before enlistment.

ADMISSION OF TERRITORIES

We favor the admission of the Territories of New Mexico, Arizona and Oklahoma into the Union as States, and we favor the early admission of all the Territories, having the necessary population and resources to entitle them to Statehood, and, while they remain Territories, we hold that the officials appointed to administer the government of any Territory, together with the District of Columbia and Alaska, should be *bona-fide* residents of the Territory or District in which their duties are to be performed. The Democratic party believes in home rule and that all public lands of the United States should be appropriated to the establishment of free homes for American citizens.

We recommend that the Territory of Alaska be granted a delegate in Congress and that the general land and timber laws of the United States be extended to said Territory.

SYMPATHY FOR CUBA

The Monroe doctrine, as originally declared, and as interpreted by succeeding Presidents, is a permanent part of the foreign policy of the United States, and must at all times be maintained.

We extend our sympathy to the people of Cuba in their heroic struggle for liberty and independence.

CIVIL-SERVICE LAWS

We are opposed to life tenure in the public service, except as provided in the Constitution. We favor appointments based on merit, fixed terms of office, and such an administration of the civil-service laws as will afford equal opportunities to all citizens of ascertained fitness.

THIRD-TERM RESOLUTION

We declare it to be the unwritten law of this Republic, established by custom and usage of 100 years, and sanctioned by the examples of the greatest and wisest of those who founded and have maintained our Government that no man should be eligible for a third term of the Presidential office.

IMPROVEMENT OF WATERWAYS

The Federal Government should care for and improve the Mississippi River and other great waterways of the Republic, so as to secure for the interior States easy and cheap transportation to tidewater. When any waterway of the Republic is of sufficient importance to demand aid of the Government such aid should be extended upon a definite plan of continuous work until permanent improvement is secured.

CONCLUSION

Confiding in the justice of our cause and the necessity of its success at the polls, we submit the foregoing declaration of principles and purposes to the considerate judgment of the American people. We invite the support of all citizens who approve them and who desire to have them made effective through legislation, for the relief of the people and the restoration of the country's prosperity.

National Platform of 1896

The National party, recognizing God as the Author of All just power in government, presents the following declaration of principles, which it pledges itself to enact into effective legislation when given the power to do so.

1. The suppression of the manufacture and sale, importation, exportation, and transportation of intoxicating liquors for beverage purposes. We utterly reject all plans for regulating or compromising with this traffic, whether such plans be called local option, taxation, license, or public control. The sale of liquors for medicinal and other legitimate uses should be conducted by the State, without profit, and with such regulations as will prevent fraud or evasion.

2. No citizen should be denied the right to vote on account of sex.

3. All money should be issued by the General Government only, and without the intervention of any private citizen, corporation, or banking institution. It should be based upon the wealth, stability, and integrity of the nation. It should be a full legal tender for all debts, public and private, and should be of full volume to meet the demands of the legitimate business interests of the country. For the purpose of honestly liquidating our outstanding coin obligations, we favor the free and unlimited coinage of both silver and gold, at the ratio 16 to 1, without consulting any other nation.

4. Land is the common heritage of the people and should be preserved from monopoly and speculation. All unearned grants of land, subject to forfeiture should be reclaimed by the Government, and no portion of the public domain should hereafter be granted except to actual settlers, continuous use being essential to tenure.

5. Railroads, telegraphs, and other natural monopolies should be owned and operated by the Government, giving to the people the benefit of the service at actual cost.

6. The National Constitution should be so amended as to allow the National revenue to be raised by equitable adjustment of taxation on the properties and incomes of the people, and import duties should be levied as a means of securing equitable commercial relations with other nations.

7. The contract convict labor system, through which speculators are enriched at the expense of the State, should be abolished.

8. All citizens should be protected by law in their right to one day of rest in seven, without oppressing any who conscientiously observe any other than the first day of the week.

9. The American public schools, taught in the English language, should be maintained, and no public funds should be appropriated for sectarian institutions.

10. The President, Vice-President, and United States Senators should be elected by direct vote of the people.

11. Ex-soldiers and sailors of the United States Army and Navy, their widows and minor children, should receive liberal pensions, granted on disability and term of service, not merely as a debt of gratitude, but for service rendered in the preservation of the Union.

12. Our immigration laws should be so revised as to exclude paupers and criminals. None but citizens of the United States should be allowed to vote in any State, and naturalized citizens should not vote until one year after naturalization papers have been issued.

13. The initiative and referendum, and proportional representation, should be adopted.

14. Having herein presented our principles and purposes, we invite the co-operation and support of all citizens who are with us substantially agreed.

National Democratic Platform of 1896

This convention has assembled to uphold the principles upon which depend the honor and welfare of the American people in order that Democrats throughout the Union may unite their patriotic efforts to avert disaster from their country and ruin from their party.

The Democratic party is pledged to equal and exact justice to all men of every creed and condition; to the largest freedom of the individual consistent with good government; to the preservation of the Federal government in its constitutional vigor, and to the support of the States in all their just rights; to economy in the public expenditures; to the maintenance of the public faith and sound money; and it is opposed to paternalism and all class legislation.

Chicago Platform Condemned

The declarations of the Chicago convention attack individual freedom, the right of private contract, the independence of the judiciary and the authority of the President to enforce Federal laws. They advocate a reckless attempt to increase the price of silver by legislation to the debasement of our monetary standard, and threaten unlimited issues of paper money by the government. They abandon for Republican allies the Democratic cause of tariff reform to court the favor of protectionists to their fiscal heresy.

In view of these and other grave departures from Democratic principles, we cannot support the candidates of that convention nor be bound by its acts. The Democratic party has survived defeats, but could not survive a victory won in behalf of the doctrine and policy proclaimed in its name at Chicago.

The conditions, however, which made possible such utterances from a national convention are the direct result of class-legislation by the Republican party. It still proclaims, as it has for years, the power and duty of government to raise and maintain prices by law; and it proposes no remedy for existing evils except oppressive and unjust taxation.

Democratic Principles

The National Democracy here reconvened, therefore renews its declaration of faith in Democratic principles, especially as applicable to the conditions of the times.

Taxation, tariff, excise or direct, is rightfully imposed only for public purposes, and not for private gain. Its amount is justly measured by public expenditures, which should be limited by scrupulous economy. The sum derived by the treasury from tariff and excise levies is affected by the state of trade and volume of consumption. The amount required by the treasury is determined by the appropriations made by Congress. The demand of the Republican party for an increase in tariff taxation has its pretext in the deficiency of the revenue, which has its causes in the stagnation of trade and reduced consumption, due entirely to the loss of confidence that has followed the Populist threat of free coinage and depreciation of our money and the Republican practice of extravagant appropriations beyond the needs of good government. We arraign and condemn the Populistic conventions of Chicago and St. Louis for their co-operation with the Republican party in creating these conditions, which are pleaded in justification of a heavy increase of the burdens of the people by a further resort to protection. We, therefore, denounce protection and its ally, free coinage of silver, as schemes for the personal profit of a few at the expense of the masses, and oppose the two parties which stand for these schemes as hostile to the people of the Republic, whose food and shelter, comfort and prosperity are attacked by higher taxes and depreciated money.

TARIFF

In fine, we reaffirm the historic Democratic doctrine of tariff for revenue only.

We demand that henceforth modern and liberal policies toward American shipping shall take the place of our imitation of the restricted statutes of the eighteenth century, which were long ago abandoned by every maritime power but the United States, and which, to the nation's humiliation, has driven American capital and enterprise to the use of alien flags and alien crews, have made the stars and stripes an almost unknown emblem in foreign ports, and have virtually extinguished the race of American seamen. We oppose the pretense that discriminating duties will promote shipping; that scheme is an invitation to commercial warfare upon the United States, un-American in the light of our great commercial treaties, offering no gain whatever to American shipping, while greatly increasing ocean freights on our agricultural and manufactured products.

FOR A GOLD STANDARD

The experience of mankind has shown that by reason of their natural qualities gold is the necessary money of the large affairs of commerce and business, while silver is conveniently adapted to minor transactions, and the most beneficial use of both together can be insured only by the adoption of the former as a standard of monetary measure, and the maintenance of silver at a parity with gold by its limited coinage under suitable safeguards of law. Thus the largest possible enjoyment of both metals is gained with a value universally accepted throughout the world, which constitutes the only practical bimetallic currency, assuring the most stable standard, and especially the best and safest money for all who earn their livelihood by labor or the produce of husbandry. They cannot suffer when paid in the best money known to man, but are the peculiar and most defenseless victims of a debased and fluctuating currency, which offers continual profits to the money-changer at their cost.

Realizing these truths, demonstrated by long public inconvenience and loss, the Democratic party, in the interests of the masses and of equal justice to all, practically established by the legisla-

tion of 1834 and 1853 the gold standard of monetary measurement, and likewise entirely divorced the government from banking and currency issues. To this long-established Democratic policy we adhere, and insist upon the maintenance of the gold standard and of the parity therewith of every dollar issued by the government, and are firmly opposed to the free and unlimited coinage of silver and to the compulsory purchase of silver bullion. But we denounce also the further maintenance of the present costly patchwork system of national paper currency as a constant source of injury and peril.

We assert the necessity of such intelligent currency reform as will confine the government to its legitimate functions, completely separated from the banking business, and afford to all sections of our country a uniform, safe and elastic bank currency under governmental supervision, measured in volume by the needs of business.

THE ADMINISTRATION

The fidelity, patriotism and courage with which President Cleveland has fulfilled his great public trust, the high character of his administration, its wisdom and energy in the maintenance of civil order and the enforcement of the laws, its equal regard for the rights of every class and every section, its firm and dignified conduct of foreign affairs, and its sturdy persistence in upholding the credit and honor of the nation, are fully recognized by the Democratic party, and will secure to him a place in history beside the Fathers of the Republic.

We also commend the administration for the great progress made in the reform of the public service, and we indorse its efforts to extend the merit system still further. We demand that no backward step be taken, but that the reform be supported and advanced until the un-Democratic spoils system of appointments shall be eradicated.

OTHER AFFAIRS

We demand strict economy in the appropriations and in the administration of the government.

We favor arbitration for the settlement of international disputes.

We favor a liberal policy of pensions to deserving soldiers and sailors of the United States.

The Supreme Court of the United States was

wisely established by the framers of our Constitution as one of the three co-ordinate branches of the government. Its independence and authority to interpret the law of the land, without fear or favor, must be maintained. We condemn all efforts to degrade that tribunal, or impair the confidence and respect which it has deservedly held.

The Democratic party ever has maintained, and ever will maintain, the supremacy of law, the independence of its judicial administration, the inviolability of contracts, and the obligations of all good citizens to resist every illegal trust, combination or attempt against the just rights of property and the good order of society, in which are bound up the peace and happiness of our people.

Believing these principles to be essential to the well-being of the Republic, we submit them to the consideration of the American people.

National Silver Platform of 1896

We, the national silver party, in convention assembled, hereby adopt the following declaration of principles:

First. The paramount issue at this time in the United States is indisputably the money question. It is between the gold standard, gold bonds, and bank currency on the one side, and the bimetallic standard, no bonds, and government currency on the other.

On this issue we declare ourselves to be in favor of a distinctively American financial system.

We are unalterably opposed to single gold standard, and demand an immediate return to the constitutional standard of gold and silver, by restoration by this government, independently of any foreign power, of the unrestricted coinage of both gold and silver into standard money at a ratio of 16 to 1, and upon terms of exact equality as they existed prior to 1873; the silver coin to be a full legal tender equally with gold, for all debts and dues, public and private.

We favor such legislation as will prevent for the future the demonetization of any kind of legal-tender by private contract. We hold the power to control and regulate paper currency is inseparable from the power to coin money, and hence all currency intended to circulate as money should be issued and its volume controlled by the general government only and should be legal tender.

We are unalterably opposed to the issue by the United States of interest-bearing bonds in time of peace, and we denounce as a blunder worse than a crime, the present treasury policy, concurred in by a republican house, of plunging the country in debt by hundreds of millions in a vain attempt to maintain the gold standard by borrowing gold.

We demand the payment of all coin obligations of the United States as provided by existing laws, in either gold or silver coin, at the option of the government, and not at the option of the creditor.

The demonetization of silver of 1873 enormously increased the demand for gold, enhancing its purchasing power and lowering all prices measured by that standard, and since that unjust indefensible act, the prices of American products have fallen, upon an average of nearly 50 per cent., carrying down with them, proportionately, the money value of all other forms of property.

Such a fall of prices destroyed the profits of legitimate industry, injuring the producer for the benefit of the non-producer, increasing the burden of the debtor, swelling the gains of creditors, paralyzing the productive energies of the American people, relegating to idleness vast numbers of willing workers, sending shadows of despair into the home of the honest toiler, filling the land with tramps and paupers, and building up colossal fortunes at the money centers to maintain the gold standard. The country has within the last two years, in a time of profound peace and plenty been loaded down with $262,000,000 additional interest-bearing debt, under such circumstances as to allow a syndicate of native and foreign bankers to realize a net profit of millions on a single deal.

It stands confessed that a gold standard can only be upheld by so depleting our paper currency as to force the prices of our products below the European and even below the Asiatic level, to enable us to sell in foreign markets, thus aggravating the very evils of which our people so bitterly complain, degrading American labor and striking at the foundations of our civilization itself.

Advocates of gold standard persistently claim that the cause of our distress is overproduction— that we have produced so much that it made us poor—which implies that the true remedy is to close the factory, abandon the farm and throw a multitude of people out of employment, a doctrine that leaves us unnerved and disheartened, and absolutely without hope for the future. We affirm it to be unquestioned that there can be no such economic paradox as overproduction and at the same time tens of thousands of our fellow citizens remain half clothed and half fed, and who are piteously clamoring for the common necessities of life.

Second. That over and above all other questions of policy, we are in favor of restoring to the people of the United States the time-honored money of the Constitution—gold and silver, not one, but both—the money of Washington, Hamilton, Jefferson, Monroe, Jackson, and Lincoln, to the end that the American people may receive honest pay for an honest product; that an American debtor may pay his just obligations in honest standard, and not in a standard that has appreciated one hundred per cent above all the great staples of the country, and to the end, further, that silver standard countries may be deprived of the unjust advantage they now enjoy in the difference in exchange between gold and silver—an advantage which tariff legislation alone cannot overcome.

We, therefore, confidently appeal to the people of the United States to leave in abeyance for the moment all other questions, however important and even momentous though they may be, to sunder, if need be, all former party ties and affiliations, and unite in one supreme effort to free themselves and their children from the domination of the money power—a power more destructive than any which has ever been fastened upon the civilized men of any race or in any age, and upon the consummation of our desires and efforts we invoke the aid of all patriotic American citizens, and the gracious favor of Divine Providence.

Inasmuch as the patriotic majority of the Chicago convention embodied in the financial plank of its platform the principles enunciated in the platform of the American bimetallic party, promulgated at Washington, D. C., January 22, 1896, and herein reiterated, which is not only the paramount, but the only real issue in the pending campaign, therefore, recognizing that their nominees embody these patriotic principles, we recommend that this Convention nominate William J. Bryan, of Nebraska, for President, and Arthur Sewall, of Maine, for Vice-President.

People's Platform of 1896

The People's Party, assembled in National Convention, reaffirms its allegiance to the principles declared by the founders of the Republic, and also to the fundamental principles of just government as enunciated in the platform of the party in 1892.

We recognize that through the connivance of the present and preceding Administrations the country has reached a crisis in its National life, as predicted in our declaration four years ago, and that prompt and patriotic action is the supreme duty of the hour.

We realize that, while we have political independence, our financial and industrial independence is yet to be attained by restoring to our country the Constitutional control and exercise of the functions necessary to a people's government, which functions have been basely surrendered by our public servants to corporate monopolies. The influence of European moneychangers has been more potent in shaping legislation than the voice of the American people. Executive power and patronage have been used to corrupt our legislatures and defeat the will of the people, and plutocracy has thereby been enthroned upon the ruins of democracy. To restore the Government intended by the fathers, and for the welfare and prosperity of this and future generations, we demand the establishment of an economic and financial system which shall make us masters of our own affairs and independent of European control, by the adoption of the following declaration of principles:

THE FINANCES

1. We demand a National money, safe and sound, issued by the General Government only, without the intervention of banks of issue, to be a full legal tender for all debts, public and private; a just, equitable, and efficient means of distribution, direct to the people, and through the lawful disbursements of the Government.

2. We demand the free and unrestricted coinage of silver and gold at the present legal ratio of 16 to 1, without waiting for the consent of foreign nations.

3. We demand that the volume of circulating medium be speedily increased to an amount sufficient to meet the demand of the business and

population, and to restore the just level of prices of labor and production.

4. We denounce the sale of bonds and the increase of the public interest-bearing debt made by the present Administration as unnecessary and without authority of law, and demand that no more bonds be issued, except by specific act of Congress.

5. We demand such legislation as will prevent the demonetization of the lawful money of the United States by private contract.

6. We demand that the Government, in payment of its obligation, shall use its option as to the kind of lawful money in which they are to be paid, and we denounce the present and preceding Administrations for surrendering this option to the holders of Government obligations.

7. We demand a graduated income tax, to the end that aggregated wealth shall bear its just proportion of taxation, and we regard the recent decision of the Supreme Court relative to the income-tax law as a misinterpretation of the Constitution and an invasion of the rightful powers of Congress over the subject of taxation.

8. We demand that postal savings-banks be established by the Government for the safe deposit of the savings of the people and to facilitate exchange.

RAILROADS AND TELEGRAPHS

1. Transportation being a means of exchange and a public necessity, the Government should own and operate the railroads in the interest of the people and on a non-partisan basis, to the end that all may be accorded the same treatment in transportation, and that the tyranny and political power now exercised by the great railroad corporations, which result in the impairment, if not the destruction of the political rights and personal liberties of the citizens, may be destroyed. Such ownership is to be accomplished gradually, in a manner consistent with sound public policy.

2. The interest of the United States in the public highways built with public moneys, and the proceeds of grants of land to the Pacific railroads, should never be alienated, mortgaged, or sold, but guarded and protected for the general welfare, as provided by the laws organizing such railroads. The foreclosure of existing liens of the United States on these roads should at once follow default in the payment thereof by the debtor

companies; and at the foreclosure sales of said roads the Government shall purchase the same, if it becomes necessary to protect its interests therein, or if they can be purchased at a reasonable price; and the Government shall operate said railroads as public highways for the benefit of the whole people, and not in the interest of the few, under suitable provisions for protection of life and property, giving to all transportation interests equal privileges and equal rates for fares and freight.

3. We denounce the present infamous schemes for refunding these debts, and demand that the laws now applicable thereto be executed and administered according to their intent and spirit.

4. The telegraph, like the Post Office system, being a necessity for the transmission of news, should be owned and operated by the Government in the interest of the people.

THE PUBLIC LANDS

1. True policy demands that the National and State legislation shall be such as will ultimately enable every prudent and industrious citizen to secure a home, and therefore the land should not be monopolized for speculative purposes. All lands now held by railroads and other corporations in excess of their actual needs should by lawful means be reclaimed by the Government and held for actual settlers only, and private land monopoly, as well as alien ownership, should be prohibited.

2. We condemn the land grant frauds by which the Pacific railroad companies have, through the connivance of the Interior Department, robbed multitudes of *bona-fide* settlers of their homes and miners of their claims, and we demand legislation by Congress which will enforce the exemption of mineral land from such grants after as well as before the patent.

3. We demand that *bona-fide* settlers on all public lands be granted free homes, as provided in the National Homestead Law, and that no exception be made in the case of Indian reservations when opened for settlement, and that all lands not now patented come under this demand.

THE REFERENDUM

We favor a system of direct legislation through the initiative and referendum, under proper Constitutional safeguards.

Direct Election of President and Senators by the People

We demand the election of President, Vice-President, and United States Senators by a direct vote of the people.

Sympathy for Cuba

We tender to the patriotic people of Cuba our deepest sympathy for their heroic struggle for political freedom and independence, and we believe the time has come when the United States, the great Republic of the world, should recognize that Cuba is, and of right ought to be, a free and independent state.

The Territories

We favor home rule in the Territories and the District of Columbia, and the early admission of the Territories as States.

Public Salaries

All public salaries should be made to correspond to the price of labor and its products.

Employment to Be Furnished by Government

In times of great industrial depression, idle labor should be employed on public works as far as practicable.

Arbitrary Judicial Action

The arbitrary course of the courts in assuming to imprison citizens for indirect contempt and ruling by injunction should be prevented by proper legislation.

Pensions

We favor just pensions for our disabled Union soldiers.

A Fair Ballot

Believing that the elective franchise and an untrammeled ballot are essential to a government of, for, and by the people, the People's party condemns the wholesale system of disfranchisement adopted in some States as unrepublican and undemocratic, and we declare it to be the duty of the several State legislatures to take such action as will secure a full, free and fair ballot and an honest count.

The Financial Question "The Pressing Issue"

While the foregoing propositions constitute the platform upon which our party stands, and for the vindication of which its organization will be maintained, we recognize that the great and pressing issue of the pending campaign, upon which the present election will turn, is the financial question, and upon this great and specific issue between the parties we cordially invite the aid and co-operation of all organizations and citizens agreeing with us upon this vital question.

Prohibition Platform of 1896

We the members of the Prohibition party, in National Convention assembled, renewing our acknowledgment of allegiance to Almighty God as the Rightful Ruler of the Universe, lay down the following as our declaration of political purpose:

Platform

The Prohibition party, in National Convention assembled, declares its firm conviction that the manufacture, exportation, importation and sale of alcoholic beverages has produced such social, commercial, industrial, and political wrongs, and is now so threatening the perpetuity of all our social and political institutions that the suppression of the same by a National party organized therefor, is the greatest object to be accomplished by the voters of our country, and is of such importance that it, of right, ought to control the political actions of all our patriotic citizens until such suppression is accomplished.

The urgency of this cause demands the union without further delay of all citizens who desire the prohibition of the liquor traffic; therefore,

Resolved, That we favor the legal prohibition by State and National legislation of the manufacture, importation, exportation, and interstate transportation and sale of alcoholic beverages; that we declare our purpose to organize and unite all the friends of prohibition into one party, and in order to accomplish this end we deem it but right to leave every Prohibitionist the freedom of his own convictions upon all other political questions, and trust our representatives to take such action upon other political questions as the change occasioned by prohibition and the welfare of the whole people shall demand.

Republican Platform of 1896

The Republicans of the United States, assembled by their representatives in National Convention, appealing for the popular and historical justification of their claims to the matchless achievements of thirty years of Republican rule, earnestly and confidently address themselves to the awakened intelligence, experience and conscience of their countrymen in the following declaration of facts and principles:

For the first time since the civil war the American people have witnessed the calamitous consequence of full and unrestricted Democratic control of the government. It has been a record of unparalleled incapacity, dishonor and disaster. In administrative management it has ruthlessly sacrificed indispensable revenue, entailed an unceasing deficit, eked out ordinary current expenses with borrowed money, piled up the public debt by $262,000,000 in time of peace, forced an adverse balance of trade, kept a perpetual menace hanging over the redemption fund, pawned American credit to alien syndicates and reversed all the measures and results of successful Republican rule. In the broad effect of its policy it has precipitated panic, blighted industry and trade with prolonged depression, closed factories, reduced work and wages, halted enterprise and crippled American production, while stimulating foreign production for the American market. Every consideration of public safety and individual interest demands that the government shall be wrested from the hands of those who have shown themselves incapable of conducting it without disaster at home and dishonor abroad and shall be restored to the party which for thirty years administered it with unequaled success and prosperity. And in this connection, we heartily endorse the wisdom, patriotism and success of the administration of Benjamin Harrison. We renew and emphasize our allegiance to the policy of protection, as the bulwark of American industrial independence, and the foundation of American development and prosperity. This true American policy taxes foreign products and encourages home industry. It puts the burden of revenue on foreign goods; it secures the American market for the American producer. It upholds the American standard of wages for the American workingman; it puts the factory by the side of the farm and makes the American farmer less dependent on foreign demand and price; it diffuses general thrift, and founds the strength of all on the strength of each. In its reasonable application it is just, fair and impartial, equally opposed to foreign control and domestic monopoly to sectional discrimination and individual favoritism.

We denounce the present tariff as sectional, injurious to the public credit and destructive to business enterprise. We demand such an equitable tariff on foreign imports which come into competition with the American products as will not only furnish adequate revenue for the necessary expenses of the Government, but will protect American labor from degradation and the wage level of other lands. We are not pledged to any particular schedules. The question of rates is a practical question, to be governed by the conditions of time and of production. The ruling and uncompromising principle is the protection and development of American labor and industries. The country demands a right settlement, and then it wants rest.

We believe the repeal of the reciprocity arrangements negotiated by the last Republican Administration was a National calamity, and demand their renewal and extension on such terms as will equalize our trade with other nations, remove the restrictions which now obstruct the sale of American products in the ports of other countries, and secure enlarged markets for the products of our farms, forests, and factories.

Protection and Reciprocity are twin measures of American policy and go hand in hand. Democratic rule has recklessly struck down both, and both must be re-established. Protection for what we produce; free admission for the necessaries of life which we do not produce; recriprocal agreement of mutual interests, which gain open markets for us in return for our open markets for others. Protection builds up domestic industry and trade and secures our own market for ourselves; reciprocity builds up foreign trade and finds an outlet for our surplus. We condemn the present administration for not keeping pace [faith] with the sugar producers of this country. The Republican party favors such protection as will lead to the production on American soil of all the sugar which the American people use, and for which they pay other countries more than one hundred million dollars annually. To all our products; to those of the mine and the fields, as well as to those of the shop and the factory, to hemp and wool, the product of the great industry sheep husbandry; as well as to the foundry, as to the mills, we promise the most ample protection. We favor the early American policy of discriminating duties for the upbuilding of our merchant marine. To the protection of our shipping in the foreign-carrying trade, so that American ships, the product of American labor, employed in American ship-yards, sailing under the stars and stripes, and manned, officered and owned by Americans, may regain the carrying of our foreign commerce.

The Republican party is unreservedly for sound money. It caused the enactment of a law providing for the redemption [resumption] of specie payments in 1879. Since then every dollar has been as good as gold. We are unalterably opposed to every measure calculated to debase our currency or impair the credit of our country. We are therefore opposed to the free coinage of silver, except by international agreement with the leading commercial nations of the earth, which agreement we pledge ourselves to promote, and until such agreement can be obtained the existing gold standard must be maintained. All of our silver and paper currency must be maintained at parity with gold, and we favor all measures designated to maintain inviolable the obligations of the United States, of all our money, whether coin or paper, at the present standard, the standard of most enlightened nations of the earth.

The veterans of the Union Armies deserve and should receive fair treatment and generous recognition. Whenever practicable they should be given the preference in the matter of employment. And they are entitled to the enactment of such laws as are best calculated to secure the fulfillment of the pledges made to them in the dark days of the country's peril.

We denounce the practice in the pension bureau so recklessly and unjustly carried on by the present Administration of reducing pensions and arbitrarily dropping names from the rolls, as deserving the severest condemnation of the American people.

Our foreign policy should be at all times firm, vigorous and dignified, and all our interests in the western hemisphere should be carefully watched and guarded.

The Hawaiian Islands should be controlled by the United States, and no foreign power should be permitted to interfere with them. The Nicaragua Canal should be built, owned and operated by the United States. And, by the purchase of the Danish Islands we should secure a much needed Naval station in the West Indies.

The massacres in Armenia have aroused the deep sympathy and just indignation of the American people, and we believe that the United States should exercise all the influence it can properly exert to bring these atrocities to an end. In Turkey, American residents have been exposed to gravest [grievous] dangers and American property destroyed. There, and everywhere, American citizens and American property must be absolutely protected at all hazards and at any cost.

We reassert the Monroe Doctrine in its full extent, and we reaffirm the rights of the United States to give the Doctrine effect by responding to the appeal of any American State for friendly intervention in case of European encroachment.

We have not interfered and shall not interfere, with the existing possession of any European power in this hemisphere, and to the ultimate union of all the English speaking parts of the continent by the free consent of its inhabitants; from the hour of achieving their own independence the people of the United States have regarded with sympathy the struggles of other American peoples to free themselves from European domination. We watch with deep and abiding interest the heroic battles of the Cuban patriots against cruelty and oppression, and best hopes go out for the full success of their determined contest for liberty. The government of Spain, having lost control of Cuba, and being unable to protect the property or lives of resident American citizens, or to comply with its Treaty obligations, we believe that the government of the United States should actively use its influence and good offices to restore peace and give independence to the Island.

The peace and security of the Republic and the maintenance of its rightful influence among the nations of the earth demand a naval power commensurate with its position and responsibilities. We, therefore, favor the continued enlargement of the navy, and a complete system of harbor and sea-coast defenses.

For the protection of the equality of our American citizenship and of the wages of our workingmen, against the fatal competition of low priced labor, we demand that the immigration laws be thoroughly enforced, and so extended as to exclude from entrance to the United States those who can neither read nor write.

The civil service law was placed on the statute book by the Republican party which has always sustained it, and we renew our repeated declarations that it shall be thoroughly and heartily, and honestly enforced, and extended wherever practicable.

We demand that every citizen of the United States shall be allowed to cast one free and unrestricted ballot, and that such ballot shall be counted and returned as cast.

We proclaim our unqualified condemnation of the uncivilized and preposterous [barbarous] practice well known as lynching, and the killing of human beings suspected or charged with crime without process of law.

We favor the creation of a National Board of Arbitration to settle and adjust differences which may arise between employers and employed engaged in inter-State commerce.

We believe in an immediate return to the free homestead policy of the Republican party, and urge the passage by Congress of a satisfactory free homestead measure which has already passed the House, and is now pending in the senate.

We favor the admission of the remaining Territories at the earliest practicable date having due regard to the interests of the people of the Territories and of the United States. And the Federal officers appointed for the Territories should be selected from the *bona-fide* residents thereof, and the right of self-government should be accorded them as far as practicable.

We believe that the citizens of Alaska should have representation in the Congress of the United States, to the end that needful legislation may be intelligently enacted.

We sympathize fully with all legitimate efforts to lessen and prevent the evils of intemperance and promote morality. The Republican party is mindful of the rights and interests of women, and believes that they should be accorded equal opportunities, equal pay for equal work, and protection to the home. We favor the admission of women to wider spheres of usefulness and welcome their co-operation in rescuing the country from Democratic and Populist mismanagement and misrule.

Such are the principles and policies of the Republican party. By these principles we will apply it to those policies and put them into execution. We rely on the faithful and considerate judgment of the American people, confident alike of the history of our great party and in the justice of our cause, and we present our platform and our candidates in the full assurance that their selection will bring victory to the Republican party, and prosperity to the people of the United States.

Socialist Labor Platform of 1896

The Socialist Labor Party of the United States, in Convention assembled, re-asserts the inalienable right of all men to life, liberty, and the pursuit of happiness.

With the founders of the American Republic, we hold that the purpose of government is to secure every citizen in the enjoyment of this right; but in the light of our social conditions, we hold furthermore, that no such right can be exercised under a system of economic inequality, essentially destructive of life, of liberty, and of happiness.

With the founders of this Republic, we hold that the true theory of politics is that the machinery of government must be owned and controlled by the whole people; but in the light of our industrial development we hold, furthermore, that the true theory of economics is that the machinery of production must likewise belong to the people in common.

To the obvious fact that our despotic system of economics is the direct opposite of our democratic system of politics, can plainly be traced the existence of a privileged class, the corruption of government by that class, the alienation of public property, public franchises and public functions to that class, and the abject dependence of the mightiest of nations upon that class.

Again, through the perversion of democracy to the ends of plutocracy, labor is robbed of the wealth which it alone produces, is denied the means of self-employment, and, by compulsory idleness in wage slavery, is even deprived of the necessaries of life.

Human power and natural forces are thus wasted, that the plutocracy may rule.

Ignorance and misery, with all their concomitant evils, are perpetuated, that the people may be kept in bondage.

Science and invention are diverted from their humane purpose, to the enslavement of women and children.

Against such a system the Socialist Labor Party once more enters its protest. Once more it reiterates its fundamental declaration that private property in the natural sources of production and in the instruments of labor is the obvious cause of all economic servitude and political dependence.

The time is fast coming, when, in the natural course of social evolution, this system, through the destructive action of its failures and crises on one hand, and the constructive tendencies of its trusts and other capitalistic combinations on the other hand, shall have worked out its own downfall.

We, therefore, call upon the wage-workers of the United States, and upon all other honest citizens, to organize under the banner of the Socialist Labor Party into a class-conscious body, aware of its rights and determined to conquer them by taking possession of the public powers, so that, held together by an indomitable spirit of solidarity under the most trying conditions of the present class struggle, we may put a summary end to that barbarous struggle by the abolition of classes, the restoration of the land and of all the means of production, transportation and distribution to the people as a collective body, and the substitution of the Co-operative Commonwealth for the present state of planless production, industrial war, and social disorder; a commonwealth in which every worker shall have the free exercise and full benefit of his faculties, multiplied by all modern factors of civilization.

RESOLUTIONS

With a view to immediate improvement in the condition of labor we present the following demands:

1. Reduction of the hours of labor in proportion to the progress of production.

2. The United States to obtain possession of the mines, railroads, canals, telegraphs, telephones, and all other means of public transportation and communication; the employees to operate the same co-operatively under control of the Federal Government and to elect their own superior officers, but no employee shall be discharged for political reasons.

3. The municipalities to obtain possession of the local railroads, ferries, water-works, gas-works, electric plants, and all industries requiring municipal franchises; the employees to operate the same co-operatively under control of the municipal administration and to elect their own superior officers, but no employees shall be discharged for political reasons.

4. The public land to be declared inalienable. Revocation of all land grants to corporations or individuals, the conditions of which have not been complied with.

5. The United States to have the exclusive right to issue money.

6. Congressional legislation providing for the scientific management of forests and waterways, and prohibiting the waste of the natural resources of the country.

7. Inventions to be free to all; the inventors to be remunerated by the nation.

8. Progressive income tax and tax on inheritances; the smaller incomes to be exempt.

9. School education of all children under fourteen years of age to be compulsory, gratuitous and accessible to all by public assistance in meals, clothing, books, etc., where necessary.

10. Repeal of all pauper, tramp, conspiracy, and sumptuary laws. Unabridged right of combination.

11. Prohibition of the employment of children of school age and the employment of female labor in occupations detrimental to health or morality. Abolition of the convict labor contract system.

12. Employment of the unemployed by the public authorities (county, city, State and Nation).

13. All wages to be paid in lawful money of the United States. Equalization of women's wages to those of men where equal service is performed.

14. Laws for the protection of life and limb in

all occupations, and an efficient employer's liability law.

15. The people to have the right to propose laws and to vote upon all measures of importance, according to the referendum principle.

16. Abolition of the veto power of the Executive (National, State, or Municipal), wherever it exists.

17. Abolition of the United States Senate and all upper legislative chambers.

18. Municipal self-government.

19. Direct vote and secret ballots in all elections. Universal and equal right of suffrage without regard to color, creed, or sex. Election days to be legal holidays. The principle of proportional representative [sic] to be introduced.

20. All public officers to be subject to recall by their respective constituencies.

21. Uniform civil and criminal law throughout the United States. Administration of justice to be free of charge. Abolition of capital punishment.

In 1900 there were the two major parties and the well-established minor parties, namely,—the Prohibitionists and the Socialist Labor Party. The Prohibitionists called themselves the National Prohibition Party, but the word "National" does not appear to be a true part of the name. In addition, a new socialistic group appeared, calling itself the Social Democratic Party. It was a forerunner of the regular Socialist Party. A Silver Republican Party appeared, composed of Republicans who approved free silver. The People's Party was split. One faction, known as the "Fusionists," joined the Democratic Party. The other faction refused to do so, and was known as the "Middle-of-the-Road" Faction.

Democratic Platform of 1900

We, the representatives of the Democratic party of the United States assembled in National Convention, on the Anniversary of the adoption of the Declaration of Independence, do reaffirm our faith in that immortal proclamation of the inalienable rights of man, and our allegiance to the Constitution framed in harmony therewith by the fathers of the Republic. We hold with the United States Supreme Court that the Declaration of Independence is the spirit of our government, of which the Constitution is the form and letter.

We declare again that all governments instituted among men derive their just powers from the consent of the governed; that any government not based upon the consent of the governed is a tyranny; and that to impose upon any people a government of force is to substitute the methods of imperialism for those of a republic. We hold

that the Constitution follows the flag, and denounce the doctrine that an Executive or Congress deriving their existence and their powers from the Constitution can exercise lawful authority beyond it or in violation of it. We assert that no nation can long endure half republic and half empire, and we warn the American people that imperialism abroad will lead quickly and inevitably to despotism at home.

Believing in these fundamental principles, we denounce the Porto Rican law, enacted by a Republican Congress against the protest and opposition of the Democratic minority, as a bold and open violation of the nation's organic law and a flagrant breach of the national good faith. It imposes upon the people of Porto Rico a government without their consent and taxation without representation. It dishonors the American people by repudiating a solemn pledge made in their behalf by the Commanding General of our Army, which the Porto Ricans welcomed to a peaceful and unresisted occupation of their land. It dooms to poverty and distress a people whose helplessness appeals with peculiar force to our justice and magnanimity. In this, the first act of its imperialistic programme, the Republican party seeks to commit the United States to a colonial policy, inconsistent with republican institutions and condemned by the Supreme Court in numerous decisions.

We demand the prompt and honest fulfillment of our pledge to the Cuban people and the world that the United States has no disposition nor intention to exercise sovereignty jurisdiction, or control over the Island of Cuba, except for its pacification. The war ended nearly two years ago, profound peace reigns over all the island, and still the administration keeps the government of the island from its people, while Republican carpet-bag officials plunder its revenues and exploit the colonial theory, to the disgrace of the American people.

We condemn and denounce the Philippine policy of the present administration. It has involved the Republic in an unnecessary war, sacrificed the lives of many of our noblest sons, and placed the United States, previously known and applauded throughout the world as the champion of freedom, in the false and un-American position of crushing with military force the efforts of our former allies to achieve liberty and self-government. The Filipinos cannot be citizens without endangering our civilization; they cannot be subjects without imperiling our form of government; and as we are not willing to surrender our civilization nor to convert the Republic into an empire, we favor an immediate declaration of the nation's purpose to give the Filipinos, first, a stable form of government; second, independence; and third, protection from outside interference, such as has been given for nearly a century to the republics of Central and South America.

The greedy commercialism which dictated the Philippine policy of the Republican administration attempts to justify it with the plea that it will pay; but even this sordid and unworthy plea fails when brought to the test of facts. The war of "criminal aggression" against the Filipinos, entailing an annual expense of many millions, has already cost more than any possible profit that could accrue from the entire Philippine trade for years to come. Furthermore, when trade is extended at the expense of liberty, the price is always too high.

We are not opposed to territorial expansion when it takes in desirable territory which can be erected into States in the Union, and whose people are willing and fit to become American citizens. We favor trade expansion by every peaceful and legitimate means. But we are unalterably opposed to seizing or purchasing distant islands to be governed outside the Constitution, and whose people can never become citizens.

We are in favor of extending the Republic's influence among the nations, but we believe that that influence should be extended not by force and violence, but through the persuasive power of a high and honorable example.

The importance of other questions, now pending before the American people is no wise diminished and the Democratic party takes no backward step from its position on them, but the burning issue of imperialism growing out of the Spanish war involves the very existence of the Republic and the destruction of our free institutions. We regard it as the paramount issue of the campaign.

The declaration in the Republican platform adopted at the Philadelphia Convention, held in June, 1900, that the Republican party "steadfastly adheres to the policy announced in the Monroe Doctrine" is manifestly insincere and deceptive. This profession is contradicted by the avowed policy of that party in opposition to the spirit of the Monroe Doctrine to acquire and hold sovereignty over large areas of territory and large numbers of people in the Eastern Hemisphere. We insist on the strict maintenance of the Monroe Doctrine in all its integrity, both in letter and in spirit, as necessary to prevent the extension of European authority on this Continent and as essential to our supremacy in American affairs. At the same time we declare that no American people shall ever be held by force in unwilling subjection to European authority.

We oppose militarism. It means conquest abroad and intimidation and oppression at home. It means the strong arm which has ever been fatal to free institutions. It is what millions of our citizens have fled from in Europe. It will impose upon our peace loving people a large standing army and unnecessary burden of taxation, and will be a constant menace to their liberties. A small standing army and a well-disciplined state militia are amply sufficient in time of peace. This republic has no place for a vast military establishment, a sure forerunner of compulsory military service and conscription. When the nation is in danger the volunteer soldier is his country's best defender. The National Guard of the United States should ever be cherished in the patriotic hearts of a free people. Such organizations are ever an element of strength and safety. For the first time in our history, and coeval with the Philippine conquest, has there been a wholesale departure from our time honored and approved system of volunteer organization. We denounce it as un-American, un-Democratic, and un-Republican, and as a subversion of the ancient and fixed principles of a free·people.

Private monopolies are indefensible and intolerable. They destroy competition, control the price of all material, and of the finished product, thus robbing both producer and consumer. They lessen the employment of labor, and arbitrarily fix the terms and conditions thereof; and deprive individual energy and small capital of their opportunity of betterment.

They are the most efficient means yet devised for appropriating the fruits of industry to the benefit of the few at the expense of the many, and unless their insatiate greed is checked, all wealth will be aggregated in a few hands and the Republic destroyed. The dishonest paltering with the trust evil by the Republican party in State and national platforms is conclusive proof of the truth of the charge that trusts are the legitimate product of Republican policies, that they are fostered by Republican laws, and that they are protected by the Republican administration, in return for campaign subscriptions and political support.

We pledge the Democratic party to an unceasing warfare in nation, State and city against private monopoly in every form. Existing laws against trusts must be enforced and more stringent ones must be enacted providing for publicity as to the affairs of corporations engaged in inter-State commerce requiring all corporations to show, before doing business outside the State of their origin, that they have no water in their stock, and that they have not attempted, and are not attempting, to monopolize any branch of business or the production of any articles of merchandise;

and the whole constitutional power of Congress over inter-State commerce, the mails and all modes of inter-State communication, shall be exercised by the enactment of comprehensive laws upon the subject of trusts. Tariff laws should be amended by putting the products of trusts upon the free list, to prevent monopoly under the plea of protection. The failure of the present Republican administration, with an absolute control over all the branches of the national government, to enact any legislation designed to prevent or even curtail the absorbing power of trusts and illegal combinations, or to enforce the anti-trust laws already on the statute-books proves that insincerity of the high-sounding phrases of the Republican platform.

Corporations should be protected in all their rights and their legitimate interests should be respected, but any attempt by corporations to interfere with the public affairs of the people or to control the sovereignty which creates them, should be forbidden under such penalties as will make such attempts impossible.

We condemn the Dingley tariff law as a trust breeding measure, skillfully devised to give the few favors which they do not deserve, and to place upon the many burdens which they should not bear.

We favor such an enlargement of the scope of the inter-State commerce law as will enable the commission to protect individuals and communities from discrimination, and the public from unjust and unfair transportation rates.

We reaffirm and indorse the principles of the National Democratic Platform adopted at Chicago in 1896, and we reiterate the demand of that platform for an American financial system made by the American people for themselves, and which shall restore and maintain a bi-metallic price-level, and as part of such system the immediate restoration of the free and unlimited coinage of silver and gold at the present legal ratio of 16 to 1, without waiting for the aid or consent of any other nation.

We denounce the currency bill enacted at the last session of Congress as a step forward in the Republican policy which aims to discredit the sovereign right of the National Government to issue all money, whether coin or paper, and to bestow upon national banks the power to issue and control the volume of paper money for their own benefit. A permanent national bank currency, secured by government bonds, must have a permanent debt to rest upon, and, if the bank currency is to increase with population and business, the debt must also increase. The Republican currency scheme is, therefore, a scheme for fastening upon the taxpayers a perpetual and growing debt for the benefit of the banks. We are opposed to this private corporation paper circulated as money, but without legal tender qualities, and demand the retirement of national bank notes as fast as government paper or silver certificates can be substituted for them.

We favor an amendment to the Federal Constitution, providing for the election of United States Senators by direct vote of the people, and we favor direct legislation wherever practicable.

We are opposed to government by injunction; we denounce the blacklist, and favor arbitration as a means of settling disputes between corporations and their employees.

In the interest of American labor and the uplifting of the workingman, as the cornerstone of the prosperity of our country, we recommend that Congress create a Department of Labor, in charge of a secretary, with a seat in the Cabinet, believing that the elevation of the American laborer will bring with it increased production and increased prosperity to our country at home and to our commerce abroad.

We are proud of the courage and fidelity of the American soldiers and sailors in all our wars; we favor liberal pensions to them and their dependents, and we reiterate the position taken in the Chicago platform of 1896, that the fact of enlistment and service shall be deemed conclusive evidence against disease and disability before enlistment.

We favor the immediate construction, ownership and control of the Nicaraguan Canal by the United States, and we denounce the insincerity of the plank in the Republican National Platform for an Isthmian Canal in face of the failure of the Republican majority to pass the bill pending in Congress.

We condemn the Hay-Pauncefote treaty as a surrender of American rights and interests not to be tolerated by the American people.

We denounce the failure of the Republican party to carry out its pledges to grant statehood to the territories of Arizona, New Mexico and Oklahoma, and we promise the people of those territories immediate statehood and home rule during their condition as territories, and we favor home rule and a territorial form of government for Alaska and Porto Rico.

We favor an intelligent system of improving the arid lands of the West, storing the waters for the purpose of irrigation, and the holding of such lands for actual settlers.

We favor the continuance and strict enforcement of the Chinese exclusion law, and its application to the same classes of all Asiatic races.

Jefferson said: "Peace, commerce and honest friendship with all nations; entangling alliance with none." We approve this wholesome doctrine, and earnestly protest against the Republican departure which has involved us in so-called world politics, including the diplomacy of Europe and the intrigue and land-grabbing of Asia, and we especially condemn the ill-concealed Republican alliance with England, which must mean discrimination against other friendly nations, and which has already stifled the nation's voice while liberty is being strangled in Africa.

Believing in the principles of self-government and rejecting, as did our forefathers, the claim of monarchy, we view with indignation the purpose of England to overwhelm with force the South African Republics. Speaking, as we believe, for the entire American nation, except its Republican office-holders and for all freemen everywhere, we extend our sympathies to the heroic burghers in their unequal struggle to maintain their liberty and independence.

We denounce the lavish appropriations of recent Republican Congresses, which have kept taxes high and which threaten the perpetuation of the oppressive war levies. We oppose the accumulation of a surplus to be squandered in such barefaced frauds upon the taxpayers as the shipping subsidy bill, which, under the false pretense of prospering American shipbuilding, would put unearned millions into the pockets of favorite contributors to the Republican campaign fund. We favor the reduction and speedy repeal of the war taxes, and a return to the time-honored Democratic policy of strict economy in governmental expenditures.

Believing that our most cherished institutions are in great peril, that the very existence of our constitutional republic is at stake, and that the decision now to be rendered will determine whether or not our children are to enjoy these blessed privileges of free government, which have made the United States great, prosperous and honored, we earnestly ask for the foregoing declaration of principles, the hearty support of the liberty-loving American people, regardless of previous party affiliations.

People's (Fusion Faction) Platform of 1900

The People's party of the United States, in convention assembled, congratulating its supporters on the wide extension of its principles in all directions, does hereby reaffirm its adherence to the fundamental principles proclaimed in its two prior platforms and calls upon all who desire to avert the subversion of free institutions by corporate and imperialistic power to unite with it in bringing the Government back to the ideals of Washington, Jefferson, Jackson, and Lincoln.

It extends to its allies in the struggle for financial and economic freedom, assurances of its loyalty to the principles which animate the allied forces and the promise of honest and hearty cooperation in every effort for their success.

To the people of the United States we offer the following platform as the expression of our unalterable convictions:

That we denounce the act of March 14, 1900, as the culmination of a long series of conspiracies to deprive the people of their constitutional rights over the money of the nation and relegate to a gigantic money trust the control of the purse and hence of the people.

We denounce this act, first, for making all money obligations, domestic and foreign, payable in gold coin or its equivalent, thus enormously increasing the burdens of the debtors and enriching the creditors.

For refunding "coin bonds" not to mature for years into long-time gold bonds, so as to make their payment improbable and our debt perpetual.

For taking from the Treasury over $50,000,000 in a time of war and presenting it, at a premium, to bond-holders, to accomplish the refunding of bonds not due.

For doubling the capital of bankers by returning to them the face value of their bonds in current money notes so that they may draw one interest from the Government and another from the people.

For allowing banks to expand and contract their circulation at pleasure, thus controlling prices of all products.

For authorizing the Secretary of the Treasury to issue new gold bonds to an unlimited amount whenever he deems it necessary to replenish the gold hoard, thus enabling usurers to secure more bonds and more bank currency by drawing gold from the Treasury, thereby creating an "endless chain" for perpetually adding to a perpetual debt.

For striking down the greenback in order to force the people to borrow $346,000,000 more from the banks at an annual cost of over $20,000,-000.

While barring out the money of the Constitution this law opens the printing mints of the Treasury to the free coinage of bank paper money, to enrich the few and impoverish the many.

We pledge anew the People's party never to cease the agitation until this great financial conspiracy is blotted from the statute-books, the Lincoln greenback restored, the bonds all paid, and all corporation money forever retired.

We affirm the demand for the reopening of the mints of the United States to the free and unlimited coinage of silver and gold at the present legal ratio of 16 to 1, the immediate increase in the volume of silver coins and certificates thus created to be substituted, dollar for dollar, for the bank notes issued by private corporations under special privilege granted by law of March 14, 1900, and prior National banking laws, the remaining portion of the bank notes to be replaced with full legal-tender Government paper money, and its volume so controlled as to maintain at all times a stable money market and a stable price-level.

We demand a graduated income and inheritance tax, to the end that aggregated wealth shall bear its just proportion of taxation.

We demand that postal savings banks be established by the Government for the safe deposit of the savings of the people and to facilitate exchange.

With Thomas Jefferson we declare the land, including all natural sources of wealth, the inalienable heritage of the people. Government should so act as to secure homes for the people and prevent land monopoly. The original homestead policy should be enforced, and future settlers upon the public domain should be entitled to a free homestead, while all who have paid an acreage price to the Government under existing laws should have their homestead rights restored.

Transportation being a means of exchange and a public necessity, the Government should own and operate the railroads in the interest of the people and on a non-partisan basis, to the end that all may be accorded the same treatment in transportation, and that the extortion, tyranny, and political power now exercised by the great railroad corporations, which result in the impairment, if not the destruction, of the political rights and personal liberties of the citizen, may be destroyed. Such ownership is to be accomplished in a manner consistent with sound public policy.

Trusts, the overshadowing evil of the age, are the result and culmination of the private ownership and control of the three great instruments of commerce—money, transportation, and the means of transmission of information—which instruments of commerce are public functions, and which our forefathers declared in the Constitution should be controlled by the people through their Congress for the public welfare. The one remedy for the trusts is that the ownership and control be assumed and exercised by the people.

We further demand that all tariffs on goods controlled by a trust shall be abolished.

To cope with the trust evil, the people must act directly, without the intervention of representatives, who may be controlled or influenced. We therefore demand direct legislation, giving the people the law-making and veto power under the initiative and referendum. A majority of the people can never be corruptly influenced.

Applauding the valor of our army and navy in the Spanish war, we denounce the conduct of the Administration in changing a war for humanity into a war of conquest. The action of the Administration in the Philippines is in conflict with all the precedents of our National life; at war with the Declaration of Independence, the Constitution, and the plain precepts of humanity. Murder and arson have been our response to the appeals of the people who asked only to establish a free government in their own land. We demand a stoppage of this war of extermination by the assurance to the Philippines of independence and protection under a stable government of their own creation.

The Declaration of Independence, the Constitution, and the American flag are one and inseparable. The island of Porto Rico is a part of the territory of the United States, and by levying special and extraordinary customs duties on the commerce of that island the Administration has violated the Constitution, abandoned the fundamental principles of American liberty, and has striven to give the lie to the contention of our forefathers that there should be no taxation without representation.

Out of the Imperialism which would force an undesired domination on the people of the Philippines springs the un-American cry for a large standing army. Nothing in the character or purposes of our people justifies us in ignoring the plain lesson of history and putting our liberties in jeopardy by assuming the burden of militarism, which is crushing the people of the Old World. We denounce the Administration for its sinister efforts to substitute a standing army for the citizen soldiery, which is the best safeguard of the Republic.

We extend to the brave Boers of South Africa our sympathy and moral support in their patriotic struggle for the right of self-government, and we are unalterably opposed to any alliance, open or covert, between the United States and any other nation that will tend to the destruction of human liberty.

And a further manifestation of imperialism is to be found in the mining districts of Idaho. In the Cœur d'Alene soldiers have been used to overawe miners striving for a greater measure of industrial independence. And we denounce the State Government of Idaho and the Federal Government for employing the military arm of the Government to abridge the civil rights of the people, and to enforce an infamous permit system which denies to laborers their inherent liberty and compels them to forswear their manhood and their right before being permitted to seek employment.

The importation of Japanese and other laborers under contract to serve monopolistic corporations is a notorious and flagrant violation of the immigration laws. We demand that the Federal Government shall take cognizance of this menacing evil and repress it under existing laws. We further pledge ourselves to strive for the enactment of more stringent laws for the exclusion of Mongolian and Malayan immigration.

We indorse municipal ownership of public utilities, and declare that the advantages which have accrued to the public under that system would be multiplied a hundredfold by its extension to natural inter-State monopolies.

We denounce the practice of issuing injunctions in the cases of dispute between employers and employees, making criminal acts by organizations which are not criminal when performed by individuals, and demand legislation to restrain the evil.

We demand that United States Senators and all other officials as far as practicable be elected by direct vote of the people, believing that the elective franchise and untrammeled ballot are essential to a government for and by the people.

The People's party condemns the wholesale system of disfranchisement by coercion and intimidation, adopted in some States, as un-republican and un-democratic. And we declare it to be the duty of the several State Legislatures to take such action as will secure a full, free, and fair ballot, and an honest count.

We favor home rule in the Territories and the District of Columbia, and the early admission of the Territories as States.

We denounce the expensive red-tape system, political favoritism, cruel and unnecessary delay and criminal evasion of the statutes in the management of the Pension Office, and demand the simple and honest execution of the law, and the fulfillment by the nation of its pledges of service pension to all its honorably discharged veterans.

People's (Middle-of-the-Road Faction) Platform of 1900

The People's party of the United States, assembled in National Convention this 10th day of May, 1900, affirming our unshaken belief in the cardinal tenets of the People's party as set forth in the Omaha platform, and pledging ourselves anew to continue advocacy of those grand principles of human liberty, until right shall triumph over might and love over greed, do adopt and proclaim this declaration of faith:

We demand the initiative and referendum, and the imperative mandate for such changes of existing fundamental and statute law as will enable the people in their sovereign capacity to propose and compel the enactment of such laws as they desire, to reject such as they deem injurious to their interests, and to recall unfaithful public servants.

We demand the public ownership and operation of those means of communication, transportation, and production which the people may elect, such as railroads, telegraph and telephone lines, coal mines, etc.

The land, including all natural sources of wealth, is a heritage of the people and should not be monopolized for speculative purposes, and alien ownership of land should be prohibited. All lands now held by railroads and other corporations in excess of their actual needs, and all lands now owned by aliens, should be reclaimed by the Government and held for actual settlers only.

A scientific and absolute paper money, based upon the entire wealth and population of the nation, not redeemable in any specific commodity, but made a full legal tender for all debts, and receivable for all taxes and public dues, and issued by the Government only without the intervention of banks, and in sufficient quantity to meet the demands of commerce, is the best currency that can be devised, but until such a financial system is secured, which we shall press for adoption, we favor the free and unlimited coinage of both silver and gold at the legal ratio of 16 to 1.

We demand the levy and collection of a graduated tax on incomes and inheritances, and a constitutional amendment to secure the same, if necessary.

We demand the election of President, Vice-President, Federal Judges, and United States Senators by direct vote of the people.

We are opposed to trusts, and declare the contention between the old parties on the monopoly question is a sham battle, and that no solution of this mighty problem is possible without the adoption of the principles of public ownership of public utilities.

Prohibition Platform of 1900

PREAMBLE

The National Prohibition party, in convention represented, at Chicago, June 27 and 28, 1900, acknowledge Almighty God as the Supreme Source of all just government. Realizing that this Republic was founded upon Christian principles and can endure only as it embodies justice and righteousness, and asserting that all authority should seek the best good of all the governed, to this end wisely prohibiting what is wrong and permitting only what is right, hereby records and proclaims:

First—We accept and assert the definition given by Edmund Burke, that "a party is a body of men joined together for the purpose of promoting, by their joint endeavor, the national interest upon some particular principle upon which they are all agreed."

We declare that there is no principle now advocated, by any other party, which could be made a fact in government with such beneficent moral and material results as the principle of prohibition, applied to the beverage liquor traffic; that the national interest could be promoted in no other way so surely and widely as by its adoption and assertion through a National policy, and the co-operation therein by every State, forbidding the manufacture, sale, exportation, importation, and transportation of intoxicating liquors for beverage purposes; that we stand for this as the only principle, proposed by any party anywhere, for the settlement of a question greater and graver than any other before the American people, and involving more profoundly than any other their moral future, and financial welfare; and that all the patriotic citizenship of this country, agreed upon this principle, however much disagreement there may be as to minor considerations and issues, should stand together at the ballot-box, from this time forward, until prohibition is the established policy of the United States, with a party in power to enforce it and to insure its moral and material benefits.

We insist that such a party, agreed upon this principle and policy, having sober leadership, without any obligation for success to the saloon vote and to those demoralizing political combinations of men and money now allied therewith and suppliant thereto, can successfully cope with all other and lesser problems of government, in legislative halls and in the executive chair, and that it is useless for any party to make declarations in its platforms as to any questions concerning which there may be serious differences of opinion

in its own membership, and as to which, because of such differences, the party could legislate only on a basis of mutual concessions when coming into power.

We submit that the Democratic and Republican parties are alike insincere in their assumed hostility to trusts and monopolies. They dare not and do not attack the most dangerous of them all, the liquor power. So long as the saloon debauches the citizens and breeds the purchasable voter, money will continue to buy its way to power. Break down this traffic, elevate manhood, and a sober citizenship will find a way to control dangerous combinations of capital.

We propose as a first step in the financial problems of the nation to save more than a billion of dollars every year, now annually expended to support the liquor traffic and to demoralize our people. When that is accomplished, conditions will have so improved that, with a clearer atmosphere, the country can address itself to the questions as to the kind and quantity of currency needed.

Second—We reaffirm as true indisputably the declaration of William Windom when Secretary of the Treasury in the cabinet of President Arthur, that "Considered socially, financially, politically, or morally, the licensed liquor traffic is or ought to be the overwhelming issue in American politics," and that "the destruction of this iniquity stands next on the calendar of the world's progress." We hold that the existence of our party presents this issue squarely to the American people, and lays upon them the responsibility of choice between liquor parties, dominated by distillers and brewers, with their policy of saloon-perpetuation, breeding waste, wickedness, woe, pauperism, taxation, corruption and crime, and our one party of patriotic and moral principle, with a policy which defends it from domination by corrupt bosses and which insures it forever against the blighting control of saloon politics.

We face with sorrow, shame, and fear the awful fact that this liquor traffic has a grip on our Government, municipal, State, and National, through the revenue system and saloon sovereignty, which no other party dares to dispute; a grip which dominates the party now in power, from caucus to Congress, from policeman to President, from the rumshop to the White House; a grip which compels the executive to consent that law shall be nullified in behalf of the brewer, that the canteen shall curse our army and spread intemperance across the seas, and that our flag shall wave as the symbol of partnership, at home and abroad, between this Government and the men who defy and defile it for their unholy gain.

Third—We charge upon President McKinley, who was elected to his high office by appeal to Christian sentiment and patriotism almost unprecedented and by a combination of moral influences never before seen in this country, that, by his conspicuous example as a wine-drinker at public banquets and a wine-serving host in the White House, he has done more to encourage the liquor business, to demoralize the temperance habits of young men, and to bring Christian practices and requirements into disrepute, than any other President this republic has had. We further charge upon President McKinley responsibility for the army canteen, with all its dire brood of disease, immorality, sin, and death, in this country, in Cuba, in Porto Rico, and the Philippines; and we insist that by his attitude concerning the canteen, and his apparent contempt for the vast number of petitions and petitioners protesting against it, he has outraged and insulted the moral sentiment of this country in such a manner and to such a degree as calls for its righteous uprising and his indignant and effective rebuke.

We challenge denial of the fact that our Chief Executive, as commander in chief of the military forces of the United States, at any time prior to or since March 2, 1899, could have closed every army saloon, called a canteen, by executive order, as President Hayes in effect did before him, and should have closed them, for the same reasons which actuated President Hayes; we assert that the act of Congress passed March 2, 1899, forbidding the sale of liquor "in any post-exchange or canteen," by any "officer or private soldier" or by "any other person on any premises used for military purposes in the United States," was and is as explicit an act of prohibition as the English language can frame.

We declare our solemn belief that the Attorney-General of the United States in his interpretation of that law, and the Secretary of War in his acceptance of that interpretation and his refusal to enforce the law, were and are guilty of treasonable nullification thereof, and that President McKinley, through his assent to and indorsement of such interpretation and refusal, on the part of officials appointed by and responsible to him, shares responsibility in their guilt; and we record our conviction that a new and serious peril confronts our country, in the fact that its President, at the behest of the beer power, dares and does abrogate a law of Congress, through subordinates removable at will by him and whose acts become his, and thus virtually confesses that laws are to be administered or to be nullified in the interest of a law-defying business, by an Administration under mortgage to such business for support.

Fourth—We deplore the fact that an Administration of this Republic claiming the right and power to carry our flag across seas, and to conquer and annex new territory, should admit its lack of power to prohibit the American saloon on subjugated soil, or should openly confess itself subject to liquor sovereignty under that flag. We are humiliated, exasperated and grieved, by the evidence painfully abundant, that this Administration's policy of expansion is bearing so rapidly its first fruits of drunkenness, insanity, and crime under the hot-house sun of the tropics; and when the president of the first Philippine commission said: "It was unfortunate that we introduced and established the saloon there, to corrupt the natives and to exhibit the vices of our race," we charge the inhumanity and unchristianity of this act upon the Administration of William McKinley and upon the party which elected and would perpetuate the same.

Fifth—We declare that the only policy which the government of the United States can of right uphold as to the liquor traffic, under the national Constitution, upon any territory under the military or civic control of that Government, is the policy of prohibition; that "to establish justice, insure domestic tranquillity, provide for the common defense, promote the general welfare, and secure the blessings of liberty to ourselves and our posterity," as the Constitution provides, the liquor traffic must neither be sanctioned nor tolerated, and that the revenue policy, which makes our Government a partner with distillers and brewers and barkeepers, is a disgrace to our civilization, an outrage upon humanity, and a crime against God.

We condemn the present Administration at Washington because it has repealed the prohibitory laws in Alaska, and has given over the partly civilized tribes there to be the prey of the American grog-shop; and because it has entered upon a license policy in our new possessions by incorporating the same in the recent act of Congress in the code of laws for the government of the Hawaiian Islands.

We call general attention to the fearful fact that exportation of liquors from the United States to the Philippine Islands increased from $337 in 1898 to $467,198 in the first ten months of the fiscal year ending June 30, 1900; and that while our exportation of liquors to Cuba never reached $30,000 a year previous to American occupation of that island, our exports of such liquors to Cuba during the fiscal year of 1899 reached the sum of $629,855.

Sixth—One great religious body (the Baptist) having truly declared of the liquor traffic "that it has no defensible right to exist, that it can never be reformed, and that it stands condemned by its unrighteous fruits as a thing un-Christian, un-American, and perilous utterly to every interest in life"; another great religious body (the Methodist) having as truly asserted, and reiterated that "no political party has a right to expect, nor should receive, the votes of Christian men so long as it stands committed to the license system, or refuses to put itself on record in an attitude of open hostility to the saloon"; other great religious bodies having made similar deliverances, in language plain and unequivocal, as to the liquor traffic and the duty of Christian citizenship in opposition thereto; and the fact being plain and undeniable that the Democratic party stands for license, the saloon, and the canteen, while the Republican party, in policy and administration, stands for the canteen, the saloon and revenue therefrom, we declare ourselves justified in expecting that Christian voters everywhere shall cease their complicity with the liquor curse by refusing to uphold a liquor party, and shall unite themselves with the only party which upholds the prohibition policy, and which for nearly thirty years has been the faithful defender of the church, the State, the home, and the school, against the saloon, its expanders and perpetrators, their actual and persistent foes.

We insist that no differences of belief as to any other question or concern of government should stand in the way of such a union of moral and Christian citizenship as we hereby invite, for the speedy settlement of this paramount moral, industrial, financial and political issue, which our party presents; and we refrain from declaring ourselves upon all minor matters, as to which differences of opinion may exist, that hereby we may offer to the American people a platform so broad that all can stand upon it who desire to see sober citizenship actually sovereign over the allied hosts of evil, sin, and crime, in a government of the people, by the people, and for the people.

We declare that there are but two real parties to-day concerning the liquor traffic—Perpetuationists and Prohibitionists—and that patriotism, Christianity, and every interest of genuine republicanism and of pure democracy, besides the loyal demands of our common humanity, require the speedy union, in one solid phalanx at the ballot-box, of all who oppose the liquor traffic's perpetuation, and who covet endurance for this Republic.

Republican Platform of 1900

The Republicans of the United States, through their chosen representatives, met in National Convention, looking back upon an unsurpassed record of achievement and looking forward into a great field of duty and opportunity, and appealing to the judgment of their countrymen, make these declarations:

The expectation in which the American people, turning from the Democratic party, intrusted power four years ago to a Republican Chief Magistrate and a Republican Congress, has been met and satisfied. When the people then assembled at the polls, after a term of Democratic legislation and administration, business was dead, industry paralyzed and the National credit disastrously impaired. The country's capital was hidden away and its labor distressed and unemployed. The Democrats had no other plan with which to improve the ruinous conditions which they had themselves produced than to coin silver at the ratio of sixteen to one. The Republican party, denouncing this plan as sure to produce conditions even worse than those from which relief was sought, promised to restore prosperity by means of two legislative measures—a protective tariff and a law making gold the standard of value. The people by great majorities issued to the Republican party a commission to enact these laws. This commission has been executed, and the Republican promise is redeemed. Prosperity more general and more abundant than we have ever known has followed these enactments. There is no longer controversy as to the value of any Government obligations. Every American dollar is a gold dollar or its assured equivalent, and American credit stands higher than that of any other nation. Capital is fully employed and labor everywhere is profitably occupied. No single fact can more strikingly tell the story of what Republican Government means to the country than this— That while during the whole period of one hundred and seven years from 1790 to 1897 there was an excess of exports over imports of only $383,028,497, there has been in the short three years of the present Republican administration an excess of exports over imports in the enormous sum of $1,483,537,094.

And while the American people, sustained by this Republican legislation, have been achieving these splendid triumphs in their business and commerce, they have conducted and in victory concluded a war for liberty and human rights. No thought of National aggrandizement tarnished the high purpose with which American standards were unfurled. It was a war unsought and patiently resisted, but when it came the American Government was ready. Its fleets were cleared for action. Its armies were in the field, and the quick and signal triumph of its forces on land and sea bore equal tribute to the courage of American soldiers and sailors, and to the skill and foresight of Republican statesmanship. To ten millions of the human race there was given "a new birth of freedom," and to the American people a new and noble responsibility.

We indorse the administration of William McKinley. Its acts have been established in wisdom and in patriotism, and at home and abroad it has distinctly elevated and extended the influence of the American nation. Walking untried paths and facing unforeseen responsibilities, President McKinley has been in every situation the true American patriot and the upright statesman, clear in vision, strong in judgment, firm in action, always inspiring and deserving the confidence of his countrymen.

In asking the American people to indorse this Republican record and to renew their commission

to the Republican party, we remind them of the fact that the menace to their prosperity has always resided in Democratic principles, and no less in the general incapacity of the Democratic party to conduct public affairs. The prime essential of business prosperity is public confidence in the good sense of the Government and in its ability to deal intelligently with each new problem of administration and legislation. That confidence the Democratic party has never earned. It is hopelessly inadequate, and the country's prosperity, when Democratic success at the polls is announced, halts and ceases in mere anticipation of Democratic blunders and failures.

We renew our allegiance to the principle of the gold standard and declare our confidence in the wisdom of the legislation of the Fifty-sixth Congress, by which the parity of all our money and the stability of our currency upon a gold basis has been secured. We recognize that interest rates are a potent factor in production and business activity, and for the purpose of further equalizing and of further lowering the rates of interest, we favor such monetary legislation as will enable the varying needs of the season and of all sections to be promptly met in order that trade may be evenly sustained, labor steadily employed and commerce enlarged. The volume of money in circulation was never so great per capita as it is to-day. We declare our steadfast opposition to the free and unlimited coinage of silver. No measure to that end could be considered which was without the support of the leading commercial countries of the world. However firmly Republican legislation may seem to have secured the country against the peril of base and discredited currency, the election of a Democratic President could not fail to impair the country's credit and to bring once more into question the intention of the American people to maintain upon the gold standard the parity of their money circulation. The Democratic party must be convinced that the American people will never tolerate the Chicago platform.

We recognize the necessity and propriety of the honest co-operation of capital to meet new business conditions and especially to extend our rapidly increasing foreign trade, but we condemn all conspiracies and combinations intended to restrict business, to create monopolies, to limit production, or to control prices; and favor such legislation as will effectively restrain and prevent all such abuses, protect and promote competition and secure the rights of producers, laborers, and all who are engaged in industry and commerce.

We renew our faith in the policy of Protection to American labor. In that policy our industries have been established, diversified and maintained. By protecting the home market competition has been stimulated and production cheapened. Opportunity to the inventive genius of our people has been secured and wages in every department of labor maintained at high rates, higher now than ever before, and always distinguishing our working people in their better conditions of life from those of any competing country. Enjoying the blessings of the American common school, secure in the right of self-government and protected in the occupancy of their own markets, their constantly increasing knowledge and skill have enabled them to finally enter the markets of the world. We favor the associated policy of reciprocity so directed as to open our markets on favorable terms for what we do not ourselves produce in return for free foreign markets.

In the further interest of American workmen we favor a more effective restriction of the immigration of cheap labor from foreign lands, the extension of opportunities of education for working children, the raising of the age limit for child labor, the protection of free labor as against contract convict labor, and an effective system of labor insurance.

Our present dependence upon foreign shipping for nine-tenths of our foreign carrying is a great loss to the industry of this country. It is also a serious danger to our trade, for its sudden withdrawal in the event of European war would seriously cripple our expanding foreign commerce. The National defense and naval efficiency of this country, moreover, supply a compelling reason for legislation which will enable us to recover our former place among the trade-carrying fleets of the world.

The Nation owes a debt of profound gratitude to the soldiers and sailors who have fought its battles, and it is the Government's duty to provide for the survivors and for the widows and orphans of those who have fallen in the country's wars. The pension laws, founded in this just sentiment, should be liberally administered, and preference should be given wherever practicable with respect to employment in the public service, to soldiers and sailors and to their widows and orphans.

We commend the policy of the Republican party in maintaining the efficiency of the civil service. The Administration has acted wisely in its efforts to secure for public service in Cuba, Puerto Rico, Hawaii, and the Philippine Islands, only those whose fitness has been determined by training and experience. We believe that employment in the public service in these territories should be confined as far as practicable to their inhabitants.

It was the plain purpose of the fifteenth amendment to the Constitution, to prevent discrimination on account of race or color in regulating the elective franchise. Devices of State governments, whether by statutory or constitutional enactment, to avoid the purpose of this amendment are revolutionary, and should be condemned.

Public movements looking to a permanent improvement of the roads and highways of the country meet with our cordial approval, and we recommend this subject to the earnest consideration of the people and of the Legislatures of the several states.

We favor the extension of the Rural Free Delivery service wherever its extension may be justified.

In further pursuance of the constant policy of the Republican party to provide free homes on the public domain, we recommend adequate national legislation to reclaim the arid lands of the United States, reserving control of the distribution of water for irrigation to the respective States and territories.

We favor home rule for, and the early admission to statehood of the Territories of New Mexico, Arizona, and Oklahoma.

The Dingley Act, amended to provide sufficient revenue for the conduct of the war, has so well performed its work that it has been possible to reduce the war debt in the sum of $40,000,000. So ample are the Government's revenues and so great is the public confidence in the integrity of its obligations that its newly-funded two per cent bonds sell at a premium. The country is now justified in expecting, and it will be the policy of the Republican party to bring about, a reduction of the war taxes.

We favor the construction, ownership, control and protection of an Isthmian Canal by the Government of the United States. New markets are necessary for the increasing surplus of our farm products. Every effort should be made to open and obtain new markets, especially in the Orient, and the Administration is warmly to be commended for its successful efforts to commit all trading and colonizing nations to the policy of the open door in China.

In the interest of our expanding commerce we recommend that Congress create a Department of Commerce and Industries, in the charge of a Secretary with a seat in the Cabinet. The United States Consular system should be reorganized under the supervision of this new Department upon such a basis of appointment and tenure as will render it still more serviceable to the Nation's increasing trade.

The American Government must protect the person and property of every citizen wherever they are wrongfully violated or placed in peril.

We congratulate the women of America upon their splendid record of public service in the volunteer aid association and as nurses in camp and hospital during the recent campaigns of our armies in the East and West Indies, and we appreciate their faithful co-operation in all works of education and industry.

President McKinley has conducted the foreign affairs of the United States with distinguished credit to the American people. In releasing us from the vexatious conditions of a European alliance for the government of Samoa, his course is especially to be commended. By securing to our undivided control the most important island of the Samoan group and the best harbor in the Southern Pacific, every American interest has been safeguarded.

We approve the annexation of the Hawaiian Islands to the United States.

We commend the part taken by our Government in the Peace Conference at The Hague. We assert our steadfast adherence to the policy announced in the Monroe Doctrine. The provisions of The Hague Convention were wisely regarded when President McKinley tendered his friendly offices in the interest of peace between Great Britain and the South African Republic. While the American Government must continue the policy prescribed by Washington, affirmed by every succeeding President and imposed upon us by The Hague treaty, of non-intervention in

European controversies, the American people earnestly hope that a way may soon be found, honorable alike to both contending parties, to terminate the strife between them.

In accepting by the Treaty of Paris the just responsibility of our victories in the Spanish war, the President and the Senate won the undoubted approval of the American people. No other course was possible than to destroy Spain's sovereignty throughout the West Indies and in the Philippine Islands. That course created our responsibility before the world, and with the unorganized population whom our intervention had freed from Spain, to provide for the maintenance of law and order, and for the establishment of good government and for the performance of international obligations. Our authority could not be less than our responsibility; and wherever sovereign rights were extended it became the high duty of the Government to maintain its authority, to put down armed insurrection and to confer the blessings of liberty and civilization upon all the rescued peoples.

The largest measure of self-government consistent with their welfare and our duties shall be secured to them by law.

To Cuba independence and self-government were assured in the same voice by which war was declared, and to the latter this pledge shall be performed.

The Republican party, upon its history, and upon this declaration of its principles and policies confidently invokes the considerate and approving judgment of the American people.

Silver Republican Platform of 1900

We, the Silver Republican party, in National Convention assembled, declare these as our principles and invite the co-operation of all who agree therewith:

We recognize that the principles set forth in the Declaration of Independence are fundamental and everlastingly true in their application to governments among men. We believe the patriotic words of Washington's farewell to be the words of soberness and wisdom, inspired by the spirit of right and truth. We treasure the words of Jefferson as priceless gems of American statesmanship.

We hold in sacred remembrance the broad philanthropy and patriotism of Lincoln, who was the great interpreter of American history and the great apostle of human rights and of industrial freedom; and we declare, as was declared by the convention that nominated the great emancipator, that the maintenance of the principles promulgated in the Declaration of Independence and embodied in the Federal Constitution, "that all men are created equal; that they are endowed by their Creator with certain inalienable rights; that among these are life, liberty, and the pursuit of happiness; that to secure these rights governments are instituted among men, deriving their just powers from the consent of the governed," is essential to the preservation of our republican institutions.

We declare our adherence to the principle of bimetallism as the right basis of a monetary system under our National Constitution, a principle that found place repeatedly in Republican platforms, from the demonetization of silver in 1873 to the St. Louis Republican Convention in 1896.

Since that convention a Republican Congress and a Republican President, at the dictation of the trusts and money power, have passed and approved a currency bill which in itself is a repudiation of the doctrine of bimetallism advocated theretofore by the President and every great leader of his party.

This currency law destroys the full money power of the silver dollar, provides for the payment of all government obligations and the redemption of all forms of paper money in gold alone; retires the time-honored and patriotic greenbacks, constituting one-sixth of the money in circulation, and surrenders to banking corporations a sovereign function of issuing all paper money, thus enabling these corporations to control the prices of labor and property by increasing or diminishing the volume of money in circulation, thus giving the banks power to create panics and bring disaster upon business enterprises.

The provisions of this currency law making the bonded debt of the Republic payable in gold alone, change the contract between the Government and the bond-holders to the advantage of the latter, and is in direct opposition to the declaration of the Matthews resolution passed by Congress in 1878, for which resolution the present Republican President, then a member of Congress, voted, as did also all leading Republicans, both in the House and Senate.

We declare it to be our intention to lend our efforts to the repeal of this currency law, which not only repudiates ancient and time-honored principles of the American people before the Constitution was adopted, but is violative of the principles of the Constitution itself, and we shall not cease our efforts until there has been established in its place a monetary system based upon the free and unlimited coinage of silver and gold into money at the present legal ratio of 16 to 1 by the independent action of the United States, under which system all paper money shall be issued by the Government and all such money coined or issued shall be a full legal tender in payment of all debts, public and private, without exception.

We are in favor of a graduated tax upon incomes, and if necessary to accomplish this we favor an amendment to the Constitution.

We believe that United States Senators ought to be elected by a direct vote of the people, and we favor such amendment of the Constitution and such legislation as may be necessary to that end.

We favor the maintenance and the extension wherever practicable of the merit system in the public service, appointments to be made according to fitness, competitively ascertained, and public servants to be retained in office only so long as shall be compatible with the efficiency of the service.

Combinations, trusts, and monopolies contrived and arranged for the purpose of controlling the prices and quantity of articles supplied to the public are unjust, unlawful, and oppressive.

Not only do these unlawful conspiracies fix the prices of commodities in many cases, but they invade every branch of the State and National Government with their polluting influence and control the actions of their employees and dependents in private life until their influence actually imperils society and the liberty of the citizen.

We declare against them. We demand the most stringent laws for their destruction and the most severe punishment of their promoters and maintainers and the energetic enforcement of such laws by the courts.

We believe the Monroe doctrine to be sound in principle and a wise National policy, and we demand a firm adherence thereto. We condemn acts inconsistent with it and that tend to make us parties to the interest and to involve us in the controversies of European nations and to recognition by pending treaty, of the right of England to be considered in the construction of an interoceanic canal. We declare that such a canal when constructed ought to be controlled by the United States in the interests of American nations.

We observe with anxiety and regard with disapproval the increasing ownership of American lands by aliens, and their growing control over international transportation, natural resources, and public utilities. We demand legislation to protect our public domain, our natural resources, our franchises, and our internal commerce and to keep them free and maintain their independence of all foreign monopolies, institutions, and influences, and we declare our opposition to the leasing of the public lands of the United States whereby corporations and syndicates will be able to secure control thereof and thus monopolize the public domain, the heritage of the people.

We are in favor of the principles of direct legislation. In view of the great sacrifice made and patriotic services rendered, we are in favor of liberal pensions to deserving soldiers, their widows, orphans, and other dependents. We believe that enlistment and service should be accepted as conclusive proof that the soldier was free from disease and disability at the time of his enlistment. We condemn the present administration of the pension laws.

We tender to the patriotic people of the South African Republic our sympathy and express our admiration for them in their heroic attempts to preserve their political freedom and maintain their national independence. We declare the destruction of those republics and the subjugation of their people to be a crime against civilization.

We believe this sympathy should have been voiced by the American Congress, as was done in the case of the French, the Greeks, the Hungarians, the Polanders, the Armenians, and the Cubans, and as the traditions of this country would have dictated. We declare the Porto Rican Tariff law to be not only a serious but a dangerous departure from the principles of our form of government. We believe in a republican form of government and are opposed to monarchy and to the whole theory of imperialistic control.

We believe in self-government—a government by the consent of the governed—and are unaltera-

bly opposed to a government based upon force. It is clear and certain that the inhabitants of the Philippine archipelago cannot be made citizens of the United States without endangering our civilization. We are, therefore, in favor of applying to the Philippine archipelago the principle we are solemnly and publicly pledged to observe in the case of Cuba.

There no longer being any necessity for collecting war taxes, we demand the repeal of the war taxes levied to carry on the war with Spain.

We favor the immediate admission into the Union of States the Territories of Arizona, New Mexico, and Oklahoma.

We demand that our nation's promises to Cuba shall be fulfilled in every particular.

We believe the National Government should lend every aid, encouragement, and assistance toward the reclamation of the arid lands of the United States, and to that end we are in favor of a comprehensive survey thereof and an immediate ascertainment of the water supply available for such reclamation, and we believe it to be the duty of the General Government to provide for the construction of storage reservoirs and irrigation works so that the water supply of the arid region may be utilized to the greatest possible extent in the interests of the people, while preserving all rights of the State.

Transportation is a public necessity and the means and methods of it are matters of public concern. Railway companies exercise a power over industries, business, and commerce which they ought not to do, and should be made to serve the public interests without making unreasonable charges of unjust discrimination.

We observe with satisfaction the growing sentiment among the people in favor of the public ownership and operation of public utilities.

We are in favor of expanding our commerce in the interests of American labor and for the benefit of all our people, by every honest and peaceful means. Our creed and our history justify the nations of the earth in expecting that wherever the American flag is unfurled in authority human liberty and political freedom will be found. We protest against the adoption of any policy that will change in the thought of the world, the meaning of our flag.

We are opposed to the importation of Asiatic laborers in competition with American labor, and favor a more rigid enforcement of the laws relating thereto.

The Silver Republican party of the United States, in the foregoing principles, seeks to perpetuate the spirit and to adhere to the teachings of Abraham Lincoln.

Social Democratic Platform of 1900

The Social Democratic Party of the United States, in convention assembled, reaffirms its allegiance to the revolutionary principles of International Socialism and declares the supreme political issue in America to-day to be the contest between the working class and the capitalist class for the possession of the powers of government. The party affirms its steadfast purpose to use those powers, once achieved, to destroy wage slavery, abolish the institution of private property in the means of production, and establish the Co-operative Commonwealth.

In the United States, as in all other civilized countries, the natural order of economic development has separated society into two antagonistic classes—the capitalists, a comparatively small class, the possessors of all the means of production and distribution (land, mines, machinery, and means of transportation and communication), and the large and ever-increasing class of wage workers, possessing no means of production.

This economic supremacy has secured to the dominant class the full control of the government, the pulpit, the schools, and the public press; it has thus made the capitalist class the arbiters of the fate of the workers, whom it is reducing to a condition of dependence, economically exploited and oppressed, intellectually and physically crippled and degraded, and their political equality rendered a bitter mockery.

The contest between these two classes grows ever sharper. Hand in hand with the growth of monopolies goes the annihilation of small industries and of the middle class depending upon them; ever larger grows the multitude of destitute wage workers and of the unemployed, and ever fiercer the struggle between the class of the exploiter and the exploited, the capitalists and the wage workers.

The evil effects of capitalist production are intensified by the recurring industrial crises which render the existence of the greater part of the population still more precarious and uncertain.

These facts amply prove that the modern means of production have outgrown the existing social order based on production for profit.

Human energy and natural resources are wasted for individual gain.

Ignorance is fostered that wage slavery may be perpetuated. Science and invention are perverted to the exploitation of men, women, and children.

The lives and liberties of the working class are recklessly sacrificed for profit.

Wars are fomented between nations; indiscriminate slaughter is encouraged; the destruction of whole races is sanctioned, in order that the capitalist class may extend its commercial dominion abroad and enhance its supremacy at home.

The introduction of a new and higher order of society is the historic mission of the working class. All other classes, despite their apparent or actual conflicts, are interested in upholding the system of private ownership in the means of production. The Democratic, Republican, and all other parties which do not stand for the complete overthrow of the capitalist system of production, are alike the tools of the capitalist class.

The workers can most effectively act as a class in their struggle against the collective power of the capitalist class only by constituting themselves into a political party, distinct and opposed to all parties formed by the propertied classes.

We, therefore, call upon the wage-workers of the United States, without distinction of color, race, sex, or creed, and upon all citizens in sympathy with the historic mission of the working class, to organize under the banner of the Social Democratic Party as a party truly representing the interests of the toiling masses and uncompromisingly waging war upon the exploiting class, until the system of wage slavery shall be abolished and the Co-operative Commonwealth established. Pending the accomplishment of this our ultimate purpose, we pledge every effort of the Social Democratic Party for the immediate improvement of the condition of labor and for the securing of its progressive demands.

IMMEDIATE DEMANDS

As steps in that direction, we make the following demands:

First—Revision of our federal constitution, in order to remove the obstacles to complete control of Government by the people irrespective of sex.

Second—The public ownership of all industries controlled by monopolies, trusts, and combines.

Third—The public ownership of all railroads, telegraphs, and telephones; all means of transportation and communication; all water-works, gas and electric plants, and other public utilities.

Fourth—The public ownership of all gold, silver, copper, lead, iron, coal, and other mines, and all oil and gas wells.

Fifth—The reduction of the hours of labor in proportion to increasing facilities of production.

Sixth—The inauguration of a system of public works and improvements for the employment of the unemployed, the public credit to be utilized for that purpose.

Seventh—Useful inventions to be free, the inventors to be remunerated by the public.

Eighth—Labor legislation to be national, instead of local, and international when possible.

Ninth—National insurance of working people against accidents, lack of employment, and want in old age.

Tenth—Equal civic and political rights for men and women, and the abolition of all laws discriminating against women.

Eleventh—The adoption of the initiative and referendum, proportional representation, and the right of recall of representatives by the voters.

Twelfth—Abolition of war and the introduction of international arbitration.

Socialist Labor Platform of 1900

The Socialist Labor Party of the United States in Convention assembled, reasserts the inalienable right of all men to life, liberty, and the pursuit of happiness.

With the founders of the American Republic we hold that the purpose of government is to secure every citizen in the enjoyment of this right; but in the light of our social conditions we hold, furthermore, that no such right can be exercised under a system of economic inequality, essentially destructive of life, of liberty, and of happiness.

With the founders of this Republic, we hold that the true theory of politics is that the machinery of government must be owned and con-

trolled by the whole people; but in the light of our industrial development we hold, furthermore, that the true theory of economics is that the machinery of production must likewise belong to the people in common.

To the obvious fact that our despotic system of economics is the direct opposite of our democratic system of politics, can plainly be traced the existence of a privileged class, the corruption of government by that class, the alienation of public property, public franchises and public functions to that class, and the abject dependence of the mightiest of nations upon that class.

Again, through the perversion of democracy to the ends of plutocracy, labor is robbed of the wealth which it alone produces, is denied the means of self-employment, and, by compulsory idleness in wage slavery, is even deprived of the necessaries of life.

Human power and natural forces are thus wasted, that the plutocracy may rule.

Ignorance and misery, with all their concomitant evils, are perpetuated, that the people may be kept in bondage.

Science and invention are diverted from their humane purpose to the enslavement of women and children.

Against such a system the Socialist Labor Party once more enters its protest. Once more it reiterates its fundamental declaration that private property in the natural sources of production and in the instruments of labor is the obvious cause of all economic servitude and political dependence.

The time is fast coming when, in the natural course of social evolution, this system, through the destructive action of its failures and crises on the one hand, and the constructive tendencies of its trusts and other capitalistic combinations on the other hand, shall have worked out its own downfall.

We, therefore, call upon the wage workers of the United States, and upon all other honest citizens, to organize under the banner of the Socialist Labor Party into a class-conscious body, aware of its rights and determined to conquer them by taking possession of the public powers; so that, held together by an indomitable spirit of solidarity under the most trying conditions of the present class struggle, we may put a summary end to that barbarous struggle by the abolition of classes, the restoration of the land and of all the means of production, transportation and distribution to the people as a collective body, and the substitution of the Co-operative Commonwealth for the present state of planless production, industrial war and social disorder; a commonwealth in which every worker shall have the free exercise and full benefit of his faculties, multiplied by all the modern factors of civilization.

☒ CAMPAIGN OF 1904

In 1904 there were the two major parties, the factions having been absorbed. The Social Democratic Party of 1900 now appears as the Socialist Party, along with the other well-established minor parties,—the Prohibitionists and the Social Labor Party. The People's Party of this year was the Middle-of-the-Road Faction of 1900.

Democratic Platform of 1904

The Democratic party of the United States, in National Convention assembled, declares its devotion to the essential principles of the Democratic faith which bring us together in party communion.

Under these principles local self-government and National unity and prosperity were alike established. They underlaid our independence, the structure of our free Republic, and every Democratic expansion from Louisiana to California, and Texas to Oregon, which preserved faithfully in all the States the tie between taxation and representation. They yet inspirit the masses of our people, guarding jealously their rights and liberties, and cherishing their fraternity, peace and orderly development. They remind us of our duties and responsibilities as citizens and impress upon us, particularly at this time, the necessity of reform and the rescue of the administration of Government from the headstrong, arbitrary and spasmodic methods which distract business by uncertainty, and pervade the public mind with dread, distrust and perturbation.

FUNDAMENTAL PRINCIPLES

The application of these fundamental principles to the living issues of the day constitutes the first step toward the assured peace, safety and progress of our nation. Freedom of the press, of conscience, and of speech; equality before the law of all citizens; right of trial by jury; freedom of the person defended by the Writ of Habeas Corpus; liberty of personal contract untrammeled by sumptuary laws; supremacy of the civil over military authority; a well-disciplined militia; separation of Church and State; economy in expenditures; low taxes, that labor may be lightly burdened; prompt and sacred fulfillment of public and private obligations; fidelity to treaties; peace and friendship with all nations, entangling alliances with none; absolute acquiescence in the will of the majority, the vital principle of Republics — these are doctrines which Democracy has established as proverbs of the Nation, and they should be constantly invoked, and enforced.

ECONOMY OF ADMINISTRATION

Large reductions can easily be made in the annual expenditures of the Government without impairing the efficiency of any branch of the public service, and we shall insist upon the strictest economy and frugality compatible with vigorous and efficient civil, military and naval administration as a right of the people, too clear to be denied or withheld.

HONESTY IN THE PUBLIC SERVICE

We favor the enforcement of honesty in the public service, and to that end a thorough legislative investigation of those executive departments of the Government already known to teem with corruption, as well as other departments suspected of harboring corruption, and the punishment of ascertained corruptionists without fear or favor or regard to persons. The persistent and deliberate refusal of both the Senate and House of Representatives to permit such investigation to be made demonstrates that only by a change in the executive and in the legislative departments can complete exposure, punishment and correction be obtained.

FEDERAL GOVERNMENT CONTRACTS WITH TRUSTS

We condemn the action of the Republican party in Congress in refusing to prohibit an executive department from entering into contracts with convicted trusts or unlawful combinations in restraint of inter-State trade. We believe that one of the best methods of procuring economy and honesty in the public service is to have public officials, from the occupant of the White House down to the lowest of them, return, as nearly as may be, to Jeffersonian simplicity of living.

EXECUTIVE USURPATION

We favor the nomination and election of a President imbued with the principles of the Constitution, who will set his face sternly against executive usurpation of legislative and judicial functions, whether that usurpation be veiled under the guise of executive construction of existing laws, or whether it take refuge in the tyrant's plea of necessity or superior wisdom.

IMPERIALISM

We favor the preservation, so far as we can, of an open door for the world's commerce in the Orient without unnecessary entanglement in Oriental and European affairs, and without arbitrary, unlimited, irresponsible and absolute government anywhere within our jurisdiction. We oppose, as fervently as did George Washington, an indefinite, irresponsible, discretionary and vague absolutism and a policy of colonial exploitation, no matter where or by whom invoked or exercised. We believe with Thomas Jefferson and John Adams, that no Government has a right to make one set of laws for those "at home" and another and a different set of laws, absolute in their character, for those "in the colonies." All men under the American flag are entitled to the protection of the institutions whose emblem the flag is; if they are inherently unfit for those institutions, then they are inherently unfit to be members of the American body politic. Wherever there may exist a people incapable of being governed under American laws, in consonance with the American Constitution, the territory of that people ought not to be part of the American domain.

We insist that we ought to do for the Filipinos what we have done already for the Cubans, and it is our duty to make that promise now, and upon suitable guarantees of protection to citizens of our own and other countries resident there at the time of our withdrawal to set the Filipino people upon their feet, free and independent, to work out their own destiny.

The endeavor of the Secretary of War, by pledging the Government's endorsement for "promoters" in the Philippine Islands to make the United States a partner in speculative exploitation of the archipelago, which was only temporarily held up by the opposition of Democratic Senators in the last session, will, if successful, lead to entanglements from which it will be difficult to escape.

TARIFF

The Democratic party has been, and will continue to be, the consistent opponent of that class of tariff legislation by which certain interests have been permitted, through Congressional favor, to draw a heavy tribute from the American people. This monstrous perversion of those equal opportunities which our political institutions were established to secure, has caused what may once have been infant industries to become the greatest combinations of capital that the world has ever known. These special favorites of the Government have, through trust methods, been converted into monopolies, thus bringing to an end domestic competition, which was the only alleged check upon the extravagant profits made possible by the protective system. These industrial combinations, by the financial assistance they can give, now control the policy of the Republican party.

We denounce protectionism as a robbery of

the many to enrich the few, and we favor a tariff limited to the needs of the Government economically, effectively and constitutionally administered and so levied as not to discriminate against any industry, class or section, to the end that the burdens of taxation shall be distributed as equally as possible.

We favor a revision and a gradual reduction of the tariff by the friends of the masses and for the common weal, and not by the friend of its abuses, its extortions and its discriminations, keeping in view the ultimate end of "equality of burdens and equality of opportunities," and the constitutional purpose of raising a revenue by taxation, to wit: the support of the Federal Government in all its integrity and virility, but in simplicity.

Trusts and Unlawful Combinations

We recognize that the gigantic trusts and combinations designed to enable capital to secure more than its just share of the joint product of capital and labor, and which have been fostered and promoted under Republican rule, are a menace to beneficial competition and an obstacle to permanent business prosperity.

A private monopoly is indefensible and intolerable.

Individual equality of opportunity and free competition are essential to a healthy and permanent commercial prosperity; and any trust, combination or monopoly tending to destroy these by controlling production, restricting competition or fixing prices and wages, should be prohibited and punished by law. We especially denounce rebates and discriminations by transportation companies as the most potent agency in promoting and strengthening these unlawful conspiracies against trade.

We demand an enlargement of the powers of the Interstate Commerce Commission, to the end that the traveling public and shippers of this country may have prompt and adequate relief from the abuses to which they are subjected in the matter of transportation. We demand a strict enforcement of existing civil and criminal statutes against all such trusts, combinations and monopolies; and we demand the enactment of such further legislation as may be necessary effectually to suppress them.

Any trust or unlawful combination engaged in inter-State commerce which is monopolizing any branch of business or production, should not be permitted to transact business outside of the State of its origin, whenever it shall be established in any court of competent jurisdiction that such monopolization exists. Such prohibition should be enforced through comprehensive laws to be enacted on the subject.

Capital and Labor

We favor the enactment and administration of laws giving labor and capital impartially their just rights. Capital and labor ought not to be enemies. Each is necessary to the other. Each has its rights, but the rights of labor are certainly no less "vested," no less "sacred" and no less "inalienable" than the rights of capital.

We favor arbitration of differences between corporate employers and their employees and a strict enforcement of the eight hour law on all Government work.

We approve the measure which passed the United States Senate in 1896, but which a Republican Congress has ever since refused to enact, relating to contempts in Federal courts and providing for trial by jury in cases of indirect contempt.

Constitutional Guaranties

Constitutional guaranties are violated whenever any citizen is denied the right to labor, acquire and enjoy property or reside where interest or inclination may determine. Any denial thereof by individuals, organizations or governments should be summarily rebuked and punished.

We deny the right of any executive to disregard or suspend any constitutional privilege or limitation. Obedience to the laws and respect for their requirements are alike the supreme duty of the citizen and the official.

The military should be used only to support and maintain the law. We unqualifiedly condemn its employment for the summary banishment of citizens without trial, or for the control of elections.

Waterways

We favor liberal appropriations for the care and improvement of the waterways of the country. When any waterway like the Mississippi River is of sufficient importance to demand the special aid of the Government, such aid should be extended with a definite plan of continuous work until permanent improvement is secured.

We oppose the Republican policy of starving home development in order to feed the greed for conquest and the appetite for national "prestige" and display of strength.

Reclamation of Arid Lands and Domestic Development

We congratulate our Western citizens upon the passage of the measure known as the Newlands Irrigation Act for the irrigation and reclamation of the arid lands of the West—a measure framed by a Democrat, passed in the Senate by a non-partisan vote, and passed in the House against the opposition of almost all the Republican leaders by a vote the majority of which was Democratic. We call attention to this great Democratic measure, broad and comprehensive as it is, working automatically throughout all time without further action of Congress, until the reclamation of all the lands in the arid West capable of reclamation, is accomplished, reserving the lands reclaimed for homeseekers in small tracts and rigidly guarding against land monopoly, as an evidence of the policy of domestic development contemplated by the Democratic party, should it be placed in power.

The Isthmian Canal

The Democracy when entrusted with power will construct the Panama Canal speedily, honestly and economically, thereby giving to our people what Democrats have always contended for—a great inter-oceanic canal, furnishing shorter and cheaper lines of transportation, and broader and less trammeled trade relations with the other peoples of the world.

American Citizenship

We pledge ourselves to insist upon the just and lawful protection of our citizens at home and abroad, and to use all proper measures to secure for them, whether native born or naturalized, and without distinction of race or creed, the equal protection of laws and the enjoyment of all rights and privileges open to them under the covenants of our treaties of friendship and commerce; and if under existing treaties the right of travel and sojourn is denied to American citizens or recognition is withheld from American passports by any countries on the ground of race or creed, we favor

the beginning of negotiations with the governments of such countries to secure by new treaties the removal of these unjust discriminations.

We demand that all over the world a duly authenticated passport issued by the Government of the United States to an American citizen shall be proof of the fact that he is an American citizen and shall entitle him to the treatment due him as such.

Election of Senators by the People

We favor the election of United States Senators by direct vote of the people.

Statehood for Territories

We favor the admission of the Territory of Oklahoma and the Indian Territory. We also favor the immediate admission of Arizona and New Mexico, as separate States, and territorial governments for Alaska and Porto Rico.

We hold that the officials appointed to administer the government of any Territory, as well as the District of Alaska, should be *bona-fide* residents at the time of their appointment of the Territory or district in which their duties are to be performed.

Condemnation of Polygamy

We demand the extermination of polygamy within the jurisdiction of the United States, and the complete separation of Church and State in political affairs.

Merchant Marine

We denounce the ship subsidy bill recently passed by the United States Senate as an iniquitous appropriation of public funds for private purposes and a wasteful, illogical and useless attempt to overcome by subsidy the obstructions raised by Republican legislation to the growth and development of American commerce on the sea.

We favor the upbuilding of a merchant marine without new or additional burdens upon the people and without bounties from the public treasury.

Reciprocity

We favor liberal trade arrangements with Canada, and with peoples of other countries where they can be entered into with benefit to American agriculture, manufactures, mining or commerce.

Monroe Doctrine

We favor the maintenance of the Monroe Doctrine in its full integrity.

Army

We favor the reduction of the Army and of Army expenditures to the point historically demonstrated to be safe and sufficient.

Pensions. Our Soldiers and Sailors

The Democracy would secure to the surviving soldiers and sailors and their dependents generous pensions, not by an arbitrary executive order, but by legislation which a grateful people stand ready to enact.

Our soldiers and sailors who defend with their lives the Constitution and the laws have a sacred interest in their just administration. They must, therefore, share with us the humiliation with which we have witnessed the exaltation of court favorites, without distinguished service, over the scarred heroes of many battles, or aggrandizement by executive appropriations out of the treasuries of prostrate peoples in violation of the act of Congress which fixes the compensation of allowance of the military officers.

Civil Service

The Democratic party stands committed to the principles of civil service reform, and we demand their honest, just and impartial enforcement.

We denounce the Republican party for its continuous and sinister encroachments upon the spirit and operation of civil service rules, whereby it has arbitrarily dispensed with examinations for office in the interest of favorites, and employed all manner of devices to overreach and set aside the principles upon which the Civil Service is based.

Sectional and Race Agitation

The race question has brought countless woes to this country. The calm wisdom of the American people should see to it that it brings no more.

To revive the dead and hateful race and sectional animosities in any part of our common country means confusion, distraction of business, and the reopening of wounds now happily healed. North, South, East and West have but recently stood together in line of battle from the walls of Pekin to the hills of Santiago, and as sharers of a common glory and a common destiny, we should share fraternally the common burdens.

We therefore deprecate and condemn the Bourbon-like selfish, and narrow spirit of the recent Republican Convention at Chicago which sought to kindle anew the embers of racial and sectional strife, and we appeal from it to the sober common sense and patriotic spirit of the American people.

The Republican Administration

The existing Republican administration has been spasmodic, erratic, sensational, spectacular and arbitrary. It has made itself a satire upon the Congress, courts, and upon the settled practices and usages of national and international law.

It summoned the Congress in hasty and futile extra session and virtually adjourned it, leaving behind in its flight from Washington uncalled calendars and unaccomplished tasks.

It made war, which is the sole power of Congress, without its authority, thereby usurping one of its fundamental prerogatives. It violated a plain statute of the United States as well as plain treaty obligations, international usages and constitutional law; and has done so under pretense of executing a great public policy which could have been more easily effected lawfully, constitutionally and with honor.

It forced strained and unnatural constructions upon statutes, usurping judicial interpretation, and substituting for congressional enactment executive decree.

It withdrew from the Congress its customary duties of investigation which have heretofore made the representatives of the people and the States the terror of evildoers.

It conducted a secretive investigation of its own, and boasting of a few sample convicts, it threw a broad coverlet over the bureaus which had been their chosen field of operative abuses, and kept in power the superior officers under whose administration the crimes had been committed.

It ordered assault upon some monopolies, but paralyzed by a first victory, it flung out the flag of truce and cried out that it would not "run amuck"; leaving its future purposes beclouded by its vacillations.

Appeal to the People

Conducting the campaign upon this declaration of our principles and purposes, we invoke for our candidates the support not only of our great and time-honored organization, but also the active assistance of all of our fellow citizens who, disregarding past differences, desire the perpetuation of our constitutional Government as framed and established by the fathers of the Republic.

People's Platform of 1904

The People's party reaffirms its adherence to the basic truths of the Omaha platform of 1892, and of the subsequent platforms of 1896 and 1900. In session in its fourth national convention on July 4, 1904, in the city of Springfield, Ill., it draws inspiration from the day that saw the birth of the nation as well as its own birth as a party, and also from the soul of him who lives at its present place of meeting. We renew our allegiance to the old-fashioned American spirit that gave this nation existence, and made it distinctive among the peoples of the earth. We again sound the key-note of the Declaration of Independence that all men are created equal in a political sense, which was the sense in which that instrument, being a political document, intended that the utterance should be understood. We assert that the departure from this fundamental truth is responsible for the ills from which we suffer as a nation, that the giving of special privileges to the few has enabled them to dominate the many, thereby tending to destroy the political equality which is the corner-stone of democratic government.

Holding fast to the truths of the fathers we vigorously protest against the spirit of mammonism and of thinly veiled monarchy that is invading certain sections of our national life, and of the very administration itself. This is a nation of peace, and we deplore the appeal to the spirit of force and militarism which is shown in ill-advised and vainglorious boasting and in more harmful ways in the denial of the rights of man under martial law.

A political democracy and an industrial despotism cannot exist side by side; and nowhere is this truth more plainly shown than in the gigantic transportation monopolies which have bred all sorts of kindred trusts, subverted the governments of many of the States, or established their official agents in the National Government. We submit that it is better for the Government to own the railroads than for the railroads to own the Government, and that one or the other alternative seems inevitable.

We call the attention of our fellow-citizens to the fact that the surrender of both of the old parties to corporative influences leaves the People's party the only party of reform in the nation.

Therefore we submit the following platform of principles to the American people:—

The issuing of money is a function of government, and should never be delegated to corporations or individuals. The Constitution gives to Congress alone power to issue money and regulate its value.

We therefore demand that all money shall be issued by the Government in such quantity as shall maintain a stability in prices, every dollar to be full legal tender, none of which shall be a debt redeemable in other money.

We demand that postal-savings banks be established by the Government for the safe deposit of the savings of the people.

We believe in the right of labor to organize for the benefit and protection of those who toil; and pledge the efforts of the People's party to preserve this right inviolate. Capital is organized and has no right to deny to labor the privilege which it claims for itself. We feel that intelligent organization of labor is essential; that it raises the standard of workmanship; promotes the efficiency, intelligence, independence and character of the wage earner. We believe with Abraham Lincoln that labor is prior to capital, and is not its slave, but its companion, and we plead for that broad spirit of toleration and justice which will promote industrial peace through the observance of the principles of voluntary arbitration.

We favor the enactment of legislation looking to the improvement of conditions for wage earners, the abolition of child labor, the suppression of sweat shops, and of convict labor in competition with free labor, and the exclusion from American shores of foreign pauper labor.

We favor the shorter work day, and declare that if eight hours constitute a day's labor in Government service, that eight hours should constitute a day's labor in factories, workshops and mines.

As a means of placing all public questions directly under the control of the people, we demand that legal provision be made under which the people may exercise the initiative, referendum and proportional representation and direct vote for all public officers with the right of recall.

Land, including all the natural sources of wealth, is a heritage of all the people, and should not be monopolized for speculative purposes, and alien ownership of land should be prohibited.

We demand a return to the original interpretation of the Constitution and a fair and impartial enforcement of laws under it, and denounce government by injunction and imprisonment without the right of trial by jury.

To prevent unjust discrimination and monopoly the Government should own and control the railroads, and those public utilities which in their nature are monopolies. To perfect the postal service, the Government should own and operate the general telegraph and telephone systems and provide a parcels post.

As to these trusts and monopolies which are not public utilities or natural monopolies, we demand that those special privileges which they now enjoy, and which alone enables them to exist, should be immediately withdrawn. Corporations being the creatures of government should be subjected to such governmental regulations and control as will adequately protect the public. We demand the taxation of monopoly privileges, while they remain in private hands, to the extent of the value of the privileges granted.

We demand that Congress shall enact a general law uniformly regulating the power and duties of all incorporated companies doing interstate business.

Prohibition Platform of 1904

The Prohibition party, in national convention assembled, at Indianapolis, June 30, 1904, recognizing that the chief end of all government is the establishment of those principles of righteousness and justice which have been revealed to men as the will of the ever-living God, desiring His blessing upon our national life, and believing in the perpetuation of the high ideals of government of the people, by the people and for the people, established by our fathers, makes the following declaration of principles and purposes:

The widely prevailing system of the licensed and legalized sale of alcoholic beverages is so ruinous to individual interests, so inimical to public welfare, so destructive of national wealth and so subversive of the rights of great masses of our citizenship, that the destruction of the traffic is, and for years has been, the most important question in American politics.

We denounce the lack of statesmanship exhibited by the leaders of the Democratic and Republican parties in their refusal to recognize the paramount importance of this question, and the cowardice with which the leaders of these parties have courted the favor of those whose selfish interests are advanced by the continuation and augmentation of the traffic, until to-day the influence of the liquor traffic practically dominates national, State and local government throughout the nation.

We declare the truth, demonstrated by the experience of half a century, that all methods of dealing with the liquor traffic which recognize its right to exist, in any form, under any system of license or tax or regulation, have proved powerless to remove its evils, and useless as checks upon its growth, while the insignificant public revenues which have accrued therefrom have seared the public conscience against a recognition of its iniquity.

We call public attention to the fact, proved by the experience of more than fifty years, that to secure the enactment and enforcement of prohibitory legislation, in which alone lies the hope of the protection of the people from the liquor traffic, it is necessary that the legislative, executive and judicial branches of government should be in the hands of a political party in harmony with the prohibition principle, and pledged to its embodiment in law, and to the execution of those laws.

We pledge the Prohibition party, wherever given power by the suffrages of the people, to the enactment and enforcement of laws prohibiting and abolishing the manufacture, importation, transportation and sale of alcoholic beverages.

We declare that there is not only no other issue of equal importance before the American people to-day, but that the so-called issues upon which the Democratic and Republican parties seek to divide the electorate of the country are, in large part, subterfuges under the cover of which they wrangle for the spoils of office.

Recognizing that the intelligent voters of the country may properly ask our attitude upon other questions of public concern, we declare ourselves in favor of:

The impartial enforcement of all law.

The safeguarding of the people's rights by a rigid application of the principles of justice to all combinations and organizations of capital and labor.

The recognition of the fact that the right of suffrage should depend upon the mental and moral qualifications of the citizen.

A more intimate relation between the people and government, by a wise application of the principle of the initiative and referendum.

Such changes in our laws as will place tariff schedules in the hands of an omnipartisan commission.

The application of uniform laws to all our country and dependencies.

The election of United States Senators by vote of the people.

The extension and honest administration of the civil service laws.

The safeguarding of every citizen in every place under the government of the people of the United States, in all the rights guaranteed by the laws and the Constitution.

International arbitration, and we declare that our nation should contribute, in every manner consistent with national dignity, to the permanent establishment of peace between all nations.

The reform of our divorce laws, the final extirpation of polygamy, and the total overthrow of the present shameful system of the illegal sanction of the social evil, with its unspeakable traffic in girls, by the municipal authorities of almost all our cities.

Republican Platform of 1904

Fifty years ago the Republican party came into existence dedicated among other purposes to the great task of arresting the extension of human slavery. In 1860 it elected its first President. During twenty-four years of the forty-four which have elapsed since the election of Lincoln the Republican party has held complete control of the government. For eighteen more of the forty-four years it has held partial control through the possession of one or two branches of the government, while the Democratic party during the same period has had complete control for only two years. This long tenure of power by the Republican party is not due to chance. It is a demonstration that the Republican party has commanded the confidence of the American people for nearly two generations to a degree never equalled in our history, and has displayed a high capacity for rule and government which has been made even more conspicuous by the incapacity and infirmity of purpose shown by its opponents.

The Republican party entered upon its present period of complete supremacy in 1897. We have every right to congratulate ourselves upon the work since then accomplished, for it has added lustre even to the traditions of the party which carried the government through the storms of civil war.

We then found the country after four years of Democratic rule in evil plight, oppressed with misfortune, and doubtful of the future. Public credit had been lowered, the revenues were declining, the debt was growing, the administration's attitude toward Spain was feeble and mortifying, the standard of values was threatened and uncertain, labor was unemployed, business was sunk in the depression which had succeeded the panic of 1893, hope was faint and confidence was gone.

We met these unhappy conditions vigorously, effectively, and at once. We replaced a Democratic tariff law based on free trade principles and garnished with sectional protection by a consistent protective tariff, and industry, freed from oppression and stimulated by the encouragement of wise laws, has expanded to a degree never before known, has conquered new markets, and has created a volume of exports which has surpassed imagination. Under the Dingley tariff labor has been fully employed, wages have risen, and all industries have revived and prospered.

We firmly established the gold standard which was then menaced with destruction. Confidence returned to business, and with confidence an unexampled prosperity.

For deficient revenues, supplemented by improvident issues of bonds, we gave the country an income which produced a large surplus and which enabled us only four years after the Spanish War had closed to remove over one hundred millions of annual war taxes, reduce the public debt, and lower the interest charges of the Government.

The public credit which had been so lowered that in time of peace a Democratic administration made large loans at extravagant rates of interest in order to pay current expenditures, rose under Republican administration to its highest point and enabled us to borrow at 2 per cent even in time of war.

We refuse to palter longer with the miseries of Cuba. We fought a quick and victorious war with Spain. We set Cuba free, governed the island for three years, and then gave it to the Cuban people with order restored, with ample revenues, with education and public health established, free from debt, and connected with the United States by wise provisions for our mutual interests.

We have organized the government of Porto Rico, and its people now enjoy peace, freedom, order, and prosperity.

In the Philippines we have suppressed insurrection, established order, and given to life and property a security never known there before. We have organized civil government, made it effective and strong in administration, and have conferred upon the people of those islands the largest civil liberty they have ever enjoyed.

By our possession of the Philippines we were enabled to take prompt and effective action in the relief of the legations at Peking and a decisive part in preventing the partition and preserving the integrity of China.

The possession of a route for an Isthmian canal, so long the dream of American statesmanship, is now an accomplished fact. The great work of connecting the Pacific and Atlantic by a canal is at last begun, and it is due to the Republican party.

We have passed laws which will bring the arid lands of the United States within the area of cultivation.

We have reorganized the army and put it in the highest state of efficiency.

We have passed laws for the improvement and support of the militia.

We have pushed forward the building of the navy, the defence and protection of our honor and our interests.

Our administration of the great departments of the Government has been honest and efficient, and wherever wrongdoing has been discovered, the Republican administration has not hesitated to probe the evil and bring offenders to justice without regard to party or political ties.

Laws enacted by the Republican party which the Democratic party failed to enforce and which were intended for the protection of the public against the united discrimination or the illegal encroachment of vast aggregations of capital, have been fearlessly enforced by a Republican President, and new laws insuring reasonable publicity as to the operations of great corporations, and providing additional remedies for the prevention of discrimination in freight rates, have been passed by a Republican Congress.

In this record of achievement during the past eight years may be read the pledges which the Republican party has fulfilled. We promise to continue these policies, and we declare our constant adherence to the following principles:

Protection, which guards and develops our industries, is a cardinal policy of the Republican party. The measure of protection should always at least equal the difference in the cost of production at home and abroad. We insist upon the maintenance of the principle of protection, and therefore rates of duty should be readjusted only when conditions have so changed that the public interest demands their alteration, but this work cannot safely be committed to any other hands than those of the Republican party. To intrust it to the Democratic party is to invite disaster. Whether, as in 1892, the Democratic party declares the protective tariff unconstitutional, or whether it demands tariff reform or tariff revision, its real object is always the destruction of the protective system. However specious the name, the purpose is ever the same. A Democratic tariff has always been followed by business adversity: a Republican tariff by business prosperity. To a Republican Congress and a Republican President this great question can be safely intrusted. When the only free trade country among the great nations agitates a return to protection, the chief protective country should not falter in maintaining it.

We have extended widely our foreign markets, and we believe in the adoption of all practicable methods for their further extension, including commercial reciprocity wherever reciprocal arrangements can be effected consistent with the principles of protection and without injury to

American agriculture, American labor, or any American industry.

We believe it to be the duty of the Republican party to uphold the gold standard and the integrity and value of our national currency. The maintenance of the gold standard, established by the Republican party, cannot safely be committed to the Democratic party which resisted its adoption and has never given any proof since that time of belief in it or fidelity to it.

While every other industry has prospered under the fostering aid of Republican legislation, American shipping engaged in foreign trade in competition with the low cost of construction, low wages and heavy subsidies of foreign governments, has not for many years received from the Government of the United States adequate encouragement of any kind. We therefore favor legislation which will encourage and build up the American merchant marine, and we cordially approve the legislation of the last Congress which created the Merchant Marine Commission to investigate and report upon this subject.

A navy powerful enough to defend the United States against any attack, to uphold the Monroe Doctrine, and watch over our commerce, is essential to the safety and the welfare of the American people. To maintain such a navy is the fixed policy of the Republican party.

We cordially approve the attitude of President Roosevelt and Congress in regard to the exclusion of Chinese labor, and promise a continuance of the Republican policy in that direction.

The Civil Service Law was placed on the statute books by the Republican party, which has always sustained it, and we renew our former declarations that it shall be thoroughly and honestly enforced.

We are always mindful of the country's debt to the soldiers and sailors of the United States, and we believe in making ample provision for them, and in the liberal administration of the pension laws.

We favor the peaceful settlement of international differences by arbitration.

We commend the vigorous efforts made by the Administration to protect American citizens in foreign lands, and pledge ourselves to insist upon the just and equal protection of all of our citizens abroad. It is the unquestioned duty of the government to procure for all our citizens, without distinction, the rights of travel and sojourn in friendly countries, and we declare ourselves in favor of all proper efforts tending to that end.

Our great interests and our growing commerce in the Orient render the condition of China of high importance to the United States. We cordially commend the policy pursued in that direction by the administrations of President McKinley and President Roosevelt.

We favor such Congressional action as shall determine whether by special discrimination the elective franchise in any State has been unconstitutionally limited, and, if such is the case, we demand that representation in Congress and in the electoral college shall be proportionately reduced as directed by the Constitution of the United States.

Combinations of capital and of labor are the results of the economic movement of the age, but neither must be permitted to infringe upon the rights and interests of the people. Such combinations, when lawfully formed for lawful purposes, are alike entitled to the protection of the laws, but both are subject to the laws and neither can be permitted to break them.

The great statesman and patriotic American, William McKinley, who was re-elected by the Republican party to the Presidency four years ago, was assassinated just at the threshold of his second term. The entire nation mourned his untimely death and did that justice to his great qualities of mind and character which history will confirm and repeat.

The American people were fortunate in his successor, to whom they turned with a trust and confidence which have been fully justified. President Roosevelt brought to the great responsibilities thus sadly forced upon him a clear hand, a brave heart, and earnest patriotism, and high ideals of public duty and public service. True to the principles of the Republican party and to the policies which that party had declared, he has also shown himself ready for every emergency and has met new and vital questions with ability and with success.

The confidence of the people in his justice, inspired by his public career, enabled him to render personally an inestimable service to the country by bringing about a settlement of the coal strike, which threatened such disastrous results at the opening of Winter in 1902.

Our foreign policy under his administration has not only been able, vigorous, and dignified, but in the highest degree successful.

The complicated questions which arose in Venezuela were settled in such a way by President Roosevelt that the Monroe doctrine was signally vindicated, and the cause of peace and arbitration greatly advanced.

His prompt and vigorous action in Panama, which we commend in the highest terms, not only secured to us the canal route, but avoided foreign complications which might have been of a very serious character.

He has continued the policy of President McKinley in the Orient, and our position in China, signalized by our recent commercial treaty with that empire, has never been so high.

He secured the tribunal by which the vexed and perilous question of the Alaskan boundary was finally settled.

Whenever crimes against humanity have been perpetrated which have shocked our people, his protest has been made, and our good offices have been tendered, but always with due regard to international obligations.

Under his guidance we find ourselves at peace with all the world, and never were we more respected or our wishes more regarded by foreign nations.

Pre-eminently successful in regard to our foreign relations, he has been equally fortunate in dealing with domestic questions. The country has known that the public credit and the national currency were absolutely safe in the hands of his administration. In the enforcement of the laws he has shown not only courage, but the wisdom which understands that to permit laws to be violated or disregarded opens the door to anarchy, while the just enforcement of the law is the soundest conservatism. He has held firmly to the fundamental American doctrine that all men must obey the law; that there must be no distinction between rich and poor, between strong and weak, but that justice and equal protection under the law must be secured to every citizen without regard to race, creed, or condition.

His administration has been throughout vigorous and honorable, high minded and patriotic. We commend it without reservation to the considerate judgment of the American people.

Socialist Platform of 1904

1. The Socialist Party, in convention assembled, makes its appeal to the American people as the defender and preserver of the idea of liberty and self-government, in which the nation was born; as the only political movement standing for the program and principles by which the liberty of the individual may become a fact; as the only political organization that is democratic, and that has for its purpose the democratizing of the whole of society.

To this idea of liberty the Republican and Democratic parties are equally false. They alike struggle for power to maintain and profit by an industrial system which can be preserved only by the complete overthrow of such liberties as we already have, and by the still further enslavement and degradation of labor.

Our American institutions came into the world in the name of freedom. They have been seized upon by the capitalist class as the means of rooting out the idea of freedom from among the people. Our state and national legislatures have become the mere agencies of great propertied interests. These interests control the appointments and decisions of the judges of our courts. They have come into what is practically a private ownership of all the functions and forces of government. They are using these to betray and conquer foreign and weaker peoples, in order to establish new markets for the surplus goods which the people make, but are too poor to buy. They are gradually so invading and restricting the right of suffrage as to take away unawares the right of the worker to a vote or voice in public affairs. By enacting new and misinterpreting old laws, they are preparing to attack the liberty of the individual even to speak or think for himself, or for the common good.

By controlling all the sources of social revenue, the possessing class is able to silence what might be the voice of protest against the passing of liberty and the coming of tyranny. It completely controls the university and public school, the pulpit and the press, and the arts and literatures. By making these economically dependent upon itself, it has brought all the forms of public teaching into servile submission to its own interests.

Our political institutions are also being used as

the destroyers of that individual property upon which all liberty and opportunity depend. The promise of economic independence to each man was one of the faiths upon which our institutions were founded. But, under the guise of defending private property, capitalism is using our political institutions to make it impossible for the vast majority of human beings ever to become possessors of private property in the means of life.

Capitalism is the enemy and destroyer of essential private property. Its development is through the legalized confiscation of all that the labor of the working class produces, above its subsistence-wage. The private ownership of the means of employment grounds society in an economic slavery which renders intellectual and political tyranny inevitable.

Socialism comes so to organize industry and society that every individual shall be secure in that private property in the means of life upon which his liberty of being, thought and action depend. It comes to rescue the people from the fast increasing and successful assault of capitalism upon the liberty of the individual.

2. As an American socialist party, we pledge our fidelity to the principles of international socialism, as embodied in the united thought and action of the socialists of all nations. In the industrial development already accomplished, the interests of the world's workers are separated by no national boundaries. The condition of the most exploited and oppressed workers, in the most remote places of the earth, inevitably tends to drag down all the workers of the world to the same level. The tendency of the competitive wage system is to make labor's lowest condition the measure or rule of its universal condition. Industry and finance are no longer national but international, in both organization and results. The chief significance of national boundaries, and of the so-called patriotisms which the ruling class of each nation is seeking to revive, is the power which these give to capitalism to keep the workers of the world from uniting, and to throw them against each other in the struggles of contending capitalist interests for the control of the yet unexploited markets of the world, or the remaining sources of profit.

The socialist movement, therefore, is a world-movement. It knows of no conflicts of interests between the workers of one nation and the workers of another. It stands for the freedom of the workers of all nations; and, in so standing, it makes for the full freedom of all humanity.

3. The socialist movement owes its birth and growth to that economic development or world-process which is rapidly separating a working or producing class from a possessing or capitalist class. The class that produces nothing possesses labor's fruits, and the opportunities and enjoyments these fruits afford, while the class that does the world's real work has increasing economic uncertainty, and physical and intellectual misery, for its portion.

The fact that these two classes have not yet become fully conscious of their distinctions from each other, the fact that the lines of division and interest may not yet be clearly drawn, does not change the fact of the class conflict.

This class struggle is due to the private ownership of the means of employment, or the tools of production. Wherever and whenever man owned his own land and tools, and by them produced only the things which he used, economic independence was possible. But production, or the making of goods, has long ceased to be individual. The labor of scores, or even thousands, enters into almost every article produced. Production is now social or collective. Practically everything is made or done by many men—sometimes separated by seas or continents—working together for the same end. But this co-operation in production is not for the direct use of the things made by the workers who make them, but for the profit of the owners of the tools and means of production; and to this is due the present division of society into two classes; and from it have sprung all the miseries, inharmonies and contradictions of our civilization.

Between these two classes there can be no possible compromise or identity of interest, any more than there can be peace in the midst of war, or light in the midst of darkness. A society based upon this class division carries in itself the seeds of its own destruction. Such a society is founded in fundamental injustice. There can be no possible basis for social peace, for individual freedom, for mental and moral harmony, except in the conscious and complete triumph of the working class as the only class that has the right or power to be.

4. The socialist program is not a theory imposed upon society for its acceptance or rejection. It is but the interpretation of what is, sooner or later, inevitable. Capitalism is already struggling to its destruction. It is no longer competent to organize or administer the work of the world, or even to preserve itself. The captains of industry are appalled at their own inability to control or direct the rapidly socializing forces of industry. The so-called trust is but a sign and form of the developing socialization of the world's work. The universal increase of the uncertainty of employment, the universal capitalist determination to break down the unity of labor in the trades unions, the widespread apprehensions of impending change, reveal that the institutions of capitalist society are passing under the power of inhering forces that will soon destroy them.

Into the midst of the strain and crisis of civilization, the socialist movement comes as the only conservative force. If the world is to be saved from chaos, from universal disorder and misery, it must be by the union of the workers of all nations in the socialist movement. The socialist party comes with the only proposition or program for intelligently and deliberately organizing the nation for the common good of all its citizens. It is the first time that the mind of man has ever been directed toward the conscious organization of society.

Socialism means that all those things upon which the people in common depend shall by the people in common be owned and administered. It means that the tools of employment shall belong to their creators and users; that all production shall be for the direct use of the producers; that the making of goods for profit shall come to an end; that we shall all be workers together; and that all opportunities shall be open and equal to all men.

5. To the end that the workers may seize every possible advantage that may strengthen them to gain complete control of the powers of government, and thereby the sooner establish the co-operative commonwealth, the Socialist Party pledges itself to watch and work, in both the economic and the political struggle, for each successive immediate interest of the working class; for shortened days of labor and increases of wages; for the insurance of the workers against accident, sickness and lack of employment; for pensions for aged and exhausted workers; for the public ownership of the means of transportation, communication and exchange; for the graduated taxation of incomes, inheritances, franchises and land values, the proceeds to be applied to the public employment and improvement of the conditions of the workers; for the complete education of children, and their freedom from the workshop; for the prevention of the use of the military against labor in the settlement of strikes; for the free administration of justice; for popular government, including initiative, referendum, proportional representation, equal suffrage of men and women, municipal home rule, and the recall of officers by their constituents; and for every gain or advantage for the workers that may be wrested from the capitalist system, and that may relieve the suffering and strengthen the hands of labor. We lay upon every man elected to any executive or legislative office the first duty of striving to procure whatever is for the workers' most immediate interest, and for whatever will lessen the economic and political powers of the capitalist, and increase the like powers of the worker.

But, in so doing, we are using these remedial measures as means to the one great end of the co-operative commonwealth. Such measures of relief as we may be able to force from capitalism are but a preparation of the workers to seize the whole powers of government, in order that they may thereby lay hold of the whole system of industry, and thus come into their rightful inheritance.

To this end we pledge ourselves, as the party of the working class, to use all political power, as fast as it shall be entrusted to us by our fellow-workers, both for their immediate interests and for their ultimate and complete emancipation. To this end we appeal to all the workers of America, and to all who will lend their lives to the service of the workers in their struggle to gain their own, and to all who will nobly and disinterestedly give their days and energies unto the workers' cause, to cast in their lot and faith with the socialist party. Our appeal for the trust and suffrages of our fellow-workers is at once an appeal for their common good and freedom, and for the freedom and blossoming of our common humanity. In pledging ourselves, and those we represent, to be faithful to the appeal which we make, we believe that we are but preparing the soil of that economic freedom from which will spring the freedom of the whole man.

Socialist Labor Platform of 1904

The Socialist Labor Party of America, in convention assembled, reasserts the inalienable right of man to life, liberty and the pursuit of happiness.

We hold that the purpose of government is to secure to every citizen the enjoyment of this right: but taught by experience we hold furthermore that such right is illusory to the majority of the people, to wit, the working class, under the present system of economic inequality that is essentially destructive to *their* life, *their* liberty and *their* happiness.

We hold that the true theory of politics is that the machinery of government must be controlled by the whole people; but again taught by experience we hold furthermore that the true theory of economics is that the means of production must likewise be owned, operated and controlled by the people in common. Man cannot exercise his right of life, liberty and the pursuit of happiness without the ownership of the land on and the tool with which to work. Deprived of these, his life, his liberty and his fate fall into the hands of the class that owns those essentials for work and production.

We hold that the existing contradiction between the theory of democratic government and the fact of a despotic economic system—the private ownership of the natural and social opportunities—divides the people into two classes, the capitalist class and the working class; throws society into the convulsions of the Class Struggle, and perverts government to the exclusive benefit of the Capitalist Class.

Thus labor is robbed of the wealth which it alone produces, is denied the means of self-employment, and, by compulsory idleness in wage slavery, is even deprived of the necessaries of life.

Against such a system the Socialist Labor Party raises the banner of revolt, and demands the unconditional surrender of the Capitalist Class.

The time is fast coming when, in the natural course of social evolution, this system, through the destructive action of its failures and crises on the one hand, and the constructive tendencies of its trusts and other capitalist combinations on the other hand, will have worked out its own downfall.

We, therefore, call upon the wage workers of America to organize under the banner of the Socialist Labor Party into a class-conscious body, aware of its rights and determined to conquer them.

And we also call upon all other intelligent citizens to place themselves squarely upon the ground of Working Class interests, and join us in this mighty and noble work of human emancipation, so that we may put summary end to the existing barbarous class conflict by placing the land and all the means of production, transportation and distribution into the hands of the people as a collective body, and substituting the co-operative commonwealth for the present state of planless production, industrial war and social disorder—a commonwealth in which every worker shall have the free exercise and full benefit of his faculties, multiplied by all the modern factors of civilization.

In 1908 there were, in addition to the two major parties, the well-established minor parties, namely, — the People's Party, the Prohibition Party, the Socialist Party, and the Socialist Labor Party. An entirely new party appeared also. It announced itself as the Independence Party. It was an outgrowth of the Independence League, led by Mr. William R. Hearst of New York.

Democratic Platform of 1908

We, the representatives of the Democracy of the United States, in National Convention assembled, reaffirm our belief in, and pledge our loyalty to, the principles of the party.

We rejoice at the increasing signs of an awakening throughout the country. The various investigations have traced graft and political corruption to the representatives of the predatory wealth, and laid bare the unscrupulous methods by which they have debauched elections and preyed upon a defenseless public through the subservient officials whom they have raised to place and power.

The conscience of the nation is now aroused to free the Government from the grip of those who have made it a business asset of the favor-seeking corporations. It must become again a people's government, and be administered in all its departments according to the Jeffersonian maxim, "equal rights to all; special privileges to none."

"Shall the people rule?" is the overshadowing issue which manifests itself in all the questions now under discussion.

INCREASE OF OFFICE-HOLDERS

Coincident with the enormous increase in expenditures is a like addition to the number of office-holders. During the past year 23,784 were added, costing $16,156,000, and in the past six years of Republican administration the total number of new offices created, aside from many commissions, has been 99,319, entailing an additional expenditure of nearly $70,000,000 as against only 10,279 new offices created under the Cleveland and McKinley administrations, which involved an expenditure of only $6,000,000. We denounce this great and growing increase in the number of office-holders as not only unnecessary and wasteful, but also as clearly indicating a deliberate purpose on the part of the Administration to keep the Republican party in power at public expense by thus increasing the number of its retainers and dependents. Such procedure we declare to be no less dangerous and corrupt than the open purchase of votes at the polls.

ECONOMY IN ADMINISTRATION

The Republican Congress in the session just ended made appropriations amounting to $1,008,-000,000, exceeding the total expenditures of the past fiscal year by $90,000,000 and leaving a deficit of more than $60,000,000 for the fiscal year just ended. We denounce the heedless waste of the people's money which has resulted in this appalling increase as a shameful violation of all prudent considerations of government and as no less than a crime against the millions of working men and women, from whose earnings the great proportion of these colossal sums must be extorted through excessive tariff exactions and other indirect methods. It is not surprising that in the face of this shocking record the Republican platform contains no reference to economical administration or promise thereof in the future. We demand that a stop be put to this frightful extravagance, and insist upon the strictest economy in every department compatible with frugal and efficient administration.

ARBITRARY POWER—THE SPEAKER

The House of Representatives was designed by the fathers of the Constitution to be the popular branch of our Government, responsive to the public will.

The House of Representatives, as controlled in recent years by the Republican party, has ceased to be a deliberative and legislative body, responsive to the will of a majority of its members, but has come under the absolute domination of the Speaker, who has entire control of its deliberations and powers of legislation.

We have observed with amazement the popular branch of our Federal Government helpless to obtain either the consideration or enactment of measures desired by a majority of its members.

Legislative control becomes a failure when one member in the person of the Speaker is more powerful than the entire body.

We demand that the House of Representatives shall again become a deliberative body, controlled by a majority of the people's representatives, and not by the Speaker; and we pledge ourselves to adopt such rules and regulations to govern the House of Representatives as will enable a majority of its members to direct its deliberations and control legislation.

MISUSE OF PATRONAGE

We condemn as a violation of the spirit of our institutions the action of the present Chief Executive in using the patronage of his high office to secure the nomination for the Presidency of one of his Cabinet officers. A forced succession to the Presidency is scarcely less repugnant to public sentiment than is life tenure in that office. No good intention on the part of the Executive, and no virtue in the one selected, can justify the establishment of a dynasty. The right of the people freely to select their officials is inalienable and cannot be delegated.

PUBLICITY OF CAMPAIGN CONTRIBUTIONS

We demand Federal legislation forever terminating the partnership which has existed between corporations of the country and the Republican party under the expressed or implied agreement that in return for the contribution of great sums of money wherewith to purchase elections, they should be allowed to continue substantially unmolested in their efforts to encroach upon the rights of the people.

Any reasonable doubt as to the existence of this relation has been forever dispelled by the sworn testimony of witnesses examined in the insurance investigation in New York, and the open admission of a single individual—unchallenged by the Republican National Committee—that he himself at the personal request of the Republican candidate for the Presidency raised over a quarter of a million dollars to be used in a single State during the closing hours of the last campaign. In order that this practice shall be stopped for all time, we demand the passage of a statute punishing by imprisonment any officer of a corporation who shall either contribute on behalf of, or consent to the contribution by, a corporation, of any money or thing of value to be used in furthering the election of a President or Vice-President of the United States or of any member of the Congress thereof.

We denounce the Republican party, having complete control of the Federal Government, for their failure to pass the bill, introduced in the last Congress, to compel the publication of the names of contributors and the amounts contributed toward campaign funds, and point to the evidence of their insincerity when they sought by an absolutely irrelevant and impossible amendment to defeat the passage of the bill. As a further evidence of their intention to conduct their campaign in the coming contest with vast sums of money wrested from favor-seeking corporations, we call attention to the fact that the recent Republican National Convention at Chicago refused, when the issue was presented to it, to declare against such practices.

We pledge the Democratic party to the enactment of a law prohibiting any corporation from contributing to a campaign fund and any individual from contributing an amount above a reasonable maximum, and providing for the publication before election of all such contributions.

THE RIGHTS OF THE STATES

Believing, with Jefferson, in "the support of the State governments in all their rights as the most competent administrations for our domestic concerns, and the surest bulwarks against anti-republican tendencies," and in "the preservation of the General Government in its whole constitutional vigor, as the sheet anchor of our peace at home and safety abroad," we are opposed to the centralization implied in the suggestion, now frequently made, that the powers of the General Government should be extended by judicial construction. There is no twilight zone between the Nation and the State in which exploiting interests can take refuge from both; and it is as necessary that the Federal Government shall exercise the powers delegated to it as it is that the State governments shall use the authority reserved to them; but we insist that Federal remedies for the regulation of interstate commerce and for the prevention of private monopoly shall be added to, not substituted for, State remedies.

TARIFF

We welcome the belated promise of tariff reform now offered by the Republican party in tardy recognition of the righteousness of the Democratic position on this question; but the people cannot safely entrust the execution of this important work to a party which is so deeply obligated to the highly protected interests as is the Republican party. We call attention to the significant fact that the promised relief is postponed until after the coming election—an election to succeed in which the Republican party must have that same support from the beneficiaries of the high protective tariff as it has always heretofore received from them; and to the further fact that during years of uninterrupted power no action whatever has been taken by the Republican Congress to correct the admittedly existing tariff iniquities.

We favor immediate revision of the tariff by the reduction of import duties. Articles entering into competition with trust-controlled products should be placed upon the free list, and material reductions should be made in the tariff upon the necessaries of life, especially upon articles competing with such American manufactures as are sold abroad more cheaply than at home; and gradual reductions should be made in such other schedules as may be necessary to restore the tariff to a revenue basis.

Existing duties have given to the manufacturers of paper a shelter behind which they have organized combinations to raise the price of pulp and of paper, thus imposing a tax upon the spread of knowledge. We demand the immediate repeal of the tariff on wood pulp, print paper, lumber, timber and logs, and that these articles be placed upon the free list.

TRUSTS

A private monopoly is indefensible and intolerable. We therefore favor the vigorous enforcement of the criminal law against guilty trust magnates and officials, and demand the enactment of such additional legislation as may be necessary to make it impossible for a private monopoly to exist in the United States. Among the additional remedies we specify three: First, a law preventing a duplication of directors among competing corporations; second, a license system which will, without abridging the right of each State to create corporations, or its right to regulate as it will foreign corporations doing business within its limits, make it necessary for a manufacturing or trading corporation engaged in interstate commerce to take out a Federal license before it shall be permitted to control as much as twenty-five per cent of the product in which it deals, the license to protect the public from watered stock and to prohibit the control by such corporation of more than fifty per cent of the total amount of any product consumed in the United States; and, third, a law compelling such licensed corporations to sell to all purchasers in all parts of the country on the same terms, after making due allowance for cost of transportation.

RAILROAD REGULATION

We assert the right of Congress to exercise complete control over interstate commerce and the right of each State to exercise like control over commerce within its borders.

We demand such enlargement of the powers of the Interstate Commerce Commission as may be necessary to enable it to compel railroads to perform their duties as common carriers and prevent discrimination and extortion.

We favor the efficient supervision and rate regulation of railroads engaged in interstate commerce. To this end we recommend the valuation of railroads by the Interstate Commerce Commission, such valuation to take into consideration the physical value of the property, the original cost of production, and all elements of value that will render the valuation fair and just.

We favor such legislation as will prohibit the railroads from engaging in business which brings them into competition with their shippers; also legislation which will assure such reduction in transportation rates as conditions will permit, care being taken to avoid reduction that would compel a reduction of wages, prevent adequate service, or do injustice to legitimate investments.

We heartily approve the laws prohibiting the pass and the rebate, and we favor any further necessary legislation to restrain, correct and prevent such abuses.

We favor such legislation as will increase the power of the Interstate Commerce Commission, giving to it the initiative with reference to rates and transportation charges put into effect by the railroad companies, and permitting the Interstate Commerce Commission, on its own initiative, to declare a rate illegal and as being more than should be charged for such service. The present law relating thereto is inadequate, by reason of the fact that the Interstate Commerce Commission is without power to fix or investigate a rate until complaint has been made to it by the shipper.

We further declare in favor of a law providing that all agreements of traffic or other associations of railway agents affecting interstate rates, service or classification, shall be unlawful, unless filed with and approved by the Interstate Commerce Commission.

We favor the enactment of a law giving to the Interstate Commerce Commission the power to inspect proposed railroad tariff rates or schedules before they shall take effect, and, if they be found to be unreasonable, to initiate an adjustment thereof.

Banking

The panic of 1907, coming without any legitimate excuse, when the Republican party had for a decade been in complete control of the Federal government, furnishes additional proof that it is either unwilling or incompetent to protect the interests of the general public. It has so linked the country to Wall street that the sins of the speculators are visited upon the whole people. While refusing to rescue the wealth producers from spoliation at the hands of the stock gamblers and speculators in farm products, it has deposited Treasury funds, without interest and without competition, in favorite banks. It has used an emergency for which it is largely responsible to force through Congress a bill changing the basis of bank currency and inviting market manipulation, and has failed to give to the 15,000,000 depositors of the country protection in their savings.

We believe that in so far as the needs of commerce require an emergency currency, such currency should be issued and controlled by the Federal Government, and loaned on adequate security to National and State banks. We pledge ourselves to legislation under which the national banks shall be required to establish a guarantee fund for the prompt payment of the depositors of any insolvent national bank, under an equitable system which shall be available to all State banking institutions wishing to use it.

We favor a postal savings bank if the guaranteed bank can not be secured, and that it be constituted so as to keep the deposited money in the communities where it is established. But we condemn the policy of the Republican party in providing postal savings banks under a plan of conduct by which they will aggregate the deposits of the rural communities and redeposit the same while under Government charge in the banks of Wall street, thus depleting the circulating medium of the producing regions and unjustly favoring the speculative markets.

Income Tax

We favor an income tax as part of our revenue system, and we urge the submission of a constitutional amendment specifically authorizing Congress to levy and collect a tax upon individual and corporate incomes, to the end that wealth may bear its proportionate share of the burdens of the Federal Government.

Labor and Injunctions

The courts of justice are the bulwark of our liberties, and we yield to none in our purpose to maintain their dignity. Our party has given to the bench a long line of distinguished judges, who have added to the respect and confidence in which this department must be jealously maintained. We resent the attempt of the Republican party to raise a false issue respecting the judiciary. It is an unjust reflection upon a great body of our citizens to assume that they lack respect for the courts.

It is the function of the courts to interpret the laws which the people create, and if the laws appear to work economic, social or political injustice, it is our duty to change them. The only basis upon which the integrity of our courts can stand is that of unswerving justice and protection of life, personal liberty and property. If judicial processes may be abused, we should guard them against abuse.

Experience has proved the necessity of a modification of the present law relating to injunctions, and we reiterate the pledge of our national platforms of 1896 and 1904 in favor of the measure which passed the United States Senate in 1896, but which a Republican Congress has ever since refused to enact, relating to contempts in Federal courts and providing for trial by jury in cases of indirect contempt.

Questions of judicial practice have arisen especially in connection with industrial disputes. We deem that the parties to all judicial proceedings should be treated with rigid impartiality, and that injunctions should not be issued in any cases in which injunctions would not issue if no industrial dispute were involved.

The expanding organization of industry makes it essential that there should be no abridgement of the right of wage earners and producers to organize for the protection of wages and the improvement of labor conditions, to the end that such labor organizations and their members should not be regarded as illegal combinations in restraint of trade.

We favor the eight hour day on all Government work.

We pledge the Democratic party to the enactment of a law by Congress, as far as the Federal jurisdiction extends, for a general employer's liability act covering injury to body or loss of life of employes.

We pledge the Democratic party to the enactment of a law creating a Department of Labor, represented separately in the President's Cabinet, in which Department shall be included the subject of mines and mining.

MERCHANT MARINE

We believe in the upbuilding of the American merchant marine without new or additional burdens upon the people and without bounties from the public treasury.

THE NAVY

The constitutional provision that a navy shall be provided and maintained means an adequate navy, and we believe that the interests of this country would be best served by having a navy sufficient to defend the coasts of this country and protect American citizens wherever their rights may be in jeopardy.

PROTECTION OF AMERICAN CITIZENS

We pledge ourselves to insist upon the just and lawful protection of our citizens at home and abroad, and to use all proper methods to secure for them, whether native born or naturalized, and without distinction of race or creed, the equal protection of the law and the enjoyment of all rights and privileges open to them under our treaties; and if, under existing treaties, the right of travel and sojourn is denied to American citizens, or recognition is withheld from American passports by any countries on the ground of race or creed, we favor prompt negotiations with the governments of such countries to secure the removal of these unjust discriminations.

We demand that all over the world a duly authenticated passport issued by the Government of the United States to an American citizen, shall be proof of the fact that he is an American citizen and shall entitle him to the treatment due him as such.

CIVIL SERVICE

The laws pertaining to the civil service should be honestly and rigidly enforced, to the end that merit and ability shall be the standard of appointment and promotion rather than services rendered to a political party.

PENSIONS

We favor a generous pension policy, both as a matter of justice to the surviving veterans and their dependents, and because it tends to relieve the country of the necessity of maintaining a large standing army.

Health Bureau

We advocate the organization of all existing national public health agencies into a national bureau of public health with such power over sanitary conditions connected with factories, mines, tenements, child labor and other such subjects as are properly within the jurisdiction of the Federal government and do not interfere with the power of the States controlling public health agencies.

Agricultural and Mechanical Education

The Democratic party favors the extension of agricultural, mechanical and industrial education. We therefore favor the establishment of district agricultural experiment stations and secondary agricultural and mechanical colleges in the several States.

Popular Election of Senators

We favor the election of United States Senators by direct vote of the people, and regard this reform as the gateway to other national reforms.

Oklahoma

We welcome Oklahoma to the sisterhood of States and heartily congratulate her upon the auspicious beginning of a great career.

Panama Canal

We believe that the Panama Canal will prove of great value to our country, and favor its speedy completion.

Arizona and New Mexico

The National Democratic party has for the last sixteen years labored for the admission of Arizona and New Mexico as separate States of the Federal Union, and recognizing that each possesses every qualification successfully to maintain separate State governments, we favor the immediate admission of these Territories as separate States.

Grazing Lands

The establishment of rules and regulations, if any such are necessary, in relation to free grazing upon the public lands outside of forest or other reservations, until the same shall eventually be disposed of, should be left to the people of the States respectively in which such lands may be situated.

Waterways

Water furnishes the cheaper means of transportation, and the National Government, having the control of navigable waters, should improve them to their fullest capacity. We earnestly favor the immediate adoption of a liberal and comprehensive plan for improving every water course in the Union which is justified by the needs of commerce; and, to secure that end, we favor, when practicable, the connection of the Great Lakes with the navigable rivers and with the Gulf through the Mississippi River, and the navigable rivers with each other, and the rivers, bays and sounds of our coasts with each other, by artificial canals, with a view of perfecting a system of inland waterways to be navigated by vessels of standard draught.

We favor the co-ordination of the various services of the Government connected with waterways in one service, for the purpose of aiding in the completion of such a system of inland waterways; and we favor the creation of a fund ample for continuous work, which shall be conducted under the direction of a commission of experts to be authorized by law.

Post Roads

We favor Federal aid to State and local authorities in the construction and maintenance of post roads.

Telegraph and Telephone

We pledge the Democratic party to the enactment of a law to regulate, under the jurisdiction of the Interstate Commerce Commission, the rates and services of telegraph and telephone companies engaged in the transmission of messages between the States.

Natural Resources

We repeat the demand for internal development and for the conservation of our natural resources contained in previous platforms, the enforcement of which Mr. Roosevelt has vainly sought from a reluctant party; and to that end we insist upon the preservation, protection and replacement of needed forests, the preservation of the public domain for home seekers, the protection of the national resources in timber, coal, iron and oil against monopolistic control, the development of our waterways for navigation and every other useful purpose, including the irrigation of arid lands, the reclamation of swamp lands, the clarification of streams, the development of water power, and the preservation of electric power, generated by this natural force, from the control of monopoly; and to such end we urge the exercise of all powers, national, State and municipal, both separately and in co-operation.

We insist upon a policy of administration of our forest reserves which shall relieve it of the abuses which have arisen thereunder, and which shall, as far as practicable, conform to the police regulations of the several States wherein the reserves are located, which shall enable homesteaders as of right to occupy and acquire title to all portions thereof which are especially adapted to agriculture, and which shall furnish a system of timber sales available as well to the private citizen as to the larger manufacturer and consumer.

Hawaii

We favor the application of the principles of the land laws of the United States to our newly acquired territory, Hawaii, to the end that the public lands of that territory may be held and utilized for the benefit of *bona-fide* homesteaders.

The Philippines

We condemn the experiment in imperialism as an inexcusable blunder which has involved us in enormous expense, brought us weakness instead of strength, and laid our nation open to the charge of abandoning a fundamental doctrine of self-government. We favor an immediate declaration of the nation's purpose to recognize the independence of the Philippine Islands as soon as a stable government can be established, such independence to be guaranteed by us as we guarantee the independence of Cuba, until the neutralization of the islands can be secured by treaty with other powers. In recognizing the independence of the Philippines our Government should retain such land as may be necessary for coaling stations and naval bases.

Alaska and Porto Rico

We demand for the people of Alaska and Porto Rico the full enjoyment of the rights and privileges of a territorial form of government, and that the officials appointed to administer the government of all our territories and the District of Columbia should be thoroughly qualified by previous *bona-fide* residence.

Pan-American Relations

The Democratic party recognizes the importance and advantage of developing closer ties of Pan-American friendship and commerce between the United States and her sister nations of Latin America, and favors the taking of such steps, consistent with Democratic policies, for better acquaintance, greater mutual confidence, and larger exchange of trade as will bring lasting benefit not only to the United States, but to this group of American Republics, having constitutions, forms of government, ambitions and interests akin to our own.

Asiatic Immigration

We favor full protection, by both National and State governments within their respective spheres, of all foreigners residing in the United States under treaty, but we are opposed to the admission of Asiatic immigrants who can not be amalgamated with our population, or whose presence among us would raise a race issue and involve us in diplomatic controversies with Oriental powers.

Foreign Patents

We believe that where an American citizen holding a patent in a foreign country is compelled to manufacture under his patent within a certain time, similar restrictions should be applied in this country to the citizens or subjects of such a country.

Conclusion

The Democratic party stands for Democracy; the Republican party has drawn to itself all that is aristocratic and plutocratic.

The Democratic party is the champion of equal rights and opportunities to all; the Republican party is the party of privilege and private monopoly. The Democratic party listens to the voice of the whole people and gauges progress by the prosperity and advancement of the average man; the Republican party is subservient to the comparatively few who are the beneficiaries of governmental favoritism. We invite the co-operation of all, regardless of previous political affiliation or past differences, who desire to preserve a government of the people, by the people and for the people and who favor such an administration of the government as will insure, as far as human wisdom can, that each citizen shall draw from society a reward commensurate with his contribution to the welfare of society.

Independence Platform of 1908

We, independent American citizens, representing the Independence party in forty-four States and two Territories, have met in national convention to nominate, absolutely independent of all other political parties, candidates for President and Vice-President of the United States.

Our action is based upon a determination to wrest the conduct of public affairs from the hands of selfish interests, political tricksters and corrupt bosses, and make the Government, as the founders intended, an agency for the common good.

At a period of unexampled national prosperity and promise a staggering blow was dealt to legitimate business by the unmolested practice of stock watering and dishonest financiering. Multitudes of defenceless investors, thousands of honest business men, and an army of idle workingmen are paying the penalty. Year by year, fostered by wasteful and reckless governmental extravagance, by the manipulation of trusts and by a privilege creating tariff, the cost of living mounts higher and higher. Day by day the control of the Government drifts further away from the people and more firmly into the grip of machine politicians and party bosses.

The Republican and Democratic parties are not only responsible for these conditions, but are committed to their indefinite continuance. Prodigal of promises, they are so barren of performance that to a new party of independent voters the country must look for the establishment of a new policy and a return to genuine popular government.

Our object is not to introduce violent innovations or startlingly new features. We of the Independence party look back as Lincoln did, to the Declaration of Independence as the fountain-head of all political inspiration. It is not our purpose to attempt to revolutionize the American system of government, but to restore the action of the Government to the principles of Washington and

Jefferson and Lincoln. It is not our purpose, either, to effect a radical change in the American system of government, but to conserve for the citizens of the United States their privileges and liberties won for them by the founders of this Government and to perpetuate the principles and policies upon which the nation's greatness has been built.

The Independence party is, therefore, a conservative force in American politics, devoted to the preservation of American liberty and independence, to honesty in elections, to opportunity in business and to equality before the law.

Those who believe in the Independence party and work with it are convinced that a genuine democracy should exist; that a true republican form of government should continue; that the power of government should rest with the majority of the people, and that the Government should be conducted for the benefit of the whole citizenship, rather than for the special advantage of any particular class.

As of first importance in order to restore the power of government to the people, to make their will supreme in the primaries, in the elections and in the control of public officials after they have been elected, we declare for direct nominations, the initiative and referendum and the right of recall.

It is idle to cry out against the evil of bossism while we perpetuate a system under which the boss is inevitable. The destruction of the individual boss is of little value. The people in their politics must establish a system which will eliminate not only an objectionable boss but the system of bossism. Representative government is made a mockery by the system of modern party conventions dominated by the bosses and controlled by cliques. We demand the natural remedy of direct nominations by which the people not only elect, but which is far more important, select their representatives.

We believe in the principle of the initiative and referendum, and we particularly demand that no franchise grant go into operation until the terms and conditions have been approved by popular vote in the locality interested.

We demand for the people the right to recall public officials from the public service. The power to make officials reside in the people, and in them also should reside the power to unmake and remove from office any official who demonstrates his unfitness or betrays the public trust.

Of next importance in destroying the power of selfish special interests and the corrupt political bosses whom they control is to wrest from their hands their main weapon—the corruption fund. We demand severe and effective legislation against all forms of corrupt practices at elections, and advocate prohibiting the use of any money at elections except for meetings, literature and the necessary travelling expenses of the candidates. Bidding for votes the Republican and Democratic candidates are making an outcry about publicity of contributions, although both the Republican and Democratic parties have for years consistently blocked every effort to pass a corrupt practices act. Publicity of contributions is desirable and should be required, but the main matter of importance is the use to which contributions are put. We believe that the dishonest use of money in the past, whether contributed by individuals or by corporations, has been chiefly responsible for the corruption which has undermined our system of popular government.

We demand honest conduct of public office and business alike and an economical administration of public affairs, and we condemn the gross extravagance of Federal administration and its appalling annual increase in appropriations. Unnecessary appropriations mean unnecessary taxes, and unnecessary taxes, whether direct or indirect, are paid by the people, and add to the ever increasing cost of living.

We condemn the evil of overcapitalization. Modern industrial conditions make the corporation and stock company a necessity, but overcapitalization in corporations is as harmful and criminal as is personal dishonesty in an individual. Compelling the payment of dividends upon great sums that have never been invested, upon masses of watered stock not justified by the property, overcapitalization prevents the better wages, the better public service and the lower cost that should result from American inventive genius and that wide organization which is replacing costly individual competition. The collapse of dishonestly inflated enterprises robs investors, closes banks, destroys confidence and engenders panics. The Independence party advocates as a primary necessity for sounder business conditions and improved public service the enactment of laws, State and national, to prevent watering of stock, dishonest issues of bonds and other forms of corporation frauds.

We denounce the so-called labor planks of the Republican and Democratic platforms as political buncombe and contemptible claptrap, unworthy of national parties claiming to be serious and sincere.

The Republican declaration that "no injunction or temporary or restraining order should not be issued without notice, except where irreparable injury would result from delay," is empty verbiage, for a showing of irreparable injury can always be made and is always made in ex parte affidavits.

The Democratic declaration that "injunctions should not be issued in any case in which injunctions should not issue if no industrial dispute were involved" is meaningless and worthless.

Such insincere and meaningless declarations place a low estimate upon the intelligence of the average American workingman and exhibit either ignorance of or indifference to the real interest of labor.

The Independence party condemns the arbitrary use of the writ of injunction and contempt proceedings as a violation of the fundamental American right of trial by jury.

From the foundation of our Government down to 1872 the Federal Judiciary act prohibited the issue of any injunction without reasonable notice until after a hearing. We assert that in all actions growing out of a dispute between employers and employés concerning terms or conditions of employment no injunction should issue until after a trial upon the merits, that such trial should be held before a jury, and that in no case of alleged contempt should any person be deprived of liberty without a trial by jury.

The Independence party believes that the distribution of wealth is as important as the creation of wealth, and indorses these organizations among farmers and workers which tend to bring about a just distribution of wealth through good wages for workers and good prices for farmers, and which protect the employer and the consumer through equality of price for labor and for product, and we favor such legislation as will remove them from the operation of the Sherman antitrust law.

We indorse the eight hour work day, favor its application to all Government employés, and demand the enactment of laws requiring that all work done for the Government, whether Federal or State, and whether done directly or indirectly through contractors or sub-contractors shall be done on an eight hour basis.

We favor the enactment of a law defining as illegal any combination or conspiracy to black-list employés.

We demand protection for workmen through enforced use of standard safety appliances and provisions of hygienic conditions in the operation of factories, railways, mills, mines and all industrial undertakings.

We advocate State and Federal inspection of railways to secure a greater safety for railway employés and for the travelling public. We call for the enactment of stringent laws fixing employers' liabilities, and a rigid prohibition of child labor through co-operation between the State governments and the National Government.

We condemn the manufacture and sale of prison-made goods in the open market in competition with free labor manufactured goods. We demand that convicts shall be employed direct by the different States in the manufacture of products for use in State institutions and in making good roads and in no case shall convicts be hired out to contractors or sub-contractors.

We favor the creation of a Department of Labor, including mines and mining, the head of which shall be a member of the President's Cabinet.

The great abuses of grain inspection, by which the producers are plundered, demand immediate and vigorous correction. To that end we favor Federal inspection under a strict civil service law.

The Independence party declares the right to issue money is inherent in the Government, and it favors the establishment of a central governmental bank, through which the money so issued shall be put into general circulation.

We demand a revision of the tariff, not by the friends of the tariff, but by the friends of the people, and declare for a gradual reduction of tariff duties, with just consideration for the rights of the consuming public and of established industry. There should be no protection for oppressive trusts which sell cheaply abroad and take advantage of the tariff at home to crush competition, raise prices, control production and limit work and wages.

The railroads must be kept open to all upon exactly equal terms. Every form of rebate and discrimination in railroad rates is a crime against business and must be stamped out. We demand adequate railroad facilities and advocate a bill empowering shippers in time of need to compel railroads to provide sufficient cars for freight and passenger traffic and other railroad facilities through summary appeal to the courts. We favor the creation of an Interstate Commerce Court, whose sole function it shall be to review speedily and enforce summarily the orders of the Interstate Commerce Commission. The Interstate Commerce Commission has the power to initiate investigation into the reasonableness of rates and practices and no increase in rates should be put into effect until opportunity for such investigation is afforded. The Interstate Commerce Commission should proceed at once with a physical valuation of railroads engaged in interstate commerce.

We believe that legitimate organizations in business designed to secure an economy of operation and increased production are beneficial wherever the public participates in the advantages which result. We denounce all combinations for restraint of trade and for the establishment of monopoly in all products of labor, and declare that such combinations are not combinations for production, but for extortion, and that activity in this direction is not industry, but robbery.

In case of infractions of the Anti-Trust law or of the Interstate Commerce act, we believe in the enforcement of a prison penalty against the guilty and responsible individuals controlling the management of the offending corporations, rather than a fine imposed upon stockholders.

We advocate the extension of the principle of public ownership of public utilities, including railroads, as rapidly as municipal, State, or National Government shall demonstrate ability to conduct public utilities for the public benefit. We favor specifically government ownership of the telegraphs, such as prevails in every other civilized country in the world, and demand as an immediate measure that the Government shall purchase and operate the telegraphs in connection with the postal service.

The parcels post system should be rapidly and widely extended and Government postal savings banks should be established where the people's deposits will be secure, the money to be loaned to the people in the locality of the several banks at a rate of interest to be fixed by the Government.

We favor the immediate development of a national system of good roads connecting all States, and national aid to States in the construction and maintenance of post roads.

We favor a court of review of the censorship and arbitrary rulings of the Post-Office Department.

We favor the admission of Arizona and New Mexico to separate Statehood.

We advocate such legislation, both State and national, as will suppress the bucket shop and prohibit the fictitious selling of farm products for future delivery.

We favor the creation of a national department of public health, to be presided over by a member of the medical profession, this department to exercise such authority over matters of public health, hygiene, and sanitation which come properly within the jurisdiction of the National Government and does not interfere with the rights of states or municipalities.

We oppose Asiatic immigration which does not amalgamate with our population, creates race issues and un-American conditions, and which reduces wages and tends to lower the high standard of living and the high standard of morality which American civilization has established.

We demand the passage of an exclusion act which shall protect American workingmen from competition with Asiatic cheap labor and which shall protect American civilization from the contamination of Asiatic conditions.

The Independence party declares for peace and against aggression, and will promote the movement for the settlement of international disputes by arbitration.

We believe, however, that a small navy is poor economy and that a strong navy is the best protection in time of war and the best preventive of war. We, therefore, favor the speedy building of a navy sufficiently strong to protect at the same time both the Atlantic and Pacific Coasts of the United States.

We rejoice in the adoption by both the Democratic and Republican platforms of the demand of the Independence party for improved national waterways and the Mississippi inland deep-waters

project, to complete a ship canal from the Gulf to the Great Lakes. We favor the extension of this system to the tributaries of the Mississippi by means of which thirty States shall be served and 20,000 miles added to the coast line of the United States. The reclamation of arid land should be continued and the irrigation programme now contemplated by the Government extended and steps taken for the conservation of the country's natural resources, which should be guarded not only against devastation and waste, but against falling into the control of the monopoly. The abuses growing out of the administration of our forest preserves must be corrected and provisions should be made for free grazing from public lands outside of forest or other reservations. In behalf of the people residing in arid portions of our Western States we protest vigorously against the policy of the Federal Government in selling the exclusive use of water and electric power derived from public works to private corporations, thus creating a monopoly and subjecting citizens living in those sections to exorbitant charges for light and power, and diverting enterprises originally started for public benefit into channels for corporate greed and oppression, and we demand that no more exclusive contracts be made.

American citizens abroad, whether native born or naturalized, and of whatever race or creed, must be secured in the enjoyment of all rights and privileges under our treaties, and wherever such rights are withheld by any country on the ground of race or religious faith, steps should be taken to secure the removal of such unjust discrimination.

We advocate the popular election of United States Senators and of judges, both State and Federal, and favor a graduated income tax and any constitutional amendment necessary to these ends.

Equality of opportunity, the largest measure of individual liberty consistent with equal rights, the overthrow of the rule of special interest and the restoration of government by the majority exercised for the benefit of the whole community; these are the purposes to which the Independence party is pledged, and we invite the co-operation of all patriots and progressive citizens, irrespective of party, who are in sympathy with these principles and in favor of their practical enforcement.

People's Platform of 1908

The People's Party of the United States, in convention assembled, at St. Louis, Mo., this 2d day of April, 1908, with increased confidence in its contentions, reaffirms the declarations made by its first national convention at Omaha, in 1892.

The admonitions of Washington's farewell address; the state papers of Jefferson, and the words of Lincoln, are the teachings of our greatest apostles of human rights and political liberty. There has been a departure from the teaching of these great patriots during recent administrations. The Government has been controlled so as to place the rights of property above the rights of humanity, and has brought the country to a condition that is full of danger to our national wellbeing. Financial combinations have had too much power over Congress, and too much influence with the administrative departments of the Government.

Prerogatives of government have been unwisely and often corruptly surrendered to corporate monopoly and aggregations of predatory wealth. The supreme duty of the hour is for the people to insist that these functions of government be exercised in their own interest. Not the giver of the "thirty pieces of silver" has been condemned, but the "Judas" who received them, has been execrated through the ages. The sycophants of monopoly deserve no better fate.

The issuance of money is a function of government and should not be delegated to corporation or individual. The Constitution gives Congress alone the power to issue money and regulate the value thereof; we, therefore, demand that all money shall be issued by the Government direct to the people without the intervention of banks, and shall be a full legal tender for all debts, public and private, and in quantity sufficient to supply the needs of the country.

The issuance and distribution of full legal tender money from the Treasury, shall not be through private banks, preferred or otherwise, but direct to the people without interest, for the construction and purchase of Federal and internal improvements and utilities, and for the employment of labor.

We demand that postal savings banks be established by the Government for the safe deposit of the savings of the people.

The public domain is a sacred heritage of all the people and should be held for homesteads for actual settlers only. Alien ownership should be forbidden, and lands now held by aliens or by corporations, who have violated the conditions of their grants, should be restored to the public domain.

To prevent unjust discrimination and monopoly, the Government should own and control the railroads and those public utilities, which in their nature are monopolies. To perfect the postal service, the Government should own and operate the general telegraph and telephone systems and provide a parcels post.

As to those trusts and monopolies which are not public utilities or national monopolies, we demand that those special privileges which they now enjoy, and which alone enable them to exist, shall be immediately withdrawn.

Corporations being the creatures of government, should be subjected to such governmental regulation and control as will adequately protect the public.

We demand the taxation of monopoly privileges while they remain in private hands, to the extent of the value of the privilege granted.

We demand that Congress shall enact a general law uniformly regulating the powers and duties of all incorporated companies doing interstate business.

As a means of placing all public questions directly under the control of the people, we demand that legal provision be made under which the people may exercise the initiative and referendum, proportional representation, and direct vote for all public officers, with the right of recall.

We recommend a Federal statute that will recognize the principle of the initiative and referendum, and thereby restore to the voters the right to instruct their national representatives.

We believe in the right of those who labor, to organize for their mutual protection and benefit, and pledge the efforts of the People's Party to preserve this right inviolate.

We condemn the recent attempt to destroy the power of trades union through the unjust use of the Federal injunction, substituting government by injunction for free government.

We favor the enactment of legislation looking to the improvement of conditions for wage earners.

We demand the abolition of child labor in factories and mines, and the suppression of sweatshops.

We oppose the use of convict labor in competition with free labor.

We demand the exclusion from American shores of foreign pauper labor, imported to beat down the wages of intelligent American workingmen.

We favor the eight hour work day, and legislation protecting the lives and limbs of workmen through the use of safety appliances.

We demand the enactment of an employer's liability act within constitutional bounds.

We declare against the continuation of the criminal carelessness in the operation of mines, through which thousands of miners have lost their lives to increase the dividends of stockholders, and demand the immediate adoption of precautionary measures to prevent a repetition of such horrible catastrophes.

We declare that in times of depression, when workingmen are thrown into enforced idleness, that works of public improvement should be at once inaugurated and work provided for those who cannot otherwise secure employment.

We especially emphasize the declaration of the Omaha platform, that "Wealth belongs to him who creates it and every dollar taken from industry without a just equivalent is robbery."

We congratulate the farmers of the country upon the enormous growth of their splendid organizations, and the good already accomplished through them, securing higher prices for farm products and better conditions generally, for those engaged in agricultural pursuits. We urge the importance of maintaining these organizations and extending their power and influence.

We condemn all unwarranted assumption of authority by inferior Federal courts, in annulling, by injunction, the laws of the States, and demand legislative action by Congress, which will prohibit such usurpation, and will restrict to the Supreme Court of the United States, the exercise of power in cases involving State legislation.

We are opposed to gambling in futures.

We present to all people the foregoing declaration of principles and policies as our deep, earnest and abiding convictions; and now, before the country and in the name of the great moral, but eternal power in the universe, that makes for right thinking and right living and determines the destiny of nations, this convention pledges that the People's Party will stand by these principles and policies in success and in defeat; that never again will the party by the siren songs and false promises of designing politicians, be tempted to change its course, or be drawn again upon the treacherous rocks of fusion.

Prohibition Platform of 1908

The Prohibition Party of the United States, assembled in convention at Columbus, Ohio, July 15-16, 1908, expressing gratitude to Almighty God for the victories of our principles in the past, for encouragement at present, and for confidence in early and triumphant success in the future, makes the following declaration of principles, and pledges their enactment into law when placed in power:—

1. The submission by Congress to the several States, of an amendment to the Federal constitution prohibiting the manufacture, sale, importation, exportation, or transportation of alcoholic liquors for beverage purposes.

2. The immediate prohibition of the liquor traffic for beverage purposes in the District of Columbia, in the Territories, and all places over which the National Government has jurisdiction; the repeal of the internal revenue tax on alcoholic liquors and the prohibition of interstate traffic therein.

3. The election of United States Senators by direct vote of the people.

4. Equitable graduated income and inheritance taxes.

5. The establishment of postal savings banks and the guaranty of deposits in banks.

6. The regulation of all corporations doing an interstate commerce business.

7. The creation of a permanent tariff commission.

8. The strict enforcement of law instead of official tolerance and practical license of the social evil which prevails in many of our cities, with its unspeakable traffic in girls.

9. Uniform marriage and divorce laws.

10. An equitable and constitutional employers liability act.

11. Court review of Post-Office Department decisions.

12. The prohibition of child labor in mines, workshops, and factories.

13. Legislation basing suffrage only upon intelligence and ability to read and write the English language.

14. The preservation of the mineral and forest resources of the country, and the improvement of the highways and waterways.

Believing in the righteousness of our cause and the final triumph of our principles, and convinced of the unwillingness of the Republican and Democratic parties to deal with these issues, we invite to full party fellowship all citizens who are with us agreed.

Republican Platform of 1908

Once more the Republican Party, in National Convention assembled, submits its cause to the people. This great historic organization, that destroyed slavery, preserved the Union, restored credit, expanded the national domain, established a sound financial system, developed the industries and resources of the country, and gave to the nation her seat of honor in the councils of the world, now meets the new problems of government with the same courage and capacity with which it solved the old.

Republicanism Under Roosevelt

In this greatest era of American advancement the Republican party has reached its highest service under the leadership of Theodore Roosevelt. His administration is an epoch in American history. In no other period since national sovereignty was won under Washington, or preserved under Lincoln, has there been such mighty progress in those ideals of government which make for justice, equality and fair dealing among men. The highest aspirations of the American people have found a voice. Their most exalted servant represents the best aims and worthiest purposes of all his countrymen. American manhood has been lifted to a nobler sense of duty and obligation. Conscience and courage in public station and higher standards of right and wrong in private life have become cardinal principles of political faith; capital and labor have been brought into closer relations of confidence and interdependence, and the abuse of wealth, the tyranny of power, and all the evils of privilege and favoritism have been put to scorn by the simple, manly virtues of justice and fair play.

The great accomplishments of President Roosevelt have been, first and foremost, a brave and impartial enforcement of the law, the prosecution of illegal trusts and monopolies, the exposure and punishment of evil-doers in the public service; the more effective regulation of the rates and service of the great transportation lines; the complete overthrow of preferences, rebates and discriminations; the arbitration of labor disputes; the amelioration of the condition of wage-workers everywhere; the conservation of the natural resources of the country; the forward step in the improvement of the inland waterways; and always the earnest support and defence of every wholesome safeguard which has made more secure the guarantees of life, liberty and property.

These are the achievements that will make for Theodore Roosevelt his place in history, but more than all else the great things he has done will be an inspiration to those who have yet greater things to do. We declare our unfaltering adherence to the policies thus inaugurated, and pledge their continuance under a Republican administration of the Government.

Equality of Opportunity

Under the guidance of Republican principles the American people have become the richest nation in the world. Our wealth to-day exceeds that of England and all her colonies, and that of France and Germany combined. When the Republican Party was born the total wealth of the country was $16,000,000,000. It has leaped to $110,000,000,000 in a generation, while Great Britain has gathered but $60,000,000,000 in five hundred years. The United States now owns one-fourth of the world's wealth and makes one-third of all modern manufactured products. In the great necessities of civilization, such as coal, the motive power of all activity; iron, the chief basis of all industry; cotton, the staple foundation of all fabrics; wheat, corn and all the agricultural products that feed mankind, America's supremacy is undisputed. And yet her great natural wealth has been scarcely touched. We have a vast domain of 3,000,000 square miles, literally bursting with latent treasure, still waiting the magic of capital and industry to be converted to the practical uses of mankind; a country rich in soil and climate, in the unharnessed energy of its rivers and in all the varied products of the field, the forest and the factory. With gratitude for God's bounty, with pride in the splendid productiveness of the past and with confidence in the plenty and prosperity of the future, the Republican party declares for the principle that in the development and enjoyment of wealth so great and blessings so benign there shall be equal opportunity for all.

THE REVIVAL OF BUSINESS

Nothing so clearly demonstrates the sound basis upon which our commercial, industrial and agricultural interests are founded, and the necessity of promoting their continued welfare through the operation of Republican policies, as the recent safe passage of the American people through a financial disturbance which, if appearing in the midst of Democratic rule or the menace of it, might have equalled the familiar Democratic panics of the past. We congratulate the people upon this renewed evidence of American supremacy and hail with confidence the signs now manifest of a complete restoration of business prosperity in all lines of trade, commerce and manufacturing.

RECENT REPUBLICAN LEGISLATION

Since the election of William McKinley in 1896, the people of this country have felt anew the wisdom of intrusting to the Republican party, through decisive majorities, the control and direction of national legislation.

The many wise and progressive measures adopted at recent sessions of Congress have demonstrated the patriotic resolve of Republican leadership in the legislative department to keep step in the forward march toward better government.

Notwithstanding the indefensible filibustering of a Democratic minority in the House of Representatives during the last session, many wholesome and progressive laws were enacted, and we especially commend the passage of the emergency currency bill; the appointment of the national monetary commission; the employer's and Government liability laws, the measures for the greater efficiency of the Army and Navy; the widow's pension bill; the child labor law for the District of Columbia; the new statutes for the safety of railroad engineers and firemen, and many other acts conserving the public welfare.

REPUBLICAN PLEDGES FOR THE FUTURE

Tariff

The Republican party declares unequivocally for a revision of the tariff by a special session of Congress immediately following the inauguration of the next President, and commends the steps already taken to this end in the work assigned to the appropriate committees of Congress, which are now investigating the operation and effect of existing schedules.

In all tariff legislation the true principle of protection is best maintained by the imposition of such duties as will equal the difference between the cost of production at home and abroad, together with a reasonable profit to American industries. We favor the establishment of maximum and minimum rates to be administered by the President under limitations fixed in the law, the maximum to be available to meet discriminations by foreign countries against American goods entering their markets, and the minimum to represent the normal measure of protection at home; the aim and purpose of the Republican policy being not only to preserve, without excessive duties, that security against foreign competition to which American manufacturers, farmers and producers are entitled, but also to maintain the high standard of living of the wage-earners of this country, who are the most direct beneficiaries of the protective system. Between the United States and the Philippines we believe in a free interchange of products with such limitations as to sugar and tobacco as will afford adequate protection to domestic interests.

Currency

We approve the emergency measures adopted by the Government during the recent financial disturbance, and especially commend the passage by Congress, at the last session of the law designed to protect the country from a repetition of such stringency. The Republican party is committed to the development of a permanent currency system, responding to our greater needs; and the appointment of the National Monetary

Commission by the present Congress, which will impartially investigate all proposed methods, insures the early realization of this purpose. The present currency laws have fully justified their adoption, but an expanding commerce, a marvellous growth in wealth and population, multiplying the centres of distribution, increasing the demand for the movement of crops in the West and South, and entailing periodic changes in monetary conditions, disclose the need of a more elastic and adaptable system. Such a system must meet the requirements of agriculturists, manufacturers, merchants and business men generally, must be automatic in operation, minimizing the fluctuations of interest rates, and above all, must be in harmony with that Republican doctrine, which insists that every dollar shall be based upon, and as good as, gold.

Postal Savings

We favor the establishment of a postal savings bank system for the convenience of the people and the encouragement of thrift.

Trusts

The Republican-party passed the Sherman Anti-trust law over Democratic opposition, and enforced it after Democratic dereliction. It has been a wholesome instrument for good in the hands of a wise and fearless administration. But experience has shown that its effectiveness can be strengthened and its real objects better attained by such amendments as will give to the Federal Government greater supervision and control over, and secure greater publicity in, the management of that class of corporations engaged in interstate commerce having power and opportunity to effect monopolies.

Railroads

We approve the enactment of the railroad rate law and the vigorous enforcement by the present administration of the statutes against rebates and discriminations, as a result of which the advantages formerly possessed by the large shipper over the small shipper have substantially disappeared; and in this connection we commend the appropriation by the present Congress to enable the Interstate Commerce Commission to thoroughly investigate, and give publicity to, the accounts of interstate railroads. We believe, however, that the interstate commerce law should be further amended so as to give railroads the right to make and publish tariff agreements, subject to the approval of the Commission, but maintaining always the principle of competition between naturally competing lines and avoiding the common control of such lines by any means whatsoever. We favor such national legislation and supervision as will prevent the future over-issue of stocks and bonds by interstate carriers.

Railroad and Government Employees

The enactment in constitutional form at the present session of Congress of the employer's liability law; the passage and enforcement of the safety appliance statutes, as well as the additional protection secured for engineers and firemen; the reduction in the hours of labor of trainmen and railroad telegraphers; the successful exercise of the powers of mediation and arbitration between interstate railroads and their employes, and the law making a beginning in the policy of compensation for injured employes of the Government, are among the most commendable accomplishments of the present administration. But there is further work in this direction yet to be done, and the Republican party pledges its continued devotion to every cause that makes for safety and the betterment of conditions among those whose labor contributes so much to the progress and welfare of the country.

Wage-Earners Generally

The same wise policy which has induced the Republican party to maintain protection to American labor; to establish an eight hour day in the construction of all public works; to increase the list of employes who shall have preferred claims for wages under the bankruptcy laws; to adopt a child labor statute for the District of Columbia; to direct an investigation into the condition of working women and children, and later, of employes of telephone and telegraph companies engaged in interstate business; to appropriate $150,000 at the recent session of Congress in order to secure a thorough inquiry into the causes of catastrophes and loss of life in the mines; and to amend and strengthen the laws prohibiting the importation of contract labor, will be pursued in every legitimate direction within Federal authority to lighten the burdens and increase the opportunity for happiness and advancement of all who toil. The Republican party recognizes the special needs of wage-workers generally, for their well-being means the well-being of all. But more important than all other considerations is that of good citizenship and we especially stand for the needs of every American, whatever his occupation, in his capacity as a self-respecting citizen.

Court Procedure

The Republican party will uphold at all times the authority and integrity of the courts, State and Federal, and will ever insist that their powers to enforce their process and to protect life, liberty and property shall be preserved inviolate. We believe, however, that the rules of procedure in the Federal Courts with respect to the issuance of the writ of injunction should be more accurately defined by statute, and that no injunction or temporary restraining order should be issued without notice, except where irreparable injury would result from delay, in which case a speedy hearing thereafter should be granted.

The American Farmer

Among those whose welfare is as vital to the welfare of the whole country as is that of the wage-earner, is the American farmer. The prosperity of the country rests peculiarly upon the prosperity of agriculture. The Republican party during the last twelve years has accomplished extraordinary work in bringing the resources of the National Government to the aid of the farmer, not only in advancing agriculture itself, but in increasing the conveniences of rural life. Free rural mail delivery has been established; it now reaches millions of our citizens, and we favor its extension until every community in the land receives the full benefits of the postal service. We recognize the social and economical advantages of good country roads, maintained more and more largely at public expense, and less and less at the expense of the abutting owner. In this work we commend the growing practice of State aid, and we approve the efforts of the National Agricultural Department by experiments and otherwise to make clear to the public the best methods of road construction.

Rights of the Negro

The Republican party has been for more than fifty years the consistent friend of the American Negro. It gave him freedom and citizenship. It wrote into the organic law the declarations that proclaim his civil and political rights, and it believes to-day that his noteworthy progress in intelligence, industry and good citizenship has earned the respect and encouragement of the nation. We demand equal justice for all men, without regard to race or color; we declare once more, and without reservation, for the enforcement in letter and spirit of the Thirteenth, Fourteenth and Fifteenth amendments to the Constitution which were designed for the protection and advancement of the negro, and we condemn all devices that have for their real aim his disfranchisement for reasons of color alone, as unfair, un-American and repugnant to the Supreme law of the land.

Natural Resources and Waterways

We indorse the movement inaugurated by the administration for the conservation of natural resources; we approve all measures to prevent the waste of timber; we commend the work now going on for the reclamation of arid lands, and reaffirm the Republican policy of the free distribution of the available areas of the public domain to the landless settler. No obligation of the future is more insistent and none will result in greater blessings to posterity. In line with this splendid undertaking is the further duty, equally imperative, to enter upon a systematic improvement upon a large and comprehensive plan, just to all portions of the country, of the waterways, harbors, and Great Lakes, whose natural adaptability to the increasing traffic of the land is one of the greatest gifts of a benign Providence.

The Army and Navy

The 60th Congress passed many commendable acts increasing the efficiency of the Army and Navy; making the militia of the States an integral part of the national establishment; authorizing joint manœuvres of army and militia; fortifying new naval bases and completing the construction of coaling stations; instituting a female nurse corps for naval hospitals and ships, and adding two new battleships, ten torpedo boat destroyers, three steam colliers, and eight submarines to the strength of the Navy. Although at peace with all the world, and secure in the consciousness that the American people do not desire and will not provoke a war with any other country, we nevertheless declare our unalterable devotion to a policy that will keep this Republic ready at all times to defend her traditional doctrines, and assure her appropriate part in promoting permanent tranquillity among the nations.

Protection of American Citizens Abroad

We commend the vigorous efforts made by the administration to protect American citizens in foreign lands, and pledge ourselves to insist upon the just and equal protection of all our citizens abroad. It is the unquestioned duty of the Government to procure for all our citizens, without distinction, the rights of travel and sojourn in friendly countries, and we declare ourselves in favor of all proper efforts tending to that end.

Extension of Foreign Commerce

Under the administration of the Republican party, the foreign commerce of the United States has experienced a remarkable growth, until it has a present annual valuation of approximately $3,000,000,000, and gives employment to a vast amount of labor and capital which would otherwise be idle. It has inaugurated, through the recent visit of the Secretary of State to South America and Mexico a new era of Pan-American commerce and comity, which is bringing us into closer touch with our twenty sister American republics, having a common historical heritage, a republican form of government, and offering us a limitless field of legitimate commercial expansion.

Arbitration and The Hague Treaties

The conspicuous contributions of American statesmanship to the great cause of international peace so signally advanced in the Hague conferences, are an occasion for just pride and gratification. At the last session of the Senate of the United States eleven Hague conventions were ratified, establishing the rights of neutrals, laws of war on land, restriction of submarine mines, limiting the use of force for the collection of contractual debts, governing the opening of hostilities, extending the application of Geneva principles and, in many ways, lessening the evils of war and promoting the peaceful settlement of international controversies. At the same session twelve arbitration conventions with great nations were confirmed, and extradition, boundary and neutralization

treaties of supreme importance were ratified. We indorse such achievements as the highest duty a people can perform and proclaim the obligation of further strengthening the bonds of friendship and good-will with all the nations of the world.

Merchant Marine

We adhere to the Republican doctrine of encouragement to American shipping and urge such legislation as will revive the merchant marine prestige of the country, so essential to national defence, the enlargement of foreign trade and the industrial prosperity of our own people.

Veterans of the Wars

Another Republican policy which must ever be maintained is that of generous provision for those who have fought the country's battles, and for the widows and orphans of those who have fallen. We commend the increase in the widows' pensions, made by the present Congress, and declare for a liberal administration of all pension laws, to the end that the people's gratitude may grow deeper as the memories of heroic sacrifice grow more sacred with the passing years.

Civil Service

We reaffirm our former declarations that the civil service laws, enacted, extended, and enforced by the Republican party, shall continue to be maintained and obeyed.

Public Health

We commend the efforts designed to secure greater efficiency in National Public Health agencies and favor such legislation as will effect this purpose.

Bureau of Mines and Mining

In the interest of the great mineral industries of our country, we earnestly favor the establishment of a Bureau of Mines and Mining.

Cuba, Porto Rico, Philippines, and Panama

The American Government, in Republican hands, has freed Cuba, given peace and protection to Porto Rico and the Philippines under our flag, and begun the construction of the Panama Canal. The present conditions in Cuba vindicate the wisdom of maintaining, between that Republic and this, imperishable bonds of mutual interest, and the hope is now expressed that the Cuban people will soon again be ready to assume complete sovereignty over their land.

In Porto Rico the Government of the United States is meeting loyal and patriotic support; order and prosperity prevail, and the well-being of the people is in every respect promoted and conserved.

We believe that the native inhabitants of Porto Rico should be at once collectively made citizens of the United States, and that all others properly qualified under existing laws residing in said island should have the privilege of becoming naturalized.

In the Philippines insurrection has been suppressed, law is established and life and property made secure. Education and practical experience are there advancing the capacity of the people for government, and the policies of McKinley and Roosevelt are leading the inhabitants step by step to an ever-increasing measure of home rule.

Time has justified the selection of the Panama route for the great Isthmian Canal, and events have shown the wisdom of securing authority over the zone through which it is to be built. The work is now progressing with a rapidity far beyond expectation, and already the realization of the hopes of centuries has come within the vision of the near future.

New Mexico and Arizona

We favor the immediate admission of the Territories of New Mexico and Arizona as separate States in the Union.

Centenary of the Birth of Lincoln

February 12, 1909, will be the 100th anniversary of the birth of Abraham Lincoln, an immortal spirit whose fame has brightened with the receding years, and whose name stands among the first of those given to the world by the great Republic. We recommend that this centennial anniversary be celebrated throughout the confines of the nation, by all the people thereof, and especially by the public schools, as an exercise to stir the patriotism of the youth of the land.

Democratic Incapacity for Government

We call the attention of the American people to the fact that none of the great measures here advocated by the Republican party could be enacted, and none of the steps forward here proposed could be taken under a Democratic administration or under one in which party responsibility is divided. The continuance of present policies, therefore, absolutely requires the continuance in power of that party which believes in them and which possesses the capacity to put them into operation.

Fundamental Differences Between Democracy and Republicanism

Beyond all platform declarations there are fundamental differences between the Republican party and its chief opponent which make the one worthy and the other unworthy of public trust.

In history, the difference between Democracy and Republicanism is that the one stood for debased currency, the other for honest currency; the one for free silver, the other for sound money; the one for free trade, the other for protection; the one for the contraction of American influence, the other for its expansion; the one has been forced to abandon every position taken on the great issues before the people, the other has held and vindicated all.

In experience, the difference between Democracy and Republicanism is that one means adversity, while the other means prosperity; one means low wages, the other means high; one means doubt and debt, the other means confidence and thrift.

In principle, the difference between Democracy and Republicanism is that one stands for vacillation and timidity in government, the other for strength and purpose; one stands for obstruction, the other for construction; one promises, the other performs, one finds fault, the other finds work.

The present tendencies of the two parties are even more marked by inherent differences. The trend of Democracy is toward socialism, while the Republican party stands for a wise and regulated individualism. Socialism would destroy wealth, Republicanism would prevent its abuse. Socialism would give to each an equal right to take; Republicanism would give to each an equal right to earn. Socialism would offer an equality of possession which would soon leave no one anything to possess, Republicanism would give equality of opportunity which would assure to each his share of a constantly increasing sum of possessions. In line with this tendency the Democratic party of to-day believes in Government ownership, while the Republican party believes in Government regulation. Ultimately Democracy would have the nation own the people, while Republicanism would have the people own the nation.

Upon this platform of principles and purposes, reaffirming our adherence to every Republican doctrine proclaimed since the birth of the party, we go before the country, asking the support not only of those who have acted with us heretofore, but of all our fellow citizens who, regardless of past political differences, unite in the desire to maintain the policies, perpetuate the blessings and make secure the achievements of a greater America.

Socialist Platform of 1908

PRINCIPLES

Human life depends upon food, clothing and shelter. Only with these assured are freedom, culture and higher human development possible. To produce food, clothing or shelter, land and machinery are needed. Land alone does not satisfy human needs. Human labor creates machinery and applies it to the land for the production of raw materials and food. Whoever has control of land and machinery controls human labor, and with it human life and liberty.

To-day the machinery and the land used for industrial purposes are owned by a rapidly decreasing minority. So long as machinery is simple and easily handled by one man, its owner cannot dominate the sources of life of others. But when machinery becomes more complex and expensive, and requires for its effective operation the organized effort of many workers, its influence reaches over wide circles of life. The owners of such machinery become the dominant class.

In proportion as the number of such machine owners compared to all other classes decreases, their power in the nation and in the world increases. They bring ever larger masses of working people under their control, reducing them to the point where muscle and brain are their only productive property. Millions of formerly self-employing workers thus become the helpless wage slaves of the industrial masters.

As the economic power of the ruling class grows it becomes less useful in the life of the nation. All the useful work of the nation falls upon the shoulders of the class whose only property is its manual and mental labor power — the wage worker—or of the class who have but little land and little effective machinery outside of their labor power — the small traders and small farmers. The ruling minority is steadily becoming useless and parasitic.

A bitter struggle over the division of the products of labor is waged between the exploiting propertied classes on the one hand and the exploited, propertyless class on the other. In this struggle the wage-working class cannot expect adequate relief from any reform of the present order at the hands of the dominant class.

The wage-workers are therefore the most determined and irreconcilable antagonists of the ruling class. They suffer most from the curse of class rule. The fact that a few capitalists are permitted to control all the country's industrial resources and social tools for their individual profit, and to make the production of the necessaries of life the object of competitive private enterprise and speculation is at the bottom of all the social evils of our time.

In spite of the organization of trusts, pools and combinations, the capitalists are powerless to regulate production for social ends. Industries are largely conducted in a planless manner. Through periods of feverish activity the strength and health of the workers are mercilessly used up, and during periods of enforced idleness the workers are frequently reduced to starvation.

The climaxes of this system of production are the regularly recurring industrial depressions and crises which paralyze the nation every fifteen or twenty years.

The capitalist class, in its mad race for profits, is bound to exploit the workers to the very limit of their endurance and to sacrifice their physical, moral and mental welfare to its own insatiable greed. Capitalism keeps the masses of workingmen in poverty, destitution, physical exhaustion and ignorance. It drags their wives from their homes to the mill and factory. It snatches their children from the playgrounds and schools and grinds their slender bodies and unformed minds into cold dollars. It disfigures, maims and kills hundreds of thousands of workingmen annually in mines, on railroads and in factories. It drives millions of workers into the ranks of the unemployed, and forces large numbers of them into beggary, vagrancy and all forms of crime and vice.

To maintain their rule over their fellow men the capitalists must keep in their pay all organs of the public powers, public mind and public conscience. They control the dominant parties and, through them, the elected public officials. They select the executives, bribe the legislatures and corrupt the courts of justice. They own and censor the press. They dominate the educational institutions. They own the nation politically and intellectually just as they own it industrially.

The struggle between wage-workers and capitalists grows ever fiercer, and has now become the only vital issue before the American people. The wage-working class, therefore, has the most direct interest in abolishing the capitalist system. But in abolishing the present system, the workingmen will free not only their own class, but also all other classes of modern society. The small farmer, who is to-day exploited by large capital more indirectly but not less effectively than is the wage laborer; the small manufacturer and trader, who is engaged in a desperate and losing struggle for economic independence in the face of the all-conquering power of concentrated capital; and even the capitalist himself, who is the slave of his wealth rather than its master. The struggle of the working class against the capitalist class, while it is a class struggle, is thus at the same time a struggle for the abolition of all classes and class privileges.

The private ownership of the land and means of production used for exploitation, is the rock upon which class rule is built; political government is its indispensable instrument. The wage-workers cannot be freed from exploitation without conquering the political power and substituting collective for private ownership of the land and means of production used for exploitation.

The basis for such transformation is rapidly developing within present capitalist society. The factory system, with its complex machinery and minute division of labor, is rapidly destroying all vestiges of individual production in manufacture. Modern production is already very largely a collective and social process. The great trusts and monopolies which have sprung up in recent years have organized the work and management of the principal industries on a national scale, and have fitted them for collective use and operation.

The Socialist Party is primarily an economic and political movement. It is not concerned with matters of religious belief.

In the struggle for freedom the interests of the modern workers are identical. The struggle is not only national, but international. It embraces the world and will be carried to ultimate victory by the united workers of the world.

To unite the workers of the nation and their allies and sympathizers of all other classes to this end, is the mission of the Socialist party. In this battle for freedom the Socialist party does not strive to substitute working class rule for capitalist class rule, but by working class victory, to free all humanity from class rule and to realize the international brotherhood of man.

PLATFORM FOR 1908

The Socialist party, in national convention assembled, again declares itself as the party of the working class, and appeals for the support of all workers of the United States and of all citizens who sympathize with the great and just cause of labor.

We are at this moment in the midst of one of those industrial breakdowns that periodically paralyze the life of the nation. The much-boasted era of our national prosperity has been followed by one of general misery. Factories, mills and mines are closed. Millions of men, ready, willing and able to provide the nation with all the necessaries and comforts of life are forced into idleness and starvation.

Within recent years the trusts and monopolies have attained an enormous and menacing development. They have acquired the power to dictate the terms upon which we shall be allowed to live. The trusts fix the prices of our bread, meat and sugar, of our coal, oil and clothing, of our raw material and machinery, of all the necessities of life.

The present desperate condition of the workers has been made the opportunity for a renewed onslaught on organized labor. The highest courts of the country have within the last year rendered decision after decision depriving the workers of rights which they had won by generations of struggle.

The attempt to destroy the Western Federation of Miners, although defeated by the solidarity of organized labor and the Socialist movement, revealed the existence of a far-reaching and unscrupulous conspiracy by the ruling class against the organization of labor.

In their efforts to take the lives of the leaders of the miners the conspirators violated state laws and the federal constitution in a manner seldom equaled even in a country so completely dominated by the profit-seeking class as is the United States.

The Congress of the United States has shown its contempt for the interests of labor as plainly and unmistakably as have the other branches of government. The laws for which the labor organizations have continually petitioned have failed to pass. Laws ostensibly enacted for the benefit of labor have been distorted against labor.

The working class of the United States cannot expect any remedy for its wrongs from the present ruling class or from the dominant parties. So long as a small number of individuals are permitted to control the sources of the nation's wealth for their private profit in competition with each other and for the exploitation of their fellowmen, industrial depressions are bound to occur at certain intervals. No currency reforms or other legislative measures proposed by capitalist reformers can avail against these fatal results of utter anarchy in production.

Individually competition leads inevitably to combinations and trusts. No amount of government regulation, or of publicity, or of restrictive legislation will arrest the natural course of modern industrial development.

While our courts, legislatures and executive officers remain in the hands of the ruling classes and their agents, the government will be used in the interests of these classes as against the toilers.

Political parties are but the expression of economic class interests. The Republican, the Democratic, and the so-called "Independence" parties and all parties other than the Socialist party, are financed, directed and controlled by the representatives of different groups of the ruling class.

In the maintenance of class government both the Democratic and Republican parties have been equally guilty. The Republican party has had control of the national government and has been directly and actively responsible for these wrongs. The Democratic party, while saved from direct responsibility by its political impotence, has shown itself equally subservient to the aims of the capitalist class whenever and wherever it has been in power. The old chattel slave-owning aristocracy of the south, which was the backbone of the Democratic party, has been supplanted by a child slave plutocracy. In the great cities of our country the Democratic party is allied with the criminal element of the slums as the Republican party is allied with the predatory criminals of the palace in maintaining the interests of the possessing class.

The various "reform" movements and parties which have sprung up within recent years are but the clumsy expression of widespread popular discontent. They are not based on an intelligent understanding of the historical development of civilization and of the economic and political needs of our time. They are bound to perish as the numerous middle class reform movements of the past have perished.

PROGRAM

As measures calculated to strengthen the working class in its fight for the realization of this ultimate aim, and to increase its power of resistance against capitalist oppression, we advocate and pledge ourselves and our elected officers to the following program:

GENERAL DEMANDS

1—The immediate government relief for the unemployed workers by building schools, by reforesting of cutover and waste lands, by reclamation of arid tracts, and the building of canals, and by extending all other useful public works. All persons employed on such works shall be employed directly by the government under an eight hour work day and at the prevailing union wages. The government shall also loan money to states and municipalities without interest for the purpose of carrying on public works. It shall contribute to the funds of labor organizations for the purpose of assisting their unemployed members, and shall take such other measures within its power as will lessen the widespread misery of the workers caused by the misrule of the capitalist class.

2—The collective ownership of railroads, telegraphs, telephones, steamship lines and all other means of social transportation and communication, and all land.

3—The collective ownership of all industries which are organized on a national scale and in which competition has virtually ceased to exist.

4—The extension of the public domain to include mines, quarries, oil wells, forests and water-power.

5—The scientific reforestation of timber lands, and the reclamation of swamp lands. The land so reforested or reclaimed to be permanently retained as a part of the public domain.

6—The absolute freedom of press, speech and assemblage.

Industrial Demands

7—The improvement of the industrial condition of the workers,

(a) By shortening the workday in keeping with the increased productiveness of machinery.

(b) By securing to every worker a rest period of not less than a day and a half in each week.

(c) By securing a more effective inspection of workshops and factories.

(d) By forbidding the employment of children under sixteen years of age.

(e) By forbidding the interstate transportation of the products of child labor, of convict labor and of all uninspected factories.

(f) By abolishing official charity and substituting in its place compulsory insurance against unemployment, illness, accident, invalidism, old age and death.

Political Demands

8—The extension of inheritance taxes, graduated in proportion to the amount of the bequests and the nearness of kin.

9—A graduated income tax.

10—Unrestricted and equal suffrage for men and women, and we pledge ourselves to engage in an active campaign in that direction.

11—The initiative and referendum, proportional representation and the right of recall.

12—The abolition of the senate.

13—The abolition of the power usurped by the supreme court of the United States to pass upon the constitutionality of legislation enacted by Congress. National laws to be repealed or abrogated only by act of Congress or by a referendum of the whole people.

14—That the constitution be made amendable by majority vote.

15—The enactment of further measures for general education and for the conservation of health. The bureau of education to be made a department. The creation of a department of public health.

16—The separation of the present bureau of labor from the department of commerce and labor, and the establishment of a department of labor.

17—That all judges be elected by the people for short terms, and that the power to issue injunctions shall be curbed by immediate legislation.

18—The free administration of justice.

Such measures of relief as we may be able to force from capitalism are but a preparation of the workers to seize the whole power of government, in order that they may thereby lay hold of the whole system of industry and thus come to their rightful inheritance.

Socialist Labor Platform of 1908

The Socialist Labor Party of America, in convention assembled, reasserts the inalienable right of man to life, liberty and the pursuit of happiness.

We hold that the purpose of government is to secure to every citizen the enjoyment of this right: but taught by experience we hold furthermore that such right is illusory to the majority of the people, to wit, the working class, under the present system of economic inequality that is essentially destructive of *their* life, *their* liberty, and *their* happiness.

We hold that the true theory of politics is that the machinery of government must be controlled by the whole people; but again taught by experience we hold furthermore that the true theory of economics is that the means of production must likewise be owned, operated and controlled by the people in common. Man cannot exercise his right of life, liberty and the pursuit of happiness without the ownership of the land on and the tool with which to work. Deprived of these, his life, his liberty and his fate fall into the hands of the class that owns those essentials for work and production.

We hold that the existing contradiction between the theory of democratic government and the fact of a despotic economic system—the private ownership of the natural and social opportunities—divides the people into two classes, the Capitalist Class and the Working Class; throws society into the convulsions of the Class Struggle, and perverts Government to the exclusive benefit of the Capitalist Class.

Thus labor is robbed of the wealth which it

alone produces, is denied the means of self-employment, and, by compulsory idleness in wage slavery, is even deprived of the necessaries of life.

Against such a system the Socialist Labor party raises the banner of revolt, and demands the unconditional surrender of the Capitalist Class.

The time is fast coming when, in the natural course of social evolution, this system, through the destructive action of its failures and crises on the one hand, and the constructive tendencies of its trusts and other capitalist combinations on the other hand, will have worked out its own downfall.

We, therefore, call upon the wage workers of America to organize under the banner of the Socialist Labor Party into a class-conscious body, aware of its rights and determined to conquer them.

And we also call upon all other intelligent citizens to place themselves squarely upon the ground of Working Class interests, and join us in this mighty and noble work of human emancipation, so that we may put summary end to the existing barbarous class conflict by placing the land and all the means of production, transportation and distribution into the hands of the people as a collective body, and substituting the co-operative commonwealth for the present state of planless production, industrial war and social disorder—a commonwealth in which every worker shall have the free exercise and full benefit of his faculties, multiplied by all the modern factors of civilization.

☒ CAMPAIGN OF 1912

In this year there were the two major parties and three well-established minor parties,—the Prohibitionists, the Socialists, and the Socialist Labor Party.

But the year 1912 is marked chiefly by the advent of a very powerful minor party which broke away from the Republicans. They adopted the name Progressive Party.

It is to be observed that the People's Party disappeared at this time.

Democratic Platform of 1912

We, the representatives of the Democratic party of the United States, in national convention assembled, reaffirm our devotion to the principles of Democratic government formulated by Thomas Jefferson and enforced by a long and illustrious line of Democratic Presidents.

TARIFF REFORM

We declare it to be a fundamental principle of the Democratic party that the Federal government, under the Constitution, has no right or power to impose or collect tariff duties, except for the purpose of revenue, and we demand that the collection of such taxes shall be limited to the necessities of government honestly and economically administered.

The high Republican tariff is the principal cause of the unequal distribution of wealth; it is a system of taxation which makes the rich richer and the poor poorer; under its operations the American farmer and laboring man are the chief sufferers; it raises the cost of the necessaries of life to them, but does not protect their product or wages. The farmer sells largely in free markets and buys almost entirely in the protected markets. In the most highly protected industries, such as cotton and wool, steel and iron, the wages of the laborers are the lowest paid in any of our industries. We denounce the Republican pretence on that subject and assert that American wages are established by competitive conditions, and not by the tariff.

We favor the immediate downward revision of the existing high and in many cases prohibitive tariff duties, insisting that material reductions be speedily made upon the necessaries of life. Articles entering into competition with trust-controlled products and articles of American manufacture which are sold abroad more cheaply than at home should be put upon the free list.

We recognize that our system of tariff taxation is intimately connected with the business of the country, and we favor the ultimate attainment of the principles we advocate by legislation that will not injure or destroy legitimate industry.

We denounce the action of President Taft in vetoing the bills to reduce the tariff in the cotton, woolen, metals, and chemical schedules and the Farmers' free bill, all of which were designed to give immediate relief to the masses from the exactions of the trusts.

The Republican party, while promising tariff revision, has shown by its tariff legislation that such revision is not to be in the people's interest, and having been faithless to its pledges of 1908, it should not longer enjoy the confidence of the nation. We appeal to the American people to support us in our demand for a tariff for revenue only.

HIGH COST OF LIVING

The high cost of living is a serious problem in every American home. The Republican party, in its platform, attempts to escape from responsibility for present conditions by denying that they are due to a protective tariff. We take issue with them on this subject, and charge that excessive prices result in a large measure from the high tariff laws enacted and maintained by the Republican party and from trusts and commercial conspiracies fostered and encouraged by such laws, and we assert that no substantial relief can be secured for the people until import duties on the necessaries of life are materially reduced and these criminal conspiracies broken up.

ANTI-TRUST LAW

A private monopoly is indefensible and intolerable. We therefore favor the vigorous enforcement of the criminal as well as the civil law against trusts and trust officials, and demand the enactment of such additional legislation as may be necessary to make it impossible for a private monopoly to exist in the United States.

We favor the declaration by law of the conditions upon which corporations shall be permitted to engage in interstate trade, including, among others, the prevention of holding companies, of interlocking directors, of stock watering, of discrimination in price, and the control by any one corporation of so large a proportion of any industry as to make it a menace to competitive conditions.

We condemn the action of the Republican administration in compromising with the Standard Oil Company and the tobacco trust and its failure to invoke the criminal provisions of the anti-trust law against the officers of those corporations after the court had declared that from the undisputed facts in the record they had violated the criminal provisions of the law.

We regret that the Sherman anti-trust law has received a judicial construction depriving it of much of its efficiency and we favor the enactment of legislation which will restore to the statute the strength of which it has been deprived by such interpretation.

RIGHTS OF THE STATES

We believe in the preservation and maintenance in their full strength and integrity of the three co-ordinate branches of the Federal government— the executive, the legislative, and the judicial— each keeping within its own bounds and not encroaching upon the just powers of either of the others.

Believing that the most efficient results under our system of government are to be attained by the full exercise by the States of their reserved sovereign powers, we denounce as usurpation the efforts of our opponents to deprive the States of any of the rights reserved to them, and to enlarge and magnify by indirection the powers of the Federal government.

We insist upon the full exercise of all the powers of the Government, both State and national, to protect the people from injustice at the hands of those who seek to make the government a private asset in business. There is no twilight zone between the nation and the State in which exploiting interests can take refuge from both. It is as necessary that the Federal government shall exercise the powers delegated to it as it is that the States shall exercise the powers reserved to them, but we insist that Federal remedies for the regulation of interstate commerce and for the prevention of private monopoly, shall be added to, and not substituted for State remedies.

INCOME TAX AND POPULAR ELECTION OF SENATORS

We congratulate the country upon the triumph of two important reforms demanded in the last national platform, namely, the amendment of the Federal Constitution authorizing an income tax, and the amendment providing for the popular election of senators, and we call upon the people of all the States to rally to the support of the pending propositions and secure their ratification.

We note with gratification the unanimous sentiment in favor of publicity, before the election, of campaign contributions—a measure demanded in our national platform of 1908, and at that time opposed by the Republican party—and we commend the Democratic House of Representatives for extending the doctrine of publicity to recommendations, verbal and written, upon which presidential appointments are made, to the ownership and control of newspapers, and to the expenditures made by and in behalf of those who aspire to presidential nominations, and we point for additional justification for this legislation to the enormous expenditures of money in behalf of the President and his predecessor in the recent contest for the Republican nomination for President.

PRESIDENTIAL PRIMARY

The movement toward more popular government should be promoted through legislation in each State which will permit the expression of the preference of the electors for national candidates at presidential primaries.

We direct that the National Committee incorporate in the call for the next nominating convention a requirement that all expressions of preference for Presidential candidates shall be given and the selection of delegates and alternates made through a primary election conducted by the party organization in each State where such expression and election are not provided for by State law. Committeemen who are hereafter to constitute the membership of the Democratic National Committee, and whose election is not provided for by law, shall be chosen in each State at such primary elections, and the service and authority of committeemen, however chosen, shall begin immediately upon the receipt of their credentials, respectively.

CAMPAIGN CONTRIBUTIONS

We pledge the Democratic party to the enactment of a law prohibiting any corporation from contributing to a campaign fund and any individual from contributing any amount above a reasonable maximum.

TERM OF PRESIDENT

We favor a single Presidential term, and to that end urge the adoption of an amendment to the Constitution making the President of the United States ineligible to reëlection, and we pledge the candidates of this Convention to this principle.

DEMOCRATIC CONGRESS

At this time, when the Republican party, after a generation of unlimited power in its control of the Federal Government, is rent into factions, it is opportune to point to the record of accomplishment of the Democratic House of Representatives in the Sixty-second Congress. We indorse its action and we challenge comparison of its record with that of any Congress which has been controlled by our opponents.

We call the attention of the patriotic citizens of our country to its record of efficiency, economy and constructive legislation.

It has, among other achievements, revised the rules of the House of Representatives so as to give to the Representatives of the American people freedom of speech and of action in advocating, proposing and perfecting remedial legislation.

It has passed bills for the relief of the people and the development of our country; it has endeavored to revise the tariff taxes downward in the interest of the consuming masses and thus to reduce the high cost of living.

It has proposed an amendment to the Federal Constitution providing for the election of United States Senators by the direct vote of the people.

It has secured the admission of Arizona and New Mexico as two sovereign States.

It has required the publicity of campaign expenses both before and after election and fixed a limit upon the election expenses of United States Senators and Representatives.

It has passed a bill to prevent the abuse of the writ of injunction.

It has passed a law establishing an eight hour day for workmen on all national public work.

It has passed a resolution which forced the President to take immediate steps to abrogate the Russian treaty.

And it has passed the great supply bills which lessen waste and extravagance, and which reduce the annual expenses of the government by many millions of dollars.

We approve the measure reported by the Democratic leaders in the House of Representatives for the creation of a council of national defence, which will determine a definite naval program with a view to increased efficiency and economy.

The party that proclaimed and has always enforced the Monroe Doctrine, and was sponsor for the new navy, will continue faithfully to observe the constitutional requirements to provide and maintain an adequate and well-proportioned navy sufficient to defend American policies, protect our citizens and uphold the honor and dignity of the nation.

REPUBLICAN EXTRAVAGANCE

We denounce the profligate waste of the money wrung from the people by oppressive taxation through the lavish appropriations of recent Republican Congresses, which have kept taxes high and reduced the purchasing power of the people's toil. We demand a return to that simplicity and economy which befits a Democratic government and a reduction in the number of useless offices, the salaries of which drain the substance of the people.

RAILROADS, EXPRESS COMPANIES, TELEGRAPH AND TELEPHONE LINES

We favor the efficient supervision and rate regulation of railroads, express companies, telegraph and telephone lines engaged in interstate commerce. To this end we recommend the valuation of railroads, express companies, telegraph and telephone lines by the Interstate Commerce Commission, such valuation to take into consideration the physical value of the property, the original cost, the cost of reproduction, and any element of value that will render the valuation fair and just.

We favor such legislation as will effectually prohibit the railroads, express, telegraph and telephone companies from engaging in business which brings them into competition with their shippers or patrons; also legislation preventing the overissue of stocks and bonds by interstate railroads, express companies, telegraph and telephone lines, and legislation which will assure such reduction in transportation rates as conditions will permit, care being taken to avoid reduction that would compel a reduction of wages, prevent adequate service, or do injustice to legitimate investments.

BANKING LEGISLATION

We oppose the so-called Aldrich bill or the establishment of a central bank; and we believe our country will be largely freed from panics and consequent unemployment and business depres-

sion by such a systematic revision of our banking laws as will render temporary relief in localities where such relief is needed, with protection from control of dominion by what is known as the money trust.

Banks exist for the accommodation of the public, and not for the control of business. All legislation on the subject of banking and currency should have for its purpose the securing of these accommodations on terms of absolute security to the public and of complete protection from the misuse of the power that wealth gives to those who possess it.

We condemn the present methods of depositing government funds in a few favored banks, largely situated in or controlled by Wall Street, in return for political favors, and we pledge our party to provide by law for their deposit by competitive bidding in the banking institutions of the country, national and State, without discrimination as to locality, upon approved securities and subject to call by the Government.

RURAL CREDITS

Of equal importance with the question of currency reform is the question of rural credits or agricultural finance. Therefore, we recommend that an investigation of agricultural credit societies in foreign countries be made, so that it may be ascertained whether a system of rural credits may be devised suitable to conditions in the United States; and we also favor legislation permitting national banks to loan a reasonable proportion of their funds on real estate security.

We recognize the value of vocational education, and urge Federal appropriations for such training and extension teaching in agriculture in co-operation with the several States.

WATERWAYS

We renew the declaration in our last platform relating to the conservation of our natural resources and the development of our waterways. The present devastation of the Lower Mississippi Valley accentuates the movement for the regulation of river flow by additional bank and levee protection below, and the diversion, storage and control of the flood waters above, their utilization for beneficial purposes in the reclamation of arid and swamp lands and the development of water power, instead of permitting the floods to continue, as heretofore, agents of destruction.

We hold that the control of the Mississippi River is a national problem. The preservation of the depth of its waters for the purpose of navigation, the building of levees to maintain the integrity of its channel and the prevention of the overflow of the land and its consequent devastation, resulting in the interruption of interstate commerce, the disorganization of the mail service, and the enormous loss of life and property impose an obligation which alone can be discharged by the general government.

To maintain an adequate depth of water the entire year, and thereby encourage water transportation, is a consummation worthy of legislative attention, and presents an issue national in its character. It calls for prompt action on the part of Congress, and the Democratic party pledges itself to the enactment of legislation leading to that end.

We favor the co-operation of the United States and the respective States in plans for the comprehensive treatment of all waterways with a view of co-ordinating plans for channel improvement, with plans for drainage of swamp and overflowed lands, and to this end we favor the appropriation by the Federal Government of sufficient funds to make surveys of such lands, to develop plans for draining of the same, and to supervise the work of construction.

We favor the adoption of a liberal and comprehensive plan for the development and improvement of our inland waterways, with economy and efficiency, so as to permit their navigation by vessels of standard draft.

Post Roads

We favor national aid to State and local authorities in the construction and maintenance of post roads.

Rights of Labor

We repeat our declarations of the platform of 1908, as follows:

"The courts of justice are the bulwarks of our liberties, and we yield to none in our purpose to maintain their dignity. Our party has given to the bench a long line of distinguished justices who have added to the respect and confidence in which this department must be jealously maintained. We resent the attempt of the Republican party to raise a false issue respecting the judiciary. It is

an unjust reflection upon a great body of our citizens to assume that they lack respect for the courts.

"It is the function of the courts to interpret the laws which the people enact, and if the laws appear to work economic, social or political injustice, it is our duty to change them. The only basis upon which the integrity of our courts can stand is that of unswerving justice and protection of life, personal liberty, and property. As judicial processes may be abused, we should guard them against abuse.

"Experience has proved the necessity of a modification of the present law relating to injunction, and we reiterate the pledges of our platforms of 1896 and 1904 in favor of a measure which passed the United States Senate in 1898, relating to contempt in Federal Courts, and providing for trial by jury in cases of indirect contempt.

"Questions of judicial practice have arisen especially in connection with industrial disputes. We believe that the parties to all judicial proceedings should be treated with rigid impartiality, and that injunctions should not be issued in any case in which an injunction would not issue if no industrial dispute were involved.

"The expanding organization of industry makes it essential that there should be no abridgement of the right of the wage earners and producers to organize for the protection of wages and the improvement of labor conditions, to the end that such labor organizations and their members should not be regarded as illegal combinations in restraint of trade.

"We pledge the Democratic party to the enactment of a law creating a department of labor, represented separately in the President's cabinet in which department shall be included the subject of mines and mining."

We pledge the Democratic party, so far as the Federal jurisdiction extends, to an employés' compensation law providing adequate indemnity for injury to body or loss of life.

Conservation

We believe in the conservation and the development, for the use of all the people, of the natural resources of the country. Our forests, our sources of water supply, our arable and our mineral lands, our navigable streams, and all the other material resources with which our country has been so lavishly endowed, constitute the foundation of our national wealth. Such additional legislation as may be necessary to prevent their being wasted or absorbed by special or privileged interests, should be enacted and the policy of their conservation should be rigidly adhered to.

The public domain should be administered and disposed of with due regard to the general welfare. Reservations should be limited to the purposes which they purport to serve and not extended to include land wholly unsuited therefor. The unnecessary withdrawal from sale and settlement of enormous tracts of public land, upon which tree growth never existed and cannot be promoted, tends only to retard development, create discontent, and bring reproach upon the policy of conservation.

The public land laws should be administered in a spirit of the broadest liberality toward the settler exhibiting a *bona-fide* purpose to comply therewith, to the end that the invitation of this government to the landless should be as attractive as possible, and the plain provisions of the forest reserve act permitting homestead entries to be made within the national forests should not be nullified by administrative regulations which amount to a withdrawal of great areas of the same from settlement.

Immediate action should be taken by Congress to make available the vast and valuable coal deposits of Alaska under conditions that will be a perfect guarantee against their falling into the hands of monopolizing corporations, associations or interests.

We rejoice in the inheritance of mineral resources unequalled in extent, variety, or value, and in the development of a mining industry unequalled in its magnitude and importance. We honor the men who, in their hazardous toil underground, daily risk their lives in extracting and preparing for our use the products of the mine, so essential to the industries, the commerce, and the comfort of the people of this country. And we pledge ourselves to the extension of the work of the bureau of mines in every way appropriate for national legislation with a view to safeguarding the lives of the miners, lessening the waste of essential resources, and promoting the economic development of mining, which, along with agriculture, must in the future, even more than in the past, serve as the very foundation of our national prosperity and welfare, and our international commerce.

AGRICULTURE

We believe in encouraging the development of a modern system of agriculture and a systematic effort to improve the conditions of trade in farm products so as to benefit both consumer and producer. And as an efficient means to this end we favor the enactment by Congress of legislation that will suppress the pernicious practice of gambling in agricultural products by organized exchanges or others.

MERCHANT MARINE

We believe in fostering, by constitutional regulation of commerce, the growth of a merchant marine, which shall develop and strengthen the commercial ties which bind us to our sister republics of the south, but without imposing additional burdens upon the people and without bounties or subsidies from the public treasury.

We urge upon Congress the speedy enactment of laws for the greater security of life and property at sea; and we favor the repeal of all laws, and the abrogation of so much of our treaties with other nations, as provide for the arrest and imprisonment of seamen charged with desertion, or with violation of their contract of service.

Such laws and treaties are un-American, and violate the spirit, if not the letter, of the Constitution of the United States.

We favor the exemption from tolls of American ships engaged in coastwise trade passing through the Panama canal.

We also favor legislation forbidding the use of the Panama Canal by ships owned or controlled by railroad carriers engaged in transportation competitive with the canal.

PURE FOOD AND PUBLIC HEALTH

We reaffirm our previous declarations advocating the union and strengthening of the various governmental agencies relating to pure foods, quarantine, vital statistics and human health. Thus united, and administered without partiality to or discrimination against any school of medicine or system of healing, they would constitute a single health service, not subordinated to any commercial or financial interests, but devoted exclusively to the conservation of human life and efficiency. Moreover, this health service should co-operate with the health agencies of our various States and cities, without interference with their prerogatives, or with the freedom of individuals to employ such medical or hygienic aid as they may see fit.

CIVIL SERVICE LAW

The law pertaining to the civil service should be honestly and rigidly enforced, to the end that merit and ability shall be the standard of appointment and promotion, rather than service rendered to a political party; and we favor a reorganization of the civil service, with adequate compensation commensurate with the class of work performed for all officers and employés; and also favor the extension to all classes of civil service employés of the benefits of the provisions of the employers' liability law. We also recognize the right of direct petition to Congress by employés for the redress of grievances.

LAW REFORM

We recognize the urgent need of reform in the administration of civil and criminal law in the United States, and we recommend the enactment of such legislation and the promotion of such measures as will rid the present legal system of the delays, expense, and uncertainties incident to the system as now administered.

THE PHILIPPINES

We reaffirm the position thrice announced by the Democracy in national convention assembled against a policy of imperialism and colonial exploitation in the Philippines or elsewhere. We condemn the experiment in imperialism as an inexcusable blunder, which has involved us in enormous expense, brought us weakness instead of strength, and laid our nation open to the charge of abandonment of the fundamental doctrine of self-government. We favor an immediate declaration of the nation's purpose to recognize the independence of the Philippine Islands as soon as a stable government can be established, such independence to be guaranteed by us until the neutralization of the islands can be secured by treaty with other Powers.

In recognizing the independence of the Philippines, our government should retain such land as may be necessary for coaling stations and naval bases.

ARIZONA AND NEW MEXICO

We welcome Arizona and New Mexico to the sisterhood of States, and heartily congratulate them upon their auspicious beginnings of great and glorious careers.

ALASKA

We demand for the people of Alaska the full enjoyment of the rights and privileges of a Territorial form of government, and we believe that the officials appointed to administer the government of all our Territories and the District of Columbia should be qualified by previous *bona-fide* residence.

THE RUSSIAN TREATY

We commend the patriotism of the Democratic members of the Senate and House of Representatives which compelled the termination of the Russian treaty of 1832, and we pledge ourselves anew to preserve the sacred rights of American citizenship at home and abroad. No treaty should receive the sanction of our government which does not recognize the equality of all of our citizens, irrespective of race or creed, and which does not expressly guarantee the fundamental right of expatriation.

The constitutional rights of American citizens should protect them on our borders and go with them throughout the world, and every American citizen residing or having property in any foreign country is entitled to and must be given the full protection of the United States government, both for himself and his property.

PARCELS POST AND RURAL DELIVERY

We favor the establishment of a parcels post or postal express, and also the extension of the rural delivery system as rapidly as practicable.

PANAMA CANAL EXPOSITION

We hereby express our deep interest in the great Panama Canal Exposition to be held in San Francisco in 1915, and favor such encouragement as can be properly given.

PROTECTION OF NATIONAL UNIFORM

We commend to the several States the adoption of a law making it an offence for the proprietors of places of public amusement and entertainment to discriminate against the uniform of the United States, similar to the law passed by Congress applicable to the District of Columbia and the Territories in 1911.

PENSIONS

We renew the declaration of our last platform relating to a generous pension policy.

RULE OF THE PEOPLE

We direct attention to the fact that the Democratic party's demand for a return to the rule of the people expressed in the national platform four years ago, has now become the accepted doctrine of a large majority of the electors. We again remind the country that only by a larger exercise of the reserved power of the people can they protect themselves from the misuse of delegated power and the usurpation of government instrumentalities by special interests. For this reason the National Convention insisted on the overthrow of Cannonism and the inauguration of a system by which United States Senators could be elected by direct vote. The Democratic party offers itself to the country as an agency through which the complete overthrow and extirpation of corruption, fraud, and machine rule in American politics can be effected.

CONCLUSION

Our platform is one of principles which we believe to be essential to our national welfare. Our pledges are made to be kept when in office, as well as relied upon during the campaign, and we invite the co-operation of all citizens, regardless of party, who believe in maintaining unimpaired the institutions and traditions of our country.

Progressive Platform of 1912

The conscience of the people, in a time of grave national problems, has called into being a new party, born of the nation's sense of justice. We of the Progressive party here dedicate ourselves to the fulfillment of the duty laid upon us by our fathers to maintain the government of the people, by the people and for the people whose foundations they laid.

We hold with Thomas Jefferson and Abraham Lincoln that the people are the masters of their Constitution, to fulfill its purposes and to safeguard it from those who, by perversion of its intent, would convert it into an instrument of injustice. In accordance with the needs of each generation the people must use their sovereign powers to establish and maintain equal opportunity and industrial justice, to secure which this Government was founded and without which no republic can endure.

This country belongs to the people who inhabit it. Its resources, its business, its institutions and its laws should be utilized, maintained or altered in whatever manner will best promote the general interest.

It is time to set the public welfare in the first place.

THE OLD PARTIES

Political parties exist to secure responsible government and to execute the will of the people.

From these great tasks both of the old parties have turned aside. Instead of instruments to promote the general welfare, they have become the tools of corrupt interests which use them impartially to serve their selfish purposes. Behind the ostensible government sits enthroned an invisible government owing no allegiance and acknowledging no responsibility to the people.

To destroy this invisible government, to dissolve the unholy alliance between corrupt business and corrupt politics is the first task of the statesmanship of the day.

The deliberate betrayal of its trust by the Republican party, the fatal incapacity of the Democratic party to deal with the new issues of the new time, have compelled the people to forge a new instrument of government through which to give effect to their will in laws and institutions.

Unhampered by tradition, uncorrupted by power, undismayed by the magnitude of the task, the new party offers itself as the instrument of the people to sweep away old abuses, to build a new and nobler commonwealth.

A COVENANT WITH THE PEOPLE

This declaration is our covenant with the people, and we hereby bind the party and its candidates in State and Nation to the pledges made herein.

The Rule of the People

The National Progressive party, committed to the principles of government by a self-controlled democracy expressing its will through representatives of the people, pledges itself to secure such alterations in the fundamental law of the several States and of the United States as shall insure the representative character of the government.

In particular, the party declares for direct primaries for the nomination of State and National officers, for nation-wide preferential primaries for candidates for the presidency; for the direct election of United States Senators by the people; and we urge on the States the policy of the short ballot, with responsibility to the people secured by the initiative, referendum and recall.

Amendment of Constitution

The Progressive party, believing that a free people should have the power from time to time to amend their fundamental law so as to adapt it progressively to the changing needs of the people, pledges itself to provide a more easy and expeditious method of amending the Federal Constitution.

Nation and State

Up to the limit of the Constitution, and later by amendment of the Constitution, it found necessary, we advocate bringing under effective national jurisdiction those problems which have expanded beyond reach of the individual States.

It is as grotesque as it is intolerable that the several States should by unequal laws in matter of common concern become competing commercial agencies, barter the lives of their children, the health of their women and the safety and well being of their working people for the benefit of their financial interests.

The extreme insistence on States' rights by the Democratic party in the Baltimore platform demonstrates anew its inability to understand the world into which it has survived or to administer the affairs of a union of States which have in all essential respects become one people.

Equal Suffrage

The Progressive party, believing that no people can justly claim to be a true democracy which denies political rights on account of sex, pledges itself to the task of securing equal suffrage to men and women alike.

Corrupt Practices

We pledge our party to legislation that will compel strict limitation of all campaign contributions and expenditures, and detailed publicity of both before as well as after primaries and elections.

Publicity and Public Service

We pledge our party to legislation compelling the registration of lobbyists; publicity of committee hearings except on foreign affairs, and recording of all votes in committee; and forbidding federal appointees from holding office in State or National political organizations, or taking part as officers or delegates in political conventions for the nomination of elective State or National officials.

The Courts

The Progressive party demands such restriction of the power of the courts as shall leave to the people the ultimate authority to determine fundamental questions of social welfare and public policy. To secure this end, it pledges itself to provide:

1. That when an Act, passed under the police power of the State, is held unconstitutional under the State Constitution, by the courts, the people, after an ample interval for deliberation, shall have an opportunity to vote on the question whether they desire the Act to become law, notwithstanding such decision.

2. That every decision of the highest appellate court of a State declaring an Act of the Legislature unconstitutional on the ground of its violation of the Federal Constitution shall be subject to the same review by the Supreme Court of the United States as is now accorded to decisions sustaining such legislation.

Administration of Justice

The Progressive party, in order to secure to the people a better administration of justice and by that means to bring about a more general respect for the law and the courts, pledges itself to work unceasingly for the reform of legal procedure and judicial methods.

We believe that the issuance of injunctions in cases arising out of labor disputes should be prohibited when such injunctions would not apply when no labor disputes existed.

We also believe that a person cited for contempt in labor disputes, except when such contempt was committed in the actual presence of the court or so near thereto as to interfere with the proper administration of justice, should have a right to trial by jury.

SOCIAL AND INDUSTRIAL JUSTICE

The supreme duty of the Nation is the conservation of human resources through an enlightened measure of social and industrial justice. We pledge ourselves to work unceasingly in State and Nation for:

Effective legislation looking to the prevention of industrial accidents, occupational diseases, overwork, involuntary unemployment, and other injurious effects incident to modern industry;

The fixing of minimum safety and health standards for the various occupations, and the exercise of the public authority of State and Nation, including the Federal Control over interstate commerce, and the taxing power, to maintain such standards;

The prohibition of child labor;

Minimum wage standards for working women, to provide a "living wage" in all industrial occupations;

The general prohibition of night work for women and the establishment of an eight hour day for women and young persons;

One day's rest in seven for all wage workers;

The eight hour day in continuous twenty-four-hour industries;

The abolition of the convict contract labor system; substituting a system of prison production for governmental consumption only; and the application of prisoners' earnings to the support of their dependent families;

Publicity as to wages, hours and conditions of labor; full reports upon industrial accidents and diseases, and the opening to public inspection of all tallies, weights, measures and check systems on labor products;

Standards of compensation for death by industrial accident and injury and trade disease which will transfer the burden of lost earnings from the families of working people to the industry, and thus to the community;

The protection of home life against the hazards of sickness, irregular employment and old age through the adoption of a system of social insurance adapted to American use;

The development of the creative labor power of America by lifting the last load of illiteracy from American youth and establishing continuation schools for industrial education under public control and encouraging agricultural education and demonstration in rural schools;

The establishment of industrial research laboratories to put the methods and discoveries of science at the service of American producers;

We favor the organization of the workers, men and women, as a means of protecting their interests and of promoting their progress.

DEPARTMENT OF LABOR

We pledge our party to establish a department of labor with a seat in the cabinet, and with wide jurisdiction over matters affecting the conditions of labor and living.

COUNTRY LIFE

The development and prosperity of country life are as important to the people who live in the cities as they are to the farmers. Increase of prosperity on the farm will favorably affect the cost of living, and promote the interests of all who dwell in the country, and all who depend upon its products for clothing, shelter and food.

We pledge our party to foster the development of agricultural credit and co-operation, the teaching of agriculture in schools, agricultural college extension, the use of mechanical power on the farm, and to re-establish the Country Life Commission, thus directly promoting the welfare of the farmers, and bringing the benefits of better farming, better business and better living within their reach.

HIGH COST OF LIVING

The high cost of living is due partly to worldwide and partly to local causes; partly to natural and partly to artificial causes. The measures proposed in this platform on various subjects such as the tariff, the trusts and conservation, will of themselves remove the artificial causes.

There will remain other elements such as the tendency to leave the country for the city, waste, extravagance, bad system of taxation, poor methods of raising crops and bad business methods in marketing crops.

To remedy these conditions requires the fullest information and based on this information, effective government supervision and control to remove all the artificial causes. We pledge ourselves to such full and immediate inquiry and to immediate action to deal with every need such inquiry discloses.

HEALTH

We favor the union of all the existing agencies of the Federal Government dealing with the public health into a single national health service without discrimination against or for any one set of therapeutic methods, school of medicine, or school of healing with such additional powers as may be necessary to enable it to perform efficiently such duties in the protection of the public from preventable diseases as may be properly undertaken by the Federal authorities, including the executing of existing laws regarding pure food, quarantine and cognate subjects, the promotion of vital statistics and the extension of the registration area of such statistics, and co-operation with the health activities of the various States and cities of the Nation.

BUSINESS

We believe that true popular government, justice and prosperity go hand in hand, and, so believing, it is our purpose to secure that large measure of general prosperity which is the fruit of legitimate and honest business, fostered by equal justice and by sound progressive laws.

We demand that the test of true prosperity shall be the benefits conferred thereby on all the citizens, not confined to individuals or classes, and that the test of corporate efficiency shall be the ability better to serve the public; that those who profit by control of business affairs shall justify that profit and that control by sharing with the public the fruits thereof.

We therefore demand a strong National regulation of inter-State corporations. The corporation is an essential part of modern business. The concentration of modern business, in some degree, is both inevitable and necessary for national and international business efficiency. But the existing concentration of vast wealth under a corporate system, unguarded and uncontrolled by the Nation, has placed in the hands of a few men enor-

mous, secret, irresponsible power over the daily life of the citizen—a power insufferable in a free Government and certain of abuse.

This power has been abused, in monopoly of National resources, in stock watering, in unfair competition and unfair privileges, and finally in sinister influences on the public agencies of State and Nation. We do not fear commercial power, but we insist that it shall be exercised openly, under publicity, supervision and regulation of the most efficient sort, which will preserve its good while eradicating and preventing its ill.

To that end we urge the establishment of a strong Federal administrative commission of high standing, which shall maintain permanent active supervision over industrial corporations engaged in inter-State commerce, or such of them as are of public importance, doing for them what the Government now does for the National banks, and what is now done for the railroads by the Inter-State Commerce Commission.

Such a commission must enforce the complete publicity of those corporation transactions which are of public interest; must attack unfair competition, false capitalization and special privilege, and by continuous trained watchfulness guard and keep open equally all the highways of American commerce.

Thus the business man will have certain knowledge of the law, and will be able to conduct his business easily in conformity therewith; the investor will find security for his capital; dividends will be rendered more certain, and the savings of the people will be drawn naturally and safely into the channels of trade.

Under such a system of constructive regulation, legitimate business, freed from confusion, uncertainty and fruitless litigation, will develop normally in response to the energy and enterprise of the American business man.

We favor strengthening the Sherman Law by prohibiting agreement to divide territory or limit output; refusing to sell to customers who buy from business rivals; to sell below cost in certain areas while maintaining higher prices in other places; using the power of transportation to aid or injure special business concerns; and other unfair trade practices.

PATENTS

We pledge ourselves to the enactment of a patent law which will make it impossible for patents to be suppressed or used against the public welfare in the interests of injurious monopolies.

INTER-STATE COMMERCE COMMISSION

We pledge our party to secure to the Inter-State Commerce Commission the power to value the physical property of railroads. In order that the power of the commission to protect the people may not be impaired or destroyed, we demand the abolition of the Commerce Court.

CURRENCY

We believe there exists imperative need for prompt legislation for the improvement of our National currency system. We believe the present method of issuing notes through private agencies is harmful and unscientific.

The issue of currency is fundamentally a Government function and the system should have as basic principles soundness and elasticity. The control should be lodged with the Government and should be protected from domination or manipulation by Wall Street or any special interests.

We are opposed to the so-called Aldrich currency bill, because its provisions would place our currency and credit system in private hands, not subject to effective public control.

COMMERCIAL DEVELOPMENT

The time has come when the Federal Government should co-operate with manufacturers and producers in extending our foreign commerce. To this end we demand adequate appropriations by Congress, and the appointment of diplomatic and consular officers solely with a view to their special fitness and worth, and not in consideration of political expediency.

It is imperative to the welfare of our people that we enlarge and extend our foreign commerce.

In every way possible our Federal Government should co-operate in this important matter. Germany's policy of co-operation between government and business has, in comparatively few years, made that nation a leading competitor for the commerce of the world.

CONSERVATION

The natural resources of the Nation must be promptly developed and generously used to supply the people's needs, but we cannot safely allow them to be wasted, exploited, monopolized or controlled against the general good. We heartily favor the policy of conservation, and we pledge our party to protect the National forests without hindering their legitimate use for the benefit of all the people.

Agricultural lands in the National forests are, and should remain, open to the genuine settler. Conservation will not retard legitimate development. The honest settler must receive his patent promptly, without hindrance, rules or delays.

We believe that the remaining forests, coal and oil lands, water powers and other natural resources still in State or National control (except agricultural lands) are more likely to be wisely conserved and utilized for the general welfare if held in the public hands.

In order that consumers and producers, managers and workmen, now and hereafter, need not pay toll to private monopolies of power and raw material, we demand that such resources shall be retained by the State or Nation, and opened to immediate use under laws which will encourage development and make to the people a moderate return for benefits conferred.

In particular we pledge our party to require reasonable compensation to the public for water power rights hereafter granted by the public.

We pledge legislation to lease the public grazing lands under equitable provisions now pending which will increase the production of food for the people and thoroughly safeguard the rights of the actual homemaker. Natural resources, whose conservation is necessary for the National welfare, should be owned or controlled by the Nation.

GOOD ROADS

We recognize the vital importance of good roads and we pledge our party to foster their extension in every proper way, and we favor the early construction of National highways. We also favor the extension of the rural free delivery service.

ALASKA

The coal and other natural resources of Alaska should be opened to development at once. They are owned by the people of the United States, and are safe from monopoly, waste or destruction only while so owned.

We demand that they shall neither be sold nor

given away, except under the Homestead Law, but while held in Government ownership shall be opened to use promptly upon liberal terms requiring immediate development.

Thus the benefit of cheap fuel will accrue to the Government of the United States and to the people of Alaska and the Pacific Coast; the settlement of extensive agricultural lands will be hastened; the extermination of the salmon will be prevented and the just and wise development of Alaskan resources will take the place of private extortion or monopoly.

We demand also that extortion or monopoly in transportation shall be prevented by the prompt acquisition, construction or improvement by the Government of such railroads, harbor and other facilities for transportation as the welfare of the people may demand.

We promise the people of the Territory of Alaska the same measure of legal self-government that was given to other American territories, and that Federal officials appointed there shall be qualified by previous *bona-fide* residence in the Territory.

WATERWAYS

The rivers of the United States are the natural arteries of this continent. We demand that they shall be opened to traffic as indispensable parts of a great Nation-wide system of transportation, in which the Panama Canal will be the central link, thus enabling the whole interior of the United States to share with the Atlantic and Pacific seaboards in the benefit derived from the canal.

It is a National obligation to develop our rivers, and especially the Mississippi and its tributaries, without delay, under a comprehensive general plan covering each river system from its source to its mouth, designed to secure its highest usefulness for navigation, irrigation, domestic supply, water power and the prevention of floods.

We pledge our party to the immediate preparation of such a plan, which should be made and carried out in close and friendly co-operation between the Nation, the States and the cities affected.

Under such a plan, the destructive floods of the Mississippi and other streams, which represent a vast and needless loss to the Nation, would be controlled by forest conservation and water stor-

age at the headwaters, and by levees below; land sufficient to support millions of people would be reclaimed from the deserts and the swamps, water power enough to transform the industrial standings of whole States would be developed, adequate water terminals would be provided, transportation by river would revive, and the railroads would be compelled to co-operate as freely with the boat lines as with each other.

The equipment, organization and experience acquired in constructing the Panama Canal soon will be available for the Lakes-to-the-Gulf deep waterway and other portions of this great work, and should be utilized by the Nation in co-operation with the various States, at the lowest net cost to the people.

PANAMA CANAL

The Panama Canal, built and paid for by the American people, must be used primarily for their benefit.

We demand that the canal shall be so operated as to break the transportation monopoly now held and misused by the transcontinental railroads by maintaining sea competition with them; that ships directly or indirectly owned or controlled by American railroad corporations shall not be permitted to use the canal, and that American ships engaged in coastwise trade shall pay no tolls.

The Progressive party will favor legislation having for its aim the development of friendship and commerce between the United States and Latin-American nations.

TARIFF

We believe in a protective tariff which shall equalize conditions of competition between the United States and foreign countries, both for the farmer and the manufacturer, and which shall maintain for labor an adequate standard of living.

Primarily the benefit of any tariff should be disclosed in the pay envelope of the laborer. We declare that no industry deserves protection which is unfair to labor or which is operating in violation of Federal law. We believe that the presumption is always in favor of the consuming public.

We demand tariff revision because the present tariff is unjust to the people of the United States. Fair dealing toward the people requires an immediate downward revision of those schedules wherein duties are shown to be unjust or excessive.

We pledge ourselves to the establishment of a non-partisan scientific tariff commission, reporting both to the President and to either branch of Congress, which shall report, first, as to the costs of production, efficiency of labor, capitalization, industrial organization and efficiency and the general competitive position in this country and abroad of industries seeking protection from Congress; second, as to the revenue producing power of the tariff and its relation to the resources of Government; and, third, as to the effect of the tariff on prices, operations of middlemen, and on the purchasing power of the consumer.

We believe that this commission should have plenary power to elicit information, and for this purpose to prescribe a uniform system of accounting for the great protected industries. The work of the commission should not prevent the immediate adoption of acts reducing these schedules generally recognized as excessive.

We condemn the Payne-Aldrich bill as unjust to the people. The Republican organization is in the hands of those who have broken, and cannot again be trusted to keep, the promise of necessary downward revision.

The Democratic party is committed to the destruction of the protective system through a tariff for revenue only—a policy which would inevitably produce widespread industrial and commercial disaster.

We demand the immediate repeal of the Canadian Reciprocity Act.

Inheritance and Income Tax

We believe in a graduated inheritance tax as a National means of equalizing the obligations of holders of property to Government, and we hereby pledge our party to enact such a Federal law as will tax large inheritances, returning to the States an equitable percentage of all amounts collected.

We favor the ratification of the pending amendment to the Constitution giving the Government power to levy an income tax.

Peace and National Defense

The Progressive party deplores the survival in our civilization of the barbaric system of warfare among nations with its enormous waste of resources even in time of peace, and the consequent impoverishment of the life of the toiling masses. We pledge the party to use its best endeavors to substitute judicial and other peaceful means of settling international differences.

We favor an international agreement for the limitation of naval forces. Pending such an agreement, and as the best means of preserving peace, we pledge ourselves to maintain for the present the policy of building two battleships a year.

Treaty Rights

We pledge our party to protect the rights of American citizenship at home and abroad. No treaty should receive the sanction of our Government which discriminates between American citizens because of birthplace, race, or religion, or that does not recognize the absolute right of expatriation.

The Immigrant

Through the establishment of industrial standards we propose to secure to the able-bodied immigrant and to his native fellow workers a larger share of American opportunity.

We denounce the fatal policy of indifference and neglect which has left our enormous immigrant population to become the prey of chance and cupidity.

We favor Governmental action to encourage the distribution of immigrants away from the congested cities, to rigidly supervise all private agencies dealing with them and to promote their assimilation, education and advancement.

Pensions

We pledge ourselves to a wise and just policy of pensioning American soldiers and sailors and their widows and children by the Federal Government. And we approve the policy of the southern States in granting pensions to the ex-Confederate soldiers and sailors and their widows and children.

Parcel Post

We pledge our party to the immediate creation of a parcel post, with rates proportionate to distance and service.

Civil Service

We condemn the violations of the Civil Service Law under the present administration, including the coercion and assessment of subordinate employés, and the President's refusal to punish such violation after a finding of guilty by his own commission; his distribution of patronage among subservient congressmen, while withholding it from those who refuse support of administration measures; his withdrawal of nominations from the Senate until political support for himself was secured, and his open use of the offices to reward those who voted for his renomination.

To eradicate these abuses, we demand not only the enforcement of the civil service act in letter and spirit, but also legislation which will bring under the competitive system postmasters, collectors, marshals, and all other non-political officers, as well as the enactment of an equitable retirement law, and we also insist upon continuous service during good behavior and efficiency.

GOVERNMENT BUSINESS ORGANIZATION

We pledge our party to readjustment of the business methods of the National Government and a proper co-ordination of the Federal bureaus, which will increase the economy and efficiency of the Government service, prevent duplications, and secure better results to the taxpayers for every dollar expended.

GOVERNMENT SUPERVISION OVER INVESTMENTS

The people of the United States are swindled out of many millions of dollars every year, through worthless investments. The plain people, the wage earner and the men and women with small savings, have no way of knowing the merit of concerns sending out highly colored prospectuses offering stock for sale, prospectuses that make big returns seem certain and fortunes easily within grasp.

We hold it to be the duty of the Government to protect its people from this kind of piracy. We, therefore, demand wise, carefully thought out legislation that will give us such Governmental supervision over this matter as will furnish to the people of the United States this much-needed protection, and we pledge ourselves thereto.

CONCLUSION

On these principles and on the recognized desirability of uniting the Progressive forces of the Nation into an organization which shall unequivocally represent the Progressive spirit and policy we appeal for the support of all American citizens, without regard to previous political affiliations.

Prohibition Platform of 1912

The Prohibition Party in National Convention at Atlantic City, N. J., July 10, 1912, recognizing God as the source of all governmental authority, makes the following declarations of principles and policies:

1. The alcoholic drink traffic is wrong; is the most serious drain on the wealth and resources of the nation; is detrimental to the general welfare and destructive of the inalienable rights of life, liberty and the pursuit of happiness. All laws taxing or licensing a traffic which produces crime, poverty and political corruption, and spreads disease and death should be repealed. To destroy such a traffic there must be elected to power a political party which will administer the government from the standpoint that the alcoholic drink traffic is a crime and not a business, and we pledge that the manufacture, importation, exportation, transportation and sale of alcoholic beverages shall be prohibited.

We favor:

2. Suffrage for women on the same terms as for men.

3. A uniform marriage and divorce law. The extermination of polygamy. And the complete suppression of the traffic in girls.

4. Absolute protection of the rights of labor, without impairment of the rights of capital.

5. The settlement of all international disputes by arbitration.

6. The abolition of child labor in mines, workshops and factories, with the rigid enforcement of the laws now flagrantly violated.

7. The election of United States Senators by direct vote of the people.

8. A Presidential term of six years, and one term only.

9. Court review of Post Office and other departmental decisions and orders; the extension of the Postal Savings Bank system, and of Rural Delivery, and the establishment of an efficient parcels post.

10. The initiative, referendum and recall.

11. As the tariff is a commercial question it should be fixed on the scientific basis of accurate knowledge, secured by means of a permanent, omni-partisan tariff commission, with ample powers.

12. Equitable graduated income and inheritance taxes.

13. Conservation of our forest and mineral reserves, and the reclamation of waste lands. All mineral and timber lands, and water powers, now owned by the government, should be held perpetually, and leased for revenue purposes.

14. Clearly defined laws for the regulation and control of corporations transacting an inter-State business.

15. Efficiency and economy in governmental administration.

16. The protection of one day in seven as a day of rest.

To these fundamental principles, the National Prohibition Party renews its long allegiance, and on these issues invites the co-operation of all good citizens, to the end that the true object of government may be attained, namely, equal and exact justice for all.

Republican Platform of 1912

The Republican party, assembled by its representatives in National Convention, declares its unchanging faith in government of the people, by the people, for the people. We renew our allegiance to the principles of the Republican party and our devotion to the cause of Republican institutions established by the fathers.

It is appropriate that we should now recall with a sense of veneration and gratitude the name of our first great leader, who was nominated in this city, and whose lofty principles and superb devotion to his country are an inspiration to the party he honored—Abraham Lincoln.

In the present state of public affairs we should be inspired by his broad statesmanship and by his tolerant spirit toward men.

The Republican party looks back upon its record with pride and satisfaction, and forward to its new responsibilities with hope and confidence. Its achievements in government constitute the most luminous pages in our history. Our greatest national advance has been made during the years of its ascendancy in public affairs. It has been genuinely and always a party of progress; it has never been either stationary or reactionary. It has gone from the fulfilment of one great pledge to the fulfilment of another in response to the public need and to the popular will.

We believe in our self-controlled representative democracy which is a government of laws, not of men, and in which order is the prerequisite of progress.

The principles of constitutional government, which make provisions for orderly and effective expression of the popular will, for the protection of civil liberty and the rights of man, and for the interpretation of the law by an untrammelled and independent judiciary, have proved themselves capable of sustaining the structure of a government which, after more than a century of development, embraces one hundred millions of people, scattered over a wide and diverse territory, but bound by common purpose, common ideals and common affection to the Constitution of the United States. Under the Constitution and the principles asserted and vitalized by it, the United States has grown to be one of the great civilized and civilizing powers of the earth. It offers a home and an opportunity to the ambitious and the industrious from other lands. Resting upon the broad basis of a people's confidence and a people's support, and managed by the people themselves, the government of the United States will meet the problems of the future as satisfactorily as it has solved those of the past.

The Republican party is now, as always, a party of advanced and constructive statemanship. It is prepared to go forward with the solution of those new questions, which social, economic and political development have brought into the forefront of the nation's interest. It will strive, not only in the nation but in the several States, to enact the necessary legislation to safeguard the public health; to limit effectively the labor of women and children, and to protect wage earners engaged in dangerous occupations; to enact comprehensive and generous workman's compensation laws in place of the present wasteful and unjust system of employers' liability; and in all possible ways to satisfy the just demand of the people for the study and solution of the complex and constantly changing problems of social welfare.

In dealing with these questions, it is important that the rights of every individual to the freest possible development of his own powers and resources and to the control of his own justly acquired property, so far as those are compatible with the rights of others, shall not be interfered with or destroyed. The social and political structure of the United States rests upon the civil liberty of the individual; and for the protection of that liberty the people have wisely, in the National and State Constitutions, put definite limitations upon themselves and upon their governmental officers and agencies. To enforce these limitations, to secure the orderly and coherent exercise of governmental powers, and to protect the rights of even the humblest and least favored individual are the function of independent Courts of Justice.

The Republican party reaffirms its intention to uphold at all times the authority and integrity of the Courts, both State and Federal, and it will ever insist that their powers to enforce their process and to protect life, liberty and property shall be preserved inviolate. An orderly method is provided under our system of government by which the people may, when they choose, alter or amend the constitutional provisions which underlie that government. Until these constitutional provisions are so altered or amended, in orderly fashion, it is the duty of the courts to see to it that when challenged they are enforced.

That the Courts, both Federal and State, may bear the heavy burden laid upon them to the complete satisfaction of public opinion, we favor legislation to prevent long delays and the tedious and costly appeals which have so often amounted to a denial of justice in civil cases and to a failure to protect the public at large in criminal cases.

Since the responsibility of the Judiciary is so great, the standards of judicial action must be always and everywhere above suspicion and reproach. While we regard the recall of judges as unnecessary and unwise, we favor such action as may be necessary to simplify the process by which any judge who is found to be derelict in his duty may be removed from office.

Together with peaceful and orderly development at home, the Republican party earnestly favors all measures for the establishment and protection of the peace of the world and for the development of closer relations between the various nations of the earth. It believes most earnestly in the peaceful settlement of international disputes and in the reference of all justiciable controversies between nations to an International Court of Justice.

Monopoly and Privilege

The Republican party is opposed to special privilege and to monopoly. It placed upon the statute-book the interstate commerce act of 1887, and the important amendments thereto, and the anti-trust act of 1890, and it has consistently and successfully enforced the provisions of these laws. It will take no backward step to permit the reestablishment in any degree of conditions which were intolerable.

Experience makes it plain that the business of the country may be carried on without fear or without disturbance and at the same time without resort to practices which are abhorrent to the common sense of justice. The Republican party favors the enactment of legislation supplementary to the existing anti-trust act which will define as criminal offences those specific acts that uniformly mark attempts to restrain and to monopolize trade, to the end that those who honestly intend to obey the law may have a guide for their action and those who aim to violate the law may the more surely be punished. The same certainty should be given to the law prohibiting combinations and monopolies that characterize other provisions of commercial law; in order that no part of the field of business opportunity may be restricted by monopoly or combination, that business success honorably achieved may not be converted into crime, and that the right of every man to acquire commodities, and particularly the necessaries of life, in an open market uninfluenced by the manipulation of trust or combination, may be preserved.

Federal Trade Commission

In the enforcement and admistration of Federal Laws governing interstate commerce and enterprises impressed with a public use engaged therein, there is much that may be committed to a Federal trade commission, thus placing in the hands of an administrative board many of the functions now necessarily exercised by the courts. This will promote promptness in the administration of the law and avoid delays and technicalities incident to court procedure.

The Tariff

We reaffirm our belief in a protective tariff. The Republican tariff policy has been of the greatest benefit to the country, developing our resources, diversifying our industries, and protecting our workmen against competition with cheaper labor abroad, thus establishing for our wage-earners the American standard of living. The protective tariff is so woven into the fabric of our industrial and agricultural life that to substitute for it a tariff for revenue only would destroy many industries and throw millions of our people out of employment. The products of the farm and of the mine should receive the same measure of protection as other products of American labor.

We hold that the import duties should be high enough, while yielding a sufficient revenue, to protect adequately American industries and wages. Some of the existing import duties are too high, and should be reduced. Readjustment should be made from time to time to conform to changing conditions and to reduce excessive rates, but without injury to any American industry. To accomplish this correct information is indispensable. This information can best be obtained by an expert commission, as the large volume of useful facts contained in the recent reports of the Tariff Board has demonstrated.

The pronounced feature of modern industrial life is its enormous diversification. To apply tariff rates justly to these changing conditions requires closer study and more scientific methods than ever before. The Republican party has shown by its creation of a Tariff Board its recognition of this situation, and its determination to be equal to it. We condemn the Democratic party for its failure either to provide funds for the continuance of this board or to make some other provision for securing the information requisite for intelligent tariff legislation. We protest against the Democratic method of legislating on these vitally important subjects without careful investigation.

We condemn the Democratic tariff bills passed by the House of Representatives of the Sixty-second Congress as sectional, as injurious to the public credit, and as destructive to business enterprise.

Cost of Living

The steadily increasing cost of living has become a matter not only of national but of world-wide concern. The fact that it is not due to the protective tariff system is evidenced by the existence of similar conditions in countries which have a tariff policy different from our own, as well as by the fact that the cost of living has increased while rates of duty have remained stationary or been reduced.

The Republican party will support a prompt scientific inquiry into the causes which are operative, both in the United States and elsewhere, to increase the cost of living. When the exact facts are known, it will take the necessary steps to remove any abuses that may be found to exist, in order that the cost of the food, clothing and shelter of the people may in no way be unduly or artificially increased.

Banking and Currency

The Republican party has always stood for a sound currency and for safe banking methods. It is responsible for the resumption of specie payments and for the establishment of the gold standard. It is committed to the progressive development of our banking and currency systems. Our banking arrangements to-day need further revision to meet the requirements of current conditions. We need measures which will prevent the recurrence of money panics and financial disturbances and which will promote the prosperity of business and the welfare of labor by producing constant employment. We need better currency facilities for the movement of crops in the West and South. We need banking arrangements under American auspices for the encouragement and better conduct of our foreign trade. In attaining these ends, the independence of individual banks, whether organized under national or State charters, must be carefully protected, and our banking and currency system must be safeguarded from any possibility of domination by sectional, financial, or political interests.

It is of great importance to the social and economic welfare of this country that its farmers have facilities for borrowing easily and cheaply the money they need to increase the productivity of their land. It is as important that financial machinery be provided to supply the demand of farmers for credit as it is that the banking and currency systems be reformed in the interest of general business. Therefore, we recommend and urge an authoritative investigation of agricultural credit societies and corporations in other countries and the passage of State and Federal laws for the establishment and capable supervision of organizations having for their purpose the loaning of funds to farmers.

The Civil Service

We reaffirm our adherence to the principle of appointment to public office based on proved fitness, and tenure during good behavior and efficiency. The Republican party stands committed to the maintenance, extension and enforcement of the Civil Service Law, and it favors the passage of legislation empowering the President to extend the competitive service as far as practicable. We favor legislation to make possible the equitable retirement of disabled and superannuated members of the Civil Service in order that a higher standard of efficiency may be maintained.

We favor the amendment of the Federal Employers' Liability Law so as to extend its provisions to all government employés, as well as to provide a more liberal scale of compensation for injury and death.

CAMPAIGN CONTRIBUTIONS

We favor such additional legislation as may be necessary more effectually to prohibit corporations from contributing funds, directly or indirectly, to campaigns for the nomination or election of the President, the Vice-President, Senators, and Representatives in Congress.

We heartily approve the recent Act of Congress requiring the fullest publicity in regard to all campaign contributions, whether made in connection with primaries, conventions, or elections.

CONSERVATION POLICY

We rejoice in the success of the distinctive Republican policy of the conservation of our National resources, for their use by the people without waste and without monopoly. We pledge ourselves to a continuance of such a policy.

We favor such fair and reasonable rules and regulations as will not discourage or interfere with actual *bona-fide* homeseekers, prospectors and miners in the acquisition of public lands under existing laws.

PARCELS POST

In the interest of the general public, and particularly of the agricultural or rural communities, we favor legislation looking to the establishment, under proper regulations, of a parcels post, the postal rates to be graduated under a zone system in proportion to the length of carriage.

PROTECTION OF AMERICAN CITIZENSHIP

We approve the action taken by the President and the Congress to secure with Russia as with other countries, a treaty that will recognize the absolute right of expatriation and that will prevent all discrimination of whatever kind between American citizens, whether native-born or aliens, and regardless of race, religion or previous political allegiance. The right of asylum is a precious possession of the people of the United States, and it is to be neither surrendered nor restricted.

THE NAVY

We believe in the maintenance of an adequate navy for the National defence, and we condemn the action of the Democratic House of Representatives in refusing to authorize the construction of additional ships.

MERCHANT MARINE

We believe that one of the country's most urgent needs is a revived merchant marine. There should be American ships, and plenty of them, to make use of the great American Inter-Oceanic canal now nearing completion.

FLOOD PREVENTION IN THE MISSISSIPPI VALLEY

The Mississippi River is the nation's drainage ditch. Its flood waters, gathered from thirty-one States and the Dominion of Canada, constitute an overpowering force which breaks the levees and pours its torrents over many millions of acres of the richest land in the Union, stopping mails, impeding commerce, and causing great loss of life and property. These floods are national in scope, and the disasters they produce seriously affect the general welfare. The States unaided cannot cope with this giant problem; hence, we believe the Federal Government should assume a fair proportion of the burden of its control, so as to prevent the disasters from recurring floods.

RECLAMATION

We favor the continuance of the policy of the government with regard to the reclamation of arid lands; and for the encouragement of the speedy settlement and improvement of such lands we favor an amendment to the law that will reasonably extend the time within which the cost of any reclamation project may be repaid by the landowners under it.

RIVERS AND HARBORS

We favor a liberal and systematic policy for the improvement of our rivers and harbors. Such improvements should be made upon expert information and after a careful comparison of cost and prospective benefits.

ALASKA

We favor a liberal policy toward Alaska to promote the development of the great resources of that district, with such safeguards as will prevent waste and monopoly.

We favor the opening of the coal lands to development through a law leasing the lands on such terms as will invite development and provide fuel for the navy and the commerce of the Pacific Ocean, while retaining title in the United States to prevent monopoly.

PHILIPPINE POLICY

The Philippine policy of the Republican party has been and is inspired by the belief that our duty toward the Filipino people is a national obligation which should remain entirely free from partisan politics.

IMMIGRATION

We pledge the Republican party to the enactment of appropriate laws to give relief from the constantly growing evil of induced or undesirable immigration, which is inimical to the progress and welfare of the people of the United States.

SAFETY AT SEA

We favor the speedy enactment of laws to provide that seamen shall not be compelled to endure involuntary servitude, and that life and property at sea shall be safeguarded by the ample equipment of vessels with lifesaving appliances and with full complements of skilled, able-bodied seamen to operate them.

REPUBLICAN ACCOMPLISHMENT

The approaching completion of the Panama Canal, the establishment of a Bureau of Mines, the institution of postal savings banks, the increased provision made in 1912 for the aged and infirm soldiers and sailors of the Republic and for their widows, and the vigorous administration of laws relating to Pure Foods and Drugs, all mark the successful progress of Republican administration, and are additional evidences of its effectiveness.

ECONOMY AND EFFICIENCY IN GOVERNMENT

We commend the earnest effort of the Republican administration to secure greater economy and increased efficiency in the conduct of government business; extravagant appropriations and the creation of unnecessary offices are an injustice to the taxpayer and a bad example to the citizen.

CIVIC DUTY

We call upon the people to quicken their interest in public affairs, to condemn and punish lynchings and other forms of lawlessness, and to strengthen in all possible ways a respect for law and the observance of it. Indifferent citizenship is an evil against which the law affords no adequate protection and for which legislation can provide no remedy.

ARIZONA AND NEW MEXICO

We congratulate the people of Arizona and New Mexico upon the admission of those States, thus merging in the Union in final and enduring form the last remaining portion of our continental territory.

We retify [ratify] in all its parts the platform of 1908 respecting citizenship for the people of Porto Rico.

REPUBLICAN ADMINISTRATION

We challenge successful criticism of the sixteen years of Republican administration under Presidents McKinley, Roosevelt, and Taft. We heartily reaffirm the indorsement of President McKinley contained in the platforms of 1900 and of 1904, and that of President Roosevelt contained in the Platforms of 1904 and 1908.

We invite the intelligent judgment of the American people upon the administration of William H. Taft. The country has prospered and been at peace under his Presidency. During the years in which he had the co-operation of a Republican Congress an unexampled amount of constructive legislation was framed and passed in the interest of the people and in obedience to their wish. That legislation is a record on which any administration might appeal with confidence to the favorable judgment of history.

We appeal to the American Electorate upon the record of the Republican party, and upon this declaration of its principles and purposes. We are confident that under the leadership of the candidates here to be nominated our appeal will not be in vain; that the Republican party will meet every just expectation of the people whose servant it is; that under its administration and its laws our nation will continue to advance; that peace and prosperity will abide with the people;

and that new glory will be added to the great Republic.

Socialist Platform of 1912

The Socialist party declares that the capitalist system has outgrown its historical function, and has become utterly incapable of meeting the problems now confronting society. We denounce this outgrown system as incompetent and corrupt and the source of unspeakable misery and suffering to the whole working class.

Under this system the industrial equipment of the nation has passed into the absolute control of a plutocracy which exacts an annual tribute of hundreds of millions of dollars from the producers. Unafraid of any organized resistance, it stretches out its greedy hands over the still undeveloped resources of the nation—the land, the mines, the forests and the water-powers of every State in the Union.

In spite of the multiplication of labor-saving machines and improved methods in industry which cheapen the cost of production, the share of the producers grows ever less, and the prices of all the necessities of life steadily increase. The boasted prosperity of this nation is for the owning class alone. To the rest it means only greater hardship and misery. The high cost of living is felt in every home. Millions of wage-workers have seen the purchasing power of their wages decrease until life has become a desperate battle for mere existence.

Multitudes of unemployed walk the streets of our cities or trudge from State to State awaiting the will of the masters to move the wheels of industry.

The farmers in every state are plundered by the increasing prices exacted for tools and machinery and by extortionate rents, freight rates and storage charges.

Capitalist concentration is mercilessly crushing the class of small business men and driving its members into the ranks of propertyless wage-workers. The overwhelming majority of the people of America are being forced under a yoke of bondage by this soulless industrial despotism.

It is this capitalist system that is responsible for the increasing burden of armaments, the poverty, slums, child labor, most of the insanity, crime and prostitution, and much of the disease that afflicts mankind.

Under this system the working class is exposed to poisonous conditions, to frightful and needless perils to life and limb, is walled around with court decisions, injunctions and unjust laws, and is preyed upon incessantly for the benefit of the controlling oligarchy of wealth. Under it also, the children of the working class are doomed to ignorance, drudging toil and darkened lives.

In the face of these evils, so manifest that all thoughtful observers are appalled at them, the legislative representatives of the Republican and Democratic parties remain the faithful servants of the oppressors. Measures designed to secure to the wage-earners of this Nation as humane and just treatment as is already enjoyed by the wage-earners of all other civilized nations have been smothered in committee without debate, and laws ostensibly designed to bring relief to the farmers and general consumers are juggled and transformed into instruments for the exaction of further tribute. The growing unrest under oppression has driven these two old parties to the enactment of a variety of regulative measures, none of which has limited in any appreciable degree the power of the plutocracy, and some of which have been perverted into means for increasing that power. Anti-trust laws, railroad restrictions and regulations, with the prosecutions, indictments and investigations based upon such legislation, have proved to be utterly futile and ridiculous.

Nor has this plutocracy been seriously restrained or even threatened by any Republican or Democratic executive. It has continued to grow in power and insolence alike under the administration of Cleveland, McKinley, Roosevelt and Taft.

In addition to this legislative juggling and this executive connivance, the courts of America have sanctioned and strengthened the hold of this plutocracy as the Dred Scott and other decisions strengthened the slave-power before the civil war. They have been used as instruments for the oppression of the working class and for the suppression of free speech and free assembly.

We declare, therefore, that the longer sufferance of these conditions is impossible, and we purpose to end them all. We declare them to be the product of the present system in which industry is carried on for private greed, instead of for the welfare of society. We declare, furthermore, that for these evils there will be and can be no remedy and no substantial relief except through Socialism under which industry will be carried on for the common good and every worker receive the full social value of the wealth he creates.

Society is divided into warring groups and classes, based upon material interests. Fundamentally, this struggle is a conflict between the two main classes, one of which, the capitalist class, owns the means of production, and the other, the working class, must use these means of production on terms dictated by the owners.

The capitalist class, though few in numbers, absolutely controls the government—legislative, executive and judicial. This class owns the machinery of gathering and disseminating news through its organized press. It subsidizes seats of learning—the colleges and schools—and even religious and moral agencies. It has also the added prestige which established customs give to any order of society, right or wrong.

The working class, which includes all those who are forced to work for a living, whether by hand or brain, in shop, mine or on the soil, vastly outnumbers the capitalist class. Lacking effective organization and class solidarity, this class is unable to enforce its will. Given such a class solidarity and effective organization, the workers will have the power to make all laws and control all industry in their own interest.

All political parties are the expression of economic class interests. All other parties than the Socialist party represent one or another group of the ruling capitalist class. Their political conflicts reflect merely superficial rivalries between competing capitalist groups. However they result, these conflicts have no issue of real value to the workers. Whether the Democrats or Republicans win politically, it is the capitalist class that is victorious economically.

The Socialist party is the political expression of the economic interests of the workers. Its defeats have been their defeats and its victories their victories. It is a party founded on the science and laws of social development. It proposes that, since all social necessities to-day are socially produced, the means of their production and distribution shall be socially owned and democratically controlled.

In the face of the economic and political aggressions of the capitalist class the only reliance left the workers is that of their economic organizations and their political power. By the intelligent and class-conscious use of these, they may resist successfully the capitalist class, break the fetters of wage-slavery, and fit themselves for the future society, which is to displace the capitalist system. The Socialist party appreciates the full significance of class organization and urges the wage-earners, the working farmers and all other useful workers to organize for economic and political action, and we pledge ourselves to support the toilers of the fields as well as those in the shops, factories and mines of the nation in their struggles for economic justice.

In the defeat or victory of the working class party in this new struggle for freedom lies the defeat or triumph of the common people of all economic groups, as well as the failure or triumph of popular government. Thus the Socialist party is the party of the present-day revolution which marks the transition from economic individualism to socialism, from wage slavery to free co-operation, from capitalist oligarchy to industrial democracy.

Working Program

As measures calculated to strengthen the working class in its fight for the realization of its ultimate aim, the co-operative commonwealth, and to increase its power of resistance against capitalist oppression, we advocate and pledge ourselves and our elected officers to the following programme:

Collective Ownership

1. The collective ownership and democratic management of railroads, wire and wireless telegraphs and telephones, express service, steamboat lines, and all other social means of transportation and communication and of all large-scale industries.

2. The immediate acquirement by the municipalities, the states or the federal government of all grain elevators, stock yards, storage warehouses, and other distributing agencies, in order to reduce the present extortionate cost of living.

3. The extension of the public domain to include mines, quarries, oil wells, forests and water power.

4. The further conservation and development

of natural resources for the use and benefit of all the people:

(a) By scientific forestation and timber protection.

(b) By the reclamation of arid and swamp tracts.

(c) By the storage of flood waters and the utilization of water power.

(d) By the stoppage of the present extravagant waste of the soil and of the products of mines and oil wells.

(e) By the development of highway and waterway systems.

5. The collective ownership of land wherever practicable, and in cases where such ownership is impracticable, the appropriation by taxation of the annual rental value of all land held for speculation or exploitation.

6. The collective ownership and democratic management of the banking and currency system.

Unemployment

The immediate government relief of the unemployed by the extension of all useful public works. All persons employed on such works to be engaged directly by the government under a work day of not more than eight hours and at not less than the prevailing union wages. The government also to establish employment bureaus; to lend money to states and municipalities without interest for the purpose of carrying on public works, and to take such other measures within its power as will lessen the widespread misery of the workers caused by the misrule of the capitalist class.

Industrial Demands

The conservation of human resources, particularly of the lives and well-being of the workers and their families:

1. By shortening the work day in keeping with the increased productiveness of machinery.

2. By securing to every worker a rest period of not less than a day and a half in each week.

3. By securing a more effective inspection of workshops, factories and mines.

4. By forbidding the employment of children under sixteen years of age.

5. By the co-operative organization of the industries in the federal penitentiaries for the benefit of the convicts and their dependents.

6. By forbidding the interstate transportation of the products of child labor, of convict labor and of all uninspected factories and mines.

7. By abolishing the profit system in government work and substituting either the direct hire of labor or the awarding of contracts to co-operative groups of workers.

8. By establishing minimum wage scales.

9. By abolishing official charity and substituting a non-contributory system of old age pensions, a general system of insurance by the State of all its members against unemployment and invalidism and a system of compulsory insurance by employers of their workers, without cost to the latter, against industrial diseases, accidents and death.

Political Demands

1. The absolute freedom of press, speech and assemblage.

2. The adoption of a graduated income tax, the increase of the rates of the present corporation tax and the extension of inheritance taxes, graduated in proportion to the value of the estate and to nearness of kin—the proceeds of these taxes to be employed in the socialization of industry.

3. The abolition of the monopoly ownership of patents and the substitution of collective ownership, with direct rewards to inventors by premiums or royalties.

4. Unrestricted and equal suffrage for men and women.

5. The adoption of the initiative, referendum and recall and of proportional representation, nationally as well as locally.

6. The abolition of the Senate and of the veto power of the President.

7. The election of the President and Vice-President by direct vote of the people.

8. The abolition of the power usurped by the Supreme Court of the United States to pass upon the constitutionality of the legislation enacted by Congress. National laws to be repealed only by act of Congress or by a referendum vote of the whole people.

9. Abolition of the present restrictions upon the amendment of the constitution, so that instrument may be made amendable by a majority of the voters in a majority of the States.

10. The granting of the right of suffrage in the District of Columbia with representation in Congress and a democratic form of municipal government for purely local affairs.

11. The extension of democratic government to all United States territory.

12. The enactment of further measures for general education and particularly for vocational education in useful pursuits. The Bureau of Education to be made a Department.

13. The enactment of further measures for the conservation of health. The creation of an independent bureau of health, with such restrictions as will secure full liberty to all schools of practice.

14. The separation of the present Bureau of Labor from the Department of Commerce and Labor and its elevation to the rank of a department.

15. Abolition of all federal district courts and the United States circuit courts of appeals. State courts to have jurisdiction in all cases arising between citizens of the several states and foreign corporations. The election of all judges for short terms.

16. The immediate curbing of the power of the courts to issue injunctions.

17. The free administration of the law.

18. The calling of a convention for the revision of the constitution of the United States.

Such measures of relief as we may be able to force from capitalism are but a preparation of the workers to seize the whole powers of government, in order that they may thereby lay hold of the whole system of socialized industry and thus come to their rightful inheritance.

Socialist Labor Platform of 1912

The Socialist Labor Party of the United States of America in National Convention assembled in New York on April 10th, 1912, re-affirming its previous platform pronouncements, and in accord with the International Socialist Movement, declares:—

Social conditions, as illustrated by the events that crowded into the last four years, have ripened so fast that each and all the principles, hitherto proclaimed by the Socialist Labor Party, and all and each of the methods that the Socialist Labor Party has hitherto advocated, stand to-day most conspicuously demonstrated.

The Capitalist Social System has wrought its own destruction. Its leading exponents, the present incumbent in the presidential chair, and his "illustrious predecessor," however, seemingly at war with each other on principles, cannot conceal the identity of their political views. The oligarchy proclaimed by the tenets of the one, the monarchy proclaimed by the tenets of the other, jointly proclaim the conviction of the foremost men of the Ruling Class that the Republic of Capital is at the end of its tether.

True to the economic laws from which Socialism proceeds, dominant wealth has to such an extent concentrated into the hands of a select few, the Plutocracy, that the lower layers of the Capitalist Class feel driven to the ragged edge, while the large majority of the people, the Working Class, are being submerged.

True to the sociologic laws, by the light of which Socialism reads its forecasts, the Plutocracy is breaking through its republic-democratic shell and is stretching out its hands towards Absolutism in government; the property-holding layers below it are turning at bay; the proletariat is awakening to its consciousness of class, and thereby to the perception of its historic mission.

In the midst of this hurly, all the colors of the rainbow are being projected upon the social mists from the prevalent confusion of thought.

From the lower layers of the Capitalist Class the bolder, yet foolhardy, portion bluntly demands that "the Trust be smashed."

Even if the Trust could, it should not be smashed; even if it should, it cannot. The law of social progress pushes toward a system of production that shall crown the efforts of man, without arduous toil, with an abundance of the necessaries for material existence, to the end of allowing leisure for mental and spiritual expansion. The Trust is a mechanical contrivance wherewith to solve the problem. To smash the contrivance were to re-introduce the days of small-fry competition, and set back the hands of the dial of time. The mere thought is foolhardy. He who undertakes the feat might as well brace himself against the cascade of Niagara. The cascade of Social Evolution would whelm him.

The less bold among the smaller property-holding element proposes to "curb" the Trust with a variety of schemes. The very forces of social evolution that propel the development of the Trust stamp the "curbing" schemes, whether political or economic, as childish. They are attempts to hold back a runaway horse by the tail. The laws by which the attempt has been tried strew the path of the runaway. They are splintered to pieces with its kicks, and serve only to furnish a livelihood for the Corporation and the Anti-Corporation lawyer.

From still lower layers of the same property-holding class, social layers that have sniffed the breath of Socialism and imagine themselves Socialists, comes the iridescent theory of capturing the Trust for the people by the ballot only. The "capture of the Trust for the people" implies the Social Revolution. To imply the Social Revolution with the ballot only, without the means to enforce the ballot's fiat, in case of Reaction's attempt to override it, is to fire blank cartridges at a foe. It is worse. It is to threaten his existence without the means to carry out the threat. Threats of revolution, without provisions to carry them out, result in one of two things only—either the leaders are bought out, or the revolutionary class, to which the leaders appeal and which they succeed in drawing after themselves, are led like cattle to the shambles. The Commune disaster of France stands a monumental warning against the blunder.

An equally iridescent hue of the rainbow is projected from a still lower layer, a layer that lies almost wholly within the submerged class—the theory of capturing the Trust for the Working Class with the fist only. The capture of the Trust for the people implies something else besides revolution. It implies revolution carried on by the masses. For reasons parallel to those that decree the day of small-fry competition gone by, mass-revolutionary conspiracy is, to-day, an impossibility. The Trust-holding Plutocracy may successfully put through a conspiracy of physical force. The smallness of its numbers makes a successful conspiracy possible on its part. The hugeness of the numbers requisite for a revolution against the Trust-holding Plutocracy excludes Conspiracy from the arsenal of the Revolution. The idea of capturing the Trust with physical force only is a wild chimera.

Only two programs—the program of the Plutocracy and the programme of the Socialist Labor Party—grasp the situation.

The Political State, another name for the Class State, is worn out in this, the leading capitalist nation of the world, most prominently. The Industrial or Socialist State is throbbing for birth. The Political State, being a Class State, is govern-ment separate and apart from the productive energies of the people; it is government mainly for holding the ruled class in subjection. The Industrial or Socialist State, being the denial of the Class State, is government that is part and parcel of the productive energies of the people.

As their functions are different, so are the structures of the two States different.

The structure of the Political State contemplates territorial "representation" only; the structure of the Industrial State contemplates representation of industries, of useful occupations only.

The economic or industrial evolution has reached that point where the Political State no longer can maintain itself under the forms of democracy. While the Plutocracy has relatively shrunk, the enemies it has raised against itself have become too numerous to be dallied with. What is still worse, obedient to the law of its own existence the Political State has been forced not merely to multiply enemies against itself; it has been forced to recruit and group the bulk of these enemies, the revolutionary bulk, at that.

The Working Class of the land, the historically revolutionary element, is grouped by the leading occupations, agricultural as well as industrial, in such manner that the "autonomous craft union" one time the palladium of the workers, has become a harmless scarecrow upon which the capitalist birds roost at ease, while the Industrial Unions cast ahead of them the constituencies of the government of the future, and, jointly, point to the Industrial State.

Nor yet is this all. Not only has the Political State raised its own enemies; not only has itself multiplied them; not only has itself recruited and drilled them; not only has itself grouped them into shape and form to succeed it; it is, furthermore, driven by its inherent necessities, prodding on the Revolutionary Class by digging ever more fiercely into its flanks the harpoon of exploitation.

With the purchasing power of wages sinking to ever lower depths; with certainty of work hanging on ever slenderer threads; with an ever more gigantically swelling army of the unemployed; with the needs of profits pressing the Plutocracy harder and harder recklessly to squander the workers' limbs and life; what with all this and the parallel process of merging the workers of all industries into one interdependent solid mass, the final break-up is rendered inevitable and at hand.

No wild schemes and no rainbow-chasing will stead in the approaching emergency. The Plutocracy knows this—and so does the Socialist Labor Party—and logical is the programme of each.

The programme of the Plutocracy is feudalic Autocracy, translated into Capitalism. Where a Social Revolution is pending, and, for whatever reason, is not enforced, *reaction* is the alternative.

The programme of the Socialist Labor Party is *revolution*—the Industrial or Socialist Republic, the Social Order where the Political State is overthrown; where the Congress of the land consists of the representatives of the useful occupations of the land; where, accordingly, a government is an essential factor in production; where the blessings to man that the Trust is instinct with, are freed from the trammels of the private ownership that now turn the potential blessings into a curse; where, accordingly, abundance can be the patrimony of all who work; and the shackles of wage slavery are no more.

In keeping with the goals of the different programmes are the means of their execution.

The means in contemplation by *reaction* is the bayonet. To this end *reaction* is seeking, by means of the police spy and other agencies, to lash the proletariat into acts of violence that may give a color to the resort to the bayonet. By its manœuvres, it is egging the Working Class on to deeds of fury. The capitalist press echoes the policy, while the pure and simple political Socialist Party press, generally, is snared into the trap.

On the contrary, the means firmly adhered to by the Socialist Labor Party is the constitutional method of political action, backed by the industrially and class-consciously organized proletariat, to the exclusion of Anarchy, and all that thereby hangs.

At such a critical period in the Nation's existence the Socialist Labor Party calls upon the Working Class of America, more deliberately serious than ever before to rally at the polls under the Party's banner. And the Party also calls upon all intelligent citizens to place themselves squarely upon the ground of Working Class interests, and join us in this mighty and noble work of human emancipation, so that we may put summary end to the existing barbarous class conflict by placing the land and all the means of production, transportation and distribution into the hands of the people as a collective body, and substituting for the present state of planless production, industrial war, and social disorder, the Social or Industrial Commonwealth—a commonwealth in which every worker shall have the free exercise and full benefit of his faculties, multiplied by all the modern factors of civilization.

☒ CAMPAIGN OF 1916

In 1916 there were the two major parties and three minor parties, namely,—the Prohibitionists, the Socialists, and the Socialist Labor Party.

The Progressives disappeared in 1916. Mr. Roosevelt refused to be their candidate and they did not name another. Some irreconcilables attempted to keep up the organization and stayed in the field with a candidate for vice-president only.

Democratic Platform of 1916

The Democratic Party, in National Convention assembled, adopts the following declaration to the end that the people of the United States may both realize the achievements wrought by four years of Democratic administration and be apprised of the policies to which the party is committed for the further conduct of National affairs.

I. RECORD OF ACHIEVEMENT

We endorse the administration of Woodrow Wilson. It speaks for itself. It is the best exposition of sound Democratic policy at home and abroad.

We challenge comparison of our record, our keeping of pledges and our constructive legislation, with those of any party of any time.

We found our country hampered by special privilege, a vicious tariff, obsolete banking laws and an inelastic currency. Our foreign affairs were dominated by commercial interests for their selfish ends. The Republican Party, despite repeated pledges, was impotent to correct abuses which it had fostered. Under our Administration, under a leadership which has never faltered, these abuses have been corrected, and our people have been freed therefrom.

Our archaic banking and currency system, prolific of panic and disaster under Republican administrations,—long the refuge of the money trust,—has been supplanted by the Federal Reserve Act, a true democracy of credit under government control, already proved a financial bulwark in a world crisis, mobilizing our resources, placing abundant credit at the disposal of legitimate industry and making a currency panic impossible.

We have created a Federal Trade Commission to accommodate perplexing questions arising under the anti-trust laws, so that monopoly may be strangled at its birth and legitimate industry encouraged. Fair competition in business is now assured.

We have effected an adjustment of the tariff, adequate for revenue under peace conditions, and fair to the consumer and to the producer. We have adjusted the burdens of taxation so that swollen incomes bear their equitable share. Our revenues have been sufficient in times of world stress, and will largely exceed the expenditures for the current fiscal year.

We have lifted human labor from the category of commodities and have secured to the workingman the right of voluntary association for his protection and welfare. We have protected the rights of the laborer against the unwarranted issuance of writs of injunction, and have guaranteed to him the right of trial by jury in cases of alleged contempt committed outside the presence of the court.

We have advanced the parcel post to genuine efficiency, enlarged the postal savings system, added ten thousand rural delivery routes and extensions, thus reaching two and one-half millions additional people, improved the postal service in every branch, and for the first time in our history, placed the post-office system on a self-supporting basis, with actual surplus in 1913, 1914 and 1916.

II. ECONOMIC FREEDOM

The reforms which were most obviously needed to clear away special privilege, prevent unfair discrimination and release the energies of men of all ranks and advantages, have been effected by recent legislation. We must now remove, as far as possible, every remaining element of unrest and uncertainty from the path of the business men of America, and secure for them a continued period of quiet, assured and confident prosperity.

III. TARIFF

We reaffirm our belief in the doctrine of a tariff for the purpose of providing sufficient revenue for the operation of the government economically administered, and unreservedly endorse the Underwood tariff law as truly exemplifying that doctrine. We recognize that tariff rates are necessarily subject to change to meet changing conditions in the world's productions and trade. The events of the last two years have brought about many momentous changes. In some respects their effects are yet conjectural and wait to be disclosed, particularly in regard to our foreign trade. Two years of a war which has directly involved most of the chief industrial nations in the world, and which has indirectly affected the life and industry of all nations are bringing about economic changes more varied and far-reaching than the world has ever before experienced. In order to ascertain just what those changes may be, the Democratic Congress is providing for a non-partisan tariff commission to make impartial and thorough study of every economic fact that may throw light either upon our past or upon our future fiscal policy with regard to the imposition of taxes on imports or with regard to the changed and changing conditions under which our trade is carried on. We cordially endorse this timely proposal and declare ourselves in sympathy with the principle and purpose of shaping legislation within that field in accordance with clearly established facts rather than in accordance with the demands of selfish interests or upon information provided largely, if not exclusively, by them.

IV. AMERICANISM

The part that the United States will play in the new day of international relationships that is now upon us will depend upon our preparation and our character. The Democratic party, therefore, recognizes the assertion and triumphant demonstration of the indivisibility and coherent strength of the nation as the supreme issue of this day in which the whole world faces the crisis of manifold change. It summons all men of whatever origin or creed who would count themselves Americans, to join in making clear to all the world the unity and consequent power of America. This is an issue of patriotism. To taint it with partisanship would be to defile it. In this day of test, America must show itself not a nation of partisans but a nation of patriots. There is gathered here in America the best of the blood, the industry and the genius of the whole world, the elements of a great race and a magnificent society to be welded into a mighty and splendid Nation. Whoever, actuated by the purpose to promote the interest of a foreign power, in disregard of our own country's welfare or to injure this government in its foreign relations or cripple or destroy its industries at home, and whoever by arousing prejudices of a racial, religious or other nature creates discord and strife among our people so as to obstruct the wholesome process of unification, is faithless to the trust which the privileges of citizenship repose in him and is disloyal to his country. We therefore condemn as subversive to this Nation's unity and integrity, and as destructive of its welfare, the activities and designs of every group or organization, political or otherwise, that has for its object the advancement of the interest of a foreign power, whether such object is promoted by intimidating the government, a political party, or representatives of the people, or which is calculated and tends to divide our people into antagonistic groups and thus to destroy that complete agreement and solidarity of the people and that unity of sentiment and purpose so essential to the perpetuity of the Nation and its free institutions. We condemn all alliances and combinations of individuals in this country, of whatever nationality or descent, who agree and conspire together for the purpose of embarrassing or weakening our government or of improperly influencing or coercing our public representatives in dealing or negotiating with any foreign power. We charge that such conspiracies among a limited number exist and have been instigated for the purpose of advancing the interests of foreign countries to the prejudice and detriment of our own country. We condemn any political party which, in view of the activity of such conspirators, surrenders its integrity or modifies its policy.

V. Preparedness

Along with the proof of our character as a Nation must go the proof of our power to play the part that legitimately belongs to us. The people of the United States love peace. They respect the rights and covet the friendship of all other nations. They desire neither any additional territory nor any advantage which cannot be peacefully gained by their skill, their industry, or their enterprise; but they insist upon having absolute freedom of National life and policy, and feel that they owe it to themselves and to the rôle of spirited independence which it is their sole ambition to play that they should render themselves secure against the hazard of interference from any quarter, and should be able to protect their rights upon the seas or in any part of the world. We therefore favor the maintenance of an army fully adequate to the requirements of order, of safety, and of the protection of the nation's rights, the fullest development of modern methods of seacoast defence and the maintenance of an adequate reserve of citizens trained to arms and prepared to safeguard the people and territory of the United States against any danger of hostile action which may unexpectedly arise; and a fixed policy for the continuous development of a navy, worthy to support the great naval traditions of the United States and fully equal to the international tasks which this Nation hopes and expects to take a part in performing. The plans and enactments of the present Congress afford substantial proof of our purpose in this exigent matter.

VI. International Relation

The Democratic administration has throughout the present war scrupulously and successfully held to the old paths of neutrality and to the peaceful pursuit of the legitimate objects of our National life which statesmen of all parties and creeds have prescribed for themselves in America since the beginning of our history. But the circumstances of the last two years have revealed necessities of international action which no former generation can have foreseen. We hold that it is the duty of the United States to use its power, not only to make itself safe at home, but also to make secure its just interests throughout the world, and, both for this end and in the interest of humanity, to assist the world in securing settled peace and justice. We believe that every people has the right to choose the sovereignty under which it shall live; that the small states of the world have a right to enjoy from other nations the same respect for their sovereignty and for their territorial integrity that great and powerful nations expect and insist upon; and that the world has a right to be free from every disturbance of its peace that has its origin in aggression or disregard of the rights of people and nations; and we believe that the time has come when it is the duty of the United States to join the other nations of the world in any feasible association that will effectively serve those principles, to maintain inviolate the complete security of the highway of the seas for the common and unhindered use of all nations.

The present Administration has consistently sought to act upon and realize in its conduct of the foreign affairs of the Nation the principle that should be the object of any association of the nations formed to secure the peace of the world and the maintenance of national and individual rights. It has followed the highest American traditions. It has preferred respect for the fundamental rights of smaller states even to property interests, and has secured the friendship of the people of these States for the United States by refusing to make a more material interest an excuse for the assertion of our superior power against the dignity of their sovereign independence. It has regarded the lives of its citizens and the claims of humanity as of greater moment than material rights, and peace as the best basis for the just settlement of commercial claims. It has made the honor and ideals of the United States its standard alike in negotiation and action.

VII. Pan-American Concord

We recognize now, as we have always recognized, a definite and common interest between the United States and the other peoples and republics of the Western Hemisphere in all matters of National independence and free political development. We favor the establishment and maintenance of the closest relations of amity and mutual helpfulness between the United States and the other republics of the American continents for the support of peace and the promotion of a common prosperity. To that end we favor all measures which may be necessary to facilitate intimate intercourse and promote commerce between the United States and her neighbors to the south of us, and such international understandings as may be practicable and suitable to accomplish these ends.

We commend the action of the Democratic administration in holding the Pan-American Financial Conference at Washington in May, 1915, and organizing the International High Commission, which represented the United States in the recent meeting of representatives of the Latin-American Republics at Buenos Aires, April, 1916, which have so greatly promoted the friendly relations between the people of the Western Hemisphere.

VIII. Mexico

The Monroe Doctrine is reasserted as a principle of Democratic faith. That doctrine guarantees the independent republics of the two Americas against aggression from another continent. It implies, as well, the most scrupulous regard upon our part for the sovereignty of each of them. We court their good will. We seek not to despoil them. The want of a stable, responsible government in Mexico, capable of repressing and punishing marauders and bandit bands, who have not only taken the lives and seized and destroyed the property of American citizens in that country, but have insolently invaded our soil, made war upon and murdered our people thereon, has rendered it necessary temporarily to occupy, by our armed forces, a portion of the territory of that friendly state. Until, by the restoration of law and order therein, a repetition of such incursions is improbable, the necessity for their remaining will continue. Intervention, implying as it does, military subjugation, is revolting to the people of the United States, notwithstanding the provocation

to that course has been great and should be resorted to, if at all, only as a last recourse. The stubborn resistance of the President and his advisers to every demand and suggestion to enter upon it, is creditable alike to them and to the people in whose name he speaks.

IX. Merchant Marine

Immediate provision should be made for the development of the carrying trade of the United States. Our foreign commerce has in the past been subject to many unnecessary and vexatious obstacles in the way of legislation of Republican Congresses. Until the recent Democratic tariff legislation, it was hampered by unreasonable burdens of taxation. Until the recent banking legislation, it had at its disposal few of the necessary instrumentalities of international credit and exchange. Until the formulation of the pending act to promote the construction of a merchant marine, it lacked even the prospect of adequate carriage by sea. We heartily endorse the purposes and policy of the pending shipping bill and favor all such additional measures of constructive or remedial legislation as may be necessary to restore our flag to the seas and to provide further facilities for our foreign commerce, particularly such laws as may be requisite to remove unfair conditions of competition in the dealings of American merchants and producers with competitors in foreign markets.

X. Conservation

For the safeguarding and quickening of the life of our own people, we favor the conservation and development of the natural resources of the country through a policy which shall be positive rather than negative, a policy which shall not withhold such resources from development but which, while permitting and encouraging their use, shall prevent both waste and monopoly in their exploitation, and we earnestly favor the passage of acts which will accomplish these objects, reaffirming the declaration of the platform of 1912 on this subject.

The policy of reclaiming our arid lands should be steadily adhered to.

XI. The Administration and the Farmer

We favor the vigorous prosecution of investigations and plans to render agriculture more profitable and country life more healthful, comfortable and attractive, and we believe that this should be a dominant aim of the nation as well as of the States. With all its recent improvement, farming still lags behind other occupations in development as a business, and the advantages of an advancing civilization have not accrued to rural communities in a fair proportion. Much has been accomplished in this field under the present administration, far more than under any previous administration. In the Federal Reserve Act of the last Congress, and the Rural Credits Act of the present Congress, the machinery has been created which will make credit available to the farmer constantly and readily, placing him at last upon a footing of equality with the merchant and the manufacturer in securing the capital necessary to carry on his enterprises. Grades and standards necessary to the intelligent and successful conduct of the business of agriculture have also been established or are in the course of establishment by law. The long-needed Cotton Futures Act, passed by the Sixty-Third Congress, has now been in successful operation for nearly two years. A Grain Grades Bill, long needed, and a permissive Warehouse Bill, intended to provide better storage facilities and to enable the farmer to obtain certificates upon which he may secure advances of money have been passed by the House of Representatives, have been favorably reported to the Senate, and will probably become law during the present session of the Congress. Both Houses have passed a good-roads measure, which will be of far reaching benefit to all agricultural communities. Above all, the most extraordinary and significant progress has been made, under the direction of the Department of Agriculture, in extending and perfecting practical farm demonstration work which is so rapidly substituting scientific for empirical farming. But it is also necessary that rural activities should be better directed through co-operation and organization, that unfair methods of competition should be eliminated and the conditions requisite for the just, orderly and economical marketing of farm products created. We approve the Democratic administration for having emphatically directed attention for the first time to the essential interests of agriculture involved in farm marketing and finance, for creating the Office of Markets and Rural Organization in connection with the De-

partment of Agriculture, and for extending the co-operative machinery necessary for conveying information to farmers by means of demonstration. We favor continued liberal provision, not only for the benefit of production, but also for the study and solution of problems of farm marketing and finance and for the extension of existing agencies for improving country life.

XII. GOOD ROADS

The happiness, comfort and prosperity of rural life, and the development of the city, are alike conserved by the construction of public highways. We, therefore, favor national aid in the construction of post roads and roads for like purposes.

XIII. GOVERNMENT EMPLOYMENT

We hold that the life, health and strength of the men, women and children of the Nation are its greatest asset and that in the conservation of these the Federal Government, wherever it acts as the employer of labor, should both on its own account and as an example, put into effect the following principles of just employment:

1. A living wage for all employees.

2. A working day not to exceed eight hours, with one day of rest in seven.

3. The adoption of safety appliances and the establishment of thoroughly sanitary conditions of labor.

4. Adequate compensation for industrial accidents.

5. The standards of the "Uniform Child Labor Law," wherever minors are employed.

6. Such provisions for decency, comfort and health in the employment of women as should be accorded the mothers of the race.

7. An equitable retirement law providing for the retirement of superannuated and disabled employees of the civil service, to the end that a higher standard of efficiency may be maintained.

We believe also that the adoption of similar principles should be urged and applied in the legislation of the States with regard to labor within their borders and that through every possible agency the life and health of the people of the nation should be conserved.

XIV. LABOR

We declare our faith in the Seamen's Act, passed by the Democratic Congress, and we promise our earnest continuance of its enforcement.

We favor the speedy enactment of an effective Federal Child Labor Law and the regulation of the shipment of prison-made goods in interstate commerce.

We favor the creation of a Federal Bureau of Safety in the Department of Labor, to gather facts concerning industrial hazards, and to recommend legislation to prevent the maiming and killing of human beings.

We favor the extension of the powers and functions of the Federal Bureau of Mines.

We favor the development upon a systematic scale of the means already begun under the present administration, to assist laborers throughout the Nation to seek and obtain employment, and the extension of the Federal Government of the same assistance and encouragement as is now given to agricultural training.

We heartily commend our newly established Department of Labor for its fine record in settling strikes by personal advice and through conciliating agents.

XV. Public Health

We favor a thorough reconsideration of the means and methods by which the Federal Government handles questions of public health to the end that human life may be conserved by the elimination of loathsome disease, the improvement of sanitation and the diffusion of a knowledge of disease prevention.

We favor the establishment by the Federal Government of tuberculosis sanitariums for needy tubercular patients.

XVI. Senate Rules

We favor such alteration of the rules of procedure of the Senate of the United States as will permit the prompt transaction of the Nation's legislative business.

XVII. Economy and the Budget

We demand careful economy in all expenditures for the support of the government, and to that end favor a return by the House of Representatives to its former practice of initiating and preparing all appropriation bills through a single committee chosen from its membership, in order that responsibility may be central, expenditures standardized and made uniform, and waste and duplication in the public service as much as possible avoided. We favor this as a practicable first step towards a budget system.

XVIII. Civil Service

We reaffirm our declarations for the rigid enforcement of the civil service laws.

XIX. Philippine Islands

We heartily endorse the provisions of the bill, recently passed by the House of Representatives, further promoting self-government in the Philippine Islands as being in fulfillment of the policy declared by the Democratic Party in its last national platform, and we reiterate our endorsement of the purpose of ultimate independence for the Philippine Islands, expressed in the preamble of that measure.

XX. Woman Suffrage

We recommend the extension of the franchise to the women of the country by the States upon the same terms as to men.

XXI. Protection of Citizens

We again declare the policy that the sacred rights of American citizenship must be preserved at home and abroad, and that no treaty shall receive the sanction of our Government which does not expressly recognize the absolute equality of all our citizens irrespective of race, creed or previous nationality, and which does not recognize the right of expatriation. The American Government should protect American citizens in their rights, not only at home but abroad, and any country having a government should be held to strict accountability for any wrongs done them, either to person or property. At the earliest practical opportunity our country should strive earnestly for peace among the warring nations of Europe and seek to bring about the adoption of the fundamental principle of justice and humanity, that all men shall enjoy equality of right and freedom from discrimination in the lands wherein they dwell.

XXII. Prison Reform

We demand that the modern principles of prison reform be applied in our Federal Penal System. We favor such work for prisoners as shall give them training in remunerative occupations so that they may make an honest living when released from prison; the setting apart of the net wages of the prisoner to be paid to his dependent family or to be reserved for his own use upon his release; the liberal extension of the principles of the Federal Parole Law, with due regard both to the welfare of the prisoner and the interests of society; the adoption of the Probation System especially in the case of first offenders not convicted of serious crimes.

XXIII. PENSIONS

We renew the declarations of recent Democratic platforms relating to generous pensions for soldiers and their widows, and call attention to our record of performance in this particular.

XXIV. WATERWAYS AND FLOOD CONTROL

We renew the declaration in our last two platforms relating to the development of our waterways. The recent devastation of the lower Mississippi Valley and several other sections by floods accentuates the movement for the regulation of river flow by additional bank and levee protection below, and diversion, storage and control of the flood waters above, and their utilization for beneficial purposes in the reclamation of arid and swamp lands and development of waterpower, instead of permitting the floods to continue as heretofore agents of destruction. We hold that the control of the Mississippi River is a National problem. The preservation of the depth of its waters for purposes of navigation, the building of levees and works of bank protection to maintain the integrity of its channel and prevent the overflow of its valley resulting in the interruption of interstate commerce, the disorganization of the mail service, and the enormous loss of life and property, impose an obligation which alone can be discharged by the National Government.

We favor the adoption of a liberal and comprehensive plan for the development and improvement of our harbors and inland waterways with economy and efficiency so as to permit their navigation by vessels of standard draft.

XXV. ALASKA

It has been and will be the policy of the Democratic party to enact all laws necessary for the speedy development of Alaska and its great natural resources.

XXVI. TERRITORIES

We favor granting to the people of Alaska, Hawaii and Porto Rico the traditional territorial government accorded to the territories of the United States since the beginning of our government, and we believe that the officials appointed to administer the government of those several territories should be qualified by previous *bona-fide* residence.

XXVII. CANDIDATES

We unreservedly endorse our President and Vice-President, Woodrow Wilson, of New Jersey, and Thomas Riley Marshall of Indiana, who have performed the functions of their great offices faithfully and impartially and with distinguished ability.

In particular, we commend to the American people the splendid diplomatic victories of our great President, who has preserved the vital interests of our Government and its citizens, and kept us out of war.

Woodrow Wilson stands to-day the greatest American of his generation.

XXVIII. CONCLUSION

This is a critical hour in the history of America, a critical hour in the history of the world. Upon the record above set forth, which shows great constructive achievement in following out a consistent policy for our domestic and internal development; upon the record of the Democratic administration, which has maintained the honor, the dignity and the interests of the United States, and, at the same time, retained the respect and friendship of all the nations of the world; and upon the great policies for the future strengthening of the life of our country, the enlargement of our National vision and the ennobling of our international relations, as set forth above, we appeal with confidence to the voters of the country.

Prohibition Platform of 1916

The Prohibition Party, assembled in its Twelfth National Convention in the city of St. Paul, Minnesota, on this Twentieth day of July, 1916, grateful to Almighty God for the blessings of liberty, for our institutions and the multiplying signs of early victory for the cause for which the Party stands in order that the people may know the source of its faith and the basis of its action, should it be clothed with governmental power, challenges the attention of the Nation and asks the votes of the people on this Declaration of principles.

We denounce the traffic in intoxicating liquors. We believe in its abolition. It is a crime—not a business—and should not have governmental sanction.

We demand—and if given power, we will effectuate the demand—that the manufacture, importation, exportation, transportation and sale of alcoholic beverage purposes shall be prohibited.

To the accomplishment of that end, we pledge the exercise of all governmental power and amendment of statutes and the amendment of constitutions, State and National. Only by a political party committed to this purpose can such policy be made effective. We call upon all voters, so believing, to place the Prohibition Party in power upon this issue as a necessary step in the solution of the liquor problem.

The right of citizens of the United States to vote should not be denied or abridged by the United States or by any State on account of sex. We declare in favor of the enfranchisement of women by amendments to State and Federal Constitutions.

We condemn the Republican and Democratic parties for their failure to submit an equal suffrage amendment to the National Constitution. We remind the four million women voters that our Party was the first to declare for their political rights, which it did in 1872. We invite their co-operation in electing the Prohibition Party to power.

We are committed to the policy of peace and friendliness with all nations. We are unalterably opposed to the wasteful military programme of the Democratic Republican Parties. Militarism protects no worthy institution. It endangers them all. It violates the high principles which have brought us as a Nation to the present hour. We are for a constructive programme in preparedness for peace. We declare for and will promote a world court, to which national differences shall be submitted, so maintained as to give its decrees binding force.

We will support a compact among nations to dismantle navies and disband armies, but until such court and compact are established we pledge ourselves to maintain an effective army and navy and to provide coast defenses entirely adequate for national protection.

We are opposed to universal military service, and to participation in the rivalry that has brought Europe to the shambles and now imperils the civilization of the race.

Private profit, so far as constitutionally possible, should be taken out of the manufacture of war munitions and all war equipment.

In normal times we favor the employment of the army in vast reclamation plans, in reforesting hills and mountains, in building State and National highways, in the construction of an inland waterway from Florida to Maine, in the opening of Alaska and in unnumbered other projects which will make our soldiers constructive builders of peace. For such service there should be paid an adequate individual wage.

Those units of our navy which are capable of being converted into merchantmen and passenger vessels should be constructed with that purpose in view, and chiefly so utilized in times of peace.

We condemn the political parties, which for more than thirty years have allowed munition and war equipment manufacturers to plunder the people and to jeopardize the highest interest of the Nation by furnishing honey-combed armour plate and second rate battleships which the Navy League now declares are wholly inadequate.

We will not allow the country to forget that the first step toward physical, economic, moral and political preparedness is the enactment of National Prohibition.

The countries at war are preparing for a fierce industrial struggle to follow the cessation of hostilities. As a matter of commercial economy, international friendliness, business efficiency, and as a help to peace, we demand that reciprocal trade treaties be negotiated with all nations with which we have trade relations. A Commission of specialists, free from the control of any party, should be appointed with power to gather full information of all phases of the questions of tariff and reciprocity, and to recommend such legislation as it deems necessary for the welfare of American business and labor.

The necessity of legislation to enable American ship builders or owners to meet foreign competition, on the most favorable terms, is obvious.

Materials for construction should be admitted free of duty.

The purchase of ships abroad, when low prices invite, should be allowed and, when so purchased, should be admitted to American registry.

Harbor rules and charges and navigation laws should not be onerous, but favorable to the highest degree.

Liberal payment should be made by the Government for the carrying of mails or for transport services.

All shipping from the United States to any of our possessions should be reserved to ships of American registry.

The people should not overlook the fact that the effect of Nationwide Prohibition, on labor and industry generally, will be such as to lower the cost of ship building per unit, and at the same time permit the payment of higher wages. The increased volume of trade and commerce, which will result, when the wastage of the liquor traffic is stopped, will quicken our shipping on every sea and send our flag on peaceful missions into every port. This is urged as an incidental effect of wise action on the liquor question, but is none the less to be desired and will aid in the solution of the problem of our merchant marine.

Mexico needs not a conqueror, but a good Samaritan. We are opposed to the violation of the sovereignty of the Mexican people, and we will countenance no war of aggression against them. We pledge the help of this country in the suppression of lawless bands of marauders and murderers, who have taken the lives of American citizens, on both sides of the border, as well as of Mexicans in their own country.

The lives and property of our citizens, when about their lawful pursuits, either in the United States or in Mexico, must and will be protected. In the event of a break-down of government across the border, we would use, in the interests of civilization, the force necessary for the establishment of law and order.

In this connection we affirm our faith in the Monroe Doctrine, proclaimed in the early days of the Nation's life and unswervingly maintained for nearly a hundred years.

We cannot claim the benefits of the Doctrine and refuse to assume or discharge the responsibility and the duties which inhere therein and flow therefrom.

Those duties have long been unmet in Mexico. We should meet them now, acting, not for territory, not for conquest or for ourselves alone, but for and with all the nations of North and South America.

The Democratic party has blundered, and four years ago the Republican party evaded and passed on the problem it now asks the opportunity to solve.

The abandonment of the Philippines at this time would be an injustice to them and a violation of our plain duty. As soon as they are prepared for self-government, by education and training, they should be granted their independence on terms just to themselves and us.

We reaffirm our declaration in favor of conservation of forests, water power and other natural resources.

Departmental decisions ought not to be final, but the rights of the people should be protected by provision for court review.

In order that the public service may be of the highest standard, the government should be a model employer in all respects. To enforce the civil service law in spirit as well as in letter, all promotions should be non-political, based only upon proven fitness; all recommendations for demotions or removals from the service should be subjected to the review of a non-partisan board or commission.

The merit system should be extended to cover all postmasters, collectors of revenue, marshals and other such public officials whose duties are purely administrative.

We reaffirm our allegiance to the principle of secure tenure of office, during good behavior and capable effort, as the means of obtaining expert service. We declare for the enactment of an equitable retirement law for disabled and superannuated employees, in return for faithful service rendered, to maintain a high degree of efficiency in public office.

We stand for Americanism. We believe this country was created for a great mission among the nations of the earth. We rejoice in the fact that it has offered asylum to the oppressed of other lands and for those, more fortunately situated, who yet wished to improve their condition. It is the land of all peoples and belongs not to any one—it is the heritage of all. It should come first in the affections of every citizen, and he who loves another land more than this is not fit for citizenship here, but he is a better citizen who, loving his country, has reverence for the land of his fathers and gains from its history and traditions that which inspires him to nobler service to the one in which he lives.

The Federal Government should interest itself in helping the newcomer into that vocation and locality where he shall most quickly become an American. Those fitted by experience and training for agricultural pursuits should be encouraged to develop the millions of acres of rich and idle land.

We favor uniform marriage and divorce laws, the extermination of polygamy and the complete suppression of the traffic in women and girls.

Differences between capital and labor should be settled through arbitration, by which the rights of the public are conserved as well as those of the disputants. We declare for the prohibition of child labor in factories, mines and workshops; an eight hour maximum day, with one day of rest in seven; for more rigid sanitary requirements and such working conditions as shall foster the physical and moral well-being of the unborn; for the protection of all who toil, by the extension of Employers' Liability Acts; for the adoption of safety appliances for the safeguarding of labor; and for laws that will promote the just division of the wealth which labor and capital jointly produce. Provision should be made for those who suffer from industrial accidents and occupational diseases.

We pledge a business-like administration of the Nation's affairs; the abolition of useless offices, bureaus and commissions; economy in the expenditure of public funds; efficiency in governmental service; and the adoption of the budget system. The president should have power to veto any single item or items of an appropriation bill.

We condemn, and agree when in power to remedy, that which is known as "pork barrel" legislation, by which millions of dollars have been appropriated for rivers where there is no commerce, harbors where there are no ships and public buildings where there is no need.

We are in favor of a single presidential term of six years.

Public utilities and other resources that are natural monopolies are at the present time exploited for personal gain under a monopolistic system. We demand the public ownership or control of all such utilities by the people and their operation and administration in the interests of all the people.

We stand for the preservation and development of our free institutions and for absolute separation of church and state with the guaranty of full religious and civil liberty.

We stand for the rights, safety, justice and development of humanity; we believe in the equality of all before the law; in old-age pensions and insurance against unemployment and in help for needy mothers, all of which could be provided from what is now wasted for drink.

We favor the initiative, referendum and recall.

While it is admitted that grain and cotton are fundamental factors in our national life, it cannot be denied that proper assistance and protection are not given these commodities at terminal markets, in the course of inter-state commerce.

We favor and pledge our efforts to obtain grain elevators at necessary terminal markets, such elevators to be owned and operated by the Federal Government; also to secure Federal grain inspection under a system of civil service and to secure the abolition of any Board of Trade, Chamber of Commerce, or other place of gambling in grain or trading in "options" or "futures" or "short-selling," or any other form of so-called speculation wherein products are not received or delivered, but wherein so-called contracts are settled by the payment of "margins" or "differences" through clearing houses or otherwise.

This Party stands committed to free and open markets based upon legitimate supply and demand, absolutely free from questionable practices of market manipulation. We also favor government warehouses for cotton at proper terminals where the interests of producers require the same; and the absolute divorce of all railroad elevators or warehouses owned by railroad companies, either public or private, from operation and control of private individuals in competition with the public in merchandising grain, cotton or other farm products.

We furthermore endorse all proper methods among producers of those means of co-operative mutual enterprise, which tend toward broader and better markets for both producer and consumer.

This is the day of opportunity for the American

people. The triumph of neither old political party is essential to our safety or progress. The defeat of either will be no public misfortune. They are one party. By age and wealth, by membership and traditions, by platforms and in the character of their candidates, they are the Conservative Party of the United States. The Prohibition Party as the promoter of every important measure of social justice presented to the American people in the last two generations, and as the originator of nearly all such legislation, remains now the only great Progressive Party.

The patriotic voters, who compose the Republican and Democratic parties, can, by voting the Prohibition ticket this year, elect the issue of National Prohibition.

To those, in whatever party, who have the vision of a land redeemed from drink, we extend a cordial invitation to join with us in carrying the banner of Prohibition to Nationwide victory.

Republican Platform of 1916

In 1861 the Republican party stood for the Union. As it stood for the Union of States, it now stands for a united people, true to American ideals, loyal to American traditions, knowing no allegiance except to the Constitution, to the Government, and to the Flag of the United States. We believe in American policies at home and abroad.

PROTECTION OF AMERICAN RIGHTS

We declare that we believe in and will enforce the protection of every American citizen in all the rights secured to him by the Constitution, by treaties and the laws of nations, at home and abroad, by land and by sea. These rights, which in violation of the specific promise of their party made at Baltimore in 1912, the Democratic President and the Democratic Congress have failed to defend, we will unflinchingly maintain.

FOREIGN RELATIONS

We desire peace, the peace of justice and right, and believe in maintaining a strict and honest neutrality between the belligerents in the great war in Europe. We must perform all our duties and insist upon all our rights as neutrals without fear and without favor. We believe that peace and neutrality, as well as the dignity and influence of the United States, cannot be preserved by shifty expedients, by phrase-making, by performances in language, or by attitudes ever changing in an effort to secure votes or voters. The present Administration has destroyed our influence abroad and humiliated us in our own eyes. The Republican party believes that a firm, consistent, and courageous foreign policy, always maintained by Republican Presidents in accordance with American traditions, is the best, as it is the only true way, to preserve our peace and restore us to our rightful place among the nations.

We believe in the pacific settlement of international disputes, and favor the establishment of a world court for that purpose.

MEXICO

We deeply sympathize with the fifteen million people of Mexico who, for three years have seen their country devastated, their homes destroyed, their fellow citizens murdered and their women outraged, by armed bands of desperadoes led by self-seeking, conscienceless agitators who when temporarily successful in any locality have neither sought nor been able to restore order or establish and maintain peace.

We express our horror and indignation at the outrages which have been and are being perpetrated by these bandits upon American men and women who were or are in Mexico by invitation of the laws and of the government of that country and whose rights to security of person and property are guaranteed by solemn treaty obligations. We denounce the indefensible methods of interference employed by this Administration in the internal affairs of Mexico and refer with shame to its failure to discharge the duty of this country as next friend to Mexico, its duty to other powers who have relied upon us as such friend, and its duty to our citizens in Mexico, in permitting the continuance of such conditions, first by failure to act promptly and firmly, and second, by lending its influence to the continuation of such conditions through recognition of one of the factions responsible for these outrages.

We pledge our aid in restoring order and maintaining peace in Mexico. We promise to our citizens on and near our border, and to those in Mexico, wherever they may be found, adequate and absolute protection in their lives, liberty, and property.

Monroe Doctrine

We reaffirm our approval of the Monroe Doctrine, and declare its maintenance to be a policy of this country essential to its present and future peace and safety and to the achievement of its manifest destiny.

Latin America

We favor the continuance of Republican policies which will result in drawing more and more closely the commercial, financial and social relations between this country and the countries of Latin America.

Philippines

We renew our allegiance to the Philippine policy inaugurated by McKinley, approved by Congress, and consistently carried out by Roosevelt and Taft. Even in this short time it has enormously improved the material and social conditions of the Islands, given the Philippine people a constantly increasing participation in their government, and if persisted in will bring still greater benefits in the future.

We accepted the responsibility of the Islands as a duty to civilization and the Filipino people. To leave with our task half done would break our pledges, injure our prestige among nations, and imperil what has already been accomplished.

We condemn the Democratic administration for its attempt to abandon the Philippines, which was prevented only by the vigorous opposition of Republican members of Congress, aided by a few patriotic Democrats.

Right of Expatriation

We reiterate the unqualified approval of the action taken in December, 1911, by the President and Congress to secure with Russia, as with other countries, a treaty that will recognize the absolute right of expatriation and prevent all discrimination of whatever kind between American citizens whether native-born or alien, and regardless of race, religion or previous political allegiance. We renew the pledge to observe this principle and to maintain the right of asylum, which is neither to be surrendered nor restricted, and we unite in the cherished hope that the war which is now desolating the world may speedily end, with a complete and lasting restoration of brotherhood among the nations of the earth and the assurance of full equal rights, civil and religious, to all men in every land.

Protection of the Country

In order to maintain our peace and make certain the security of our people within our own borders the country must have not only adequate but thorough and complete national defence ready for any emergency. We must have a sufficient and effective Regular Army and a provision for ample reserves, already drilled and disciplined, who can be called at once to the colors when the hour of danger comes.

We must have a Navy so strong and so well proportioned and equipped, so thoroughly ready and prepared, that no enemy can gain command of the sea and effect a landing in force on either our Western or our Eastern coast. To secure these results we must have a coherent continuous policy of national defence, which even in these perilous days the Democratic party has utterly failed to develop, but which we promise to give to the country.

Tariff

The Republican party stands now, as always, in the fullest sense for the policy of tariff protection to American industries and American labor and does not regard an anti-dumping provision as an adequate substitute.

Such protection should be reasonable in amount but sufficient to protect adequately American industries and American labor and so adjusted as to prevent undue exactions by monopolies or trusts. It should, moreover, give special attention to securing the industrial independence of the United States as in the case of dye-stuffs.

Through wise tariff and industrial legislation our industries can be so organized that they will become not only a commercial bulwark but a powerful aid to national defence.

The Underwood tariff act is a complete failure in every respect. Under its administration imports have enormously increased in spite of the fact that intercourse with foreign countries has been largely cut off by reason of the war, while the revenues of which we stand in such dire need have been greatly reduced.

Under the normal conditions which prevailed prior to the war it was clearly demonstrated that this Act deprived the American producer and the

American wage earner of that protection which enabled them to meet their foreign competitors, and but for the adventitious conditions created by the war, would long since have paralyzed all forms of American industry and deprived American labor of its just reward.

It has not in the least degree reduced the cost of living, which has constantly advanced from the date of its enactment. The welfare of our people demands its repeal and its substitution of a measure which in peace as well as in war will produce ample revenue and give reasonable protection to all forms of American production in mine, forest, field and factory.

We favor the creation of a tariff commission with complete power to gather and compile information for the use of Congress in all matters relating to the tariff.

BUSINESS

The Republican party has long believed in the rigid supervision and strict regulation of the transportation and of the great corporations of the country. It has put its creed into its deeds, and all really effective laws regulating the railroads and the great industrial corporations are the work of Republican Congresses and Presidents. For this policy of regulation and supervision the Democrats, in a stumbling and piecemeal way, are within the sphere of private enterprise and in direct competition with its own citizens, a policy which is sure to result in waste, great expense to the taxpayer and in an inferior product.

The Republican party firmly believes that all who violate the laws in regulation of business, should be individually punished. But prosecution is very different from persecution, and business success, no matter how honestly attained, is apparently regarded by the Democratic party as in itself a crime. Such doctrines and beliefs choke enterprise and stifle prosperity. The Republican party believes in encouraging American business as it believes in and will seek to advance all American interests.

RURAL CREDITS

We favor an effective system of Rural Credits as opposed to the ineffective law proposed by the present Democratic Administration.

RURAL FREE DELIVERY

We favor the extension of the Rural Free De-livery system and condemn the Democratic administration for curtailing and crippling it.

MERCHANT MARINE

In view of the policies adopted by all the maritime nations to encourage their shipping interest, and in order to enable us to compete with them for the ocean-carrying trade, we favor the payment to ships engaged in the foreign trade of liberal compensation for services actually rendered in carrying the mails, and such further legislation as will build up an adequate American Merchant Marine and give us ships which may be requisitioned by the Government in time of national emergency.

We are utterly opposed to the Government ownership of vessels as proposed by the Democratic party, because Government-owned ships, while effectively preventing the development of the American Merchant Marine by private capital, will be entirely unable to provide for the vast volume of American freights and will leave us more helpless than ever in the hard grip of foreign syndicates.

TRANSPORTATION

Interstate and intrastate transportation have become so interwoven that the attempt to apply two and often several sets of laws to its regulation has produced conflicts of authority, embarrassment in operation and inconvenience and expense to the public.

The entire transportation system of the country has become essentially national. We, therefore, favor such action by legislation, or, if necessary, through an amendment to the Constitution of the United States, as will result in placing it under complete Federal control.

ECONOMY AND A NATIONAL BUDGET

The increasing cost of the national government and the need for the greatest economy of its resources in order to meet the growing demands of the people for government service call for the severest condemnation of the wasteful appropriations of this democratic administration, of its shameless raids on the treasury, and of its opposition to and rejection of President Taft's oft-repeated proposals and earnest efforts to secure economy and efficiency through the establishment of a simple businesslike budget system to which we pledge our support and which we hold to be necessary to effect a real reform in the administration of national finance.

CONSERVATION

We believe in a careful husbandry of all the natural resources of the nation—a husbandry which means development without waste; use without abuse.

CIVIL SERVICE REFORM

The Civil Service Law has always been sustained by the Republican party, and we renew our repeated declarations that it shall be thoroughly and honestly enforced and extended wherever practicable. The Democratic party has created since March 4, 1913, thirty thousand offices outside of the Civil Service Law at an annual cost of forty-four million dollars to the taxpayers of the country.

We condemn the gross abuse and the misuse of the law by the present Democratic Administration and pledge ourselves to a reorganization of this service along lines of efficiency and economy.

TERRITORIAL OFFICIALS

Reaffirming the attitude long maintained by the Republican party, we hold that officials appointed to administer the government of any territory should be *bona-fide* residents of the territory in which their duties are to be performed.

LABOR LAWS

We pledge the Republican party to the faithful enforcement of all Federal laws passed for the protection of labor. We favor vocational education, the enactment and rigid enforcement of a Federal child labor law; the enactment of a generous and comprehensive workmen's compensation law, within the commerce power of Congress, and an accident compensation law covering all Government employees. We favor the collection and collation, under the direction of the Department of Labor, of complete data relating to industrial hazards for the information of Congress, to the end that such legislation may be adopted as may be calculated to secure the safety, conservation and protection of labor from the dangers incident to industry and transportation.

SUFFRAGE

The Republican party, reaffirming its faith in government of the people, by the people, for the people, as a measure of justice to one-half the adult people of this country, favors the extension of the suffrage to women, but recognizes the right of each state to settle this question for itself.

CONCLUSION

Such are our principles, such are our "purposes and policies." We close as we began. The times are dangerous and the future is fraught with peril. The great issues of the day have been confused by words and phrases. The American spirit, which made the country and saved the union, has been forgotten by those charged with the responsibility of power. We appeal to all Americans, whether naturalized or native-born, to prove to the world that we are Americans in thought and in deed, with one loyalty, one hope, one aspiration. We call on all Americans to be true to the spirit of America, to the great traditions of their common country, and above all things, to keep the faith.

Socialist Platform of 1916

In the midst of the greatest crisis and bloodiest struggle of all history the socialist party of America re-affirms its steadfast adherence to the principles of international brotherhood, world peace and industrial democracy.

The great war which has engulfed so much of civilization and destroyed millions of lives is one of the natural results of the capitalist system of production.

The socialist party, as the political expression of the economic interests of the working class, calls upon them to take a determined stand on the question of militarism and war, and to recognize the opportunity which the great war has given them of forcing disarmament and furthering the cause of industrial freedom.

An armed force in the hands of the ruling class serves two purposes: to protect and further the policy of imperialism abroad and to silence by force the protest of the workers against industrial despotism at home. Imperialism and militarism plunged Europe into this world war. America's geographical and industrial situation has kept her out of the cataclysm. But Europe's extremity has been the opportunity of America's ruling class to amass enormous profits. As a result there is a surfeit of capital which demands the policy of imperialism to protect and further investments abroad. Hence the frenzy of militarism into which the ruling class has made every attempt to force the United States.

The workers in Europe were helpless to avert the war because they were already saddled with the burden of militarism. The workers of the United States are yet free from this burden and have the opportunity of establishing a working class policy and program against war. They can compel the government of the United States to lead the way in an international movement for disarmament and to abandon the policy of imperialism which is forcing the conquest of Mexico and must, if carried out, eventually plunge the United States into a world war.

The working class must recognize the cry of preparedness against foreign invasion as a mere cloak for the sinister purpose of imperialism abroad and industrial tyranny at home. The class struggle, like capitalism, is international. The proletariat of the world has but one enemy, the capitalist class, whether at home or abroad. We must refuse to put into the hands of this enemy an armed force even under the guise of a "democratic army," as the workers of Australia and Switzerland have done.

Therefore the socialist party stands opposed to military preparedness, to any appropriations of men or money for war or militarism, while control of such forces through the political state rests in the hands of the capitalist class. The socialist party stands committed to the class war, and urges upon the workers in the mines and forests, on the railways and ships, in factories and fields, the use of their economic and industrial power, by refusing to mine the coal, to transport soldiers, to furnish food or other supplies for military purposes, and thus keep out of the hands of the ruling class the control of armed forces and economic power, necessary for aggression abroad and industrial despotism at home.

The working class must recognize militarism as the greatest menace to all efforts toward industrial freedom, and regardless of political or industrial affiliations must present a united front in the fight against preparedness and militarism.

Hideous as they are, the horrors of the far-stretched battle field of the old world are dwarfed by the evil results of the capitalist system, even in normal times. Instead of being organized to provide all members of society with an abundance of food, clothing and shelter, and the highest attainable freedom and culture, industry is at present organized and conducted for the benefit of a parasite class. All the powers of government and all our industrial genius are directed to the end of securing to the relatively small class of capital investors the largest amount of profits which can be wrung from the labor of the ever-increasing class whose only property is muscle and brain, manual and mental labor power.

The dire consequences of this system are everywhere apparent. The workers are oppressed and deprived of much that makes for physical, mental and moral well-being. Year by year poverty and industrial accidents destroy more lives than all the armies and navies in the world.

To preserve their privilege and power is the most vital interest of the possessing class, while it is the most vital interest of the working class to resist oppression, improve its position and struggle to obtain security of life and liberty. Hence there exists a conflict of interests, a social war within the nation, which can know neither truce nor compromise. So long as the few own and control the economic life of the nation the many must be enslaved, poverty must coexist with riotous luxury and civil strife prevail.

The socialist party would end these conditions by reorganizing the life of the nation upon the basis of socialism. Socialism would not abolish private property, but greatly extend it. We believe that every human being should have and own all the things which he can use to advantage, for the enrichment of his own life, without imposing disadvantage or burden upon any other human being. Socialism admits the private ownership and individual direction of all things, tools, economic processes and functions which are individualistic in character, and requires the collective ownership and democratic control and direction of those which are social or collectivistic in character.

We hold that this country cannot enjoy happiness and prosperity at home and maintain lasting peace with other nations so long as its industrial wealth is monopolized by a capitalist oligarchy. In this, as in every other campaign, all special issues arising from temporary situations, whether domestic or foreign, must be subordinated to the major issue—the need of such a reorganization of our economic life as will remove the land, the mines, forests, railroads, mill and factories, all the things required for our physical existence, from the clutches of industrial and financial freebooters and place them securely and permanently in the hands of the people.

If men were free to labor to satisfy their desires there could be in this country neither poverty nor involuntary unemployment. But the men in this country are not free to labor to satisfy their desires. The great industrial population can labor only when the capitalist class who own the industries believe they can market their product at a profit. The needs of millions are subordinated to the greeds of a few. The situation is not unlike that of a pyramid balanced upon its apex. Oftentimes this pyramid tumbles and industrial depression comes. There was such a crash in 1907. If the capitalist owners had been willing to get out of the way, industry could have been revived in a day. But the capitalist owners are never willing to get out of the way. Their greeds come first—the people's needs, if at all, afterwards. Therefore, business did not quickly revive after the industrial depression in 1907. Mr. Taft was elected to bring good times, but in four years failed to bring them. Mr. Wilson was elected to bring good times, but not all of the measures he advocated had the slightest effect upon industry. The European war has brought to this country tremendous orders for military supplies and has created a period of prosperity for the few. For the masses of the people there is but an opportunity to work hard for a bare living, which is not prosperity, but slavery. As against the boast of the present national administration that its political program, now fully in force, had brought prosperity to the masses, we call attention to the statement of the federal public health service that $800 is required a year to enable a family to avoid physical deterioration through lack of decent living conditions, that more than half of the families of working men receive less than that amount, that nearly a third receive less than $500 a year, and that one family in twelve received less than $300 a year.

The capitalist class for a great many years has been trying to saddle upon this country a great army and a greater navy. A greater army is desired to keep the working class of the United States in subjection. A greater navy is desired to safeguard the foreign investments of American capitalists and to "back-up" American diplomacy in its efforts to gain foreign markets for American capitalists. The war in Europe, which diminished and is still diminishing the remote possibility of European attack upon the United States, was nevertheless seized upon by capitalists and by unscrupulous politicians as a means of spreading fear throughout the country, to the end that, by false pretenses, great military establishments might be obtained. We denounce such "preparedness" as both false in principle, unnecessary in character and dangerous in its plain tendencies toward militarism. We advocate that sort of social preparedness which expresses itself in better homes, better bodies and better minds, which are alike the products of plenty and the necessity of effective defense in war.

The socialist party maintains its attitude of unalterable opposition to war.

We reiterate the statement that the competitive nature of capitalism is the cause of modern war and that the co-operative nature of socialism is alone adapted to the task of ending war by removing its causes. We assert, however, that, even under the present capitalist order, additional measures can be taken to safeguard peace, and to this end we demand:

MEASURES TO INSURE PEACE

1. That all laws and appropriations for the increase of the military and naval forces of the United States shall be immediately repealed.

2. That the power be taken from the president to lead the nation into a position which leaves no escape from war. No one man, however exalted in official station, should have the power to decide the question of peace or war for a nation of a hundred millions. To give one man such power is neither democratic nor safe. Yet the president exercises such power when he determines what shall be the nation's foreign policies and what shall be the nature and tone of its diplomatic intercourse with other nations. We, therefore, demand that the power to fix foreign policies and conduct diplomatic negotiations shall be lodged in congress and shall be exercised publicly, the people reserving the right to order congress, at any time, to change its foreign policy.

3. That no war shall be declared or waged by the United States without a referendum vote of

the entire people, except for the purpose of re-pelling invasion.

4. That the Monroe doctrine shall be immediately abandoned as a danger so great that even its advocates are agreed that it constitutes perhaps our greatest single danger of war. The Monroe doctrine was originally intended to safeguard the peace of the United States. Though the doctrine has changed from a safeguard to a menace, the capitalist class still defends it for the reason that our great Capitalists desire to retain South and Central America as their private trade preserve. We favor the cultivation of social, industrial and political friendship with all other nations in the western hemisphere, as an approach to a world confederation of nations, but we oppose the Monroe doctrine because it takes from our hands the peace of America and places it in the custody of any nation, that would attack the sovereignty of any state in the western world.

5. That the independence of the Philippine Islands be immediately recognized as a measure of justice both to the Philippines and to ourselves. The Filipinos are entitled to self-government, we are entitled to be freed from the necessity of building and maintaining enough dreadnoughts to defend them in the event of war.

6. The government of the United States shall call a congress of all neutral nations to mediate between the belligerent powers in an effort to establish an immediate and lasting peace without indemnities or forcible annexation of territory and based on a binding and enforcible international treaty, which shall provide for concerted disarmament on land and at sea and for an international congress with power to adjust all disputes between nations and which shall guarantee freedom and equal rights to all oppressed nations and races.

WORKING PROGRAM

As general measures calculated to strengthen the working class in its fight for the realization of its ultimate aim the co-operative commonwealth, and to increase its power of resistance against capital oppression, we advocate and pledge ourselves and our elected officers to the following program.

Political Demands

1. Unrestricted and equal suffrage for men and women.
2. The immediate adoption of the so-called "Susan B. Anthony amendment" to the constitution of the United States granting the suffrage to women on equal terms with men.

3. The adoption of the initiative, referendum and recall and of proportional representation, nationally as well as locally.

4. The abolition of the senate and of the veto power of the president.

5. The election of the president and the vice-president by direct vote of the people.

6. The abolition of the present restriction upon the amendment of the constitution so that that instrument may be made amendable by a majority of the voters in the country.

7. The calling of a convention for the revision of the constitution of the United States.

8. The abolition of the power usurped by the Supreme Court of the United States to pass upon the constitutionality of legislation enacted by congress. National laws to be repealed only by act of congress or by a referendum vote of the whole people.

9. The immediate curbing of the power of the courts to issue injunctions.

10. The election of all judges of the United States courts for short terms.

11. The free administration of the law.

12. The granting of the right of suffrage in the District of Columbia with representation in congress and a democratic form of municipal government for purely local affairs.

13. The extension of democratic government to all United States territory.

14. The freedom of press, speech and assemblage.

15. The increase of the rates of the present income tax and corporation tax and the extension of inheritance taxes, graduated in proportion to the value of the estate and to nearness of kin— the proceeds of these taxes to be employed in the socialization of industry.

16. The enactment of further measures for general education in useful pursuits. The bureau of education to be made a department.

17. The enactment of further measures for the conservation of health and the creation of an independent department of health.

18. The abolition of the monopoly ownership of patents and the substitution of collective ownership, with direct rewards to inventors by premiums or royalties.

Collective Ownership

1. The collective ownership and democratic management of railroads, telegraphs and telephones, express service, steamboat lines and all other social means of transportation and communication and of all large-scale industries.

2. The immediate acquirement by the municipalities, and the states of the federal government of all grain elevators, stock yards, storage warehouses and other distributing agencies, in order to relieve the farmer from the extortionate charges of the middlemen and to reduce the present high cost of living.

3. The extension of the public domain to include mines, quarries, oil wells, forests and water power.

4. The further conservation and development of natural resources for the use and benefit of all the people:

(a) By scientific afforestation and timber protection.

(b) By the reclamation of arid and swamp tracts.

(c) By the storage of flood waters and the utilization of water power.

(d) By the stoppage of the present extravagant waste of the soil and the products of mines and oil wells.

(e) By the development of highway and waterway systems.

5. The collective ownership of land wherever practicable, and, in cases where such ownership is impracticable, the appropriation by taxation of the annual rental value of all lands held for speculation or exploitation.

6. All currency shall be issued by the government of the United States and shall be legal tender for the payment of taxes and impost duties and for the discharge of public and private debts. The government shall lend money on bonds to counties and municipalities at a nominal rate of interest for the purpose of taking over or establishing public utilities and for building or maintaining public roads or highways and public schools —up to 25 per cent of the assessed valuation of such counties or municipalities. Said bonds are to be repaid in twenty equal and annual installments, and the currency issued for that purpose by the government is to be canceled and destroyed seriatim as the debt is paid. All banks and banking institutions shall be owned by the government of the United States or by the states.

7. Government relief of the unemployed by the extension of all useful public works. All persons employed on such work to be engaged directly by the government under a work day of not more than eight hours and at not less than the prevailing union wages. The government also to establish employment bureaus; to lend money to states and municipalities without interest for the purpose of carrying on public works; to contribute money to unemployment funds of labor unions and other organizations of workers, and to take such other measures within its power as will lessen the widespread misery of the workers caused by the misrule of the capitalist class.

Industrial Demands

The conservation of human resources, particularly of the lives and well-being of the workers and their families:

1. By shortening the work-day in keeping with the increased productiveness of machinery.

2. By securing to every worker a rest period of not less than a day and a half in each week.

3. By securing the freedom of political and economic organization and activities.

4. By securing a more effective inspection of workshops, factories and mines.

5. By forbidding the employment of children under eighteen years of age.

6. By forbidding the interstate transportation of the products of child labor and of all uninspected factories and mines.

7. By establishing minimum wage scales.

8. By abolishing official charity and substituting a non-contributory system of old age pensions, a general system of insurance by the state against invalidism, and a system of compulsory insurance by employers of their workers, without cost to the latter, against industrial diseases, accidents and death.

9. By establishing mothers' pensions.

Socialist Labor Platform of 1916

The Socialist Labor Party, in national convention assembled, reaffirming its previous platform declarations, reasserts the right of man to life, liberty, and the pursuit of happiness.

We hold that the purpose of government is to secure to every citizen the enjoyment of this right; but taught by experience we hold furthermore that such right is illusory to the majority of the people, to wit, the working class, under the present system of economic inequality that is essentially destructive of *their* life, *their* liberty, and *their* happiness.

We hold that the true theory of economics is that the means of production must be owned, operated, and controlled by the people in common. Man cannot exercise his right of life, liberty, and the pursuit of happiness without the ownership of the land on, and the tool with which to work. Deprived of these, his life, his liberty, and his fate fall into the hands of that class which owns these essentials for work and production.

We hold that the existing contradiction between social production and capitalist appropriation—the latter resulting from the private ownership of the natural and social opportunities—divides the people into two classes: the Capitalist Class and the Working Class; throws society into the convulsions of the Class Struggle; and perverts government in the interests of the Capitalist Class.

Thus Labor is robbed of the wealth it alone produces, is denied the means of self-employment, and by compulsory idleness in wage-slavery, is even deprived of the necessaries of life.

Against such a system the Socialist Labor Party raises the banner of revolt, and demands the unconditional surrender of the Capitalist Class.

In place of such a system the Socialist Labor Party aims to substitute a system of social ownership of the means of production, industrially administered by the Working Class—the workers to assume control and direction as well as operation of their industrial affairs.

This solution of necessity requires the organization of the Working Class as a class upon revolutionary political and industrial lines.

We therefore call upon the wage workers to organize themselves into a revolutionary political organization under the banner of the Socialist Labor Party; and to organize themselves likewise upon the industrial field into a revolutionary industrial union in keeping with their political aims.

And we also call upon all other intelligent citizens to place themselves squarely upon the ground of Working Class interests, and join us in this mighty and noble work of human emancipation, so that we may put summary end to the existing barbarous class conflict by placing the land and all the means of production, transportation, and distribution into the hands of the people as a collective body, and substituting the Cooperative Commonwealth for the present state of planless production, industrial war, and social disorder—a Commonwealth in which every worker shall have the free exercise and full benefit of his faculties, multiplied by all the factors of modern civilization.

☒ **CAMPAIGN OF 1920**

In 1920, there were the two major parties and three minor parties, namely the Prohibitionists, the Socialists, and the Socialist Labor Party.

In addition a new party appeared which adopted the name Farmer-Labor Party.

Democratic Platform of 1920

The Democratic Party, in its National Convention now assembled, sends greetings to the President of the United States, Woodrow Wilson, and hails with patriotic pride the great achievements for country and the world wrought by a Democratic administration under his leadership.

It salutes the mighty people of this great republic, emerging with imperishable honor from the severe tests and grievous strains of the most tragic war in history, having earned the plaudits and the gratitude of all free nations.

It declares its adherence to the fundamental progressive principles of social, economic and industrial justice and advance, and purposes to resume the great work of translating these principles into effective laws, begun and carried far by the Democratic administration and interrupted only when the war claimed all the national energies for the single task of victory.

League of Nations

The Democratic Party favors the League of Nations as the surest, if not the only, practicable means of maintaining the permanent peace of the world and terminating the insufferable burden of great military and naval establishments. It was for this that America broke away from traditional isolation and spent her blood and treasure to crush a colossal scheme of conquest. It was upon this basis that the President of the United States, in prearrangement with our allies, consented to a suspension of hostilities against the Imperial German Government; the Armistice was granted and a Treaty of Peace negotiated upon the definite assurance to Germany, as well as to the powers pitted against Germany, that "a general association of nations must be formed, under specific covenants, for the purpose of affording mutual guarantees of political independence and territorial integrity to great and small states alike." Hence, we not only congratulate the President on the vision manifested and the vigor exhibited in the prosecution of the war; but we felicitate him and his associates on the exceptional achievement at Paris involved in the adoption of a league and treaty so near akin to previously expressed American ideals and so intimately related to the aspirations of civilized peoples everywhere.

We commend the President for his courage and his high conception of good faith in steadfastly standing for the covenant agreed to by all the associated and allied nations at war with Germany, and we condemn the Republican Senate for its refusal to ratify the treaty merely because it was the product of Democratic statesmanship, thus interposing partisan envy and personal hatred in the way of the peace and renewed prosperity of the world.

By every accepted standard of international morality the President is justified in asserting that the honor of the country is involved in this business; and we point to the accusing fact that, before it was determined to initiate political antagonism to the treaty, the now Republican chairman of the Senate Foreign Relations Committee himself publicly proclaimed that any proposition for a separate peace with Germany, such as he and his party associates thereafter reported to the Senate, would make us "guilty of the blackest crime."

On May 15 last the Knox substitute for the Versailles Treaty was passed by the Republican Senate; and this Convention can contrive no more fitting characterization of its obloquy than that made in the *Forum* magazine of December, 1918, by Henry Cabot Lodge, when he said:

"If we send our armies and young men abroad to be killed and wounded in northern France and Flanders with no result but this, our entrance into war with such an intention was a crime which nothing can justify. The intent of Congress and the intent of the President was that there could be no peace until we could create a situation where no such war as this could recur.

"We cannot make peace except in company with our allies.

"It would brand us with everlasting dishonor and bring ruin to us also if we undertook to make a separate peace."

Thus, to that which Mr. Lodge, in saner moments, considered "the blackest crime" he and his party in madness sought to give the sanctity of law; that which eighteen months ago was of "everlasting dishonor," the Republican Party and its candidates to-day accept as the essence of faith.

We endorse the President's view of our international obligations and his firm stand against reservations designed to cut to pieces the vital provisions of the Versailles Treaty and we commend the Democrats in Congress for voting against resolutions for separate peace which would disgrace the nation.

We advocate the immediate ratification of the treaty without reservations which would impair its essential integrity; but do not oppose the acceptance of any reservations making clearer or more specific the obligations of the United States to the league associates. Only by doing this may we retrieve the reputation of this nation among the powers of the earth and recover the moral leadership which President Wilson won and which Republican politicians at Washington sacrificed. Only by doing this may we hope to aid effectively in the restoration of order throughout the world and to take the place which we should assume in the front rank of spiritual, commercial and industrial advancement.

We reject as utterly vain, if not vicious, the Republican assumption that ratification of the treaty and membership in the League of Nations would in any wise impair the integrity or independence of our country. The fact that the covenant has been entered into by twenty-nine nations, all as jealous of their independence as we of ours, is a sufficient refutation of such a charge. The President repeatedly has declared, and this Convention reaffirms, that all our duties and obligations as a member of the league must be fulfilled in strict conformity with the Constitution of the United States, embodied in which is the fundamental requirement of declaratory action by the Congress before this nation may become a participant in any war.

Senate Rules

We favor such alteration of the rules of procedure of the Senate of the United States as will permit the prompt transaction of the nation's legislative business.

Conduct of the War

During the war President Wilson exhibited the very broadest conception of liberal Americanism. In his conduct of the war, as in the general administration of his high office, there was no semblance of partisan bias. He invited to Washington as his councilors and coadjutors hundreds of the most prominent and pronounced Republicans in the country. To these he committed responsibilities of the gravest import and most confidential nature. Many of them had charge of vital activities of the government.

And yet, with the war successfully prosecuted and gloriously ended, the Republican Party in Congress, far from applauding the masterly leadership of the President and felicitating the country on the amazing achievements of the American government, has meanly requited the considerate course of the chief magistrate by savagely defaming the Commander-in-Chief of the Army and Navy and by assailing nearly every public officer of every branch of the service intimately concerned in winning the war abroad and preserving the security of the government at home.

We express something that the Republican Convention omitted to express—we express to the soldiers and sailors of America the admiration of their fellow countrymen. Guided by the genius of such commanders as General John J. Pershing, the armed forces of America constituted a decisive factor in the victory and brought new lustre to the flag.

We commend the patriotic men and women, who sustained the efforts of their government in the crucial hours of the war, and contributed to the brilliant administrative success, achieved under the broad-visioned leadership of the President.

Financial Achievements

A review of the record of the Democratic Party during the administration of Woodrow Wilson presents a chapter of substantial achievements unsurpassed in the history of the republic. For fifty years before the advent of this administration periodical convulsions had impeded the industrial progress of the American people and caused unestimatable loss and distress. By the enactment of the Federal Reserve Act the old system, which bred panics, was replaced by a new system, which insured confidence. It was an indispensable factor in winning the war, and to-day it is the hope and inspiration of business. Indeed, one vital danger against which the American people should keep constantly on guard, is the commitment of this system to partisan enemies who struggled against its adoption and vainly attempted to retain in the hands of speculative bankers a monopoly of the currency and credits of the nation. Already there are well defined indications of an assault upon the vital principles of the system in the event of Republican success at the elections in November.

Under Democratic leadership the American people successfully financed their stupendous part in the greatest war of all time. The Treasury wisely insisted during the war upon meeting an adequate portion of the war expenditure from current taxes and the bulk of the balance from popular loans, and, during the first full fiscal year after fighting stopped, upon meeting current expenditures from current receipts notwithstanding the new and unnecessary burdens thrown upon the Treasury by the delay, obstruction and extravagance of a Republican Congress.

The non-partisan Federal Reserve authorities have been wholly free of political interference or motive; and, in their own time and their own way, have used courageously, though cautiously, the instruments at their disposal to prevent undue expansion of credit in the country. As a result of these sound Treasury and Federal Reserve policies, the inevitable war inflation has been held down to a minimum, and the cost of living has been prevented from increasing in this country in proportion to the increase in other belligerent countries and in neutral countries which are in close contact with the world's commerce and exchanges.

After a year and a half of fighting in Europe, and despite another year and a half of Republican obstruction at home, the credit of the Government of the United States stands unimpaired, the Federal Reserve note is the unit of value throughout all the world; and the United States is the one great country in the world which maintains a free gold market.

We condemn the attempt of the Republican party to deprive the American people of their legitimate pride in the financing of the war—an achievement without parallel in the financial history of this or any other country, in this or any other war. And in particular we condemn the pernicious attempt of the Republican Party to create discontent among the holders of the bonds of the Government of the United States and to drag our public finance and our banking and currency system back into the arena of party politics.

Tax Revision

We condemn the failure of the present Congress to respond to the oft-repeated demand of the President and the Secretaries of the Treasury to revise the existing tax laws. The continuance in force in peace times of taxes devised under pressure of imperative necessity to produce a revenue for war purposes is indefensible and can only result in lasting injury to the people. The Republican Congress persistently failed, through sheer political cowardice, to make a single move toward a readjustment of tax laws which it denounced before the last election and was afraid to revise before the next election.

We advocate reform and a searching revision of the War Revenue Acts to fit peace conditions so that the wealth of the nation may not be withdrawn from productive enterprise and diverted to wasteful or non-productive expenditure.

We demand prompt action by the next Congress for a complete survey of existing taxes and their modification and simplification with a view to secure greater equity and justice in the tax burden and improvement in administration.

PUBLIC ECONOMY

Claiming to have effected great economies in Government expenditures, the Republican Party cannot show the reduction of one dollar in taxation as a corollary of this false pretense. In contrast, the last Democratic Congress enacted legislation reducing taxes from eight billions, designed to be raised, to six billions for the first year after the Armistice, and to four billions thereafter; and there the total is left undiminished by our political adversaries. Two years after Armistice Day a Republican Congress provides for expending the stupendous sum of $5,403,390,327.30, and wouldn't even lop off the thirty cents.

Affecting great paper economies by reducing departmental estimates of sums which would not have been spent in any event, and by reducing formal appropriations, the Republican statement of expenditures omits the pregnant fact that the Congress authorized the use of one and a half billion dollars in the hands of various departments and bureaus, which otherwise would have been covered back into the Treasury, and which should be added to the Republican total of expenditures.

HIGH COST OF LIVING

The high cost of living and the depreciation of bond values in this country are primarily due to the war itself, to the necessary governmental expenditures for the destructive purposes of war, to private extravagance, to the world shortage of capital, to the inflation of foreign currencies and credits, and, in large degree, to conscienceless profiteering.

The Republican Party is responsible for the failure to restore peace and peace conditions in Europe, which is a principal cause of post-armistice inflation the world over. It has denied the demand of the President for necessary legislation to deal with secondary and local causes. The sound policies pursued by the Treasury and the Federal Reserve system have limited in this country, though they could not prevent, the inflation which was worldwide. Elected upon specific promises to curtail public expenditures and to bring the country back to a status of ef-

fective economy, the Republican Party in Congress wasted time and energy for more than a year in vain and extravagant investigations, costing the tax-payers great sums of money, while revealing nothing beyond the incapacity of Republican politicians to cope with the problems. Demanding that the President, from his place at the Peace Table, call the Congress into extraordinary session for imperative purposes of readjustment, the Congress when convened spent thirteen months in partisan pursuits, failing to repeal a single war statute which harassed business or to initiate a single constructive measure to help business. It busied itself making a pre-election record of pretended thrift, having not one particle of substantial existence in fact. It raged against profiteers and the high cost of living without enacting a single statute to make the former afraid or doing a single act to bring the latter within limitations.

The simple truth is that the high cost of living can only be remedied by increased production, strict governmental economy and a relentless pursuit of those who take advantage of post-war conditions and are demanding and receiving outrageous profits.

We pledge the Democratic Party to a policy of strict economy in government expenditures, and to the enactment and enforcement of such legislation as may be required to bring profiteers before the bar of criminal justice.

THE TARIFF

We reaffirm the traditional policy of the Democratic Party in favor of a tariff for revenue only and confirm the policy of basing tariff revisions upon the intelligent research of a non-partisan commission, rather than upon the demands of selfish interests, temporarily held in abeyance.

BUDGET

In the interest of economy and good administration, we favor the creation of an effective budget system, that will function in accord with the principles of the Constitution. The reform should reach both the executive and legislative aspects of the question. The supervision and preparation of the budget should be vested in the Secretary of the Treasury as the representative of the President. The budget, as such, should not be increased by the Congress except by a two-thirds vote, each House, however, being free to exercise its constitutional privilege of making appropriations through independent bills. The appropriation bills should be considered by single Committees of the House and Senate. The audit system should be consolidated and its powers expanded so as to pass upon the wisdom of, as well as the authority for, expenditures.

A budget bill was passed in the closing days of the second session of the Sixty-sixth Congress which, invalidated by plain constitutional defects and defaced by considerations of patronage, the President was obliged to veto. The House amended the bill to meet the Executive objection. We condemn the Republican Senate for adjourning without passing the amended measure, when by devoting an hour or two more to this urgent public business a budget system could have been provided.

AGRICULTURAL INTERESTS

To the great agricultural interests of the country, the Democratic Party does not find it necessary to make promises. It already is rich in its record of things actually accomplished. For nearly half a century of Republican rule not a sentence was written into the Federal Statutes affording one dollar of bank credits to the farming interests of America. In the first term of this Democratic administration the National Bank Act was so altered as to authorize loans of five years' maturity on improved farm lands. Later was established a system of farm loan banks, from which the borrowings already exceed three hundred millions of dollars; and under which the interest rate to farmers has been so materially reduced as to drive out of business the farm loan sharks who formerly subsisted by extortion upon the great agricultural interests of the country.

Thus it was a Democratic Congress in the administration of a Democratic President which enabled the farmers of America for the first time to obtain credit upon reasonable terms and insured their opportunity for the future development of the nation's agricultural resources. Tied up in Supreme Court proceedings, in a suit by hostile interests, the Federal Farm Loan System, originally opposed by the Republican candidate for the Presidency, appealed in vain to a Republican Congress for adequate financial assistance to tide over the interim between the beginning and the

ending of the current year, awaiting a final decision of the highest court on the validity of the contested act. We pledge prompt consistent support of sound and effective measures to sustain, to amplify and to perfect the rural Credits Statutes and thus to check and reduce the growth and course of farm tenancy.

Not only did the Democratic Party put into effect a great Farm Loan system of land mortgage banks, but it passed the Smith-Lever agricultural extension act, carrying to every farmer in every section of the country, through the medium of trained experts and by demonstration farms, the practical knowledge acquired by the Federal Agricultural Department in all things relating to agriculture, horticulture and animal life; it established the Bureau of Markets, the Bureau of Farm Management, and passed the Cotton Futures Act, the Grain Grades Bill, the Co-operative Farm Administration Act, and the Federal Warehouse Act.

The Democratic Party has vastly improved the rural mail system and has built up the parcel post system to such an extent as to render its activities and its practical service indispensable to the farming community. It was this wise encouragement and this effective concern of the Democratic Party for the farmers of the United States that enabled this great interest to render such essential service in feeding the armies of America and the allied nations of the war and succoring starving populations since Armistice Day.

Meanwhile the Republican leaders at Washington have failed utterly to propose one single measure to make rural life more tolerable. They have signalized their fifteen months of Congressional power by urging schemes which would strip the farms of labor; by assailing the principles of the Farm Loan system and seeking to impair its efficiency; by covertly attempting to destroy the great nitrogen plant at Mussel Shoals upon which the government has expended $70,-000,000 to supply American farmers with fertilizers at reasonable cost; by ruthlessly crippling nearly every branch of agricultural endeavor, literally starving the productive mediums through which the people must be fed.

We favor such legislation as will confirm to the primary producers of the nation the right of collective bargaining, and the right of co-operative handling and marketing of the products of the workshop and the farm and such legislation as will facilitate the exportation of our farm products.

We favor comprehensive studies of farm production costs and the uncensored publication of facts found in such studies.

LABOR AND INDUSTRY

The Democratic Party is now, as ever, the firm friend of honest labor and the promoter of progressive industry. It established the Department of Labor at Washington and a Democratic President called to his official council board the first practical workingman who ever held a cabinet portfolio. Under this administration have been established employment bureaus to bring the man and the job together; have been peaceably determined many bitter disputes between capital and labor; were passed the Child-Labor Act, the Workingman's Compensation Act (the extension of which we advocate so as to include laborers engaged in loading and unloading ships and in interstate commerce), the Eight-Hour Law, the act for Vocational Training, and a code of other wholesome laws affecting the liberties and bettering the conditions of the laboring classes. In the Department of Labor the Democratic administration established a Woman's Bureau, which a Republican Congress destroyed by withholding appropriations.

Labor is not a commodity; it is human. Those who labor have rights, and the national security and safety depend upon a just recognition of those rights and the conservation of the strength of the workers and their families in the interest of sound-hearted and sound-headed men, women and children. Laws regulating hours of labor and conditions under which labor is performed, when passed in recognition of the conditions under which life must be lived to attain the highest development and happiness, are just assertions of the national interest in the welfare of the people.

At the same time, the nation depends upon the products of labor; a cessation of production means loss and, if long continued, means disaster. The whole people, therefore, have a right to insist that justice shall be done to those who work, and in turn that those whose labor creates the necessities upon which the life of the nation depends must recognize the reciprocal obligation between the worker and the state.

They should participate in the formulation of sound laws and regulations governing the conditions under which labor is performed, recognize and obey the laws so formulated, and seek their amendment when necessary by the processes ordinarily addressed to the laws and regulations affecting the other relations of life.

Labor, as well as capital, is entitled to adequate compensation. Each has the indefeasible right of organization, of collective bargaining and of speaking through representatives of their own selection. Neither class, however, should at any time nor in any circumstances take action that will put in jeopardy the public welfare. Resort to strikes and lockouts which endanger the health or lives of the people is an unsatisfactory device for determining disputes, and the Democratic Party pledges itself to contrive, if possible, and put into effective operation a fair and comprehensive method of composing differences of this nature.

In private industrial disputes, we are opposed to compulsory arbitration as a method plausible in theory, but a failure in fact. With respect to government service, we hold distinctly that the rights of the people are paramount to the right to strike. However, we profess scrupulous regard for the conditions of public employment and pledge the Democratic Party to instant inquiry into the pay of government employees and equally speedy regulations designed to bring salaries to a just and proper level.

WOMAN'S SUFFRAGE

We endorse the proposed 19th Amendment of the Constitution of the United States granting equal suffrage to women. We congratulate the legislatures of thirty-five states which have already ratified said amendment and we urge the Democratic Governors and Legislatures of Tennessee, North Carolina and Florida and such states as have not yet ratified the Federal Suffrage Amendment to unite in an effort to complete the process of ratification and secure the thirty-sixth state in time for all the women of the United States to participate in the fall election.

We commend the effective advocacy of the measure by President Wilson.

WELFARE OF WOMEN AND CHILDREN

We urge co-operation with the states for the protection of child life through infancy and maternity care; in the prohibition of child labor and by adequate appropriations for the Children's

Bureau and the Woman's Bureau in the Department of Labor.

EDUCATION

Co-operative Federal assistance to the states is immediately required for the removal of illiteracy, for the increase of teachers' salaries and instruction in citizenship for both native and foreign-born; increased appropriation for vocational training in home economics; re-establishment of joint Federal and state employment service with women's departments under the direction of technically qualified women.

WOMEN IN INDUSTRY

We advocate full representation of women on all commissions dealing with women's work or women's interests and a reclassification of the Federal Civil Service free from discrimination on the ground of sex; a continuance of appropriations for education in sex hygiene; Federal legislation which shall insure that American women resident in the United States, but married to aliens, shall retain their American citizenship, and that the same process of naturalization shall be required for women as for men.

DISABLED SOLDIERS

The Federal government should treat with the utmost consideration every disabled soldier, sailor, and marine of the world war, whether his disability be due to wounds received in line of action or to health impaired in service; and for the dependents of the brave men who died in line of duty the government's tenderest concern and richest bounty should be their requital. The fine patriotism exhibited, the heroic conduct displayed, by American soldiers, sailors and marines at home and abroad, constitute a sacred heritage of posterity, the worth of which can never be recompensed from the Treasury and the glory of which must not be diminished by any such expedients.

The Democratic administration wisely established a War Risk Insurance Bureau, giving four and a half millions of enlisted men insurance at unprecedentedly low rates and through the medium of which compensation of men and women injured in service is readily adjusted, and hospital facilities for those whose health is impaired are abundantly afforded.

The Federal Board for Vocational Education should be made a part of the War Risk Insurance Bureau, in order that the task may be treated as a whole, and this machinery of protection and assistance must receive every aid of law and appropriation necessary to full and effective operation.

We believe that no higher or more valued privilege can be afforded to an American citizen than to become a freeholder in the soil of the United States, and to that end we pledge our party to the enactment of soldier settlements and home aid legislation which will afford to the men who fought for America the opportunity to become land and home owners under conditions affording genuine government assistance unencumbered by needless difficulties of red tape or advance financial investment.

THE RAILROADS

The railroads were subjected to Federal control as a war measure, without other idea than the swift transport of troops, munitions and supplies. When human life and national hopes were at stake profits could not be considered and were not. Federal operation, however, was marked by an intelligence and efficiency that minimized loss and resulted in many and marked reforms. The equipment taken over was not only grossly inadequate but shamefully outworn. Unification practices overcame these initial handicaps and provided additions, betterments and improvements. Economies enabled operation without the rate raises that private control would have found necessary, and labor was treated with an exact justice that secured the enthusiastic co-operation that victory demanded. The fundamental purpose of Federal control was achieved fully and splendidly, and at far less cost to the taxpayer than would have been the case under private operation. Investments in railroad properties were not only saved by government operation, but government management returned these properties vastly improved in every physical and executive detail. A great task was greatly discharged.

The President's recommendation of return to private ownership gave the Republican majority a full year in which to enact the necessary legislation. The House took six months to formulate its ideas, and another six months was consumed by the Republican Senate in equally vague debate. As a consequence, the Esch-Cummins Bill went to the President in the closing hours of Congress, and he was forced to a choice between the chaos of a veto and acquiescence in the measure submitted, however grave may have been his objections to it.

There should be a fair and complete test of the law until careful and mature action by Congress may cure its defects and insure a thoroughly effective transportation system under private ownership without government subsidy at the expense of the taxpayers of the country.

IMPROVED HIGHWAYS

Improved roads are of vital importance not only to commerce and industry but also to agriculture and rural life. The Federal Road Act of 1916, enacted by a Democratic Congress, represented the first systematic effort of the government to insure the building of an adequate system of roads in this country. The act, as amended, has resulted in placing the movement for improved highways on a progressive and substantial basis in every State in the Union and in bringing under actual construction more than 13,000 miles of roads suited to the traffic needs of the communities in which they are located.

We favor a continuance of the present Federal aid plan under existing Federal and State agencies, amended so as to include as one of the elements in determining the ratio in which the several states shall be entitled to share in the fund, the area of any public lands therein.

Inasmuch as the postal service has been extended by the Democratic Party to the door of practically every producer and every consumer in the country (rural free delivery alone having been provided for 6,000,000 additional patrons within the past eight years without materially added cost), we declare that this instrumentality can and will be used to the maximum of its capacity to improve the efficiency of distribution and reduce the cost of living to consumers while increasing the profitable operations of producers.

We strongly favor the increased use of the motor vehicle in the transportation of the mails and urge the removal of the restrictions imposed by the Republican Congress on the use of motor devices in mail transportation in rural territories.

THE POSTAL SERVICE

The efficiency of the Post Office Department has been vindicated against a malicious and designing assault, by the efficiency of its operation. Its record refutes its assailants. Their voices are silenced and their charges have collapsed.

We recommend the work of the Joint Commission on the reclassification of salaries of postal employes, recently concluded, which commission was created by a Democratic administration. The Democratic Party has always favored and will continue to favor the fair and just treatment of all government employes.

FREE SPEECH AND PRESS

We resent the unfounded reproaches directed against the Democratic administration for alleged interference with the freedom of the press and freedom of speech.

No utterance from any quarter has been assailed, and no publication has been repressed, which has not been animated by treasonable purposes, and directed against the nation's peace, order and security in time of war.

We reaffirm our respect for the great principles of free speech and a free press, but assert as an indisputable proposition that they afford no toleration of enemy propaganda or the advocacy of the overthrow of the government of the state or nation by force or violence.

INLAND WATERWAYS

We call attention to the failure of the Republican National Convention to recognize in any way the rapid development of barge transportation on our inland waterways, which development is the result of the constructive policies of the Democratic administration. And we pledge ourselves to the further development of adequate transportation facilities on our rivers and to the further improvement of our inland waterways, and we recognize the importance of connecting the Great Lakes with the sea by way of the Mississippi River and its tributaries, as well as by the St. Lawrence River. We favor an enterprising Foreign Trade policy with all nations, and in this connection we favor the full utilization of all Atlantic, Pacific, and Gulf ports, and an equitable distribution of shipping facilities between the various ports.

Transportation remains an increasingly vital problem in the continued development and prosperity of the nation.

Our present facilities for distribution by rail are inadequate and the promotion of transportation by water is imperative.

We therefore favor a liberal and comprehensive

policy for the development and utilization of our harbors and interior waterways.

Merchant Marine

We desire to congratulate the American people upon the rebirth of our Merchant Marine which once more maintains its former place in the world. It was under a Democratic administration that this was accomplished after seventy years of indifference and neglect, thirteen million tons having been constructed since the act was passed in 1916. We pledge the policy of our party to the continued growth of our Merchant Marine under proper legislation so that American products will be carried to all ports of the world by vessels built in American yards, flying the American flag.

Reclamation of Arid Lands

By wise legislation and progressive administration, we have transformed the government reclamation projects, representing an investment of $100,000,000, from a condition of impending failure and loss of confidence in the ability of the government to carry through such large enterprises, to a condition of demonstrated success, whereby formerly arid and wholly unproductive lands now sustain 40,000 prosperous families and have an annual crop production of over $70,000,-000, not including the crops grown on a million acres outside the projects supplied with storage water from government works.

We favor ample appropriations for the continuation and extension of this great work of home-building and internal improvement along the same general lines, to the end that all practical projects shall be built, and waters now running to waste shall be made to provide homes and add to the food supply, power resources, and taxable property, with the government ultimately reimbursed for the entire outlay.

Flood Control

We commend the Democratic Congress for the redemption of the pledge contained in our last platform by the passage of the Flood Control Act of March 1st, 1917, and point to the successful control of the floods of the Mississippi River and the Sacramento River, California, under the policy of that law, for its complete justification. We favor the extension of this policy to other flood control problems wherever the Federal interest involved justified the expenditure required.

The Trade Commission

The Democratic Party heartily endorses the creation and work of the Federal Trade Commission in establishing a fair field for competitive business, free from restraints of trade and monopoly and recommends amplification of the statutes governing its activities so as to grant it authority to prevent the unfair use of patents in restraint of trade.

Live Stock Markets

For the purpose of insuring just and fair treatment in the great interstate live stock market, and thus instilling confidence in growers through which production will be stimulated and the price of meats to consumers be ultimately reduced, we favor the enactment of legislation for the supervision of such markets by the national government.

Port Facilities

The urgent demands of the war for adequate transportation of war material as well as for domestic need, revealed the fact that our port facilities and rate adjustments were such as to seriously affect the whole country in times of peace as well as war.

We pledge our party to stand for equality of rates, both import and export, for the ports of the country, to the end that there may be adequate and fair facilities and rates for the mobilization of the products of the country offered for shipment.

Petroleum

The Democratic Party recognizes the importance of the acquisition by Americans of additional sources of supply of petroleum and other minerals and declares that such acquisition both at home and abroad should be fostered and encouraged. We urge such action, legislative and executive, as may secure to American citizens the same rights in the acquirement of mining rights in foreign countries as are enjoyed by the citizens or subjects of any other nation.

Mexico

The United States is the neighbor and friend

of the nations of the three Americas. In a very special sense, our international relations in this hemisphere should be characterized by good will and free from any possible suspicion as to our national purpose.

The administration, remembering always that Mexico is an independent nation and that permanent stability in her government and her institutions could come only from the consent of her own people to a government of their own making, has been unwilling either to profit by the misfortunes of the people of Mexico or to enfeeble their future by imposing from the outside a rule upon their temporarily distracted councils. (a) As a consequence, order is gradually reappearing in Mexico; at no time in many years have American lives and interests been so safe as they are now; peace reigns along the border and industry is resuming.

When the new government of Mexico shall have given ample proof of its ability permanently to maintain law and order, signified its willingness to meet its international obligations and written upon its statute books just laws under which foreign investors shall have rights as well as duties, that government should receive our recognition and sympathetic assistance. Until these proper expectations have been met, Mexico must realize the propriety of a policy that asserts the right of the United States to demand full protection for its citizens.

Ireland

The great principle of national self-determination has received constant reiteration as one of the chief objectives for which this country entered the war and victory established this principle.

Within the limitations of international comity and usage, this Convention repeats the several previous expressions of the sympathy of the Democratic Party of the United States for the aspirations of Ireland for self-government.

Armenia

We express our deep and earnest sympathy for the unfortunate people of Armenia, and we believe that our government, consistent with its Constitution and principles, should render every possible and proper aid to them in their efforts to establish and maintain a government of their own.

Porto Rico

We favor granting to the people of Porto Rico the traditional territorial form of government, with a view to ultimate statehood, accorded to all territories of the United States since the beginning of our government, and we believe that the officials appointed to administer the government of such territories should be qualified by previous *bona-fide* residence therein.

Alaska

We commend the Democratic administration for inaugurating a new policy as to Alaska, as evidenced by the construction of the Alaska railroad and opening of the coal and oil fields.

We declare for the modification of the existing coal land law, to promote development without disturbing the features intended to prevent monopoly.

For such changes in the policy of forestry control as will permit the immediate initiation of the paper pulp industry.

For relieving the territory from the evils of long-distance government by arbitrary and interlocking bureaucratic regulation, and to that end we urge the speedy passage of a law containing the essential features of the Land-Curry Bill now pending, co-ordinating and consolidating all Federal control of natural resources under one department to be administered by a non-partisan board permanently resident in the territory.

For the fullest measure of territorial self-government with the view of ultimate statehood, with jurisdiction over all matters not of purely Federal concern, including fisheries and game, and for an intelligent administration of Federal control we believe that all officials appointed should be qualified by previous *bona-fide* residence in the territory.

For a comprehensive system of road construction with increased appropriations and the full extension of the Federal Road Aid Act to Alaska.

For the extension to Alaska of the Federal Farm Loan Act.

The Philippines

We favor the granting of independence without unnecessary delay to the 10,500,000 inhabitants of the Philippine Islands.

Hawaii

We favor a liberal policy of homesteading public lands in Hawaii to promote a larger middle-class citizen population, with equal rights to all citizens.

The importance of Hawaii as an outpost on the western frontier of the United States, demands adequate appropriations by Congress for the development of our harbors and highways there.

New Nations

The Democratic Party expresses its active sympathy with the people of China, Czecho-Slovakia, Finland, Poland, Persia, Jugo-Slavia and others who have recently established representative governments and who are striving to develop the institutions of true Democracy.

Asiatic Immigrants

The policy of the United States with reference to the non-admission of Asiatic immigrants is a true expression of the judgment of our people, and to the several states, whose geographical situation or internal conditions make this policy, and the enforcement of the laws enacted pursuant thereto, of particular concern, we pledge our support.

Republican Corruption

The shocking disclosure of the lavish use of money by aspirants for the Republican nomination for the highest office in the gift of the people, has created a painful impression throughout the country. Viewed in connection with the recent conviction of a Republican Senator from the State of Michigan for the criminal transgression of the law limiting expenditures on behalf of a candidate for the United States Senate, it indicates the re-entry, under Republican auspices, of money as an influential factor in elections, thus nullifying the letter and flaunting the spirit of numerous laws, enacted by the people, to protect the ballot from the contamination of corrupt practices. We deplore these delinquencies and invoke their stern popular rebuke, pledging our earnest efforts to a strengthening of the present statutes against corrupt practices, and their rigorous enforcement.

We remind the people that it was only by the return of a Republican Senator in Michigan, who is now under conviction and sentence for the criminal misuse of money in his election, that the present organization of the Senate with a Republican majority was made possible.

Conclusion

Believing that we have kept the Democratic faith, and resting our claims to the confidence of the people not upon grandiose promises, but upon the solid performances of our party, we submit our record to the nation's consideration and ask that the pledges of this platform be appraised in the light of that record.

Farmer-Labor Platform of 1920

Preamble

The American Declaration of Independence, adopted July 4, 1776, states that governments are instituted to secure to the people the rights of life, liberty and pursuit of happiness and that governments derive their just powers from the consent of the governed.

Democracy cannot exist unless all power is preserved to the people. The only excuse for the existence of government is to serve, not to rule, the people.

In the United States of America, the power of government, the priceless and inalienable heritage of the people, has been stolen from the people—has been seized by a few men who control the wealth of the nation and by the tools of these men, maintained by them in public office to do their bidding.

The administrative offices of the government and congress are controlled by the financial barons —even the courts have been prostituted—and the people as a result of this usurpation have been reduced to economic and industrial servitude.

Under the prevailing order in the United States, wealth is monopolized by a few and the people are kept in poverty, while costs of living mount until the burden of providing the necessaries of life is well-nigh intolerable.

Having thus robbed the people first of their power and then of their wealth, the wielders of financial power, seeking new fields of exploitation, have committed the government of the United States, against the will of the people, to imperialistic policies and seek to extend these enterprises to such lengths that our nation to-day stands in danger of becoming an empire instead of a republic.

Just emerging from a war which we said we fought to extend democracy to the ends of the earth, we find ourselves helpless while the masters of our government, who are also the masters of industry and commerce, league themselves with the masters of other nations to prevent self-determination by helpless people and to exploit and rob them, notwithstanding that we committed ourselves to guaranty of self-government for all such peoples.

Following the greedy spectacle of the peace conference, the money-masters feared an awakening of the people which threatened to exact for mankind those benefits for which the war was said to have been fought. Thereupon these masters, in the United States, through their puppets in public office, in an effort to stifle free discussion, stripped from the inhabitants of this land, rights and liberties guaranteed under American doctrines on which this country was founded and guaranteed also by the federal constitution.

These rights and liberties must be restored to the people.

More than this must be done. All power to govern this nation must be restored to the people. This involved industrial freedom, for political democracy is only an empty phrase without industrial democracy. This can not be done by superficial, palliative measures such as are, from time to time, thrown as sops to the voters by the Republican and Democratic parties. Patchwork cannot repair the destruction of democracy wrought by these two old parties. Reconstruction is necessary.

The invisible government of the United States maintains the two old parties to confuse the voters with false issues. These parties, therefore, can not seriously attempt reconstruction, which, to be effective, must smash to atoms the money power of the proprietors of the two old parties.

Into this breach step the amalgamated groups of forward looking men and women who perform useful work with hand and brain, united in the Farmer-Labor Party of the United States by a spontaneous and irresistible impulse to do righteous battle for democracy against its despoilers, and more especially determined to function together because of the exceptionally brazen defiance shown by the two old parties in the selection of their candidates and the writing of their platforms in this campaign. This party, financed by its rank and file and not by big business, sets about the task of fundamental reconstruction of democracy in the United States, to restore all power to the people and to set up a governmental structure that will prevent seizure, henceforth, of that power by a few unscrupulous men.

The reconstruction proposed is set forth in the following platform of national issues, to which all candidates of the Farmer-Labor Party are pledged:

1. 100 Per Cent Americanism

Restoration of civil liberties and American doctrines and their preservation inviolate, including free speech, free press, free assemblage, right of asylum, equal opportunity, and trial by jury; return of the Department of Justice to the functions for which it was created, to the end that laws may be enforced without favor and without discrimination; amnesty for all persons imprisoned because of their patriotic insistence upon their constitutional guaranties, industrial activities or religious beliefs; repeal of all so-called "espionage," "sedition," and "criminal syndicalist," laws; protection of the right of all workers to strike, and stripping from the courts of powers unlawfully usurped by them and used to defeat the people and foster big business, especially the power to issue anti-labor injunctions and to declare unconstitutional laws passed by Congress.

To Americanize the federal courts, we demand that federal judges be elected for terms not to exceed four years, subject to recall.

As Americanism means democracy, suffrage should be universal. We demand immediate ratification of the nineteenth amendment and full, unrestricted political rights for all citizens, regardless of sex, race, color or creed, and for civil service employes.

Democracy demands also that the people be equipped with the instruments of the initiative, referendum and recall, with the special provision that war may not be declared except in cases of actual military invasion, before referring the question to a direct vote of the people.

2. Abolish Imperialism at Home and Abroad

Withdrawal of the United States from further participation (under the treaty of Versailles) in the reduction of conquered peoples to economic or political subjection to the small groups of men who manipulate the bulk of the world's wealth; refusal to permit our government to aid in the exploitation of the weaker people of the earth by these men; refusal to permit use of the agencies of our government (through dollar diplomacy or other means) by the financial interests of our country to exploit other peoples, including emphatic refusal to go to war with Mexico at the behest of Wall Street; recognition of the elected government of the Republic of Ireland and of the government established by the Russian people; denial of assistance financial, military, or otherwise, for foreign armies invading these countries, and an embargo on the shipment of arms and ammunition to be used against the Russian or Irish people; instant lifting of the blockade against Russia; recognition of every government set up by people who wrest their sovereignty from oppressors, in accordance with the right of self-determination for all peoples; abolition of secret treaties and prompt publication of all diplomatic documents received by the State Department; withdrawal from imperialistic enterprises upon which we already have embarked (including the dictatorship we exercise in varying degrees over the Philippines, Hawaii, Haiti, the Dominican Republic, Porto Rico, Cuba, Samoa and Guam); and prevention of the imposition upon the people of the United States of any form whatever of conscription, military or industrial, or of military training.

We stand committed to a league of free peoples, organized and pledged to destruction of autocracy, militarism and economic imperialism throughout the world and to bring about a world-wide disarmament and open diplomacy, to the end that there shall be no more kings and no more wars.

3. Democratic Control of Industry

The right of labor to an increasing share in the responsibilities and management of industry; application of this principle to be developed in accordance with the experience of actual operation.

4. Public Ownership and Operation

Immediate repeal of the Esch-Cummins Law; public ownership and operation, with democratic operation of the railroads, mines and natural resources, including stock-yards, large abattoirs, grain-elevators, water-power, and coal-storage and terminal warehouses; government ownership and democratic operation of the railroads, mines and of such natural resources as are in whole or in part bases of control by special interests of basic industries and monopolies such as lands containing coal, iron, copper, oil, large water-power and commercial timber tracts; pipe lines and oil tanks; telegraph and telephone lines; and establishment of a public policy that no land (including natural resources) and no patents shall be held out of use for speculation or to aid monopoly; establishment of national and state owned banks where the money of the government must, and that of individuals may, be deposited; granting of credit to individuals or groups according to regulations laid down by Congress which will safe-guard deposits.

We denounce the attempt to scuttle our great government-owned merchant marine and favor bringing ocean-going commerce to our inland ports.

5. Promotion of Agricultural Prosperity

Legislation that will effectively check and reduce the growth and evils of farm tenancy; establishment of public markets; extension of the federal farm loan system, making personal credit readily available and cheap to farmers; maintenance of dependable transportation for farm products; organization of a state and national service that will furnish adequate advice and guidance to applicants for farms and to farmers already on the land; legislation to promote and protect farmers' and consumers' co-operative organizations conducted for mutual benefit; comprehensive studies of costs of production of farm and staple manufactured products and uncensored publication of facts found in such studies.

6. Government Finance

We demand that economy in governmental expenditures shall replace the extravagance that has run riot under the present administration. The governmental expenditures of the present year of peace, as already disclosed, exceed $6,000,000,-000—or six times the annual expenditures of the pre-war period. We condemn and denounce the system that has created one war-millionaire for every three American soldiers killed in the war in France, and we demand that this war-acquired wealth shall be taxed in such a manner as to prevent the shifting of the burden of taxation to the shoulders of the poor in the shape of higher prices and of increased living costs.

We are opposed, therefore, to consumption taxes and to all indirect taxation for support of current operations of the government. For support of such current operations, we favor steeply graduated income taxes, exempting individual incomes amounting to less than $3,000 a year, with a further exemption allowance of $300 for every child under 18 and also for every child over 18 who may be pursuing an education to fit himself for life. In the case of state governments and of local governments we favor taxation of land value, but not of improvements or of equipment, and also sharply graduated taxes on inheritance.

7. REDUCE THE COST OF LIVING

Stabilization of currency so that it may not fluctuate as at present, carrying the standard of living of all the people down with it when it depreciates; federal control of the meat packing industry; extension and perfection of the Parcel Post system to bring producer and consumer closer together; enforcing existing laws against profiteers, especially the big and powerful ones.

8. JUSTICE TO THE SOLDIERS

We favor paying the soldiers of the late war as a matter of right and not as charity, a sufficient sum to make their war-pay not less than civilian earnings. We denounce the delays in payment, and the inadequate compensation to disabled soldiers and sailors and their dependents, and we pledge such changes as will promptly and adequately give sympathetic recognition of their services and sacrifices.

9. LABOR'S BILL OF RIGHTS

During the years that Labor has tried in vain to obtain recognition of the rights of the workers at the hands of the government through the agencies of the Republican and Democrat parties, the principal demands of Labor have been catalogued and presented by the representatives of Labor, who have gone to convention after convention of the old parties—to Congress after Congress of old-party office-holders. Those conventions and sessions of Congress have, from time to time, included in platforms and laws a few fragments of Labor's program, carefully rewritten, however,

to interpose no interference with the oppression of Labor by private wielders of the power of capital. It remains for the Farmer-Labor Party, the people's own party, financed by the people themselves, to pledge itself to the entire Bill of Rights of Labor, the conditions enumerated therein to be written into the laws of the land to be enjoyed by the workers, organized or unorganized, without the amelioration of a single word in the program. Abraham Lincoln said: "Labor is the superior of Capital, and deserves the highest consideration."

We pledge the application of this fundamental principle in the enactment and administration of legislation.

(a) The unqualified right of all workers, including civil service employes, to organize and bargain collectively with employers through such representatives of their unions as they choose.

(b) Freedom from compulsory arbitration and all other attempts to coerce workers.

(c) A maximum standard 8-hour day and 44-hour week.

(d) Old age and unemployment payments and workmen's compensation to insure workers and their dependents against accident and disease.

(e) Establishment and operation, through periods of depression, of governmental work on housing, road-building, reforestation, reclamation of cut-over timber, desert and swamp lands and development of ports, waterways and water-power plants.

(f) Re-education of the cripples of industry as well as the victims of war.

(g) Abolition of employment of children under sixteen years of age.

(h) Complete and effective protection for women in industry, with equal pay for equal work.

(i) Abolition of private employment, detective and strike-breaking agencies and extension of the federal free employment service.

(j) Prevention of exploitation of immigration and immigrants by employers.

(k) Vigorous enforcement of the Seamen's Act, and the most liberal interpretation of its provisions. The present provisions for the protection of seamen and for the safety of the traveling public, must not be minimized.

(l) Exclusion from interstate commerce of the products of convict labor.

(m) A federal department of education to advance democracy and effectiveness in all public school systems throughout the country, to the end that the children of workers in industrial and rural communities may have maximum opportunity of training to become unafraid, well-informed citizens of a free country.

Prohibition Platform of 1920

The Prohibition Party assembled in National Convention in the city of Lincoln, Nebraska, on this twenty-second day of July, 1920, expresses its thanks to Almighty God for the victory over the beverage liquor traffic which crowns fifty years of consecrated effort. The principles which we have advocated throughout our history have been so far recognized that the manufacture and traffic in intoxicating drink have been forever prohibited in the fundamental law of the land; Congress has rightly interpreted the Eighteenth Amendment in laws enacted for its enforcement; and the Supreme Court has upheld both the Amendment and the law.

Asking that it be clothed with governmental power, the Prohibition Party challenges the attention of the Nation and requests the votes of the people on this Declaration of Principles.

NULLIFICATION CONDEMNED

The organized liquor traffic is engaged in a treasonable attempt to nullify the Amendment by such modification of the enforcement act as will increase the alcoholic content in beer and wine and thus thwart the will of the people as constitutionally expressed.

In the face of this open threat the Republican and Democratic parties refused to make platform declarations in favor of law enforcement, though petitioned so to do by multitudes of people. Thus the Prohibition Party remains the sole political champion of National Prohibition.

The Prohibition Party in its platform in 1872 declared. "There can be no greater peril to the nation than the existing party competition for the liquor vote; any party not openly opposed to the traffic, experience shows, will engage in this competition, will court the favor of the criminal classes, will barter away the public morals, the purity of the ballot, and every object of good government for party success." Notwithstanding

the liquor traffic is now outlawed by the Constitution this fitly describes the present political attitude of the old parties.

The issue is not only the ENFORCEMENT but also the MAINTENANCE of the law to make the Amendment effective.

The proposed increase in the alcoholic content of beverages would be fraught with grave danger in that it would mean the return of the open saloon with all its attendant evils.

THE LEAGUE OF NATIONS

The League of Nations is now in existence and is functioning in world affairs. We favor the entrance of the United States into the League by the immediate ratification of the treaty of peace, not objecting to reasonable reservations interpreting American understanding of the covenant. The time is past when the United States can hold aloof from the affairs of the world. Such course is short-sighted and only invites disaster.

PEACE

We stand for a constitutional amendment providing that treaties of peace shall be ratified by a majority of both Houses of Congress.

We stand by our declaration of 1916 against militarism and universal military training. Without it our boys were in a short time trained to whip the greatest army ever assembled and with national prohibition to make sure the most virile manhood in the world we should encourage universal disarmament and devotion to the acts of peace.

EDUCATION

We stand for compulsory education with instruction in the English language, which, if given in private or parochial schools, must be equivalent to that afforded by the public schools, and be under state supervision.

SUFFRAGE

The Prohibition Party has long advocated the enfranchisement of women. Suffrage should not be conditioned upon sex. We congratulate the women upon the freedom which the Party has helped them to achieve.

WOMAN AND THE HOME

We approve and adopt the program of the

National League of Women Voters providing for:

The prohibition of child labor;

Adequate appropriation for the Children's Bureau;

Protection for infant life through a federal program for maternity and infancy care;

A Federal department of education, Federal aid for the removal of illiteracy and the increase of teachers' salaries;

Instruction of the youth and the newcomer to our shores in the duties and ideals of citizenship;

Vocational training in home economics;

Federal supervision of the marketing and distribution of food, the enactment and enforcement of such measures as will open the channels of trade, prevent excess profits, and eliminate unfair competition and control of the necessities of life;

The establishment of a Woman's Bureau in the Department of Labor to determine standards and policies which will improve working conditions for women and increase their efficiency;

The appointment of women in the mediation and conciliation service and on any industrial commissions and tribunals which may be created;

The establishment of a joint Federal and State employment service with women's departments under the direction of qualified women;

The merit system in the Civil Service free from discrimination on account of sex with a wage scale determined by skill demanded for the work and in no wise below the cost of living as established by official investigation;

Appropriation to carry on a campaign against venereal diseases and for public education in sex hygiene;

Federal legislation permitting an American born woman to retain her citizenship while resident in the United States, though married to an alien;

And further, that an alien woman who marries an American citizen must take the obligation of citizenship before she can become a citizen.

Economy in Administration

We believe in the Budget system and we stand for economy in governmental administration. There should be a reduction in boards, committees, commissions and offices which consume taxes and increase expenses.

Labor and Industry

We stand for Industrial Peace. We believe the

time has come for the government to assume responsibility for the protection of the public against the waste and terror of industrial warfare, and to that end we demand legislation defining the rights of labor and the creation of industrial courts, which will guarantee to labor and employing capital equal and exact justice, and to the general public protection against the paralysis of industry due to this warfare.

Profiteering

The prohibition Party pledges the nation to rid it of the profiteer and to close the door against his return. It will endeavor to eliminate all unnecessary middlemen by the encouragement of organizations among producers that will bring those who sell and those who use nearer together. It will enact and enforce laws needful to effectively prevent excessive charges by such middlemen. To this end it will demand legislation subjecting to the penalties of the criminal law all corporate officers and employees who give or carry out instructions that result in extortion; it will make it unlawful for anyone engaged in Interstate Commerce to make the sale of one article dependent upon the purchase of another article and it will require such corporation to disclose to customers the difference between cost price and selling price or limit the profit that can be legally charged as the rate of interest is now limited.

Agriculture

We pledge our aid to the farmer in working out a plan to equalize prices, to secure labor, and to organize a system of co-operative marketing, including public terminals, mills and storage for the purpose of encouraging agriculture and securing for the farmer such return as will tend to increase production.

We favor such extension of the parcel post as will further facilitate the direct traffic between the producer and consumer.

Presidential Qualifications

The qualifications for President stated in the Constitution have to do with age and citizenship. We call attention to the fact that of greater importance are those not so stated referring to moral, intellectual and spiritual endowments. The President of the United States in his daily life, his home and family relationships and in his official career is expected to typify the finest and best the country can produce. He is the leader of the nation. The moral force and power of his example are immeasurable. No man or woman should ever be elected to the high office who is out of harmony with the purposes of the people or who lacks sympathy with their highest and holiest ideals, and with the Christian principles upon which the nation was founded.

Law and Order

A crying evil of the day is the general lax enforcement of law. Without obedience to law and maintenance of order our American institutions must perish.

The Prohibition Party now, as ever, pledges impartial enforcement of all law.

Conclusion

In this national and world crisis the Prohibition Party reminds the people of its long time faithfulness and its wisdom, proved by the many reforms which it was the first to advocate; and on its record as the oldest minority party—one which has never sold its birthright for a mess of pottage but throughout the years has stood for the best interests of the country—it asks the favorable consideration of the voters, believing that by its support they can make it necessary for all political organizations to come up to a higher level and to render a finer quality of service.

It pledges itself resolutely to stand for the right and oppose the wrong and dauntlessly to lead in the advocacy of righteous and patriotic principles. On its record and on this Declaration of Principles it submits its case to the American people.

Republican Platform of 1920

The Republican party, assembled in representative national convention, reaffirms its unyielding devotion to the Constitution of the United States, and to the guaranties of civil, political and religious liberty therein contained. It will resist all attempts to overthrow the foundations of the government or to weaken the force of its controlling principles and ideals, whether these attempts be made in the form of international policy or domestic agitation.

For seven years the national government has been controlled by the Democratic party. During that period a war of unparalleled magnitude has shaken the foundations of civilization, decimated the population of Europe, and left in its train economic misery and suffering second only to the war itself.

The outstanding features of the Democratic administration have been complete unpreparedness for war and complete unpreparedness for peace.

Unpreparedness for War

Inexcusable failure to make timely preparations is the chief indictment against the Democratic administration in the conduct of the war. Had not our associates protected us, both on land and sea, during the first twelve months of our participation and furnished us to the very day of the armistice with munitions, planes, and artillery, this failure would have been punished with disaster. It directly resulted in unnecessary losses to our gallant troops, in the imperilment of victory itself, and in an enormous waste of public funds, literally poured into the breach created by gross neglect. To-day it is reflected in our huge tax burdens and in the high cost of living.

Unpreparedness for Peace

Peace found the administration as unprepared for peace as war found it unprepared for war. The vital need of the country demanded the early and systematic return of a peace time basis.

This called for vision, leadership, and intelligent planning. All three have been lacking. While the country has been left to shift for itself, the government has continued on a wartime basis. The administration has not demobilized the army of place holders. It continued a method of financing which was indefensible during the period of reconstruction. It has used legislation passed to meet the emergency of war to continue its arbitrary and inquisitorial control over the life of the people in the time of peace, and to carry confusion into industrial life. Under the despot's plea of necessity or superior wisdom, executive usurpation of legislative and judicial function still undermines our institutions. Eighteen months after the armistice, with its wartime powers unabridged, its wartime departments undischarged, its wartime army of place holders still mobilized, the administration still continues to flounder helplessly.

The demonstrated incapacity of the Democratic party has destroyed public confidence, weakened the authority of the government, and produced a feeling of distrust and hesitation so universal as to increase enormously the difficulty of readjustment and to delay the return to normal conditions.

Never has our nation been confronted with graver problems. The people are entitled to know in definite terms how the parties purpose solving these problems. To that end, the Republican party declares its policy and programme to be as follows:

Constitutional Government

We undertake to end executive autocracy and restore to the people their constitutional government.

The policies herein declared will be carried out by the Federal and State governments, each acting within its constitutional powers.

Foreign Relations

The foreign policy of the Administration has been founded upon no principle and directed by no definite conception of our nation's rights and obligations. It has been humiliating to America and irritating to other nations, with the result that after a period of unexampled sacrifice, our motives are suspected, our moral influence impaired, and our Government stands discredited and friendless among the nations of the world.

We favor a liberal and generous foreign policy founded upon definite moral and political principle, characterized by a clear understanding of and a firm adherence to our own rights, and unfailing respect for the rights of others. We should afford full and adequate protection to the life, liberty, property and all international rights of every American citizen, and should require a proper respect for the American flag; but we should be equally careful to manifest a just regard for the rights of other nations. A scrupulous observance of our international engagements when lawfully assumed is essential to our own honor and self-respect, and the respect of other nations. Subject to a due regard for our international obligations, we should leave our country free to develop its civilization along lines most conducive to the happiness and welfare of its people, and to cast its influence on the side of justice and right should occasion require.

(a) Mexico

The ineffective policy of the present Administration in Mexican matters has been largely responsible for the continued loss of American lives in that country and upon our border; for the enormous loss of American and foreign property; for the lowering of American standards of morality and social relations with Mexicans, and for the bringing of American ideals of justice, national honor and political integrity into contempt and ridicule in Mexico and throughout the world.

The policy of wordy, futile written protests against the acts of Mexican officials, explained the following day by the President himself as being meaningless and not intended to be considered seriously, or enforced, has but added in degree to that contempt, and has earned for us the sneers and jeers of Mexican bandits, and added insult upon insult against our national honor and dignity.

We should not recognize any Mexican government, unless it be a responsible government willing and able to give sufficient guarantees that the lives and property of American citizens are respected and protected; that wrongs will be promptly corrected and just compensation will be made for injury sustained. The Republican party pledges itself to a consistent, firm and effective policy towards Mexico that shall enforce respect for the American flag and that shall protect the rights of American citizens lawfully in Mexico to security of life and enjoyment of property, in accordance with established principles of international law and our treaty rights.

The Republican party is a sincere friend of the Mexican people. In its insistence upon the maintenance of order for the protection of American citizens within its borders a great service will be rendered the Mexican people themselves; for a continuation of present conditions means disaster to their interests and patriotic aspirations.

(b) Mandate for Armenia

We condemn President Wilson for asking Congress to empower him to accept a mandate for Armenia. We commend the Republican Senate for refusing the President's request to empower him to accept the mandate for Armenia. The acceptance of such mandate would throw the United States into the very maelstrom of European quarrels. According to the estimate of the Harbord Commission, organized by authority of President Wilson, we would be called upon to send 59,000 American boys to police Armenia and to expend $276,000,000 in the first year and $756,000,000 in five years. This estimate is made upon the basis that we would have only roving bands to fight; but in case of serious trouble with the Turks or with Russia, a force exceeding 200,000 would be necessary.

No more striking illustration can be found of President Wilson's disregard of the lives of American boys or of American interests.

We deeply sympathize with the people of Armenia and stand ready to help them in all proper ways, but the Republican party will oppose now and hereafter the acceptance of a mandate for any country in Europe or Asia.

(c) League of Nations

The Republican party stands for agreement among the nations to preserve the peace of the world. We believe that such an international association must be based upon international justice, and must provide methods which shall maintain the rule of public right by the development of law and the decision of impartial courts, and which shall secure instant and general international conference whenever peace shall be threatened by political action, so that the nations pledged to do and insist upon what is just and fair may exercise their influence and power for the prevention of war.

We believe that all this can be done without the compromise of national independence, without depriving the people of the United States in advance of the right to determine for themselves what is just and fair when the occasion arises, and without involving them as participants and not as peacemakers in a multitude of quarrels, the merits of which they are unable to judge.

The covenant signed by the President at Paris failed signally to accomplish this great purpose, and contains stipulations, not only intolerable for an independent people, but certain to produce the injustice, hostility and controversy among nations which it proposed to prevent.

That covenant repudiated, to a degree wholly unnecessary and unjustifiable, the time-honored policies in favor of peace declared by Washington, Jefferson, and Monroe, and pursued by all American administrations for more than a century, and it ignored the universal sentiment of America for generations past in favor of international law and arbitration, and it rested the hope of the future upon mere expediency and negotiation.

The unfortunate insistence of the President upon having his own way, without any change and without any regard to the opinions of a majority of the Senate, which shares with him in the treaty-making power, and the President's demand that the Treaty should be ratified without any modification, created a situation in which Senators were required to vote upon their consciences and their oaths according to their judgment against the Treaty as it was presented, or submit to the commands of a dictator in a matter where the authority and the responsibility under the Constitution were theirs, and not his.

The Senators performed their duty faithfully. We approve their conduct and honor their courage and fidelity. And we pledge the coming Republican administration to such agreements with the other nations of the world as shall meet the full duty of America to civilization and humanity, in accordance with American ideals, and without surrendering the right of the American people to exercise its judgment and its power in favor of justice and peace.

Congress and Reconstruction

Despite the unconstitutional and dictatorial course of the President and the partisan obstruction of the Democratic congressional minority, the Republican majority has enacted a program of constructive legislation which in great part, however, has been nullified by the vindictive vetoes of the President.

The Republican Congress has met the problems presented by the administration's unpreparedness for peace. It has repealed the greater part of the vexatious war legislation. It has enacted a transportation act making possible the rehabilitation of the railroad systems of the country, the operation of which, under the present Democratic administration, has been wasteful, extravagant, and inefficient in the highest degree. The transportation act made provision for the peaceful settlement of wage disputes, partially nullified, however, by the President's delay in appointing the wage board created by the Act. This delay precipitated the outlaw railroad strike.

We stopped the flood of public treasure, recklessly poured into the lap of an inept shipping board, and laid the foundations for the creation of a great merchant marine; we took from the incompetent Democratic administration the administration of the telegraph and telephone lines of the country and returned them to private ownership; we reduced the cost of postage and increased the pay of the postal employes—the poorest paid of all public servants; we provided pensions for superannuated and retired civil servants; and for an increase in pay of soldiers and sailors we reorganized the Army on a peace footing and provided for the maintenance of a powerful and efficient navy.

The Republican Congress established by law a permanent woman's bureau in the Department of Labor; we submitted to the country the constitutional amendment for woman suffrage, and furnished twenty-nine of the thirty-five legislatures which have ratified it to date.

Legislation for the relief of the consumers of print paper, for the extension of the powers of the government under the Food Control Act, for broadening the scope of the War Risk Insurance Act, better provision for the dwindling number of aged veterans of the Civil War and for the better support of the maimed and injured of the great war, and for making practical the vocational rehabilitation act, has been enacted by the Republican Congress.

We passed an oil leasing and water power bill to unlock for the public good the great pent-up resources of the country; we have sought to check the profligacy of the administration, to realize upon the assets of the government and to husband the revenues derived from taxation. The Republicans in Congress have been responsible for cuts in the estimates for government expenditure of nearly $3,000,000,000 since the signing of the armistice.

We enacted a national executive budget law; we strengthened the Federal Reserve Act to permit banks to lend needed assistance to farmers; we authorized financial incorporations to develop export trade; and finally, amended the rules of the Senate and House, which will reform evils in procedure and guarantee more efficient and responsible government.

AGRICULTURE

The farmer is the backbone of the nation. National greatness and economic independence demand a population distributed between industry and the farm, and sharing on equal terms the prosperity which it holds is wholly dependent upon the efforts of both. Neither can prosper at the expense of the other without inviting joint disaster.

The crux of the present agricultural condition lies in prices, labor and credit.

The Republican party believes that this condition can be improved by: practical and adequate farm representation in the appointment of governmental officials and commissions; the right to form co-operative associations for marketing their products, and protection against discrimination; the scientific study of agricultural prices and farm production costs, at home and abroad, with a view to reducing the frequency of abnormal fluctuation; the uncensored publication of such reports; the authorization of associations for the extension of personal credit; a national inquiry on the co-ordination of rail, water and motor transportation with adequate facilities for receiving, handling and marketing food; the encouragement of our export trade; and end to unnecessary price-fixing and ill-considered efforts arbitrarily to reduce prices of farm products which invariably result to the disadvantage both of producer and consumer; and the encouragement of the production and importation of fertilizing material and of its extensive use.

The Federal Farm Loan Acts should be so administered as to facilitate the acquisition of farm land by those desiring to become owners and proprietors and thus minimize the evils of farm tenantry, and to furnish such long time credits as farmers may need to finance adequately their larger and long time production operations.

INDUSTRIAL RELATIONS

There are two different conceptions of the relations of capital and labor. The one is contractual and emphasizes the diversity of interest of employer and employé. The other is that of co-partnership in a common task.

We recognize the justice of collective bargaining as a means of promoting good will, establishing closer and more harmonious relations between employers and employés and realizing the true ends of industrial justice.

The strike or the lockout, as a means of settling industrial disputes, inflicts such loss and suffering on the community as to justify government initiative to reduce its frequency and limit its consequences. We denied the right to strike against the government; but the rights and interests of all government employés must be safeguarded by impartial laws and tribunals.

In public utilities we favor the establishment of an impartial tribunal to make an investigation of the facts and to render decision to the end that there may be no organized interruption of service necessary to the lives and health and welfare of the people. The decisions of the tribunal to be morally but not legally binding, and an informed public sentiment be relied on to secure their acceptance. The tribunals, however, should refuse to accept jurisdiction except for the purpose of investigation as long as the public service be interrupted. For public utilities we favor the type of tribunal provided for in the Transportation Act of 1920.

In private industries we do not advocate the principle of compulsory arbitration, but we favor impartial commissions and better facilities for voluntary mediation, conciliation and arbitration supplemented by the full publicity which will enlist the influence of an aroused public opinion. The government should take the initiative in inviting the establishment of tribunals or commissions for the purpose of voluntary arbitration and of investigation of disputed issues.

We demand the exclusion from interstate commerce of the products of convict labor.

NATIONAL ECONOMY

A Republican Congress reduced the estimates submitted by the Administration almost three billion dollars. Greater economies could have been effected had it not been for the stubborn refusal of the Administration to co-operate with Congress in an economy program. The universal demand for an executive budget is a recognition of the incontrovertible fact that leadership and sincere assistance on the part of the executive departments are essential to effective economy and constructive retrenchment.

The Overman Act invested the President of the United States with all the authority and power necessary to restore the Federal Government to a normal peace basis and to reorganize, retrench and demobilize. The dominant fact is that eight-een months after the armistice, the United States Government is still on a war time basis, and the expenditure program of the Executive reflects war time extravagance rather than rigid peace time economy.

As an example of the failure to retrench which has characterized the post war time administration we cite the fact that not including the war and navy departments, the executive departments and other establishments at Washington actually record an increase subsequent to the armistice of 2,184 employés. The net decrease in pay roll costs contained in the 1921 demands submitted by the Administration is only one per cent below that of 1920. The annual expenses of Federal operations can be reduced hundreds of millions of dollars without impairing the efficiency of the public service.

We pledge ourselves to a carefully planned readjustment on a peace time basis and to a policy of rigid economy, to the better co-ordination of departmental activities, to the elimination of unnecessary officials and employés, and to the raising of the standard of individual efficiency.

THE EXECUTIVE BUDGET

We congratulate the Republican Congress on the enactment of a law providing for the establishment of an Executive Budget as a necessary instrument for a sound and business-like administration of the national finances; and we condemn the veto of the President which defeated this great financial reform.

REORGANIZATION OF FEDERAL DEPARTMENTS AND BUREAUS

We advocate a thorough investigation of the present organization of the Federal departments and bureaus, with a view to securing consolidation, a more business-like distribution of functions, the elimination of duplication, delays and overlapping of work and the establishment of an up-to-date and efficient administrative organization.

WAR POWERS OF THE PRESIDENT

The President clings tenaciously to his autocratic war time powers. His veto of the resolution declaring peace and his refusal to sign the bill repealing war time legislation, no longer necessary, evidenced his determination not to restore to the Nation and to the State the form of government provided for by the Constitution. This usurpation is intolerable and deserves the severest condemnation.

Taxation

The burden of taxation imposed upon the American people is staggering; but in presenting a true statement of the situation we must face the fact that, while the character of the taxes can and should be changed, an early reduction of the amount of revenue to be raised is not to be expected. The next Republican Administration will inherit from its Democratic predecessor a floating indebtedness of over three billion dollars—the prompt liquidation of which is demanded by sound financial consideration. Moreover, the whole fiscal policy of the Government must be deeply influenced by the necessity of meeting obligations in excess of five billion dollars which mature in 1923. But sound policy equally demands the early accomplishment of that real reduction of the tax burden which may be achieved by substituting simple for complex tax laws and procedure, prompt and certain determination of the tax liability for delay and uncertainty, tax laws which do not, for tax laws which do, excessively mulct the consumer or needlessly repress enterprise and thrift.

We advocate the issuance of a simplified form of income return; authorizing the Treasury Department to make changes in regulations effective only from the date of their approval empowering the Commissioner of Internal Revenue, with the consent of the taxpayers, to make final and conclusive settlements of tax claims and assessments barring fraud, the creation of a Tax Board consisting of at least three representatives of the taxpaying public and the heads of the principal divisions of the Bureau of Internal Revenue to act as a standing committee on the simplification of forms, procedure and law and to make recommendations to the Congress.

Banking and Currency

The fact is that the war to a great extent, was financed by a policy of inflation, through certificate borrowings from the banks, and bonds issued at artificial rates sustained by the low discount rates established by the Federal Reserve Board. The continuance of this policy since the armistice lays the administration open to severe criticism. Almost up to the present time the practices of the Federal Reserve Board as to credit control have been frankly dominated by the convenience of the Treasury.

The results have been a greatly increased war cost, a serious loss to the millions of people who, in good faith, bought liberty bonds and victory notes at par, and extensive post war speculation followed to-day by a restricted credit for legitimate industrial expansion and as a matter of public policy, we urge all banks to give credit preference to essential industry.

The Federal Reserve System should be free from political influence, which is quite as important as its independence of domination by financial combinations.

The High Cost of Living

The prime cause of the "High Cost of Living" has been first and foremost, a fifty per cent depreciation in the purchasing power of the dollar, due to a gross expansion of our currency and credit. Reduced production, burdensome taxation, swollen profits, and the increased demand for goods arising from a fictitious but enlarged buying power, have been contributing forces in a greater or less degree. We condemn the unsound fiscal policies of the Democratic Administration which have brought these things to pass, and their attempts to impute the consequences to minor and secondary causes. Much of the injury wrought is irreparable. There is no short way out, and we decline to deceive the people with vain promises or quack remedies. But as the political party that throughout its history has stood for honest money and sound finance, we pledge ourselves to earnest and consistent attack upon the high cost of living, by rigorous avoidance of further inflation in war government borrowing, by courageous and intelligent deflation of over-expanded credit and currency, by encouragement of heightened production of goods and services, by prevention of unreasonable profits, by exercise of public economy and stimulation of private thrift and by revision of war imposed taxes unsuited to peace time economy.

Profiteering

We condemn the Democratic Administration for failure impartially to enforce the Anti-Profiteering Laws enacted by the Republican Congress.

RAILROADS

We are opposed to government ownership and operation or employé operation of the Railroads. In view of the conditions prevailing in this country, the experience of the last two years, and the conclusion which may fairly be drawn from an observation of the transportation systems of other countries it is clear that adequate transportation service both for the present and future can be furnished more certainly, economically and efficiently through private ownership and operation under proper regulation and control.

There should be no speculative profit in rendering the service of transportation; but in order to do justice to the capital already invested in railway enterprise, to restore railway credit, to induce future investment at a reasonable rate, and to furnish a large facility to meet the requirements of the constantly increasing development and distribution a fair return upon actual value of the railway property used in transportation should be made reasonably sure, and at the same time to provide constant employment to those engaged in transportation service, with fair hours and favorable working conditions, at wages or compensation at least equal to those prevailing in similar lines of industry.

We endorse the transportation act of 1920 enacted by the Republican Congress as a most constructive legislative achievement.

WATERWAYS

We declare it to be our policy to encourage and develop water transportation service and facilities in connection with the commerce of the United States.

REGULATION OF INDUSTRY AND COMMERCE

We approve in general the existing Federal Legislation against monopoly and combinations in restraint of trade, but since the known certainty of a law is the safety of all, we advocate such amendment as will provide American business men with better means of determining in advance whether a proposed combination is or is not unlawful. The Federal Trade Commission, under a Democratic Administration, has not accomplished the purpose for which it was created. This commission properly organized and its duties efficiently administered should afford protection to the public and legitimate business interests. There should be no persecution of honest business; but to the extent that circumstances warrant we pledge ourselves to strengthen the law against unfair practices.

We pledge the party to an immediate resumption of trade relations with every nation with which we are at peace.

INTERNATIONAL TRADE AND TARIFF

The uncertain and unsettled condition of international balances, the abnormal economic and trade situation of the world, and the impossibility of forecasting accurately even the near future, preclude the formulation of a definite program to meet conditions a year hence. But the Republican party reaffirms its belief in the protective principles and pledges itself to a revision of the tariff as soon as conditions shall make it necessary for the preservation of the home market for American labor, agriculture and industry.

MERCHANT MARINE

The National defense and our foreign commerce require a merchant marine of the best type of modern ship, flying the American flag, and manned by American seamen, owned by private capital, and operated by private energy. We endorse the sound legislation recently enacted by the Republican Congress that will insure the promotion and maintenance of the American Merchant Marine.

We favor the application of the workmen's compensation act to the Merchant Marine.

We recommend that all ships engaged in coastwise trade and all vessels of the American Merchant Marine shall pass through the Panama Canal without payment of tolls.

IMMIGRATION

The standard of living and the standard of citizenship of a nation are its most precious possessions, and the preservation and the elevation of those standards is the first duty of our government. The immigration policy of the U. S. should be such as to insure that the number of foreigners in the country at any one time shall not exceed that which can be assimilated with reasonable rapidity, and to favor immigrants whose standards are similar to ours.

The selective tests that are at present applied should be improved by requiring a higher physical standard, a more complete exclusion of mental defectives and of criminals, and a more effective inspection applied as near the source of immigration as possible, as well as at the port of entry. Justice to the foreigner and to ourselves demands provision for the guidance, protection and better economic distribution of our alien population. To facilitate government supervision, all aliens should be required to register annually until they become naturalized.

The existing policy of the United States for the practical exclusion of Asiatic immigrants is sound, and should be maintained.

NATURALIZATION

There is urgent need of improvement in our naturalization law. No alien should become a citizen until he has become genuinely American, and adequate tests for determining the alien's fitness for American citizenship should be provided for by law.

We advocate, in addition, the independent naturalization of married women. An American woman, resident in the United States, should not lose her citizenship by marriage to an alien.

FREE SPEECH AND ALIEN AGITATION

We demand that every American citizen shall enjoy the ancient and constitutional right of free speech, free press and free assembly and the no less sacred right of the qualified voted [sic] to be represented by his duly chosen representatives; but no man may advocate resistance to the law, and no man may advocate violent overthrow of the government.

Aliens within the jurisdiction of the United States are not entitled of right to liberty of agitation directed against the government of American institutions.

Every government has the power to exclude and deport those aliens who constitute a real menace to its peaceful existence. But in view of the large numbers of people affected by the immigration acts and in view of the vigorous malpractice of the Departments of Justice and Labor, an adequate public hearing before a competent administrative tribunal should be assured to all.

LYNCHING

We urge Congress to consider the most effective means to end lynching in this country which continues to be a terrible blot on our American civilization.

PUBLIC ROADS AND HIGHWAYS

We favor liberal appropriations in co-operation with the States for the construction of highways, which will bring about a reduction in transportation costs, better marketing of farm products, improvement in rural postal delivery, as well as meet the needs of military defense.

In determining the proportion of Federal aid for road construction among the States, the sums lost in taxation to the respective States by the setting apart of large portions of their area as forest reservations should be considered as a controlling factor.

CONSERVATION

Conservation is a Republican policy. It began with the passage of the Reclamation Act signed by President Roosevelt. The recent passage of the coal, oil and phosphate leasing act by a Republican Congress and the enactment of the water-power bill fashioned in accordance with the same principle, are consistent landmarks in the development of the conservation of our national resources. We denounce the refusal of the President to sign the waterpower bill, passed after ten years of controversy. The Republican party has taken an especially honorable part in saving our national forests and in the effort to establish a national forest policy. Our most pressing conservation question relates to our forests. We are using our forest resources faster than they are being renewed. The result is to raise unduly the cost of forest products to consumers and especially farmers, who use more than half the lumber produced in America, and in the end to create a timber famine. The Federal Government, the States and private interests must unite in devising means to meet the menace.

RECLAMATION

We favor a fixed and comprehensive policy of reclamation to increase national wealth and production.

We recognize in the development of reclamation through Federal action with its increase of production and taxable wealth a safeguard for the nation.

We commend to Congress a policy to reclaim

lands and the establishment of a fixed national policy of development of natural resources in relation to reclamation through the now designated government agencies.

ARMY AND NAVY

We feel the deepest pride in the fine courage, the resolute endurance, the gallant spirit of the officers and men of our army and navy in the World War. They were in all ways worthy of the best traditions of the nation's defenders, and we pledge ourselves to proper maintenance of the military and naval establishments upon which our national security and dignity depend.

THE SERVICE MEN

We hold in imperishable remembrance the valor and the patriotism of the soldiers and sailors of America who fought in the great war for human liberty, and we pledge ourselves to discharge to the fullest the obligations which a grateful nation justly should fulfill, in appreciation of the services rendered by its defenders on sea and on land.

Republicans are not ungrateful. Throughout their history they have shown their gratitude toward the nation's defenders. Liberal legislation for the care of the disabled and infirm and their dependents has ever marked Republican policy toward the soldier and sailor of all the wars in which our country has participated. The present Congress has appropriated generously for the disabled of the World War.

The amounts already applied and authorized for the fiscal year 1920-21 for this purpose reached the stupendous sum of $1,180,571,893. The legislation is significant of the party's purpose in generously caring for the maimed and disabled men of the recent war.

CIVIL SERVICE

We renew our repeated declaration that the civil service law shall be thoroughly and honestly enforced and extended wherever practicable. The recent action of Congress in enacting a comprehensive civil service retirement law and in working out a comprehensive employment and wage policy that will guarantee equal and just treatment to the army of government workers, and in centralizing the administration of the new and progressive employment policy in the hands of the Civil Service Commission is worthy of all praise.

POSTAL SERVICE

We condemn the present administration for its destruction of the efficiency of the postal service, and the telegraph and telephone service when controlled by the government and for its failure to properly compensate employés whose expert knowledge is essential to the proper conduct of the affairs of the postal system. We commend the Republican Congress for the enactment of legislation increasing the pay of postal employés, who up to that time were the poorest paid in the government service.

WOMAN SUFFRAGE

We welcome women into full participation in the affairs of government and the activities of the Republican Party. We earnestly hope that Republican legislatures in states which have not yet acted on the Suffrage Amendment will ratify the amendment, to the end that all of the women of the nation of voting age may participate in the election of 1920 which is so important to the welfare of our country.

SOCIAL PROGRESS

The supreme duty of the nation is the conservation of human resources through an enlightened measure of social and industrial justice. Although the federal jurisdiction over social problems is limited, they affect the welfare and interest of the nation as a whole. We pledge the Republican party to the solution of these problems through national and state legislation in accordance with the best progressive thought of the country.

EDUCATION AND HEALTH

We endorse the principle of Federal aid to the States for the purpose of vocational and agricultural training.

Wherever Federal money is devoted to education, such education must be so directed as to awaken in the youth the spirit of America and a sense of patriotic duty to the United States.

A thorough system of physical education for all children up to the age of 19, including adequate health supervision and instruction, would remedy conditions revealed by the draft and would add to the economic and industrial strength of the nation. National leadership and stimulation will be necessary to induce the States to adopt a wise system of physical training.

The public health activities of the Federal government are scattered through numerous departments and bureaus, resulting in inefficiency, duplication and extravagance. We advocate a greater centralization of the Federal functions, and in addition urge the better co-ordination of the work of the Federal, State and local health agencies.

Child Labor

The Republican party stands for a Federal child labor law and for its rigid enforcement. If the present law be found unconstitutional or ineffective, we shall seek other means to enable Congress to prevent the evils of child labor.

Women in Industry

Women have special problems of employment which make necessary special study. We recommend Congress for the permanent establishment of the Women's Bureau in the United States Department of Labor to serve as a source of information to the States and to Congress.

The principle of equal pay for equal service should be applied throughout all branches of the Federal government in which women are employed.

Federal aid for vocational training should take into consideration the special aptitudes and needs of women workers.

We demand Federal legislation to limit the hours of employment of women engaged in intensive industry, the product of which enters into interstate commerce.

Housing

The housing shortage has not only compelled careful study of ways of stimulating building, but it has brought into relief the unsatisfactory character of the housing accommodations of large numbers of the inhabitants of our cities. A nation of home owners is the best guaranty of the maintenance of those principles of liberty, law and order upon which our government is founded. Both National and State governments should encourage in all proper ways the acquiring of homes by our citizens. The United States Government should make available the valuable information on housing and town planning collected during the war. This information should be kept up to date and made currently available.

Hawaii

For Hawaii we recommend Federal assistance in Americanizing and educating their greatly disproportionate foreign population; home rule; and the rehabilitation of the Hawaiian race.

Pointing to its history and relying on its fundamental principles, we declare that the Republican party has the genius, courage and constructive ability to end executive usurpation and restore constitutional government; to fulfill our world obligations without sacrificing our national independence; to raise the national standards of education, health and general welfare; to re-establish a peace time administration and to substitute economy and efficiency for extravagance and chaos; to restore and maintain the national credit; to reform unequal and burdensome taxes; to free business from arbitrary and unnecessary official control; to suppress disloyalty without the denial of justice; to repel the arrogant challenge of any class and to maintain a government of all the people as contrasted with government for some of the people, and finally, to allay unrest, suspicion and strife, and to secure the co-operation and unity of all citizens in the solution of the complex problems of the day; to the end that our country, happy and prosperous, proud of its past, sure of itself and of its institutions, may look forward with confidence to the future.

Socialist Platform of 1920

In the national campaign of 1920 the Socialist Party calls upon all American workers of hand and brain, and upon all citizens who believe in political liberty and social justice, to free the country from the oppressive misrule of the old political parties, and to take the government into their own hands under the banner and upon the program of the Socialist Party.

The outgoing administration, like Democratic and Republican administrations of the past, leave behind it a disgraceful record of solemn pledges unscrupulously broken and public confidence ruthlessly betrayed.

It obtained the suffrage of the people on a

platform of peace, liberalism and social betterment, but drew the country into a devastating war, and inaugurated a régime of despotism, reaction and oppression unsurpassed in the annals of the republic.

It promised to the American people a treaty which would assure to the world a reign of international right and true democracy. It gave its sanction and support to an infamous pact formulated behind closed doors by predatory elder statesmen of European and Asiatic imperialism. Under this pact territories have been annexed against the will of their populations and cut off from their sources of sustenance; nations seeking their freedom in the exercise of much heralded right of self-determination have been brutally fought with armed force, intrigue and starvation blockades.

To the millions of young men, who staked their lives on the field of battle, to the people of the country who gave unstintingly of their toil and property to support the war, the Democratic administration held out the sublime ideal of a union of the peoples of the world organized to maintain perpetual peace among nations on the basis of justice and freedom. It helped create a reactionary alliance of imperialistic governments, banded together to bully weak nations, crush working-class governments and perpetuate strife and warfare.

While thus furthering the ends of reaction, violence and oppression abroad, our administration suppressed the cherished and fundamental rights and civil liberties at home.

Upon the pretext of war-time necessity, the Chief Executive of the republic and the appointed heads of his administration were clothed with dictatorial powers (which were often exercised arbitrarily), and Congress enacted laws in open and direct violation of the constitutional safeguards of freedom of expression.

Hundreds of citizens who raised their voices for the maintenance of political and industrial rights during the war were indicted under the Espionage Law, tried in an atmosphere of prejudice and hysteria and are now serving inhumanly long jail sentences for daring to uphold the traditions of liberty which once were sacred in this country.

Agents of the Federal government unlawfully raided homes and meeting places and prevented or broke up peaceable gatherings of citizens.

The postmaster-general established a censorship of the press more autocratic than that ever tolerated in a régime of absolutism, and has harassed and destroyed publications on account of their advanced political and economic views, by excluding them from the mails.

And after the war was in fact long over, the administration has not scrupled to continue a policy of repression and terrorism under the shadow and hypocritical guise of war-time measures.

It has practically imposed involuntary servitude and peonage on a large class of American workers by denying them the right to quit work and coercing them into acceptance of inadequate wages and onerous conditions of labor. It has dealt a foul blow to the traditional American right of asylum by deporting hundreds of foreign born workers by administrative order, on the mere suspicion of harboring radical views, and often for the sinister purpose of breaking labor strikes.

In the short span of three years our self-styled liberal administration has succeeded in undermining the very foundation of political liberty and economic rights which this republic has built up in more than a century of struggle and progress.

Under the cloak of a false and hypocritical patriotism and under the protection of governmental terror the Democratic administration has given the ruling classes unrestrained license to plunder the people by intensive exploitation of labor, by the extortion of enormous profits and by increasing the cost of all necessities of life. Profiteering has become reckless and rampant, billions have been coined by the capitalists out of the suffering and misery of their fellow men. The American financial oligarchy has become a dominant factor in the world, while the condition of the American workers has grown more precarious.

The responsibility does not rest upon the Democratic party alone. The Republican party, through its representatives in Congress and otherwise, has not only openly condoned the political misdeeds of the last three years, but has sought to outdo its Democratic rival in the orgy of political reaction and repression. Its criticism of the Democratic administrative policy is that it is not reactionary and drastic enough.

America is now at the parting of the roads. If the outraging of political liberty and concentration of economic power into the hands of the few is permitted to go on, it can have only one consequence, the reduction of the country to a state of absolute capitalist despotism.

We particularly denounce the militaristic policy of both old parties, of investing countless hundreds of millions of dollars in armaments after the victorious completion of what was to have been the "last war." We call attention to the fatal results of such a program in Europe, carried on prior to 1914, and culminating in the Great War; we declare that such a policy, adding unbearable burdens to the working class and to all the people, can lead only to the complete Prussianization of the nation, and ultimately to war; and we demand immediate and complete abandonment of this fatal program.

The Socialist Party sounds the warning. It calls upon the people to defeat both parties at the polls, and to elect the candidates of the Socialist Party to the end of restoring political democracy and bringing about complete industrial freedom.

The Socialist Party of the United States therefore summons all who believe in this fundamental doctrine to prepare for a complete reorganization of our social system, based upon public ownership of public necessities; upon government by representatives chosen from occupational as well as from geographical groups in harmony with our industrial development, and with citizenship based on service; that we may end forever the exploitation of class by class.

To achieve this end the Socialist Party pledges itself to the following program:

1. Social

1. All business vitally essential for the existence and welfare of the people, such as railroads, express service, steamship lines, telegraphs, mines, oil wells, power plants, elevators, packing houses, cold storage plants and all industries operating on a national scale, should be taken over by the nation.

2. All publicly owned industries should be administered jointly by the government and representatives of the workers, not for revenue or profit, but with the sole object of securing just compensation and humane conditions of employment to the workers and efficient and reasonable service to the public.

3. All banks should be acquired by the government, and incorporated in a unified public banking system.

4. The business of insurance should be taken over by the government, and should be extended to include insurance against accident, sickness, invalidity, old age and unemployment, without contribution on the part of the worker.

5. Congress should enforce the provisions of the Thirteenth, Fourteenth and Fifteenth Amendments with reference to the Negroes, and effective federal legislation should be enacted to secure to the Negroes full civil, political, industrial and educational rights.

2. Industrial

1. Congress should enact effective laws to abolish child labor, to fix minimum wages, based on an ascertained cost of a decent standard of life, to protect migratory and unemployed workers from oppression, to abolish detective and strike-breaking agencies and to establish a shorter work-day in keeping with increased industrial productivity.

3. Political

1. The constitutional freedom of speech, press and assembly should be restored by repealing the Espionage Law and all other repressive legislation, and by prohibiting the executive usurpation of authority.

2. All prosecutions under the Espionage Law should be discontinued, and all persons serving prison sentences for alleged offenses growing out of religious beliefs, political views or industrial activities should be fully pardoned and immediately released.

3. No alien should be deported from the United States on account of his political views or participation in labor struggles, nor in any event without proper trial on specific charges. The arbitrary power to deport aliens by administrative order should be repealed.

4. The power of the courts to restrain workers in their struggles against employers by the Writ of Injunction or otherwise, and their power to nullify congressional legislation, should be abrogated.

5. Federal judges should be elected by the people and be subject to recall.

6. The President and the Vice-President of the United States should be elected by direct

popular election, and be subject to recall. All members of the Cabinet should be elected by Congress and be responsible at all times to the vote thereof.

7. Suffrage should be equal and unrestricted in fact as well as in law for all men and women throughout the nation.

8. Because of the strict residential qualification of suffrage in this country, millions of citizens are disfranchised in every election; adequate provision should be made for the registration and voting of migratory workers.

9. The Constitution of the United States should be amended to strengthen the safeguards of civil and political liberty, and to remove all obstacles to industrial and social reform and reconstruction, including the changes enumerated in this program, in keeping with the will and interest of the people. It should be made amendable by a majority of the voters of the nation upon their own initiative, or upon the initiative of Congress.

4. Foreign Relations

1. All claims of the United States against allied countries for loans made during the war should be canceled upon the understanding that all war debts among such countries shall likewise be canceled. The largest possible credit in food, raw materials and machinery should be extended to the stricken nations of Europe in order to help them rebuild the ruined world.

2. The Government of the United States should initiate a movement to dissolve the mischievous organization called the "League of Nations" and to create an international parliament, composed of democratically elected representatives of all nations of the world based upon the recognition of their equal rights, the principles of self-determination, the right to national existence of colonies and other dependencies, freedom of international trade and trade routes by land and sea, and universal disarmament, and be charged with revising the Treaty of Peace on the principles of justice and conciliation.

3. The United States should immediately make peace with the Central Powers and open commercial and diplomatic relations with Russia under the Soviet Government. It should promptly recognize the independence of the Irish Republic.

4. The United States should make and proclaim it a fixed principal in its foreign policy that American capitalists who acquire concessions or make investments in foreign countries do so at their own risk, and under no circumstances should our government enter into diplomatic negotiations or controversies or resort to armed conflicts on account of foreign property-claims of American capitalists.

5. Fiscal

1. All war debts and other debts of the Federal Government should immediately be paid in full, the funds for such payment to be raised by means of a progressive property tax, whose burden should fall upon the rich and particularly upon great fortunes made during the war.

2. A standing progressive income tax and a graduated inheritance tax should be levied to provide for all needs of the government, including the cost of its increasing social and industrial functions.

3. The unearned increment of land should be taxed; all land held out of use should be taxed at full rental value.

Socialist Labor Platform of 1920

The world stands upon the threshold of a new social order. The capitalist system of production and distribution is doomed; capitalist appropriation of labor's produce forces the bulk of mankind into wage slavery, throws society into the convulsions of the class struggle, and momentarily threatens to engulf humanity in chaos and disaster. At this crucial period in history the Socialist Labor Party of America, in 15th National Convention assembled, reaffirming its former platform declarations, calls upon the workers to rally around the banner of the Socialist Labor Party, the only party in this country that blazes the trail to the Workers' Industrial Republic.

Since the advent of civilization human society has been divided into classes. Each new form of society has come into being with a definite purpose to fulfill in the progress of the human race. Each has been born, has grown, developed, prospered, become old, outworn, and has finally been overthrown. Each society has developed within itself the germs of its own destruction as well as the germs which went to make up the society of the future.

The capitalist system rose during the seventeenth, eighteenth, and nineteenth centuries, by the overthrow of feudalism. Its great and all-important mission in the development of man was to improve, develop, and concentrate the means of production and distribution, thus creating a system of co-operative production. This work was completed in advanced capitalist countries about the beginning of the 20th century. That moment capitalism had fulfilled its historic mission, and from that moment the capitalist class became a class of parasites.

In the course of human progress mankind has passed through class rule, private property, and individualism in production and exchange, from the enforced and inevitable want, misery, poverty, and ignorance of savagery and barbarism to the affluence and high productive capacity of civilization. For all practical purposes, co-operative production has now superseded individual production.

Capitalism no longer promotes the greatest good of the greatest number. Private production carries with it private ownership of the products. Production is carried on, not to supply the needs of humanity, but for the profit of the individual owner, the company, or the trust. The worker, not receiving the full product of his labor, can not buy back all he produces. The capitalist wastes part in riotous living; the rest must find a foreign market. By the opening of the twentieth century the capitalist world—England, America, Germany, France, Japan, China, etc.—was producing at a mad rate for the world market. A capitalist deadlock of market brought on in 1914 the capitalist collapse popularly known as the World War. The capitalist world can not extricate itself out of the débris. America to-day is choking under the weight of her own gold and products.

This situation has brought on the present stage of human misery—starvation, want, cold, disease, pestilence, and war. This state is brought about in the midst of plenty, when the earth can be made to yield hundred-fold, when the machinery of production is made to multiply human energy and ingenuity by the hundred. The present state of misery exists solely because the mode of production rebels against the mode of exchange.

Private property in the means of life has become a social crime. The land was made by no man; the modern machines are the result of the combined ingenuity of the human race from time immemorial; the land can be made to yield and the machines can be set in motion only by the collective effort of the workers. Progress demands the collective ownership of the land on and the tools with which to produce the necessities of life. The owner of the means of life to-day partakes of the nature of a highwayman; he stands with his gun before society's temple; it depends upon him whether the million mass may work, earn, eat, and live. The capitalist system of production and exchange must be supplanted if progress is to continue.

In place of the capitalist system the Socialist Labor Party aims to substitute a system of social ownership of the means of production, industrially administered by the workers, who assume control and direction as well as operation of their industrial affairs.

We therefore call upon the wage workers to organize themselves into a revolutionary political organization under the banner of the Socialist Labor Party; and to organize themselves likewise upon the industrial field into a Socialist industrial union, as now exemplified by the Workers' International Industrial Union, in keeping with their political aims.

And we also call upon all other intelligent citizens to place themselves squarely upon the ground of working class interests, and join us in this mighty and noble work of human emancipation, so that we may put summary end to the existing barbarous class conflict by placing the land and all the means of production, transportation, and distribution into the hands of the people as a collective body, and substituting Industrial Self-Government for the present state of planless production, industrial war and social disorder—a government in which every worker shall have the free exercise and full benefit of his faculties, multiplied by all the modern factors of civilization.

☒ CAMPAIGN OF 1924

In 1924, in addition to the Democratic and Republican parties, the Prohibition Party, the Socialist Labor Party, and the Workers' (Communist) Party published platforms and appeared on the ballots in more than a quarter of the states. Senator Robert M. La Follette was nominated for the presidency by a Conference for Progressive Political Action which met in Cleveland, Ohio in July of 1924, but he also ran as an independent in several states. The platform and resolutions committee of the Conference submitted a platform which was adopted, and at a later date Mr. La Follette published a platform of his own. Both platforms are included in this volume. The Socialist Party published only a Declaration of Principles instead of a platform, and supported La Follette in the election.

Democratic Platform of 1924

We, the representatives of the democratic party, in national convention assembled, pay our profound homage to the memory of Woodrow Wilson. Our hearts are filled with gratitude that American democracy should have produced this man, whose spirit and influence will live on through the ages; and that it was our privilege to have co-operated with him in the advancement of ideals of government which will serve as an example and inspiration for this and future generations. We affirm our abiding faith in those ideals and pledge ourselves to take up the standard which he bore and to strive for the full triumph of the principles of democracy to which he dedicated his life.

DEMOCRATIC PRINCIPLES

The democratic party believes in equal rights to all and special privilege to none. The republican party holds that special privileges are essential to national prosperity. It believes that national prosperity must originate with the special interests and seep down through the channels of trade to the less favored industries to the wage earners and small salaried employes. It has accordingly enthroned privilege and nurtured selfishness.

The republican party is concerned chiefly with material things; the democratic party is concerned chiefly with human rights. The masses, burdened by discriminating laws and unjust administration, are demanding relief. The favored special interests, represented by the republican party, contented with their unjust privileges, are demanding that no change be made. The democratic party stands for remedial legislation and progress. The republican party stands still.

Comparison of Parties

We urge the American people to compare the record of eight unsullied years of democratic administration with that of the republican administration. In the former there was no corruption. The party pledges were faithfully fulfilled and a democratic congress enacted an extraordinary number of constructive and remedial laws. The economic life of the nation was quickened.

Tariff taxes were reduced. A federal trade commission was created. A federal farm loan system was established. Child labor legislation was enacted. A good roads bill was passed. Eight hour laws were adopted. A secretary of labor was given a seat in the cabinet of the president. The Clayton amendment to the Sherman anti-trust act was passed, freeing American labor and taking it from the category of commodities. By the Smith-Lever bill improvement of agricultural conditions was effected. A corrupt practice act was adopted. A well-considered warehouse act was passed. Federal employment bureaus were created, farm loan banks were organized and the federal reserve system was established. Privilege was uprooted. A corrupt lobby was driven from the national capital. A higher sense of individual and national duty was aroused. America enjoyed an unprecedented period of social and material progress.

During the time which intervened between the inauguration of a democratic administration on March 4, 1913, and our entrance into the world war, we placed upon the statute-books of our country more effective constructive and remedial legislation than the republican party had placed there in a generation.

During the great struggle which followed we had a leadership that carried America to greater heights of honor and power and glory than she had ever known before in her entire history.

Transition from this period of exalted democratic leadership to the sordid record of the last three and a half years makes the nation ashamed. It marks the contrast between a high conception of public service and an avid purpose to distribute spoils.

G. O. P. Corruption

Never before in our history has the government been so tainted by corruption and never has an administration so utterly failed. The nation has been appalled by the revelations of political de-pravity which have characterized the conduct of public affairs. We arraign the republican party for attempting to limit inquiry into official delinquencies and to impede if not to frustrate the investigations to which in the beginning the republican party leaders assented, but which later they regarded with dismay.

These investigations sent the former secretary of the interior to Three Rivers in disgrace and dishonor. These investigations revealed the incapacity and indifference to public obligation of the secretary of the navy, compelling him by force of public opinion to quit the cabinet. These investigations confirmed the general impression as to the unfitness of the attorney general by exposing an official situation and personal contacts which shocked the conscience of the nation and compelled his dismissal from the cabinet.

These investigations disclosed the appalling conditions of the veterans bureau with its fraud upon the government and its cruel neglect of the sick and disabled soldiers of the world war. These investigations revealed the criminal and fraudulent nature of the oil leases which caused the congress, despite the indifference of the executive, to direct recovery of the public domain and the prosecution of the criminal.

Such are the exigencies of partisan politics that republican leaders are teaching the strange doctrine that public censure should be directed against those who expose crime rather than against criminals who have committed the offenses. If only three cabinet officers out of ten are disgraced, the country is asked to marvel at how many are free from taint. Long boastful that it was the only party "fit to govern," the republican party has proven its inability to govern even itself. It is at war with itself. As an agency of government it has ceased to function.

This nation cannot afford to entrust its welfare to a political organization that cannot master itself, or to an executive whose policies have been rejected by his own party. To retain in power an administration of this character would inevitably result in four years more of continued disorder, internal dissension and governmental inefficiency. A vote for Coolidge is a vote for chaos.

Issues

The dominant issues of the campaign are created by existing conditions. Dishonesty, discrimination, extravagances and inefficiency exist in government. The burdens of taxation have become unbearable. Distress and bankruptcy in agriculture, the basic industry of our country, is affecting the happiness and prosperity of the whole people. The cost of living is causing hardship and unrest.

The slowing down of industry is adding to the general distress. The tariff, the destruction of our foreign markets and the high cost of transportation are taking the profit out of agriculture, mining and other raw material industries. Large standing armies and the cost of preparing for war still cast their burdens upon humanity. These conditions the existing republican administration has proven itself unwilling or unable to redress.

The democratic party pledges itself to the following program:

Honest government.

We pledge the democratic party to drive from public places all which make barter of our national power, its resources or the administration of its laws; to punish those guilty of these offenses.

To put none but the honest in public office; to practice economy in the expenditure of public money; to reverence and respect the rights of all under the constitution.

To condemn and destroy government by the spy and blackmailer which was by this republican administration both encouraged and practiced.

Tariff and Taxation

The Fordney-McCumber tariff act is the most unjust, unscientific and dishonest tariff tax measure ever enacted in our history. It is class legislation which defrauds the people for the benefit of a few, it heavily increases the cost of living, penalizes agriculture, corrupts the government, fosters paternalism and, in the long run, does not benefit the very interests for which it was intended.

We denounce the republican tariff laws which are written, in great part, in aid of monopolies and thus prevent that reasonable exchange of commodities which would enable foreign countries to buy our surplus agricultural and manufactured products with resultant profit to the toilers and producers of America.

Trade interchange, on the basis of reciprocal advantages to the countries participating is a time-honored doctrine of democratic faith. We declare our party's position to be in favor of a tax on commodities entering the customs house that will promote effective competition, protect against monopoly and at the same time produce a fair revenue to support the government.

The greatest contributing factor in the increase and unbalancing of prices is unscientific taxation. After having increased taxation and the cost of living by $2,000,000,000 under the Fordney-McCumber tariff, all that the republican party could suggest in the way of relief was a cut of $300,000,000 in direct taxes; and that was to be given principally to those with the largest incomes.

Although there was no evidence of a lack of capital for investment to meet the present requirements of all legitimate industrial enterprises and although the farmers and general consumers were bearing the brunt of tariff favors already granted to special interests, the administration was unable to devise any plan except one to grant further aid to the few. Fortunately this plan of the administration failed and under democratic leadership, aided by progressive republicans, a more equitable one was adopted, which reduces direct taxes by about $450,000,000.

The issue between the president and the democratic party is not one of tax reduction or of the conservation of capital. It is an issue of relative burden of taxation and of the distribution of capital as affected by the taxation of income. The president still stands on the so-called Mellon plan, which his party has just refused to indorse or mention in its platform.

The income tax was intended as a tax upon wealth. It was not intended to take from the poor any part of the necessities of life. We hold that the fairest tax with which to raise revenue for the federal government is the income tax. We favor a graduated tax upon incomes, so adjusted as to lay the burdens of government upon the taxpayers in proportion to the benefits they enjoy and their ability to pay.

We oppose the so-called nuisance taxes, sales taxes and all other forms of taxation that unfairly shift to the consumer the burdens of taxation. We refer to the democratic revenue measure passed by the last congress as distinguished from the Mellon tax plan as an illustration of the policy of the democratic party. We first made a flat reduction of 25 per cent upon the tax of all incomes payable this year and then we so changed the proposed Mellon plan as to eliminate taxes upon the poor, reducing them upon moderate incomes and, in a lesser degree, upon the incomes of multi-millionaires. We hold that all taxes are unnecessarily high and pledge ourselves to further reductions.

We denounce the Mellon plan as a device to relieve multi-millionaires at the expense of other taxpayers, and we accept the issue of taxation tendered by President Coolidge.

AGRICULTURE

During the four years of republican government the economic condition of the American farmer has changed from comfort to bankruptcy, with all its attendant miseries. The chief causes for this are:

(a) The republican party policy of isolation in international affairs has prevented Europe from getting back to its normal balance, and, by leaving unsolved the economic problems abroad, has driven the European city population from industrial activities to the soil in large numbers in order to earn the mere necessaries of life. This has deprived the American farmer of his normal export trade.

(b) The republican policy of a prohibitive tariff, exemplified in the Fordney-McCumber law, which has forced the American farmer, with his export market debilitated, to buy manufactured goods at sustained high domestic levels, thereby making him the victim of the profiteer.

(c) The republican policy of high transportation rates, both rail and water, which has made it impossible for the farmer to ship his produce to market at even a living profit.

To offset these policies and their disastrous results, and to restore the farmer again to economic equality with other industrialists, we pledge ourselves:

(a) To adopt an international policy of such co-operation by direct official, instead of indirect and evasive unofficial means, as will re-establish the farmers' export market by restoring the industrial balance in Europe and the normal flow of international trade with the settlement of Europe's economic problems.

(b) To adjust the tariff so that the farmer and all other classes can buy again in a competitive manufacturers' market.

(c) To readjust and lower rail and water rates which will make our markets, both for the buyer and the seller, national and international instead of regional and local.

(d) To bring about the early completion of international waterway systems for transportation and to develop our water powers for cheaper fertilizer and use on our farms.

(e) To stimulate by every proper governmental activity the progress of the co-operative marketing movement and the establishment of an export marketing corporation or commission in order that the exportable surplus may not establish the price of the whole crop.

(f) To secure for the farmer credits suitable for his needs.

(g) By the establishment of these policies and others naturally supplementary thereto, to reduce the margin between what the producer receives for his products and the consumer has to pay for his supplies, to the end that we secure an equality for agriculture.

RAILROADS

The sponsors for the Esch-Cummins transportation act of 1920, at the time of its presentation to congress, stated that it had for its purposes the reduction of the cost of transportation, the improvement of service, the bettering of labor conditions, the promotion of peaceful co-operation between employer and employe, and at the same time the assurance of a fair and just return to the railroads upon their investment.

We are in accord with these announced purposes, but contend that the act has failed to accomplish them. It has failed to reduce the cost of transportation. The promised improvement in service has not been realized. The labor provisions of the act have proven unsatisfactory in settling differences between employer and employes. The so-called recapture clause has worked out to the advantage of the strong and has been of no benefit to the weak. The pronouncement in the act for the development of both rail and water transportation has proved futile. Water transportation upon our inland waterways has not been encouraged, the limitation of our coastwise trade is threatened by the administration of the act. It has unnecessarily interfered with the power of the states to regulate purely intrastate transportation. It must therefore be so rewritten that the high purpose which the public welfare demands may be accomplished.

Railroad freight rates should be so readjusted as to give the bulky basic, low-priced raw commodities, such as agricultural products, coal and ores the lowest rates, placing the higher rates upon more valuable and less bulky manufactured products.

Muscle Shoals

We reaffirm and pledge the fulfillment of the policy, with reference to Muscle Shoals, as declared and passed by the democratic majority of the sixty-fourth congress in the national defense act of 1916, "for the production of nitrates or other products needed for munitions of war and useful in the manufacture of fertilizers."

We hold that the production of cheaper and high grade fertilizers is essential to agricultural prosperity. We demand prompt action by congress for the operation of the Muscle Shoals plants to maximum capacity in the production, distribution and sale of commercial fertilizers to the farmers of the country and we oppose any legislation that limits the production of fertilizers at Muscle Shoals by limiting the amount of power to be used in their manufacture.

Credit and Currency

We denounce the recent cruel and unjust contraction of legitimate and necessary credit and currency, which was directly due to the so-called deflation policy of the republican party, as declared in its national platform of June, 1920, and in the speech of acceptance of its candidate for the presidency. Within eighteen months after the election of 1920 this policy resulted in withdrawing bank loans by over $5,000,000,000 and in contracting our currency by over $1,500,000,000.

The contraction bankrupted hundreds of thousands of farmers and stock growers in America and resulted in widespread industrial depression and unemployment. We demand that the federal reserve system be so administered as to give stability to industry, commerce and finance, as was intended by the democratic party, which gave the federal reserve system to the nation.

Reclamation

The democratic party was foremost in urging reclamation for the immediate arid and semiarid lands of the west. The lands are located in the public land states, and, therefore, it is due to the government to utilize their resources by reclamation. Homestead entrymen under reclamation projects have suffered from the extravagant inefficiencies and mistakes of the federal government.

The reclamation act of 1924, recommended by the fact finding commission and added as an amendment to the second deficiency appropriation bill at the last session of congress, was eliminated from that bill by the republican conferees in the report they presented to congress one hour before adjournment. The democratic party pledges itself actively, efficiently and economically to carry on the reclamation projects, and to make equitable adjustment for the mistakes the government has made.

Conservation

We pledge recovery of the navy's oil reserves, and all other parts of the public domain which have been fraudulently or illegally leased or otherwise wrongfully transferred to the control of private interests; vigorous prosecution of all public officials, private citizens and corporations that participated in these transactions; revision of the water power act, the general leasing act and all other legislation relating to public domain, that may be essential to its conservation and honest and efficient use on behalf of the people of the country.

We believe that the nation should retain title to its water power and we favor the expeditious creation and development of our water power. We favor strict public control and conservation of all the nation's natural resources, such as coal, iron, oil and timber, and their use in such manner as may be to the best interest of our citizens.

The conservation of migratory birds, the establishment of game preserves, and the protection and conservation of wild life is of importance to agriculturists as well as sportsmen. Our disappearing national natural resources of timber calls for a national policy of reforestation.

Improved Highways

Improved roads are of vital importance, not only to commerce and industry, but also to agriculture and natural life. We call attention to the record of the democratic party in this matter and favor continuance of federal aid under existing federal and state agencies.

Mining

Mining is one of the basic industries of this country. We produce more coal, iron, copper and silver than any other country. The value of our mineral production is second only to agriculture.

Mining has suffered like agriculture and from the same causes. It is the duty of our government to foster this industry and to remove the restrictions that destroy its prosperity.

MERCHANT MARINE

The democratic party condemns the vacillating policy of the republican administration in the failure to develop an American flag shipping policy. There has been a marked decrease in the volume of American commerce carried in American vessels as compared to the record under a democratic administration.

We oppose as illogical and unsound all efforts to overcome by subsidy the handicap to American shipping and commerce imposed by republican policies.

We condemn the practice of certain American railroads in favoring foreign ships, and pledge ourselves to correct such discriminations. We declare for an American owned merchant marine, American built and manned by American crews, which is essential for naval security in war and is a protection to the American farmer and manufacturer against excessive ocean freight charges on products of farm and factory.

We declare that the government should own and operate such merchant ships as will insure the accomplishment of these purposes and to continue such operation so long as it may be necessary without obstructing the development and growth of a privately owned American flag shipping.

NECESSITIES OF LIFE

We pledge the democratic party to regulate by governmental agencies the anthracite coal industry and all other corporations controlling the necessaries of life where public welfare has been subordinated to private interests.

EDUCATION

We believe with Thomas Jefferson and founders of the republic that ignorance is the enemy of freedom and that each state, being responsible for the intellectual and moral qualifications of its citizens and for the expenditure of the moneys collected by taxation for the support of its schools, shall use its sovereign right in all matters pertaining to education. The federal government should offer to the states such counsel, advice and aid as may be made available through the federal agencies for the general improvement of our schools in view of our national needs.

CIVIL SERVICE

We denounce the action of the republican administration in its violations of the principles of civil service by its partisan removals and manipulation of the eligible lists in the postoffice department and other governmental departments; by its packing the civil service commission so that commission became the servile instrument of the administration in its wish to deny to the former service men their preferential rights under the law and the evasion of the requirements of the law with reference to appointments in the department.

We pledge the democratic party faithfully to comply with the spirit as well as the regulation of civil service; to extend its provisions to internal revenue officers and to other employes of the government not in executive positions, and to secure to former service men preference in such appointments.

POSTAL EMPLOYES

We declare in favor of adequate salaries to provide decent living conditions for postal employes.

POPULAR ELECTIONS

We pledge the democratic party to a policy which will prevent members of either house who fail of re-election from participating in the subsequent sessions of congress. This can be accomplished by fixing the days for convening the congress immediately after the biennial national election; and to this end we favor granting the right to the people of the several states to vote on proposed constitutional amendments on this subject.

PROBATION

We favor the extension of the probation principle to the courts of the United States.

ACTIVITIES OF WOMEN

We welcome the women of the nation to their rightful place by the side of men in the control of the government whose burdens they have always shared.

The democratic party congratulates them upon the essential part which they have taken in the progress of our country, and the zeal with which they are using their political power to aid the enactment of beneficial laws and the exaction of fidelity in the public service.

Veterans of Wars

We favor generous appropriations, honest management and sympathetic care and assistance in the hospitalization, rehabilitation and compensation of the veterans of all wars and their dependents. The humanizing of the veterans' bureau is imperatively required.

Contributions

The nation now knows that the predatory interests have, by supplying republican campaign funds, systematically purchased legislative favors and administrative immunity. The practice must stop; our nation must return to honesty and decency in politics.

Elections are public affairs conducted for the sole purpose of ascertaining the will of the sovereign voters. Therefore, we demand that national elections shall hereafter be kept free from the poison of excessive private contributions. To this end, we favor reasonable means of publicity, at public expense, so that candidates, properly before the people for federal offices, may present their claims at a minimum of cost. Such publicity should precede the primary and the election.

We favor the prohibition of individual contributions, direct and indirect, to the campaign funds of congressmen, senators or presidential candidates, beyond a reasonable sum to be fixed in the law, for both individual contributions and total expenditures, with requirements for full publicity. We advocate a complete revision of the corrupt practice act to prevent Newberryism and the election evils disclosed by recent investigations.

Narcotics

Recognizing in narcotic addiction, especially the spreading of heroin addiction among the youth, a grave peril to America and to the human race, we pledge ourselves vigorously to take against it all legitimate and proper measures for education, for control and for suppression at home and abroad.

Prohibition Law

The republican administration has failed to enforce the prohibition law; is guilty of trafficking in liquor permits, and has become the protector of violators of this law.

The democratic party pledges itself to respect and enforce the constitution and all laws.

Rights of States

We demand that the states of the union shall be preserved in all their vigor and power. They constitute a bulwark against the centralizing and destructive tendencies of the republican party.

We condemn the efforts of the republican party to nationalize the functions and duties of the states.

We oppose the extension of bureaucracy, the creation of unnecessary bureaus and federal agencies and the multiplication of offices and office-holders.

We demand a revival of the spirit of local self-government essential to the preservation of the free institutions of our republic.

Asiatic Immigration

We pledge ourselves to maintain our established position in favor of the exclusion of Asiatic immigration.

Philippines

The Filipino peoples have succeeded in maintaining a stable government and have thus fulfilled the only condition laid down by congress as a prerequisite to the granting of independence. We declare that it is now our liberty and our duty to keep our promise to these people by granting them immediately the independence which they so honorably covet.

Alaska

The maladministration of affairs in Alaska is a matter of concern to all our people. Under the republican administration, development has ceased and the fishing industry has been seriously impaired. We pledge ourselves to correct the evils which have grown up in the administration of that rich domain.

An adequate form of local self-government for Alaska must be provided and to that end we favor the establishment of a full territorial form of government for that territory similar to that enjoyed by all the territories except Alaska during the last century of American history.

HAWAII

We believe in a policy for continuing the improvements of the national parks, the harbors and breakwaters, and the federal roads of the territory of Hawaii.

VIRGIN ISLANDS

We recommend legislation for the welfare of the inhabitants of the Virgin islands.

LAUSANNE TREATY

We condemn the Lausanne treaty. It barters legitimate American rights and betrays Armenia, for the Chester oil concessions.

We favor the protection of American rights in Turkey and the fulfillment of President Wilson's arbitral award respecting Armenia.

DISARMAMENT

We demand a strict and sweeping reduction of armaments by land and sea, so that there shall be no competitive military program or naval building. Until international agreements to this end have been made we advocate an army and navy adequate for our national safety.

Our government should secure a joint agreement with all nations for world disarmament and also for a referendum of war, except in case of actual or threatened attack.

Those who must furnish the blood and bear the burdens imposed by war should, whenever possible, be consulted before this supreme sacrifice is required of them.

GREECE

We welcome to the sisterhood of republics the ancient land of Greece which gave to our party its priceless name. We extend to her government and people our cordial good wishes.

WAR

War is a relic of barbarism and it is justifiable only as a measure of defense.

In the event of war in which the man power

of the nation is drafted, all other resources should likewise be drafted. This will tend to discourage war by depriving it of its profits.

PERSONAL FREEDOM

The democratic party reaffirms its adherence and devotion to those cardinal principles contained in the constitution and the precepts upon which our government is founded, that congress shall make no laws respecting the establishment of religion, or prohibiting the free exercises thereof, or abridging the freedom of speech or of the press or of the right of the people peaceably to assemble and to petition the government for a redress of grievances, that the church and the state shall be and remain separate, and that no religious test shall ever be required as a qualification to any office of public trust under the United States. These principles, we pledge ourselves ever to defend and maintain. We insist at all times upon obedience to the orderly processes of the law and deplore and condemn any effort to arouse religious or racial dissension.

LEAGUE OF NATIONS

The democratic party pledges all its energies to the outlawing of the whole war system. We refuse to believe that the wholesale slaughter of human beings on the battlefield is any more necessary to man's highest development than is killing by individuals.

The only hope for world peace and for economic recovery lies in the organized efforts of sovereign nations co-operating to remove the causes of war and to substitute law and order for violence.

Under democratic leadership a practical plan was devised under which fifty-four nations are now operating, and which has for its fundamental purpose the free co-operation of all nations in the work of peace.

The government of the United States for the last four years has had no foreign policy, and consequently it has delayed the restoration of the political and economic agencies of the world. It has impaired our self-respect at home and injured our prestige abroad. It has curtailed our foreign markets and ruined our agricultural prices.

It is of supreme importance to civilization and to mankind that America be placed and kept on the right side of the greatest moral question of all time, and therefore the democratic party renews its declarations of confidence in the idea of world peace, the league of nations and the world court of justice as together constituting the supreme effort of the statesmanship and religious conviction of our time to organize the world for peace.

Further, the democratic party declared that it will be the purpose of the next administration to do all in its power to secure for our country that moral leadership in the family of nations which, in the providence of God, has been so clearly marked out for it. There is no substitute for the league of nations as an agency working for peace, therefore, we believe, that, in the interest of permanent peace, and in the lifting of the great burdens of war from the backs of the people, and in order to establish a permanent foreign policy on these supreme questions, not subject to change with change of party administration, it is desirable, wise and necessary to lift this question out of party politics and to that end to take the sense of the American people at a referendum election, advisory to the government, to be held officially, under act of congress, free from all other questions and candidacies, after ample time for full consideration and discussion throughout the country, upon the question, in substance, as follows:

"Shall the United States become a member of the league of nations upon such reservations or amendments to the covenant of the league as the president and the senate of the United States may agree upon."

Immediately upon an affirmative vote we will carry out such mandate.

WATERWAYS

We favor and will promote deep waterways from the great lakes to the gulf and to the Atlantic ocean.

FLOOD CONTROL

We favor a policy for the fostering and building of inland waterways and the removal of discrimination against water transportation. Flood control and the lowering of flood levels is essential to the safety of life and property, the productivity of our lands, the navigability of our streams and the reclaiming of our wet and overflowed lands and the creation of hydro-electric power. We favor the expeditious construction of flood relief works on the Mississippi and Colorado rivers and also such reclamation and irrigation projects upon the Colorado river as may be found to be feasible and practical.

We favor liberal appropriations for prompt coordinated surveys by the United States to determine the possibilities of general navigation improvements and water power development on navigable streams and their tributaries, to secure reliable information as to the most economical navigation improvement, in combination with the most efficient and complete development of water power.

We favor suspension of the granting of federal water power licenses by the federal water power committee until congress has received reports from the water power commission with regard to applications for such licenses.

PRIVATE MONOPOLIES

The federal trade commission has submitted to the republican administration numerous reports showing the existence of monopolies and combinations in restraint of trade, and has recommended proceedings against these violators of the law. The few prosecutions which have resulted from this abundant evidence furnished by this agency created by the democratic party, while proving the indifference of the administration to the violations of law by trusts and monopolies and its friendship for them, nevertheless demonstrate the value of the federal trade commission.

We declare that a private monopoly is indefensible and intolerable, and pledge the democratic party to vigorous enforcement of existing laws against monopoly and illegal combinations, and to the enactment of such further measures as may be necessary.

FRAUDULENT STOCK SALE

We favor the immediate passage of such legislation as may be necessary to enable the states efficiently to enforce their laws relating to the gradual financial strangling of innocent investors, workers and consumers, caused by the indiscriminate promotion, refinancing and reorganizing of corporations on an inflated and over-capitalized basis, resulting already in the undermining and collapse of many railroads, public service and industrial corporations, manifesting itself in unemployment, irreparable loss and waste and which constitute a serious menace to the stability of our economic system.

AVIATION

We favor a sustained development of aviation by both the government and commercially.

LABOR, CHILD WELFARE

Labor is not a commodity. It is human. We favor collective bargaining and laws regulating hours of labor and conditions under which labor is performed. We favor the enactment of legislation providing that the product of convict labor shipped from one state to another shall be subject to the laws of the latter state exactly as though they had been produced therein. In order to mitigate unemployment attending business depression, we urge the enactment of legislation authorizing the construction and repair of public works be initiated in periods of acute unemployment.

We pledge the party to co-operate with the state governments for the welfare, education and protection of child life and all necessary safeguards against exhaustive debilitating employment conditions for women.

Without the votes of democratic members of congress the child labor amendment would not have been submitted for ratification.

LATIN-AMERICA

From the day of their birth, friendly relations have existed between the Latin-American republics and the United States. That friendship grows stronger as our relations become more intimate. The democratic party sends to these republics its cordial greeting; God has made us neighbors— justice shall keep us friends.

La Follette's Platform of 1924

The great issue before the American people today is the control of government and industry by private monopoly.

For a generation the people have struggled patiently, in the face of repeated betrayals by successive administrations, to free themselves from this intolerable power which has been undermining representative government.

Through control of government, monopoly has steadily extended its absolute dominion to every basic industry.

In violation of law, monopoly has crushed competition, stifled private initiative and independent enterprise, and without fear of punishment now exacts extortionate profits upon every necessity of life consumed by the public.

The equality of opportunity proclaimed by the Declaration of Independence and asserted and defended by Jefferson and Lincoln as the heritage of every American citizen has been displaced by special privilege for the few, wrested from the government of the many.

FUNDAMENTAL RIGHTS IN DANGER

That tyrannical power which the American people denied to a king, they will no longer endure from the monopoly system. The people know they cannot yield to any group the control of the economic life of the nation and preserve their political liberties. They know monopoly has its representatives in the halls of Congress, on the Federal bench, and in the executive departments; that these servile agents barter away the nation's natural resources, nullify acts of Congress by judicial veto and administrative favor, invade the people's rights by unlawful arrests and unconstitutional searches and seizures, direct our foreign policy in the interests of predatory wealth, and make wars and conscript the sons of the common people to fight them.

The usurpation in recent years by the federal courts of the power to nullify laws duly enacted by the legislative branch of the government is a plain violation of the Constitution. Abraham Lincoln, in his first inaugural address, said: "The candid citizen must confess that if the policy of the government, upon vital questions affecting the whole people, is to be irrevocably fixed by decisions of the Supreme Court, the people will have ceased to be their own rulers, having to that extent practically resigned their government into the hands of that eminent tribunal." The Constitution specifically vests all legislative power in the Congress, giving that body power and authority to override the veto of the president. The federal courts are given no authority under the Constitution to veto acts of Congress. Since the federal courts have assumed to exercise such veto power, it is essential that the Constitution shall give the Congress the right to override such judicial veto, otherwise the Court will make itself master over the other coordinate branches of the government. The people themselves must approve or disapprove the present exercise of legislative power by the federal courts.

DISTRESS OF AMERICAN FARMERS

The present condition of American agriculture constitutes an emergency of the gravest character. The Department of Commerce report shows that during 1923 there was a steady and marked increase in dividends paid by the great industrial corporations. The same is true of the steam and electric railways and practically all other large corporations. On the other hand, the Secretary of Agriculture reports that in the fifteen principal wheat growing states more than 108,000 farmers since 1920 have lost their farms through foreclosure or bankruptcy; that more than 122,000 have surrendered their property without legal proceedings, and that nearly 375,000 have retained possession of their property only through the leniency of their creditors, making a total of more than 600,000 or 26 per cent of all farmers who have virtually been bankrupted since 1920 in these fifteen states alone.

Almost unlimited prosperity for the great corporations and ruin and bankruptcy for agriculture is the direct and logical result of the policies and legislation which deflated the farmer while extending almost unlimited credit to the great corporations; which protected with exorbitant tariffs the industrial magnates, but depressed the prices of the farmers' products by financial juggling while greatly increasing the cost of what he must buy; which guaranteed excessive freight rates to the railroads and put a premium on wasteful management while saddling an unwarranted burden on to the backs of the American farmer; which permitted gambling in the products of the farm by grain speculators to the great detriment of the farmer and to the great profit of the grain gambler.

A COVENANT WITH THE PEOPLE

Awakened by the dangers which menace their freedom and prosperity the American people still retain the right and courage to exercise their sovereign control over their government. In order to destroy the economic and political power of monopoly, which has come between the people and their government, we pledge ourselves to the following principles and policies:

THE HOUSE CLEANING

1. We pledge a complete housecleaning in the Department of Justice, the Department of the Interior, and the other executive departments. We demand that the power of the Federal Government be used to crush private monopoly, not to foster it.

NATURAL RESOURCES

2. We pledge recovery of the navy's oil reserves and all other parts of the public domain which have been fraudulently or illegally leased, or otherwise wrongfully transferred, to the control of private interests; vigorous prosecution of all public officials, private citizens and corporations that participated in these transactions; complete revision of the water-power act, the general leasing act, and all other legislation relating to the public domain. We favor public ownership of the nation's water power and the creation and development of a national super-water-power system, including Muscle Shoals, to supply at actual cost light and power for the people and nitrate for the farmers, and strict public control and permanent conservation of all the nation's resources, including coal, iron and other ores, oil and timber lands, in the interest of the people.

RAILROADS

3. We favor repeal of the Esch-Cummins railroad law and the fixing of railroad rates upon the basis of actual, prudent investment and cost of service. We pledge speedy enactment of the Howell-Barkley Bill for the adjustment of controversies between railroads and their employees, which was held up in the last Congress by joint action of reactionary leaders of the Democratic and Republican parties. We declare for public ownership of railroads with definite safeguards against bureaucratic control, as the only final solution of the transportation problem.

TAX REDUCTION

4. We favor reduction of Federal taxes upon individual incomes and legitimate business, limiting tax exactions strictly to the requirements of the government administered with rigid economy,

particularly by curtailment of the eight hundred million dollars now annually expended for the army and navy in preparation for future wars; by the recovery of the hundreds of millions of dollars stolen from the Treasury through fraudulent war contracts and the corrupt leasing of the public resources; and by diligent action to collect the accumulated interest upon the eleven billion dollars owing us by foreign governments.

We denounce the Mellon tax plan as a device to relieve multi-millionaires at the expense of other tax payers, and favor a taxation policy providing for immediate reductions upon moderate incomes, large increases in the inheritance tax rates upon large estates to prevent the indefinite accumulation by inheritance of great fortunes in a few hands; taxes upon excess profits to penalize profiteering, and complete publicity, under proper safeguards, of all Federal tax returns.

The Courts

5. We favor submitting to the people, for their considerate judgment, a constitutional amendment providing that Congress may by enacting a statute make it effective over a judicial veto.

We favor such amendment to the constitution as may be necessary to provide for the election of all Federal Judges, without party designation, for fixed terms not exceeding ten years, by direct vote of the people.

The Farmers

6. We favor drastic reduction of the exhorbitant duties on manufactures provided in the Fordney-McCumber tariff legislation, the prohibiting of gambling by speculators and profiteers in agricultural products; the reconstruction of the Federal Reserve and Federal Farm Loan Systems, so as to eliminate control by usurers, speculators and international financiers, and to make the credit of the nation available upon fair terms to all and without discrimination to business men, farmers and home-builders. We advocate the calling of a special session of Congress to pass legislation for the relief of American agriculture. We favor such further legislation as may be needful or helpful in promoting and protecting cooperative enterprises. We demand that the Interstate Commerce Commission proceed forthwith to reduce by an approximation to pre-war levels the present freight rates on agricultural products, including live stock, and upon the materials required upon American farms for agricultural purposes.

Labor

7. We favor abolition of the use of injunctions in labor disputes and declare for complete protection of the right of farmers and industrial workers to organize, bargain collectively through representatives of their own choosing, and conduct without hindrance cooperative enterprises.

We favor prompt ratification of the Child Labor amendment, and subsequent enactment of a Federal law to protect children in industry.

Postal Service

8. We believe that a prompt and dependable postal service is essential to the social and economic welfare of the nation; and that as one of the most important steps toward establishing and maintaining such a service, it is necessary to fix wage standards that will secure and retain employees of character, energy and ability.

We favor the enactment of the postal salary adjustment measure (S. 1898) for the employees of the postal service, passed by the first session of the 68th Congress, vetoed by the President and now awaiting further consideration by the next session of Congress.

We endorse liberalizing the Civil Service Retirement Law along the lines of S. 3011 now pending in Congress.

War Veterans

9. We favor adjusted compensation for the veterans of the late war, not as charity, but as a matter of right, and we demand that the money necessary to meet this obligation of the government be raised by taxes laid upon wealth in proportion to the ability to pay, and declare our opposition to the sales tax or any other device to shift this obligation onto the backs of the poor in higher prices and increased cost of living. We do not regard the payment at the end of a long period of a small insurance as provided by the law recently passed as in any just sense a discharge of the nation's obligations to the veterans of the late war.

Great Lakes to Sea

10. We favor a deep waterway from the Great Lakes to the sea. The government should, in conjunction with Canada, take immediate action to

give the northwestern states an outlet to the ocean for cargoes, without change in bulk, thus making the primary markets on the Great Lakes equal to those of New York.

POPULAR SOVEREIGNTY

11. Over and above constitutions and statutes and greater than all, is the supreme sovereignty of the people, and with them should rest the final decision of all great questions of national policy. We favor such amendments to the Federal Constitution as may be necessary to provide for the direct nomination and election of the President, to extend the initiative and referendum to the federal government, and to insure a popular referendum for or against war except in cases of actual invasion.

PEACE ON EARTH

12. We denounce the mercenary system of foreign policy under recent administrations in the interests of financial imperialists, oil monopolists and international bankers, which has at times degraded our State Department from its high service as a strong and kindly intermediary of defenseless governments to a trading outpost for those interests and concession-seekers engaged in the exploitations of weaker nations, as contrary to the will of the American people, destructive of domestic development and provocative of war. We favor an active foreign policy to bring about a revision of the Versailles treaty in accordance with the terms of the armistice, and to promote firm treaty agreements with all nations to outlaw wars, abolish conscription, drastically reduce land, air and naval armaments, and guarantee public referendum on peace and war.

Conference for Progressive Political Action Platform, 1924

For 148 years the American people have been seeking to establish a government for the service of all and to prevent the establishment of a government for the mastery of the few. Free men of every generation must combat renewed efforts of organized force and greed to destroy liberty. Every generation must wage a new war for freedom against new forces that seek through new devices to enslave mankind.

Under our representative democracy the people protect their liberties through their public agents.

The test of public officials and public polities alike must be: Will they serve or will they exploit the common need?

The reactionary continues to put his faith in mastery for the solution of all problems. He seeks to have what he calls the strong men and best minds rule and impose their decisions upon the masses of their weaker brethren.

The progressive, on the contrary, contends for less autocracy and more democracy in government, for less power of privilege and greater obligations of service.

Under the principle of ruthless individualism and competition, that government is deemed best which offers to the few the greatest chance of individual gain.

Under the progressive principle of cooperation, that government is deemed best which offers to the many the highest level of average happiness and well being.

It is our faith that we all go up or down together—that class gains are temporary delusions and that eternal laws of compensation make every man his brother's keeper.

PROGRAM OF PUBLIC SERVICE

In that faith we present our program of public service:

(1) The use of the power of the federal government to crush private monopoly, not to foster it.

(2) Unqualified enforcement of the constitutional guarantees of freedom of speech, press, and assemblage.

(3) Public ownership of the nation's water power and creation of a public super-power system. Strict public control and permanent conservation of all natural resources, including coal, iron, and other ores, oil, and timber lands in the interest of the people. Promotion of public works in times of business depression.

(4) Retention of surtax on swollen incomes, restoration of the tax on excess profits, taxation of stock dividends, profits undistributed to evade taxes, rapidly progressive taxes on large estates and inheritances, and repeal of excessive tariff duties, especially on trust-controlled necessities of life and of nuisance taxes on consumption, to relieve the people of the present unjust burden of taxation and compel those who profited by the war to pay their share of the war's cost, and to provide the funds for adjusted compensation

solemnly pledged to the veterans of the World War.

(5) Reconstruction of the federal reserve and federal farm loan systems to provide for direct public control of the nation's money and credit to make it available on fair terms to all, and national and state legislation to permit and promote co-operative banking.

(6) Adequate laws to guarantee to farmers and industrial workers the right to organize and bargain collectively through representatives of their own choosing for the maintenance or improvement of their standard of life.

(7) Creation of a government marketing corporation to provide a direct route between farm producer and city consumer and to assure farmers fair prices for their products, and protect consumers from the profiteers in foodstuffs and other necessaries of life. Legislation to control the meat-packing industry.

(8) Protection and aid of cooperative enterprises by national and state legislation.

(9) Common international action to effect the economic recovery of the world from the effects of the World War.

(10) Repeal of the Cummins-Esch law. Public ownership of railroads, with democratic operation, and with definite safeguards against bureaucratic control.

(11) Abolition of the tyranny and usurpation of the courts, including the practice of nullifying legislation in conflict with the political, social or economic theories of the judges. Abolition of injunctions in labor disputes and of the power to punish for contempt without trial by jury. Election of all federal judges without party designation for limited terms.

(12) Prompt ratification of the child labor amendment and subsequent enactment of a federal law to protect children in industry. Removal of legal discriminations against women by measures not prejudicial to legislation necessary for the protection of women and for the advancement of social welfare.

(13) A deep waterway from the great lakes to the sea.

(14) We denounce the mercenary system of degraded foreign policy under recent administrations in the interests of financial imperialists, oil monopolists, and international bankers, which has at times degraded our State Department from its high service as a strong and kindly intermediary of defenseless governments to a trading outpost for those interests and concession seekers engaged in the exploitation of weaker nations, as contrary to the will of the American people, destructive of domestic development and provocative of war. We favor an active foreign policy to bring about a revision of the Versailles treaty in accordance with the terms of the armistice, and to promote firm treaty agreements with all nations to outlaw wars, abolish conscription, drastically reduce land, air and naval armaments and guarantee public referendum on peace and war.

In supporting this program we are applying to the needs of today the fundamental principles of American democracy, opposing equally the dictatorship of plutocracy and the dictatorship of the proletariat.

We appeal to all Americans without regard to partisan affiliation and we raise the standards of our faith so that all of like purpose may rally and march in this campaign under the banners of progressive union.

The nation may grow rich in the vision of greed. The nation will grow great in the vision of service.

Prohibition Platform of 1924

The Prohibition Party in National Convention at Columbus, Ohio, this sixth day of June, 1924, recognizing Almighty God as the source of all governmental authority and that the principles enunciated by His Son, Jesus Christ, should guide in all matters pertaining to government, makes the following declaration of principles:

OUR PARTY AND ITS PHILOSOPHY

Four years of nullification of the Eighteenth Amendment by the Democratic and Republican officials have demonstrated the soundness of the philosophy of the Prohibition party that a law conferring a right will enforce itself, but a law prohibiting a wrong, financially and politically entrenched, requires a party thoroughly committed to its maintenance and enforcement. Little or no improvement can be expected so long as the friends of the prohibitory law divide themselves among political parties seeking the votes of the law violators and the nullificationists, which votes are regarded to be as necessary to the success of those political parties as are the votes of the law-abiders.

The astounding revelations of corruption and maladministration in government, extending to the Cabinet itself, are but the inevitable consequences of the moral bankruptcy of a political party which, perpetuating the old liquor régime, is dependent upon the wet vote for its margin of plurality.

INTERNATIONAL RELATIONS

The time is past when the United States can hold aloof from the affairs of the World. We support the proposal for the entry of this Country into the Court of International Justice, as an important step for substituting law for force in the settlement of international disputes.

LABOR, CAPITAL AND THE GENERAL PUBLIC

While adhering to our time honored position of demanding justice for both Labor and Capital, we declare that the interests of the general public are paramount to both. Therefore, we favor the speedy enactment by Congress and the several state Legislatures, each in its respective jurisdiction, of such legislation as shall impartially protect all three of these classes.

AGRICULTURE

In the constantly increasing trend of population from the country into the towns and cities, with the constant abandonment of the farms, this country faces a grave peril. It is self-evident that the farmer, with his investment in his lands, buildings, live-stock, machinery, tools, and labor, ought to receive more than one-half of the dollar paid by the consumer for the products of the farm, where no process of manufacture intervenes. If given power, we will by appropriate legislation endeavor to secure to the farmer his just share of the proceeds of his toil.

CONSERVATION

All natural resources, including mineral, oil, and timber lands, water powers and other wealth still remaining to the United States after the wasteful and profligate administration of corrupt old party officials, should be held perpetually and operated to produce revenue for the use of the Government. They must not be ruthlessly squandered by men or corporations for their own enrichment, nor must they become the collateral of political parties for promissory notes issued for value received.

UNJUST BALLOT LAWS

We denounce the enactment by the Republican and Democratic parties in many states of unjust and discriminatory election laws, that make it almost, and in some states entirely impossible for minor parties to retain their place on the official ballot, or for new parties to be formed, and we demand their repeal.

THE BIBLE IN THE SCHOOLS

The Bible is the Magna Charta of human liberty and national safety and is of highest educational value. Therefore it should have a large place in our public schools.

AMERICANIZATION OF ALIENS

Recognizing the fact that there are large numbers of unassimilated aliens now in this country who, in their present condition and environment, are incapable of assimilation, and are therefore a menace to our institutions, we declare for an immediate, scientific investigation, looking forward to a constructive program for Americanizing these aliens.

SEPARATION OF DEPARTMENTS OF GOVERNMENT

We deplore the prevailing disregard of the parties in power of the Constitutional division of governmental powers into Legislative, Executive, and Judicial branches, and when placed in authority we pledge strict observance of such division.

WOMAN AND THE HOME

We approve and adopt the program of the National League of Women Voters for public welfare in government in so far as a strict regard for the division of powers under our dual form of government will permit.

CIVIL SERVICE

We favor the extension of the merit system to all the agencies of the Executive branch of our government.

FREE INSTITUTIONS

We favor freedom of speech, a free press, our free public school system, and compulsory attendance in our public schools. We are unalterably opposed to public monies being used for sectarian purposes. We favor keeping open to public inspection all places where public wards are cared for.

CONCLUSION

On this record of principles, and on its record of long-time faithfulness and vision, proved by the many reforms which it was the first to advocate, the National Prohibition Party summons all those who favor suppression of the liquor traffic, the enforcement of law, the maintenance of constitutional government, the purification of our politics, honesty and efficiency in administration, and the building of a better citizenship, to join with us in a new alignment in a political party to achieve these transcendent objectives.

Republican Platform of 1924

We the delegates of the republican party in national convention assembled, bow our heads in reverent memory of Warren G. Harding.

We nominated him four years ago to be our candidate; the people of the nation elected him their president. His human qualities gripped the affections of the American people. He was a public servant unswerving in his devotion to duty.

A staunch republican, he was first of all a true patriot, who gave unstintingly of himself during a trying and critical period of our national life.

His conception and successful direction of the limitation of armaments conference in Washington was an accomplishment which advanced the world along the path toward peace.

As delegates of the republican party, we share in the national thanksgiving that in the great emergency created by the death of our great leader there stood forth fully equipped to be his successor one whom we had nominated as vice-president—Calvin Coolidge, who as vice-president and president by his every act has justified the faith and confidence which he has won from the nation.

He has put the public welfare above personal considerations. He has given to the people practical idealism in office. In his every act, he has won without seeking the applause of the people

of the country. The constantly accumulating evidence of his integrity, vision and single minded devotion to the needs of the people of this nation strengthens and inspires our confident faith in his continued leadership.

SITUATION IN 1921

When the republican administration took control of the government in 1921, there were four and a half million unemployed; industry and commerce were stagnant; agriculture was prostrate; business was depressed; securities of the government were selling below their par values.

Peace was delayed; misunderstanding and friction characterized our relations abroad. There was a lack of faith in the administration of government resulting in a growing feeling of distrust in the very principles upon which our institutions are founded.

To-day industry and commerce are active; public and private credits are sound; we have made peace; we have taken the first step toward disarmament and strengthened our friendship with the world powers, our relations with the rest of the world are on a firmer basis, our position was never better understood, our foreign policy never more definite and consistent. The tasks to which we have put our hands are completed. Time has been too short for the correction of all the ills we received as a heritage from the last democratic administration, and the notable accomplishments under republican rule warrant us in appealing to the country with entire confidence.

PUBLIC ECONOMY

We demand and the people of the United States have a right to demand rigid economy in government. A policy of strict economy enforced by the republican administration since 1921 has made possible a reduction in taxation and has enabled the government to reduce the public debt by $2,500,000,000. This policy vigorously enforced has resulted in a progressive reduction of public expenditures until they are now two billions dollars per annum less than in 1921. The tax burdens of the people have been relieved to the extent of $1,250,000,000 per annum. Government securities have been increased in value more than $3,000,000,000. Deficits have been converted in surpluses. The budget system has been firmly established and the number of federal employes has been reduced more than one hundred thousand. We commend the firm insistence of President Coolidge upon rigid government economy and pledge him our earnest support to this end.

FINANCE AND TAXATION

We believe that the achievement of the republican administration in reducing taxation by $1,250,000,000 per annum; reducing of the public debt by $2,432,000,000; installing a budget system; reducing the public expenditures from $5,500,000,000 per annum to approximately $3,-400,000,000 per annum, thus reducing the ordinary expenditures of the government to substantially a pre-war basis, and the complete restoration of public credit; the payment or refunding of $7,500,000,000 of public obligations without disturbance of credit or industry—all during the short period of three years—presents a record unsurpassed in the history of public finance.

The assessment of taxes wisely and scientifically collected and the efficient and economical expenditure of the money received by the government are essential to the prosperity of our nation.

Carelessness in levying taxes inevitably breeds extravagance in expenditures. The wisest of taxation rests most rightly on the individual and economic life of the country. The public demand for a sound tax policy is insistent.

Progressive tax reduction should be accomplished through tax reorganization. It should not be confined to less than 4,000,000 of our citizens who pay direct taxes, but is the right of more than 100,000,000 who are daily paying their taxes through their living expenses. Congress has in the main confined its work to tax reduction. The matter of tax reform is still unsettled and is equally essential.

We pledge ourselves to the progressive reduction of taxes of all the people as rapidly as may be done with due regard for the essential expenditures for the government administered with rigid economy and to place our tax system on a sound peace time basis.

We endorse the plan of President Coolidge to call in November a national conference of federal and state officials for the development of the effective methods of lightening the tax burden of our citizens and adjusting questions of taxation as between national and state governments.

We favor the creation by appropriate legislation of a non-partisan federal commission to make a comprehensive study and report upon the tax system of the states and federal government with a view to an intelligent reformation of our systems of taxation to a more equitable basis and a proper adjustment of the subjects of taxation as between the national and state governments with justice to the taxpayer and in conformity with the sound economic principles.

REORGANIZATION

We favor a comprehensive reorganization of the executive departments and bureaus along the line of the plan recently submitted by a joint committee of the congress which has the unqualified support of President Coolidge.

CIVIL SERVICE

Improvement in the enforcement of the merit system both by legislative enactment and executive action since March 4, 1921, has been marked and effective. By executive order the appointment of presidential postmasters has been placed on the merit basis similar to that applying to the classified service.

We favor the classification of postmasters in first, second and third class postoffices and the placing of the prohibition enforcement field forces within the classified civil service without necessarily incorporating the present personnel.

FOREIGN DEBTS

In fulfillment of our solemn pledge in the national platform of 1920 we have steadfastly refused to consider the cancellation of foreign debts. Our attitude has not been that of an oppressive creditor seeking immediate return and ignoring existing financial conditions, but has been based on the conviction that a moral obligation such as was incurred should not be disregarded.

We stand for settlements with all debtor countries, similar in character to our debt agreement with Great Britain. That settlement achieved under a republican administration, was the greatest international financial transaction in the history of the world. Under the terms of the agreement the United States now receives an annual return upon four billion six hundred million dollars owing to us by Great Britain with a definite obligation of ultimate payment in full.

The justness of the basis employed has been formally recognized by other debtor nations.

Great nations cannot recognize or admit the principle of repudiation. To do so would undermine the integrity essential for international trade, commerce and credit. Thirty-five per cent of the total foreign debt is now in process of liquidation.

The Tariff

We reaffirm our belief in the protective tariff to extend needed protection to our productive industries. We believe in protection as a national policy, with due and equal regard to all sections and to all classes. It is only by adherence to such a policy that the well being of the consumers can be safeguarded that there can be assured to American agriculture, to American labor and to American manufacturers a return to perpetuate American standards of life. A protective tariff is designed to support the high American economic level of life for the average family and to prevent a lowering to the levels of economic life prevailing in other lands.

In the history of the nation the protective tariff system has ever justified itself by restoring confidence, promoting industrial activity and employment, enormously increasing our purchasing power and bringing increased prosperity to all our people.

The tariff protection to our industry works for increased consumption of domestic agricultural products by an employed population instead of one unable to purchase the necessities of life. Without the strict maintenance of the tariff principle our farmers will need always to compete with cheap lands and cheap labor abroad and with lower standards of living.

The enormous value of the protective principle has once more been demonstrated by the emergency tariff act of 1921 and the tariff act of 1922.

We assert our belief in the elastic provision adopted by congress in the tariff act of 1922 providing for a method of readjusting the tariff rates and the classifications in order to meet changing economic conditions when such changed conditions are brought to the attention of the president by complaint or application.

We believe that the power to increase or decrease any rate of duty provided in the tariff furnishes a safeguard on the one hand against excessive taxes and on the other hand against too high customs charges.

The wise provisions of this section of the tariff act afford ample opportunity for tariff duties to be adjusted after a hearing in order that they may cover the actual differences in the cost of production in the United States and the principal competing countries of the world.

We also believe that the application of this provision of the tariff act will contribute to business stability by making unnecessary general disturbances which are usually incident to general tariff revisions.

Foreign Relations

The republican party reaffirmed its stand for agreement among the nations to prevent war and preserve peace. As an immediate step in this direction we endorse the permanent court of international justice and favor the adherence of the United States to this tribunal as recommended by President Coolidge. This government has definitely refused membership in the league of nations or to assume any obligations under the covenant of the league. On this we stand.

While we are unwilling to enter into political commitments which would involve us in the conflict of European politics, it should be the purpose and high privilege of the United States to continue to co-operate with other nations in humanitarian efforts in accordance with our cherished traditions. The basic principles of our foreign policy must be independence without indifference to the rights and necessities of others and co-operation without entangling alliances. The policy overwhelmingly approved by the people has been vindicated since the end of the great war.

America's participation in world affairs under the administration of President Harding and President Coolidge has demonstrated the wisdom and prudence of the national judgment. A most impressive example of the capacity of the United States to serve the cause of the world peace without political affiliations was shown in the effective and beneficent work of the Dawes commission toward the solution of the perplexing question of German reparations.

The first conference of great powers in Washington called by President Harding accomplished the limitation of armaments and the readjustment of the relations of the powers interested in the far east. The conference resulted in an agreement to reduce armaments, relieved the competitive nations involved from the great burdens of taxation arising from the construction and maintenance of capital battleships; assured a new, broader and better understanding in the far east; brought the assurance of peace in the region of the Pacific and formally adopted the policy of the open door for trade and commerce in the great markets of the far east.

This historic conference paved the way to avert the danger of renewed hostilities in Europe, and to restore the necessary economic stability. While the military forces of America have been restored to a peace footing, there has been an increase in the land and air forces abroad which constitutes a continual menace to the peace of the world and a bar to the return of prosperity.

We firmly advocate the calling of a conference on the limitation of land forces, the use of submarines and poison gas, as proposed by President Coolidge, when, through the adoption of a permanent reparations plan the conditions in Europe will make negotiations and co-operation opportune and possible.

By treaties of peace, safeguarding our rights and without derogating those of our former associates in arms, the republican administration ended the war between this country and Germany and Austria. We have concluded and signed with other nations during the past three years more than fifty treaties and international agreements in the furtherance of peace and good will.

New sanctions and new proofs of permanent accord have marked our relations with all Latin-America. The long standing controversy between Chile and Peru has been advanced toward settlement by its submission to the president of the United States as arbitrator and with the helpful co-operation of this country a treaty has been signed by the representatives of sixteen American republics which will stabilize conditions on the American continent and minimize the opportunities for war.

Our difficulties with Mexico have happily yielded to a most friendly adjustment. Mutual confidence has been restored and a pathway for that friendliness and helpfulness which should exist between this government and the government of our neighboring republic has been marked. Agreements have been entered into for the determination by judicial commissions of the claims of the citizens of each country against the respective governments. We can confidently look forward to more permanent and more stable re-

lations with this republic that joins for so many miles our southern border.

Our policy, now well defined, of giving practical aid to other peoples without assuming political obligations has been conspicuously demonstrated. The ready and generous response of America to the needs of the starving in Russia and the suddenly stricken people of Japan gave evidence of our helpful interest in the welfare of the distressed in other lands.

The work of our representatives in dealing with subjects of such universal concern as the traffic in women and children, the production and distribution of narcotic drugs, the sale of arms and in matters affecting public health and morals, demonstrates that we can effectively do our part for humanity and civilization without forfeiting, limiting or restricting our national freedom of action.

The American people do cherish their independence, but their sense of duty to all mankind will ever prompt them to give their support, service and leadership to every cause which makes for peace and amity among the nations of the world.

Agriculture

In dealing with agriculture the republican party recognizes that we are faced with a fundamental national problem, and that the prosperity and welfare of the nation as a whole is dependent upon the prosperity and welfare of our agricultural population.

We recognize our agricultural activities are still struggling with adverse conditions that have brought about distress. We pledge the party to take whatever steps are necessary to bring back a balanced condition between agriculture, industry and labor, which was destroyed by the democratic party through an unfortunate administration of legislation passed as war-time measures.

We affirm that under the republican administration the problems of the farm have received more serious consideration than ever before both by definite executive action and by congressional action not only in the field of general legislation but also in the enactment of laws to meet emergency situations.

The restoration of general prosperity and the purchasing power of our people through tariff protection has resulted in an increased domestic consumption of food products while the price of many agricultural commodities are above the war price level by reason of direct tariff protection.

Under the leadership of the president at the most critical time, a corporation was organized by private capital making available $100,000,000 to assist the farmers of the northwest.

In realization of the disturbance in the agricultural export market, the result of the financial depression in Europe, and appreciating that the export field would be enormously improved by economic rehabilitation and the resulting increased consuming power, a sympathetic support and direction was given to the work of the American representatives on the European reparations commission.

The revival in 1921 of the war finance corporation with loans of over $300,000,000 averted in 1921 a complete collapse in the agricultural industry.

We have established new intermediate credit banks for agriculture and increased the capital of the federal farm loan system. Emergency loans have been granted to drought stricken areas. We have enacted into law the co-operative marketing act, the grain futures and packer control acts; given to agriculture direct representation on the federal reserve board and on the federal aid commission. We have greatly strengthened our foreign marketing service for the disposal of our agricultural products.

The crux of the problem from the standpoint of the farmer is the net profit he receives after his outlay. The process of bringing the average prices of what he buys and what he sells closer together can be promptly expedited by reduction in taxes, steady employment in industry and stability in business.

This process can be expedited directly by lower freight rates, by better marketing through co-operative efforts and a more scientific organization of the physical human machinery of distribution and by a greater diversification of farm products.

We promise every assistance in the reorganization of the market system on sounder and more economical lines and where diversification is needed government assistance during the period of transition. Vigorous efforts of this administration toward broadening our exports market will be continued. The republican party pledges itself to the development and enactment of measures which will place the agricultural interests of America on a basis of economic equality with other industries to assure its prosperity and success. We favor adequate tariff protection to such of our agriculture products as are threatened by competition. We favor, without putting the government into business, the establishment of a federal system of organization for co-operative marketing of farm products.

Highways

The federal aid road act, adopted by the republican congress in 1921 has been of inestimable value to the development of the highway systems of the several states and of the nation. We pledge a continuation of this policy of federal co-operation with the states in highway building.

We favor the construction of roads and trails in our national forests necessary to their protection and utilization. In appropriations, therefore, the taxes which these lands would pay if taxable, should be considered as a controlling factor.

Labor

The increasing stress of industrial life, the constant and necessary efforts because of world competition to increase production and decrease costs has made it specially incumbent on those in authority to protect labor from undue exactions.

We commend congress for having recognized this possibility in its prompt adoption of the recommendation of President Coolidge for a constitutional amendment authorizing congress to legislate on the subject of child labor, and we urge the prompt consideration of that amendment by the legislatures of the various states.

There is no success great enough to justify the employment of women in labor under conditions which will impair their natural functions.

We favor high standards for wage, working and living conditions among the women employed in industry. We pledge a continuance of the successful efforts of the republican administration to eliminate the seven-day, twelve-hour day industry.

We regard with satisfaction the elimination of the twelve-hour day in the steel industry and the agreement eliminating the seven-day work week of alternate thirteen and eleven hours accomplished through the efforts of Presidents Harding and Coolidge.

We declare our faith in the principle of the eight-hour day.

We pledge a continuation of the work of rehabilitating workers in industry as conducted by the federal board for vocational education, and favor adequate appropriations for this purpose.

We favor a broader and better system of vocational education, a more adequate system of federal free employment agencies with facilities for assisting the movements of seasonal and migratory labor, including farm labor, with ample organization for bringing the man and his job together.

RAILROADS

We believe that the demand of the American people for improved railroad service at cheaper rates is justified and that it can be fulfilled by the consolidation of the railroads into a lesser number of connecting systems with the resultant operating economy. The labor board provision should be amended to meet the requirements made evident by experience gained from its actual creation.

Collective bargaining, voluntary mediation and arbitration are the most important steps in maintaining peaceful labor relations. We do not believe in compulsory action at any time. Public opinion must be the final arbiter in any crisis which so vitally affects public welfare as the suspension of transportation. Therefore, the interests of the public require the maintenance of an impartial tribunal which can in any emergency make an investigation of the fact and publish its conclusions. This is accepted as a basis of popular judgment.

GOVERNMENT CONTROL

The prosperity of the American nation rests on the vigor of private initiative which has bred a spirit of independence and self-reliance. The republican party stands now, as always, against all attempts to put the government into business.

American industry should not be compelled to struggle against government competition. The right of the government to regulate, supervise and control public utilities and public interests, we believe, should be strengthened, but we are firmly opposed to the nationalization or government ownership of public utilities.

COAL

The price and a constant supply of this essential commodity are of vital interest to the public. The government has no constitutional power to regulate prices, but can bring its influence to bear by the powerful instrument afforded by full publicity. When through industrial conflict, its supply is threatened, the president should have authority to appoint a commission to act as mediators and as a medium for voluntary arbitration. In the event of a strike, the control of distribution must be invoked to prevent profiteering.

MERCHANT MARINE

The republican party stands for a strong and permanent merchant marine built by Americans, owned by Americans and manned by Americans to secure the necessary contact with world markets for our surplus agricultural products and manufactures; to protect our shippers and importers from exorbitant ocean freight rates, and to become a powerful arm of our national defense.

That part of the merchant marine now owned by the government should continue to be improved in its economic and efficient management, with reduction of the losses now paid by the government through taxation until it is finally placed on so sound a basis that, with ocean freight rates becoming normal, due to improvement in international affairs, it can be sold to American citizens.

WATERWAYS

Fully realizing the vital importance of transportation in both cost and service to all of our people, we favor the construction of the most feasible waterways from the Great Lakes to the Atlantic seaboard and the Gulf of Mexico, and the improvement and development of rivers, harbors and waterways, inland and coastwise, to the fullest extent justified by the present and potential tonnage available.

We favor a comprehensive survey of the conditions under which the flood waters of the Colorado river may be controlled and utilized for the benefit of the people of the states which border thereon.

The federal water power act establishes a national water power policy and the way has thereby been opened for the greatest water power development in history under conditions which preserve initiative of our people, yet protect the public interest.

WORLD WAR VETERANS

The republican party pledges a continual and increasing solicitude for all those suffering any disability as a result of service to the United States in time of war. No country and no administration has ever shown a more generous disposition in the care of its disabled, or more thoughtful consideration in providing a sound administration for the solution of the many problems involved in making intended benefits fully, directly and promptly available to the veterans.

The confusion, inefficiency and maladministration existing heretofore since the establishment of this government agency has been cured, and plans are being actively made looking to a further improvement in the operation of the bureau by the passage of new legislation. The basic statute has been so liberalized as to bring within its terms 100,000 additional beneficiaries. The privilege of hospitalization in government hospitals, as recommended by President Coolidge, has been granted to all veterans irrespective of the origin of disability, and over $50,000,000 has been appropriated for hospital construction which will provide sufficient beds to care for all. Appropriations totalling over $1,100,000,000, made by the republican congress for the care of the disabled, evidence the unmistakable purpose of the government not to consider costs when the welfare of these men is at stake. No legislation for the benefit of the disabled soldiers proposed during the last four years by veterans' organizations has failed to receive consideration.

We pledge ourselves to meet the problems of the future affecting the care of our wounded and disabled in a spirit of liberality, and with that thoughtful consideration which will enable the government to give to the individual veteran that full measure of care guaranteed by an effective administrative machinery.

CONSERVATION

We believe in the development, effective and efficient, whether of oil, timber, coal or water power resources of this government only as needed and only after the public needs have become a matter of public record, controlled with a scrupulous regard and ever-vigilant safeguards against waste, speculation and monopoly.

The natural resources of the country belong to all the people and are a part of an estate belonging to generations yet unborn. The government policy should be to safeguard, develop and utilize these possessions. The conservation policy of the nation originated with the republican party under the inspiration of Theodore Roosevelt.

We hold it a privilege of the republican party to build as a memorial to him on the foundation which he laid.

EDUCATION AND RELIEF

The conservation of human resources is one of the most solemn responsibilities of government. This is an obligation which cannot be ignored and which demands that the federal government shall, as far as lies in its power, give to the people and the states the benefit of its counsel.

The welfare activities of the government connected with the various departments are already numerous and important, but lack the co-ordination which is essential to effective action. To meet these needs we approve the suggestion for the creation of a cabinet post of education and relief.

WAR-TIME MOBILIZATION

We believe that in time of war the nation should draft for its defense not only its citizens but also every resource which may contribute to success. The country demands that should the United States ever again be called upon to defend itself by arms the president be empowered to draft such material resources and such service as may be required, and to stabilize the prices of services and essential commodities, whether used in actual warfare or private activities.

COMMERCIAL AVIATION

We advocate the early enactment of such legislation and the taking of such steps by the government as will tend to promote commercial aviation.

ARMY AND NAVY

There must be no further weakening of our regular army and we advocate appropriations sufficient to provide for the training of all members of the national guard, the citizens' military training camps, the reserve officers' training camps and the reserves who may offer themselves for service. We pledge ourselves for service. We pledge ourselves to round out and maintain the navy to the full strength provided the United States by the letter and spirit of the limitation of armament conference.

THE NEGRO

We urge the congress to enact at the earliest possible date a federal anti-lynching law so that the full influence of the federal government may be wielded to exterminate this hideous crime. We believe that much of the misunderstanding which now exists can be eliminated by humane and sympathetic study of its causes. The president has recommended the creation of a commission for the investigation of social and economic conditions and the promotion of mutual understanding and confidence.

ORDERLY GOVERNMENT

The republican party reaffirms its devotion to orderly government under the guarantees embodied in the constitution of the United States. We recognize the duty of constant vigilance to preserve at all times a clean and honest government and to bring to the bar of justice every defiler of the public service in or out of office.

Dishonesty and corruption are not political attributes. The recent congressional investigations have exposed instances in both parties of men in public office who are willing to sell official favors and men out of office who are willing to buy them in some cases with money and others with influence.

The sale of influence resulting from the holding of public position or from association while in public office or the use of such influence for private gain or advantage is a perversion of public trust and prejudicial to good government. It should be condemned by public opinion and forbidden by law.

We demand the speedy, fearless and impartial prosecution of all wrong doers, without regard for political affiliations; but we declare no greater wrong can be committed against the people than the attempt to destroy their trust in the great body of their public servants. Admitting the deep humiliation which all good citizens share that our public life should have harbored some dishonest men, we assert that these undesirables do not represent the standard of our national integrity.

The government at Washington is served to-day by thousands of earnest, conscientious and faithful officials and employés in every department.

It is a grave wrong against these patriotic men and women to strive indiscriminately to besmirch the names of the innocent and undermine the confidence of the people in the government under which they live. It is even a greater wrong when this is done for partisan purposes or for selfish exploitation.

IMMIGRATION

The unprecedented living conditions in Europe following the world war created a condition by which we were threatened with mass immigration that would have seriously disturbed our economic life. The law recently enacted is designed to protect the inhabitants of our country, not only the American citizen, but also the alien already with us who is seeking to secure an economic foothold for himself and family from the competition that would come from unrestricted immigration. The administrative features of the law represent a great constructive advance, and eliminate the hardships suffered by immigrants under emergency statute.

We favor the adoption of methods which will exercise a helpful influence among the foreign born population and provide for the education of the alien in our language, customs, ideals and standards of life. We favor the improvement of naturalization laws.

Socialist Labor Platform of 1924

The world stands upon the threshold of a new social order. The capitalist system of production and distribution is doomed; capitalist appropriation of labor's product forces the bulk of mankind into wage slavery, throws society into the convulsions of the class struggle, and momentarily threatens to engulf humanity in chaos and disaster. At this crucial period in history the Socialist Labor Party of America, in 16th National Convention assembled, reaffirming its former platform declarations, calls upon the workers to rally around the banner of the Socialist Labor Party, the only party in this country that blazes the trail to the Worker's Industrial Republic.

Since the advent of civilization human society has been divided into classes. Each new form of society has come into being with a definite purpose to fulfill in the progress of the human race. Each has been born, has grown, developed, prospered, become old, outworn, and has finally been overthrown. Each society has developed within itself the germs of its own destruction as well as the germs which went to make up the society of the future.

The capitalist system rose during the seventeenth, eighteenth, and nineteenth centuries by the overthrow of feudalism. Its great and all-important mission in the development of man was to improve, develop, and concentrate the means of production and distribution, thus creating a system of co-operative production. This work was completed in advanced capitalist countries about the beginning of the 20th century. That moment capitalism had fulfilled its historic mission, and from that moment the capitalist class became a class of parasites.

In the course of human progress mankind has passed, through class rule, private property, and individualism in production and exchange, from the enforced and inevitable want, misery, poverty, and ignorance of savagery and barbarism to the affluence and high productive capacity of civilization. For all practical purposes, co-operative production has now superseded individual production.

Capitalism no longer promotes the greatest good of the greatest number. It no longer spells progress, but reaction. Private production carries with it private ownership of the products. Production is carried on, not to supply the needs of humanity, but for the profit of the individual owner, the company, or the trust. The worker, not receiving the full product of his labor, cannot buy back all he produces. The capitalist wastes part in riotous living; the rest must find a foreign market. By the opening of the twentieth century the capitalist world—England, America, Germany, France, Japan, China, etc.—was producing at a mad rate for the world market. A capitalist deadlock of markets brought on in 1914 the capitalist collapse popularly known as the World War. The capitalist world can not extricate itself out of the débris. America to-day is choking under the weight of her own gold and products.

This situation has brought on the present stage of human misery—starvation, want, cold, disease, pestilence, and war. This state is brought about in the midst of plenty, when the earth can be made to yield hundred-fold, when the machinery of production is made to multiply human energy and ingenuity by the hundred. The present state of misery exists solely because the mode of production rebels against the mode of exchange. Private property in the means of life has become a social crime. The land was made by no man; the modern machines are the result of the combined ingenuity of the human race from time immemorial; the land can be made to yield and the machines can be set in motion only by the collective effort of the workers. Progress demands the collective ownership of the land on and the tools with which to produce the necessities of life. The owner of the means of life to-day partakes of the nature of a highwayman; he stands with his gun before society's temple; it depends upon him whether the million mass may work, earn, eat, and live. The capitalist system of production and exchange must be supplanted if progress is to continue.

In place of the capitalist system the Socialist Labor Party aims to substitute a system of social ownership of the means of production, industrially administered by the workers, who assume control and direction as well as operation of their industrial affairs.

We therefore call upon the wage workers to organize themselves into a revolutionary political organization under the banner of the Socialist Labor Party; and to organize themselves likewise upon the industrial field into a Socialist industrial union, in order to consolidate the material power necessary for the establishment of the Socialist Industrial Republic.

We also call upon all intelligent citizens to place themselves squarely upon the ground of working class interest, and join us in this mighty and noble work of human emancipation, so that we may put summary end to the existing barbarous class conflict by placing the land and all the means of production, transportation, and distribution into the hands of the people as a collective body, and substituting Industrial Self-Government for the present state of planless production, industrial war and social disorder—a government in which every worker shall have the free exercise and full benefit of his faculties, multiplied by all the modern factors of civilization.

Workers' Party Platform, 1924

The workers and exploited farmers of the United States face the question of how to organize and use their political power in the coming election. Before deciding this question every industrial worker, agricultural worker and exploited farmer should give fundamental consideration to the situation which exists in this country.

IN THE GRIP OF THE EXPLOITERS

The United States is the wealthiest country in the world. We have natural resources which supply us with raw materials and a great industrial organization which can turn these raw materials into the finished products which satisfy human needs. With the raw materials available and the tremendous machinery of production we have the means of giving a high standard of life —good food, good clothing, good homes, the opportunity for education and recreation—to every person in this country. This high standard of life is denied the workers and exploited farmers of the United States. Millions of these producers of wealth are able to secure for their labor only the means for a bare existence. Millions of workers must work long hours, under bad working conditions, for low wages. Millions are periodically unemployed, as at present, with all the consequent misery and suffering for themselves and their families. In order to keep these conditions from growing worse, millions of industrial workers are periodically compelled to go on strike to fight back the greedy employers. Millions of farmers have been driven into bankruptcy and from the land because of inability to earn enough for a living.

These conditions prevail in a country in which we have the means of supplying a high standard of life to every person because a relatively small class has fastened its grip upon the raw materials and industries and uses these to enrich itself at the expense of the producers. Through theft, fraud, corruption, bribery, and the capitalist system of profit taking, this capitalist class has become the owner of the land, raw material and machinery of production upon which the workers and farmers are dependent for a livelihood.

The raw materials and industries of the United States are owned by the Garys, Morgans, Rockefellers, Fords, McCormicks, and other great capitalists. The workers and farmers alike pay tribute to these capitalists. They are compelled to accept a low standard of living in order that the capitalists may amass even greater fortunes for themselves.

It is this system of capitalist ownership of industry which gives the wealth produced to the few, that denies the millions of industrial workers, agricultural workers and exploited farmers the enjoyment of that high standard of life which their labor and the wealth they produce make possible in this country.

It is this system of capitalist ownership of industry which is the basis of the class struggle between the workers, fighting for more of what they produce, and the capitalists, ever bent on securing greater and greater profits for themselves.

HOW THE CAPITALISTS USE THE GOVERNMENT

The government of the United States is and has been a government of, by, and for the capitalists. It is through the government and use of the governmental power that the capitalists maintain their grip on the industries and their power to rob the industrial workers, agricultural workers, and farmers.

During the war, with the connivance of government officials, the capitalists looted the country of billions of wealth. Since the war the shipping board deals, the war veterans' board corruption, the Teapot Dome exposures, have shown how the capitalists fill their pockets at the expense of the working and farming masses.

Governmental legislation is framed so as to yield the capitalists more and more profits. Tariff laws, taxation laws, agrarian bank laws, are all framed so as to enable the bankers and industrial magnates to take more and more of what the workers produce.

To prevent the workers from securing better wages and working conditions through strikes, the capitalists use the government to destroy these strikes. The disgraceful Daugherty injunction against the railway shopmen, the use of troops against miners in their strike in 1922, the use of the Railway Labor Board against the railroad workers, are only outstanding examples of the continual use of the governmental power by the capitalists to protect themselves in taking greater and greater profits out of the labor of the workers.

The government is a dictatorship of the capitalists and their instrument for the oppression and exploitation of the workers. Although the workers are permitted to vote, the capitalists are able, through their control of the means of information and through their economic power, to completely dominate the government, national, state and local.

THE ELECTION THIS YEAR

It is these conditions which the workers and exploited farmers must consider in using their political power in the election this year.

The capitalist dictatorship has named two candidates, the Republican, strikebreaker Coolidge, and the Morgan-Rockefeller lawyer Davis. Both are agents of the capitalist class. They, and the other candidates of the two old parties, will loyally serve the capitalists if returned to power—as they have done in the past.

La Follette, who is running as an independent, progressive Republican, is equally a supporter of the capitalist system of exploitation. The only difference between La Follette and Coolidge and Davis is that La Follette represents the independent manufacturers, bankers and merchants, who are seeking greater power and profit for themselves and are trying to use the workers and farmers to attain that end.

La Follette is the representative of little business against big business, but not the representative of the workers and exploited farmers in their struggle against the capitalists. La Follette's platform is not a workers' and farmers' platform, but a little business men's platform with some bait thrown in for sections of the skilled workers.

Against these three candidates of the capitalist system of exploitation, big and little, the Workers' (Communist) Party presents working class candidates—Foster and Gitlow—and a working class platform.

THE WORKERS MUST RULE

There is only one way in which the exploitation of the workers and farmers of this country can be ended. That is through the workers organizing their mass power, ending the capitalist dictatorship and establishing the Workers' and Farmers' Government.

In place of the capitalist dictatorship there must be established the rule of the workers. The governmental power must be used in the interest of the workers and farmers as it is now used by the capitalist dictatorship in the interest of the capitalist class.

The Russion workers and peasants have established their rule in the form of the Soviet government and are using their power against the capitalists and for themselves—to build a Communist social system which will give the workers and farmers the fruits of their toil.

The Workers' party is fighting for the rule of the 30,000,000 workers and their families in the United States. This rule will be established through a proletarian revolution which will create a Soviet government and the dictatorship of the proletariat.

This Workers' and Farmers' Government will wrest out of the hands of the capitalists the raw material and great industries and operate them for the happiness and well-being of the producers. It will build in place of the capitalist system of production a Communist system of production.

The Workers' Party calls upon workers and exploited farmers to join it in the struggle to establish the Workers' and Farmers' Government in the United States. It urges them to demonstrate their support of the program of the Workers' Party by voting against the three capitalist candidates and for the Communist candidates—Foster and Gitlow.

IMMEDIATE PROGRAM

1. For a Mass Farmer-Labor Party

The Workers' Party has for two years carried on a consistent campaign for the formation of a mass Farmer-Labor Party to unite the industrial workers and exploited farmers for independent political action. The betrayal of the Conference for Progressive Political Action in accepting the independent candidacy of La Follette, the betrayal of the Farmer-Labor Party by the Socialist Party and the La Follette supporters among the workers and farmers, the attack upon the Farmer-Labor Party by La Follette, who does not want a party of workers and farmers, made the achievement of this goal impossible in this election campaign. The Workers' party declares its purpose to continue the struggle to mobilize the workers and exploited farmers for independent political action through a mass Farmer-Labor Party.

2. Nationalization of Industry and Workers' Control

The Workers' Party declares itself in favor of the immediate nationalization of all large-scale industries, such as railroads, mines, super-power plants, and means of communication and transportation, and for the organization of the workers in these industries for participation in the management and direction of the industries nationalized, thus developing industrial democracy, until industry comes under the control of those who produce the wealth of the nation, subject only to such general control as will protect the interest of the producers as a whole.

3. Compel Industry and the Government to Pay Wages to the Unemployed

Industry in the United States is slowing down and the workers face another period of industrial crisis with millions of unemployed unable to earn a living. The Workers' Party declares that industry must support the unemployed to whom it cannot give work. The government must take the accumulated profits of industry. It must levy excess profit and inheritance taxes to create an unemployment fund, to be administered by the workers, for payment of union wages to workers without jobs. The Workers' Party will initiate the organization of unemployment councils to fight for these demands.

4. Down with Injunctions and the Use of Police and Soldiers Against Workers

The Workers' Party calls upon the workers and exploited farmers to fight with it against the use of injunctions in labor disputes, intimidation of strikers through police and soldiers, and the use of criminal syndicalist laws to suppress the demands of the revolutionary workers, as well as other infringements of the rights of the workers.

5. Release All Political and Class War Prisoners

The Workers' Party will fight for the immediate and unconditional release of all workers imprisoned because of their political or economic views and for participation in the class struggle.

6. Land for the Users—Nationalize the Farmers' Marketing Industries

Land was created for all the people and we demand a system of land tenure which will eliminate landlordism and tenantry and will secure the land to the users thereof. We demand the nationalization of all means of transportation and industries engaged in the preparation and distribution of farm products, with participation of the farmers in the management of these industries.

7. Down with Militarism and Imperialist Wars

The World War and its slaughter of millions and destruction of billions of wealth was the product of capitalist imperialism. The capitalist government of the United States is already preparing for a new war. It is using its power to oppress weaker nations in the interest of the capitalists, as in Haiti, Santo Domingo, and Central America. It is holding the Philippine Islands in subjection. It is aiding to force the Dawes plan upon Germany in order to enslave the workers of that country. The Workers' Party will fight against militarism and imperialist wars and the use of the governmental power for the exploitation of weaker nations. It demands freedom for the Philippines and the right of self-determination for all colonies and territories of the United States.

8. Recognize the Workers' and Peasants' Government of Russia

The Union of Soviet Socialist Republics is the only workers' and farmers' government in the world. The capitalist government of the United States refuses it recognition and the restoration of full trade relations. The Workers' Party will rally the workers for immediate, unconditional recognition of the Union of Soviet Socialist Republics.

The measures outlined here are measures for immediate struggle and mobilization of the workers against the capitalist class and the capitalist dictatorship in the United States. The end of the glaring evils of capitalist society can only come with the victory of the workers and the establishment of the Workers' and Peasants' government through which capitalism will be abolished and the Communist society created. The Workers' Party will carry on the struggle until this goal is achieved.

In 1928, the Republican and Democratic parties received ninety-nine per cent of the votes. The minor parties offering candidates for the presidency included the Socialist Party, the Workers' Party, the Socialist Labor Party, the Prohibitionist Party and the Farmer Labor Party.

Democratic Platform for 1928

We, the Democratic Party in convention assembled, pause to pay our tribute of love and respect to the memory of him who in his life and in his official actions voiced the hopes and aspirations of all good men and women of every race and clime, the former President of the United States, Woodrow Wilson. His spirit moves on and his example and deeds will exalt those who come after us as they have inspired us.

We are grateful that we were privileged to work with him and again pay tribute to his high ideals and accomplishments.

We reaffirm our devotion to the principles of Democratic government formulated by Jefferson and enforced by a long and illustrious line of Democratic Presidents.

We hold that government must function not to centralize our wealth but to preserve equal opportunity so that all may share in our priceless resources; and not confine prosperity to a favored few. We, therefore, pledge the Democratic Party to encourage business, small and great alike; to conserve human happiness and liberty; to break the shackles of monopoly and free business of the nation; to respond to the popular will.

The function of a national platform is to declare general principles and party policies. We do not, therefore, assume to bind our party respecting local issues or details of legislation.

We, therefore, declare the policy of the Democratic Party with regard to the following dominant national issues:

The Rights of the States

We demand that the constitutional rights and powers of the states shall be preserved in their full vigor and virtue. These constitute a bulwark against centralization and the destructive tendencies of the Republican Party.

We oppose bureaucracy and the multiplication of offices and officeholders.

We demand a revival of the spirit of local self-government, without which free institutions cannot be preserved.

Republican Corruption

Unblushingly the Republican Party offers as its record agriculture prostrate, industry depressed, American shipping destroyed, workmen without employment; everywhere disgust and suspicion, and corruption unpunished and unafraid.

Never in the entire history of the country has there occurred in any given period of time or, indeed, in all time put together, such a spectacle of sordid corruption and unabashed rascality as that which has characterized the administration of federal affairs under eight blighting years of Republican rule. Not the revels of reconstruction, nor all the compounded frauds succeeding that evil era, have approached in sheer audacity the shocking thieveries and startling depravities of officials high and low in the public service at Washington. From cabinet ministers, with their treasonable crimes, to the cheap vendors of official patronage, from the purchasers of seats in the United States Senate to the vulgar grafters upon alien trust funds, and upon the hospital resources of the disabled veterans of the World War; from the givers and receivors of stolen funds for Republican campaign purposes to the public men who sat by silently consenting and never revealing a fact or uttering a word in condemnation, the whole official organization under Republican rule has become saturated with dishonesty defiant of public opinion and actuated only by a partisan desire to perpetuate its control of the government.

As in the time of Samuel J. Tilden, from whom the presidency was stolen, the watchword of the day should be: "Turn the rascals out." This is the appeal of the Democratic Party to the people of the country. To this fixed purpose should be devoted every effort and applied every resource of the party; to this end every minor difference on non-essential issues should be put aside and a determined and a united fight be made to rescue the government from those who have betrayed their trust by disgracing it.

ECONOMY AND REORGANIZATION

The Democratic Party stands for efficiency and economy in the administration of public affairs and we pledge:

(a) Business-like reorganization of all the departments of the government.

(b) Elimination of duplication, waste and overlapping.

(c) Substitution of modern business-like methods for existing obsolete and antiquated conditions.

No economy resulted from the Republican Party rule. The savings they claim take no account of the elimination of expenditures following the end of the World War, the large sums realized from the sale of war materials, nor its failure to supply sufficient funds for the efficient conduct of many important governmental activities.

FINANCING AND TAXATION

(a) The Federal Reserve system, created and inaugurated under Democratic auspices, is the greatest legislative contribution to constructive business ever adopted. The administration of the system for the advantage of stock market speculators should cease. It must be administered for the benefit of farmers, wage earners, merchants, manufacturers and others engaged in constructive business.

(b) The taxing function of governments, free or despotic, has for centuries been regarded as the power above all others which requires vigilant scrutiny to the end that it be not exercised for purposes of favor or oppression.

Three times since the World War the Democrats in Congress have favored a reduction of the tax burdens of the people in face of stubborn opposition from a Republican administration; and each time these reductions have largely been made for the relief of those least able to endure the exactions of a Republican fiscal policy. The tax bill of the session recently ended was delayed by Republican tactics and juggled by partisan considerations so as to make impossible a full measure of relief to the greater body of taxpayers. The moderate reductions afforded were grudgingly conceded and the whole proceeding in Congress, dictated as far as possible from the White House and the treasury, denoted the proverbial desire of the Republican Party always to discriminate against the masses in favor of privileged classes.

The Democratic Party avows its belief in the fiscal policy inaugurated by the last Democratic Administration, which provided a sinking fund sufficient to extinguish the nation's indebtedness within a reasonable period of time, without harassing the present and next succeeding generations with tax burdens which, if not unendurable, do in fact check initiative in enterprise and progress in business. Taxes levied beyond the actual requirements of the legally established sinking fund are but an added burden upon the American people, and the surplus thus accumulated in the federal treasury is an incentive to the increasingly extravagant expenditures which have characterized Republican administrations. We, therefore, favor a further reduction of the internal taxes of the people.

TARIFF

The Democratic tariff legislation will be based on the following policies:

(a) The maintenance of legitimate business

and a high standard of wages for American labor.

(b) Increasing the purchasing power of wages and income by the reduction of those monopolistic and extortionate tariff rates bestowed in payment of political debts.

(c) Abolition of log-rolling and restoration of the Wilson conception of a fact-finding tariff commission, quasi-judicial and free from the executive domination which has destroyed the usefulness of the present commission.

(d) Duties that will permit effective competition, insure against monopoly and at the same time produce a fair revenue for the support of government. Actual difference between the cost of production at home and abroad, with adequate safeguard for the wage of the American laborer must be the extreme measure of every tariff rate.

(e) Safeguarding the public against monopoly created by special tariff favors.

(f) Equitable distribution of the benefits and burdens of the tariff among all.

Wage-earner, farmer, stockman, producer and legitimate business in general have everything to gain from a Democratic tariff based on justice to all.

Civil Service

Grover Cleveland made the extension of the merit system a tenet of our political faith. We shall preserve and maintain the civil service.

Agriculture

Deception upon the farmer and stock raiser has been practiced by the Republican Party through false and delusive promises for more than fifty years. Specially favored industries have been artificially aided by Republican legislation. Comparatively little has been done for agriculture and stock raising, upon which national prosperity rests. Unsympathetic inaction with regard to this problem must cease. Virulent hostility of the Republican administration to the advocates of farm relief and denial of the right of farm organizations to lead in the development of farm policy must yield to Democratic sympathy and friendliness.

Four years ago the Republican Party, forced to acknowledge the critical situation, pledged itself to take all steps necessary to bring back a balanced condition between agriculture and other industries and labor. Today it faces the country not only with that pledge unredeemed but broken by the acts of a Republican President, who is primarily responsible for the failure to offer a constructive program to restore equality to agriculture.

While he has had no constructive and adequate program to offer in its stead, he has twice vetoed farm relief legislation and has sought to justify his disapproval of agricultural legislation partly on grounds wholly inconsistent with his acts, making industrial monopolies the beneficiaries of government favor; and in endorsing the agricultural policy of the present administration the Republican Party, in its recent convention, served notice upon the farmer that the so-called protective system is not meant for him; that while it offers protection to the privileged few, it promises continued world prices to the producers of the chief cash crops of agriculture.

We condemn the policy of the Republican Party which promises relief to agriculture only through a reduction of American farm production to the needs of the domestic market. Such a program means the continued deflation of agriculture, the forcing of additional millions from the farms, and the perpetuation of agricultural distress for years to come, with continued bad effects on business and labor throughout the United States.

The Democratic Party recognizes that the problems of production differ as between agriculture and industry. Industrial production is largely under human control, while agricultural production, because of lack of co-ordination among the 6,500,000 individual farm units, and because of the influence of weather, pests and other causes, is largely beyond human control. The result is that a large crop frequently is produced on a small acreage and a small crop on a large acreage; and, measured in money value, it frequently happens that a large crop brings less than a small crop.

Producers of crops whose total volume exceeds the needs of the domestic market must continue at a disadvantage until the government shall intervene as seriously and as effectively in behalf of the farmer as it has intervened in behalf of labor and industry. There is a need of supplemental legislation for the control and orderly handling of agricultural surpluses, in order that the price of the surplus may not determine the price of the whole crop. Labor has benefited by collective bargaining and some industries by tariff. Agriculture must be as effectively aided.

The Democratic Party in its 1924 platform pledged its support to such legislation. It now reaffirms that stand and pledges the united efforts of the legislative and executive branches of government, as far as may be controlled by the party, to the immediate enactment of such legislation, and to such other steps as are necessary to establish and maintain the purchasing power of farm products and the complete economic equality of agriculture.

The Democratic Party has always stood against special privilege and for common equality under the law. It is a fundamental principle of the party that such tariffs as are levied must not discriminate against any industry, class or section. Therefore, we pledge that in its tariff policy the Democratic Party will insist upon equality of treatment between agriculture and other industries.

Farm relief must rest on the basis of an economic equality of agriculture with other industries. To give this equality a remedy must be found which will include among other things:

(a) Credit aid by loans to co-operatives on at least as favorable a basis as the government aid to the merchant marine.

(b) Creation of a federal farm board to assist the farmer and stock raiser in the marketing of their products, as the Federal Reserve Board has done for the banker and business man. When our archaic banking and currency system was revised after its record of disaster and panic under Republican administrations, it was a Democratic Congress in the administration of a Democratic President that accomplished its stabilization through the Federal Reserve Act creating the Federal Reserve Board, with powers adequate to its purpose. Now, in the hour of agriculture's need, the Democratic Party pledges the establishment of a new agricultural policy fitted to present conditions, under the direction of a farm board vested with all the powers necessary to accomplish for agriculture what the Federal Reserve Board has been able to accomplish for finance, in full recognition of the fact that the banks of the country, through voluntary co-operation, were never able to stabilize the financial system of the country until the government powers were invoked to help them.

(c) Reduction through proper government agencies of the spread between what the farmer and stock raiser gets and the ultimate consumer pays, with consequent benefits to both.

(d) Consideration of the condition of agriculture in the formulation of government financial and tax measures.

We pledge the party to foster and develop co-operative marketing associations through appropriate governmental aid. We recognize that experience has demonstrated that members of such associations alone can not successfully assume the full responsibility for a program that benefits all producers alike. We pledge the party to an earnest endeavor to solve this problem of the distribution of the cost of dealing with crop surpluses over the marketed units of the crop whose producers are benefited by such assistance. The solution of this problem would avoid government subsidy, to which the Democratic Party has always been opposed. The solution of this problem will be a prime and immediate concern of a Democratic administration.

We direct attention to the fact that it was a Democratic Congress, in the administration of a Democratic President, which established the federal loan system and laid the foundation for the entire rural credits structure, which has aided agriculture to sustain in part the shock of the policies of two Republican administrations; and we promise thorough-going administration of our rural credits laws, so that the farmers in all sections may secure the maximum benefits intended under these acts.

MINING

Mining is one of the basic industries of this country. We produce more coal, iron and copper than any other country. The value of our mineral production is second only to agriculture. Mining has suffered like agriculture, and from similar causes. It is the duty of our government to foster this industry and to remove the restrictions that destroy its prosperity.

FOREIGN POLICY

The Republican administration has no foreign policy; it has drifted without plan. This great nation can not afford to play a minor role in world politics. It must have a sound and positive foreign policy, not a negative one. We declare for a constructive foreign policy based on these principles:

(a) Outlawry of war and an abhorrence of militarism, conquest and imperialism.

(b) Freedom from entangling political alliances with foreign nations.

(c) Protection of American lives and rights.

(d) Non-interference with the elections or other internal political affairs of any foreign nation. This principle of non-interference extends to Mexico, Nicaragua and all other Latin-American nations. Interference in the purely internal affairs of Latin-American countries must cease.

(e) Rescue of our country from its present impaired world standing and restoration to its former position as a leader in the movement for international arbitration, conciliation, conference and limitation of armament by international agreement.

(f) International agreements for reduction of all armaments and the end of competitive war preparations, and, in the meantime, the maintenance of an army and navy adequate for national defense.

(g) Full, free and open co-operation with all other nations for the promotion of peace and justice throughout the world.

(h) In our foreign relations this country should stand as a unit, and, to be successful, foreign policies must have the approval and the support of the American people.

(i) Abolition of the practice of the President of entering into and carrying out agreements with a foreign government, either de facto or de jure, for the protection of such government against revolution or foreign attack, or for the supervision of its internal affairs, when such agreements have not been advised and consented to by the Senate, as provided in the Constitution of the United States, and we condemn the administration for carrying out such an unratified agreement that requires us to use our armed forces in Nicaragua.

(j) Recognition that the Monroe Doctrine is a cardinal principle of this government promulgated for the protection of ourselves and our Latin-American neighbors. We shall seek their friendly co-operation in the maintenance of this doctrine.

(k) We condemn the Republican administration for lack of statesmanship and efficiency in negotiating the 1921 treaty for the limitation of armaments, which limited only the construction of battleships and ships of over ten thousand tons. Merely a gesture towards peace, it accomplished

no limitation of armament, because it simply substituted one weapon of destruction for another. While it resulted in the destruction of our battleships and the blueprints of battleships of other nations, it placed no limitation upon construction of aircraft, submarines, cruisers, warships under ten thousand tons, poisonous gases or other weapons of destruction. No agreement was ratified with regard to submarines and poisonous gases. The attempt of the President to remedy the failure of 1921 by the Geneva Conference of 1928 was characterized by the same lack of statesmanship and efficiency and resulted in entire failure.

In consequence, the race between nations in the building of unlimited weapons of destruction still goes on and the peoples of the world are still threatened with war and burdened with taxation for additional armament.

WATERPOWER, WATERWAYS AND FLOOD CONTROL

The federal government and state governments, respectively, now have absolute and exclusive sovereignty and control over enormous waterpowers, which constitute one of the greatest assets of the nation. This sovereign title and control must be preserved respectively in the state and federal governments, to the end that the people may be protected against exploitation of this great resource and that water powers may be expeditiously developed under such regulations as will insure to the people reasonable rates and equitable distribution.

We favor and will promote deep waterways from the Great Lakes to the Gulf and to the Atlantic Ocean.

We favor the fostering and building up of water transportation through improvement of inland waterways and removal of discrimination against water transportation. Flood control and the lowering of flood levels are essential to the safety of life and property, and the productivity of our lands, the navigability of our streams, the reclaiming of our wet and overflowed lands. We favor expeditious construction of flood relief works on the Mississippi and Colorado rivers and such reclamation and irrigation projects upon the Colorado River as may be found feasible.

We favor appropriations for prompt co-ordinated surveys by the United States to determine the possibilities of general navigation improvements and waterpower development on navigable streams and their tributaries and to secure reliable information as to the most economical navigation improvement, in combination with the most efficient and complete development of waterpower.

We favor the strict enforcement of the Federal Waterpower Act, a Democratic act, and insist that the public interest in waterpower sites, ignored by two Republican administrations, be protected.

Being deeply impressed by the terrible disasters from floods in the Mississippi Valley during 1927, we heartily endorse the Flood Control Act of last May, which recognizes that the flood waters of the Mississippi River and its tributaries constitute a national problem of the gravest character and makes provision for their speedy and effective control. This measure is a continuation and expansion of the policy established by a Democratic Congress in 1917 in the act of that year for controlling floods on the Mississippi and Sacramento rivers. It is a great piece of constructive legislation, and we pledge our party to its vigorous and early enforcement.

Conservation and Reclamation

We shall conserve the natural resources of our country for the benefit of the people and to protect them against waste and monopolization. Our disappearing resources of timber call for a national policy of reforestation. The federal government should improve and develop its public lands so that they may go into private ownership and become subjected to taxation for the support of the states wherein they exist. The Democratic administration will actively, efficiently and economically carry on reclamation projects and make equitable adjustments with the homestead entrymen for the mistakes the government has made, and extend all practical aid to refinance reclamation and drainage projects.

Transportation

Efficient and economical transportation is essential to the prosperity of every industry. Cost of transportation controls the income of every human being and materially affects the cost of living. We must, therefore, promote every form of transportation to a state of highest efficiency. Recognizing the prime importance of air transportation, we shall encourage its development by every possible means. Improved roads are of vital importance not only to commerce and industry, but also to agriculture and rural life. The federal government should construct and maintain at its own expense roads upon its public lands. We reaffirm our approval of the Federal Roads Law, enacted by a Democratic administration. Common carriers, whether by land, water or rail, must be protected in an equal opportunity to compete, so that governmental regulations against exorbitant rates and inefficiency will be aided by competition.

Labor

(a) We favor the principle of collective bargaining, and the Democratic principle that organized labor should choose its own representatives without coercion or interference.

(b) Labor is not a commodity. Human rights must be safeguarded. Labor should be exempt from the operation of anti-trust laws.

(c) We recognize that legislative and other investigations have shown the existence of grave abuse in the issuance of injunctions in labor disputes. No injunctions should be granted in labor disputes except upon proof of threatened irreparable injury and after notice and hearing and the injunction should be confined to those acts which do directly threaten irreparable injury. The expressed purpose of representatives of capital, labor and the bar to devise a plan for the elimination of the present evils with respect to injunctions must be supported and legislation designed to accomplish these ends formulated and passed.

(d) We favor legislation providing that products of convict labor shipped from one state to another shall be subject to laws of the latter state, as though they had been produced therein.

Unemployment

Unemployment is present, widespread and increasing. Unemployment is almost as destructive to the happiness, comfort, and well-being of human beings as war. We expend vast sums of money to protect our people against the evils of war, but no governmental program is anticipated to prevent the awful suffering and economic losses of unemployment. It threatens the well-being of millions of our people and endangers the prosperity of the nation. We favor the adoption by the government, after a study of this subject, of a scientific plan whereby during periods of unemployment appropriations shall be made available for the construction of necessary public works and the lessening, as far as consistent with public interests, of government construction work when labor is generally and satisfactorily employed in private enterprise.

Study should also be made of modern methods of industry and a constructive solution found to absorb and utilize the surplus human labor released by the increasing use of machinery.

Accident Compensation to Government Employees

We favor legislation making fair and liberal compensation to government employees who are injured in accident or by occupational disease and to the dependents of such workers as may die as a result thereof.

Federal Employees

Federal employees should receive a living wage based upon American standards of decent living. Present wages are, in many instances, far below that standard. We favor a fair and liberal retirement law for government employees in the classified service.

Veterans

Through Democratic votes, and in spite of two Republican Presidents' opposition, the Congress has maintained America's traditional policy to generously care for the veterans of the World War. In extending them free hospitalization, a statutory award for tuberculosis, a program of progressive hospital construction, and provisions for compensation for the disabled, the widows and orphans, America has surpassed the record of any nation in the history of the world. We pledge the veterans that none of the benefits heretofore accorded by the Wilson administration and the votes of Democrat members of Congress shall be withdrawn; that these will be added to more in accordance with the veterans' and their dependents' actual needs. Generous appropriations, honest management, the removal of vexatious administration delays, and sympathetic assistance for the veterans of all wars, is what the Democratic Party demands and promises.

Women and Children

We declare for equality of women with men in all political and governmental matters.

Children are the chief asset of the nation. Therefore their protection through infancy and childhood against exploitation is an important national duty.

The Democratic Party has always opposed the exploitation of women in industry and has stood for such conditions of work as will preserve their health and safety.

We favor an equal wage for equal service; and likewise favor adequate appropriations for the women's and children's bureau.

Immigration

Laws which limit immigration must be preserved in full force and effect, but the provisions contained in these laws that separate husbands from wives and parents from infant children are inhuman and not essential to the purpose or the efficacy of such laws.

Radio

Government supervision must secure to all the people the advantage of radio communication and likewise guarantee the right of free speech. Official control in contravention of this guarantee should not be tolerated. Governmental control must prevent monopolistic use of radio communication and guarantee equitable distribution and enjoyment thereof.

Coal

Bituminous coal is not only the common base of manufacture, but it is a vital agency in our interstate transportation. The demoralization of this industry, its labor conflicts and distress, its waste of a national resource and disordered public service, demand constructive legislation that will allow capital and labor a fair share of prosperity, with adequate protection to the consuming public.

Congressional Election Reform

We favor legislation to prevent defeated members of both houses of Congress from participating in the sessions of Congress by fixing the date for convening the Congress immediately after the biennial national election.

Law Enforcement

The Republican Party, for eight years in complete control of the government at Washington, presents the remarkable spectacle of feeling compelled in its national platform to promise obedience to a provision of the federal Constitution, which it has flagrantly disregarded and to apologize to the country for its failure to enforce laws enacted by the Congress of the United States. Speaking for the national Democracy, this convention pledges the party and its nominees to an honest effort to enforce the eighteenth amendment and all other provisions of the federal Constitution and all laws enacted pursuant thereto.

CAMPAIGN EXPENDITURES

We condemn the improper and excessive use of money in elections as a danger threatening the very existence of democratic institutions. Republican expenditures in senatorial primaries and elections have been so exorbitant as to constitute a national scandal. We favor publicity in all matters affecting campaign contributions and expenditures. We shall, beginning not later than August 1, 1928, and every thirty days thereafter, the last publication and filing being not later than five days before the election, publish in the press and file with the appropriate committees of the House and Senate a complete account of all contributions, the names of the contributors, the amounts expended and the purposes for which the expenditures are made, and will, at all times, hold open for public inspection the books and records relating to such matters. In the event that any financial obligations are contracted and not paid, our National Committee will similarly report and publish, at least five days before the election, all details respecting such obligations.

We agree to keep and maintain a permanent record of all campaign contributions and expenditures and to insist that contributions by the citizens of one state to the campaign committees of other states shall have immediate publicity.

MERCHANT MARINE

We reaffirm our support of an efficient, dependable American merchant marine for the carriage of the greater portion of our commerce and for the national defense.

The Democratic Party has consistently and vigorously supported the shipping services maintained by the regional United States Shipping Board in the interest of all ports and all sections of our country, and has successfully opposed the discontinuance of any of these lines. We favor the transfer of these lines gradually to the local private American companies, when such companies can show their ability to take over and permanently maintain the lines. Lines that can not now be transferred to private enterprise should continue to be operated as at present and should be kept in an efficient state by remodeling of some vessels and replacement of others.

We are unalterably opposed to a monopoly in American shipping and are opposed to the operation of any of our services in a manner that would retard the development of any ports or section of our country.

We oppose such sacrifices and favoritism as exhibited in the past in the matter of alleged sales, and insist that the primary purpose of legislation upon this subject be the establishment and maintenance of an adequate American merchant marine.

ARMENIA

We favor the most earnest efforts on the part of the United States to secure the fulfillment of the promises and engagements made during and following the World War by the United States and the allied powers to Armenia and her people.

EDUCATION

We believe with Jefferson and other founders of the Republic that ignorance is the enemy of freedom and that each state, being responsible for the intellectual and moral qualifications of its citizens and for the expenditure of the moneys collected by taxation for the support of its schools, shall use its sovereign right in all matters pertaining to education.

The federal government should offer to the states such counsel, advice, results of research and aid as may be made available through the federal agencies for the general improvement of our schools in view of our national needs.

MONOPOLIES AND ANTI-TRUST LAWS

During the last seven years, under Republican rule, the anti-trust laws have been thwarted, ignored and violated so that the country is rapidly becoming controlled by trusts and sinister monopolies formed for the purpose of wringing from the necessaries of life an unrighteous profit. These combinations are formed and conducted in violation of law, encouraged, aided and abetted in their activities by the Republican administration and are driving all small tradespeople and small industrialists out of business. Competition is one of the most sacred, cherished and economic rights of the American people. We demand the strict enforcement of the anti-trust laws and the enactment of other laws, if necessary, to control this great menace to trade and commerce, and thus to preserve the right of the small merchant and manufacturer to earn a legitimate profit from his business.

Dishonest business should be treated without influence at the national capitol. Honest business, no matter its size, need have no fears of a Democratic administration. The Democratic Party will ever oppose illegitimate and dishonest business. It will foster, promote, and encourage all legitimate enterprises.

Canal Zone

We favor the employment of American citizens in the operation and maintenance of the Panama Canal in all positions above the grade of messenger and favor as liberal wages and conditions of employment as prevailed under previous Democratic administrations.

Alaska—Hawaii

We favor the development of Alaska and Hawaii in the traditional American way, through self-government. We favor the appointment of only bona fide residents to office in the territories. We favor the extension and improvement of the mail, air mail, telegraph and radio, agricultural experimenting, highway construction, and other necessary federal activities in the territories.

Porto Rico

We favor granting to Porto Rico such territorial form of government as would meet the present economic conditions of the island, and provide for the aspirations of her people, with the view to ultimate statehood accorded to all territories of the United States since the beginning of our government, and we believe any officials appointed to administer the government of such territories should be qualified by previous bona fide residence therein.

Philippines

The Filipino people have succeeded in maintaining a stable government and have thus fulfilled the only condition laid down by the Congress as a prerequisite to the granting of independence. We declare that it is now our duty to keep our promise to these people by granting them immediately the independence which they so honorably covet.

Public Health

The Democratic Party recognizes that not only the productive wealth of the nation but its contentment and happiness depends upon the health of its citizens. It, therefore, pledges itself to enlarge the existing Bureau of Public Health and to do all things possible to stamp out communicable and contagious diseases, and to ascertain preventive means and remedies for these diseases, such as cancer, infantile paralysis and others which heretofore have largely defied the skill of physicians.

We pledge our party to spare no means to lift the apprehension of diseases from the minds of our people, and to appropriate all moneys necessary to carry out this pledge.

Conclusion

Affirming our faith in these principles, we submit our cause to the people.

Farmer-Labor Platform of 1928

1. We believe in using governmental powers to utilize the labor-saving features of our trusts and corporations in the interests of the people instead of for the profit of the few.

2. Unqualified enforcement of the constitutional guaranties of freedom of speech, press and assemblage.

3. Public ownership and permanent conservation under democratic public management of all natural resources, including coal, iron and other ores, oil, timber lands and all means of production and distribution, including railroads, super-power such as Muscle Shoals and Boulder Dam, or any industry that may become a monopoly.

4. Direct government issue of money paid into circulation and government operation of banking and exchange in the common interest.

5. Guaranteed public employment for all whom private industry does not employ, and unemployment insurance.

6. We believe in the enforcement of all laws.

7. Adequate farm relief by applying the prin-

ciple of an equalization fee and the acquisition by genuine co-operative societies as well as government ownership of grain elevators, storage and distributing agencies on a nonprofit basis, in the equitable interest of the farmer, city worker and consumer.

8. We favor abolition of the use of injunctions in labor disputes and declare for complete protection of the right of farmers' facilities.

9. We favor the ratification of the passed child labor amendment.

10. We favor a deep waterway from the great lakes to the sea. The government should, in conjunction with Canada, take immediate action to give the northwestern states an outlet to the ocean for cargoes without changing bulk, thus making the primary markets on the great lakes equal to those of New York.

11. We are opposed to exploitation and imperialism in all forms, and we favor the scrapping of all implements of warfare and the withdrawal of military forces from Nicaragua, and in non-interference in the local affairs of Mexico, Latin America, China or any other country.

12. We favor recognizing the Soviet Russian government and the establishment of trade relations.

13. Abolition of bureaus, commissions, committees or other like organizations exercising legislative or judicial powers.

14. We favor adequate pensions to the aged, to victims of war and industry, to widows and all indigents.

15. We demand that all men and women who served as welfare workers overseas be federalized, thereby making them eligible to pensions and hospitalization, and also they and the veterans choose their own method of treatment and choice of practitioner.

16. We believe in the calling of a constitutional convention to consider a throrough revision of our organic law in line with modern principles of human welfare.

17. We favor independence of the Philippines, autonomy for Porto Rico and civil government for the Virgin Islands.

18. We favor revision of tax laws so that large incomes and inheritances may be made to carry the burden of the cost of government and social insurance.

19. We favor proper legislation to assure economic reforestation, reclamation and irrigation, with particular consideration of the southern farmers' problems, also flood prevention and flood relief.

20. We favor the restoration of the franchise and complete self-government to citizens of the District of Columbia. We also favor legislation that will provide means for every adult citizen regardless of race or nationality to vote for national officers regardless of where one may be in the nation on election day, also to abolish the electoral college and "lame duck" sessions of congress, and election of president and vice-president by direct vote of the people.

Prohibition Platform for 1928 [1]

The Prohibition party contemplates with gratitude and solemn joy the triumphs of the great cause, of which, in partisan matters it has been the champion for threescore years, yet for the common victory we would not withhold recognition due the many thousands in times past and the unnumbered millions now, though not affiliated with our party, who firmly stood and now stand ardently for national prohibition.

We note in review that among political parties the Prohibition party is the only one in the last fifty years whose majority issue has triumphed. For half a century it was the lone sponsor of two policies now imbedded in the Constitution, viz: Prohibition and Woman Suffrage. Both are parts of our basic law and believed in by an overwhelming majority of the people. Forty-six of the forty-eight states have ratified Prohibition. The government is no longer a partner in the liquor traffic and no more takes tribute from the iniquitous trade in return for legal protection.

THE MAJOR PARTIES

We are glad to believe and declare that nullifi-

[1] A lengthy Prohibition Party Platform for 1928 was submitted by the party's Platform Committee to the party's national convention.

The convention was hopelessly split over whether or not to offer Prohibition Party candidates or to endorse the Republican candidate, Herbert Hoover. The delegates finally adopted this short platform together with a set of resolutions which provided that the Prohibition candidates would withdraw from the campaign if such a request were made by the party's Executive Committee.

cation of Federal provisions for enforcement of prohibition is not a tenet of the Democratic or Republican parties, but that all nullification is the act of liquor sympathizers whose disregard of all laws in conflict with their desires is common knowledge confirmed by heaped up precedents. Nullification was blasted by Andrew Jackson, the Democrat, in his day, and resisted to the death by Abraham Lincoln, the Republican. We deprecate the custom of political parties in their platforms charging all sins and shortcomings to each other. Oft-repeated folly does not thereby become wisdom, and falsehood frequently stated does not become the truth. We appeal to their sense of shame and intellectual pride for reform in this regard. A greater circumspection in putting officials in office will lessen the necessity of a call to turn the rascals out.

RESOLUTIONS ADOPTED BY THE PROHIBITION NATIONAL CONVENTION, CHICAGO, ILLINOIS, JULY 12, 1928

First: That the supreme objective of all good citizens of America in this campaign is to annihilate the beverage liquor traffic and maintain our Constitution which objective is opposed by the wet Tammany candidate;

Second: That the activities of the Prohibition party in this campaign shall be dominated by the purpose to promote the above objective;

Third: That we carry on a vigorous and effective campaign in behalf of the principle of National Prohibition of which our party was the pioneer champion;

Fourth: That we join with the good citizens of all parties in a union of forces to prevent the threatened calamity of the election of the wet Tammany candidate;

Fifth: That no separate presidential electors be placed upon the ballot in any state where the nomination of such electors will contribute to the election of said candidate;

Sixth: That in all states where we are an official party we nominate state and local candidates and carry on an aggressive campaign;

Seventh: That the Nominees of this Convention shall withdraw on request of the Executive Committee, at any time prior to September first next, and the said Committee is authorized and empowered to substitute other candidates supporting the objective named above.

Republican Platform of 1928

The Republican Party in national convention assembled presents to the people of the Nation this platform of its principles, based on a record of its accomplishments, and asks and awaits a new vote of confidence. We reaffirm our devotion to the Constitution of the United States and the principles and institution of the American system of representative government.

THE NATIONAL ADMINISTRATION

We endorse without qualification the record of the Coolidge administration.

The record of the Republican Party is a record of advancement of the nation. Nominees of Republican National conventions have for 52 of the 72 years since the creation of our party been the chief executives of the United States. Under Republican inspiration and largely under Republican executive direction the continent has been bound with steel rails, the oceans and great rivers have been joined by canals, waterways have been deepened and widened for ocean commerce, and with all a high American standard of wage and living has been established.

By unwavering adherence to sound principles, through the wisdom of Republican policies, and the capacity of Republican administrations, the foundations have been laid and the greatness and prosperity of the country firmly established.

Never has the soundness of Republican policies been more amply demonstrated and the Republican genius for administration been better exemplified than during the last five years under the leadership of President Coolidge.

No better guaranty of prosperity and contentment among all our people at home, no more reliable warranty of protection and promotion of American interests abroad can be given than the pledge to maintain and continue the Coolidge policies. This promise we give and will faithfully perform.

Under this Administration the country has been lifted from the depths of a great depression to a level of prosperity. Economy has been raised to the dignity of a principle of government. A standard of character in public service has been established under the chief Executive, which has given to the people of the country a feeling of stability and confidence so all have felt encouraged to proceed on new undertakings in trade and commerce. A foreign policy based on the traditional American position and carried on with wisdom and steadfastness has extended American influence throughout the world and everywhere promoted and protected American interests.

The mighty contribution to general well-being which can be made by a government controlled by men of character and courage, whose abilities are equal to their responsibilities, is self-evident, and should not blind us to the consequences which its loss would entail. Under this administration a high level of wages and living has been established and maintained. The door of opportunity has been opened wide to all. It has given to our people greater comfort and leisure, and the mutual profit has been evident in the increasingly harmonious relations between employers and employees, and the steady rise by promotion of the men in the shops to places at the council tables of the industries. It has also been made evident by the increasing enrollments of our youth in the technical schools and colleges, the increase in savings and life insurance accounts, and by our ability, as a people, to lend the hand of succor not only to those overcome by disasters in our own country but in foreign lands. With all there has been a steady decrease in the burden of Federal taxation, releasing to the people the greatest possible portion of the results of their labor from Government exactions.

For the Republican Party we are justified in claiming a major share of the credit for the position which the United States occupies today as the most favored nation on the globe, but it is well to remember that the confidence and prosperity which we enjoy can be shattered, if not destroyed, if this belief in the honesty and sincerity of our government is in any way affected. A continuation of this great public peace of mind now existing, which makes for our material well being, is only possible by holding fast to the plans and principles which have marked Republican control.

The record of the present Administration is a guaranty of what may be expected of the next. Our words have been made deeds. We offer not promises but accomplishments.

Public Economy

The citizen and taxpayer has a natural right to be protected from unnecessary and wasteful expenditures. This is a rich but also a growing nation with constantly increasing legitimate demands for public funds. If we are able to spend wisely and meet these requirements, it is first necessary that we save wisely. Spending extravagantly not only deprives men through taxation of the fruits of their labor, but oftentimes means the postponement of vitally important public works. We commend President Coolidge for his establishment of this fundamental principle of sound administration and pledge ourselves to live up to the high standard he has set.

Finance and Taxation

The record of the United States Treasury under Secretary Mellon stands unrivalled and unsurpassed. The finances of the nation have been managed with sound judgment. The financial policies have yielded immediate and substantial results.

In 1921 the credit of our government was at a low ebb. We were burdened with a huge public debt, a load of war taxes, which in variety and weight exceeded anything in our national life, while vast unfunded intergovernmental debts disorganized the economic life of the debtor nations and seriously affected our own by reason of the serious obstacles which they presented to commercial intercourse. This critical situation was evidenced by a serious disturbance in our own life which made for unemployment.

Today all these major financial problems have been solved.

The Public Debt

In seven years the public debt has been reduced by $6,411,000,000. From March 1921 to September 1928 over eleven billion dollars of securities, bearing high rates of interest, will have been retired or refunded into securities bearing a low rate of interest, while Liberty Bonds, which were selling below par, now command a premium. These operations have resulted in an annual saving in interest charges of not less than $275,000,-000, without which the most recent tax reduction measure would not have been made possible. The Republican Party will continue to reduce our National debt as rapidly as possible and in accordance with the provision of existing laws and the present program.

TAX REDUCTION

Wise administrative management under Republican control and direction has made possible a reduction of over a billion eight hundred million dollars a year in the tax bill of the American people. Four separate tax reduction measures have been enacted, and millions of those least able to pay have been taken from the tax rolls.

Excessive and uneconomic rates have been radically modified, releasing for industrial and payroll expansion and development great sums of money which formerly were paid in taxes to the Federal government.

Practically all the war taxes have been eliminated and our tax system has been definitely restored to a peace time basis.

We pledge our party to a continuation of these sound policies and to such further reduction of the tax burden as the condition of the Treasury may from time to time permit.

TARIFF

We reaffirm our belief in the protective tariff as a fundamental and essential principle of the economic life of this nation. While certain provisions of the present law require revision in the light of changes in the world competitive situation since its enactment, the record of the United States since 1922 clearly shows that the fundamental protective principle of the law has been fully justified. It has stimulated the development of our natural resources, provided fuller employment at higher wages through the promotion of industrial activity, assured thereby the continuance of the farmer's major market, and further raised the standards of living and general comfort and well-being of our people. The great expansion in the wealth of our nation during the past fifty years, and particularly in the past decade, could not have been accomplished without a protective tariff system designed to promote the vital interests of all classes.

Nor have these manifest benefits been restricted to any particular section of the country. They are enjoyed throughout the land either directly or indirectly. Their stimulus has been felt in industries, farming sections, trade circles, and communities in every quarter. However, we realize that there are certain industries which cannot now successfully compete with foreign producers because of lower foreign wages and a lower cost of living abroad, and we pledge the next Republican Congress to an examination and where necessary a revision of these schedules to the end that American labor in these industries may again command the home market, may maintain its standard of living, and may count upon steady employment in its accustomed field.

Adherence to that policy is essential for the continued prosperity of the country. Under it the standard of living of the American people has been raised to the highest levels ever known. Its example has been eagerly followed by the rest of the world whose experts have repeatedly reported with approval the relationship of this policy to our prosperity, with the resultant emulation of that example by other nations.

A protective tariff is as vital to American agriculture as it is to American manufacturing. The Republican Party believes that the home market, built up under the protective policy, belongs to the American farmer, and it pledges its support of legislation which will give this market to him to the full extent of his ability to supply it. Agriculture derives large benefits not only directly from the protective duties levied on competitive farm products of foreign origin, but also, indirectly, from the increase in the purchasing power of American workmen employed in industries similarly protected. These benefits extend also to persons engaged in trade, transportation, and other activities.

The Tariff Act of 1922 has justified itself in the expansion of our foreign trade during the past five years. Our domestic exports have increased from 3.8 billions of dollars in 1922 to 4.8 billions in 1927. During the same period imports have increased from 3.1 billions to 4.4 billions. Contrary to the prophesies of its critics, the present tariff law has not hampered the natural growth in the exportation of the products of American agriculture, industry, and mining, nor has it restricted the importation of foreign commodities which this country can utilize without jeopardizing its economic structure.

The United States is the largest customer in the world today. If we were not prosperous and able to buy, the rest of the world also would suffer. It is inconceivable that American labor will ever consent to the abolition of protection which would bring the American standard of living down to the level of that in Europe, or that the American farmer could survive if the enormous consuming power of the people in this country were curtailed and its market at home, if not destroyed, at least seriously impaired.

FOREIGN DEBTS

In accordance with our settled policy and platform pledges, debt settlement agreements have been negotiated with all of our foreign debtors with the exception of Armenia and Russia. That with France remains as yet unratified. Those with Greece and Austria are before the Congress for necessary authority. If the French Debt Settlement be included, the total amount funded is eleven billion five hundred twenty-two million three hundred fifty-four thousand dollars. We have steadfastly opposed and will continue to oppose cancellation of foreign debts.

We have no desire to be oppressive or grasping, but we hold that obligations justly incurred should be honorably discharged. We know of no authority which would permit public officials, acting as trustees, to shift the burden of the War from the shoulders of foreign taxpayers to those of our own people. We believe that the settlements agreed to are fair to both the debtor nation and to the American taxpayer. Our Debt Commission took into full consideration the economic condition and resources of the debtor nations, and were ever mindful that they must be permitted to preserve and improve their economic position, to bring their budgets into balance, to place their currencies and finances on a sound basis, and to improve the standard of living of their people. Giving full weight to these considerations, we know of no fairer test than ability to pay, justly estimated.

The people can rely on the Republican Party to adhere to a foreign debt policy now definitely established and clearly understood both at home and abroad.

SETTLEMENT OF WAR CLAIMS

A satisfactory solution has been found for the question of War Claims. Under the Act, approved by the President on March 10, 1928, a provision was made for the settlement of War Claims of the United States and its citizens against the German, Austrian and Hungarian Governments, and of the claims of the nationals of these governments against the United States; and for the return to its owners of the property seized by the Alien Property Custodian during the War, in accordance with our traditional policy of respect for private property.

FOREIGN POLICIES

We approve the foreign policies of the Administration of President Coolidge. We believe they express the will of the American people in working actively to build up cordial international understanding that will make world peace a permanent reality. We endorse the proposal of the Secretary of State for a multilateral treaty proposed to the principal powers of the world and open to the signatures of all nations, to renounce war as an instrument of national policy and declaring in favor of pacific settlement of international disputes, the first step in outlawing war. The idea has stirred the conscience of mankind and gained widespread approval, both of governments and of the people, and the conclusion of the treaty will be acclaimed as the greatest single step in history toward the conservation of peace.

In the same endeavor to substitute for war the peaceful settlement of international disputes the administration has concluded arbitration treaties in a form more definite and more inclusive than ever before and plans to negotiate similar treaties with all countries willing in this manner to define their policy peacefully to settle justiciable disputes. In connection with these, we endorse the Resolution of the Sixth Pan American Conference held at Havana, Cuba, in 1928, which called a conference on arbitration and conciliation to meet in Washington during the year and express our earnest hope that such conference will greatly further the principles of international arbitration. We shall continue to demand the same respect and protection for the persons and property of American citizens in foreign countries that we cheerfully accord in this country to the persons and property of aliens.

The commercial treaties which we have negotiated and those still in the process of negotiation are based on strict justice among nations, equal opportunity for trade and commerce on the most-favored-nation principle and are simplified so as to eliminate the danger of misunderstanding. The object and the aim of the United States is to further the cause of peace, of strict justice between nations with due regard for the rights of others in all international dealings. Out of justice grows peace. Justice and consideration have been and will continue to be the inspiration of our nation.

The record of the Administration toward Mexico has been consistently friendly and with equal consistency have we upheld American rights. This firm and at the same time friendly policy has brought recognition of the inviolability of legally acquired rights. This condition has been reached without threat or without bluster, through a calm support of the recognized principles of international law with due regard to the rights of a sister sovereign state. The Republican Party will continue to support American rights in Mexico, as elsewhere in the world, and at the same time to promote and strengthen friendship and confidence.

There has always been, as there always will be, a firm friendship with Canada. American and Canadian interests are in a large measure identical. Our relationship is one of fine mutual understanding and the recent exchange of diplomatic officers between the two countries is worthy of commendation.

The United States has an especial interest in the advancement and progress of all the Latin American countries. The policy of the Republican Party will always be a policy of thorough friendship and co-operation. In the case of Nicaragua, we are engaged in co-operation with the government of that country upon the task of assisting to restore and maintain peace, order and stability, and in no way to infringe upon her sovereign rights. The Marines, now in Nicaragua, are there to protect American lives and property and to aid in carr 'ng out an agreement whereby we have undertaken to do what we can to restore and maintain order and to insure a fair and free election. Our policy absolutely repudiates any idea of conquest or exploitation, and is actuated solely by an earnest and sincere desire to assist a friendly and neighboring state which has appealed for aid in a great emergency. It is the same policy the United States has pursued in other cases in Central America.

The Administration has looked with keen sympathy on the tragic events in China. We have avoided interference in the internal affairs of that unhappy nation merely keeping sufficient naval and military forces in China to protect the lives of the Americans who are there on legitimate business and in still larger numbers for nobly humanitarian reasons. America has not been stampeded into making reprisals but, on the other hand, has consistently taken the position of leadership among the nations in a policy of wise moderation. We shall always be glad to be of assistance to China when our duty is clear.

The Republican Party maintains the traditional American policy of non-interference in the political affairs of other nations. This government has definitely refused membership in the League of Nations and to assume any obligations under the covenant of the League.

On this we stand.

In accordance, however, with the long established American practice of giving aid and assistance to other peoples, we have most usefully assisted by co-operation in the humanitarian and technical work undertaken by the League, without involving ourselves in European politics by accepting membership.

The Republican Party has always given and will continue to give its support to the development of American foreign trade, which makes for domestic prosperity. During this administration extraordinary strides have been made in opening up new markets for American produce and manufacture. Through these foreign contacts a mutually better international understanding has been reached which aids in the maintenance of world peace.

The Republican Party promises a firm and consistent support of American persons and legitimate American interests in all parts of the world. This support will never contravene the rights of other nations. It will always have in mind and support in every way the progressive development of international law, since it is through the operation of just laws, as well as through the growth of friendly understanding, that world peace will be made permanent. To that end the Republican Party pledges itself to aid and assist in the perfection of principles of international law and the settlement of international disputes.

CIVIL SERVICE

The merit system in government service originated with and has been developed by the Republican Party. The great majority of our public service employees are now secured through and maintained in the government service rules. Steps have already been taken by the Republican Congress to make the service more attractive as to wages and retirement privileges, and we commend what has been done, as a step in the right direction.

AGRICULTURE

The agricultural problem is national in scope and, as such, is recognized by the Republican Party which pledges its strength and energy to the solution of the same. Realizing that many farmers are facing problems more difficult than those which are the portion of many other basic industries, the party is anxious to aid in every way possible. Many of our farmers are still going through readjustments, a relic of the years directly following the great war. All the farmers are being called on to meet new and perplexing conditions created by foreign competition, the complexities of domestic marketing, labor problems, and a steady increase in local and state taxes.

The general depression in a great basic industry inevitably reacts upon the conditions in the country as a whole and cannot be ignored. It is a matter of satisfaction that the desire to help in the correction of agricultural wrongs and conditions is not confined to any one section of our country or any particular group.

The Republican Party and the Republican Administration, particularly during the last five years, have settled many of the most distressing problems as they have arisen, and the achievements in aid of agriculture are properly a part of this record. The Republican Congresses have been most responsive in the matter of agricultural appropriations, not only to meet crop emergencies, but for the extension and development of the activities of the Department of Agriculture.

The protection of the American farmer against foreign farm competition and foreign trade practices has been vigorously carried on by the Department of State. The right of the farmers to engage in collective buying and co-operative selling as provided for by the Capper-Volstead Act of 1922 has been promulgated through the Department of Agriculture and the Department of Justice, which have given most valuable aid and assistance to the heads of the farm organizations. The Treasury Department and the proper committees of Congress have lightened the tax burden on farming communities, and through the Federal

Farm Loan System there has been made available to the farmers of the nation one billion eight hundred fifty millions of dollars for loaning purposes at a low rate of interest, and through the Intermediate Credit Banks six hundred fifty-five million dollars of short term credits have been made available to the farmers. The Post Office Department has systematically and generously extended the Rural Free Delivery routes into even the most sparsely settled communities.

When a shortage of transportation facilities threatened to deprive the farmers of their opportunity to reach waiting markets overseas, the President, appreciative and sensitive of the condition and the possible loss to the communities, ordered the reconditioning of Shipping Board vessels, thus relieving a great emergency.

Last, but not least, the Federal Tariff Commission has at all times shown a willingness under the provisions of the Flexible Tariff Act to aid the farmers when foreign competition, made possible by low wage scales abroad, threatened to deprive our farmers of their domestic markets. Under this Act the President has increased duties on wheat, flour, mill feed, and dairy products. Numerous other farm products are now being investigated by the Tariff Commission.

We promise every assistance in the reorganization of the marketing system on sounder and more economical lines and, where diversification is needed, Government financial assistance during the period of transition.

The Republican Party pledges itself to the enactment of legislation creating a Federal Farm Board clothed with the necessary powers to promote the establishment of a farm marketing system of farmer-owned-and-controlled stabilization corporations or associations to prevent and control surpluses through orderly distribution.

We favor adequate tariff protection to such of our agricultural products as are affected by foreign competition.

We favor, without putting the Government into business, the establishment of a Federal system of organization for co-operative and orderly marketing of farm products.

The vigorous efforts of this Administration towards broadening our exports market will be continued.

The Republican Party pledges itself to the development and enactment of measures which will place the agricultural interests of America on a basis of economic equality with other industries to insure its prosperity and success.

MINING

The money value of the mineral products of the country is second only to agriculture. We lead the countries of the world in the production of coal, iron, copper and silver. The nation suffers as a whole from any disturbance in the securing of any one of these minerals, and particularly when the coal supply is affected. The mining industry has always been self-sustaining, but we believe that the Government should make every effort to aid the industry by protection by removing any restrictions which may be hampering its development, and by increased technical and economic research investigations which are necessary for its welfare and normal development. The Party is anxious, hopeful, and willing to assist in any feasible plan for the stabilization of the coal mining industry, which will work with justice to the miners, consumers and producers.

HIGHWAYS

Under the Federal Aid Road Act, adopted by the Republican Congress in 1921, and supplemented by generous appropriations each year, road construction has made greater advancement than for many decades previous. Improved highway conditions is a gauge of our rural developments and our commercial activity. We pledge our support to continued appropriations for this work commensurate with our needs and resources.

We favor the construction of roads and trails in our national forests necessary to their protection and utilization. In appropriations therefor the taxes which these lands would pay if taxable should be considered as a controlling factor.

LABOR

The Labor record of the Republican Party stands unchallenged. For 52 of the 72 years of our national existence Republican Administrations have prevailed. Today American labor enjoys the highest wage and the highest standard of living throughout the world. Through the saneness and soundness of Republican rule the American workman is paid a "real wage" which allows comfort for himself and his dependents, and an opportunity and leisure for advancement. It is not surpris-

ing that the foreign workman, whose greatest ambition still is to achieve a "living wage," should look with longing towards America as the goal of his desires.

The ability to pay such wages and maintain such a standard comes from the wisdom of the protective legislation which the Republican Party has placed upon the national statute books, the tariff which bars cheap foreign-made goods from the American market and provides continuity of employment for our workmen and fair profits for the manufacturers, the restriction of immigration which not only prevents the glutting of our labor market, but allows to our newer immigrants a greater opportunity to secure a footing in their upward struggle.

The Party favors freedom in wage contracts, the right of collective bargaining by free and responsible agents of their own choosing, which develops and maintains that purposeful co-operation which gains its chief incentive through voluntary agreement.

We believe that injunctions in labor disputes have in some instances been abused and have given rise to a serious question for legislation.

The Republican Party pledges itself to continue its efforts to maintain this present standard of living and high wage scale.

RAILROADS

Prompt and effective railroad service at the lowest rates which will provide for its maintenance and allow a reasonable return to the investor so they may be encouraged to advance new capital for acquired developments, has long been recognized by the Republican Party as a necessity of national existence.

We believe that the present laws under which our railroads are regulated are soundly based on correct principles, the spirit of which must always be preserved. Because, however, of changes in the public demands, trade conditions and of the character of the competition, which even the greatest railroads are now being called upon to meet, we feel that in the light of this new experience possible modifications or amendments, the need of which is proved, should be considered.

The Republican Party initiated and set in operation the Interstate Commerce Commission. This body has developed a system of railroad control and regulation which has given to the transportation public an opportunity not only to make suggestions for the improvement of railroad service, but to protest against discriminatory rates or schedules. We commend the work which that body is accomplishing under mandate of law in considering these matters and seeking to distribute equitably the burden of transportation between commodities based on their ability to bear the same.

MERCHANT MARINE

The Republican Party stands for the American-built, American-owned, and American-operated merchant marine. The enactment of the White-Jones Bill is in line with a policy which the party has long advocated.

Under this measure, substantial aid and encouragement are offered for the building in American yards of new and modern ships which will carry the American flag.

The Republican Party does not believe in government ownership or operation, and stands specifically for the sale of the present government vessels to private owners when appropriate arrangements can be made. Pending such a sale, and because private owners are not ready as yet to operate on certain of the essential trade routes, the bill enacted allows the maintenance of these necessary lines under government control till such transfer can be made.

MISSISSIPPI FLOOD RELIEF AND CONTROL

The Mississippi Valley flood in which seven hundred thousand of our fellow citizens were placed in peril of life, and which destroyed hundreds of million of dollars' worth of property, was met with energetic action by the Republican Administration.

During this disaster the President mobilized every public and private agency under the direction of Secretary Hoover of the Department of Commerce and Dwight Davis, the Secretary of War. Thanks to their joint efforts, a great loss of life was prevented and everything possible was done to rehabilitate the people in their homes and to relieve suffering and distress.

Congress promptly passed legislation authorizing the expenditure of $325,000,000 for the construction of flood control works, which it is believed will prevent the recurrence of such a disaster.

RADIO

We stand for the administration of the radio facilities of the United States under wise and expert government supervision which will

(1) Secure to every home in the nation, whether city or country, the great educational and inspirational values of broadcast programs, adequate in number and varied in character, and

(2) Assign the radio communication channels, regional, continental, and transoceanic,—in the best interest of the American business man, the American farmer, and the American public generally.

WATERWAYS

Cheaper transportation for bulk goods from the midwest agricultural sections to the sea is recognized by the Republican Party as a vital factor for the relief of agriculture. To that end we favor the continued development in inland and in intra-coastal waterways as an essential part of our transportation system.

The Republican Administration during the last four years initiated the systematic development of the Mississippi system of inland transportation lanes, and it proposes to carry on this modernization of transportation to speedy completion. Great improvements have been made during this administration in our harbors, and the party pledges itself to continue these activities for the modernization of our national equipment.

VETERANS

Our country is honored whenever it bestows relief on those who have faithfully served its flag. The Republican Party, appreciative of this solemn obligation and honor, has made its sentiments evident in Congress. Our expenditures for the benefit of all our veterans now aggregate 750 million dollars annually. Increased hospital facilities have been provided, payments in compensation have more than doubled, and in the matter of rehabilitations, pensions, and insurance, generous provision has been made. The administration of laws dealing with the relief of veterans and their dependents has been a difficult task, but every effort has been made to carry service to the veteran and bring about not only a better and generous interpretation of the law, but a sympathetic consideration of the many problems of the veteran. Full and adequate relief for our disabled veterans is our aim, and we commend the action of Congress in further liberalizing the laws applicable to veterans' relief.

PUBLIC UTILITIES

Republican Congresses and Administrations have steadily strengthened the Interstate Commerce Commission. The protection of the public from exactions or burdens in rates for service by reason of monopoly control, and the protection of the smaller organizations from suppression in their own field, has been a fundamental idea in all regulatory enactments. While recognizing that at times Federal regulations might be more effective than State regulations in controlling intrastate utilities, the Party favors and has sustained State regulations, believing that such responsibility in the end will create a force of State public opinion which will be more effective in preventing discriminations and injustices.

CONSERVATION

We believe in the practical application of the conservation principle by the wise development of our natural resources. The measure of development is our national requirement, and avoidance of waste so that future generations may share in this natural wealth. The Republican policy is to prevent monopolies in the control and utilization of natural resources. Under the General Leasing Law, enacted by a Republican Congress, the ownership of the mineral estate remains in the Government, but development occurs through private capital and energy. Important for the operation of this law is the classification and appraisement of public lands according to their mineral content and value. Over five hundred million acres of public land have been thus classified.

To prevent wasteful exploitation of our oil products, President Coolidge appointed an Oil Conservation Board, which is now conducting an inquiry into all phases of petroleum production, in the effort to devise a national policy for the conservation and proper utilization of our oil resources.

The Republican Party has been forehanded in assuring the development of water power in accordance with public interest. A policy of permanent public retention of the power sites on public land and power privileges in domestic and international navigable streams, and one-third of the potential water power resources in the United States on public domain, has been assured by the Federal Water Powers Act, passed by a Republican Congress.

LAW ENFORCEMENT

We reaffirm the American Constitutional Doctrine as announced by George Washington in his "Farewell Address," to-wit:

"The Constitution which at any time exists until changed by the explicit and authentic act by the whole people is sacredly obligatory upon all."

We also reaffirm the attitude of the American people toward the Federal Constitution as declared by Abraham Lincoln:

"We are by both duty and inclination bound to stick by that Constitution in all its letter and spirit from beginning to end. I am for the honest enforcement of the Constitution. Our safety, our liberty, depends upon preserving the Constitution of the United States, as our forefathers made it inviolate."

The people through the method provided by the Constitution have written the Eighteenth Amendment into the Constitution. The Republican Party pledges itself and its nominees to the observance and vigorous enforcement of this provision of the Constitution.

HONESTY IN GOVERNMENT

We stand for honesty in government, for the appointment of officials whose integrity cannot be questioned. We deplore the fact that any official has ever fallen from this high standard and that certain American citizens of both parties have so far forgotten their duty as citizens as to traffic in national interests for private gain. We have prosecuted and shall always prosecute any official who subordinates his public duty to his personal interest.

The Government today is made up of thousands of conscientious, earnest, self-sacrificing men and women, whose single thought is service to the nation.

We pledge ourselves to maintain and, if possible, to improve the quality of this great company of Federal employees.

Campaign Expenditures

Economy, honesty, and decency in the conduct of political campaigns are a necessity if representative government is to be preserved to the people and political parties are to hold the respect of the citizens at large.

The Campaign of 1924 complied with all these requirements. It was a campaign, the expenses of which were carefully budgeted in advance, and, which, at the close, presented a surplus and not a deficit.

There will not be any relaxing of resolute endeavor to keep our elections clean, honest and free from taint of any kind. The improper use of money in governmental and political affairs is a great national evil. One of the most effective remedies for this abuse is publicity in all matters touching campaign contributions and expenditures. The Republican Party, beginning not later than August 1, 1928, and every 30 days thereafter,—the last publication being not later than five days before the election—will file with the Committees of the House and Senate a complete account of all contributions, the names of the contributors, the amounts expended, and for what purposes, and will at all times hold its records and books touching such matters open for inspection.

The party further pledges that it will not create, or permit to be created, any deficit which shall exist at the close of the campaign.

Reclamation

Federal reclamation of arid lands is a Republican policy, adopted under President Roosevelt, carried forward by succeeding Republican Presidents, and put upon a still higher plane of efficiency and production by President Coolidge. It has increased the wealth of the nation and made the West more prosperous.

An intensive study of the methods and practices of reclamation has been going on for the past four years under the direction of the Department of the Interior in an endeavor to create broader human opportunities and their financial and economic success. The money value of the crops raised on reclamation projects is showing a steady and gratifying increase as well as the number of farms and people who have settled on the lands.

The continuation of a surplus of agricultural products in the selling markets of the world has influenced the Department to a revaluation of plans and projects. It has adopted a ten-year program for the completion of older projects and will hold other suggestions in abeyance until the surveys now under way as to the entire scope of the work are completed.

Commercial Aviation

Without governmental grants or subsidies and entirely by private initiative, the nation has made extraordinary advances in the field of commercial aviation. Over 20,000 miles of air mail service privately operated are now being flown daily, and the broadening of this service is an almost weekly event. Because of our close relations with our sister republics on the south and our neighbor on the north, it is fitting our first efforts should be to establish an air communication with Latin-America and Canada.

The achievements of the aviation branches of the Army and Navy are all to the advantage of commercial aviation, and in the Mississippi flood disaster the work performed by civil and military aviators was of inestimable value.

The development of a system of aircraft registration, inspection and control is a credit to the Republican Administration, which, quick to appreciate the importance of this new transportation development, created machinery for its safeguarding.

Immigration

The Republican Party believes that in the interest of both native and foreign-born wage-earners, it is necessary to restrict immigration. Unrestricted immigration would result in widespread unemployment and in the breakdown of the American standard of living. Where, however, the law works undue hardships by depriving the immigrant of the comfort and society of those bound by close family ties, such modification should be adopted as will afford relief.

We commend Congress for correcting defects for humanitarian reasons and for providing an effective system of examining prospective immigrants in their home countries.

Naturalization

The priceless heritage of American citizenship is our greatest gift to our friends of foreign birth.

Only those who will be loyal to our institutions, who are here in conformity with our laws, and who are in sympathy with our national traditions, ideals, and principles, should be naturalized.

NAVY

We pledge ourselves to round out and maintain the Navy in all types of combatant ships to the full ratio provided for the United States by the Washington Treaty for the Limitation of Naval Armament and any amendment thereto.

HAWAII-ALASKA

We favor a continuance for the Territory of Hawaii of Federal assistance in harbor improvements, the appropriation of its share of federal funds and the systematic extension of the settlement of public lands by the Hawaiian race.

We indorse the policy of the present administration with reference to Alaska and favor a continuance of the constructive development of the territory.

WOMEN AND PUBLIC SERVICE

Four years ago at the Republican National Convention in Cleveland women members of the National Committee were welcomed into full association and responsibility in party management. During the four years which have passed they have carried with their men associates an equal share of all responsibilities and their contribution to the success of the 1924 campaign is well recognized.

The Republican Party, which from the first has sought to bring this development about, accepts wholeheartedly equality on the part of women, and in the public service it can present a record of appointments of women in the legal, diplomatic, judicial, treasury and other governmental departments. We earnestly urge on the women that they participate even more generally than now in party management and activity.

NATIONAL DEFENSE

We believe that in time of war the nation should draft for its defense not only its citizens but also every resource which may contribute to success. The country demands that should the United States ever again be called upon to defend itself by arms, the President be empowered to draft such material resources and such services as may

be required, and to stabilize the prices of services and essential commodities, whether utilized in actual warfare or private activity.

OUR INDIAN CITIZENS

National citizenship was conferred upon all native born Indians in the United States by the General Indian Enfranchisement Act of 1924. We favor the creation of a Commission to be appointed by the President including one or more Indian citizens to investigate and report to Congress upon the existing system of the administration of Indian affairs and to report any inconsistencies that may be found to exist between that system and the rights of the Indian citizens of the United States. We also favor the repeal of any law and the termination of any administrative practice which may be inconsistent with Indian citizenship, to the end that the Federal guardianship existing over the persons and properties of Indian tribal communities may not work a prejudice to the personal and property rights of Indian citizens of the United States. The treaty and property rights of the Indians of the United States must be guaranteed to them.

THE NEGRO

We renew our recommendation that the Congress enact at the earliest possible date a Federal Anti-Lynching Law so that the full influence of the Federal Government may be wielded to exterminate this hideous crime.

HOME RULE

We believe in the essential unity of the American people. Sectionalism in any form is destructive of national life. The Federal Government should zealously protect the national and international rights of its citizens. It should be equally zealous to respect and maintain the rights of the States and territories and to uphold the vigor and balance of our dual system of government. The Republican party has always given its energies to supporting the Government in this direction when any question has arisen.

There are certain other well-defined Federal obligations such as interstate commerce, the development of rivers and harbors, and the guarding and conservation of national resources. The effort, which, however, is being continually made to have the Federal Government move into the field of state activities, has never had, and never will have the support of the Republican Party. In the majority of the cases state citizens and officers are most pressing in their desire to have the Federal Government take over these state functions. This is to be deplored for it weakens the sense of initiative and creates a feeling of dependence which is unhealthy and unfortunate for the whole body politic.

There is a real need of restoring the individual and local sense principles; there is a real need of restoring the individual and local sense of responsibility and self-reliance; there is a real need for the people once more to grasp the fundamental fact that under our system of government they are expected to solve many problems themselves through their municipal and State governments, and to combat the tendency that is all too common to turn to the Federal Government as the easiest and least burdensome method of lightening their own responsibilities.

Socialist Party National Platform, 1928

Preamble

We Americans are told that we live in the most prosperous country in the world. Certainly, our natural resources, our mechanical equipment, our physical power, the technical capacity of our engineers and the skill of our workers in farm and factory make it possible for us to attain a level of well-being of which our fathers never dared to dream.

Yet poverty abounds. The owners of our natural resources and industrial equipment and the government which they have made virtually their tool have not given us plenty, freedom or peace in any such degree as we have the right and duty to demand.

Men are hungry while farmers go bankrupt for lack of effective demand for food. Tenant farming has reached a proportion of almost 40 per cent; more than 40 per cent of the value of farm lands is covered by mortgages. Industrial workers are scarcely better off. In good years there are at least 1,000,000 unemployed. By a conservative estimate in these times of stock market prosperity the number has arisen to 4,000,000. About ⅓ of those of our population 65 years of age and upward are at least partially dependent upon some form of charity. While real wages have risen for

certain groups they have risen scarcely more than half the increase of productive power of the workers. And what gains have been made are far from universal as the misery of textile workers and the tragedy of the coal fields—to cite only two examples—abundantly prove. In fact, at the present time a majority of workers obtain a wage insufficient to maintain themselves and families in health and decency. Furthermore the rapid increase in the use of machinery and the growing intensity of work are leading to quicker exhaustion and greater insecurity.

Unions Bereft of Rights by Class Justice

Meanwhile the owning class has been using the government to curtail the power of the workers whose organized might, especially through their unions, has been chiefly responsible for whatever material gains they have made. To curb the workers, civil liberties are denied, injunctions are invoked against union activities and the courts are made the instruments of that class justice of which the Mooney case and the legalized murder of Sacco and Vanzetti were conspicuous examples.

Not only plenty and freedom but peace is endangered by this system under which the many are exploited for the profit of the few. Sons of the workers now die in President Coolidge's infamous little imperialist war in Nicaragua, as they died in President Wilson's similar wars in Haiti, Santo Domingo and Mexico, and above all in that great imperialistic war born of the trade and financial rivalries of the nations which cost our country forty billion dollars and hundreds of thousands of lives.

From the wars, waste and cruelty of a system where the rightful heritage of the workers is the private property of the few only the united efforts of farmers and workers of hand and brain, through their cooperatives, unions and political party, can save us. We must make government in cities, states and nation the servant of the people. That requires our own political party. We cannot place our trust in "good men" or political Messiahs. Bitter experience has proved that we cannot trust the alternate rule of the Republican and Democratic parties. They belong to the landlords, bankers, oil speculators, coal and power barons, in short to the capitalist class which finances them. Under their control the government by what it does and leaves undone, by its calculated inefficiency as well as its repression and corruption, makes our alleged democracy largely an illusion. Corruption is natural under parties which are the tools of the forces of privilege. It has become accepted even by the men who are victims of it.

Labor's Weapon in the Class Struggle

These things need not be. The Socialist Party offers itself as the political party of the producing classes, the workers in farm, factory, mine or office. It is our political weapon in the class struggle and in its triumph lies our hope of ending that struggle. Our record proves our good faith. As the only democratic labor party in the United States, we stand now as always, in America and in all lands, for the collective ownership of natural resources and basic industries and their democratic management for the use and benefit of all instead of the private profit of the privileged few.

With this ultimate aim in view, the Socialist Party enters the presidential campaign of 1928 with the following program:

Public Ownership and Conservation

To recover the rightful heritage of the people we propose:

1. Nationalization of our natural resources, beginning with the coal mines and water sites, particularly at Boulder Dam and Muscle Shoals.

2. A publicly owned giant power system under which the federal government shall cooperate with the states and municipalities in the distribution of electrical energy to the people at cost. Only when public agencies have full control over the generation, transmission and distribution of electrical power can the consumers be guaranteed against exploitation by the great electrical interests of the country. Public ownership of these and other industries must include employee representation in the management and the principle of collective bargaining must be recognized.

3. National ownership and democratic management of railroads and other means of transportation and communication.

4. An adequate national program for flood control, flood relief, reforestation, irrigation and reclamation.

Unemployment Relief

To relieve the tragic misery of millions of unemployed workers and their families we propose:

1. Immediate governmental relief of the unemployed by the extension of all public works and a program of long range planning of public works following the present depression. All persons thus employed to be engaged at hours and wages fixed by bona-fide labor unions.

2. Loans to states and municipalities without interest for the purpose of carrying on public works and the taking of such other measures as will lessen widespread misery.

3. A system of unemployment insurance.

4. The nation-wide extension of public employment agencies in cooperation with city federations of labor.

Labor Legislation

The lives and well-being of the producers and their families should be the first charge on society. We therefore urge:

1. A system of health and accident insurance and of old age pension as well as unemployment insurance. As long as workers are dependent primarily upon their employers rather than on the community for protection against the exigencies of old age, sickness, accident and unemployment, employers hostile or indifferent to the labor movement will be able to use their private insurance schemes as powerful weapons against organized labor.

2. Shortening the workday in keeping with the steadily increasing productivity of labor due to improvements in machinery and methods.

3. Securing to every worker a rest period of no less than two days in each week.

4. Enacting of an adequate federal anti-child labor amendment.

5. Abolition of the brutal exploitation of convicts under the contract system and substitution of a cooperative organization of industries in penitentiaries and workshops for the benefit of convicts and their dependents, the products to be used in public institutions, and the convict workers to be employed at wages current in the industry.

Taxation

For the proper support of government and as a step toward social justice we propose:

1. Increase of taxation on high income levels, of corporation taxes and inheritance taxes, the proceeds to be used for old age pensions and other forms of social insurance.

2. Appropriation by taxation of the annual rental value of all land held for speculation.

CIVIL LIBERTIES

To secure to the people the civil rights without which democracy is impossible, we demand:

1. Federal legislation to enforce the first amendment to the constitution so as to guarantee effectually freedom of speech, press and assembly, and to penalize any official who interferes with the civil rights of any citizen.

2. Abolition of injunctions in labor disputes.

3. Repeal of the espionage law and of other repressive legislation and restoration of civil and political rights to those unjustly convicted under war time laws with reimbursement for time served.

4. Legislation protecting foreign born workers from deportation and refusal of citizenship on account of political opinions.

5. Modification of immigration laws to permit the reuniting of families and to offer a refuge for those fleeing from political or religious persecution.

6. Abolition of detective agencies engaged in interstate business.

ANTI-LYNCHING

As a measure of protection for the oppressed, especially for our Negro fellow citizens, we propose:

Enactment of the Berger anti-lynching bill making participation in lynching a felony.

POLITICAL DEMOCRACY

The constitution of the United States was drafted in 1787 and was designed to meet conditions utterly different from those prevailing today. In order to make our form of government better suited to exigencies of the times, we propose the immediate calling of a constitutional convention. A modernized constitution should provide, among other things, for the election of the President and Vice-President by direct popular vote of the people, for reduction of the representation in Congress of those states where large sections of the citizens are disfranchised by force or fraud, and proportional representation, and for the abolition of the usurped power of the Supreme Court to pass upon the constitutionality of legislation enacted by Congress.

CREDIT AND BANKING

For our emancipation from the money trust, we propose:

Nationalization of the banking and currency system, beginning with extension of the service of the postal savings banks to cover every department of the banking business.

FARM RELIEF

The Socialist Party believes that the farmer is entitled to special consideration because of the importance of agriculture, because of the farmers' present economic plight and because the farmer is unable to control the prices of what he buys and what he sells. Many of the party's demands, including public development of electrical energy, nationalization of coal and railroads, and reform of the credit system will be of distinct benefit to the farmer.

As a further means of agricultural relief, we propose:

1. Acquisition by bona fide cooperative societies and by federal, state and municipal governments of grain elevators, stockyards, storage warehouses and other distributing agencies and the conduct of these services on a non-profit basis.

2. Encouragement of farmers' cooperative purchasing and marketing societies and of credit agencies.

3. Social insurance against losses due to adverse weather conditions, such as hail, drought, cyclone and flood.

INTERNATIONAL RELATIONS

We are unalterably opposed to imperialism and militarism. Therefore we propose:

1. Immediate withdrawal of American forces from Nicaragua and abandonment of the policy of military intervention in Central America and other countries.

2. That all private loans and investments of American citizens in foreign countries shall be made at the sole risk of the bondholders and investors. The United States government shall not resort to any military or other coercive intervention with foreign governments for the protection of such loans and investments.

3. Cancellation of all war debts due the United States from its former associated powers on condition of a simultaneous cancellation of all inter-allied debts and a corresponding remission of the

reparation obligations of the Central Powers and on the further condition that our debtors reduce their military expenditures below pre-war level. The Socialist Party especially denounces the debt settling policy of our government in favoring the Fascist dictatorship of Italy and thereby helping to perpetuate the political enslavement of the Italian nation.

4. Recognizing both the services and the limitations of the League of Nations, the need of revision of its convenant and the Treaty of Versailles, we unite with the workers of Europe in demanding that the League be made all inclusive and democratic, and that the machinery for the revision of the peace treaty under article 19 of the covenant be elaborated and made effective. We favor the entry of the United States at the time and under conditions which will further these clauses and promote the peace of the world.

5. The recognition of the Russian government.

6. Aggressive activity against militarism, against the large navy and army program of our present administration, and in behalf of international disarmament.

7. Treaties outlawing war and the substitution of peaceful methods for the settlement of international disputes.

8. Independence of the Philippines on terms agreed upon in negotiations with the Filipinos; autonomy for Porto Rico and civil government for the Virgin Islands.

Platform of the Socialist Labor Party

The Socialist Labor Party of the United States of America in National Convention assembled in New York on May 13, 1928, reaffirming its previous platform pronouncements, and in accord with international Socialist principles, declares:

Social conditions, as illustrated by events crowded into the last few years, have ripened so fast that the principles, hitherto proclaimed by the Socialist Labor Party, as well as the methods that the Socialist Labor Party has hitherto advocated, stands conspiciously demonstrated.

The Capitalist Social System has wrought its own destruction. Its leading exponents, even when seemingly at war on principles, cannot conceal the identity of their political views. The absence of dividing lines between the two leading political clearing houses of capitalism—the Republican and Democratic parties; the supineness, almost exultant readiness with which the leading politicians—aspirants for the presidency and other important posts in the Political State—yield themselves to the needs of ultra-capitalism, to the exclusion of the needs of the producing masses, proclaim the inner conviction of the foremost men of the Ruling Class that the Republic of Capital is at the end of its tether.

True to economic laws, from which Socialism proceeds, dominant wealth has to such an extent concentrated into the hands of a select few, the modern industrial autocracy, that the lower layers of the capitalist class feel driven to the ragged edge, while the large majority of the people, the working class, are being submerged.

True to sociologic laws, by the light of which Socialism reads its forecasts, the industrial autocracy is breaking through its republican-democratic shell and is stretching out its hands towards abolutism in government; the property-holding layers below it are turning at bay; the proletariat is awakening to its consciousness of class, and thereby to the perception of its historic mission.

In the midst of this hurly-burly, and the resulting confusion of thought, all the colors of the rainbow are being projected upon the social mists.

From the lower layers of the capitalist class issue demands for reforms designed to check the logical tendencies of capitalism, demands covering the entire range of social visionariness. Overwhelmed by gigantic combinations in industry and finance, the middle and lower sections of the capitalist class clamor for a return of the age of competition. But even if such a return were possible it should not be effected; even if it should it cannot. To the thinker it is self-evident that the system neither can nor will return to what the Industrial Revolution has been gradually sloughing off during a century of progress.

The law of social progress pushes toward a system of production that shall crown the efforts of man—a system which without arduous toil, with an abundance of necessaries for material existence, will allow leisure for mental and spiritual expansion. The gigantic machine of modern production is a mechanical contrivance which is solving the problem of material needs which has confronted mankind from its infancy. To smash this contrivance and to reintroduce the days of small-fry competition would set back the hands of the dial of time. The mere thought is foolhardy.

He who undertakes the feat might as well brace himself against the cascade of Niagara. The cascade of Social Evolution would overwhelm him.

From the lowest layers of the property-holding class—layers that have sniffed the breath of Socialism and imagine themselves Socialists—comes the iridescent theory of capturing the machinery of production for the people by the ballot only, with a vague idea of government ownership and operation as the aim. But the "capture of the machinery of production for the people" implies the Social Revolution. To imply the Social Revolution with the ballot, without the means of enforcing the fiat of the ballot in case the Reaction attempts to override it, is to fire blank cartridges at a foe. It is worse. It is to threaten his existence without the means to carry out the threat, which can result in only one of two things—either the leaders are bought out, or the revolutionary class, to which they appeal and which they succeed in drawing along, are led like cattle to the shambles.

An equally iridescent hue of the rainbow is projected from a layer that lies almost wholly within the submerged class—the theory of capturing the machinery of production for the working class with physical force only and through underground conspiracies. The capture of the machinery of production for the people implies something strikingly different from all previous revolutions. It implies revolution carried on by the masses. For sociologic reasons mass-revolutionary conspiracy is, today, an impossibility, even an absurdity. The trust-holding autocracy may successfully put through a conspiracy of physical force. The smallness of its numbers make conspiracy possible. The hugeness of the numbers, requisite for a revolution against the trustholding autocracy, excludes conspiracy from the arsenal of the Revolution, and just as that autocracy at one point of the social circle boldly aims for absolutism and dictatorship in government, so this all but submerged layer at the merging point proclaims its aim to be dictatorship, thus closing the circle.

All these groups have one thing in common: they plant themselves upon the presumption of a continuation of the Political State—a presumption that is at war with logic and social evolution.

Only two programs—the program of Industrial Top-Capitalism and the program of the Socialist Labor Party grasp the situation.

The Political State, the instrument of class rule and oppression, is worn out in this, the leading capitalist nation of the world. The Socialist or Industrial Government is throbbing for birth. The Political State, being a class state, is government separate and apart from the productive energies of the people; it is government mainly for holding the ruled class in subjection. The Socialist or Industrial Government, being the denial of the class state, is government that is an integral part of the productive energies of the people.

As their functions differ, so are the structures of the two "States" different.

The structure of the Political State is based on territorial representation; the structure of the Industrial Government demands representation by industries and useful occupations.

The economic or industrial evolution has reached that point where the Political State no longer can maintain itself under the forms of democracy. While the Industrial Autocracy has relatively shrunk, the enemies it is raising against itself are becoming numerous. Moreover, obedient to the law of its existence, the Political State not only multiplies its enemies; it has been forced to recruit and group the bulk of these enemies, and the revolutionary bulk at that.

The working class of the land, the historically revolutionary element, is grouped by occupations, agricultural as well as industrial, in such manner that—while the "autonomous craft union," at one time the palladium of workers, has become a harmless scarecrow upon which the capitalist birds roost at ease—the Revolutionary Industrial Unions will spring logically from the modern organization of industry itself and, casting ahead of them the constituencies of the government of the future, point to the Industrial Governmental Organization.

Nor is this all. Not only has the Political State raised its own enemies; not only has it multiplied them; not only has it recruited and drilled them; not only has it grouped them into shape to succeed it; it is, furthermore, driven by its inherent necessities to prodding on the revolutionary class by digging ever more fiercely into its flanks the harpoon of exploitation.

With the purchasing power of wages sinking to ever lower depths; with certainty of work hanging on ever slenderer threads; with an ever more gigantically swelling army of the unemployed; with the need of profits pressing the Industrial Autocracy harder and harder to squander recklessly the workers' limbs and lives; what with all this and the parallel process of merging the workers of all industries into one interdependent solid mass, the final break-up is rendered inevitable.

No wild schemes and no rainbow-chasing will stead in the approaching emergency. The Industrial Autocracy knows this—and so does the Socialist Labor Party—and logical is the program of each.

The program of the Industrial Autocracy is Industrial Feudalism. Where a Social Revolution is pending and for whatever reason is not accomplished, REACTION is the alternative.

The program of the Socialist Labor Party is REVOLUTION—the Industrial or Socialist Republic, the social order where the Political State is overthrown; where the "Congress" of the land, the legislative and executive central directing authority, consists of representatives of the useful occupations; where, accordingly, the government will be an essential factor in production; where the gigantic machines are freed from the trammels of the private ownership that now turn into a curse the blessings which these machines are instinct with; where, accordingly, abundance can be the patrimony of all who work; where the shackles of wage slavery are no more.

In keeping with the goals of the different programs are the means of their execution.

The means in contemplation by REACTION is forcible repression. To this end REACTION is seeking, by means of industrial spies and other agencies, to lash the proletariat into acts of violence that may give color to a resort to physical force. By its maneuvers, it is egging the working class on to deeds of fury. The capitalist press echoes the policy, while the pure and simple reformers, pure and simple trade unionists, and "revolutionary" visionaries generally, are snared into the trap.

To the contrary, the means firmly adhered to by the Socialist Labor Party is the constitutional method of political action, backed by the industrially and classconsciously organized proletariat, to the exclusion of anarchy, underground conspiracies, and all that thereby hangs.

At such a critical period in the nation's existence the Socialist Labor Party calls upon the working class of America, more deliberately serious than ever before, to rally at the polls under the Party's banner. And the Party also calls upon all intelligent citizens to place themselves squarely upon the ground of working class interests, and join us in this mighty and noble work of human emancipation, so that we may put summary end to the existing barbarous class conflict by placing the land and all the means of production, transportation and distribution into the hands of the people as a collective body, and substituting for the present state of planless production, industrial war and social disorder, the Socialist or Industrial Commonwealth—a commonwealth in which every worker shall have the free exercise and full benefit of his faculties, multiplied by all the modern factors of civilization.

National Platform of the Workers (Communist) Party, 1928

I. AMERICA TODAY

President Coolidge said to the big bankers and manufacturers in Philadelphia: "We hold a great treasure which must be protected." In the name of the working class and the exploited farmers of this country the Workers (Communist) Party raises the question: *Who owns the "great treasure," in whose interests must it be protected, and who bears the burden of its protection?* And our answer is: The "great treasure" is owned by a handful of powerful bankers, manufacturers, and railroad magnates. The only share of it the workers and working farmers receive is exploitation and poverty, and all the burden of defense of the "great treasure" of American imperialism rests on the shoulders of the industrial and agricultural workers.

America is today the most powerful country in the world. America's wealth, the "great treasure," mounts up to 400 billion dollars. Half of the gold of the world is now in the possession of the United States. With but seven per cent of the world's total population America controls the bulk of the world's resources: 44 per cent of the world's coal, 70 per cent of the oil produced, 52 out of every 100 tons of steel, 60 per cent of the cotton and corn, and half of the world's railways, copper and pig iron.

A gigantic accumulation and concentration of capital is going on. The total amount of bank deposits is now over 56 billion dollars. There are over 1,000 factories in America employing more than 1,000 workers each, with a total of about 2½ million workers. Of all wage-earners in manufacturing over 56 per cent work in those 10,000 factories each of which turns out annually products to the amount of a million dollars or over.

Trustification is asserting itself with irresistible power. Consolidations of railways, big combines and mergers in all industries are the order of the day. The United States Steel Corporation has a capital of 1.4 billion dollars. A food trust is attempting to combine 2 billion dollars into one powerful corporation. The recent consolidation of the Brooklyn Edison Company and the Consolidated Gas Company of New York resulted in a merger of over one billion dollars. Five powerful companies control almost half of the whole national output of water power, and eleven groups control 80 per cent. Eight companies control three-fourths of the anthracite coal. Two companies exercise control over half of the copper resources of the country.

A process of centralization similar to that in *production* is going on in the field of *distribution*. There are today 3,893 chain store organizations controlling 101,536 retail outlets in thirty merchandise fields. These chains realized in 1927 a volume of business estimated at almost six billion dollars or 16 per cent of the total retail business of the country. The anti-trust laws function today not as instruments of "trust-busting" but as a means of trustification.

The United States is the leading country in respect to capitalist rationalization. The productive power of American industries has increased tremendously. In a decade productivity per employee in American manufacturing has increased 33 per cent, cost of management has decreased 12 per cent, but wages per unit of production have increased only 2 per cent. Overdevelopment of industrial productive capacity is one of the basic features of American imperialism.

Finance capital is almighty today. *Banks and industries are merged.* The climax of this development was marked by the fact that J. P. Morgan, head of American finance capital, became the head of the United States Steel Corporation, the country's biggest industrial company. Hand in hand with the trustification of industry goes the trustification of State power. *The Government of the United States is today an administration of finance capital.* The identity of the dominating personnel in finance capital and government administration is complete. Finance capital sends its direct representatives to the Cabinet as well as ambassadors to foreign countries.

Trustification, high tariff, monopoly, merger of trusts and State power, growing export of capital —this is the picture of American imperialism today.

The stabilization of European industries and the decline of British imperialism have increased competition on a world scale. United States imperialism is in a growing measure dependent on the world market, and it struggles for world hegemony in every corner of the world—from Latin America to China. It is engaged in murderous competition for the Russian market as well as for the markets of the British Empire.

Increased competition, increased struggle for the resources of raw material and for the export of capital, high tariff walls, and ever-larger armies and navies create a growing menace of war. *A second world war is inevitable.* Wars on a smaller scale are going on today in a period which the spokesmen of imperialism call the era of "world peace." American imperialism is conducting a war of extermination against Nicaragua, is participating in interventions in China, and is an active accomplice of the capitalist conspiracy against Soviet Russia.

Two main antagonisms lead today towards a world conflagration. One is the chief capitalist antagonism between British and American imperialism, which has taken the place of the prewar British-German rivalry. The other one is the general capitalist conspiracy against the Union of Socialist Soviet Republics.

Although British imperialism is today the most reactionary force in world politics, American imperialism is the leading power and represents the most dangerous, most aggressive force of world capitalism. There is an ever-clearer crystallization of the *two poles:* on the one hand, *the counter-revolutionary pole* under the leadership of the United States to defend capitalism against the growing revolt of the colonial peoples and the working masses of the capitalist countries; on the other hand, *the revolutionary pole* under the leadership of Soviet Russia, around which all the oppressed peoples of the colonies and all the exploited workers of the world rally.

Wealth and Poverty

The United States is the richest country in the world. "Uncle Shylock" is the creditor of all countries. The world owes the United States today not less than 23½ billion dollars. The yearly income of the United States from foreign investments amounts today to the huge sum of one billion dollars. The number of millionaires is growing fast. In 1919 there were only 65 incomes over a million; in 1926 there were 228. In 1919 there were only 189 incomes between $500,000 and $1,000,000; in 1926 the number was 465.

In his 1926 address to Congress President Coolidge said: "The wealth of our country is not public wealth but private wealth. It does not belong to the Government; it belongs to the people." The prodigious wealth of the country is private wealth, but the "people" who own it are not the workers and exploited farmers. They are the few millionaires. The country is growing richer, but the share of the millions of working people in the wealth of the country is decreasing and the share of the few powerful millionaires is increasing with amazing speed. One per cent of all recipients of any income in this country receive not less than 20 per cent of the whole national income and get not less than 86.2 per cent of all corporate dividends. *One per cent of the population possesses today not less than 33 per cent of all wealth; 10 per cent own 64 per cent; and the poorest 25 per cent possess only 3½ per cent.* The overwhelming majority of the "people" to whom President Coolidge refers are born poor and die poor. The Federal Trade Commission states that "about one per cent of the estimated number of decedents owned about 59 per cent of the estimated wealth, and more than 90 per cent was owned by about 13 per cent of the decedents."

The accumulated wealth is not distributed equally. *Hand in hand with the growing fortunes of the few millionaires goes the growing exploitation and poverty of the unskilled workers, Negroes, and exploited farmers.* Even President Coolidge was forced to admit in his Hammond dedication speech that there is a *"considerable class of unskilled workers who have not come into full participation in the wealth of the nation."* The share of the wage-earners in the national income has decreased. The manufacturing wage-earners received only 40.1 per cent of the "value product" in 1925 as against 44.8 per cent in 1921. The wages of the shamelessly exploited four million agricultural workers amounted in 1920 to 2.3 per cent of the national income and in 1926 to only 1.4 per cent. *The "democratization" of wealth is only a capitalist myth.* Bankers and industrial magnates own the big corporations. The workers do not possess more than one per cent of all stocks and bonds. "High American wages" is today the most popular publicity stunt of American and international capitalism, but high wages embrace only a thin aristocratic stratum of the working class. The overwhelming majority of wage-earners is not able to earn even sufficient to fulfill the most elementary needs of a decent life. In the middle of the most advertised prosperity, in the summer of 1926, the Federal Bureau of Labor Statistics estimated that the average wages for "common labor" were 42.6 cents an hour. The United States Department of Labor was forced to admit that huge sections of the working class are receiving wages of only $10.34 a week.

President Coolidge made the bold declaration that *"the people are prosperous,"* but reality shows that the overwhelming majority of the people work on starvation wages, that nearly 60 per cent of the workers still work more than 48 hours a week, that women and children, Negro and foreign-born unskilled workers are exploited at least as mercilessly as the most exploited strata of the European working class. *The prosperity of the "people" is best illustrated by the miserable shacks of the Southern cotton fields and the poverty-stricken slums of the Eastern cities.* In his 1926 address to Congress President Coolidge said: "The power of the purse is the power over liberty." A handful of millionaires exercise power over the purse, and they exercise power over the liberty of the overwhelming majority of the people of the United States. A handful of powerful millionaires own all the means of production—the factories, machinery, mines, railroads, water power—of this country, and are thus in a position to force the overwhelming majority of the people into wage slavery. *The wealth of the few is the poverty of the many; the liberty of the few is the bondage of the masses.*

Indictment of American Capitalism

Overproduction and starvation, overtime and unemployment, accumulation of wealth and accumulation of poverty—these are the features of capitalist prosperity for the workers and working farmers. The very fact that there can be such a thing as overproduction as long as the needs of every member of society are still unsatisfied is the most terrible indictment against capitalist society. Cyclones of periodic crises sweep over the whole capitalist economy. Capitalist society is unable to control its own forces of production. As the President of the United States Chamber of Commerce put it in his speech of May 10, 1928, there has been an *"economic thunderbolt of increasing production unloosed by industry."*

Unemployment is a permanent phenomenon in capitalist society. There is at any time 1½ million unemployed. The constant industrial reserve army is one of the props of capitalist society. The present depression with its 4 to 5 million unemployed workers brings untold misery. The labor of hundreds of thousands of children is one of the basic institutions of capitalism. Peonage, no better than chattel slavery, Jim Crowism and lynching are regular accompaniments of present-day capitalist prosperity. The shameless exploitation of the unskilled foreign-born workers and the oppression of whole races are parts of the capitalist system. The modern industrial serfdom of company towns is in existence to the glory of the "freest" constitution in the world. Capitalist industry conducts in the form of industrial accidents a bloody war of extermination against the working class. The infamous speed-up system causes the workers to age prematurely. Old workers are thrown away like slack, like useless by-products. Not less than 1,800,000 old people are forced to live the life of "dependents." Sickness and early death are the punishment for poverty. The United States Public Health Service states: "Both sickness and death are much more frequent among those with low incomes than among those with incomes adequate to comfortable living."

Capitalist decency and morality is symbolized by almshouses, brothels, slums, and bootleg saloons. Prostitution of science, literature, and art is on the same level as prostitution of women. Capitalist "justice" is equivalent to frame-ups, third degree, filling the penitentiaries with political prisoners, execution of working-class fighters like Sacco and Vanzetti. There is a crusade against the "crime wave," against petty larceny by the poor, conducted by those who are guilty of large-scale corruption and lobbying. With the exception of backward and impoverished China and India the powerful and rich and civilized United States is the only country which does not have any social legislation. The latest "achievement" of American imperialist civilization is the appearance of a *rentier* class completely divorced from the process of production and foisting its parasitic existence upon the toiling masses. Jingoism, militarism, robber wars against Nicaragua and China—these are the results of American capitalism.

President Coolidge summed up in the following way his picture of American capitalism: *"Those are some of the economic results which have accrued from the American principles of reliance upon the initiative and the freedom of the individual. It is the very antithesis of Communism."* And President Coolidge is right. American capitalism as it is—with all its economic, political, and moral results—is the very antithesis of Communism. There is no other altenative. *The issue is capitalism or Communism.* The Workers (Communist) Party of America declares itself the deadly enemy of capitalism. It has as its aim the overthrow of capitalism, the establishment of a workers' and farmers' government, the establishment of a Communist society in which the means of production will not be the private property of the few, a society which will not be based on profit but on labor, which will not be founded on class divisions, which will eradicate both imperialist wars and class wars, which will be able to eliminate poverty.

The Parties of Big and Small Business

With the exception of the Workers (Communist) Party all political parties and groups are defenders of the present capitalist society.

The two old capitalist parties, the Republican and Democratic, are twin brothers in the expression of the interests of the bosses.

The *Republican Party,* which in the interests of

the then revolutionary capitalism conducted a war against chattel slavery, is today working in the interests of the now counter-revolutionary capitalism for the perpetuation of wage slavery. The Republican Party of today is nothing but the party of trusts, of finance capital, of the biggest business interests of the country.

The *Democratic Party* was in the early stages of its history the party of slavery, against Northern capitalism and in the interests of the Southern plantation owners. Today, though many times masked with phrases of liberalism, it stands for the perpetuation of the peonage of Negroes in the South and for the maintenance of wage slavery throughout the country.

There are no real political differences between the two big political parties. Both are parties of capitalism; both are the enemies of the working class. The very existence of the two-party system is the most reactionary factor in American politics, is one of the factors which are responsible for the lack of an independent mass political party of the working class. Both capitalist parties try to put up the semblance of being defenders of the farmers, vying with each other in putting forward fake "farm relief" measures. *The "struggle" between the Republican and Democratic Parties is a staged fight, a mock struggle. There are no political issues between these two parties.* On the question of tariff, prohibition, taxation, imperialist war, farm relief, League of Nations, and all other discussed political issues there is much more division *within* each party than *between* the two parties.

The main slogan of the Republican Party today is "Prosperity." But reality shows depression and unemployment. The main slogan of the Democratic Party is: "Honesty in Government." But reality shows at least as much corruption on the part of the Democrats as on that of the Republicans. Tammany Hall can successfully compete in corruption with Teapot Dome.

There are several classes combined in each of these parties. Both still mirror in many respects the old sectional and regional groupings of the country, but in both there is an outspoken, decisive dominance of finance capital. *Both are one on the basic issues: the oppression of the working class, the maintenance of the exploitation of the workers and working farmers, and the robber policies against the colonies and semi-colonies of American imperialism.*

The group of so-called *Progressives* is by no means better than the Republican "Old Guard" or the Democratic heroes of Tammany Hall and the "solid" South. In 1924, the bulk of the so-called progressive group supported the LaFollette movement, which betrayed the interests of the working class and the working farmers, dissipating the discontent of the masses and leading them back to the capitalist parties.

In 1928 the attitude of the so-called Progressives is still more cowardly. They have even deserted the idea of a third party, and have gone back meekly into the old capitalist parties. Senator Wheeler came out openly in support of Al Smith, who is the embodiment of the new Tammany Hall and the hero of the labor-smashing policies in the needle trades. Senators Borah and Norris and their Republican colleagues are equally untrustworthy. Borah's empty gesture of "outlawing" war serves only as a cover for Kellogg's imperialist wars and war preparations. Senator Shipstead, who still usurps the name of a Farmer-Laborite, is betraying the interests of the workers and exploited farmers in the most shameless way. He upholds the Nicaraguan war, and gives his support to the anti-labor injunction policies of the courts by introducing a fake anti-injunction bill. These "progressive" Senators and Congressmen are in many respects more dangerous enemies of the workers and working farmers than the official spokesmen of big business, because they hide their capitalist face and create illusions in the minds of the masses. *All these Progressives and semi-Progressives serve as a prop of the present capitalist society and must be combatted by all honest workers and farmers.*

The official leadership of the *American Federation of Labor* is today part and parcel of American imperialism. Under the leadership of the most corrupt trade-union bureaucracy in the world the A. F. of L. has become mainly an organization of the labor aristocracy, an instrument of class collaboration with the bosses instead of a means of struggle against big business. The capitalists are conducting the most murderous offensive of the open shop and wage cuts against the workers. The answer of the leaders of the A. F. of L. is a joint proposal with the American Bar Association for a Federal anti-strike law. *The trade-union bureaucrats are today the partners of the bosses.* They are trying to wrench the weapon of the strike from the hands of the workers. The whole infamous system of labor banks and trade-union insurance —trade-union capitalism—is nothing but the most elaborate system of class betrayal. The leadership of the A. F. of L. does not conduct any struggle against wage cuts or for higher wages and shorter hours. The trade-union bureaucracy sabotages the great task of organizing the unorganized. The worthy heirs of Gompers—Green, Woll and Co.—are the advocates of the *"Monroe Doctrine of Labor," are the spokesmen of a "labor imperialism."* They have come out openly for a policy of common exploitation of all Latin-American peoples by the capitalists and workers of the United States. The B. and O. plan, the Mitten plan, compulsory arbitration, the transformation of the trade unions into semi-Fascist and semi-company unions —is today the policy of the A. F. of L. These corrupt misleaders of labor are helping to keep the workers in the camp of the old capitalist parties by maintaining the sterile and treacherous policy of "reward your friends and punish your enemies" within the capitalist parties. There cannot be successful struggles of the working class against its exploiters without a systematic struggle against the whole edifice of the labor aristocracy and its corrupt bureaucratic leadership.

The *Socialist Party of America,* which still claims to be a working-class party, is in fact a party of the lower middle class. Its leadership has become part of the bureaucracy of the A. F. of L. Its whole ambition is to inherit the traditions of the LaFollette third-party movement. The militant spirit of Eugene Debs has been completely wiped out from the Socialist Party. In Wisconsin the Socialist Party is an official party of the capitalist administration. In New York the Socialist Party has substituted the red-white-and-blue flag of patriotism for the red flag of revolution. In Reading the city officials of the Socialist Party have pledged themselves to *"understand that their responsibilities will be those of capitalist officials rather than of Socialist Party members."* James H. Maurer, one of the councilmen elected by the Socialists in Reading and vice-Presidential candidate of the Socialist Party, declared: "We are going to give the workers a typical working-class government, but *if there is a strike in Reading while we are in power, the capitalist employer will have his property and life protected as he never had it before."*

The presidential candidate of the Socialist Party, Norman Thomas, is the worst kind of pacifist, a typical preacher, who performs the greatest service for American imperialism by creating illusions about the League of Nations, about the possibility of preventing wars by peaceful means. The Socialist Party today is an advocate of the League of Nations, and is a supporter of the hypocritical "peace offensive" of Secretary of State Kellogg. The Socialist Party is uttering some critical phrases about the war in Nicaragua not because it is an imperialist war in the interests of Wall Street but only because it is "unauthorized and unsanctioned by the people or Congress."

The Socialist Party of today is for the protection of capitalist law and order, is against revolution, is against the working-class government of Soviet Russia, and supports every measure of the A. F. of L. bureaucracy for class collaboration. The Socialist Party has transformed its party organization from a membership organization into a ward organization of voters. It has shifted its class basis from the working class entirely and definitely to the lower middle class. The last national convention of the Socialist Party in April, 1928, went so far as to drop the class struggle pledge that applicants for membership had to sign in the past.

The small sects, the *Socialist Labor Party* and the *Proletarian Party,* have become completely fossilized, and do not play any role in the political life of the country or in any of the struggles of the working class.

The Workers (Communist) Party is today the only genuine working-class party. It is the sole party which has a program for the workers and working farmers. It is the only party which conducts a relentless struggle against capitalism, against the old parties of the bosses and against the corrupt labor bureaucracy and the treacherous Socialist Party.

The Workers (Communist) Party is the party of the class struggle. It is the deadly enemy of class collaboration because it is the deadly enemy of capitalism. It is the revolutionary party of the working class. The Workers (Communist) Party is the champion of the interests of the working class and the working farmers. It is the advocate of the most exploited stratum of the working class, of the unskilled workers. It is the champion of the oppressed Negro race. It is the organizer of the struggle against imperialism, against imperialist wars.

The Workers (Communist) Party is the only

party which fights for the interests of the working class, working farmers, and the oppressed Negro race; and that is the very reason why *all the forces of the old capitalist parties, the bureaucrats of the A. F. of L and the leaders of the Socialist Party are united against the Communists.* The Republicans, Democrats, Socialists, and labor bureaucrats have a common platform. That platform is Red-baiting, anti-Communism.

In its 1928 election campaign the Workers (Communist) Party offers the *following program against trustified capital* and in the interests of the working class, working farmers, and oppressed Negro race:

II. The Curse of Unemployment

There is a heavy economic depression over the country with a very heavy unemployment in its wake. Bread-lines are long. Hypocritical "charity" is in its flower. Even conservative Senators estimate the number of unemployed at four million.

The curse of unemployment is the most terrible plight of the working class. The cyclical crises of capitalist industry bring with them time and again the untold sufferings of mass unemployment. But there is unemployment not only at times of crises; it is here at all times. Unemployment on a mass scale is a *"normal"* phenomenon of this glorious capitalist society.

The very technical progress—the development of new machinery, the increased productivity of labor — becomes under capitalist conditions a source of growing unemployment. The introduction of new machines has decreased the number of workers. The opening up of new markets cannot keep pace with the speedy development of technique. The introduction of machinery makes the skill of the workers superfluous. Large masses of *unskilled* workers can take the place of the skilled. The time of apprenticeship is being greatly shortened. *Young workers* and even *children* can take the place of adults. A growing number of *women* are entering into industry.

The introduction of machinery creates the basis for mass production. Mass production with its murderous competition ruins the *lower middle class* and drives its members as workers into the industries. Monopoly capitalism ruins the *farmers* and forces them to sell their labor power as industrial workers in the cities. Mass production opens up hitherto backward agrarian regions industrially.

A large-scale industrialization of the South is taking place, and has driven hundreds of thousands of *Negroes* into the industries. Despite all prohibition of *immigration* there is an annual influx of hundreds of thousands of workers from other countries.

Under present capitalist conditions it is inevitable that there should be a constant industrial reserve army of jobless. Even in the best periods of prosperity the number of jobless is estimated at one and a half million. In 1927, the factories produced 26 per cent more than in 1919. During this same period the number of wage-earners employed in *manufacturing* decreased by not less than 980,000. Eleven per cent fewer wage-earners than in 1919 produced in manufacturing in 1927 26 per cent more products. In other words, each worker produced 42 per cent more. The same tendency manifests itself everywhere. The *railways* had in 1927 almost 200,000 less workers than in 1919. The number of *"superfluous"* miners is near to a quarter of a million. In manufacturing, mining and railroading, there were almost one and a half million fewer workers employed by the end of 1927 than in 1919. During the last few years there has been a continuous movement of population from the *farms* to the cities: in 1925, 834,000 in 1926, 1,020,000, in 1927, 604,-000 more persons left the farms for the cities than the cities for the farms. A large proportion of these bankrupt and ruined farmers became industrial workers or rather tried to become industrial workers. Even Secretary of Labor Davis has been forced to raise the question:

"Is automatic machinery driven by relentless power going to leave on our hands a state of chronic and increasing unemployment? Is the machinery that turns out our wealth also to create poverty? Is it giving us a permanent jobless class?"

A capitalist writer characterizes the present unemployment as a "technological unemployment, not cyclical—an unemployment developing gradually, almost unawares, *like creeping paralysis,* in the midst of unprecedented prosperity, the by-product of improved technological efficiency."

Unemployment is indeed the "creeping paralysis" of capitalist society. It represents the most vicious contradiction of the present economic order. The more machinery, the higher the productivity of labor, the more unemployed. Labor itself produces unemployment. Unemployment of one part produces overtime for the other part of the working class. The pressure of unemployment forces wage-earners to accept jobs at lower wages and longer hours. The fear of unemployment is the most powerful chain which binds the workers to wage slavery. The fear of unemployment increases competition among the workers. Unemployment lowers the power of resistance of the workers on the job. The working wage-earners are forced to accept overtime. Overtime again makes new masses of wage-earners superfluous. *Unemployment creates overtime, and overtime creates unemployment.* The bigger the factories, the more expensive the machinery, the greater is the tendency of the capitalists to lengthen the working times instead of increasing the number of workers. Hand in hand with the increasing accumulation of capital goes a relative and today even an absolute decrease in the number of workers.

The hypocritical advocates of capitalism lament about the existence of unemployment and call it the "greatest blot on our capitalist system" (Owen D. Young), but in fact the existence of a constant industrial reserve army is not a hindrance to capitalism. Quite the contrary. It is one of the basic conditions for the existence and maintenance of capitalism. Technical development, new inventions, the introduction of new labor-saving machinery will not cease. The opening up of new markets will not go on at the same speed as heretofore. The industrialization of the colonies, the increasing competition with Europe, the existence of non-capitalistic Soviet Russia, and the revolt of the colonial peoples are the narrowing limitations.

The present depression is not an "accident." It has been brought about by prosperity itself. Disproportion between production and consumption, which is a part of the general anarchy of capitalist production, is responsible for cyclical crises. Saturation of the automobile and building construction markets, over-production of oil, the world coal crisis, the migration of the textile industry to the South, the limits of installment buying, the restriction of the farmers' market, the effects of American export of capital and of the stabilization of Europe, the increased competition with Europe—these are the basic features of the present economic depression. Neither the existence of huge monopolies and trusts nor the "interventions" of the Federal Reserve Bank are able to prevent the occurrence of economic crises.

There is no cure for unemployment under capitalism.

Shortening of the working day alone would not do away with unemployment. A general shortening of the working day would result in general part-time work, in perpetual overproduction, would bring about a crisis in permanence.

High wages alone cannot cure unemployment. It is futile to try to "convince" the capitalists to increase wages for the purpose of increasing the purchasing power of the workers. The capitalists will never sacrifice a portion of their profits, by transforming it into wages, for the purpose of broadening the home market. Just the opposite is the policy of imperialist capitalism. It is cutting wages everywhere, and trying to increase its exports for the foreign markets.

Neither can *public works alone* cure unemployment. Public works would tend to increase the forces of production, and would in the long run tend to reproduce unemployment on a larger scale. Higher wages, shorter hours, and public works would not cure unemployment, but might bring about a certain limited and temporary relief.

An especially dangerous illusion is created in the minds of the workers by a whole string of efficiency experts and economists of capitalism who predict a so-called capitalist efficiency "socialism." These capitalist engineers and experts try to make the workers believe that it is possible not only to cure unemployment but to liquidate capitalism itself by social insurance, profit-sharing and employee stock-buying plans, by technical improvements, by elimination of waste, increased mass production, or various forms of State capitalism. This capitalist efficiency "socialism" is the more harmful because its real aim is not the liquidation of capitalism but the liquidation of the every-day struggles of the workers to improve their living and working conditions and the wiping out of all revolutionary movements of the working class.

Unemployment is a world phenomenon today. The constant industrial reserve army has always been in existence, but the present chronic unemployment has assumed such proportions that it is no longer a prop of capitalism but an *organic defect,* one of the basic sicknesses of post-war capitalism. Unemployment is a horrible curse upon the working class. It is the most powerful weapon in the hands of the bosses. It chains the worker to wage slavery. It brings tormenting uncertainty into the life of every wage-earner. It breaks up the family of the worker by driving the women and children into the factories. It brings about moral degradation, creates a slum proletariat. There follows in its wake a growing criminality. It is the foundation of prostitution. In other words, it embodies and sums up capitalism as a whole.

Demands

1. Unemployment insurance. A federal system of unemployment insurance should be established. A federal law must be enacted immediately by Congress providing for unemployment insurance for all wage-earners without any exceptions or disqualifications. The amount of compensation should be full wages for the entire period of unemployment, up to $30 per week. An unemployment insurance fund should be created, fifty per cent to be contributed by the employers and fifty per cent by the State. The amount contributed by the State should be raised by special taxes levied against inheritance, high incomes and corporation profits. The administration of unemployment insurance should be carried out by unemployment insurance commissions, composed of representatives of trade unions, organizations of the unemployed, and factory committees.

2. Immediate enactment of a federal law providing for a general 40-hour, 5-day week working time and forbidding all overtime.

3. A federal law should be enacted providing for immediate emergency help for all workers who have been unemployed two months or more, consisting of eight weeks' wages for each worker. The average wage received during the last four weeks of employment should serve as the basis.

4. Establishment of public kitchens by municipalities to provide free meals for all unemployed workers and their families.

5. Municipal provision for supplying free medical treatment, medicine and hospital care to all unemployed.

6. Public works. The federal, state and city governments should devise schemes for improving the roads and bridges of the country, improving the rivers, canals, docks and harbors, setting up electric power stations, reforestation, land drainage and land reclamation, extension and electrification of railways. On all public works trade union wages and conditions must be guaranteed by law.

7. Immediate abolition of all vagrancy laws. Protection of unemployed workers from arrest on charges of vagrancy.

III. THE OFFENSIVE OF THE BOSSES

The working class of this country is facing a great crisis. A general offensive of the bosses is being conducted against the workers, an offensive to smash the whole trade-union movement, to lower the standard of living of all workers.

The trustification of capital, the erection of huge monopolies, the all embracing rationalization have increased the power of the bosses tremendously.

The capitalists are using all methods of rationalization mercilessly. Wage-cuts everywhere —in the shoe, textile, automobile and rubber industries and in mining. A whole system of speed-up has been put in operation. The stop-watch, group piece work, bonus system, efficiency engineering, the conveyor or travelling-belt system increase mass production and intensify the exploitation of the workers. Concentration of industries, Fordization, technical innovations, and the wholesale introduction of new machinery is the order of the day. The lengthening of working hours is attempted everywhere, with especially disastrous results for the unskilled workers. An injunction mania raves against every movement of the workers to resist the effects of rationalization. All the forces of the Government—the police, the state constabulary, the coal and iron police, the most infamous spy system—are mobilized against the workers. The open-shop drive, the "American Plan," is today the official policy of the capitalist class on the whole front. Company unions are being set up by the bosses, and strenuous attempts are being made to company-unionize all existing trade unions. All the combined forces of the bosses and their government are concentrated to prevent the organization of the unorganized masses in the basic industries.

The trade union bureaucracy of the A. F. of L. has met the general offensive of the bosses—by a general surrender. There has never been in the history of labor such a shameful capitulation as the treachery of the A. F. of L. leadership and of the Socialist Party in the present grave situation of the American labor movement. Instead of fighting the harmful effects of capitalist rationalization, these misleaders try to cooperate in introducing speed-up systems and capitalist efficiency. They put forward the "union-management cooperation" policy. They babble about "industrial democracy." They have elaborated the "higher strategy of labor," the notorious theory of Matthew Woll about the three stages of the American labor movement: the stage of conflict, of collective bargaining, and of worker-employer cooperation. They proclaim the passing of *war* and *truce* and the coming of the age of *permanent peace* between the bosses and the workers. The trade union bureaucracy has dropped the last semblance of any resistance to company-unionizing the trade unions. They have come out openly for the Watson-Parker Bill and for a federal anti-strike law. They have dropped their previous petty-bourgeois trust-busting program and have become the high apostles of "efficient" trusts.

The result of the offensive of the bosses and the treachery of the trade union bureaucrats is *the growing crisis in the labor movement.* Trustified industry is out for a general open shop. The trade unions have been driven out from all basic industries. For the first time in the history of the A. F. of L. the number of organized workers has deceased even during a period of prosperity. The climax of the struggle was reached in the present fight of the United Mine Workers of America. This most powerful and most militant unit of the American labor movement has now been broken to pieces and delivered to the mercy of the operators.

The present depression has ruthlessly exposed the notorious formula of the trade union bureaucracy about "mass production, high wages and low prices" as the foundation of permanent prosperity. Millions of workers are jobless, desperately walking the streets. The crisis in the labor movement and the depression have exposed the true meaning of all class-collaboration plans. They show up the so-called profit-sharing, employee stock-buying, group insurance, B. and O. plan, Mitten scheme, and other systems of "union-management cooperation." The smash-up of the labor bank of the Brotherhood of Locomotive En-

gineers is beginning to open the eyes of the workers to the disastrous effects of trade-union capitalism.

Despite all the treachery of the labor bureaucrats, the workers are beginning to resist. The long struggle of the textile workers in Passaic, the Haverhill shoe strike, the battle of the Colorado miners, the firm and solid front of the needle trades workers in New York, the strike struggle of the textile workers in New Bedford and Fall River, and heroic struggle of the Pennsylvania and Ohio miners, who have already maintained their fight against the whole world for fourteen months, are the first powerful signs of the defensive struggle of the working class. Despite all the sabotage of the misleaders of labor, the vast masses of unorganized workers are beginning to organize themselves. The first attempts to organize the automobile workers have been made. The needle trades workers and the textile workers are being organized into new unions. *The mill committee movement of the textile workers, the shop chairman movement of the needle trades, the Save-the-Union movement of the miners, etc., constitute the basis and means for a consolidation of fighting unions in these industries and are the most promising signs of a militant future.*

The Workers (Communist) Party of America considers it its duty to mobilize the masses for a relentless struggle against all harmful effects of capitalist rationalization. The workers must understand that rationalization in a capitalist society, with the means of production in private hands, can only intensify the exploitation of the workers. Rationalization in the interests of the whole of society can be carried out only in a Communist society in which the means of production are the property of the whole nation.

Demands

1. Shorter hours of labor. A 5-day, 40-hour week. A minimum of 48 consecutive hours rest in seven days.

2. Fight for high wages. Strike against wage cuts.

3. Fight for the protection of the workers from the bad effects of capitalist rationalization, of the technical advances of mass production. Struggle against the speed-up system.

4. Organize the unorganized. Organize new unions in the unorganized industries. The Ameri-

can working class cannot successfully resist the power of the trusts without building up a powerful organization of the workers in the basic industries.

5. Destroy company unions. Abolish the B. and O. and Mitten plans. Eradicate trade-union capitalism.

6. Save the unions from the onslaught of the bosses and the treachery of the bureaucrats. Amalgamation of craft unions into industrial unions. Democratization of the trade unions. The present corrupt leadership must be driven out.

7. Trade-union methods alone cannot wage a successful fight. Trade-union struggle must be supplemented by political struggle.

IV. THE HEROIC STRUGGLE OF THE MINERS

There has never been a more heroic struggle than the present strike of the hundreds of thousands of miners. They are fighting against the whole capitalist world. They are not only up against the coal operators, who are in close alliance with the big railroad companies and banks and are backed by the government, but are also betrayed by their own leaders.

There is a deep-going crisis in the mining industry. The industry is unorganized. Production is in a chaotic state. Each of the 7,000 coal companies produces as much as it can. There is a murderous competition for markets. The mines are able to produce twice as much coal today as industry and consumers can absorb. The operators are closing down mine after mine, creating heavy unemployment. At the same time, new labor-saving machinery is being introduced, aggravating the unemployment situation everywhere. The miners are being forced to increase their daily output by speed-up and longer working hours, thus making themselves in growing numbers superfluous. *The operators say that the industry is faced with the problem: either it must get rid of its superfluous coal or its superfluous miners. They are driving out 250,000 miners from the industry.*

The government has exposed itself frankly as the instrument of the operators in the present struggle. It has mobilized everything against the miners. Courts, injunctions, the national guard, state constabulary, judges and sheriffs are at the service of the operators. Every miner must now clearly see that the government is but the organization of the bosses. *The operators themselves sit in the government.* The Secretary of the Treasury, Mellon, a member of President Coolidge's cabinet, is one of the biggest shareholders of the most unscrupulous Pittsburgh Coal Company. The governor of Pennsylvania, Fisher, was a member of the Board of Directors of the Clearfield Coal Company. The officials of the government are either the bosses themselves or their paid agents. In the company towns the coal operators exercise directly State power in the form of coal and iron police and company gunmen. The coal operators there own everything— land, streets, buildings, stores. The local judges and sheriffs are paid by the operators, as has been proved by the Senate Investigating Committee. The Senate Investigating Committee itself is nothing but a smoke screen to deceive the workers, to create illusions in the minds of the miners. *The miners have no constitutional rights in the "freest" country in the world.* And there cannot be any real democracy and freedom in a society in which the few own everything and the masses do not own anything.

The scores of thousands of Pennsylvania and Ohio miners are engaged in a bitter, desperate strike struggle for higher wages, better conditions, and the right to organize. But to win their struggle—which will require a whole series of battles against the employers, the Government, and the Lewis bureaucracy, and which will be directed against the deadly effects of the rationalization drive of the capitalists and for higher wages and union conditions—they must completely defeat the Lewis bureaucracy and build up a new militant union in the mining industry. The Lewis machine is nothing but the agent of the bosses in the union. It sold out the struggle of the miners to the operators and to the government. The Lewis machine does not want to win the strike. Its whole history is but an uninterrupted betrayal of all the fights of the miners. It betrayed the miners in 1919, in 1922, in 1925, and it has betrayed them in the most shameless way in the present struggle.

District after district was lost for the United Mine Workers under the leadership of the Lewis machine. In 1919 the miners' strike tied up 70 per cent of production; the present strike only 20 per cent. Lewis and the operators have broken up the U. M. W. A. The Lewis machine criminally neglected the necessary preparations for the strike. It sabotaged the organization of the unorganized. It has signed up individual agree-ments. It has betrayed the cause of a national agreement. It has split the movement by ousting everybody from the union who wants a militant struggle. It is cutting off relief from every strik-ing miner who dares to criticize it. It is trying to enforce a yellow dog pledge of starvation. The last vestiges of democracy have been eradicated from the union. Lewis stole the elections. *The Lewis machine is not a leadership set up by the rank and file, but a leadership set up with the aid of the bosses over the rank and file.* From June to December, 1927, while the striking miners were starving on a dollar or two a week relief, Lewis drew $11,093.66 in salary and personal expenses.

The mining industry is in a crisis. The issue is: Who shall pay the expenses of the crisis? Shall it be solved at the cost of the operators or of the miners? The miners, and with them the whole labor movement, must multiply their efforts to combat the onslaught of the operators. *The de-feat of the miners would be a defeat for the whole labor movement.*

Demands

1. Lewis and the whole reactionary machine must go. The rank and file must take over the organization to build a new militant union in the industry, to organize the unorganized, to re-estab-lish union conditions, to fight for a national agree-ment.

2. The unorganized miners must be organized. The big organization drive must be intensified and speeded up.

3. Support the Pennsylvania and Ohio strike. Fight against wage cuts and for the Jacksonville scale. Mass picketing and mass violation of in-junctions against the workers. Mass resistance to evictions.

4. It is the duty of the whole labor movement to organize relief for the starving and struggling miners.

5. Railroad workers, don't haul scab coal!

V. Colonies and Imperialist War

Increasing rivalry with the other imperialist powers and brutal exploitation of the economically weaker, more backward peoples—these two fea-tures characterize the foreign policy of United States imperialism at present.

Wall Street's dollars and marines are extending their domination over ever greater sections of the world. Wherever there is a revolutionary up-heaval United States imperialism is on hand and ready to crush it. United States imperialism is in a conspiracy with Great Britain against the Russian revolution. It cooperates with Japan and England in the interventions against China. *United States imperialism supported Great Brit-ain in her infamous Nanking policies, and it now supports Japan in her ruthless intervention in Shantung.* All talk about the United States as the "friend of China" is mere babble in view of the fact that America supports Japan's domination over Manchuria in order to protect her own vast financial investments there. Japanese intervention in China today promotes the striving of the United States for financial hegemony in the Far East. American-British-Japanese cooperation in the dis-memberment of China includes at the same time growing possibilities of a clash between the rival interests of these three leading imperialist pow-ers on the Pacific. United States warships and thousands of marines are "pacifying" China, and Washington admits that Admiral Bristol is em-powered to call out the whole Pacific fleet against China if United States imperialist policy requires it. The conquest of the tremendous Chinese market is in a growing degree one of the foremost aims of United States imperialism. United States imperialism goes hand in hand with Japanese im-perialism in Shantung against the armies of Chiang Kai-Shek, but at the same time its repre-sentative, Admiral Bristol, cooperates with Chiang Kai-Shek in crushing Soviet Canton, suppressing all revolutionary movements of the Chinese work-ers and peasants.

The military dictatorship of United States im-perialism is exercised more ruthlessly than ever before over the Philippines, Hawaii, Porto Rico, the Panama Canal Zone and the Virgin Islands. Cuba, Haiti, Panama and Liberia are today re-duced to vassal states of United States imperial-ism. *The independence of all the Caribbean and Central American republics has become nothing more than a tragic farce in view of their increased bondage to Wall Street.* The Havana Conference, which was called in the name of Pan-American-ism, was only the instrument of United States imperialism. The Monroe Doctrine, which once served as a defense against European powers, is today the most aggressive means to conquer all America for the United States. The pressure of Wall Street forced Mexico to surrender her oil and land resources to dollar imperialism. The appointment of Morrow, the employee of Morgan, as United States Ambassador to Mexico exposes the whole Latin-American policy of the United States as the policy of finance capital and big business. The fake "good will" flights of Colonel Lindbergh tried to exploit the sentimental illusions of the North American masses for the conquest of Latin America. Large parts of Central and South America have already been reduced to a state of semi-colonies of United States imperialism, and Wall Street and its White House agency are trying to transform them into true colonies.

The most disgraceful action of United States imperialism is its robber war against Nicaragua. President Coolidge disclosed in his speech of the 10th of January, 1927, the true meaning of the Nicaraguan war: *"If the revolution in Nicaragua continues, American investments and business interests will be in danger."* The infamous, bloody crusade against Nicaragua is as naked an imperialist profit-war as any ever conducted.

United States imperialism cooperates with British imperialism against China, against Soviet Russia, against Nicaragua; but at the same time there is a murderous competition and increasing imperialist rivalry between the two robber powers. *There is hardly any part of the world in which there is no open or covert struggle between British and American imperialism.* United States imperialism is breaking up the British Empire by catering to Canada and Australia. United States imperialism has successfully challenged Great Britain's financial hegemony. There is a permanent rubber struggle and oil war going on between America and Great Britain. The fiasco of the Three-Power Naval Limitation Conference in Geneva and the American slogan for a "second to none" navy show the irreconcilable nature of this imperialist antagonism. *The present cooperation of the United States Government with Japan in China has in it the germs of future conflicts on the Pacific.*

The recent "peace offensive" of Secretary of State Kellogg under the slogan to "outlaw war" is nothing but an imperialist maneuver to counteract the genuine struggles for peace of the Soviet Union. United States imperialism aims through the Kellogg treaty to diminish the power of the League of Nations, which is the organization of the European big powers, and tries to render futile any attempt of the European powers to build a bloc against United States imperialism. At the same time the Kellogg treaty tries to unite all the capitalist powers, not under the leadership of the League of Nations, but under the leadership of United States imperialism against the Soviet Union. Despite all empty talk about "outlawing" war, imperialist antagonisms are steadily growing, and there is *increasing resistance* against the aggressive imperialist policies of the United States. The growing competition with Europe, the organization of European trusts and cartels, the tariff issues with Germany, Great Britain and France, the questions of the war debts and the Dawes Plan, the domination over the Pacific, the growing revolt of the Latin-American countries— all these conflicts are pregnant with future imperialistic wars.

The whole policy of United States imperialism is today a policy of preparedness for imperialist wars. The entire country is bristling with bayonets. The United States has never before had such a big army and navy. No other country in the world has spent as much for its navy as this country. In 1926-27 Japan spent $119,000,000, the British Empire $299,000,000 and the United States $334,000,000 for navy purposes. In 1928 the appropriation for the United States navy has already reached $363,000,000 and for the army $394,000,000, totalling $757,000,000. In his last message to Congress President Coolidge came out openly for the big navy program. On December 14, 1927, the big navy program was introduced in the House of Representatives, appropriating not less than $725,000,000. Federal government expenses for past and future wars amounted to 82 cents out of every dollar spent in 1927. *It is estimated that in 1928 Congress will directly or indirectly vote about two billion dollars for military purposes on land and sea and in the air.*

United States imperialism is making the most elaborate preparations for war. *The workers and working farmers must know that wars under capitalism are inevitable.* "Small" wars are going on all the time, even today, and the next big imperialist world war is already looming up. The next world war will be even more devastating than the first one. The whole life of the entire country will be subordinated to war purposes. The whole population will be mobilized. The whole country will be turned into a huge munition factory. The phrase about "outlawing war," the promise about preventing war by arbitration, and the babbling of the Socialist Party about democratizing the League of Nations of the European robber powers are only designed for one purpose—to distract the attention of the masses from the war danger, from the real revolutionary struggle against imperialistic wars. Disarmament is impossible under capitalism. Compulsory arbitration is a reactionary utopia and delusion. Only the proletarian revolution can be the way out from the present situation.

Demands

1. Not a man, not a gun, not a cent for the imperialist army and navy!

2. Down with the imperialist war against Nicaragua! Defeat Wall Street's war in Nicaragua! Marines sent to Nicaragua must refuse to fight against the National Liberation Army. American marines in Nicaragua and China, go over to the side of the Nicaraguan and Chinese revolutions!

3. Immediate withdrawal of all American troops from Latin America and from the colonies of the Pacific. Immediate withdrawal of United States warships and marines from China.

4. Complete and immediate independence for all American colonies and semi-colonies.

5. Hands off Mexico!

6. Abolition of the regimes of United States Customs control or "supervision" of finances in Latin America. Withdrawal of support from the puppet governments subsidized by United States imperialism, such as those of Gomez of Venezuela, Leguía of Peru, and Ibañez of Chile.

7. Abolition of all extra-territoriality privileges of the United States in Asia, Africa and Latin America.

8. Abolition of the present mercenary army and navy and State militia, and struggle for a toilers' militia. Election of officers by the soldiers and sailors. Full right to vote and hold office for the members of the military forces.

9. Fight for the abolition of the whole system of infamous imperialist "peace" treaties. Down with the Dawes Plan! Cancellation of all debts of the last imperialist world war. Immediate withdrawal from the World Court and refusal to enter into the League of Nations.

VI. Defense of the Soviet Union

The whole world is under capitalist domination. The Socialist Republic of the Soviet Union is the sole country in which there is a Workers' and Farmers' Government.

The very existence of the Soviet Union is the best proof that it is possible to overthrow capitalism and emancipate the working class. The example of Soviet Russia shows that socialism is not a dream. It is a fact—and a fact that looms big in the history of mankind—that under the leadership of the Russian workers, a nation of 150 million, not less than one-sixth of the earth, has been able to free itself from the yoke of capitalism and establish a workers' republic which has maintained power for over ten years in spite of all the capitalists of the world.

The capitalist countries are carrying out a ruthless rationalization at the expense of the workers. *Only the Soviet Union is carrying out a socialist rationalization for the benefit of the nation as a whole.* The proletarian dictatorship in the Soviet Union expropriated the capitalists and big land-owners. The workers control the industries. The working farmers received the land of the big land-owners. Soviet Russia is building socialism now, and is taking the first steps toward a higher, a collective type of agriculture. *There is the most complete system of labor protection and social insurance in Soviet Russia.* One of the first steps of the proletarian revolution was the introduction of the 8-hour day, and at the tenth anniversary of the existence of the Soviet Republic the Soviet Government established the 7-hour day. While the courts and the government of this country are smashing the unions in the name of the Constitution, the Code of Labor Laws, Paragraph 155, of the Soviet Union runs:

"In accordance with Statute 16 of the Constitution of the Soviet Union, all organs of the State must render to the industrial unions and their organizations every assistance, place at their disposal fully equipped premises to be used as Palaces of Labor and trade-union halls; charge reduced rates for public services, such as posts, telegraphs, telephones, railroad and shipping rates, etc."

There is a sinister conspiracy of all capitalist powers against the Socialist Soviet Union. Great Britain is the leader of the imperialist coalition, but the United States Government is actively participating in it. The United States Government refuses to recognize the Soviet Government, to recognize the very existence of one of the most powerful countries in the world, for the sole reason that the workers and not the capitalists run that country. The United States Government and its officials seize upon every opportunity to fight the Soviet Union. Ambassador Herrick's shameful statements in Paris, the American loans to finance the anti-Soviet policies of Poland and Finland, and the rejection of the gold bullion sent to the United States are convincing proofs of the hostile policy of United States imperialism toward Soviet Russia.

The Soviet Union is the only power which has reduced its military forces. It made the historic offer at the last international conference at Geneva for an immediate and complete disarmament of all countries. The capitalist governments refused to accept the proposal of the Soviet Union, because the very nature of capitalism is aggression, oppression, and war. All capitalist armies are deadly enemies of the working class, but the Red Army of workers and peasants of the Soviet Union is the defender of the working class of the whole world. *The solidarity of the working class of all countries must be with the only Workers' Republic in the world.*

Demands

1. Defend the Socialist Republic of the Soviet Union, the champion of the cause of the working class of all countries, against the conspiracies of the capitalist powers.

2. Immediate recognition of the Soviet Government by the United States Government.

3. Promotion of trade with the Union of Socialist Soviet Republics by the granting of sufficient credits by the Federal Government, as a means of stimulating American industry and absorbing the unemployed.

4. Establishment of direct connections between the American and Russian working class.

VII. CAPITALIST DEMOCRACY AND THE GOVERNMENT-STRIKEBREAKER

Many workers foster illusions as to the possibility of achieving their emancipation from the oppression and exploitation of capitalism through the election of a majority of the members of the legislative bodies and executive officials of the capitalist government. The American Federation of Labor and the Socialist Party help to maintain these dangerous and futile illusions. The national platform of the Socialist Party states: *"By intelligent use of the ballot, aided if need be by indus-trial action, all class divisions and class rule can be abolished."* It is one of the foremost duties of the Communists to destroy such illusions and to expose all those yellow Socialist misleaders of the workers who help to create these illusions.

The present government is a government of the capitalists. It cannot be transformed into a government of the working class, and its sole purpose is to defend the interests of private property and oppress the workers, working farmers, the Negro masses, and the colonial peoples.

The Constitution of the United States was drawn up by the bankers, big landowners, and rich merchants of 1787, admittedly against the working masses. As Madison, the "Father of the Constitution," put it, the Government ought *"to protect the minority of the opulent against the majority."* It is an illusion to think that the *majority* of the people of the United States can change the Constitution. The vote of two-thirds of the members of the legislative bodies of three-fourths of the forty-eight States is required to initiate any movement for an amendment. On this basis one-fourth of the States, which may be the smallest ones and in which there may live only one-fourteenth of the population, can prevent any change of the so-called "democratic" Constitution.

The Constitution contains a whole series of notorious "checks and balances" for the sole purpose of making it impossible for a majority antagonistic to the ruling class to make its will effective. The members of the House of Representatives are elected every two years, the President every four years, and the members of the Senate every six years, so that a complete change of Government can be made only through elections spread over six years. The elections are not at the same time, because the Fathers of the Constitution wanted to give a chance for the "cooling off" of any mass discontent which might express itself in the elections. The Senate has a veto over the decisions of the House. A special joker of the Constitution is that a newly elected Congress cannot come into session until thirteen months after its election, thus giving a chance to the repudiated Congress to intrench its will by new legislation. The President can veto the actions of both houses of Congress, and over and above the House, the Senate, and the President stands the Supreme Court, which can nullify laws which all three have passed, declaring these laws unconstitutional.

Only a minority of the people entitled to vote participate in the elections, and large sections of the population of voting age are disfranchised. In the South the 5.7 million Negroes of voting age are today as much disfranchised as in the darkest days of chattel slavery. The 6.3 million foreign-born unnaturalized workers of voting age are disfranchised because they are "aliens." The disfranchised Negroes and foreign-born workers together constitute almost 20 per cent of the population of voting age. The youth between the ages of 18 and 21 is entirely disfranchised. The hundreds of thousands of migratory workers, who cannot comply with the residential qualifications, are likewise robbed of their elementary political rights.

The *two-party system,* which in the South is in reality only a one-party system, is also one of the props of American democracy, preventing the splitting-off of the bulk of the working class and working farmers from the parties of big business.

Elections are very expensive in this country. Campaign funds are huge; they run into millions, and big business is able to buy as many and as high offices as it likes. On the other hand, working-class parties, which rely only on the support of the exploited workers and farmers, are poor and are not able to compete with the rich capitalist parties.

Big business controls thousands of *newspapers.* Thirty million copies of poisonous capitalist propaganda every day fill the minds of the masses. *Big business has a monopoly of the schools, churches, moving picture theatres, radio, and the whole machinery of propaganda and agitation.*

And when, despite all obstacles and barriers, some representatives elected by the votes of the working class get into the legislative bodies, big business prevents their functioning by simply kicking them out. This was done in the case of the Socialist members of the Cleveland City Council because they protested against the imperialist war. The same procedure was repeated in the case of the Socialist Assemblymen of New York State.

Under such circumstances to prate about "democracy" is hypocrisy and conscious betrayal of the working class. *The present big business democracy of the United States is in reality nothing but a dictatorship of the capitalists.* The 1928

election platform of the Socialist Party, which accepts the present Constitution as a basis and demands only a "modernized Constitution," is thereby accepting the present capitalist State and the perpetuation of the oppression of the working class.

And if there is anything big business is unable to push through by "constitutional" means, it does it unscrupulously by *unconstitutioinal* means. *Corruption is inseparable from capitalist government.* There are very few countries in the world which show such a clear picture of governmental corruption. The Teapot Dome scandal, the Sinclair-Burns affair, the open purchases of elections by Vare and Smith, the Fall-Doheny affair, the dirty deals of Daugherty and the other members of the Harding-Coolidge cabinet, and the campaign funds of the Republican Hoover and the Democrat Al Smith are but a few examples of the venality of leading politicians. And if any of them are caught, there are still judges and fixed juries to save them. Few rich men are convicted in this country.

Democracy, corruption, and naked force and violence are the chief methods of capitalist dictatorship. Government by injunction, raids and deportations, penitentiaries for political prisoners, troops crushing strikes, frame-ups and lynchings—these are the realities of the unwritten Constitution. Today what George Washington, the first President of the United States, said is more true than ever before: "Government is not reason; it is not eloquence—it is force."

With imperialism the Government has grown into a mammoth monster of centralization. *The country has never had such a huge governmental apparatus.* In 1884 the number of Federal civil service employees was only 13,780; by 1912 it had mounted to 278,000; while today the figure (exclusive of army and navy forces) is not less than 559,138. The number of Government employees—Federal, State and local—in the whole country today mounts up to a total of three million. *This gigantic apparatus of bureaucracy is entirely in the hands of the capitalists.* There is a complete merger of trustified capital and government. The leaders of big business—Hoover, the efficiency expert; Mellon, one of the richest men in the country; Dawes, the banker; Morrow, the errand boy of Morgan; Hughes, of Standard Oil; Coolidge, the strikebreaker; Fall and Daugherty, the kept men of the oil magnates—have or had seats in the Government. Governmental power is being concentrated more and more in the hands of the executive and judicial departments at the expense of the elected legislative bodies. *The President, above all, has assumed almost unlimited power.* He has control over appropriations of funds, over tariff, runs the foreign policy of the country, and decides questions of war and peace. *The actual constitutional form of the "freest" democracy in the world is today that of an unconstitutional monarchy.*

The working class in its struggle for emancipation cannot reform or "take over" the present apparatus of government. The proletarian revolution will destroy this apparatus, and will build its own based on the factories as units of production and not on territorial congressional districts. The State form of the rule of the working class will be the councils of the workers, which will serve not as "talking shops" but as working bodies uniting legislative and executive power. This Soviet form of government constitutes the only real democracy for the overwhelming majority of the people, for the toiling masses.

Demands

1. Abrogation of government by injunction.
2. Prohibition of the use of guards, gunmen, deputy sheriffs, militia or Federal troops in labor struggles.
3. Unrestricted right to organize, to strike, and to picket. Unrestricted right of free speech, free press, and free assemblage for the working class.
4. Abolition of the Senate, of the Supreme Court, and of the veto power of the President.
5. Judges should not be appointed. They should be elected by the working people, and should be removable at any time. Legal aid should be gratis for all wage-earners.
6. Franchise for all foreign-born and migratory workers and for the youth between the ages of 18 and 21. Enforcement of the franchise for the Negroes.
7. Abolition of the anti-syndicalist laws and the Espionage Act.
8. Repeal of all industrial court laws.
9. Abolition of secret anti-labor organizations.
10. Abolition of censorship over moving pictures, theatres, radio.
11. Immediate release of all political prisoners.

VIII. A Labor Party

There are many strikes and labor struggles in this country, but there is no political *mass* party of the working class in the United States which can today rally *millions of wage-earners.* America is the only highly developed industrial country in the world in which the bulk of the working class is not yet politically independent.

It is a most vital necessity that the masses of workers should understand that the economic struggle must be supplemented by political struggle. Without economic fights, without building unions and conducting strikes, the workers would be unable to improve their living conditions, hours, and wages. But no permanent gain can be achieved by the weapon of a mere economic struggle. *The most powerful trade union can be paralyzed by the almighty Government of the bosses,* by its troops and injunctions. The workers may even be robbed of the results of a successful strike, because the *increasing cost of living* can nullify higher wages.

Mere economic struggle cannot free the workers from exploitation and oppression. Political struggle is also necessary. But it must be political struggle in the interests of the working class and carried on by political organizations of the working class. Many workers participate in political struggles but on the side of the bosses. Today the bulk of the workers—even those who economically, in their trade unions, by their strikes, fight the bosses—support the political parties of the same bosses, the Republican and Democratic parties. This is a fatal mistake, because it means that the workers themselves help the capitalists to hold their grip on the State power. *Those workers who still remain in the camps of the Republican and Democratic parties are helping the capitalists to be the bosses of the courts, to use injunctions and armed forces to crush the trade unions and to paralyze the strike movements of the workers.*

The workers have made several attempts to link up their trade unions and other labor organizations into a Labor Party. In certain places Farmer Labor parties are now in existence. The Workers (Communist) Party supports the formation of those labor parties which are based on trade unions and other organizations of the working class. It is willing to participate in the formation of such labor parties, because it considers this the *first decisive step toward independent political action* by the working class, the first step of the workers to break away from the parties of the bosses. At the same time the Communist Party considers it its duty to tell the workers frankly that a Labor Party has its limitations and that it will not be able to lead the workers in their final struggle for their emancipation. Only a Communist Party can do that. Only under the leadership of the Communist Party can the American working class emancipate itself from the double yoke of capitalist exploitation and oppression.

It is to the interest of the workers to participate in all election struggles. *It is necessary to fight for the election of workers to the various legislative bodies.* It is necessary to run workers' candidates for offices. *But it is a dangerous illusion to think that the workers can assume power by electing more and more members of Congress or executive officials.* The workers can never seize power by the mere means of the ballot. Only by revolution can the working class swing into power. The most important aim of participation in election campaigns is the mobilization of the working masses for the struggle against the bosses and for the political organization of the working class in preparation for the struggle for power. The chief usefulness of representatives in legislative bodies consists in securing a public tribune for the cause of the working class, from whence it is possible to expose the actions of the bosses and arouse the militancy of the masses. The workers must know that political struggle is much broader than mere election struggle. They must know that political struggle is in the interests of the working class only if it is conducted in the form of a politically independent working-class party. The notorious *"non-partisan" policy of the A. F. of L.,* which calls upon the workers "to reward their friends and punish their enemies" within the capitalist parties, amounts in fact to unqualified support of the capitalist parties and capitalism itself. The policy of the *Socialist Party,* which promises the workers that they can assume power, abolish classes, and control the industries by the "intelligent use of the ballot" is an equally base betrayal of the working class. The *I. W. W.,* which restricts itself to mere "industrial action" because it is afraid that through political activities it will lose its revolutionary integrity, has actually become a sectarian and reactionary organization.

Demands

1. Independent political action of the working class. Formation of a Labor Party on a national, state and local scale and an alliance between the Labor Party and the exploited farmers for a common political struggle against capitalism.

2. A genuine Labor Party must be based on trade unions and other labor organizations, and on factory, mill, and mine committees of the unorganized workers. A genuine Labor Party must exclude all politicians of big and small business, and must include as a true federated body all sections of the working class, without any discrimination, which accept the general principle of the class struggle and are willing to fight for the interests of the workers and exploited farmers.

3. We call upon every worker: Affiliate your trade union to the Labor Party and you yourself join the Workers (Communist) Party.

IX. SOCIAL LEGISLATION

There is hardly any labor protection and even less social insurance in this country. The aim of labor protection is the safeguarding of the workers from the harmful conditions of production. The aim of the United States government today is the safeguarding of the capitalist from the "harmful" effects of trade-union organization. There is no law setting a maximum to the working day or against overtime. No law guarantees a weekly rest for the workers. No legal yearly holiday is assured the wage-earners. Very few compulsory rules exist or are enforced for safety and sanitation. Labor inspection is ineffective.

America is the leading country of the world in the field of industrial accidents. In industry there occur annually 25,000 fatal accidents and 2½ million accidents causing temporary disability. In 1927 there were no less than 2,224 fatalities on the mining field of battle. New York State alone had in 1926-27 in structural iron work not less than 21,606 accident cases which required compensation. In the metal mines there were 2,865 accidents per 10,000 workers. In other words, one worker out of every four was the victim of an accident.

There is no social insurance deserving the name in the United States. No care is taken of the *unemployed,* of the *sick,* of the *old,* of *invalids* and *cripples.* No help is given to families of deceased workers. The A. F. of L., with its narrow craft attitude against any social legislation, and the Socialist Party, with its parliamentary idiocy, share with the capitalists the responsibility for this complete lack of social legislation. The workers must understand that social legislation can be brought about only as a by-product of revolutionary struggle.

As substitutes for social legislation there are only the voluntary organizations of fraternal societies. Some of the trade unions try to build up some insurance schemes. All these small-scale organizations are very limited in their effect and mean an additional burden for the workers. The group insurance of the employers means the enslavement of the workers to a certain corporation. The private insurance companies are fleecing the working masses. There is a general lack of security in the life of the working class of America. No worker grows old as fast as the American worker. Speed-up and lack of labor protection drive him to premature old age. Scores of poisons, extreme heat and dampness and dust, and lack of sanitary measures ruin the health of the toilers.

The lack of labor protection and social insurance in the United States, in the richest capitalist country in the world, is brought out in bold relief by *comparison with the Workers' Republic of the Soviet Union.* The Socialist Republic of Soviet Russia has the most complete system of labor protection and social insurance. Her social insurance provides the following benefits: temporary disability benefits; benefits for child-birth, infant nursing, burial of insured persons and members of their families; pensions for widows; permanent disability benefits; pensions to family in event of bread-winner's death; unemployed benefits; maintenance of rest homes, sanatoria, and health resorts for workers; free medical aid.

In Soviet Russia all forms of social insurance are under the management of the workers and are maintained at the expense of the State. Factory inspection and all State protection of labor organs are under the direct control of the trade unions. Compulsory yearly vacations on pay are assured. The 7-hour day is guaranteed by law. The law forbids systematic overtime. There is a legal weekly rest of 42 hours. Special protection of women and children in industry has been enacted. A large range of sanitation and safety measures in all factories has been instituted.

There is a world of difference between the lack of labor protection and social insurance in the United States of America and the complete system of labor protection and social insurance in the United States of Socialist Russia—*the difference between a capitalist and a socialist country.*

Demands

1. Federal law for social insurance in the case of sickness, accident, old age, and unemployment for all wage-earners. The administration of all social insurance measures should be in the hands of the workers. The expenses should be covered by the State and the employers.

2. Federal law for the enactment of the 40-hour, 5-day week, forbidding all overtime. The law to provide for a six-hour working day in especially dangerous industries. Immediate enactment of a federal law providing for 48 consecutive hours of weekly rest for all wage-earners.

3. Federal law for compulsory rules and technical measures for safety and sanitation.

4. Establishment of effective labor inspection; inspectors to be elected by the workers themselves.

5. Free medical treatment, medicine, and hospital care for all wage-earners.

X. TARIFF AND TAXATION

The propaganda agencies of the bosses are spreading the fallacy that the workers do not pay taxes. *In reality the workers and working farmers are the classes of society which bear the burden of the bulk of all taxation.*

Direct and indirect taxation and tariff revenues weigh down upon the shoulders of the working masses. Taxes are the basis of public expenditures. Public expenditures, however, are nothing but the cost of maintenance of the state apparatus of big business. The collection of taxes from the masses is a method by which the exploited are forced to pay the expenses for the upkeep of the system of exploitation and oppression.

Both parties of big business have been vying with each other for years to lighten as much as possible the burden of taxation for the big capitalists, transferring the burden of taxation to the backs of the workers and exploited farmers. The various tax-reduction plans of the government have had only one single aim: to cut the taxes of the rich and to cut even more the taxes of the richest. Secretary of the Treasury Mellon, who himself is one of the richest men in the country, is brazenly following the policy of cutting down the super-tax on high incomes, and declares that he is against tax exemption of low incomes, on the ground that the payment of taxes creates for people with low incomes "a sense of part ownership in the government." The most outrageous privileges are enjoyed by the parasitic owners of federal, state and municipal securities. This *rentier* class, which is completely divorced from the process of production and whose only connection with industry is coupon-clipping, owns today no less than 16 billion dollars of such securities, which are wholly exempt from all taxation.

The most vicious form of indirect taxation is the tariff. The tariff raises the cost of living for the working class, and increases the price of industrial goods bought by the farmers. The United States has the highest tariffs in the world, despite the fact that the industries of this country are the most highly developed and enjoy the strongest position.

Trust monopoly and tariff go together in the United States. *The chief function of tariff is to secure unlimited monopoly to the trusts.* The tariff helps to exclude foreign competition. It makes it possible for the trusts to raise the prices of their products to the buyers of this country by an amount nearly equal to that of the tariff. At the same time it makes it possible for the trusts to sell their goods below cost price in foreign countries, thanks to the surplus profits they make in this country.

Trust monopoly and high tariff are the most dangerous factors working for new imperialist wars. The larger the territory "protected" by tariff, the greater the amount of super-profit. The trust monopolies, therefore, have a tendency to expand the territory of the United States, to occupy new regions. That can be done only by conquest, through threat of war, and war.

The high tariff wall around this country forces the other countries likewise to "protect" themselves by tariff walls. This hinders or even prevents the export of American products to other countries. But accumulation of capital is going on with increasing speed, and American big business, instead of exporting goods, is exporting capital on an ever greater scale. The next step is the "defense" of the investments of American bankers in foreign countries. A strong army and a "second to none" navy are necessary. War

threats, war danger, and wars are the order of the day. *The "protective," "defensive" tariff is in reality the most offensive weapon in the hands of big business.*

The tariff policy of both parties of big business exposes the emptiness of their so-called struggle against each other.

The Republican Party was originally the party of tariff, because it represented the growing manufacturing interests of the North. The Democratic Party was originally the party against tariff, because it expressed the interests of the large plantation owners of the South. But with the change in economic conditions both parties are altering their positions on tariff. The industrialization of the South has created a powerful capitalist section in that part of the country, too, and caused a portion of the Democrats to come out as advocates of high tariff. On the other hand, the international bankers of the North—who have invested billions in Europe and are afraid that Europe will not be able to pay her debts, if she cannot export industrial products to this country—are now in favor of the lowering or abolition of the tariff and are making their influence felt more and more in the high councils of the Republican Party which they dominate.

The interests of the working class are against high tariff. At the same time it would be an illusion to think that "free trade" would be a permanent relief for the toiling masses. Free trade under capitalist conditions is as much a capitalist institution as high tariff.

Demands

1. Abolition of all indirect taxes.

2. Exemption from all kinds of taxation for all wage-earners.

3. Tax-exemption for all working and exploited farmers.

4. Graduated income tax, starting with incomes above $5,000 and increasing gradually, so that all incomes over $25,000 per year are confiscated.

5. All tax exemptions on bonds, stocks and securities must be abolished.

6. Graduated inheritance and gift taxes on great fortunes must be introduced.

7. Tariff on all necessities of the working class and on all goods used by the farmers must be abolished.

XI. The Plight of the Farmers

For two decades the conditions of the farmers have been growing steadily worse. The working farmer is becoming poorer and poorer. Millions have been driven away from their farms. Other millions are bankrupt and are only nominally owners of their farms. Tenancy is growing. The standard of living for the farmer and his family is becoming lower and lower. Hardships, suffering and poverty are features of the life of the working farmer.

The working farmer is today in an increasing measure only nominally the owner of the land. The mortgages and other debts are an unbearable burden on the exploited farmer. The product of his labor no longer belongs to him but to his creditors. The total amount of debts of the farmers (mortgage, personal and commercial) is the stupendous sum of 15 billion dollars, which at 6 per cent means *an annual tribute of 900 million dollars to the bankers, merchants and other leeches of capitalism.* The number of exploiting absentee owners is steadily increasing. In 1880 tenant farmers were 25.6 per cent of all farmers; in 1925 they were 38.6 per cent. Farmers are forced into bankruptcy by hundreds of thousands. In the Middle West between 1920 and 1923 no less than 22.5 per cent of all farm owners and 35 per cent of all tenants lost their farms by bankruptcy, by foreclosure, or retained them only—as the Government expresses it—by the "leniency" of their creditors.

At least 40 per cent of the whole agricultural population, 4.2 million people, are neither owners nor tenant farmers but simply agricultural workers, who own nothing but their labor power. *The agricultural workers have the lowest standard of living, are forced to work the longest working day and under the worst conditions in the whole country.* Their wages are actually decreasing. The introduction of new machinery is replacing them by tens of thousands. They are unorganized, isolated, and completely at the mercy of their employers and the State power. The agricultural workers are part of the American working class and must be embraced by its economic and political organizations in the struggle against capitalism.

The working farmers are in the most disastrous condition, because they are up against trust monopoly. The farmers are forced to pay the highest percentage of taxation. *The taxes of the farmers have been increased in a most alarming fashion.* They amounted in 1913 to $624,000,000; today to $1,436,000,000. The general property tax is directed chiefly against the farmer rather than against other property owners. The local taxes increase the burden of the working farmer to an intolerable degree. Even Secretary of Agriculture Jardine was forced to admit that the *farmers spend not less than 30 per cent of their net income for taxes.*

Mechanization of agriculture is another reason for the ruin of the farmers. The number of tractors, which in 1920 was 229,000, by 1925 had grown to 506,000, and in 1927 amounted to 700,-000. The use of combines is spreading, each of them displacing three harvest hands. The poor farmer is too poor to buy expensive machinery. His farm is too small to utilize machinery to its full extent.

Industry is trustified and by virtue of its monopoly is able to control the prices of machinery and all the other goods the farmer must buy. At the same time big business is able to dictate the prices of all products the farmer must sell. There is a whole series of special forms of exploitation to which the farmer is subjected. He is at the mercy of the powerful capitalist agencies of distribution of farm products, the railroads, meat packers, milk trusts, huge elevator combines, gamblers and cotton brokers, banks, and the government farm credit system.

The basic reason for the bankruptcy of the working farmers is trust monopoly, is capitalism.

All agricultural credit is in the hands of the banks. The cooperative organizations of the farmers are chained to capitalism by means of credit. Tariff, which is supposed to "protect" not only industrial products but agricultural products as well, operates only in the interests of the big trusts. All the promises of the Republican and Democratic parties have amounted only to betrayal of the farmers, and have only been in the interests of the bigger landowners and farm banks.

The big lesson the working and exploited farmers must learn from their own desperate situation is that they must break off their alliance with the bankers and other factors of big business and must form an alliance with the working class. The fate of the McNary-Haugen "farm relief" bill and the McFadden branch banking bill is the best proof of the futility of any alliance of the farmers with the bankers. The farm bloc in Congress—which speaks in the name of the working farmers, but is in fact the expression of the interests of the big landowners, farmer-capitalists, and farm bankers—made a bargain with the representatives of Wall Street to the end that both bills should pass jointly in Congress. Indeed, both bills passed. But President Coolidge, as the highest exponent of big business in the Government, signed only the McFadden banking bill and vetoed the McNary-Haugen "farm relief" bill. All the so-called friends of the farmers — banker Dawes, millionaire Lowden, the farm bloc, the "Progressives," such as LaFollette, Norris, Shipstead and their ilk—are only enemies of the exploited farmers in the disguise of friends.

The working and exploited farmers and the industrial and agricultural workers must fight shoulder to shoulder against their common enemies: against big business, against the trusts and against the government of capitalism.

Demands

1. A five-year moratorium on farm mortgage debts, including debts on chattels.

2. Protection of the working farmer against monopoly prices. Essential lowering of the prices of all trust products which the farmer uses.

3. Protection of the farmer against special exploitation by distributing agencies of production, by railroads, meat packers, milk trusts and grain elevator combines.

4. Federal law for the creation of a special farm relief fund of $1,000,000,000 to relieve the conditions of the tenant and mortgaged farmers, the fund to be administered by organizations of working farmers.

5. Federal law against forced farm foreclosures.

6. Abolition of all federal and local taxes on working and tenant farmers.

7. The land to belong to its users.

8. Complete freedom to organize and strike for the agricultural workers. Federal law to guarantee a seven-hour maximum working day and a 48-hour weekly rest for all agricultural workers. Yearly vacation with pay for all farm laborers. Extension to agricultural workers of all benefits of social insurance and labor protection legislation demanded for industrial workers.

XII. Oppression of the Negroes

American white imperialism oppresses in the most terrific way the ten million Negroes who constitute not less than one-tenth of the total population. White capitalist prejudice considers the Negroes a "lower race," the born servants of the lofty white masters. The *racial caste system* is a fundamental feature of the social, industrial and political organization of this country. The Communist Party declares that it considers itself not only the party of the working class generally but also the champion of the Negroes as an oppressed race, and especially the organizer of the Negro working-class elements. *The Communist Party is the party of the liberation of the Negro race from all white oppression.*

There is a "new Negro" in process of development. The social composition of the Negro race is changing. Formerly the Negro was the cotton farmer in the South and domestic help in the North. The industrialization of the South, the concentration of a new Negro working-class population in the big cities of the East and North, and the entrance of the Negroes into the basic industries on a mass scale have changed the whole social composition of the Negro race. *The appearance of a genuine Negro industrial proletariat creates an organizing force for the whole Negro race,* furnishes a new working-class leadership to all Negro race movements, and strengthens immensely the fighting possibilities for the emancipation of the race.

The Negro tenant farmers and share-croppers of the South are still, despite all the pompous phrases about freeing the slaves, in the status of virtual slavery. They have not the slightest prospect of ever acquiring possession of the land on which they work. By means of an usurious credit system they are chained to the plantation owners as securely as chattel slaves. Peonage and contract labor are the fate of the Negro cotton farmer. The landowners, who are at the same time the merchants and government of the South, rule over the Negroes with a merciless dictatorship.

There is the most dishonest and disgraceful "gentleman's agreement" between the two capitalist parties against the political rights of the Negroes. The famous Fourteenth and Fifteenth Amendments of the Constitution amount but to a scrap of paper. They were never carried out for a moment. The Supreme Court has upheld State laws which disfranchised the Negroes. Sheer force prevents the Negro from exercising his so-called political rights. The Federal Government has never made any attempt to reduce the representation of those Southern States which violate the Constitution, as Section Two of the Fourteenth Amendment of the Constitution provides. The Republican Party, the party of Lincoln, has sunk so low that it has provided for measures to segregate the Negro delegates in its 1928 Kansas City nominating convention. *Lynch law is the law over the Negroes. The terror of the Ku Klux Klan is the constitution for the Negroes.* They are burned alive, whipped to death, hunted to death with dogs in the name of white civilization.

There is a general segregation policy against the Negro race. Separate residential sections; Jim Crow cars; separate schools for Negro children; exclusion from "white" hotels, restaurants, theatres and railway waiting rooms; exclusion of Negroes from juries which try Negroes. Negro teachers cannot teach in most white schools. *The white masters try to reduce the Negroes to illiteracy.* According to the 1920 census, there were 4 per cent illiterates among the whites and 22.9 per cent among the Negroes. The Southern States spend hardly any money for the education of Negro children.

In the cotton States the Negro farmers are compelled to live in miserable shacks under conditions destructive of life and health. In the cities the Negroes do the unskilled, the most disagreeable, most hazardous work, and are crowded into the worst sections of the city. The death rate of the Negroes is much higher than that of the whites. In 1925 it was 11.8 per thousand for the whites and 18.2 for the Negroes.

The Southern plantation owners and their Government have tried to keep the Negro farmers and agricultural workers in the Southern cotton fields by force. But even their brutal terror has not been able to check the mighty migration from these cotton plantations to the industrial centers of the Northern and Eastern States. This migration is an "unarmed, Spartacan uprising" against slavery and oppression by a capitalist and feudal oligarchy.

The Negro fled from the South, but what has he found in the North? He has found in the company towns and industrial cities of the North and East a wage slavery virtually no better than the contract labor in the South. He has found crowded, unsanitary slums. He has exchanged the old segregation for a new segregation. He is doing the most dangerous, worst paid work in the steel, coal and packing industries. He has found the racial prejudices of a narrow, white labor aristocracy, which refuses to recognize the unskilled Negro worker as its equal. *He has found the treachery of the bureaucracy of the A. F. of L. which refuses to organize the Negroes into trade unions.* The lynchings of the South are replaced by the race riots of the East. The employing class deliberately arouses the racial hatred and prejudice of the white workers against the Negro workers with the sinister aim to split and divide the ranks of the working class, thereby maintaining the oppression and exploitation of white and Negro workers. What Marx said about the United States is still true: "Labor in a white skin cannot emancipate itself as long as labor in a dark skin is branded." The Negro worker must learn to utilize to the fullest extent the possibilities created by modern capitalism for organization and struggle against wage slavery in alliance with the workers of other races.

The Communist Party considers it as its historic duty to unite all workers regardless of their color against the common enemy, against the master class. The Negro race must understand that capitalism means racial oppression and Communism means social and racial equality.

Demands

1. Abolition of the whole system of race discrimination. Full racial, political, and social equality for the Negro race.

2. Abolition of all laws which result in segregation of Negroes. Abolition of all Jim Crow laws. The law shall forbid all discrimination against Negroes in selling or renting houses.

3. Abolition of all laws which disfranchise the Negroes.

4. Abolition of laws forbidding intermarriage of persons of different races.

5. Abolition of all laws and public administration measures which prohibit, or in practice prevent, Negro children or youth from attending general public schools or universities.

6. Full and equal admittance of Negroes to all railway station waiting rooms, restaurants, hotels, and theatres.

7. Federal law against lynching and the protection of the Negro masses in their right of self-defense.

8. Abolition of discriminatory practices in courts against Negroes. No discrimination in jury service.

9. Abolition of the convict lease system and of the chain gang.

10. Abolition of all Jim Crow distinctions in the army, navy, and civil service.

11. Immediate removal of all restrictions in all trade unions against the membership of Negro workers.

12. Equal opportunity for employment, wages, hours, and working conditions for Negro and white workers. Equal pay for equal work for Negro and white workers.

XIII. THE FOREIGN-BORN WORKERS

Next to the Negroes the foreign-born workers in the basic industries are the most exploited, most persecuted stratum of the toiling masses of this country. There are almost 14 million foreign-born in the United States. The overwhelming majority belong to the working class. *Nearly half of all the foreign-born are toiling in the manufacturing and mechanical industries. The majority of all industrial workers of America, not less than 58 per cent of the total employed in American industries, are foreign-born.* Steel, coal, textile, automobile—all these industries are based on the sweat of the foreign-born workers. Cut off by differences in language and customs, the foreign-born workers are an easy prey of the employing class. Their fate is the longest hours, the lowest wages, the worst housing, the poorest schooling. *Scores of state and federal laws discriminate against the foreign-born workers.* There is hardly a State in the United States which has no special laws discriminating against the foreign-born workers. According to the law of some States, the foreign-born person has no right to read newspapers or books not printed in English. He has no right to keep dogs or a gun or a rifle. He cannot teach in public schools. According to the laws of nine States, a foreign-born worker cannot be employed on public works. Some States do not allow public meetings to be conducted except in the English language.

But all this discrimination is not enough for 100 per cent Americanism. *The Coolidge administration is carrying out an offensive against the foreign-born workers as part of the open-shop drive of the bosses, is planning a whole series of vicious measures against them.* The foreign-born workers are to be registered. They are to be finger-printed and photographed like criminals. If naturalized, they are to have their citizenship papers taken from them if their conduct does not suit the bosses. They are to be deported if they participate in strikes or make speeches in strike meetings. The Chairman of the House Immigration Committee, Albert Johnson, during the powerful demonstrations demanding freedom for Sacco and Vanzetti, uttered the threat: "Aliens domiciled in America should remember that if they partake in anti-government demonstrations here they are liable to deportation under the 1919 Act."

There is a whole series of bills before Congress which are aimed against the foreign-born workers. The Brand Bill, the Hawes Bill, the Ashwell Bill, and other products of American Fascism try to reduce the foreign-born workers to modern industrial serfs. The Brand Bill would compel all foreign-born not only to register but "to report at such times and such places" when "in the judgment of the President the interests of the national defense so require." The same Act would decree that "whenever any alien is *temporarily* absent from the district in which he is registered, he shall report at such times and places and give such information in regard to his movements as may be required."

The *immigration laws* which restrict the freedom of movement of the foreign-born workers and discriminate against the peoples of Asia are part and parcel of the system of American imperialism. The newest demand of the bosses, as expressed in the notorious Brand Bill, is to give full authority to the President to regulate, restrict or enlarge the immigration quotas according to the actual needs of the different industries. The apostles of 100-percentism are not the enemies of the foreign-born workers, if they can use them as strikebreakers, as helpers "in industrial needs."

The labor aristocracy, under the leadership of the A. F. of L. bureaucracy, shares with big business the profits derived from high tariffs and restriction of immigration. High tariff is the material basis for the prohibition of immigration. The platform of the Socialist Party for 1928 shows the true colors of this renegade party in not demanding unrestricted freedom of immigration and the repeal of the infamous immigration laws, but calling only for the *"modification of the immigration laws to permit the reuniting of families."*

The Workers (Communist) Party of America is equally the party of the native-born, the foreign-born, and the Negro workers. It is the party of the whole working class. It fights the offensive of the bosses against the foreign-born workers. It fights against nationalist prejudices which divide the ranks of the workers. *Its slogan is: Workers of all languages and races in America unite!*

Demands

1. All workers must unite against the common enemy, the capitalist class, to prevent the enactment of new laws (to register, fingerprint, and photograph) against foreign-born workers and to abolish all existing laws of discrimination.

2. All workers must wage an active campaign to uproot the prejudices fostered by the employing class against the foreign-born workers and to draw the millions of foreign-born workers more and more into the political life of the country and the class struggle.

3. Immediate repeal of the immigration laws. Abolition of all restrictions on immigration.

4. Equal pay for equal work for native and foreign-born workers.

XIV. WORKING WOMEN

The number of working women is steadily growing. There are today in this country 8½ million working women over the age of ten.

The capitalists are the apostles of the family, but they do not hesitate to break up the family life of the working class, if the needs of industry make it necessary. They cannot resist the call of profits. The number of adult and married women in industry is growing fast. It had reached in 1920 almost two million. Manufacturers prefer women, because they offer less resistance than male workers to capitalist oppression. Male workers are often replaced by women, because the introduction of new machinery makes the skill of male workers superfluous. *As a general rule, women work in less well-paid occupations and receive lower wages for identical work.* The logic of capitalism is that working women need more

protection, they are weaker than the male workers; therefore, *they get less protection and are subjected to greater exploitation than male workers.*

The Communist Party is by no means against women working in industry. It is of the opinion that in entering industry working women can become more effective participants in the struggle of the working class against capitalist exploitation. But it calls on the workers to fight the harmful effects of industrial work on women and to struggle for the adequate protection of working women. Only a Communist society can lift the double burden of housekeeping and factory work from the women of the working class.

Demands

1. Prohibition by law of night work, overtime and job work for working women.

2. The law shall provide for an allowance throughout the period of pregnancy and childbirth to the amount of full working wages.

3. Legal enactment of a special allowance for working women during the nursing period of nine months. Nursing mothers shall have a half hour's leave every three hours for child feeding in nurseries provided by employers at all working places.

4. The organization of working women into trade unions and elimination of all restrictions and discriminations against women in trade unions.

5. Equal pay for equal work for male and female workers.

XV. YOUTH, CHILD LABOR AND EDUCATION

Exploitation of children and young workers is one of the pillars of American capitalist society. Children's blood and young boys' and girls' sweat are a growing source of profit for big business. According to the 1920 census, which greatly underestimates the number of child laborers, there were over one million working children between the ages of 10 and 15. To increase the shame there were 378,000 toiling children between the ages of 10 and 13. There are no statistics on the work of children under the age of 10 —that is the sole reason why there is no report about the scores of thousands of the smallest children of the working class slaving to the glory of our dollar civilization.

There are almost four million young workers

and at least one million boys and girls in industry alone. Steel and iron, coal and textile factories are the chief "playgrounds" of our working-class youth. *Technical progress means progress of youth and child labor.* It is one of the biggest achievements of American "democracy" that the Supreme Court of the United States, that notorious guardian of American "liberties," declared any laws forbidding child labor unconstitutional.

The propaganda agencies of capitalism boast about the wonderful progress in education. They forget only that the sole aim of the education of the children of the working class is to implant in their minds as early as possible a feeling of awe towards capitalist society. *Education is class education in this country.* Higher education is too expensive for the children of the working class. Primary education is conducted in the spirit of jingoism and religious prejudice. According to official statistics, in 1920 only 73 per cent of the pupils reached the sixth and only 58 per cent the eighth grade. In other words, almost half of the children did not even graduate from the elementary school. The schools are overcrowded. Anti-evolution laws prevent the teaching of natural science in many States. In the South, Jim Crow education prevails. The famous "academic" freedom is only a legend.

Under capitalism education is a monopoly of the master class. Only a Communist society, which will combine the participation in production with vocational training and general education, will break this monopoly and will abolish the class character of education, transforming it into social education, making it compulsory, universal and equal.

Demands

1. Compulsory abolition by law of child labor under the age of 16, and State maintenance of all children at present employed. Abolition of underground work, night work, overtime, and work in dangerous occupations for all young workers. Six-hour working day and the five-day week for all young workers between the ages of 16 and 18.

2. A $20 minimum wage for young workers.

3. Establishment of work-schools in factories for the training of young workers in industry. These work-schools should be modeled on the work-schools in the Soviet Union, should be under the control of the young workers belonging to trade unions and workers' factory committees. Young workers to receive full wages while attending work-schools, and the hours attending school should be included in the general hours of work.

4. Immediate utilization of schools as feeding centers for children of unemployed workers, whether of school age or below it. These stations should be under labor-parent control. Free clothing and free medical treatment by the schools for the children of the unemployed.

5. Every young person 18 years of age or over must be given the right to vote. Old enough to work—old enough to vote.

6. In schools at present: (a) free and equal education from the elementary schools through the universities; (b) immediate relief from overcrowding by building new schools; (c) abolition of religious and jingoist instruction; abolition of anti-evolution laws; (d) abolition of Jim Crow education; (e) no discrimination against teachers on account of "subversive" political opinions; right of teachers and students to organize.

XVI. HOUSING

Nothing brings out into bolder relief "equality" under capitalist conditions than the matter of housing. The members of the master class dwell in the finest apartments, in the most luxurious palaces. They monopolize the clean, broad streets of the "respectable" residential sections. *The workers are segregated in the most disagreeable unsanitary sections of the crowded cities.*

Congested tenements, miserable slums are the main quarters for proletarian homes. Death has a bigger toll in the working-class sections, especially among the children. Rent is unbearably high for workers. On the average the worker is compelled to spend more than 25 per cent of his wages on rent. According to the law of social justice in capitalist society, the higher the income the lower relatively the rent.

The Government—federal, state and municipal governments alike—are doing nothing to relieve the housing shortage and to reduce the high rents. Building speculators do not construct homes for the workers, because the poorly-paid wage-earner is not able to pay the high rent demanded. Scores of thousands of workers are forced to live in lightless rooms without adequate plumbing and heating, with insufficient ventilation and water supply.

In striking contrast to the criminal attitude of the American capitalist Government toward the housing situation are the measures of the Workers' Government of the Soviet Union. The Workers' Government of the Soviet Union nationalized all dwellings of the employing class. It turned over all the palaces and villas of the capitalists to the workers. It lowered the rent for wage-earners so much that unskilled workers pay only a nominal rent. The building of homes for workers is an essential part of the whole constructive program of the Soviet Government, which spends millions yearly to erect houses for wage-earners.

Demands

1. Municipal fixing of low rents for workers. Rent for wage-earners should not amount to more than 10 per cent of their wages.

2. Municipally built houses should be rented to the workers without profit.

3. Immediate enactment of state laws providing for abolition of the right of eviction by landlords against wage-earner tenants.

4. Compulsory repair by the landlords of all working-class homes in bad condition.

5. Immediate establishment by municipalities of homes to shelter the unemployed.

6. Municipal aid to workers' building co-operatives.

XVII. PROHIBITION

Prohibition, as it is "enforced" and violated in this country, is one of the most outstanding examples of capitalist corruption and hypocrisy.

The Workers (Communist) Party takes the following stand on the prohibition issue:

Prohibition was introduced in the interests of the manufacturers. As the *Pennsylvania Manufacturers' Journal* put it: "We believe there is no question of greater importance to American manufacturers, the great employers of labor, than prohibition." The prohibition of the consumption of liquor decreases the needs of the worker, and thus tends to decrease the price of his labor power. *The introduction of prohibition was part and parcel of the big rationalization campaign of the employing class.* It makes the worker more efficient, more adaptable to the machinery. It is a link in the chain of the general speed-up. The enforcement of prohibition is a typical class measure. Rich people are exempt from its enforcement. Its whole burden falls upon the proletarian elements.

Prohibition embodies in the most classic manner the basic views of the employers toward the workers. The worker gives his life not only during the working hours but all day and all the time to the capitalist. Eating, drinking and sleeping, the worker serves only one purpose: the maintenance of his labor power for the capitalists. The very fact that the worker consumes the food which he buys for his wages forces him to sell his labor power again. It *does* concern the capitalist how the worker eats and drinks. If the worker spends his wages for liquor, if he gets drunk Sunday night, if he is not fit for work Monday morning—that concerns the capitalist not because it is a violation of the interests of the worker, not because it helps to destroy him physically and mentally, but because it constitutes high crime against capital, since it "defrauds" the capitalist of the labor power which belongs to him.

These are the views of the capitalists concerning the "private" life of the workers. Prohibition is nothing but the realization of these views.

On the other hand, the driving force behind the movement against the enforcement of prohibition, for the repeal of the Eighteenth Amendment and the Volstead Act, is the *powerful alcohol capital* which still has tremendous vested interests in the liquor industry.

The "enforcement" of prohibition has created a *huge governmental machine* of prosecutors, spies, provocateurs and courts. This machine tends to increase the power of the capitalist government and is a virtual part of its strikebreaking apparatus.

The lack of enforcement of capitalist prohibition has created a *powerful bootlegging industry* with a capital of hundreds of millions of dollars. The hazards of this industry are compensated by extremely high profits. An elaborate system of an underground capitalist world is hiding itself under the surface of respectable capitalist society. It has its own spies, provocateurs and gunmen, who are often utilized against the labor movement, against striking workers. *The combination of the twin brothers, capitalist prohibition enforcement and capitalist bootlegging, has created an unheard-of amount of corruption, crime and hypocrisy.*

The stand of the Republican and Democratic parties on the prohibition issue is a model example of capitalist demagogy. It is not an issue between the two parties but rather one within both. Very often from wet throats issue dry voices. The playing up of prohibition as a major political issue serves only one purpose. It covers up the lack of any real difference between the capitalist parties, and distracts the attention of the workers **from the real major class issues of the toiling masses.**

Especially shameful is the position of the Socialist Party of America on the prohibition issue. Its platform is against the present prohibition enforcement, because "further persistence in this tragic farce threatens a complete breakdown of law and order." This exposes the Socialist Party in its true role as the upholder of capitalist law and order. Many members of the employing class also, who favor prohibition from the point of view of capitalist efficiency, are against strict enforcement, because they realize its impossibility under present conditions and likewise are concerned lest the faith of the masses in "law and order" be shaken.

Alcoholism is one of the most terrible social diseases of capitalist society. Alcoholism is caused by capitalism itself. Insecurity of life, the monotony of standardized factory work, the low cultural level of the masses and desperate poverty are the reasons for this social disease. Only a Communist society can cure alcoholism by elevating the cultural level of the masses, by diversifying labor, by putting an end to insecurity of life, and by eradicating poverty. The struggle against alcoholism, which must be conducted by the Communists in the most energetic fashion, is a part of the general struggle against capitalism. *Only the overthrow of capitalism will sweep away the despicable bootlegging industry and the equally despicable, corrupt, hypocritical capitalist prohibition enforcement.*

Demands

1. The Workers (Communist) Party favors the repeal of the Volstead Act and the Eighteenth Amendment.

2. Dissolution of the federal and state prohibition enforcement apparatus.

3. Energetic propaganda against alcoholism as one of the most malignant social diseases under capitalism.

XVIII. FORWARD TO A WORKERS AND FARMERS GOVERNMENT

This is the platform of the class struggle. These are the demands the Workers (Communist) Party puts forward in the present Presidential election campaign. But none of these demands, and not even the total of demands, exhausts the program of the Communist Party. We call upon the workers to rally around the Communist Party in a relentless struggle for these demands which, realized, would protect the toiling masses against the most harmful effects of trustified capitalism. But even the realization of all these demands would not liberate the working class from the double yoke of capitalist exploitation and oppression. Only the full realization of the entire program of the Communist Party can bring about the emancipation of the working class. The Communist Party has the following aims:

The formation of the proletariat into a class; its separation from other classes; the development of its consciousness, organization, and fighting capacity;

The organization of a mass Communist Party to lead the struggles of the working class against all capitalist parties;

The representation of the most general international interests of the working class as a whole as expressed in the principles and practice of the Communist International;

The overthrow of capitalist rule;

The conquest of political power by the working class and the establishment of the Dictatorship of the Proletariat.

American imperialism is very powerful. Capitalism in this country is still on its upward grade, but it is becoming more and more part and parcel of world capitalism, which on the whole has entered into the last declining stage of its development.

United States imperialism will not be able to bribe broad sections of the working class for many more years. It is not the sole workshop in the world as Great Britain was for decades. There are other mighty imperialist powers limiting the expansion of United States imperialism, competing with it on every front. The menace of new imperialist wars is looming up ever bigger on the horizon.

The very existence of the Socialist Republic of the Soviet Union, which freed one-sixth of the earth from capitalist influence and expansion, is a limitation to the growth of United States imperialism. *The forces of the proletarian revolution are gathering in other countries, too.* The more than three million votes of the Communist Party of Germany, the over one million votes of the Communist Party of France, the election victories of the Communist Party of Poland, which, though driven underground, was able to rally the majority of the Polish working class—are so many indices of the growth of the legions of the working-class revolution.

The struggle for liberation of the oppressed peoples of Asia and the growing resistance of the suffering peoples of Latin America constitute another limitation to the upward development of United States imperialism. There are *inherent contradictions within American imperialism* which work with irresistible force to break up the whole system. The anarchy created by the private ownership of the means of production results inevitably in murderous competition, crises and wars. The class character of American capitalist society must lead without fail to class wars. The sharpening contradictions within American capitalism will arouse gigantic forces which will be strong enough to overthrow it. The alliance of the 17 million industrial workers, the 4 million agricultural workers, the 10 million Negroes, and the millions of exploited tenant farmers will constitute a powerful bloc which will be able to crush the present dictatorship of the bosses.

These exploited and oppressed masses will rise up and establish a workers' and farmers' govern-ment, will organize their own State apparatus in the form of workers' councils, and will break the monopoly of the capitalists over the means of production.

A genuine Workers' and Farmers' Government of the United States will expropriate all large-scale industries, railroads, super-power plants, meat-packing plants, grain elevator combines. It will nationalize all large land estates; it will establish huge collective State farms, and will satisfy the land needs of the mortgaged and tenant farmers. It will nationalize all banks and commercial institutions. A Workers' and Farmers' Government of the United States will free all American colonies immediately, will grant the right of full self-determination to all Latin-American peoples, will realize full social equality for Negroes. It will disarm the master class and will arm the working masses.

Forward to a Workers' and Farmers' Government! Forward by means of relentless class struggle! The Workers (Communist) Party is the party of the class struggle. It is the deadly enemy of capitalist society. It fights for the complete unity of the working class, for the united struggle of native-born, foreign-born, and Negro workers against the common enemy: trustified capital.

The Workers (Communist) Party calls upon all workers and exploited farmers to leave the old capitalist parties.

Workers and exploited farmers, vote for and join the Workers (Communist) Party!

Rally around the platform of the class struggle!

Down with capitalist rule!

Forward to a Workers' and Farmers' Government!

THE END.

⊠ CAMPAIGN OF 1932

In the year 1932 seven parties offered candidates for the presidency. Together with the Republican and Democratic parties, the Socialist, Socialist Labor, Prohibition, Farm Labor, and Communist parties presented candidates and platforms.

The Communist Party Platform

The Communist party is the political party of the oppressed masses of the people—the industrial workers, the persecuted Negroes, the toiling farmers.

The Communist party enters this election campaign explicitly to rally the toilers of city and country, Negro and white, in a united struggle for jobs and bread, for the fight against imperialist war.

The Communist party calls upon all workers to resist the attacks of the bosses and to fight to maintain and improve their living standards.

The Communist party calls upon the oppressed masses to rally under Communist leadership in the revolutionary struggle to overthrow capitalism and to establish a government in the United States of workers and farmers.

CAPITALISM CANNOT FEED THE PEOPLE

Capitalism has shown its inability to feed the people. The political parties of capitalism which rule the country—Republican and Democratic—have exposed their complete bankruptcy in this period of severe crisis.

Fifteen million workers, ready and anxious to work, and capable of producing the food, clothing and other goods so urgently needed by the people, are suffering enforced idleness.

Those workers who still desperately cling to their jobs have been forced to accept one drastic wage cut after another, until in some cases their wages are now 50 per cent below their former income.

Hoover's "stagger plan" has brought almost universal part-time work with great reductions in the weekly earnings of the workers. Only 15 per cent of the employed workers now have full time jobs. Eighty-five per cent of these workers are only working a few days per week.

The ruthless robbery of the farmers by the big banks, railroads and manufacturers, which has been going on for the past fifteen years, has during the crisis increased a hundredfold. Farmers, like the workers, are starving; they are being evicted from their homes; their farms are being grabbed by the parasite bankers.

Unemployment, part-time work and wage cuts have resulted in a lowering of the living standards of the entire working class by more than 50 per cent, bringing the American workers down to the level of the poorly-paid European workers.

PROMISES, BUT NO FOOD

The frequent promises of Hoover and his Republican and Democratic supporters about "returning prosperity" are being completely refuted by these undeniable facts. Instead of "returning prosperity," we find only that the suffering of the workers and farmers and of their wives and children becomes steadily worse.

What have the capitalist politicians—Republicans and Democrats—done about it? Warehouses are bursting with unused food and clothing. Hundreds of thousands of houses are standing empty. Idle factories are capable of producing all the goods the people need and more. Yet have these politicians taken any steps to start the factories going again, to open up the empty houses for the evicted workers, or to distribute the food and clothing now stacked up in the warehouses among the starving? Not a step!

Starvation in the midst of plenty. This is what is presented to the workers and toiling farmers of the United States by the ruling class, by the bankers, manufacturers, lawyers, publicists, politicians and their political parties.

THE CAPITALIST WAY OUT OF THE CRISIS

The capitalists and their political henchmen remain coldly unconcerned about the suffering of the masses. They think only about the profits of the rich. Their way out of the crisis is a way that will bring permanent poverty and misery to the workers and poor farmers, while the few rich bankers and manufacturers who control the country become still richer and still more powerful.

Their way out of the crisis—the capitalist way out—firstly, means direct help, not to the poor, but to the rich.

Under the guise of "economy" they categorically refuse unemployment insurance at the expense of the State and the employers. They refuse to appropriate money for a far-reaching public works program. They refuse to appropriate money for immediate relief for the starving workers and farmers. They refuse to pay the bonus to the ex-servicemen of the last war, most of whom are now unemployed or working only part-time.

In their opinion, the slop from the restaurants and hotels and the miserable charity system is good enough for the hungry masses. The employed workers, themselves suffering from part-time work and wage cuts, are being forced to pay for even the charity system. The abominable "block-aid," "community chest," and "family-help-family" systems, by means of forced collections in the factories and neighborhoods, are placing the burdens of charity also on the hungry masses and taking it off the rich who alone can afford to pay.

Yet the Republicans and Democrats, who control the National and State governments, despite their "economy" talk where the masses are concerned, have plenty of funds to aid the bankers and manufacturers and to provide huge amounts for graft and corruption.

The last session of Congress, the Democratic control of the House and with the approval of Hoover, appropriated billions of dollars for direct aid to the rich. Hoover's "Reconstruction Corporation" alone made $2,000,000,000 available for the big bankers. Changes in the banking, tariff and taxation laws, not only placed the burden of the huge government deficit on the middle class and chiefly on the broad masses, but paved the way for further trustification of industry, more firm control of industries and railroads by the Wall Street banks, and for still greater profits by the biggest and most powerful capitalists.

The capitalist way out of the crisis—secondly—embodies a further direct and brutal attack on the living standards of the toilers.

Workers' wages are being even more drastically slashed. The speed-up in the factories and mines is daily increased. More factories are being shut down; more workers are thrown into the streets to join the ranks of the unemployed. The miserable charity rations are being further reduced and the burdens of the charity system are being placed on the already breaking backs of the toilers. In this way the capitalists try to escape from the crisis—to maintain their bloated profits, while the workers are being forced nearer and nearer to the starvation level and even below.

MURDEROUS POLICE ATTACKS

When the workers, by strikes and demonstrations, fight to maintain their living standards and to resist these attacks of the bosses, they meet the sharpest terror. Their political rights guaranteed by the Constitution are denied them. Meetings, demonstrations and picket lines are ruthlessly smashed. Foreign-born workers are torn from their families and callously deported. The attack on the foreign-born is directed against the entire working class with the aim of dividing native and foreign-born workers. Workers are clubbed and gassed by the police on the instruction of the capitalists and their political hirelings. The Negro masses are Jim-Crowed and lynched. Workers are shot down and killed.

This terror is not the monopoly of one capitalist, one politician or one party. The Republican, Hoover, orders the gassing and brutal clubbing of the workers in Washington. The "liberal" Republican, Pinchot, orders the clubbing and murder of the Pennsylvania coal strikers. The Democratic Mayor Cermak orders the beating, gassing and killing of Negro workers on Chicago's South Side. Ford and his "progressive" henchman, Murphy, carries through the murder of four Detroit workers at Dearborn. The Socialist Mayor Hoan, backed by the progressive Republican LaFollette, orders the same attacks on the Milwaukee workers.

All the capitalists and all their parties are determined to force through the lowering of the workers' living standard and the maintenance of their own profits by an unprecedented and growing terror.

The capitalist way out of the crisis—thirdly— provides for intense preparation for and the immediate launching of a new imperialist war in which the workers and farmers will be called upon to serve as cannon fodder.

In their greedy desire for greater profits the capitalists set out to wrest new markets from their imperialist rivals by armed force, and to further oppress the people of Latin America, of China, of the Philippines, etc., and rob them of their territory and natural resources.

In preparation for this war the terror against the workers is being carried through to crush all militancy among the workers' organizations; billions of dollars are spent for naval and military armaments, while the people starve.

Efforts are being made to herd the masses— workers, farmers, students — into military and auxiliary organizations in an effort to make them the cannon fodder to be ruthlessly slaughtered on the battlefields. All this is done behind the screen of fake peace talk and fake disarmament proposals.

War in the Far East

The imperialist war has already started in the East, on the borders of the Soviet Union, with the robber attacks of Japanese imperialism on the Chinese people in Manchuria and Shanghai, with actual warfare against the Soviet Union daily threatened.

The Hoover-Stimson tools of Wall Street are openly preparing to throw the American workers into this war, and in the first place, into a war against the Soviet Union. The battle fleet has been concentrated in the Pacific Ocean where the most gigantic and demonstrative maneuvers are being carried out.

The call to war has already been sounded in the Far East. War in the interests of Wall Street and the imperialist master class threatens to engulf the workers of America and other countries. Increased hunger and misery for the masses, terror and war—this is the capitalist way out of the crisis. The election programs of Republicans, Democrats and Socialists, no matter how skilfully concealed, reflect only the differences between these parties on how to carry through this capitalist way out, how to get the masses to accept hunger, terror and war.

Persecution of Negroes

The Negro people, always hounded, persecuted, disfranchised and discriminated against in capitalist America, are, during this period of crisis, oppressed as never before. They are the first to be fired when lay-offs take place. They are discriminated against when charity rations are handed out to the unemployed. They are cheated and robbed by the Southern white landlords and evicted from their land and homes when their miserable income does not enable them to pay rent. When they protest against this unbearable oppression and persecution they are singled out for police attacks in the North and for lynch victims in the South. Over 150 Negroes have been barbarously lynched at the instigation of the white ruling class since the crisis began. The Negro reformist misleaders are shamelessly aiding the white master class in these vicious attacks.

Every day of the crisis, every new effort of the bosses to find a capitalist way out of the crisis, brings new misery and new acts of terror to confront the oppressed Negro people.

Workers Must Militantly Resist Bosses' Attacks

Against these attacks of the employers, against these efforts of the capitalists to enrich themselves at the expense of the toilers, the workers, the farmers, Negro and white, must fight. They must rally all their forces for the most uncompromising class struggle against every effort of the capitalists to terrorize them into accepting worsened conditions, or to force them into another world imperialist slaughter.

The capitalists will never voluntarily yield an inch to the workers. They will continue ever more ruthlessly to maintain and increase their own profits and wealth by forcing the workers and farmers into greater misery. They will never voluntarily relax their pressure on the masses, nor will they cease for one moment their war preparations, particularly for a bloody war to crush the Soviet Union.

There is only one way out of the crisis for the workers. That is the way of mass struggles. A militant mass struggle can force concessions from the parasite ruling class. Such a struggle will lead to the final liberation from the horrors of capitalism.

In order to carry out this struggle, the workers and poor farmers, Negro and white, must organize. They must build powerful, fighting trade unions and unemployed councils and strong organizations of poor farmers. Under the leadership of the Communist party, the workers in such class organizations can defend their interests to-day, while fighting for the revolutionary way out of the crisis, for the overthrow of capitalism.

The most relentless struggle, now and through the election campaign, for the following demands —the demands of the Communist party—alone offers to the workers the means of defending their interests against the bosses' attack.

1. *Unemployment and social insurance at the expense of the state and employers.*

2. Against Hoover's wage-cutting policy.

3. Emergency relief for the impoverished farmers without restrictions by the government and banks; exemption of impoverished farmers from taxes, and no forced collection of rents or debts.

4. Equal rights for the Negroes and self-determination for the Black Belt.

5. Against capitalist terror; against all forms of suppression of the political rights of the workers.

6. Against imperialist war; for the defense of the Chinese people and of the Soviet Union.

WORKERS' AND FARMERS' GOVERNMENT WILL END MISERY

The Communist party calls upon the millions of workers and farmers, Negro and white, and particularly those rank and file workers who are now misled by the leaders of the Socialist party and the American Federation of Labor, to rally to fight for these demands. The mass fight for the demands can alone develop effective resistance to the starvation and war program of the capitalists.

The fight for these demands, as proposed by the Communist party, means even more. It is the starting point for the struggle for final victory of the toilers, for the establishment of the workers' and farmers' government in the United States. This is the workers' way out—the revolutionary way out of the crisis.

The Communist party proposes an organized mass struggle for the above immediate demands of the workers, as the first step toward the establishment of a *workers' and farmers' government.*

Such a *revolutionary government* alone can fully free the masses from misery and slavery, by taking over and operating the big industries, trusts, railroads and banks. Only such a government will open up every idle factory, mill and mine, and put the workers on their jobs again producing the goods which are needed for a hungry, starving population. Such a government will immediately seize and distribute to the hungry masses enormous stores of foodstuffs now kept locked up in the warehouses, thus caring for the masses and creating a demand for new production. It will open the millions of houses, now held empty by greedy private landlords, and provide comfortable housing for the million now living in the cellars, sewers, disgraceful public lodging houses and the terrible "Hoover cities" of the homeless unemployed. *It will immediately feed, clothe and house all the workers and put them busily at work reproducing all things necessary.*

There is plenty and to spare for all.

It is held away from the toilers by the capitalists and their private property and for their private profit. Only a revolutionary workers' and farmers' government can break through this paralysis of the capitalist crisis and start economic activity going full speed for the benefit of the masses of workers and farmers.

Moreover, such a revolutionary workers' and farmers' government alone can enforce full and complete equality for the oppressed Negro masses and grant unconditional independence to Hawaii, the Philippines and other colonial peoples now enslaved by Wall Street.

This is proven by the experiences of the Soviet Union. There the workers seized power in the revolution of 1917. With the government in their hands the last remnant of capitalism is being uprooted, Socialism is being built. The first Five-Year Plan is now being successfully completed; unemployment has been completely eliminated; wages are being steadily raised; the material and cultural level of the masses is being raised; no crisis such as in capitalist countries has affected their progress; the second Five-Year Plan is about to begin.

The Soviet Union stands out as proof that the workers can rule, not only in their own interests, but in the interests of all those who are oppressed by capitalism.

OLD PARTIES SERVE CAPITALISTS

The capitalist parties—Republican, Democratic and Socialist—together with their American Federation of Labor henchmen—will each appear in this election campaign in different garb; each will pretend to offer a way out of the crisis beneficial to the masses; each will freely promise jobs and plenty to workers when elected.

But behind all their false promises and all of their apparent differences, the workers must see their reactionary actions while in office, their brutal attacks on the workers and their protection of the rich. The workers must see that these parties have been and are now the defenders of the capitalists and the bitter enemies of the workers.

Leading the attack against the workers is the Hoover government, with its bi-partisan coalition of Republican-Democratic parties, composed of rapacious profit-seekers, loyal agents of Wall Street, corporation promoters, and the biggest capitalists themselves, as Mellon, Hoover, Smith, Raskob, and Young.

In order to trick those workers and farmers who are no longer fooled by two-party fakery— new demagogy and promises are being indulged in to make the masses choose "Progressives" and "Reactionaries" within the two old capitalist parties.

The difference between progressive and reactionary is merely on the surface, for the purpose of demagogy, to hide the same basic program of the capitalist way out of the crisis.

Openly supporting the Hoover program, is the officialdom of the American Federation of Labor. It fights against the workers and for the capitalists on every essential point. It fights against unemployment insurance, against the bonus for the ex-soldiers. It tries to stifle strikes and carries on strike-breaking where the workers take up the fight against the bosses' offensive. It fights for huge grants of money to the corporations and taxation of the masses; it supports new laws to help build greater monopolies, it helps prepare imperialist war, especially war against the Soviet Union. Through its deceitful "nonpartisan" policy of "reward friends and punish enemies," it delivers the workers gagged and bound to the Republicans and Democrats, "Progressives" and "Reactionaries," in order to further confuse and divide the working class. It decks itself out in "victories" like the so-called anti-injunction law which fastens injunctions and "yellow dog contracts" ever more firmly upon the workers than ever before.

The reactionary officialdom of the American Federation of Labor is an agency of capitalism among the workers for putting over the capitalist way out of the crisis.

THE SOCIALIST PARTY—THE AGENT OF THE BOSSES

The Socialist party, together with its self-styled "left-wing"—the Muste group—is the little brother of the American Federation of Labor. Its special task is to cover up the same program with the mask of Socialist phrases, and thus to prevent the awakening workers from organizing for a really effective struggle. It supports capitalistic monopoly and trustification under the hypocritical slogans of "nationalization of banks, railroads and mines" through the capitalist "nation." It covers the worst capitalist robberies as "steps toward socialism." It fights against the Workers' Unemployment Insurance Bill, and puts forth its own demagogical emasculated proposals to keep the workers from fighting for their own bill. Its leaders in trade unions help sign wage-cutting agreements, and break the strikes of workers who resist.

The Socialist party and the Farmer-Labor party of Minnesota carry through the same policies in America, as their brother party, the Labor party in England, which launched the wage-cutting campaign, cut down the unemployed insurance, raised high tariffs and taxes on the masses, and carried through inflation. They support and operate on the same principle as their brother party in Germany, the Social Democracy, which is in coalition with the monarchist Hindenburg and supports his emergency decrees which cut wages, destroyed social services, halved unemployment relief, and threw the burden of taxation upon the masses, carrying through the Fascist suppression of the working class and preparation for the open Fascist government.

The Socialist party in Milwaukee and in Reading, when it is in power, carries out the capitalist program of hunger and terror as their big brothers of the Republican and Democratic parties.

They support the pacifist swindle of the League of Nations and especially help prepare war on the Soviet Union, one of their principle occupations being daily slander against the workers' republic.

Rally Against Starvation and War

Against all these parties which openly or hiddenly attempt to force through the capitalist way out of the crisis, the Communist party calls upon the workers and farmers of America, white and Negro, to rally for the struggle against starvation and war, for the immediate demands stated above, for the revolutionary way out of the crisis.

These measures represent what a large majority of workers and farmers *wish to have now*. These things can only be gotten by fighting for them. They cut across the capitalist way [sic] of the crisis, because they do not take into account capitalist profits, for which the capitalists and their lieutenants will fight to the death.

It was the Communist party alone which forewarned the workers of the approaching crisis long before the crisis began; it was the Communist party which alone raised the banner of mass struggle against unemployment, lynching, police terror, wage cuts and imperialist war.

The great hunger marches and demonstration of the unemployed in hundreds of cities; the strikes of the miners in Western Pennsylvania, Eastern Ohio, West Virginia and Kentucky; the textile strikes in Paterson, Lawrence and many other cities; the mass mobilization against terror in Chicago, Detroit, Harlan, etc.; the strong fight against lynching, for the defense of the Scottsboro boys; all these struggles of the masses, in which the Communist party played the leading role, are the best proof that the Communist party alone deserves the confidence of the workers.

The Socialist party and its "left" ally, the Muste group, especially has tried in the past and tries now to break up the workers' fight for the program put forward by the Commuists, by bringing forward its own substitute of "something just as good," by making its fake program look as much as possible "like the Communists," by talking "revolutionary," by arguing for a choice of "the lesser evil," by putting themselves forth as "the same thing only more practical."

But all their demagogic claims are given the lie by the capitalist class itself, which takes the Socialist party and its leaders, especially its darlings, Norman Thomas, the respectable churchman, and Morris Hillquit, millionaire lawyer, to its heart.

The Socialist party is openly recognized by the capitalist press as the third capitalist party, which more and more becomes equally respectable in capitalist society with the other parties, as the capitalists more and more need it to fool and trick the awakening workers. Even to force concessions *now* from the three capitalist parties, there is no weapon so powerful as a militant daily struggle against the capitalist enemies and a strong vote for the Communist party.

For a United States of Soviet America

In the election campaign of the Communist party, there is room for the organized participation and support of every worker in America, man and woman, white and Negro, without regard to whether he is a member of the Communist party or not.

Every worker and workers' organization which is ready to fight for the *immediate demands* is invited to be represented in the *Communist Campaign Committees* which will organize and conduct this campaign.

Support the Communist Election Campaign! Rally behind its platform and candidates! Make this the starting point of a gigantic mass movement against starvation, terror and war! Resist with all your energy and strength the brutal attacks of the capitalists! Fight for unemployment insurance against wage cuts, for relief for the farmers, for equality for the Negroes, against the murderous capitalist terror and against the plans for a new bloody imperialist war. Resist the carrying through of the capitalist way out of the crisis! Fight for the workers' way—for the revolutionary way out of the crisis—for the United States of Soviet America! Vote for the workers' candidates—the Communist candidates! Vote Communist!

Democratic Platform for 1932

In this time of unprecedented economic and social distress the Democratic Party declares its conviction that the chief causes of this condition were the disastrous policies pursued by our government since the World War, of economic isolation, fostering the merger of competitive businesses into monopolies and encouraging the indefensible expansion and contraction of credit for private profit at the expense of the public.

Those who were responsible for these policies have abandoned the ideals on which the war was won and thrown away the fruits of victory, thus rejecting the greatest opportunity in history to bring peace, prosperity, and happiness to our people and to the world.

They have ruined our foreign trade; destroyed the values of our commodities and products, crippled our banking system, robbed millions of our people of their life savings, and thrown millions more out of work, produced wide-spread poverty and brought the government to a state of financial distress unprecedented in time of peace.

The only hope for improving present conditions, restoring employment, affording permanent relief to the people, and bringing the nation back to the proud position of domestic happiness and of financial, industrial, agricultural and commercial leadership in the world lies in a drastic change in economic governmental policies.

We believe that a party platform is a covenant with the people to have [sic] faithfully kept by the party when entrusted with power, and that the people are entitled to know in plain words the terms of the contract to which they are asked to subscribe. We hereby declare this to be the platform of the Democratic Party:

The Democratic Party solemnly promises by appropriate action to put into effect the principles, policies, and reforms herein advocated, and to eradicate the policies, methods, and practices herein condemned. We advocate an immediate and drastic reduction of governmental expenditures by abolishing useless commissions and offices, consolidating departments and bureaus, and

eliminating extravagance to accomplish a saving of not less than twenty-five per cent in the cost of the Federal Government. And we call upon the Democratic Party in the states to make a zealous effort to achieve a proportionate result.

We favor maintenance of the national credit by a federal budget annually balanced on the basis of accurate executive estimates within revenues, raised by a system of taxation levied on the principle of ability to pay.

We advocate a sound currency to be preserved at all hazards and an international monetary conference called on the invitation of our government to consider the rehabilitation of silver and related questions.

We advocate a competitive tariff for revenue with a fact-finding tariff commission free from executive interference, reciprocal tariff agreements with other nations, and an international economic conference designed to restore international trade and facilitate exchange.

We advocate the extension of federal credit to the states to provide unemployment relief wherever the diminishing resources of the states makes it impossible for them to provide for the needy; expansion of the federal program of necessary and useful construction effected [sic] with a public interest, such as adequate flood control and waterways.

We advocate the spread of employment by a substantial reduction in the hours of labor, the encouragement of the shorter week by applying that principle in government service; we advocate advance planning of public works.

We advocate unemployment and old-age insurance under state laws.

We favor the restoration of agriculture, the nation's basic industry; better financing of farm mortgages through recognized farm bank agencies at low rates of interest on an amortization plan, giving preference to credits for the redemption of farms and homes sold under foreclosure.

Extension and development of the Farm Cooperative movement and effective control of crop surpluses so that our farmers may have the full benefit of the domestic market.

The enactment of every constitutional measure that will aid the farmers to receive for their basic farm commodities prices in excess of cost.

We advocate a Navy and an Army adequate for national defense, based on a survey of all facts affecting the existing establishments, that the people in time of peace may not be burdened by an expenditure fast approaching a billion dollars annually.

We advocate strengthening and impartial enforcement of the anti-trust laws, to prevent monopoly and unfair trade practices, and revision thereof for the better protection of labor and the small producer and distributor.

The conservation, development, and use of the nation's water power in the public interest.

The removal of government from all fields of private enterprise except where necessary to develop public works and natural resources in the common interest.

We advocate protection of the investing public by requiring to be filed with the government and carried in advertisements of all offerings of foreign and domestic stocks and bonds true information as to bonuses, commissions, principal invested, and interests of the sellers.

Regulation to the full extent of federal power, of

(a) Holding companies which sell securities in interstate commerce;

(b) Rates of utilities companies operating across State lines;

(c) Exchanges in securities and commodities.

We advocate quicker methods of realizing on assets for the relief of depositors of suspended banks, and a more rigid supervision of national banks for the protection of depositors and the prevention of the use of their moneys in speculation to the detriment of local credits.

The severance of affiliated security companies from, and the divorce of the investment banking business from, commercial banks, and further restriction of federal reserve banks in permitting the use of federal reserve facilities for speculative purposes.

We advocate the full measure of justice and generosity for all war veterans who have suffered disability or disease caused by or resulting from actual service in time of war and for their dependents.

We advocate a firm foreign policy, including peace with all the world and the settlement of international disputes by arbitration; no interference in the internal affairs of other nations; and sanctity of treaties and the maintenance of good faith and of good will in financial obligations;

adherence to the World Court with appending reservations; the Pact of Paris abolishing war as an instrument of national policy, to be made effective by provisions for consultation and conference in case of threatened violations of treaties.

International agreements for reduction of armaments and cooperation with nations of the Western Hemisphere to maintain the spirit of the Monroe Doctrine.

We oppose cancelation of the debts owing to the United States by foreign nations.

Independence for the Philippines; ultimate statehood for Porto Rico.

The employment of American citizens in the operation of the Panama Canal.

Simplification of legal procedure and reorganization of the judicial system to make the attainment of justice speedy, certain, and at less cost.

Continuous publicity of political contributions and expenditures; strengthening of the Corrupt Practices Act and severe penalties for misappropriation of campaign funds.

We advocate the repeal of the Eighteenth Amendment. To effect such repeal we demand that the Congress immediately propose a Constitutional Amendment to truly represent [sic] the conventions in the states called to act solely on that proposal; we urge the enactment of such measures by the several states as will actually promote temperance, effectively prevent the return of the saloon, and bring the liquor traffic into the open under complete supervision and control by the states.

We demand that the Federal Government effectively exercise its power to enable the states to protect themselves against importation of intoxicating liquors in violation of their laws.

Pending repeal, we favor immediate modification of the Volstead Act; to legalize the manufacture and sale of beer and other beverages of such alcoholic content as is permissable under the Constitution and to provide therefrom a proper and needed revenue.

We condemn the improper and excessive use of money in political activities.

We condemn paid lobbies of special interests to influence members of Congress and other public servants by personal contact.

We condemn action and utterances of high public officials designed to influence stock exchange prices.

We condemn the open and covert resistance of

administrative officials to every effort made by Congressional Committees to curtail the extravagant expenditures of the Government and to revoke improvident subsidies granted to favorite interests.

We condemn the extravagance of the Farm Board, its disastrous action which made the Government a speculator in farm products, and the unsound policy of restricting agricultural products to the demands of domestic markets.

We condemn the usurpation of power by the State Department in assuming to pass upon foreign securities offered by international bankers as a result of which billions of dollars in questionable bonds have been sold to the public upon the implied approval of the Federal Government.[1]

And in conclusion, to accomplish these purposes and to recover economic liberty, we pledge the nominees of this convention the best efforts of a great Party whose founder announced the doctrine which guides us now in the hour of our country's need: equal rights to all; special privilege to none.

The Farmer-Labor Party Platform

BANKING, CURRENCY, GOLD STANDARD AND ECONOMIC BALANCE

The fifth clause of Section 8 of Article I of the United States Constitution provides:

"The Congress shall have power to coin money, regulate the value thereof, and of foreign coin, and fix the standard of weights and measures."

"To coin money" means to print money for the use of the Nation, States, counties, townships, cities, towns, villages, school districts, and for the people, at cost of printing and service.

"Regulate the value thereof" means the Congress gives by an act, authority and debt-paying power to foreign coin (money) coming into the United States, the same as that which it authorizes to be coined or printed.

---

[1] Inadvertently omitted from the reading of the platform, and later included, was the following statement:

"We condemn the Hawley-Smoot Tariff Law, the prohibitive rates of which have resulted in retaliatory action by more than forty countries, created international economic hostilities, destroyed international trade, driven our factories into foreign countries, robbed the American farmer of his foreign markets, and increased the cost of production."

The United States Supreme Court decided:

"Congress is authorized to establish a national currency either in coin or in paper and to make that currency lawful money for all purposes as regards the National government of private individuals."

Organized Banking and Currency System

(a) We demand legislation to abolish the Federal Reserve Banking System (Fiscal Agent of the United States), private ownership of the United States Banking and Currency System, by repealing the present unconstitutional banking laws on that subject, and then placing them in the hands of the Communities, i.e., the Federal, State, and local governmental bodies, so that the profits, if any, shall accrue to the people's governments, thereby preventing panics, depressions and crises, and private control of money.

Postal Savings Banks

(b) As a step to that goal, we demand a law to authorize Postal Savings Banks in each post-office to accept deposits and permit checking accounts without limit in amount, make loans at uniform interest rate of 2 per cent per annum.

Currency and Free Coinage of Silver

(c) We demand laws providing for the issuance of sound money, full legal tender currency, by the Federal government. And we favor the opening of the mints to the free coinage of silver produced in the United States at its present weight and fineness, but only as coordinate money with that sound money currency, and not as redeemable money. All such money to be redeemable in service rendered by the government, and said money and credit based on same to be properly regulated as to volume in circulation.

Payment of International Debts

(d) Germany should print 11½ billions of full legal tender currency, pay it to discharge the reparations due foreign nations that are indebted in like amount to the United States, each nation making it full legal tender and to tender such money in the United States in full payment of their debts; the United States Congress shall then make it full legal tender in the United States, and authorize the Secretary of the Treasury to accept it in full payment of such foreign nation's debts, place it in the Treasury and use it to pay, as they mature, bonds, compensation certificates in full, Treasury deficits and other indebtedness of the government. Additional issues of international currency can be created by international governmental agreement, free from control by or dictation from the international bankers.

Guarantee to Farmers

(e) (1) We favor a Federal and State government guarantee to the farmers of such prices for their products as will return to them the average cost of production plus a reasonable profit, which will give them a proper return upon their investment as well as a reasonable living. As a step to that goal, we favor the immediate enactment of a law based on the principles of the Bill H.R. 7797, now before Congress, the title of which reads: "*A Bill to abolish the Federal Farm Board. To secure to the farmer a price for agricultural products, at least equal to the cost of production thereof, and for other purposes.*"

Refinancing of Mortgages

(e) (2) For the benefit of farmers and other real estate owners, we favor the immediate enactment of a law based on the principles of the Bill S.F. 1197, now before Congress, the title of which reads: "*A bill to liquidate and refinance agricultural indebtedness,* and to encourage and promote agriculture, commerce, and industry, by establishing an efficient credit system, through which unjust and unequal burdens placed upon agriculture, during the period of price fixing and deflation, may be lightened by providing for the liquidating and refinancing of farm mortgages, . . . and creating a Board of Agriculture to supervise same."

(f) We demand Federal and State government guarantees to the laborers of an opportunity to work at a living wage, or failing, which they shall be paid unemployment insurance benefits by a Federal and State Unemployment Insurance Plan.

Limit Speculation

(g) We favor effective legislation to prohibit gambling in securities or commodities.

Public Works Measures

(h) (1) We favor a three billion dollar annual appropriation by the Federal government for a period of five years if necessary, for the employment of labor on public works over the entire United States, the money to be issued by the government and paid for services rendered, but not to bear interest, namely modern homes for workers, bridge and highway construction, waterways, farm-to-market roads, abolition of toll gates, grade crossings, reforestation, rural school buildings, public grain elevators, water power development, public buildings, recreation facilities, including public parks, etc.

Local Improvements

(h) (2) That can be partially accomplished by the communities depositing with the Federal government their non-interest-bearing 25-year bonds as security for an equal amount of legal tender Federal government money which can be paid by such communities to employ millions of the unemployed on public works and improvements, to be redeemed through taxation, 4 per cent of the principal annually in accordance with H.R. 5857.

Redemption of Bonds

(i) Liberty bonds and all other Federal government bond issues to be redeemed by the Federal government legal tender currency within a period of five years in equal annual proportions and further Federal bond issues to be prohibited by law.

UNEMPLOYMENT, VETERANS' BONUS, DEBTORS AND OTHER RELIEF

We favor measures to accomplish the following:

(a) Temporary immediate aid to unemployed by Federal and State appropriations until—

Unemployment Insurance

(b) An intermediate system of the Unemployment Insurance is set in operation with funds to be provided by (1) Federal government, (2) State government, (3) Employers, and (4) Employees, based on percentages of the pay rolls, which system will remain in operation for ten to twenty years or until permanent relief is attained by other means.

Cash Soldier Bonus

(c) The Federal government to issue two and one-half billion dollars full legal tender Treasury

Notes, good for all debts, public and private, to pay the veterans their unpaid balance of compensation already voted to them.

Old-Age Pensions

(d) A Federal and State system of indigent, accident, sickness, maternity and old-age pensions for the needy.

Moratorium

(e) A five-year moratorium on the foreclosure of real estate mortgages, so worded that the debtor who claims inability to pay will have his property rights properly protected. Federal land banks to refinance such small interest-bearing debts as are required for the necessities of life of the creditor.

Flood Relief, Etc.

(f) A Federal commission to be created and funds appropriated by Congress in advance, to take care of sufferers from floods and other catastrophies, so that immediate relief can be given without calling Congress to meet in special session.

Exclusion of Immigrants

(g) Total exclusion of all immigrants until the period of unemployment has terminated.

PUBLIC AND PRIVATE OWNERSHIP

Government Ownership

We demand public ownership of all monopolies.
(a) The community to gradually assume ownership and operation of:
(I) Railroads and other means of transportation, telegraph, telephone and cable lines, all by the Federal government.
(II) Other public utilities, including power, light, heat and water, by local or State authorities, or where necessary by the Federal government.

Provide Means to Distribute Profits and Surplus

(b) All other producing, distributing and retailing business to be privately owned and operated, but to pay all profits in excess of a certain percentage, to be fixed by Congress, on invested capital, to the government as taxes.

Patents

(c) The life of patents to be limited to ten years.

Compensation

(d) We favor the payment of a reasonable compensation for all property taken by the government bodies.

LABOR

We favor measures to accomplish the following:

Public Works and Six-Hour Day-Minimum Wage

(a) On public works establish a six-hour day, and a minimum wage of one dollar per hour for common labor, to be paid in full legal tender money issued by Congress.

Construct Mississippi River Waterway

(b) In order to control the overflow of the Mississippi River and to furnish work for unemployed, we favor the issuance of two billion dollars of full legal tender money to be issued to construct a one mile wide Mississippi channel from Cairo, Illinois, to the Gulf of Mexico, with concrete highways the full length of the 600-mile course on both sides of the waterway.

Reduce Working Hours

(c) Establish a reduced number of working hours per day in private industry in order to reduce unemployment.

Convict Labor

(d) Abolish exploitation of convict labor.

Stop Yellow-Dog Contracts

(e) No yellow-dog contract shall be enforceable in the courts, Federal or State.
(f) Prohibit by law injunctions in labor disputes.

TAXATION

We favor measures to accomplish the following:

Higher Income Tax

(a) Increase income taxes on incomes over $10,000.
(b) Reduce all taxes. Balance the budget by

paying all interest-bearing debts with full legal tender currency. This will abolish 50 per cent of our present burdensome taxation. Repeal the Garner-Hoover Sales Tax.

Higher Inheritance Tax

(c) Increase inheritance taxes in higher brackets.

Abolish Tax Exemptions

(d) Abolish all tax exemptions on property except homesteads up to the amount of $3,000.00, and personal property up to the amount of $1,000.00.

(e) Prohibit the tax on labor to pay debts and support war.

AMENDMENTS TO CONSTITUTION

We favor the calling of a Constitutional Convention to act on amendments as follows:

Lame Duck Congress

(a) Norris Act, abolishing lame duck sessions of Congress, and President to take office in January following election.

Election by Direct Vote

(b) Abolish the electoral college and decide presidential elections by popular vote.

Elect Federal Judges

(c) All Federal judges to be elected by popular vote for six years, on non-partisan ballot, provide for recall.

Exclude Aliens

(d) The exclusion of all aliens in the determination of the representation in Congress.

Child Labor

(e) Complete abolition of labor by child wage earners.

Initiative, Referendum and Recall

(f) Provide for a National Initiative and Referendum and Recall, on any subject, including prohibition and the Eighteenth Amendment.

(g) The establishment of a one-house legislative body in order to fix responsibility of government.

THE TARIFF—FOREIGN AFFAIRS AND NATIONAL DEFENSE

In view of the present improbability of getting International Agreement for several years to come, we favor the following principles until International Agreements are reached, or compelled by other circumstances, to abolish the tariffs and to adopt a sound economic system, and to preserve peace on earth.

The Tariff

(a) (1) The gradual reduction of all tariffs by International Agreement, except temporarily on those selected commodities the United States prices of which will be controlled and standardized as the result of the provisions of Plank No. 1 (e).

(a) (2) Until such International Agreement is reached we favor the maintenance of the present tariff rates until January 1, 1937, except those which are now or may before that date be fostering exorbitant profits.

(a) (3) If no International Agreement is reached before January 1, 1937, we favor thereafter the reduction of the United States tariff rates then existing by 10 per cent per annum until January 1, 1944.

Tariff on Oil

(a) (4) We favor an immediate tariff duty on oil and such other products as may be necessary to protect our independent producers in the meantime.

Disarmament, Foreign Affairs and National Defense

(b) (1) General disarmament by International Agreement.

League of Nations

(b) (2) United States shall not enter League of Nations or World Court, nor shall it voluntarily cancel the foreign inter-governmental debts.

Philippine Islands

(b) (3) Independence of the Philippine Islands, to be accomplished within a period of ten years.

Air, Army and Navy

(b) (4) A Department of National Defense

under one head with three Assistant Secretaries: of Air, Army, and Navy.

(b) (5) Build up the Navy to the treaty limits immediately and provide an adequate Army.

PEOPLE'S RIGHTS

"We demand equality before the law, political and religious freedom, and restore the economic rights of labor."

Workmen's Compensation Act

(a) Repeal the Federal Employer's Liability Act provision which now disfranchises the rights of railroad men by compelling them to prove negligence where, under State Workmen's Acts, negligence is presumed.

Contempt of Court

(b) Permit trial by jury in all contempt cases with right to change of venue in all courts, State or Federal.

Free Speech

(c) The full observance by Courts, police and other government officers of the constitutional rights of free speech, in schools and other public places, free press, freedom of assembly, and impartial access to the use of movies and radio by minority groups.

Abolish Third Degree

(d) The Courts should be prohibited from receiving evidence unlawfully obtained whether by "third degree" or unlawful search and seizure, or otherwise, or by tapping of wires or other means of communication.

Outlaw Holding Companies

(e) Prohibit by law trust companies, holding companies, corporation farms and chain stores. Strict enforcement of the anti-trust law.

Abolish Bureaucracy

(f) The abolition of Government Bureaus, Commissions, Committees, exercising legislative or judicial powers of either Federal, State or local governments.

Prisoners' Compensation

(g) All prisoners should be compensated for their labor.

Treatment of Patients

(h) All United States hospitals shall permit the patients the kind of treatment and the practitioners the patients desire, whether they be allopathic, homeopathic, osteopathic, Christian Science, chiropractic, or any other practitioners.

Women's Equal Rights

We demand the repeal of all laws, that deny to women equal rights and liberty to earn a living, freedom of occupation, with the same opportunities for economic advancement as offered to men; that marriage or sex shall not exclude or discriminate against women in any occupation, profession or employment; or likewise in the rates of pay, hours of labor or working conditions, and that women shall enjoy equal protection of the law.

OATH TO SUPPORT PLATFORM

Candidates' Oaths

All candidates for National Office, standing on this platform and party, shall be sworn to before a Notary Public in the presence of two members of the party, to support this platform in every respect.

Prohibition Party Platform of 1932

PREAMBLE

We, the representatives of the National Prohibition Party in National Convention assembled at Indianapolis, July 6, 1932, devoutly recognize the supreme authority and just government of Almighty God in the affairs of men and nations and declare that, only by obedience to the principles enunciated by the Prince of Peace, can our Country hope for deliverance from the tribulations now upon us as a people. Upon this basis we make the following declarations:

PROHIBITION

The liquor traffic never willingly obeyed any restrictive measures before prohibition, has not obeyed the law under prohibition, nor can it be expected to obey any restrictive measures should the Eighteenth Amendment be repealed or modified. The difficulty of enforcing any such restrictive measures would be greater than that now experienced.

We unequivocally oppose the repeal or weakening of the Eighteenth Amendment or of the laws enacted thereunder, and insist upon the strengthening of such laws. Being unanimously agreed upon the principle, having within our ranks no voter opposed thereto, this party if placed in power by voters of like mind, can and will coordinate all the powers of government, Federal, State and local, strictly to enforce, by adequate and unescapable punishment of all violators, this wise and beneficent law. Concurrently with such enforcement activities a constructive and comprehensive educational campaign will be conducted, stressing the evil effects of alcoholic beverages.

We indict and condemn the Republican and Democratic parties for the continued nullification of the Eighteenth Amendment and their present determination to repeal that amendment on the excuse that it cannot be enforced, and reiterate that adequate enforcement cannot be had from a party dependent on pro-liquor votes for success at the polls.

ECONOMIC RELIEF

The country finds itself in the depths of the most severe depression in its history. As a result of unemployment, the orgy of gambling on the stock exchanges, bank failures and consequent loss of confidence, millions of dollars have been withdrawn from banks and hoarded. The banks, in their turn are hoarding untold millions in their vaults, refusing to lend even on prime security. Thus a severe contraction of the currency actually in circulation, and of credit based thereon, has taken place with the consequent fall in prices and general business stagnation usually following such contraction. To stop this contraction, now constantly growing greater, and to restore the amount of money in actual circulation to normal proportions, with consequent expansion of credit, we advocate the purchase by the government of legally issued bonds of States and subdivisions thereof, now unable to market same through banks and bank-controlled agencies, to an amount sufficient to accomplish this purpose, paying therefor by the issue of legal-tender treasury notes, directly to the people through such States and subdivisions without the intermediary of the banking system, such bonds to be gradually retired by repayment to the government.

WOULD SET UP COUNCIL

To further restore and maintain normal prosperity, an economic council will be created to be composed of the best and most sincere leaders in the fields of economics, agriculture, labor, finance, commerce, and industry, for the consideration and development of further measures such as:

1. Regulation of stock exchange and boards of trade;

2. Rehabilitation of wage schedules and hours of labor;

3. Revision of tariff schedules;

4. Revision of the banking system to assure safety of deposits;

5. Development of a comprehensive economic plan to stabilize industry;

6. Relief of the destitute and unfortunate;

7. Governmental unemployment and other insurance;

8. The revaluation of all utilities, transportation systems and basic industries in order to disclose actual values so that earnings may be freed to pay a just schedule of wages and increase employment;

9. Any other related measures designed to assure economic security.

TAXATION

We pledge an economical administration of government. Waste, extravagance, duplication in public office, unnecessary commissions and bureaus, padded payrolls and graft cost more than the amount required to pay the soldiers' bonus and feed the poor. We condemn the plan of the old political parties to raise revenue on beer, wine and whisky as being a scheme to tax the poor and exempt the rich. Vast increase in revenue can be obtained by compelling the payment of taxes of huge amounts of property now escaping taxation.

AGRICULTURE

To aid agriculture, we favor the principle of the equalization fee, or such other measure as may be agreed upon by the leading farm organizations of the United States.

CONSERVATION

We condemn the prodigal waste and criminal exploitation of the nation's coal, timber, oil, water power and other natural resources by private interests. All such remaining resources should be utilized and developed under government control for the benefit of all the people.

REFORM OF JUDICIAL PROCEDURE

We pledge a comprehensive reform in judicial procedure to eliminate legal technicalities and to secure speedy and substantial justice, and the abolition of unjust injunctions.

FOREIGN REPRESENTATIVES

All representatives of the United States Government in foreign nations should be required to observe the principles of the Eighteenth Amendment, and we condemn the negligence of the present administration in not requiring such observance. We also demand that representatives of foreign nations in this country shall not be permitted liquor concessions denied to American citizens.

MOTION PICTURES

We favor Federal control at the source of the output of the motion picture industry to prevent the degrading influence of immoral pictures and insidious propaganda connected therewith.

UNJUST BALLOT LAWS

We denounce the enactment by the Republican and Democratic parties in many States of unjust and discriminatory election laws that make it almost impossible for minor parties to retain their place on the official ballot, or for new parties to be formed.

PEACE

We declare our abhorrence of war and favor continued efforts for peaceful settlement of international differences, the reduction of military armaments and the entrance of our country into the World Court.

ALIEN REPRESENTATION

Representation in State and Federal legislative bodies should be based on citizenship and not on population.

FREE INSTITUTIONS

We reiterate our position in favor of free speech and a free press.

CHILD LABOR

We favor the abolition of all child labor in mills, factories, and other industries, that their places may be taken by adult laborers.

PUBLIC UTILITIES

We favor the governmental ownership of all public utilities which can be owned and operated by the Federal government, all proceeds above the cost of operation to be applied to the support of the Federal government.

CONCLUSION

On these principles the national Prohibition party invites all those who favor suppression of the liquor traffic, the enforcement of law, honesty and efficiency in administration, and the building of a better citizenship to join with us in a new political alignment to achieve these great objectives.

Republican Platform of 1932

We, the representatives of the Republican Party, in convention assembled, renew our pledge to the principles and traditions of our party and dedicate it anew to the service of the nation.

We meet in a period of widespread distress and of an economic depression that has swept the world. The emergency is second only to that of a great war. The human suffering occasioned may well exceed that of a period of actual conflict.

The supremely important problem that challenges our citizens and government alike is to break the back of the depression, to restore the economic life of the nation and to bring encouragement and relief to the thousands of American families that are sorely afflicted.

The people themselves, by their own courage, their own patient and resolute effort in the readjustments of their own affairs, can and will work out the cure. It is our task as a party, by leadership and a wise determination of policy, to assist that recovery.

To that task we pledge all that our party possesses in capacity, leadership, resourcefulness and ability. Republicans, collectively and individually, in nation and State, hereby enlist in a war which will not end until the promise of American life is once more fulfilled.

LEADERSHIP

For nearly three years the world has endured an economic depression of unparalleled extent and severity. The patience and courage of our people have been severely tested, but their faith in themselves, in their institutions and in their future remains unshaken. When victory comes, as it will, this generation will hand on to the next a great heritage unimpaired.

This will be due in large measure to the quality of the leadership that this country has had during this crisis. We have had in the White House a leader—wise, courageous, patient, understanding, resourceful, ever present at his post of duty, tireless in his efforts and unswervingly faithful to American principles and ideals.

At the outset of the depression, when no man could foresee its depth and extent, the President succeeded in averting much distress by securing agreement between industry and labor to maintain wages and by stimulating programs of private and governmental construction. Throughout the depression unemployment has been limited by the systematic use of part-time employment as a substitute for the general discharge of employees. Wage scales have not been reduced except under compelling necessity. As a result there have been fewer strikes and less social disturbance than during any similar period of hard times.

The suffering and want occasioned by the great drought of 1930 were mitigated by the prompt mobilization of the resources of the Red Cross and of the government. During the trying winters of 1930-31 and 1931-32 a nation-wide organization to relieve distress was brought into being under the leadership of the President. By the Spring of 1931 the possibility of a business upturn in the United States was clearly discernible when, suddenly, a train of events was set in motion in Central Europe which moved forward with extraordinary rapidity and violence, threatening the credit structure of the world and eventually dealing a serious blow to this country.

The President foresaw the danger. He sought to avert it by proposing a suspension of intergovernmental debt payments for one year, with the purpose of relieving the pressure at the point of greatest intensity. But the credit machinery of the nations of Central Europe could not withstand the strain, and the forces of disintegration continued to gain momentum until in September Great Britain was forced to depart from the gold standard. This momentous event, followed by a tremendous raid on the dollar, resulted in a series of bank suspensions in this country, and the hoarding of currency on a large scale.

Again the President acted. Under his leadership the National Credit Association came into being. It mobilized our banking resources, saved scores of banks from failure, helped restore confidence and proved of inestimable value in strengthening the credit structure.

By the time the Congress met the character of our problems was clearer than ever. In his message to Congress the President outlined a constructive and definite program which in the main has been carried out; other portions may yet be carried out.

The Railroad Credit Corporation was created. The capital of the Federal Land Banks was increased. The Reconstruction Finance Corporation came into being and brought protection to millions of depositors, policy holders and others.

Legislation was enacted enlarging the discount facilities of the Federal Reserve System, and, without reducing the legal reserves of the Federal Reserve Banks, releasing a billion dollars of gold, a formidable protection against raids on the dollar and a greatly enlarged basis for an expansion of credit.

An earlier distribution to depositors in closed banks has been brought about through the action of the Reconstruction Finance Corporation. Above all, the national credit has been placed in an impregnable position by provision for adequate revenue and a program of drastic curtailment of expenditures. All of these measures were designed to lay a foundation for the resumption of business and increased employment.

But delay and the constant introduction and consideration of new and unsound measures has kept the country in a state of uncertainty and fear, and offset much of the good otherwise accomplished.

The President has recently supplemented his original program to provide for distress, to stimulate the revival of business and employment, and to improve the agricultural situation, he recommended extending the authority of the Reconstruction Finance Corporation to enable it:

(a) To make loans to political subdivisions

of public bodies or private corporations for the purpose of starting construction of income-producing or self-liquidating projects which will at once increase employment;

(b) To make loans upon security of agricultural commodities so as to insure the carrying of normal stocks of those commodities, and thus stabilize their loan value and price levels:

(c) To make loans to the Federal Farm Board to enable extension of loans to farm cooperatives and loans for export of agricultural commodities to quarters unable to purchase them;

(d) To loan up to $300,000,000 to such States as are unable to meet the calls made on them by their citizens for distress relief.

The President's program contemplates an attack on a broad front, with far-reaching objectives, but entailing no danger to the budget. The Democratic program, on the other hand, contemplates a heavy expenditure of public funds, a budget unbalanced on a large scale, with a doubtful attainment of at best a strictly limited objective.

We strongly endorse the President's program.

UNEMPLOYMENT AND RELIEF

True to American traditions and principles of government, the administration has regarded the relief problem as one of State and local responsibility. The work of local agencies, public and private has been coordinated and enlarged on a nation-wide scale under the leadership of the President.

Sudden and unforeseen emergencies such as the drought have been met by the Red Cross and the Government. The United States Public Health Service has been of inestimable benefit to stricken areas.

There has been magnificent response and action to relieve distress by citizens, organizations and agencies, public and private throughout the country.

PUBLIC ECONOMY

Constructive plans for financial stabilization cannot be completely organized until our national, State and municipal governments not only balance their budgets but curtail their current expenses as well to a level which can be steadily and economically maintained for some years to come.

We urge prompt and drastic reduction of public expenditure and resistance to every appropriation not demonstrably necessary to the performance of government, national or local.

The Republican Party established and will continue to uphold the gold standard and will oppose any measure which will undermine the government's credit or impair the integrity of our national currency. Relief by currency inflation is unsound in principle and dishonest in results. The dollar is impregnable in the marts of the world today and must remain so. An ailing body cannot be cured by quack remedies. This is no time to experiment upon the body politic or financial.

BANKS AND THE BANKING SYSTEM

The efficient functioning of our economic machinery depends in no small measure on the aid rendered to trade and industry by our banking system. There is need of revising the banking laws so as to place our banking structure on a sounder basis generally for all concerned, and for the better protection of the depositing public there should be more stringent supervision and broader powers vested in the supervising authorities. We advocate such a revision.

One of the serious problems affecting our banking system has arisen from the practice of organizing separate corporations by the same interests as banks, but participating in operations which the banks themselves are not permitted legally to undertake. We favor requiring reports of and subjecting to thorough and periodic examination all such affiliates of member banks until adequate information has been acquired on the basis of which this problem may definitely be solved in a permanent manner.

INTERNATIONAL CONFERENCE

We favor the participation by the United States in an international conference to consider matters relating to monetary questions, including the position of silver, exchange problems, and commodity prices, and possible cooperative action concerning them.

HOME LOAN DISCOUNT BANK SYSTEM

The present Republican administration has initiated legislation for the creation of a system of Federally supervised home loan discount banks, designed to serve the home owners of all parts of the country and to encourage home ownership by making possible long term credits for homes on more stable and more favorable terms.

There has arisen in the last few years a disturbing trend away from home ownership. We believe that everything should be done by Governmental agencies, national State and local, to reverse this tendency; to aid home owners by encouraging better methods of home financing; and to relieve the present inequitable tax burden on the home. In the field of national legislation we pledge that the measures creating a home loan discount system will be pressed in Congress until adopted.

AGRICULTURE

Farm distress in America has its root in the enormous expansion of agricultural production during the war, the deflation of 1919, 1920 and the dislocation of markets after the war. There followed, under Republican Administrations, a long record of legislation in aid of the cooperative organization of farmers and in providing farm credit. The position of agriculture was gradually improved. In 1928 the Republican Party pledged further measures in aid of agriculture, principally tariff protection for agricultural products and the creation of a Federal Farm Board "clothed with the necessary power to promote the establishment of a farm marketing system of farmer-owned and controlled stabilization corporations."

Almost the first official act of President Hoover was the calling of a special session of Congress to redeem these party pledges. They have been redeemed.

The 1930 tariff act increased the rates on agricultural products by 30 per cent, upon industrial products only 12 per cent. That act equalized, so far as legislation can do so, the protection afforded the farmer with the protection afforded industry, and prevented a vast flood of cheap wool, grain, livestock, dairy and other products from entering the American market.

By the Agricultural Marketing Act, the Federal Farm Board was created and armed with broad powers and ample funds. The object of that act, as stated in its preamble, was:

"To promote the effective merchandising of agricultural commodities in interstate and foreign commerce so that ° ° ° agriculture will be placed on the basis of economic equality with other industries ° ° ° By encouraging the organization of producers into effective association for their own

control ° ° ° and by promoting the establishment of a farm marketing system of producer-owned and producer-controlled cooperative associations."

The Federal Farm Board, created by the agricultural marketing act, has been compelled to conduct its operations during a period in which all commodity prices, industrial as well as agricultural, have fallen to disastrous levels. A period of decreasing demand and of national calamities such as drought and flood has intensified the problem of agriculture.

Nevertheless, after only a little more than two years' efforts, the Federal Farm Board has many achievements of merit to its credit. It has increased the membership of the cooperative farms marketing associations to coordinate efforts of the local associations. By cooperation with other Federal agencies, it has made available to farm marketing associations a large value of credit, which, in the emergency, would not have otherwise been available. Larger quantities of farm products have been handled cooperatively than ever before in the history of the cooperative movement. Grain crops have been sold by the farmer through his association directly upon the world market.

Due to the 1930 tariff act and the agricultural marketing act, it can truthfully be stated that the prices received by the American farmer for his wheat, corn, rye, barley, oats, flaxseed, cattle, butter and many other products, cruelly low though they are, are higher than the prices received by the farmers of any competing nation for the same products.

The Republican Party has also aided the American farmer by relief of the sufferers in the drought-stricken areas, through loans for rehabilitation and through road building to provide employment, by the development of the inland waterway system, by the perishable product act, by the strengthening of the extension system, and by the appropriation of $125,000,000 to recapitalize the Federal land banks and enable them to extend time to worthy borrowers.

The Republican Party pledges itself to the principle of assistance to cooperative marketing associations, owned and controlled by the farmers themselves, through the provisions of the agricultural marketing act, which will be promptly amended or modified as experience shows to be necessary to accomplish the objects set forth in the preamble of that act.

TARIFF AND THE MARKETING ACT

The party pledges itself to make such revision of tariff schedules as economic changes require to maintain the parity of protection to agriculture with other industry.

The American farmer is entitled not only to tariff schedules on his products but to protection from substitutes therefor.

We will support any plan which will help to balance production against demand, and thereby raise agricultural prices, provided it is economically sound and administratively workable without burdensome bureaucracy.

The burden of taxation borne by the owners of farm land constitutes one of the major problems of agriculture.

President Hoover has aptly and truly said, "Taxes upon real property are easiest to enforce and are the least flexible of all taxes. The tendency under pressure of need is to continue these taxes unchanged in times of depression, despite the decrease in the owner's income. Decreasing price and decreasing income results in an increasing burden upon property owners * * * which is now becoming almost unbearable. The tax burden upon real estate is wholly out of proportion to that upon other forms of property and income. There is no farm relief more needed today than tax relief."

The time has come for a reconsideration of our tax systems, Federal, State and local, with a view to developing a better coordination, reducing duplication and relieving unjust burdens. The Republican Party pledges itself to this end.

More than all else, we point to the fact that, in the administration of executive departments, and in every plan of the President for the coordination of national effort and for strengthening our financial structure, for expanding credit, for rebuilding the rural credit system and laying the foundations for better prices, the President has insisted upon the interest of the American farmer.

The fundamental problem of American agriculture is the control of production to such volume as will balance supply with demand. In the solution of this problem the cooperative organization of farmers to plan production, and the tariff, to hold the home market for American farmers,

are vital elements. A third element equally as vital is the control of the acreage of land under cultivation, as an aid to the efforts of the farmer to balance production.

We favor a national policy of land utilization which looks to national needs, such as the administration has already begun to formulate. Such a policy must foster reorganization of taxing units in areas beset by tax delinquency and divert lands that are submarginal for crop production to other uses. The national welfare plainly can be served by the acquisition of submarginal lands for watershed protection, grazing, forestry, public parks and game preserves. We favor such acquisition.

THE TARIFF

The Republican Party has always been the staunch supporter of the American system of a protective tariff. It believes that the home market, built up under that policy, the greatest and richest market in the world, belongs first to American agriculture, industry and labor. No pretext can justify the surrender of that market to such competition as would destroy our farms, mines and factories, and lower the standard of living which we have established for our workers.

Because many foreign countries have recently abandoned the gold standard, as a result of which the costs of many commodities produced in such countries have, at least for the time being, fallen materially in terms of American currency, adequate tariff protection is today particularly essential to the welfare of the American people.

The Tariff Commission should promptly investigate individual commodities so affected by currency depreciation and report to the President any increase in duties found necessary to equalize domestic with foreign costs of production.

To fix the duties on some thousands of commodities, subject to highly complex conditions, is necessarily a difficult technical task. It is unavoidable that some of the rates established by legislation should, even at the time of their enactment, to be too low or too high. Moreover, a subsequent change in costs or other conditions may render obsolete a rate that was before appropriate. The Republican Party has, therefore, long supported the policy of a flexible tariff, giving power to the President, after investigation by an impartial commission and in accordance with prescribed principles, to modify the rates named by the Congress.

We commend the President's veto of the measure, sponsored by Democratic Congressmen, which would have transferred from the President to Congress the authority to put into effect the findings of the Tariff Commission. Approval of the measure would have returned tariff making to politics and destroyed the progress made during ten years of effort to lift it out of log-rolling methods. We pledge the Republican Party to a policy which will retain the gains made and enlarge the present scope of greater progress.

We favor the extension of the general Republican principle of tariff protection to our natural resource industries, including the products of our farms, forests, mines and oil wells, with compensatory duties on the manufactured and refined products thereof.

VETERANS

Our country is honored whenever it bestows relief on those who have faithfully served its flag. The Republican Party, appreciative of this solemn obligation and honor, has made its sentiments evident in Congress.

Increased hospital facilities have been provided, payments in compensation have more than doubled and in the matter of rehabilitations, pensions and insurance, generous provision has been made.

The administration of laws dealing with the relief of the veterans and their dependents has been a difficult task, but every effort has been made to carry service to the veterans and bring about not only a better and generous interpretation of the law but a sympathetic consideration of the many problems of the veteran.

We believe that every veteran incapacitated in any degree by reason of illness should be cared for and compensated, so far as compensation is possible, by a grateful nation, and that the dependents of those who lost their lives in war or whose death since the war in which service was rendered is traceable to service causes, should be provided for adequately. Legislation should be in accord with this principle.

Disability from causes subsequent and not attributable to war and the support of dependents of deceased veterans whose death is unconnected with war have been to some measure accepted

obligations of the nation as a part of the debt due.

A careful study should be made of existing veterans' legislation with a view to elimination of inequalities and injustices and effecting all possible economies, but without departing from our purpose to provide on a sound basis full and adequate relief for our service disabled men, their widows and orphans.

FOREIGN AFFAIRS

Our relations with foreign nations have been carried on by President Hoover with consistency and firmness, but with mutual understanding and peace with all nations. The world has been overwhelmed with economic strain which has provoked extreme nationalism in every quarter, has overturned many governments, stirred the springs of suspicion and distrust and tried the spirit of international cooperation, but we have held to our own course steadily and successfully.

The party will continue to maintain its attitude of protecting our national interests and policies wherever threatened but at the same time promoting common understanding of the varying needs and aspirations of other nations and going forward in harmony with other peoples without alliances or foreign partnerships.

The facilitation of world intercourse, the freeing of commerce from unnecessary impediments, the settlement of international difficulties by conciliation and the methods of law and the elimination of war as a resort of national policy have been and will be our party program.

FRIENDSHIP AND COMMERCE

We believe in and look forward to the steady enlargement of the principles of equality of treatment between nations great and small, the concessions of sovereignty and self-administration to every nation which is capable of carrying on stable government and conducting sound orderly relationships with other peoples, and the cultivation of trade and intercourse on the basis of uniformity of opportunity of all nations.

In pursuance of these principles, which have steadily gained favor in the world, the administration has asked no special favors in commerce, has protested discriminations whenever they arose, and has steadily cemented this procedure by reciprocal treaties guaranteeing equality for trade and residence.

The historic American plan known as the most-favored-nation principle has been our guiding program, and we believe that policy to be the only one consistent with a full development of international trade, the only one suitable for a country having as wide and diverse a commerce as America, and the one most appropriate for us in view of the great variety of our industrial, agricultural and mineral products and the traditions of our people.

Any other plan involves bargains and partnerships with foreign nations, and as a permanent policy is unsuited to America's position.

Conditions on the Pacific

Events in the Far East, involving the employment of arms on a large scale in a controversy between Japan and China, have caused worldwide concern in the past year and sorely tried the bulwarks erected to insure peace and pacific means for the settlement of international disputes.

The controversy has not only threatened the security of the nations bordering the Pacific but has challenged the maintenance of the policy of the open door in China and the administrative and political integrity of that people, programs which upon American initiation were adopted more than a generation ago and secured by international treaty.

The President and his Secretary of State have maintained throughout the controversy a just balance between Japan and China, taking always a firm position to avoid entanglements in the dispute, but consistently upholding the established international policies and the treaty rights and interests of the United States, and never condoning developments that endangered the obligation of treaties or the peace of the world.

Throughout the controversy our government has acted in harmony with the governments represented in the League of Nations, always making it clear that American policy would be determined at home, but always lending a hand in the common interest of peace and order.

In the application of the principles of the Kellogg pact the American Government has taken the lead, following the principle that a breach of the pact or a threat of infringement thereof was a matter of international concern wherever and however brought about.

As a further step the Secretary of State, upon the instruction of the President, adopted the principle later enlarged upon in his letter to the chairman of the Committee on Foreign Relations of the Senate that this government would not recognize any situation, treaty or agreement brought about between Japan and China by force and in defiance of the covenants of the Kellogg pact.

This principle, associated as it is with the name of President Hoover, was later adopted by the Assembly of the League of Nations at Geneva as a rule for the conduct of all those governments. The principle remains today as an important contribution to international law and a significant moral and material barrier to prevent a nation obtaining the fruits of aggressive warfare. It thus opens a new pathway to peace and order.

We favor enactment by Congress of a measure that will authorize our government to call or participate in an international conference in case of any threat of non-fulfillment of Article 2 of the Treaty of Paris (Kellogg-Briand pact).

Latin-America

The policy of the administration has proved to our neighbors of Latin-America that we have no imperialistic ambitions, but that we wish only to promote the welfare and common interest of the independent nations in the western hemisphere.

We have aided Nicaragua in the solution of its troubles and our country, in greatly reduced numbers, at the request of the Nicaraguan Government only to supervise the coming election. After that they will all be returned to the United States.

In Haiti, in accord with the recommendations of the Forbes commission, appointed by the President, the various services of supervision are being rapidly withdrawn, and only those will be retained which are mandatory under the treaties.

Throughout Latin America the policy of the government of the United States has been and will, under Republican leadership, continue to be one of frank and friendly understanding.

World Court

The acceptance by America of membership in the World Court has been approved by three successive Republican Presidents and we commend this attitude of supporting in this form the settlement of international disputes by the rule of law. America should join its influence and gain a voice in this institution, which would offer us a safer, more judicial and expeditious instrument for the constantly recurring questions between us and other nations than is now available by arbitration.

REDUCTION OF ARMAMENT

Conscious that the limitation of armament will contribute to security against war, and that the financial burdens of military preparation have been shamefully increased throughout the world, the Administration under President Hoover has made steady efforts and marked progress in the direction of proportional reduction of arms by agreement with other nations.

Upon his initiative a treaty between the chief naval powers at London in 1930, following the path marked by the Washington Conference of 1922, established a limitation of all types of fighting ships on a proportionate basis as between the three great naval powers. For the first time, a general limitation of a most costly branch of armament was successfully accomplished.

In the Geneva disarmament conference, now in progress, America is an active participant and a representative delegation of our citizens is laboring for progress in a cause to which this country has been an earnest contributor. This policy will be pursued.

Meanwhile maintenance of our navy on the basis of parity with any nation is a fundamental policy to which the Republican Party is committed. While in the interest of necessary government retrenchment, humanity and relief of the taxpayer we shall continue to exert our full influence upon the nations of the world in the cause of reduction of arms, we do not propose to reduce our navy defenses below that of any other nation.

NATIONAL DEFENSE

Armaments are relative and, therefore, flexible and subject to changes as necessity demands. We believe that in time of war every material resource in the nation should bear its proportionate share of the burdens occasioned by the public need and that it is a duty of government to perfect plans in time of peace whereby this objective may be attained in war.

We support the essential principles of the National Defense Act as amended in 1920 and by the Air Corps Act of 1926, and believe that the army of the United States has, through successive reductions accomplished in the last twelve years, reached an irreducible minimum consistent with the self-reliance, self-respect and security of this country.

WAGES AND WORK

We believe in the principle of high wages.

We favor the principle of the shorter working week and shorter work day with its application to government as well as to private employment, as rapidly and as constructively as conditions will warrant.

We favor legislation designed to stimulate, encourage and assist in home building.

IMMIGRATION

The restriction of immigration is a Republican policy. Our party formulated and enacted into law the quota system, which for the first time has made possible an adequate control of foreign immigration.

Rigid examination of applicants in foreign countries prevented the coming of criminals and other undesirable classes, while other provisions of the law have enabled the President to suspend immigration of foreign wage-earners who otherwise, directly or indirectly, would have increased unemployment among native-born and legally resident foreign-born wage-earners in this country. As a result, immigration is now less than at any time during the past one hundred years.

We favor the continuance and strict enforcement of our present laws upon this subject.

DEPARTMENT OF LABOR

We commend the constructive work of the United States Department of Labor.

LABOR

Collective bargaining by responsible representatives of employers and employes of their own choice, without the interference of any one, is recognized and approved.

Legislation, such as laws, prohibiting alien contract labor, peonage labor and the shanghaiing of sailors; the eight-hour law on government contracts and in government employment; provision for railroad safety devices, of methods of conciliation, mediation and arbitration in industrial labor disputes, including the adjustment of railroad disputes; the providing of compensation for injury to government employes (the forerunner of Federal workers' compensation acts), and other laws to aid and protect labor are of Republican origin, and have had and will continue to have the unswerving support of the party.

EMPLOYMENT

We commend the constructive work of the United States Employment Service in the Department of Labor. This service was enlarged and its activities extended through an appropriation made possible by the President with the cooperation of the Congress. It has done high service for the unemployed in the ranks of civil life and in the ranks of the former soldiers of the World War.

FREEDOM OF SPEECH

Freedom of speech, press and assemblages are fundamental principles upon which our form of government rests. These vital principles should be preserved and protected.

PUBLIC UTILITIES

Supervision, regulation and control of interstate public utilities in the interest of the public is an established policy of the Republican Party, to the credit of which stands the creation of the Interstate Commerce Commission, with its authority to assure reasonable transportation rates, sound railway finance and adequate service.

As proof of the progress made by the Republican Party in government control of public utilities, we cite the reorganization under this administration of the Federal Power Commission, with authority to administer the Federal water power act. We urge legislation to authorize this commission to regulate the charges for electric current when transmitted across State lines.

TRANSPORTATION

The promotion of agriculture, commerce and industry requires coordination of transportation by rail, highway, air and water. All should be subjected to appropriate and constructive regulation.

The public will, of course, select the form of transportation best fitted to its particular service, but the terms of competition fixed by public au-

thority should operate without discrimination, so that all common carriers by rail, highway, air and water shall operate under conditions of equality.

INLAND WATERWAYS

The Republican Party recognizes that low cost transportation for bulk commodities will enable industry to develop in the midst of agriculture in the Mississippi Valley, thereby creating a home market for farm products in that section. With a view to aiding agriculture in the middle west the present administration has pushed forward as rapidly as possible the improvement of the Mississippi waterway system, and we favor the continued vigorous prosecution of these works to the end that agriculture and industry in that great area may enjoy the benefits of these improvements at the earliest possible date.

The railroads constitute the backbone of our transportation system and perform an essential service for the country. The railroad industry is our largest employer of labor and the greatest consumer of goods. The restoration of their credit and the maintenance of their ability to render adequate service are of paramount importance to the public, to their many thousands of employes and to savings banks, insurance companies and other similar institutions, to which the savings of the people have been entrusted.

We should continue to encourage the further development of the merchant marine under American registry and ownership.

Under the present administration the American merchant fleet has been enlarged and strengthened until it now occupies second place among the merchant marines of the world.

By the gradual retirement of the government from the field of ship operations and marked economies in costs, the United States Shipping Board will require no appropriation for the fiscal year 1933 for ship operations.

ST. LAWRENCE SEAWAY

The Republican Party stands committed to the development of the Great Lakes-St. Lawrence seaway. Under the direction of President Hoover negotiation of a treaty with Canada for this development is now at a favorable point. Recognizing the inestimable benefits which will accrue to the nation from placing the ports of the Great Lakes on an ocean base, the party reaffirms allegiance to this great project and pledges its best efforts to secure its early completion.

HIGHWAYS

The Federal policy to cooperate with the States in the building of roads was thoroughly established when the Federal highway act of 1921 was adopted under a Republican Congress. Each year since that time appropriations have been made which have greatly increased the economic value of highway transportation and helped to raise the standards and opportunities of rural life.

We pledge our support to the continuation of this policy in accordance with our needs and resources.

CRIME

We favor the enactment of rigid penal laws that will aid the States in stamping out the activities of gangsters, racketeers and kidnappers. We commend the intensive and effective drive made upon these public enemies by President Hoover and pledge our party to further efforts to the same purpose.

NARCOTICS

The Republican Party pledges itself to continue the present relentless warfare against the illicit narcotic traffic and the spread of the curse of drug addiction among our people. This administration has by treaty greatly strengthened our power to deal with this traffic.

CIVIL SERVICE

The merit system has been amply justified since the organization of the Civil Service by the Republican Party. As a part of our governmental system it is now unassailable. We believe it should remain so.

THE EIGHTEENTH AMENDMENT

The Republican Party has always stood and stands today for obedience to and enforcement of the law as the very foundation of orderly government and civilization. There can be no national security otherwise. The duty of the President of the United States and the officers of the law is clear. The law must be enforced as they find it enacted by the people. To these courses of action we pledge our nominees.

The Republican Party is and always has been the party of the Constitution. Nullification by non-observance by individuals or State action threatens the stability of government.

While the Constitution makers sought a high degree of permanence, they foresaw the need of changes and provided for them. Article V limits the proposals of amendments to two methods: (1) Two-thirds of both houses of Congress may propose amendments or (2) on application of the Legislatures of two-thirds of the States a national convention shall be called by Congress to propose amendments. Thereafter ratification must be had in one of two ways: (1) By the Legislatures of three-fourths of the several States or (2) by conventions held in three-fourths of the several States. Congress is given power to determine the mode of ratification.

Referendums without constitutional sanction cannot furnish a decisive answer. Those who propose them innocently are deluded by false hopes; those who propose them knowingly are deceiving the people.

A nation-wide controversy over the Eighteenth Amendment now distracts attention from the constructive solution of many pressing national problems. The principle of national prohibition as embodied in the amendment was supported and opposed by members of both great political parties. It was submitted to the States by members of Congress of different political faith and ratified by State Legislatures of different political majorities. It was not then and is not now a partisan political question.

Members of the Republican Party hold different opinions with respect to it and no public official or member of the party should be pledged or forced to choose between his party affiliations and his honest convictions upon this question.

We do not favor a submission limited to the issue of retention or repeal, for the American nation never in its history has gone backward, and in this case the progress which has been thus far made must be preserved, while the evils must be eliminated.

We therefore believe that the people should have an opportunity to pass upon a proposed amendment the provision of which, while retaining in the Federal Government power to preserve the gains already made in dealing with the evils inherent in the liquor traffic, shall allow the States to deal with the problem as their citizens may determine, but subject always to the power of the Federal Government to protect those States where prohibition may exist and safeguard our citizens everywhere from the return of the saloon and attendant abuses.

Such an amendment should be promptly submitted to the States by Congress, to be acted upon by State conventions called for that sole purpose in accordance with the provisions of Article V of the Constitution and adequately safeguarded so as to be truly representative.

CONSERVATION

The wise use of all natural resources freed from monopolistic control is a Republican policy, initiated by Theodore Roosevelt. The Roosevelt, Coolidge and Hoover reclamation projects bear witness to the continuation of that policy. Forestry and all other conservation activities have been supported and enlarged.

The conservation of oil is a major problem to the industry and the nation. The administration has sought to bring coordination of effort through the States, the producers and the Federal Government. Progress has been made and the effort will continue.

THE NEGRO

For seventy years the Republican Party has been the friend of the American Negro. Vindication of the rights of the Negro citizen to enjoy the full benefits of life, liberty and the pursuit of happiness is traditional in the Republican Party, and our party stands pledged to maintain equal opportunity and rights for Negro citizens. We do not propose to depart from that tradition nor to alter the spirit or letter of that pledge.

HAWAII

We believe that the existing status of self-government which for many years has been enjoyed by the citizens of the Territory of Hawaii should be maintained, and that officials appointed to administer the government should be bona-fide residents of the Territory.

PUERTO RICO

Puerto Rico being a part of the United States and its inhabitants American citizens, we believe that they are entitled to a good-faith recognition of the spirit and purposes of their organic act.

We, therefore, favor the inclusion of the island in all legislative and administrative measures enacted or adopted by Congress or otherwise for the economic benefit of their fellow-citizens of the mainland.

We also believe that, in so far as possible, all officials appointed to administer the affairs of the island government should be qualified by at least five years of bona-fide residence therein.

ALASKA

We favor the policy of giving to the people of Alaska the widest possible territorial self-government and the selection so far as possible of bona-fide residents for positions in that Territory and the placing of its citizens on an equality with those in the several States.

WELFARE WORK AND CHILDREN

The children of our nation, our future citizens, have had the most solicitous thought of our President. Child welfare and protection has been a major effort of this administration. The organization of the White House Conference on Child Health and Protection is regarded as one of the outstanding accomplishments of this administration.

Welfare work in all its phases has had the support of the President and aid of the administration. The work of organized agencies—local, State and Federal—has been advanced and an increased impetus given by that recognition and help. We approve and pledge a continuation of that policy.

INDIANS

We favor the fullest protection of the property rights of the American Indians and the provision for them of adequate educational facilities.

REORGANIZATION OF GOVERNMENT BUREAUS

Efficiency and economy demand reorganization of government bureaus. The problem is non-partisan and must be so treated if it is to be solved. As a result of years of study and personal contact with conflicting activities and wasteful duplication of effort, the President is particularly fitted to direct measures to correct the situation. We favor legislation by Congress which will give him the required authority.

DEMOCRATIC FAILURE

The vagaries of the present Democratic House of Representatives offer characteristic and appalling proof of the existing incapacity of that party for leadership in a national crisis. Individualism running amuck has displaced party discipline and has trampled under foot party leadership. A bewildered electorate has viewed the spectacle with profound dismay and deep misgivings.

Goaded to desperation by their confessed failure, the party leaders have resorted to "pork barrel" legislation to obtain a unity of action which could not otherwise be achieved. A Republican President stands resolutely between the helpless citizen and the disaster threatened by such measures; and the people, regardless of party, will demand his continued service.

Many times during his useful life has Herbert Hoover responded to such a call, and his response has never disappointed. He will not disappoint us now.

PARTY GOVERNMENT

The delays and differences which recently hampered efforts to obtain legislation imperatively demanded by prevailing critical conditions strikingly illustrate the menace to self-government brought about by the weakening of party ties and party fealty.

Experience has demonstrated that coherent political parties are indispensable agencies for the prompt and effective operation of the functions of our government under the Constitution.

Only by united party action can consistent, well-planned and wholesome legislative programs be enacted. We believe that the majority of the Congressmen elected in the name of a party have the right and duty to determine the general policies of that party requiring Congressional action, and that Congressmen belonging to that party are, in general, bound to adhere to such policies. Any other course inevitably makes of Congress a body of detached delegates which, instead of representing the collective wisdom of our people, become the confused voices of a heterogeneous group of unrelated local prejudices.

We believe that the time has come when Senators and Representatives of the United States should be impressed with the inflexible truth that their first concern should be the welfare of the United States and the well-being of all of its people, and that stubborn pride of individual opinion is not a virtue, but an obstacle to the orderly and successful achievement of the objects of representative government.

Only by cooperation can self-government succeed. Without it election under a party aegis becomes a false pretense.

We earnestly request that Republicans throughout the Union demand that their representatives in the Congress pledge themselves to these principles, to the end that the insidious influences of party disintegration may not undermine the very foundations of the Republic.

CONCLUSION

In contrast with the Republican policies and record, we contrast those of the democratic as evidenced by the action of the House of Representatives under Democratic leadership and control, which includes:

1. The issuance of fiat currency.

2. Instructions to the Federal Reserve Board and the Secretary of the Treasury to attempt to manipulate commodity prices.

3. The guarantee of bank deposits.

4. The squandering of the public resources and the unbalancing of the budget through pork-barrel appropriations which bear little relation to distress and would tend through delayed business revival to decrease rather than increase employment.

Generally on economic matters we pledge the Republican Party:

1. To maintain unimpaired the national credit.

2. To defend and preserve a sound currency and an honest dollar.

3. To stand steadfastly by the principle of a balanced budget.

4. To devote ourselves fearlessly and unremittingly to the task of eliminating abuses and extravagance and of drastically cutting the cost of government so as to reduce the heavy burden of taxation.

5. To use all available means consistent with sound financial and economic principles to promote an expansion of credit to stimulate business and relieve unemployment.

6. To make a thorough study of the conditions which permitted the credit and the credit machinery of the country to be made available, with-

out adequate check, for wholesale speculation in securities, resulting in ruinous consequences to millions of our citizens and to the national economy, and to correct those conditions so that they shall not recur.

Recognizing that real relief to unemployment must come through a revival of industrial activity and agriculture, to the promotion of which our every effort must be directed, our party in State and nation undertakes to do all in its power that is humanly possible to see that distress is fully relieved in accordance with American principles and traditions.

No successful solution of the problems before the country today can be expected from a Congress and a President separated by partisan lines or opposed in purposes and principles. Responsibility cannot be placed unless a clear mandate is given by returning to Washington a Congress and a Chief Executive united in principles and program.

The return to power of the Republican Party with that mandate is the duty of every voter who believes in the doctrines of the party and its program as herein stated. Nothing else, we believe, will insure the orderly recovery of the country and that return to prosperous days which every American so ardently desires.

The Republican Party faces the future unafraid!

With courage and confidence in ultimate success, we will strive against the forces that strike at our social and economic ideals, our political institutions.

Socialist Party Platform of 1932

"The Socialist party calls upon the nation's workers and all progressive citizens to unite with it in a mighty movement in behalf of justice, peace and freedom."

We are facing a breakdown of the capitalist system. This situation the Socialist Party has long predicted. In the last campaign it warned the people of the increasing insecurity in American life and urged a program of action which, if adopted, would have saved millions from their present tragic plight.

To-day in every city of the United States jobless men and women by the thousands are fighting the grim battle against want and starvation while factories stand idle and food rots on the ground. Millions of wage earners and salaried workers are hunting in vain for jobs while other millions are only partly employed.

Unemployment and poverty are inevitable products of the present system. Under capitalism the few own our industries. The many do the work. The wage earners and farmers are compelled to give a large part of the product of their labor to the few. The many in the factories, mines, shops, offices, and on the farms obtain but a scanty income and are able to buy back only a part of the goods that can be produced in such abundance by our mass industries.

Goods pile up. Factories close. Men and women are discharged. The Nation is thrown into a panic. In a country with natural resources, machinery, and trained labor sufficient to provide security and plenty for all, masses of people are destitute.

Capitalism spells not only widespread economic disaster but class strife. It likewise carries with it an ever-present threat of international war. The struggle of the capitalist class to find world markets and investment areas for their surplus goods and capital was a prime cause of the World War. It is to-day fostering those policies of militarism and imperialism which, if unchecked, will lead to another world conflict.

From the poverty, insecurity, unemployment, the economic collapse, the wastes, and the wars of our present capitalistic order, only the united efforts of workers and farmers, organized in unions and cooperatives, and above all in a political party of their own, can save the nation.

The Republican and Democratic Parties, both controlled by the great industrialists and financiers, have no plan or program to rescue us from the present collapse. In this crisis their chief purpose and desire has been to help the railroads, banks, insurance companies, and other capitalist interests.

The Socialist Party is to-day the one democratic party of the workers whose program would remove the causes of class struggles, class antagonisms, and social evils inherent in the capitalist system.

It proposes to transfer the principal industries of the country from private ownership and autocratic, cruelly inefficient management to social ownership and democratic control. Only by these means will it be possible to organize our industrial life on a basis of planned and steady operation, without periodic breakdowns and disastrous crises.

It proposes the following measures:

UNEMPLOYMENT AND LABOR LEGISLATION

1. A Federal appropriation of $5,000,000,000 for immediate relief for those in need to supplement State and local appropriations.

2. A Federal appropriation of $5,000,000,000 for public works and roads, reforestation, slum clearance, and decent homes for the workers, by Federal Government, States and cities.

3. Legislation providing for the acquisition of land, buildings, and equipment necessary to put the unemployed to work producing food, fuel, and clothing and for the erection of houses for their own use.

4. The 6-hour day and the 5-day week without reduction of wages.

5. A comprehensive and efficient system of free public employment agencies.

6. A compulsory system of unemployment compensation with adequate benefits, based on contributions by the Government and by employers.

7. Old-age pensions for men and women 60 years of age and over.

8. Health and maternity insurance.

9. Improved system of workmen's compensation and accident insurance.

10. The abolition of child labor.

11. Government aid to farmers and small home-owners to protect them against mortgage foreclosures and moratorium on sales for non-payment of taxes by destitute farmers and unemployed workers.

12. Adequate minimum wage laws.

SOCIAL OWNERSHIP

1. Public ownership and democratic control of mines, forests, oil, and power resources; public utilities dealing with light and power, transportation and communication, and of all other basic industries.

2. The operation of these publicly owned industries by boards of administration on which the wageworker, the consumer, and the technician are adequately represented; the recog-

nition in each industry of the principles of collective bargaining and civil service.

BANKING

1. Socialization of our credit and currency system and the establishment of a unified banking system, beginning with the complete governmental acquisition of the Federal reserve banks and the extension of the services of postal savings banks to cover all departments of the banking business and the transference of this department of the post office to a Government-owned banking corporation.

TAXATION

1. Steeply increased inheritance taxes and income taxes on the higher incomes and estates of both corporations and individuals.

2. A constitutional amendment authorizing the taxation of all government securities.

AGRICULTURE

Many of the foregoing measures for socializing the power, banking, and other industries, for raising living standards among the city workers, etc., would greatly benefit the farming population.

As special measures for agricultural upbuilding, we propose:

1. The reduction of tax burdens, by a shift from taxes on farm property to taxes on incomes, inheritance, excess profits, and other similar forms of taxation.

2. Increased Federal and State subsidies to road building and education and social services for rural communities.

3. The creation of a Federal marketing agency for the purchase and marketing of agricultural products.

4. The acquisition by bona fide cooperative societies and by governmental agencies of grain elevators, stockyards, packing houses, and warehouses and the conduct of these services on a nonprofit basis. The encouragement of farmers' cooperative societies and of the consumers' cooperatives in the cities, with a view of eliminating the middleman.

5. The socialization of Federal land banks and the extension by these banks of long-term credit to farmers at low rates of interest.

6. Social insurance against losses due to adverse weather conditions.

7. The creation of national, regional, and State land utilization boards for the purpose of discovering the best uses of the farming land of the country, in view of the joint needs of agriculture, industry, recreation, water supply, reforestation, etc., and to prepare the way for agricultural planning on a national and, ultimately, on a world scale.

Constitutional Changes

1. Proportional representation.

2. Direct election of the President and Vice President.

3. The initiative and referendum.

4. An amendment to the Constitution to make constitutional amendments less cumbersome.

5. Abolition of the power of the Supreme Court to pass upon the constitutionality of legislation enacted by Congress.

6. The passage of the Socialist Party's proposed Worker's rights amendment to the Constitution empowering Congress to establish national systems of unemployment, health and accident insurance and old age pensions, to abolish child labor, establish and take over enterprises in manufacture, commerce, transportation, banking, public utilities, and other business and industries to be owned and operated by the Government, and generally, for the social and economic welfare of the workers of the United States.

7. Repeal the 18th amendment and take over the liquor industry under government ownership and control with the right of local option for each state to maintain prohibition within its borders.

Civil Liberties

1. Federal legislation to enforce the first amendment to the Constitution so as to guarantee freedom of speech, press, and assembly, and to penalize officials who interfere with the civil rights of citizens.

2. The abolition of injunctions in labor disputes, the outlawing of "yellow-dog" contracts and the passing of laws enforcing the rights of workers to organize into unions.

3. The immediate repeal of the espionage law and other repressive legislation, and the restoration of civil and political rights to those unjustly convicted under wartime laws.

4. Legislation protecting aliens from being excluded from this country or from citizenship or from being deported on account of their political, social, or economic beliefs, or on account of activities engaged in by them which are not illegal for citizens.

5. Modification of the immigration laws to permit the reuniting of families and to offer a refuge to those fleeing from political or religious persecution.

The Negro

The enforcement of constitutional guarantees of economic, political, and legal equality for the Negro.

The enactment and enforcement of drastic antilynching laws.

International Relations

While the Socialist Party is opposed to all wars, it believes that there can be no permanent peace until Socialism is established internationally. In the meanwhile, we will support all measures that promise to promote good will and friendship among the nations of the world, including:

1. The reduction of armaments, leading to the goal of total disarmament by international agreement, if possible; but, if that is not possible, by setting an example ourselves. Soldiers, sailors, and workers unemployed by reason of disarmament to be absorbed, where desired, in a program of public works, to be financed in part by the savings due to disarmament. The abolition of conscription, of military training camps, and the Reserve Officers' Training Corps.

2. The recognition of the Soviet Union and the encouragement of trade and industrial relations with that country.

3. The cancellation of war debts due from the allied governments as part of a program for wiping out war debts and reparations, provided that such cancellation does not release money for armaments, but promotes disarmament.

4. The entrance of the United States into the World Court.

5. The entrance of the United States into the League of Nations under conditions which will make it an effective instrument for world peace and renewed cooperation with the working-class parties abroad to the end that the League may be transformed from a league of imperialist powers to a democratic assemblage representative of the aspirations of the common people of the world.

6. The creation of international economic organizations on which labor is adequately represented, to deal with problems of raw material, investments, money, credit, tariffs, and living standards from the viewpoint of the welfare of the masses throughout the world.

7. The abandonment of every degree of military intervention by the United States in the affairs of other countries. The immediate withdrawal of military forces from Haiti and Nicaragua.

8. The withdrawal of United States military and naval forces from China and the relinquishment of American extraterritorial privileges.

9. The complete independence of the Philippines and the negotiation of treaties with other nations safeguarding the sovereignty of these islands.

10. Prohibition of the sales of munitions to foreign powers.

Committed to this constructive program, the Socialist Party calls upon the Nation's workers and upon all fair-minded and progressive citizens to unite with it in a mighty movement against the present drift into social disaster and in behalf of sanity, justice, peace, and freedom.

Platform of the Socialist Labor Party

Social systems and their corresponding forms of government come into being as results of social forces making for social progress. The purpose of governments is ostensibly to insure life, liberty and the pursuit of happiness of the useful members of society.

Whenever a society fails in or becomes destructive of these ends, it has self-evidently outlived its usefulness, rendering it imperative for the exploited and oppressed class to organize its forces to put an end to the outworn social system.

Such a crucial period of history is facing humanity today, and in view of this the Socialist Labor Party in National Convention assembled, May 1, 1932, reaffirms its former platform declarations and in accord with the international Socialist principles declares:

The history of mankind has been a struggle for progress, taking the form of struggles for power between contending classes. Whenever a ruling class had fulfilled its mission, and its interests ceased to be in harmony with social interests, it was supplanted by the class below, which, by increasing economic and political powers, attained its revolutionary goal. This class, in turn, became a carrier of social progress until it had outlived its usefulness and, becoming reactionary and a stumbling block in the path of humanity, had to give way before the combined forces of social progress and a new revolutionary class.

With capitalism there remain in society just two contending classes, the capitalist class and the working class—the capitalist class, the owner of the means of production, which ownership today is wholly destructive of the life, liberty and happiness of the mass of the people; and the working class whose interests demand the abolition of private ownership in the means of life.

The interests of the working class demand the institution of collective ownership and control, guaranteeing to all the right to work, and by securing to all the full fruits of their labor, ending for all time the destructive class wars which have up to now torn humanity asunder.

For forty years the Socialist Labor Party has been moving upward toward this historic moment.

The capitalist system is now creaking and breaking in every joint and cranny. It is no more "on trial" than a horse-drawn vehicle is on trial beside a powerful motor van. Capitalism is outworn, obsolete, ready for the museum of social history. A mere glance at the world situation should suffice to convince even the dullest of this forceful fact.

Economic bonds have snapped; social bonds are dissolving. As a result, factories are closing down, machinery stands idle and rusts, until from ten to twelve million working men and women of this country are idle and they and their dependents stand bereft of food, clothing and shelter. The million mass of the people, the world over, are starving and dying, surrounded by tremendous wealth created by their own labor. Workers are unable to find work, to secure the necessities of life.

The Socialist Labor Party has ceaselessly pointed out the inevitable doom of the capitalist system of production and distribution:

has pointed to the fact that "free" competition—one of the beatitudes of the system—was inevitably leading to the elimination of the small, and gradually not so small either, business men and manufactures;

has shown that the cumulative effect of the gigantic machines of production in fewer and fewer hands would be so tremendous as to get beyond the possibility of control by the few industries;

has demonstrated beyond doubt that the capitalist profit system was built and could exist only on the exploitation of labor;

that this exploitation with the aid of the machines was becoming so tremendous that it would eventually become absolutely impossible for the capitalist expropriators to dispose of this surplus in either domestic or foreign markets;

that this "stolen goods" would eventually accumulate and lie like an incubus on the chest of humanity, preventing it from breathing and living while a multi-million army of unemployed would tramp the streets and highways unable to find the wherewithal to live.

This state of social dissolution is now upon us. When a social system has reached the point of utter dissolution, when the bonds that held it together are snapping, ruling class interests eagerly offer palliatives and reforms to stave off the impending doom of the system. It is so with capitalism. In various disguises, but moved with one purpose, various agents of capitalism appear, holding out alluring promises of reform ostensibly to bring relief to the workers. But there can be no relief to a revolutionary class within a social system that is doomed.

Where a social revolution is pending and, for whatever reason, is not accomplished, reaction is the alternative. Every reform granted by capi-

talism is a concealed measure of reaction. He who says reform says preservation, and he who says that reforms under capitalism are possible and worth while thereby declares that a continuation of capitalism is possible and worth while. But capitalism has grown into an all-destroying and all-devouring monster that must be destroyed if humanity is to live.

At this crucial moment the Socialist Labor Party calls upon the working class of America, more deliberately serious than ever before, to rally at the polls under the Party's banner.

The Socialist Labor Party also calls upon all other intelligent citizens to place themselves squarely upon the ground of working class interests, and join us in this mighty and noble work of human emancipation, so that we may put summary end to the existing barbarous class conflict and insane contradictions between unlimited wealth and wealth production, and the poverty and wretchedness suffered by those whose labor created all this wealth.

We call upon them to place the land and all the means of production, transportation and distribution in the hands of the useful producers as an organized industrial body, under a national industrial administration to take the place of the present outworn political or territorial government. And we further call upon the workers to hasten this work of social and human regeneration to the end that a speedy termination may be put to the present state of planless production, industrial war and social disorder, substituting for it the Socialist or Industrial Commonwealth of Emancipated Labor—a commonwealth in which every worker shall have the free exercise and full benefit of his faculties, multiplied by all the factors of modern civilization.

☒ CAMPAIGN OF 1936

Seven candidates conducted campaigns for the presidency in 1936. The Democratic and Republican candidates polled more than ninety-seven per cent of the votes, and the Socialists, Communists, Prohibitionists, and Socialist Laborites also presented candidates and platforms. The new party in 1936, the Union Party, received nearly 900,000 votes.

The Election Platform of the Communist Party

The American people today face the greatest crisis since the Civil War. Extreme reaction threatens the country, driving toward Fascism and a new world war.

To meet this danger to our liberties and welfare, we must unite our ranks. In common action we must go forward to overcome this crisis in an American way, in the spirit of 1776, in the interests of our people and of our country.

The collapse of the Hoover-Republican prosperity destroyed our boasted American standards of living. The New Deal failed to protect and restore our living standards. American capitalism is unable to provide the American people with the simple necessities of life.

Over 12,000,000 able-bodied and willing workers are without jobs. For a majority of these there is no hope of jobs.

The income of the working people has been cut in half. Half our farmers have lost their land. They are being converted into a pauperized peasantry.

Millions of young people face a future without hope, with no prospect of ever being able to establish a home or rear a family.

The Negro people suffer doubly. Most ex-ploited of working people, they are also victims of jim-crowism and lynching. They are denied the right to live as human beings.

Civil rights are being systematically attacked and curtailed. The Supreme Court has usurped the power of Congress. It is destroying all labor and social legislation.

Reactionary forces, roused and organized by Hearst and the Liberty League, are striving to seize the government fully. They want to saddle the entire burden of the crisis upon the people, to establish a fascist régime and move toward war on the side of Hitler, the butcher of the German people and the chief maker of war.

The peace, freedom, and security of the people are at stake. Democracy or Fascism, progress or reaction—this is the central issue of 1936.

At the head of the camp of reaction stands the Republican party—the party of Wall Street, the party of the banks and monopolies. Landon and Knox are supported by the barons of steel, oil, auto, and munitions; by Morgan, the du Ponts; and by that arch-enemy of all decency, William Randolph Hearst. They are the candidates of the Liberty League, the National Association of Manufacturers, the American Bankers' Association, the United States Chamber of Commerce, the Ku Klux Klan, and the Black Legion.

Roosevelt is bitterly attacked by the camp of reaction. But he does not fight back these attacks. Roosevelt compromises. He grants but small concessions to the working people, while making big concessions to Hearst, to Wall Street, to the reactionaries.

The working people must organize themselves *independently,* under their own banner, with their own leadership and program. They must organize a great Farmer-Labor Party to fight for and establish a people's government—a government of, for, and by the people. They must unite the forces of progress against the forces of reaction.

The secretly formed Union party of Lemke and Coughlin is not the new party for which the people are looking. It is the creature of Landon, Hearst, and the Liberty League. Under cover of radical sounding words, its program contains essentially the some proposals as the Republican platform. It is deceiving its followers. It is the tool of the reactionaries.

But a real people's party is arising. Organized by the workers and farmers themselves, the Farmer-Labor party is growing in the majority of states. Unable to put up a presidential ticket this year, it is organizing on a national scale. It fights for local, state and Congressional offices. It is the most hopeful sign in American political life. It is cooperating with the powerful trade unions in the new Labor's Non-Partisan League against the Republicans. It will undoubtedly be a major contender in the presidential elections of 1940. The Communist party unconditionally supports the building of the Farmer-Labor party. It pledges itself to work to bring the trade unions and all progressive forces into its ranks. The Socialist party, on a national scale, is withholding its cooperation with all other groups. It conducts a harmful policy of isolation. It gives little help to the people's struggle against reaction. We appeal to the Socialist party to change its course. We urge it to unite with us and the mass of the toilers against reaction.

In this situation the Communist party comes forward with its own presidential ticket and its own platform. It enters the campaign to defend and promote the unity of the working people. It pledges to fight for their interests, to defeat the reactionaries, to build the Farmer-Labor party, and, finally, to win the masses to the banner of socialism. The chief aim of the Communist party today is to defeat the Landon-Hearst-Liberty League reaction, to defeat the forces of Wall Street.

The Communist party and its candidates stand on the following platform, which expresses the immediate interests of the majority of the population of our country.

I. PUT AMERICA BACK TO WORK. PROVIDE JOBS AND A LIVING WAGE FOR ALL.

Open the closed factories—we need all that our industries can produce. If the private employers will not or cannot do so, then the government must open and operate the factories, mills and mines for the benefit of the people.

Industry and the productive powers of our nation must be used to give every working man and woman a real, American standard of living, with a minimum annual wage guaranteed by law.

We demand equal opportunity for women in industry and in all spheres of life. We favor legislative measures for the improvement of the wages and working conditions of women.

We demand a 30-hour week without reduction in earnings, at trade union rates and conditions, in private industry and on public works.

We oppose the present railroad consolidation policy which results in the discharge of hundreds of thousands of workers.

We demand higher wages and vacations with pay. We demand the abolition of the wage differential between the North and the South.

II. PROVIDE UNEMPLOYMENT INSURANCE, OLD AGE PENSIONS, AND SOCIAL SECURITY FOR ALL.

It is the obligation of the American government to establish an adequate system of social insurance for the unemployed, the aged, the disabled and the sick, as provided in the Frazier-Lundeen Bill. This bill provides compensation to all unemployed without exception, and pensions for the aged from 60 years, at rates equal to former earnings, but in no case less than $15 per week. Make the Frazier-Lundeen Bill the law of the land!

We favor a federal system of maternity and health insurance.

We stand for adequate relief standards for all unemployed. We demand a stop to all relief cuts. The federal government must continue and extend the W. P. A. We favor an extensive Federal Works Program, to provide housing at low rentals, schools, hospitals, health and recreational facilities, as provided for in the proposed six billion dollar appropriation of the Marcantonio Relief Standards Bill.

We support the demands of the veterans for uniform pension laws and for adequate hospitalization.

III. Save the Young Generation!

Our country can and must provide opportunity, education, and work for the youth of America. These demands of the young people as embodied in the American Youth Act—the Benson-Amlie Bill—must be enacted into law.

This bill provides for jobs, educational opportunities, and vocational training for all young people between the ages of 16 and 25.

The National Youth Administration budget must be maintained and enlarged.

Military training in the C. C. C. and schools must be abolished.

Free education and financial assistance to the youth and the children must be guaranteed by both federal and state appropriations.

Child labor must once and for all be abolished and made unconstitutional.

IV. Free the Farmers From Debts, Unbearable Tax Burdens and Foreclosures. Guarantee the Land to Those Who Till the Soil.

We declare that the American government is obligated to save the American farmers from distress and ruin, to guarantee the farmers and tenants their inalienable rights to possession of their land, their homes and their chattels. We demand for this purpose the immediate refinancing of the farmers' debts with government loans at nominal interest.

We demand a halt to evictions and foreclosures, a long-term moratorium on all needy farmers' debts, and the adoption of measures to provide land for the landless farmers.

We favor immediate relief to the drought-stricken farmers by the government. We favor a graduated land tax to prevent the accumulation of large land holdings in the hands of the insurance companies, private and government banks, and other absentee owners.

We favor exemption from taxation of small operating farmers and farm cooperatives.

We are unalterably opposed to the policy of crop destruction and curtailment.

We support government regulation of farm prices with the aim of guaranteeing to the farmer his cost of production. We urge scientific soil conservation under supervision of the elected representatives of farmers' organizations, with compensation to farmer-owners and tenants for loss of income.

V. The Rich Hold the Wealth of Our Country; Make the Rich Pay.

We demand that social and labor legislation shall be financed and the budget balanced by taxation of the rich. We are opposed to sales taxes in any form, including processing taxes, and call for their immediate repeal. The main source of government finance must be a system of sharply graduated taxation upon incomes of over $5,000 a year, upon corporate profits and surpluses, as well as taxation upon the present tax-exempt securities and large gifts and inheritances. The people of small income, small property, and home owners must be protected against foreclosures and seizures and from burdensome taxes and high interest rates.

We are unconditionally opposed to inflationary policies which bring catastrophe and ruin to the workers, farmers, and middle classes, and enrich the speculators.

We favor nationalization of the entire banking system.

VI. Defend and Extend Democratic Rights and Civil Liberties! Curb the Supreme Court!

We support a Constitutional Amendment to put an end to the dictatorial and usurped powers of the Supreme Court. We demand further that Congress immediately reassert its Constitutional powers to enact social and labor legislation and to curb the Supreme Court usurpation.

We champion the unrestricted freedom of speech, press, radio and assembly and the right to organize and strike. We call upon the people to safeguard these traditional liberties.

We stand for federal legislation which will establish labor's full right to collective bargaining, which will outlaw the company unions, the spy and stool pigeon systems, and all other coercion by employers.

We demand heavy penalties and imprisonment for employers guilty of discharging workers for union or political activities.

We demand the abolition of poll taxes and all other limitations on the right to vote.

We demand the release of political prisoners, among whom Tom Mooney, Angelo Herndon, and the Scottsboro Boys are but the outstanding examples.

The infamous policy of deportation of foreign-born workers must be stopped. The traditional American right of asylum for political refugees must be reestablished. Anti-Semitic propaganda must be prohibited by law.

VII. FULL RIGHTS FOR THE NEGRO PEOPLE

We demand that the Negro people be guaranteed complete equality, equal rights to jobs, equal pay for equal work, the full right to organize, vote, serve on juries, and hold public office. Segregation and discrimination against Negroes must be declared a crime. Heavy penalties must be established against mob rule, floggers, and kidnappers, with the *death penalty for lynchers*. We demand the enforcement of the Thirteenth, Fourteenth and Fifteenth Amendments to the Constitution.

VIII. KEEP AMERICA OUT OF WAR BY KEEPING WAR OUT OF THE WORLD!

We declare that peace must be maintained and defended at all costs. We declare in favor of strengthening all measures for collective security. We favor effective financial and economic measures to this end by the League of Nations, against Hitler Germany, Italian Fascism and Japanese imperialism. These measures should be supported by the United States government.

We consider the expenditure of billions for armaments and war preparations unnecessary and provocative, contributing to the danger of a new world war.

Instead of ever greater armaments, we believe that the United States should develop an American Peace Policy in close collaboration with the Soviet Union, based on complete prohibition of the sale or delivery of goods, or the granting of loans to nations engaged in a foreign war contrary to the provisions of the Kellogg Peace Pact. The huge funds now spent for armament should be turned to the support of the suffering people.

We demand the nationalization of the entire munitions industry.

We demand an end to American intervention in the internal affairs of the Latin-American countries and the Philippines.

We demand the strict non-recognition of the Japanese conquests in Manchuria and China, and the Italian conquest of Ethiopia.

We support the Puerto Rican demand for independence.

We support the complete independence and self-determination of all oppressed nations.

This platform represents the life needs of the majority of workers, farmers, and middle classes today. These demands can be won even under the present capitalist system. This is being conclusively proved by the victories of the People's Front in France. We appeal to all members of the American Federation of Labor and farm organizations, to our comrades in the Socialist party, to all who toil with hand or brain, Negro and white, to unite in a determined fight to achieve the demands of the people and to beat back the sinister forces of reaction.

The fight for those demands will organize and strengthen the people. It will give them deeper political experience and understanding. It will prepare them for the great decisions to come when it will be necessary to move forward to socialism.

Today the immediate issue is Democracy or Fascism. But the consistent fight for Democracy in the conditions of declining capitalism will finally bring us to the necessary choice of the socialist path.

Our land is the richest in the world. It has the largest and most skilled working class. Everything is present to provide a rich and cultured life for the whole population. Yet millions starve. The whole nation suffers, because capitalism is breaking down, because profits are the first law and are put above human needs—and the capitalist rulers are turning to Fascism and war.

The Communist party prepares the people to bring an end to this crucifixion of humanity. Our economy must be taken from the incompetent and greedy hands of Wall Street. It must be made the common property of the whole people. It must be operated fully for the benefit of all who work. This will be socialism. Only when socialism will be established, as today in the Soviet Union, will there be no crisis, no poverty, no unemployment—but abundance and security for all, with the gates of progress open to humanity.

Reactionaries of all shades cry out against socialism. They say it is revolutionary. True, the change to socialism will be revolutionary; but since when is revolution un-American? On the contrary, revolution is the proudest tradition of our people who have always been among the most revolutionary peoples of the world.

Communism is Twentieth-century Americanism. The Communist party continues the traditions of 1776, of the birth of our country, of the revolutionary Lincoln, who led the historic struggle that preserved our nation. In the greater crisis of today only the Communist party shows a way to a better life now, and to the future of peace, freedom, and security for all.

By supporting, working with, and voting for the Communist party in the November elections; by organizing the mass-production industries into powerful industrial unions, in a united American Federation of Labor, by independent political action and by building the American people's front—the Farmer-Labor party—the toilers of America can best fight for the realization of their aims in 1936.

Forward to a progressive, free, prosperous, and happy America.

VOTE COMMUNIST!

Democratic Platform of 1936

We hold this truth to be self-evident—that the test of a representative government is its ability to promote the safety and happiness of the people.

We hold this truth to be self-evident—that 12 years of Republican leadership left our Nation sorely stricken in body, mind, and spirit; and that three years of Democratic leadership have put it back on the road to restored health and prosperity.

We hold this truth to be self-evident—that 12 years of Republican surrender to the dictatorship of a privileged few have been supplanted by a Democratic leadership which has returned the people themselves to the places of authority, and has revived in them new faith and restored the hope which they had almost lost.

We hold this truth to be self-evident—that this three-year recovery in all the basic values of life and the reestablishment of the American way of living has been brought about by humanizing the policies of the Federal Government as they affect the personal, financial, industrial, and agricultural well-being of the American people.

We hold this truth to be self-evident—that government in a modern civilization has certain inescapable obligations to its citizens, among which are:

(1) Protection of the family and the home.

(2) Establishment of a democracy of opportunity for all the people.

(3) Aid to those overtaken by disaster.

These obligations, neglected through 12 years of the old leadership, have once more been recognized by American Government. Under the new leadership they will never be neglected.

FOR THE PROTECTION OF THE FAMILY AND THE HOME

(1) We have begun and shall continue the successful drive to rid our land of kidnappers and bandits. We shall continue to use the powers of government to end the activities of the malefactors of great wealth who defraud and exploit the people.

Savings and Investment

(2) We have safeguarded the thrift of our citizens by restraining those who would gamble with other peoples savings, by requiring truth in the sale of securities; by putting the brakes upon the use of credit for speculation; by outlawing the manipulation of prices in stock and commodity markets; by curbing the overweening power and unholy practices of utility holding companies; by insuring fifty million bank accounts.

Old Age and Social Security

(3) We have built foundations for the security of those who are faced with the hazards of unemployment and old age; for the orphaned, the crippled, and the blind. On the foundation of the Social Security Act we are determined to erect a structure of economic security for all our people, making sure that this benefit shall keep step with the ever-increasing capacity of America to provide a high standard of living for all its citizens.

Consumer

(4) We will act to secure to the consumer fair value, honest sales and a decreased spread between the price he pays and the price the producer receives.

Rural Electrification

(5) This administration has fostered power rate yardsticks in the Tennessee Valley and in several other parts of the Nation. As a result, electricity has been made available to the people at a lower rate. We will continue to promote plans for rural electrification and for cheap power by means of the yardstick method.

Housing

(6) We maintain that our people are entitled to decent, adequate housing at a price which they can afford. In the last three years, the Federal Government, having saved more than two million homes from foreclosure, has taken the first steps in our history to provide decent housing for people of meagre incomes. We believe every encouragement should be given to the building of new homes by private enterprise; and that the Government should steadily extend its housing program toward the goal of adequate housing for those forced through economic necessities to live in unhealthy and slum conditions.

Veterans

(7) We shall continue just treatment of our war veterans and their dependents.

FOR THE ESTABLISHMENT OF A DEMOCRACY OF OPPORTUNITY

Agriculture

We have taken the farmers off the road to ruin.

We have kept our pledge to agriculture to use all available means to raise farm income toward its pre-war purchasing power. The farmer is no longer suffering from 15-cent corn, 3-cent hogs, 2½-cent beef at the farm, 5-cent wool, 30-cent wheat, 5-cent cotton, and 3-cent sugar.

By Federal legislation, we have reduced the farmer's indebtedness and doubled his net income. In cooperation with the States and through the farmers' own committees, we are restoring the fertility of his land and checking the erosion of his soil. We are bringing electricity and good roads to his home.

We will continue to improve the soil conservation and domestic allotment program with payments to farmers.

We will continue a fair-minded administration of agricultural laws, quick to recognize and meet new problems and conditions. We recognize the gravity of the evils of farm tenancy, and we pledge the full cooperation of the Government in the refinancing of farm indebtedness at the lowest possible rates of interest and over a long term of years.

We favor the production of all the market will absorb, both at home and abroad, plus a reserve supply sufficient to insure fair prices to consumers; we favor judicious commodity loans on seasonal surpluses; and we favor assistance within Federal authority to enable farmers to adjust and balance production with demand, at a fair profit to the farmers.

We favor encouragement of sound, practical farm cooperatives.

By the purchase and retirement of ten million acres of sub-marginal land, and assistance to those attempting to eke out an existence upon it, we have made a good beginning toward proper land use and rural rehabilitation.

The farmer has been returned to the road to freedom and prosperity. We will keep him on that road.

Labor

We have given the army of America's industrial workers something more substantial than the Republicans' dinner pail full of promises. We have increased the worker's pay and shortened his hours; we have undertaken to put an end to the sweated labor of his wife and children; we have written into the law of the land his right to collective bargaining and self-organization free from the interference of employers; we have provided Federal machinery for the peaceful settlement of labor disputes.

We will continue to protect the worker and we will guard his rights, both as wage-earner and consumer, in the production and consumption of all commodities, including coal and water power and other natural resource products.

The worker has been returned to the road to

freedom and prosperity. We will keep him on that road.

Business

We have taken the American business man out of the red. We have saved his bank and given it a sounder foundation; we have extended credit; we have lowered interest rates; we have undertaken to free him from the ravages of cutthroat competition.

The American business man has been returned to the road to freedom and prosperity. We will keep him on that road.

Youth

We have aided youth to stay in school; given them constructive occupation; opened the door to opportunity which 12 years of Republican neglect had closed.

Our youth have been returned to the road to freedom and prosperity. We will keep them on that road.

MONOPOLY AND CONCENTRATION OF ECONOMIC POWER

Monopolies and the concentration of economic power, the creation of Republican rule and privilege, continue to be the master of the producer, the exploiter of the consumer, and the enemy of the independent operator. This is a problem challenging the unceasing effort of untrammeled public officials in every branch of the Government. We pledge vigorously and fearlessly to enforce the criminal and civil provisions of the existing anti-trust laws, and to the extent that their effectiveness has been weakened by new corporate devices or judicial construction, we propose by law to restore their efficacy in stamping out monopolistic practices and the concentration of economic power.

AID TO THOSE OVERTAKEN BY DISASTER

We have aided and will continue to aid those who have been visited by widespread drought and floods, and have adopted a Nation-wide flood-control policy.

Unemployment

We believe that unemployment is a national problem, and that it is an inescapable obligation of our Government to meet it in a national way.

Due to our stimulation of private business, more than five million people have been reemployed; and we shall continue to maintain that the first objective of a program of economic security is maximum employment in private industry at adequate wages. Where business fails to supply such employment, we believe that work at prevailing wages should be provided in cooperation with State and local governments on useful public projects, to the end that the national wealth may be increased, the skill and energy of the worker may be utilized, his morale maintained, and the unemployed assured the opportunity to earn the necessities of life.

The Constitution

The Republican platform proposes to meet many pressing national problems solely by action of the separate States. We know that drought, dust storms, floods, minimum wages, maximum hours, child labor, and working conditions in industry, monopolistic and unfair business practices cannot be adequately handled exclusively by 48 separate State legislatures, 48 separate State administrations, and 48 separate State courts. Transactions and activities which inevitably overflow State boundaries call for both State and Federal treatment.

We have sought and will continue to seek to meet these problems through legislation within the Constitution.

If these problems cannot be effectively solved by legislation within the Constitution, we shall seek such clarifying amendment as will assure to the legislatures of the several States and to the Congress of the United States, each within its proper jurisdiction, the power to enact those laws which the State and Federal legislatures, within their respective spheres, shall find necessary, in order adequately to regulate commerce, protect public health and safety and safeguard economic security. Thus we propose to maintain the letter and spirit of the Constitution.

THE MERIT SYSTEM IN GOVERNMENT

For the protection of government itself and promotion of its efficiency, we pledge the immediate extension of the merit system through the classified civil service—which was first established and fostered under Democratic auspices—to all non-policy-making positions in the Federal service.

We shall subject to the civil service law all continuing positions which, because of the emergency, have been exempt from its operation.

CIVIL LIBERTIES

We shall continue to guard the freedom of speech, press, radio, religion and assembly which our Constitution guarantees; with equal rights to all and special privileges to none.

GOVERNMENT FINANCE

The Administration has stopped deflation, restored values and enabled business to go ahead with confidence.

When national income shrinks, government income is imperilled. In reviving national income, we have fortified government finance. We have raised the public credit to a position of unsurpassed security. The interest rate on Government bonds has been reduced to the lowest point in twenty-eight years. The same Government bonds which in 1932 sold under 83 are now selling over 104.

We approve the objective of a permanently sound currency so stabilized as to prevent the former wide fluctuations in value which injured in turn producers, debtors, and property owners on the one hand, and wage-earners and creditors on the other, a currency which will permit full utilization of the country's resources. We assert that today we have the soundest currency in the world.

We are determined to reduce the expenses of government. We are being aided therein by the recession in unemployment. As the requirements of relief decline and national income advances, an increasing percentage of Federal expenditures can and will be met from current revenues, secured from taxes levied in accordance with ability to pay. Our retrenchment, tax and recovery programs thus reflect our firm determination to achieve a balanced budget and the reduction of the national debt at the earliest possible moment.

FOREIGN POLICY

In our relationship with other nations, this Government will continue to extend the policy of the Good Neighbor. We reaffirm our opposition to war as an instrument of national policy, and declare that disputes between nations should be settled by peaceful means. We shall continue to observe a true neutrality in the disputes of others; to be prepared, resolutely to resist aggression against ourselves; to work for peace and to take the profits out of war; to guard against being drawn, by political commitments, international banking or private trading, into any war which may develop anywhere.

We shall continue to foster the increase in our foreign trade which has been achieved by this administration; to seek by mutual agreement the lowering of those tariff barriers, quotas and embargoes which have been raised against our exports of agricultural and industrial products; but continue as in the past to give adequate protection to our farmers and manufacturers against unfair competition or the dumping on our shores of commodities and goods produced abroad by cheap labor or subsidized by foreign governments.

THE ISSUE

The issue in this election is plain. The American people are called upon to choose between a Republican administration that has and would again regiment them in the service of privileged groups and a Democratic administration dedicated to the establishment of equal economic opportunity for all our people.

We have faith in the destiny of our nation. We are sufficiently endowed with natural resources and with productive capacity to provide for all a quality of life that meets the standards of real Americanism.

Dedicated to a government of liberal American principles, we are determined to oppose equally, the despotism of Communism and the menace of concealed Fascism.

We hold this final truth to be self-evident— that the interests, the security and the happiness of the people of the United States of America can be perpetuated only under democratic government as conceived by the founders of our nation.

Prohibition Party Platform of 1936

PREAMBLE

After three and a half years of Republican administration, and three and a half years of Democratic administration since the depression, we find our gravest problems unsolved, the morals of the people greatly undermined and the national morals broken down to an incredible extent.

It is plain that the crass materialism of our dominant parties; their abandonment of moral precepts; their flouting of the majesty of the law; their double dealing; their supreme self interest must be replaced by a return to the early American principles of dependence upon Almighty God as the source of all just government and to a following of the principles of the Prince of Peace.

The conclusion is inevitable that the prosperity and progress of the nation can come only through the spiritual and moral regeneration of the people manifested in government.

PROHIBITION

We denounce the bipartisan conspiracy by which the Eighteenth Amendment was removed from the Constitution and the nation reopened to the exploitation of the people by a legalized liquor traffic.

Respect for this great moral provision of our Constitution had been weakened by the maladministration to which it was subjected by the two old parties. Both parties are organically incapable of effective enforcement by reason of the two-sided "wet-dry" character of each party and their dominant leadership.

Eighty years' history of non-partisan prohibition in three great prohibition waves has demonstrated that the great obstacles to the maintenance and effectiveness of prohibition has been the lack of a united party behind it.

We seek to unite the opponents of the liquor traffic and then marshal all the powers of government for the complete suppression of that traffic.

We present a sane, liberal and comprehensive program on the great problems of our time.

WORLD PEACE

We pledge ourselves to use every possible means to promote world peace and the settlement of international misunderstandings by arbitration.

TAXES

Must be reduced. Unnecessary governmental functions must be curtailed and the multitude of political jobs abolished. Taxes should be levied in accordance with ability to pay.

Assessments should be uniform and without favor. There should be no tax exemptions.

CRIME

We seek to diminish crime, first by suppressing the traffics in alcoholics and other narcotics, which pervert the brains of the people; second, by bringing about a re-alignment of politics which shall unite the anti-crime voters and overcome the alliance of the underworld with the political machines; third, by effective enforcement of the law, and fourth, by the reform and modernization of antiquated and outmoded system of judicial procedure.

OLD AGE PENSIONS

Our party was the first party to declare for old age pensions. We acknowledge the responsibility of government to adequately care for those handicapped by advanced age or other disabilities.

UNEMPLOYMENT

We must continue to accept responsibility for taking care of the unemployed until such time as industry is able to re-employ them.

DISTRIBUTION

We seek a better distribution of economic goods so that the increased consumption of the products of factory and farm may produce complete employment of labor without interruption.

CURRENCY

The privately owned Federal Reserve Banks should no longer have the special privilege of issuing the currency of the United States and of profiting financially thereby. Congress should resume the exercise of its constitutional right to coin money and fix the value thereof.

We favor a sound legal tender currency, issued directly by the United States government to the people, through the several States and subdivisions thereof, in exchange for an equal amount of legally issued bonds of such States and subdivisions, the funds thus obtained to be used partially for the construction of necessary public works, but chiefly in retiring present tax exempt bonds, as soon as the same shall become due and callable. To prevent undue expansion of bank credit based on such increased emission of currency, we favor a proportionate increase in the cash reserve requirements behind such credit. No further tax exempt securities whatever should be issued, and all those now outstanding whether

Federal, State or local, should be retired and cancelled as soon as practicable.

Thus we would substitute for the present irredeemable paper money a sound currency redeemable dollar for dollar in good and valid bonds, the interest on which would furnish the Treasury most, if not all, the revenues needed for the ordinary expenses of government, economically administered. This would greatly lessen the burden of Federal taxation. Furthermore, because the holders of present tax exempt securities would have to seek some other way to earn an income from their capital, this would contribute in large measure to increased employment and business recovery.

Movie Censorship

We stand for federal supervision of the creation of motion picture films at the source of production so that the public effect may be beneficial and uplifting.

Gambling

We are opposed to the legalization of lotteries, gambling and all other forms of exploitation of the people.

Constitution

We stand for loyalty to the principles of the Constitution and for the preservation of our system of government against the assaults of communism and of fascism, and the subversive influences exerted by the alliance of the old parties with predatory wealth, organized crime and the liquor power.

We invite the support of all patriotic Americans to help build a political party united in its loyalty to the best interests of the nation.

Resolution

Adopted by the National Prohibition Convention. We appeal to the youth of the land with their idealism and enthusiasm to meet the challenge of the hour, and join with us in the solving of the great problems involving the preservation and integrity of American institutions.

Republican Platform for 1936

America is in peril. The welfare of American men and women and the future of our youth are at stake. We dedicate ourselves to the preservation of their political liberty, their individual opportunity and their character as free citizens, which today for the first time are threatened by Government itself.

For three long years the New Deal Administration has dishonored American traditions and flagrantly betrayed the pledges upon which the Democratic Party sought and received public support.

The powers of Congress have been usurped by the President.

The integrity and authority of the Supreme Court have been flouted.

The rights and liberties of American citizens have been violated.

Regulated monopoly has displaced free enterprise.

The New Deal Administration constantly seeks to usurp the rights reserved to the States and to the people.

It has insisted on the passage of laws contrary to the Constitution.

It has intimidated witnesses and interfered with the right of petition.

It has dishonored our country by repudiating its most sacred obligations.

It has been guilty of frightful waste and extravagance, using public funds for partisan political purposes.

It has promoted investigations to harass and intimidate American citizens, at the same time denying investigations into its own improper expenditures.

It has created a vast multitude of new offices, filled them with its favorites, set up a centralized bureaucracy, and sent out swarms of inspectors to harass our people.

It has bred fear and hesitation in commerce and industry, thus discouraging new enterprises, preventing employment and prolonging the depression.

It secretly has made tariff agreements with our foreign competitors, flooding our markets with foreign commodities.

It has coerced and intimidated voters by withholding relief to those opposing its tyrannical policies.

It has destroyed the morale of our people and made them dependent upon government.

Appeals to passion and class prejudice have replaced reason and tolerance.

To a free people, these actions are insufferable. This campaign cannot be waged on the traditional differences between the Republican and Democratic parties. The responsibility of this election transcends all previous political divisions. We invite all Americans, irrespective of party, to join us in defense of American institutions.

CONSTITUTIONAL GOVERNMENT AND FREE ENTERPRISE

We pledge ourselves:

1. To maintain the American system of Constitutional and local self government, and to resist all attempts to impair the authority of the Supreme Court of the United States, the final protector of the rights of our citizens against the arbitrary encroachments of the legislative and executive branches of government. There can be no individual liberty without an independent judiciary.

2. To preserve the American system of free enterprise, private competition, and equality of opportunity, and to seek its constant betterment in the interests of all.

REEMPLOYMENT

The only permanent solution of the unemployment problem is the absorption of the unemployed by industry and agriculture. To that end, we advocate:

Removal of restrictions on production.

Abandonment of all New Deal policies that raise production costs, increase the cost of living, and thereby restrict buying, reduce volume and prevent reemployment.

Encouragement instead of hindrance to legitimate business.

Withdrawal of government from competition with private payrolls.

Elimination of unnecessary and hampering regulations.

Adoption of such other policies as will furnish a chance for individual enterprise, industrial expansion, and the restoration of jobs.

RELIEF

The necessities of life must be provided for the needy, and hope must be restored pending recovery. The administration of relief is a major failing of the New Deal. It has been faithless to those who must deserve our sympathy. To end confusion, partisanship, waste and incompetence, we pledge:

1. The return of responsibility for relief administration to non-political local agencies familiar with community problems.

2. Federal grants-in-aid to the States and territories while the need exists, upon compliance with these conditions: (a) a fair proportion of the total relief burden to be provided from the revenues of States and local governments; (b) all engaged in relief administration to be selected on the basis of merit and fitness; (c) adequate provision to be made for the encouragement of those persons who are trying to become self-supporting.

3. Undertaking of Federal public works only on their merits and separate from the administration of relief.

4. A prompt determination of the facts concerning relief and unemployment.

SECURITY

Real security will be possible only when our productive capacity is sufficient to furnish a decent standard of living for all American families and to provide a surplus for future needs and contingencies. For the attainment of that ultimate objective, we look to the energy, self-reliance and character of our people, and to our system of free enterprise.

Society has an obligation to promote the security of the people, by affording some measure of protection against involuntary unemployment and dependency in old age. The New Deal policies, while purporting to provide social security, have, in fact, endangered it.

We propose a system of old age security, based upon the following principles:

1. We approve a pay-as-you-go policy, which requires of each generation the support of the aged and the determination of what is just and adequate.

2. Every American citizen over sixty-five should receive the supplementary payment necessary to provide a minimum income sufficient to protect him or her from want.

3. Each state and territory, upon complying with simple and general minimum standards, should receive from the federal government a

graduated contribution in proportion to its own, up to a fixed maximum.

4. To make this program consistent with sound fiscal policy the Federal revenues for this purpose must be provided from the proceeds of a direct tax widely distributed. All will be benefited and all should contribute.

We propose to encourage adoption by the states and territories of honest and practical measures for meeting the problems of unemployment insurance.

The unemployment insurance and old age annuity sections of the present Social Security Act are unworkable and deny benefits to about two-thirds of our adult population, including professional men and women and all those engaged in agriculture and domestic service, and the self employed while imposing heavy tax burdens upon all. The so-called reserve fund estimated at forty-seven billion dollars for old age insurance is no reserve at all, because the fund will contain nothing but the Government's promise to pay, while the taxes collected in the guise of premiums will be wasted by the Government in reckless and extravagant political schemes.

LABOR

The welfare of labor rests upon increased production and the prevention of exploitation. We pledge ourselves to:

Protect the right of labor to organize and to bargain collectively through representatives of its own choosing without interference from any source.

Prevent governmental job holders from exercising autocratic powers over labor.

Support the adoption of state laws and interstate compacts to abolish sweatshops and child labor, and to protect women and children with respect to maximum hours, minimum wages and working conditions. We believe that this can be done within the Constitution as it now stands.

AGRICULTURE

The farm problem is an economic and social, not a partisan problem, and we propose to treat it accordingly. Following the wreck of the restrictive and coercive A.A.A., the New Deal Administration has taken to itself the principles of the Republican Policy of soil conservation and land retirement. This action opens the way for a non-political and permanent solution. Such a solution cannot be had under a New Deal Administration which misuses the program to serve partisan ends, to promote scarcity and to limit by coercive methods the farmer's control over his own farm.

Our paramount object is to protect and foster the family type of farm, traditional in American life, and to promote policies which will bring about an adjustment of agriculture to meet the needs of domestic and foreign markets. As an emergency measure, during the agricultural depression, federal benefits payments or grants-in-aid when administered within the means of the Federal government are consistent with a balanced budget.

We propose:

1. To facilitate economical production and increased consumption on a basis of abundance instead of scarcity.

2. A national land-use program, including the acquisition of abandoned and non-productive farm lands by voluntary sale or lease, subject to approval of the legislative and executive branches of the States concerned, and the devotion of such land to appropriate public use, such as watershed protection and flood prevention, reforestation, recreation, and conservation of wild life.

3. That an agricultural policy be pursued for the protection and restoration of the land resources, designed to bring about such a balance between soil-building and soil-depleting crops as will permanently insure productivity, with reasonable benefits to cooperating farmers on family-type farms, but so regulated as to eliminate the New Deal's destructive policy towards the dairy and live-stock industries.

4. To extend experimental aid to farmers developing new crops suited to our soil and climate.

5. To promote the industrial use of farm products by applied science.

6. To protect the American farmer against the importation of all live stock, dairy, and agricultural products, substitutes thereof, and derivatives therefrom, which will depress American farm prices.

7. To provide effective quarantine against imported live-stock, dairy and other farm products from countries which do not impose health and sanitary regulations fully equal to those required of our own producers.

8. To provide for ample farm credit at rates as low as those enjoyed by other industries, including commodity and live-stock loans, and preference in land loans to the farmer acquiring or refinancing a farm as a home.

9. To provide for decentralized, non-partisan control of the Farm Credit Administration and the election by National Farm Loan Associations of at least one-half of each Board of Directors of the Federal Land Banks, and thereby remove these institutions from politics.

10. To provide in the case of agricultural products of which there are exportable surpluses, the payment of reasonable benefits upon the domestically consumed portion of such crops in order to make the tariff effective. These payments are to be limited to the production level of the family type farm.

11. To encourage and further develop co-operative marketing.

12. To furnish Government assistance in disposing of surpluses in foreign trade by bargaining for foreign markets selectively by countries both as to exports and imports. We strenuously oppose so-called reciprocal treaties which trade off the American farmer.

13. To give every reasonable assistance to producers in areas suffering from temporary disaster, so that they may regain and maintain a self-supporting status.

Tariff

Nearly sixty percent of all imports into the United States are now free of duty. The other forty percent of imports compete directly with the product of our industry. We would keep on the free list all products not grown or produced in the United States in commercial quantities. As to all commodities that commercially compete with our farms, our forests, our mines, our fisheries, our oil wells, our labor and our industries, sufficient protection should be maintained at all times to defend the American farmer and the American wage earner from the destructive competition emanating from the subsidies of foreign governments and the imports from low-wage and depreciated-currency countries.

We will repeal the present Reciprocal Trade Agreement Law. It is futile and dangerous. Its effect on agriculture and industry has been de-structive. Its continuation would work to the detriment of the wage earner and the farmer.

We will restore the principle of the flexible tariff in order to meet changing economic conditions here and abroad and broaden by careful definition the powers of the Tariff Commission in order to extend this policy along non-partisan lines.

We will adjust tariffs with a view to promoting international trade, the stabilization of currencies, and the attainment of a proper balance between agriculture and industry.

We condemn the secret negotiations of reciprocal trade treaties without public hearing or legislative approval.

Monopolies

A private monopoly is indefensible and intolerable. It menaces and, if continued, will utterly destroy constitutional government and the liberty of the citizen.

We favor the vigorous enforcement of the criminal laws, as well as the civil laws, against monopolies and trusts and their officials, and we demand the enactment of such additional legislation as is necessary to make it impossible for private monopoly to exist in the United States.

We will employ the full powers of the government to the end that monopoly shall be eliminated and that free enterprise shall be fully restored and maintained.

Regulation of Business

We recognize the existence of a field within which governmental regulation is desirable and salutary. The authority to regulate should be vested in an independent tribunal acting under clear and specific laws establishing definite standards. Their determinations on law and facts should be subject to review by the Courts. We favor Federal regulation, within the Constitution, of the marketing of securities to protect investors. We favor also Federal regulation of the interstate activities of public utilities.

Civil Service

Under the New Deal, official authority has been given to inexperienced and incompetent persons. The Civil Service has been sacrificed to create a national political machine. As a result the Federal

Government has never presented such a picture of confusion and inefficiency.

We pledge ourselves to the merit system, virtually destroyed by New Deal spoilsmen. It should be restored, improved and extended.

We will provide such conditions as offer an attractive permanent career in government service to young men and women of ability, irrespective of party affiliations.

GOVERNMENT FINANCE

The New Deal Administration has been characterized by shameful waste, and general financial irresponsibility. It has piled deficit upon deficit. It threatens national bankruptcy and the destruction through inflation of insurance policies and savings bank deposits.

We pledge ourselves to:

Stop the folly of uncontrolled spending.

Balance the budget—not by increasing taxes but by cutting expenditures, drastically and immediately.

Revise the federal tax system and coordinate it with state and local tax systems.

Use the taxing power for raising revenue and not for punitive or political purposes.

MONEY AND BANKING

We advocate a sound currency to be preserved at all hazards.

The first requisite to a sound and stable currency is a balanced budget.

We oppose further devaluation of the dollar.

We will restore to the Congress the authority lodged with it by the Constitution to coin money and regulate the value thereof by repealing all the laws delegating this authority to the Executive.

We will cooperate with other countries toward stabilization of currencies as soon as we can do so with due regard for our National interests and as soon as other nations have sufficient stability to justify such action.

FOREIGN AFFAIRS

We pledge ourselves to promote and maintain peace by all honorable means not leading to foreign alliances or political commitments.

Obedient to the traditional foreign policy of America and to the repeatedly expressed will of the American people, we pledge that America shall not become a member of the League of Nations nor of the World Court nor shall America take on any entangling alliances in foreign affairs.

We shall promote, as the best means of securing and maintaining peace by the pacific settlement of disputes, the great cause of international arbitration through the establishment of free, independent tribunals, which shall determine such disputes in accordance with law, equity and justice.

NATIONAL DEFENSE

We favor an army and navy, including air forces, adequate for our National Defense.

We will cooperate with other nations in the limitation of armaments and control of traffic in arms.

BILL OF RIGHTS

We pledge ourselves to preserve, protect and defend, against all intimidation and threat, freedom of religion, speech, press and radio; and the right of assembly and petition and immunity from unreasonable searches and seizures.

We offer the abiding security of a government of laws as against the autocratic perils of a government of men.

FURTHERMORE

1. We favor the construction by the Federal Government of head-water storage basins to prevent floods, subject to the approval of the legislative and executive branches of the government of the States whose lands are concerned.

2. We favor equal opportunity for our colored citizens. We pledge our protection of their economic status and personal safety. We will do our best to further their employment in the gainfully occupied life of America, particularly in private industry, agriculture, emergency agencies and the Civil Service.

We condemn the present New Deal policies which would regiment and ultimately eliminate the colored citizen from the country's productive life, and make him solely a ward of the federal government.

3. To our Indian population we pledge every effort on the part of the national government to ameliorate living conditions for them.

4. We pledge continuation of the Republican

policy of adequate compensation and care for veterans disabled in the service of our country and for their widows, orphans and dependents.

5. We shall use every effort to collect the war debt due us from foreign countries, amounting to $12,000,000—one-third of our national debt. No effort has been made by the present administration even to reopen negotiations.

6. We are opposed to legislation which discriminates against women in Federal and State employment.

CONCLUSION

We assume the obligations and duties imposed upon Government by modern conditions. We affirm our unalterable conviction that, in the future as in the past, the fate of the nation will depend, not so much on the wisdom and power of government, as on the character and virtue, self-reliance, industry and thrift of the people and on their willingness to meet the responsibilities essential to the preservation of a free society.

Finally, as our party affirmed in its first Platform in 1856: "Believing that the spirit of our institutions as well as the Constitution of our country guarantees liberty of conscience and equality of rights among our citizens we oppose all legislation tending to impair them," and "we invite the affiliation and cooperation of the men of all parties, however differing from us in other respects, in support of the principles herein declared."

The acceptance of the nomination tendered by the Convention carries with it, as a matter of private honor and public faith, an undertaking by each candidate to be true to the principles and program herein set forth.

Socialist Party Platform Adopted in Cleveland, Ohio, on May 26, 1936

The Socialist Party of the United States pledges itself anew to the task of building a society under which the industries of the country shall be socially owned and democratically managed for the common good; a society under which security, plenty, peace, and freedom shall be the heritage of all.

THE OLD DEAL FAILS

Eight years ago the people of this country voted to continue the capitalist Old Deal. The purpose of this deal was to preserve the rights of the few who own most of the Nation's wealth. Under the Old Deal the economic machine was plunged into the worst depression in our history.

THE NEW DEAL FAILS

Four years ago the voters of the United States threw their support to the New Deal. They elected to office Franklin D. Roosevelt and the Democratic Party. The New Deal, like the Old Deal, has utterly failed. Under it big business was given almost unheard-of powers. Untold wealth was destroyed. Prices rose. Profits advanced. Wages lagged. Twelve million men and women are still jobless, and hunger and destitution exist throughout the land.

Under the New Deal attacks have been made on our civil liberties more vicious than at any period since the days immediately following the World War. Gag and loyalty bills have been rushed through our legislatures. Labor organizers have been seized, kidnapped, maltreated, killed.

The militia has been used to crush attempts of labor to organize. Lynching, race discrimination, and the development of Fascist trends have continued unabated. Against these infringements of human rights the Democratic administration has kept an ominous silence.

Under the New Deal we are now spending on our Army and Navy three times as much as before the World War.

CAPITALISM MEANS INSECURITY

Under the capitalist Old Deal and the capitalist New Deal America has drifted increasingly toward insecurity, suppression, and war.

Insecurity is but the logical result of the workings of capitalism. For under capitalism, new and old, the many work for the owners of the machines and land. The owners will not employ the workers unless they expect to extract a profit. Labor is forced to divide up its earning with the owning group.

With their scanty wages, the workers are able to buy only a part of the goods which they create. Goods pile up. Factories close. Workers are discharged. The country finds itself face to face with another depression.

In the past after a period of hard times we could depend upon the settlement of the West, the development of new foreign markets, and the rapid expansion of our population to revive industry. These forces can no longer be depended upon, as formerly, to keep the system going while our gross and unjust inequality of wealth, our monopoly prices, and our growing debt structure are sowing the seeds of more tragic depressions in the days ahead.

Capitalism Sows Seeds of Dictatorship

Our capitalist system is also sowing the seeds of dictatorship. As unemployment increases under capitalism the masses, to save themselves from starvation, are compelled to make even greater demands on the Government for relief and for public jobs. These demands are resisted by the propertied classes, fearful of higher taxes. Restlessness grows.

Demand for greater appropriations increase. The struggle between the House of Have and the House of Want becomes ever more intense. Big business seeks to deny the masses their constitutional rights. Fascist trends develop, trends that only a powerful and militant labor movement on the economic and political fields can successfully stay.

Capitalism Brings War

Militarism, likewise, under a declining capitalism, becomes an ever greater menace. As unrest increases, the masters of industry seek to use the military forces as the bulwark of reaction at home. They support higher military budgets. They look toward imperialist adventures abroad as a means of diverting attention from the unrest at home, and of gaining new markets, new investment areas, new sources of raw material.

A race begins that can have but one ending— an international war. The Japanese seizure of Manchuria and Italy's invasion of Ethiopia are but examples of the forces at work under capitalism. These adventures may well be the forerunners of another world conflict.

Socialism Provides Only Solution

In socialism and in socialism alone will we find the solution of our problem. Under socialism the socially necessary industries would be socially owned and democratically administered by workers, consumers, and technicians. The farmer working his own farm would be secure in its possession. The workers would no longer be forced to pay tribute to private owners. They would be able to buy back the goods they created.

Socialism and the Good Life

Industry, finding a market for these goods, would run to capacity without periodic breakdowns. Unemployment and the wastes of unplanned industry would cease. Our national income would double or treble. Every useful worker would be assured of high living standards, short hours, freedom of thought and action, and a chance to live the good life. The young would be guaranteed an opportunity for a well-rounded education. The old, the sick, the invalided would be assured the necessaries of life. Industrial autocracy and war would pass. An economy of scarcity would give way to an economy of abundance.

Such a society cannot be obtained without a mighty struggle. That struggle must be made both by workers and farmers, organized on the economic and political fields and dedicated to the creation of a cooperative commonwealth.

In their fight for power and socialism the workers and farmer must gain new strength and unity by their daily struggle against poverty and exploitation. To improve the conditions of life and labor and thereby to weld together the strength and solidarity of the masses, the Socialist Party pledges itself to fight for a number of immediate proposals in legislative halls and side by side with labor in field and factory and office.

1. Constitutional changes

We propose the adaptation of the Constitution to the needs of the times through the farmers' and workers' rights amendment, ending the usurped power of the Supreme Court to declare social legislation unconstitutional and reaffirming the right of Congress to acquire and operate industries. We also propose to change the Constitution so as to make future amendments less difficult and pledge our continued support of the child-labor amendment.

2. Social ownership

We propose the social ownership and democratic control of mines, railroads, the power industry, and other key industries and the recognition of public industries of the right of collective bargaining.

3. Relief, insurance, jobs

We propose an immediate appropriation by Congress of $6,000,000,000 to continue Federal relief to the unemployed for the coming year; the continuance of W. P. A. projects at union wages; the inauguration of a public-housing program for the elimination of the Nation's slums and the building of modern homes for the workers at rents they can afford to pay; a Federal system of unemployment insurance and of old-age pensions for persons 60 years of age and over, with contributions for such social-insurance systems to be raised from taxes on incomes and inheritances, as provided in the Frazier-Lundeen bill; and adequate medical care of the sick and injured as a social duty, not as a private or public charity. Such services should be financed by taxation and should be democratically administered.

4. Youth

We propose the passage of the American Youth Act to meet the immediate educational and economic needs of young people; adequate Federal appropriations for public schools and free city colleges with a view to making possible a full education for all young people; and the abolition of the C. C. C., the National Youth Administration and other governmental agencies dealing with the youth problem which threaten the wage and the living standards of organized labor.

5. Taxation

We propose a drastic increase of income and inheritance taxes on the higher income levels and of excess-profits taxes and wide experimentation in land-value taxation.

6. Labor legislation

We propose the establishment of the 30-hour week; the abolition of injunctions in labor disputes; the prohibition of company unions, company spying, and private guards and gunmen; and the prohibition of the use of police, deputy sheriffs, and militia and Federal troops in labor disputes.

7. Agriculture

We propose the abolition of tenant and corporation farming and the substitution of the use-and-occupancy title for family-sized farms and the conversion of plantations and corporation farms into cooperative farms. We propose that the marketing, processing, and distribution of farm products be taken over by bona-fide cooperatives and other agencies to be created for this purpose. We propose that farm prices be stabilized at cost of production to the working farmer, such stabilization to be made by representatives of organized working farmers and consumers.

While these changes are taking place we urge:

a. That immediate relief be provided for debt-laden working farmers by advancing Government credit on such terms as do not threaten the farmer with the loss of his farm.

b. That social insurance be provided against crop failures.

8. Civil liberties

We urge the abolition of all laws that interfere with the right of free speech, free press, free assembly, and the peaceful activities of labor in its struggle for organization and power; the enforcement of constitutional guaranties of economic, political, legal, and social equality for the Negro and all other oppressed minorities; and the enactment and enforcement of a Federal antilynching law.

9. Militarism and war

Not a penny, not a man to the military arms of the Government. We reaffirm our opposition to any war engaged in by the American Government. We propose the elimination of military training from our schools; the abandonment of imperialistic adventures of a military or economic nature abroad; the maintenance of friendly relations with Soviet Russia; and the strengthening of neutrality laws, to the end that we may ward off immediate wars while fighting for the attainment of a social order which will eliminate the chief causes of war.

10. Cooperation

We recognize the importance of the consumers' cooperative movement, though realizing that it alone cannot be depended upon to achieve a Socialist cooperative commonwealth. We urge the Socialist and the organized-labor movement to give their support to consumers' cooperatives to the end that it may become a valuable auxiliary to labor on the economic and political fields, and that it may help lay the foundation for a new economic order. We urge the encouragement by the Federal Government by every legitimate means of genuine consumers' cooperation.

The Socialist Party calls upon the workers, farmers, and all advocates of social justice to join with it in its struggle to widen the channels through which may be made peaceful, orderly, and democratic progress; to resist all trends toward insecurity, fascism, and war; to strengthen labor in its battles for better conditions, and for increasing power; to refuse to support the parties of capitalism, or any of their candidates, and to unite with it in its historic struggle toward a cooperative world.

Platform of the Socialist Labor Party

The capitalist system has outlived its usefulness. If progress is to be the order of society in the future as in the past, this outworn system MUST give way to a new social order. Social development points in but one direction—to an Industrial Union Government, an administration of things in place of a political rule over men.

The avowed purpose of governments is to insure life, liberty, and the pursuit of happiness to the useful members of society. Whenever a given social system, and its corresponding government, fails in or becomes destructive of these ends, it has outlived its usefulness, rendering it imperative for the exploited and oppressed class to organize its forces to put an end to the outworn economic and political system. This historic duty and necessity now confront the working class of America.

Social systems and their corresponding forms of government come into being as results of social and economic forces. The history of mankind has been the history of class struggles, with Progress ever as the aim. Ancient autocracies fell before ancient republics, the slave labor systems gave way to feudalism, feudalism broke down before the onslaught of capitalism. Capitalism, with its concomitant—wage slavery—is the world system which has been the vanguard of progress through the eighteenth and nineteenth centuries. In the United States of America capitalism has reached the highest point of development; here also may be traced the most rapid decay.

When a ruling class can no longer live and exploit as previously, and the exploited class can no longer be fed and cared for while rendering useful social service, *the hour of Social Revolution has struck*.

At this crucial period, accordingly, the Socialist Labor Party, in National Convention assembled, April 27, 1936, reaffirms its former platform pronouncements and, in accord with international Socialist principles, declares:

For close to a decade now, millions of the working class have had to be fed by the exploiting masters, instead of, as heretofore, feeding and keeping the masters in luxury. The richest country in the world, with the highest degree of productivity in the world, has been turned into a gigantic poorhouse, with vast numbers of its useful and able workers turned into mendicants, suppliants for a handout to keep body and soul together. History's pages record no greater disgrace than this.

A decaying system creates nothing so surely as its own gravediggers. The germs of destruction are active within American capitalism. Competition is the very life of capitalism; markets constitute the indispensable condition for its continued existence.

The early termination of capitalism was clearly indicated when the fact was revealed that a few giant corporations virtually control the entire production and distribution machinery of the nation. "Rugged individualism" has gone by the board. There is no possibility for the "average man" to become a capitalist. The small farmer, the small manufacturer, and the business man with small capital who still hangs on, are perpetually on the verge of bankruptcy. In most cases the farmer is but a tenant farmer or a "sharecropper" working for some banking house; the small business man is but a repair man or an agent of some large corporation.

The markets, foreign and domestic, are becoming extinct. A social system will flourish only while there is room within it for expansion. The possibilities for expansion in the United States of America seemed unlimited during its first 150 years. Ships, canals, railroads, bridges, roads, farms, machinery of all sorts were the crying need of expanding and progressing capitalism. This called for millions of workers, skilled and unskilled, in mines, mills, factories, on railroads, on the land, in shops, stores, offices and the technical trades. This, in turn, opened a tremendous market for other commodities — houses, furniture, clothing, food, and the so-called public service industries. "Prosperity" ruled; capitalism was in its full flower.

With the beginning of the twentieth century reaction had already set in. The frontier had gone; internal improvements were approaching a limit and commenced to slacken; American capitalism for a decade had been on a sharp look-out for foreign markets. The era of imperialism was at hand.

In the world market America encountered Great Britain, a formidable rival, the erstwhile "workshop of the world." Germany, France, Japan were stepping up, with Italy and Russia in the offing. The World War brought the rivals together with a clash. World expansion turned into a battle of "survival of the fittest," with every one struggling with the view of destruction of all rivals. The *progress* of capitalism had stopped; decay and degeneration had definitely set in.

There was one avenue, however, where progress under capitalism DID NOT STOP, for that avenue and that alone leads to the future, viz., the invention and perfection of machinery. The World War gave this a tremendous impetus which has not relaxed since. As a result, production is keyed up tremendously. The increased productive capacity of the system demands more markets, and when no markets are forthcoming, the abundance of products results in social degeneration and decay.

To bolster up market prices by creating artificial scarcity, millions of dollars' worth of products have been destroyed—plowed under, or allowed to rot, or burnt or dumped in the ocean—and this was done while millions of workers were poorly housed, underfed and insufficiently clothed. Decay and degeneration of a social system cannot go further than that.

Ever more and better machinery is the demand of capitalism. As the machines go into a factory, the workers go out. Millions of those who are unemployed today will never again under capitalism have regular, useful employment.

The Socialist Revolutionary hour in America is at hand. For forty-five years the Socialist Labor Party has been moving upward to this historic opportunity. The working class of America cannot afford to, must not, at the peril of its own existence, and that of future generations, allow to slip by this moment of opportunity to free the world from wage slavery.

Where a social revolution is pending and, for whatever reason, is not accomplished, reaction is the alternative. Every reform granted by capitalism is a concealed measure of reaction, exemplified by the NRA, AAA, TVA, CCC, WPA, etc.

He who says reform says preservation, and he who says that reforms under capitalism are possible and worth while thereby declares that a continuation of capitalism is possible and worth while. But capitalism has grown into an all-destroying and all-devouring monster that must itself be destroyed if humanity is to live. Fascism, Nazism, Absolutism in government — in short, Industrial Feudalism—are but means in the attempts to preserve capitalism.

American capitalism, along with capitalism in the rest of the world today, is trembling in the balance between decay or progress, reaction or revolution. THIS IS THE HISTORIC HOUR OF THE AMERICAN WORKING CLASS.

The class struggle, which rages today, is destined to be the last. There is no exploited or enslaved class below that of the exploited working class. When the workers take possession of the government and the social means of production, they are bound to do so in the name of society as a whole. That means the abolition of all classes, the abolition of private property and the inauguration of a Socialist Industrial Republic, where the means of production will be the collective property of society, operated by all able workers, for the benefit of all. Social or collective ownership —administered by an Industrial Union Government of, by and for the workers—of the already socially operated means of production will be the fulfillment of the promise implicit in social evolution throughout the ages!

At this crucial moment in history, the Socialist Labor Party of America, earnestly and deliberately, calls upon the working class of America to rally at the polls under the banner of the Socialist Labor Party, the only Party with a program that meets the needs of the hour, i.e., a progressive and revolutionary program.

The Socialist Labor Party also calls upon all other intelligent citizens to place themselves squarely upon the ground of working class interests, and join in this mighty and noble work of human emancipation, so that we may put summary end to the existing barbarous class conflict and insane contradictions between unlimited wealth and wealth production, and the poverty and wretchedness suffered by those whose labor created all this wealth.

We, therefore, call upon the workers of America to organize into Socialist Revolutionary Industrial Unions in shop, mine, mill and factory, and on the land, to provide a lever to place the land and the means of production and distribution in the hands of the useful producers as a body organized into a national Industrial Union Administration to take the place of the present outworn political or territorial government.

So shall come into being the Socialist Industrial Commonwealth of Emancipated Labor—a commonwealth in which every worker shall have the free exercise and full benefit of his faculties, multiplied by all the factors of modern civilization.

Union Party Platform of 1936

1. America shall be self-contained and self-sustained—no foreign entanglements, be they political, economic, financial or military.

2. Congress and Congress alone shall coin and issue the currency and regulate the value of all money and credit in the United States through a central bank of issue.

3. Immediately following the establishment of the central bank of issue Congress shall provide for the retirement of all tax-exempt, interest-bearing bonds and certificates of indebtedness of the Federal Government and shall refinance all the present agricultural mortgage indebtedness for the farmer and all the home mortgage indebtedness for the farmer and all the home mortgage indebtedness for the city owner by the use of its money and credit which it now gives to the private bankers.

4. Congress shall legislate that there will be an assurance of a living annual wage for all laborers capable of working and willing to work.

5. Congress shall legislate that there will be an assurance of production at a profit for the farmer.

6. Congress shall legislate that there will be assurance of reasonable and decent security for the aged, who, through no fault of their own, have been victimized and exploited by an unjust economic system which has so concentrated wealth in the hands of a few that it has impoverished great masses of our people.

7. Congress shall legislate that American agricultural, industrial, and commercial markets will be protected from manipulation of foreign moneys and from all raw material and processed goods produced abroad at less than a living wage.

8. Congress shall establish an adequate and perfect defense for our country from foreign aggression either by air, by land, or by sea, but with the understanding that our naval, air, and military forces must not be used under any consideration in foreign fields or in foreign waters either alone or in conjunction with any foreign power. If there must be conscription, there shall be a conscription of wealth as well as a conscription of men.

9. Congress shall so legislate that all Federal offices and positions of every nature shall be distributed through civil-service qualifications and not through a system of party spoils and corrupt patronage.

10. Congress shall restore representative government to the people of the United States to preserve the sovereignty of the individual States of the United States by the ruthless eradication of bureaucracies.

11. Congress shall organize and institute Federal works for the conservation of public lands, waters, and forests, thereby creating billions of dollars of wealth, millions of jobs at the prevailing wage, and thousands of homes.

12. Congress shall protect small industry and private enterprise by controlling and decentralizing the economic domination of monopolies to the end that these small industries and enterprises may not only survive and prosper but that they may be multiplied.

13. Congress shall protect private property from confiscation through unnecessary taxation with the understanding that the human rights of the masses take precedence over the financial rights of the classes.

14. Congress shall set a limitation upon the net income of any individual in any one year and a limitation of the amount that such an individual may receive as a gift or as an inheritance, which limitation shall be executed through taxation.

15. Congress shall reestablish conditions so that the youths of the Nation, as they emerge from schools and colleges, will have the opportunity to earn a decent living while in the process of perfecting and establishing themselves in a trade or profession.

☒ CAMPAIGN OF 1940

In 1940 there were, in addition to the two major parties, four well-established minor parties, the Socialist Party, the Prohibition Party, the Communist Party, and the Socialist Labor Party. In this election, the minor parties received approximately one-half of one per cent of the votes cast.

Communist Platform of 1940

The life, liberty and the pursuit of happiness of the American people are now endangered as never before since our revolutionary forefathers one hundred and sixty-four years ago proclaimed these rights to be inalienable for all mankind.

For the flower of American youth, the right to life itself is challenged by those who claim the privilege to conscript them and to throw them into reactionary wars for the benfit of the propertied classes.

For the American people as a whole, their liberty is challenged by projects of conscription of even the civilian population, of tens of millions of workers of factories and farms—ostensibly for the security of the country, but really for the purpose of setting aside the sacred guarantees of our Bill of Rights and placing the civilian population under military law, to free the hands of ruling financiers for military adventures and conquest abroad.

For our country, as for the peoples of all the world, the pursuit of happiness can be realized only with work, with security against unemployment, against poverty in old age, with guaranteed education for the youth—and with a genuine policy of peace. But with 11,000,000 Americans unemployed, the Democratic Party Administration is sacrificing all social legislation, unemployment relief, unemployment and old-age insurance, and educational guarantees for the youth, in order to pour all resources of the nation as well as the blood of our people into the scramble of monopoly capital for domination of the world.

WALL STREET WANTS WAR

The predatory war unleashed by the imperialist ruling classes of Berlin, London, Paris, Rome and Tokyo is a worldwide struggle for the division of the world among imperialist bandits—a struggle for the right of capitalist imperialist exploitation of the world by sacrificing the freedom of all peoples and the national independence of all nations.

Therefore the richest and most predatory of international bankers and trust heads of the whole world—those of Wall Street—are determined to enter into this worldwide, military contest in order to claim for themselves a share in proportion to their gigantic wealth. While their war profits pile high they deliberately seek to prolong the war and feverishly prepare to enter it. They have already transformed our country into an arsenal for one side of the predatory European conflict, and into a chief source of war materials for the Japanese adventures in Asia — thus making the United States, while still a non-belligerent, nevertheless a participant in the worldwide military conflict.

The warmongers of Wall Street are feverishly

preparing to establish through military might the exclusive role of American finance capital over the two American continents at the sacrifice of the independence of twenty republics of Latin America. They are striving to strengthen their imperialist positions in China and aim toward control of the Dutch East Indies (Indonesia) in struggle for mastery of the Pacific.

Aspiring for world domination, the American finance capitalists strive to drag the American people into the European war on the side of Great Britain. They work for a continuation and extension of that war and share guilt for the fate of those countries already conquered in Europe, Asia and Africa. But the same American imperialists have not closed the door to possible temporary agreements with the German and Japanese conquerors for establishment of the "new orders" in Europe and Asia, if only the terms be advantageous to the bankers of Wall Street.

Just as the American imperialists applauded and supported the betrayal of the democracy of Europe in the Pact of Munich, so are they ready now, on the promise of a gain to themselves, to betray the people of the United States, the peoples of the twenty Latin American republics, and those of Asia and of all of Europe and Africa to new imperialist agreements—if only they can secure their monopolist domination through the suppression of American democracy under blanket conscription and M-Day laws.

The Democratic and Republican parties—twin parties of the financiers of Wall Street—are seeking in this election to goad the people into a war hysteria, into panic and confusion, and to induce the people to agree to a surrender of constitutional democracy to a virtual military dictatorship in time of peace. All war plans are dressed in the disguise of peace plans. All plans for dangerous military adventures are given the gentle name of "national security." All projects for military aggression are entitled "national defense plans." All imperialist ventures for subjecting the Latin American republics are entitled "protecting the Western Hemisphere." Every prospective imperialist venture and "Munich" arrangement designed to throw the American people into war and to sacrifice the independence of Latin American peoples are brought forward under slogans of "peace" and "democracy" as was the treaty of Munich.

The People Want Peace

All domestic policies defended or proposed in this election by the Democratic and Republican parties are domestic policies subordinated to and completely dominated by the common purpose of American finance capital, the economic royalists, to plunge this country into a worldwide military struggle for conquest. This fundamental and decisive agreement between the Sixty Families of Wall Street that control both the Democratic and Republican parties, on a foreign policy of aggressive and militaristic imperialism, has brought the Democratic and the Republican parties to strangely harmonious positions on domestic policies. Both have common class interests and objectives. The differences between the two parties arise from specific secondary rivalries and conflicts among great financial interests, as to division of the spoils, as well as from the traditional rivalry between the Ins and the Outs, and from partisan bureaucratic interests incidental to the two-party system of American capitalism.

The bogus Socialist Party and other Social-Democratic groups and leaders, like their counterparts in Europe, Blum, Citrine and Tanner, play the role of treacherous agents of the warmongers in labor's ranks. They beat the drums for war and strive to paralyze labor toward this goal, they lead the reactionary pack for a "holy crusade" against the land of socialism and peace, the Soviet Union. They perform a special task for reaction in its assault upon the democratic rights of our people.

The top leadership of the A. F. of L., the Hillman wing of the C. I. O. leadership and the leadership of the Railroad Brotherhoods have committed themselves to the "defense" program of the Roosevelt Administration and are attempting to subordinate the labor movement to Wall Street's war program.

All these parties are in opposition to the will of the majority of the American people. The overwhelming majority of our people are opposed to the entrance of our country into this predatory war. The overwhelming majority stand for the preservation and enlarging of social and progressive legislation, for unemployment insurance, old-age pensions, public works, farmer and youth aid, and for full civil liberties.

Only the Communist Party, among the political parties participating in the 1940 elections, fights on the side of and in harmony with the deepest desires of the majority of the people. The Communist Party alone of all political parties fights against the imperialist war, combats its prolongation and spread, and seeks to bring an end to the war.

Only the Communist Party opposes the imperialist policies of the economic royalists, their government and parties. The Communist Party is for a people's peace, and opposed to an imperialist peace based upon terror, annexations and oppression.

We want to keep our country out of the imperialist war. We want to ensure jobs and social security for all. We want to protect the Bill of Rights. We are opposed to imperialist ventures abroad, against M-Day plans and the militarization of our country.

The economic royalists once again have full domination over the Republican and Democratic parties.

In the name of "national unity" and "national defense" the Roosevelt Democrats have surrendered to the economic royalists. The ruling class is attempting to suppress the people's opposition to its war program through terror, attacks upon organized labor and with vicious alien and sedition laws.

The Roosevelt Democrats make every effort to retain support of the people on grounds of progressive labor and social legislation enacted in the past seven years, but the Roosevelt Administration has thrown overboard even the meager popular gains of the New Deal and has embraced the program of the Liberty League which was roundly rejected by the people in the 1936 election. This has been done on the ground that all national resources must be poured into war preparations, and in order to put through this unpopular war they find it necessary to fight the people's demands.

While playing for popular support with ambiguous phrases about differences, the Willkie-Hoover Republicans have joined hands with the reactionary Democratic Party leadership in championing the pro-war foreign policy and undemocratic domestic measures of the Roosevelt Administration. Republican advocacy of the interests of Wall Street may be more open and outspoken, but it is not more effective than that of the Roosevelt Democrats.

The gains which labor and the American people won by organization and struggle during the New Deal period are now under a concerted attack.

After eight years of New Deal "liberalism," just as in 1933 after twelve years of Republican "rugged individualism," the misery and poverty of the working people under capitalism is growing.

Eleven million Americans are denied the right to work. A huge armaments program for imperialist conquest and war has been substituted for the former meager work and relief program.

Millions of small farmers, sharecroppers and tenant farmers are impoverished, and are being driven from their land by banks and insurance companies, and by the Federal and state governments.

Big business strives to crush the labor and anti-war movements by F. B. I. and Dies Committee persecutions, by attacks upon the National Labor Relations Act, the Wages and Hours Law and through a renewed open-shop offensive.

The youth of America, deprived of a decent education and the right to work, face conscription and being turned into cannon fodder by the merchants of death.

The Negro people, most exploited of the toilers, suffering from lynching and Jim Crowism, robbed of their constitutional rights, are being prepared to fight another war for "democracy" in order to further enslave them.

Millions of innocent and industrious foreign-born immigrants, who have given their all to the development of America, are being harassed and persecuted with fingerprinting and registration as if common criminals.

Wall Street girds for war by striving to destroy the Bill of Rights, by attacking the civil rights of Communists and other anti-war fighters, by promoting red-baiting, labor disunity and religious prejudices, by smearing as "fifth columnists" and "foreign agents" all who love peace, liberty and democracy.

This is the plight of the common people under the rule of the Sixty Families. This is the type of "democracy" represented by the Democratic and Republican parties.

A People's Program

In this grave hour of crisis, the Communist Party calls upon the working class and toilers to close ranks, organize and unite around a common program of action to protect and advance the peace, liberties and welfare of our people, to defend the interests of our nation, the interests of the American people.

The Communist Party calls upon all opponents of imperialist war and capitalist reaction to establish unity of action, under labor's leadership, around a people's program to defend our country, for peace, jobs, security and civil liberties. Towards this end the Communist Party enters the election campaign with the following program of action:

KEEP AMERICA OUT OF THE IMPERIALIST WAR!

HALT THE WAR PREPARATIONS AND IMPERIALIST ADVENTURES OF WALL STREET AND THE GOVERNMENT!

AGAINST THE MILITARIZATION OF THE NATION!

FOR A PEOPLE'S PEACE!

1. Combat the imperialist policies and acts of the President, the State Department, Congress, the Democratic and Republican parties to spread the war and involve the United States in it. No aid to the imperialist war-makers in London, Berlin, Tokyo, Rome or to their satellites. Oppose all war loans and credits to the warring imperialist powers. Stop the sale and shipment of munitions and armaments to the imperialist belligerents.

2. Defeat Wall Street's imperialist policy of economic and political domination, and miltary adventures in Latin America, China, and the Dutch East Indies (Indonesia). Full solidarity with the anti-imperialist struggles of the peoples of Mexico, Cuba, and all other Latin American countries. For the immediate and complete national independence of the Philippines and Puerto Rico. Maximum support for the great Chinese people in their heroic struggle for national liberation. Halt the anti-Soviet policies and incitements of the government and Wall Street. For friendship and collaboration for peace between the two great peoples of the United States and the Soviet Union.

3. No armaments or American soldiers for imperialist wars or adventures. Democratize the armed forces. Protect the freedom and independence of the trade unions. Make the rich pay the costs of the war preparations and the economic crisis for which they are responsible. Fight against war profiteering.

4. Against a peace of "appeasement." Against an imperialist peace of violence and oppression. For solidarity with and support to the peoples in the warring nations in their struggle for a democratic people's peace.

PROTECT AND EXTEND CIVIL LIBERTIES!

FULL RIGHTS FOR THE NEGRO PEOPLE!

1. For the unrestricted freedom of speech, press, radio, assembly and worship, and the full right to organize, strike and picket. Defeat the anti-labor drive under the Sherman anti-trust law. Pass the La-Follette-Thomas Oppressive Labor Practices Bill without reactionary amendments. Stop the attacks upon labor by the F. B. I. and the Department of Justice.

2. Pass the Geyer Anti-Poll Tax Bill to give the vote to the Negro and white masses in the South. For full civil rights and the right to vote for all men in the armed services, migratory workers and seafaring men.

3. Guarantee the Negro people complete equality, equal rights to jobs, equal pay for equal work, the full right to organize, serve on juries and hold public office. Pass the Anti-Lynching Bill. Demand the death penalty for lynchers. Enforce the 13th, 14th and 15th Amendments to the United States Constitution.

4. End the dictatorial powers of the Dies and other Congressional anti-labor investigating committees. Repeal the vicious anti-alien and sedition laws that are a blot on the statute books of a free people. Put an end to anti-Semitism. Guarantee the traditional American right of asylum to all victims of imperialist war and oppression, especially to the refugees from Franco Spain.

5. Guarantee the civil rights and freedom of action of labor, including the Communists, and all other anti-war, anti-imperialist organizations. Against all reactionary measures requiring the registration, incorporation or Federal control of working class political organizations, trade unions and other popular organizations. For the freedom of all working class political prisoners now languishing in Federal and state prisons. Defend the Bill of Rights against the reactionaries and warmakers.

JOBS, SECURITY AND AN AMERICAN STANDARD OF LIVING FOR ALL TOILERS!

PROTECT THE FARMERS FROM WALL STREET!

PROTECT THE RIGHTS AND INTERESTS OF THE AMERICAN YOUTH!

CURB THE MONOPOLISTS!

1. For the organization of the unorganized. For higher wages and the thirty-hour week without reduction in pay. For equal rights for Negro workers, the foreign born, women and youth labor. Abolish the wage differential between North and South. Abolish child labor. Cancel all government orders to those employers who fail to comply with labor legislation.

2. For a Federal housing program providing for building a minimum of a million homes annually for the low-income groups. Expand W. P. A. to provide work for all unemployed with a minimum of 3,000,000 jobs to be provided immediately on socially beneficial projects, at union wage rates. Increase the present wage scale by 30 percent and make as minimum payment for any classification $70 monthly. Extend unemployment insurance to cover domestic, agricultural and all wage earners not now covered by the law. Increase minimum benefit payments to $10 weekly. Increase maximum payments from one-half to two-thirds of wages earned. Extend the period of unemployment compensation payments from the present maximum of thirteen weeks to twenty-six weeks.

3. Establish an *old-age pension* system providing $60 monthly for all over sixty. Enact an adequate Federal health program and a system of maternity insurance. Guarantee free education to all youth and children, Negro and white, by extending Federal and state appropriations.

4. Guarantee to all farmers their land, equipment, and livestock free from seizure. Free the working farmers and sharecroppers from debt, tax burdens and foreclosures. Provide a high homestead tax-exemption and heavier taxes on large farms. For a Homestead Act for Today to return all lands confiscated by the Federal, state, and local governments, by the banks and insurance companies to all small farmers, tenants and sharecroppers dispossessed from the land and who wish to engage in farming. Develop an adequate program of tenant rehabilitation, soil conservation and drought relief. Guarantee the cost of production to the family-sized farm. Provide Federal funds for direct farm relief so that no farm family shall lack the necessities of life. Establish a ten-year debt moratorium for the small-income farmers.

5. Extend the N. Y. A. and the C. C. C. under civilian control and on civilian projects at trade union standards. Adopt the American Youth Act.

6. Prosecute the trusts and monopolies for profiteering, monopoly practices, nullifying labor legislation, evading taxes and violating the laws of the land. Establish a heavy excess profits tax and a steeply graduated income tax on the higher brackets. Abolish tax-exempt securities. Confiscate all war profits. Repeal the provisions of the new tax laws hitting the low-income groups. Abolish all direct and indirect taxes on articles of mass consumption.

For a National Farmer-Labor Party

This is an anti-imperialist program of struggle for peace, real national defense, and social security. It can be realized by labor and the toiling people through organization and united struggle, by building and strengthening the trade unions and other progressive organizations of labor, and by promoting independent political action of labor and the common people, leading towards the building up of a united mass party—a national Farmer-Labor Party, an anti-imperialist third party of the people.

The struggle for such a united people's party for peace, security and civil liberties can be actively promoted in the November elections by voting for and supporting the Communist Party. It can be effectively developed by establishing unity of action by the workers in all unions and industries in defense of their immediate economic and political demands. It can be strengthened by supporting tested anti-war and labor candidates for Congress and state legislatures.

Capitalism has brought our people only tyranny, hunger, degradation and war. Capitalism has given us an ever-deepening crisis, with millions permanently unemployed. Capitalism is destroying the cultural achievements and constitutional guarantees of freedom provided in the Bill of Rights. Under capitalism the people face a hopeless future. Only when capitalism is abolished, when socialism is established, as today in the U. S. S. R., will there be no wars, no unemployment, no social retrogression. Under socialism there will be abundance and security for the toiling people. To make our country really free, united and prosperous—to make it possible for all the people to benefit from the tremendous resources of our country—demands a new social order in which the national economy will belong to the people—a socialist society. Only in a nation free from its monopoly and financial overlords and freed of bondage to the few who have seized its wealth and oppress its people can our people live and flourish.

The Communist Party fights for the immediate interests of the working class, as well as its socialist future. We pledge to continue our struggle for our socialist aim, the common goal of all progressive mankind, already triumphant over one-sixth of the earth.

Vote Communist!

Workers! Toilers! The Democratic Party is the party of the Roosevelts and Dies, of the Garners and Woodrums, of the du Ponts and Cromwells, of the Boss Hagues and Kelleys, of Tammany and K. K. K. It is the party of "liberal" promises and reactionary deeds.

The Republican Party is the party of the Willkies and Hoovers, the Vandenbergs and Fords, of the Insulls, Weirs and Girdlers. It is the party of the Associated Farmers and the open shoppers.

The Morgans, Rockefellers and du Ponts are the Interlocking Directorate and Holding Company of both the Democratic and Republican parties. That is why *both* parties are war parties, M-Day parties, parties of imperialism, reaction and hunger.

This is why labor and the people cannot and must not vote for nor support the Democratic or the Republican parties, or their little brother, the Socialist Party.

This is why the working class and toilers should vote for and support the Communist Party.

A vote for the Communist Party is a vote against the imperialist war, against Wall Street's imperialist adventures and war preparations, for safeguarding the peace of America and defending the national interests of the American people.

A vote for the Communist Party is a vote for peace, freedom and socialism. Vote Communist! Vote for Browder and Ford!

Democratic Platform of 1940

Preamble

The world is undergoing violent change. Humanity, uneasy in this machine age, is demanding a sense of security and dignity based on human values.

No democratic government which fails to recognize this trend—and take appropriate action—can survive.

That is why the Government of this nation has moved to keep ahead of this trend; has moved with speed incomprehensible to those who do not see this trend.

Outside the Americas, established institutions are being overthrown and democratic philosophies are being repudiated by those whose creed recognizes no power higher than military force, no values other than a false efficiency.

What the founding fathers realized upon this continent was a daring dream, that men could have not only physical security, not only efficiency, but something else in addition that men had never had before—the security of the heart that comes with freedom, the peace of mind that comes from a sense of justice.

To this generation of Americans it is given to defend this democratic faith as it is challenged by social maladjustment within and totalitarian greed without. The world revolution against which we prepare our defense is so threatening that not until it has burned itself out in the last corner of the earth will our democracy be able to relax its guard.

In this world crisis, the purpose of the Democratic Party is to defend against external attack and justify by internal progress the system of government and way of life from which the Democratic Party takes its name.

Fulfilling American Ideal

Toward the modern fulfillment of the American ideal, the Democratic Party, during the last seven years, has labored successfully:

1. *To strengthen democracy by defensive preparedness against aggression, whether by open attack or secret infiltration;*

2. *To strengthen democracy by increasing our economic efficiency; and*

3. *To strengthen democracy by improving the welfare of the people.*

These three objectives are one and inseparable. No nation can be strong by armaments alone. It must possess and use all the necessary resources for producing goods plentifully and distributing them effectively. It must add to these factors of material strength the unconquerable spirit and energy of a contented people, convinced that there are no boundaries to human progress and happiness in a land of liberty.

Our faith that these objectives can be attained is made unshakable by what has already been done by the present Administration—in stopping the waste and exploitation of our human and natural resources, in restoring to the average man and woman a stake in the preservation of our democracy, in enlarging our national armaments, and in achieving national unity.

We shall hold fast to these gains. We are proud of our record. Therefore the Party in convention assembled endorses wholeheartedly the brilliant and courageous leadership of President Franklin D. Roosevelt and his statesmanship and that of the Congress for the past seven trying years. And to our President and great leader we send our cordial greetings.

WE MUST STRENGTHEN DEMOCRACY AGAINST AGGRESSION

The American people are determined that war, raging in Europe, Asia and Africa, shall not come to America.

We will not participate in foreign wars, and we will not send our army, naval or air forces to fight in foreign lands outside of the Americas, except in case of attack. We favor and shall rigorously enforce and defend the Monroe Doctrine.

The direction and aim of our foreign policy has been, and will continue to be, the security and defense of our own land and the maintenance of its peace.

For years our President has warned the nation that organized assaults against religion, democracy and international good faith threatened our own peace and security. Men blinded by partisanship brushed aside these warnings as war-mongering and officious intermeddling. The fall of twelve nations was necessary to bring their belated approval of legislative and executive action that the President had urged and undertaken with the full support of the people. It is a tribute to the President's foresight and action that our defense forces are today at the peak of their peacetime effectiveness.

Weakness and unpreparedness invite aggression. We must be so strong that no possible combination of powers would dare to attack us. We propose to provide America with an invincible air force, a navy strong enough to protect all our seacoasts and our national interests, and a fully-equipped and mechanized army. We shall continue to coordinate these implements of defense with the necessary expansion of industrial productive capacity and with the training of appropriate personnel. Outstanding leaders of industry and labor have already been enlisted by the Government to harness our mighty economic forces for national defense.

Experience of other nations gives warning that total defense is necessary to repel attack, and that partial defense is no defense.

We have seen the downfall of nations accomplished through internal dissension provoked from without. We denounce and will do all in our power to destroy the treasonable activities of disguised anti-democratic and un-American agencies which would sap our strength, paralyze our will to defend ourselves, and destroy our unity by inciting race against race, class against class, religion against religion and the people against their free institutions.

To make America strong, and to keep America free, every American must give of his talents and treasure in accordance with his ability and his country's needs. We must have democracy of sacrifice as well as democracy of opportunity.

To insure that our armaments shall be implements of peace rather than war, we shall continue our traditional policies of the good neighbor; observe and advocate international respect for the rights of others and for treaty obligations; cultivate foreign trade through desirable trade agreements; and foster economic collaboration with the Republics of the Western Hemisphere.

In self-defense and in good conscience, the world's greatest democracy cannot afford heartlessly or in a spirit of appeasement to ignore the peace-loving and liberty-loving peoples wantonly attacked by ruthless aggressors. We pledge to extend to these peoples all the material aid at our command, consistent with law and not inconsistent with the interests of our own national self-defense —all to the end that peace and international good faith may yet emerge triumphant.

We do not regard the need for preparedness a warrant for infringement upon our civil liberties, but on the contrary we shall continue to protect them, in the keen realization that the vivid contrast between the freedom we enjoy and the dark repression which prevails in the lands where liberty is dead, affords warning and example to our people to confirm their faith in democracy.

WE MUST STRENGTHEN DEMOCRACY BY INCREASING OUR ECONOMIC EFFICIENCY

The well-being of the land and those who work upon it is basic to the real defense and security of America.

The Republican Party gives its promises to the farmer and its allegiance to those who exploit him.

Since 1932 farm income has been doubled; *six million* farmers, representing more than 80 per cent of all farm families, have participated in an effective soil conservation program; the farm debt and the interest rate on farm debt have been reduced, and farm foreclosures have been drastically curtailed; rural highways and farm-to-market roads have been vastly improved and extended; the surpluses on the farms have been used to feed the needy; low cost electricity has been brought to five million farm people as a result of the rural electrification program; thousands of impoverished farm families have been rehabilitated; and steps have been taken to stop the alarming growth of farm tenancy, to increase land ownership, and to mitigate the hardships of migratory farm labor.

The Land and the Farmer

We pledge ourselves

To make parity as well as soil conservation payments until such time as the goal of parity income for agriculture is realized.

To extend and enlarge the tenant-purchase program until every deserving tenant farmer has a real opportunity to have a farm of his own.

To refinance existing farm debts at lower interest rates and on longer and more flexible terms.

To continue to provide for adjustment of production through democratic processes to the extent that excess surpluses are capable of control.

To continue the program of rehabilitation of farmers who need and merit aid.

To preserve and strengthen the ever-normal granary on behalf of the national defense, the consumer at home and abroad, and the American farmer.

To continue to make commodity loans to maintain the ever-normal granary and to prevent destructively low prices.

To expand the domestic consumption of our surpluses by the food and cotton stamp plan, the free school lunch, low-cost milk and other plans for bringing surplus farm commodities to needy consumers.

To continue our substantially increased appropriations for research and extension work through the land-grant colleges, and for research laboratories established to develop new outlets for farm products.

To conserve the soil and water resources for the benefit of farmers and the nation. In such conservation programs we shall, so far as practicable, bring about that development in forests and other permanent crops as will not unduly expand livestock and dairy production.

To safeguard the farmer's foreign markets and expand his domestic market for all domestic crops.

To enlarge the rural electrification *[sic]*.

To encourage farmer-owned and controlled cooperatives.

To continue the broad program launched by this Administration for the coordinated development of our river basins through reclamation and irrigation, flood control, reforestation and soil conservation, stream purification, recreation, fish and game protection, low-cost power, and rural industry.

To encourage marketing agreements in aid of producers of dairy products, vegetables, fruits and specialty crops for the purpose of orderly marketing and the avoidance of unfair and wasteful practices.

To extend crop insurance from wheat to other crops as rapidly as experience justifies such extension.

To safeguard the family-sized farm in all our programs.

To finance these programs adequately in order that they may be effective.

In settling new lands reclaimed from desert by projects like Grand Coulee, we shall give priority to homeless families who have lost their farms. As these new lands are brought into use, we shall continue by Federal purchase to retire from the plow submarginal lands so that an increased percentage of our farmers may be able to live and work on good land.

These programs will continue to be in the hands of locally-elected farmer committees to the largest extent possible. In this truly democratic way, we will continue to bring economic security to the farmer and his family, while recognizing the dignity and freedom of American farm life.

Industry and the Worker

Under Democratic auspices, more has been done in the last seven years to foster the essential freedom, dignity and opportunity of the American worker than in any other administration in the nation's history. In consequence, labor is today taking its rightful place as a partner of management in the common cause of higher earnings, industrial efficiency, national unity and national defense.

A far-flung system of employment exchanges has brought together millions of idle workers and available jobs. The workers' right to organize and bargain collectively through representatives of their own choosing is being enforced. We have enlarged the Federal machinery for the mediation of labor disputes. We have enacted an effective wage and hour law. Child labor in factories has been outlawed. Prevailing wages to workers employed on Government contracts have been assured.

We pledge to continue to enforce fair labor standards; to maintain the principles of the National Labor Relations Act; to expand employment training and opportunity for our youth, older workers, and workers displaced by technological changes; to strengthen the orderly processes of collective bargaining and peaceful settlement of labor disputes; and to work always for a just distribution of our national income among those who labor.

We will continue our efforts to achieve equality of opportunity for men and women without impairing the social legislation which promotes true equality by safeguarding the health, safety and economic welfare of women workers. The right to work for compensation in both public and private employment is an inalienable privilege of

women as well as men, without distinction as to marital status.

The production of coal is one of our most important basic industries. Stability of production, employment, distribution and price are indispensable to the public welfare. We pledge continuation of the Federal Bituminous Coal Stabilization Act, and sympathetic consideration of the application of similar legislation to the anthracite coal industry, in order to provide additional protection for the owners, miners and consumers of hard coal.

We shall continue to emphasize the human element in industry and strive toward increasingly wholehearted cooperation between labor and industrial management.

Capital and the Business Man

To make democracy strong, our system of business enterprise and individual initiative must be free to gear its tremendous productive capacity to serve the greatest good of the greatest number.

We have defended and will continue to defend all legitimate business.

We have attacked and will continue to attack unbridled concentration of economic power and the exploitation of the consumer and the investor.

We have attacked the kind of banking which treated America as a colonial empire to exploit; the kind of securities business which regarded the Stock Exchange as a private gambling club for wagering other people's money; the kind of public utility holding companies which used consumers' and investors' money to suborn a free press, bludgeon legislatures and political conventions, and control elections against the interest of their customers and their security holders.

We have attacked the kind of business which levied tribute on all the rest of American business by the extortionate methods of monopoly.

We did not stop with attack—we followed through with the remedy. The American people found in themselves, through the democratic process, ability to meet the economic problems of the average American business where concentrated power had failed.

We found a broken and prostrate banking and financial system. We restored it to health by strengthening banks, insurance companies and other financial institutions. We have insured 62 million bank accounts, and protected millions of small investors in the security and commodity markets. We have thus revived confidence, safeguarded thrift, and opened the road to all honorable business.

We have made credit at low interest rates available to small-business men, thus unfastening the oppressive yoke of a money monopoly, and giving the ordinary citizen a chance to go into business and stay in business.

We recognize the importance of small business concerns and new enterprises in our national economy, and favor the enactment of constructive legislation to safeguard the welfare of small business. Independent small-scale enterprise, no less than big business, should be adequately represented on appropriate governmental boards and commissions, and its interests should be examined and fostered by a continuous research program.

We have provided an important outlet for private capital by stimulating home building and low-rent housing projects. More new homes were built throughout the nation last year than in any year since 1929.

We have fostered a well-balanced American merchant marine and the world's finest system of civil aeronautics, to promote our commerce and our national defense.

We have steered a steady course between a bankruptcy-producing deflation and a thrift-destroying inflation, so that today the dollar is the most stable and sought-after currency in the world —a factor of immeasurable benefit in our foreign and domestic commerce.

We shall continue to oppose barriers which impede trade among the several states. We pledge our best efforts in strengthening our home markets, and to this end we favor the adjustment of freight rates so that no section or state will have undue advantage over any other.

To encourage investment in productive enterprise, the tax-exempt privileges of future Federal, state and local bonds should be removed.

We have enforced the anti-trust laws more vigorously than at any time in our history, thus affording the maximum protection to the competitive system.

We favor strict supervision of all forms of the insurance business by the several states for the protection of policyholders and the public.

The full force of our policies, by raising the national income by thirty billion dollars from the low of 1932, by encouraging vast reemployment, and by elevating the level of consumer demand, has quickened the flow of buying and selling through every artery of industry and trade.

With mass purchasing power restored and many abuses eliminated, American business stands at the threshold of a great new era, richer in promise than any we have witnessed—an era of pioneering and progress beyond the present frontiers of economic activity—in transportation, in housing, in industrial expansion, and in the new utilization of the products of the farm and the factory.

We shall aid business in redeeming America's promise.

Electric Power

During the past seven years the Democratic Party has won the first major victories for the people of the nation in their generation-old contest with the power monopoly.

These victories have resulted in the recognition of certain self-evident principles and the realization of vast benefits by the people. These principles, long opposed by the Republican Party, are:

That the power of falling water is a gift from God, and consequently belongs not to a privileged few, but to all the people, who are entitled to enjoy its benefits;

That the people have the right through their government to develop their own power sites and bring low-cost electricity to their homes, farms and factories;

That public utility holding companies must not be permitted to serve as the means by which a few men can pyramid stocks upon stocks for the sole purpose of controlling vast power empires.

We condemn the Republican policies which permitted the victimizing of investors in the securities of private power corporations, and the exploitation of the people by unnecessarily high utility costs.

We condemn the opposition of utility power interests which delayed for years the development of national defense projects in the Tennessee Valley, and which obstructed river basin improvements and other public projects bringing low-cost electric power to the people. The successful power developments in the Tennessee and Columbia River basins show the wisdom of the Democratic Party in establishing government-owned and operated hydro-electric plants in the interests of power and light consumers.

Through these Democratic victories, whole regions have been revived and restored to prosperous habitation. Production costs have been reduced. Industries have been established which employ men and capital. Cheaper electricity has brought vast economic benefits to thousands of homes and communities.

These victories of the people must be safeguarded. They will be turned to defeat if the Republican Party should be returned to power. We pledge our Party militantly to oppose every effort to encroach upon the inherent right of our people to be provided with this primary essential of life at the lowest possible cost.

The nomination of a utility executive by the Republican Party as its presidential candidate raises squarely the issue, whether the nation's water power shall be used for all the people or for the selfish interests of a few. We accept that issue.

Developments of Western Resources

We take satisfaction in pointing out the incomparable development of the public land states under the wise and constructive legislation of this Administration. Mining has been revived, agriculture fostered, reclamation extended and natural resources developed as never before in a similar period. We pledge the continuance of such policies, based primarily on the expansion of opportunity for the people, as will encourage the full development, free from financial exploitation, of the great resources—mineral, agricultural, livestock, fishing and lumber—which the West affords.

Radio

Radio has become an integral part of the democratically accepted doctrine of freedom of speech, press, assembly and religion. We urge such legislative steps as may be required to afford the same protection from censorship that is now afforded the press under the Constitution of the United States.

WE MUST STRENGTHEN DEMOCRACY BY IMPROVING THE WELFARE OF THE PEOPLE

We place human resources first among the assets of a democratic society.

Unemployment

The Democratic Party wages war on unemployment, one of the gravest problems of our times, inherited at its worst from the last Republican administration. Since we assumed office, nine million additional persons have gained regular employment in normal private enterprise. All our policies—financial, industrial and agricultural—will continue to accelerate the rate of this progress.

By public action, where necessary to supplement private reemployment, we have rescued millions from idleness that breeds weakness, and given them a real stake in their country's well being. We shall continue to recognize the obligation of Government to provide work for deserving workers who cannot be absorbed by private industry.

We are opposed to vesting in the states and local authorities the control of Federally-financed work relief. We believe that this Republican proposal is a thinly disguised plan to put the unemployed back on the dole.

We will continue energetically to direct our efforts toward the employment in private industry of all those willing to work, as well as the fullest employment of money and machines. This we pledge as our primary objective. To further implement this objective, we favor calling, under the direction of the President, a national unemployment conference of leaders of government, industry, labor and farm groups.

There is work in our factories, mines, fields, forests and river basins, on our coasts, highways, railroads and inland waterways. There are houses to be built to shelter our people. Building a better America means work and a higher standard of living for every family, and a richer and more secure heritage for every American.

Social Security

The Democratic Party, which established social security for the nation, is dedicated to its extension. We pledge to make the Social Security Act increasingly effective, by covering millions of persons not now protected under its terms; by strengthening our unemployment insurance system and establishing more adequate and uniform benefits, through the Federal equalization fund principle; by progressively extending and increasing the benefits of the old-age and survivors insurance system, including protection of the permanently disabled; and by the early realization of a minimum pension for all who have reached the age of retirement and are not gainfully employed.

Health

Good health for all the people is a prime requisite of national preparedness in its broadest sense. We have advanced public health, industrial hygiene, and maternal and child care. We are coordinating the health functions of the Federal Government. We pledge to expand these efforts, and to provide more hospitals and health centers and better health protection wherever the need exists, in rural and urban areas, all through the cooperative efforts of the Federal, state and local governments, the medical, dental, nursing and other scientific professions, and the voluntary agencies.

Youth and Education

Today, when the youth of other lands is being sacrificed in war, this nation recognizes the full value of the sound youth program established by the Administration. The National Youth Administration and Civilian Conservation Corps have enabled our youth to complete their education, have maintained their health, trained them for useful citizenship, and aided them to secure employment.

Our public works have modernized and greatly expanded the nation's schools. We have increased Federal aid for vocational education and rehabilitation, and undertaken a comprehensive program of defense-industry training. We shall continue to bring to millions of children, youths and adults, the educational and economic opportunities otherwise beyond their reach.

Slum-Clearance and Low-Rent Housing

We have launched a soundly conceived plan of loans and contributions to rid America of overcrowded slum dwellings that breed disease and crime, and to replace them by low-cost housing projects within the means of low-income families. We will extend and accelerate this plan not only in the congested city districts, but also in the small towns and farm areas, and we will make it a powerful arm of national defense by supplying housing for the families of enlisted personnel and for workers in areas where industry is expanding to meet defense needs.

Consumers

We are taking effective steps to insure that, in this period of stress, the cost of living shall not be increased by speculation and unjustified price rises.

Negroes

Our Negro citizens have participated actively in the economic and social advances launched by this Administration, including fair labor standards, social security benefits, health protection, work relief projects, decent housing, aid to education, and the rehabilitation of low-income farm families. We have aided more than half a million Negro youths in vocational training, education and employment. We shall continue to strive for complete legislative safeguards against discrimination in government service and benefits, and in the national defense forces. We pledge to uphold due process and the equal protection of the laws for every citizen, regardless of race, creed or color.

Veterans

We pledge to continue our policy of fair treatment of America's war veterans and their dependents, in just tribute to their sacrifices and their devotion to the cause of liberty.

Indians

We favor and pledge the enactment of legislation creating an Indian Claims Commission for the special purpose of entertaining and investigating claims presented by Indian groups, bands and tribes, in order that our Indian citizens may have their claims against the Government considered, adjusted, and finally settled at the earliest possible date.

Civil Service

We pledge the immediate extension of a genuine system of merit to all positions in the executive branch of the Federal Government except actual bona fide policy-making positions. The competitive method of selecting employes shall be improved until experience and qualification shall be the sole test in determining fitness for employment in the Federal service. Promotion and tenure in Federal service shall likewise depend upon fitness, experience and qualification. Arbitrary and unreasonable rules as to academic training shall be abolished, all to the end that a genuine system of efficiency and merit shall prevail throughout the entire Federal service.

Territories and District of Columbia

We favor a larger measure of self-government leading to statehood, for Alaska, Hawaii and Puerto Rico. We favor the appointment of residents to office, and equal treatment of the citizens of each of these three territories. We favor the prompt determination and payment of any just claims by Indian and Eskimo citizens of Alaska against the United States.

We also favor the extension of the right of suffrage to the people of the District of Columbia.

TRUE FIRST LINE OF DEFENSE

We pledge to continue to stand guard on our true first line of defense—the security and welfare of the men, women and children of America.

OUR DEMOCRATIC FAITH

Democracy is more than a political system for the government of a people. It is the expression of a people's faith in themselves as human beings. If this faith is permitted to die, human progress will die with it. We believe that a mechanized existence, lacking the spiritual quality of democracy, is intolerable to the free people of this country.

We therefore pledge ourselves to fight, as our fathers fought, for the right of every American to enjoy freedom of religion, speech, press, assembly, petition, and security in his home.

It is America's destiny, in these days of rampant despotism, to be the guardian of the world heritage of liberty and to hold aloft and aflame the torch of Western civilization.

The Democratic Party rededicates itself to this faith in democracy, to the defense of the American system of government, the only system under which men are masters of their own souls, the only system under which the American people, composed of many races and creeds, can live and work, play and worship in peace, security and freedom.

Firmly relying upon a continuation of the blessings of Divine Providence upon all our righteous endeavors to preserve forever the priceless heritage of American liberty and peace, we appeal to all the liberal-minded men and women of the nation to approve this platform and to go forward with us by wholeheartedly supporting the candidates who subscribe to the principles which it proclaims.

Prohibition Party Platform of 1940

We, the representatives of the National Prohibition Party, in convention assembled at Chicago, May 9, 1940, recognizing Almighty God as the source of all good government, make the following declaration of principles and purposes:

MORAL ISSUES

We realize the permanent progress does not come merely by prohibiting certain things, but that prohibition of that which is evil must go hand in hand with the promotion of that which is good. Since all evils which are undermining character stand in the way of such promotion they should be prohibited. Among these evils we name specifically the liquor traffic, harmful narcotics, commercialized gambling, indecent publications, debasing moving pictures and the block booking thereof, deceptive radio broadcasting, political graft, and injustices of all kinds. We commend the work of those combating these and other evils.

ECONOMIC AND OTHER ISSUES

We are vitally interested in, and pledge ourselves to enact measures for the purpose of purifying government, reducing debt and taxation, conserving natural resources both human and material, aiding farmers who occupy and till the soil, encouraging employers engaged in honest and useful business, assuring workers and consumers a fair share of industry's profits and products, preventing unfit persons or unfair goods entering this country, but applying to all nations equitable immigration and tariff policies, avoiding war by maintaining friendly relations and providing adequate defense, providing proper aid to the worthy youth and aged, and of securing tolerance to all, while insisting that governmental changes be made only in accordance with existing constitutional methods.

NEED OF SPIRITUAL AWAKENING

We believe that to accomplish these and other worthy ends there must be a change in the purposes, motives and lives of our people. Such a spiritual awakening requires both encouraging churches and freeing schools and other forces of education from politics. The development of character—integrity, industry, self-control, initiative, a desire to be of service and a willingness to make sacrifices—must be the first aim of parents and teachers. Such a change in the hearts of employers, wage workers and consumers would so develop confidence as to restore real estate values, eliminate unemployment, and assure equal opportunities to all. We therefore, especially pledge ourselves to better and more useful public schools, and the teaching therein of fundamental moral precepts.

A COALITION PARTY

While both of the major political parties are performing useful service in emphasizing different needs, entangling alliances with corrupt interests, necessary to their success, make it impossible for these parties to take a definite stand on moral issues, even though these issues today are fundamental in solving our nation's problems. Therefore, there must be a union of church people and others who stand first for righteousness, into a Third Party. The NEW Prohibition Party serves such a purpose.

CONCLUSION

We, the members of this Party, are the one political group which has learned from sad experience that legislation alone—whether Old Deal or New Deal—is insufficient. We know that the solution of all problems—from liquor to unemployment—depends upon character, and the election to power of a political party committed to these principles. To this end we invite the cooperation and the votes of like minded men and women.

Republican Platform for 1940

INTRODUCTION

The Republican party, in representative Convention assembled, submits to the people of the United States the following declaration of its principles and purposes:

We state our general objectives in the simple and comprehensive words of the Preamble to the Constitution of the United States.

Those objectives as there stated are these:

"To form a more perfect Union; establish justice; insure domestic tranquility; provide for the common defense, promote the general welfare and secure the blessings of liberty to ourselves and our posterity."

Meeting within the shadow of Independence Hall where those words were written we solemnly reaffirm them as a perfect statement of the ends for which we as a party propose to plan and to labor.

The record of the Roosevelt Administration is a record of failure to attain any one of those essential objectives.

Instead of leading us into More Perfect Union the Administration has deliberately fanned the flames of class hatred.

Instead of the Establishment of Justice the Administration has sought the subjection of the Judiciary to Executive discipline and domination.

Instead of insuring Domestic Tranquility the Administration has made impossible the normal friendly relation between employers and employees and has even succeeded in alienating both the great divisions of Organized Labor.

Instead of Providing for the Common Defense the Administration, notwithstanding the expenditure of billions of our dollars, has left the Nation unprepared to resist foreign attack.

Instead of promoting the General Welfare the Administration has Domesticated the Deficit, Doubled the Debt, Imposed Taxes where they do the greatest economic harm, and used public money for partisan political advantage.

Instead of the Blessings of Liberty the Administration has imposed upon us a Regime of Regimentation which has deprived the individual of his freedom and has made of America a shackled giant.

Wholly ignoring these great objectives, as solemnly declared by the people of the United States, the New Deal Administration has for seven long years whirled in a turmoil of shifting, contradictory and overlapping administrations and policies. Confusion has reigned supreme. The only steady undeviating characteristic has been the relentless expansion of the power of the Federal government over the everyday life of the farmer, the industrial worker and the business man. The emergency demands organization—not confusion. It demands free and intelligent cooperation—not incompetent domination. It demands a change.

The New Deal Administration has failed America.

It has failed by seducing our people to become continuously dependent upon government, thus weakening their morale and quenching the traditional American spirit.

It has failed by viciously attacking our industrial system and sapping its strength and vigor.

It has failed by attempting to send our Congress home during the world's most tragic hour, so that we might be eased into the war by word of deed during the absence of our elected representatives from Washington.

It has failed by disclosing military details of our equipment to foreign powers over protests by the heads of our armed defense.

It has failed by ignoring the lessons of fact concerning modern, mechanized, armed defense.

In these and countless other ways the New Deal Administration has either deliberately deceived the American people or proved itself incompetent longer to handle the affairs of our government.

The zero hour is here. America must prepare at once to defend our shores, our homes, our lives and our most cherished ideals.

To establish a first line of defense we must place in official positions men of faith who put America first and who are determined that her governmental and economic system be kept unimpaired.

Our national defense must be so strong that no unfriendly power shall ever set foot on American soil. To assure this strength our national economy, the true basis of America's defense, must be free of unwarranted government interference.

Only a strong and sufficiently prepared America can speak words of reassurance and hope to the liberty-loving peoples of the world.

NATIONAL DEFENSE

The Republican Party is firmly opposed to involving this Nation in foreign war.

We are still suffering from the ill effects of the last World War: a war which cost us a twenty-four billion dollar increase in our national debt, billions of uncollectible foreign debts, and the complete upset of our economic system, in addition to the loss of human life and irreparable damage to the health of thousands of our boys.

The present National Administration has already spent for all purposes more than fifty-four billion dollars;—has boosted the national debt and current federal taxes to an all-time high; and yet by the President's own admission we are still wholly unprepared to defend our country, its institutions and our individual liberties in a war that threatens to engulf the whole world; and this in spite of the fact that foreign wars have been in progress for two years or more and that military information concerning these wars and the re-armament programs of the warring nations has been at all times available to the National Administration through its diplomatic and other channels.

The Republican Party stands for Americanism, preparedness and peace. We accordingly fasten upon the New Deal full responsibility for our unpreparedness and for the consequent danger of involvement in war.

We declare for the prompt, orderly and realistic building of our national defense to the point at which we shall be able not only to defend the United States, its possessions, and essential outposts from foreign attack, but also efficiently to uphold in war the Monroe Doctrine. To this task the Republican party pledges itself when entrusted with national authority. In the meantime we shall support all necessary and proper defense measures proposed by the Administration in its belated effort to make up for lost time; but we deplore explosive utterances by the President directed at other governments which serve to imperil our peace; and we condemn all executive acts and proceedings which might lead to war without the authorization of the Congress of the United States.

Our sympathies have been profoundly stirred by invasion of unoffending countries and by disaster to nations whole ideals most closely resemble our own. We favor the extension to all peoples fighting for liberty, or whose liberty is threatened, of such aid as shall not be in violation of international law or inconsistent with the requirements of our own national defense.

We believe that the spirit which should animate our entire defensive policy is determination to preserve not our material interests merely, but those liberties which are the priceless heritage of America.

RE-EMPLOYMENT

The New Deal's failure to solve the problem of unemployment and revive opportunity for our youth presents a major challenge to representative government and free enterprise. We propose to recreate opportunity for the youth of America and put our idle millions back to work in private industry, business, and agriculture. We propose to eliminate needless administrative restrictions, thus restoring lost motion to the wheels of individual enterprise.

Relief

We shall remove waste, discrimination, and politics from relief—through administration by the States with federal grants-in-aid on a fair and non-political basis, thus giving the man and woman on relief a larger share of the funds appropriated.

Social Security

We favor the extension of necessary old age benefits on an ear-marked pay-as-you-go basis to the extent that the revenues raised for this purpose will permit. We favor the extension of the un-employment compensation provisions of the Social Security Act, wherever practicable, to those groups and classes not now included. For such groups as may thus be covered we favor a system of unemployment compensation with experience rating provisions, aimed at protecting the worker in the regularity of his employment and providing adequate compensation for reasonable periods when that regularity of employment is interrupted. The administration should be left with the States with a minimum of Federal control.

Labor Relations

The Republican party has always protected the American worker.

We shall maintain labor's right of free organization and collective bargaining.

We believe that peace and prosperity at home require harmony, teamwork, and understanding in all relations between worker and employer. When differences arise, they should be settled directly and voluntarily across the table.

Recent disclosures respecting the administration of the National Labor Relations Act require that this Act be amended in fairness to employers and all groups of employees so as to provide true freedom for, and orderliness in self-organization and collective bargaining.

Agriculture

A prosperous and stable agriculture is the foundation of our economic structure. Its preservation is a national and non-political social problem not yet solved, despite many attempts. The farmer is entitled to a profit-price for his products. The Republican party will put into effect such governmental policies, temporary and permanent, as will establish and maintain an equitable balance between labor, industry, and agriculture by expanding industrial and business activity, eliminating unemployment, lowering production costs, thereby creating increased consumer buying power for agricultural products.

Until this balance has been attained, we propose to provide benefit payments, based upon a widely-applied, constructive soil conservation program free from government-dominated production control, but administered, as far as practicable, by farmers themselves; to restrict the major benefits of these payments to operators of family-type farms; to continue all present benefit payments until our program becomes operative; and to eliminate the present extensive and costly bureaucratic interference.

We shall provide incentive payments, when necessary, to encourage increased production of agricultural commodities, adaptable to our soil and climate, not now produced in sufficient quantities for our home markets, and will stimulate the use and processing of all farm products in industry as raw materials.

We shall promote a cooperative system of adequate farm credit, at lowest interest rates commensurate with the cost of money, supervised by an independent governmental agency, with ultimate farmer ownership and control; farm commodity loans to facilitate orderly marketing and stabilize farm income; the expansion of sound, farmer-owned and farmer-controlled cooperative associations; and the support of educational and extension programs to achieve more efficient production and marketing.

We shall foster Government refinancing, where necessary, of the heavy Federal farm debt load through an agency segregated from cooperative credit.

We shall promote a national land use program for Federal acquisition, without dislocation of local tax returns, of non-productive farm lands by voluntary sale or lease subject to approval of the States concerned; and the disposition of such lands to appropriate public uses including watershed protection and flood prevention, reforestation, recreation, erosion control, and the conservation of wild life.

We advocate a foreign trade policy which will end one-man tariff making, afford effective protection to farm products, regain our export markets, and assure an American price level for the domestically consumed portion of our export crops.

We favor effective quarantine against imported livestock, dairy, and other farm products from countries which do not impose health and sanitary standards equal to our own domestic standards.

We approve the orderly development of reclamation and irrigation, project by project and as conditions justify.

We promise adequate asistance to rural communities suffering disasters from flood, drought, and other natural causes.

We shall promote stabilization of agricultural income through intelligent management of accumulated surpluses, and through the development of outlets by supplying those in need at home and abroad.

Tariff and Reciprocal Trade

We are threatened by unfair competition in world markets and by the invasion of our home markets, especially by the products of state-controlled foreign economies.

We believe in tariff protection for Agriculture, Labor, and Industry, as essential to our American standard of living. The measure of the protection shall be determined by scientific methods with due regard to the interest of the consumer.

We shall explore every possibility of reopening the channels of international trade through negotiations so conducted as to produce genuine reciprocity and expand our exports.

We condemn the manner in which the so-called reciprocal trade agreements of the New Deal have been put into effect without adequate hearings, with undue haste, without proper consideration of our domestic producers, and without Congressional approval. These defects we shall correct.

Money

The Congress should reclaim its constitutional powers over money, and withdraw the President's arbitrary authority to manipulate the currency, establish bimetallism, issue irredeemable paper money, and debase the gold and silver coinage. We shall repeal the Thomas Inflation Amendment of 1933 and the (foreign) Silver Purchase Act of 1934, and take all possible steps to preserve the value of the Government's huge holdings of gold and re-introduce gold into circulation.

Jobs and Idle Money

Believing it possible to keep the securities market clean without paralyzing it, we endorse the principle of truth in securities in the Securities Act. To get billions of idle dollars and a multitude of idle men back to work and to promote national defense, these acts should be revised and the policies of the Commission changed to encourage the flow of private capital into industry.

Taxation

Public spending has trebled under the New Deal, while tax burdens have doubled. Huge taxes are necessary to pay for New Deal waste and for neglected national defense. We shall revise the tax system and remove those practices which impede recovery and shall apply policies which stimulate enterprise. We shall not use the taxing power as an instrument of punishment or to secure objectives not otherwise obtainable under existing law.

Public Credit

With urgent need for adequate defense, the people are burdened by a direct and contingent debt exceeding fifty billion dollars. Twenty-nine billion of this debt has been created by New Deal borrowings during the past seven years. We pledge ourselves to conserve the public credit for all essential purposes by levying taxation sufficient to cover necessary civil expenditure, a substantial part of the defense cost, and the interest and retirement of the national debt.

Public Spending

Millions of men and women still out of work after seven years of excessive spending refute the New Deal theory that "deficit spending" is the way to prosperity and jobs. Our American system of private enterprise, if permitted to go to work, can rapidly increase the wealth, income, and standard of living of all the people. We solemnly pledge that public expenditures, other than those required for full national defense and relief, shall be cut to levels necessary for the essential services of government.

EQUAL RIGHTS

We favor submission by Congress to the States of an amendment to the Constitution providing for equal rights for men and women.

NEGRO

We pledge that our American citizens of Negro descent shall be given a square deal in the economic and political life of this nation. Discrimination in the civil service, the army, navy, and all other branches of the Government must cease. To enjoy the full benefits of life, liberty and pursuit of happiness universal suffrage must be made effective for the Negro citizen. Mob violence shocks the conscience of the nation and legislation to curb this evil should be enacted.

UN-AMERICAN ACTIVITIES

We vigorously condemn the New Deal encouragement of various groups that seek to change the American form of government by means outside the Constitution. We condemn the appointment of members of such un-American groups to high positions of trust in the national Government. The development of the treacherous so-called Fifth Column, as it has operated in war-stricken countries, should be a solemn warning to America. We pledge the Republican Party to get rid of such borers from within.

IMMIGRATION

We favor the strict enforcement of all laws controlling the entry of aliens. The activities of undesirable aliens should be investigated and those who seek to change by force and violence the American form of government should be deported.

VETERANS

We pledge adequate compensation and care for veterans disabled in the service of our country, and for their widows, orphans, and dependents.

INDIANS

We pledge an immediate and final settlement of all Indian claims between the government and the Indian citizenship of the nation.

HAWAII

Hawaii, sharing the nation's obligations equally with the several States, is entitled to the fullest measure of home rule; and to equality with the several States in the rights of her citizens and in the application of our national laws.

PUERTO RICO

Statehood is a logical aspiration of the people of Puerto Rico who were made citizens of the United States by Congress in 1917; legislation affecting Puerto Rico, in so far as feasible, should be in harmony with the realization of that aspiration.

GOVERNMENT AND BUSINESS

We shall encourage a healthy, confident, and growing private enterprise, confine Government activity to essential public services, and regulate business only so as to protect consumer, employee, and investor and without restricting the production of more and better goods at lower prices.

MONOPOLY

Since the passage of the Sherman Anti-trust Act by the Republican party we have consistently fought to preserve free competition with regulation to prevent abuse. New Deal policy fosters Government monopoly, restricts production, and fixes prices. We shall enforce anti-trust legislation without prejudice or discrimination. We condemn the use or threatened use of criminal indictments to obtain through consent decrees objectives not contemplated by law.

GOVERNMENT COMPETITION

We promise to reduce to the minimum Federal competition with business. We pledge ourselves to establish honest accounting and reporting by every agency of the Federal Government and to continue only those enterprises whose maintenance is clearly in the public interest.

FREE SPEECH

The principles of a free press and free speech, as established by the Constitution, should apply to the radio. Federal regulation of radio is necessary in view of the natural limitations of wave lengths, but this gives no excuse for censorship. We oppose the use of licensing to establish arbitrary controls. Licenses should be revocable only when, after public hearings, due cause for cancellation is shown.

Small Business

The New Deal policy of interference and arbitrary regulation has injured all business, but especially small business. We promise to encourage the small business man by removing unnecessary bureaucratic regulation and interference.

Stock and Commodity Exchanges

We favor regulation of stock and commodity exchanges. They should be accorded the fullest measure of self-control consistent with the discharge of their public trust and the prevention of abuse.

Insurance

We condemn the New Deal attempts to destroy the confidence of our people in private insurance institutions. We favor continuance of regulation of insurance by the several States.

Government Reorganization

We shall reestablish in the Federal Civil Service a real merit system on a truly competitive basis and extend it to all non-policy-forming positions.

We pledge ourselves to enact legislation standardizing and simplifying quasi-judicial and administrative agencies to insure adequate notice and hearing, impartiality, adherence to the rules of evidence and full judicial review of all questions of law and fact.

Our greatest protection against totalitarian government is the American system of checks and balances. The constitutional distribution of legislative, executive, and judicial functions is essential to the preservation of this system. We pledge ourselves to make it the basis of all our policies affecting the organization and operation of our Republican form of Government.

Third Term

To insure against the overthrow of our American system of government we favor an amendment to the Constitution providing that no person shall be President of the United States for more than two terms.

A Pledge of Good Faith

The acceptance of the nominations made by this Convention carries with it, as a matter of private honor and public faith, an undertaking by each candidate to be true to the principles and program herein set forth.

We earnestly urge all patriotic men and women, regardless of former affiliations, to unite with us in the support of our declaration of principles to the end that "government of the people, by the people and for the people shall not perish from this earth."

Socialist Platform of 1940

We Take Our Stand!

Every American knows that we have the resources and the machinery, the workers and the skill to conquer poverty. Every American knows that poverty and insecurity, the more unendurable because they are unnecessary, curse this most fortunate of lands.

That the situation has not already led to worse suffering and graver menace to our imperfect democracy is due to social legislation originating in Socialist immediate demands. The best of what goes by the New Deal name; social insurance, minimum wage laws, guarantees of the right to collective bargaining, public power projects were first demanded by the Socialist Party.

But these things, for reasons that Socialists have always proclaimed, have not averted the multiplying ills of a dying private capitalism nor given any assurance that out of its failure we shall not get the slavery of state capitalism under a fascist or totalitarian government.

Today more than 20 per cent of our people have no place in the social economic order; for ten years we have had an army of 10,000,000 unemployed. Two out of three American families must live on less than $1,500 a year.

Why? Because our private capitalism by its very nature exploits the mass of workers with hand and brain, in town and country, to provide profits for the few. And these profits are dependent on relative scarcity from which the whole community suffers. What planning there is, is not primarily for use, but for the profits of an owning class.

Neither old party offers any adequate remedy.

The Republicans want a qualified, and impossible, return to the system which brought us to ruin at the end of 1929. The Democrats as a party have never accepted the New Deal and the New Deal administration itself has turned from its failure to conquer poverty at home to armament economics and the hope of war-time profits.

Under these circumstances democratic Socialism becomes an immediate demand; the one road to plenty, peace and freedom. For the producing and consuming masses of America to recognize this fact and turn their faces while there is yet time to a deliberate harnessing of our machinery to peace, not war, abundance for all, not profit for the few is the one chance of our escape from fascism and war.

This means socialization. Socialization is social ownership and democratic control of industry, substituting the principle of public service or social usefulness for the system of private profit, preserving workers' free choice of occupation, consumers' free choice of goods and freedom of association for all functional groups.

Socialism Is Necessary

Wherever private exploitation of a limited natural resource is highly wasteful, as in the oil, coal and timber industries, there socialization is required in the interest of this as well as of future generations.

Wherever concentration of financial power leads to the restriction of the expansive forces of our economy, as in insurance and investment banking, we propose socialization.

Wherever private monopoly, in the drive for monopoly profit, restricts production to less than is justified by the social usefulness of the product, as in the steel and cement industries, the principle of socialization should be applied.

Wherever concentration of economic power creates a political interest which is too powerful for a democracy to tolerate in private hands, we should put this power in public hands.

Wherever natural monopoly has consumers at its mercy, as in the aluminum industry, socialization is both practical and necessary.

Wherever, as in the railroads, private operation cannot or will not undertake socially-needed investment, socialization becomes the order of the day.

Wherever, as in many large-scale corporations, ownership has lost its management function and the business is managed by hired men, these managers should be working for the public instead of for private owners.

Wherever one or more of these conditions exist it means that the private profit principle is destroying the very basis of living; that business must be taken over by the public.

This is a program of immediate socialization. It is the program of the Socialist Party. It is the only program capable of solving the economic plight of America, of putting men and machines to work, of giving abundance and plenty to all.

This is a program which is the only valid alternative to armament economics and war. Hysterical concern for the kind of defense which seems a threat to our neighbors is the first escape for a government and a system which cannot end unemployment.

War and Totalitarianism

To furnish supplies for other people's wars is, to the profit seekers, a welcome alternative to supplying our own people with their daily bread. But the search for war profits and armament economics leads straight to war. War and frantic preparation for war mean the totalitarian state, not Socialist freedom.

To the whole world let America say:

"We will not share in the collective suicide of your wars. We will, to the best of our ability, aid the victims of war and oppression. We will co-operate in disarmament and in all economic arrangements which will lessen the strain of insecurity and exploitation upon the peoples of all the world."

Other Campaign Issues

In its platform the Socialist Party presents a carefully considered, all-embracing program to build a free, secure and warless America. In this supplementary material, we present our stand on other issues of this campaign.

Socialism and Democracy mean the same thing. "Government of the people, by the people and for the people" cannot exist so long as we have government of industry by the bosses for the profits of an owning class.

The Socialist Party opposes dictatorship and the concept of party-state, either Fascist or Communist. The tragedy of Russia has shown that political and industrial democracy are inseparable, and without such democracy, economic collectivism becomes a new form of slavery.

Socialism means freedom. A Socialist state must serve the common good of the individual. Under true Socialism, our civil liberties will not only be preserved but extended.

Unemployment and Social Security

Under the Roosevelt administration, public works and housing have too often become a political football. Projects have been proposed for political prestige and then abandoned through false economy. The Socialist Party proposes reduction of the administration's huge and planless armament-building program and use of armament funds for a public works program which would provide low-rent housing, organized on a cooperative basis wherever possible, for millions of American families in rural and city slums.

We favor expansion of the WPA, NYA, and CCC. The unemployed are society's responsibility so long as we tolerate an economic system which denies them the right to work. We oppose any conspiracy to place the CCC, either partially or wholly, under military control. We advocate the provision by the government of useful jobs for young people at prevailing wages.

The Socialist Party proposes federal old-age pensions supplemented by a voluntary annuity system. We would extend unemployment benefits to all workers now unprotected, particularly agricultural, domestic and maritime workers, and provide more liberal benefits and shorter waiting periods. We propose a complete health and disability insurance program.

We favor a broad federal program for aid to education. For the first time in our history, children in many districts are receiving less schooling than their parents. Such federal aid must be given on terms which eliminate discrimination against Negroes and other minority groups. In all our educational programs, academic freedom, democratic control with teacher representation, and the principle of separation of church and state must be upheld.

Agriculture

Half of the farmer's problem is in the city. If every American had what the U. S. Bureau of Home Economics calls a "decent diet," we should need more rather than less of every important farm product except wheat. We have no genuine farm surpluses—merely market surpluses resulting from the inability of the people to buy what they sorely need. The Socialist program of economic expansion will bring industrial production up to the level of farm production instead of dragging farm production down to the level of restricted industry.

But while industry is catching up with agriculture, the farmers must not be penalized for being able to feed the people better than the people can afford. Direct and large-scale government action is required to maintain farmers' income. We must continue and extend the government program to buy up the so-called farm surpluses for the people who need them.

The soil conservation program must be continued with long range planning, keyed to an expanding standard of living. In the local planning of the farm program, low-income farmers and tenants, Negroes as well as Whites, must take part.

We are utterly opposed to the present practice of using government subsidies to preserve the plantation peonage system. No benefit payments should be made to plantation owners unless there are rigorous provisions to prevent the diversion of those payments from tenants and sharecroppers. Plantation and ranch owners employing day and migratory labor on a large scale must be required to accept federal minimum wage standards as the basis for receiving benefit payments.

For the increasing number of migratory families, a wide program of camp relief and resettlement must be carried out by the federal government.

The Socialist Party is opposed to the brutal regimentation of agriculture employed by Stalin in Russia. We believe that no single type of farm organization is applicable to the whole country, and that the farmers themselves in democratic fashion should reach decisions on agricultural practice.

Clearly, however, the absentee ownership of farm lands conflicts with the interest of the public in general and of the farmers in particular. Therefore, the Socialist Party favors the use of land taxation and, where necessary, public purchase to abolish absentee landlordship.

In some cases the solution for sharecropping

and "factories in the field" will be cooperative collective farms. In other cases the answer to absentee land-owning will be by settling farm families on their own land under conditions which will establish the principle that their title rests upon occupancy and use.

Dwellers in farm areas as well as in towns and cities should receive the benefits of all social security legislation.

Labor Legislation

The Socialist Party is steadfastly opposed to any effort to weaken or destroy protection for collective bargaining either through the vicious Smith amendments or the underhanded slashing of the already meager appropriations for the proper enforcement of the law. We propose immediate extension of the Wages and Hours law to all lines of employment and the raising of the minimum wage level. Technological progress makes possible steady reduction of hours as a necessary safeguard against technological unemployment. Civil service employees must be allowed full economic and civil rights, including adequate machinery for dealing with grievance and dismissals.

As a political party which fights side by side with labor, we call upon the unions to end the civil war in labor's ranks. This conflict not only endangers the progress made by labor during the past half-century but threatens to block further advancement.

Socialists condemn as anti-democratic and anti-social the administration's use of anti-trust legislation against the unions. If labor is to prevent government intervention, however, it must eliminate bureaucratic and racketeering trends in its ranks. Democracy in public life must have, as a basic example, democracy in the ranks of labor.

Taxation, Tariffs and the Fiscal System

In federal, state and local taxation, now chaotic and mismanaged, we favor simplification and co-ordination.

We condemn all taxes on consumption and especially general sales and payroll taxes, which bear most heavily on those with the lowest income and thus restrict production and employment by reducing the demand for goods.

Primarily, reliance must be placed on graduated income and inheritance taxes as a source of fed-eral and state revenue. The application of this principle requires tax increases, especially on incomes from $5,000 up which now escape their fair share of taxation. Tax-exempt securities must be abolished. Undistributed corporate income which is not reinvested in productive equipment should be subject to surtax.

Taxation on unimproved real estate should be increased to discourage land speculation. In most cities, drastic revision of real estate taxes is a necessary aid to any housing program. Slum land appraisals must be written down. We oppose any increase of taxes on farms and homes.

We renew our endorsement of a scientifically graduated capital levy for reduction of the national debt and as an aid toward socialization.

We condemn action of states under various pretexts in levying imports duties, taxes or license fees which restrict free trade within the United States.

We favor encouragement of trade with peaceful peoples but not in materials of war.

Our present fiscal system, particularly in respect to gold and silver purchases, imposes a tax—disguised but enormous—upon the people, gives foreign nations, including Japan, a gigantic subsidy for their wars, and lays a basis for inflation of astronomical proportions. The gold purchase policy is particularly dangerous and should be abandoned as fast as possible without panic. In general, it is the Socialist Party's purpose to achieve a fiscal system protected against the evils both of inflation and deflation, and a system from which neither a small class of private bankers nor of gold and silver owners shall derive huge profits at public expense.

Civil Liberties and Political Rights

We renew our pledge for the maintenance and increase of civil liberty for all groups, regardless of race, color or creed. We support everywhere the fight against poll taxes, undemocratic laws, and all limitations of suffrage.

Citizens of the District of Columbia should have the same right to local self-government and the same voice in national elections as other citizens.

Discrimination against Negroes must be abolished. Anti-Semitism or any form of racial, religious or group intolerance must be rigorously combatted as paving the road to fascism.

We oppose alien and sedition legislation as directed toward the abridgment of civil liberty.

We commend the methods and aim of the La-Follette Committee which has been investigating civil liberty and condemn, by contrast, the methods employed by the Dies Committee and particularly by its chairman.

We condemn the use of immigration laws to return, directly or indirectly, refugees to the tyranny of totalitarian states and favor a more generous treatment of them. America must be kept the land of political asylum.

INTERNATIONAL FRIENDSHIP

The Socialist Party favors active cooperation with all forces, particularly labor, farm and cooperative organizations in other lands which seek freedom, peace and justice. We pledge unstinted aid to the heroic underground movement in Germany and other totalitarian countries.

In order to establish an honest fraternal relationship between the nations of the western hemisphere, we demand withdrawal of economic dictation by the United States over Latin-American countries. We pledge full support to all forces in Latin-America which seek the establishment of working democracies.

SOCIALISTS, LABOR UNIONS AND COOPERATIVES

The Socialist Party calls upon its members and friends to be active in labor unions of their industry and trade, to seek democratically within them to advance an understanding and acceptance of the principles of Socialism, but not to seek control over them by power politics. We seek organization of the unorganized and of the unemployed.

The Socialist Party renews its endorsement of the cooperative movement. We rejoice in the sound progress made by this movement in recent years and note with especial approval the formation of farmer-labor cooperative councils in such an important farm state as Wisconsin.

We urge young people to seek a solution to their pressing economic problems in alliance with labor, farmers, unemployed and cooperatives.

Throughout its existence, the Socialist Party has endorsed and participated in genuine farmer-labor political parties and leagues. In 1940, however, Socialists see no sign whatever of any possibility of building a genuine farmer-labor party on a national scale. It will be too late for effective and constructive action by protesting groups which wait until after the old party conventions. Believers in a farmer-labor party will advance their cause by supporting the Socialist ticket.

WAR

Summary of Resolution Adopted by Socialist National Convention, Washington, D. C., April 7, 1940.

The present European war presents to the American workers a challenge that can be met only by hard thinking and great emotional self-control. Vast armies are being hurled at each other across devastated lands. Shall Americans plunge into the abyss?

The cause for which Hitler has hurled the German masses into war is one of ruthless brutality. Its record has horrified all decent men and women. But that does not mean that the Allied war itself will produce the kind of democratic world in which peace and security will be assured. Indeed, the very existence of the Hitler regime is based on the kind of peace that the Allies effected at the close of the World War.

Like war, fascism has its origin in capitalism. Both war and fascism spring from the failure of the capitalist economy to solve domestic problems and provide security for the masses of the people. Fascism has its roots in the breakdown of the national economy, the desperate turning of the frustrated people to a messiah who promises all. Like capitalism, it uses war in the competition among nations for the control of the world market, as dictated by the need for expansion. But war has its own dynamics, accelerates economic breakdown and itself leads to the further entrenchment of reaction and fascism.

Defeat of Hitler will be welcomed by all anti-fascists. But defeat of Hitler will mean the defeat of Hitlerism and a victory for democracy only if the roots of fascism and the war system are destroyed. The United States cannot contribute toward that end nor vindicate real democracy if it loses itself in the processes of war.

If America enters the war, we shall be subjected to military dictatorship, the regimentation of labor and ultimate economic collapse that must follow war. In an effort to "save democracy," we shall have destroyed its only remaining citadel.

The first demand of the American people must

now be: Keep America Out of War! That means a refusal to take any of those "steps short of war"—which by very definition are steps in the direction of war. The alternatives are few. Economic participation, by every test of past experience, must lead to military participation. However hard the decision, the American people must resolutely determine to avoid all roads to war and pursue only the paths of peace.

To drive war out of the world, we must first keep America out of war!

THE SOCIALIST CANDIDATES

In its candidate for President, the Socialist Party presents a distinguished American whose entire life has been devoted to the cause of the oppressed. As a thinker and writer, as a man of action, a fighter for civil liberties and against every manifestation of class, racial and religious prejudice, he has won the respect and admiration of all progressive forces throughout the nation.

Norman Thomas was born in Marion, Ohio, and lives in New York City, but he is at home wherever labor's cause and democracy in general are threatened—in Indiana, where he defied McNutt's martial law, in Florida where he fought and exposed the Ku Klux Klan, in Arkansas where he faced planter mobs in behalf of the share-croppers, in New Jersey where he fought and licked Boss Hague on the issue of free speech.

Norman Thomas joined the Socialist Party in 1917, when less courageous men were leaving it and when it was the only political force in the country actively opposing our participation in the first World War. Today, when we are threatened with participation in the second World War, he is America's leader in the fight against militarism, the fight to keep America out of war and to build a genuine democracy in this country. Alone, of all presidential candidates, he has taken an uncompromising stand against American participation, economic or military, in the European conflict.

Maynard C. Krueger, the Socialist candidate for Vice-President, is one of a rising school of American economists which is challenging our present economic and social order. Born 35 years ago on a Missouri farm, he completed his high school course at the age of 15 and entered the University of Missouri. He has since risen rapidly in academic circles and is now teaching at the University of Chicago.

Mr. Krueger is known to millions of radio listeners as a participant in the University of Chicago Round Table Sunday Afternoon Discussions where he has at all times upheld social progress for America. His fellow-teachers have thrice honored him by electing him vice-president of the American Federation of Teachers, A. F. of L.

His work among the coal miners of Illinois and West Virginia, among the unemployed and the farmers of the Mid-West has given him an intimate understanding of the problems of America. Representative of a new generation, Maynard C. Krueger is an ideal choice as running mate for Norman Thomas.

VOTE SOCIALIST!

Platform of the Socialist Labor Party

Socialism or Capitalism—that is the crucial issue confronting the workers of America!

Shall we institute a society of collective property, production for use, plenty for all and international peace, or shall we allow predatory capitalism to drag society back into a new dark ages?

The Socialist Labor Party of America, at its 20th National Convention in the City of New York, April 29, 1940, reiterates that capitalism cannot be amended, but must be ended. Indisputable evidence of hopeless social decay is apparent nationally in the concentration of wealth and power, on the one hand, and perpetual mass unemployment, and insecurity among the workers, on the other. Internationally the breakdown of capitalism reveals itself in world chaos—a desperate death struggle between capitalist nations over the world's markets and spheres of influence.

We hold that the existing contradiction between the theory of democratic government and the fact of a despotic economic system—the private ownership of the natural and social opportunities—divides the nation into two classes: the non-producing, but owning, Capitalist Class, and the producing but propertiless Working Class; throws society into the convulsions of the Class Struggle; and invariably perverts government to the uses and benefit of the Capitalist Class.

The incompetence of the Capitalist Class and its unfitness to rule any longer stand conspicuously demonstrated. Capitalist Class rule has created slums in the cities faster than it has torn them down. It has thrown millions of workers on the industrial scrap-heap barely to exist on the degrading pittance of relief. Its minimum wage has placed the stamp of approval on a starvation wage and in great industrial areas the "minimum wage" has become the *maximum* wage. In its insane efforts to raise prices and create scarcity, it has hailed drouths as blessings and bumper crops as a curse. Through its executive committee, the Political State, it has wantonly destroyed the surplus while millions were ill fed.

Capitalist political henchmen have placated the workers with sops and relief and the promise of jobs with the restoration of production. But when production soared above the 1929 peak, in December, 1939, its staunchest apologists admitted that higher production had been effected without reducing unemployment. In spite of billions spent for relief and additional billions spent to "prime the pump," in spite of scores of reforms acclaimed as "victories" for the workers, in spite of prodigious programs for rehousing, reclamation, resettlement, and work relief—unemployment and insecurity among the workers are as rampant as ever.

To swell its profits, the capitalist class seeks in the laboratory still newer means of cheapening commodities, new methods of eliminating workers, thus consigning them to permanent unemployment.

Private ownership stands as a solid wall between the useful producers and the product of their labor. The Socialist Labor Party declares that this wall shall be battered down and the wealth of the nation be made available to all who perform useful labor. Under Socialism, machines, collectively owned and operated for the benefit of society, can be made to fulfill the promise of the age and bring an end to unemployment and poverty. Instead of eliminating workers, socially owned and constantly improved machinery will eliminate hours from the working day, giving leisure and affluence to all.

Unable to solve the problems at home, the capitalist class diverts attention from its failures to the anarchy abroad. The long anticipated war is now an irrevocable fact. Capitalist democracy is perishing in its flames. The belligerents which boasted the broadest liberties have scrapped the conquests of centuries of struggle for freedom over night. Perceptibly America is being drawn into the bloody vortex. Its exports have shifted from grain, fruit and plows to war-planes, guns and munitions. On this grim traffic is its "prosperity" based. War feeds on commerce; commerce feeds on war. Under the pretext of "national defense" and to a chorus of declarations for peace, its statesmen, New Deal, old deal, liberal and conservative alike, gird the nation for its fateful role. Punchinello-like, the political henchmen of the capitalist class move as their masters pull the strings.

War referendums, pacifism and anti-war resolutions are futile, childish gestures. We hold that, given the capitalist system with its mutual antagonisms and relentless struggle for markets, American involvement in the European war is inescapable. Capitalism means war; one plank of capitalism means the whole of capitalism. To oppose one plank only is to leave all others standing and thus render abortive all seeming success against the monster. It is the capitalist system itself which must be destroyed!

Against this insane social system the Socialist Labor Party raises the banner of revolution and calls upon the working class to organize politically and industrially for the conquest of power.

POLITICAL ORGANIZATION

The Constitution of the United States provides for its own amendment. The Constitution thereby recognizes and legalizes revolution. Our people hold the government in the hollow of their hand. We propose, therefore, that the revolutionary change be effected by the peaceful and civilized means of the ballot.

In presenting the issue—Socialism or Capitalism —and a program for its solution, the Socialist Labor Party stands alone. All other parties, whether Republican, Democratic, "Socialist," "Labor," "Progressive," or "Communist," propose reforms which tend to preserve capitalism but fail to improve the lot of the workers. Therefore, we call upon the toilers of America, in order to implement their hope for life, liberty and the pursuit of happiness, to cast their ballot for the Socialist

Labor Party, for the abolition of the capitalist system.

ECONOMIC ORGANIZATION

Recognizing the simple truth that RIGHT without the MIGHT to support it is useless and meaningless, we call upon the workers of America to organize themselves into integral Socialist Industrial Unions to enforce the demand for collective ownership proclaimed through the ballot. But we at the same time caution the workers that such unions *must be organized,* for none now exist. The C.I.O., A.F. of L., and similar organizations are agencies of capitalism for the reason that they are pledged to maintain the system of private property, and structurally they lend themselves preeminently to the furthering of capitalist interests.

Organized *as a class,* along industrial lines, the workers can act instantaneously, and with such momentum that no power on earth can stop them. Only the thoroughly integrated Socialist Industrial Unions can block a brutal reaction, should the outvoted, expropriated capitalists rebel against the explicit decision of the majority.

SOCIALIST ADMINISTRATION

More than an invincible force behind Labor's ballot, the Socialist Industrial Union organizes the workers intelligently *to carry on production,* thus avoiding a chaotic period of transition. Finally, the Socialist Industrial Union becomes *the Government of the Socialist Republic,* supplanting the outworn, reactionary and inefficient capitalist Political State. *Democratically elected representatives* of the industrial constituencies will form an Industrial Union Congress, the duties of which will be the simple ones of directing, coordinating and supervising production for the benefit of all.

Workers of America! The issue of our age can no longer be postponed! Vote for the Socialist Republic! Organize the Socialist Industrial Union NOW to put a speedy end to barbarous capitalism. Unite under the banner of the Socialist Labor Party NOW to demand—

THE WORKSHOPS TO THE WORKERS!
THE PRODUCT TO THE PRODUCERS!
ALL POWER TO THE SOCIALIST
INDUSTRIAL UNION!

☒ CAMPAIGN OF 1944

In the 1944 campaign, candidates were nominated by the Republican Party, the Democratic Party, the Socialist Party, the National Prohibition Party, and the Socialist Labor Party. In May of 1944, the Communist Party dissolved and its place was taken by a "Communist Political Association" which did not nominate a presidential candidate.

Democratic Platform of 1944

The Democratic Party stands on its record in peace and in war.

To speed victory, establish and maintain peace, guarantee full employment and provide prosperity —this is its platform.

We do not here detail scores of planks. We cite action.

Beginning March, 1933, the Democratic Administration took a series of actions which saved our system of free enterprise.

It brought that system out of collapse and thereafter eliminated abuses which had imperiled it.

It used the powers of government to provide employment in industry and to save agriculture.

It wrote a new Magna Carta for labor.

It provided social security, including old age pensions, unemployment insurance, security for crippled and dependent children and the blind. It established employment offices. It provided federal bank deposit insurance, flood prevention, soil conservation, and prevented abuses in the security markets. It saved farms and homes from foreclosure, and secured profitable prices for farm products.

It adopted an effective program of reclamation, hydro-electric power, and mineral development.

It found the road to prosperity through production and employment.

We pledge the continuance and improvement of these programs.

Before war came, the Democratic Administration awakened the Nation, in time, to the dangers that threatened its very existence.

It succeeded in building, in time, the best-trained and equipped army in the world, the most powerful navy in the world, the greatest air force in the world, and the largest merchant marine in the world.

It gained for our country, and it saved for our country, powerful allies.

When war came, it succeeded in working out with those allies an effective grand strategy against the enemy.

It set that strategy in motion, and the tide of battle was turned.

It held the line against wartime inflation.

It ensured a fair share-and-share-alike distribution of food and other essentials.

It is leading our country to certain victory.

The primary and imperative duty of the United States is to wage the war with every resource available to final triumph over our enemies, and we pledge that we will continue to fight side by side with the United Nations until this supreme objective shall have been attained and thereafter to secure a just and lasting peace.

That the world may not again be drenched in blood by international outlaws and criminals, we pledge:

To join with the other United Nations in the establishment of an international organization based on the principle of the sovereign equality of all peace-loving states, open to membership by all such states, large and small, for the prevention of aggression and the maintenance of international peace and security.

To make all necessary and effective agreements and arrangements through which the nations would maintain adequate forces to meet the needs of preventing war and of making impossible the preparation for war and which would have such forces available for joint action when necessary.

Such organization must be endowed with power to employ armed forces when necessary to prevent aggression and preserve peace.

We favor the maintenance of an international court of justice of which the United States shall be a member and the employment of diplomacy, conciliation, arbitration and other like methods where appropriate in the settlement of international disputes.

World peace is of transcendent importance. Our gallant sons are dying on land, on sea, and in the air. They do not die as Republicans. They do not die as Democrats. They die as Americans. We pledge that their blood shall not have been shed in vain. America has the opportunity to lead the world in this great service to mankind. The United States must meet the challenge. Under Divine Providence, she must move forward to her high destiny.

We pledge our support to the Atlantic Charter and the Four Freedoms and the application of the principles enunciated therein to the United Nations and other peace-loving nations, large and small.

We shall uphold the good-neighbor policy, and extend the trade policies initiated by the present administration.

We favor the opening of Palestine to unrestricted Jewish immigration and colonization, and such a policy as to result in the establishment there of a free and democratic Jewish commonwealth.

We favor legislation assuring equal pay for equal work, regardless of sex.

We recommend to Congress the submission of a Constitutional amendment on equal rights for women.

We favor Federal aid to education administered by the states without interference by the Federal Government.

We favor Federal legislation to assure stability of products, employment, distribution and prices in the bituminous coal industry, to create a proper balance between consumer, producer and mine worker.

We endorse the President's statement recognizing the importance of the use of water in arid land states for domestic and irrigation purposes.

We favor non-discriminatory transportation charges and declare for the early correction of inequalities in such charges.

We favor enactment of legislation granting the fullest measure of self-government for Alaska, Hawaii and Puerto Rico, and eventual statehood for Alaska and Hawaii.

We favor the extension of the right of suffrage to the people of the District of Columbia.

We offer these postwar programs:

A continuation of our policy of full benefits for ex-servicemen and women with special consideration for the disabled. We make it our first duty to assure employment and economic security to all who have served in the defense of our country.

Price guarantees and crop insurance to farmers with all practical steps:

To keep agriculture on a parity with industry and labor.

To foster the success of the small independent farmer.

To aid the home ownership of family-sized farms.

To extend rural electrification and develop broader domestic and foreign markets for agricultural products.

Adequate compensation for workers during demobilization.

The enactment of such additional humanitarian, labor, social and farm legislation as time and experience may require, including the amendment or repeal of any law enacted in recent years which has failed to accomplish its purpose.

Promotion of the success of small business.

Earliest possible release of wartime controls.

Adaptation of tax laws to an expanding peacetime economy, with simplified structure and wartime taxes reduced or repealed as soon as possible.

Encouragement of risk capital, new enterprise, development of natural resources in the West and other parts of the country, and the immediate reopening of the gold and silver mines of the West as soon as manpower is available.

We reassert our faith in competitive private enterprise, free from control by monopolies, cartels, or any arbitrary private or public authority.

We assert that mankind believes in the Four Freedoms.

We believe that the country which has the greatest measure of social justice is capable of the greatest achievements.

We believe that racial and religious minorities have the right to live, develop and vote equally with all citizens and share the rights that are guaranteed by our Constitution. Congress should exert its full constitutional powers to protect those rights.

We believe that without loss of sovereignty, world development and lasting peace are within humanity's grasp. They will come with the greater enjoyment of those freedoms by the peoples of the world, and with the freer flow among them of ideas and goods.

We believe in the world right of all men to write, send and publish news at uniform communication rates and without interference by governmental or private monopoly and that right should be protected by treaty.

To these beliefs the Democratic Party subscribes.

These principles the Democratic Party pledges itself in solemn sincerity to maintain.

Finally, this Convention sends its affectionate greetings to our beloved and matchless leader and President, Franklin Delano Roosevelt.

He stands before the nation and the world, the champion of human liberty and dignity. He has rescued our people from the ravages of economic disaster. His rare foresight and magnificent courage have saved our nation from the assault of international brigands and dictators. Fulfilling the ardent hope of his life, he has already laid the foundation of enduring peace for a troubled world and the well being of our nation. All mankind is his debtor. His life and services have been a great blessing to humanity.

That God may keep him strong in body and in spirit to carry on his yet unfinished work is our hope and our prayer.

Prohibition Party Platform of 1944

Preamble

We, the representatives of the Prohibition Party in National Convention at Indianapolis, Indiana, November 10, 11, 12, 1943, recognizing Almighty God as the source of all just Government and with faith in the teachings of the Prince of Peace, do solemnly promise that if chosen to administer the affairs of the nation, we will use all the power placed in our hands to serve the people of the United States, and that we will hold their interests above those of ourselves and our party. To do this requires the effective carrying out of the following program of Government.

A Constitutional Party

Pledge of Loyalty:

In this time of our national crises we pledge our loyalty to the Constitutional Government of the United States, to our flag and to the Republic for which it stands. We have supreme confidence in this basic law of the United States to meet ever-changing national and world conditions. Believing this, we are utterly opposed to the violation of the Bill of Rights, and to the rapidly growing tendency toward totalitarian Government in the United States.

State Rights:

We will confine the power of the executive department of the Government within the limits provided by the Constitution, will decentralize the national administration and restore to the several states their constitutional place in Government.

The support of state government in all its constitutional rights is the current bulwark against tyranny and dictatorship. We condemn the present administration for its extreme concentration in Washington of control over minor affairs.

Abolition of Bureaucracy:

We will do away with all bureaucratic devices with overlapping functions which are causing enormous waste of public funds and manpower, and will conduct Government by means of constitutional methods.

No administrative board or agency should be at the same time accuser, jury, judge and hangman. Departmental decisions ought not to be final. All decisions of administrative boards or agencies should be reviewable by our courts to preserve our liberties.

Law Enforcement:

We will maintain the integrity of democracy by enforcing the laws enacted by elected representatives of the people or by popular vote.

Money:

We believe that the Constitutional provision for the issuance of money and determination of the value thereof is a sound and feasible monetary policy.

Taxes and Government Economy:

We pledge a reduction in taxes. We condemn most vigorously the administration's extravagance and maladministration of Government funds since long before the War. We stand for radical reduction in Government expenditures. In the States we favor the effort to limit the tax rate to one percent of full value of property, in order to prevent foreclosure and confiscation, and assist the home owner, farmer, real estate owner, and others to preserve their property. But there can be no reduction in taxes unless we abolish the present increasingly expensive paternalistic bureaucracy.

Ballot Law Reform:

We demand the repeal of the many state ballot laws which have been enacted to make the two-party system impregnable, and which now deny to independent voters and minority groups the fundamental right of free political expression.

Moral Issues Supreme:

Moral and spiritual considerations, as well as economic should determine national policies. Therefore, we pledge to give them first place. To this end we will strengthen and enforce laws against gambling, narcotics, and commercialized vice now so openly violated and nullified by inaction of the parties in power.

Prevent Juvenile Delinquency:

In the interests of the moral well-being of children, youth, and the public, we urge the necessity of higher standards of decency in the enactment and enforcement of laws concerning the radio, moving pictures, literature and the stage. Since the motion pictures and the radio have become such powerful factors in the character formation of our youth, we pledge that all public officials concerned will enforce adequate laws to prevent obscenity, profanity and education tending to crime as now current in movie and radio. As a fundamental protection for youth, we will strengthen the teaching of moral precepts in the public schools and will establish and effectively enforce in the public school system scientific education on alcohol and other narcotics.

A Party of Service, Not Spoils:

The two dominant parties are committed to the spoils system and when in office have prostituted governmental power to serve their own selfish party interests instead of the whole people. That system has led to excessive government expenditures, higher taxes, and a scandalous alliance of crime with politics. We pledge ourselves to an honest, efficient and economical administration.

Social Security and Old Age Pensions:

We will extend the Social Security Act so as not to exclude any groups from its provisions, and will include a system of insurance for all aged persons, and administer it so as to preserve the incentives of initiative and thrift.

Co-operatives:

Co-operative and profit sharing enterprises are a natural outgrowth of democracy. Government under our administration will encourage such enterprises.

Labor and Capital:

We commend organized labor for its constructive contributions to the general welfare, but steps should be taken to protect labor unions from invasion and exploitation by racketeers. We would require unions to keep their records open to members and to government inspection and to file periodic financial reports, the same as corporations.

Because we stand for Industrial Peace and National Security, we believe the time has come for the Government to assume responsibility for the protection of itself and the public against the waste and terror of industrial warfare, and to that end we will enact and enforce legislation granting and defining the rights of labor to bargain individually or collectively, to negotiate, arbitrate and to establish courts of industrial relations as the final tribunal for all industrial disputes, which will seek for both labor and employing capital equal justice, and to the nation and the general public protection against the paralysis of industry due to their warfare.

Presidential Term:

American traditions will best be served by limiting the presidential office to a single term of six years.

Church and State:

The Constitutional separation of Church and State must be maintained. We will not tax church or religious activities. This, however, should not exempt individuals engaged in religious work who, as citizens, are subject to taxation.

Crime:

We seek to diminish crime, first by suppressing the traffic in alcoholic beverages and other narcotics which pervert the people; second, by bringing about a realignment of politics which shall unite the moral-minded citizens and overcome the alliance of the underworld with the political machines; third, by effective enforcement of the law; and, fourth, by the general adoption of those systems of judicial procedure which have proved most efficient and progressive.

Monopoly:

Monopolies have not ceased to exist but have become an increasing public evil. Government under our administration, in order to safeguard the rights of the common citizen, will be alert to prevent combinations of trade or of wealth which would monopolize any branch of industry or our natural resources.

No Racial Discrimination:

Recognizing that "God created of one blood all nations to dwell upon the face of the earth," we declare in favor of full justice and equal opportunity for all people, whatever their religion; racial or national origin.

Agriculture:

Believing that more people should be attracted to agriculture we favor an equitable, stable price structure for farm products. We will develop a sound program for the maintenance of individual ownership of farms.

Marriage and Divorce:

To maintain the sanctity of the home we favor the enactment of uniform marriage and divorce laws.

Freedom in Fact:

It is falsely said we should not criticize the administration in time of War. "We do not need less criticism in time of War, but more. It is to be hoped such criticism will be constructive, but better unfair attack than autocratic repression. HONESTY AND COMPETENCE REQUIRE NO SHIELD OF SECRECY," nor need fear criticism, dishonesty and fraud. Those who would usurp our rights while paying lip service to our ideals should not be shielded from it.

Domestic Post-War Problems:

The nation must accept responsibility for an adequate national program to provide opportunity for employment in suitable and satisfactory occupations not only for all men and women in the military service but also those civilians who have been employed in discontinued war industries. This program should provide special training for the disabled and unskilled. We pledge ourselves to utilize the services of public-spirited men and women representing labor, industry, and the general public, to join in a thorough-going honest effort to work out a solution of this complex problem.

World Co-operation:

Recognizing the supreme challenge and opportunity which confronts America to help secure a more just and permanent peace following this War, we insist upon preparation for that responsibility by setting up righteous standards which will guarantee to all people more equal opportunities and the rights to life, liberty, and the pursuit of happiness. To this end we advocate constructive co-operation and collaboration with all nations in some form of world organization but military alliance with none.

True Use of the Ballot:

We pledge our support to the original purpose of the ballot, which is to register the individual voter's conviction on principle, and not merely to elect persons to office. We recognize church leaders, pastors, church officials, members and editors of Christian literature as very influential on behalf of higher standards of political action, and we urge them to recognize and teach the true use of the ballot for principle. We urge them to unite in this party, which upholds righteousness as implied in the Ten Great Commandments and the Golden Rule.

The Liquor Problem:

Right thinking people are alarmed at the rapidly growing peril of the liquor power as now manifested:

1. Inflicting the alcoholic appetite upon millions of girls and women.
2. In multiplying juvenile delinquency.
3. In increasing gambling, vice and all kinds of crime.
4. In combating the efforts of the church and other moral forces.
5. In dominating our great organs of public opinion.
6. In subjecting political leaders and parties to its control.
7. In delaying, if not endangering, the success of our war effort.

The re-legalizing of the liquor traffic has brought about the worst moral reaction of modern times. Present conditions are due directly to the action of Government in restoring the liquor power through repeal of the Eighteenth Amendment, and repeal was due directly to the platform pledges of both the old parties in the 1932 presidential campaign.

Of all the wrongs committed by Government none has been worse than the authorizing of the liquor traffic to degenerate our own citizenship.

There is no higher duty of Government than to overcome the forces of evil. This cannot be done by political parties who are subservient to liquor votes. Parties dependent upon wet support are incapable of furnishing a solution.

We urge the realignment of voters and the union of good citizens in a political party not dependent upon the liquor traffic for votes. The Prohibition Party is that party.

A political party committed to prohibition (as a party principle) is the only adequate method for marshalling the agencies of Government to overcome the liquor power.

We urge all good citizens who believe in these principles, to cast their votes for them by supporting with their ballots this progressive program of government.

Republican Platform for 1944

INTRODUCTION

The tragedy of the war is upon our country as we meet to consider the problems of government and our people. We take this opportunity to render homage and enduring gratitude to those brave members of our armed forces who have already made the supreme sacrifice, and to those who stand ready to make the same sacrifice that the American course of life may be secure.

Mindful of this solemn hour and humbly conscious of our heavy responsibilities, the Republican Party in convention assembled presents herewith its principles and makes these covenants with the people of our Nation.

THE WAR AND THE PEACE

We pledge prosecution of the war to total victory against our enemies in full cooperation with the United Nations and all-out support of our Armies and the maintenance of our Navy under the competent and trained direction of our General Staff and Office of Naval Operations without civilian interference and with every civilian resource. At the earliest possible time after the cessation of hostilities we will bring home all members of our armed forces who do not have unexpired enlistments and who do not volunteer for further overseas duty.

We declare our relentless aim to win the war against all our enemies: (1) for our own American security and welfare; (2) to make and keep the Axis powers impotent to renew tyranny and attack; (3) for the attainment of peace and freedom based on justice and security.

We shall seek to achieve such aims through organized international cooperation and not by joining a World State.

We favor responsible participation by the United States in post-war cooperative organization among sovereign nations to prevent military aggression and to attain permanent peace with organized justice in a free world.

Such organization should develop effective cooperative means to direct peace forces to prevent or repel military aggression. Pending this, we pledge continuing collaboration with the United Nations to assure these ultimate objectives.

We believe, however, that peace and security do not depend upon the sanction of force alone, but should prevail by virtue of reciprocal interests and spiritual values recognized in these security agreements. The treaties of peace should be just; the nations which are the victims of aggression should be restored to sovereignty and self-government; and the organized cooperation of the nations should concern itself with basic causes of world disorder. It should promote a world opinion to influence the nations to right conduct, develop international law and maintain an international tribunal to deal with justiciable disputes.

We shall seek, in our relations with other nations, conditions calculated to promote world-wide economic stability, not only for the sake of the world, but also to the end that our own people may enjoy a high level of employment in an increasingly prosperous world.

We shall keep the American people informed concerning all agreements with foreign nations. In all of these undertakings we favor the widest consultation of the gallant men and women in our armed forces who have a special right to speak with authority in behalf of the security and liberty for which they fight. We shall sustain the Constitution of the United States in the attainment of our international aims; and pursuant to the Constitution of the United States any treaty or agreement to attain such aims made on behalf of the United States with any other nation or any association of nations, shall be made only by and with the advice and consent of the Senate of the United States provided two-thirds of the Senators present concur.

We shall at all times protect the essential interests and resources of the United States.

Western Hemisphere Relations

We shall develop Pan-American solidarity. The citizens of our neighboring nations in the Western Hemisphere are, like ourselves, Americans. Cooperation with them shall be achieved through mutual agreement and without interference in the internal affairs of any nation. Our policy should be a genuine Good Neighbor policy, commanding their respect, and not one based on the reckless squandering of American funds by overlapping agencies.

Postwar Preparedness

We favor the maintenance of postwar military forces and establishments of ample strength for the successful defense and the safety of the United States, its possessions and outposts, for the maintenance of the Monroe Doctrine, and for meeting any military commitments determined by Congress. We favor the peacetime maintenance and strengthening of the National Guards under State control with the Federal training and equipment as now provided in the National Defense Act.

Domestic Policy

We shall devote ourselves to re-establishing liberty at home.

We shall adopt a program to put men to work in peace industry as promptly as possible and with special attention to those who have made sacrifice by serving in the armed forces. We shall take government out of competition with private industry and terminate rationing, price fixing and all other emergency powers. We shall promote the fullest stable employment through private enterprise.

The measures we propose shall avoid federalization of government activities, to the end that our States, schools and cities shall be freed; shall avoid delegation of legislative and judicial power to administrative agencies, to the end that the people's representatives in Congress shall be independent and in full control of legislative policy; and shall avoid, subject to war necessities, detailed regulation of farmers, workers, businessmen and consumers, to the end that the individual shall be free. The remedies we propose shall be based on intelligent cooperation between the Federal Government, the States and local government and the initiative of civic groups—not on the panacea of Federal cash.

Four more years of New Deal policy would centralize all power in the President, and would daily subject every act of every citizen to regulation by his henchmen; and this country could remain a Republic only in name. No problem exists which cannot be solved by American methods. We have no need of either the communistic or the fascist technique.

Security

Our goal is to prevent hardship and poverty in America. That goal is attainable by reason of the productive ability of free American labor, industry and agriculture, if supplemented by a system of social security on sound principles.

We pledge our support of the following:

1. Extension of the existing old-age insurance and unemployment insurance systems to all employees not already covered.

2. The return of the public employment-office system to the States at the earliest possible time, financed as before Pearl Harbor.

3. A careful study of Federal-State programs for maternal and child health, dependent children, and assistance to the blind, with a view to strengthening these programs.

4. The continuation of these and other programs relating to health, and the stimulation by Federal aid of State plans to make medical and hospital service available to those in need without disturbing doctor-patient relationships or socializing medicine.

5. The stimulation of State and local plans to provide decent low-cost housing properly financed by the Federal Housing Administration, or otherwise, when such housing cannot be supplied or financed by private sources.

LABOR

The Republican Party is the historical champion of free labor. Under Republican administrations American manufacturing developed, and American workers attained the most progressive standards of living of any workers in the world. Now the Nation owes those workers a debt of gratitude for their magnificent productive effort in support of the war.

Regardless of the professed friendship of the New Deal for the workingman, the fact remains that under the New Deal American economic life is being destroyed.

The New Deal has usurped selfish and partisan control over the functions of Government agencies where labor relationships are concerned. The continued perversion of the Wagner Act by the New Deal menaces the purposes of the law and threatens to destroy collective bargaining completely and permanently.

The long series of Executive orders and bureaucratic decrees reveal a deliberate purpose to substitute for contractual agreements of employers and employees the political edicts of a New Deal bureaucracy. Labor would thus remain organized only for the convenience of the New Deal in enforcing its orders and inflicting its whims upon labor and industry.

We condemn the conversion of administrative boards, ostensibly set up to settle industrial disputes, into instruments for putting into effect the financial and economic theories of the New Deal.

We condemn the freezing of wage rates at arbitrary levels and the binding of men to their jobs as destructive to the advancement of a free people. We condemn the repeal by Executive order of the laws secured by the Republican party to abolish "contract labor" and peonage. We condemn the gradual but effective creation of a Labor Front as but one of the New Deal's steps toward a totalitarian state.

We pledge an end to political trickery in the administration of labor laws and the handling of labor disputes; and equal benefits on the basis of equality to all labor in the administration of labor controls and laws, regardless of political affiliation.

The Department of Labor has been emasculated by the New Deal. Labor bureaus, agencies and committees are scattered far and wide, in Washington and throughout the country, and have no semblance of systematic or responsible organization. All governmental labor activities must be placed under the direct authority and responsibility of the Secretary of Labor. Such labor bureaus as are not performing a substantial and definite service in the interest of labor must be abolished.

The Secretary of Labor should be a representative of labor. The office of the Secretary of Labor was created under a Republican President, William Howard Taft. It was intended that a representative of labor should occupy this Cabinet office. The present administration is the first to disregard this intention.

The Republican Party accepts the purposes of the National Labor Relations Act, the Wage and Hour Act, the Social Security Act and all other Federal statutes designed to promote and protect the welfare of American working men and women, and we promise a fair and just administration of these laws.

American well-being is indivisible. Any national program which injures the national economy inevitably injures the wage-earner. The American labor movement and the Republican Party, while continuously striving for the betterment of labor's status, reject the communistic and New Deal concept that a single group can benefit while the general economy suffers.

AGRICULTURE

We commend the American farmers, their wives and families for their magnificent job of wartime production and their contribution to the war effort, without which victory could not be assured. They have accomplished this in spite of labor shortages, a bungled and inexcusable machinery program and confused, unreliable, impractical price and production administration.

Abundant production is the best security against inflation. Governmental policies in war and in peace must be practical and efficient with freedom from regimentation by an impractical Washington bureaucracy in order to assure independence of operation and bountiful production, fair and equitable market prices for farm products, and a sound program for conservation and use of our soil and natural resources. Educational progress and the social and economic stability and well-being of the farm family must be a prime national purpose.

For the establishment of such a program we propose the following:

1. A Department of Agriculture under practical and experienced administration, free from regimentation and confusing government manipulation and control of farm programs.

2. An American market price to the American farmer and the protection of such price by means of support prices, commodity loans, or a combination thereof, together with such other economic means as will assure an income to agriculture that is fair and equitable in comparison with labor, business and industry. We oppose subsidies as a substitute for fair markets.

3. Disposition of surplus war commodities in an orderly manner without destroying markets or continued production and without benefit to speculative profiteers.

4. The control and disposition of future surpluses by means of (a) new uses developed through constant research, (b) vigorous development of foreign markets, (c) efficient domestic distribution to meet all domestic requirements, and (d) arrangements which will enable farmers to make necessary adjustments in production of any given basic crop only if domestic surpluses should become abnormal and exceed manageable proportions.

5. Intensified research to discover new crops, and new and profitable uses for existing crops.

6. Support of the principle of bona fide farmer-owned and farmer-operated cooperatives.

7. Consolidation of all government farm credit under a non-partisan board.

8. To make life more attractive on the family type farm through development of rural roads, sound extension of rural electrification service to the farm and elimination of basic evils of tenancy wherever they exist.

9. Serious study of and search for a sound program of crop insurance with emphasis upon establishing a self-supporting program.

10. A comprehensive program of soil, forest, water and wildlife conservation and development, and sound irrigation projects, administered as far as possible at State and regional levels.

BUSINESS AND INDUSTRY

We give assurance now to restore peacetime industry at the earliest possible time, using every care to avoid discrimination between different sections of the country, (a) by prompt settlement of war contracts with early payment of government obligations and disposal of surplus inventories, and (b) by disposal of surplus government plants, equipment, and supplies, with due consideration to small buyers and with care to prevent monopoly and injury to existing agriculture and industry.

Small business is the basis of American enterprise. It must be preserved. If protected against discrimination and afforded equality of opportunity throughout the Nation, it will become the most potent factor in providing employment. It must also be aided by changes in taxation, by eliminating excessive and repressive regulation and government competition, by the enforcement of laws against monopoly and unfair competition, and by providing simpler and cheaper methods for obtaining venture capital necessary for growth and expansion.

For the protection of the public, and for the security of millions of holders of policies of insurance in mutual and private companies, we insist upon strict and exclusive regulation and supervision of the business of insurance by the several States where local conditions are best known and where local needs can best be met.

We favor the re-establishment and maintenance, as early as military considerations will permit, of a sound and adequate American Merchant Marine under private ownership and management.

The Republican Party pledges itself to foster the development of such strong privately owned air transportation systems and communications systems as will best serve the interests of the American people.

The Federal Government should plan a program for flood control, inland waterways and other economically justifiable public works, and prepare the necessary plans in advance so that construction may proceed rapidly in emergency and in times of reduced employment. We urge that States and local governments pursue the same policy with reference to highways and other public works within their jurisdiction.

Taxation and Finance

As soon as the war ends the present rates of taxation on individual incomes, on corporations, and on consumption should be reduced as far as is consistent with the payment of the normal expenditures of government in the postwar period. We reject the theory of restoring prosperity through government spending and deficit financing.

We shall eliminate from the budget all wasteful and unnecessary expenditures and exercise the most rigid economy.

It is essential that Federal and State tax structures be more effectively coordinated to the end that State tax sources be not unduly impaired.

We shall maintain the value of the American dollar and regard the payment of government debt as an obligation of honor which prohibits any policy leading to the depreciation of the currency. We shall reduce that debt as soon as economic conditions make such reduction possible.

Control of the currency must be restored to Congress by repeal of existing legislation which gives the President unnecessary powers over our currency.

Foreign Trade

We assure American farmers, livestock producers, workers and industry that we will establish and maintain a fair protective tariff on competitive products so that the standards of living of our people shall not be impaired through the importation of commodities produced abroad by labor or producers functioning upon lower standards than our own.

If the postwar world is to be properly organized, a great extension of world trade will be necessary to repair the wastes of war and build an enduring peace. The Republican Party, always remembering that its primary obligation, which must be fulfilled, is to our own workers, our own farmers and our own industry, pledges that it will join with others in leadership in every cooperative effort to remove unnecessary and destructive barriers to international trade. We will always bear in mind that the domestic market is America's greatest market and that tariffs which protect it against foreign competition should be modified only by reciprocal bilateral trade agreements approved by Congress.

Relief and Rehabilitation

We favor the prompt extension of relief and emergency assistance to the peoples of the liberated countries without duplication and conflict between government agencies.

We favor immediate feeding of the starving children of our Allies and friends in the Nazi-dominated countries and we condemn the New Deal administration for its failure, in the face of humanitarian demands, to make any effort to do this.

We favor assistance by direct credits in reasonable amounts to liberated countries to enable them to buy from this country the goods necessary to revive their economic systems.

Bureaucracy

The National Administration has become a sprawling, overlapping bureaucracy. It is undermined by executive abuse of power, confused lines of authority, duplication of effort, inadequate fiscal controls, loose personnel practices and an attitude of arrogance previously unknown in our history.

The times cry out for the restoration of harmony in government, for a balance of legislative and executive responsibility, for efficiency and economy, for pruning and abolishing unnecessary agencies and personnel, for effective fiscal and personnel controls, and for an entirely new spirit in our Federal Government.

We pledge an administration wherein the President, acting in harmony with Congress, will effect these necessary reforms and raise the Federal service to a high level of efficiency and competence.

We insist that limitations must be placed upon spending by government corporations of vast sums never appropriated by Congress but made available by directives, and that their accounts should be subject to audit by the General Accounting Office.

TWO-TERM LIMIT FOR PRESIDENT

We favor an amendment to the Constitution providing that no person shall be President of the United States for more than two terms of four years each.

EQUAL RIGHTS

We favor submission by Congress to the States of an amendment to the Constitution providing for equal rights for men and women. We favor job opportunities in the postwar world open to men and women alike without discrimination in rate of pay because of sex.

VETERANS

The Republican Party has always supported suitable measures to reflect the Nation's gratitude and to discharge its duty toward the veterans of all wars.

We approve, have supported and have aided in the enactment of laws which provide for re-employment of veterans of this war in their old positions, for mustering-out-pay, for pensions for widows and orphans of such veterans killed or disabled, for rehabilitation of disabled veterans, for temporary unemployment benefits, for education and vocational training, and for assisting veterans in acquiring homes and farms and in establishing themselves in business.

We shall be diligent in remedying defects in veterans' legislation and shall insist upon efficient administration of all measures for the veteran's benefit.

RACIAL AND RELIGIOUS INTOLERANCE

We unreservedly condemn the injection into American life of appeals to racial or religious prejudice.

We pledge an immediate Congressional inquiry to ascertain the extent to which mistreatment, segregation and discrimination against Negroes who are in our armed forces are impairing morale and efficiency, and the adoption of corrective legislation.

We pledge the establishment by Federal legislation of a permanent Fair Employment Practice Commission.

ANTI-POLL TAX

The payment of any poll tax should not be a condition of voting in Federal elections and we favor immediate submission of a Constitutional amendment for its abolition.

ANTI-LYNCHING

We favor legislation against lynching and pledge our sincere efforts in behalf of its early enactment.

INDIANS

We pledge an immediate, just and final settlement of all Indian claims between the Government and the Indian citizenship of the Nation. We will take politics out of the administration of Indian affairs.

PROBLEMS OF THE WEST

We favor a comprehensive program of reclamation projects for our arid and semi-arid States, with recognition and full protection of the rights and interests of those States in the use and control of water for present and future irrigation and other beneficial consumptive uses.

We favor (a) exclusion from this country of livestock and fresh and chilled meat from countries harboring foot and mouth disease or Rinderpest; (b) full protection of our fisheries whether by domestic regulation or treaties; (c) consistent with military needs, the prompt return to private ownership of lands acquired for war purposes; (d) withdrawal or acquisition of lands for establishment of national parks, monuments, and wildlife refuges, only after due regard to local problems and under closer controls to be established by the Congress; (e) restoration of the long established public land policy which provides opportunity of ownership by citizens to promote the highest land use; (f) full development of our forests on the basis of cropping and sustained yield; cooperation with private owners for conservation and fire protection; (g) the prompt reopening of mines which can be operated by miners and workers not subject to military service and which have been closed by bureaucratic denial of labor or material; (h) adequate stockpiling of war minerals and metals for possible future emergencies; (i) continuance, for tax purposes, of adequate depletion allowances on oil, gas and minerals; (j) administration of laws relating to oil and gas on the public domain to encourage exploratory operations to meet the public need; (k) continuance of present Federal laws on mining claims on the public domain, good faith administration thereof, and we state our opposition to the plans of the Secretary of the Interior to substitute a leasing system; and (l) larger representation in the Federal Government of men and women especially familiar with Western problems.

Hawaii

Hawaii, which shares the Nation's obligations equally with the several States, is entitled to the fullest measure of home rule looking toward statehood; and to equality with the several States in the rights of her citizens and in the application of all our national laws.

Alaska

Alaska is entitled to the fullest measure of home rule looking toward statehood.

Puerto Rico

Statehood is a logical aspiration of the people of Puerto Rico who were made citizens of the United States by Congress in 1917; legislation affecting Puerto Rico, in so far as feasible, should be in harmony with the realization of that aspiration.

Palestine

In order to give refuge to millions of distressed Jewish men, women and children driven from their homes by tyranny, we call for the opening of Palestine to their unrestricted immigration and land ownership, so that in accordance with the full intent and purpose of the Balfour Declaration of 1917 and the Resolution of a Republican Congress in 1922, Palestine may be constituted as a free and democratic Commonwealth. We condemn the failure of the President to insist that the mandatory of Palestine carry out the provision of the Balfour Declaration and of the mandate while he pretends to support them.

Free Press and Radio

In times like these, when whole peoples have found themselves shackled by governments which denied the truth, or, worse, dealt in half-truths or withheld the facts from the public, it is imperative to the maintenance of a free America that the press and radio be free and that full and complete information be available to Americans. There must be no censorship except to the extent required by war necessity.

We insistently condemn any tendency to regard the press or the radio as instruments of the Administration and the use of government publicity agencies for partisan ends. We need a new radio law which will define, in clear and unmistakable language, the role of the Federal Communications Commission.

All channels of news must be kept open with equality of access to information at the source. If agreement can be achieved with foreign nations to establish the same principles, it will be a valuable contribution to future peace.

Vital facts must not be withheld.

We want no more Pearl Harbor reports.

Good Faith

The acceptance of the nominations made by this Convention carries with it, as a matter of private honor and public faith, an undertaking by each candidate to be true to the principles and program herein set forth.

Conclusion

The essential question at trial in this nation is whether men can organize together in a highly industrialized society, succeed, and still be free. That is the essential question at trial throughout the world today.

In this time of confusion and strife, when moral values are being crushed on every side, we pledge ourselves to uphold with all our strength the Bill of Rights, the Constitution and the law of the land. We so pledge ourselves that the American tradition may stand forever as the beacon light of civilization.

Socialist Platform of 1944

Freedom for All

In their struggle for freedom, peace and plenty,

the American people face four paramount and closely interrelated issues: (1) the winning of the earliest possible peace that will last; (2) the provision of economic security for every American, with the preservation and increase of liberty; (3) the establishment of fraternity among all races, with equality of rights and obligations; (4) the improvement of the techniques of democratic political action.

On this platform for dealing with these issues, the Socialist Party, confident that the development of a strong party with mass support is essential to the struggle against fascism and the winning of the kind of world we want, seeks the support of the American people.

1. WINNING OF THE PEACE

The winning of the peace cannot be the result of appeasement of Nazism or of any other aggressive imperialisms.

Neither can it be the consequence of the "unconditional surrender" of the Germans and Japanese to the rulers of the USSR, Great Britain and the United States of America. Shouting that slogan the Roosevelt administration is prolonging this war and inviting the next by underwriting with the lives of our sons the restoration and maintenance of the British, Dutch and French empires in the Far East, and the Balkanization of Europe between Moscow and London.

Averting New Wars

New war will not be averted by a triple alliance of the major powers—with China as a "poor relation"—even though such an alliance with its already obvious rivalries may be masked behind a plan for a vague association of nations. Yet this is the pattern for the future which most Republican as well as Democratic leaders accept.

The alternative to an uneasy and impermanent triple alliance for policing and exploiting the world is not an America first or isolationist imperialism equally dangerous to democracy and peace. But toward one or the other of these forms of imperialism and the fascism which accompanies it the policies of both old parties inexorably lead us.

Against so dire a fate, we summon the American people and the people of our allies to demand an immediate political peace offensive

based on the offer of an armistice to the people of the Axis nations on the following conditions:

Conditions for Peace

1. The peace should be organized on the acceptance of two fundamental principles: (a) the equal rights of all peoples of every race to order their lives without subjection to any race or nation; (b) the necessity that self-determination be accompanied by organized co-operation, from which no people, enemy, neutral or colonial, shall be excluded, and the establishment of political and economic arrangements for removing the causes of war, settling disputes, guaranteeing security and conquering poverty.

2. As a guarantee of good faith and a condition of armistice, the German and Japanese people must: (a) replace governments guilty of gross deceit and cruel aggression by governments in whose good faith reasonable confidence may be reposed; (b) withdraw their military forces from all occupied territory and rapidly disarm; and (c) wherever possible, restore loot and give refugees a new economic start.

3. The United Nations, on their part, must pledge themselves specifically (a) to free the European nations overrun by Germany; (b) to help them guarantee their independence through a United States of Europe or strong regional federations to supplement a world federation; (c) to refrain from interference in the internal affairs of nations thus freed; (d) to extend material aid for immediate relief and reconstruction of devastated countries without using such aid as a weapon for political domination; (e) to reject all demands for Axis slave labor in the postwar world; (f) to decide boundary questions which do not yield to negotiation by plebiscite under international authority; (g) to turn away from imperialism by guaranteeing speedy self-government, not only to lands now occupied by Japan, but to colonial territories under white rule. Where guidance to such independence is necessary, it shall be under international authority.

4. As a guarantee of good faith and a condition of the success of any federation, the United Nations must pledge themselves after the establishment of peace to follow the disarmament of the enemy countries by ending their own competitive armaments and military conscription and working out international guarantees of mutual security.

These points together comprise a peace offensive capable of inspiring revolt against the Axis dictators, winning the confidence of their victims and saving thousands of American lives.

2. ECONOMIC SECURITY WITH LIBERTY

The people of America fear the joblessness and depression which they think that the great boon of peace will bring. They remember that on the eve of the war boom, 23% of them were dependent on made work or relief and 40% lived just on, or below, the level of proper subsistence in respect to food.

In spite of this fear, what can be done in war can be better and more democratically done in peace, but only if we will plan for plenty for all as we have planned to meet the insatiable appetites of the god of war.

Poverty and joblessness cannot be conquered by private capitalism under the false alias of "free enterprise," which is extolled today, ignorantly or hypocritically, by such diverse groups as the Republicans, the Democrats, the Communists, Wall Street monopolists, little business, farmers—and even labor leaders.

Planning for plenty is wholly incompatible with a return of the control over our great productive machinery to private owners—very largely absentee owners—while the government commits itself to overcome the periodic crisis of a scarcity economy by maintaining the unemployed at subsistence levels. This has been and is the economic program of the New Deal.

Socialists pioneered in the advocacy of social insurance. We favor its extension and improvement. We endorse all possible help to returning veterans. We demand that the new public domain —the war plants now owned by the government— be used in the struggle against unemployment and not handed over to big business.

But that is not enough. Only profound social and economic reorganization will enable men to use our marvelous technological resources for the complete conquest of poverty.

Democracy—Not Bureaucracy

The commanding heights of our economic order; our system of money, banking and credit; our natural resources; our public utilities and all monopolies, semi-monopolies, and other exploitive industries, must be socially controlled. To be effective that requires social ownership, but not autocratic administration by agents of a bureaucratic state. We do not need to exchange "government of the workers, by the bosses, for the profits of absentee owners" for "government of the workers, by the bureaucrats, for the glory and power of the military state."

Two forms of administration of socialized enterprise will go far to protect us against this danger: (1) public corporations operated for the people's benefit through directors representing consumers and the various categories of workers with hand and brain in each such industry; and (2) growth of consumers' co-operatives on the Rochdale Plan.

The democratic state can further play its part by the proper control of the fiscal system and by taxation based on the two principles of the ability to pay and the encouragement of production, both of which exclude the sales tax. A postwar tax program must not be used to support the big business system and hinder the growth of social enterprise. Taxes on the rental value of land should be used to end absentee landlordism; sharply graduated inheritance taxes should prevent the perpetuation of vast estates and a carefully proportioned capital levy tax should aid socialization. Such taxation will also be found necessary to prevent enormous and growing national debt from leading us into financial disaster.

As against exploitation by private owners or the state, the right of workers to organize and to bargain collectively must be restored and protected. We oppose in war or peace the conscription of labor and the outlawry of the right to strike. Free labor is essential to a free America.

There is no more essential function of labor than the raising of food and fibre. We pledge our support to all measures looking to the conservation of our soil and the production of abundance with adequate reward to American farmers. We pledge our aid to the working farmers against exploitation by absentee landlords, bankers and middlemen. We recognize the principle of occupancy and use as the only rightful title to farm land.

Where family farming has already been replaced by great plantations and company farms, or where modern technology forces large scale farming, we demand the social ownership and co-operative operation of such land plus the use of the most modern techniques and tools. Where conditions favor family farming we encourage the security of such farmers through cooperative credit, purchasing and marketing. We reject the compulsory collectivization of family farms along Russian lines.

We advocate the extension of social insurance to farm workers and provision of social security for farmers and farm workers displaced by age or technological changes. We advocate planning for full and balanced production of food and fibre in a hungry world. We advocate the further development of government agencies essential to carrying out these proposals, including the upbuilding of a Bureau of Cooperatives in the Department of Agriculture. We oppose the subversion—often the illegal subversion—of government agencies, especially the extension service of the Department of Agriculture, and agricultural colleges, to promote the profit and power of special interest groups now so dominant in the farm bloc.

3. Equality and Fraternity of Races

Democracy requires the application of the principle that each person is to be accorded social, political and economic equality, and judged solely on the basis of his own deeds, rather than by his race, religion, or national origin.

Specifically, we pledge ourselves to work for American hospitality to war refugees and the end of the exclusion of certain Asiatic peoples. The law applying to the Chinese the general provisions concerning immigration and admitting them to citizenship, should be extended to all Asiatic countries.

We demand the complete restoration of their rights as citizens to the 70,000 Americans of Japanese origin on the West Coast who were evacuated en masse, without trial or even hearing, and confined in centers which, however humanely run, are concentration camps.

We condemn anti-Semitism, Jim-Crowism, and every form of race discrimination and segregation in the armed forces as well as civil life. We urge the passage of anti-lynching and anti-poll tax laws and the prompt enactment of legislation to set up a permanent federal Fair Employment Practice Committee.

We reaffirm our historic opposition to any doctrine or practice of a master or favored race, not only in the realm of law, but in such labor unions —fortunately a minority—churches, political parties, and other basic social organizations as today countenance it. One of the conditions that will help make permanent the end of racial prejudice is the maintenance of full employment.

4. Democratic Political Action

Year after year, by law and custom, the two old parties tighten their monopoly of the ballot. They are divided by no principles, but only by tradition and desire for office. Their platforms consist of generalities which are designed to prevent intelligent discussion and clear decision of issues. In consequence, pressure groups are the principal effective agencies in legislation and a situation is created which will aid the rise of a fascist demagogue in a period of postwar reaction.

The situation cries aloud for a democratic socialist party with mass support, such as our Canadian neighbors have developed in their Cooperative Commonwealth Federation.

Labor in the United States must establish its independence of current governmental control if it is to bargain freely with employers and government. The interests of a free labor movement are going to be better served as it severs its connections with the old parties, and unites with farm and consumer groups and minority groups seeking justice, to build a new kind of political party.

The issues here discussed are basic; they affect the lives of us all and the destiny of America. They cannot be solved separately.

An America disgraced by racial tensions which occasionally find expression in lynchings and race riots cannot lead the way to a peace which depends upon worldwide reconciliation of races on the basis of equality of right.

An America which cannot or will not provide useful jobs for its own people will easily be led into militarism, imperialism, and new war itself as palliatives for unemployment.

An America which cannot or will not perfect the tools of democracy will be relatively defenseless against a rising fascism.

Platform of the Socialist Labor Party

Our society stands where the road forks. The signs are plainly marked.

One points to a continuation of capitalism. It leads to a postwar world of chronic economic crisis, of idle factories and idle men, of spreading anti-Semitism and racism, of fascist controls and Statism, and of perpetual struggle and war.

The other points to Socialism—a world of social ownership, democratic management of the industries, jobs and plenty for all, human brotherhood, and enduring peace.

The Socialist Labor Party of America, at its 21st National Convention in the City of New York, May 1, 1944, in placing its program for a Socialist reconstruction of society before the American workers, declares this to be the issue that confronts them: Either society moves onward and upward to peace and plenty via collective ownership of the industries, or it continues under the economic despotism of private property to a new dark age. There is no middle way.

The present global war—the greatest crisis ever to face civilized man—grew out of the prewar struggle among the capitalist powers for the markets and resources of the world. The chaos it has wrought is evidence of the breakdown of the capitalist system, of its inability to manage for the benefit of society the immensely productive machinery created under it.

Capitalism could not solve the problems besetting society before the war began; it cannot solve the immensely greater problems which will arise when the war ends.

For more than a decade prior to the outbreak of World War II the factories stood idle or operated part-time, while the army of unemployed workers numbered millions. The reason is self-evident. The capitalists, owning the instruments of production and using them to exploit the propertiless workers, could not find markets for labor's product. Only one "market" could absorb the abundant output of our fields and factories. That market is war.

What the New Deal failed to do—after spending billions of dollars in a vain attempt to prime the pump of business—war did. Production has soared to unprecedented heights. But note this: We *could* have produced just as much for peace in 1939 as we produce for war in 1944. We *could* have built new factories then, factories that would turn out just as many kitchen gadgets, automobiles, refrigerators, etc., as the shells, warplanes and guns our new plants are turning out today. We did not do this because the capitalists who own the factories and decide what shall be produced, or shall not be produced, could not find markets for more than a fraction of labor's actual or potential product.

The capitalists could not find a market for labor's product before the war began; how can they sell the immensely greater product when the war ends? The capitalists themselves stand appalled before the magnitude of this problem. Their desperation is reflected in their preoccupation, in the very midst of war, with *postwar* markets and the *postwar* struggle for markets. The war has intensified and multiplied the problems confronting the capitalist class—it has, therefore, merely delayed, it has not averted, the collapse of capitalism.

The capitalist class turns more and more to the State as an agency to prolong its existence as the ruling class. Internationally the American capitalist State has become a huge cartel which utilizes the nation's military and economic might to the furtherance of capitalist aims. Domestically the State is called upon to control the forces unleashed by competitive capitalism—for the benefit of the capitalist proprietors. If private property remains the basis of society, and the capitalists are left in control of affairs, we may expect them to do precisely what the capitalists of Germany and Italy did when their rule was threatened—attempt to preserve dominion over the workers by putting totalitarian shackles upon them.

Signs of the capitalist reaction abound. The policy of dealing with fascists abroad is paralleled at home by the demand for fascist-pioneered controls over the workers—conscription of labor, for example, in open contempt of the Constitutional ban on involuntary servitude. Hardly less ominous are the demands to continue wartime controls into the postwar era, the establishment of permanent military conscription, the anti-strike laws, the creation of a huge State bureaucracy, and the spread of anti-Semitism and racism.

Anticipating unprecedented postwar unemployment and social unrest, the capitalist class and its reformer henchmen advance numerous schemes to appease the workers. Foremost among these are a vast postwar public works program and the extension of "social security"—a patent misnomer under a system which, by its very nature, dictates insecurity for the useful producers. From these proposals it is abundantly clear that what the capitalists envision is a condition of servility wherein the unemployed are held in reserve by the State in a huge public works reservoir.

Against this insane social system of capitalism, the Socialist Labor Party raises its voice in emphatic protest and unqualified condemnation, and calls upon the working class to organize politically and industrially to put an end to capitalism, and to establish the Socialist Industrial Commonwealth of Labor.

Socialism and Socialism alone is the hope of humanity! If the vast potentialities of this technological age are to be realized, capitalism must be destroyed. The industries and the land of the nation must become the collective property of society. Thus only can an end be put to unemployment, poverty, the scourge of racism and anti-Semitism, and the barbarity of war.

The Constitution of the United States provides for its own amendment. The Constitution thereby recognizes and legalizes revolution. The working class, the majority, holds the government in the hollow of its hand. We propose, accordingly, that the revolutionary change be effected by the peaceful and civilized means of the ballot.

In presenting the issue—the *only* issue, Socialism or Capitalism—and a program for its solution, the Socialist Labor Party stands alone. All other parties, whatever their names or claims, propose to reform and to preserve the criminal, and crime-breeding, capitalist system. Recognizing the simple truth that RIGHT without MIGHT to support it is useless and meaningless, we call upon the workers of America to organize themselves into integral Socialist Industrial Unions to enforce the demand for collective ownership proclaimed through the ballot. Such unions must be organized, for none now exist adequate to the great task, the existing unions—A. F. of L., C.I.O. and kindred bodies—being avowed supporters and agencies of the capitalist class and their despotic social system.

Organized along Socialist industrial lines, the working class can act instantaneously, and with such momentum that no power on earth can stop it. Only the thoroughly integrated Socialist Industrial Unions could block a brutal reaction should the outvoted, expropriated capitalists rebel against the ballot-box decision of the majority.

More than an invincible force behind Labor's ballot, the Socialist Industrial Union organizes the workers intelligently *to carry on production,* thus averting chaos. Finally, the Socialist Industrial Union becomes the *Government of the Socialist Republic,* supplanting the outworn and reactionary capitalist political State. *Democratically elected* representatives of the industrial constituencies will form an Industrial Union Congress, the duties of which will be the simple ones of directing and coordinating production for the benefit of all.

Workers of America! Repudiate the barbarous social system that exploits the mass of useful producers for the benefit of the few who merely own! Repudiate the political representatives of capitalism, be they Republican, Democratic, so-called "Socialist" or "Communist" or "Labor," who preach the criminal falsity that capitalism can be reformed and that it is worth reforming. Vote for the candidates of the Socialist Labor Party! Unite with us to demand the termination of the social system which dooms us to a lifelong tenure of wage slavery, with unemployment, poverty and wars as inseparable and ever recurrent features. Unite with us to establish the Socialist Brotherhood of Man, the Republic of Peace, Plenty and International Fraternity.

In 1948, the Democrats and Republicans received only ninety-two per cent of the electoral votes. This situation was due to a bolt from the Democratic National Convention of delegates from several southern states who protested the strong civil rights plank in the Democratic platform. These delegates formed a States' Rights or "Dixiecrat" Party which received the thirty-eight electoral votes of Alabama, Louisiana, Mississippi, South Carolina, and one vote from Tennessee. Moreover, 1948 saw the rise of a new Progressive Party which polled over a million popular votes. In addition, the Socialists, National Prohibitionists, the Christian Nationalists, Socialist Workers and Socialist Laborites presented candidates for the presidency. The Communist Party issued a party platform but did not nominate candidates for the position of Chief Executive.

The Platform of the Christian Nationalist Party, 1948

1. CHRISTIANITY

As a political party, we recognize the fact that only Christianity embraces the principle, the ethics and the spiritual dynamic fundamental to the establishment of a party equal to the present crisis.

We reassert the belief of our Founding Fathers that at all times the organic substance of the church and the organic substance of the state must be separate and distinct entities, but we hold the conviction that the righteousness of Christianity must characterize our social and political leadership if America is to survive.

All questions of dogma and doctrine are the responsibility of the organized church, but we boldly assert that the United States of America was founded as a Christian nation, dedicated to Christian principle. We believe that it is our duty to re-instate militant Christianity as a positive factor in the political, economic and national life of our country. We call all members of the Christian clergy to a realization of the fact that the same forces which crucified our Lord Jesus Christ are now attempting to crucify the civilization that grew from His teachings.

We believe that the Cross of Christ should stand beside the Stars and Stripes in the legislative halls, the schools and the courts of the land —"*Lift high the Cross, unfurl the Flag; may they forever stand united in our hearts and hopes, God and our native land.*"

2. COMMUNISM

The Christian Nationalist Party recognizes the fog of materialism that is descending upon mankind as the greatest threat to continued existence of American liberty and American security. We further recognize the Internationalist Communist movement as one of the prime manifestations of satanic materialism. Having full knowledge that the aim of the Communist movement is to destroy Christianity and overrun America, we pledge ourselves to unending warfare against every phase and facet of atheistic Communism and dictatorial Marxism. It is our ambition to finally obliterate Communism from the face of the world.

It is well known that Communist forces first infiltrate, then weaken, that which they wish to destroy. They have infiltrated the "old" political parties and government offices of the United States. They have weakened the United States Government by instituting an economic program of state socialism; by a program of Communist appeasement in our foreign relations; by continuing to allow Communists to organize politically inside the United States. For the safeguarding of our country we demand that all members of the Communist Party, all members of Communist-front organizations, all supporters of Communism be removed from the Federal payrolls and from all positions in Government service.

J. Edgar Hoover, Director of the F. B. I., has stated that the backbone of the Communist Party in America is composed of aliens and foreign born. We, therefore, demand the immediate deportation of every alien who is a member of the Communist Party, a member of a Communist-front organization, or supporters of Communism.

Further, we believe that all persons naturalized within the past 15 years should have their citizenship applications re-examined for the purpose of deporting those persons who are members of the Communist Party, members of Communist-front organizations, or supporters of Communism.

For the purpose of declaring to the world our opposition to Communism; for the purpose of alerting the citizens of our country to the evil inherent in Communism; for the purpose of protecting the United States from the insidious destructiveness of Communism we demand the arrest of all members of the Communist Party as agents of a foreign power and the outlawing of the Communist Party in America as a conspiracy to overthrow the Constitution and the government of the United States.

3. THE JEW

The power of the Jew has become America's problem. His influence, brought about by the manipulation of minority votes, international and domestic finance, has created an intolerable situation in America. He has coerced and intimidated the old parties and all political parties to the point where no existing American political party dares challenge his authority. This circumstance is one of the chief fundamentals which make necessary the formation of the Christian Nationalist Party.

The Jew now exercises this authority and power in numerous ways contrary to natural sentiment, public good, Christian principle and American tradition.

Our indictment of the organized Jew grows out of numerous situations that have recently developed in our national life, including the following:

Political Zionism

An overwhelming majority of all Jews in America are obviously committed to political Zionism which calls for the establishment of a Jewish state. This commitment involves dual citizenship. We hold that these Jews cannot be loyal Americans and political Zionists at the same time. We believe that anyone claiming to be an American citizen and holding allegiance to a foreign state should be deported. Therefore, we call for the immediate deportation of all supporters of the political Zionist movement. We demand that this international political machine and all its activity be outlawed in the United States. We take this position in order that we may defend ourselves from an obvious plot to make the United States subservient to a Jewish state with international headquarters in Jerusalem.

Jewish Gestapo Organizations

The Jewish international state would destroy the independence of our nation. At the same time, the Jewish gestapo tends to destroy the peace and happiness and the liberty of the individual Christian American citizen. Jewish-operated, Jewish-controlled and Jewish-financed gestapo organizations now exist in America for the purpose of controlling, intimidating, coercing, punishing, boycotting and abusing in general individuals who hold the express frank and accurate opinions concerning the Jew.

Even beyond this, we find these organizations operating with unlimited sums of money in an attempt to discredit all men who are out-spoken in their defense of Christianity, of Nationalism and American tradition.

We call for the dissolution of such organizations as the so-called Anti-Defamation League, the American Jewish Congress, the so-called Non-Sectarian Anti-Nazi League, the self-styled Friends of Democracy and all other organizations that spy on, threaten, coerce and smear American citizens. These organizations are un-American in spirit and criminal in practice.

The Jew and Communism

We assert, and eventually all intelligent American citizens must admit, that behind Communism stands the organized Jew. It now becomes increasingly obvious that the power and support of the International Jewish cabal has been given to the various forms of Communism growing out of the teachings of the Jew, Karl Marx.

These powers of support have exercised themselves in numerous ways, including the following: Their journals have been used to make Communism seem good to our people. Their power in the realm of the radio and motion picture has been definitely exerted in support of the atheistic, Christ-hating philosophies of Marx and his disciples. Their financial, political and organizational power has brought Communism into the American home and American school and even into certain of the American churches. This power, exerted in defense of civilization's worst enemy, must be broken and it can only be broken by putting Christian Nationalists in control of the Government of the United States.

4. IMMIGRATION

All immigration of Asiatics, including Jews, and members of the colored races must be stopped by law.

We favor a program of constructive immigration which would include the Christian peoples of Europe, such as the Scandinavians, the Anglo-Saxons and the Germanic groups. These people and their types almost without exception become constructive citizens in the development of a Christian community and a Christian nation.

Millions of undesirables now reside within the borders of the United States who have entered this country illegally or have been admitted because of loosely-drawn and loosely-enforced immigration laws. These individuals furnish most of the membership of Marxist organizations and supply most of the destructive agitation now menacing our Nation. We advocate the deportation of these undesirables.

5. THE NEGRO

The enemies of America are missing no opportunity to organize and exploit the American Negro. This exploitation takes on three forms of abuse. The Communists would make the Negro a revolutionary backlog for an era of bloodshed and slaughter. The organized Jew is attempting to use the American Negro to break down the influence and power of the white man's leadership. Numerous Jewish pressure groups encourage intermarriage, mongrelization and social intermixture. The political demagogue is using the Negro vote in doubtful states as a pawn in his greed for power.

The Negro, without his knowledge, is being used to destroy the Nation that exposed him to Christian civilization. We condemn the original enslavement of the Negro. We brand it as a crime of which Northern and Southern interests were equally guilty. We must atone for that crime but not by the destruction of our Nation.

Therefore, the Christian Nationalist Party supports the Abraham Lincoln Plan for the Negro—a homeland in Africa. We believe that this homeland should be opened to all American Negroes and that $5,000 per family should be set aside for Negroes willing to migrate to this homeland where all public officials shall be Negroes and where only Negroes shall be eligible for office. We accept the philosophy of Abraham Lincoln expressed in his address to the free Negroes of Washington when he said: "You and we are a different race. We have between us a broader difference than exists between almost any other two races. It is better for us both, therefore, to be separated."

Segregation

In the light of the historic fact that the intermarriage of the black and white races invariably spells the destruction of a civilization, we Christian Nationals shall support an amendment to the Constitution of the United States which would require the segregation of the black and white races and which would outlaw intermarriage and make of same a Federal crime. Pending such a time as the American people can atone for the crime of slavery by the establishment of a Negro homeland, immediate steps must be taken to prevent the destruction of our Nation by mongrelization.

6. Relationship to Other Nations

We shall support constructive Nationalism wherever it exists. We shall support the doctrine of self-determination, intelligent self-interest and national pride wherever it exists. Our intercourse with these nations would rest upon the philosophy expounded by the father of our country, George Washington, who said: "Friendship with all nations; trade with all nations; entangling alliances with none."

The United Nations

The United Nations is a Jewish-Communist instrument for the destruction of the sovereignty of all nations. America should withdraw from it and lend its influence to its complete destruction. Steps must be taken to remove this embryonic super-state and its agencies from American soil.

Secret Commitment

We denounce, and demand the publication and repudiation of, all secret promises and agreements entered into by the late Franklin D. Roosevelt, Josef Stalin, their cohorts and advisors.

Bi-Partisan Plan

This is a betrayal of the American people. It is a conspiracy to end intelligent discussion and open debate on all matters pertaining to our relationship to other nations. This conspiracy of agreement made it possible for Internationalists to put over the Marshall Plan, UNRRA and the Truman doctrine without exposing the electorate to intelligent discussion and debate.

Marshall Plan

We favor a policy of encouraging the anti-Communist forces of the various European countries, and we favor extending humanitarian aid to all starving people. We condemn, however, the appeasement of the Socialist politicians who are thriving on the fear and hunger of Europe; we condemn the rank hypocrisy and graft of the "Marshall Plan"—whereby we are spending mil-

lions of dollars for liquor and tobacco, millions of dollars to repay Mussolini's debts to international financiers, millions of dollars to American newspapers and magazines—we condemn the treason that allowed export of American materials to the Communist dominated states of Europe. Money-wasting enterprises such as the Marshall Plan, designed to fatten the purses and the financial empires of international bankers must be ended.

Spain

We recognize the fact that Stalin, the International Jew and all Marxist forces have attempted to destroy the present Spanish Government. We recognize further that it has proved to be an uncompromising bulwark against Communist aggression. We advocate a development of friendly relations with this courageous people.

Germany

We favor the immediate and absolute end of the satanic Morgenthau policy of starving and enslaving the innocent women and children of Germany merely to satisfy the blood-lust of certain power-mad, sadistic, Christ-hating International Jews. We challenge the clergy and the Christian leadership of the world to help build a strong Christian Germany to help us contain the Communist beast, to prevent the invasion of Western Europe by the Red Army of Josef Stalin.

Russia

We recognize the fact that Russia is ruled by savages. It has no moral capacity to complete agreements or to fulfill treaties. It has fattened and become powerful through the exploitation of secret and pro-Russian commitments made by Franklin D. Roosevelt. We advocate that all diplomatic relations with the present Russian government be broken and that ways and means be devised for encouraging white Russians all over the world and anti-Communist Russians within Russia to rise and rebuild a Christian nation.

Palestine

The political Zionists in cooperation with the forces of Russia as well as by the favor and consent of President Truman, Thomas E. Dewey and others have driven 300,000 Arabs out of their homes and away from their own land where they now starve on the desert. We oppose this abortive state which the Jews named "the New Israel." We refuse to endorse this savage policy in its attempt to exploit the Christian's faith in the destiny of Jerusalem. We deny that it is in harmony with Christian teaching to steal land and slaughter innocents. This the Jews have done. We oppose the partition of Palestine. It is our conviction that it is a political Zionist plot for establishing headquarters for world control.

China

The Nationalists of China should be encouraged. We recognize the fact that were it not for the Nationalists of China, now led by General Chiang Kai-shek, Stalin could mobilize 400 million Chinese against the Christian world. We strongly urge the encouragement of Chiang Kai-shek on the sound basis of intelligent self-interest and constructive American Nationalism.

Japan, Korea, and Kindred Communities

Postwar policy in Japan should encourage all anti-communist forces and should be alert to all attempts being made by materialistic elements to exploit our victory to the disadvantage of Christianity and the best interests of America.

7. War Criminals

It is a matter of common knowledge that prior to and during World War II men high in office, including the late Franklin D. Roosevelt, committed crimes against our people which tax the imagination of even the most enlightened. The Pearl Harbor attack was precipitated. The Pearl Harbor investigation was a hypocritical whitewash. The Morgenthau Plan was a sadistic plot to liquidate 100 million Christians. Certain high officials, including the war-time President, actually plotted the continuation of the war unnecessarily. The American armies were actually ordered to withdraw from Berlin in favor of the Russian forces. It is our belief that a thorough investigation by a Congressional Committee would reveal scores of high crimes which would call for the punishment of the culprits who precipitated such crimes.

8. Atomic Energy

Control of the atom bomb and atomic energy must be removed immediately from the hands of the Lilienthal committee and returned to the control of the military. All who know the secret of atomic energy should be kept under surveillance by the FBI, the Military Intelligency and the Secret Service for the remainder of their lives. Inasmuch as it is the belief of certain students of world affairs that important information concerning atomic energy has been taken from America to Russia and others, those guilty of this act should be brought to justice immediately and double safeguards should be thrown around all atomic energy information from this moment forward.

9. National Defense

We believe that citizenship carries with it the responsibility to defend the Nation whenever invasion threatens or the menace of international revolution appears. The military power of the nation at all times must be sufficiently strong to guarantee the preservation of our national self-respect and to support pronounced policies of a true Nationalist state. It is our belief that a wage scale for a peace-time army comparable to the wage scale of American industry would supply the necessary peace-time personnel.

10. Economic Stability

We believe that the constant alternating between periods of perilous depression and wild inflation (with the slaughtering of livestock and plowing under of foodstuffs on the one hand, and the siphoning off of our production to maintain a world-wide WPA on the other) is a planned program to keep the American people in a state of economic insecurity. By removing the control of our monetary system from private banking houses and returning it to Congress, by instituting an economy of abundance and full-production we can free our citizens from the threat of economic slavery and provide security through the abolition of speculation and usury.

11. Price Control

We denounce all price controls and all forms of rationing as forms of bureaucratic regimentation. Such practices menace the system of private enterprise and fatten the purses of the Jewish black marketeers who grew fat during the recent war. We believe in an economy of abundance. The available supply of necessities would be greatly increased and prices greatly reduced if American production could be reserved for Americans first. If Marshall Plan waste could be checked, if mysteriously accumulated American currency now flooding this country in the hands of refugees could be recalled, the purchase power of the American housewife would be greatly enhanced.

12. HOUSING

We recognize the shortage of houses. We propose the solution of this problem by certain direct and simple steps.

a. Vacate and make available to veterans and citizens all housing units now occupied by illegal immigrants and non-citizens.

b. Declare vacant and make available to American citizens all housing units now occupied by non-citizens.

c. Destroy the power of the labor racketeer who refuses to permit the introduction of assembly-line science and labor-saving methods necessary to effect inexpensive and speedy housing construction. It is now a matter of common knowledge that houses could be constructed twice as rapidly and for one-half the cost if the above mentioned practices could be introduced.

d. Bureaucratic controls over construction and rentals should be abolished and avoided in order that private enterprise may be given the maxium encouragement in solving our housing problem.

e. As these aliens vacate American houses to be made available for American people, they should be extended humanitarian treatment and provided with temporary shelter in quickly constructed public camps during the time they are being screened for deportation as undesirables. Following the screening, desirable aliens will then be free to qualify for citizenship.

13. THE AGED AND THE INFIRM

Improvement in our mode of living has extended the age of the American citizen ten years in the past generation. Labor saving devices will continue to retire the average man from productive labor at an increasingly younger age. Our senior citizens must be made the benefactors of this progress, not the victims. A simple but effective system must be provided whereby the children of one generation can provide well for those of the passing generation. We favor a pension that will guarantee a self-respecting and in-dependent standard of living for all regardless of their economic standing, just as veterans compensations are paid to all regardless of economic standing. Monetary reforms which will remove our money system from the hands of the money changers and establish Constitutional controls will go a long way toward solving this important problem. To specify an amount for a pension is demagoguery unless our economy stabilizes the purchase power of the amount paid.

14. CITIZENSHIP

Our plan for naturalizing citizens should be re-examined and requirements should be made more stringent. In light of the fact that a phenomenal number of aliens have entered this country illegally, the time has come for us to demand that a roster of all citizens be made available to every community and be open to inspection in every county court house. Non-citizens who have dwelt within the borders of the USA for some time without attempting to become citizens should be viewed with suspicion.

15. PRIVATE ENTERPRISE

Private enterprise has made America the richest nation on earth. It has developed a strong middle class which has kept our people relatively free from regimentation and monopoly. The two greatest enemies of private enterprise are: regimentation and monopoly control. As long as private enterprise is permitted to operate in an atmosphere of health and freedom, the humblest plough-hand and the son of the most obscure worker has the opportunity to become a citizen of prominence and abundance.

16. LABOR

The Christian Nationalist Party is determined that American citizens who perform common and skilled labor shall be freed from the exploitation of the revolutionist and labor racketeer and the feudal lord. The men and women who perform the necessary task in the field of skilled and unskilled labor must be freed from bureaucratic interference to the end that they may establish a free, unhampered relationship between themselves and their employers. Incentive systems must be encouraged and all constructive steps must be taken necessary to create a situation where the laborer shall be paid in proportion to the labor he performs. The Marxist system of levelling all workers under a uniform, union scale where the competent and efficient are paid no more than the lazy and inefficient, must be discouraged and wherever possible abolished.

17. Agriculture

The prices of farm crops must be stabilized in such a way as to guarantee the cost of production, plus a reasonable profit. Upon these stable prices freed from tyranny and uncertainty of speculation and money-changing tactics, the farmer will be rewarded for abundance, not scarcity; for the ingenuity of production and not the ingenuity of destruction. Wealth under a Nationalist administration would be determined by the production of the soil and not the arbitrary price of an ounce of metal subject to the whims of the money changers. Under all circumstances, the great American market must be reserved exclusively for the American farmer.

18. Veterans

The two world wars were fought by citizen armies which drew on the youth of the Nation. The recent war took 13 million men. We hold that the following fundamental principles must be observed in relation to the veterans of all wars.

  a. Totally disabled men must be guaranteed a self-respecting and generous livelihood for themselves and their families.
  b. Impaired men suffering from wounds and sickness due to war must have every modern facility necessary to the maximum amount of comfort, and their compensation must be generous and consistent with their impairment.
  c. Able-bodied men who returned in sound health will naturally share in the abundance and opportunity which will be guaranteed to all citizens in a regime of Christian Nationalism.
  d. Veterans of all wars should be given priority in jobs and houses over non-citizens. Whenever unemployment appears, non-citizens should surrender their jobs and make them available to veterans. In the same manner houses occupied by aliens should be vacated and made available to veterans.

Conclusion

We who have framed and adopted this plat-form are realistic. We are conscious of the fact that evil and materialistic forces will oppose the fulfillment of this Platform with every power at their command. It is our conviction that deep in the hearts of millions of American citizens—Yes, more than a majority of our citizens—is a pronounced hunger for the moral courage and the Christian statesmanship necessary to enforce the ideals expressed in this Platform. The summary of the whole matter is: Shall the lovers of Jesus Christ or the enemies of Jesus Christ determine the destiny of America. The time has come for all citizens of our Nation to take their stand. There is no middle ground. Believing that the teaching and the spirit of Jesus Christ constitute the dynamic with which this party must be built, we recognize the fact that only through the help of Divine Power can the maximum victory be accomplished.

It is agreed by this Convention assembled that this Platform be reproduced in print and made available to all members of the Party and interested friends and observers.

Communist Party Platform, 1948

In this crucial 1948 election the American people have a fateful decision to make: Shall America follow the path of peace or war, democracy or fascism?

Our boys returned from World War II with the hope that their wartime sacrifices had not been in vain.

Remember the promises:

Fascism would be wiped out.

The great-power unity that brought war victory would bring enduring peace.

An economic bill of rights would provide every American with security.

These promises have been broken.

Instead of peace, there is war—in Greece, in China, in Israel.

Instead of peace, we witness feverish preparations for a new world war.

Instead of peace, American boys are being regimented for war with the enactment of the peacetime draft.

Instead of security and abundance, we have sky-rocketing prices, lowered living standards and the shadow of an impending economic crash with mass unemployment. Farmers fear the inevitable collapse of farm prices. After three years our veterans are still denied housing. Our youth face a future of insecurity and new wars.

Instead of greater democracy, we have lynch law, mounting Jim-Crowism and anti-Semitism, and a conspiracy to undermine our sacred democratic heritage. We have anti-Communist witch-hunts, the arrest and conviction of anti-fascist leaders, the harassment and intimidation of writers, artists and intellectuals. We have phony spy scares, the hounding of government employees and former Roosevelt associates, the persecution of foreign-born workers, and the adoption of anti-labor legislation, attempts to outlaw the Communist Party through Mundt-Nixon Bills, and now the indictment of the twelve Communist leaders on the trumped-up charge of "force and violence." These are the methods by which the American people are step by step being driven down the road to a police state and fascism.

These are the chief issues of the 1948 elections.

America is a great and beautiful land, endowed with immense natural resources and a people skilled in producing abundance. Why then the fear of insecurity?

We are today threatened by no outside force. We are in no danger of attack from any nation. Why then the war hysteria?

The answer lies in this simple fact—250 giant corporations, operating through a handful of banks, control the economic life of the United States. These in turn are largely owned by a few plutocratic families—Morgan, Rockefeller, Mellon, du Pont and Ford.

The nation's industries are not operated for the public welfare, but for the private gain and power of the multi-millionaire ruling class. Prices continue to rise because of vast military expenditures and because the monopolies, through price-fixing agreements and other devious devices, extract exorbitant profits.

They make huge profits from war and from armaments. They extract super-profits abroad by forcing other nations into economic dependence upon Wall Street. This drive for foreign markets, for Wall Street domination of the world, is at the bottom of the war hysteria and war preparations. Big Business strives to crush the growth and advance of democracy and socialism throughout the world, in order to protect and swell its profits.

Big Business seeks to re-establish the old Nazi cartels and to use Germany and Japan as military bases for new aggression. But the failures of the bipartisan policy to achieve its main aim of world conquest have increased the frenzy with which Wall Street seeks to plunge the nation into fascism and World War III.

War and Peace . . .

Neither the American people nor the Soviet Union is responsible for the sharpening tension in international relations. The responsibility rests squarely on Wall Street and the bipartisan Truman-Dewey atomic diplomacy. Only the capitalists trusts want war. The Soviet Union is a socialist country. It has no trusts, no I. G. Farben or du Pont cartels to profit from wars. That is why the Soviet Union is the most powerful force for peace in the world.

The Communist Party calls upon the labor movement and all progressive, peace-loving Americans to struggle for the realization of the following peace program:

End the "cold war," the draft, and the huge military budget.

Restore American-Soviet friendship, the key to world peace and the fulfillment of the people's hope in the United Nations.

Conclude a peace settlement for a united, democratic Germany and Japan based on the Yalta and Potsdam agreements. Guarantee the complete democratization and demilitarization of these Countries.

Stop military aid and intervention in China, Korea and Greece.

Break diplomatic and economic ties with Franco Spain.

Scrap the Marshall Plan and the Truman Doctrine. Furnish large-scale economic assistance to the war-ravaged victims of fascist attack. Give this aid through the United Nations without political strings.

Lift the embargo on, and extend full recognition to Israel.

Give immediate, unconditional independence to Puerto Rico.

Aid the economic development of the colonial and semi-colonial countries of Asia, Africa and Latin America on the basis of full support to their fight for their national independence. De-

feat the Truman Arms Standardization Plan.

Abandon economic, political and military pressures on the countries of Latin America.

The Attack on Labor and Our Living Standards

The trusts have inflated prices and battered down the real wages of American workers to 16 per cent below 1944.

Huge war expenditures amount to 15 billion dollars this year—one-third of the entire national budget. The American people are already paying dearly for this "cold war economy," through a heavy tax burden, speed-up and reduction in real wages. We will pay still more heavily as the inflationary boom speeds the day of the oncoming economic bust.

Big Business has decreed that labor's hands be tied and its rights destroyed. The Taft-Hartley Law and strike-breaking injunctions are weapons against the people's resistance to the monopoly drive towards war and fascism.

To defend the labor movement and the vital economic interests of the overwhelming majority of the American people, labor and all progressives should unite in stubborn and militant struggle for the following demands:

Repeal the Taft-Hartley Law and end strike-breaking injunctions. Adopt a code of Federal labor legislation including the best features of the Wagner Act and the Norris-LaGuardia Anti-Injunction Law.

Restore price control and roll back prices, without any wage freeze.

Enact an extensive program for Federally-financed low-rent public housing, minimum wage legislation, old-age pensions, adequate health insurance, and increased aid to education.

Provide increased security for the working farmers through up-to-date parity price and income guarantees, based on unlimited farm production. Such income guarantees require farm subsidies, effective crop insurance and sharp curbs on the giant food trusts and their marketing agencies. Carry out a program of planned conservation and River Valley projects. Extend the Federal minimum wage and social security laws to agricultural workers, including seasonal and migratory labor.

We call for heavier taxation on high incomes and excess profits, with increased exemption for the low brackets. We demand a capital levy on big fortunes and corporations to finance essential social legislation.

We support all steps to curb the power of the trusts, the source of reaction, fascism and war. The American people can make gains, even under capitalism, by mass resistance to the monopolies.

We support measures to nationalize the basic industries, banks and insurance companies, but point out that such measures can only be useful as part of the fight to realize a people's democratic government in the United States. Democratic nationalization of trustified industries requires guarantees of democratic controls and the right of labor to organize, bargain collectively and strike. This can only be accomplished by a people's government dedicated to curbing the power of the trusts.

We point out that capitalism cannot become "progressive" even by curbing the excesses of the monopolies. The basic causes of unemployment, economic crisis, fascism and war can only be removed by the establishment of Socialism through the democratic will of the majority of the American people.

Civil Rights . . .

The destruction of the rights of the Communists is the classical first step down the road to fascism. The tragedy of Germany and Italy proves this. Therefore, it is incumbent upon the working class and all Americans who hate fascism to defend the rights of the Communists, and to help explode the myth that Communists are foreign agents or advocate force and violence.

We Communists are no more foreign agents than was Jefferson who was also accused of being a foreign agent by the Tories of his day. We follow in the best traditions of the spokesmen of labor, science and culture whose contributions to human progress knew no national boundaries. We follow in the tradition of Abraham Lincoln, who said: "The strongest bond of human sympathy, outside of the family relation, should be one uniting all working people, of all nations and tongues, and kindreds."

It is the monopolists who advocate and practice force and violence, not the Communists. Reaction has always resorted to force and violence to thwart the democratic aspirations of the people.

In 1776, force and violence were the weapons of King George against the American colonists seeking national independence. In 1861, force and violence were used by the Southern slave owners in an attempt to overthrow the democratic republic headed by Lincoln. Today the people suffer the violence of the K.K.K., the lynch mobs, the fascist hoodlum gangs and police brutality.

We are Marxists, not adventurers or conspirators. We condemn and reject the policy and practice of terror and assassination and repudiate the advocates of force and violence. We Communists insist upon our right to compete freely in the battle of ideas. We Communists insist upon our right to organize and bring our program to the people. Let the people judge our views and activities on their merits.

We call upon the American people to fight with all their strength against the danger of fascism to resist every fascist measure, to defend every democratic right.

End the witch-hunts, loyalty orders and phony spy scares.

Abolish the Un-American Committee. Withdraw the indictments against the twelve Communist leaders and the contempt citations against the anti-fascist victims of Congressional inquisitions.

Stop the campaign of terror and intimidation against labor leaders, intellectuals and people of the professions.

End persecution and deportation of the foreign born and lift the undemocratic bars to citizenship.

Outlaw all forms of anti-Semitism, anti-Catholicism, and every other expression of racial and religious bigotry.

End all discrimination against the Mexican-American people in the Southwest.

The Communist party calls for an end to any and all political, social, and economic inequalities practiced against women and demands the maintenance and extension of existing protective legislation.

Extend the suffrage. Remove the bars directed against minority parties. Lower the voting age to 18 years in every state.

NEGRO RIGHTS . . .

The hypocrisy of the democratic pretensions of Wall Street and the Administration are shattered by the reality of the Jim-Crow system in America. The most shameful aspect of American life is the Jim-Crowism, the terror and violence imposed upon the Negro people, especially in the South. Discrimination in employment, only slightly relaxed during the war, is once again widespread.

The Communist Party, which has pioneered in fighting for full political, economic and social equality for the Negro people, calls for an end to the policies of the Federal and state governments which give official sanction to the Jim-Crow system in the United States.

We call upon all progressives, especially white progressives, to carry on an unceasing day-to-day struggle to outlaw the poll tax, lynchings, segregation, job discrimination and all other forms of Jim-Crowism, official and unofficial, and to give their full support to the rising national liberation movement of the Negro people. This is vital to the Negro people, to the white workers, and to the whole fight for democracy in America.

We demand a national F.E.P.C. law, to be vigorously and fully enforced.

We demand that the Ingram family be freed and adequately compensated for the ordeals to which they have been subjected.

We demand that the Ku Klux Klan and all other hate-and-terror organizations be outlawed.

We condemn President Truman's cynical evasion of the issue of segregation in the armed forces. We demand that he immediately issue an Executive Order ending every form of segregation and discrimination in the armed forces and the government services.

We defend the right of the Negro people to full representation in government, and demand Federal enforcement of the 13th, 14th, and 15th Amendments, so that the Negro people, North and South, may participate freely and fully in the 1948 elections and all elections thereafter.

We call for a democratic agricultural program which will give land and other forms of assistance to millions of Negro and white tenants and sharecroppers in the South, and thereby help put an end to the semi-feudal plantation system.

Such reforms will help provide the material basis for the Negro people's advance towards full liberation from their national oppression, towards their full political, economic and social equality.

THE TWO-PARTY SYSTEM . . .

Millions of American working people have come to realize the futility of any further support for the bankrupt two-party system of Big Business. Both major parties are committed to the bipartisan war program, reflected in both the Truman Doctrine and its New Look version, the Marshall Plan. Both major parties are united in this program of fattening the billionaires and bleeding the people.

Both major parties are responsible for runaway inflation. Both the Democratic Administration and the Republican Congress have done nothing to curb the powers of the trusts to hoard food, rig markets, boost prices and gouge consumers.

Both major parties are responsible for the atrocities committed against the Bill of Rights. Both helped pass the Taft-Hartley Law. Both the Democratic Congressional leaders and the cynical Dewey-Warren-Taft Republican leadership are responsible for the failure to enact civil rights legislation. Neither the Democratic platform nor President Truman's demagogy will fool any enlightened American. The President's deeds belie his words. He has refused to end segregation in the armed forces and the government and fire from his cabinet those who maintain it.

Both major parties are responsible for the Hitler-like hysteria expressed in spy scares, loyalty probes, government witch-hunts and the arrest and indictment of Americans whose "crime" it is to oppose the Wall Street war plans. The Democratic-controlled Department of Justice and the Republican-controlled Un-American Committee are equally guilty of subverting the Bill of Rights.

Chief allies of the twin parties of Big Business in the ranks of labor and the progressive organizations of the people are those who pretend to criticize the corruption and decay of the two old parties while, in fact, keeping the people tied hand and foot to the two-party system. These include the top officialdom of the A.F.L., C.I.O. and R.R. Brotherhoods and groups like the Americans for Democratic Action and such Social-Democrats as Norman Thomas and David Dubinsky.

THE NEW PARTY . . .

Millions of Americans, disillusioned with the two-party system, have joined to found a new people's party.

The new Progressive Party is an inescapable historic necessity for millions who want a real choice now between peace and war, democracy and fascism, security and poverty.

The Communists, who support every popular progressive movement, naturally welcome this new people's party. We supported the progressive features of Roosevelt's policies, domestic and foreign. We helped organize the C.I.O. in the 1930's. We have supported every democratic movement since the Communists of Lincoln's generation fought in the Union cause during the Civil War.

On most immediate questions before the people of the country the Progressive Party has offered detailed platform planks around which all forward-looking people can unite. Our support of the Progressive Party policies and campaign does not alter the fact that we have fundamental as well as some tactical differences with Henry Wallace and related third-party forces.

The Communist Party is not nominating a Presidential ticket in the 1948 elections. In 1944 we Communists supported Roosevelt to help win the anti-Axis war. Similarly, in 1948 we Communists join with millions of other Americans to support the Progressive Party ticket to help win the peace. The Communist Party will enter its own candidates only in those districts where the people are offered no progressive alternatives to the twin parties of Wall Street.

The Progressive Party is by its very nature a great coalition of labor, farmers, the Negro people, youth, and professional and small business people. It is anti-monopoly, anti-fascist, anti-war. By its very nature it is not an anti-capitalist party. It is not a Socialist or a Communist Party and we are not seeking to make it one. It is and should develop as a united front, broad, mass people's party.

There is only one Marxist Party in America, one party dedicated to replacing the capitalist system with Socialism—and that is the Communist Party.

Our firm conviction that only a Socialist reorganization of society will bring permanent peace, security and prosperity is no barrier to cooperation with all other progressive Americans, in helping create a great new coalition in order to save our people from the twin horrors of war and fascism.

We seek no special position in this movement and will, of course, oppose any attempt to discriminate against us because of our Socialist aims.

We Communists are dedicated to the proposition that the great American dream of life, liberty and pursuit of happiness, will be realized only under Socialism, a society in which the means of production will be collectively owned and operated under a government led by the working class. Only such a society can forever banish war, poverty and race hatred. Only in such a society can there be the full realization of the dignity of man and the full development of the individual. Only such a society can permanently protect the integrity of the home and family. Only a Socialist society can realize in life the vision of the brotherhood of man.

Fellow Americans:

We live in times of great danger.

Fascism and war now threaten our country.

But the common people of America, and in the first place the working people, can defeat these dangers. They can turn our country to the path of democracy and peace, to the path of social progress.

The 1948 elections will help decide which way America will go.

Your united action in this election, your determined defense of your rights, can become powerful forces for peace and progress. The future of our country is in your hands.

Democratic Party Platform 1948

The Democratic Party adopts this platform in the conviction that the destiny of the United States is to provide leadership in the world toward a realization of the Four Freedoms.

We chart our future course as we charted our course under the leadership of Franklin D. Roosevelt and Harry S. Truman in the abiding belief that democracy—when dedicated to the service of all and not to a privileged few—proves its superiority over all other forms of government.

Our party record of the past is assurance of its policies and performance in the future.

Ours is the party which was entrusted with responsibility when twelve years of Republican neglect had blighted the hopes of mankind, had squandered the fruits of prosperity and had plunged us into the depths of depression and despair.

Ours is the party which rebuilt a shattered economy, rescued our banking system, revived our agriculture, reinvigorated our industry, gave labor strength and security, and led the American people to the broadest prosperity in our history.

Ours is the party which introduced the spirit of humanity into our law, as we outlawed child labor and the sweatshop, insured bank deposits, protected millions of home-owners and farmers from foreclosure, and established national social security.

Ours is the party under which this nation before Pearl Harbor gave aid and strength to those countries which were holding back the Nazi and Fascist tide.

Ours is the party which stood at the helm and led the nation to victory in the war.

Ours is the party which, during the war, prepared for peace so well that when peace came reconversion promptly led to the greatest production and employment in this nation's life.

Ours is the party under whose leadership farm owners' income in this nation increased from less than $2.5 billions in 1933 to more than $18 billions in 1947; independent business and professional income increased from less than $3 billions in 1933 to more than $22 billions in 1947; employees' earnings increased from $29 billions in 1933 to more than 128 billions in 1947; and employment grew from 39 million jobs in 1933 to a record of 60 million jobs in 1947.

Ours is the party under which the framework of the world organization for peace and justice was formulated and created.

Ours is the party under which were conceived the instruments for resisting Communist aggression and for rebuilding the economic strength of the democratic countries of Europe and Asia—the Truman Doctrine and the Marshall Plan. They are the materials with which we must build the peace.

Ours is the party which first proclaimed that the actions and policies of this nation in the foreign field are matters of national and not just party concern. We shall go forward on the course charted by President Roosevelt and President Truman and the other leaders of Democracy.

We reject the principle—which we have always rejected, but which the Republican 80th Congress enthusiastically accepted—that government exists for the benefit of the privileged few.

To serve the interests of all and not the few; to assure a world in which peace and justice can prevail; to achieve security, full production, and full employment—this is our platform.

OUR FOREIGN POLICY

We declared in 1944 that the imperative duty of the United States was to wage the war to final triumph and to join with the other United Nations in the establishment of an international organization for the prevention of aggression and the maintenance of international peace and security.

Under Democratic leadership, those pledges were gloriously redeemed.

When the United States was treacherously and savagely attacked, our great Democratic President, Franklin D. Roosevelt, and a Democratic Congress preserved the nation's honor, and with high courage and with the invincible might of the American people, the challenge was accepted. Under his inspiring leadership, the nation created the greatest army that ever assembled under the flag, the mightiest air force, the most powerful navy on the globe, and the largest merchant marine in the world.

The nation's gallant sons on land, on sea, and in the air, ended the war in complete and overwhelming triumph. Armed aggression against peaceful peoples was resisted and crushed. Arrogant and powerful war lords were vanquished and forced to unconditional surrender.

Before the end of the war the Democratic administration turned to the task of establishing measures for peace and the prevention of aggression and the threat of another war. Under the leadership of a Democratic President and his Secretary of State, the United Nations was organized at San Francisco. The charter was ratified by an overwhelming vote of the Senate. We support the United Nations fully and we pledge our whole-hearted aid toward its growth and development. We will continue to lead the way toward curtailment of the use of the veto. We shall favor such amendments and modifications of the charter as experience may justify. We will continue our efforts toward the establishment of an international armed force to aid its authority. We advocate the grant of a loan to the United Nations recommended by the President, but denied by the Republican Congress, for the construction of the United Nations headquarters in this country.

We pledge our best endeavors to conclude treaties of peace with our former enemies. Already treaties have been made with Italy, Hungary, Bulgaria and Rumania. We shall strive to conclude treaties with the remaining enemy states, based on justice and with guarantees against the revival of aggression, and for the preservation of peace.

We advocate the maintance of an adequate Army, Navy and Air Force to protect the nation's vital interests and to assure our security against aggression.

We advocate the effective international control of weapons of mass destruction, including the atomic bomb, and we approve continued and vigorous efforts within the United Nations to bring about the successful consummation of the proposals which our Government has advanced.

The adoption of these proposals would be a vital and most important step toward safe and effective world disarmament and world peace under a strengthened United Nations which would then truly constitute a more effective parliament of the world's peoples.

Under the leadership of a Democratic President, the United States has demonstrated its friendship for other peace-loving nations and its support of their freedom and independence. Under the Truman doctrine vital aid has been extended to China, to Greece, and to Turkey. Under the Marshall Plan generous sums have been provided for the relief and rehabilitation of European nations striving to rebuild their economy and to secure and strengthen their safety and freedom. The Republican leadership in the House of Representatives, by its votes in the 80th Congress, has shown its reluctance to provide funds to support this program, the greatest move for peace and recovery made since the end of World War II.

We pledge a sound, humanitarian administration of the Marshall Plan.

We pledge support not only for these principles—we pledge further that we will not withhold necessary funds by which these principles can be achieved. Therefore, we pledge that we will implement with appropriations the commitments which are made in this nation's foreign program.

We pledge ourselves to restore the Reciprocal Trade Agreements program formulated in 1934 by Secretary of State Cordell Hull and operated successfully for 14 years—until crippled by the Republican 80th Congress. Further, we strongly endorse our country's adherence to the International Trade Organization.

A great Democratic President established the Good Neighbor Policy toward the nations of the Western Hemisphere. The Act of Chapultepec was negotiated at Mexico City under Democratic leadership. It was carried forward in the Western Hemisphere defense pact concluded at Rio de Janeiro, which implemented the Monroe Doctrine and united the Western Hemisphere in behalf of peace.

We pledge continued economic cooperation with the countries of the Western Hemisphere. We pledge continued support of regional arrangements within the United Nations Charter, such as the Inter-American Regional Pact and the developing Western European Union.

President Truman, by granting immediate recognition to Israel, led the world in extending friendship and welcome to a people who have long sought and justly deserve freedom and independence.

We pledge full recognition to the State of Israel. We affirm our pride that the United States under the leadership of President Truman played a leading role in the adoption of the resolution of November 29, 1947, by the United Nations General Assembly for the creation of a Jewish State.

We approve the claims of the State of Israel to the boundaries set forth in the United Nations resolution of November 29th and consider that modifications thereof should be made only if fully acceptable to the State of Israel.

We look forward to the admission of the State of Israel to the United Nations and its full participation in the international community of nations. We pledge appropriate aid to the State of Israel in developing its economy and resources.

We favor the revision of the arms embargo to accord to the State of Israel the right of self-defense. We pledge ourselves to work for the modification of any resolution of the United Nations to the extent that it may prevent any such revision.

We continue to support, within the framework of the United Nations, the internationalization of Jerusalem and the protection of the Holy Places in Palestine.

The United States has traditionally been in sympathy with the efforts of subjugated countries to attain their independence, and to establish a democratic form of government. Poland is an outstanding example. After a century and a half of subjugation, it was resurrected after the first World War by our great Democratic President, Woodrow Wilson. We look forward to development of these countries as prosperous, free, and democratic fellow members of the United Nations.

OUR DOMESTIC POLICIES

The Republican 80th Congress is directly responsible for the existing and ever increasing high cost of living. It cannot dodge that responsibility. Unless the Republican candidates are defeated in the approaching elections, their mistaken policies will impose greater hardships and suffering on large numbers of the American people. Adequate food, clothing and shelter—the bare necessities of life—are becoming too expensive for the average wage earner and the prospects are more frightening each day. The Republican 80th Congress has lacked the courage to face this vital problem.

We shall curb the Republican inflation. We shall put a halt to the disastrous price rises which have come as a result of the failure of the Republican 80th Congress to take effective action on President Truman's recommendations, setting forth a comprehensive program to control the high cost of living.

We shall enact comprehensive housing legislation, including provisions for slum clearance and low-rent housing projects initiated by local agencies. This nation is shamed by the failure of the Republican 80th Congress to pass the vitally needed general housing legislation as recommended by the President. Adequate housing will end the need for rent control. Until then, it must be continued.

We pledge the continued maintenance of those sound fiscal policies which under Democratic leadership have brought about a balanced budget and reduction of the public debt by $28 billion since the close of the war.

We favor the reduction of taxes, whenever it is possible to do so without unbalancing the nation's economy, by giving a full measure of relief to those millions of low-income families on whom the wartime burden of taxation fell most heavily. The form of tax reduction adopted by the Republican 80th Congress gave relief to those who need it least and ignored those who need it most.

We shall endeavor to remove tax inequities and to continue to reduce the public debt.

We are opposed to the imposition of a general federal sales tax.

We advocate the repeal of the Taft-Hartley Act. It was enacted by the Republican 80th Congress over the President's veto. That act was proposed with the promise that it would secure "the legitimate rights of both employees and employers in their relations affecting commerce." It has failed. The number of labor-management disputes has increased. The number of cases before the National Labor Relations Board has more than doubled since the Act was passed, and efficient and prompt administration is becoming more and more difficult. It has encouraged litigation in labor disputes and undermined the established American policy of collective bargaining. Recent decisions by the courts prove that the Act was so poorly drawn that its application is uncertain, and that it is probably, in some provisions, unconstitutional.

We advocate such legislation as is desirable to establish a just body of rules to assure free and effective collective bargaining, to determine, in the public interest, the rights of employees and employers, to reduce to a minimum their conflict of interests, and to enable unions to keep their membership free from communistic influences.

We urge that the Department of Labor be rebuilt and strengthened, restoring to it the units, including the Federal Mediation and Conciliation Service and the United States Employment Service, which properly belong to it, and which the Republican 80th Congress stripped from it over the veto of President Truman. We urge that the Department's facilities for collecting and disseminating economic information be expanded, and that a Labor Education Extension Service be established in the Department of Labor.

We favor the extension of the coverage of the Fair Labor Standards Act as recommended by President Truman, and the adoption of a minimum wage of at least 75 cents an hour in place of the present obsolete and inadequate minimum of 40 cents an hour.

We favor legislation assuring that the workers of our nation receive equal pay for equal work, regardless of sex.

We favor the extension of the Social Security program established under Democratic leadership, to provide additional protection against the hazards of old age, disability, disease or death. We believe that this program should include:

Increases in old-age and survivors' insurance benefits by at least 50 percent, and reduction of the eligibility age for women from 65 to 60 years; extension of old-age and survivors' and unemployment insurance to all workers not now covered; insurance against loss of earnings on account of illness or disability; improved public assistance for the needy.

We favor the enactment of a national health program for expanded medical research, medical education, and hospitals and clinics.

We will continue our efforts to aid the blind and other handicapped persons to become self-supporting.

We will continue our efforts to expand maternal care, improve the health of the nation's children, and reduce juvenile delinquency.

We approve the purposes of the Mental Health Act and we favor such appropriations as may be necessary to make it effective.

We advocate federal aid for education administered by and under the control of the states. We vigorously support the authorization, which was so shockingly ignored by the Republican 80th Congress, for the appropriation of $300 million as a beginning of Federal aid to the states to assist them in meeting the present educational needs. We insist upon the right of every American child to obtain a good education.

The nation can never discharge its debt to its millions of war veterans. We pledge ourselves to the continuance and improvement of our national program of benefits for veterans and their families.

We are proud of the sound and comprehensive program conceived, developed and administered under Democratic leadership, including the GI Bill of Rights, which has proved beneficial to many millions.

The level of veterans' benefits must be constantly re-examined in the light of the decline in the purchasing power of the dollar brought about by inflation.

Employment and economic security must be

afforded all veterans. We pledge a program of housing for veterans at prices they can afford to pay.

The disabled veteran must be provided with medical care and hospitalization of the highest possible standard.

We pledge our efforts to maintain continued farm prosperity, improvement of the standard of living and the working conditions of the farmer, and to preserve the family-size farm.

Specifically, we favor a permanent system of flexible price supports for agricultural products, to maintain farm income on a parity with farm operating costs; an intensified soil conservation program; an extended crop insurance program; improvement of methods of distributing agricultural products; development and maintenance of stable export markets; adequate financing for the school lunch program; the use of agricultural surpluses to improve the diet of low-income families in case of need; continued expansion of the rural electrification program; strengthening of all agricultural credit programs; intensified research to improve agricultural practices, and to find new uses for farm products.

We strongly urge the continuance of maximum farmer participation in all these programs.

We favor the repeal of the discriminatory taxes on the manufacture and sale of oleomargarine.

We will encourage farm cooperatives and oppose any revision of federal law designed to curtail their most effective functioning as a means of achieving economy, stability and security for American agriculture.

We favor provisions under which our fishery resources and industry will be afforded the benefits that will result from more scientific research and exploration.

We recognize the importance of small business in a sound American economy. It must be protected against unfair discrimination and monopoly, and be given equal opportunities with competing enterprises to expand its capital structure.

We favor non-discriminatory transportation charges and declare for the early correction of inequalities in such charges.

We pledge the continued full and unified regional development of the water, mineral, and other natural resources of the nation, recognizing that the progress already achieved under the initiative of the Democratic Party in the arid and semi-arid states of the West, as well as in the Tennessee Valley, is only an indication of still greater results which can be accomplished. Our natural resources are the heritage of all our people and must not be permitted to become the private preserves of monopoly.

The irrigation of arid land, the establishment of new, independent, competitive business and the stimulation of new industrial opportunities for all of our people depends upon the development and transmission of electric energy in accordance with the program and the projects so successfully launched under Democratic auspices during the past sixteen years.

We favor acceleration of the Federal Reclamation Program, the maximum beneficial use of water in the several states for irrigation and domestic supply. In this connection, we propose the establishment and maintenance of new family-size farms for veterans and others seeking settlement opportunities, the development of hydroelectric power and its widespread distribution over publicly owned transmission lines to assure benefits to the water users in financing irrigation projects, and to the power users for domestic and industrial purposes, with preference to public agencies and R.E.A. cooperatives.

These are the aims of the Democratic Party which in the future, as in the past, will place the interest of the people as individual citizens first.

We will continue to improve the navigable waterways and harbors of the nation.

We pledge to continue the policy initiated by the Democratic Party of adequate appropriations for flood control for the protection of life and property.

In addition to practicing false economy on flood control, the Republican-controlled 80th Congress was so cruel as even to deny emergency federal funds for the relief of individuals and municipalities victimized by recent great floods, tornadoes and other disasters.

We shall expand our programs for forestation, for the improvement of grazing lands, public and private, for the stockpiling of strategic minerals and the encouragement of a sound domestic mining industry. We shall carry forward experiments for the broader utilization of mineral resources in the highly beneficial manner already demonstrated in the program for the manufacture of synthetic liquid fuel from our vast deposits of coal and oil shale and from our agricultural resources.

We pledge an intensive enforcement of the anti-trust laws, with adequate appropriations.

We advocate the strengthening of existing anti-trust laws by closing the gaps which experience has shown have been used to promote concentration of economic power.

We pledge a positive program to promote competitive business and to foster the development of independent trade and commerce.

We support the right of free enterprise and the right of all persons to work together in cooperatives and other democratic associations for the purpose of carrying out any proper business operations free from any arbitrary and discriminatory restrictions.

The Democratic Party is responsible for the great civil rights gains made in recent years in eliminating unfair and illegal discrimination based on race, creed or color.

The Democratic Party commits itself to continuing its efforts to eradicate all racial, religious and economic discrimination.

We again state our belief that racial and religious minorities must have the right to live, the right to work, the right to vote, the full and equal protection of the laws, on a basis of equality with all citizens as guaranteed by the Constitution.

We highly commend President Harry S. Truman for his courageous stand on the issue of civil rights.

We call upon the Congress to support our President in guaranteeing these basic and fundamental American Principles: (1) the right of full and equal political participation; (2) the right to equal opportunity of employment; (3) the right of security of person; (4) and the right of equal treatment in the service and defense of our nation.[1]

We pledge ourselves to legislation to admit a minimum of 400,000 displaced persons found eligible for United States citizenship without discrimination as to race or religion. We condemn the undemocratic action of the Republican 80th

Congress in passing an inadequate and bigoted bill for this purpose, which law imposes un-American restrictions based on race and religion upon such admissions.

We urge immediate statehood for Hawaii and Alaska; immediate determination by the people of Puerto Rico as to their form of government and their ultimate status with respect to the United States; and the maximum degree of local self-government for the Virgin Islands, Guam and Samoa.

We recommend to Congress the submission of a constitutional amendment on equal rights for women.

We favor the extension of the right of suffrage to the people of the District of Columbia.

We pledge adherence to the principle of non-partisan civilian administration of atomic energy, and the development of atomic energy for peaceful purposes through free scientific inquiry for the benefit of all the people.

We urge the vigorous promotion of world-wide freedom in the gathering and dissemination of news by press, radio, motion pictures, newsreels and television, with complete confidence that an informed people will determine wisely the course of domestic and foreign policy.

We believe the primary step toward the achievement of world-wide freedom is access by all peoples to the facts and the truth. To that end, we will encourage the greatest possible vigor on the part of the United Nations Commission on Human Rights and the United Nations Economic and Social Council to establish the foundations on which freedom can exist in every nation.

We deplore the repeated attempts of Republicans in the 80th Congress to impose thought control upon the American people and to encroach on the freedom of speech and press.

We pledge the early establishment of a national science foundation under principles which will guarantee the most effective utilization of public and private research facilities.

We will continue our efforts to improve and strengthen our federal civil service, and provide adequate compensation.

We will continue to maintain an adequate American merchant marine.

We condemn Communism and other forms of totalitarianism and their destructive activity overseas and at home. We shall continue to build firm

---

[1] When this platform was presented to the Convention, this section stated: "We again call upon the Congress to exert its full authority to the limit of its constitutional powers to assure and protect these rights." The last two paragraphs in the text above were inserted as an amendment to the platform by a vote of 651½ to 582½.

defenses against Communism by strengthening the economic and social structure of our own democracy. We reiterate our pledge to expose and prosecute treasonable activities of anti-democratic and un-American organizations which would sap our strength, paralyze our will to defend ourselves, and destroy our unity, inciting race against race, class against class, and the people against free institutions.

We shall continue vigorously to enforce the laws against subversive activities, observing at all times the constitutional guarantees which protect free speech, the free press and honest political activity. We shall strengthen our laws against subversion to the full extent necessary, protecting at all times our traditional individual freedoms.

We recognize that the United States has become the principal protector of the free world. The free peoples of the world look to us for support in maintaining their freedoms. If we falter in our leadership, we may endanger the peace of the world—and we shall surely endanger the welfare of our own nation. For these reasons it is imperative that we maintain our military strength until world peace with justice is secure. Under the leadership of President Truman, our military departments have been united and our Government organization for the national defense greatly strengthened. We pledge to maintain adequate military strength, based on these improvements, sufficient to fulfill our responsibilities in occupation zones, defend our national interests, and to bolster those free nations resisting Communist aggression.

This is our platform. These are our principles. They form a political and economic policy which has guided our party and our nation.

The American people know these principles well. Under them, we have enjoyed greater security, greater prosperity, and more effective world leadership than ever before.

Under them and with the guidance of Divine Providence we can proceed to higher levels of prosperity and security; we can advance to a better life at home; we can continue our leadership in the world with ever-growing prospects for lasting peace.

Progressive Party Platform, 1948

PREAMBLE

Three years after the end of the second world war, the drums are beating for a third. Civil liberties are being destroyed. Millions cry out for relief from unbearably high prices. The American way of life is in danger.

The root cause of this crisis is Big Business control of our economy and government.

With toil and enterprise the American people have created from their rich resources the world's greatest productive machine. This machine no longer belongs to the people. Its ownership is concentrated in the hands of a few and its product used for their enrichment.

Never before have so few owned so much at the expense of so many.

Ten years ago Franklin Delano Roosevelt warned: "The liberty of a democracy is not safe if the people tolerate the growth of private power to a point where it becomes stronger than their democratic state. That, in its essence, is fascism."

Today that private power has constituted itself an invisible government which pulls the strings of its puppet Republican and Democratic parties. Two sets of candidates compete for votes under the outworn emblems of the old parties. But both represent a single program—a program of monopoly profits through war preparations, lower living standards, and suppression of dissent.

For generations the common man of America has resisted this concentration of economic and political power in the hands of a few. The greatest of America's political leaders have led the people into battle against the money power, the railroads, the trusts, the economic royalists.

We of the Progressive Party are the present-day descendants of these people's movements and fighting leaders. We are the political heirs of Jefferson, Jackson and Lincoln — of Frederick Douglass, Altgeld and Debs—of "Fighting Bob" LaFollette, George Norris, and Franklin Roosevelt.

Throughout our history new parties have arisen when the old parties have betrayed the people. As Jefferson headed a new party to defeat the reactionaries of his day, and as Lincoln led a new party to victory over the slave-owners, so today the people, inspired and led by Henry Wallace, have created a new party to secure peace, freedom, and abundance.

With the firm conviction that the principles of the Declaration of Independence and of the Constitution of the United States set forth all fundamental freedoms for all people and secure the safety and well being of our country, the Progressive Party pledges itself to safeguard these principles to the American people.

Betrayal by the Old Parties

The American people want peace. But the old parties, obedient to the dictates of monopoly and the military, prepare for war in the name of peace.

They refuse to negotiate a settlement of differences with the Soviet Union.

They reject the United Nations as an instrument for promoting world peace and reconstruction.

They use the Marshall Plan to rebuild Nazi Germany as a war base and to subjugate the economies of other European countries to American Big Business.

They finance and arm corrupt, fascist governments in China, Greece, Turkey, and elsewhere, through the Truman Doctrine, wasting billions in American resources and squandering America's heritage as the enemy of despotism.

They encircle the globe with military bases which other peoples cannot but view as threats to their freedom and security.

They protect the war-making industrial and financial barons of Nazi Germany and imperial Japan, and restore them to power.

They stockpile atomic bombs.

They pass legislation to admit displaced persons, discriminating against Catholics, Jews, and other victims of Hitler.

They impose a peacetime draft and move toward Universal Military Training.

They fill policy-making positions in government with generals and Wall Street bankers.

Peace cannot be won—but profits can—by spending ever-increasing billions of the people's money in war preparations.

Yet these are the policies of the two old parties —policies profaning the name of peace.

The American people cherish freedom.

But the old parties, acting for the forces of special privilege, conspire to destroy traditional American freedoms.

They deny the Negro people the rights of citizenship. They impose a universal policy of Jim Crow and enforce it with every weapon of terror. They refuse to outlaw its most bestial expression—the crime of lynching.

They refuse to abolish the poll tax, and year after year they deny the right to vote to Negroes and millions of white people in the South.

They aim to reduce nationality groups to a position of social, economic, and political inferiority.

They connive to bar the Progressive Party from the ballot.

They move to outlaw the Communist Party as a decisive step in their assault on the democratic rights of labor, of national, racial, and political minorities, and of all those who oppose their drive to war. In this they repeat the history of Nazi Germany, Fascist Italy, and Franco Spain.

They support the House Committee on Un-American Activities in its vilification and persecution of citizens in total disregard of the Bill of Rights.

They build the Federal Bureau of Investigation into a political police with secret dossiers on millions of Americans.

They seek to regiment the thinking of the American people and to suppress political dissent.

They strive to enact such measures as the Mundt-Nixon Bill which are as destructive of democracy as were the Alien and Sedition Laws against which Jefferson fought.

They concoct a spurious "loyalty" program to create an atmosphere of fear and hysteria in government and industry.

They shackle American labor with the Taft-Hartley Act at the express command of Big Business, while encouraging exorbitant profits through uncontrolled inflation.

They restore the labor injunction as a weapon for breaking strikes and smashing unions.

This is the record of the two old parties—a record profaning the American ideal of freedom.

The American people want abundance.

But the old parties refuse to enact effective price and rent controls, making the people victims of a disastrous inflation which dissipates the savings of millions of families and depresses their living standards.

They ignore the housing problem, although more than half the nation's families, including millions of veterans, are homeless or living in rural and urban slums.

They refuse social security protection to millions and allow only meagre benefits to the rest.

They block national health legislation even

though millions of men, women, and children are without adequate medical care.

They foster the concentration of private economic power.

They replace progressive government officials, the supporters of Franklin Roosevelt, with spokesmen of Big Business.

They pass tax legislation for the greedy, giving only insignificant reductions to the needy.

These are the acts of the old parties—acts profaning the American dream of abundance.

No glittering party platforms or election promises of the Democratic and Republican parties can hide their betrayal of the needs of the American people.

Nor can they act otherwise. For both parties, as the record of the 80th Congress makes clear, are the champions of Big Business.

The Republican platform admits it.

The Democratic platform attempts to conceal it.

But the very composition of the Democratic leadership exposes the demogogy of its platform. It is a party of machine politicians and Southern Bourbons who veto in Congress the liberal planks "won" in convention.

Such platforms, conceived in hypocrisy and lack of principle, deserve nothing but contempt.

PRINCIPLES OF THE PROGRESSIVE PARTY

The Progressive Party is born in the deep conviction that the national wealth and natural resources of our country belong to the people who inhabit it and must be employed in their behalf; that freedom and opportunity must be secured equally to all; that the brotherhood of man can be achieved and scourge of war ended.

The Progressive Party holds that basic to the organization of world peace is a return to the purpose of Franklin Roosevelt to seek areas of international agreement rather than disagreement. It was his conviction that within the framework of the United Nations different social and economic systems can and must live together. If peace is to be achieved capitalist United States and communist Russia must establish good relations and work together.

The Progressive Party holds that it is the first duty of a just government to secure for all the people, regardless of race, creed, color, sex, national background, political belief, or station in life, the inalienable rights proclaimed in the Declaration of Independence and guaranteed by the Bill of Rights. The government must actively protect these rights against the encroachments of public and private agencies.

The Progressive Party holds that a just government must use its powers to promote an abundant life for its people. This is the basic idea of Franklin Roosevelt's Economic Bill of Rights. Heretofore every attempt to give effect to this principle has failed because Big Business dominates the key sectors of the economy. Anti-trust laws and government regulation cannot break this domination. Therefore the people, through their democratically elected representatives, must take control of the main levers of the economic system. Public ownership of these levers will enable the people to plan the use of their productive resources so as to develop the limitless potential of modern technology and to create a true American-Commonwealth free from poverty and insecurity.

The Progressive Party believes that only through peaceful understanding can the world make progress toward reconstruction and higher standards of living; that peace is the essential condition for safe-guarding and extending our traditional freedoms; that only by preserving liberty and by planning an abundant life for all can we eliminate the sources of world conflict. Peace, freedom, and abundance—the goals of the Progressive Party—are indivisible.

Only the Progressive Party can destroy the power of private monopoly and restore the government to the American people. For ours is a party uncorrupted by privilege, committed to no special interests, free from machine control, and open to all Americans of all races, colors, and creeds.

The Progressive Party is a party of action. We seek through the democratic process and through day-by-day activity to lead the American people toward the fulfillment of these principles.

We ask support for the following program:

PEACE

American-Soviet Agreement

Henry Wallace in his open letter suggested, and Premier Stalin in his reply accepted, a basis for sincere peace discussions. The exchange showed that specific areas of agreement can be found if the principles of non-interference in the internal affairs of other nations and acceptance of the right of peoples to choose their own form of government and economic system are mutually respected.

The Progressive Party therefore demands negotiation and discussion with the Soviet Union to find areas of agreement to win the peace.

The Progressive Party believes that enduring peace among the peoples of the world community is possible only through world law. Continued anarchy among nations in the atomic age threatens our civilization and humanity itself with annihilation. The only ultimate alternative to war is the abandonment of the principle of the coercion of sovereignties by sovereignties and the adoption of the principle of the just enforcement upon individuals of world federal law, enacted by a world federal legislature with limited but adequate powers to safeguard the common defense and the general welfare of all mankind.

Such a structure of peace through government can be evolved by making of the United Nations an effective agency of cooperation among nations. This can be done by restoring the unity of the Great Powers as they work together for common purposes. Since the death of Franklin Roosevelt, this principle has been betrayed to a degree which not only paralyzes the United Nations but threatens the world with another war in which there can be no victors and few survivors.

Beyond an effective United Nations lies the further possibility of genuine world government. Responsibility for ending the tragic prospect of war is a joint responsibility of the Soviet Union and the United States. We hope for more political liberty and economic democracy throughout the world. We believe that war between East and West will mean fascism and death for all. We insist that peace is the prerequisite of survival.

We believe with Henry Wallace that "there is no misunderstanding or difficulty between the USA and USSR which can be settled by force or fear and there is no difference which cannot be settled by peaceful, hopeful negotiation. There is no American principle of public interest, and there is no Russian principle of public interest, which would have to be sacrificed to end the cold war and open up the Century of Peace which the Century of the Common Man demands."

We denounce anti-Soviet hysteria as a mask for monopoly, militarism, and reaction. We demand that a new leadership of the peace-seeking people of our nation—which has vastly greater responsibility for peace than Russia because it has vastly greater power for war—undertake in good faith and carry to an honorable conclusion, without appeasement or sabre-rattling on either side, a determined effort to settle current controversies and enable men and women everywhere to look forward with confidence to the common task of building a creative and lasting peace for all the world.

End the Drive to War

The Progressive Party calls for the repeal of the peacetime draft and the rejection of Universal Military Training.

We call for the immediate cessation of the piling up of armament expenditures beyond reasonable peacetime requirements for national defense.

We demand the repudiation of the Truman Doctrine and an end to military and economic intervention in support of reactionary and fascist regimes in China, Greece, Turkey, the Middle East, and Latin America. We demand that the United States completely sever diplomatic and economic relations with Franco Spain.

We call for the abandonment of military bases designed to encircle and intimidate other nations.

We demand the repeal of the provisions of the National Security Act which are mobilizing the nation for war, preparing a labor draft, and organizing a monopoly-militarist dictatorship.

These measures will express the American people's determination to avoid provocation and aggression. They will be our contribution to the reduction of mistrust and the creation of a general atmosphere in which peace can be established.

United Nations

The Progressive Party will work to realize Franklin Roosevelt's ideal of the United Nations as a world family of nations, by defending its Charter and seeking to prevent its transformation into the diplomatic or military instrument of any one power or group of powers.

We call for the establishment of a United Nations Reconstruction and Development Fund to promote international recovery by providing assistance to the needy nations of Europe, Africa and Asia, without political conditions and with priorities to those peoples that suffered most from Axis aggression.

We call for the repudiation of the Marshall Plan.

We urge the full use of the Economic and Social Council and other agencies of the United Nations to wipe out disease and starvation, to promote the development of culture and science, and to develop the peaceful application of atomic energy.

We demand that the United States delegation to the United Nations stop protecting fascist Spain and press for effective economic and diplomatic sanctions against Franco's dictatorship.

Disarmament

The Progressive Party will work through the United Nations for a world disarmament agreement to outlaw the atomic bomb, bacteriological warfare, and all other instruments of mass destruction; to destroy existing stockpiles of atomic bombs and to establish United Nations controls, including inspection, over the production of atomic energy; and to reduce conventional armaments drastically in accordance with resolutions already passed by the United Nations General Assembly.

Germany and Japan

The Progressive Party calls for cooperation with our wartime allies to conclude peace treaties promptly with a unified Germany and with Japan. The essentials for a German settlement are denazification and democratization, punishment of war criminals, land reform, decartelization, nationalization of heavy industry, Big-Four control of the Ruhr, reparations to the victims of Nazi aggression, and definitive recognition of the Oder-Neisse line as the Western boundary of Poland. On this basis, we advocate the speedy conclusion of a peace treaty and a simultaneous withdrawal of all occupation troops.

Similar principles should govern a settlement with Japan.

State of Israel

The Progressive Party demands the immediate de jure recognition of the State of Israel.

We call for admission of Israel to the United Nations.

We call for a Presidential proclamation lifting the arms embargo in favor of the State of Israel.

We pledge our support for and call upon the Government of the United States to safeguard the sovereignty, autonomy, political independence, and territorial integrity of the State of Israel in accordance with the boundaries laid down by the Resolution of the General Assembly of the United Nations of November 29, 1947.

We support the prompt extension to Israel of generous financial assistance without political conditions.

We oppose any attempt to interfere with Israel in its sovereign right to control its own immigration policy.

We call upon the United States Government to provide immediate shipping and other facilities for the transportation of Jewish displaced persons in Europe who desire to emigrate to Israel.

We support, within the framework of the United Nations, the internationalization of Jerusalem and the protection of the Holy Places.

We appeal to the Arab workers, farmers and small merchants to accept the United Nations decision for a Jewish and Arab state as being in their best interest. We urge them not to permit themselves to be used as tools in a war against Israel on behalf of British and American monopolies, for the latter are the enemies of both Arabs and Jews.

The Far East

The Progressive Party supports the struggle of the peoples of Asia to achieve independence and to move from feudalism into the modern era. We condemn the bipartisan policy of military and economic intervention to crush these people's movements. World peace and prosperity cannot be attained unless the people of China, Indonesia, Indo-China, Malaya and Asian lands win their struggle for independence and take their place as equals in the family of nations.

We call for the immediate withdrawal of American troops and abandonment of bases in China.

We demand cessation of financial and military aid to the Chiang Kai-shek dictatorship.

We follow the policy of Franklin Roosevelt in encouraging the creation of a democratic coalition government in China. We urge support for and the granting of large scale economic assistance to such a government.

We support the efforts of the people of Korea to establish national unity and the kind of government they desire. We demand an early joint withdrawal of occupation troops.

Colonial and Dependent Peoples

We believe that people everywhere in the world have the right to self-determination. The people of Puerto Rico have the right to independence. The people of the United States have an obligation toward the people of Puerto Rico to see that they are started on the road toward economic security and prosperity.

We demand the repeal of the Bell Trade Act relating to the Philippines and the abrogation of other unequal trade treaties with economically weaker peoples.

We urge action by the people of the United States and cooperation with other countries in the United Nations to abolish the colonial system in all its forms and to realize the principle of self-determination for the peoples of Africa, Asia, the West Indies, and other colonial areas.

We support the aspirations for unified homelands, of traditionally oppressed and dispersed people such as the Irish and Armenians.

Latin America

The Progressive Party urges a return to, and the strengthening of, Franklin Roosevelt's good-neighbor policy in our relations with republics to the South.

We demand the abandonment of the inter-American military program.

We call for economic assistance without political conditions to further the independent economic development of the Latin American and Caribbean countries.

Displaced Persons

The Progressive Party calls for the repeal of the anti-Catholic, anti-semitic Displaced Persons Act of 1948 which permits the entry into the United States of fascists and collaborators. We call for the enactment of legislation to open our doors in the true American tradition to the victims of fascist persecution.

FREEDOM

End Discrimination

The Progressive Party condemns segregation and discrimination in all its forms and in all places.

We demand full equality for the Negro people, the Jewish people, Spanish-speaking Americans, Italian Americans, Japanese Americans, and all other nationality groups.

We call for a Presidential proclamation ending segregation and all forms of discrimination in the armed services and Federal employment.

We demand Federal anti-lynch, anti-discrimination, and fair-employment-practices legislation, and legislation abolishing segregation in interstate travel.

We call for immediate passage of anti-poll tax legislation, enactment of a universal suffrage law to permit all citizens to vote in Federal elections, and the full use of Federal enforcement powers to assure free exercise of the right to franchise.

We call for a Civil Rights Act for the District of Columbia to eliminate racial segregation and discrimination in the nation's capital.

We demand the ending of segregation and discrimination in the Panama Canal Zone and all territories, possessions and trusteeships.

We demand that Indians, the earliest Americans, be given full citizenship rights without loss of reservation rights and be permitted to administer their own affairs.

We will develop special programs to raise the low standards of health, housing, and educational facilities for Negroes, Indians and nationality groups, and will deny Federal funds to any state or local authority which withholds opportunities or benefits for reasons of race, creed, color, sex or national origin.

We will initiate a Federal program of education, in cooperation with state, local, and private agencies to combat racial and religious prejudice.

We support the enactment of legislation making it a Federal crime to disseminate anti-Semitic, anti-Negro, and all racist propaganda by mail, radio, motion picture or other means of communication.

We call for a Constitutional amendment which will effectively prohibit every form of discrimination against women—economic, educational, legal, and political.

We pledge to respect the freedom of conscience

of sincere conscientious objectors to war. We demand amnesty for conscientious objectors imprisoned in World War II.

The Right of Political Association and Expression

The Progressive Party will fight for the constitutional rights of Communists and all other political groups to express their views as the first line in the defense of the liberties of a democratic people.

We oppose the use of violence or intimidation, under cover of law or otherwise, by any individual or group, including the violence and intimidation now being committed by those who are attempting to suppress political dissent.

We pledge an all-out fight against the Mundt-Nixon Bill and all similar legislation designed to impose thought control, restrict freedom of opinion, and establish a police state in America.

We demand the abolition of the House Un-American Activities Committee and similar State Committees, and we mean to right the wrongs which these committees have perpetrated upon thousands of loyal Americans working for the realization of democratic ideals.

We pledge to eliminate the current "Loyalty" purge program and to reestablish standards for government service that respect the rights of Federal employees to freedom of association and opinion and to engage in political activity.

We demand the full right of teachers and students to participate freely and fully in the social, civic and political life of the nation and of the local community.

We demand that the Federal Bureau of Investigation and other Government agencies desist from investigating, or interfering with, the political beliefs and lawful activities of Americans.

We demand an end to the present practices of Congressional Committees — such as the House Labor Committee — in persecuting trade unionists and political leaders at the behest of Big Business.

We demand an end to the present campaign of deportation against foreign-born trade unionists and political leaders, and will actively protect the civil rights of naturalized citizens and the foreign born.

Nationality Groups

The Progressive Party recognizes the varied contributions of all nationality groups to American cultural, economic, and social life, and considers them a source of strength for the democratic development of our country.

We advocate the right of the foreign born to obtain citizenship without discrimination.

We advocate the repeal of discriminatory immigration laws based upon race, national origin, religion, or political belief.

We recognize the just claims of the Japanese Americans for indemnity for the losses suffered during their wartime internment, which was an outrageous violation of our fundamental concepts of justice.

We support legislation facilitating naturalization of Filipinos, Koreans, Japanese, Chinese, and other national groups now discriminated against by law.

We support legislation facilitating naturalization of merchant seamen with a record of war service.

Democracy in the Armed Forces

The Progressive Party demands abolition of Jim Crow in the armed forces.

We demand abolition of social inequalities between officers and enlisted personnel.

We call for basic revision in the procedure of military justice, including the more adequate participation of enlisted men in courts-martial.

We urge that admission to West Point and Annapolis be based on the candidates' qualifications, determined by open competitive examinations, and that an increasing percentage of young men admitted be drawn from the ranks.

Representative Government

The Progressive Party proposes a constitutional amendment providing for the direct election of the President and Vice President by popular vote.

We call for Home Rule and the granting of full suffrage to the disfranchised citizens of the District of Columbia.

We favor the immediate admission of Hawaii and Alaska as the 49th and 50th states of the Union.

We urge that all general and primary election days be declared holidays to enable all citizens to vote.

Separation of Church and State

The Progressive Party intends to maintain the traditional American separation of church and state and protect the freedom of secular education.

ABUNDANCE

High Cost of Living

The living standards of the American people are under bipartisan attack through uncontrolled inflation. The only effective method of combating inflation is to take the profits out of inflation.

The Progressive Party calls for legislation which will impose controls that will reduce and keep down the prices of food, shelter, clothing, other essentials of life, and basic materials. Such controls should squeeze out excessive profits, provide for the payment of subsidies to farmers wherever necessary to maintain fair agricultural prices, and allocate materials and goods in short supply.

We call for removal by the President of the Housing Expediter who is administering rent control in the interests of the real estate lobby.

We call for strengthening rent control, providing protection against evictions, and eliminating the present "hardship" regulations which are a bonanza for the large realty interests.

Economic Planning

The Progressive Party believes in the principle of democratic economic planning and rejects the boom-and-bust philosophy of the old parties.

We mean to establish a Council of Economic Planning to develop plans for assuring high production, full employment, and a rising standard of living.

We mean to develop, on the TVA pattern, regional planning authorities in the major river-valleys the country over to achieve cheap power, rural electrification, soil conservation, flood control and reforestation, and to accelerate the growth of undeveloped areas, particularly in the South and West.

We mean to promote, through public ownership and long-range planning, the peaceful use of atomic energy to realize its great potential as a source of power and as a tool in science, medicine, and technology.

Only through the planned development of all our resources will the full benefit of the nation's wealth and productivity be secured for the people.

Breaking the Grip of Monopoly

Monopoly's grip on the economy must be broken if democracy is to survive and economic planning become possible. Experience has shown that anti-trust laws and government regulation are not by themselves sufficient to halt the growth of monopoly. The only solution is public ownership of key areas of the economy.

The Progressive Party will initiate such measures of public ownership as may be necessary to put into the hands of the people's representatives the levers of control essential to the operation of an economy of abundance. As a first step, the largest banks, the railroads, the merchant marine, the electric power and gas industry, and industries primarily dependent on government funds or government purchases such as the aircraft, the synthetic rubber and synthetic oil industries must be placed under public ownership.

We mean to strengthen and vigorously enforce the anti-trust laws to curb monopoly in the rest of the economy.

We call for the immediate abolition of discriminatory freight rates, which help to keep the South and West in bondage to Wall Street.

Tideland oil resources belong to the people, and we fight the efforts of the oil companies to steal them. We support Federal control of such resources.

We demand the repeal of the Bulwinkle law which exempts railroads from anti-trust prosecution.

We call for the repeal of the Miller-Tydings legislation which eliminated retail competition in branded goods, excluding these from the coverage of the Anti-trust laws.

Labor

The Progressive Party recognizes that from the earliest period of its history the organized labor movement has taken leadership in the struggle for democratic and humanitarian objectives. Organized labor remains the mainspring of America's democratic striving, and the just needs of labor are of special concern to the Progressive Party.

We hold that every American who works for a living has an inalienable right to an income sufficient to provide him and his family with a high standard of living. Unless the rights of labor to organize, to bargain collectively, and to strike are secure, a rising standard of living cannot be realized.

We demand the immediate repeal of the Taft-Hartley Act and the reinstatement of the principles of the Wagner and Norris-LaGuardia acts. These last measures are essential to restore labor's equality in collective bargaining and to prevent business from using government to establish a dictatorship over labor by injunction.

We will demand the right for employees in publicly owned industries to organize, to bargain collectively, and to strike.

We call for the establishment of collective bargaining machinery for Federal employees.

We support the legitimate demands of all wage and salary earners, including Federal employees, for wage and salary increases and improved working conditions. We demand the enactment of a minimum wage of $1 an hour, extension of the Fair Labor Standards Act to cover all workers, enforcement of equal pay for equal work regardless of age or sex, and the elimination of any regional wage differential.

We oppose governmental strike-breaking through seizure of struck industries under the pretext of Federal operation, while profits continue to go to private employers.

We urge the enactment and stringent enforcement of Federal and State laws establishing adequate safety and health standards for miners, longshoremen, railroad workers, merchant seamen, and all other workers in hazardous industries.

We pledge drastic amendment of the Railway Labor Act to make certain that the railroad workers enjoy genuine collective bargaining and the right to strike. We call for amendment of the Railroad Retirement Act to grant railroad workers pensions of $100 minimum after 30 years' service or when they become 60 years old.

We call for Federal legislation to improve railroad working conditions by establishing a 40-hour, 5-day week for non-operating and terminal employees, and a six-hour day for roadmen, and train limit and full crew provisions.

We actively support measures to repair and improve the living standards of the 12 million white collar and professional employees, who have suffered particularly under the inflation.

We call for an end to the second-class citizenship of our nation's two and a half million agricultural wage workers, and the thousands of food-processing workers who are excluded from the protection of social and labor legislation. We stand for legislation to protect the right of agricultural workers to bargain collectively. We call for extension of social security and fair labor standards coverage to all agricultural and food-processing workers.

We demand an immediate end to the arbitrary security orders issued by the Department of National Defense which blacklist employees in private industries under government contracts.

Agriculture

The Progressive Party recognizes that the welfare of farmers is closely tied to the living standards of consumers. We reject the "eat-less" policy of the old parties and proclaim our intention to develop within the framework of an economy of planned abundance, a long-range program of full agricultural production, combined with necessary safeguards for the security of farmers and for the conservation of our natural resources.

We stand for the family-type farm as the basic unit of American agriculture. The Farmer's Home Administration, (formerly, Farm Security Administration) must be expanded to provide ample low-cost credit to assist tenants, sharecroppers, and returned veterans to become farm-owners. Marginal farmers must be assisted to become efficient producers. Where farming is incapable of yielding an adequate family income, supplementary employment on needed conservation and public works projects must be provided.

We propose as a major goal of Federal farm programs that all farm families be enabled to earn an income of not less than $3000 a year. We repudiate the program of Big Business which would eliminate as many as two-thirds of the nation's farmers.

We call for a 5-year program of price-supports for all major crops at not less than 90 percent of parity—parity to be calculated according to an up-to-date formula. Dairy products and certain specialties should be supported at higher rates than 90 percent.

We demand that all essential crops be insured against hazards which are beyond the control of the individual farmer.

We support the principle of direct payments to farmers for soil conservation practices, crop adjustment, and rodent control.

We favor the principle of compensating payments and production subsidies when needed to encourage a high level of consumption without jeopardizing farm income. We also call for assistance to low-income consumers through such programs as the food stamp plan and the school hot-lunch program.

We favor international commodity agreements

and a World Food Board under the United Nations Food and Agriculture Organization to stabilize world markets and to move farm surpluses to deficient areas.

We call for a long-range national land policy designed to discourage the growth of corporation farms and absentee ownership. This policy is especially important in the South to promote the proper development of its resources and to provide land for the landless. Priority in the purchase of land made available by river-valley projects must be given to tenants, sharecroppers, and small farmers.

We regard it as of utmost importance that programs of conservation, production, marketing, and price-support be administered by democratically-elected farmer committeemen, as in the Triple-A program.

We stand for the principle of a graduated land tax and for the 160-acre limitation in the use of public irrigation.

We support farmer and consumer cooperatives as a highly important answer to the problem of monopoly control over markets and supplies. We oppose the tax drive being staged by Big Business against cooperatives.

We favor immediate flood control projects and universal electrification of all farms. REA lines and generating facilities should be rapidly expanded, and river-valley projects for power and irrigation should be undertaken as promptly as possible.

Independent Business

The Progressive Party believes that independent businessmen can survive only in an economy free from monopoly domination, where workers and farmers receive incomes sufficient to permit them to purchase the goods they need.

We propose to encourage and safeguard independent business by providing adequate working capital and development loans at low interest rates, granting tax relief, and giving independent and small business a fair share of government contracts. We propose to make available to independent business, through an expanded government research program, the know-how essential to efficient operation.

Housing

The Progressive Party charges that private enterprise, under monopoly control, has failed to house the American people. It is the responsibility of democratic government to guarantee the right of every family to a decent home at a price it can afford to pay.

We demand a Federal emergency housing program to build within the next two years four million low-rent and low-cost dwellings for homeless and doubled-up families, with priority to veterans.

We recognize that to accomplish this objective it will be necessary to curb non-essential construction, to allocate scarce materials, and to reduce the cost of land, money, and building materials.

We pledge an attack on the chronic housing shortage and the slums through a long-range program to build 25 million new homes during the next ten years. This program will include public subsidized housing for low-income families.

We pledge that as a part of our general program of economic planning the building industry will be reorganized and rationalized, capacity to produce presently scarce materials will be expanded, and year-round employment will be guaranteed to workers in the building trades.

Government—Federal, state and local—has the responsibility to insure that communities are well-planned, with homes conveniently located near places of employment and with adequate provision for health, education, recreation, and culture.

We pledge the abolition of discrimination and segregation in housing.

Security and Health

The Progressive Party demands the extension of social security protection to every man, woman and child in the United States.

We recognize the service which the Townsend Plan has performed in bringing to national attention the tragic plight of the senior citizens of America, and we condemn the bipartisan conspiracy in Congress over the past ten years against providing adequate old-age pensions.

We pledge our active support for a national old-age pension of $100 a month to all persons at 60 years of age, based on right and not on a pauperizing need basis.

We call for a Federal program of adequate disability and sickness benefits and increased unemployment benefits, protecting all workers and their standards of living.

We call for maternity benefits for working mothers for thirteen weeks, including the period before and after childbirth, and the granting of children's allowances to families with children under 18.

We favor adequate public assistance for all persons in need, with Federal grants-in-aid proportionate to the needs and financial ability of the states, pending the enactment of a comprehensive Federal Social Security program.

We support the right of every American to good health through a national system of health insurance, giving freedom of choice to patient and practitioner, and providing adequate medical and dental care for all.

We favor the expenditure of Federal funds in support of an effective program for public health and preventive medicine and a program of dental care.

We favor the expenditure of Federal funds for the promotion of medical and dental education and research.

We look forward to the eventual transfer of the entire cost of the security and health program to the government as an essential public service.

Women

The Progressive Party proposes to secure the rights of women and children and to guarantee the security of the American family as a happy and democratic unit and as the mainstay of our nation.

We propose to raise women to first-class citizens by removing all restrictions—social, economic, and political—without jeopardizing the existing protective legislation vital to women as mothers or future mothers.

We propose to extend fair labor standards for women, to guarantee them healthful working conditions, equal job security with men, and their jobs back after the birth of children.

We propose to guarantee medical care for mother and child prior to, during and after birth, through a national system of health insurance.

We propose a program of Federal assistance for the establishment of day care centers for all children.

Young People

The Progressive Party believes young people are the nation's most valuable asset; their full potentialities can be realized only by implementing our complete program for peace, freedom and abundance. We challenge the failure of the old parties to meet the special problems of youth.

We call for the right to vote at eighteen.

We call for the enforcement and extension of child labor laws.

We call for Federal and state expenditures for recreational facilities, particularly in needy rural communities.

Veterans

The Progressive Party recognizes the veterans' special sacrifices and contributions in the nation's most critical period.

We demand priority for veterans in obtaining homes.

We call for a Federal bonus to veterans based on length of service.

We demand the expansion of the Veterans Administration program and increased G. I. benefits and allowances and the elimination of discrimination.

We demand that the coverage of the GI Bill of Rights and other servicemen's benefits be extended to war widows and to merchant seamen with war service.

We call for the prompt refund of the overcharges collected from veterans by National Service Life Insurance.

We demand that the government enforce the right of Negro veterans in the South to file terminal leave applications and to collect their benefits.

We call for increased benefits for disabled veterans and a program to guarantee them jobs at decent wages.

Taxation

The Progressive Party demands the overhaul of the tax structure according to the democratic principle of ability to pay. We propose to employ taxation as a flexible instrument to promote full employment and economic stability.

We propose to exempt from personal income taxes all families and individuals whose income falls below the minimum required for a decent standard of living. We propose that income from capital gains, be taxed at the same graduated rate as ordinary income.

We propose to enact effective excess profits and undistributed profits taxation.

We propose to curb tax-dodging by closing existing loopholes.

We propose to work towards the progressive elimination of Federal excise taxes on the basic necessities of life.

We oppose all state and local sales taxes.

We propose to close existing loopholes in estate and gift taxes and establish an integrated system of estate and gift taxation.

Education

The Progressive Party proposes to guarantee, free from segregation and discrimination, the inalienable right to a good education to every man, woman, and child in America. Essential to good education are the recognized principles of academic freedom—in particular, the principle of free inquiry into and discussion of controversial issues by teachers and students.

We call for the establishment of an integrated Federal grant-in-aid program to build new schools, libraries, raise teachers' and librarians' salaries, improve primary and secondary schools, and assist municipalities and states to establish free colleges.

We call for a system of Federal scholarships, fellowships, and cost-of-living grants, free from limitations or quotas based on race, creed, color, sex or national origin, in order to enable all those with necessary qualifications but without adequate means of support to obtain higher education in institutions of their own choice.

We call for a national program of adult education in cooperation with state and local authorities.

We oppose segregation in education and support legal action on behalf of Negro students and other minorities aimed at securing their admission to state-supported graduate and professional schools which now exclude them by law.

We call for a Department of Education with a Secretary of Cabinet rank.

Culture

The Progressive Party recognizes culture as a potentially powerful force in the moral and spiritual life of a people and through the people, in the growth of democracy and the preservation of peace, and realizes that the culture of a democracy must, like its government, be of, by, and for the people.

We pledge ourselves to establish a department of government that shall be known as the Department of Culture, whose function shall be the promotion of all the arts as an expression of the spirit of the American people, and toward the enrichment of the people's lives, to make the arts available to all.

Promotion of Science

The Progressive Party calls for the enactment of legislation to promote science, including human and social sciences, so that scientific knowledge may be enlarged and used for the benefit of all people.

We condemn the militarization of science and the imposition of military control over scientific expression and communication.

We support measures for public control of patents and licensing provisions to insure that new inventions will be used for the benefit of the people.

The Progressive Party has taken root as the party of the common man. It has arisen in response to, and draws growing strength from, the demand of millions of men and women for the simple democratic right to vote for candidates and a program which satisfy their needs. It gives voters a real choice.

Purposeful and deeply meant, the program of the Progressive Party carries forward the policies of Franklin Roosevelt and the aspirations of Wendell Willkie and holds forth the promise of a reborn democracy ready to play its part in one world. The American people want such a program. They will support it.

Under the leadership of Henry A. Wallace and Glen H. Taylor, a great new people's movement is on the march. Under the guidance of Divine Providence, the Progressive Party, with strong and active faith, moves forward to peace, freedom and abundance.

1948 Platform of the Prohibition Party

PREAMBLE

We, the representatives of the Prohibition Party, assembled in national convention at Winona Lake, Indiana, June 26, 27, 28, 1947, recognizing Almighty God as the source of all just government and with faith in the teachings of the Prince of Peace, do solemnly promise that, if our party is chosen to administer the affairs of this nation, we will use all the power of our administration to serve the people of the United States.

World Peace and Order

We believe in World peace, and universal brotherhood.

Having united with other national groups to restore world order and preserve world peace, our nation should lead them all in submerging selfish interests for the common good of all.

This is a severe test for American statesmen and the men to be intrusted with the task should be men whose dependence is upon a Higher Power for wisdom and guidance.

Atomic Energy

We favor the development of a constructive plan for the international control of atomic energy, involving a system of international inspection of the manufacture of atomic energy and punishment for violation of regulations.

Universal Military Training

Believing that peacetime military training in our country does not represent a safeguard for world peace, that it is contrary in principle to our American way of life, that it places an unnecessary burden upon our peacetime economy, that it could lead only to military dictatorship, and that it would, under existing conditions, lead to the moral and spiritual deterioration of our youth, we declare our opposition to any program of peacetime military conscription.

Constitutional Government

We renew our loyalty to the Constitution of the United States and have supreme confidence in this form of government to meet ever-changing national and world conditions.

We are opposed to Nazism, Communism and Fascism and all other forms of totalitarianism. We are convinced that the best and only safeguard against these dangerous doctrines is to protect the rights and guard the welfare of our citizens.

War spending has set an extravagant example of wasteful government operation. The time is here for rigid curtailment. We believe that for any government to take nearly one-third of its citizen's income to pay the expenses of government is a most unjust, immoral act. We believe the only way to materially reduce the cost of government is to reduce the number of functions performed by government. Hence, in accordance with the principle which we believe to be the basis of all sound government—namely, that government ought not to do what the people, without government intervention, can do. We promise, if elected to power, to reorganize the federal government in accordance with this principle, discarding all departments, bureaus or other unnecessary personnel that cannot qualify as legitimate when measured by this principle.

Taxes

With proper economy, government will cost less and thus make it possible to steadily reduce the public debt and gradually lift the tax load from the average citizen.

In the states we favor the effort to limit the tax rate whenever possible to one percent of full value of property, in order to prevent foreclosure and confiscation, and assist the home owner, farmer, and others to preserve their property.

Enforcement of Law

We are opposed to nullification of law by nonenforcement, and will maintain the integrity of democracy by enforcing the Constitution and the laws enacted under it by elected representatives of the people or by popular vote.

Ballot Law Reform

We demand the repeal of the many state ballot laws which have been enacted to make the two-party system a bi-partisan political monopoly and which now deny to independent voters and minority groups the fundamental right of free political expression as guaranteed by the Constitution.

Church and State

The Constitutional separation of Church and State must be maintained. We will not tax church or religious activities, except those operated for profit. We are opposed to the appropriation of public money for any sectarian purposes.

Monopoly

Because monopolies, whether by capital, labor or any other group or individual are harmful in result, wrong in principle and tend to dictatorship, we shall enact and enforce laws to break them up and prevent their operations.

PUBLIC MORALITY

Moral and spiritual considerations should be primary factors in determining national policies. We will strengthen and enforce laws against gambling, narcotics and commercialized vice now so openly violated and nullified by the inaction of the parties in power, and thus prevent further disintegration of the public morals.

MONEY

The Constitution provides for the issuance of money and the determination of the value thereof by Congress. This is a sound and feasible monetary policy, which we shall enforce.

NO RACIAL DISCRIMINATION

Recognizing that "God created of one blood all nations to dwell upon the face of the earth," we declare in favor of full justice and equal opportunity for all people, whatever their religion, or racial or national origin.

MARRIAGE AND DIVORCE

To maintain the sanctity of the home we favor the enactment of uniform marriage and divorce laws.

LABOR AND INDUSTRY

Labor organizations are entitled to great credit for improving the status of the workers, and for their constructive contributions to the general welfare. It is our purpose to give the public good paramount consideration. Neither capital nor labor can be permitted to dominate at the expense of the other or the public welfare.

SOCIAL SECURITY AND OLD AGE PENSIONS

We will extend the Social Security Act so as to include all employed groups in its provisions. We will also develop a system of annuity insurance for aged persons and so administer it as to preserve the incentives of initiative and thrift.

HOME OWNERSHIP

We greatly deprecate the fact that so many ex-service men are without sufficient housing facilities for themselves and families.

It should be possible for every American family that desires to do so to own its own house. We favor such legislation as may facilitate the realization of this objective.

CO-OPERATIVES

Co-operatives and profit sharing enterprises are a natural outgrowth of democracy. Government under our administration will encourage such enterprises.

A PARTY OF SERVICE, NOT SPOILS

The two dominant parties are committed to the spoils system and when in office have prostituted government to serve their own selfish party interests instead of serving the whole people. That policy has led to excessive government expenditures, and higher taxes. We pledge ourselves to an honest, efficient and economical administration.

PROHIBITION

No self governing nation can survive the mass alcoholization of its voters and the mass perversion of the judgments of its citizens.

As the result of the repeal of the 18th Amendment our government has authorized and empowered the liquor traffic to derange the minds and pervert the judgment of a multitude of American citizens both young and old.

No political issue confronting our citizens compares in magnitude with the necessity for suppressing the alcohol beverage traffic.

The present liquor conditions, which are far worse than ever before, are due directly to the joint action of the two major parties when they adopted platform planks to destroy the 18th Amendment.

The moral forces have to contend with the liquor power which is highly capitalized, strongly organized, and is promoting liquor sales by every possible means to create an ever growing appetite in youth, men and women. This power dominates our politics and government. It controls large numbers of voters. Every saloon is a center for mobilizing and controlling votes. Both parties are subservient to the liquor power. So long as good citizens continue to give their votes to liquor parties, so long as they continue to be yoked by party membership with the liquor interests and the underworld, so long will they be incapable of making moral principles prevail.

What is needed is a re-alignment of voters and the union of good citizens in a party unitedly committed to the principles of Prohibition—a party not dependent upon votes wielded and delivered by the liquor power. American government is party government. There are constitutional reasons why this is so. To overcome the liquor power it is necessary to employ the agency of a political party unitedly committed to Prohibition.

We summon the voters of America to help elect the Prohibition party to power. We will then marshal the resources of the government, legislative, executive and judicial, to overcome the liquor power.

Republican Party Platform of 1948

I

DECLARATION OF PRINCIPLES

To establish and maintain peace, to build a country in which every citizen can earn a good living with the promise of real progress for himself and his family, and to uphold as a beacon light for mankind everywhere, the inspiring American tradition of liberty, opportunity and justice for all—that is the Republican platform.

To this end we propose as a guide to definite action the following principles:

Maximum voluntary cooperation between citizens and minimum dependence on law; never, however, declining courageous recourse to law if necessary.

Our competitive system furnishes vital opportunity for youth and for all enterprising citizens; it makes possible the productive power which is the unique weapon of our national defense; and is the mainspring of material well-being and political freedom.

Government, as the servant of such a system, should take all needed steps to strengthen and develop public health, to promote scientific research, to provide security for the aged, and to promote a stable economy so that men and women need not fear the loss of their jobs or the threat of economic hardships through no fault of their own.

The rights and obligations of workers are commensurate with the rights and obligations of employers and they are interdependent; these rights should be protected against coercion and exploitation from whatever quarter and with due regard for the general welfare of all.

The soil as our basic natural resource must be conserved with increased effectiveness; and farm prices should be supported on a just basis.

Development of the priceless national heritage which is in our West is vital to our nation.

Administration of government must be economical and effective.

Faulty governmental policies share an important responsibility for the present cruelly high cost of living. We pledge prompt action to correct these policies. There must be decent living at decent wages.

Our common defense must be strengthened and unified.

Our foreign policy is dedicated to preserving a free America in a free world of free men. This calls for strengthening the United Nations and primary recognition of America's self-interest in the liberty of other peoples. Prudently conserving our own resources, we shall cooperate on a self-help basis with other peace-loving nations.

Constant and effective insistence on the personal dignity of the individual, and his right to complete justice without regard to race, creed or color, is a fundamental American principle.

We aim always to unite and to strengthen; never to weaken or divide. In such a brotherhood will we Americans get results. Thus we will overcome all obstacles.

II

In the past eighteen months, the Republican Congress, in the face of frequent obstruction from the Executive Branch, made a record of solid achievement. Here are some of the accomplishments of this Republican Congress:

The long trend of extravagant and ill-advised Executive action reversed;

the budget balanced;

taxes reduced;

limitation of Presidential tenure to two terms passed;

assistance to veterans, their widows and orphans provided;

assistance to agriculture and business enacted;

elimination of the poll tax as a requisite to soldier voting;

a sensible reform of the labor law, protecting all rights of Labor while safeguarding the entire community against those breakdowns in essential industries which endanger the health and livelihood of all;

a long-range farm program enacted;

unification of the armed services launched;

a military manpower law enacted;

the United Nations fostered;

a haven for displaced persons provided;

the most far-reaching measures in history adopted to aid the recovery of the free world on a basis of self-help and with prudent regard for our own resources;

and, finally, the development of intelligent plans and party teamwork for the day when the American people entrust the Executive as well as the Legislative branch of our National Government to the Republican Party.

We shall waste few words on the tragic lack of foresight and general inadequacy of those now in charge of the Executive Branch of the National Government; they have lost the confidence of citizens of all parties.

III

Present cruelly high prices are due in large part to the fact that the government has not effectively used the powers it possesses to combat inflation, but has deliberately encouraged higher prices.

We pledge an attack upon the basic causes of inflation, including the following measures:

progressive reduction of the cost of government through elimination of waste;

stimulation of production as the surest way to lower prices;

fiscal policies to provide increased incentives for production and thrift;

a sound currency;

reduction of the public debt.

We pledge further, that in the management of our National Government, we shall achieve the abolition of overlapping, duplication, extravagance, and excessive centralization;

the more efficient assignment of functions within the government;

and the rooting out of Communism wherever found.

These things are fundamental.

IV

We must, however, do more.

The Constitution gives us the affirmative mandate "to establish justice."

In Lincoln's words: The dogmas of the quiet past are inadequate to the stormy present. The occasion is piled high with difficulty and we must rise with the occasion. As our case is new, so we must think anew and act anew.

The tragic experience of Europe tells us that popular government disappears when it is ineffective and no longer can translate into action the aims and the aspirations of the people.

Therefore, in domestic affairs, we propose:

The maintenance of armed services for air, land and sea, to a degree which will insure our national security; and the achievement of effective unity in the Department of National Defense so as to insure maximum economy in money and manpower, and maximum effectiveness in case of war. We favor sustained effective action to procure sufficient manpower for the services, recognizing the American principle that every citizen has an obligation of service to his country.

An adequate privately operated merchant marine, the continued development of our harbors and waterways, and the expansion of privately operated air transportation and communication systems.

The maintenance of Federal finances in a healthy condition and continuation of the efforts so well started by the Republican Congress to reduce the enormous burden of taxation in order to provide incentives for the creation of new industries and new jobs, and to bring relief from inflation. We favor intelligent integration of Federal-State taxing and spending policies designed to eliminate wasteful duplication, and in order that the State and local governments may be able to assume their separate responsibilities, the Federal government shall as soon as practicable withdraw or reduce those taxes which can be best administered by local governments, with particular consideration of excise and inheritance taxes; and we favor restoring to America a working federalism.

Small business, the bulwark of American enterprise, must be encouraged through aggressive anti-monopoly action, elimination of unnecessary controls, protection against discrimination, correction of tax abuses, and limitation of competition by governmental organizations.

Collective bargaining is an obligation as well as a right, applying equally to workers and employers; and the fundamental right to strike is subordinate only to paramount considerations of public health and safety. Government's chief function in this field is to promote good will, encourage cooperation, and where resort is had to intervention, to be impartial, preventing violence and requiring obedience to all law by all parties involved. We pledge continuing study to improve labor-management legislation in the light of experience and changing conditions.

There must be a long-term program in the interest of agriculture and the consumer which should include: An accelerated program of sounder soil conservation; effective protection of reasonable market prices through flexible support prices, commodity loans, marketing agreements, together with such other means as may be necessary, and the development of sound farm credit; encouragement of family-size farms; intensified research to discover new crops, new uses for existing crops, and control of hoof and mouth and other animal diseases and crop pests; support of the principle of bona fide farmer-owned and farmer-operated cooperatives, and sound rural electrification.

We favor progressive development of the Nation's water resources for navigation, flood control and power, with immediate action in critical areas.

We favor conservation of all our natural resources and believe that conservation and stockpiling of strategic and critical raw materials is indispensable to the security of the United States.

We urge the full development of our forests on the basis of cropping and sustained yield with cooperation of States and private owners for conservation and fire protection.

We favor a comprehensive reclamation program for arid and semi-arid areas with full protection of the rights and interests of the States in the use and control of water for irrigation, power development incidental thereto and other beneficial uses; withdrawal or acquisition of lands for public purposes only by Act of Congress and after due consideration of local problems; development of processes for the extraction of oil and other substances from oil shale and coal; adequate representation of the West in the National Administration.

Recognizing the Nation's solemn obligation to all veterans, we propose a realistic and adequate adjustment of benefits on a cost-of-living basis for service-connected disabled veterans and their dependents, and for the widows, orphans and dependents of veterans who died in the service of their country. All disabled veterans should have ample opportunity for suitable, self-sustaining employment. We demand good-faith compliance with veterans preference in Federal service with simplification and codification of the hundreds of piecemeal Federal laws affecting veterans, and efficient and businesslike management of the Veterans Administration. We pledge the highest possible standards of medical care and hospitalization.

Housing can best be supplied and financed by private enterprise; but government can and should encourage the building of better homes at less cost. We recommend Federal aid to the States for local slum clearance and low-rental housing programs only where there is a need that cannot be met either by private enterprise or by the States and localities.

Consistent with the vigorous existence of our competitive economy, we urge: extension of the Federal Old Age and Survivors' Insurance program and increase of the benefits to a more realistic level; strengthening of Federal-State programs designed to provide more adequate hospital facilities, too improve methods of treatment for the mentally ill, to advance maternal and child health and generally to foster a healthy America.

Lynching or any other form of mob violence anywhere is a disgrace to any civilized state, and we favor the prompt enactment of legislation to end this infamy.

One of the basic principles of this Republic is the equality of all individuals in their right to life, liberty, and the pursuit of happiness. This principle is enunciated in the Declaration of Independence and embodied in the Constitution of the United States; it was vindicated on the field of battle and became the cornerstone of this Republic. This right of equal opportunity to work and to advance in life should never be limited in any individual because of race, religion, color, or country of origin. We favor the enactment and just enforcement of such Federal legislation as may be necessary to maintain this right at all times in every part of this Republic.

We favor the abolition of the poll tax as a requisite to voting.

We are opposed to the idea of racial segregation in the armed services of the United States.

V

We pledge a vigorous enforcement of existing laws against Communists and enactment of such new legislation as may be necessary to expose the treasonable activities of Communists and defeat their objective of establishing here a godless dictatorship controlled from abroad.

We favor a revision of the procedure for the election of the President and Vice President which will more exactly reflect the popular vote.

We recommend to Congress the submission of a constitutional amendment providing equal rights for women.

We favor equal pay for equal work regardless of sex.

We propose a well-paid and efficient Federal career service.

We favor the elimination of unnecessary Federal bureaus and of the duplication of the functions of necessary governmental agencies.

We favor equality of educational opportunity for all and the promotion of education and educational facilities.

We favor restoration to the States of their historic rights to the tide and submerged lands, tributary waters, lakes, and streams.

We favor eventual statehood for Hawaii, Alaska and Puerto Rico. We urge development of Alaskan land communications and natural resources.

We favor self-government for the residents of the nation's capital.

VI

We dedicate our foreign policy to the preservation of a free America in a free world of free men. With neither malice nor desire for conquest, we shall strive for a just peace with all nations.

America is deeply interested in the stability, security and liberty of other independent peoples. Within the prudent limits of our own economic welfare, we shall cooperate, on a basis of self-help and mutual aid, to assist other peace-loving nations to restore their economic independence and the human rights and fundamental freedoms for which we fought two wars and upon which dependable peace must build. We shall insist on businesslike and efficient administration of all foreign aid.

We welcome and encourage the sturdy progress toward unity in Western Europe.

We shall erect our foreign policy on the basis of friendly firmness which welcomes cooperation but spurns appeasement. We shall pursue a consistent foreign policy which invites steadiness and reliance and which thus avoids the misunderstandings from which wars result. We shall protect the future against the errors of the Democrat Administration, which has too often lacked clarity, competence or consistency in our vital international relationships and has too often abandoned justice.

We believe in collective security against aggression and in behalf of justice and freedom. We shall support the United Nations as the world's best hope in this direction, striving to strengthen it and promote its effective evolution and use. The United Nations should progressively establish international law, be freed of any veto in the peaceful settlement of international disputes, and be provided with the armed forces contemplated by the Charter. We particularly commend the value of regional arrangements as prescribed by the Charter; and we cite the Western Hemispheric Defense Pact as a useful model.

We shall nourish these Pan-American agreements in the new spirit of cooperation which implements the Monroe Doctrine.

We welcome Israel into the family of nations and take pride in the fact that the Republican Party was the first to call for the establishment of a free and independent Jewish Commonwealth. The vacillation of the Democrat Administration on this question has undermined the prestige of the United Nations. Subject to the letter and spirit of the United Nations Charter, we pledge to Israel full recognition, with its boundaries as sanctioned by the United Nations and aid in developing its economy.

We will foster and cherish our historic policy of friendship with China and assert our deep interest in the maintenance of its integrity and freedom.

We shall seek to restore autonomy and self-sufficiency as rapidly as possible in our post-war occupied areas, guarding always against any rebirth of aggression.

We shall relentlessly pursue our aims for the

universal limitation and control of arms and implements of war on a basis of reliable disciplines against bad faith.

At all times safeguarding our own industry and agriculture, and under efficient administrative procedures for the legitimate consideration of domestic needs, we shall support the system of reciprocal trade and encourage international commerce.

We pledge that under a Republican Administration all foreign commitments shall be made public and subject to constitutional ratification. We shall say what we mean and mean what we say. In all of these things we shall primarily consult the national security and welfare of our own United States. In all of these things we shall welcome the world's cooperation. But in none of these things shall we surrender our ideals or our free institutions.

We are proud of the part that Republicans have taken in those limited areas of foreign policy in which they have been permitted to participate. We shall invite the Minority Party to join us under the next Republican Administration in stopping partisan politics at the water's edge.

We faithfully dedicate ourselves to peace with justice.

VII

Guided by these principles, with continuing faith in Almighty God; united in the spirit of brotherhood; and using to the full the skills, resources and blessings of liberty with which we are endowed; we, the American people, will courageously advance to meet the challenge of the future.

Socialist Party Platform—1948

PREAMBLE

Mankind is haunted by new fears. In the crowded metropolis and on the distant farm, men ask themselves whether, under freedom, depression can be avoided, poverty vanquished and war uprooted.

Starvation stalks much of the world, and in our own land men dread the insecurity that tomorrow may bring. While millions go in rags, the world's looms are again knitting the uniforms that will shroud new victims to be offered on the altars of nationalism, imperialism and tyranny.

In 1948, we face the elemental question of survival. The atomic revolution has burst upon the world and a new unity has been forged among the human race: men who have refused to be brothers one of another may now become children of a common doom.

. . . Unless we learn to reorganize our society for survival and not for mutual extinction;

. . . Unless we learn new techniques of co-operation to replace the old policies of competition;

. . . Unless we move rapidly toward socialization by which alone the individual can be preserved in the inter-dependent world of the turbine, the plane, the steel mill and the uranium pile;

. . . Unless we move rapidly to a world order without greed, profit and hate.

The American people, because of the accidents of geography, will make the decision for mankind. Our mines and factories were not devastated by the physical havoc of the last war. For America, and consequently the world, it is not too late.

Three forces today are competing for the loyalty of men. And in this race, the stakes are the survival of mankind.

On the one hand, an economic system calling itself "free enterprise" asserts that it can lead to the salvation of humanity. It has brought us repeatedly to depressions and wars, yet its spokesmen in the Democratic and Republican Parties still pretend they have solutions.

They have, in fact, betrayed the promises with which they woo the American people every four years. They offered prosperity and delivered depression. They pledged peace and delivered war. They promised to increase our standard of living and are now raising the cost of living. They promised freedom to organized labor and hobbled it with new bonds.

They have sought partisan advantage and jeopardized national welfare. The dominant wings in their parties have combined to destroy price control and give us inflation, to undermine restraints on greed and give us shortage, to favor the rich and deny the poor, to cut the taxes of the wealthy and insult the common man with a crumb.

There is a second force in the world—which promises security and speaks of freedom but delivers only economic bondage and dictatorship. It is the force of totalitarianism. Yesterday its most sinister front was Fascism; today it is Communism.

In the United States, it marches under masked

banners. It calls itself a "new party" and has pushed into the forefront well-meaning liberals who do not know the purposes of their Communist allies. And this alliance, though speaking for civil liberties at home, defends the most powerful tyranny in the modern world. It speaks of peace but is blind to the most aggressive imperialism of the present day. It speaks of one world but works for two spheres of influence. It urges the brotherhood of man but sanctifies the divisive principle of national sovereignty.

As against these forces, the Socialist Party of the United States speaks for the Third Force—democratic socialism, the principles of democratic planning and international order. This socialist program for the United States today includes these major goals:

Basic Socialist Demands

1. The natural resources of the nation—minerals, oil, electric and atomic power—are the property of the people. Their preservation for future generations and their management by the people for social purposes can be achieved democratically under socialism.

2. The basic industries, public utilities, banking and credit institutions—all the economic facilities needed for the satisfaction of the fundamental requirements of the people—must be socially owned and democratically managed.

3. Socialism will democratize the economic life of the nation by the joint representation of workers, the working management and the consuming public, in the management of socialized enterprises; by the guarantee of popular control of enterprise through the maximum decentralization economically feasible and the use of various types of organization, particularly the public corporation and the voluntary cooperative; and by the preservation of the freedom of labor organization and of consumer choice.

With such control we can have democratic planning. The lessons of the last war have taught that only by planning, by large-scale government investment, by decisive national action, can production be increased to meet the goals set by the nation. In place of the destructive ends sought in wartime, the nation must now fix its peacetime goals—food for the ill-fed, clothing for the ill-clothed, homes for the ill-housed.

A nation that could fill the skies with planes and the oceans with warships can fill its streets and avenues with homes, schools and hospitals; swell its granaries and storehouses; bring joy to its people and the world. In the light of this Socialist program for democratic planning, we offer this platform to the American people in the 1948 elections. It can be achieved.

Domestic Program

1. Raise the Standard of Living

It must be the constant task of the nation to raise the standard of living of its people. This can be effected only by a continually rising trend in production and wage levels, the stabilization of prices, and the immediate elimination of profits as the determining factor in production. In a period of inflation wage increases without price controls are delusions.

2. Expand the Productive Facilities of the Nation

The American standard of living and the needs of world economic rehabilitation make it essential that our national production be rapidly expanded. An economy based on profit will not expand so long as scarcity is profitable and inflation an easy road to gain.

The Socialist Party calls for government action to assure investment in new plant capacity through the establishment of public corporations for the production of ever-mounting quantities of steel, oil and other raw materials, and the utilization of the nation's water resources for the development of cheaper and more abundant electric power. A far-flung program of Tennessee Valley Administrations, Missouri Valley Administrations and Rural Electrification Administration cooperatives can effect the electrification of whole areas that are lagging far behind their agricultural and industrial potential. Only by planned growth in our national output of civilian goods can we end the menace of inflation, which is now dangerously increased by our enormous expenditures on arms.

3. Expand Social Legislation

The intricacies of twentieth century living and the potentialities of modern technology have at last made it possible to guarantee a national minimum standard of living for the population. The Socialist Party advocates:

a. Expansion of unemployment insurance and social security. Millions of workers are as yet uncovered by the unemployment and social security provisions. The present law discriminates against farm labor, domestic servants and other working groups despite the constitutional guarantee of the "equal protection of the laws." Even so, the Democratic-Republican coalition in Congress has been whittling down the number of workers protected by the existing law at a time when extension of coverage should be the order of the day.

The age at which workers become eligible for old age pensions should be promptly reduced to 60, and the system should be financed by net progressive income taxation rather than by the regressive payroll tax. The benefits—now drastically cut by the current inflation—should be raised.

The Social Security law should be amended to include family allowances. The proper care of children is at least as important as the care of the aged.

b. Minimum Wage. The present legal minimum wage under the Wage-Hour Law should be immediately raised to the 75 cents an hour demanded by organized labor, with progressive increases to occur periodically.

The number of employees protected by the Act must be increased by a redefinition of coverage; and the present reactionary drive to reduce the coverage must be defeated.

c. Health services. Legislation for comprehensive medical and hospital care, financed by a national contributory system of health insurance, must be enacted by Congress. The Democratic-Republican coalition has successfully blocked the health insurance bill. In contrast, the Taft health bill will not provide comprehensive medical care nor remove the economic barriers now depriving millions of proper medical service.

Only a national health insurance program can guarantee free access to medical care, freedom of doctors' choice and freedom for the medical profession within a framework of public responsibility.

Neither a fee-for-service system nor voluntary prepayment plans can bring the benefits of modern medical science to all the people, regardless of race, color, creed, geography or economic condition.

Federal tax funds should be used to supplement an insurance program in creating a fully rounded national health service.

Public health services must be increased; the construction of new hospitals and clinics must be pushed. Federal action must be taken to stimulate research and public preventive medicine in cancer, heart diseases, mental illness, alcoholism and other ailments, as was done in the field of atomic fission. The maternal and child services provided by the Social Security Act must be extended.

d. Education. It is a national disgrace that the richest nation in the world does not have the best possible educational program from the nursery school to the university. America has subjected its children and youth to a shameful chronic emergency in this field. Higher standards of teacher training, enlarged and improved facilities, curricula better designed to meet pupil needs, adequate salaries, attractive conditions for superior professional work—all require that Federal contributions to public education be vastly multiplied without reducing local community initiative and existing State responsibilities.

At the same time, legislative efforts to divert public funds to private sectarian schools must be defeated. The principle of separation of church and state must be consistently applied in the use of public educational funds.

We propose passage of State and Federal laws aimed at eliminating racial, cultural and religious discrimination and segregation in education.

e. Veterans. Because of the special hardships war worked upon the veterans and conscientious objectors, we favor legislation to provide them substantial and adequate benefits in the form of education, medical care and loans; and full care for the families of those who did not return. We demand immediate steps to end the vicious discrimination and outright fraud now being practiced against Negro, Nisei, Spanish- or Mexican-American veterans by prejudiced local employees of the Veterans Administration, particularly in the South and Southwest.

4. Expand the Nation's Housing Facilities

Private enterprise has failed dismally to meet the challenge of housing the American people. Its boast that the lifting of controls on new construction would stimulate large-scale building has proved hollow. The lower income groups most desperately in need of housing, the young people —particularly our veterans—and the inhabitants of our ever-growing slums, are not in a position to buy or rent the facilities that private contractors are willing or able to erect.

The Taft-Ellender-Wagner Bill should be passed —but only as the merest fraction of a beginning, precisely because its major reliance is on the private construction industry.

The Socialist Party proposes the creation of a Home Loan Bank to finance the purchase of homes, a Public Supply and Fabricating Corporation to set up factory units needed to produce materials and to develop large-scale prefabricated housing; the expansion of public housing activities in the field of low-income multiple dwellings; the expansion of publicly built, cooperative tenant-operated housing; the integration of national and local housing plans, including revision of municipal building codes; the development of a government program of bona fide collective bargaining with the building and construction unions, providing for a guaranteed annual wage to remove one of the worst evils of the building industry and for the development of apprentice-training programs.

We favor the extension and strengthening of rent control for the duration of the housing emergency. The people of America must call to account those legislators who are destroying rent controls, permitting eviction of tenants by subterfuge and so contributing to disastrous inflation in the field of housing.

5. Protect the Nation's Title to Atomic Energy Pending Internationalization

The United States has made a good beginning in reserving to the nation, rather than ceding to business, the ownership of atomic energy. But this principle is already being undermined by cost-plus contracts, granted to private corporations to exploit this new storehouse of power for profit as coal, oil and other resources have been in the past. Nuclear fission was not the product of private enterprise. It was financed by the nation and was achieved by cooperative scientific effort operating in complete disregard of the profit motive. As the peace-time uses of atomic energy begin to emerge, it becomes increasingly important that the constructive applications of atomic power be utilized only through non-profit public corporations.

6. Strengthen Civil and Political Liberties

Civil and political liberties are in serious danger today. The Socialist Party calls for greater vigilance and specifically demands:

a. Repeal of the Taft-Hartley Act which undermines the right to strike, the right to organize, the right to sign contracts guaranteeing union security and furthering the economic interests of organized workers; and which permits the power of the state to be used in behalf of employers and against workers with just grievances. The Socialist Party pledges its full support to organized labor in its effort to repeal the Taft-Hartley Act and similar state laws.

b. Elimination of the Committee on Un-American Activities which has pursued the dishonest tradition of the Dies Committee. The Committee has abused the legitimate democratic function of Congress to investigate and collect data on matters of national importance.

c. Defeat of any legislation that would force the Communist Party further underground and that would appear to give moral justification to its conspiratorial policies. The right to free expression of political views must not be impaired. But the existing laws against overt acts should be vigorously enforced.

d. Elimination of poll taxes and opening of the ballot to citizens regardless of income.

e. Full amnesty and restoration of civil rights for war objectors, several hundred of whom are still in prison and thousands of whom have lost citizenship.

7. Establish Racial Equality

Democracy cannot tolerate two classes of citizenship. Complete political economic and social equality, regardless of race, religion or national origin must be established.

a. Segregation must be abolished in the armed forces, in all public institutions and in housing.

b. Legislation for a Fair Employment Practices Committee, long overdue, should be passed.

c. Anti-lynching legislation must be enacted to wipe out the worst blot on the American scene.

d. Naturalization rights should be granted to Japanese immigrants who have demonstrated their loyalty, and indemnification should be given to Japanese immigrants and their American descendants who suffered property losses because of government policy during World War II.

e. All forms of discriminating barriers against immigration on grounds of race, color or national origin must be abolished.

f. Guarantee the right to vote to many citizens now robbed of suffrage. The 14th Amendment of the Constitution, depriving states of representation in Congress in proportion to the number of citizens deprived of the right to vote by virtue of race, color, or previous condition of servitude, should be promptly enforced.

8. Safeguard American Agriculture

The Socialist Party opposes the absentee ownership of farms and its attendant tenancy in America. We reaffirm our position that occupancy and use should be the only rightful title to farmland. Where conditions favor family farming, the security of such farmers should be strengthened through cooperative credit purchasing and marketing, aided by government financing. Where modern techniques and specialization require large-scale farm enterprises, we call for social ownership and cooperative operation to replace the corporation farm which threatens both the security and freedom of farm workers.

We disapprove of the New Deal idea of agricultural scarcity, aimed at keeping prices up by limiting production. Our domestic needs and those of the world require an agricultural program based on maximum production.

We urge the continuation and expansion of the present conservation program to check destruction by floods, erosion of topsoil and depletion of farm fertility. Our obligation to our grandchildren demands a greater concern with the heritage we leave in productive farmland.

The proper distribution and marketing of food and fiber does not require gambling. Our present Board of Trade pricing of farm produce, with its poker game practices of buying on futures, must be ended.

9. Establish a Progressive Tax System

The Tax Law of 1948 is legislation for the direct and immediate benefit of the wealthiest group in the country. Their taxes have been drastically lowered without any real assurance that corresponding economic benefits in the form of additional equity capital for new production will result. The tax reduction for those in the lower income brackets is petty, and will disappear altogether after November if a Democratic or Republican Congress is elected.

We Propose:

a. Raising the present exemption levels to equal the amounts necessary to sustain minimum standards of living.

b. Restoring the earned Income Credit in such form that it grants a tax benefit (with an appropriate maximum) to income from wages and salary in contrast to income from investment.

c. Tightening of the provisions of the Estate Tax section of the Internal Revenue Code by increasing the rates, lowering the exemption and plugging the loop-holes by which inherited wealth can be passed on for two and sometimes more generations, by means of trusts, without paying succession taxes. Corresponding changes must be made in the Gift Tax section.

d. Modification of the Internal Revenue Code's favored treatment of speculative and gambling profits, and encouragement of new equity capital for production by revision of the treatment of Capital Assets.

e. Financing of extraordinary government expenses through a capital levy, especially on the increase in private capital since 1939, so that those who benefited directly from World War II will bear the burden of the nation's war deficit.

f. We condemn the fraudulent joint-return provision of the new tax law as a device which enables the wealthy to minimize their share of the tax burden.

10. Financing the Socialist Program

The American people will be told that it is impossible to finance this program for economic security. The cost of World War II to the American people was some 350 billion dollars. It is fantastic to assert that we cannot afford to devote a fraction of that sum to the peace and happiness of the nation. On the basis of the program submitted to Congress by the Armed Forces, it is apparent that our military budget alone in 1952 will equal the present total national budget. The path to plenty lies in expanding our production and in reallocating our budget in the service of life and peace.

FOREIGN POLICY

Victory by the U. S. and its allies in two world wars has not established justice or peace. A third world war fought with atom bombs and bacteria will complete the ruin of mankind.

The major, but by no means the only threat of war, lies in the aggression of the Soviet empire and the international communist movement. That aggression has been invited and encouraged by the blunders of American policy from the Cairo and Teheran through the Yalta and Potsdam conferences. Disregard for those principles of peace which the Socialist Party has steadily urged since the campaign of 1944 has contributed directly to the present crisis. The problem of peace cannot be solved by any attainable superiority of American military might. The bi-partisan effort in Washington to achieve such superiority and the hysteria which accompanies it make war more likely, and threaten our internal democracy with a dangerous American militarism.

The road to peace lies neither through the policy of appeasement laid down at Yalta and now supported by Henry Wallace, nor through the confused military commitments of the Truman doctrine. Neither of these contradictory policies can defeat international communism or the conditions that breed it.

A far better approach is the European Economic Recovery Program. It is a significant recognition that cooperative economic action must be taken if the European continent is not to pass into chaos and so into communist hands. But the helpful economic cooperation necessary to peace cannot be confined to Western Europe. In Europe itself vigilance is necessary lest the Recovery Program be subverted into an attempt to re-establish capitalist reaction or fascism, or to promote an American economic imperialism.

In addition to the proper conduct of the ERP a policy looking to the winning of lasting peace must include the following proposals:

1. Conscription

The representatives of the United States should immediately propose to the United Nations that peacetime conscription be outlawed by all nations. We are opposed to all forms of peacetime conscription in the U. S. Conscription contributed greatly to the growth of totalitarianism in Europe and has been sharply criticized as unnecessary even from the military standpoint.

2. Disarmament

The United States should propose the rigid limitation and international control of all armaments, to be followed by universal—not unilateral —disarmament; all such measures to be accom-

panied by the unlimited right of inspection through an authorized agency of the United Nations. The principle of unlimited international inspection must be recognized as a fundamental safeguard of world security.

3. World Government

The achievement of true democratic federal world government is the ultimate structure of peace. The U. N. as we have repeatedly pointed out is not by its nature such a government. Yet in the critical years before us it may serve a great interim usefulness if its constructive agencies are strengthened and if it is given power to deal with aggression by abolition of the veto in the Security Council. To the rapid achievement of these ends the Socialist Party pledges itself.

4. Atomic Control

The United States should renew its efforts for United Nations adoption of the Majority Plan, based on the Baruch proposals; a campaign of unceasing world education on the contents of the plan should be launched immediately; and meanwhile production of atomic bombs should be halted.

5. Raw Materials

All peoples of the world must be assured access to the raw materials now controlled by international, private, and state monopolies. For this, the area of operation of the world Food and Agriculture Organization, in cooperation with the International Trade Organization where necessary, must be extended. At the same time, world planning is necessary to allocate materials in short supply on the basis of need. World production must be planned to meet the needs of world, not national, markets.

6. International Waterways

The United States should offer to join in the internationalization and demilitarization of the strategic waterways of the world, e.g. Panama, Suez, the Danube, the Dardanelles, Gibraltar, the Baltic, the Black Sea, the Arctic, etc., as part of the general program of world disarmament.

7. Police Force

The organization of world peace requires the existence of an international police or security force. Along with the principle of unlimited international inspection, an international police force is indispensable for the solution of such problems as Palestine, Kashmir, and other crises which may arise.

8. Colonialism

The United States should urge immediate action to begin the permanent liquidation of all colonialism—whether resting on military might, economic domination or political infiltration. The United Nations should establish commissions to supervise an early transition to self-government.

9. Trade Barriers

The United States should support all efforts to establish customs unions as a first step in the direction of a world-wide outlawry of trade barriers.

10. Refugees

The United States, whose greatness has been built by the creativity of generations of immigrants from all parts of the world, must open its doors to those displaced persons who have no home. At the very least, 400,000 such persons can be admitted under unused immigration quotas from the war years. Full support for the International Refugee Organization is essential as long as the present emergency exists, but the goal must be the free and unrestricted movement of peoples, according to their own choice, throughout the world.

11. Palestine

The present disastrous situation has been precipitated by the monstrous Nazi terror, conflicting promises to Jews and Arabs, and repeated betrayal of a pledged word. It is now the duty of the United Nations, with the wholehearted support of the United States, to establish order, to guarantee to the Jewish community in Palestine full self-government, and to protect the right of immigration since it has not reached a saturation point. Whether the political structure necessary to establish these rights is partition or a federation of cantons somewhat on the Swiss model, the civil rights of minorities must be preserved within each district. In no event can immigration into Palestine be considered a complete and adequate answer to the problem of anti-semitism. Every country must be made a desirable homeland for those who live in it, regardless of race, creed or color.

12. Occupied Countries

Military occupation of conquered peoples is by nature inimical to democracy. American armies are now in occupation in Germany, Japan, Korea and various island outposts. Any attempts to use such occupation for economic advantage to American businessmen or for strategic military moves and counter-moves must be defeated. The encouragement of democratic self-government and functioning economies controlled by the people is the responsibility of occupying government, and as soon as this is done it must withdraw. Plans for fifty-year occupations have been mentioned; they must be defeated and dates for withdrawal set.

13. Economic Rehabilitation

The American government must increase its economic aid in the rehabilitation or development of all countries accepting the principles of political freedom, irrespective of the economic direction they choose for themselves in a free expression at the ballot box. Not only Europe but Asia, Africa and Latin America are in need of U. S. assistance.

INTERNATIONAL ORGANIZATION

Above all, it is essential that the United States use its great resources to hasten the world on the road to democratic international organization. Even if any other power rejects the concept of a world sovereignty and continues to assert the outmoded principle of individual national sovereignty, the United States must continue to press toward the goal. It should invite all nations that agree with the program described here to join in a close and effective organization, leaving the door open to the others to participate at a later date.

In 1948, the American people will decide their course. A spirit of defeatism now will result only in defeat. A willingness to vote for your convictions and hopes can start America and the world on the road to peace, to freedom and to plenty.

Socialist Labor Party Platform 1948

The crucial issue of our age is written in gigantic letters across the social sky.

It is: *Capitalist Despotism* or *Socialist Freedom*.

The Socialist Labor Party of America, at its last National Convention in the City of New York, in placing its program for a Socialist reconstruction of society before the American workers, declares this to be the issue that confronts them:

Either the working class takes control of affairs out of the hands of the capitalist class, ends the system of capitalist private ownership, and rebuilds our society on the basis of social ownership of the means of production, democratic management and production for use;

Or, as surely as night follows day, the capitalist system will lead us down the road to a third world war, totalitarian dictatorship and imperialist barbarism.

The Socialist Labor Party earnestly asks you to consider the facts of the present situation:

With the invention of atomic bombs and guided missiles, and the development of germ warfare, war at last looms as the potential destroyer of the human race. Despite this portentous fact and its frightful implications, the plutocratic masters of this country are preparing for another global war.

Through the press, radio and motion pictures, they are conditioning the country psychologically for a war with America's imperialist rival, Soviet Russia.

They have launched a huge rearmament program that will divert the energies of millions of workers from the tasks of peace.

Flouting America's traditional hostility to militarism, they are scheming to enact a system of permanent military conscription.

By means of fabulous subsidies voted by Congress for military research, they are reducing science and education to mere tools of an exalted military machine.

They have drafted plans for total war and the regimentation of industry.

They have brazenly acknowledged their intention to flout the Constitution. In plain violation of the Thirteenth Amendment they are scheming to conscript industrial manpower, and thus to reduce the workers to involuntary servitude.

Their politicians and spokesmen say this huge militarization program is for peace, but everyone in his senses knows that it is for war, and that if matters are allowed to drift, sooner or later there will be war.

Why is the plutocracy taking this desperate and suicidal course?

The Socialist Labor Party declares that the capitalists who guide America's policies are acting in response to their material and class interests, and that the real cause of war is not "bad men," but an outmoded, predatory social system. The logic of this is easily explained:

The international rivalries that erupt in war are a direct result of the system of wage labor—of the fact that the workers receive in wages only a fraction of the value of their product, hence can buy back only a fraction. Of the surplus, a part is consumed by the capitalist class in extravagant living, a part is wasted, a part is employed in expanding industry, and another part goes down the huge drain of the bureaucratic political State.

All of this represents wealth of which labor is robbed, and which in no manner or sense accrues to the benefit of the producing workers or contributes to social progress. That which remains after these deductions must be sold in foreign markets to relieve the glut at home. It is competition for these markets and for spheres of economic influence and sources of raw materials that makes the recurrence of war inevitable as long as the capitalist principle prevails as the basis of society.

It follows that attempts to insure peace via the United Nations are doomed to fail. Sooner or later, every world-organization edifice that is built on the foundation of capitalist dry rot must collapse.

Socialism alone supplies a sound foundation for peace and for the free cultural and material intercourse among the peoples of the world. Socialism does this by destroying the parent evil —the exploitation of wage labor—and thereby ending the problem of "unsold surpluses." Capitalism has everything standing on its head. Under capitalism surpluses are a curse. Under Socialism, which puts things right side up, there will be *production for use* instead of *production for sale and profit,* and surpluses, should they occur, will be a blessing. There can be no lasting peace without Socialism!

War is one consequence of prolonging the outmoded capitalist system; another is the scrapping of the Bill of Rights and the Statification of society.

In recent years the capitalists have turned more

and more to the State as an agency to break the back of working class resistance to increased exploitation, and to prolong their existence as a ruling, privileged class.

Signs of the capitalist reaction abound.

One is the enactment by a pliant capitalist Congress of the labor-shackling Taft-Hartley Law and the revival of the medieval weapon of the court injunction.

Another is the attempt, typical of the police State, to intimidate the workers and break their spirit by launching a Gestapo-like "disloyalty" witch hunt among them.

Still another is the ominous spread of police brutality and officially condoned mob violence and terrorism, and the alarming growth of race prejudice.

Finally, and most conspicuous of all, is the rapid militarization of the country and the corresponding rise in the influence and power of the anti-democratic military caste.

The Socialist Labor Party holds this reaction to be but a manifestation of an irreconcilable class struggle that rages in capitalist society.

One aim of the capitalist class is to hold wages down during the period of brisk demand for labor, to intensify exploitation, and thus to insure higher profits for itself.

A second aim is to reduce labor to the status of unresisting industrial serfs, thus evolving a labor-shackling system that corresponds to the needs of the present huge concentrations of feudalistic corporate capital.

The Socialist Labor Party warns the American workers that they are unprepared, ideologically and organizationally, to block this reaction or to prevent its success. Their present unions (A. F. of L., C.I.O. and kindred bodies), by reason of their pro-capitalist philosophy, treacherous labor-faker leadership and job-trust character, are, like the German trade unions (which were taken over by the Nazis and converted into the Labor Front), preeminently capitalist weapons to bridle the working class.

To remove the menace of fascism and industrial feudalism, the American workers must scrap the unions that accept capitalism as a finality. They must build a new union based on their class interests, and one that will consciously fight for the Socialist goal. They must organize the all-embracing Socialist Industrial Union—the workers' power!

The Socialist Labor Party appeals to you to accept the logic of these facts:

WAR, FASCISM AND POVERTY AMIDST PLENTY ARE THE EVIL BROOD OF CAPITALISM. No worker who reaches this conclusion can, without consciously aligning himself with the forces of reaction, support the parties that have as their aim the preservation of capitalism. In this category, besides the Republicans and Democrats, we include the "Third Party Progressives" (who acclaim "progressive capitalism"), and the "Liberal," "Labor," "Socialist" and "Communist" reformers. To speak of "progressive capitalism" today is as nonsensical as it would have been to speak of "progressive slavery" in 1860. And to propose capitalist reforms is to help prolong the capitalist cause of war and fascism. The logic of this is inescapable.

The Socialist Labor Party, therefore, calls upon the American workers, and all other enlightened citizens, to repudiate the parties of capitalism, and to support its program for a Socialist reconstruction of society.

The goal of the Socialist Labor Party is an Industrial Republic of Labor—a system based on collective ownership by the people of the land and all the instruments of wealth production, and one in which the workers will manage industry democratically through socially integrated Socialist Industrial Union Councils.

To bring to birth this society of peace, abundance and boundless human happiness, the Socialist Labor Party appeals to the working class, and to all other enlightened citizens, to support the principles of the Socialist Labor Party, and prepare now to help build the Socialist Industrial Union to back up the Socialist ballot. Unite with us to end the social system that dooms us to a lifelong tenure of wage slavery, with unemployment, poverty and wars as inseparable and ever recurrent features. Unite with us to establish the free Socialist Republic of Peace, Plenty and International Brotherhood!

Socialist Workers Party Platform—1948

Our vast natural resources and productive plant, the unexampled skill and energy of our workers, farmers and technicians, are the essential elements for abolishing poverty and creating a rational and harmonious society.

At the same time, never have the American people viewed the future with so much uncertainty and fear. For our generation, war and depression are the outstanding memories of the past and the imminent perspectives of the future.

The price of a loaf of bread or a pound of meat, the right to speak freely without persecution, questions of war and peace, every aspect of life presents the mass of our people with perpetual insecurity and unending crisis.

What are the reasons our rulers give for this ruinous condition? Since 1914 Democrats and Republicans alike have been reduced to diverting the people's wrath to a foreign enemy, the Kaiser and German militarism, Hitler and German fascism, and now Stalin and the "Iron Curtain."

This explanation is repeated by politicians and the government, by the press, the pulpit and the radio, taught in schools and universities, hammered into the heads of the population by every technical resource at the command of our capitalist masters. It can no longer deceive the people.

Gone are the days when individuals could carve out wealth for themselves and at the same time develop the country's economy. Today huge monopolies choke our splendid industrial resources.

But capitalism has not only created these monstrous monopolies. It has also brought into being the working class comprising tens of millions of people, with a high standard of education, great technical skills and long traditions of democracy and social equality.

Shaken by the collapse of 1929, this working class has already shown its tremendous capabilities by its organization of the CIO and the rapid growth of industrial unionism.

The workers are becoming increasingly aware of capitalist inefficiency in the use of resources. They are beginning to see through the warmongering of the imperialists. They resent the capitalist cheating of the people by inflation. They know that the Sixty Richest Families of the United States, like their counterparts abroad, will abandon democracy for fascism at any serious threat to their profits, privileges and power.

The irrepressible conflict between the monopolists and the workers shakes America with ever-growing convulsions and inexorably extends into a battle for rulership of the country.

The middle classes, the great mass of agricultural workers and small farmers, are ravaged by the anarchy of the profit system.

Millions of women bear the burden of a double oppression. Exploited and abused like all workers, they are also discriminated against and often denied jobs in industry, as well as having upon them the burden of the home.

The generations of the youth face the prospect of serving in permanent conscript armies and providing the fodder for a new war. Capitalist corruption bears down with increasing force upon the high ideals of the professions of medicine, journalism, education and upon the workers in the arts, sciences and engineering.

Far from seeing any end to segregation, the Negro people have seen the Federal Government of Roosevelt and Henry Wallace carry the infamy of a Jim Crow Army to every quarter of the globe.

Tormented by these conditions, the oppressed classes and groups are looking for a way out. There is no way out for them except to follow the leadership of organized labor. On the day when the working class can assure them of its determination to end capitalist anarchy and chaos, the rule of the capitalists is doomed.

The capitalists know this. That is why they concentrate all their power and energy to crush the growing challenge of the working class. The Taft-Hartley Act, the Mundt Bill, the Committee on un-American Activities, the preparation for transforming the FBI into a Gestapo, militarization of the country, the strangling of liberties traditional in the United States since the beginning of the Republic—this long train of abuses and usurpations reveals that their aim is to subject the working class to an absolute despotism, the sole guarantee of capitalist rule in its period of decay.

Twice our people have faced a similar threat. Twice they have known how to meet it.

In 1776 the farmers, mechanics and artisans, led by revolutionists such as Sam Adams, Jefferson and Washington, destroyed the power of the British ruling class who sought to crush the birth of a new nation.

In 1860 William Lloyd Garrison and Wendell Phillips, John Brown and Frederick Douglass, Abraham Lincoln and Thaddeus Stevens, personified the forces which waged merciless war against the slaveowners' attempt to perpetuate their outmoded system, halt the expansion of our economy and destroy the liberties of our people.

The Socialist Workers Party, in these years of

decision, comes forward as the continuator of these revolutionary traditions. The socialist revolution is even more imperative for the salvation of the U.S. than was the Civil War and the War for Independence.

The Socialist Workers Party warns the people that the present struggle is so deeply rooted in a bankrupt economic system that it must end either in the complete destruction of civilization or in the socialist reconstruction of society under the leadership of the working class.

Let him who dares, face the workers and farmers and tell them that they do not possess the knowledge, the will, the physical and intellectual resources, and the political capacity to pull this country back from the brink of the abyss to which monopoly capitalism has led it. The Socialist Workers Party bases itself upon its supreme confidence in the creative capacities of the working people.

The Socialist Workers Party presents itself under the banner of Marx and Engels, Lenin and Trotsky, Debs and Haywood. Their banner is our banner. These great leaders of international socialism were animated by the conviction that unless the tremendous powers of modern industry were taken over by the workers of the world, society would collapse into barbarism. The state of the world today is proof of how correct they were.

Genuine labor politics, however, can have nothing in common with the politics of the Democratic and Republican parties. Against the background of national and international crisis, increasing numbers of the American people view their antics with indignation and disgust. These parties are bi-partisan in foreign policy, bi-partisan in their devotion to capitalism, bi-partisan in their incapacity to cure its evils, bi-partisan in their assault upon the working class and the civil liberties of the American people. The only difference between them is the dispute over who can best secure the privileges and the pilfering which fall to those who administer the capitalist government.

These two parties would long ago have been repudiated and abandoned by the working men and women except for the treacherous and opportunist practices of the top union leaders, who are tied to the apron strings of the capitalist politicians and act as apologists, recruiters and vote-solicitors for them in the ranks of the workers.

The party of Henry Wallace represents nothing but an attempt to exploit the disgust of the people with the Democrats and the Republicans. The Wallace party is the unashamed champion of decaying capitalism. Claiming support as an anti-war party, its leader, Wallace, has betrayed the struggle in advance by declaring his readiness to support the projected war when it breaks out. Wallace's stock-in-trade is a recitation of evils without one single concrete proposal to mobilize labor's strength against monopoly capitalism, the source of all the evils he criticizes.

The Communist Party (Stalinists), which is supporting the Wallace party in this year's election, is interested in the class struggle only insofar as it can be exploited to advance the interests of the arch-reactionary Stalinist bureaucracy in the Kremlin. When it serves Stalin's purposes, as it did during the period of the Stalin-Hitler Pact, the American Stalinists talk class struggle, support strikes, pay lip-service to the need for socialism, etc. And similarly, when it serves Stalin's purposes, as it did during the wartime period of the Washington-Moscow alliance, the American Stalinists advocate class collaboration, "national unity," cessation of labor and Negro struggles, strikebreaking, etc. In their case they remain instruments of Stalin's reactionary foreign policy and must be seen as enemies of the workers' true class interests and revolutionary socialism.

The Socialist Party of Norman Thomas pretends that war can be stopped by the United Nations just as it pretended that the war could be stopped by the League of Nations. While denouncing war in general it is no less ready to support World War III than it was to support World War II. It seeks to reform and not to abolish capitalism.

The Socialist Workers Party alone consistently and unconditionally champions the interests of the workers in their struggles against capitalism, and works to organize them for its abolition. This goal is expressed and concretized in the Socialist Workers Party's fundamental objective in the 1948 campaign—the mobilization of the masses for a Workers and Farmers Government.

Such a government, based on direct representation from democratically elected councils of workers, farmers, housewives, soldiers and minority groups, will initiate the reign of real and complete democracy in every sphere of life. It will take over the means of production, expand and coordinate them in a planned economy, and create the conditions for permanent prosperity. It will end the rule of coupon-clippers and put the former capitalists to work at honest toil. Its victory will bring peace and harmony to the United States by doing away with the material cause of class divisions and therefore of class conflicts. The victory of socialism in the most powerful country will serve as an inspiring example to be quickly followed by the rest of the world.

Only a Workers and Farmers Government can reorganize our crumbling society on a rational basis and bring that new birth of freedom and prosperity which is socialism.

Only a Workers and Farmers Government, pledged to irreconcilable opposition to every vestige of monopoly capitalism, can prevent a Third World War.

The program, the platform, the policies and the methods which we advocate will be realized through the formation of a great independent party, led and organized by the working class, including all those tens of millions whose basic hostility to capitalism needs only this leadership to achieve full consciousness and resolute action. Such a party, embracing the productive, social and political activity of the vast majority of the nation, is today the guarantee of democracy. By its mere existence it will be an invincible safeguard against totalitarianism in any form.

The platform of the Socialist Workers Party is not designed to patch up the dying capitalist system, but to protect the interests of the toilers against the brutal aggressions of their capitalist enemies. It is an election platform, to be supported by the ballot on election day, but it is more than that—it is also a program of action to unite and guide the struggles of the workers on a year-round basis. Its effectiveness depends not only on the support it receives in Congress and other legislative bodies, but even more on the extent to which it receives support from the masses in their daily struggles in the factories, in the unions, etc. Its aim is to organize and mobilize the working people for the part they are destined to play in the march to a better world.

In line with these fundamental objectives, the Socialist Workers Party advocates this platform:

1. FOREIGN POLICY

Take the war-making powers out of the hands of Congress! Let the people vote through nationwide referendum on the question of war or peace! No secret diplomacy! Withdraw all troops from foreign soil! For the complete independence of the colonial peoples! No confidence whatever in the United Nations, dominated by despots of every variety and designed to spread the illusion that peace is possible under capitalism! Full solidarity with the revolutionary struggles of workers and farmers in all lands—those dominated by American imperialism as well as those dominated by reactionary Stalinism! For the Socialist United States of the World!

2. LABOR'S STANDARD OF LIVING

For the inclusion in all union contracts of an escalator clause (also known as the sliding scale of wages or automatic cost-of-living bonus) to meet the rising cost of living, with the safeguard that wages shall not fall below the basic rates established in the contract! For the application of this principle to wages of all government employes, veterans' allotments, old-age allowances, old-age pensions and social security! For the establishment of price control, to be regulated and enforced by mass consumers committees of housewives, unionists, working farmers and small shopkeepers! For the 6-hour day, 30-hour week, with no reduction in pay! For unemployment insurance equal to trade union wages!

3. LABOR AND CIVIL RIGHTS

Repeal the Taft-Hartley Act! No government interference in union affairs! No restrictions on the right to organize, strike and picket! No compulsory arbitration! Repeal all anti-labor laws! Down with government by injunction!

An end to red-baiting, witch hunts and political persecution! Withdraw the "subversive" blacklists used for political persecution of government and other employees! Abolish the House Committee on un-American Activities! Defeat the Mundt Bill and all other measures to totalitarianize American politics! Liberalize the election laws which discriminate against minority parties through excessive petition requirements and subject them to arbitrary exclusion from the ballot! Old enough to be drafted, old enough to vote! Safeguard and extend the Bill of Rights!

4. RIGHTS OF MINORITY GROUPS

Smash the Jim Crow system! Full economic, political and social equality for the Negro people and other minorities! Pass and enforce legislation to punish lynching, abolish the poll tax, establish a Fair Employment Practices Committee with power to root out discriminatory practices, eliminate segregation wherever it exists! Combat anti-Semitism in all its forms! Wipe out discriminatory immigration policies and open the doors of the U.S. to refugees! Unite the workers of all races for the common struggle against their exploiters!

5. FARM POLICY

Establish a federal farm program to guarantee the cost of production to working farmers and to be operated under the control of their own representatives! Expand rural electrification! No limitation on crops! A federal program for soil conservation and flood control! No taxes on savings of cooperatives! A federal ban on all speculation in farm commodities! Abolish sharecropping and landlordism! The land to those who work it!

6. MILITARY POLICY

Against a permanent conscript army! It is necessary to establish a system of military training, financed and equipped by the government, but operating under the control and discipline of the trade union movement! Abolish the officer caste system in the armed forces! Full democratic rights for the ranks in all the services, including their right to participate in politics and public life, to elect their own officers, to organize along union lines and engage in collective bargaining! Abolish race segregation in the armed forces! Trade union wages for the servicemen!

7. HOUSING

The Federal government must be forced to declare a state of national housing emergency and to initiate a program to erect 25 million permanent low-cost, low-rent housing units! Nationalize and operate under workers' control all feeder industries which provide building materials! Operate this housing program through a government planning board of outstanding architects, engineers and representatives of the workers in the building trades! Finance the program with the billions now spent for war preparations! Homes, not atom bombs! Clear the slums! Restore rent control, under supervision of tenants committees!

8. TAXATION

Repeal all payroll taxes! Abolish all sales taxes! No taxes on incomes under $5,000 a year! A 100% tax on incomes over $25,000 a year! Tax the rich, not the poor!

9. GOVERNMENT OWNERSHIP OF INDUSTRY

Nationalize the basic industries, all war plants, all natural resources, and operate them in the interests of the producers and consumers by democratically-elected committees of workers and technicians! Nationalize the banks! Institute a planned economy of abundance, based on production for use, not for profit!

10. INDEPENDENT POLITICAL ACTION

Labor must break all ties with the capitalist parties—Democratic, Republican, Wallaceite! For an Independent Labor Party based on the trade unions and embracing the working farmers, Negroes and veterans! For a United Labor Conference, with representation from all unions, to launch labor's own party and run labor's own candidates for office!

For a Workers and Farmers Government!

States' Rights Platform of 1948

We affirm that a political party is an instrumentality for effectuating the principles upon which the party is founded; that a platform of principles is a solemn covenant with the people and with the members of the party; that no leader of the party, in temporary power, has the right or privilege to proceed contrary to the fundamental principles of the party, or the letter or spirit of the Constitution of the United States; that to act contrary to these principles is a breach of faith, a usurpation of power, and a forfeiture of the party name and party leadership.

We believe that the protection of the American people against the onward march of totalitarian government requires a faithful observance of Article X of the American Bill of Rights which provides that: "The powers not delegated to the United States by the Constitution, nor prohibited by it to the states, are reserved to the states respectively, or to the people."

THE PRINCIPLE OF STATES' RIGHTS

We direct attention to the fact that the first platform of the Democratic Party, adopted in 1840, resolved that: "Congress has no power under the Constitution to interfere with or control the domestic institutions of the several states, and that such states are the sole and proper judges of everything appertaining to their own affairs not prohibited by the Constitution."

Such pronouncement is the cornerstone of the Democratic Party. A long train of abuses and usurpations of power by unfaithful leaders who are alien to the Democratic parties of the states here represented has become intolerable to those who believe in the preservation of constitutional government and individual liberty in America.

The Executive Department of the government is promoting the gradual but certain growth of a totalitarian state by domination and control of a politically minded Supreme Court. As examples of the threat to our form of government, the Executive Department, with the aid of the Supreme Court, has asserted national dominion and control of submerged oil-bearing lands in California, schools in Oklahoma and Missouri, primary elections in Texas, South Carolina and Louisiana, restrictive covenants in New York and the District of Columbia, and other jurisdictions, as well as religious instruction in Illinois.

Peril to Basic Rights

By asserting paramount Federal rights in these instances, a totalitarian concept has been promulgated which threatens the integrity of the states and the basic rights of their citizens.

We have repeatedly remonstrated with the leaders of the national organization of our party but our petitions, entreaties and warnings have been treated with contempt. The latest response to our entreaties was a Democratic convention in Philadelphia rigged to embarrass and humiliate the South.

This alleged Democratic assembly called for a civil-rights law that would eliminate segregation of every kind from all American life, prohibit all forms of discrimination in private employment, in public and private instruction and administration and treatment of students; in the operation of public and private health facilities; in all transportation, and require equal access to all places of public accommodation for persons of all races, colors, creeds and national origin.

Proposed FBI Powers

This infamous and iniquitous program calls for the reorganization of the civil rights section of the Department of Justice with a substantial increase in a bureaucratic staff to be devoted exclusively to the enforcement of the civil rights program; the establishment within the FBI of a special unit of investigators and a police state in a totalitarian, centralized, bureaucratic government.

This convention hypocritically denounced totalitarianism abroad but unblushingly proposed and approved it at home. This convention would strengthen the grip of a police state upon a liberty-loving people by the imposition of penalties upon local public officers who failed or refused to act in accordance with its ideas in suppressing mob violence.

We point out that if a foreign power undertook to force upon the people of the United States the measures advocated by the Democratic convention in Philadelphia, with respect to civil rights, it would mean war and the entire nation would resist such effort.

The convention that insulted the South in the party platform advocated giving the Virgin Islands and other dependencies of the United States "the maximum degree of local self-government."

When an effort was made to amend this part of the platform so as to make it read that the party favored giving the Virgin Islands and the several states the maximum degree of local self-government, the amendment adding the words "these several states" was stricken out and the sovereign states were denied the rights that the party favors giving the Virgin Islands.

Past Loyalty

We point out that the South, with clock-like regularity, has furnished the Democratic Party approximately 50 per cent of the votes necessary to nominate a President every four years for nearly a century. In 1920 the only states in the union that went Democratic were the eleven Southern states.

Notwithstanding this rugged loyalty to the party, the masters of political intrigue now allow Republican states in which there is scarcely a Democratic office holder to dominate and control the party and fashion its policies.

New Policy

As Democrats who are irrevocably committed to democracy as defined and expounded by Thomas Jefferson, Andrew Jackson and Woodrow

Wilson, and who believe that all necessary steps must be taken for its preservation, we declare to the people of the United States as follows:

1. We believe that the Constitution of the United States is the greatest charter of human liberty ever conceived by the mind of man.

2. We oppose all efforts to invade or destroy the rights vouchsafed by it to every citizen of this republic.

3. We stand for social and economic justice, which we believe can be vouchsafed to all citizens only by a strict adherence to our Constitution and the avoidance of any invasion or destruction of the constitutional rights of the states and individuals. We oppose the totalitarian, centralized, bureaucratic government and the police state called for by the platforms adopted by the Democratic and Republican conventions.

4. We stand for the segregation of the races and the racial integrity of each race; the constitutional right to choose one's associates; to accept private employment without governmental interference, and to earn one's living in any lawful way. We oppose the elimination of segregation employment by Federal bureaucrats called for by the misnamed civil rights program. We favor home rule, local self-government and a minimum interference with individual rights.

5. We oppose and condemn the action of the Democratic convention in sponsoring a civil rights program calling for the elimination of segregation, social equality by Federal fiat, regulation of private employment practices, voting and local law enforcement.

6. We affirm that the effective enforcement of such a program would be utterly destructive of the social, economic and political life of the Southern people, and of other localities in which there may be differences in race, creed or national origin in appreciable numbers.

7. We stand for the checks and balances provided by the three departments of our Government. We oppose the usurpation of legislative functions by the executive and judicial departments. We unreservedly condemn the effort to establish nation-wide a police state in this republic that would destroy the last vestige of liberty enjoyed by a citizen.

8. We demand that there be returned to the people, to whom of right they belong, those powers needed for the preservation of human rights and the discharge of our responsibility as Democrats for human welfare. We oppose a denial of those rights by political parties, a barter or sale of those rights by a political convention, as well as any invasion or violation of those rights by the Federal Government.

We call upon all Democrats and upon all other loyal Americans who are opposed to totalitarianism at home and abroad to unite with us in ignominiously defeating Harry S. Truman and Thomas E. Dewey, and every other candidate for public office who would establish a police state in the United States of America.

In 1952, the candidates of the Republican and Democratic parties received the highest popular vote for a winner and loser respectively in the history of presidential elections in the United States. The States' Rights Party had dissolved shortly after the 1948 election, and the Progressive Party was less prominent in 1952 than it had been four years previously. In addition to the Progressives, the minor parties which presented candidates were the Socialist Workers, the Socialist Laborites, the Socialists, the Prohibitionists, and the Christian Nationalists (in nine states).

Christian Nationalist Party

1952 PLATFORM

This is an era characterized by a universal sentiment of nationalism.

In this day of gathering storms, as the moral deterioration of political power spreads its growing infection, it is essential that every spiritual force be mobilized to defend and preserve the religious base upon which this nation was founded. For it is that base which has been the motivating impulse to our moral and national growth. History fails to record a single precedent in which nations subject to moral decay have not passed into political and economic decline. There has been either a spiritual reawakening to overcome the moral lapse, or a progressive deterioration leading to ultimate national disaster.

Our people are desperate for a plan which will revive hope and restore faith as they feel the oppressive burden of the tax levy upon every source of revenue and upon every property transaction; as they see the astronomically rising public debt heavily mortgaging the industry, the well-being and the opportunity of our children and our children's children; as they observe the rising costs of the necessities of life impairing the effectiveness of pensions, insurance and other fixed incomes and reducing the aged and infirm to appalling circumstances.

They look to their leaders, but their protests are silenced by the grim warnings of the disaster of a possible total war. They see no sign of concern, hear no words of encouragement, find no basis for easing fear. Their every expression of hope for reduction in the tax burden is met by the angry rejoinder that taxes must go even higher. There is no plan to transform extravagance into frugality, no desire to regain economic and fiscal stability, no prospect of return to the rugged idealism and collective tranquility of our fathers.

Perhaps it is unnecessary here to indict the present administration for all of its tragic blunders. For that indictment has already found full expression in the resentments which have poured from the hearts of the American people from north to south, from east to west. Many who thus register their resentments do not fully comprehend the

469

nature and degree of the policy misdirection which has brought us to fiscal instability, political insecurity and military weakness.

The issues which today confront the nation are clearly defined and so fundamental as to directly involve the very survival of the Republic.

Are we going to preserve the religious base to our origin, our growth and our progress or yield to the devious assaults of atheistic or other antireligious forces?

Are we going to maintain our present course toward State Socialism with Communism just beyond or reverse the present trend and regain our hold upon our heritage of liberty and freedom?

Are we going to squander our limited resources to the point of our own inevitable exhaustion or adopt commonsense policies of frugality which will insure financial stability in our time and a worth-while heritage in that of our progeny?

Are we going to continue to yield personal liberties and community autonomy to the steady and inexorable centralization of all political power or restore the Republic to constitutional direction, regain our personal liberties and reassume the individual State's primary responsibility and authority in the conduct of local affairs?

Are we going to permit a continuing decline in public and private morality or re-establish a high ethical standard as the means of regaining a diminishing faith in the integrity of our public and private institutions?

Are we going to continue to permit the pressure of alien doctrines to strongly influence the orientation of foreign and domestic policy or regain trust in our own traditions, experience and free institutions and the wisdom of our own people?

Other issues which deeply stir the conscience of the American people are many and varied, but all stem from irresponsibility in leadership. Domestic policy is largely dictated by the political expediencies of the moment. Foreign policy is as shifting as the sands before the winds and tides. Spendthriftness and waste have lost us our heritage of stability; weakness and vacillation, the moral leadership of the world.

In short, is American life of the future to be characterized by freedom or by servitude, strength or weakness. The answer must be clear and unequivocal if we are to avoid the pitfalls toward which we are now heading with such certainty.

DOMESTIC POLICY

Our government now differs substantially from the design of our forefathers as laid down in the Constitution. In this march away from our traditional standards, few of our former liberties have been left unimpaired. Rights and powers specifically reserved to State, community and individual by constitutional mandate have been ruthlessly suppressed by Federal authority. Our economic stature built under the incentives of free enterprise is imperiled by our drift through the back door of confiscatory taxation toward State Socialism. We find ourselves already past the point where higher taxes might be expected to produce higher revenue.

Expenditure upon expenditure, extravagance upon extravagance have so burdened our people with taxation and fed the forces of infiltration that our traditionally high standard of life has become largely fictitious and illusory.

As always, it is the great masses of the people, not the rich or prosperous, but the farmer, the laborer, and the average office worker who suffer the most.

Some of these penalties are now obscured by the reckless extravagance of government spending which creates a false sense of security, but the day of reckoning is inevitable.

The great bulwark of the Republic, individual and collective self-reliance, is under constant threat through a carefully designed paternalism which renders both community and individual increasingly dependent upon the support of the Federal Government. In all areas of private welfare, the Socialist planners seek to inject the Federal hand to produce a progressive weakening of the structure of individual character.

This process is sapping the initiative and energies of the people and leaves little incentive for the assumption of those risks which are inherent and unescapable in the forging of progress under the system of free enterprise. Worst of all, it is throwing its tentacles around the low income bracket sector of our society from whom is now exacted the major share of the cost of government.

The so-called "forgotten man" of the early thirties now is indeed no longer forgotten as the government levies upon his income as the main remaining source to defray reckless spendthrift policies.

More and more we work not for ourselves but for the State. In time, if permitted to continue, this trend cannot fail to be destructive. For no nation may survive in freedom once its people become the servants of the State, a condition to which we are now pointed with dreadful certainty. Labor, as always, will be the first to feel its frightful consequence.

But our failures in domestic policy can be overcome, for government takes its tone, its character, even its general efficiency from its leadership. Sound leadership can restore integrity to the public service; can economize in the public administration; can eliminate disloyal elements from public authority; can purge our educational system of subversive and immoral influence; can restore to youth its rightful heritage; can strengthen the fabric of our free economy; can raise the dollar to its true value; can reduce the tax burden on individual and industry; can regain the course of constitutional direction; can recapture personal liberties now impaired; can correct social inequities; can strengthen the position of both worker and owner in private industry, even while protecting the public interest; can fortify the initiative, energy and enterprise of the farmer so as to insure the adequacy of the production of food in lean years and its distribution in those of plenty, without being crippled by the unwarranted interference and domination of government; and can rearm the nation without undue burden upon the people. The correction of domestic evils and lapses would not be too difficult provided the will to do so firmly exists.

Foreign Policy

Foreign policy has been as tragically in error as has domestic policy. We practically invited Soviet dominance over the free peoples of Eastern Europe through strategic dispositions of Soviet force at the close of the European war; we deliberately withdrew our armies from thousands of square miles of hard-won territory, permitting the advance of Soviet forces to the west to plant the Red flag of Communism on the ramparts of Berlin, Vienna and Prague, capitals of western civilization; we recklessly yielded effective control over areas of vast uranium deposits without which the Soviet might never have developed the threat of atomic power.

We foolishly permitted the encirclement of Berlin by Soviet forces, rendering almost inevitable the tragically high cost we have had to pay to secure open lines of supply and communication between our zones of occupation there and in West Germany; we authored, sponsored or approved policies under which the German industrial plant was subjected to major postwar dismantling and destruction; we turned over to the Soviet for slave labor hundreds of thousands of German prisoners of war in violation of every humanitarian concept and tradition; we failed to protest the murder by the Soviet of the flower of the Polish nation, and, even after victory had been achieved, we continued to supply the Soviet with quantities of war material, despite the clear and inescapable warnings of the Soviet threat to future peace.

In the East we gave over to Soviet control the industrial resources of Manchuria, the area of North Korea, and the sword pointed at the heart of the Japanese home islands. We condemned our faithful wartime ally, the Chinese people, to the subjugation of Communist tyranny. And, in the course of these moves we proceeded with precipitate haste to divest ourselves of our own military strength. Despite the threat to our security then clearly apparent, our executive flaunted and ignored the judgment and will of the Congress which appropriated funds for the expansion of our air arm which he arbitrarily refused to expend for such purpose.

Then, suddenly, with our military strength standing at possibly the lowest relativity in history —our divisions in Japan reduced from three to two regiments, our regiments from three to two battalions, our battalions from three to two companies —without protection withdrawn from South Korea as a militarily indefensible peninsula, we there and then plunged our forces into war to defend it.

We defeated the North Korean armies; but, when the Communist armies of China struck, our leaders lacked the courage to fight to a military decision, even though victory was then readily within our grasp—a victory which would not only have discharged our commitment to the Korean people but which in the long run might well have saved continental Asia from Red domination. And, after discarding victory as the military objective and thereby condemning our forces to a stalemated struggle of attrition and the Korean nation and people to progressive obliteration, we again yielded to Communist intrigue and entered into protracted armistice negotiations even though every lesson of experience had clearly shown such negotiations to be but the means whereby such an enemy gains time to reinforce his military capabilities.

We have yielded to selfish pressures both at home and abroad and, in so doing, have unduly directed the distribution of our wealth into privileged channels, have taken sides in international disputes which were fundamentally none of our affair, and have endeavored to impose our will on other nations' purely domestic problems in an imperialistic manner. We have ignored traditional friends while showering our favors on others, and we have lost that sense of judicial fairness which formerly characterized our relations abroad.

In our preoccupation with Europe, we have tended to discard from our concern, those great people of Asia and the Middle East who historically have sought not our wealth, but our friendship and understanding. Our "good neighbor" policy with respect to the people of Central and South America—of greater strategic concern than all others—has been largely subordinated. Through the paternalistic attitude which has dominated our material asistance abroad, we have promoted as much weakness as strength, as much resentment as friendship.

PRESERVATION OF OUR REPUBLIC

It is not of any external threat that we chiefly concern ourselves but rather of insidious forces working from within which have already so drastically altered the character of our free institutions—those institutions which formerly we hailed as beyond question or challenge.

Foremost of these forces is the scourge of Communism—but they have many allies, who, blind to reality, ardently support the Communist aims while denying violently that they do so. They have infiltrated into positions of public trust and responsibility—into journalism, the press, the radio and the schools. They seek to pervert the truth, impair respect for moral values, suppress human freedom and representative government.

They first make traitors among those of high degree and through them seek to destroy nations and bend peoples to its malevolent will. Their plan is to abolish private property and free enterprise in order to secure that degree of power over material things necessary to render absolute their power to suppress the spiritual things.

This evil force, with neither spiritual base nor moral standard, rallies the abnormal and subnormal elements among our citizenry and applies internal pressure against all things we hold decent and all things that we hold right—the type of pressure which has caused many Christian Nations abroad to fall.

Our need for patriotic fervor and religious devotion was never more impelling. There can be no compromise with atheistic Communism. Any complacent tolerance of this destructive force of evil should be replaced by an implacable and uncompromising determination to resist its every threat to basic and traditional ideals.

As a counter-balance to those forces is the deep spiritual urge in the hearts of our people—a spiritual urge capable of arousing and directing a decisive and impelling public opinion. This, indeed, is the greatest safeguard and resource of America. It is an infallible reminder that our greatest hope and faith rests upon two mighty symbols—the Cross and the Flag; the one based upon those immutable teachings which provide the spiritual strength to persevere along the course which is just and right—the other based upon the invincible will that human freedom shall not perish from the earth.

We must unite in the high purpose that the liberties etched upon the design of our lives be unimpaired and that we maintain the moral courage and spiritual leadership to preserve inviolate that mighty bulwark of all freedom, our Christian faith.

CONCLUSION

We stand today at a critical moment of history —at a vital crossroad. In one direction is the path of courageous patriots seeking in humility but the opportunity to serve their country; the other that of those selfishly seeking to entrench autocratic power. The one group stands for implacable resistance against Communism; the other for compromising with Communism. The one stands for our traditional system of government and freedom; the other for a Socialist State and slavery. The one boldly speaks the truth; the other spreads propaganda, fear and deception. The one denounces excessive taxation, bureaucratic government and corruption; the other seeks more taxes, more bureaucratic power and shields corruption.

Our leaders must throw off the complacent belief that the only threat to our survival is from without. All freedoms lost since war's end have been the result of internal pressures rather than external assault.

To free ourselves from the greatest internal menace, we must end invisible government based upon propaganda and restore truly representative government based upon truth.

Despite failures in leadership, they have it in their power to rise to that stature which befits their lofty heritage of spiritual and material strength; to reject the Socialist policies covertly and by devious means being forced upon us; to stamp out Communist influence which has played so ill-famed a part in the past misdirection of our public administration; to reorganize our government under a leadership invincibly obedient to our Constitutional mandates. To re-enforce existing safeguards to our economy of free-enterprises; to reassert full protection for freedom of speech and expression and those other freedoms now threatened; to regain State and community autonomy; to renounce undue alien interference in the shaping of American public policy; and to re-establish our governmental process upon a foundation of faith in our American institutions, American traditions, and the time-tested adequacy of American vision.

Many pessimistic voices are being raised today throughout the land. But the times are full of hope, if the vision and courage and faith of the early pioneer continue to animate the American people in the discharge of their sovereign responsibilities.

The people have it in their hands to restore morality, wisdom and vision to the direction of our foreign and domestic affairs and regain the religious base which in times past assured general integrity in public and private life.

Not for a moment do we doubt the decision or that it will guide the nation to a new and fuller greatness.

In this unusual assignment we feel a deep consciousness of the nature and gravity of the crusade upon which we now embark—a crusade to which all sound and patriotic Americans, irrespective of party, may well dedicate their hearts and minds and fullest effort. Only thus can our beloved country restore its spiritual and temporal strength and regain once again the universal respect.

Democratic Party Platform of 1952

PREAMBLE

Our nation has entered into an age in which Divine Providence has permitted the genius of man to unlock the secret of the atom.

No system of government can survive the challenge of an atomic era unless its administration is committed to the stewardship of a trustee imbued with a democratic faith, a buoyant hope for the future, the charity of brotherhood, and the vision to translate these ideals into the realities of human government. The Government of the United States, administered by the Democratic Party, is today so entrusted.

The free choice of the Democratic Party by the people of America as the instrument to achieve that purpose will mean world peace with honor, national security based on collective pacts with other free nations, and a high level of human dignity. National survival demands that these goals be attained, and the endowments of the Democratic Party alone can assure their attainment.

For twenty years, under the dedicated guidance of Franklin Delano Roosevelt and Harry S. Truman, our country has moved steadily along the road which has led the United States of America to world leadership in the cause of freedom.

We will not retreat one inch along that road. Rather, it is our prayerful hope that the people, whom we have so faithfully served, will renew the mandate to continue our service and that Almighty God may grant us the wisdom to succeed.

TWENTY YEARS OF PROGRESS

Achieving Prosperity

An objective appraisal of the past record clearly demonstrates that the Democratic Party has been the chosen American instrument to achieve prosperity, build a stronger democracy, erect the structure of world peace, and continue on the path of progress.

Democratic Party policies and programs rescued American business from total collapse—from the fatal economic consequences of watered stock, unsound banks, useless and greedy holding companies, high tariff barriers, and predatory business practices, all of which prevailed under the last Republican administrations. Democratic policies have enabled the Federal Government to help all business, small and large, to achieve the highest rate of productivity, the widest domestic and world markets, and the largest profits in the history of the Nation.

The simple fact is that today there are more than four million operating business enterprises in this country, over one million more than existed in 1932. Corporate losses in that fateful year were over three billion dollars; in 1951, corporate profits, after taxes, reached the staggering total of eighteen billion.

Democratic policies and programs rescued American agriculture from the economic consequences of blight, drought, flood and storm, from oppressive and indiscriminate foreclosures, and from the ruinous conditions brought about by the bungling incompetence and neglect of the preceding twelve years of Republican maladministration. Economic stability, soil conservation, rural electrification, farm dwelling improvement, increased production and efficiency and more than sevenfold increase in cash income have been the return to farmers for their faith in the Democratic Party.

Democratic labor policies have rescued the wage earners in this country from mass unemployment and from sweatshop slavery at starvation wages. Under our Democratic administrations, decent hours, decent wages, and decent working conditions have become the rule rather than the exception.

Self organizations of labor unions and collective bargaining, both of which are the keystone to labor management, peace and prosperity, must be encouraged, for the good of all.

Unemployment is now less than 3 per cent of the labor force, compared with almost 25 per cent in 1932. Trade union membership has reached a total of 16 million, which is more than five times the total of 1932.

The welfare of all economic and social groups in our society has been promoted by the sound, progressive and humane policies of the Democratic Party.

Strengthening Democracy

We are convinced that lasting prosperity must be founded upon a healthy democratic society respectful of the rights of all people.

Under Democratic Party leadership more has been done in the past twenty years to enhance the sanctity of individual rights than ever before in our history. Racial and religious minorities have progressed further toward real equality than during the preceding 150 years.

Governmental services, Democratically administered, have been improved and extended. The efficiency, economy, and integration of Federal operations have been advocated and effectuated through sound programs and policies. Through cooperative programs of Federal aid, State and local governments have been encouraged and enabled to provide many more services.

The Democratic Party has been alert to the corroding and demoralizing effects of dishonesty and disloyalty in the public service. It has exposed and punished those who would corrupt the integrity of the public service, and it has always championed honesty and morality in government. The loyalty program of President Truman has served effectively to prevent infiltration by subversive elements and to protect honest and loyal public servants against unfounded and malicious attacks.

We commend the relentless and fearless actions of Congressional Committees which, under vigorous Democratic leadership, have exposed dereliction in public service, and we pledge our support to a continuance of such actions as conditions require them.

The administration of our government by the Democratic Party has been based upon principles of justice and equity, and upon the American tradition of fair play. Men who are elected to high political office are entrusted with high responsibilities. Slander, defamation of character, deception and dishonesty are as truly transgressions of God's commandments, when resorted to by men in public life, as they are for all other men.

Building Peace with Honor

The Democratic Party has worked constantly for peace—lasting peace, peace with honor, freedom, justice and security for all nations.

The return of the Democratic Party to power in 1933 marked the end of a tragic era of isolationism fostered by Republican Administrations which had deliberately and callously rejected the golden opportunity created by Woodrow Wilson for collective action to secure the peace.

This folly contributed to the second World War. Victory in that war has presented the nations of the world a new opportunity which the Democratic Party is determined shall not be lost.

We have helped establish the instrumentalities through which the hope of mankind for universal world peace can be realized. Under Democratic leadership, our Nation has moved promptly and effectively to meet and repel the menace to world peace by Soviet imperialism.

Progress in the New Era

The Democratic Party believes that past progress is but a prelude to the human aspirations which may be realized in the future.

Under Democratic Party leadership, America has accepted each new challenge of history and has found practical solutions to meet and overcome them. This we have done without departing from the principles of our basic philosophy, that is, the destiny of man to achieve his earthly ends in the spirit of brotherhood.

A great Democrat—Franklin Delano Roosevelt—devised the programs of the New Deal to meet the pressing problems of the 1930s. Another great Democrat—Harry S. Truman—devised the programs of the Fair Deal to meet the complex problems of America in the 1940s. The Democratic Party is ready to face and solve the challenging problems of the 1950s. We dedicate ourselves to the magnificent work of these great Presidents and to mould and adapt their democratic principles to the new problems of the years ahead.

In this spirit we adopt and pledge ourselves to this, the Democratic platform for 1952:

Our Goal Is Peace with Honor

Peace with honor is the greatest of all our goals.

We pledge our unremitting efforts to avert another world war. We are determined that the people shall be spared that frightful agony.

We are convinced that peace and security can be safeguarded if America does not deviate from the practical and successful policies developed under Democratic leadership since the close of World War II. We will resolutely move ahead with the constructive task of promoting peace.

The Democratic Program for Peace and National Security

Supporting the United Nations

Under Democratic leadership, this country sponsored and helped create the United Nations and became a charter member and staunchly supports its aims.

We will continue our efforts to strengthen the United Nations, improve its institutions as experience requires, and foster its growth and development.

The Communist aggressor has been hurled back from South Korea. Thus, Korea has proved, once and for all, that the United Nations will resist aggression. We urge continued effort, by every honorable means, to bring about a fair and effective peace settlement in Korea in accordance with the principles of the United Nations' charter.

Strong National Defense

Our Nation has strengthened its national defenses against the menace of Soviet aggression.

The Democratic Party will continue to stand unequivocally for the strong, balanced defense forces for this country—land, sea and air. We will continue to support the expansion and maintenance of the military and civil defense forces required for our national security. We reject the defeatist view of those who say we cannot afford the expense and effort necessary to defend ourselves. We express our full confidence in the Joint Chiefs of Staff. We voice complete faith in the ability and valor of our armed forces, and pride in their accomplishments.

Collective Strength for the Free World

We reject the ridiculous notions of those who would have the United States face the aggressors alone. That would be the most expensive—and the most dangerous—method of seeking security. This nation needs strong allies, around the world, making their maximum contribution to the common defense. They add their strength to ours in the defense of freedom.

The Truman Doctrine in 1947, the organization of hemisphere defense at Rio de Janeiro that same year, the Marshall Plan in 1948, the North Atlantic Treaty in 1949, the Point IV program, the resistance to Communist aggression in Korea, the Pacific Security pacts in 1951, and the Mutual Security programs now under way—all stand as landmarks of America's progress in mobilizing the strength of the free world to keep the peace.

Encouraging European Unity

We encourage the economic and political unity of free Europe and the increasing solidarity of the nations of the North Atlantic Community.

We hail the Schuman Plan to pool the basic resources of industrial Western Europe, and the European Defense Community. We are proud of America's part in carrying these great projects forward, and we pledge our continuing support until they are established.

Support for Free Germany

We welcome the German Federal Republic into the company of free nations. We are determined that Germany shall remain free and continue as a good neighbor in the European community. We sympathize with the German people's wish for unity and will continue to do everything we can by peaceful means to overcome the Kremlin's obstruction of that rightful aim.

Support for the Victims of Soviet Imperialism

We will not abandon the once-free peoples of Central and Eastern Europe who suffer now under the Kremlin's tyranny in violation of the Soviet Union's most solemn pledges at Tehran, Yalta, and Potsdam. The United States should join other nations in formally declaring genocide to be an international crime in time of peace as well as war. This crime was exposed once more by the shocking revelations of Soviet guilt as disclosed in the report filed in Congress by the special committee investigating the Katyn Forest massacre. We look forward to the day when the liberties of Poland and the other oppressed Soviet satellites, including Czechoslovakia, Hungary, Rumania, Bulgaria, Albania, Lithuania, Estonia and Latvia and other nations in Asia under Soviet domination, will be restored to them and they can again take their rightful place in the community of free nations. We will carry forward and expand the vital and effective program of the "Voice of America" for penetration of the "Iron Curtain," bringing truth and hope to all the people subjugated by the Soviet Empire.

Support for the Nations of the Middle East

We seek to enlist the people of the Middle East to work with us and with each other in the de-velopment of the region, the lifting of health and living standards, and the attainment of peace. We favor the development of integrated security arrangements for the Middle East and other assistance to help safeguard the independence of the countries in the area.

We pledge continued assistance to Israel so that she may fulfill her humanitarian mission of providing shelter and sanctuary for her homeless Jewish refugees while strengthening her economic development.

We will continue to support the tripartite declaration of May 1950, to encourage Israel and the Arab States to settle their differences by direct negotiation, to maintain and protect the sanctity of the Holy Places and to permit free access to them.

We pledge aid to the Arab States to enable them to develop their economic resources and raise the living standards of their people. We support measures for the relief and reintegration of the Palestine refugees, and we pledge continued assistance to the reintegration program voted by the General Assembly of the United Nations in January 1952.

South Asia: A Testing Ground for Democracy

In the subcontinent of South Asia, we pledge continuing support for the great new countries of India and Pakistan in their efforts to create a better life for their people and build strong democratic governments to stand as bastions of liberty in Asia, secure against the threat of Communist subversion.

Collective Security in the Pacific

We welcome free Japan as a friendly neighbor and an ally in seeking security and progress for the whole Pacific area. America's security pacts with Japan and with the Philippines, Australia, and New Zealand are indispensable steps toward comprehensive mutual security arrangements in that area. Our military and economic assistance to the Nationalist Government of China on Formosa has strengthened that vital outpost of the free world, and will be continued.

Strengthening the Americas

In the Western Hemisphere, we pledge ourselves to continue the policy of the good neighbor. We will strive constantly to strengthen the bonds of friendship and cooperation with our Latin

American allies who are joined with us in the defense of the Americas.

Disarmament Remains the Goal

The free world is rearming to secure the peace. Under Democratic leadership, America always stands prepared to join in a workable system for foolproof inspection and limitation of all armaments, including atomic weapons. This Nation has taken the leadership in proposing concrete, practical plans for such a system. We are determined to carry on the effort for real, effective disarmament.

We look forward to the day when a great share of the resources now devoted to the armaments program can be diverted into the channels of peaceful production to speed the progress of America and of the underdeveloped regions of the world.

Helping Other People to Help Themselves

Even though we cannot now disarm, we will go forward as rapidly as possible in developing the imaginative and farsighted concept of President Truman embodied in the Point IV program.

We will continue to encourage use of American skills and capital in helping the people of underdeveloped lands to combat disease, raise living standards, improve land tenure and develop industry and trade. The continuance of ever stronger and more vigorous Point IV programs—sponsored both by this country and by the United Nations—is an indispensable element in creating a peaceful world.

Upholding the Principle of Self-Determination

In an era when the "satellite state" symbolizes both the tyranny of the aggressor nations and the extinction of liberty in small nations, the Democratic Party reasserts and reaffirms the Wilsonian principle of the right of national self-determination. It is part of the policy of the Democratic Party, therefore, to encourage and assist small nations and all peoples in the peaceful and orderly achievement of their legitimate aspirations toward political, geographical and ethnic integrity so that they may dwell in the family of sovereign nations with freedom and dignity.

Expanding World Trade

The Democratic Party has always stood for expanding trade among free nations. We reassert that stand today. We vigorously oppose any restrictive policies which would weaken the highly successful reciprocal trade program fathered by Cordell Hull.

Since 1934, the United States has taken the lead in fostering the expansion and liberalization of world trade.

Our own economy requires expanded export markets for our manufactured and agricultural products and a greater supply of essential imported raw materials. At the same time, our friends throughout the world will have opportunity to earn their own way to higher living standards with lessened dependence on our aid.

Progressive Immigration Policies

Solution of the problem of refugees from communism and over-population has become a permanent part of the foreign policy program of the Democratic Party. We pledge continued cooperation with other free nations to solve it.

We pledge continued aid to refugees from communism and the enactment of President Truman's proposals for legislation in this field. In this way we can give hope and courage to the victims of Soviet brutality and can carry on the humanitarian tradition of the Displaced Persons Act.

Subversive elements must be screened out and prevented from entering our land, but the gates must be left open for practical numbers of desirable persons from abroad whose immigration to this country provides an invigorating infusion into the stream of American life, as well as a significant contribution to the solution of the world refugee and over-population problems.

We pledge continuing revision of our immigration and naturalization laws to do away with any unjust and unfair practices against national groups which have contributed some of our best citizens. We will eliminate distinctions between nativeborn and naturalized citizens. We want no "second-class" citizens in free America.

OUR DOMESTIC POLICY

Economic Opportunity and Growth

The United States is today a land of boundless opportunity. Never before has it offered such a large measure of prosperity, security and hope for all its people.

Horizons of even greater abundance and opportunity lie before us under a Democratic Administration responsive to the will of the people.

The Democratic Administration has had a guiding principle since taking office 20 years ago: that the prosperity and growth of this Nation are indivisible. Every step we have taken to help the farmers has also helped the workers and business. Every improvement in the status of the worker has helped both farmers and business. Every expansion of business has provided more jobs for workers and greater demand for farm products.

A STABILIZED ECONOMY

Combatting Inflation

The Democratic Administration early recognized that defense production would limit the amount of goods in civilian markets, and subject our economy to heavy inflationary pressure. To prevent this from resulting in ruinous inflation, the Administration proposed pay-as-we-go taxation to keep the national debt as low as possible and to prevent excess money pressure on scarce goods and services.

Direct controls were also proposed to channel scarce materials into highly essential defense production, and to keep prices down.

In 1951 and 1952 Republican Congressmen demonstrated their attitude toward these necessary measures when they sponsored amendments which would have destroyed all controls.

Prices

We shall strive to redress the injury done to the American people—especially to white collar workers and fixed-income families—by the weakening amendments which the Republicans in Congress have forced into our anti-inflation laws.

We pledge continuance of workable controls so long as the emergency requires them. We pledge fair and impartial enforcement of controls and their removal as quickly as economic conditions allow.

Rents

We strongly urge continued federal rent control in critical defense areas and in the many other localities still suffering from a substantial shortage of adequate housing at reasonable prices.

Full Employment

The Democratic Administration prudently passed the Employment Act of 1946 declaring it to be national policy never again to permit large-scale unemployment to stalk the land. We will assure the transition from defense production to peace-time production without the ravages of unemployment. We pledge ourselves at all times to the maintenance of maximum employment, production, and purchasing power in the American economy.

Integrity in Government Finances

We solemnly pledge the preservation of the financial strength of the Government. We have demonstrated our ability to maintain and enhance the nation's financial strength. In the six full fiscal years since V-J Day, our fiscal policy has produced a $4 billion budget surplus. We have reduced the public debt $17 billion from the postwar peak.

We have demonstrated our ability to make fiscal policy contribute in a positive way to economic growth and the maintenance of high-level employment. The policies which have been followed have given us the greatest prosperity in our history. Sustained economic expansion has provided the funds necessary to finance our defense and has still left our people with record high consumer incomes and business with a record volume of investment. Employment and personal incomes are at record levels. Never have Americans enjoyed a higher standard of living and saved more for contingencies and old age.

Federal Taxes

We believe in fair and equitable taxation. We oppose a Federal general sales tax. We adhere to the principle of ability to pay. We have enacted an emergency excess profits tax to prevent profiteering from the defense program and have vigorously attacked special tax privileges.

Tax Reductions

In the future, as in the past, we will hold firm to policies consistent with sound financing and continuing economic progress. As rapidly as defense requirements permit, we favor reducing taxes, especially for people with lower incomes. But we will not imperil our Nation's security by making reckless promises to reduce taxes. We deplore irresponsible assertions that national security can be achieved without paying for it.

Closing Tax Loopholes

Justice requires the elimination of tax loopholes

which favor special groups. We pledge continued efforts to the elimination of remaining loopholes.

Government Expenditures

We believe in keeping government expenditures to the lowest practicable level. The great bulk of our national budget consists of obligations incurred for defense purposes. We pledge ourselves to a vigilant review of our expenditures in order to reduce them as much as possible.

THE AMERICAN FARMER AND AGRICULTURE

We know that national prosperity depends upon a vigorous, productive and expanding agriculture.

We take great pride in our Party's record of performance and in the impressive gains made by American agriculture in the last two decades. Under programs of Democratic Administrations the net agricultural income has increased from less than two billion dollars to almost fifteen billion dollars. These programs must be continued and improved.

Resource Conservation

The soil resources of our country have been conserved and strengthened through the Soil Conservation Service, the Agricultural Conservation Program, the Forestry and the Research programs, with their incentives to increased production through sound conservation farming. These programs have revolutionized American agriculture and must be continued and expanded. We will accelerate programs of upstream flood prevention, watershed protection, and soil, forest and water conservation in all parts of the country. These conservation measures are a national necessity; they are invaluable to our farmers, and add greatly to the welfare of all Americans and of generations yet unborn.

Grass Roots Administration

We will continue the widest possible farmer participation through referenda, farmer-elected committees, local soil conservation districts, and self-governing agencies in the conduct and administration of these truly democratic programs, initiated and developed under Democratic adminstrations.

Price Supports

Under the present farm program, our farmers have performed magnificently and have achieved unprecedented production. We applaud the recent Congressional action in setting aside the "sliding scale" for price support through 1954, and we will continue to protect the producers of basic agricultural commodities under the terms of a mandatory price support program at not less than ninety percent of parity. We continue to advocate practical methods for extending price supports to other storables and to the producers of perishable commodities, which account for three-fourths of all farm income.

Abundant Production

We will continue to assist farmers in providing abundant and stable supplies of agricultural commodities for the consumers at reasonable prices, and in assuring the farmer the opportunity to earn a fair return commensurate with that enjoyed by other segments of the American economy.

The agricultural adjustment programs encourage the production of abundant supplies while enabling producers to keep supply in line with consumer demand, preventing wide fluctuations and bringing stability to the agricultural income of the Nation. We pledge retention of such programs.

We pledge continued efforts to provide adequate storage facilities for grain and other farm products with sufficient capacity for needed reserves for defense, and other emergency requirements, in order to protect the integrity of the farm price support programs.

Research

We are justly proud of the outstanding achievements of our agricultural research. We favor a greatly expanded research and education program for American agriculture in order that both production and distribution may more effectively serve consumers and producers alike, and thus meet the needs of the modern world. We favor especial emphasis on the development of new crops and varieties, on crop and livestock disease and pest control, and on agricultural statistics and marketing services.

Marketing

We must find profitable markets for the products of our farms, and we should produce all that these markets will absorb. To this end we will continue our efforts to reduce trade barriers, both at home and abroad, to provide better marketing and inspection facilities, and to find new uses and outlets for our foods and fibers both in domestic and foreign markets.

Farm Credit

We have provided credit facilities for all agriculture, including means by which young men, veterans of military service, and farm tenants have been encouraged to become farmers and farm home-owners, and through which low-income farmers have been assisted in establishing self-sustaining and fully productive farm units. We will not waver in our efforts to provide such incentives.

Crop Insurance

Crop insurance to protect farmers against loss from destruction of their crops by natural causes has been created and developed under Democratic Administrations into a sound business operation. This program should be expanded as rapidly as experience justifies, in order that its benefits may be made available to every farmer.

Rural Electrification

Democratic Administrations have established the great Rural Electrification Program, which has brought light and power to the rural homes of our Nation. In 1935, only 10% of the farm homes of America had the benefits of electricity. Today 85% of our rural homes enjoy the benefits of electric light and power. We will continue to fight to make electricity available to all rural homes, with adequate facilities for the generation and transmission of power. Through the Rural Telephone Program, inaugurated by the Democratic 81st Congress, we will provide the opportunity for every farm home to have this modern essential service. We pledge support of these self-liquidating farm programs.

Cooperatives

We will continue to support the sound development and growth of bona fide farm cooperatives and to protect them from punitive taxation.

Defense Needs

We will continue to recognize agriculture as an essential defense industry, and to assist in providing all the necessary tools, machinery, fertilizer, and manpower needed by farmers in meeting production goals.

Family Farming

The family farm is the keystone of American agriculture. We will strive unceasingly to make the farm homes of our country healthier and happier places in which to live. We must see that our youth continues to find attractive opportunity in the field of agriculture.

The Republican Party platform is loud in its criticism of our great farm programs. We challenge Republicans and other enemies of farm progress to justify their opposition to the program now in operation, to oppose the improvements here proposed, or to advocate repeal of a single vital part of our program.

A FAIR DEAL FOR WORKERS

Good Incomes

There can be no national prosperity unless our working men and women continue to prosper and enjoy rising living standards. The rising productivity of American workers is a key to our unparalleled industrial progress. Good incomes for our workers are the secret of our great and growing consumer markets.

Labor-Management Relations

Good labor-management relations are essential to good incomes for wage earners and rising output from our factories. We believe that to the widest possible extent consistent with the public interest, management and labor should determine wage rates and conditions of employment through free collective bargaining.

Taft-Hartley Act

We strongly advocate the repeal of the Taft-Hartley Act.

The Taft-Hartley Act has been proved to be inadequate, unworkable, and unfair. It interferes in an arbitrary manner with collective bargaining, tipping the scales in favor of management against labor.

The Taft-Hartley Act has revived the injunction as a weapon against labor in industrial relations. The Act has arbitrarily forbidden traditional hiring practices which are desired by both management and labor in many industries. The Act has forced workers to act as strikebreakers against their fellow unionists. The Act has served to interfere with one of the most fundamental rights of American workers—the right to organize in unions of their own choosing.

We deplore the fact that the Taft-Hartley Act provides an inadequate and unfair means of meeting with national emergency situations. We advocate legislation that will enable the President to deal fairly and effectively with cases where a breakdown in collective bargaining seriously threatens the national safety or welfare.

In keeping with the progress of the times, and based on past experiences, a new legislative approach toward the entire labor management problem should be explored.

Fair Labor Standards

We pledge to continue our efforts so that government programs designed to establish improved fair labor standards shall prove a means of assuring minimum wages, hours and protection to workers, consistent with present-day progress.

Equal Pay for Equal Work

We believe in equal pay for equal work, regardless of sex, and we urge legislation to make that principle effective.

The Physically-Handicapped

We promise to further the program to afford employment opportunities both in government and in private industry for physically handicapped persons.

Migratory Workers

We advocate prompt improvement of employment conditions of migratory workers and increased protection of their safety and health.

Strengthening Free Enterprise

The free enterprise system has flourished and prospered in America during these last twenty years as never before. This has been made possible by the purchasing power of all our people and we are determined that the broad base of our prosperity shall be maintained.

Small and Independent Business

Small and independent business is the backbone of American free enterprise. Upon its health depends the growth of the economic system whose competitive spirit has built this Nation's industrial strength and provided its workers and consumers with an incomparably high standard of living.

Independent business is the best offset to monopoly practices. The Government's role is to insure that independent business receives equally fair treatment with its competitors.

Congress has established the permanent Small Business Committee of the Senate and the Special Small Business Committee of the House, which have continued to render great service to this important segment of our economy. We favor continuance of both these committees with all the powers to investigate and report conditions, correct discriminations, and propose needed legislation.

We pledge ourselves to increased efforts to assure that small business be given equal opportunity to participate in Government contracts, and that a suitable proportion of the dollar volume of defense contracts be channeled into independent small business. The Small Defense Plants Administration, which our Party caused to be established, should retain its independent status and be made a continuing agency, equipped with sufficient lending powers to assist qualified small business in securing defense contracts.

We urge the enactment of such laws as will provide favorable incentives to the establishment and survival of independent businesses, especially in the provision of tax incentives and access to equity or risk capital.

Enforcement of Anti-Trust Laws

Free competitive enterprise must remain free and competitive if the productive forces of this Nation are to remain strong. We are alarmed over the increasing concentration of economic power in the hands of a few.

We reaffirm our belief in the necessity of vigorous enforcement of the laws against trusts, combinations, and restraints of trade, which laws are vital to the safeguarding of the public interest and of small competitive business men against predatory monopolies. We will seek adequate appropriations for the Department of Justice and the Federal Trade Commission for vigorous investigation and for enforcement of the anti-trust laws. We support the right of all persons to work together in cooperatives and other democratic associations for the purpose of carrying out any proper business operations free from any arbitrary and discriminatory restrictions.

Protection of Investors and Consumers

We must avoid unnecessary business controls. But we cannot close our eyes to the special problems which require Government surveillance. The Government must continue its efforts to stop unfair selling practices which deceive investors, and unfair trade practices which deceive consumers.

Transportation

In the furtherance of national defense and commerce, we pledge continued Government support, on a sound financial basis, for further development of the Nation's transportation systems, land, sea and air. We endorse a policy of fostering the safest and most reliable air transportation system of the world. We favor fair, nondiscriminatory freight rates to encourage economic growth in all parts of the country.

Highways

In cooperation with State and local governmental units, we will continue to plan, coordinate, finance, and encourage the expansion of our road and highway network, including access roads, for the dual purposes of national defense and efficient motor transportation. We support expansion of farm-to-market roads.

Rivers and Harbors

We pledge continued development of our harbors and waterways.

Merchant Marine

We will continue to encourage and support an adequate Merchant Marine.

Our Natural Resources

The United States has been blessed with the richest natural resources of any nation on earth.

Yet, unless we redouble our conservation efforts we will become a "have-not" nation in some of the most important raw materials upon which depend our industries, agriculture, employment and high standard of living. This can be prevented by a well rounded and nation-wide conservation effort.

Land and Water Resources

We favor sound, progressive development of the Nation's land and water resources for flood control, navigation, irrigation, power, drainage, soil conservation and creation of new, small family-sized farms, with immediate action in critical areas.

We favor the acceleration of all such projects, including construction of transmission facilities to load centers for wider and more equitable distribution of electric energy at the lowest cost to the consumer with continuing preference to public agencies and REA Cooperatives.

The Democratic Party denounces all obstructionist devices designed to prevent or retard utilization of the Nation's power and water resources for the benefit of the people, their enterprises and interests.

The wise policy of the Democratic Party in encouraging multipurpose projects throughout the country is responsible for America's productive superiority over any nation in the world and is one of the greatest single factors leading toward the accomplishment of world peace. Without these projects our atomic weapons program could never have been achieved, and without additional such projects it cannot be expanded.

The Democratic Party is dedicated to a continuation of the natural resources development policy inaugurated and carried out under the administrations of Presidents Roosevelt and Truman, and to the extension of that policy to all parts of the Nation—North, South, East, Midwest, West and the territories to the end that the Nation and its people receive maximum benefits from these resources to which they have an inherent right.

The Democratic Party further pledges itself to protect these resources from destructive monopoly and exploitation.

River Basin Development

We pledge the continued full and unified regional development of the water, mineral and other natural resources of the nation, recognizing that the progress already achieved under the initiative of the Democratic Party in the arid and semi-arid States of the West, as well as in the Tennessee Valley, is only an indication of still greater results which can be accomplished.

Fertilizer Development

Great farming areas, particularly of the Midwest and West, are in acute need of low-cost commercial fertilizers. To meet this demand, we favor the opening of the Nation's phosphate rock deposits in the West, through prompt provision of sufficient low-cost hydro-electric power to develop this great resource.

Forests and Public Lands

We seek to establish and demonstrate such successful policies of forest and land management on Federal property as will materially assist State and private owners in their conservation efforts. Conservation of forest and range lands is vital to the strength and welfare of the Nation. Our forest and range lands must be protected and used wisely in order to produce a continuing supply of basic raw materials for industry; to reduce damaging floods; and to preserve the sources of priceless water. With adequate appropriations to carry out feasible projects, we pledge a program of forest protection, reforestation projects and sound practices of production and harvesting which will promote sustained yields of forest crops.

We propose to increase forest access roads in order to improve cutting practices on both public and private lands.

On the public land ranges we pledge continuance of effective conservation and use programs, including the extension of water pond construction and restoration of forage cover.

Arid Areas

In many areas of the Nation assistance is needed to provide water for irrigation, domestic and industrial purposes. We pledge that in working out programs for rational distribution of water from Federal sources we will aid in delivering this essential of life cheaply and abundantly.

Minerals and Fuels

The Nation's minerals and fuels are essential to the national defense and development of our country. We pledge the adoption of policies which will further encourage the exploration and development of additional reserves of our mineral resources. We subscribe to the principles of the Stockpiling Act and will lend our efforts to strengthening and expanding its provisions and those of the Defense Production Act to meet our military and civilian needs. Additional access roads should be constructed with Government aid. Our synthetic fuels, including monetary metals, research program should go forward. Laws to aid and assist these objectives will be advocated.

Domestic Fisheries

We favor increased research and exploration for conserving and better utilizing fishery resources; expanded research and education to promote new fishery products and uses and new markets; promotion of world trade in fish products; a public works and water policy providing adequate protection for domestic fishery resources; and treaties with other nations for conservation and better utilization of international fisheries.

Wildlife Recreations

In our highly complex civilization, outdoor recreation has become essential to the health and happiness of our people.

The Democratic Party has devoted its efforts to the preservation, restoration and increase of the bird, animal and fish life which abound in this Nation. State, local and private agencies have cooperated in this worthy endeavor. We have extended and vastly improved the parks, forests, beaches, streams, preserves and wilderness areas across the land.

To the 28,000,000 of our citizens who annually purchase fishing and hunting licenses, we pledge continued efforts to improve all recreational areas.

Atomic Energy

In the field of atomic energy, we pledge ourselves:

(1) to maintain vigorous and non-partisan civilian administrations, with adequate security safeguards;

(2) to promote the development of nuclear energy for peaceful purposes in the interests of America and mankind;

(3) to build all the atomic and hydrogen firepower needed to defend our country, deter aggression, and promote world peace;

(4) To exert every effort to bring about bona

fide international control and inspection of all atomic weapons.

SOCIAL SECURITY

Our national system of social security, conceived and developed by the Democratic Party, needs to be extended and improved.

Old Age and Survivors Insurance

We favor further strengthening of old age and survivors insurance, through such improvements as increasing benefits, extending them to more people and lowering the retirement age for women.

We favor the complete elimination of the work clause for the reason that those contributing to the Social Security program should be permitted to draw benefits, upon reaching the age of eligibility, and still continue to work.

Unemployment Insurance

We favor a stronger system of unemployment insurance, with broader coverage and substantially increased benefits, including an allowance for dependents.

Public Assistance

We favor further improvements in public assistance programs for the blind, the disabled, the aged and children in order to help our less fortunate citizens meet the needs of daily living.

Private Plans

We favor and encourage the private endeavors of social agencies, mutual associations, insurance companies, industry-labor groups, and cooperative societies to provide against the basic hazards of life through mutually agreed upon benefit plans designed to complement our present social security program.

Needs of Our Aging Citizens

Our older citizens constitute an immense reservoir of skilled, mature judgment and ripened experience. We pledge ourselves to give full recognition to the right of our older citizens to lead a proud, productive and independent life throughout their years.

In addition to the fundamental improvements in Old Age and Survivors Insurance, which are outlined above, we pledge ourselves, in coopera-tion with the States and private industry, to encourage the employment of older workers. We commend the 82nd Congress for eliminating the age restriction on employment in the Federal Government.

Health

We will continue to work for better health for every American, especially our children. We pledge continued and wholehearted support for the campaign that modern medicine is waging against mental illness, cancer, heart disease and other diseases.

Research

We favor continued and vigorous support, from private and public sources, of research into the causes, prevention and cure of disease.

Medical Education

We advocate Federal aid for medical education to help overcome the growing shortages of doctors, nurses, and other trained health personnel.

Hospitals and Health Centers

We pledge continued support for Federal aid to hospital construction. We pledge increased Federal aid to promote public health through preventive programs and health services, especially in rural areas.

Cost of Medical Care

We also advocate a resolute attack on the heavy financial hazard of serious illness. We recognize that the costs of modern medical care have grown to be prohibitive for many millions of people. We commend President Truman for establishing the non-partisan Commission on the Health Needs of the Nation to seek an acceptable solution of this urgent problem.

Housing

We pledge ourselves to the fulfillment of the programs of private housing, public low-rent housing, slum clearance, urban redevelopment, farm housing and housing research as authorized by the Housing Act of 1949.

We deplore the efforts of special interests groups, which themselves have prospered through Government guarantees of housing mortgages, to destroy those programs adopted to assist families of low-income.

Additional Legislation

We pledge ourselves to enact additional legislation to promote housing required for defense workers, middle income families, aged persons and migratory farm laborers.

Veterans' Housing

We pledge ourselves to provide special housing aids to veterans and their families.

EDUCATION

Every American child, irrespective of color, national origin, economic status or place of residence should have every educational opportunity to develop his potentialities.

Local, State and Federal governments have shared responsibility to contribute appropriately to the pressing needs of our educational system. We urge that Federal contributions be made available to State and local units which adhere to basic minimum standards.

The Federal Government should not dictate nor control educational policy.

We pledge immediate consideration for those school systems which need further legislation to provide Federal aid for new school construction, teachers' salaries and school maintenance and repair.

We urge the adoption by appropriate legislative action of the proposals advocated by the President's Commission on Higher Education, including Federal scholarships.

We will continue to encourage the further development of vocational training which helps people acquire skills and technical knowledge so essential to production techniques.

Child Welfare

The future of America depends on adequate provision by Government for the needs of those of our children who cannot be cared for by their parents or private social agencies.

Maternity, Child Health and Welfare Services

The established national policy of aiding States and localities, through the Children's Bureau and other agencies, to insure needed maternity, child health and welfare services should be maintained and extended. Especially important are the detection and treatment of physical defects and diseases which, if untreated, are reflected in adult life in draft rejections and as handicapped workers. The Nation, as a whole, should provide maternity and health care for the wives, babies and pre-school children of those who serve in our armed forces.

School Lunches

We will enlarge the school lunch program which has done so much for millions of American school children and charitable institutions while at the same time benefiting producers.

Day Care Facilities

Since several million mothers must now be away from their children during the day, because they are engaged in defense work, facilities for adequate day care of these children should be provided and adequately financed.

Children of Migratory Workers

The Nation, as a whole, has a responsibility to support health, educational, and welfare services for the children of agricultural migratory workers who are now almost entirely without such services while their parents are engaged in producing essential crops.

Veterans

The Democratic Party is determined to advance the welfare of all the men and women who have seen service in the armed forces. We pledge ourselves to continue and improve our national program of benefits for veterans and their families, to provide the best possible medical care and hospitalization for the disabled veteran, and to help provide every veteran an opportunity to be a productive and responsible citizen with an assured place in the civilian community.

STRENGTHENING DEMOCRATIC GOVERNMENT

Streamlining the Federal Government

The public welfare demands that our government be efficiently and economically operated and that it be reorganized to meet changing needs. During the present Democratic Administration, more reorganization has been accomplished than by all its predecessors. We pledge our support to continuing reorganization wherever improvements can be made. Only constant effort by the Executive, the Congress, and the public will enable our Government to render the splendid service to which our citizens are entitled.

Improving the Postal Service

We pledge a continuing increase in the services of the United States Postal Service. Through efficient handling of mail, improved working conditions for postal employees, and more frequent services, the Democratic Party promises its efforts to provide the greatest communication system in the world for the American people.

Strengthening the Civil Service

Good government requires a Civil Service high in quality and prestige. We deplore and condemn smear attacks upon the character and reputations of our Federal workers. We will continue our fight against partisan political efforts to discredit the Federal service and undermine American principles of justice and fair play.

Under President Truman's leadership, the Federal Civil Service has been extended to include a greater proportion of positions than ever before. He has promoted a record number of career appointees to top level policy positions. We will continue to be guided by these enlightened policies, and we will continue our efforts to provide Federal service with adequate pay, sound retirement provisions, good working conditions, and an opportunity for advancement.

We will use every proper means to eliminate pressure by private interests seeking undeserved favors from the Government. We advocate the strongest penalties against those who try to exert improper influence, and against any who may yield to it.

Democracy in Federal Elections

We advocate new legislation to provide effective regulation and full disclosure of campaign expenditures in elections to Federal office, including political advertising from any source.

We recommend that Congress provide for a non-partisan study of possible improvements in the methods of nominating and electing Presidents and in the laws relating to Presidential succession. Special attention should be given to the problem of assuring the widest possible public participation in Presidential nominations.

Strengthening Basic Freedoms

We will continue to press strongly for worldwide freedom in the gathering and dissemination of news and for support to the work of the United Nations Commission on Human Rights in furthering this and other freedoms.

Equal Rights Amendment

We recommend and endorse for submission to the Congress a constitutional amendment providing equal rights for women.

Puerto Rico

Under Democratic Party leadership, a new status has been developed for Puerto Rico. This new status is based on mutual consent and common devotion to the United States, formalized in a new Puerto Rican Constitution. We welcome the dignity of the new Puerto Rican Commonwealth and pledge our support of the Commonwealth, its continued development and growth.

Alaska and Hawaii

By virtue of their strategic geographical locations, Alaska and Hawaii are vital bastions in the Pacific. These two territories have contributed greatly to the welfare and economic development of our country and have become integrated into our economic and social life. We, therefore, urge immediate statehood for these two territories.

Other Territories and Possessions

We favor increased self-government for the Virgin Islands and other outlying territories and the trust territory of the Pacific.

District of Columbia

We favor immediate home rule and ultimate national representation for the District of Columbia.

American Indians

We shall continue to use the powers of the Federal Government to advance the health, education and economic well-being of our American Indian citizens, without impairing their cultural traditions. We pledge our support to the cause of fair and equitable treatment in all matters essential to and desirable for their individual and tribal welfare.

The American Indian should be completely integrated into the social, economic and political life of the nation. To that end we shall move to secure the prompt final settlement of Indian claims and to remove restrictions on the rights of Indians individually and through their tribal councils to handle their own fiscal affairs.

We favor the repeal of all acts or regulations that deny to Indians rights or privileges held by citizens generally.

Constitutional Government

The Democratic Party has demonstrated its belief in the Constitution as a charter of individual freedom and an effective instrument for human progress. Democratic Administrations have placed upon the statute books during the last twenty years a multitude of measures which testify to our belief in the Jeffersonian principle of local control, even in general legislation involving nation-wide programs. Selective service, Social Security, Agricultural Adjustment, Low Rent Housing, Hospital, and many other legislative programs have placed major responsibilities in States and counties and provide fine examples of how benefits can be extended through Federal-State cooperation.

In the present world crisis with new requirements of Federal action for national security, and accompanying provision for public services and individual rights related to defense, constitutional principles must and will be closely followed. Our record and our clear commitments, in this platform, measure our strong faith in the ability of constitutional government to meet the needs of our times.

Improving Congressional Procedures

In order that the will of the American people may be expressed upon all legislative proposals, we urge that action be taken at the beginning of the 83rd Congress to improve Congressional procedures so that majority rule prevails and decisions can be made after reasonable debate without being blocked by a minority in either House.

Civil Rights

The Democratic Party is committed to support and advance the individual rights and liberties of all Americans.

Our country is founded on the proposition that all men are created equal. This means that all citizens are equal before the law and should enjoy equal political rights. They should have equal opportunities for education, for economic advancement, and for decent living conditions.

We will continue our efforts to eradicate discrimination based on race, religion or national origin.

We know this task requires action, not just in one section of the Nation, but in all sections. It requires the cooperative efforts of individual citizens and action by State and local governments. It also requires Federal action. The Federal Government must live up to the ideals of the Declaration of Independence and must exercise the powers vested in it by the Constitution.

We are proud of the progress that has been made in securing equality of treatment and opportunity in the Nation's armed forces and the civil service and all areas under Federal jurisdiction. The Department of Justice has taken an important part in successfully arguing in the courts for the elimination of many illegal discriminations, including those involving rights to own and use real property, to engage in gainful occupations and to enroll in publicly supported higher educational institutions. We are determined that the Federal Government shall continue such policies.

At the same time, we favor Federal legislation effectively to secure these rights to everyone: (1) the right to equal opportunity for employment; (2) the right to security of persons; (3) the right to full and equal participation in the Nation's political life, free from arbitrary restraints. We also favor legislation to perfect existing Federal civil rights statutes and to strengthen the administrative machinery for the protection of civil rights.

Conclusion

Under the guidance, protection, and help of Almighty God we shall succeed in bringing to the people of this Nation a better and more rewarding life and to the peoples of the entire world, new hope and a lasting, honorable peace.

Progressive Party Platform

Preamble

Cease Fire in Korea at Once—No Ifs,
Ands or Buts

The American people want peace.

In recognition of this universal desire, each

political party will claim to be the peace party in 1952.

There is one touchstone by which every voter can test the sincerity of these claims: Does the party have a program for ending the fighting in Korea? Has it any proposal to stop a useless and senseless war which has already cost over 110,000 American casualties and untold suffering to the Korean people, and under cover of which the people are being robbed of their freedom and their substance?

Judged by this acid test, the professions of peace made by the Democratic and Republican candidates are a fraud and a pretense. They may differ on how the war in Korea should be fought and vie with each other in reckless acts and proposals that threaten to spread it beyond Korea's borders, engulfing the world. But neither old party and none of its candidates—be they generals, bankers or politicians—has any realistic plan for ending it.

Only the Progressive Party opposed the Korean War from its outset. Only the Progressive Party has a program for its immediate termination.

The Progressive Party is the only genuine party of peace.

For more than two years before the fighting started in Korea the Progressive Party warned that the Truman-Dulles cold war would inevitably lead to a shooting war. It has consistently opposed each cold war step taken by the two old parties: Truman Doctrine, Marshall Plan, North Atlantic Pact, the huge arms program at home, the arming of Western Germany and Japan, alliances with Franco and Chiang Kai-shek, the support of reaction, renascent fascism and dying colonialism in Europe, Asia, Africa and Latin America.

Even if the fighting were to end in Korea tomorrow, there are other Koreas in the making, in areas of international tension, particularly in a divided Germany. These must be averted before they result in the catastrophe of total war. Civilized negotiations among the powers can avert them.

We recognize the integral link between the bi-partisan war drive and the racist violence which seeks to suppress by napalm bombs and other atrocities the mighty upsurge of the peoples of Korea, South Africa, Indo-China, Malaya, the Philippines, India and Japan in the assertion of their inherent right to determine their own destinies.

The Progressive Party has steadfastly demanded a return to the Roosevelt-Willkie policy of One World that proved itself in the victory over fascism and held out the promise of an enduring peace.

That glorious promise can still be redeemed by the American people. The Progressive Party enters the 1952 election campaign dedicated to its redemption.

DEFEND THE RIGHTS OF LABOR; PROTECT THE LIVING STANDARDS OF THE AMERICAN PEOPLE

The Democratic and Republican parties offer no end to the war in Korea because that war, and the billions spent in preparation for an even bigger war, have been profitable business for the giant corporations which these parties serve, netting them 150 billion dollars in profits and tax-free new plants in the past four years.

These fabulous profits have been extracted from the people.

Expenditures for war are taxing away one-third of the average worker's income and have cut the purchasing power of the farmer by one-third. The cost of living stands at the highest point in our history. Yet, in the name of a so-called national emergency, the right of the trade unions to secure just wage increases is being wrecked. Even as they scuttle price controls and clamp a tighter freeze on wages, the bi-partisans are legislating out of existence the right to bargain and to strike.

The promise of prosperity through a war economy is fading before the harsh reality of growing layoffs and unemployment in the automobile and other industries geared for war as well as in textiles and consumer industries. At the same time, a rigid cold-war embargo shuts off the limitless peace-time markets of China, the Soviet Union and Eastern Europe to the products of American workers and farmers.

The need for housing, schools and playgrounds, the protection of the people's health, for harnessing our river valleys and conserving our soil resources, for assuring our senior citizens a decent income on retirement, for providing our young people with education and peace-time jobs, are all sacrificed in the race for bigger and deadlier weapons. This year the bi-partisans propose to spend 65 billion dollars for arms while less than one-tenth of that amount has been appropriated for the people's welfare.

FULL AND EQUAL RIGHTS FOR THE NEGRO PEOPLE—NOW

The war program of the bi-partisans has been accompanied by the intensification of racist acts and practices against the Negro people, the Mexican-American people, the Puerto Rican people and the Jewish people.

In Korea, American bombs are wiping out the villages and snuffing out the lives of a colored people. Here at home, the terror-weapon of the bomb is turned upon the Negro people in an attempt to stem the rising militancy of their struggle for full equality and freedom. But bombs, violence and terror will not halt the Negro people in their march to full liberation. Nor will they be put off by the pious repetition of platform promises by the two old parties which have shamelessly betrayed their pledges of anti-lynch and anti-poll tax legislation and an F.E.P.C. The magnificent struggle of the Negro people for equality and full representation at every level of government is making a vital contribution to the fight for the peace and freedom of all Americans.

RESTORE THE BILL OF RIGHTS FOR ALL AMERICANS

Under the pretense of the so-called national emergency, American democratic liberties are being destroyed. Free speech and assembly, the right to counsel, to bail, to a fair hearing—the Bill of Rights itself are nullified by Taft-Hartley, Smith and McCarran Acts, McCarthyism and McCarranism, with the support of both old parties, and the participation of every arm of government, executive, legislative and judicial. The example of the Federal government has been followed by a rash of similar legislation in almost every state.

Workers, teachers, authors, actors, government employees, small business men and professional people, are hounded, harassed, denied passports, driven from their jobs, terrorized and blacklisted for daring to express political criticism. Men and women are victimized and jailed on the unsupported testimony of stool-pigeons and paid informers or on the charges of nameless accusers brought by the FBI.

Foreign born non-citizens are deported or jailed indefinitely. Naturalized Americans are having their citizenship revoked for their political opinions.

This nullification of constitutional freedom was at first ostensibly directed against the Communists alone. Now, inevitably, all Americans—and organized labor foremost—are the victims. The so-called "emergency" used to justify the conviction of Communists under the Smith Act is invoked to destroy labor's basic right to bargain collectively through the use of injunctions, governmental seizures and the wage freeze. Not content with these measures, the bi-partisans are now pushing further legislation in Congress, sponsored by the author of the Smith Act itself, which would completely outlaw the right to strike.

The events of the past four years have fully confirmed our platform statement in 1948 that defense of the constitutional rights of Communists and all other political groups to express their views is the first line in the defense of the liberties of a democratic people.

THE BIGGEST GRAFT OF ALL: THE WAR-RACKET

The only liberty guaranteed by both old parties is the liberty to pilfer the public purse. The tax graft, the police graft, the mink coat scandals have revolted all honest Americans. But these are penny-ante games compared to the big racket—the war racket. Billions are made in the deals arrived at in the Pentagon and in the very halls of Congress. Tideland oil, natural gas, pipelines, extravagant ship subsidies, control over railroad ratemaking, control of the air waves, rapid tax write-offs, tax loopholes—these mean billions to the profit-mad backers of the two old parties.

It is clear that in 1952, neither Democrats nor Republicans can offer the people anything but more war in Korea, more spending for war, and the consequences of war spending: a tighter belt on the living standards and liberties of our people. Neither party offers any alternative. Both disclaim responsibility for this grim outlook. They blame Soviet aggression. Yet, the generals and politicians have themselves punctured the carefully nurtured myth of aggressive Soviet intentions by stating in unguarded moments that they don't believe the USSR will start a war now or at any time. As the Chicago Tribune—no friend of Communism—observed, if Soviet Russia did not exist, it would be necessary for the war spenders to invent her.

THE KEY TO PEACE: AMERICAN-SOVIET UNDERSTANDING AND CO-OPERATION

American-Soviet understanding and cooperation still remain the key to peace. Despite the differences in political and economic viewpoints between the United States and the Soviet Union, whatever mistakes each may have made, whatever the shortcomings of each great country may be, they can and must work together on the basis of mutual self-interest and the dictates of survival, for world peace, far-reaching disarmament and normal international trade.

The Progressive Party asserts that the real threat to American security comes, not from without, but from within: from the policies of the bipartisans themselves. Those policies have not protected our national security but undermined it. They have debased the living standards and are destroying the freedoms of the American people, on which our national security rests.

The tremendous armaments program that the Truman Administration has forced upon Western Europe, together with its disruption of East-West trade, have steadily lowered living standards in England, France and Italy; and are bringing those countries to the brink of economic disaster. America's get-tough policy is also tough on the hard-pressed peoples of Western Europe. It is tough, too, on the people of Turkey and Greece who suffer under a fascist government and a decaying monarchy, supported by American dollars.

The devastation our weapons have wrought in Korea and the repression of the colonial liberation movements in Asia and Africa have earned us the enmity of the colored peoples. The rearming of Germany and Japan is not only a gross violation of our war-time agreements, but is alienating the freedom-loving people of the world who fought beside us to extirpate the scourge of fascism.

The reservoir of good will for America, filled to overflowing under Franklin Roosevelt, has run dry. We stand today without firm friends or stable allies anywhere.

THE AMERICAN PEOPLE ARE FIGHTING BACK

The American people have not remained silent. They are voicing a powerful mandate for a cease-fire in Korea at once; labor is standing up in aroused strength against the wage-freeze, injunctions, and anti-union shackles. A militant Negro people is splendidly asserting its right to full citizenship and all mankind. Such an America—and only such an America—can be a secure America.

To restore such an America, we offer the following platform:

In offering it, we reaffirm our belief in the validity of the democratic process. "Freedom is the right to choose." We dedicate ourselves to the preservation and extension of that basic right. So long as that right is secured to the American people, we are confident that the program for which we stand can be obtained through the exercise of the processes guaranteed by the Constitution, and we will vigorously oppose any group that would subvert the democratic process and seek its objectives by any other means.

Our platform and our candidates give to every voter, whatever his political affiliation, the opportunity to use his precious ballot as part of a people's referendum for peace, security and freedom.

I. PEACE: THE MANDATE OF THE PEOPLE

The Progressive Party was founded in the belief that the way to peace is through negotiation of differences among nations.

The events of the past four years now cry out clearly and urgently that this is the only alternative to world destruction.

The Progressive Party rejects the idea that war is inevitable.

We reaffirm that peaceful co-existence of the Soviet Union and the United States is both possible and essential, without the sacrifice of a single interest of the American people, based upon peaceful competition between the two systems in the service of humanity.

We reject the idea of the stockpiling of A-bombs and H-bombs and the militarization of our country is needed to defend America. We reaffirm that the best defense of America is peaceful understanding and peaceful relations with all the nations of the world.

The conference table for peace must replace the battlefields of war.

Toward these ends, the Progressive Party submits the following program:

1. Agree to a cease-fire in Korea today, without any ifs, ands or buts. Propose an immediate

armistice at the agreed upon demarcation line; all disputed questions, including the exchange of war prisoners, to be settled by civilian representatives of all nations involved in the war after the fighting stops.

2. Stop the rearmament and renazification of a disunited Germany. We must work out an agreement at the conference table with England, France and the Soviet Union to make Germany a united and disarmed neutral. We also oppose the rearming of Japan and call for a conference of all the former belligerents against Japan for the renegotiation of a peace treaty.

3. Negotiate an international agreement outlawing the use of the A-bomb, and the H-bomb, with effective control and inspection of atomic stockpiles and installations. Ratify the Geneva Protocol outlawing the use of germ warfare. Take action in the UN for progressive universal disarmament, starting with an immediate and substantial reduction in the arms of all nations.

4. Contribute to a United Nations fund of $50 billion for working with the peoples of the underprivileged areas of the world in the development by them of their own resources and the improvement of their own living standards, without any political or economic interference.

5. Provide full representation in the United Nations by admitting all present applicant nations, including the People's Republic of China. Recognize the People's Republic of China; and withdraw recognition from fascist Spain.

6. Defeat any bill for Universal Military Training. Repeal the Draft Law.

7. Abolish the trade barriers to peaceful trade between America and the Soviet Union, China and Eastern Europe.

8. Support the demands for independence and freedom of colonial peoples all over the world. Stop support for fascist and racist regimes such as the Malan government in South Africa and all other imperialisms which hold African and Asian peoples in colonial bondage. Support democratic movements in Latin America and reverse the present policy of support to South American dictatorships. Repeal all laws imposing restrictions on the economic and political independence of the Philippines.

9. Grant the Puerto Rican people the right to full and immediate independence, and extend them economic assistance.

10. Extend full statehood to the territories of Alaska and Hawaii.

11. Proceed to hold a conference of the five great powers, as the only peaceful means for securing an over-all settlement of differences.

II. JOBS AND SECURITY FOR AMERICA

A prompt return to a peacetime economy is the only real guarantee of economic security for the American people. The old parties offer war and a war economy as the only way to have prosperity and stave off a depression.

The fact is that production for war has meant soaring prices, crushing taxes, frozen wages, mounting unemployment and sharply reduced living standards.

Production for peace would mean millions of lasting new jobs, decent wages, lower prices, lower taxes, improved social security and higher living standards.

In the midst of a so-called war boom, 5½ million Americans are on relief, some 40 million Americans try to make ends meet on incomes of less than $2,000.00 a year and one out of every four American children live in want and bitter poverty. The overwhelming majority of our people are unable to meet the costs of sickness and a third of the illnesses of the low-income groups goes without medical care. We lack almost 1,000,000 hospital beds. More than one-half the nation's families live in rural or urban slums which blight our country. Not a city or county in our country has sufficient teachers, schools, facilities or books. Not only do we waste and endanger our basic resources, the health and welfare of our people, but we waste and endanger our natural resources as well. We suffer periodic disasters and floods which are entirely within our power to prevent.

The richest nation in the world, we have the resources to assure all Americans against want, to build all the houses, schools, hospitals we need. A fraction of what we waste on insane war preparations could provide an adequate social welfare program.

Only through the planned development of all our resources will the full benefit of the Nation's wealth and productivity be secured for all of the people. Farmer and laborer, housewife and shopkeeper, all remember and urgently seek the Economic Bill of Rights first put forth by Franklin Delano Roosevelt.

The Progressive Party urges the following program to make that Economic Bill of Rights a reality today:

1. Strict Federal dollar and cents price ceilings and restoration of Federal Rent Control at pre-Korea levels.

2. End of wage-freeze. Return to free collective bargaining.

3. Repeal the Taft-Hartley Act and re-enact the Wagner Act. Defeat the Smith Anti-labor bill.

4. Launch a national housing program to provide 2.5 million low-rent homes a year, with public subsidies to make low rents possible. Wipe out the slums and provide all Americans with decent homes, without descrimination or segregation.

5. Tax exemption for families of four whose income is below $4000 and individuals whose income is below $2000. Allow tax deductions to working mothers for the cost of child care. Raise corporation taxes. Defeat the proposed Federal sales tax. Repeal the excise tax on necessities. Provide tax relief for small business.

6. A comprehensive Federal system of old-age, unemployment and disability compensation, guaranteeing to every American, without discrimination, benefits equal to a minimum decent standard of living. For the aged, not less than $150 monthly; for the unemployed or disabled, not less than $40 weekly, with additional dependency allowances. Extend the Social Security Act to all workers and all who are self-employed, including the farmer.

7. Provide family allowance of $3 weekly per child. Virtually every industrial nation, except ours, pays a weekly or monthly grant to the parent of every child, to assure a basic minimum standard of living for children.

8. A system of national health insurance, guaranteeing to all Americans as a matter of right, and not as charity, and without discrimination, adequate dental and medical care, together with a hospital and health center construction program and an expanded program of medical education and research. Provide dependency benefits to working mothers equal to the unemployment compensation. We are now the only industrial Nation in the world without a system of health insurance.

9. Enact a comprehensive farm program, providing that the prices to be paid farmers will be agreed upon and set well in advance of the production season. So long as necessary, the market place returns to farmers should be supplemented by production payments at national expense—and with no nonsense about basic and non-basic farm commodities and with all working farmers receiving equal and equitable treatment. The total return to farmers for their products should be such as to enable them to adopt and enjoy living standards on a parity with the rest of the population and, in addition, to finance soil conservation practices and the restoration of soil fertility. Participation should be voluntary, conditioned upon performance, and limited to family type farmers with corporate and large scale operations excluded as a matter of public policy. Only through such a program can the long standing inequities between agriculture on the one hand and industry and commerce on the other be corrected, scarcity abolished, abundance assured, and the agricultural threat to our national survival removed. To that end, we call for the following:

(1) 100 per cent parity prices for all farm commodities on the basis of a revised and modernized parity formula. We condemn the shameful betrayal of the Brannan Plan by the Truman Administration, which lifted this program from the Progressive Party's program of 1948, and reaffirm our support for these principles, without dilution or demagogy.

(2) Halt the draft of our farm youth.

(3) Use production payments to encourage food production and reduce farm-to-market price spreads. Provide government credit at low rates to working farmers and enact a farm debt moratorium law.

(4) Provide federal development and conservatism of soil, water and power resources on an integrated basin-wide scale, including the St. Lawrence seaway, to provide publicly owned low-cost power and irrigation water and protect against the ravages of flood and drought. Develop and conserve harbors and fisheries.

(5) Reduce taxes on working farmers and eliminate federal income taxes on farm cooperatives.

(6) Recognize the elementary right of agricultural workers and sharecroppers to organize and bargain collectively and end sharecropper peonage in the South. Enact a tenant purchase program. Provide full coverage of agricultural workers under Workmen's Compensation, Unemployment Insurance, and Social Security legislation. Establish minimum federal standards for

the protection of agricultural workers, including all who come from Mexico, Puerto Rico, and the British West Indies.

10. Appropriate ten billion dollars for a 10 year program of federally financed school construction; immediate appropriation of one billion dollars for federal aid for public schools to raise teachers' salaries, employ additional needed teachers and provide essential materials and services for the children. Eliminate segregation and all forms of discrimination in education.

11. Increase to $1.25 the minimum hourly wage under the Fair Labor Standards Act, with overtime pay for work in excess of 30 hours in any work week.

12. Empower the Federal Bureau of Mines to fine or close down mines not conforming to Government standards of safety.

13. Provide and guarantee equal job opportunities and job training for Negroes, Mexican-Americans, Puerto Ricans and other minority groups.

14. Establish a system of nation-wide job training centers for youth; full social security protection for youth. Federal scholarships and cost-of-living grants, free from discrimination by reason of race, color, creed or national origin, to insure full educational opportunities. Grant the right to vote to 18 year olds.

15. We demand for all women all of the economic rights of first class citizens. We urge legislation forbidding discrimination against women, guaranteeing them equal pay and job security and removing all social and economic restrictions upon women, without jeopardizing existing protective legislation.

16. Enact a GI Bill of Rights for all veterans since World War II, providing all the benefits granted to World War II veterans. Increase all veterans' benefits in amounts which reflect the increased cost of living. Extend all veterans' benefits to merchant seamen with war service.

17. Establish a Federally subsidized arts and theatre program.

III. END AMERICA'S SHAME; GUARANTEE FULL CIVIL RIGHTS FOR THE NEGRO PEOPLE AND OTHER MINORITIES; END SEGREGATION

The deliberate official policy of government on all levels which denies full equality of rights to sixteen million Negro Americans is responsible for the evils of segregation, discrimination, police brutality, terror, lynching and second-class citizenship.

That policy has shortened the average life span of the Negro people in America to eight years less than the life span of whites. It sanctions violence and murder against Negroes solely because they are Negroes—and this violence is being wrought on so mounting a scale that it approaches what is defined as "genocide" under the United Nations Convention against genocide.

An aroused and determined Negro people properly insist on their protection, on their full status as American citizens, and on full representation in the political life of the nation.

In vigorous and uncompromising support of these aims and steps toward stamping out every form of discrimination against the Negro people, the Mexican-American people, the Puerto Rican people, the Jewish people and other minority groups, the Progressive Party calls for:

1. A Federal Fair Employment Practices Law with effective enforcement powers to guarantee equality in job opportunities and training for the Negro people, Puerto Ricans, Mexican-Americans and all other minorities.

2. A Federal anti-poll tax law together with Federal legislation to guarantee to the Negro people, Puerto Ricans, Mexican-Americans and other minorities the right to register and to vote in primary and general elections for Federal office. Revise Senate cloture rules to make filibusters impossible.

3. A Federal anti-lynch law to direct the full power of the Federal government against lynchers.

4. The immediate issuance of an Executive Order by the President to prohibit discrimination in employment, under any contract entered into by the Federal government or any of its agencies.

5. The immediate issuance of an Executive Order by the President for effective prosecution under the Federal civil rights statutes of the violation of the civil rights of Negro citizens and other minorities.

6. End segregation and discrimination in housing; replace Jim Crow ghettos with low-rent, unsegregated housing.

7. The immediate issuance of an Executive Order to end segregation and discrimination in the armed forces, in all Federal departments and agencies, and in the Panama Canal Zone.

8. Real Home Rule for the District of Colum-

bia and Congressional legislation to prohibit every form of segregation and discrimination in the nation's capital.

9. Full representation of the Negro and Puerto Rican and Mexican-American people in Congress, in State legislatures and all levels of public office, elective and appointive.

10. Provide that all Federal laws appropriating Federal monies for any public purpose contain a specific provision prohibiting the use of any such funds in a manner which discriminates against the Negro people, Puerto Ricans, Mexican-Americans or any other minorities.

11. Full citizenship for the American Indians and the right to administer their own affairs without loss of Reservation rights. Adequate compensation for loss of tribal land rights.

IV. RESTORE FREEDOM TO ALL AMERICANS

The right freely to petition, to speak, to think, to write, to travel, to assemble peacefully, to vote for candidates of one's own choice,—these are the bedrocks of American democracy. We support these freedoms of all individuals and groups in our American community, for those with whom we disagree as well as those with whom we agree. Only a nation which guarantees and implements these freedoms can find the path of social progress and develop science, art and other fields of creative endeavor in the peaceful service of the people.

The Progressive Party calls for a great national crusade to restore the full meaning of the Bill of Rights to all Americans.

1. Repeal the Smith, McCarran, and the new McCarran-Walter Acts. No concentration camps in America.

2. End all prosecution under the Smith Act, stop the proceedings under the McCarran Act, grant unconditional pardons and restore full civil rights to all persons convicted under the Smith Act.

3. Stop the persecution, deportation and imprisonment of native or foreign-born Americans because of their trade union of political activities or opinions.

4. Guarantee the freedom of advocacy for lawyers and the right of accused to counsel of their own choice. Free the lawyers who have courageously defended advocates of minority opinion and causes.

5. Abolish the House Committee on un-American Activities, and the McCarran Committees of the Senate on Internal Security. Establish fair and equitable procedures for all legislative investigating committees.

6. End the "loyalty" and "screening" programs and the Attorney-General's subversive list which affect millions of government workers, teachers, members of the arts and professions, and millions more in private industry. Repeal the Magnusson Act providing for the screening of maritime workers. Restore all those fired under these procedures to their jobs.

7. Maintain the traditional American principle of separation of church and state and protect the freedom of public education.

8. Provide compulsory public hearings on major legislation; end government by secret star chamber proceedings; insure public knowledge of the public business. End government by secrecy and censorship.

9. Ratify the UN Convention on Genocide and the UN Convention on Human Rights.

10. Stop attempts to impose thought control on teachers and pupils and the use of the public schools to promote war hysteria.

Prohibition Party—1952 Platform

PREAMBLE

We, the representatives of the Prohibition Party, assembled in national convention at Indianapolis, Indiana, November 13, 14, and 15, 1951, recognizing Almighty God as the source of all just government and with faith in the teachings of the Prince of Peace, do solemnly promise that, if our party is chosen to administer the affairs of this nation, we will use all the powers of our administration to serve the people of the United States.

We reaffirm our loyalty to the Constitution of the United States. We have supreme confidence in this form of Government to meet all changing national and world conditions.

CONSTITUTIONAL GOVERNMENT

We are strongly opposed to atheistic communism and every other form of totalitarianism. We deplore their infiltration throughout the nation. We challenge all loyal citizens to work against this menace to civilization. We are convinced that the best safeguard against these dangerous doctrines is to protect the rights of our citizens by enforcing the provisions of the Constitution and the Bill of Rights.

GOVERNMENTAL ECONOMY

Extravagant spending has set an example of wasteful governmental operation. We believe it is unjust for any government to take nearly one-third of the total income of its citizens to pay the expense of government. We believe that government ought not to do for the people what they can do for themselves. We promise to reorganize the federal government, abolishing all departments and bureaus that cannot qualify when measured by this principle.

TAXES

The constant increase in taxation is approaching the point of confiscation and economic bankruptcy. With proper economy, governmental costs will be lowered, making it possible to reduce the public debt and lighten the tax load for the average citizen.

WORLD PEACE AND ORDER

We believe in World Peace.

Having united with other nations to restore world order and preserve world peace, our nation should lead in subordinating selfish interests for the common good.

The leadership to be entrusted with this task should be men whose dependence for wisdom and guidance is upon Almighty God.

RELIGIOUS LIBERTY

We believe in religious liberty.

By religious liberty we mean the freedom of individual worship and fellowship and the right to evangelize, and educate, and establish religious institutions. When religious liberty is lost political liberty perishes with it.

UNIVERSAL MILITARY TRAINING

Believing that compulsory military training in peacetime in our country would not represent a safeguard for world peace, would be contrary in principle to our American way of life, would place an unnecessary burden upon our peacetime economy, would lead only to military dictatorship, and would, under existing conditions, lead to the moral and spiritual deterioration of our youth, we declare our opposition to any program of peacetime compulsory military training.

PUBLIC MORALITY AND LAW ENFORCEMENT

Moral and spiritual considerations should be primary factors in determining national policies. We will strengthen and enforce laws against gambling, narcotics, and commercialized vice, now so openly violated and nullified by the inaction of the parties in power, and thus prevent further disintigration of the public morals.

We oppose the present nullification of law by non-enforcement and will maintain the integrity of democracy by enforcing the Constitution and the laws enacted under it.

HONESTY IN GOVERNMENT

There is a law of cause and effect which rules in the affairs of men. With the repeal of the Eighteenth Amendment there has been a rapid decline in the moral standards of the nation, culminating in such revelations as those made by the Senate Crime Investigating Committee. We pledge ourselves to break this unholy alliance between organized crime and those in positions of trust in the government at all levels.

FREE ENTERPRISE

We deplore the current trend toward a socialistic state, with its increasing emphasis upon governmental restraint of free enterprise, regulation of our economic life, and federal interference with individual freedom. We declare ourselves in favor of freedom of opportunity, private industry financed within the structure of the present antitrust laws, and an economic program based upon sound business practice.

LABOR AND INDUSTRY

Labor organizations are entitled to great credit for improving the status of the workers and for their constructive contributions to the general welfare. It is our purpose to give the public welfare paramount consideration. Neither capital nor labor can be permitted to dominate at the expense of the other or of the common good. We favor the compulsory arbitration of labor disputes.

SOCIAL SECURITY AND OLD AGE PENSIONS

We endorse the general principle of social security, including all employed groups. We deplore, however, the widespread current abuses of its privileges and the maladministration of its provisions for political ends, and pledge ourselves to correct these evils.

Money

The Constitution provides that Congress shall have the power to "coin money" and "regulate the value thereof." This is a sound and feasible monetary policy which we promise to re-establish and enforce.

No Racial Discrimination

Recognizing that "God created of one blood all nations to dwell upon the face of the earth," we declare in favor of full justice and equal opportunity for all people, regardless of race, creed, or national origin.

Marriage and Divorce

We favor the enactment of uniform marriage and divorce laws as a help toward maintaining the sanctity of the home.

Separation of Church and State

The American principle of separation of Church and State must be maintained. We are opposed to the appropriation of public money for any sectarian purpose.

Ballot Law Reform

We demand the repeal of the many state ballot laws which have been enacted to make the two-party system a bipartisan political monopoly by keeping minor parties off the ballot, thus denying to independent voters and minority groups the fundamental right of free political expression.

Prohibition

As the result of the repeal of the Eighteenth Amendment the government now endorses an industry whose product deranges the mind of the user and whose propaganda perverts the judgment of its citizens.

We do not believe that our nation can long survive if this trend continues.

No other political issue confronting our citizens compares in magnitude with the necessity for suppressing the alcohol beverage traffic.

The present liquor conditions, which are far worse than ever before, are due in large measure to the action of the two major parties when they adopted platform planks designed to destroy the Eighteenth Amendment.

The moral forces have to contend with the liquor power which is well financed, competently organized, and is creating an ever-growing appetite for its products among youth and adults through its promotion of the sale of alcoholic beverages. This power dominates our politics and government. It controls large numbers of voters. Every saloon or tavern is a center for mobilizing and controlling votes. Both parties are subservient to the liquor power. As long as good citizens continue to give their votes to the liquor parties, as long as they continue to be yoked by party membership with the liquor interests and the underworld, they will be incapable of making moral principles prevail.

What is needed is a re-alignment of voters and the union of good citizens in a party unitedly committed to prohibition.

We summon the voters of America to help elect the Prohibition Party to power. We will then marshal the resources of the government—executive, legislative and judicial—to overthrow the liquor traffic and usher in a new day for America.

1952 Republican Platform

Preamble

We maintain that man was not born to be ruled, but that he consented to be governed; and that the reasons that moved him thereto are few and simple. He has voluntarily submitted to government because, only by the establishment of just laws, and the power to enforce those laws, can an orderly life be maintained, full and equal opportunity for all be established, and the blessings of liberty be perpetuated.

We hold that government, and those entrusted with government, should set a high example of honesty, of justice, and unselfish devotion to the public good; that they should labor to maintain tranquillity at home and peace and friendship with all the nations of the earth.

We assert that during the last twenty years, leaders of the Government of the United States under successive Democrat Administrations, and especially under this present Administration, have failed to perform these several basic duties; but, on the contrary, that they have evaded them, flouted them, and by a long succession of vicious acts, so undermined the foundations of our Republic as to threaten its existence.

We charge that they have arrogantly deprived our citizens of precious liberties by seizing powers never granted.

We charge that they work unceasingly to achieve their goal of national socialism.

We charge that they have disrupted internal tranquillity by fostering class strife for venal political purposes.

We charge that they have choked opportunity and hampered progress by unnecessary and crushing taxation.

They claim prosperity but the appearance of economic health is created by war expenditures, waste and extravagance, planned emergencies, and war crises. They have debauched our money by cutting in half the purchasing power of our dollar.

We charge that they have weakened local self-government which is the cornerstone of the freedom of men.

We charge that they have shielded traitors to the Nation in high places, and that they have created enemies abroad where we should have friends.

We charge that they have violated our liberties by turning loose upon the country a swarm of arrogant bureaucrats and their agents who meddle intolerably in the lives and occupations of our citizens.

We charge that there has been corruption in high places, and that examples of dishonesty and dishonor have shamed the moral standards of the American people.

We charge that they have plunged us into war in Korea without the consent of our citizens through their authorized representatives in the Congress, and have carried on that war without will to victory.

FOREIGN POLICY

The present Administration, in seven years, has squandered the unprecedented power and prestige which were ours at the close of World War II.

In that time, more than 500 million non-Russian people of fifteen different countries have been absorbed into the power sphere of Communist Russia, which proceeds confidently with its plan for world conquest.

We charge that the leaders of the Administration in power lost the peace so dearly earned by World War II.

The moral incentives and hopes for a better world which sustained us through World War II were betrayed, and this has given Communist Russia a military and propaganda initiative which, if unstayed, will destroy us.

They abandoned friendly nations such as Latvia, Lithuania, Estonia, Poland and Czechoslovakia to fend for themselves against the Communist aggression which soon swallowed them.

They required the National Government of China to surrender Manchuria with its strategic ports and railroads to the control of Communist Russia. They urged that Communists be taken into the Chinese Government and its military forces. And finally they denied the military aid that had been authorized by Congress and which was crucially needed if China were to be saved. Thus they substituted on our Pacific flank a murderous enemy for an ally and friend.

In all these respects they flouted our peace-assuring pledges such as the Atlantic Charter, and did so in favor of despots, who, it was well-known, consider that murder, terror, slavery, concentration camps and the ruthless and brutal denial of human rights are legitimate means to their desired ends.

Tehran, Yalta and Potsdam were the scenes of those tragic blunders with others to follow. The leaders of the Administration in power acted without the knowledge or consent of Congress or of the American people. They traded our overwhelming victory for a new enemy and for new oppressions and new wars which were quick to come.

In South Korea, they withdrew our occupation troops in the face of the aggressive, poised for action, Communist military strength on its northern border. They publicly announced that Korea was of no concern to us. Then when the Communist forces acted to take what seemed to have been invited, they committed this nation to fight back under the most unfavorable conditions. Already the tragic cost is over 110,000 American casualties.

With foresight, the Korean War would never have happened.

In going back into Korea, they evoked the patriotic and sacrificial support of the American people. But by their hampering orders they produced stalemates and ignominious bartering with our enemies, and they offer no hope of victory.

They have effectively ignored many vital areas in the face of a global threat requiring balanced handling.

The people of the other American Republics are resentful of our neglect of their legitimate aspirations and cooperative friendship.

The Middle East and much of Africa seethe with anti-American sentiment.

The peoples of the Far East who are not under Communist control find it difficult to sustain their morale as they contrast Russia's "Asia First" policy with the "Asia Last" policy of those in control of the Administration now in power.

Here at home they have exhibited corruption, incompetence, and disloyalty in public office to such an extent that the very concept of free representative government has been tarnished and has lost its idealistic appeal to those elsewhere who are confronted with the propaganda of Communism.

They profess to be following a defensive policy of "containment" of Russian Communism which has not contained it.

Those in control of the Party in power have, in reality, no foreign policy. They swing erratically from timid appeasement to reckless bluster.

The good in our foreign policies has been accomplished with Republican cooperation, such as the organization of the United Nations, the establishment of the trusteeship principle for dependent peoples, the making of peace with Japan and Germany, and the building of more solid security in Europe. But in the main the Republican Party has been ignored and its participation has not been invited.

The American people must now decide whether to continue in office the party which has presided over this disastrous reversal of our fortunes and the loss of our hopes for a peaceful world.

The Republican Party offers, in contrast to the performances of those now running our foreign affairs, policies and actions based on enlightened self-interest and animated by courage, self-respect, steadfastness, vision, purpose, competence and spiritual faith.

The supreme goal of our foreign policy will be an honorable and just peace. We dedicate ourselves to wage peace and to win it.

We shall eliminate from the State Department and from every Federal office, all, wherever they may be found, who share responsibility for the needless predicaments and perils in which we find ourselves. We shall also sever from the public payroll the hordes of loafers, incompetents and unnecessary employees who clutter the administration of our foreign affairs. The confusions, overlappings, and extravagance of our agencies abroad hold us up to the ridicule of peoples whose friendship we seek.

We shall substitute a compact and efficient organization where men of proven loyalty and ability shall have responsibility for reaching our objectives. They will reflect a dynamic initiative. Thus we can win the support and confidence which go only to those who demonstrate a capacity to define and get results.

We shall have positive peace-building objectives wherever this will serve the enlightened self-interest of our Nation and help to frustrate the enemy's designs against us.

In Western Europe we shall use our friendly influence, without meddling or imperialistic attitudes, for ending the political and economic divisions which alone prevent that vital area from being strong on its own right.

We shall encourage and aid the development of collective security forces there, as elsewhere, so as to end the Soviet power to intimidate directly or by satellites, and so that the free governments will be sturdy to resist Communist inroads.

In the balanced consideration of our problems, we shall end neglect of the Far East which Stalin has long identified as the road to victory over the West. We shall make it clear that we have no intention to sacrifice the East to gain time for the West.

The Republican Party has consistently advocated a national home for the Jewish people since a Republican Congress declared its support of that objective thirty years ago.

In providing a sanctuary for Jewish people rendered homeless by persecution, the State of Israel appeals to our deepest humanitarian instincts. We shall continue our friendly interest in this constructive and inspiring undertaking.

We shall put our influence at the service of peace between Israel and the Arab States, and we shall cooperate to bring economic and social stability to that area.

Our ties with the sister Republics of the Americas will be strengthened.

The Government of the United States, under Republican leadership, will repudiate all commitments contained in secret understandings such as those of Yalta which aid Communist enslavements. It will be made clear, on the highest authority of the President and the Congress, that United States policy, as one of its peaceful purposes, looks happily forward to the genuine independence of those captive peoples.

We shall again make liberty into a beacon light of hope that will penetrate the dark places. That program will give the Voice of America a real function. It will mark the end of the negative, futile and immoral policy of "containment" which abandons countless human beings to a despotism and godless terrorism, which in turn enables the rulers to forge the captives into a weapon for our destruction.

We shall support the United Nations and loyally help it to become what it was designed to be, a place where differences would be harmonized by honest discussion and a means for collective security under agreed concepts of justice. We shall seek real meaning and value for our regional security treaties, which implies that all parties shall contribute their loyal support and fair shares.

We shall see to it that no treaty or agreement with other countries deprives our citizens of the rights guaranteed them by the Federal Constitution.

We shall always measure our foreign commitments so that they can be borne without endangering the economic health or sound finances of the United States. Stalin said that "the moment for the decisive blow" would be when the free nations were isolated and were in a state of "practical bankruptcy." We shall not allow ourselves to be isolated and economically strangled, and we shall not let ourselves go bankrupt.

Sums available by this test, if competently used, will be more effective than vastly larger sums incompetently spent for vague and endless purposes. We shall not try to buy good will. We shall earn it by sound, constructive, self-respecting policies and actions.

We favor international exchange of students and of agricultural and industrial techniques, and programs for improvement of public health.

We favor the expansion of mutually-advanta-

geous world trade. To further this objective we shall press for the elimination of discriminatory practices against our exports, such as preferential tariffs, monetary license restrictions, and other arbitrary devices. Our reciprocal trade agreements will be entered into and maintained on a basis of true reciprocity, and to safeguard our domestic enterprises and the payrolls of our workers against unfair import competition.

The policies we espouse will revive the contagious, liberating influences which are inherent in freedom. They will inevitably set up strains and stresses within the captive world which will make the rulers impotent to continue in their monstrous ways and mark the beginning of their end.

Our nation will become again the dynamic, moral and spiritual force which was the despair of despots and the hope of the oppressed. As we resume this historic role, we ourselves will come to enjoy again the reality of peace, security and solvency, not the shabby and fleeting counterfeit which is the gift of the Administration in power.

NATIONAL DEFENSE

On the prudent assumption that Communist Russia may not accommodate our own disgracefully-lagging program for preparedness, we should develop with utmost speed a force-in-being, as distinguished from paper plans, of such power as to deter sudden attack or promptly and decisively defeat it. This defense against sudden attack requires the quickest possible development of appropriate and completely-adequate air power and the simultaneous readiness of coordinated air, land, and sea forces, with all necessary installations, bases, supplies and munitions, including atomic energy weapons in abundance.

Generally, we shall see to it that our military services are adequately supported in all ways required, including manpower, to perform their appropriate tasks in relation to the defense of this country and to meet our treaty obligations.

We shall coordinate our miltary policy with our foreign policy, always seeking universal limitation and control of armaments on a dependable basis.

We shall review our entire preparedness program and we shall strip it clean of waste, lack of coordination, inertia, and conflict between the services. We shall see that our fighting men in Korea, or wherever they may be, shall not lack the best of weapons or other supplies or services needed for their welfare.

COMMUNISM

By the Administration's appeasement of Communism at home and abroad it has permitted Communists and their fellow travelers to serve in many key agencies and to infiltrate our American life. When such infiltrations became notorious through the revelations of Republicans in Congress, the Executive Department stubbornly refused to deal with it openly and vigorously. It raised the false cry of "red herring" and took other measures to block and discredit investigations. It denied files and information to Congress. It set up boards of its own to keep information secret and to deal lightly with security risks and persons of doubtful loyalty. It only undertook prosecution of the most notorious Communists after public opinion forced action.

The result of these policies is the needless sacrifice of American lives, a crushing cost in dollars for defense, possession by Russia of the atomic bomb, the lowering of the Iron Curtain, and the present threats to world peace. Our people have been mired in fear and distrust and employees of integrity in the Government service have been cruelly maligned by the Administration's tolerance of people of doubtful loyalty.

There are no Communists in the Republican Party. We have always recognized Communism to be a world conspiracy against freedom and religion. We never compromised with Communism and we have fought to expose it and to eliminate it in government and American life.

A Republican President will appoint only persons of unquestioned loyalty. We will overhaul loyalty and security programs. In achieving these purposes a Republican President will cooperate with Congress. We pledge close coordination of our intelligence services for protecting our security. We pledge fair but vigorous enforcement of laws to safeguard our country from subversion and disloyalty. By such policies we will keep the country secure and restore the confidence of the American people in the integrity of our Government.

SMALL BUSINESS IN A FREE ECONOMY

For twenty years the Administration has praised free enterprise while actually wrecking it. Here a little, there a little, year by year, it has sought to curb, regulate, harass, restrain and punish. There is scarcely a phase of our economic and social life today in which Government does not attempt to interfere.

Such hostility deadens initiative, discourages invention and experiment, and weakens the self-reliance indispensable to the Nation's vitality. Merciless taxation, the senseless use of controls and ceaseless effort to enter business on its own account, have led the present Government to unrestrained waste and extravagance in spending, irresponsibility in decision and corruption in administration.

The anti-monopoly laws have been employed, not to preserve and foster competition, but to further the political ambitions of the men in power. Wage and price controls have been utilized, not to maintain economic stability, but to reward the friends and punish the enemies of leaders of the Party in power.

Neither small nor large business can flourish in such an atmosphere. The Republican Party will end this hostility to initiative and enterprise.

We will aid small business in every practicable way. We shall remove tax abuses and injurious price and wage controls. Efforts to plan and regulate every phase of small business activity will cease. We will maintain special committees in Congress whose chief function will be to study and review continuously the problems of small business and recommend legislation for their relief. We shall always be mindful of the importance of keeping open the channels of opportunity for young men and women.

We will follow principles of equal enforcement of the anti-monopoly and unfair-competition statutes and will simplify their administration to assist the businessman who, in good faith, seeks to remain in compliance. At the same time, we shall relentlessly protect our free enterprise system against monopolistic and unfair trade practices.

We will oppose Federal rent control except in those areas where the expansion of defense production has been accompanied by critical housing shortages. With local cooperation we shall aid slum clearance.

Our goal is a balanced budget, a reduced national debt, an economical administration and a cut in taxes. We believe in combating inflation by encouraging full production of goods and food, and not through a program of restrictions.

TAXATION AND MONETARY POLICY

Only with a sound economy can we properly carry out both the domestic and foreign policies which we advocate. The wanton extravagance and inflationary policies of the Administration in power have cut the value of the dollar in half and imposed the most confiscatory taxes in our history. These policies have made the effective control of Government expenditures impossible. If this Administration is left in power, it will further cheapen the dollar, rob the wage earner, impoverish the farmer and reduce the true value of the savings, pensions, insurance and investments of millions of our people. Further inflation must be and can be prevented. Sound tax and monetary policies are essential to this end. We advocate the following tax policies:

1. Reduction of expenditures by the elimination of waste and extravagance so that the budget will be balanced and a general tax reduction can be made.

2. An immediate study directed toward reallocation of fields of taxation between the Federal, State, and municipal governments so as to allow greater fiscal freedom to the States and municipalities, thus minimizing double taxation and enabling the various divisions of government to meet their obligations more efficiently.

3. A thorough revision and codification of the present hodge-podge of internal revenue laws.

4. Administration of the tax laws free from politics, favoritism and corruption.

We advocate the following monetary policies:

1. A Federal Reserve System exercising its functions in the money and credit system without pressure for political purposes from the Treasury or the White House.

2. To restore a domestic economy, and to use our influence for a world economy, of such stability as will permit the realization of our aim of a dollar on a fully-convertible gold basis.

AGRICULTURE

The good earth is the food storehouse for future generations. The tending of the soil is a sacred responsibility. Development of a sound farm program is a high national duty. Any program that will benefit farmers must serve the national welfare. A prosperous agriculture with free and independent farmers is fundamental to the national interest.

We charge the present Administration with seeking to destroy the farmers' freedom. We denounce the Administration's use of tax money and a multitude of Federal agencies to put agriculture under partisan political dictation and to make the farmer dependent upon government. We condemn the Brannan plan which aims to control the farmer and to socialize agriculture. We brand as unscrupulous the Administration's manipulation of grain markets during the 1948 election campaign to drive down farm prices, and its deliberate misrepresentation of laws passed by the Republican 80th Congress, which authorized a long-range farm price support program and provided for adequate grain storage.

We condemn as a fraud on both the farmer and the consumer the Brannan plan scheme to pay direct subsidies from the Federal Treasury in lieu of prices to producers.

We favor a farm program aimed at full parity prices for all farm products in the market place. Our program includes commodity loans on nonperishable products, "on-the-farm" storage, sufficient farm credit, and voluntary self-supporting crop insurance. Where government action on perishable commodities is desirable, we recommend locally-controlled marketing agreements and other voluntary methods.

Our program should include commodity loans on all non-perishable products supported at the level necessary to maintain a balanced production. We do not believe in restrictions on the American farmers' ability to produce.

We favor a bi-partisan Federal Agricultural Commission with power to review the policies and administration of our farm programs and to make recommendations.

We support a constructive and expanded soil conservation program administered through locally-controlled local districts, and which shall emphasize that payments shall be made for practices and improvements of a permanent nature.

Flood control programs should include the application of sound land use, reforestation and water-management practices on each watershed. These, so far as feasible, should be decentralized and locally-controlled to insure economy and effective soil conservation.

We recommend expanded agricultural research and education to promote new crops and uses, new markets, both foreign and domestic, more trustworthy crop and market estimates, a realistic trade program for agriculture aimed at restoring foreign markets and developing new outlets at home. Promotion of world trade must be on a basis of fair competition.

We support the principle of bona fide farmer-owned, farmer-operated co-operatives and urge the further development of rural electrification and communication, with federally-assisted production of power and facilities for distribution when these are not adequately available through private enterprise at fair rates.

We insist that an adequate supply of manpower on the farm is necessary to our national welfare and security and shall do those things required to assure this result.

The Republican Party will create conditions providing for farm prosperity and stability, safeguarding the farmers' independence and opening opportunities for young people in rural communities. We will do those things necessary to simplify and make efficient the operation of the Department of Agriculture, prevent that Department from assuming powers neither intended nor delegated by Congress, and to place the administration of farm programs as closely as possible to State and local levels.

Labor

The Republican Party believes that regular and adequate income for the employee together with uninterrupted production of goods and services, through the medium of private enterprise, are essential to a sound national economy. This can only be obtained in an era of industrial peace.

With the above in mind, we favor the retention of the Taft-Hartley Act, which guarantees:

To the Working Man:—

The right to quit his job at any time.

The right to take part in legal union activities.

The right to remain in his union so long as he pays his dues.

The right to protection against unfair practices by either employer or union officials.

The right to political activity of his own choice and freedom to contribute thereto.

The right to a job without first joining a union.

The right to a secret ballot in any election concerned with his livelihood.

The right to protection from personal financial responsibility in damage cases against his union.

To the Labor Unions:

The right to establish "union shop" contracts by agreement with management.

The right to strike.

The right to free collective bargaining.

The right to protection from rival unions during the life of union contracts.

The right to assurance from employers that they will bargain only with certified unions as a protection against unfair labor practices.

We urge the adoption of such amendments to the Taft-Hartley Act as time and experience show to be desirable, and which further protect the rights of labor, management and the public.

We condemn the President's seizure of plants and industries to force the settlement of labor disputes by claims of inherent Constitutional powers.

Natural Resources

We vigorously advocate a full and orderly program for the development and conservation of our natural resources.

We deplore the policies of the present Administration which allow special premiums to foreign producers of minerals available in the United States. We favor reasonable depletion allowances, defense procurement policies, synthetic fuels research, and public land policies, including good-faith administration of our mining laws, which will encourage exploration and development of our mineral resources consistent with our growing industrial and defense needs.

We favor stockpiling of strategic and critical raw materials and special premium incentives for their domestic exploration and development.

We favor restoration to the States of their rights to all lands and resources beneath navigable inland and offshore waters within their historic boundaries.

We favor protection of our fisheries by domestic

regulation and treaties, including safeguards against unfair foreign competition.

PUBLIC WORKS AND WATER POLICY

The Federal Government and State and local governments should continuously plan programs of economically justifiable public works.

We favor continuous and comprehensive investigations of our water resources and orderly execution of programs approved by the Congress. Authorized water projects should go forward progressively with immediate priority for those with defense significance, those in critical flood and water-shortage areas, and those substantially completed.

We favor greater local participation in the operation and control, and eventual local ownership, of federally-sponsored, reimbursable water projects.

We vigorously oppose the efforts of this national Administration, in California and elsewhere, to undermine state control over water use, to acquire paramount water rights without just compensation, and to establish all-powerful federal socialistic valley authorities.

PUBLIC LANDS

We favor restoration of the traditional Republican public land policy, which provided opportunity for ownership by citizens to promote the highest land use. We favor an impartial study of tax-free Federal lands and their uses to determine their effects on the economic and fiscal structures of our States and local communities.

In the management of public lands and forests we pledge the elimination of arbitrary bureaucratic practices. To this end we favor legislation to define the rights and privileges of grazers and other cooperators and users, to provide the protection of independent judicial review against administrative invasions of those rights and privileges, and to protect the public against corrupt or monopolistic exploitation and bureaucratic favoritism.

VETERANS

We believe that active duty in the Armed Forces of the United States of America during a state of war or national emergency constitutes a special service to our Nation, and entitles those who have so served to aid and compensation in return for this service.

Consequently we propose:

That the aid and compensation given to veterans of previous wars be extended to veterans of the Korean conflict;

That compensation be fairly and adequately adjusted to meet changes in the cost of living;

That aid be given to veterans, particularly disabled veterans, to obtain suitable employment, by providing training and education, and through strict compliance with veterans' preference laws in Federal service;

That the Veterans' Administration be maintained as a single, independent agency in full charge of all veterans' affairs, and that the Veterans' Administration manage veterans' affairs in an efficient, prompt and uniform manner;

That the Veterans' Administration should be equipped to provide and maintain medical and hospital care of the highest possible standard for all eligible veterans.

SOCIAL SECURITY

Inflation has already cut in half the purchasing power of the retirement and other benefits under the Federal Old Age and Survivors Insurance system. Sixty million persons are covered under the system and four and one-half million are now receiving benefits.

The best assurance of preserving the benefits for which the worker has paid is to stop the inflation which causes the tragic loss of purchasing power, and that we propose to do.

We favor amendment of the Old Age and Survivors Insurance system to provide coverage for those justly entitled to it but who are now excluded.

We shall work to achieve a simple, more effective and more economical method of administration.

We shall make a thorough study of universal pay-as-we-go pension plans.

HEALTH

We recognize that the health of our people as well as their proper medical care cannot be maintained if subject to Federal bureaucratic dictation. There should be a division of responsibility between government, the physician, the voluntary hospital, and voluntary health insurance. We are opposed to Federal compulsory health insurance with its crushing cost, wasteful inefficiency, bureaucratic dead weight, and debased standards of medical care. We shall support those health activities by government which stimulate the development of adequate hospital services without Federal interference in local administration. We favor support of scientific research. We pledge our continuous encouragement of improved methods of assuring health protection.

EDUCATION

The tradition of popular education, tax-supported and free to all, is strong with our people. The responsibility for sustaining this system of popular education has always rested upon the local communities and the States. We subscribe fully to this principle.

CIVIL RIGHTS

We condemn bigots who inject class, racial and religious prejudice into public and political matters. Bigotry is un-American and a danger to the Republic.

We deplore the duplicity and insincerity of the Party in power in racial and religious matters. Although they have been in office as a Majority Party for many years, they have not kept nor do they intend to keep their promises.

The Republican Party will not mislead, exploit or attempt to confuse minority groups for political purposes. All American citizens are entitled to full, impartial enforcement of Federal laws relating to their civil rights.

We believe that it is the primary responsibility of each State to order and control its own domestic institutions, and this power, reserved to the states, is essential to the maintenance of our Federal Republic. However, we believe that the Federal Government should take supplemental action within its constitutional jurisdiction to oppose discrimination against race, religion or national origin.

We will prove our good faith by:

Appointing qualified persons, without distinction of race, religion or national origin, to responsible positions in the Government.

Federal action toward the elimination of lynching.

Federal action toward the elimination of poll taxes as a prerequisite to voting.

Appropriate action to end segregation in the District of Columbia.

Enacting Federal legislation to further just and equitable treatment in the area of discriminatory employment practices. Federal action should not duplicate state efforts to end such practices; should not set up another huge bureaucracy.

CENSORSHIP

We pledge not to infringe by censorship or gag-order the right of a free people to know what their Government is doing.

EQUAL RIGHTS

We recommend to Congress the submission of a Constitutional Amendment providing equal rights for men and women.

We favor legislation assuring equal pay for equal work regardless of sex.

STATEHOOD

We favor immediate statehood for Hawaii.

We favor statehood for Alaska under an equitable enabling act.

We favor eventual statehood for Puerto Rico.

DISTRICT OF COLUMBIA

We favor self-government and national suffrage for the residents of the Nation's Capital.

INDIAN AFFAIRS

All Indians are citizens of the United States and no longer should be denied full enjoyment of their rights of citizenship.

We shall eliminate the existing shameful waste by the Bureau of Indian Affairs which has obstructed the accomplishment of our national responsibility for improving the condition of our Indian friends. We pledge to undertake programs to provide the Indians with equal opportunities for education, health protection and economic development.

The next Republican Administration will welcome the advice and counsel of Indian leaders in selecting the Indian Commissioner.

CIVIL SERVICE

We condemn the flagrant violations of the Civil Service merit system by the Party in power.

We favor a personnel program for the Federal career service comparable to the best practices of progressive private employers. Federal employees shall be selected under a strengthened and extended merit system. Civil servants of ability and integrity shall receive proper recognition, with merit the sole test for promotion.

DELIVERY OF MAIL

We pledge a more efficient and frequent mail delivery service.

GOVERNMENT REORGANIZATION

We pledge a thorough reorganization of the Federal Government in accordance with the principles set forth in the report of the Hoover Commission which was established by the Republican 80th Congress.

We denounce the duplicity in submitting to Congress for approval, reorganization plans which were represented as being in accordance with the principles of the Hoover Commission recommendations, but which in fact were actually intended to further partisan political purposes of the Administration in power.

CORRUPTION

The present Administration's sordid record of corruption has shocked and sickened the American people. Its leaders have forfeited any right to public faith by the way they transact the Federal Government's business.

Fraud, bribery, graft, favoritism and influence-peddling have come to light. Immorality and unethical behavior have been found to exist among some who were entrusted with high policy-making positions, and there have been disclosures of close alliances between the present Government and underworld characters.

Republicans exposed cases of questionable and criminal conduct and relentlessly pressed for full investigations into the cancer-like spread of corruption in the Administration. These investigations uncovered a double standard in Federal tax law enforcement—lenient treatment to political favorites including even some gangsters and crooks, but harassment and threats of prosecution for many honest taxpayers over minor discrepancies.

Besides tax fixes and scandals in the Internal Revenue Bureau, investigations have disclosed links between high officials and crime, favoritism and influence in the RFC, profiteering in grain, sale of postmasterships, tanker-ship deals in the Maritime Commission, ballot-box stuffing and thievery, and bribes and pay-offs in contract awards by officials in agencies exercising extraordinary powers and disbursing billions of dollars.

Under public pressure, the Administration took reluctant steps to clean house. But it was so eager to cover up and block more revelations that its clean-up drive launched with much fanfare ended in a farce.

The Republican Party pledges to put an end to corruption, to oust the crooks and grafters, to administer tax laws fairly and impartially, and to restore honest government to the people.

REPUBLICAN 80TH CONGRESS

The Republican Party does not rest its case upon promises alone. We have a record of performance which was grossly defamed by the Party in power. The Republican 80th Congress launched the program to stop Communism; unified the armed services; authorized a 70-group Air Force which the President blocked; enacted a national service law; balanced the budget; accumulated an eight-billion-dollar surplus; reduced taxes, with 70 per cent of the tax savings to those with incomes under $5,000; freed 7,400,000 wage earners in the lower brackets from having to pay any further income tax at all, allowed married couples to divide their incomes for tax purposes, and granted an additional $600 exemption to those over 65 years of age and to the blind; enacted the Taft-Hartley law for equitable labor-management relations; passed the first long-range agriculture program; increased social security benefits; and carried out every single pledge they made to the voters in the 1946 election.

CONCLUSION

Upon this statement of truths and this pledge of performance, the Republican Party stands confident that it expresses the hopes of the citizens of America and certain that it points out with integrity a road upon which free men may march into a new day—a new and better day—in which shall be fulfilled the decent aspirations of our people for peace, for solvency and for the fulfillment of our best welfare, under the guidance of Divine Providence.

Socialist Party—1952 Platform

PREAMBLE

Socialism has been catapulted into a major political issue in the United States today by the action of its enemies. The press, the radio, the halls of Congress, are filled with the hate and hysteria of the diehards of American capitalism who fear that they may no longer be able to dictate the economic life of the country for private profit. All the propaganda that their great fortunes can buy is unleashed in a vicious anti-socialist campaign.

What is this Socialism that the American people are asked to fear and to reject? It is any form of enterprise where public service cuts out private profit.

Public housing is under attack by the real estate lobby. Socialists were first to propose it, and they would expand it until there are decent homes for all our people.

Public power is denounced by utility monopolies. It can bring the comfort of the electric age to gladden the life of the farmer, and provide life-giving irrigation to redeem land that we need. Socialists believe that the power resources of America should serve the people, not the monopolies.

Public education, the basis of an informed citizenry and a functioning democracy, is starved out. The people's faith in our schools is constantly undermined by repeated smear attacks on teachers and text-books. Socialists insist that the wealth of the United States is great enough to provide equal educational opportunity for every child.

Public health suffers while private profit dominates medicine. Socialists demand that the people's health be protected from the inordinate greed of the drug and insurance monopolies and of the AMA.

Socialism and Liberty

Socialism, it is claimed, will destroy democracy. Nothing could be further from the truth. Socialism and democracy are one and inseparable. Socialists are in the forefront of the fight for civil liberties: freedom of speech, freedom of religion, freedom of the press, freedom to organize and vote for candidates of one's own choice. Socialism also stands for the economic freedoms of the people: the right to a job; the right to a fair wage; the right of workers to organize and strike; the right to security in old age, sickness or unemployment, and for widows and orphans.

Reaction tears down traditional civil liberties and stoops even to terror in an attack to delay progress towards racial equality. Only the great strength of organized labor has prevented the destruction of the trade union movement. An alarming trend on the domestic scene is one that the present administration has started. The witch-hunts against progressive thought are not the monopoly of the McCarthies. They are equally the responsibility of the "Fair Deal" Administration's loyalty program, and its concern with convincing the American people of its opposition to communism, which has been enlarged lately to include all non-conformist thought.

And reaction at home seeks reaction abroad as its mate. A foreign policy increasingly based on military expediency and American dominance is in the making, a policy that would embrace fascism in the name of anti-fascism.

A democratic offensive is overdue, and only Socialism can give democracy the drive it needs to win.

The industrial society that performed miracles to deepen the destructiveness of war must perform miracles to achieve abundance for all and the peace in which it can be enjoyed.

The American people, who pioneered in political democracy, must complete their democracy by taking control of their economic life.

Socialism will democratize the economic life of the nation by the joint representation of workers, the working management, and the consuming public, in the operation of socialized enterprises; by the guarantee of popular control of enterprises through the maximum decentralization economically feasible and the use of various types of organization, particularly the public corporation and the voluntary cooperative, and by the preservation of the freedom of labor organization and of consumer choice.

The basic industries, public utilities, banking and credit institutions—all the economic facilities needed for the satisfaction of the primary wants of the people—must be socially owned and democratically managed.

The natural resources of the nation—minerals, oil, atomic and electric power—are the property of the people. Their preservation for future generations and their management by the people for social purposes can be achieved democratically only under Socialism.

Planned production for use, and not for profit, in the United States will not only enrich the life of the American people. It alone can make possible the full use of American facilities, without exploitation, to raise the standard of living in underdeveloped areas and ease the economic strains that break out in war. Against the false promise of a machiavellian communism and the bankrupt incapacity of an outworn capitalism, it provides hope for a disillusioned world.

Security with liberty and peace in freedom is the goal of international Socialism, and of American Socialism. The Socialist Party urges all Americans who share this goal to join us in 1952; vote your hopes and not your fears.

Vote Socialist.

Join the Socialist Party and do your part to win this goal.

THE WORLD

The road to peace which the world's peoples desperately seek is barred by four tremendous obstacles. The greatest obstacle to enduring peace today is the aggressive imperialism of the Soviet Union, which has absorbed hundreds of millions of people into the totalitarian vise since the end of World War II. The second great obstacle to achieving peace has developed in reaction to the Communist offensive but has now become an obstacle in itself. This is the militarization of the western democracies which has resulted from the devastating arms race and the division of the world into armed camps under such tension that incidents may create war. Worse yet is the taking over of their economies for military objectives and the dictation of their foreign policy by military expediency which prevents taking constructive action for peace.

The third great obstacle to world peace and a basic cause of conflict which must be removed before we can hope to have permanent peace is the unwillingness of the privileged nations to deal fairly with the peoples of the have-not nations. The western democracies must recognize that, although colonialism has been largely overthrown, millions live at a starvation level and are oppressed by reason of color or status. They demand and deserve livelihood and liberty.

A fourth and basic obstacle to peace is capitalism, which by its nature is centered on profit, rather than on human welfare. In its international dealings, capitalism results in exploitation and injustice to the weak in every country. Aggressive totalitarianisms represent a threat to peace which must be dealt with. But Hitlers and Stalins may come and go, and—until we replace it—capitalism will still breed insecurity and resentment, new totalitarianisms and new threats of war. In the long view, the greatest single contribution the American people can make to peace is to replace an economic system dealing with the world on the basis of selfishness and conflict with a cooperative economy which can build a basic structure of economic interdependence and mutuality among ourselves and the people of the world.

The threat that Soviet aggression has hurled against the world is tragic. But just as tragic is the inability of the present government of our nation to understand its nature and to prepare to meet it with any degree of success. If we are to have permanent peace, there are some basic things that must be understood. The most important of these is that capitalism is a root cause of war and that capitalism keeps its creaking economy going through preparation for and participation in war. Therefore, the very existence of capitalism constantly threatens the world with war.

In the quest for peace, the United States under a bi-partisan foreign policy has played an equivocal role. Its war-time demand for unconditional surrender, the appeasement of the Soviet Union at Yalta, Teheran, and Potsdam, and the introduction of atomic warfare laid a foundation for permanent conflict rather than permanent peace. Yet in the early post-war period the United States pioneered generously in the rebuilding of war-devastated countries, planned expansion of aid for building up undeveloped areas, and led in the organization of a United Nations.

On the other hand, at no time did it offer the sanctuary for the dispossessed refugees of war or religious strife or to political exiles that its tradition and resources demanded of it. And recently, the rigid control of entrance into the United States has begun to approach the totalitarian pattern.

At first, the United States amazed the world by offering to subject its uniquely possessed atomic bomb to international control. Increasingly, it has placed its faith in armaments to curb Communist expansion. It is burdening our people with inflation and higher taxes. Throughout the world, in order to contain the Soviet Union, it has too often bolstered reactionary regimes that have denied the aspirations of the common people. In addition, these military efforts have also burdened the already strained economies of the democratic nations of western Europe. These increased efforts have resulted in part in the development of enmity against the United States and thus have played into the hands of Communist propagandists. Our capitalist government has failed to win the support of the peoples of the world and has sought alliances with dictators and reactionary regimes as well as with democratic governments. Both old parties share responsibility for American failure to take leadership for the crusade that might have achieved peace. And the bitterest failure is that, seven years after V-J Day, war continues.

Military influence in the American government has grown rather than declined. Military conscription continues year after year, and the pattern of the military mind grows stronger among the people. A continuing arms economy can only result in bankruptcy for our nation and the western world. In the chaos that follows, either fascism or communism is almost certain to take over. Democratic Socialism is our only hope of preserving freedom, human dignity, and justice. The gathering of people of this persuasion into a single, mighty, and organized force will furnish the strength that can overwhelm totalitarianism throughout the world, prevent a third world war, and bring peace and freedom.

A Socialist government in the United States can and will meet the threat of Soviet expansion with a foreign policy that is in keeping with the facts of political life. In this course lies the only hope that the American people have for peace, genuine prosperity, and democracy. A Socialist policy for peace, although flexible to meet changing situations, will develop from these ideas:

Internationalism

Our interdependent world, with its complex communications and transportation network supporting a vast industrial machine, has no room for isolation or economic nationalism. We are affected by developments in the far corners of the earth, as they are affected by us. The world that trans-

portation, communication, and habit have bound together cannot be separated by political differences or national boundaries. Self-preservation lies in the world-wide cooperative commonwealth of free men.

STRENGTHEN THE UNITED NATIONS

There is now only the beginning of an imperfect world organization. The present defects of the United Nations stem from the fact that the United States and the Soviet Union dominate their respective blocs in the U.N. The fact that the United States is currently able to muster the larger bloc should not blind us to the need to democratize the United Nations, as well as strengthen it to deal with aggression, by eliminating the unilateral veto in the Security Council. This should make possible the inclusion of all nations who adhere to the Charter of the United Nations.

Socialists would eliminate points of possible conflict by giving the United Nations power to handle them before trouble starts by
. . . initiating a movement for controlled and supervised disarmament, and international control and inspection of all armaments including atomic developments, as the beginning of the end of national militarism, and organizing an international police force so that the U.N. can be truly international in dealing with any disputes that may then arise.
. . . internationalizing and demilitarizing strategic waterways.
. . . ensuring access to food and raw materials to all peoples at prices fair to both producers and consumers. World planning through international agencies such as the Food and Agriculture Organization could be used to allocate materials in short supply on the basis of need, as well as to encourage expanded production where needed. Countries producing or monopolizing strategic materials, such as oil or tungsten, should be encouraged to dispose of their entire surplus, above domestic requirements, through international agencies.
. . . reducing trade barriers gradually, leading to free trade, with programs of retraining for workers in industries that are no longer protected; urging the principle of free travel, so that men as well as goods have equal access to the world.
. . . establishing a Peace Council not dominated

by the five major powers which could use good offices in tension situations (Iran or Indo-China) or act to alleviate war-breeding potentials (population pressures, racism).

. . . encouraging regional federation, which may break down artificial economic barriers and promote ideals broader than national sovereignty.

. . . insisting on international control and formulation of policy on Korea and the Korean peace.

We favor the development of the United Nations into a federal world government with careful provision to respect the rights of all countries, including the right to socialize their economies. We favor a partial world government if certain countries refuse to join the world government.

STRENGTHEN THE SOCIALIST INTERNATIONAL

Organizations of governments alone will not bring peace; and our desire for world federation does not mean that we favor the creation of the leviathan state. The unity of peoples for common goals irrespective of national boundaries can be a powerful force in developing that kinship of feeling which must be the basis of a world society. Democratic Socialism, which aims at liberating all men from every form of economic, spiritual, and political bondage, holds as primary purpose the strengthening of international democracy.

Anti-Militarism

The present arms race must be halted before it produces war by accident or subverts democracy so that war itself becomes a goal. A Socialist government would provide active American leadership to secure universal disarmament under enforceable controls, with recognition of the principle of unlimited international inspection.

Actions speak louder than words to guarantee the will to peace. A Socialist government would lead in proposing immediate outlawry of conscription by all nations, renewing the proposal for international control of atomic weapons, and taking advantage of any national offer for negotiation on disarmament to achieve that goal. It would end conscription in the United States.

The remilitarization of any other country or its participation in military pacts should not be made the condition for economic aid or other treaty arrangements. Pressure for remilitarization of Japan should be halted, and the policy of a united, demilitarized Germany advocated in Europe.

Commitments of the present foreign policy to foreign people make immediate withdrawal of American troops from abroad impossible; but the speediest withdrawal consistent with the security of the people involved should be arranged and announced as national policy.

The growing control of the military over civilian decisions in the United States must be halted. Militarization of education and the threat of permanent military training programs indoctrinate American youth to accept war as the solution to the world's problems. Military demands are wasting irreplaceable natural resources, making impossible adequate aid to less fortunate areas of the world, and threatening our standard of living. The military have overruled the state department in the demand for aid to fascist Spain and are strengthening the alliance with Chiang Kai-shek and forces of reaction the world over.

Solidarity

WORLD DEVELOPMENT

The United States, possessing so much of the industrial resources of the world, must be foremost in aid to underdeveloped areas. But this effort to build up economies, to raise the standard of living, the education and technical skills of the people, to provide the economic basis for democracy, is not a unilateral task. It should be organized through the United Nations, with a pooling of resources by all nations, and the United States contributing its fair share. Thus can the danger of exploitation, either of nation over nation or of private profiteers over underdeveloped areas, be avoided. A peace tax in the form of an income tax upon all peoples, contributed through the United Nations, would widen the basis of responsibility and participation still further.

WORLD BROTHERHOOD

The shame of racial discrimination still disfigures whole countries and oppresses millions. As we insist on the achievement of racial equality in the United States, so we also insist that the United States participate in the world-wide struggle to achieve it; that world opinion and world organization protest situations as vicious as that growing in South Africa, and stop its extension. Nor is race the only point of discrimination. Again after centuries, religious difference has become a major reason for persecution of men in millions.

And political opinion is a crime in vast areas of the world, while political asylum is too often denied. Protection for minority rights is a vital part of the Socialist recognition of the common humanity that unites us irrespective of race, creed, or color.

WORLD FREEDOM

Conscious of the failings of our own democracy, we nevertheless retain the freedom to work for its perfection and to aid democratic forces in less fortunate areas of the world. Our faith in the spirit of man insists to us that, regardless of the rigor of oppression, forces for freedom will arise and will need to be heard and to be helped throughout the world. In their natural alignment with the forces of freedom in opposition to the forces of tyranny, Socialists insist that the alternatives before the world are not simply war or communist domination; the hope of the world lies in escaping the war which would doom all people alike, and pressing the fight for freedom by methods consistent with the goal.

We recognize the enslaved peoples of the Iron Curtain countries as our friends and not our enemies. Our endeavor is: to tear down the curtain, establishing contact by radio and every means at our disposal; to pledge refuge to all those who escape; to demand no extension of slavery; to offer friendship and support to any democratic freedom movement that may develop and seek it.

Totalitarianism, though the worst, is not the only form of tyranny. Relics of colonial empire still oppress millions; to gain national freedom and the chance for individual betterment, they may take help where they find it. Time and time again, the failure of western democracies to practice democracy in Asia and Africa drives nationalist movements into the hands of communism. The victory of Stalinism in much of the world has been possible because Stalinists have been able to subvert the spirit of revolt of colonial and oppressed people where there has been no democratic alternative. Wherever there has been a strong Socialist movement, the Communists have been unable to win unless they were in a position to bring overwhelming force to bear. It is because the Stalinists have falsely identified themselves with the strivings of the people for economic advancement and political independence that they have become strong. A mighty international democratic Socialist movement is our only hope for conquering Stalinism in the political field.

Democratic Socialism rejects every form of imperialism and supports every struggle for freedom. Our one world must be a free world. The world community and the lasting peace we seek must be achieved in freedom, as it will find its fruition in fellowship.

THE NATION

American capitalism never recovered from the great collapse of the thirties when millions went hungry and homeless although the basic wealth of the country was great and unavailable for their use only because of the despotism of the private profit system. There was no recovery in the sense of devotion of the economy to human needs. Superficial prosperity returned with a war economy and the brutal and wanton destructiveness of war.

Twenty years later, the real floor under the American economy is still miltiary expenditures. 85 per cent of 1952 federal expenditures (over 61 billion dollars) are ear-marked for past, present, and future wars. By the end of 1952, 20 per cent of the total national output will be diverted to military and related production—not comparable to the 45 per cent of World War II, but with a cumulative impact on the economy that includes the previous total-war strain. At the pre-Korea spending rate, we had enough copper for only 15 years or enough high-grade iron for 30. Similarly, our other resources drain away. The only thing military expenditure can add to is the profit which private individuals manufacture out of the nation's misfortune. Capitalism has no economic equivalent for war.

Between them, the goal of profit and the acceptance of war are ruining the American economy. One-fourth of presently tillable land is in critical condition and another fourth suffering from erosion. The present annual use of timber is many times the growth. Drought in farmland and water famine in large cities have revealed dramatically a frightening condition of our watershed. The animal-carrying capacity of western grassland has been reduced by one-half (while the cattle lobby moves in on our last reserves of public land) and fishing beds are damaged by pollution.

Conservation of American resources, essential

to the life of the nation, has been neglected. But this is not all.

To the needs of the nation for flood control soil conservation, reforestation, preservation of water resources, we can add the needs of the states for development of power resources, highways and turnpikes, institutional buildings such as hospitals; and to this again, innumerable needs of local areas for improvements that local budgets can no longer afford.

The Socialist Party can and does offer a substitute for war as a motivating factor behind production. It is our internal development program framed to meet the needs of the nation.

Education

The present shortage of classrooms is 200,000. It will reach 500,000 by 1960. They can be provided at an annual expense of $1.35 billion—a little more than 2 per cent of 1952 military expenditures. Additional schools needed will take two billion dollars more. An expanded teacher-training program and adequate salary standards can change the present situation in which we graduate only one-fifth the number of qualified teachers required by our schools. An expanded scholarship program is needed to equalize educational opportunities for young people.

Health

Federal assistance in social security, health, welfare, and education costs us $4.60 per American per year. The support of one man in the armed services costs us $5,600. We can afford a national health program that will

Establish an all-inclusive health insurance plan;

Train more doctors, dentists, nurses, and other needed personnel;

Advance medical research and expand hospital building services;

Increase state maternal, child health, and crippled children's services;

Expand public health services.

Natural Resources

One year's expenditures for the cold war (estimated at $85 billion after 1952) would supply

Nine regional development projects each providing at the end of seven years

. . . irrigated land for 18,000 new family sized farms.

. . . supplemented irrigation for 53,000 farms.

. . . 3.2 million KW of new generating capacity.

An investment of three billion dollars a year for thirty years would save our land and our water and would return wealth endlessly to the people.

The Socialist Party would make this investment in America. Our resources are the basis of our strength and the first line of any defense.

Housing

The real estate lobby, which leads the national campaign against aid to people in desperate need of homes which private enterprise has failed to supply, itself accepts subsidy and makes tremendous profit out of the present FHA legislation. Recent votes in Congress to limit the low-rent public housing program to 45,000 units a year, against a national housing need for 500,000 (and an administration plan for 75,000) to prevent further deterioration of the already bad housing situation, expose the unfitness of Congressmen of both major parties.

Private industry has never been able to house the American people adequately. Public and cooperative enterprise can do so. A national budget of two billion dollars a year is not excessive. (The budget was $2.2 billion for aircraft alone in 1951, and the plan for 1952 is $6.8 billion.)

The Socialist Party would create a Home Loan Bank to finance the purchase of homes at low interest rates; a Public Supply Corporation to set up factory units needed to produce materials and develop large-scale housing; integration of national and local building plans including revision of municipal building codes; and development of a program of collective bargaining with the building and construction unions, providing a guaranteed annual wage, and the development of apprentice-training programs. For the duration of the housing emergency, rent control must be retained or restored.

Our Standard of Living

INFLATION AND DEFLATION

The standard of living of the American people is constantly threatened either by inflationary or deflationary tendencies in the economy. Either the struggle is to push up wages to the level of prices, or to maintain the level of employment at wages at or above the level of prices.

The sources of economic instability are no longer among the great mysteries of life, however. The principal lesson of the Employment Act of 1946 is that it is possible to know what is going on in the economy. The failure of this and other enactments of a similar nature is that they either make no provision or inadequate provision for meeting the problems whose existence is revealed or forecast by the agencies set up under their provisions.

The effect of the present inflation on living standards should be alleviated by price controls on essential items, but this is treating a symptom, not a disease. Taxation policy and the expansion of production can do better.

TAXATION

In the past six years, the idea of taxation according to ability to pay has been reversed in practice. The tax burden has been shifted increasingly from the rich to the poor as more and more taxes have been needed to finance the government and the armaments program. Inflation has raised costs and thus increased the load still further, unnecessarily. Low- and fixed-income groups have lost most. Merchants and speculators have profited.

The nearer we come to a pay-as-you-go tax policy, the less the ultimate cost to the people. Socialists say: pay as you go.

The more loop-holes for privileged groups can be removed, the more equally the tax burden will be shared. Socialists would abolish preferential treatment for capital gains, state and municipal bonds, percentage depletion allowances on oil and natural gas wells and other mining.

Excise taxes have two purposes. They can both raise revenue, and discourage non-essential and luxury spending. They can be increased without hurting low-income groups. We vigorously oppose sales taxes which, under the guise of equality, hit the low-income groups the hardest.

Individual-income taxation, based on ability to pay, is the fairest way to raise taxes and one of the most important. A reactionary campaign to limit taxation of high incomes (the millionaire's amendment) must be exposed and defeated.

SOCIAL SECURITY

Increases to begin to catch up with inflation are needed in social security benefits for the old and unfortunate who need this aid.

Coverage should be expanded to end discrimination against any group of workers.

The age of eligibility for old-age pensions should be reduced to 60.

Family allowances, so that the young are protected as well as the old, must be added. Four and a half million children in the United States live in families with total incomes of less than $20.00 a week.

NATIONAL INCOME

The top one-fifth of the population receive 47 per cent of the national income. Socialization would restore most of that wealth to the nation.

The bottom one-fifth of the people receive only 3 per cent of the national income. Their standard of living must be raised in many ways—through organization in trade unions; through cooperatives; through public social services. A small beginning on the part of government would be to raise the minimum wage from 75¢ to $1, and to call for progressive increases as the productivity level of the nation rises.

AGRICULTURE

The Socialist Party would halt the growing trend to absentee ownership of farms and the increase of farm tenancy. Occupancy and use should give the only rightful title to farmland. The security of family farms should be strengthened through cooperative credit purchasing and marketing, aided by government financing. Reactionary attempts to destroy rural electrification and to tax cooperatives out of existence must be defeated. Proper distribution and marketing of agricultural products does not require gambling. The present Board of Trade pricing of farm produce, with its poker-game practices of buying on futures, must be ended.

Where modern techniques and specialization require large-scale farm enterprises, we call for social ownership and cooperative operation to replace the corporation farm which threatens both the security and freedom of farm workers.

Security for all the people, and a rising standard of living, can be guaranteed by the vast resources and productive facilities of this nation. A Socialist administration will make this its first concern.

Defense of Democracy

Socialists strive to build a new society in freedom and by democratic means. We would expand the political democracy which the United States possesses to include industrial democracy and full racial equality. But the first urgent task today is to halt the destruction of political democracy which the last four years have witnessed. In the guise of defense against communist totalitarianism, the foundations of an American totalitarianism are rising.

THE RIGHT TO WORK

The Socialist Party recognizes the necessity of screening where employment of persons belonging to totalitarian organizations might endanger the security of our nation. But because civil liberties do not include the right of any person to any job without proper qualifications for fitness which may include loyalty provisions, care must be taken not to deprive individuals of the right to work at non-sensitive positions for which training and experience fit them.

DEMOCRATIC PROCEDURES

The right to hear and answer charges which may affect the livelihood, liberty, or citizenship of the individual must be protected. We ask elimination of the Committee on Un-American Activities which has abused the Congressional right of investigation. We ask the right to hear and answer charges in all security screening cases, and the inclusion of labor representation on hearing boards. We ask the elimination of loyalty oaths that totalitarians would not hesitate to swear falsely, but that discriminate against honest citizens in an increasing number of occupations. We ask recognition of the right of the individual to change his political opinions, and protest retroactive retribution for commitments made in previous years.

THE FREE BALLOT

Discrimination against minority parties through excessive requirements for gaining ballot status must be changed. The poll tax which deprives citizens of the right to vote because of income must be repealed. The growing number of states that have added to technical requirements a legal discrimination against the Communist Party— often worded with dangerous vagueness—are only driving that Party underground into illegal channels, making it more dangerous than if its ideas were exposed to the light.

FREEDOM OF OPINION

Conviction of Communist leadership under the Smith Act, which the Socialist Party has opposed from its inception, followed by the rounding up of successive layers of Communist Party leadership, is a denial of political freedom more worthy of a totalitarian nation than of a democracy. Where illegal acts have taken place—such as spying—legislation on the books, applying equally to Communist and non-Communist alike, has been successfully used in prosecution. Where overt acts take place, democracy has the ability and the duty to defend itself against the totalitarian foe from within. But persecution based on political belief and expression of political opinion must be stopped.

FREEDOM OF EDUCATION

Unwarranted censorship and pressure on teachers' opinions and of textbooks threatens free inquiry and access to full information in our schools and universities. This attacks the very basis of democratic education and scientific progress, as the exchange of ideas is impeded. Part of this pressure stems from a justifiable concern to protect children against indoctrination by Communists and fascists. Much of it comes from reactionaries such as the National Council on American Education who would turn back the clock to the economic and social practices of the last century. In some communities the pressure of organized religion imposes an unwarranted censorship. These combined efforts must be resisted on every level. Teaching must be made an attractive, not a persecuted, profession. Students must learn to discriminate among ideas through free experience with them. Adequate funds must be made available to provide equal educational opportunities for all children.

FREEDOM FOR LABOR

The Socialist Party seeks repeal of Taft-Hartley and similar state laws which undermine the right to strike, the right to organize, the right to sign contracts guaranteeing union security and furthering the economic interests of organized workers. But as we insist on freedom of action for unions on behalf of their members, so we fight for internal democracy within the union, regular and free election of officers, protection of minority rights, and racial equality.

CONSCIENTIOUS OBJECTION

We urge full amnesty and restoration of civil rights for war objectors, thousands of whom have lost voting and other citizenship rights. We ask complete exemption for absolutist objectors to war and conscription. We protest the narrowness of the present Selective Service Act which excludes many sincere conscientious objectors. We oppose re-institution of the CPS system of forced labor without pay. Any alternative service should be recompensed by accepted wage standards for the occupation and area.

RACIAL EQUALITY

Complete political, economic, and social equality, regardless of race, religion, or national origin, must be established. Equality can be achieved only after the ending of segregation practices.

Segregation must be abolished in all public or public-supported institutions, in housing, in the armed services. We shall work on a community level for abolition of segregation which cannot be handled by legislation.

Fair Employment Practices legislation must be passed nationally, and adopted on a state-wide basis in states that do not yet have it.

Anti-lynching legislation must be enacted. The Civil Rights Section of the Justice Department must move to safeguard the lives of citizens in states where "legal lynching" is protected by the state machinery.

Discriminating barriers against immigration on grounds of race, color, national origin, or political opinion, must be removed.

The right to vote must be guaranteed to all citizens. The 14th Amendment, depriving states of representation in Congress in proportion to the number of citizens deprived of the right to vote by virtue of race, color, or previous condition of servitude, should be enforced.

FULL CITIZENSHIP

The District of Columbia should be given self-government, and its citizens full citizenship rights. Statehood should be granted to Alaska and Hawaii, and to Puerto Rico if the people so desire.

THE COMMUNITY

Democratic Socialism aims at extending individual freedom on the basis of economic and social security and an increasing prosperity. While the guiding principle of capitalism is private profit, and that of totalitarianism is complete subservience of the individual to the dictatorship, the purpose of Socialism is the democratic satisfaction of human needs to liberate the full creativity of the human personality.

Socialism is thus a community as well as a world endeavor. It stresses voluntary and cooperative action in the achievement of its goal. The independent organizations of the people—unions, cooperatives, cultural and social groupings—will retain full freedom under Socialism and will guarantee the maintenance of a free society. Where social objectives are too broad for realization by individuals or private organizations, they must be undertaken by the people through government.

The forms of public ownership are not an end in themselves. Government ownership, cooperative ownership, public-authority ownership, will exist. Control is more important than ownership. It must include workers. It must include working management. It must include public or consumer representation. Under democratic control, production can be for purposes decided by the people. Under decentralized control—which Socialism will use wherever possible—bureaucracy can be limited and watched. With free consumer choice, an important economic power remains in the hands of the people.

The choice between the democratic and the authoritarian state is clarified at the local level. Civil liberties exist where men are free in their own communities. Racial justice is achieved where people live together in equality. Economic security is made real when the fear of age, of illness, of hunger, is removed from the family circle. Peace will come as the boundaries of the democratic community are extended until abundance and freedom are the property of all men.

Your vote for Socialism in this election may influence the direction of the United States. Your voice in the community in organization for a new society will bring closer the day when American policy is shaped by the Socialist objective: Humanity First.

JOIN THE SOCIALIST PARTY!
VOTE SOCIALIST IN 1952!

Socialist Labor Party—1952 Platform

The Socialist Labor Party of the United States of America, in National Convention assembled on this 4th day of May, 1952, reaffirms its previous platform pronouncements and declares:

The crisis that shakes the world today is a revolutionary crisis. It is one of those crucial turning points of history when an outmoded system is in a state of impending collapse, and a new order is waiting to be born.

The capitalist system rose on the ruins of feudalism—in this country on the transplanted feudal power of the British Crown. It had a mission to perform, the mission of establishing mass production and of organizing the workers in industry in keeping with that purpose. Its mission has been fulfilled: Abundance is now possible for all without arduous toil. But in fulfilling its historic mission the capitalist class has rendered itself useless—nay worse, it has become an encumbrance on the productive process, an incubus on society as a whole, and its continued presence as a useless class has become a menace to our very civilization.

Accordingly, the downfall of the capitalist system is certain. It is foredoomed by contradictions resulting from the division of society into classes and the exploitation of wage labor. Its economy is kept going today by rearmament and the waging of war. Without this huge, war-inciting multi-billion-dollar war-preparations program, capitalism would quickly sink in a quagmire of economic depression.

This is a permanent condition. The plutocratic rulers are committed to a permanent arms economy. In order to stave off the threatened economic breakdown, they are compelled to build and amass ever more military weapons and supplies, thereby accelerating the forces, *inherent in capitalist rivalry for world trade,* that are leading fatedly to a third world war.

Thus, decadent capitalism has brought society to the brink of catastrophe and ruin. The question now is: *Shall this doomed system be allowed to drag humanity down into the abyss? Or will the working class, in whose hands the future lies, wake up in time, organize its immense latent power, and put society on the road to safety and freedom?*

The Socialist Labor Party declares that such is the crucial nature of the crisis that grips our civilization.

The plutocratic capitalists are confused, intellectually bankrupt and divided among themselves. Although they still pay lip-service to the American tradition of civilian government, in practice they have renounced this tradition and have given professional military men a dominant role in formulating foreign and domestic policy.

The Korean war, a senseless war to all but the capitalists and Russian imperialist interests that profit from it, is a tragic consequence of ruling-class confusion and the military approach in international relations.

The frequent demands by high military leaders, and even by Cabinet members, that the United States abandon its moral scruples against "striking the first (sneak attack) blow," and that the country become the aggressor in a "preventive war" with Russia, are frightening evidence of the panic that is overtaking the American ruling class.

The Socialist Labor Party asserts that the ferocious conflict that divides the world and threatens to hurl mankind into the fiery furnace of global war is an imperialist conflict. It is basically a struggle between the plutocratic masters of the United States and the bureaucratic masters of Soviet Russia for control of the world's economic resources. Both these ruling groups must share the guilt for the appalling danger of extinction today threatening the human race.

Let no one underestimate the danger. A third world war would be an atomic war, a war of universal desolation. The Socialist Labor Party holds that peace today hangs only by a thread of fear. For the moment both imperialist rivals are deterred by the atomic bomb—the knowledge that if either attacks the other, retaliation will be swift and terrible.

In this revolutionary crisis the class struggle is becoming more intense.

The plutocratic capitalists sit uneasily on their mountains of stolen wealth. To secure their class privileges and to weaken the workers' resistance to increased exploitation, they have enacted the labor-shackling Taft-Hartley Law and revived the medieval weapon of the court injunction.

It is an incontestable fact that the workers are steadily falling behind in the race with living costs, which means, in effect, that their real wages, hence their standards of living, are being steadily reduced. By means of a wage freeze, restrictions on the right to strike and the regimentation of the workers that is accomplished through the faker-controlled, job-trust unions, the American worker is being reduced to the status of an unresisting industrial serf. Thus a new form of slavery is evolving, more in keeping with the despotic needs of the present huge concentrations of corporate capital.

By means of falsehoods and smears, whipped-up hysteria, witch-hunts and loyalty oaths, the capitalist plutocrats are attacking the very heart of American political democracy. They are imposing a "black silence of fear" on millions of once proudly independent and fearlessly outspoken Americans.

The Socialist Labor Party declares that the real target of this un-American attack is not the Communists, but the fundamental rights and civil liberties of the American people. The Communists are merely a convenient and vulnerable target. It has been said, not without logic, that if there were no Communist party in America, the capitalist reaction would organize one.

The assault on liberty and the attempted Prussianization of the country via permanent compulsory military training are, we assert, desperate efforts to prolong an outmoded and foredoomed social system.

The Socialist Labor Party appeals to you to accept the logic of these facts: WAR, FASCISM, EXPLOITATION, AND POVERTY AMIDST PLENTY ARE THE EVIL BROOD OF CAPITALISM. No person who reaches this conclusion can, without consciously aligning himself with the forces of reaction, support candidates and parties that have as their aim the reform or preservation of capitalism. In this category, besides the Republicans and Democrats, we include all other parties, whatever their designation. For one and all they follow principles of capitalism or of State despotism. One and all they preach reforms and promise improvement of conditions that are past improving. To propose reform when a fundamental social change is called for is to help prolong the capitalist cause of war, fascism and working-class exploitation. "To reform is to preserve."

The Socialist Labor Party, therefore, calls upon the American workers of brain and brawn, and all other enlightened citizens, to repudiate the parties of capitalism and to support its program for a peaceful and orderly Socialist reconstruction of society.

The Socialist Labor Party program, in line with social evolution, demands the abolition of the political State with all its organs of class coercion. Political government (based on geographic constituencies), which was suited to an age of agriculture and primitive production, has been rendered obsolete by the growth of modern industry. The goal of the Socialist Labor Party is a democratic Socialist industrial government—a society based on collective ownership of the land and all the instruments of wealth production, with the management of industry completely in the hands of the workers through socially integrated Socialist Industrial Union Councils.

To bring to birth this society of peace, abundance and freedom, the Socialist Labor Party appeals to the working class of America, and all other enlightened and social-minded citizens, to support its principles at the polls by voting for Socialist Labor Party candidates. And we call upon the workers to repudiate the present unions, which accept capitalism as a finality and are faker-controlled, and to build a new union based squarely on their working class interests and with Socialism as its goal. Build the integral Socialist Industrial Union, as the only union capable of enforcing the Socialist ballot and of assuming the administration of social production.

This program repudiates the kind of bureaucratic despotism masquerading as "Marxist" in Soviet Russia, and the reformist outfits, such as the British Labor party, falsely claiming to be "Socialist."

What Abraham Lincoln said ninety years ago, in the midst of another revolutionary crisis, applies with even greater force today. He said: "The dogmas of the quiet past are inadequate for the stormy present. . . . As our case is new, so must we think anew and act anew. We must disenthrall ourselves, and then we shall save our country."

Unite with us to save society from catastrophe—and to set an example in free, industrial self-government for all mankind! Unite with us to establish the Socialist Republic of Peace, Plenty and International Brotherhood!

Socialist Workers Party—1952 Election Platform

We are told every day that Americans live in a special "paradise-on-earth," the richest, the most peaceful, the most stable country in the world.

But the truth is we face disaster.

We stand on the brink of the most destructive of all wars. Half the peoples of the world will be ranged against us. It is doubtful that we can win such a war. But whether our generals win or lose, we, the American people, will be the losers. Millions of our sons, brothers and husbands will lose their lives on foreign battle fronts in the remotest corners of the world. Our cities will be pounded by bombs, turned into rubble as were Coventry and London, Berlin and Hamburg, Hiroshima and Nagasaki in the last war.

The military machine will devour our great national wealth and resources. Our standard of living will be driven down to the European level. Our cherished rights and liberties will be trampled underfoot by a military dictatorship. Labor will be regimented and dissenters locked up in concentration camps.

This is the tomorrow our rulers are planning for us and our children. And it is later than most of us think. In the midst of our present seeming well-being such a prospect looks like sheer madness. But it is not the common people who have lost their reason, it is not they who are plotting national suicide. It is the capitalist system under which we live, the giant banks and monopolies which dominate it and the politicians of the two major parties who serve their interest. These are the real betrayers of our country. They are the enemy within the gates.

Nothing is so frightening to them as the word "peace." There is cold calculation behind their fears.

The present prosperity is an unhealthy one. Its chief beneficiaries have been the kings of finance and industry. They have made fabulous profits running into astronomical sums.

The mass of working people have received only the crumbs of this prosperity. Every slight improvement has been undermined by higher taxes and rising prices.

Meanwhile our industrial plant has been enlarged and speeded up. We produce twice as much as we did 15 years ago. The people earn too little to consume this vast output. Each year labor gets a smaller share of the national wealth. While productivity of labor rises and profits skyrocket, wages are held back by government controls, inflation and the tax bite.

This unequal distribution of wealth has resulted in accumulation of billions upon billions of dollars by the rich, who cannot invest them at a high enough rate of profit. And there are too few dollars in the hands of the working people to purchase the goods and services of the nation's industries. These conditions caused the 10-year depression that began in 1929.

The Second World War pulled us out of that depression. Now preparations for World War III are keeping us out of a new depression. Big Business likes this war profiteering. It prefers to have the nation's wealth invested in the means of destruction instead of in a system of social insurance to provide medical care and security for everyone. It finds it more profitable to build the engines of death—atom bombs, rockets and jet planes—than to build low-cost homes within the reach of millions of slum-dwellers. It has no competitors in this business of armaments; it extorts the prices it wants from the government, which gives it free plants and tax exemptions running into billions of dollars.

To keep this boom going requires war "scares" and wars, small ones as in Korea, or a bigger war later against China, the Soviet Union and the countries of Eastern Europe. That is the reason why it has been so difficult to arrange even a truce in Korea; that is why the State Department is pushing through the rearmament of Western Germany and Japan under the old Nazi officers and war-lords, against the resistance of most of the peoples of Europe and Asia.

A war machine has a logic of its own; once set in motion it is hard to stop. In the end it must touch off the powder kegs of World War III.

There is one condition on which our monopoly-banker rulers will consider peace. It is that the people of the world permit them to establish a "dollar" empire where French, British and Dutch imperialism ruled before.

But peace is impossible on that condition. The world of imperialism is finished.

The millions of brown, yellow and black-skinned people—who constitute the majority of the human race—have thrown off the yoke of centuries of exploitation by the masters from the Old World; they will not willingly accept the new would-be master from Wall Street.

The peoples of the Soviet Union and Eastern Europe have eliminated capitalist rule and have begun the difficult climb to a planned socialist system. Despite the oppression of their dictatorial rulers, they will not willingly permit a return of the speculators, landlords and profiteers.

If they have not rid themselves of the Kremlin over-lords and the Stalinist bureaucrats, it is because they fear the threat of economic strangulation and military intervention from our financial-military oligarchy. They have in effect been told by the State Department that it plans to supplant the Stalinist dictatorship with dictatorships of the Old Regime. It plans to add foreign subjugation and economic exploitation to political tyranny. Its hue and cry against "Stalinism" is only a camouflage for the return of private profit and corporation property in areas where it has been eliminated.

We socialists are the only genuine opponents of Stalinist rule. We have fought it from the beginning as a treacherous leadership within the camp of the workers—as an aid not a foe of capitalist reaction. But we know that only the elimination of world capitalism—only a system of production for use, of economic equality between nations—will spell the doom for Stalinist dictatorship.

It is not "communism" which threatens America. It is Wall Street and the Pentagon, in their hunger for profits, investments and empire, which threatens one-third of the peoples of the world. Our so-called Atlantic "community" is a fraud. Our "allies" are a few plutocrats bought with dollars. But the people of England and the continent who are hungrier and poorer than ever, have come to hate the name of America. They don't want Washington's anti-communist crusade. They won't fight Wall Street's war. They don't believe we are fighting for "democracy" against dictatorship and totalitarianism. And they are right. They know that the only real friends of the State Department are the capitalist despots: Syngman Rhee, Chiang Kai-shek, the Greek King, the Nazi generals and the Japanese militarists.

Are we threatened by military assault from the so-called "Soviet Empire"?

The Russian army is not within 200 miles of the American border. But an American force of half a million men is within 200 miles of the Manchurian and Siberian borders.

The Russians and Chinese do not have troops and air bases in 55 foreign countries scattered around the globe. But the United States does.

The Russians and Chinese are not encircling America; but the United States, heading the greatest military alliance in history, is forging an iron ring around the borders of the Soviet Union.

It is not "communism" from afar, but reaction directed from Washington that threatens the precious liberties of the American people at home.

The Constitution and the Bill of Rights are being supplanted with a "dangerous thoughts" code.

Trial and imprisonment on accusation of advocating the 100-year old ideas of Marxism is now an everyday occurrence.

Charges of guilt by association, contrary to Anglo-Saxon law, is a customary procedure in Congress and in State Legislatures.

A sinister political police, called the FBI, conducts vast operations of prying, snooping into personal lives, making informers out of honest people, intimidating, purging workers from government jobs and even private employment.

Teachers are forbidden the right to political association outside the two major parties. Students are taught the ideological goose-step instead of being encouraged to inquire into new ideas.

The McCarran immigration law bolts the doors on racial and political grounds, against those who would come to our shores. We are not allowed to travel abroad without first being "screened" for our political views.

The Bi-Partisan Gang

The same gang that dreams of invading New China and restoring capitalism to the USSR put over the Taft-Hartley slave labor act at home, and is planning new curbs for the unions.

The same gang that has burned and bombed Korea to a wasteland is responsible for the disfranchisement and segregation of the Negro people, and the mob-and-bomb law against their most courageous leaders.

Open shop, race terror and fascism at home are the natural inclinations of the would-be masters of

China, Russia and the world. The enemy of the peoples of the world is also our enemy—and that enemy is at home.

Who are the war-makers and the witch hunters? The Democrats and Republicans are both for war. It will make little difference whether Eisenhower or Stevenson is elected; both are for the war program of Big Business.

Republicans and Democrats are also united on the witch hunt. The Democratic administration under Truman is the real inspirer of Republican witch-hunter McCarthy. Truman initiated and gave official sanction to the government "loyalty" purge, restricting and violating the democratic rights of millions.

The Democrats decreed "loyalty" oaths, and the "subversive" lists. The Republicans applauded. The Democrats object to McCarthy's character assassination only when it affects the administration itself. The truth is the Democrats have put into effect most of McCarthy's vigilante proposals.

Both old parties have aided the growing military domination of government. The Pentagon is virtually a state within a state. The military brass are in league with Big Business; together they are wasting our national resources, devouring our wealth, plundering the public treasury and plotting war on a world scale.

The Democrats brought this Brass Hat–Big Business gang into positions of power. A Republican victory would put a general in the White House and perpetuate and extend their control.

One obstacle stands on this road that leads to military dictatorship, war and catastrophe: The working people! They are the majority in the country. Through their powerful union organizations they possess tremendous strength. They don't want imperialist war or foreign conquest.

They don't want to dictate to other countries. They are not interested in the profits of the billionaire bankers and corporations, or in the glories of generals.

They want to live at peace with the peoples of the world.

They want to see the great wealth of our country and the products of its industry distributed in such a manner as to guarantee a decent standard of living to those who work, without depression or war. Only the subservience of the official union leadership, who back the war policy of the State Department, keeps the American working people politically powerless.

WE NEED A LABOR PARTY

This force of the American working people has yet to be organized in its own political party—the party of labor and the Negro people. Such a labor party could stay the hand of the war-makers; it could break the power of the race-haters; it could remove the threat of depression amid plenty; it could knit together bonds of solidarity with the peoples of the world fighting for national liberation and a better life, in keeping with our own traditions of the Revolution for Independence and the war against slavery.

The Socialist Workers Party fights for the creation of a Labor Party. It is confident it will come into being and change the whole course of American life and history.

The working people have a voice and a program in the 1952 elections—the Socialist Workers Party and its banner bearers: Farrell Dobbs for President and Myra Tanner Weiss for Vice President.

The great issue before the human race today is capitalism or socialism. Shall America join the march of history, or will it go down in ruins and poverty in a disastrous war to save the outlived dying system of capitalism? That is the burning question of our times.

The Socialist Workers Party takes its stand on the side of progress, on the side of the peoples who have taken the first step in the direction of a new society. The peoples of this new world hate their present despotic Stalinist rulers, but they hate capitalism more. The American people can aid them against oppressive Stalinist political rule and save themselves from catastrophic war only by joining the world march to socialism.

ONLY ROAD TO PEACE

The SWP urges the American people to reorganize the wealth of our country on a socialist basis, to rid ourselves of minority government of the parasites and plutocrats and to establish genuine democracy—the rule of the workers and poor farmers. That is the only road to lasting peace.

The Progressive Party fears to face this decisive issue. It cultivates the vain illusion that capitalism can be reformed into a system of peace instead of war, that the irreconcilable differences between socialism and capitalism can be compromised out of existence. Such a program cannot effectively organize the struggle against the impending counter-revolutionary war. It can only demoralize the ranks of the anti-war fighters and in the end lead to new defeats and to the victory of reaction.

The Socialist Workers Party warns the American people of the terrible future the Wall Street–Brass Hat rulers are preparing for them. We urge resistance against the threatening catastrophe, to save our vanishing democratic rights. We enter this campaign to blaze the trail for a real government of the people, a government of the majority —a Workers and Farmers Government.

The Democratic and Republican parties are war parties of the rich; the Socialist Workers Party is the party of labor, of equality for all races, of peace and a prosperous life for all under the rational human system of socialism.

Your choice is clear. Resist the imperialist war! Resist the witch hunt!

Vote the SWP ticket! Vote for Dobbs and Weiss!

1. FOREIGN POLICY

The Socialist Workers Party proposes a foreign policy of peace, friendship and assistance to the peoples of the world. Instead of military bases, we advocate the building of factories, homes, schools, dams, parks and hospitals. We propose sending men abroad with tools, knowledge and skill instead of men with guns; we propose genuine aid to the people of less favored nations without making them satellites of our Big Business oligarchy. Above all we stand for the right of all peoples to establish governments of their own choice. We propose to stop the war drive and direct our foreign policy toward building a socialist world of peace and plenty.

Withdraw all U. S. troops from foreign soil. Get out of Korea. Recognize the new Chinese government.

Let the American people vote on war or peace. Give the vote to 18-year-olds. Old enough to fight —old enough to vote.

2. DEMOCRATIC RIGHTS

The bi-partisan war bloc wants to muzzle any-one who opposes the war drive. Roosevelt started the witch hunt with the Minneapolis prosecution against the 18 leaders of the Socialist Workers Party and Teamsters Local 544. Truman continued it with the purge of government workers, prosecutions against the Communist Party under the Smith Act, and loyalty oaths and "subversive" lists. The states picked up this campaign and extended it on a local basis. The Republican party, supporting all these measures, criticizes Truman for not going far enough. Any ideas which do not conform to the official policy of Washington are in effect being outlawed.

Stop the prosecution of political minorities for mere expression of opinion. Repeal the Smith Act. Amnesty for all victims of Smith Act prosecutions.

Rescind the "loyalty" program and the "subversive" list.

Repeal the McCarran "Concentration Camp" Law. Repeal the McCarran-Walters "Race-Hate" Immigration Law. Preserve the Bill of Rights for all.

3. EQUAL RIGHTS FOR ALL

The Negro people and other minority groups were promised an effective FEPC law by Truman in 1948. This promise has been betrayed. Intimidation of minorities has assumed new and even more terrible forms. Negro families are bombed in their homes. Leaders of the Negro people, like Harry T. Moore and his wife, are murdered. Police brutality against Negroes, Mexicans and Puerto Ricans has taken scores of victims. The federal government has done nothing to stop this. Those who defend minority rights are smeared and terrorized by the witch hunters.

Full social, political and economic equality for the Negro people. Smash the Jim Crow system. Wipe out the poll tax. Enact an FEPC Law with teeth. Abolish restrictive covenants in housing. Stop segregation wherever it exists. Enact a Federal Anti-Lynch Law.

Unite workers of all races for the common struggle against their exploiters.

4. WOMEN'S RIGHTS

The war economy is effecting a revolution in the character of the American family. The improvement in living standards of sections of the working class has occurred only through its greater exploitation. Inflation and taxes have increasingly necessitated the employment of two or more members of the family.

The startling fact that 20 million women are wage earners, constituting 20% of the employed population, reveals the extent of this trend. Of these working women, almost one-fourth are mothers with children under 18 years of age.

The especially oppressed position of women is graphically illustrated by this double exploitation, with the women responsible for the family at home and at the same time working to support the family.

The Socialist Workers Party champions the struggle of women for an end to discrimination of the job. We demand:

Equal pay for equal work. Adequate Federal nursery care and Federally supported summer camps for children of working mothers.

5. Organized Labor

The two party-coalition against labor has already dealt heavy blows to unionism. The Taft-Hartley law has hamstrung the campaign to organize the unorganized. Truman has broken more strikes than any other president. The Wage Stabilization Board machinery has effectively stalled union demands in hearings dominated by Big Business. The witch-hunt has victimized union militants.

The Socialist Workers Party stands for the repeal of all laws both federal and state, restricting labor's rights. We are for the abolition of injunctions and all forms of compulsory arbitration. We are for laws guaranteeing labor's right to organize and strike without government interference.

Repeal the Taft-Hartley Law. Repeal all state anti-labor laws.

6. Inflation

Inflation is one of the major enemies of the workers' standard of living. Chief cause of this disguised wage cutting is the huge war budget, and government-sponsored profiteering. Price increases, such as the boost in steel prices, are allowed by Big Business, while wages are curbed.

Abolish the wage freeze. Produce for peace, not for war.

For committees of unionists, housewives and small merchants authorized to stop profiteering and control prices and rents.

For a compulsory cost-of-living clause covering all wages, pensions and unemployment compensation, based upon a labor-controlled cost-of-living index which would include Federal, state and local taxes in computing living costs.

7. Taxes

The government's tax policy shifts the burden of war costs to the workers and low income groups. The billionaires are allowed to continue their record-breaking profits. Workers' wages are taxed in many forms, direct and indirect. Taxation is rapidly becoming the biggest menace to the standard of living won by American workers through years of struggle. What is won on the picket line is taken away by Washington.

Tax the rich and not the poor.

Abolish all taxes on incomes below $7,500 a year. Abolish all sales taxes. Stop the war profiteers by a 100% tax on all war-goods profits.

8. Security and Welfare

The so-called "Fair Deal" welfare program promised by Truman in 1948 has been put in moth balls. It was only a campaign promise. Now it is being taken out of storage for the 1952 campaign. The Republicans and Democrats will never enact a genuine public welfare program. Their program is billions for war, not for the social benefit of the people. The Socialist Workers Party proposes to use this country's great wealth to benefit the social welfare of the majority.

For the building of 20,000,000 low-cost housing units. For a national health service to provide free medical attention and hospitalization for all. For an adequate old age pension. For a Federal education program to guarantee a college education for all youth.

9. Militarism

Militarism more and more dominates our country. The Pentagon drains the nation of its wealth and its youth. The U.S. is dragged toward war by the two-party bloc and the brass hats. We are being transformed into a garrison state.

Stop the draft. Abolish the officer caste. For full democratic rights for the ranks in all the services. No troops to be sent abroad without a referendum of the people. Union wages for all service men.

For the right of unions to investigate conditions in the armed services and to protest against all undemocratic and oppressive actions of the officers.

10. Farm Policy

Establish a federal farm program to guarantee the cost of production to working farmers and to be operated under the control of their own representatives. Expand rural electrification. No limitation on crops. A federal program for soil conservation and flood control. No taxes on savings of co-operatives. A federal ban on all speculation in farm commodities. Abolish sharecropping and landlordism. The land to those who work it!

11. Government Ownership of Industry

Today the big trusts own and control the basic wealth of America. They run the government and decide the fate of our country.

Nationalize the basic industries, all war plants, all natural resources, and operate them in the interests of the producers and consumers by democratically-elected committees of workers and technicians.

Nationalize the banks. Institute a planned economy of abundance, based on production for use, not for profit.

12. Workers and Farmers Government

Labor has no representation in Washington. The Socialist Workers Party fights for the creation of a Labor Party which can unite the working people, farmers and professional people, and put a government in power which represents the majority.

The Socialist Workers Party alone consistently and unconditionally champions the interests of the workers in their struggles against capitalism and works for its abolition. This goal is concretely expressed in the Socialist Workers Party's fundamental objective in the 1952 campaign, the mobilization of the masses for a Workers and Farmers Government.

Only a Workers and Farmers Government can reorganize our society on a rational basis, and utilize the tremendous potential wealth and strength of our country for the benefit of humanity.

For a Workers and Farmers Government that will stop the drive toward World War III and reorganize America on a socialist basis!

☒ CAMPAIGN OF 1956

In 1956 the principal parties competing for the Presidency were the Democratic, Republican, Prohibition, Socialist, Socialist-Labor, and Socialist Workers. In mid-September, 317 delegates from several splinter groups representing voters in approximately half of the States gathered in Memphis, Tennessee, to form a "National Conservative Movement." Though the delegates supported the independent candidacy of T. Coleman Andrews for President, they voted against the formation of a third party and published only a declaration of principles instead of a platform. The Progressive Party of 1948 and 1952 did not offer a candidate in 1956.

Democratic Platform 1956

PREAMBLE

In the brief space of three and one-half years, the people of the United States have come to realize, with tragic consequences, that our National Government cannot be trusted to the hands of political amateurs, dominated by representatives of special privilege.

Four years ago they were beguiled, by empty promises and pledges, to elect as President a recent convert to Republicanism. Our people have now learned that the party of Lincoln has been made captive to big businessmen with small minds. They have found that they are now ruled by a Government which they did not elect, and to which they have not given their consent. Their awareness of this fact was demonstrated in 1954 when they returned control of the legislative machinery of the Federal Government to the 84th Democratic Congress.

From the wreckage of American world leadership under a Republican Administration, this great Democratic Congress has salvaged a portion of the world prestige our Nation enjoyed under the brilliant Administrations of Franklin Delano Roosevelt and Harry S. Truman.

Our Democratic 84th Congress made one of the greatest legislative records in the history of our country. It enacted an active program of progressive, humane legislation, which has repudiated the efforts of reactionary Republicanism to stall America's progress. When we return to the halls of Congress next January, and with a Democratic President in the White House, it will be the plan and purpose of our Party to complete restoration and rehabilitation of American leadership in world affairs. We pledge return of our National Government to its rightful owners, the people of the United States.

On the threshold of an atomic age, in mid-Twentieth Century, our beloved Nation needs the vision, vigor and vitality which can be infused into it only by a government under the Democratic Party.

We approach the forthcoming election with

a firm purpose of effecting such infusion; and with the help and assistance of Divine Providence we shall endeavor to accomplish it. To the end that the people it has served so well may know our program for the return of America to the highway of progress, the Democratic Party herewith submits its platform for 1956.

I. FOREIGN POLICY AND NATIONAL DEFENSE

The Democratic Party affirms that world peace is a primary objective of human society. Peace is more than a suspension of shooting while frenzied and fearful nations stockpile armaments of annihilation.

Achievement of world peace requires political statesmanship and economic wisdom, international understanding and dynamic leadership. True peace is the tranquillity of ordered justice on a global scale. It may be destroyed without a shot being fired. It can be fostered and preserved only by the solid unity and common brotherhood of the peoples of the world in the cause of freedom.

The hopes and aspirations of the peoples of all nations for justice and peace depend largely upon the courageous and enlightened administration of the foreign and defense policies of the United States. We deplore the fact that the administration of both policies since 1953 has confused timidity with courage, and blindness with enlightenment.

The Republican Record of Confusion and Complacency Is the President's Responsibility. The world's hopes for lasting peace depend upon the conduct of our foreign policy, a function which the Constitution vests in the President of the United States and one which has not been effectively exercised by President Eisenhower. Since 1953, responsibility for foreign affairs has been President Eisenhower's, his alone, and his in full.

In the past three years, his conduct of our policies has moved us into realms where we risk grave danger. He has failed to seek peace with determination, for his disarmament policy has failed to strike hard at the institution of war. His handling of the day-by-day problems of international affairs has unnecessarily and dangerously subjected the American people to the risk of atomic world war.

Our Government Lacks Leadership. We need bold leadership, yet in the three years since Stalin's death, in the full year since President Eisenhower's meeting at the "summit," the Republican Administration has not offered a single concrete new idea to meet the new-style political and economic offensive of the Soviets, which represents, potentially, an even graver challenge than Stalin's use of force. President Eisenhower and his Secretary of State talk at cross-purposes, praising neutralism one day, condemning it the next. The Republicans seem unable either to make up their minds or to give us leadership, while the unity of the free world rapidly disintegrates.

We in America need to make our peaceful purpose clear beyond dispute in every corner of the world—yet Secretary Dulles brags of "brinks of war." We need a foreign policy which rises above jockeying for partisan position or advantage—yet, not in memory has there been so little bipartisanship in the administration of our policies, so little candor in their presentation to our people, so much pretending that things are better than they are.

The Republican Bluster and Bluff. Four years ago the Republican Party boasted of being able to produce a foreign policy which was to free the Communist satellites, unleash Chiang Kai-shek, repudiate the wartime agreements, and reverse the policy of containing Communist expansion.

Since 1953 they have done just the opposite, standing silent when the peoples rise in East Germany and Poland, and thereby weakening the positive Democratic policy of halting Communist expansion.

Our Friends Lose Faith In Us. Our friends abroad now doubt our sincerity. They have seen the solid assurance of collective security under a Democratic Administration give place to the uncertainties of personal diplomacy. They have seen the ties of our international alliances and friendship weakened by inept Republican maneuvering.

They have seen traditional action and boldness in foreign affairs evaporate into Republican complacency, retrenchment and empty posturing.

The Failure Abroad. Blustering without dynamic action will not alter the fact that the unity and strength of the free world have been drastically impaired. Witness the decline of NATO, the bitter tragedy of Cyprus, the withdrawal of French forces to North Africa, the uncertainty and dangers in the Middle East, an uncertain and insecure Germany, and resentment rising against United States leadership everywhere.

In Asia—in Burma, Ceylon, Indonesia, India—anti-Americanism grows apace, aggravated by the clumsy actions of our Government, and fanned by the inept utterances of our "statesmen."

In the Middle East, the Eisenhower Administration has dawdled and drifted. The results have been disastrous, and worse threatens. Only the good offices of the United Nations in maintaining peace between Israel and her neighbors conceal the diplomatic incapacities of the Republican Administration. The current crisis over Suez is a consequence of inept and vacillating Republican policy. Our Government's mistakes have placed us in a position in the Middle East which threatens the free world with a loss of power and prestige, potentially more dangerous than any we have suffered in the past decade.

The Failure at Home. Political considerations of budget balancing and tax reduction now come before the wants of our national security and the needs of our Allies. The Republicans have slashed our own armed strength, weakened our capacity to deal with military threats, stifled our air force, starved our army and weakened our capacity to deal with aggression of any sort save by retreat or by the alternatives, "massive retaliation" and global atomic war. Yet, while our troubles mount, they tell us our prestige was never higher, they tell us we were never more secure.

The Challenge Is For Democracy to Meet. The Democratic Party believes that "waging peace" is a monumental task to be performed honestly, forthrightly, with dedication and consistent effort.

The way to lasting peace is to forego bluster and bluff, to regain steadiness of purpose, to join again in faithful concert with the community of free nations, to look realistically at the challenging circumstances which confront us, to face them candidly and imaginatively, and to return to the Democratic policy of peace through strength.

This is a task for Democrats. This facing of new problems, this rising to new challenges, has been our Party's mission and its glory for three generations past. President Truman met and mastered Stalin's challenge a decade ago, with boldness, courage and imagination, and so will we turn to the challenge before us now, pressing the search for real and lasting peace. TO THIS WE PLEDGE:

Support for the United Nations. The United Nations is indispensable for the maintenance of world peace and for the settlement of controversies between nations small and large. We pledge our every effort to strengthen its usefulness and expand its role as guide and guardian of international security and peace. We deplore the Republicans' tendency to use the United Nations only when it suits them, ignoring or by passing it whenever they please.

We pledge determined opposition to the admission of the Communist Chinese into the United Nations. They have proven their complete hostility to the purposes of this organization. We pledge continued support to Nationalist China.

Release of American Prisoners. We urge a continuing effort to effect the release of all Americans detained by Communist China.

Support for Effective Disarmament. In this atomic age, war threatens the very survival of civilization. To eliminate the danger of atomic war, a universal, effective and enforced disarmament system must be the goal of responsible men and women everywhere. So long as we lack enforceable international control of weapons, we must maintain armed strength to avoid war. But technological advances in the field of nuclear weapons make disarmament an ever more urgent problem. Time and distance can never again protect any nation of the world. The Eisenhower Administration, despite its highly publicized proposals for aerial inspection, has made no progress toward this great objective. We pledge the Democratic Party to pursue vigorously this great goal of enforced disarmament in full awareness that irreparable injury, even total destruction, now threatens the human race.

Adequate Defense Forces. We reject the false Republican notion that this country can afford only a second-best defense. We stand for strong defense forces so clearly superior in modern weapons to those of any possible enemy that our armed strength will make an attack upon the free world unthinkable, and thus be a major force for world peace. The Republican Administration stands indicted for failing to recognize the necessity of proper living standards for the men and women of our armed forces and their families. We pledge ourselves to the betterment of the living conditions of the members of our armed services, and to a needed increase in the so-called "fringe benefits."

Training for Defense. The Democratic Party pledges itself to a bold and imaginative program devised to utilize fully the brain power of America's youth, including its talent in the scientific and technical fields.

Scholarships and loan assistance and such other steps as may be determined desirable must be employed to secure this objective. This is solely in the interest of necessary and adequate national defense.

Strengthening Civil Defense. We believe that a strong, effective civil defense is a necessary part of national defense. Advances in nuclear weapons have made existing civil defense legislation and practices obsolete.

We pledge ourselves to establish a real program for protecting the civilian population and industry of our Nation in place of the present weak and ineffective program. We believe that this is essentially a Federal responsibility.

Collective Security Arrangements. The Democratic Party inaugurated and we strongly favor collective defense arrangements, such as NATO and the Organization of American States, within the framework of the United Nations. We realize, as the Republicans have not, that mutually recognized common interests can be flexibly adapted to the varied needs and aspirations of all countries concerned.

Winning the Productivity Race. The Republican Party has not grasped one of the dominant facts of mid-century—that the growth of productive power of the Communist states presents a challenge which cannot be evaded. The Democratic Party is confident that, through the freedom we enjoy, a vast increase in productive power of our Nation and our Allies will be achieved, and by their combined capacity they will surmount any challenge.

Economic Development Abroad. We believe that, in the cause of peace, America must support the efforts of underdeveloped countries on a co-operative basis to organize their own resources and to increase their own economic productivity, so that they may enjoy the higher living standards which science and modern industry make possible. We will give renewed strength to programs of economic and technical assistance. We support a multilateral approach to these programs, wherever possible, so that burdens are shared and resources pooled among all the economically developed countries with the capital and skills to help in this great task.

Further, while recognizing the relation of our national security to the role of the United States in international affairs, the Democratic Party believes the time has come for a realistic reappraisal of the American foreign aid program, particularly as to its extent and the conditions under which it should be continued. This reappraisal will determine the standards by which further aid shall be granted, keeping in mind America's prime objective of securing world peace.

Bringing the Truth to the World. The tools of truth and candor are even more important than economic tools. The Democratic Party believes that once our Government is purged of the confusion and complacency fostered by the Republican Administration a new image of America will emerge in the world: the image of a confident America dedicated to its traditional principles, eager to work with other peoples, honest in its pronouncements, and consistent in its policies.

Freedom for Captive Nations. We condemn the Republican Administration for its heartless record of broken promises to the unfortunate victims of Communism. Candidate Eisenhower's 1952 pledges to "liberate" the captive peoples have been disavowed and dishonored.

We declare our deepest concern for the plight of the freedom-loving peoples of Central and Eastern Europe and of Asia, now under the yoke of Soviet dictatorship. The United States, under Democratic leaders, has never recognized the forcible annexation of Lithuania, Latvia, and Estonia, or condoned the extension of the Kremlin's tyranny over Poland, Bulgaria, Rumania, Czechoslovakia, Hungary, Albania and other countries.

We look forward to the day when the liberties of all captive nations will be restored to them and they can again take their rightful place in the community of free nations.

We shall press before the United Nations the principle that Soviet Russia withdraw its troops from the captive countries, so as to permit free, fair and unfettered elections in the subjugated areas, in compliance with the Atlantic Charter and other binding commitments.

Upholding the Principle of Self-Determination. We rededicate ourselves to the high principle of national self-determination, as enunciated by Woodrow Wilson, whose leadership brought freedom and independence to uncounted millions.

It is the policy of the Democratic Party, therefore, to encourage and assist small nations and all peoples, behind the Iron Curtain and outside, in the peaceful and orderly achievement of their legitimate aspirations toward political, geographical, and ethnic integrity, so that they may dwell in the family of sovereign nations with freedom and dignity. We are opposed to colonialism and Communist imperialism.

We shall endeavor to apply this principle to the desires of all peoples for self-determination.

Reciprocal Trade Among the Nations. The Democratic Party has always worked for expanding trade among free nations. Expanding world trade is necessary not only for our friends, but for ourselves; it is the way to meet America's growing need for industrial raw materials. We shall continue to support vigorously the Hull Reciprocal Trade Program.

Under Democratic Administrations, the operation of this Act was conducted in a manner that recognized equities for agriculture, industry and labor. Under the present Republican Administration, there has been a most flagrant disregard of these important segments of our economy resulting in serious economic injury to hundreds of thousands of Americans engaged in these pursuits. We pledge correction of these conditions.

Encouraging European Unity. Through the Marshall Plan, the European Economic Organization and NATO, the Democratic Party encouraged and supported efforts to achieve greater economic and political unity among the free nations of Europe, and to increase the solidarity of the nations of the North Atlantic community. We will continue those efforts, taking into account the viewpoints and aspirations of different sectors of the European community, particularly in regard to practical proposals for the unification of Germany.

Peace and Justice in the Middle East. The Democratic Party stands for the maintenance of peace in the Middle East, which is essential to the well-being and progress of all its peoples.

We will urge Israel and the Arab States to settle their differences by peaceful means, and to maintain the sanctity of the Holy Places in the Holy Land and permit free access to them.

We will assist Israel to build a sound and viable economy for her people, so that she may fulfill her humanitarian mission of providing shelter and sanctuary for her homeless Jewish refugees while strengthening her national development.

We will assist the Arab States to develop their economic resources and raise the living standards of their people. The plight of the Arab refugees commands our continuing sympathy and concern. We will assist in carrying out large-scale projects for their resettlement in countries where there is room and opportunity for them.

We support the principle of free access to the Suez Canal under suitable international auspices. The present policies of the Eisenhower Administration in the Middle East are unnecessarily increasing the risk that war will break out in this area. To prevent war, to assure peace, we will faithfully carry out our country's pledge under the Tripartite Declaration of 1950 to oppose the use or threat of force and to take such action as may be necessary in the interest of peace, both within and outside the United Nations, to prevent any violation of the frontiers of any armistice lines.

The Democratic Party will act to redress the dangerous imbalance of arms in the area resulting from the shipment of Communist arms to Egypt, by selling or supplying defensive weapons to Israel, and will take such steps, including security guarantees, as may be required to deter aggression and war in the area.

We oppose, as contrary to American principles, the practice of any government which discriminates against American citizens on grounds of race or religion. We will not countenance any arrangement or treaty with any government which by its terms or in its practical application would sanction such practices.

Support for Free Asia. The people of Asia seek a new and freer life and they are in a commendable hurry to get it. They struggle against poverty, ill health and illiteracy. In the aftermath of war, China became a victim of Communist tyranny. But many new free nations have arisen in South and Southeast Asia. South Korea remains free, and the new Japan has abandoned her former imperial and aggressive ways. America's task and interest in Asia is to help the governments of free peoples demonstrate that they have improved living standards without yielding to Communist tyranny or domination by anyone. That task will be carried out under Democratic leadership.

Support of Our Good Neighbors to the South. In the Western Hemisphere the Democratic Party will restore the policy of the "good neighbor" which has been alternately neglected and abused by the Republican Administration. We pledge ourselves to fortify the defenses of the Americas. In this respect, we will intensify our cooperation with our neighboring republics to help them strengthen their economies, improve educational opportunities, and combat disease. We will strive to make the Western Hemisphere an inspiring example of what free peoples working together can accomplish.

Progressive Immigration Policies. America's long tradition of hospitality and asylum for those seeking freedom, opportunity, and escape from oppression, has been besmirched by the delays, failures and broken promises of the Republican Administration. The Democratic Party favors prompt revision of the immigration and nationality laws to eliminate unfair provisions under which admissions to this country depend upon quotas based upon the accident of national origin. Proper safeguards against subversive elements should be provided. Our immigration procedures must reflect the principles of our Bill of Rights.

We favor eliminating the provisions of law which charge displaced persons admitted to our shores against quotas for future years. Through such "mortgages" of future quotas, thousands of qualified persons are being forced to wait long years before they can hope for admission.

We also favor more liberal admission of relatives to eliminate the unnecessary tragedies of broken families.

We favor elimination of unnecessary distinctions between native-born and naturalized citizens. There should be no "second class" citizenship in the United States.

The administration of the Refugee Relief Act of 1953 has been a disgrace to our country. Rescue has been denied to innocent, defenseless and suffering people, the victims of war and the aftermath of wars. The purpose of the Act has been defeated by Republican mismanagement.

Victims of Communist Oppression. We will continue to support programs providing succor for escapees from behind the Iron Curtain, and bringing help to the victims of war and Communist oppression.

The Challenge of the Next Four Years. Today new challenges call for new ideas and new methods.

In the coming years, our great necessity will be to pull together as a people, with true non-partisanship in foreign affairs under leaders informed, courageous and responsible.

We shall need to work closely with each other as Americans. If we here indict the Republican record, we acknowledge gratefully the efforts of individual Republicans to achieve true bipartisanship. In this spirit an affirmative, cooperative policy can be developed. We shall need to work closely, also, with others all around the world. For there is much to do—to create once more the will and the power to transform the principles of the United Nations into a living reality; to awaken ourselves and others to the effort and sacrifice which alone can win justice and peace.

II. The Domestic Policy—The Republican Reaction to 20 Years of Progress

The Democratic Bequest. Twenty years of vivid Democratic accomplishments revived and reinforced our economic system, and wrote humanity upon the statute books. All this, the current Republican Administration inherited.

The Republican Brand of Prosperity. Substituting deceptive slogans and dismal deeds for the Democratic program, the Republicans have been telling the American people that "we are now more prosperous than ever before in peacetime." For the American farmer, the small businessman and the low-income worker, the old people living on a pittance, the young people seeking an American standard of education, and the minority groups seeking full employment opportunity at adequate wages, this tall tale of Republican prosperity has been an illusion.

The evil is slowly but surely infiltrating the entire economic system. Its fever signs are evidenced by soaring monopoly profits, while wages lag, farm income collapses, and small-business failures multiply at an alarming rate.

The first time-bomb of the Republican crusade against full prosperity for all was the hard-money policy. This has increased the debt burden on depressed farms, saddled heavier costs on small business, foisted higher interest charges on millions of homeowners (including veterans), pushed up unnecessarily the cost of consumer credit, and swelled the inordinate profits of a few lenders of money. It has wrought havoc with the bond market, with resulting financial loss to the ordinary owners of Government bonds.

The Republican tax policy has joined hands in an unholy alliance with the hard-money policy.

Fantastic misrepresentation of the Government's budgetary position has been used to deny tax relief to low- and middle-income families, while tax concessions and handouts have been generously sprinkled among potential campaign contributors to Republican coffers. The disastrously reactionary farm program, the hardhearted resistance to adequate expansion of Social Security and other programs for human well-being, and favoritism in the award of Government contracts, all have watered the economic tree at the top and neglected its roots.

The Stunting of Our Economic Progress. The Republicans say that employment and production are "higher" than ever before. The fact is that our over-all rate of growth has been crippled and stunted in contrast to its faster increase during the Democratic years from 1947 to 1953, after World War II.

With production lagging behind full capacity, unemployment has grown.

The Republican claim that this stunted prosperity is the price of peace is a distortion. National-security outlays have averaged a higher part of our total production during these Republican years than during 1947-53, and yet the annual growth in total production during these Republican years has been only about 60 percent as fast as in the preceding Democratic years. The progress of low-income families toward an American standard of living, rapid during the Democratic years, has ground to a stop under the Republicans.

Federal budgetary outlays for education and health, old-age assistance and child care, slum clearance and resource development, and all the other great needs of our people have been mercilessly slashed from an annual rate of more than $57 per capita under the Democrats to $33 per capita under the Republicans, a cut of 42 percent.

The Failure of the Republican Budget-Balancers. During the Republican fiscal years 1954-1957 as a whole, the deficits have averaged larger, and the surpluses smaller, than during the Democratic fiscal years 1947-1953, financial manipulation to the contrary notwithstanding.

Democratic Principles for Full Prosperity for All:

(1) We repudiate the Republican stunting of our economic growth, and we reassert the principles of the Full Employment Act of 1946;

(2) We pledge ourselves to achieve an honest and realistic balance of the Federal Budget in a just and fully prosperous American economy;

(3) We pledge ourselves to equitable tax revisions and monetary policies designed to combine economic progress with economic justice. We condemn the Republican use of our revenue and money systems to benefit the few at the expense of the vast majority of our people;

(4) We pledge ourselves to work toward the reduction and elimination of poverty in America;

(5) We pledge ourselves to full parity of income and living standards for agriculture; to strike off the shackles which the Taft-Hartley law has unjustly imposed on labor; and to foster the more rapid growth of legitimate business enterprise by founding this growth upon the expanding consuming power of the people; and

(6) We pledge ourselves to expand world trade and to enlarge international economic cooperation, all toward the end of a more prosperous and more peaceful world.

Democratic Goals To Be Achieved During Four Years of Progress. By adhering to these principles, we shall strive to attain by 1960 the following full prosperity objectives for all American families:

(1) A 500 billion dollar national economy in real terms;

(2) An increase of 20 percent or better in the average standard of living;

(3) An increase in the annual income of American families, with special emphasis on those whose incomes are below $2000;

(4) A determined drive toward parity of incomes and living standards for those engaged in the vital pursuit of agriculture;

(5) The addition of all necessary classrooms for our primary and secondary schools; the construction of needed new homes, with a proper proportion devoted to the rehousing of low- and middle-income families in urban and rural areas; the increase of benefits under the Old Age Assistance and Old Age Survivors Insurance Programs; a substantial expansion in hospital facilities and medical research; and a doubling of our programs for resource development and conservation; and

(6) National defense outlays based upon our national needs, not permitting false economy to jeopardize our very survival.

This country of ours, in the factory, in business

and on the farm, is blessed with ever-increasing productive power. The Republicans have not permitted this potential abundance to be released for the mutual benefit of all. We reject this stunted Republican concept of America. We pledge ourselves to release the springs of abundance, to bring this abundance to all, and thus to fulfill the full promise of America.

These are our Democratic goals for the next four years. We set them forth in vivid contrast to Republican lip-service protestations that they, too, are for these goals. Their little deeds belie their large and hollow slogans. Our performance in the past gives validity to our goals for the future.

Our victory in 1956 will make way for the commencement of these four years of progress.

III. FREE ENTERPRISE

"Equal rights for all and special privileges for none," the tested Jeffersonian principle, remains today the only philosophy by which human rights can be preserved by government.

It is a sad fact in the history of the Republican Party that, under its control, our Government has always become an instrument of special privilege; not a government of the people, by the people, and for the people. We have had, instead, under Harding, Coolidge and Hoover, and now under Eisenhower, government of the many, by the few, and for the few.

We recognize monopolies and monopolistic practices as the real barriers between the people and their economic and political freedom. Monopolies act to stifle equality of opportunity and prevent the infusion of fresh blood into the lifestream of our economy. The Republican Administration has allowed giant corporate entities to dominate our economy. For example, forty thousand automobile dealers now know they were incapable of coping with these giants. They were, as the Democratic 84th Congress found, subjected to abuse and threatened with extinction. The result was passage of the O'Mahoney-Celler bill giving the automobile dealers of America economic freedom. We enacted this law, and we pledge that it shall be retained upon the statute books as a monument to the Democratic Party's concern for small business.

We pledge ourselves to the restoration of truly competitive conditions in American industry. Affirmative action within the framework of American tradition will be taken to curb corporate mergers that would contribute to the growth of economic concentration.

Small and Independent Business. In contrast to the maladministration by the Republican Party of the Federal program to assist small and independent business, we pledge ourselves—

(1) To the strict and impartial enforcement of the laws originally fostered and strengthened by the Democratic Party and designed to prevent monopolies and other concentrations of economic and financial power; and to enact legislation to close loopholes in the laws prohibiting price discrimination;

(2) To tax relief for all small and independent businesses by fair and equitable adjustments in Federal taxation which will encourage business expansion, and to the realistic application of the principle of graduated taxation to such corporate income. An option should be provided to spread Federal estate taxes over a period of years when an estate consists principally of the equity capital of a closely held small business;

(3) To adoption of all practical means of making long- and short-term credit available to small and independent businessmen at reasonable rates;

(4) To the award of a substantially higher proportion of Government contracts to independent small businesses, and to the award of a far larger percentage of military procurement, by value, after competitive bids rather than by negotiation behind closed doors. We severely condemn Republican discrimination against small and independent business;

(5) To replacement of the weak and ineffective Republican conduct of the Small Business Administration, and its reconstitution as a vigorous, independent agency which will advocate the cause of small and independent businessmen, and render genuine assistance in fulfilling their needs and solving their problems. We condemn the Republican Administration for its failure to serve this important segment of our economy.

Law Enforcement. We pledge ourselves to the fair and impartial administration of justice. The Republican Administration has degraded the great powers of law enforcement. It has not used them in the service of equal justice under law, but for concealment, coercion, persecution, political advantage and special interests.

Merchant Marine. In the interest of our national security, and of the maintenance of American standards of wages and living, and in order that our waterborne overseas commerce shall not be unfairly discriminated against by low-cost foreign competition, we pledge our continued encouragement and support of a strong and adequate American Merchant Marine.

Transportation. The public and national defense interests require the development and maintenance, under the competitive free enterprise system, of a strong, efficient and financially sound system of common-carrier transportation by water, highway, rail, and air, with each mode enabled, through sound and intelligent exercise of regulatory powers, to realize its inherent economic advantages and to reflect its full competitive capabilities. Public interest also requires, under reasonable standards, the admission of new licensees, where public convenience may be served, into the transport fields. We deplore the lack of enforcement of safety regulations for protection of life and property under the present Republican Administration, and pledge strict enforcement of such regulations.

Highways. We commend the foresight of the Democratic 84th Congress for its enactment of the greatest program in history for expansion of our highway network, and we congratulate it upon its rejection of the unsound, unworkable, inadequate and unfair roads bill proposed by the present Republican Administration. In cooperation with state and local governments, we will continue the programs developed and fostered under prior Democratic Administrations for planning, coordinating, financing and encouraging the expansion of our national road and highway network so vital to defense and transportation in the motor age. We support expansion of farm-to-market roads.

Rivers and Harbors. We pledge continued development of harbors and waterways as a vital segment of our transportation system. We denounce as capricious and arbitrary the Eisenhower pocket veto of the 1956 Rivers and Harbors bill, which heartlessly deprived the people in many sections of our country of vitally needed public works projects.

IV. A MAGNA CHARTA FOR LABOR

Labor-Management Relations. Harmonious labor-management relations are productive of good incomes for wage earners and conducive to rising output from our factories. We believe that, to the widest possible extent consistent with the public interest, management and labor should determine wage rates and conditions of employment through free collective bargaining.

The Taft-Hartley Act passed by the Republican-dominated 80th Congress seriously impaired this relationship as established in the Wagner National Labor Relations Act, enacted under the Roosevelt Administration. The Wagner Act protected, encouraged and guaranteed the rights of workers to organize, to join unions of their own choice, and to bargain collectively through these unions without coercion.

The vicious anti-union character of the Taft-Hartley Act was expressly recognized by Candidate Eisenhower during the 1952 election campaign.

At that time, he made a solemn promise to eliminate its unjust provisions and to enact a fair law. President Eisenhower and his Administration have failed utterly, however, to display any executive initiative or forcefulness toward keeping this pledge to the workers. He was further responsible for administratively amending Taft-Hartley into a more intensely anti-labor weapon by stacking the National Labor Relations Board with biased pro-management personnel who, by administrative decision, transformed the Act into a management weapon. One such decision removed millions of workers from the jurisdiction of the NLRB, which in many cases left them without protection of either State or Federal legislation.

We unequivocally advocate repeal of the Taft-Hartley Act. The Act must be repealed because State "right-to-work" laws have their genesis in its discriminatory anti-labor provisions.

It must be repealed because its restrictive provisions deny the principle that national legislation based on the commerce clause of the Constitution normally overrides conflicting State laws.

The Taft-Hartley Act has been proven to be inadequate, unworkable and unfair. It interferes in an arbitrary manner with collective bargaining, causing imbalance in the relationship between management and labor.

Upon return of our National Government to the Democratic Party, a new legislative approach toward the entire labor-management problem will be adopted, based on past experience and the principles of the Wagner National Labor Relations Act and the Norris-La Guardia Anti-Injunction Law.

Fair Labor Standards. We commend the action of the Democratic 84th Congress which raised the minimum wage from 75 cents to $1.00 an hour despite the strenuous objection of President Eisenhower and the Republicans in Congress. However, the inadequacies of the minimum wage become apparent as the cost of living increases, and we feel it imperative to raise the minimum wage to at least $1.25 an hour, in order to approximate present-day needs more closely.

We further pledge as a matter of priority to extend full protection of the Fair Labor Standards Act to all workers in industry engaged in, or affecting, interstate commerce.

Walsh-Healey Contracts Act. We pledge revision and honest administration of the Walsh-Healey Act, to restore its effectiveness and usefulness as an instrument for maintaining fair standards of wages and hours for American workers.

Equal Pay for Equal Work. We advocate legislation to provide equal pay for equal work, regardless of sex.

The Physically Handicapped. The Democratic Party has always supported legislation to benefit the disabled worker. The physically handicapped have proved their value to Government and industry. We pledge our continued support of legislation to improve employment opportunities of physically handicapped persons.

Migratory Workers. We shall support legislation providing for the protection and improvement of the general welfare of migratory workers.

Jobs for Depressed Areas. We pledge our Party to support legislation providing for an effective program to promote industry and create jobs in depressed industrial and rural areas so that such areas may be restored to economic stability.

V. AGRICULTURE

Sustained national prosperity is dependent upon a vigorous agricultural economy.

We condemn the defeatist attitude of the Eisenhower Administration in refusing to take effective action to assure the well-being of farm families. We condemn its fear of abundance, its lack of initiative in developing domestic markets, and its dismal failure to obtain for the American farmer his traditional and deserved share of the world market. Its extravagant ex-penditure of money intended for agricultural benefit, without either direction or results, is a national calamity.

The Eisenhower Administration has failed utterly to develop any programs to meet the desperate needs of farmers in the face of fantastic promises, and it has sabotaged the progressive programs inherited from prior Democratic Administrations by failing to administer them properly in the interest either of farmers or of the Nation as a whole.

Specifically, we denounce President Eisenhower's veto of the constructive legislation proposed and passed by the Democratic 84th Congress to reverse the alarming fall of farm prices and restore farmers to a position of first-class economic citizenship in the sharing of benefits from American productive ability.

We also condemn the Republican Administration for its abandonment of the true principles of soil conservation and for its destruction of the Soil Conservation Service. We pledge to support continued improvements in the soil bank program passed by the Democratic 84th Congress and originally opposed by President Eisenhower and Secretary Ezra Taft Benson. We deplore the diversion of this conservation program into a direct vote-buying scheme.

Farmers have had to struggle for three and one-half years while their net farm income has fallen more than one billion dollars a year. Their parity ratio, which under Democratic Administrations had been 100 percent or more during the eleven years prior to 1953, dropped to as low as 80 percent during the Eisenhower Administration, and the farmers' share of the consumers' food dollar shrank from 47 cents in 1952 to as low as only 38 cents. One stark fact stands out clearly for all to see—disastrously low farm prices and record high consumer prices vie with each other for the attention of responsible government. In a reduction of this incongruous spread lies the answer to some of the most vexing problems of agricultural economics.

In their courageous fight to save their homes and land, American farmers have gone deeper and deeper into debt. Last year farmers' mortgage indebtedness increased more than in any year in history with the exception of the year 1923.

The Democratic Party met similar situations forthrightly in the past with concrete remedial action. It takes legitimate pride in its consistent record of initiating and developing every constructive program designed to protect and conserve the human and natural resources so vital to our rural economy. These programs enabled consumers to obtain more abundant supplies of high-quality food and fiber at reasonable prices while maintaining adequate income for farmers and improving the level of family living in rural areas.

In order to regain the ground lost during the Eisenhower Administration, and in order better to serve both consumers and producers, the Democratic Party pledges continuous and vigorous support to the following policies:

Sponsor a positive and comprehensive program to conserve our soil, water and forest resources for future generations;

Promote programs which will protect and preserve the family-type farm as a bulwark of American life, and encourage farm-home ownership, including additional assistance to family farmers and young farmers in the form of specially designed credit and price-support programs, technical aid, and enlarged soil conservation allowances.

Maintain adequate reserves of agricultural commodities strategically situated, for national security purposes. Such stockpiles should be handled as necessary strategic reserves, so that farmers will not be penalized by depressed prices for their efficiency and diligence in producing abundance;

Promote international exchange of commodities by creating an International Food Reserve, fostering commodity agreements, and vigorously administering the Foreign Agricultural Trade Development and Assistance Act;

Undertake immediately by appropriate action to endeavor to regain the full 100 percent of parity the farmers received under the Democratic Administrations. We will achieve this by means of supports on basic commodities at 90 percent of parity and by means of commodity loans, direct purchases, direct payments to producers, marketing agreements and orders, production adjustments, or a combination of these, including legislation, to bring order and stability into the relationship between the producer, the processor and the consumer;

Develop practical measures for extending price supports to feed grains and other nonbasic storables and to the producers of perishable commodities such as meat, poultry, dairy products and the like;

Inaugurate a food-stamp or other supplemental food program administered by appropriate State or local agencies to insure that no needy family shall be denied an adequate and wholesome diet because of low income;

Continue and expand school lunch and special milk programs to meet the dietary needs of all school children;

Increase the distribution of food to public institutions and organizations and qualified private charitable agencies, and increase the distribution of food and fiber to needy people in other nations through recognized charitable and religious channels;

Devise and employ effective means to reduce the spread between producers' prices and consumers' costs, and improve market facilities and marketing practices;

Expand the program of agricultural research and education for better distribution, preservation and marketing of farm products to serve both producers and consumers, and promote increased industrial use of farm surpluses;

Provide for an increased reservoir of farm credit at lower rates, designed particularly to accommodate operators of small family-type farms, and extend crop insurance to maximum coverage and protection;

Return the administration of farm programs to farmer-elected committeemen, eliminate the deplorable political abuses in Federal employment in many agricultural counties as practiced by the Eisenhower Administration, and restore leadership to the administration of soil conservation districts;

Insure reliable and low-cost rural electric and telephone service;

Exercise authority in existing law relating to imports of price-supported agricultural commodities in raw, manufactured or processed form as part of our national policy to minimize damage to our domestic economy;

Encourage bona fide farm cooperatives which help farmers reduce the cost-price squeeze, and protect such cooperatives against punitive taxation;

Expand farm forestry marketing research and price reporting on timber products, and provide adequate credit designed to meet the needs of timber farmers; and

Enact a comprehensive farm program which, under intelligent and sympathetic Democratic administration, will make the rural homes of America better and healthier places in which to live.

VI. General Welfare

The Democratic Party believes that America can and must adopt measures to assure every citizen an opportunity for a full, healthy and happy life. To this end, we pledge ourselves to the expansion and improvement of the great social welfare programs inaugurated under Democratic Administrations.

Social Security. By lowering the retirement age for women and for disabled persons, the Democratic 84th Congress pioneered two great advances in Social Security, over the bitter opposition of the Eisenhower Administration. We shall continue our efforts to broaden and strengthen this program by increasing benefits to keep pace with improving standards of living; by raising the wage base upon which benefits depend; and by increasing benefits for each year of covered employment.

Unemployment Insurance. We shall continue to work for a stronger unemployment insurance system, with broader coverage and increased benefits consistent with rising earnings. We shall also work for the establishment of a floor to assure minimum level and duration of benefits, and fair eligibility rules.

Wage Losses Due to Illness. In 1946, a Democratic Congress enacted an insurance program to protect railroad workers against temporary wage losses due to short-term illnesses. Because this program has worked so effectively, we favor extending similar protection to other workers.

Public Assistance. We pledge improvements in the public assistance program even beyond those enacted by the Democratic 84th Congress, through increased aid for the aged, the blind, dependent children, the disabled and other needy persons who are not adequately protected by our contributory insurance programs.

Additional Needs of Our Senior Citizens. To meet the needs of the 14 million Americans aged 65 or over, we pledge ourselves to seek means of assuring these citizens greater income through expanded opportunities for employment, vocational retraining and adult education; better housing and health services for the aged; rehabilitation of the physically and mentally disabled to restore them to independent, productive lives; and intensified medical and other research aimed both at lengthening life and making the longer life more truly livable.

Health and Medical Care. The strength of our Nation depends on the health of our people. The shortage of trained medical and health personnel and facilities has impaired American health standards and has increased the cost of hospital care beyond the financial capacities of most American families.

We pledge ourselves to initiate programs of Federal financial aid, without Federal controls, for medical education.

We pledge continuing and increased support for hospital construction programs, as well as increased Federal aid to public health services, particularly in rural areas.

Medical research. Mindful of the dramatic progress made by medical research in recent years, we shall continue to support vigorously all efforts, both public and private, to wage relentless war on diseases which afflict the bodies and minds of men. We commend the Democratic Party for its leadership in obtaining greater Congressional authorizations in this field.

Housing. We pledge our Party to immediate revival of the basic housing program enacted by the Democratic Congress in 1949, to expansion of this program as our population and resources grow, and to additional legislation to provide housing for middle-income families and aged persons. Aware of the financial burdens which press upon most American communities and prevent them from taking full advantage of Federal urban redevelopment and renewal programs, we favor increasing the Federal share of the cost of these programs.

We reaffirm the goal expressed by a Democratic Congress in 1949 that every American family is entitled to a "decent home and a suitable living environment." The Republican Administration has sabotaged that goal by reducing the public housing program to a fraction of the Nation's need.

We pledge that the housing insurance and mortgage guarantee programs will be redirected in the interest of the home owner, and that the availability of low-interest housing credit will be kept consistent with the expanding housing needs of the Nation.

We favor providing aid to urban and suburban communities in better planning for their future development and redevelopment.

Education. Every American child, irrespective of race or national origin, economic status or place of residence, has full right under the law and the Constitution, without discrimination, to every educational opportunity for developing his potentialities.

We are now faced with shortages of educational facilities that threaten national security, economic prosperity and human well-being. The resources of our States and localities are already strained to the limit. Federal aid and action should be provided, within the traditional framework of State and local control.

We pledge the Democratic Party to the following:

(1) Legislation providing Federal financing to assist States and local communities to build schools, and to provide essential health and safety services for all school children;

(2) Better educational, health and welfare opportunities for children of migratory workers;

(3) Assistance to programs for training teachers of exceptional children;

(4) Programs providing for the training of teachers to meet the critical shortage in technical and scientific fields; and

(5) Expansion of the program of student, teacher and cultural exchange with other nations.

Vocational Education. We commend the 84th Congress for voting the maximum authorized funds for vocational education under the Smith-Hughes Act for the first time in the history of the Act. We pledge continuing and increased support of vocational training for youth and adults, including aid to the States and localities for area technical-vocational schools.

Child Welfare. To keep pace with the growing need for child care and welfare, we pledge an expanded program of grants to the States. We pledge continued support of adequate day care centers to care for the children of the millions of American mothers who work to help support their families.

Aid to the Physically Handicapped. There are today several million physically handicapped citizens, many of whom could become self-supporting if given the opportunity and training for rehabilitation. We pledge support to a vastly expanded rehabilitation program for these physically handicapped, including increased aid to the States, in contrast to the grossly inadequate action of the Republican Administration.

VII. FINANCIAL POLICY

Tax Adjustment. A fully expanding economy can yield enough tax revenues to meet the inescapable obligations of government, balance the Federal Budget, and lighten the tax burden. The immediate need is to correct the inequities in the tax structure which reflect the Republican determination to favor the few at the expense of the many. We favor realistic tax adjustments, giving first consideration to small independent business and the small individual taxpayer. Lower-income families need tax relief; only a Democratic victory will assure this. We favor an increase in the present personal tax exemption of $600 to a minimum of at least $800.

Debt Management. The Republican debt management policy of higher interest rates serves only to benefit a few to the detriment of the general taxpayer, the small borrower, and the small and middle-class investor in Government bonds. We pledge ourselves to a vigilant review of our debt management policy in order to reduce interest rates in the service of our common welfare.

Protection of Investors. Effective administration of the Federal securities laws has been undermined by Republican appointees with conflicting interests. Millions of investors who have bought securities with their savings are today without adequate protection. We favor vigorous administration and revision of the laws to provide investor safeguards for securities extensively traded in the over-the-counter market, for foreign securities distributed in the United States, and against proxy contest abuses.

VIII. GOVERNMENT OPERATIONS

The Democratic Party pledges that it will return the administration of our National Government to a sound, efficient, and honest basis.

Civil Service and Federal Employee Relations. The Eisenhower Administration has failed either to understand or trust the Federal employee. Its record in personnel management constitutes a grave indictment of policies reflecting prejudices and excessive partisanship to the detriment of employee morale.

Intelligent and sympathetic programs must be immediately undertaken to insure the re-establishment of the high morale and efficiency which were characteristic of the Federal worker during 20 years of Democratic Administrations.

To accomplish these objectives, we propose:

(1) Protection and extension of the merit system through the enactment of laws to specify the rights and responsibilities of workers;

(2) A more independent Civil Service Commission in order that it may provide the intelligent leadership essential in perfecting a proper Civil Service System;

(3) Promotion within the Federal Service under laws assuring advancement on merit and proven ability;

(4) Salary increases of a nature that will insure a truly competitive scale at all levels of employment;

(5) Recognition by law of the right of employee organizations to represent their members and to participate in the formulation and improvement of personnel policies and practices; and

(6) A fair and non-political loyalty program, by law, which will protect the Nation against subversion and the employee against unjust and un-American treatment.

Restoring the Efficiency of the Postal Service. The bungling policies of the Republican Administration have crippled and impaired the morale, efficiency and reputation of the U. S. Postal Service. Mail carriers and clerks and other Postal employees are compelled to work under intolerable conditions. Communication by mail and service by parcel post have been delayed and retarded with resulting hardships, business losses and inconveniences. A false concept of economy has impaired seriously the efficiency of the best communication system in the world.

We pledge ourselves to programs which will:

(1) Restore the principle that the Postal Service is a public service to be operated in the interest of improved business economy and better communication, as well as an aid to the dissemination of information and intelligence;

(2) Restore Postal employee morale through the strengthening of the merit system, with promotions by law rather than caprice or partisan politics, and payment of realistic salaries reflecting the benefits of an expanded economy;

(3) Establish a program of research and development on a scale adequate to insure the most modern and efficient handling of the mails; and

(4) Undertake modernization and construction of desperately needed Postal facilities designed to insure the finest Postal system in the world.

Conflict of Interests. Maladministration and selfish manipulation have characterized Federal Administration during the Eisenhower years. Taxpayers, paying billions of dollars each year to their Government, demand and must have the highest standards of honesty, integrity and efficiency as a minimum requirement of Federal Executive conduct. We pledge a strong merit system as a substitute for cynical policies of spoils and special favor which are now the rule of the day. We seek the constant improvement of the Federal Government apparatus to accomplish these ends.

Under certain conditions, we recognize the need for the employment of personnel without compensation in the Executive Branch of the Government. But the privileges extended these dollar-a-year men have resulted in grave abuses of power. Some of these representatives of large corporations have assumed a dual loyalty to the Government and to the corporations that pay them. These abuses under the Republican Administration have been scandalous. The Democratic Party proposes that any necessary use of non-compensated employees shall be made only after the most careful scrutiny and under the most rigidly prescribed safeguards to prevent any conflict of interests.

Freedom of Information. During recent years there has developed a practice on the part of Federal agencies to delay and withhold information which is needed by Congress and the general public to make important decisions affecting their lives and destinies. We believe that this trend toward secrecy in Government should be reversed and that the Federal Government should return to its basic tradition of exchanging and promoting the freest flow of information possible in those unclassified areas where secrets involving weapons development and bona fide national security are not involved. We condemn the Eisenhower Administration for the excesses practiced in this vital area, and pledge the Democratic Party to reverse this tendency, substituting a rule of law for that of broad claims of executive privilege.

We reaffirm our position of 1952 "to press strongly for world-wide freedom in the gathering and dissemination of news." We shall press for free access to information throughout the world for our journalists and scholars.

Clean Elections. The shocking disclosures in the last Congress of attempts by selfish interests to exert improper influence on members of Congress have resulted in a Congressional investigation now under way. The Democratic Party pledges itself to provide effective regulation and full disclosure of campaign expenditures and contributions in elections to Federal offices.

Equal Rights Amendment. We of the Democratic Party recommend and indorse for submission to the Congress a Constitutional amendment providing equal rights for women.

Veterans Administration. We are spending approximately 4¾ billion dollars per year on veterans' benefits. There are more than 22 million veterans in civil life today and approximately 4 million veterans or dependents of deceased veterans drawing direct cash benefits from the Veterans Administration. It is clear that a matter of such magnitude demands more prominence in the affairs of Government. We pledge that we will elevate the Veterans Administration to a place of dignity commensurate with its importance in national affairs.

We charge the present Administration with open hostility toward the veterans' hospital program as disclosed by its efforts to restrict severely that program in fiscal year 1954. We further charge the Administration with incompetence and gross neglect in the handling of veterans' benefits in the following particulars:

(1) The refusal to allow service connection for disabilities incurred in or aggravated by military service, and the unwarranted reduction of disability evaluations in cases where service connection has been allowed; and

(2) The failure to give proper protection to veterans purchasing homes under the VA home loan program both by inadequate supervision of the program and, in some instances, by active cooperation with unscrupulous builders, lenders and real estate brokers.

In recognition of the valiant efforts of those who served their Nation in its gravest hours, we pledge:

(1) Continuance of the Veterans Administration as an independent Federal agency handling veterans programs;

(2) Continued recognition of war veterans, with adequate compensation for the service-connected disabled and for the survivors of those who have passed away in service or from service-incurred disabilities; and with pensions for disabled and distressed veterans, and for the dependents of those who have passed on, where they are in need or unable to provide for themselves;

(3) Maintenance of the Veterans Administration hospital system, with no impairment in the high quality of medical and hospital service;

(4) Priority of hospitalization for the service-connected disabled, and the privilege of hospital care when beds are available for the non-service-connected illness of veterans who are sick and without funds or unable to procure private hospitalization;

(5) Fair administration of veterans preference laws, and employment opportunities for handicapped and disabled veterans;

(6) Full hearings for war veterans filing valid applications with the review, corrective and settlement boards of the Federal Government; and

(7) Support for legislation to obtain an extension of the current law to enable veterans to obtain homes and farms through the continuance of the GI Loan Program.

Statehood for Alaska and Hawaii. We condemn the Republican Administration for its utter disregard of the rights to statehood of both Alaska and Hawaii. These territories have contributed greatly to our national economic and cultural life and are vital to our defense. They are part of America and should be recognized as such. We of the Democratic Party, therefore, pledge immediate Statehood for these two territories. We commend these territories for the action their people have taken in the adoption of constitutions which will become effective forthwith when they are admitted into the Union.

Puerto Rico. The Democratic Party views with satisfaction the progress and growth achieved by

Puerto Rico since its political organization as a Commonwealth under Democratic Party leadership. We pledge, once again, our continued support of the Commonwealth and its development and growth along lines of increasing responsibility and authority, keeping as functions of the Federal Government only such as are essential to the existence of the compact of association adopted by the Congress of the United States and the people of Puerto Rico.

The progress of Puerto Rico under Commonwealth status has been notable proof of the great benefits which flow from self-government and the good neighbor policy which under Democratic leadership this country has always followed.

Virgin Islands. We favor increased self-government for the Virgin Islands to provide for an elected Governor and a Resident Commissioner in the Congress of the United States. We denounce the scandalous administration of the first Eisenhower-appointed Governor of the Virgin Islands.

Other Territories and Possessions. We favor increased self-government for Guam, other outlying territories and the Trust Territory of the Pacific.

District of Columbia. We favor immediate home rule and ultimate national representation for the District of Columbia.

American Indians. Recognizing that all American Indians are citizens of the United States and of the States in which they reside, and acknowledging that the Federal Government has a unique legal and moral responsibility for Indians which is imposed by the Constitution and spelled out in treaties, statutes and court decisions, we pledge:

Prompt adoption of a Federal program to assist Indian tribes in the full development of their human and natural resources, and to advance the health, education and economic well-being of Indian citizens, preserving their traditions without impairing their cultural heritage;

No alteration of any treaty or other Federal-Indian contractual relationships without the free consent of the Indian tribes concerned; reversal of the present policies which are tending toward erosion of Indian rights, reduction of their economic base through alienation of their lands, and repudiation of Federal responsibility;

Prompt and expeditious settlement of Indian claims against the United States, with full recognition of the rights of both parties; and

Elimination of all impediments to full citizenship for American Indians.

Governmental Balance. The Democratic Party has upheld its belief in the Constitution as a charter of individual rights, an effective instrument for human progress. Democratic Administrations placed upon the statute books during their last 20 years a multitude of measures which testify to our belief in the Jeffersonian principle of local control even in general legislation involving Nation-wide programs. Selective Service, Social Security, agricultural adjustment, low-rent housing, hospital, and many other legislative programs have placed major responsibilities in States and counties, and provide fine examples of how benefits can be extended through Federal-State cooperation.

While we recognize the existence of honest differences of opinion as to the true location of the Constitutional line of demarcation between the Federal Government and the States, the Democratic Party expressly recognizes the vital importance of the respective States in our Federal Union. The Party of Jefferson and Jackson pledges itself to continued support of those sound principles of local government which will best serve the welfare of our people and the safety of our democratic rights.

Improving Congressional Procedures. In order that the will of the American people may be expressed upon all legislative proposals, we urge that action be taken at the beginning of the 85th Congress to improve Congressional procedures so that majority rule prevails and decisions can be made after reasonable debate without being blocked by a minority in either House.

IX. NATURAL RESOURCES

Our national economic strength and welfare depend primarily upon the development of our land, water, mineral and energy resources, with which this Nation has been abundantly blessed.

We pledge unstinting support to a full and integrated program of development, protection, management and conservation of all of our natural resources for all of the people.

The framework of time-tested conservation and mining policy is fixed in laws under which America has developed its natural resources for the general welfare.

The Democratic 84th Congress has remained steadfast to this traditional policy. It has built upon the tremendous conservation and development achievements of the Roosevelt and Truman Administrations by undertaking the greatest program of natural resources development ever assumed by any Congress in our Nation's history.

This constructive Democratic record, embracing all resources of land, water, energy and minerals, is in sharp contrast to the faithless performance of the Eisenhower Administration which has despoiled future generations of their heritage by utter failure to safeguard natural resources. Our people will long remember this betrayal of their heritage as symbolized by the infamous Dixon-Yates contract; the Al Sarena timber scheme; the low-level Hells Canyon Dams; and for its unreasonable resistance to authorizing the Niagara Project which would benefit so many millions in the State of New York and adjacent areas.

We condemn, and will continue to decry, this pillaging of our dwindling natural resource wealth through political manipulation and administrative subversion by the Eisenhower Administration. We pledge ourselves to halt this betrayal of the people's trust.

We shall devise for the American people a dynamic, far-reaching and progressive conservation program.

The Democratic Party proposes, and will strive to secure, this comprehensive resources program for America's future.

Land. Our land will be preserved and improved for the present and future needs of our people, and not wastefully exploited to benefit special-interest groups.

Soil Conservation. In contrast to the wasteful neglect of the present Administration, soil conservation practices will be stimulated and intensified to reduce land deterioration under the vital Soil Conservation Service assistance program conceived and fostered by the Democratic Party.

National Parks, Recreation and Wildlife. We pledge adoption of an immediate and broad policy to mobilize the efforts of private and public agencies for protection of existing recreational areas, provision of new ones, and improvement of inadequate facilities. Slum conditions fostered

by Republican neglect are intolerable to the tens of millions of Americans using our national parks and forests. Democratic Administration will end this shocking situation.

Fish and game habitats will be guarded against encroachment for commercial purposes. All river basin development plans will take into full consideration their effect upon fish, wildlife, national park and wilderness areas. The Fish and Wildlife Service must and will be returned to the career status from which it was removed by the political patronage policy of the present Administration.

Recreational facilities for the millions of field and stream sportsmen of America will be conserved and expanded.

Forest and Grazing Lands. Timber on Federal commercial forest lands will be harvested and managed on a sustained-yield basis.

We propose to increase forest access roads in order to improve cutting practices on both public and private lands.

Private owners of farm, forest and range lands need and must have financial and technical assistance so that all lands will be utilized to contribute more fully to the national welfare by production of food and fiber and protection of our watersheds. Any effort to transform grazing permits from a revocable license to a vested right will be rejected.

We will vigorously advocate Federally-financed forestation, upstream erosion control and flood control programs on our public range, timber lands and small drainage basins to protect our watersheds and double the rate of forage and commercial timber growth. We will promote cooperative programs with Government assistance to reduce timber losses from fire, insects, and disease.

Prospecting and mining on unreserved Federal lands will be encouraged, but surface areas not needed in mining will be safeguarded by appropriate legislation.

Water. We pledge the resumption of rapid and orderly multiple-purpose river basin development throughout the country. This program will bring into reality the full potential benefits of flood control, irrigation and our domestic and municipal water supply from surface and underground waters. It will also materially aid low-cost power, navigation, recreation, fish and wildlife propagation and mineral development. We pledge our aid to the growing requirements of the semiarid Western States for an adequate water supply to meet the vital domestic, irrigation and industrial needs of the rapidly growing urban centers. Enhanced regional economies will strengthen the economy of the Nation as a whole.

We will take appropriate and vigorous steps to prevent comprehensive drainage basin development plans from being fragmented by single-purpose projects. The conservation of water is essential to the life of the Nation. The Democratic Party pledges itself to conservation of water in the public interest.

The Democratic 84th Congress has taken a long step toward reducing the pollution of our rivers and streams. We pledge continuation and expansion of this program, vital to every citizen.

The program of obtaining a large new source of fresh water supply from salt water was begun by the Democratic Party, but has been allowed to lapse by the Eisenhower Republican Administration. It will be resumed and accelerated.

Energy. We pledge ourselves to carry forward, under national policy, aggressive programs to provide abundant supplies of low-cost energy, including continued research for the development of synthetic liquid fuel from coal, shale and agricultural products. These we must have to feed our insatiable industrial economy, to enable our workers to develop their skills and increase their productivity, to provide more jobs at higher wages, to meet the ever-mounting demands for domestic and farm uses, including the production of lower-cost farm fertilizers and lower-cost power to consumers.

We will carry forward increased and full production of hydroelectric power on our rivers and of steam generation for the Tennessee Valley Authority to meet its peacetime and defense requirements. Such self-liquidating projects must go forward in a rapid and orderly manner, with appropriate financing plans. Integrated regional transmission systems will enhance exchange of power and encourage diversified industrial development.

We shall once more rigorously enforce the anti-monopoly and public body preference clauses, including the Holding Company Act, administratively circumvented by the Eisenhower Republican Administration. We shall preserve and strengthen the public power competitive yard-stick in power developments under TVA, REA, Bureau of Reclamation, Bonneville, Southeast and Southwest Power Administrations and other future projects, including atomic power plants, under a policy of the widest possible use of electric energy at the lowest possible cost.

Minerals. The Republican Administration has seriously neglected and ignored one of the Nation's basic industries, metal mining. We recognize that a healthy mining industry is essential to the economy of the Nation, and therefore pledge immediate efforts toward the establishment of a realistic, long-range minerals policy. The Nation's minerals and fuels are essential to the safety, security and development of our country. We pledge the adoption of policies which will further encourage the exploration and development of additional reserves of our mineral resources.

Domestic Fisheries. We will undertake comprehensive scientific and economic research programs for the conservation and better utilization of, and new markets for, fishery products. We favor and will encourage reciprocal world trade in fish products.

We pledge ourselves to a public works and water policy providing adequate protection for domestic fishery resources.

We favor treaties with other nations for conservation and better utilization of international fisheries.

Scenic Resources. To the end that the scenic beauty of our land may be preserved and maintained for this and future generations to enjoy, we pledge accelerated support of educational programs to stimulate individual responsibility and pride in clean, attractive surroundings—from big cities to rural areas.

X. ATOMIC ENERGY

The atomic era came into being and was developed under Democratic Administrations.

The genius of American scientists, engineers and workmen, supported by the vision and courage of Franklin D. Roosevelt, made possible the splitting of the atom and the development of the first atomic bomb in time to end World War II.

With the ending of the war, the supremacy of America in atomic weapons was maintained under the leadership of President Truman, and the United States pushed ahead vigorously toward utilizing this new form of energy in peaceful pursuits, particularly in the fields of medicine, agriculture and industry. By the end of the Truman Administration, the pre-eminence of the United States in the nuclear field was clearly established, and we were on the threshold of large-scale development of industrial nuclear energy at home and as an instrument of world peace.

The Eisenhower Administration promptly reversed the field and plunged the previously independent and nonpartisan Atomic Energy Commission into partisan politics. For example, President Eisenhower ordered the Commission to sign the scandalous Dixon-Yates contract. He was later forced to repudiate the same contract, after the exposure of the illegal activities of one of his own consultants with a secret office in the Bureau of the Budget.

The Republican Administration has followed the same pattern in the field of atomic energy that it has pursued in its treatment of other natural resources—lofty words, little action, but steady service to selfish interests. While the AEC and the special private interests consult and confer, the United States is lagging instead of leading in the world race for nuclear power, international prestige and world markets.

The Democrats in Congress believed that the national interest thus became imperiled, and they moved to meet the challenge both at home and abroad. They established a nonpartisan panel of eminent Americans to study the impact of the peaceful atom.

Following the comprehensive report of this panel, the Joint Congressional Committee on Atomic Energy held extensive hearings on bills to accelerate the atomic reactor demonstration program. Though the bills were reported unanimously from committee, the Republican members of Congress, under heavy pressure from the White House, insured the final defeat of this legislation in the Congress.

But the fight to bring nuclear power to the people has only begun. As the United States was first in the development of the atom as a weapon, so the United States must lead in bringing the blessings of the peaceful uses of nuclear energy to mankind.

Hence, the Democratic Party pledges itself:

(1) To restore nonpartisan administration of the vital atomic energy program and to expand and accelerate nuclear development by vigorous action:

(2) To accelerate the domestic civilian atomic power program by the construction of a variety of demonstration prototype reactors;

(3) To give reality—life and meaning—to the "Atoms for Peace" program. We will substitute deeds for words;

(4) To increase the production of fissionable material for use in a stockpile for peacetime commitments at home and abroad, and for an ever-present reserve for weapons to guarantee freedom in the world;

(5) To conduct a comprehensive survey of radiation hazards from bomb tests and reactor operations, in order to determine what additional measures are required to protect existing and future generations from these invisible dangers; and

(6) To make the maximum contribution to the defense of our Nation and the free world through the development of a balanced and flexible stockpile of nuclear weapons, containing a sufficient number and variety to support our armed services in any contingency.

XI. Civil Rights

The Democratic Party is committed to support and advance the individual rights and liberties of all Americans. Our country is founded on the proposition that all men are created equal. This means that all citizens are equal before the law and should enjoy all political rights. They should have equal opportunities for education, for economic advancement, and for decent living conditions.

We will continue our efforts to eradicate discrimination based on race, religion or national origin. We know this task requires action, not just in one section of the Nation, but in all sections. It requires the cooperative efforts of individual citizens, and action by State and local governments. It also requires Federal action. The Federal Government must live up to the ideals of the Declaration of Independence and must exercise the powers vested in it by the Constitution.

We are proud of the record of the Democratic Party in securing equality of treatment and opportunity in the nation's armed forces, the Civil

Service, and in all areas under Federal jurisdiction. The Democratic Party pledges itself to continue its efforts to eliminate illegal discriminations of all kinds, in relation to (1) full rights to vote, (2) full rights to engage in gainful occupations, (3) full rights to enjoy security of the person, and (4) full rights to education in all publicly supported institutions.

Recent decisions of the Supreme Court of the United States relating to segregation in publicly supported schools and elsewhere have brought consequences of vast importance to our Nation as a whole and especially to communities directly affected. We reject all proposals for the use of force to interfere with the orderly determination of these matters by the courts.

The Democratic Party emphatically reaffirms its support of the historic principle that ours is a government of laws and not of men; it recognizes the Supreme Court of the United States as one of the three Constitutional and coordinate branches of the Federal Government, superior to and separate from any political party, the decisions of which are part of the law of the land. We condemn the efforts of the Republican Party to make it appear that this tribunal is a part of the Republican Party.

We condemn the Republican Administration's violation of the rights of Government employees by a heartless and unjustified confusing of "security" and "loyalty" for the sole purpose of political gain and regardless of consequences to individual victims and to the good name of the United States. We condemn the Republican Administration's misrepresentation of facts and violation of individual rights in a wicked and unprincipled attempt to degrade and destroy the Democratic Party, and to make political capital for the Republican Party.

Prohibition Party Platform for 1956

PREAMBLE

We, the representatives of the Prohibition Party, assembled in National Convention at Camp Mack, Milford, Indiana, September 4, 5, and 6, 1955, recognizing Almighty God as the source of all just government and with faith in the teachings of the Prince of Peace, do solemnly promise that, if our party is chosen to administer the affairs of the nation, we will carefully use all the powers of our administration to preserve the rights, privileges and basic freedoms of the people of the United States.

CONSTITUTIONAL GOVERNMENT

We solemnly affirm our loyalty to the Constitution of the United States, to the principles of liberty enunciated in our Declaration of Independence and in the Preamble and Bill of Rights of our Constitution, our deep confidence in our form of government, and our earnest desire to serve our people with a constructive program based upon the principles of righteousness and democracy.

We are unalterably opposed to any form of totalitarianism. We challenge all loyal citizens to work against this menace to civilization. We believe that the best safeguard against these dangerous doctrines is to preserve the rights of our citizens by enforcing the provisions of the Constitution and the Bill of Rights.

We deplore the actions of any administration in exceeding its authority, through executive agreements, thereby violating the Constitutional prerogatives of our legislative bodies.

WORLD PEACE

We, in this age of atomic and hydrogen bombs (capable of destroying civilization) pledge ourselves to search for peaceful solutions of international conflicts, under an international "good neighbor" policy, call for an immediate outlawing of all weapons of annihilation, propose a progressive multi-lateral limitation of armaments and their ultimate abolition, leading to world peace and the brotherhood of man.

MILITARISM

We are opposed to the militarization of our youth, through universal military training, universal conscription, or universal reserve service.

ECONOMIC AID

Our government should give much greater emphasis to relief, rehabilitation and economic aid, especially for technical assistance, to help the people raise their own standard of living in the underdeveloped areas where widespread hunger and human misery now prepare the soil for communist propaganda.

Economy of Abundance

We pledge ourselves as opposed to the continuation of the wastage of God-given abundance, created through science, technology and the genius and labors of our people, and declare our purpose to search for means to distribute justly such abundance, as provided under our Constitution, "to promote the general welfare."

Governmental Economy

Extravagant spending has set an example of wasteful government operations. We believe it is unjust for any government to take nearly one-third of the total income of its citizens to pay the expense of government. We believe that government ought not to do for our people what they can do for themselves. We promise to reorganize the federal government, abolishing all departments and bureaus that cannot qualify when measured by this principle.

Taxes

The constant increase in taxation is approaching the point of confiscation and economic bankruptcy. With proper economy, governmental costs will be lowered, making it possible to reduce the public debt and lighten the tax load for the average citizen.

Economic Freedom

We oppose any trend toward excessive concentration of power over our economic life, whether it takes the form of unnecessary regulation by government or monopolistic control by private industry.

Co-operatives

Co-operatives and profit-sharing enterprises are a natural outgrowth of democracy. Government under our administration will encourage such enterprises.

Labor and Industry

Labor organizations are entitled to great credit for improving the status of the workers and for their constructive contributions to the general welfare. It is our purpose to give the public welfare paramount consideration. Neither capital nor labor can be permitted to dominate at the expense of the other or of the common good. We favor the compulsory arbitration of labor disputes where the public welfare is endangered.

Agriculture

We vehemently protest against the immoral policy of creating artificial scarcity by wasting or destroying farm products amid widespread hunger and want. We believe that this policy can and should be replaced by a plan which will assure every working farmer and his family an adequate income while maintaining abundant production and making it available to meet the world's needs.

Social Security and Old Age Pensions

We endorse the principle of social security, old age pensions, and unemployment compensation, including all employed groups. We deplore the abuse of its privileges, the maladministration of its provisions for political ends, and pledge ourselves to correct these evils. We propose to administer these programs in such a way as to preserve the incentives of initiative and thrift.

Money

The Constitution provides that Congress shall have the power to "coin money" and "regulate the value thereof." This is a sound and feasible monetary policy which we promise to re-establish and enforce.

Religious Liberty

We believe in religious liberty. By religious liberty we mean the freedom of individual worship and fellowship, and the right to evangelize, educate, and establish religious institutions. When religious liberty is lost political liberty perishes with it.

Separation of Church and State

We reaffirm our loyalty to the Constitutional principle of separation of Church and State, and will expose, and resist vigorously, any attempt from whatever source to weaken or subvert this fundamental principle.

Public Morality and Law Enforcement

Moral and spiritual considerations must be primary factors in determining national policies. We will strengthen and enforce laws against gambling, narcotics, and commercialized vice, now so widely violated and nullified by the political parties in power, and thus prevent further disintegration of the public morals.

We oppose the present nullification of law by non-enforcement and will maintain the integrity of democracy by enforcing the Constitution and the laws enacted under it.

HONESTY IN GOVERNMENT

There is a law of cause and effect which rules in the affairs of men. With the repeal of the Eighteenth Amendment there has come a rapid decline in the moral standards of the nation, culminating in shocking revelations of crime and political corruption. We pledge ourselves to break this unholy alliance between organized crime and those in positions of trust in the government at all levels.

NO RACIAL DISCRIMINATION

Recognizing that "God hath created of one blood all nations to dwell upon the face of the earth," we declare in favor of full justice and equal opportunity for all people, regardless of race, creed, or national origin.

MARRIAGE AND DIVORCE

We favor the enactment of uniform marriage and divorce laws as a help toward maintaining the sanctity of the home.

BALLOT LAW REFORM

We demand the repeal of the many state ballot laws which have been enacted to make the two-party system a bipartisan political monopoly by keeping minor parties off the ballot, thus denying to independent voters and minority groups the fundamental right of free political expression.

EXTENSION OF DEMOCRACY

To help perfect our political democracy and extend it to all who live under our flag we urge:

(1) The submission to the people of an amendment to the Constitution to provide for the election of the President and Vice-President directly by the people;

(2) Immediate home rule and the franchise and representation in Congress for the District of Columbia;

(3) Immediate statehood for Alaska and Hawaii;

(4) Encouraging Puerto Rico, the Virgin Islands, Guam and Samoa to advance as rapidly as possible to complete internal self-government.

(5) We recognize the right of all Indians to full citizenship.

THE ALCOHOL PROBLEM

The widespread and increasing use of alcoholic beverages since Repeal is one of the major causes of accidents, insanity, wasted manpower, poverty, broken homes, juvenile delinquency, vice, crime and political corruption.

The highly capitalized, strongly organized and socially irresponsible liquor industry out of its enormous profits, spends huge sums in promoting liquor sales by every possible means, to create a growing habitual use by youth and adults.

Both through its financial and organizational connections and through the effects of its product in weakening moral resistance, the liquor power is linked with, and supports, a nation-wide network of organized gambling, vice and crime. This power dominates our politics and government. Through its advertising it has corrupted large sections of the nation's press, and it is increasingly extending its control to radio and television.

All these social effects of the liquor industry make the beverage alcohol problem one which concerns the whole nation, and requires immediate action looking toward a solution.

Our program includes removing the cause for drinking by:

(1) Raising the economic standards of the country as outlined in this platform;

(2) Increasing psychiatric aid to treat alcoholics and help others in need of counselling;

(3) Developing community recreational programs to provide a wholesome alternative to the tavern;

(4) Publicizing scientific facts about beverage alcohol through the press, motion pictures, radio, television, the public schools and other media; and

(5) A program of publicity, education, legislation and administration leading to the elimination of the alcoholic beverage industry.

The Prohibition Party demands the repeal of all laws that legalize the liquor traffic and the enactment and enforcement of new laws which prohibit the manufacture, distribution and sale of alcoholic beverages.

An administration pledged to the above program is essential for effective steps toward solving this important problem.

CONCLUSION

What is needed is a re-alignment of voters and the union of good citizens in a party which will support only candidates of unquestioned integrity and competence, who will faithfully serve the commonwealth and set a good example of public and private morality, and who are committed to the principles of this platform.

We urge all who believe in these principles to vote their convictions and help us achieve a clean, honest and humane government "of the people, by the people, and for the people," under God.

Republican Platform 1956

DECLARATION OF FAITH

America's trust is in the merciful providence of God, in whose image every man is created . . . the source of every man's dignity and freedom.

In this trust our Republic was founded. We give devoted homage to the Founding Fathers. They not only proclaimed that the freedom and rights of men came from the Creator and not from the State, but they provided safeguards to those freedoms.

Our Government was created by the people for all the people, and it must serve no less a purpose.

The Republican Party was formed 100 years ago to preserve the Nation's devotion to these ideals.

On its Centennial, the Republican Party again calls to the minds of all Americans the great truth first spoken by Abraham Lincoln: "The legitimate object of Government is to do for a community of people whatever they need to have done but cannot do at all, or cannot so well do, for themselves in their separate and individual capacities. But in all that people can individually do as well for themselves, Government ought not to interfere."

Our great President Dwight D. Eisenhower has counseled us further: "In all those things which deal with people, be liberal, be human. In all those things which deal with people's money,

or their economy, or their form of government, be conservative."

While jealously guarding the free institutions and preserving the principles upon which our Republic was founded and has flourished, the purpose of the Republican Party is to establish and maintain a peaceful world and build at home a dynamic prosperity in which every citizen fairly shares.

We shall ever build anew, that our children and their children, without distinction because of race, creed or color, may know the blessings of our free land.

We believe that basic to governmental integrity are unimpeachable ethical standards and irreproachable personal conduct by all people in government. We shall continue our insistence on honesty as an indispensable requirement of public service. We shall continue to root out corruption whenever and wherever it appears.

We are proud of and shall continue our far-reaching and sound advances in matters of basic human needs — expansion of social security — broadened coverage in unemployment insurance —improved housing—and better health protection for all our people. We are determined that our government remain warmly responsive to the urgent social and economic problems of our people.

To these beliefs we commit ourselves as we present this record and declare our goals for the future.

Nearly four years ago when the people of this Nation entrusted their Government to President Eisenhower and the Republican Party, we were locked in a costly and stalemated war. Now we have an honorable peace, which has stopped the bitter toll in casualties and resources, ended depressing wartime restraints, curbed the runaway inflation and unleashed the boundless energy of our people to forge forward on the road to progress.

In four years we have achieved the highest economic level with the most widely shared benefits that the world has ever seen. We of the Republican Party have fostered this prosperity and are dedicated to its expansion and to the preservation of the climate in which it has thrived.

We are proud of our part in bringing into a position of unique authority in the world one who symbolizes, as can no other man, the hopes of all peoples for peace, liberty and justice. One leader in the world today towers above all others and inspires the trust, admiration, confidence and good will of all the peoples of every nation—Dwight D. Eisenhower. Under his leadership, the Republican Administration has carried out foreign policies which have enabled our people to enjoy in peace the blessings of liberty. We shall continue to work unceasingly for a just and enduring peace in a world freed of tyranny.

Every honorable means at our command has been exercised to alleviate the grievances and causes of armed conflict among nations. The advance of Communism and its enslavement of people has been checked, and, at key points, thrown back. Austria, Iran and Guatemala have been liberated from Kremlin control. Forces of freedom are at work in the nations still enslaved by Communist imperialism.

We firmly believe in the right of peoples everywhere to determine their form of government, their leaders, their destiny, in peace. Where needed, in order to promote peace and freedom throughout the world, we shall within the prudent limits of our resources, assist friendly countries in their determined efforts to strengthen their economies.

We hold high hopes for useful service to mankind in the power of the atom. We shall generously assist the International Atomic Energy Agency, now evolving from President Eisenhower's "Atoms for Peace" proposal, in an effort to find ways to dedicate man's genius not to his death, but to his life.

We maintain that no treaty or international agreement can deprive any of our citizens of Constitutional rights. We shall see to it that no treaty or agreement with other countries attempts to deprive our citizens of the rights guaranteed them by the Federal Constitution.

President Eisenhower has given the world bold proposals for mutual arms reduction and protection against aggression through flying sentinels in an "open sky."

We support this and his further offer of United States participation in an international fund for economic development financed from the savings brought by true disarmament. We approve his determined resistance to disarmament without effective inspection.

We work and pray for the day when the domination of any people from any source will have ended, and when there will be liberation and true freedom for the hundreds of millions of individuals now held in subjugation. We shall continue to dedicate our best efforts to this lofty purpose.

We shall continue vigorously to support the United Nations.

We shall continue to oppose the seating of Communist China in the United Nations.

We shall maintain our powerful military strength as a deterrent to aggression and as a guardian of the peace. We shall maintain it ready, balanced and technologically advanced for these objectives only.

Good times in America have reached a breadth and depth never before known by any nation. Moreover, it is a prosperity of a nation at peace, not at war. We shall continue to encourage the good business and sound employee relationships which have made possible for the first time in our history a productive capacity of more than $400 billion a year. Nearly 67 million people have full-time jobs, with real wages and personal income at record highs.

The farmers of America are at last able to look to the future with a confidence based on expanding peacetime markets instead of on politically contrived formulas foredoomed to fail except in a wartime economy. The objective is to insure that agriculture shares fairly and fully in our record prosperity without needless Federal meddlings and domination.

Restoration of integrity in government has been an essential element to the achievement of our unparalleled good times. We will faithfully preserve the sound financial management which already has reduced annual spending $14 billion below the budgets planned by our Democratic predecessors and made possible in 1954 a $7.4-billion tax cut, the largest one-year tax reduction in history.

We will ever fight the demoralizing influence of inflation as a national way of life. We are proud to have fulfilled our 1952 pledge to halt the skyrocketing cost of living that in the previous 13 years had cut the value of the dollar by half, and robbed millions of the full value of their wages, savings, insurance, pensions and social security.

We have balanced the budget. We believe

and will continue to prove that thrift, prudence and a sensible respect for living within income applies as surely to the management of our Government's budget as it does to the family budget.

We hold that the major world issue today is whether Government shall be the servant or the master of men. We hold that the Bill of Rights is the sacred foundation of personal liberty. That men are created equal needs no affirmation, but they must have equality of opportunity and protection of their civil rights under the law.

We hold that the strict division of powers and the primary responsibility of State and local governments must be maintained, and that the centralization of powers in the national Government leads to expansion of the mastery of our lives.

We hold that the protection of the freedom of men requires that budgets be balanced, waste in government eliminated, and taxes reduced.

In these and all other areas of proper Government concern, we pledge our best thought and whole energy to a continuation of our prized peace, prosperity and progress.

For our guidance in fulfilling this responsibility, President Eisenhower has given us a statement of principles that is neither partisan nor prejudiced, but warmly American:

The individual is of supreme importance.

The spirit of our people is the strength of our nation.

America does not prosper unless all Americans prosper.

Government must have a heart as well as a head.

Courage in principle, cooperation in practice make freedom positive.

To stay free, we must stay strong.

Under God, we espouse the cause of freedom and justice and peace for all peoples.

Embracing these guides to positive, constructive action, and in their rich spirit, we ask the support of the American people for the election of a Republican Congress and the re-election of the Nation's devoted and dedicated leader — Dwight D. Eisenhower.

DECLARATION OF DETERMINATION

In the interest of complete public understanding, elaboration of Republican aspirations and achievements is desirable in the areas of broadest public concern.

DYNAMIC ECONOMY—FREE LABOR

TAXATION AND FISCAL POLICY

The Republican Party takes pride in calling attention to the outstanding fiscal achievements of the Eisenhower Administration, several of which are mentioned in the foreword to these resolutions.

In order to progress further in correcting the unfortunate results of unwise financial management during 20 years of Democrat Administrations, we pledge to pursue the following objectives:

Further reductions in Government spending as recommended in the Hoover Commission Report, without weakening the support of a superior defense program or depreciating the quality of essential services of government to our people.

Continued balancing of the budget, to assure the financial strength of the country which is so vital to the struggle of the free world in its battle against Communism; and to maintain the purchasing power of a sound dollar, and the value of savings, pensions and insurance.

Gradual reduction of the national debt.

Then, insofar as consistent with a balanced budget, we pledge to work toward these additional objectives:

Further reductions in taxes with particular consideration for low and middle income families.

Initiation of a sound policy of tax reductions which will encourage small independent businesses to modernize and progress.

Continual study of additional ways to correct inequities in the effect of various taxes.

Consistent with the Republican Administration's accomplishment in stemming the inflation —which under five Democrat Administrations had cut the value of the dollar in half, and so had robbed the wage earner and millions of thrifty citizens who had savings, pensions and insurance—we endorse the present policy of freedom for the Federal Reserve System to combat both inflation and deflation by wise fiscal policy.

The Republican Party believes that sound money, which retains its buying power, is an essential foundation for new jobs, a higher standard of living, protection of savings, a secure national defense, and the general economic growth of the country.

BUSINESS AND ECONOMIC POLICY

The Republican Party has as a primary concern the continued advancement of the well-being of the individual. This can be attained only in an economy that, as today, is sound, free and creative, ever building new wealth and new jobs for all the people.

We believe in good business for all business—small, medium and large. We believe that competition in a free economy opens unrivaled opportunity and brings the greatest good to the greatest number.

The sound economic policies of the Eisenhower Administration have created an atmosphere of confidence in which good businesses flourish and can plan for growth to create new job opportunities for our expanding population.

We have eliminated a host of needless controls.

To meet the immense demands of our expanding economy, we have initiated the largest highway, air and maritime programs in history, each soundly financed.

We shall continue to advocate the maintenance and expansion of a strong, efficient, privately-owned and operated and soundly financed system of transportation that will serve all of the needs of our Nation under Federal regulatory policies that will enable each carrier to realize its inherent economic advantages and its full competitive capabilities.

We recognize the United States' world leadership in aviation, and we shall continue to encourage its technical development and vigorous expansion. Our goal is to support and sponsor air services and to make available to our citizens the safest and most comprehensive air transportation. We favor adequate funds and expeditious action in improving air safety, and highest efficiency in the control of air traffic.

We stand for forward-looking programs, created to replace our war-built merchant fleet with the most advanced types in design, with increased speed. Adaptation of new propulsion power units, including nuclear, must be sponsored and achieved.

We should proceed with the prompt construction of the Atomic Powered Peace Ship in order that we may demonstrate to the world, in this as in other fields, the peaceful uses of the atom.

Our steadily rising prosperity is constantly reflecting the confidence of our citizens in the policies of our Republican Administration.

SMALL BUSINESS

We pledge the continuation and improvement of our drive to aid small business. Every constructive potential avenue of improvement—both legislative and executive—has been explored in our search for ways in which to widen opportunities for this important segment of America's economy.

Beginning with our creation of the very successful Small Business Administration, and continuing through the recently completed studies and recommendations of the Cabinet Committee on Small Business, which we strongly endorse, we have focused our attention on positive measures to help small businesses get started and grow.

Small Business can look forward to expanded participation in federal procurement—valuable financing and technical aids—a continuously vigorous enforcement of anti-trust laws—important cuts in the burdens of paper work, and certain tax reductions as budgetary requirements permit.

Small business now is receiving approximately one-third, dollarwise, of all Defense contracts. We recommend a further review of procurement procedures for all defense departments and agencies with a view to facilitating and extending such participation for the further benefit of Small Business.

We favor loans at reasonable rates of interest to small businesses which have records of permanency but who are in temporary need and which are unable to obtain credit in commercial channels. We recommend an extension at the earliest opportunity of the Small Business Administration which is now scheduled to expire in mid 1957.

We also propose:

Additional technical research in problems of development and distribution for the benefit of small business;

Legislation to enable closer Federal scrutiny of mergers which have a significant or potential monopolistic connotations;

Procedural changes in the antitrust laws to facilitate their enforcement;

Simplification of wage reporting by employers for purposes of social security records and income tax withholding;

Continuance of the vigorous SEC policies which are providing maximum protection to the investor and maximum opportunity for the financing of small business without costly red tape.

LABOR

Under the Republican Administration, as our country has prospered, so have its people. This is as it should be, for as President Eisenhower said: "Labor is the United States. The men and women, who with their minds, their hearts and hands, create the wealth that is shared in this country—they are America."

The Eisenhower Administration has brought to our people the highest employment, the highest wages and the highest standard of living ever enjoyed by any nation. Today there are nearly 67 million men and women at work in the United States, 4 million more than in 1952. Wages have increased substantially over the past 3½ years; but, more important, the American wage earner today can buy more than ever before for himself and his family because his pay check has not been eaten away by rising taxes and soaring prices.

The record of performance of the Republican Administration on behalf of our working men and women goes still further. The Federal minimum wage has been raised for more than 2 million workers. Social Security has been extended to an additional 10 million workers and the benefits raised for 6½ million. The protection of unemployment insurance has been brought to 4 million additional workers. There have been increased workmen's compensation benefits for longshoremen and harbor workers, increased retirement benefits for railroad employees, and wage increases and improved welfare and pension plans for federal employees.

In addition, the Eisenhower Administration has enforced more vigorously and effectively than ever before, the laws which protect the working standards of our people.

Workers have benefited by the progress which has been made in carrying out the programs and principles set forth in the 1952 Republican plat-form. All workers have gained and unions have grown in strength and responsibility, and have increased their membership by 2 millions.

Furthermore, the process of free collective bargaining has been strengthened by the insistence of this Administration that labor and management settle their differences at the bargaining table without the intervention of the Government. This policy has brought to our country an unprecedented period of labor-management peace and understanding.

We applaud the effective, unhindered, collective bargaining which brought an early end to the 1956 steel strike, in contrast to the six months' upheaval, Presidential seizure of the steel industry and ultimate Supreme Court intervention under the last Democrat Administration.

The Eisenhower Administration will continue to fight for dynamic and progressive programs which, among other things, will:

Stimulate improved job safety of our workers, through assistance to the States, employees and employers;

Continue and further perfect its programs of assistance to the millions of workers with special employment problems, such as older workers, handicapped workers, members of minority groups, and migratory workers;

Strengthen and improve the Federal-State Employment Service and improve the effectiveness of the unemployment insurance system;

Protect by law, the assets of employee welfare and benefit plans so that workers who are the beneficiaries can be assured of their rightful benefits;

Assure equal pay for equal work regardless of sex;

Clarify and strengthen the eight-hour laws for the benefit of workers who are subject to federal wage standards on Federal and Federally-assisted construction, and maintain and continue the vigorous administration of the Federal prevailing minimum wage law for public supply contracts;

Extend the protection of the Federal minimum wage laws to as many more workers as is possible and practicable;

Continue to fight for the elimination of discrimination in employment because of race, creed, color, national origin, ancestry or sex;

Provide assistance to improve the economic

conditions of areas faced with persistent and substantial unemployment;

Revise and improve the Taft-Hartley Act so as to protect more effectively the rights of labor unions, management, the individual worker, and the public. The protection of the right of workers to organize into unions and to bargain collectively is the firm and permanent policy of the Eisenhower Administration. In 1954, 1955 and again in 1956, President Eisenhower recommended constructive amendments to this Act. The Democrats in Congress have consistently blocked these needed changes by parliamentary maneuvers. The Republican Party pledges itself to overhaul and improve the Taft-Hartley Act along the lines of these recommendations.

HUMAN WELFARE AND ADVANCEMENT

HEALTH, EDUCATION AND WELFARE

The Republican Party believes that the physical, mental, and spiritual well-being of the people is as important as their economic health. It will continue to support this conviction with vigorous action.

Republican action created the Department of Health, Education and Welfare as the first new Federal department in 40 years, to raise the continuing consideration of these problems for the first time to the highest council of Government, the President's Cabinet.

Through the White House Conference on Education, our Republican Administration initiated the most comprehensive Community-State-Federal attempt ever made to solve the pressing problems of primary and secondary education.

Four thousand communities, studying their school populations and their physical and financial resources, encouraged our Republican Administration to urge a five-year program of Federal assistance in building schools to relieve a critical classroom shortage.

The Republican Party will renew its efforts to enact a program based on sound principles of need and designed to encourage increased state and local efforts to build more classrooms.

Our Administration also proposed for the first time in history, a thorough nation-wide analysis of rapidly growing problems in education beyond the high schools.

The Republican Party is determined to press

all such actions that will help insure that every child has the educational opportunity to advance to his own greatest capacity.

We have fully resolved to continue our steady gains in man's unending struggle against disease and disability.

We have supported the distribution of free vaccine to protect millions of children against dreaded polio.

Republican leadership has enlarged Federal assistance for construction of hospitals, emphasizing low-cost care of chronic diseases and the special problems of older persons, and increased Federal aid for medical care of the needy.

We have asked the largest increase in research funds ever sought in one year to intensify attacks on cancer, mental illness, heart disease and other dread diseases.

We demand once again, despite the reluctance of the Democrat 84th Congress, Federal assistance to help build facilities to train more physicians and scientists.

We have encouraged a notable expansion and improvement of voluntary health insurance, and urge that reinsurance and pooling arrangements be authorized to speed this progress.

We have strengthened the Food and Drug Administration, and we have increased the vocational rehabilitation program to enable a larger number of the disabled to return to satisfying activity.

We have supported measures that have made more housing available than ever before in history, reduced urban slums in local-federal partnership, stimulated record home ownership, and authorized additional low-rent public housing.

We initiated the first flood insurance program in history under Government sponsorship in cooperation with private enterprise.

We shall continue to seek extension and perfection of a sound social security system.

We pledge close cooperation with State, local and private agencies to reduce the ghastly toll of fatalities on the Nation's highways.

RURAL AMERICA'S RECOVERY—AGRICULTURE

The men and women operating the farms and ranches of America have confidence in President Eisenhower and the Republican farm program. Our farmers have earned the respect and appreciation of our entire nation for their energy, resourcefulness, efficiency, and ability.

Agriculture, our basic industry, must remain free and prosperous. The Republican Party will continue to move boldly to help the farmer obtain his full share of the rewards of good business and good Government. It is committed to a program for agriculture which creates the widest possible markets and highest attainable income for our farm and ranch families. This program must be versatile and flexible to meet effectively the impact of rapidly changing conditions. It does not envision making farmers dependent upon direct governmental payments for their incomes. Our objective is markets which return full parity to our farm and ranch people when they sell their products. There is no simple, easy answer to farm problems. Our approach as ever is a many-sided, versatile and positive program to help all farmers and ranchers.

Farm legislation, developed under the Democrat Administration to stimulate production in wartime, carried a built-in mechanism for the accumulation of price-depressing surpluses in peacetime. Under laws sponsored by the Republican Administration, almost $7 billion in price-depressing surplus farm products have been moved into use, and the rate of movement is being accelerated.

Agriculture is successfully making the transition from wartime to peacetime markets, with less disruption than at any time after a great war. We are gratified by the improvement this year in farm prices and income as a result of our policies.

Our Republican Administration fostered a constructive Soil Bank Program further to reduce surpluses and to permit improvement of our soil, water and timber resources. The Democrat Party tactics of obstruction and delay have prevented our farm families from receiving the full benefits of this program in 1956.

However, by aggressive action, we now have the Soil Bank in operation, and in 3 months, half a million farmers have contracted to shift more than 10 million acres from producing more surpluses to a soil reserve for the future. For this they already have earned $225 million.

This program is a sound aid to removing the burdens of surpluses which Democrat programs placed on farmers. It is now moving into full operation.

Benefits of Social Security have been extended to farm families. Programs of loans and grants for farm families hit by flood and drought have been made operative.

Tax laws were improved to help farmers with respect to livestock, farm equipment, and conservation practices. We initiated action to refund to the farmers $60 million annually in taxes on gasoline used in machinery on the farm.

Cooperation between the U. S. Department of Agriculture, the State Departments of Agriculture and land grant colleges and universities is at an all-time high. This Republican Administration has increased support for agricultural research and education to the highest level in history. New records of assistance to farm and ranch families in soil and water conservation were attained in every year of this Republican Administration.

Convinced that the Government should ever be the farmer's helper, never his master, the Republican Party is pledged:

To establish an effective, new research program, fully and completely implemented to find and vigorously promote new uses for farm crops;

To move our agriculture commodities into use at home and abroad, and to use every appropriate and effective means to improve marketing, so that farmers can produce and sell their products to increase their income and enjoy an improving level of living;

To encourage the improvement of quality in farm products through agricultural research, education and price support differentials, thus increasing market acceptance both at home and abroad;

To further help and cooperate with the several States as co-equals with the federal government to provide needed research, education, service and regulatory programs;

To develop farm programs that are fair to all farmers;

To work toward full freedom instead of toward more regimentation, developing voluntary rather than oppressive farm programs;

To encourage agricultural producers in their efforts to seek solutions to their own production and price problems;

To provide price supports as in the Agricultural Act of 1954 that protect farmers, rather than price their products out of the market;

To continue our commodity loan and marketing agreement programs as effective marketing tools;

To make every effort to develop a more accurate measurement of farm parity;

To safeguard our precious soil and water resources for generations yet unborn;

To encourage voluntary self-supporting federal crop insurance;

To bring sympathetic and understanding relief promptly to farm and ranch families hard hit with problems of drought, flood or other natural disaster, or economic disaster, and to maintain the integrity of these programs by terminating them when the emergency is over;

To assist the young people of American farms and ranches in their development as future farmers and homemakers;

To continue and expand the Republican-sponsored school milk program, to encourage further use of the school lunch program now benefiting 11 million children, and to foster improved nutritional levels;

To provide constructive assistance by effective purchase and donation to ease temporary market surpluses, especially for the producers of perishable farm products;

To give full support to farmer-owned and farmer-operated co-operatives;

To encourage and assist adequate private and cooperative sources of credit, to provide supplemental credit through the Farmers Home Administration where needed, with an understanding of both the human and economic problems of farmers and ranchers;

To expand rural electrification through REA loans for generation and transmission, and to expand rural communication facilities;

To continue the improvement of rural mail delivery to farm families;

To promote fully the Republican-sponsored Rural-Development Program to broaden the operation and increase the income of low income farm families and help tenant farmers;

To work with farmers, ranchers and others to carry forward the Great Plains program to achieve wise use of lands in the area subject to wind erosion, so that the people of this region can enjoy a higher standard of living; and in summation:

To keep agriculture strong, free, attuned to peace and not war, to stand ready with a reserve capacity at all times as a part of our defense, based on sound agricultural economy.

We are an expanding nation. Our needs for farm products will continue to grow. Farm prices are improving and farm income is climbing.

Our farm and ranch people are confident of the future, despite efforts to frighten them into accepting economic nostrums and political panaceas. Record numbers of farms are owned by those who operate them.

The Republican Party is pledged to work for improved farm prices and farm income. We will seek that improvement boldly, in ways that protect the family farm. Our objective is a prosperous, expanding and free agriculture. We are dedicated to creating the opportunity for farmers to earn a high per-family income in a world at peace.

FEDERAL GOVERNMENT INTEGRITY

The Republican Party is wholeheartedly committed to maintaining a Federal Government that is clean, honorable and increasingly efficient. It proudly affirms that it has achieved this kind of Government and dedicated it to the service of all the people.

Our many economic and social advances of the past four years are the result of our faithful adherence to our 1952 pledge to reverse a 20-year Democratic philosophy calling for more and more power in Washington.

We have left no stone unturned to remove from Government the irresponsible and those whose employment was not clearly consistent with national security.

We believe that working for the Government is not a right but a privilege. Based on that principle we will continue a security program to make certain that all people employed by our Government are of unquestioned loyalty and trustworthiness. The Republican Party will, realistically and in conformity with constitutional safeguards for the individual, continue to protect our national security by enforcing our laws fairly, vigorously, and with certainty. We will act through the new division established to this end in the Department of Justice, and by close coordination among the intelligence services.

We promise unwavering vigilance against corruption and waste, and shall continue so to manage the public business as to warrant our people's full confidence in the integrity of their Government.

We condemn illegal lobbying for any cause and improper use of money in political activities, including the use of funds collected by compulsion for political purposes contrary to the personal desires of the individual.

Efficiency and Economy in Government. We pledge to continue our far reaching program for improving the efficiency and the effectiveness of the Federal Government in accordance with the principles set forth in the report of the Hoover Commission.

We are unalterably opposed to unwarranted growth of centralized Federal power. We shall carry forward the worthy effort of the Kestnbaum Commission on Intergovernmental Affairs to clarify Federal relationships and strengthen State and local government.

We shall continue to dispense with Federal activities wrongfully competing with private enterprise, and take other sound measures to reduce the cost of Government.

GOVERNMENTAL AFFAIRS

Postal Service. In the last four years, under direction from President Eisenhower to improve the postal service and reduce costs, we have modernized and revitalized the postal establishment from top to bottom, inside and out. We have undertaken and substantially completed the largest reorganization ever to take place in any unit of business or government:

We have provided more than 1200 badly-needed new post office buildings, and are adding two more every day. We are using the very latest types of industrial equipment where practicable; and, through a program of research and engineering, we are inventing new mechanical and electronic devices to speed the movement of mail by eliminating tedious old-fashioned methods.

We have improved service across the country in hundreds of ways. We have extended city carrier service to millions of new homes in thousands of urban and suburban communities which have grown and spread under the favorable economic conditions brought about by the Eisenhower Administration.

We have re-inspired the morale of our half-million employees through new programs of promotion based on ability, job training and safety,

and through our sponsorship of increased pay and fringe benefits.

We have adopted the most modern methods of transportation, accounting and cost control, and other operating procedures; through them we have saved many millions of dollars a year for the taxpayers while advancing the delivery of billions of letters by a day or more—all this while reducing the enormous deficit of the Department from its all time high of almost three-quarters of a billion dollars in 1952 to less than half that amount in 1955.

We pledge to continue our efforts, blocked by the Democratic leadership of the 84th Congress, for a financially sound, more nearly self-sustaining postal service—with the users of the mails paying a greater share of the costs instead of the taxpayers bearing the burden of huge postal deficits.

We pledge to continue and to complete this vitally needed program of modernization of buildings, equipment, methods and service, so that the American people will receive the kind of mail delivery they deserve—the speediest and best that American ingenuity, technology and modern business management can provide.

Civil Service. We will vigorously promote, as we have in the past, a non-political career service under the merit system which will attract and retain able servants of the people. Many gains in this field, notably pay increases and a host of new benefits, have been achieved in their behalf in less than four years.

The Republican Party will continue to fight for eagerly desired new advances for Government employees, and realistic reappraisement and adjustment of benefits for our retired civil service personnel.

Statehood for Alaska and Hawaii. We pledge immediate statehood for Alaska, recognizing the fact that adequate provision for defense requirements must be made.

We pledge immediate statehood for Hawaii.

Puerto Rico. We shall continue to encourage the Commonwealth of Puerto Rico in its political growth and economic development in accordance with the wishes of its people and the fundamental principle of self-determination.

Indian Affairs. We shall continue to pursue our enlightened policies which are now producing exceptional advances in the long struggle to help the American Indian gain the material and social advantages of his birthright and citizenship, while maintaining to the fullest extent the cultural integrity of the various tribal groups.

We commend the present administration for its progressive programs which have achieved such striking progress in preparing our Indian citizens for participation in normal community life. Health, educational and employment opportunities for Indians have been greatly expanded beyond any previous level, and we favor still further extensions of these programs.

We favor most sympathetic and constructive execution of the Federal trusteeship over Indian affairs, always in full consultation with Indians in the management of their interests and the expansion of their rights of self-government in local and tribal affairs.

We urge the prompt adjudication or settlement of pending Indian claims.

District of Columbia. We favor self-government, national suffrage and representation in the Congress of the United States for residents of the District of Columbia.

Equal Rights. We recommend to Congress the submission of a constitutional amendment providing equal rights for men and women.

EQUAL OPPORTUNITY AND JUSTICE

CIVIL RIGHTS

The Republican Party points to an impressive record of accomplishment in the field of civil rights and commits itself anew to advancing the rights of all our people regardless of race, creed, color or national origin.

In the area of exclusive Federal jurisdiction, more progress has been made in this field under the present Republican Administration than in any similar period in the last 80 years.

The many Negroes who have been appointed to high public positions have played a significant part in the progress of this Administration.

Segregation has been ended in the District of Columbia Government and in the District public facilities including public schools, restaurants, theaters and playgrounds. The Eisenhower Administration has eliminated discrimination in all federal employment.

Great progress has been made in eliminating employment discrimination on the part of those who do business with the Federal Government and secure Federal contracts. This Administration has impartially enforced Federal civil rights statutes, and we pledge that we will continue to do so. We support the enactment of the civil rights program already presented by the President to the Second Session of the 84th Congress.

The regulatory agencies under this Administration have moved vigorously to end discrimination in interstate commerce. Segregation in the active Armed Forces of the United States has been ended. For the first time in our history there is no segregation in veterans' hospitals and among civilians on naval bases. This is an impressive record. We pledge ourselves to continued progress in this field.

The Republican Party has unequivocally recognized that the supreme law of the land is embodied in the Constitution, which guarantees to all people the blessings of liberty, due process and equal protection of the laws. It confers upon all native-born and naturalized citizens not only citizenship in the State where the individual resides but citizenship of the United States as well. This is an unqualified right, regardless of race, creed or color.

The Republican Party accepts the decision of the U. S. Supreme Court that racial discrimination in publicly supported schools must be progressively eliminated. We concur in the conclusion of the Supreme Court that its decision directing school desegregation should be accomplished with "all deliberate speed" locally through Federal District Courts. The implementation order of the Supreme Court recognizes the complex and acutely emotional problems created by its decision in certain sections of our country where racial patterns have been developed in accordance with prior and longstanding decisions of the same tribunal.

We believe that true progress can be attained through intelligent study, understanding, education and good will. Use of force or violence by any group or agency will tend only to worsen the many problems inherent in the situation. This progress must be encouraged and the work of the courts supported in every legal manner by all branches of the Federal Government to the end that the constitutional ideal of equality before the law, regardless of race, creed or color, will be steadily achieved.

IMMIGRATION

The Republican Party supports an immigration policy which is in keeping with the traditions of America in providing a haven for oppressed peoples, and which is based on equality of treatment, freedom from implications of discrimination between racial, nationality and religious groups, and flexible enough to conform to changing needs and conditions.

We believe that such a policy serves our self-interest, reflects our responsibility for world leadership and develops maximum cooperation with other nations in resolving problems in this area.

We support the President's program submitted to the 84th Congress to carry out needed modifications in existing law and to take such further steps as may be necessary to carry out our traditional policy.

In that concept, this Republican Administration sponsored the Refugee Relief Act to provide asylum for thousands of refugees, expellees and displaced persons, and undertook in the face of Democrat opposition to correct the inequities in existing law and to bring our immigration policies in line with the dynamic needs of the country and principles of equity and justice.

We believe also that the Congress should consider the extension of the Refugee Relief Act of 1953 in resolving this difficult refugee problem which resulted from world conflict. To all this we give our wholehearted support.

HUMAN FREEDOM AND PEACE

Under the leadership of President Eisenhower, the United States has advanced foreign policies which enable our people to enjoy the blessings of liberty and peace.

The changes in the international scene have been so great that it is easy to forget the conditions we inherited in 1953.

Peace, so hardly won in 1945, had again been lost. The Korean War, with its tragic toll of more than an eighth of a million American casualties, seemed destined to go on indefinitely. Its material costs and accompanying inflation were undermining our economy.

Freedom was under assault, and despotism was on the march. Armed conflict continued in the Far East, and tensions mounted elsewhere.

The threat of global war increased daily.

International Communism which, in 1945, ruled the 200 million people in the Soviet Union and Baltic States, was conquering so that, by 1952, it dominated more than 700 million people in 15 once-independent nations.

Today. Now, we are at peace. The Korean War has been ended. The Communist aggressors have been denied their goals.

The threat of global war has receded.

The advance of Communism has been checked, and, at key points, thrown back. The once-monolithic structure of International Communism, denied the stimulant of successive conquests, has shown hesitancy both internally and abroad.

The Far East. The Korean War was brought to a close when the Communist rulers were made to realize that they could not win.

The United States has made a Collective Defense Treaty with the Republic of Korea which will exclude, for the future, the Communist miscalculation as to announced American interests and intentions which led to the original aggression.

The United States has made a security Treaty with the Republic of China covering Formosa and the Pescadores; and the Congress, by virtually unanimous action, has authorized the President to employ the armed forces of the United States to defend this area. As a result, the Chinese Communists have not attempted to implement their announced intention to take Formosa by force.

In Indochina, the Republics of Vietnam and Cambodia and Laos are now free and independent nations. The Republic of Vietnam, with the United States assistance, has denied the Communists the gains which they expected from the withdrawal of French forces.

The security of Southeast Asia has now been bolstered by the collective-defense system of SEATO, and its peoples encouraged by the declarations in the Pacific Charter of the principles of equal rights and self-determination of peoples.

The Middle East and Southeast Asia. The Middle East has been strengthened by the defensive unity of the four "northern tier" countries —Turkey, Iraq, Iran and Pakistan—which hold gateways to the vast oil resources upon which depend the industry and military strength of the free world. This was made possible by the liberation of Iran from the grip of the Communist Tudeh Party. Iran has again made its oil reserves available to the world under an equitable settlement negotiated by the United States.

We have maintained, and will maintain, friendly relations with all nations in this vital area, seeking to mediate differences among them, and encouraging their legitimate national aspirations.

Europe. In Western Europe, the scene has been transformed. The Federal Republic of Germany, which until 1953 was denied sovereignty and the opportunity to join the North Atlantic Treaty Organization, has now had full sovereignty restored by the Treaties of 1954, and has become a member of NATO despite the intense opposition of the Soviet Union.

NATO itself has been strengthened by developing reliance upon new weapons and retaliatory power, thus assisting the NATO countries increasingly to attain both economic welfare and adequate military defense.

On our initiative, the political aspects of NATO are being developed. Instead of being merely a military alliance, NATO will provide a means for coordinating the policies of the member states on vital matters, such as the reunification of Germany, the liberation of the satellites, and general policies in relation to the Soviet Union.

Austria has been liberated. The freedom treaty, blocked since 1947 by the Soviet Union, was signed in 1955. For the first time since the end of World War II, Red Army forces in Europe evacuated occupied lands.

The emotion-charged dispute between Italy and Yugoslavia about Trieste was settled with the active participation of the United States. The City of Trieste was restored to Italian sovereignty, and United States and British forces withdrew.

The Spanish base negotiations, which had long languished, were successfully concluded, and close working relations in this important respect established between the United States and Spain.

The Americas. Our good neighbor policy continues to prove its wisdom.

The American Republics have taken effective steps against the cancer of Communism. At the Caracas Conference of March, 1954, they agreed that if International Communism gained control of the political institutions of any American republic, this would endanger them all, and would call for collective measures to remove the danger. This new Doctrine, first proposed by the United States, extends into modern times the principles of the Monroe Doctrine.

A first fruit of the Caracas Doctrine was the expulsion of the Communist regime ruling Guatemala. Today, Guatemala is liberated from Kremlin control. The Organization of American States has grown in vigor. It has acted promptly and effectively to settle hemispheric disputes. In Costa Rica, for the first time in history, international aerial inspection was employed to maintain peace. The Panama Conference was probably the most successful in the long history of the Organization of American States in its promotion of good will, understanding and friendship.

Relations with Soviet Russia. Far-reaching steps have been taken to eliminate the danger of a third world war. President Eisenhower led the way at Geneva. There he impressed the Soviet leaders and the world with the dedication of the United States to peace, but also with its determination not to purchase peace at the price of freedom.

That Summit Conference set new forces into motion. The Soviet rulers professed to renounce the use of violence, which Stalin had made basic in the Communist doctrine. Then followed a repudiation of Stalin, the growth of doctrinal disputes within the Communist Party, and a discrediting of Party authority and its evil power. Forces of liberalism within the Soviet Bloc challenge the brutal and atheistic doctrines of Soviet Communism. For the first time, we see positive evidence that forces of freedom and liberation will inevitably prevail if the free nations maintain their strength, unity and resolution.

The future. We re-dedicate ourselves to the pursuit of a just peace and the defense of human liberty and national independence.

We shall continue vigorously to support the United Nations.

We shall continue our cooperation with our sister states of the Americas for the strengthening of our security, economic and social ties with them.

We shall continue to support the collective-security system begun in 1947 and steadily developed on a bipartisan basis. That system has joined the United States with 42 other nations in common defense of freedom. It has created a deterrent to war which cannot be nullified by Soviet veto.

Where needed, we shall help friendly countries maintain such local forces and economic strength as provide a first bulwark against Communist aggression or subversion. We shall reinforce that defense by a military capacity which, operating in accordance with the United Nations Charter, could so punish aggression that it ceases to be a profitable pursuit.

We will continue efforts with friends and allies to assist the underdeveloped areas of the free world in their efforts to attain greater freedom, independence and self-determination, and to raise their standards of living.

We recognize the existence of a major threat to international peace in the Near East. We support a policy of impartial friendship for the peoples of the Arab states and Israel to promote a peaceful settlement of the causes of tension in that area, including the human problem of the Palestine-Arab refugees.

Progress toward a just settlement of the tragic conflict between the Jewish State and the Arab nations in Palestine was upset by the Soviet Bloc sale of arms to Arab countries. But prospects of peace have now been reinforced by the mission to Palestine of the United Nations Secretary General upon the initiative of the United States.

We regard the preservation of Israel as an important tenet of American foreign policy. We are determined that the integrity of an independent Jewish State shall be maintained. We shall support the independence of Israel against armed aggression. The best hope for peace in the Middle East lies in the United Nations. We pledge our continued efforts to eliminate the obstacles to a lasting peace in this area.

We shall continue to seek the reunification of Germany in freedom, and the liberation of the satellite states—Poland, Czechoslovakia, Hungary, Rumania, Bulgaria, Latvia, Lithuania, Estonia and other, once-free countries now behind the Iron Curtain. The Republican Party stands firmly with the peoples of these countries in their just quest for freedom. We are confident that our peaceful policies, resolutely pursued, will finally restore freedom and national independence to oppressed peoples and nations.

We continue to oppose the seating of Communist China in the United Nations, thus upholding international morality. To seat a Communist China which defies, by word and deed, the principles of the United Nations Charter would be to betray the letter, violate the spirit and subvert the purposes of that charter. It would betray our friend and ally, the Republic of China. We will continue our determined efforts to free the remaining Americans held prisoner by Communist China.

Recognizing economic health as an indispensable basis of military strength and world peace, we shall strive to foster abroad and to practice at home, policies to encourage productivity and profitable trade.

Barriers which impede international trade and the flow of capital should be reduced on a gradual, selective and reciprocal basis, with full recognition of the necessity to safeguard domestic enterprises, agriculture and labor against unfair import competition. We proudly point out that the Republican Party was primarily responsible for initiating the escape clause and peril point provisions of law to make effective the necessary safeguards for American agriculture, labor and business. We pledge faithful and expeditious administration of these provisions.

We are against any trade with the Communist world that would threaten the security of the United States and our allies.

We recognize that no single nation can alone defend the liberty of all nations threatened by Communist aggression or subversion. Mutual security means effective mutual cooperation. Poverty and unrest in less developed countries make them the target for international communism. We must help them achieve the economic growth and stability necessary to attain and preserve their independence.

Technical and economic assistance programs are effective countermeasures to Soviet economic offensives and propaganda. They provide the best way to create the political and social stability essential to lasting peace.

We will strive to bring about conditions that will end the injustices of nations divided against their will, of nations held subject to foreign domination, of peoples deprived of the right of self-government.

We reaffirm the principle of freedom for all peoples, and look forward to the eventual end of colonialism.

We will overlook no opportunity that, with prudence, can be taken to bring about a progressive elimination of the barriers that interfere with the free flow of news, information and ideas, and the exchange of persons between the free peoples and the captive peoples of the world. We favor the continuance and development of the "exchange-of-persons" programs between free nations.

We approve appropriate action to oppose the imposition by foreign governments of discrimination against United States citizens, based on their religion or race.

We shall continue the bipartisan development of foreign policies. We hold this necessary if those policies are to have continuity, and be regarded by other free nations as dependable.

The Republican Party pledges itself to continue the dynamic, courageous, sound and patriotic policies which have protected and promoted the interests of the United States during the past four years.

In a world fraught with peril, peace can be won and preserved only by vigilance and inspired leadership. In such a world, we believe it is essential that the vast experience of our proven leader, President Dwight D. Eisenhower, continues to guide our country in the achievement and maintenance of a just, honorable and durable peace.

Bulwark for the Free World—Our National Defense

The military strength of the United States has been a key factor in the preservation of world peace during the past four years. We are determined to maintain that strength so long as our security and the peace of the world require it.

This Administration, within six months after President Eisenhower's inauguration, ended the war in Korea by concluding an honorable armistice. The lesson of that war and our lack of preparedness which brought it about will not be forgotten. Such mistakes must not be repeated.

As we maintain and strengthen the security of this Nation, we shall, consistent with this Administration's dedication to peace, strive for the acceptance of realistic proposals for disarmament and the humanitarian control of weapons of mass destruction.

Our country's defense posture is today a visible and powerful deterrent against attack by any enemy, from any quarter, at any time.

We *have* the strongest striking force in the world—in the air—on the sea—and a magnificent supporting land force in our Army and Marine Corps. Such visible and powerful deterrents must continue to include:

A) A jet-powered, long-range strategic air force, and a tactical air force of the fastest and very latest type aircraft, with a striking capability superior to any other;

B) The most effective guided and ballistic missiles;

C) A modern navy, with a powerful naval aircraft arm prepared to keep the sea lanes open to meet any assignment;

D) An army whose mobility and unit firepower are without equal;

E) Bases, strategically dispersed at home and around the world, essential to all these operations.

We will maintain and improve the effective strength and state of readiness of all these armed forces.

To achieve this objective, we must depend upon attracting to, and retaining in our military services vigorous and well-trained manpower, and upon continuously maintaining in reserve, an enthusiastic and well-informed group of men and women. This will require incentives that will make armed service careers attractive and rewarding. A substantial start has been made toward bolstering the rewards and benefits that accompany a military career. We must continue to provide them.

In order that American youth in our armed services shall be provided with the most modern weapons, we have supported and will continue to support an effective and well-directed program of research and development, staffed by men of the highest caliber and ability in this field. There is no substitute for the best where the lives of our men and the defense of our Nation are concerned.

We fully appreciate the importance of scientific knowledge and its application particularly in the military field.

We pledge ourselves to stimulate and encourage the education of our young people in the sciences with a determination to maintain our technological leadership.

In this age of weapons of inconceivable destructiveness, we must not neglect the protection of the civilian population by all known means, while, at the same time, preparing our armed forces for every eventuality.

We wholeheartedly agree with President Eisenhower that our military defense must be backed by a strong civil defense, and that an effective civil defense is an important deterrent against attack upon our country, and an indispensable reliance should our nation ever be attacked.

We support his proposals for strengthening civil defense, mindful that it has become an effective Government arm to deal with natural disasters.

We shall continue to carry forward, vigorously and effectively, the valued services of the Federal Bureau of Investigation, as well as all other Government intelligence agencies, so as to insure that we are protected at all times against subversive activities. We will never relax our determined efforts to keep our Government, and our people, safely guarded against all enemies from within.

We agree and assert that civilian authority and control over our defense structure and program must be maintained at all times. We believe, without qualification, that in our present Commander-in-Chief, Dwight D. Eisenhower, this Nation possesses a leader equipped by training, temperament, and experience in war and in peace, for both that personal example and that direction of our national defense in which the American people will continue to have confidence, and in which the peoples of all the free world will find an increasing sense of security and of an opportunity for peace.

Veterans

We believe that active duty in the Armed Forces during a state of war or national emergency is the highest call of citizenship constituting a special service to our nation and entitles those who have served to positive assistance to alleviate the injuries, hardships and handicaps imposed by their service.

In recognizing this principle under previous Republican Administrations we established the Veterans Administration. This Republican Administration increased compensation and pension benefits for veterans and survivors to provide more adequate levels and to off-set cost of living increases that occurred during the most recent Democratic Administration.

We have also improved quality of hospital service and have established a long-range program for continued improvement of such service. We have strengthened and extended survivors' benefits, thus affording greater security for all veterans in the interest of equity and justice.

In advancing this Republican program we pledge:

That compensation for injuries and disease arising out of service be fairly and generously provided for all disabled veterans and for their dependents or survivors;

That a pension program for disabled war veterans in need and for their widows and orphans in need be maintained as long as necessary to assure them adequate income;

That all veterans be given equal and adequate opportunity for readjustment following service, including unemployment compensation when needed, but placing emphasis on obtaining suitable employment for veterans, particularly those disabled, by using appropriate facilities of government and by assuring that Federal employment preference and re-employment rights, to which the veteran is entitled, are received;

That the Veterans Administration be continued as a single independent agency providing veterans services;

That the service-disabled continue to receive first-priority medical services of the highest standard and that non-service disabled war veterans in need receive hospital care to the extent that beds are available.

Guarding and Improving Our Resources

One of the brightest areas of achievement and progress under the Eisenhower Administration has been in resource conservation and development and in sound, long-range public works programing.

Policies of sound conservation and wise development—originally advanced half a century ago under that pre-eminent Republican conservation team of President Theodore Roosevelt and Gifford Pinchot and amplified by succeeding Republican Administrations—have been pursued by the Eisenhower Administration. While meeting the essential development needs of the people, this Administration has conserved and safeguarded our natural resources for the greatest good of all, now and in the future.

Our national parks, national forests and wildlife refuges are now more adequately financed, better protected and more extensive than ever before. Long-range improvement programs, such as Mission 66 for the National Parks system, are now under way, and studies are nearing completion for a comparable program for the National Forests. These forward-looking programs will be aggressively continued.

Our Republican Administration has modernized and vitalized our mining laws by the first major revision in more than 30 years.

Recreation, parks and wildlife. ACHIEVEMENTS: Reversed the 15-year trend of neglect of our National Parks by launching the 10-year, $785 million Mission 66 parks improvement program. Has nearly completed field surveys for a comparable forest improvement program. Obtained passage of the so-called "Week-end Miner Bill." Added more than 400,000 acres to our National Park system, and 90,000 acres to wildlife refuges. Has undertaken well-conceived measures to protect reserved areas of all types and to provide increased staffs and operating funds for public recreation agencies.

We favor full recognition of recreation as an important public use of our national forests and public domain lands.

We favor a comprehensive study of the effect upon wildlife of the drainage of our wetlands.

We favor recognition, by the States, of wildlife and recreation management and conservation as a beneficial use of water.

We subscribe to the general objectives of groups seeking to guard the beauty of our land and to promote clean, attractive surroundings throughout America.

We recognize the need for maintaining isolated wilderness areas to provide opportunity for future generations to experience some of the wilderness living through which the traditional American spirit of hardihood was developed.

Public land and forest resources. ACHIEVEMENTS: Approved conservation programs of many types, including improvement of western grazing lands through reseeding programs, water-spreading systems, and encouragement of soil- and moisture-conservation practices by range users. Returned to the States their submerged lands and resources of their coasts, out to their historical boundaries—an area comprising about one tenth of the area off the Continental Shelf and about 17 per cent of the mineral resources. Initiated leasing of the Federally owned 83 per cent of the Continental Shelf which is expected ultimately to bring from 6 to 8 billion dollars into the Treasury and already has brought in over 250 million dollars. Enacted new legislation to encourage multiple use of the public domain.

We commend the Eisenhower Administration for its administration of our public lands and for elimination of bureaucratic abuses. We recommend continuing study and evaluation of the advisability of returning unused or inadequately used public lands.

We commend the Administration for expanding forest research and access road construction.

We shall continue to improve timber conservation practices, recreational facilities, grazing management, and watershed protection of our national forests and our public domain.

Minerals. Recognizing that a vigorous and efficient mineral industry is essential to the long-term development of the United States, and to its defense, we believe the Federal Government should foster a long-term policy for the development and prudent use of domestic mineral resources, and to assure access to necessary sources abroad, without dangerously weakening the market for domestic production of defense-essential materials.

We favor reasonable depletion allowances. We favor freedom of mineral producers from unnecessary governmental regulation; expansion of government minerals exploration and research, and establishment of minerals stockpile objectives which will reduce, and, where possible, eliminate foreseeable wartime shortages.

ACHIEVEMENTS: St. Lawrence Seaway and power projects, Colorado River Storage Project, Great Lakes connecting channels, small watershed protection and flood prevention under local control, Mississippi Gulf level canal, extension of water-pollution control program, survey of power potential of Passamaquoddy Bay tides, expansion of small project development for flood control, navigation and reclamation; extension to all 48 States of water facilities act, accelerated research on saline water conversion, authorized planning surveys and construction of more than 200 navigation, flood-control, beach erosion, rivers and harbors, reclamation, and watershed projects throughout the nation, advanced partnership water resource developments in a number of states.

Water resources. Water resource development legislation enacted under the Eisenhower Administration already has ushered in one of the greatest water resource development programs this Nation has ever seen, a soundly-conceived construction program that will continue throughout this Century and beyond.

We recognize that the burgeoning growth of our Nation requires a combination of Federal, State and local water and power development—a real partnership of effort by all interested parties. In no other way can the nation meet the huge and accelerated demands for increasing generating capacity and uses of water, both by urban and agricultural areas. We also are aware that water demands have been accentuated by the ravages of drought, creating emergency conditions in many sections of our country. We commend the Eisenhower Administration for encouraging state and local governments, public agencies, and regulated private enterprise, to participate actively in comprehensive water and power development. In such partnership we are leading the way with great Federal developments such as the Upper Colorado Project and with partnership projects of great importance, some of which have been shelved by the Democratic 84th Congress.

In the marketing of federally produced power we support preference to public bodies and co-operatives under the historic policy of the Congress.

We will continue to press for co-operative solution of all problems of water supply and distribution, reclamation, pollution, flood control, and saline-water conversion.

We pledge legislative support to the arid and semi-arid states in preserving the integrity of their water laws and customs as developed out of the necessities of these regions. We affirm the historic policy of Congress recognizing State water rights, as repeatedly expressed in Federal law over the past 90 years.

We pledge an expansion in research and planning of water resource development programs, looking to the future when it may be necessary to re-distribute water from water-surplus areas to water-deficient areas.

Fisheries. ACHIEVEMENTS: Accelerated research and administrative action to rehabilitate our long-neglected fishing industry. Approval of measures for additional conservation and propagation of fish. Development of the comprehensive program for fisheries management and assistance adopted by the Congress.

We favor continuation of the Eisenhower program to rehabilitate our long-neglected domestic fishing industry.

We advocate protective treaties insuring the United States commercial-fisheries industry against unfair foreign competition.

The Republican Party is acutely aware that a foundation stone of the nation's strength is its wealth of natural resources and the high development of its physical assets. They are the basis of our great progress in 180 years of freedom and of our nation's military and economic might.

We pledge that we will continue the policies of sound conservation and wise development instituted by this Administration to insure that our resources are managed as a beneficial trust for all the people.

For a Brighter Tomorrow

Atomic Energy. The Republican Party pledges continuous, vigorous development of Atomic Energy:

for the defense of our own country and to deter aggression, and

for the promotion of world peace and the enhancement of our knowledge of basic science and its application to industry, agriculture and the healing arts.

From the passage of the first Atomic Energy Act in 1946 to the beginning of this Republican Administration, a stalemate had existed, and only an arms race with the prospect of eventual catastrophe faced the nations of the world.

President Eisenhower has inaugurated and led a strong program for developing the peaceful atom—a program which has captured the imagination of men and women everywhere with its widespread, positive achievements.

The Government and private enterprise are working together on a number of large-scale projects designed to develop substantial quantities of electric power from atomic sources. The first power reactor will be completed next year. More and more private funds are being invested as the Government monopoly is relaxed.

In relaxing its monopoly, Government can stimulate private enterprise to go ahead by taking recognition of the tremendous risks involved and the complexity of the many technical problems that will arise, and assist in those ways that will make advances possible.

The Atomic Energy Commission also is encouraging a vigorous rural electrification program by cooperatives.

Every day, radioactive isotopes are brought more and more into use on farms, in clinics and hospitals, and in industry. The use of isotopes already has resulted in annual savings of hundreds of millions of dollars and the nuclear age has only begun.

It is to the benefit of the United States, as well as to all nations everywhere, that the uses of atomic energy be explored and shared. The Republican Party pledges that it will continue this imaginative, world-embracing program. We shall continue to chart our course so as to fortify the security of the free nations and to further the prosperity and progress of all people everywhere.

DECLARATION OF DEDICATION

With utmost confidence in the future and with justifiable pride in our achievements, the Republican Party warmly greets the dawn of our second century of service in the cause of unity and progress in the Nation.

As the Party of the Young and in glowing appreciation of his dynamic leadership and inspiration, we respectfully dedicate this Platform of the Party of the Future to our distinguished President Dwight D. Eisenhower, and to the Youth of America.

Socialist Party Platform: 1956

The Socialist Party is pledged to building a new, more democratic society in the United States; a society in which human rights come before property rights; a nation which can take its place in a World Federation of Cooperative Commonwealths which will eliminate war, racial antagonism, hunger, disease, poverty and oppression.

The Socialist Party is pledged to building and

to maintaining this new society by democratic means, for without freedom there can be no true socialism and without socialism there can be no enduring freedom.

Socialism is the social ownership and democratic control of the means of production. Social ownership, which includes cooperatives, is not usually government ownership. Democratic control is not administration by the central government but control by the people most directly affected and in the interest of all the people rather than for profit. The American people have already adopted many socialist measures to serve their needs when capitalism, with its profit motive, failed them.

In a big business economy, the claim that "free enterprise" and liberty go hand-in-hand is arrant nonsense. The power of monopoly is a threat to the democratic process. The right of the few to rob the many is a flagrant denial of freedom. Not until the robbery is ended can we have liberty, equality and fraternity.

The Socialist Party is committed to a policy of forthright, deliberate, planned introduction of socialism. Creeping into socialism when capitalism fails does not promote the welfare of the people or preserve democracy and freedom.

The Socialist Party of the United States is dedicated to building socialism in this stronghold of capitalism because, even at its greatest, capitalism fails to satisfy the finest aspirations of its people. For war, it achieved great heights of productivity; for peace, it is incapable of equal performance. The development of the highest living standard in the world cannot excuse the inequality in division of wealth, which means that one family in ten receives an annual income of less than $1,000 and more than two families in ten have less than $2,000 per year. In fact, the lower half of our population receives a smaller share of the total money income of the United States now than it did early in this century.

Our program is international as well as domestic. The American people do not share fairly in the wealth they themselves create; still less have the people of the underdeveloped areas been helped to pull themselves up to the level of decency which alone can provide the stability for enduring peace. The basic purpose of socialist foreign policy is to prevent another world war. The first step is to abolish every form of colonialism, racism and imperialism, wherever it appears, and no matter upon whose toes we tread. The second step is the encouragement of the developing democratic socialism in Asia and the movements for racial justice in Africa.

These policies will have far greater appeal to the hungry and oppressed millions of Asia, Africa, Eastern Europe and Latin America than will military aid and defensive pacts which threaten to involve them in nuclear war. It will provide them with greater benefits than totalitarian Communism can offer, without any of its ugly evils. The democratic challenge to totalitarianism can be made successful only through rejecting imperialism and adopting democratic socialism, thus winning the minds and hearts of the downtrodden and oppressed everywhere. But most important of all we advocate these policies because they are morally right.

In this struggle, American Socialists find their allies around the world in the Socialist International and the Asian Socialist Conference and they look for the strengthening of the United Nations as a step in the development toward federal world government.

American foreign policy must be based on an imaginative campaign for universal disarmament, including the ending of the production of fission and thermo-nuclear weapons, under effective international supervision and control. This is absolutely essential if the living standards of the under-privileged half of the world are to be raised. As long as we spend billions for armaments there is little likelihood that large scale economic aid to underdeveloped nations will be forthcoming. The ending of thermo-nuclear tests is one way in which the United States could demonstrate its sincerity in seeking disarmament. Another way is by the abolition of peacetime military conscription.

The new society for which the Socialist Party strives would organize the American economy to produce for the welfare of the many at home and abroad rather than the profits of the favored few.

Capitalism fails to guarantee basic security to the people. We would establish social insurance with adequate provision for unemployment compensation, old-age pensions and death benefits, and provide for medical care, family allotments and sickness insurance.

Private enterprise threatens the future of the country by the waste or destruction of our irreplaceable natural resources. We would conserve these resources by the most carefully planned use under organizations like the TVA.

Private enterprise inevitably develops giant business and monopolies which threaten the economic or political welfare of the people. Socialists would step in and operate public utilities, basic industry, banks and insurance companies either by genuine cooperatives or by publicly owned and democratically managed corporations. Private enterprise inevitably encourages the recurring collapse of individual capitalist enterprises thus threatening the livelihood of the workers involved. Sectional unemployment—whether by locality or by industry—cannot be tolerated, regardless of how high the general economic level may remain. Partial measures like adequate insurance, retraining for workers, financing movement to new work, may suffice in some situations. But where private enterprise ceased to offer opportunities for productive work, social enterprise must take over and provide them. The right to a job is a basic right which should be guaranteed to all people.

In seeking greater social controls over the American economy, Socialists would guard against the substitution of irresponsible state bureaucracy for irresponsible state bureaucracy. To achieve this we propose that:

Wherever possible, the public enterprise should be at least one step removed from government control, not the patronage-run post office but the TVA is a better form.

Wherever efficient management is possible on a decentralized basis, Socialists prefer this to operation on a national basis.

Wherever the people themselves can organize the needed institution, popular participation should be given preference. Cooperatives should be aided and encouraged to expand.

Wherever a public form of enterprise is set up, various categories of workers in the industry and of consumers must be represented in its control. At all times preservation of freedom of labor organization and of consumer choice is the safeguard of liberty. Social control must extend democracy and not create a new managerial hierarchy.

.   .   .   .

While working towards these Socialist goals, Socialists are acutely aware of other pressing immediate problems which the American people must face in this presidential year.

The first of these is the achievement of full equality for all Americans, regardless of race, sex, creed, color or national origin. We applaud the Supreme Court decisions that separate but equal facilities do not provide the same opportunity for all citizens, whether in regard to education, or elsewhere. We call for the protection of the law for all citizens in exercise of their constitutional liberties, particularly the right to vote.

We oppose any action by Congress which will surrender to the individual states the right to legislate on matters which by their nature should be under the direction of the Federal Government. This includes laws on sedition, as well as legislation affecting interstate commerce.

The second is the protection and improvement of the American standard of living. The growing threat of unemployment, both from automation and from other forces, must be met primarily by increasing workers' wages but also by expanded insurance coverage and by increasing governmental action to influence investment and production. Community needs, such as schools, slum clearance, flood controls, etc., provide a wide area for useful work and stimulus to renewed productivity; we need a Point Five for America.

Taxation policies must be revised to get back to the idea of taxation in accordance with ability to pay.

We favor the establishment of government agencies or cooperatives to assist in the expansion of domestic and export consumption of farm products, to strengthen the family type farm, and to facilitate the shift from farm work to non-farm employment. But we oppose unequivocally any plan to limit the production of food or its destruction in order to keep up prices. In today's hungry world we advocate the production of more, rather than less, food.

While planning to achieve equity for the farmer, we do not forget the farm laborer or the plight of the migrant farm worker. It is essential that they be provided with steady employment, minimum wage standards, maximum hours and working conditions comparable with those of other workers and that they be provided with adequate housing and equal and identical schooling for their children.

The decline of American democracy is attested by the fact that minority parties—old or future—are being driven from the ballot by restrictive legislation; from access to the people by the incredible expense of television and new advertising techniques; and out of public favor by a manufactured conformity which stifles creative statesmanship in majority as well as minority political life.

Trade unions, too, are under attack. We continue to call for repeal of the Taft-Hartley act. So-called "right-to-work" laws passed and pending in various states, pretend to safeguard the rights of the individual to work while actually depriving him of his only real protection on the job—his union shop.

The right to work has another aspect. Where employment of persons might endanger the security of the nation, screening is a natural part of qualification for the position—and most jobs have qualifications attached. But this necessity has been distorted almost beyond recognition. Individuals must not be deprived of the right to work at non-sensitive positions for which training and experience fit them.

The right to hear and answer charges which may affect the livelihood, liberty or citizenship of the individual must be protected by law. We ask elimination of the Committee on Un-American Activities which has abused the Congressional right of investigation. We oppose any congressional investigations into areas of personal belief.

We demand repeal of the Smith Act, which we protested long before its provisions were applied to the Communist Party and when that Party supported its use against other minorities.

. . . .

Such, in brief, is the platform of the Socialist Party. This program is based on the highest ideals of human brotherhood. It will bring peace instead of war. It will replace fear and hate with goodwill and love. Death and despair will give way to life and hope.

We urge you to join with us in a call for a democratic Socialist economy with production for use, social planning for the benefit of all, equality of opportunity and full recognition of the dignity of every human being.

Socialist Labor Platform for 1956

The Socialist Labor Party of America, in National Convention assembled on the 6th day of May, 1956, reaffirms its previous platform pronouncements and declares:

Humanity stands today on the threshold of a new social order. The old order—capitalism—is doomed; it is an outmoded system shot through with fatal contradictions. For the time being, the capitalist economy is prevented from collapsing by two major props. One is the bubble of consumer credit. The other is government spending for arms—a multi-billion dollar military boondoggling program.

Sooner or later the credit bubble will burst and set in motion the forces leading to economic paralysis. Society then will be confronted by an economic crisis of the first magnitude. In this crisis the warehouses will groan with unsold surpluses while the mass of the people suffer increasing want. Unemployment among the useful producers—the working class—will be on a scale that will make the depression of the 'thirties seem mild by comparison. And business failures will spread like a plague among the petty capitalists, while the capitalist giants, the great corporate empires, concentrate even more economic power in their power-greedy hands.

H-Bomb Stalemate v. Ruling-Class Desperation

A world war that quickly consumed the piled-up surpluses enabled capitalism to extricate itself from the depression of the 'thirties. And war remains today the only real alternative the capitalists have to ultimate economic collapse. But war in 1956 means an H-bomb war, a war of annihilation and therefore a war that is suicidal not only to capitalism, but to civilization and to much, if not all, of the human race. Practically, capitalism today can postpone economic breakdown only by plunging the whole world into a veritable hell of hydrogen-bomb destructiveness and deadly radioactivity.

At the Geneva conference the political heads of the two rival imperialisms—Soviet Russia and the United States—solemnly agreed that war in these circumstances is unthinkable. Their agreement underscored the fact of atomic stalemate. But atomic stalemate, however, is no protection

against a catastrophic third World War. Ruling classes, faced with the breakdown of their system and the consequent loss of their property and class privileges, become desperate. And desperate men do desperate things. It is cause for the most sober reflection that today a few hundred top capitalists, and their military and political pawns —or their imperialist adversaries, the Russian despots—can, when their material interests so demand, set in motion fateful forces that could destroy the world.

Socialism Abolishes Bureaucracy

The Socialist Labor Party declares that the only alternative to social ruin and possible atomic war is the abolition of capitalism and all forms of class rule and the establishment of Socialism. We must add that bona fide Socialism has nothing in common with the bureaucratic despotism which, despite the "collective leadership" that has replaced Stalin's one-man rule, masquerades as "Socialism" in Soviet Russia. Nor does Socialism mean "making the politician the boss." Socialism, as Karl Marx conceived it, as Daniel De Leon, the great American Marxist, developed it, and as advocated by the Socialist Labor Party, is a society of industrial democracy in which the factories, mills, mines, railroads and land, etc., are owned collectively by all the people, where production is carried on for use instead of for sale and profit, and where the industries are operated and administered democratically by the workers themselves, organized in Socialist Industrial Unions.

In the "Iron Curtain" countries the bureaucrat is the master. In the West, too, the bureaucrat is tending to replace the capitalist as the overlord of modern society. The Socialist Industrial Union Government, as proposed by the Socialist Labor Party, is in reality the only form of social and industrial administration that eliminates both capitalists and bureaucrats and gives the workers of brain and brawn a collective mastery of their tools and products.

Socialism Will Cleanse Society!

Socialism is the answer to all social problems. Socialism is the cure for every evil spawned by the capitalist class rule:

It is the cure for recurring war because it eliminates the competition for markets and raw materials that is the basic cause of war and brings universal economic cooperation, thus creating a foundation for a durable peace.

It is the cure for recurring depression because it replaces capitalist production for sale with production for human needs, thus freeing social production from the anarchy and restrictions of private ownership and a capricious market.

It is the answer to the threat of technological unemployment—a threat underscored by the rapid spread of automation—because democratic Socialist control of industry insures that, instead of kicking workers out of their jobs, new machines will kick hours out of the working day.

It is the cure for social strife and the class struggle because Socialism terminates exploitation of man by man and creates the economic basis of collective interests essential to social harmony.

It is the cure for race prejudice because it cleanses society of the sordid material interests that profit from fomenting racism and creates the cooperative climate for human brotherhood.

Socialism is the answer to crime and juvenile delinquency, too, and to the alarming spread of mental illness, alcoholism, dope addiction, and other similar manifestations of capitalist insanity, for it will replace irrational, inhuman relationships with rational, human ones.

For a Better World!

To bring to birth this sane society of peace, abundance and freedom, the Socialist Labor Party appeals to the working class of America, and to all other enlightened and social-minded citizens, to support its principles at the polls by voting for the candidates of the Socialist Labor Party. It appeals to all enlightened elements of our population to repudiate the Republican and Democratic parties, which are the Siamese twins of capitalism. It appeals to them to repudiate the self-styled "radicals" and "liberals" whose platforms consist of reform demands, measures that are meant to sweetscent capitalist rule, and that, when granted by decadent capitalism, are in fact concealed measures of reaction.

Finally, the Socialist Labor Party appeals to the working class to repudiate the present unions. All of them accept capitalism as a finality, and are under the domination and control of labor lieutenants of the capitalist class. It calls upon the workers to build a new union based squarely on working-class interests, one which has Socialism as its goal. And it calls upon them to build the integral Socialist Industrial Union as the only power capable of enforcing the Socialist ballot and of assuming the administration of social production.

This is the peaceful and civilized way to accomplish the Socialist revolution in America.

The issue in this campaign—the burning issue confronting mankind—is Socialism v. capitalism. Until it is resolved mankind's aspirations for the abundant life, in liberty and happiness, are doomed to frustration.

Unite with us to save society from catastrophe—and to set an example in free industrial self-government for all mankind! Unite with us to establish the democratic Socialist Republic of Peace, Plenty and International Brotherhood!

Socialist Workers Party 1956 Election Platform

Mankind stands at the threshold of an era in which human culture can rise to unprecedented heights. Giant leaps in technology, ranging from the mechanization of agriculture to the control of atomic energy, have today made it possible to produce enough to meet all the needs of all the people. Now within reach are the means to eliminate human want in food, housing, health care, to satisfy all the necessities of life.

Across this brilliant prospect lies the dark shadow of a parallel leap in militarism. Nearly one-quarter of the national income is taken in taxes, mainly to create a vast war machine. Natural resources and manpower are diverted from useful production and wasted on instruments of destruction. Living standards and democratic rights stand in peril before the despotism of war. And in every mind lurks a terrible fear of the death-dealing horrors of the hydrogen bomb.

The role of militarism as the fundamental feature of American foreign policy is determined by the world conflict of rival social systems. The capitalist class wants to use America's power to prevent the birth of a world socialist order. The issue is posed: Shall capitalist exploitation of natural resources and productive labor remain dominant? Or shall mankind throw off the fetters of outlived capitalism and advance to a system of planned economy capable of eliminating human want?

COLONIAL INDEPENDENCE STRUGGLE

A universal demand for industrialization has arisen throughout the world. People everywhere seek the benefit of technological progress to improve their living standards and raise their cultural level. The main obstacle to progress in the underdeveloped countries has been the direct or indirect domination of foreign capitalist powers. Revolutionary struggles for independence, stemming from this imperialist domination, have erupted in country after country.

The indomitable determination of the colonial and semi-colonial peoples to win their independence is today typified by the heroic struggles of the people of Cyprus and Algeria. Egypt's fight for the right to nationalize the Suez Canal and to build the Aswan dam symbolizes the aspirations of the underdeveloped countries to lay new foundations for economic and social progress.

The colonial revolution can be successful only through fusion with the working class struggle against capitalism. It must gravitate toward the socialist forms of nationalized property and planned economy which open the way to rapid development of the productive forces. This tendency of the colonial revolution to become transformed into a socialist revolution has reached its highest manifestation in the case of China. Starting as an independence struggle against imperialism, the third Chinese revolution has transformed the country into an anti-capitalist world power and its rise, together with the extension of Soviet property forms to Eastern Europe, has already abolished capitalism on one-third of the globe.

TARGETS OF IMPERIALISM

At the same time the Soviet Union has rapidly risen to the status of a great industrial power, second only to the United States. Within it exists a working class almost 50 million strong, a mighty force now gaining in self-confidence and asserting its own rights against the usurping bureaucracy. The repudiation of the hated dictator Stalin and the crisis now shaking the world Stalinist movement mark the beginning of a political revolution to establish workers democracy in the

Soviet sphere. With that political transformation the way will be opened for a new upsurge in the world socialist revolution.

The anti-capitalist struggles, stemming from a fundamental drive for ever-higher living standards, for freedom and national independence, are the targets against which American foreign policy is aimed. The imperialists are arming to turn back the revolutionary tide and reconquer the world for capitalist exploitation. The bipartisan gang of Republicans and Democrats are forming military pacts with hated dictators and colonial despots. They are forging a chain of American military bases throughout the world. Never before has there been such a vast peacetime military expansion.

PUPPETS OF WALL STREET

Every alliance formed by the American capitalist government is aimed directly at the revolutionary masses abroad. In Iran the government backed by the people was forcefully overthrown with imperialist aid in order to block nationalization of the oil reserves and perpetuate exploitation of these natural resources by the capitalist oil cartel. The dictatorial Armas regime in Guatemala received thinly-veiled American support to overthrow the constitutional government by force when mass pressures began to threaten the super-profits of the United Fruit Company, an American corporation.

In country after country similarly discredited governments are imposed on the people and propped up as direct or indirect agencies of American imperialism. In return they are expected to guarantee special privileges for United States capital investments in these lands in violation of the interests of the masses. As a result the same old colonialism against which the peoples are in revolt is continued in open or concealed form. Where camouflaged forms of imperialist domination fail, resort must be had to naked force. A current example is the threat to overturn nationalization of the Suez Canal through armed intervention.

Truman's use of the United Nations as a cover in the Korean invasion revealed its true role as a front organization for imperialism and exploded the myth that the UN can serve as an instrument for peace. No less illusory is the hope that the hydrogen bomb by its very destructiveness will outlaw war.

Revolt Against Status Quo

The war drive has been slowed down primarily by the revolutionary gains abroad. World capitalism has been dealt a series of setbacks and defeats weakening its power in relation to the anti-capitalist forces. Revolutionary China has emerged as a factor of great weight in world politics. These reverses have compelled the imperialists to mask their war aims through hypocritical peace maneuvers but militarism remains the ultimate instrument of capitalist rule. In the attempt to achieve world domination American imperialism won't hesitate to risk atomic war at whatever cost to humanity.

The Kremlin bureaucrats, although forced to repudiate Stalin, nevertheless continue his basic policy. They advocate "peaceful coexistence" as the answer to war. Their aim is to preserve the status quo. But the status quo is what the masses the world over are rebelling against. They are in revolt against capitalist exploitation and oppression, as well as against the authoritarian bureaucracy in the Soviet orbit. The struggle for socialism is a continuous, uninterrupted struggle against the status quo.

In the hope of making a diplomatic deal with imperialism the Soviet rulers undertake to derail revolutions in the capitalist sphere, substituting capitalist reform policies for revolutionary socialism. Stalin's heirs seek coexistence with imperialism in order to retain their bureaucratic privileges and the power to repress the struggle for workers democracy in the Soviet sphere. Using the Communist Parties to disarm the masses politically in the struggle against capitalism, they undermine the revolutionary process which stands as the only effective obstacle to imperialist war.

SWP Fights War Program

The Socialist Workers Party opposes the war program of American imperialism. It combats the Stalinist policy of curbing the anti-capitalist struggle in an effort to appease imperialism. The foreign policy of the SWP aims to align the United States with the world social transformations now in process, mobilizing our country's full power in support of the advance to a world system of planned economy.

Such a foreign policy requires in the first instance a basic change in the United States itself. Class-collaboration with the capitalist parties must give way to independent working class political action through labor's own party. The capitalist government must be replaced by a workers and farmers government. To serve these needs the vanguard of the working class must advance a principled socialist program flowing from the economic and political realities on the world arena and within this country.

The American economy is based primarily on arms expenditures. Boom conditions have prevailed consistently in industries central to war production but mere preparations for war have not been enough to sustain capitalist production as a whole. Despite the military build-up in the cold war a serious economic decline began in 1949. Overcome temporarily by American entry into the Korean war, the slump reappeared in 1953-54 after the fighting in Korea ended.

Danger of Economic Crisis

The country has for the time being been pulled out of the slump by creating record consumer debts through installment and mortgage buying. So great is the expansion that the overall consumer debt has climbed above total personal savings and the rate of continued increase is outstripping the rise in personal income. As the workers thus go deeper into debt, the monopoly corporations are coining record profits in what for them is genuine prosperity.

War spending and credit expansion tend to increase inflationary pressures. The consumers price index stands at the highest level on record and shows every sign of a continued climb. At the same time a chronic decline has hit industries like coal, textiles and shipbuilding. Periodic slumps impair employment in such industries as auto. A sag in the farm equipment field reflects the fundamental decline in agriculture. Inflationary pressures and the threat of unemployment thus appear side by side, spelling out the danger of economic crisis as the alternative to war under capitalism.

Subcurrents of Discontent

For the present, boom conditions still predominate. A high level of employment exists despite the serious trouble spots. Most workers accept capitalism and continue to rely on the capitalist politicians in government but with anxieties as to the future. The workers fear war, yet they also fear unemployment and feel the need of war production to assure them jobs. They see their economic security being destroyed by automation, decentralization of industries, corporation mergers, runaway plants and the periodic production slumps. On the job anger is generated by the speedup.

The subcurrents of discontent within the prevailing conservative mood come to the fore when the workers are forced on strike by the corporations. Unusual militancy is shown, especially among younger workers, Negroes and other minorities and women workers who are in the least secure position, who generally have the most grievances. Some of the most determined struggles have been waged by the Southern workers who want to win union protection and end the wage differential. Industrialization of the South is having a strong economic and political impact on white and Negro workers alike. Their common class interests, sharply revealed in struggle against the corporations, will tend to cut across color lines as happened in the rise of the CIO. Foreshadowed in this process is the stormy rise of unionism below the Mason-Dixon line.

NEGRO STRUGGLE FOR EQUALITY

Also from the South has come a sharp leap in the Negro struggle for equality. The Montgomery bus boycott has produced a powerful new weapon for mass action by the Negro people in support of their democratic demands. The Montgomery freedom fighters have shown unbreakable solidarity, a grim fighting mood and tremendous staying power. Their long battle has inspired the Negro masses nationally and is producing a more militant type of leadership. Inspired by the independence struggles of the colored peoples in the colonial countries, the Negro people of America are now fighting with determination to win economic, political and social equality.

The White Citizens Councils organized to combat the Negro movement are actually the tool of the bankers, industrialists and big planters. Their white supremacist program involves more than the anti-democratic denial of Negro equality. The WCC is deliberately intensifying racial antagonisms in order to split the white and Negro workers to block unionization of the South. Taking advantage of the AFL-CIO failure to get a union drive going, the WCC uses all forms of pressure to recruit white workers in the open shop plants and indoctrinate them against giving Negroes union rights. Where unions now exist the WCC campaigns for a separate all-white Southern Federation.

The white workers of the nation therefore have a direct stake in the fight of the Negro people to win their rights, just as the Negroes need labor's aid to achieve their aims. Unionization of the South, an open-shop haven for runaway plants, is vital to labor nationally but it cannot be accomplished without the support of the Negro workers who justly demand full equality. A need therefore arises to smash the Southern political system of white supremacy and the open shop not only to win Negro equality but also for the workers to advance economically and politically. This need leads directly toward a political alliance of labor and the Negro people.

Yet another labor ally is appearing on the land. Mechanization of agriculture is putting a squeeze on the small farmers. They are caught between a rise in capital investment for mechanization and a decline in farm commodity prices due to the capitalist crisis of overproduction. The small farmer is gradually going under, farm units are getting bigger and fewer, the monopolists are expanding their holdings.

In trying to survive mechanization the small farmers feel themselves much in the same position as the industrial workers trying to hold their jobs in the face of automation. To protect themselves they seek government assistance to assure the cost of production plus a fair rate of annual income. The government has offered little more than token aid to the small farmer, solving few of his problems. For the big capitalist farmer, however, the same program provides a neat profit since his unit costs are lower because he operates on a larger scale. Government policy has veered more and more in the direction of the big operator's needs with less and less regard for the plight of the little man.

As a result the small farmers are beginning to modify their political outlook. They are breaking with the old-time farm organizations dominated by the big operators and forming new setups designed to press for a government policy meeting their own needs. They are also moving toward collaboration with organized labor and would constitute potential allies of an independent labor party.

MIGRATORY WORKERS NEED HELP

The growth of monopoly on the land has uprooted large numbers of people who have become migratory farm workers. They travel from area to area working as seasonal help on the corporation farms. Paid only a starvation wage, whole families are compelled to labor in the fields, mother and children alongside the father. Seasonal gaps in employment reduce their average earnings below $1,000 a year. Yet they are generally denied the benefits of existing social legislation.

These migratory workers badly need the help of organized labor to build the unions they have started in an effort to improve their lot. Especially they need the benefit of a labor party to compel government action for correction of the social wrongs they now suffer.

MEANING OF WITCH HUNT

The capitalist politicians are fully aware that the industrial working class, the strongest social force in the nation, would be unbeatable in a political alliance with the Negro people, agricultural labor and small farmers. They also know that for labor to break with capitalist politics would mean the doom of capitalism. To ward off this danger and maintain the capitalist monopoly in politics and in government, they have launched a witch hunt against radicalism. A political blacklist of "subversives" has been maintained to weed out anti-capitalist tendencies in the mass movement. "Loyalty" purges have been conducted as a terror device to compel mass conformity with capitalist policies. Starting against federal employees, the attack has spread to all spheres of national life.

Mounting public opposition to the witch hunt and several limited legal victories against it have slowed down the attack to a certain degree. But the laws and executive orders on which the assault is based remain in effect. Persecution of organizations and individuals continues. A new law has been enacted to undermine the Fifth Amendment. Penalties under the thought-control Smith Act have been stiffened. Passage in 1954 of the Humphrey-Butler law was intended to do more than outlaw the Communist Party. This wholly anti-democratic law, proscribing a political party for the first time in American history, also set the stage for attacks on the unions themselves as "subversive." Such strikebreaking, union-busting smears have already been hurled at two unions, the United Electrical Workers and the Mine, Mill and Smelter Workers.

NEED FOR POLITICAL ACTION

Basic to the war program are ultimate cuts in real wages and reductions in social benefits which are bound to provoke mass resistance. The capitalists are therefore moving in stages to weaken the unions through governmental attacks and direct corporation assaults. The Taft-Hartley Act restricts the economic power of the unions. Enactment of "Right to Work" laws in the states intensifies the government pressures against labor. Corporation-provoked strikes in industry, often lockouts in affect, result from rejection of moderate union demands and from corporation counterdemands intended to impair wages and conditions, weaken union job control and sharpen the speedup.

When this combined assault by the corporations and the capitalist government is intensified labor will no longer be able to defend itself through union action alone. Realizing they will have to fight on the political field, the union officials engineered the AFL-CIO merger primarily to strengthen labor politically. Then they showed their fatal weakness as working class leaders by keeping the union power tied to the Democratic Party, hoping thereby to secure a return to the New Deal days.

ROLE OF LABOR BUREAUCRACY

The union officials base their expectations on the prospects of a permanent war economy. They count on war production to prevent a deep unemployment crisis. In return for their support of the war program they expect capitalist concessions to appease the union membership. With this outlook, stemming from their social position as a privileged bureaucracy, the union officials spread capitalist ideology in labor's ranks. They retard the development of class consciousness among the workers and oppose class struggle policies in the unions.

Although most workers instinctively distrust the

Republicans as the party of Big Business, general illusions remain that they can solve their problems through the Democratic Party. Alongside these illusions, doubts about the Democratic Party are appearing as shown by a trend toward class polarization in political action.

A growing tendency has arisen among the workers to choose between the capitalist politicians as a class and to intervene in capitalist politics as a labor faction. This trend reflects an awakening political consciousness of the greatest significance. The workers realize their economic security can be guaranteed and their social welfare advanced mainly by action at the government level. They are also coming to understand their own social power if they act together politically as a class and to understand the need for them to use their power to secure government action.

For Independent Labor Party

As against the workers needs and aspirations, the Democratic Party serves the basic interests of the capitalist class. Its New Deal reputation was forced upon it in the first place out of necessity to ward off the mass radicalization following the 1929 market crash. Since the New Deal became transformed into a War Deal during the latter part of the Thirties not one major social reform has been introduced. The Democrats have broken their repeated promises to repeal the Taft-Hartley Act and pass civil rights legislation. The 1956 Democratic convention voted down a proposed pledge to enforce the Supreme Court decision against segregation. In fact the Democrats have shown real action only in their efforts to out-bid the Republicans on military appropriations for the bipartisan war program and in their support of the bi-partisan witch hunt.

Already implicit in the Democratic Party policy are the conditions leading to a union break with capitalist politics. The assault on labor has been deepening ever since the beginning of the cold war. The workers' determination to defend their living standards was dramatically revealed by the strike actions during the Korean war, conducted in defiance of the Truman administration. The conflict between capital and labor has become more and more political in character. In every showdown both the Democrats and Republicans have stood on the side of capital, their policies differing only in degree, not in basic content.

Under these conditions a class struggle program backed up by militant leadership could soon prepare the way for an advance to independent labor political action.

Communist Party Betrayal

The Communist Party policy of playing Democratic Party politics cuts squarely across this objective process. It helps tie the workers politically to the class enemy and serves to hold the Negro people in a coalition with the white supremacists. Mass demands remain limited to a capitalist reform program and the monopoly capitalists are permitted to retain unchallenged control of the government. This policy has nothing whatever in common with Leninist principles of class struggle. It violates the basic interest of the workers, Negro people and small farmers in a transparent effort to serve the Kremlin's foreign policy of "co-existence."

To enter Democratic Party politics on the pretext of helping to organize a labor faction in a capitalist party only feeds mass illusions that capitalism can be reformed and retards the break with capitalist politics. The resulting mis-education delays the fusion of the socialist program with the mass power of organized labor in an independent political party fighting for socialism.

SWP Tells the Truth

It is the duty of socialists to tell the class truth. The workers can defend their interests only outside the framework of the capitalist political parties and in class struggle against them. The toilers of America have nothing in common with the capitalist class but they have everything in common with the revolutionary masses of the world against whom capitalism is preparing a war of conquest.

To be combatted are the union bureaucracy, the conservative Negro leaders and all other elements within the mass movement who support the foreign policy of the capitalist government. To be combatted are the policies of the Communist Party seeking to preserve the status quo, thus giving outlived capitalism a new lease on life. Only those political tendencies aligning themselves against capitalism through a policy of independent working class political action are progressive and deserving of support.

In the 1956 elections only the Socialist Workers

Party presents a principle, realistic vehicle for anti-capitalist political action through support of its national ticket—Farrell Dobbs for president and Myra Tanner Weiss for vice-president—and through support of its local candidates. In line with the fundamental objectives toward which the labor and socialist movement must strive the SWP candidates are running on this platform:

1. FOREIGN POLICY

Take the war-making powers out of the hands of Congress and the President. Let the people vote through a nation-wide referendum on the question of war or peace. Withdraw all troops from foreign soil. Halt all nuclear weapons tests.

No secret diplomacy. Abolish all military alliances. Recognize the government of revolutionary China. End all trade restrictions against anti-imperialist countries. Hands off Egypt.

Support the right of all peoples to a government of their own choice, including the right to abolish capitalism and replace it with a system of planned economy.

Solidarity with all colonial and socialist revolutions against imperialism and with the struggles of the workers in the Soviet sphere for the establishment of workers democracy.

2. ECONOMIC SECURITY AND SOCIAL WELFARE

For the 30 hour week. Reduce the hours of work with no reduction in take-home pay. Jobless benefits at full union rates for the entire period of unemployment. Government operation under workers control of all production facilities made idle by mergers, decentralization, runaways and production cutbacks. Abolish the speedup through union control of production speeds by majority vote of the workers involved.

Guarantee women workers equal pay for equal work; the right to a job and full seniority rights in upgrading; maternity care and federally-financed day nurseries and summer camps for children.

Adequate old-age pensions. Free medical care and hospitalization. Full disability benefits. A government-guaranteed college education for all youth.

An escalator clause on all wages, unemployment compensation, pensions and other benefits, with taxes to be included in computing living costs.

3. DEMOCRATIC RIGHTS

Repeal the Taft-Hartley and Humphrey-Butler Acts, the "Right to Work" laws and all other federal, state and city anti-labor laws. No restrictions on the right to organize, strike and picket. No government interference in the unions.

Abolish the "subversive" list. Repeal the McCarran Internal Security and Immigration laws. Halt all deportations. Repeal the Smith Act and grant amnesty to all victims of this thought-control law. Abolish the "loyalty" oaths and "loyalty" purges. Repeal the law abridging the Fifth Amendment. Abolish the House un-American Committee and the Senate Internal Security Committee. Halt all political prosecutions for contempt and perjury based on the testimony of stool-pigeons. No political tampering with pensions or other social benefits.

Liberalize the election laws.

4. RIGHTS OF MINORITIES

Full economic, political and social equality to the Negro people and to all other minority peoples. Solidarity with all mass actions of the embattled Negro freedom fighters. For the immediate enforcement and implementation of the Supreme Court decision against segregation.

Enact and enforce legislation to abolish lynching, the poll tax and all forms of segregation. Create an FEPC with full powers of enforcement. Put a stop to police brutality.

Combat all forms of anti-Semitism.

5. FARM POLICY

Establish a federal farm program to guarantee the cost of production on all farm commodities to working farmers to be operated under the control of their own representatives. Limit government price supports to small farmers only. Set up a federal all-risk crop insurance program with the premiums to be figured in the cost-of-production program. No limitation on crops so long as a single person remains hungry. Government food subsidies for families living on sub-standard diets.

Low cost, long term government credits to small farmers for modernization of production facilities. A moratorium on repayment of distress loans until the farm problem is solved. Expand rural electrification. A federal program for soil conservation and flood control. No taxes on savings of cooperatives. A federal ban on all speculation in farm commodities.

Abolish sharecropping and landlordism; the land to those who work it.

6. Housing and Public Works

Declare a national housing emergency and initiate a program to erect 20 million low-rent housing units. Rigid rent controls under the supervision of tenants committees. Build schools, hospitals and other public needs in adequate supply. Finance all public works from funds now allocated for arms expenditures.

7. Taxation

Tax the rich, not the poor. Repeal all payroll and sales taxes. Abolish all forms of hidden taxes. No tax on incomes under $7,500 a year. A 100% tax on all incomes over $25,000 a year. A 100% tax on all profits on war goods.

8. Military Policy

Stop the draft. Abolish the officers caste. Full democratic rights to the ranks, including election of their own officers and collective bargaining in defense of their interests. Union wages for all servicemen.

9. Government Ownership of Industry

Nationalize the banks, basic industries, food trusts and all natural resources, including nuclear power. Operate all these facilities in the interests of the producers and consumers through democratically-elected committees of workers and technicians. Institute a system of planned economy.

10. Independent Political Action

Break all ties with capitalist politics. Form an independent labor party based on the unions and embracing the Negro people and working farmers. Create a Workers and Farmers government to reorganize America on a socialist basis.

☒ CAMPAIGN OF 1960

The campaign of 1960 produced the closest presidential election of the twentieth century. Of more than 68,800,000 ballots counted, the Democrats obtained approximately 49.7 per cent, while 49.6 per cent of the votes were cast for the Republicans. The comparatively permanent minor parties whose platforms for 1960 are included in this volume, the Prohibition party, the Socialist Labor party, and the Socialist Workers party, polled a total of 133,920 votes. The Socialist party adopted a platform but did not nominate a presidential candidate.

An unpledged slate of electors in Mississippi received 116,248 votes. Local parties and scattered ballots throughout the nation accounted for an additional 382,313 votes of which 227,881 were cast for Governor Orval Faubus of Arkansas in several southern states.

Democratic Platform 1960

In 1796, in America's first contested national election, our Party, under the leadership of Thomas Jefferson, campaigned on the principles of "The Rights of Man."

Ever since, these four words have underscored our identity with the plain people of America and the world.

In periods of national crisis, we Democrats have returned to these words for renewed strength. We return to them today.

In 1960, "The Rights of Man" are still the issue.

It is our continuing responsibility to provide an effective instrument of political action for every American who seeks to strengthen these rights — everywhere here in America, and everywhere in our 20th Century world.

The common danger of mankind is war and the threat of war. Today, three billion human beings live in fear that some rash act or blunder may plunge us all into a nuclear holocaust which will leave only ruined cities, blasted homes, and a poisoned earth and sky.

Our objective, however, is not the right to co-exist in armed camps on the same planet with totalitarian ideologies; it is the creation of an enduring peace in which the universal values of human dignity, truth, and justice under law are finally secured for all men everywhere on earth.

If America is to work effectively for such a peace, we must first restore our national strength—military, political, economic, and moral.

NATIONAL DEFENSE

The new Democratic Administration will recast our military capacity in order to provide forces and weapons of a diversity, balance, and mobility sufficient in quantity and quality to deter both limited and general aggressions.

When the Democratic Administration left office in 1953, the United States was the pre-eminent power in the world. Most free nations had confidence in our will and our ability to carry out our commitments to the common defense.

Even those who wished us ill respected our power and influence.

The Republican Administration has lost that position of pre-eminence. Over the past 7½ years, our military power has steadily declined relative to that of the Russians and the Chinese and their satellites.

This is not a partisan election-year charge. It has been persistently made by high officials of the Republican Administration itself. Before Congressional committees they have testified that the Communists will have a dangerous lead in intercontinental missiles through 1963 — and that the Republican Administration has no plans to catch up.

They have admitted that the Soviet Union leads in the space race — and that they have no plans to catch up.

They have also admitted that our conventional military forces, on which we depend for defense in any non-nuclear war, have been dangerously slashed for reasons of "economy" — and that they have no plans to reverse this trend.

As a result, our military position today is measured in terms of gaps — missile gap, space gap, limited-war gap.

To recover from the errors of the past 7½ years will not be easy.

This is the strength that must be erected:

1. Deterrent military power such that the Soviet and Chinese leaders will have no doubt that an attack on the United States would surely be followed by their own destruction.

2. Balanced conventional military forces which will permit a response graded to the intensity of any threats of aggressive force.

3. Continuous modernization of these forces through intensified research and development, including essential programs now slowed down, terminated, suspended, or neglected for lack of budgetary support.

A first order of business of a Democratic Administration will be a complete re-examination of the organization of our armed forces.

A military organization structure, conceived before the revolution in weapons technology, cannot be suitable for the strategic deterrent, continental defense, limited war, and military alliance requirements of the 1960s.

We believe that our armed forces should be organized more nearly on the basis of function, not only to produce greater military strength, but also to eliminate duplication and save substantial sums.

We pledge our will, energies, and resources to oppose Communist aggression.

Since World War II, it has been clear that our own security must be pursued in concert with that of many other nations.

The Democratic Administrations which, in World War II, led in forging a mighty and victorious alliance, took the initiative after the war in creating the North Atlantic Treaty Organization, the greatest peacetime alliance in history.

This alliance has made it possible to keep Western Europe and the Atlantic Community secure against Communist pressures.

Our present system of alliances was begun in a time of an earlier weapons technology when our ability to retaliate against Communist attack required bases all around the periphery of the Soviet Union. Today, because of our continuing weakness in mobile weapons systems and intercontinental missiles, our defenses still depend in part on bases beyond our borders for planes and shorter-range missiles.

If an alliance is to be maintained in vigor, its unity must be reflected in shared purposes. Some of our allies have contributed neither devotion to the cause of freedom nor any real military strength.

The new Democratic Administration will review our system of pacts and alliances. We shall continue to adhere to our treaty obligations, including the commitment of the UN Charter to resist aggression. But we shall also seek to shift the emphasis of our cooperation from military aid to economic development, wherever this is possible.

Civil Defense

We commend the work of the civil defense groups throughout the nation. A strong and effective civil defense is an essential element in our nation's defense.

The new Democratic Administration will undertake a full review and analysis of the programs that should be adopted if the protection possible is to be provided to the civilian population of our nation.

ARMS CONTROL

A fragile power balance sustained by mutual nuclear terror does not, however, constitute peace. We must regain the initiative on the entire international front with effective new policies to create the conditions for peace.

There are no simple solutions to the infinitely complex challenges which face us. Mankind's eternal dream, a world of peace, can only be built slowly and patiently.

A primary task is to develop responsible proposals that will help break the deadlock on arms control.

Such proposals should include means for ending nuclear tests under workable safeguards, cutting back nuclear weapons, reducing conventional forces, preserving outer space for peaceful purposes, preventing surprise attack, and limiting the risk of accidental war.

This requires a national peace agency for disarmament planning and research to muster the scientific ingenuity, coordination, continuity, and seriousness of purpose which are now lacking in our arms control efforts.

The national peace agency would develop the technical and scientific data necessary for serious disarmament negotiations, would conduct research in cooperation with the Defense Department and Atomic Energy Commission on methods of inspection and monitoring arms control agreements, particularly agreements to control nuclear testing, and would provide continuous technical advice to our disarmament negotiators.

As with armaments, so with disarmament, the Republican Administration has provided us with much talk but little constructive action. Representatives of the United States have gone to conferences without plans or preparation. The Administration has played opportunistic politics, both at home and abroad.

Even duing the recent important negotiations at Geneva and Paris, only a handful of people were devoting full time to work on the highly complex problem of disarmament.

More than $100 billion of the world's production now goes each year into armaments. To the extent that we can secure the adoption of effective arms control agreements, vast resources will be freed for peaceful use.

The new Democratic Administration will plan for an orderly shift of our expenditures. Long-delayed reductions in excise, corporation, and individual income taxes will then be possible. We can also step up the pace in meeting our backlog of public needs and in pursuing the promise of atomic and space science in a peaceful age.

As world-wide disarmament proceeds, it will free vast resources for a new international attack on the problem of world poverty.

THE INSTRUMENTS OF FOREIGN POLICY

American foreign policy in all its aspects must be attuned to our world of change.

We will recruit officials whose experience, humanity, and dedication fit them for the task of effectively representing America abroad.

We will provide a more sensitive and creative direction to our overseas information program. And we will overhaul our administrative machinery so that America may avoid diplomatic embarrassments and at long last speak with a single confident voice in world affairs.

The "Image" of America

First, those men and women selected to represent us abroad must be chosen for their sensitive understanding of the peoples with whom they will live. We can no longer afford representatives who are ignorant of the language and culture and politics of the nations in which they represent us.

Our information programs must be more than news broadcasts and boastful recitals of *our* accomplishments and *our* material riches. We must find ways to show the people of the world that we share the same goals — dignity, health, freedom, schools for children, a place in the sun — and that we will work together to achieve them.

Our program of visits between Americans and people of other nations will be expanded, with special emphasis upon students and younger leaders. We will encourage study of foreign languages. We favor continued support and extension of such programs as the East-West cultural center established at the University of Hawaii. We shall study a similar center for Latin America, with due consideration of the existing facilities now available in the Canal Zone.

National Policy Machinery

In the present Administration, the National Security Council has been used not to focus issues for decision by the responsible leaders of Government, but to paper over problems of policy with "agreed solutions" which avoid decisions.

The mishandling of the U-2 espionage flights — the sorry spectacle of official denial, retraction, and contradiction — and the admitted misjudging of Japanese public opinion are only two recent examples of the breakdown of the Administration's machinery for assembling facts, making decisions, and coordinating action.

The Democratic Party welcomes the study now being made by the Senate Subcommittee on National Policy Machinery. The new Democratic Administration will revamp and simplify this cumbersome machinery.

WORLD TRADE

World trade is more than ever essential to world peace. In the tradition of Cordell Hull, we shall expand world trade in every responsible way.

Since all Americans share the benefits of this policy, its costs should not be the burden of a few. We shall support practical measures to ease the necessary adjustments of industries and communities which may be unavoidably hurt by increases in imports.

World trade raises living standards, widens markets, reduces costs, increases profits, and builds political stability and international economic cooperation.

However, the increase in foreign imports involves costly adjustment and damage to some domestic industries and communities. The burden has been heavier recently because of the Republican failure to maintain an adequate rate of economic growth, and the refusal to use public programs to ease necessary adjustments.

The Democratic Administration will help industries affected by foreign trade with measures favorable to economic growth, orderly transition, fair competition, and the long-run economic strength of all parts of our nation.

Industries and communities affected by foreign trade need and deserve appropriate help through trade adjustment measures such as direct loans, tax incentives, defense contracts priority, and retraining assistance.

Our Government should press for reduction of foreign barriers to the sale of the products of American industry and agriculture. These are particularly severe in the case of fruit products. The present balance-of-payments situation provides a favorable opportunity for such action.

The new Democratic Administration will seek international agreements to assure fair competition and fair labor standards to protect our own workers and to improve the lot of workers elsewhere.

Our domestic economic policies and our essential foreign policies must be harmonious.

To sell, we must buy. We therefore must resist the temptation to accept remedies that deny American producers and consumers access to world markets and destroy the prosperity of our friends in the non-Communist world.

IMMIGRATION

We shall adjust our immigration, nationality and refugee policies to eliminate discrimination and to enable members of scattered families abroad to be united with relatives already in our midst.

The national-origins quota system of limiting immigration contradicts the founding principles of this nation. It is inconsistent with our belief in the rights of man. This system was instituted after World War I as a policy of deliberate discrimination by a Republican Administration and Congress.

The revision of immigration and nationality laws we seek will implement our belief that enlightened immigration, naturalization and refugee policies and humane administration of them are important aspects of our foreign policy.

These laws will bring greater skills to our land, reunite families, permit the United States to meet its fair share of world programs of rescue and rehabilitation, and take advantage of immigration as an important factor in the growth of the American economy.

In this World Refugee Year it is our hope to achieve admission of our fair share of refugees. We will institute policies to alleviate suffering among the homeless wherever we are able to extend our aid.

We must remove the distinctions between native-born and naturalized citizens to assure full protection of our laws to all. There is no place in the United States for "second-class citizenship."

The protections provided by due process, right of appeal, and statutes of limitation, can be extended to non-citizens without hampering the security of our nation.

We commend the Democratic Congress for the initial steps that have recently been taken toward liberalizing changes in immigration law. However, this should not be a piecemeal project and we are confident that a Democratic President in cooperation with Democratic Congresses will again implant a humanitarian and liberal spirit in our nation's immigration and citizenship policies.

To the peoples and governments beyond our shores we offer the following pledges:

THE UNDERDEVELOPED WORLD

To the non-Communist nations of Asia, Africa, and Latin America: We shall create with you working partnerships, based on mutual respect and understanding.

In the Jeffersonian tradition, we recognize and welcome the irresistible momentum of the world revolution of rising expectations for a better life. We shall identify American policy with the values and objectives of this revolution.

To this end the new Democratic Administration will revamp and refocus the objectives, emphasis and allocation of our foreign assistance programs.

The proper purpose of these programs is not to buy gratitude or to recruit mercenaries, but to enable the peoples of these awakening, developing nations to make their own free choices.

As they achieve a sense of belonging, of dignity, and of justice, freedom will become meaningful for them, and therefore worth defending.

Where military assistance remains essential for the common defense, we shall see that the requirements are fully met. But as rapidly as security considerations permit, we will replace tanks with tractors, bombers with bulldozers, and tacticians with technicians.

We shall place our programs of international cooperation on a long-term basis to permit more effective planning. We shall seek to associate other capital-exporting countries with us in promoting the orderly economic growth of the underdeveloped world.

We recognize India and Pakistan as major tests of the capacity of free men in a difficult environment to master the age-old problems of illiteracy, poverty, and disease. We will support their efforts in every practical way.

We welcome the emerging new nations of Africa to the world community. Here again we shall strive to write a new chapter of fruitful cooperation.

In Latin America we shall restore the Good Neighbor Policy based on far closer economic cooperation and increased respect and understanding.

In the Middle East we will work for guarantees to insure independence for all states. We will encourage direct Arab-Israeli peace negotiations, the resettlement of Arab refugees in lands where there is room and opportunity for them, an end to boycotts and blockades, and unrestricted use of the Suez Canal by all nations.

A billion and a half people in Asia, Africa and Latin America are engaged in an unprecedented attempt to propel themselves into the 20th Century. They are striving to create or reaffirm their national identity.

But they want much more than independence. They want an end to grinding poverty. They want more food, health for themselves and their children, and other benefits that a modern industrial civilization can provide.

Communist strategy has sought to divert these aspirations into narrowly nationalistic channels, or external troublemaking, or authoritarianism. The Republican Administration has played into the hands of this strategy by concerning itself almost exclusively with the military problem of Communist invasion.

The Democratic programs of economic cooperation will be aimed at making it as easy as possible for the political leadership in these countries to turn the energy, talent and resources of their peoples to orderly economic growth.

History and current experience show that an annual per capita growth rate of at least 2% is feasible in these countries. The Democratic Administration's assistance program, in concert with the aid forthcoming from our partners in Western Europe, Japan, and the British Commonwealth, will be geared to facilitating this objective.

The Democratic Administration will recognize that assistance to these countries is not an emergency or short-term matter. Through the Development Loan Fund and otherwise, we shall seek to assure continuity in our aid programs for periods of at least five years, in order to permit more effective allocation on our part and better planning by the governments of the countries receiving aid.

More effective use of aid and a greater confidence in us and our motives will be the result.

We shall establish priorities for foreign aid which will channel it to those countries abroad which, by their own willingness to help themselves, show themselves most capable of using it effectively.

We shall use our own agricultural productivity as an effective tool of foreign aid, and also as a vital form of working capital for economic development. We shall seek new approaches which will provide assistance without disrupting normal world markets for food and fiber.

We shall give attention to the problem of stabilizing world prices of agricultural commodities and basic raw materials on which many underdeveloped countries depend for needed foreign exchange.

We shall explore the feasibility of shipping and storing a substantial part of our food abundance in a system of "food banks" located at distribution centers in the underdeveloped world.

Such a system would be an effective means of alleviating famine and suffering in times of natural disaster, and of cushioning the effect of bad harvests. It would also have a helpful anti-inflationary influence as economic development gets under way.

Although basic development requirements like transport, housing, schools, and river development may be financed by Government, these projects are usually built and sometimes managed by private enterprise. Moreover, outside this public sector a large and increasing role remains for private investment.

The Republican Administration has done little to summon American business to play its part in this, one of the most creative tasks of our generation. The Democratic Administration will take steps to recruit and organize effectively the best business talent in America for foreign economic development.

We urge continued economic assistance to Israel and the Arab peoples to help them raise their living standards. We pledge our best efforts for peace in the Middle East by seeking to prevent an arms race while guarding against the dangers of a military imbalance resulting from Soviet arms shipments.

THE ATLANTIC COMMUNITY

To our friends and associates in the Atlantic Community: We propose a broader partnership that goes beyond our common fears to recognize the depth and sweep of our common political, economic, and cultural interests.

We welcome the recent heartening advances toward European unity. In every appropriate way, we shall encourage their further growth within the broader framework of the Atlantic Community.

After World War II, Democratic statesmen saw that an orderly, peaceful world was impossible with Europe shattered and exhausted.

They fashioned the great programs which bear their names — the Truman Doctrine and the Marshall Plan — by which the economies of Europe were revived. Then in NATO they renewed for the common defense the ties of alliance forged in war.

In these endeavors, the Democratic Administrations invited leading Republicans to full participation as equal partners. But the Republican Administration has rejected this principle of bipartisanship.

We have already seen how the mutual trust and confidence created abroad under Democratic leadership have been eroded by arrogance, clumsiness, and lack of understanding in the Republican Administration.

The new Democratic Administration will restore the former high levels of cooperation within the Atlantic Community envisaged from the beginning by the NATO treaty in political and economic spheres as well as military affairs.

We welcome the progress towards European unity expressed in the Coal and Steel Community, Euratom, the European Economic Community, the European Free Trade Association, and the European Assembly.

We shall conduct our relations with the nations of the Common Market so as to encourage the opportunities for freer and more expanded trade, and to avert the possibilities of discrimination that are inherent in it.

We shall encourage adjustment with the so-called "Outer Seven" nations so as to enlarge further the area of freer trade.

THE COMMUNIST WORLD

To the rulers of the Communist World: We confidently accept your challenge to competition in every field of human effort.

We recognize this contest as one between two radically different approaches to the meaning of life — our open society which places its highest value upon individual dignity, and your closed society in which the rights of men are sacrificed to the state.

We believe your Communist ideology to be sterile, unsound, and doomed to failure. We believe that your children will reject the intellectual prison in which you seek to confine them, and that ultimately they will choose the eternal principles of freedom.

In the meantime, we are prepared to negotiate with you whenever and wherever there is a realistic possibility of progress without sacrifice of principle.

If negotiations through diplomatic channels provide opportunities, we will negotiate.

If debate before the United Nations holds promise, we will debate.

If meetings at high level offer prospects of success, we will be there.

But we will use all the power, resources, and energy at our command to resist the further encroachment of Communism on freedom — whether at Berlin, Formosa, or new points of pressure as yet undisclosed.

We will keep open the lines of communication with our opponents. Despite difficulties in the way of peaceful agreement, every useful avenue will be energetically explored and pursued.

However, we will never surrender positions which are essential to the defense of freedom, nor will we abandon peoples who are now behind the Iron Curtain through any formal approval of the status quo.

Everyone proclaims "firmness" in support of Berlin. The issue is not the desire to be firm, but the capability to be firm. This the Democratic Party will provide as it has done before.

The ultimate solution of the situation in Berlin must be approached in the broader context of settlement of the tensions and divisions of Europe.

The good faith of the United States is pledged likewise to defending Formosa. We will carry out that pledge.

The new Democratic Administration will also reaffirm our historic policy of opposition to the establishment anywhere in the Americas of governments dominated by foreign powers, a policy now being undermined by Soviet threats to the freedom and independence of Cuba. The Government of the United States under a Democratic Administration will not be deterred from fulfilling its obligations and solemn responsibilities under its treaties and agreements with the nations of the Western Hemisphere. Nor will the United States, in conformity with its treaty obligations, permit the establishment of a regime dominated by international, atheistic Communism in the Western Hemisphere.

To the people who live in the Communist World and its captive nations: We proclaim an enduring friendship which goes beyond governments and ideologies to our common human interest in a better world.

Through exchanges of persons, cultural contacts, trade in non-strategic areas, and other non-governmental activities, we will endeavor to preserve and improve opportunities for human relationships which no Iron Curtain can permanently sever.

No political platform promise in history was more cruelly cynical than the Republican effort to buy votes in 1952 with false promises of painless liberation for the captive nations.

The blood of heroic freedom fighters in Hungary tragically proved this promise a fraud. We Democrats will never be party to such cruel cultivation of false hopes.

We look forward to the day when the men and women of Albania, Bulgaria, Czechoslovakia, East Germany, Estonia, Hungary, Latvia, Lithuania, Poland, Rumania, and the other captive nations will stand again in freedom and justice. We will hasten, by every honorable and responsible means, the arrival of the day.

We shall never accept any deal or arrangement which acquiesces in the present subjugation of these peoples.

We deeply regret that the policies and actions of the Government of Communist China have interrupted the generations of friendship between the Chinese and American peoples.

We reaffirm our pledge of determined opposition to the present admission of Communist China to the United Nations.

Although normal diplomatic relations between our Governments are impossible under present conditions, we shall welcome any evidence that the Chinese Communist Government is genuinely prepared to create a new relationship based on respect for international obligations, including the release of American prisoners.

We will continue to make every effort to effect the release of American citizens and servicemen now unjustly imprisoned in Communist China and elsewhere in the Communist empire.

The United Nations

To all our fellow members of the United Nations: We shall strengthen our commitments in this, our great continuing institution for conciliation and the growth of a world community.

Through the machinery of the United Nations, we shall work for disarmament, the establishment of an international police force, the strengthening of the World Court, and the establishment of world law.

We shall propose the bolder and more effective use of the specialized agencies to promote the world's economic and social development.

Great Democratic Presidents have taken the lead in the effort to unite the nations of the world in an international organization to assure world peace with justice under law.

The League of Nations, conceived by Woodrow Wilson, was doomed by Republican defeat of United States participation.

The United Nations, sponsored by Franklin Roosevelt, has become the one place where representatives of the rival systems and interests which divide the world can and do maintain continuous contact.

The United States' adherence to the World Court contains a so-called "self-judging reservation" which, in effect, permits us to prevent a Court decision in any particular case in which we are involved. The Democratic Party proposes its repeal.

To all these endeavors so essential to world peace, we, the members of the Democratic Party, will bring a new urgency, persistence, and determination, born of the conviction that in our thermonuclear century all of the other Rights of Man hinge on our ability to assure man's right to peace.

The pursuit of peace, our contribution to the stability of the new nations of the world, our hopes for progress and well-being at home, all these depend in large measure on our ability to release the full potential of our American economy for employment, production, and growth.

Our generation of Americans has achieved a historic technological breakthrough. Today we are capable of creating an abundance in goods and services beyond the dreams of our parents. Yet on the threshold of plenty the Republican Administration hesitates, confused and afraid.

As a result, massive human needs now exist side by side with idle workers, idle capital, and idle machines.

The Republican failure in the economic field has been virtually complete.

Their years of power have consisted of two recessions, in 1953-54 and 1957-60, separated by the most severe peacetime inflation in history.

They have shown themselves incapable of checking inflation. In their efforts to do so, they have brought on recessions that have thrown millions of Americans out of work. Yet even in these slumps, the cost of living has continued to climb, and it is now at an all-time high.

They have slowed down the rate of growth of the economy to about one-third the rate of the Soviet Union.

Over the past 7½-year period, the Republicans have failed to balance the budget or reduce the national debt. Responsible fiscal policy requires surpluses in good times to more than offset the deficits which may occur in recessions, in order to reduce the national debt over the long run. The Republican Administration has produced the deficits — in fact, the greatest deficit in any peacetime year in history, in 1958-59 — but only occasional and meager surpluses. Their first seven years produced a total deficit of nearly $19 billion.

While reducing outlays for essential public services which directly benefit our people, they have raised the annual interest charge on the national debt to a level $3 billion higher than when they took office. In the eight fiscal years of the Republican Administration, these useless higher interest payments will have cost the taxpayers $9 billion.

They have mismanaged the public debt not only by increasing interest rates, but also by failing to lengthen the average maturity of Government obligations when they had a clear opportunity to do so.

Economic Growth

The new Democratic Administration will confidently proceed to unshackle American enterprise and to free American labor, industrial leadership, and capital, to create an abundance that will outstrip any other system.

Free competitive enterprise is the most creative and productive form of economic order that the world has seen. The recent slow pace of American growth is due not to the failure of our free economy but to the failure of our national leadership.

We Democrats believe that our economy can and must grow at an average rate of 5% annually, almost twice as fast as our average annual rate since 1953. We pledge ourselves to policies that will achieve this goal without inflation.

Economic growth is the means whereby we improve the American standard of living and produce added tax resources for national security and essential public services.

Our economy must grow more swiftly in order to absorb two groups of workers: the much larger number of young people who will be reaching working age in the 1960s, and the workers displaced by the rapid pace of technological advances, including automation. Republican policies which have stifled growth could only mean increasingly severe unemployment, particularly of youth and older workers.

An End to Tight Money

As the first step in speeding economic growth, a Democratic President will put an end to the present high-interest, tight-money policy.

This policy has failed in its stated purpose — to keep prices down. It has given us two recessions within five years, bankrupted many of our farmers, produced a record number of business failures, and added billions of dollars in unnecessary higher interest charges to Government budgets and the cost of living.

A new Democratic Administration will reject this philosophy of economic slowdown. We are committed to maximum employment, at decent wages and with fair profits, in a far more productive, expanding economy.

The Republican high-interest policy has extracted a costly toll from every American who has financed a home, an automobile, a refrigerator, or a television set.

It has foisted added burdens on taxpayers of state and local governments which must borrow for schools and other public services.

It has added to the cost of many goods and services, and hence has been itself a factor in inflation.

It has created windfalls for many financial institutions.

The $9 billion of added interest charges on the national debt would have been even higher but for the prudent insistence of the Democratic Congress that the ceiling on interest rates for long-term Government bonds be maintained.

Control of Inflation

The American consumer has a right to fair prices. We are determined to secure that right.

Inflation has its roots in a variety of causes; its cure lies in a variety of remedies. Among those remedies are monetary and credit policies properly applied, budget surpluses in times of full employment, and action to restrain "administered price" increases in industries where economic power rests in the hands of a few.

A fair share of the gains from increasing productivity in many industries should be passed on to the consumer through price reductions.

The agenda which a new Democratic Administration will face next January is crowded with urgent needs on which action has been delayed, deferred, or denied by the present Administration.

A new Democratic Administration will undertake to meet those needs.

It will reaffirm the Economic Bill of Rights which Franklin Roosevelt wrote into our national conscience sixteen years ago. It will reaffirm these rights for all Americans of whatever race, place of residence, or station in life:

1. *"The right to a useful and remunerative job in the industries or shops or farms or mines of the nation."*

FULL EMPLOYMENT

The Democratic Party reaffirms its support of full employment as a paramount objective of national policy.

For nearly 30 months the rate of unemployment has been between 5 and 7.5% of the labor force. A pool of three to four million citizens, able and willing to work but unable to find jobs, has been written off by the Republican Administration as a "normal" readjustment of the economic system.

The policies of a Democratic Administration to restore economic growth will reduce current unemployment to a minimum.

Thereafter, if recessionary trends appear, we will act promptly with counter-measures, such as public works or temporary tax cuts. We will not stand idly by and permit recessions to run their course as the Republican Administration has done.

AID TO DEPRESSED AREAS

The right to a job requires action to create new industry in America's depressed areas of chronic unemployment.

General economic measures will not alone solve the problems of localities which suffer some special disadvantage. To bring prosperity to these depressed areas and to enable them to make their full contribution to the national welfare, specially directed action is needed.

Areas of heavy and persistent unemployment result from depletion of natural resources, technological change, shifting defense requirements, or trade imbalances which have caused the decline of major industries. Whole communities, urban and rural, have been left stranded in distress and despair, through no fault of their own.

These communities have undertaken valiant efforts of self-help. But mutual aid, as well as self-help, is part of the American tradition. Stricken communities deserve the help of the whole nation.

The Democratic Congress twice passed bills to provide this help. The Republican President twice vetoed them.

These bills proposed low-interest loans to private enterprise to create new industry and new jobs in depressed communities, assistance to the communities to provide public facilities necessary to encourage the new industry, and retraining of workers for the new jobs.

The Democratic Congress will again pass, and the Democratic President will sign, such a bill.

DISCRIMINATION IN EMPLOYMENT

The right to a job requires action to break down artificial and arbitrary barriers to employment based on age, race, sex, religion, or national origin.

Unemployment strikes hardest at workers over 40, minority groups, young people, and women. We will not achieve full employment until prejudice against these workers is wiped out.

COLLECTIVE BARGAINING

The right to a job requires the restoration of full support for collective bargaining and the repeal of the anti-labor excesses which have been written into our labor laws.

Under Democratic leadership a sound national policy was developed, expressed particularly by the Wagner National Labor Relations Act, which guaranteed the rights of workers to organize and to bargain collectively. But the Republican Administration has replaced this sound policy with a national anti-labor policy.

The Republican Taft-Hartley Act seriously weakened unions in their efforts to bring economic justice to the millions of American workers who remain unorganized.

By administrative action, anti-labor personnel appointed by the Republicans to the National Labor Relations Board have made the Taft-Hartley Act even more restrictive in its application than in its language.

Thus the traditional goal of the Democratic Party — to give all workers the right to organize and bargain collectively — has still not been achieved.

We pledge the enactment of an affirmative labor policy which will encourage free collective bargaining through the growth and development of free and responsible unions.

Millions of workers just now seeking to organize are blocked by Federally authorized "right-to-work" laws, unreasonable limitations on the right to picket, and other hampering legislative and administrative provisions.

Again, in the new Labor-Management Reporting and Disclosure Act, the Republican Administration perverted the constructive effort of the Democratic Congress to deal with improper activities of a few in labor and management by turning that Act into a means of restricting the legitimate rights of the vast majority of working men and women in honest labor unions. This law likewise strikes hardest at the weak or poorly organized, and it fails to deal with abuses of management as vigorously as with those of labor.

We will repeal the authorization for "right-to-work" laws, limitations on the rights to strike, to picket peacefully and to tell the public the facts of a labor dispute, and other anti-labor features of the Taft-Hartley Act and the 1959 Act. This unequivocal pledge for the repeal of the anti-labor and restrictive provisions of those laws will encourage collective bargaining and strengthen and support the free and honest labor movement.

The Railroad Retirement Act and the Railroad Unemployment Insurance Act are in need of improvement. We strongly oppose Republican attempts to weaken the Railway Labor Act.

We shall strengthen and modernize the Walsh-Healey and Davis-Bacon Acts, which protect the wage standards of workers employed by Government contractors.

Basic to the achievement of stable labor-management relations is leadership from the White House. The Republican Administration has failed to provide such leadership.

It failed to foresee the deterioration of labor-management relations in the steel industry last year. When a national emergency was obviously developing, it failed to forestall it. When the emergency came, the Administration's only solution was government-by-injunction.

A Democratic President, through his leadership and concern, will produce a better climate for continuing constructive relationships between labor and management. He will have periodic White House conferences between labor and management to consider their mutual problems before they reach the critical stage.

A Democratic President will use the vast fact-finding facilities that are available to inform himself, and the public, in exercising his leadership in labor disputes for the benefit of the nation as a whole.

If he needs more such facilities, or authority, we will provide them.

We further pledge that in the administration of all labor legislation we will restore the level of integrity, competence and sympathetic understanding required to carry out the intent of such legislation.

PLANNING FOR AUTOMATION

The right to a job requires planning for automation, so that men and women will be trained and available to meet shifting employment needs.

We will conduct a continuing analysis of the nation's manpower resources and of measures which may be required to assure their fullest development and use.

We will provide the Government leadership necessary to insure that the blessings of automation do not become burdens of widespread unemployment. For the young and the technologically displaced workers, we will provide the opportunity for training and retraining that equips them for jobs to be filled.

MINIMUM WAGES

2. *"The right to earn enough to provide adequate food and clothing and recreation."*

At the bottom of the income scale are some eight million families whose earnings are too low to provide even basic necessities of food, shelter, and clothing.

We pledge to raise the minimum wage to $1.25 an hour and to extend coverage to several million workers not now protected.

We pledge further improvements in the wage, hour and coverage standards of the Fair Labor Standards Act so as to extend its benefits to all workers employed in industries engaged in or affecting interstate commerce and to raise its standards to keep up with our general economic progress and needs.

We shall seek to bring the two million men, women and children who work for wages on the farms of the United States under the protection of existing labor and social legislation; and to assure migrant labor, perhaps the most underprivileged of all, of a comprehensive program to bring them not only decent wages but also adequate standards of health, housing, Social Security protection, education and welfare services.

AGRICULTURE

3. *"The right of every farmer to raise and sell his products at a return which will give him and his family a decent living."*

We shall take positive action to raise farm income to full parity levels and to preserve family farming as a way of life.

We shall put behind us once and for all the timidity with which our Government has viewed our abundance of food and fiber.

We will set new high levels of food consumption both at home and abroad.

As long as many Americans and hundreds of millions of people in other countries remain underfed, we shall regard these agricultural riches, and the family farmers who produce them, not as a liability but as a national asset.

Using Our Abundance

The Democratic Administration will inaugurate a national food and fiber policy for expanded use of our agricultural abundance. We will no longer view food stockpiles with alarm but will use them as powerful instruments for peace and plenty.

We will increase consumption at home. A vigorous, expanding economy will enable many American families to eat more and better food.

We will use the food stamp programs authorized to feed needy children, the aged and the unemployed. We will expand and improve the school lunch and milk programs.

We will establish and maintain food reserves for national defense purposes near important population centers in order to preserve lives in event of national disaster, and will operate them so as not to depress farm prices. We will expand research into new industrial uses of agricultural products.

We will increase consumption abroad. The Democratic Party believes our nation's capacity to produce food and fiber is one of the great weapons for waging war against hunger and want throughout the world. With wise management of our food abundance we will expand trade between nations, support economic and human development programs, and combat famine.

Unimaginative, outmoded Republican policies which fail to use these productive capacities of our farms have been immensely costly to our nation. They can and will be changed.

Achieving Income Parity

While farmers have raised their productive efficiency to record levels, Republican farm policies have forced their income to drop by 30%.

Tens of thousands of farm families have been bankrupted and forced off the land. This has happened despite the fact that the Secretary of Agriculture has spent more on farm programs than all previous Secretaries in history combined.

Farmers acting individually or in small groups are helpless to protect their incomes from sharp declines. Their only recourse is to produce more, throwing production still further out of balance with demand and driving prices down further.

This disastrous downward cycle can be stopped only by effective farm programs sympathetically administered with the assistance of democratically elected farmer committees.

The Democratic Administration will work to bring about full parity income for farmers in all segments of agriculture by helping them to balance farm production with the expanding needs of the nation and the world.

Measures to this end include production and marketing quotas measured in terms of barrels, bushels and bales, loans on basic commodities at not less than 90% of parity, production payments, commodity purchases, and marketing orders and agreements.

We repudiate the Republican administration of the Soil Bank Program, which has emphasized the retirement of whole farm units, and we pledge an orderly land retirement and conservation program.

We are convinced that a successful combination of these approaches will cost considerably less than present Republican programs which have failed.

We will encourage agricultural cooperatives by expanding and liberalizing existing credit facilities and developing new facilities if necessary to assist them in extending their marketing and purchasing activities, and we will protect cooperatives from punitive taxation.

The Democratic Administration will improve the marketing practices of the family-type dairy farm to reduce risk of loss.

To protect farmers' incomes in times of natural disaster, the Federal Crop Insurance Program, created and developed experimentally under Democratic Administrations, should be invigorated and expanded nationwide.

Improving Working and Living on Farms

Farm families have been among those victimized most severely by Republican tight-money policies.

Young people have been barred from entering agriculture. Giant corporations and other non-farmers, with readier access to credit and through vertical integration methods, have supplanted hundreds of farm families and caused the bankruptcy of many others.

The Democratic Party is committed by tradition and conviction to preservation of family agriculture.

To this end, we will expand and liberalize farm credit facilities, especially to meet the needs of family-farm agriculture and to assist beginning farmers.

Many families in America's rural counties are still living in poverty because of inadequate resources and opportunity. This blight and personal desperation should have received national priority attention long ago.

The new Democratic Administration will begin at once to eradicate long-neglected rural blight. We will help people help themselves with extended and supervised credit for farm improvement, local industrial development, improved vocational training and other assistance to those wishing to change to non-farm employment, and with the fullest development of commercial and recreational possibilities. This is one of the major objectives of the area redevelopment program, twice vetoed by the Republican President.

The rural electric cooperatives celebrate this year the twenty-fifth anniversary of the creation of the Rural Electrification Administration under President Franklin D. Roosevelt.

The Democratic Congress has successfully fought the efforts of the Republican Administration to cut off REA loans and force high-interest-rate policies on this great rural enterprise.

We will maintain interest rates for REA co-ops and public power districts at the levels provided in present law.

We deplore the Administration's failure to provide the dynamic leadership necessary for encouraging loans to rural users for generation of power where necessary.

We promise the co-ops active support in meeting the ever-growing demand for electric power and telephone service, to be filled on a complete area-coverage basis without requiring benefits for special-interest power groups.

In every way we will seek to help the men, women, and children whose livelihood comes from the soil to achieve better housing, education, health, and decent earnings and working conditions.

All these goals demand the leadership of a Secretary of Agriculture who is conversant with the technological and economic aspects of farm problems, and who is sympathetic with the objectives of effective farm legislation not only for farmers but for the best interest of the nation as a whole.

SMALL BUSINESS

4. *"The right of every businessman, large and small, to trade in an atmosphere of freedom from unfair competition and domination by monopolies at home and abroad."*

The new Democratic Administration will act to make our free economy really free — free from the oppression of monopolistic power, and free from the suffocating impact of high interest rates. We will help create an economy in which small businesses can take root, grow, and flourish.

We Democrats pledge:

1. Action to aid small business in obtaining credit and equity capital at reasonable rates. Small business which must borrow to stay alive has been a particular victim of the high-interest policies of the Republican administration.

The loan program of the Small Business Administration should be accelerated, and the independence of that agency preserved. The Small Business

Investment Act of 1958 must be administered with a greater sense of its importance and possibilities.

2. Protection of the public against the growth of monopoly.

The last 7½ years of Republican government has been the greatest period of merger and amalgamation in industry and banking in American history. Democratic Congresses have enacted numerous important measures to strengthen our anti-trust laws. Since 1950 the four Democratic Congresses have enacted laws like the Celler-Kefauver Anti-Merger Act, and improved the laws against price discriminations and tie-in sales.

When the Republicans were in control of the 80th and 83rd Congresses they failed to enact a single measure to strengthen or improve the anti-trust laws.

The Democratic Party opposes this trend to monopoly.

We pledge vigorous enforcement of the anti-trust laws.

We favor requiring corporations to file advance notice of mergers with the anti-trust enforcement agencies.

We favor permitting all firms to have access at reasonable rates to patented inventions resulting from Government-financed research and development contracts.

We favor strengthening the Robinson-Patman Act to protect small business against price discrimination.

We favor authorizing the Federal Trade Commission to obtain temporary injunctions during the pendency of administrative proceedings.

3. A more equitable share of Government contracts to small and independent business.

We will move from almost complete reliance on negotiation in the award of Government contracts toward open, competitive bidding.

Housing

5. "The right of every family to a decent home."

Today our rate of home building is less than that of ten years ago. A healthy, expanding economy will enable us to build two million homes a year, in wholesome neighborhoods, for people of all incomes.

At this rate, within a single decade we can clear away our slums and assure every American family a decent place to live.

Republican policies have led to a decline of the home building industry and the production of fewer homes. Republican high-interest policies have forced the cost of decent housing beyond the range of many families. Republican indifference has perpetuated slums.

We record the unpleasant fact that in 1960 at least 40 million Americans live in substandard housing.

One million new families are formed each year and need housing, and 300,000 existing homes are lost through demolition or other causes and need to be replaced. At present, construction does not even meet these requirements, much less permit reduction of the backlog of slum units.

We support a housing construction goal of more than two million homes a year. Most of the increased construction will be priced to meet the housing needs of middle- and low-income families who now live in substandard housing and are priced out of the market for decent homes.

Our housing programs will provide for rental as well as sales housing. They will permit expanded cooperative housing programs and sharply stepped-up rehabilitation of existing homes.

To make possible the building of two million homes a year in wholesome neighborhoods, the home building industry should be aided by special mortgage assistance, with low interest rates, long-term mortgage periods and reduced down payments. Where necessary, direct Government loans should be provided.

Even with this new and flexible approach, there will still be need for a substantial low-rent public housing program authorizing as many units as local communities require and are prepared to build.

Health

6. "The right to adequate medical care and the opportunity to achieve and enjoy good health."

Illness is expensive. Many Americans have neither incomes nor insurance protection to enable them to pay for modern health care. The problem is particularly acute with our older citizens, among whom serious illness strikes most often.

We shall provide medical care benefits for the aged as part of the time-tested Social Security insurance system. We reject any proposal which would require such citizens to submit to the indignity of a means test — a "pauper's oath."

For young and old alike, we need more medical schools, more hospitals, more research laboratories to speed the final conquest of major killers.

Medical Care for Older Persons

Fifty million Americans — more than a fourth of our people — have no insurance protection against the high cost of illness. For the rest, private health insurance pays, on the average, only about one-third of the cost of medical care.

The problem is particularly acute among the 16 million Americans over 65 years old, and among disabled workers, widows and orphans.

Most of these have low incomes and the elderly among them suffer two to three times as much illness as the rest of the population.

The Republican Administration refused to acknowledge any national responsibility for health care for elder citizens until forced to do so by an increasingly outraged demand. Then, its belated proposal was a cynical sham built around a degrading test based on means or income — a "pauper's oath."

The most practicable way to provide health protection for older people is to use the contributory machinery of the Social Security system for insurance covering hospital bills and other high-cost medical services. For those relatively few of our older people who have never been eligible for Social Security coverage, we shall provide corresponding benefits by appropriations from the general revenue.

Research

We will step up medical research on the major killers and crippling diseases — cancer, heart disease, arthritis, mental illness. Expenditures for these purposes should be limited only by the availability of personnel and promising lines of research. Today such illness costs us $35 billion annually, much of which could be avoided. Federal appropriations for medical research are barely 1% of this amount.

Heart disease and cancer together account for two out of every three deaths in this country. The Democratic President will summon to a White House conference the nation's most distinguished scientists in these fields to map a coordinated long-run program for the prevention and control of these diseases.

We will also support a cooperative program with other nations on international health research.

Hospitals

We will expand and improve the Hill-Burton hospital construction program.

Health Manpower

To ease the growing shortage of doctors and other medical personnel we propose Federal aid for constructing, expanding and modernizing schools of medicine, dentistry, nursing and public health.

We are deeply concerned that the high cost of medical education is putting this profession beyond the means of most American families. We will provide scholarships and other assistance to break through the financial barriers to medical education.

Mental Health

Mental patients fill more than half the hospital beds in the country today. We will provide greatly increased Federal support for psychiatric research and training, and community mental health programs, to help bring back thousands of our hospitalized mentally ill to full and useful lives in the community.

7. *"The right to adequate protection from the economic fears of old age, sickness, accidents, and unemployment."*

A PROGRAM FOR THE AGING

The Democratic Administration will end the neglect of our older citizens. They deserve lives of usefulness, dignity, independence, and participation. We shall assure them not only health care but employment for those who want work, decent housing, and recreation.

Already 16 million Americans — about one in ten — are over 65, with the prospect of 26 million by 1980.

Health

As stated, we will provide an effective system for paid-up medical insurance upon retirement, financed during working years through the Social Security mechanism and available to all retired persons without a means test. This has first priority.

Income

Half of the people over 65 have incomes inadequate for basic nutrition, decent housing, minimum recreation and medical care. Older people who do not want to retire need employment opportunity and those of retirement age who no longer wish to or cannot work need better retirement benefits.

We pledge a campaign to eliminate discrimination in employment due to age. As a first step we will prohibit such discrimination by Government contractors and subcontractors.

We will amend the Social Security Act to increase the retirement benefit for each additional year of work after 65, thus encouraging workers to continue on the job full time.

To encourage part-time work by others, we favor raising the $1200-a-year ceiling on what a worker may earn while still drawing Social Security benefits.

Retirement benefits must be increased generally, and minimum benefits raised from $33 a month to $50.

Housing

We shall provide decent and suitable housing which older persons can afford. Specifically we shall move ahead with the program of direct Government loans for housing for older people initiated in the Housing Act of 1959, a program which the Republican Administration has sought to kill.

Special Services

We shall take Federal action in support of state efforts to bring standards of care in nursing homes and other institutions for the aged up to desirable minimums.

We shall support demonstration and training programs to translate proven research into action in such fields as health, nutritional guidance, home care, counseling, recreational activity.

Taken together, these measures will affirm a new charter of rights for the older citizens among us — the right to a life of usefulness, health, dignity, independence and participation.

Welfare

Disability Insurance

We shall permit workers who are totally and permanently disabled to retire at any age, removing the arbitrary requirement that the worker be 50 years of age.

We shall also amend the law so that after six months of total disability, a worker will be eligible for disability benefits, with restorative services to enable him to return to work.

Physically Handicapped

We pledge continued support of legislation for the rehabilitation of physically handicapped persons and improvement of employment opportunities for them.

Public Assistance

Persons in need who are inadequately protected by social insurance are cared for by the states and local communities under public assistance programs.

The Federal Government, which now shares the cost of aid to some of these, should share in all, and benefits should be made available without regard to residence.

Unemployment Benefits

We will establish uniform minimum standards throughout the nation for coverage, duration, and amount of unemployment insurance benefits.

Equality for Women

We support legislation which will guarantee to women equality of rights under the law, including equal pay for equal work.

Child Welfare

The Child Welfare Program and other services already established under the Social Security Act should be expanded. Federal leadership is required in the nationwide campaign to prevent and control juvenile delinquency.

Intergroup Relations

We propose a Federal bureau of intergroup relations to help solve problems of discrimination in housing, education, employment, and community opportunities in general. The bureau would assist in the solution of problems arising from the resettlement of immigrants and migrants within our own country, and in resolving religious, social and other tensions where they arise.

EDUCATION

8. *"The right to a good education."*

America's young people are our greatest resource for the future. Each of them deserves the education which will best develop his potentialities.

We shall act at once to help in building the classrooms and employing the teachers that are essential if the right to a good education is to have genuine meaning for all the youth of America in the decade ahead.

As a national investment in our future we propose a program of loans and scholarship grants to assure that qualified young Americans will have full opportunity for higher education, at the institutions of their choice, regardless of the income of their parents.

The new Democratic Administration will end eight years of official neglect of our educational system.

America's education faces a financial crisis. The tremendous increase in the number of children of school and college age has far outrun the available supply of educational facilities and qualified teachers. The classroom shortage alone is interfering with the education of 10 million students.

America's teachers, parents and school administrators have striven courageously to keep up with the increased challenge of education.

So have states and local communities. Education absorbs two-fifths of all their revenue. With limited resources, private educational institutions have shouldered their share of the burden.

Only the Federal Government is not doing its part. For eight years, measures for the relief of the educational crisis have been held up by the cynical maneuvers of the Republican Party in Congress and the White House.

We believe that America can meet its educational obligations only with generous Federal financial support, within the traditional framework of local control. The assistance will take the form of Federal grants to states for educational purposes they deem most pressing, including classroom construction and teachers' salaries. It will include aid for the construction of academic facilities as well as dormitories at colleges and universities.

We pledge further Federal support for all phases of vocational education for youth and adults; for libraries and adult education; for realizing the potential of educational television; and for exchange of students and teachers with other nations.

As part of a broader concern for young people we recommend establishment of a Youth Conservation Corps, to give underprivileged young people a rewarding experience in a healthful environment.

The pledges contained in this Economic Bill of Rights point the way to a better life for every family in America.

They are the means to a goal that is now within our reach — the final eradication in America of the age-old evil of poverty.

Yet there are other pressing needs on our national agenda.

NATURAL RESOURCES

A thin layer of earth, a few inches of rain, and a blanket of air make human life possible on our planet.

Sound public policy must assure that these essential resources will be available to provide the good life for our children and future generations.

Water, timber and grazing lands, recreational areas in our parks, shores, forests and wildernesses, energy, minerals, even pure air — all are feeling the press of enormously increased demands of a rapidly growing population.

Natural resources are the birthright of all the people.

The new Democratic Administration, with the vision that built a TVA and a Grand Coulee, will develop and conserve that heritage for the use of this and future generations. We will reverse Republican policies under which America's resources have been wasted, depleted, underdeveloped, and recklessly given away.

We favor the best use of our natural resources, which generally means adoption of the multiple-purpose principle to achieve full development for all the many functions they can serve.

Water and Soil

An abundant supply of pure water is essential to our economy. This is a national problem.

Water must serve domestic, industrial and irrigation needs and inland navigation. It must provide habitat for fish and wildlife, supply the base for much outdoor recreation, and generate electricity. Water must also be controlled to prevent floods, pollution, salinity and silt.

The new Democratic Administration will develop a comprehensive national water resource policy. In cooperation with state and local governments, and interested private groups, the Democratic Administration will develop a balanced, multiple-purpose plan for each major river basin, to be revised periodically to meet changing needs. We will erase the Republican slogan of "no new starts" and will begin again to build multiple-purpose dams, hydroelectric facilities, flood-control works, navigation facilities, and reclamation projects to meet mounting and urgent needs.

We will renew the drive to protect every acre of farm land under a soil and water conservation plan, and we will speed up the small-watershed program.

We will support and intensify the research effort to find an economical way to convert salt and brackish water. The Republicans discouraged this research, which holds untold possibilities for the whole world.

Water and Air Pollution

America can no longer take pure water and air for granted. Polluted rivers carry their dangers to everyone living along their courses; impure air does not respect boundaries.

Federal action is needed in planning, coordinating and helping to finance pollution control. The states and local communities cannot go it alone. Yet President Eisenhower vetoed a Democratic bill to give them more financial help in building sewage treatment plants.

A Democratic President will sign such a bill.

Democrats will step up research on pollution control, giving special attention to:

1. the rapidly growing problem of air pollution from industrial plants, automobile exhausts, and other sources, and

2. disposal of chemical and radioactive wastes, some of which are now being dumped off our coasts without adequate knowledge of the potential consequences.

Outdoor Recreation

As population grows and the work week shortens and transportation becomes easier and speedier, the need for outdoor recreation facilities mounts.

We must act quickly to retain public access to the oceans, gulfs, rivers, streams, lakes and reservoirs, and their shorelines, and to reserve adequate camping and recreational areas while there is yet time. Areas near major population centers are particularly needed.

The new Democratic Administration will work to improve and extend recreation opportunities in national parks and monuments, forests, and river development projects, and near metropolitan areas. Emphasis will be on attractive, low-cost facilities for all the people and on preventing undue commercialization.

The National Park System is still incomplete; in particular, the few remaining suitable shorelines must be included in it. A national wilderness system should be created for areas already set aside as wildernesses. The system should be extended but only after careful consideration by the Congress of the value of areas for competing uses.

Recreational needs of the surrounding area should be given important consideration in disposing of Federally owned lands.

We will protect fish and game habitats from commercial exploitation and require military installations to conform to sound conservation practices.

Energy

The Republican Administration would turn the clock back to the days before the New Deal, in an effort to divert the benefits of the great natural energy resources from all the people to a favored few. It has followed for many years a "no new starts" policy.

It has stalled atomic energy development; it has sought to cripple rural electrification.

It has closed the pilot plant on getting oil from shale.

It has harrassed and hampered the TVA.

We reject this philosophy and these policies. The people are entitled to use profitably what they already own.

The Democratic Administration instead will foster the development of efficient regional giant power systems from all sources, including water, tidal, and nuclear power, to supply low-cost electricity to all retail electric systems, public, private, and cooperative.

The Democratic Administration will continue to develop "yardsticks" for measuring the rates of private utility systems. This means meeting the needs of rural electric cooperatives for low-interest loans for distribution, transmission and generation facilities; Federal transmission facilities, where appropriate, to provide efficient low-cost power supply; and strict enforcement of the public-preference clause in power marketing.

The Democratic Administration will support continued study and research on energy fuel resources, including new sources in wind and sun. It will push forward with the Passamaquoddy tidal power project with its great promise of cheaper power and expanded prosperity for the people of New England.

We support the establishment of a national fuels policy.

The $15 billion national investment in atomic energy should be protected as a part of the public domain.

Federal Lands and Forests

The record of the Republican Administration in handling the public domain is one of complete lethargy. It has failed to secure existing assets. In some cases, it has given away priceless resources for plunder by private corporations, as in the Al Sarena mining incident and the secret leasing of game refuges to favored oil interests.

The new Democratic Administration will develop balanced land and forest policies suited to the needs of a growing America.

This means intensive forest management on a multiple-use and sustained-yield basis, reforestation of burnt-over lands, building public access roads, range reseeding and improvement, intensive work in watershed management, concern for small business operations, and insuring free public access to public lands for recreational uses.

Minerals

America uses half the minerals produced in the entire Free World. Yet our mining industry is in what may be the initial phase of a serious long-term depression. Sound policy requires that we strengthen the domestic mining industry without interfering with adequate supplies of needed materials at reasonable costs.

We pledge immediate efforts toward the establishment of a realistic long-range minerals policy.

The new Democratic Administration will begin intensive research on scientific prospecting for mineral deposits.

We will speed up the geologic mapping of the country, with emphasis on Alaska.

We will resume research and development work on use of low-grade mineral reserves, especially oil shale, lignites, iron ore taconite, and radioactive minerals. These efforts have been halted or cut back by the Republican Administration.

The Democratic Party favors a study of the problem of non-uniform seaward boundaries of the coastal states.

Government Machinery for Managing Resources

Long-range programming of the nation's resource development is essential. We favor creation of a council of advisers on resources and conservation, which will evaluate and report annually upon our resource needs and progress.

We shall put budgeting for resources on a businesslike basis, distinguishing between operating expense and capital investment, so that the country can have an accurate picture of the costs and returns. We propose the incremental method in determining the economic justification of our river basin programs. Charges for commercial use of public lands will be brought into line with benefits received.

CITIES AND THEIR SUBURBS

A new Democratic Administration will expand Federal programs to help urban communities clear their slums, dispose of their sewage, educate their children, transport suburban commuters to and from their jobs, and combat juvenile delinquency.

We will give the city dweller a voice at the Cabinet table by bringing together within a single department programs concerned with urban and metropolitan problems.

The United States is now predominantly an urban nation.

The efficiency, comfort, and beauty of our cities and suburbs influence the lives of all Americans.

Local governments have found increasing difficulty in coping with such fundamental public problems as urban renewal, slum clearance, water supply, mass transportation, recreation, health, welfare, education and metropolitan planning. These problems are, in many cases, interstate and regional in scope.

Yet the Republican Administration has turned its back on urban and suburban America. The list of Republican vetoes includes housing, urban renewal and slum clearance, area redevelopment, public works, airports and stream pollution control. It has proposed severe cutbacks in aid for hospital construction, public assistance, vocational education, community facilities and sewage disposal.

The result has been to force communities to thrust an ever-greater tax load upon the already overburdened property taxpayer and to forgo needed public services.

The Democratic Party believes that state and local governments are strengthened — not weakened — by financial assistance from the Federal Government. We will extend such aid without impairing local administration through unnecessary Federal interference or red tape.

We propose a ten-year action program to restore our cities and provide for balanced suburban development, including the following:

1. The elimination of slums and blight and the restoration of cities and depressed areas within the next ten years.

2. Federal aid for metropolitan area planning and community facility programs.

3. Federal aid for comprehensive metropolitan transportation programs, including bus and rail mass transit, commuter railroads as well as highway programs, and construction of civil airports.

4. Federal aid in combating air and water pollution.

5. Expansion of park systems to meet the recreation needs of our growing population.

The Federal Government must recognize the financial burdens placed on local governments, urban and rural alike, by Federal installations and land holdings.

TRANSPORTATION

Over the past seven years, we have watched the steady weakening of the nation's transportation system. Railroads are in distress. Highways are congested. Airports and airways lag far behind the needs of the jet age.

To meet this challenge we will establish a national transportation policy, designed to coordinate and modernize our facilities for transportation by road, rail, water, and air.

Air

The jet age has made rapid improvement in air safety imperative. Rather than "an orderly withdrawal" from the airport grant programs as proposed by the Republican Administration, we pledge to expand the program to accommodate growing air traffic.

Water

Development of our inland waterways, our harbors, and Great Lakes commerce has been held back by the Republican President.

We pledge the improvement of our rivers and harbors by new starts and adequate maintenance.

A strong and efficient American-flag merchant marine is essential to peacetime commerce and defense emergencies. Continued aid for ship construction and operation to offset cost differentials favoring foreign shipping is essential to these goals.

Roads

The Republican Administration has slowed down, stretched out and greatly increased the costs of the interstate highway program.

The Democratic Party supports the highway program embodied in the Acts of 1956 and 1958 and the principle of Federal-state partnership in highway construction.

We commend the Democratic Congress for establishing a special committee which has launched an extensive investigation of this highway program. Continued scrutiny of this multi-billion-dollar highway program can prevent waste, inefficiency and graft and maintain the public's confidence.

Rail

The nation's railroads are in particular need of freedom from burdensome regulation to enable them to compete effectively with other forms of transportation. We also support Federal assistance in meeting certain capital needs, particularly for urban mass transportation.

SCIENCE

We will recognize the special role of our Federal Government in support of basic and applied research.

Space

The Republican Administration has remained incredibly blind to the prospects of space exploration. It has failed to pursue space programs with a sense of urgency at all close to their importance to the future of the world.

It has allowed the Communists to hit the moon first, and to launch substantially greater payloads. The Republican program is a catchall of assorted projects with no clearly defined, long-range plan of research.

The new Democratic Administration will press forward with our national space program in full realization of the importance of space accomplishments to our national security and our international prestige. We shall reorganize the program to achieve both efficiency and speedy execution. We shall bring top scientists into positions of responsibility. We shall undertake long-term basic research in space science and propulsion.

We shall initiate negotiations leading toward the international regulation of space.

Atomic Energy

The United States became pre-eminent in the development of atomic energy under Democratic Administrations.

The Republican Administration, despite its glowing promises of "Atoms for Peace," has permitted the gradual deterioration of United States leadership in atomic development both at home and abroad.

In order to restore United States leadership in atomic development, the new Democratic Administration will:

1. Restore truly nonpartisan and vigorous administration of the vital atomic energy program.

2. Continue the development of the various promising experimental and prototype atomic power plants which show promise, and provide increasing support for longer-range projects at the frontiers of atomic energy application.

3. Continue to preserve and support national laboratories and other Federal atomic installations as the foundation of technical progress and a bulwark of national defense.

4. Accelerate the Rover nuclear rocket project and auxiliary power facilities so as to achieve world leadership in peaceful outer space exploration. tion.

5. Give reality to the United States international atoms-for-peace programs, and continue and expand technological assistance to underdeveloped countries.

6. Consider measures for improved organization and procedure for radiation protection and reactor safety, including a strengthening of the role of the Federal Radiation Council, and the separation of quasi-judicial functions in reactor safety regulations.

7. Provide a balanced and flexible nuclear defense capability, including the augmentation of the nuclear submarine fleet.

Oceanography

Oceanographic research is needed to advance such important programs as food and minerals from our Great Lakes and the sea. The present Administration has neglected this new scientific frontier.

GOVERNMENT OPERATIONS

We shall reform the processes of Government in all branches — Executive, Legislative, and Judicial. We will clean out corruption and conflicts of interest, and improve Government services.

The Federal Service

Two weeks before this Platform was adopted, the difference between the Democratic and Republican attitudes toward Government employees was dramatically illustrated. The Democratic Congress passed a fully justified pay increase to bring Government pay scales more nearly into line with those of private industry.

The Republican President vetoed the pay raise.

The Democratic Congress decisively overrode the veto.

The heavy responsibilities of modern government require a Federal service characterized by devotion to duty, honesty of purpose and highest competence. We pledge the modernization and strengthening of our Civil Service system.

We shall extend and improve the employees' appeals system and improve programs for recognizing the outstanding merits of individual employees.

Ethics in Government

We reject totally the concept of dual or triple loyalty on the part of Federal officials in high places.

The conflict-of-interest statutes should be revised and strengthened to assure the Federal service of maximum security against unethical practices on the part of public officials.

The Democratic Administration will establish and enforce a Code of Ethics to maintain the full dignity and integrity of the Federal service and to make it more attractive to the ablest men and women.

Regulatory Agencies

The Democratic Party promises to clean up the Federal regulatory agencies. The acceptance by Republican appointees to these agencies of gifts, hospitality, and bribes from interests under their jurisdiction has been a particularly flagrant abuse of public trust.

We shall bring all contacts with commissioners into the open, and will protect them from any form of improper pressure.

We shall appoint to these agencies men of ability and independent judgment who understand that their function is to regulate these industries in the public interest.

We promise a thorough review of existing agency practices, with an eye toward speedier decisions, and a clearer definition of what constitutes the public interest.

The Democratic Party condemns the usurpation by the Executive of the powers and functions of any of the independent agencies and pledges the restoration of the independence of such agencies and the protection of their integrity of action.

The Postal Service

The Republican policy has been to treat the United States postal service as a liability instead of a great investment in national enlightenment, social efficiency and economic betterment.

Constant curtailment of service has inconvenienced every citizen.

A program must be undertaken to establish the Post Office Department as a model of efficiency and service. We pledge ourselves to:

1. Restore the principle that the postal service is a public service.

2. Separate the public service costs from those to be borne by the users of the mails.

3. Continue steady improvement in working conditions and wage scales, reflecting increasing productivity.

4. Establish a long-range program for research and capital improvements compatible with the highest standards of business efficiency.

Law Enforcement

In recent years, we have been faced with a shocking increase in crimes of all kinds. Organized criminals have even infiltrated into legitimate business enterprises and labor unions.

The Republican Administration, particularly the Attorney General's office, has failed lamentably to deal with this problem despite the growing power of the underworld. The new Democratic Administration will take vigorous corrective action.

Freedom of Information

We reject the Republican contention that the workings of Government are the special private preserve of the Executive.

The massive wall of secrecy erected between the Executive branch and the Congress as well as the citizen must be torn down. Information must flow freely, save in those areas in which the national security is involved.

Clean Elections

The Democratic Party favors realistic and effective limitations on contributions and expenditures, and full disclosure of campaign financing in Federal elections.

We further propose a tax credit to encourage small contributions to political parties. The Democratic Party affirms that every candidate for public office has a moral obligation to observe and uphold traditional American principles of decency, honesty and fair play in his campaign for election.

We deplore efforts to divide the United States into regional, religious and ethnic groups.

We denounce and repudiate campaign tactics that substitute smear and slander, bigotry and false accusations of bigotry, for truth and reasoned argument.

District of Columbia

The capital city of our nation should be a symbol of democracy to people throughout the world. The Democratic Party reaffirms its long-standing support of home rule for the District of Columbia, and pledges to enact legislation permitting voters of the District to elect their own local government.

We urge the legislatures of the 50 states to ratify the 23rd Amendment, passed by the Democratic Congress, to give District citizens the right to participate in Presidential elections.

We also support a Constitutional amendment giving the District voting representation in Congress.

Virgin Islands

We believe that the voters of the Virgin Islands should have the right to elect their own Governor, to have a delegate in the Congress of the United States and to have the right to vote in national elections for a President and Vice President of the United States.

Puerto Rico

The social, economic, and political progress of the Commonwealth of Puerto Rico is a testimonial to the sound enabling legislation, and to the sincerity and understanding with which the people of the 50 states and Puerto Rico are meeting their joint problems.

The Democratic Party, under whose administration the Commonwealth status was established, is entitled to great credit for providing the opportunity which the people of Puerto Rico have used so successfully.

Puerto Rico has become a show place of worldwide interest, a tribute to the benefits of the principles of self-determination. Further benefits for Puerto Rico under these principles are certain to follow.

CONGRESSIONAL PROCEDURES

In order that the will of the American people may be expressed upon all legislative proposals, we urge that action be taken at the beginning of the 87th Congress to improve Congressional procedures so that majority rule prevails and decisions can be made after reasonable debate without being blocked by a minority in either House.

The rules of the House of Representatives should be so amended as to make sure that bills reported by legislative committees reach the floor for consideration without undue delay.

CONSUMERS

In an age of mass production, distribution, and advertising, consumers require effective Government representation and protection.

The Republican Administration has allowed the Food and Drug Administration to be weakened. Recent Senate hearings on the drug industry have revealed how flagrant profiteering can be when essential facts on costs, prices, and profits are hidden from scrutiny. The new Democratic Administration will provide the money and the authority to strengthen this agency for its task.

We propose a consumer counsel, backed by a suitable staff, to speak for consumers in the formulation of Government policies and represent consumers in administrative proceedings.

The consumer also has a right to know the cost of credit when he borrows money. We shall enact Federal legislation requiring the vendors of credit to provide a statement of specific credit charges and what these charges cost in terms of true annual interest.

VETERANS AFFAIRS

We adhere to the American tradition dating from the Plymouth Colony in New England in 1636:

". . . any soldier injured in defense of the colony shall be maintained competently by the colony for the remainder of his life."

We pledge adequate compensation for those with service-connected disabilities and for the survivors of those who died in service or from service-connected disabilities. We pledge pensions adequate for a full and dignified life for disabled and distressed veterans and for needy survivors of deceased veterans.

Veterans of World War I, whose Federal benefits have not matched those of veterans of subsequent service, will receive the special attention of the Democratic Party looking toward equitable adjustments.

We endorse expanded programs of vocational rehabilitation for disabled veterans, and education for orphans of servicemen.

The quality of medical care furnished to the disabled veterans has deteriorated under the Republican Administration. We shall work for an increased availability of facilities for all veterans in need and we shall move with particular urgency to fulfill the need for expanded domiciliary and nursing-home facilities.

We shall continue the veterans home loan guarantee and direct loan programs and educational benefits patterned after the G.I. Bill of Rights.

American Indians

We recognize the unique legal and moral responsibility of the Federal Government for Indians in restitution for the injustice that has sometimes been done them. We therefore pledge prompt adoption of a program to assist Indian tribes in the full development of their human and natural resources and to advance the health, education, and economic well-being of Indian citizens while preserving their cultural heritage.

Free consent of the Indian tribes concerned shall be required before the Federal Government makes any change in any Federal-Indian treaty or other contractual relationship.

The new Democratic Administration will bring competent, sympathetic, and dedicated leadership to the administration of Indian affairs which will end practices that have eroded Indian rights and resources, reduced the Indians' land base and repudiated Federal responsibility. Indian claims against the United States can and will be settled promptly, whether by negotiation or other means, in the best interests of both parties.

The Arts

The arts flourish where there is freedom and where individual initiative and imagination are encouraged. We enjoy the blessings of such an atmosphere.

The nation should begin to evaluate the possibilities for encouraging and expanding participation in and appreciation of our cultural life.

We propose a Federal advisory agency to assist in the evaluation, development, and expansion of cultural resources of the United States. We shall support legislation needed to provide incentives for those endowed with extraordinary talent, as a worthy supplement to existing scholarship programs.

Civil Liberties

With democratic values threatened today by Communist tyranny, we reaffirm our dedication to the Bill of Rights. Freedom and civil liberties, far from being incompatible with security, are vital to our national strength. Unfortunately, those high in the Republican Administration have all too often sullied the name and honor of loyal and faithful American citizens in and out of Government.

The Democratic Party will strive to improve Congressional investigating and hearing procedures. We shall abolish useless disclaimer affidavits such as those for student educational loans. We shall provide a full and fair hearing, including confrontation of the accuser, to any person whose public or private employment or reputation is jeopardized by a loyalty or security proceeding.

Protection of rights of American citizens to travel, to pursue lawful trade and to engage in other lawful activities abroad without distinction as to race or religion is a cardinal function of the national sovereignty.

We will oppose any international agreement or treaty which by its terms or practices differentiates among American citizens on grounds of race or religion.

The list of unfinished business for America is long. The accumulated neglect of nearly a decade cannot be wiped out overnight. Many of the objectives which we seek will require our best efforts over a period of years.

Although the task is far-reaching, we will tackle it with vigor and confidence. We will substitute planning for confusion, purpose for indifference, direction for drift and apathy.

We will organize the policymaking machinery of the Executive branch to provide vigor and leadership in establishing our national goals and achieving them.

The new Democratic President will sign, not veto, the efforts of a Democratic Congress to create more jobs, to build more homes, to save family farms, to clean up polluted streams and rivers, to help depressed areas, and to provide full employment for our people.

Fiscal Responsibility

We vigorously reject the notion that America, with a half-trillion-dollar gross national product, and nearly half of the world's industrial resources, cannot afford to meet our needs at home and in our world relationships.

We believe, moreover, that except in periods of recession or national emergency, these needs can be met with a balanced budget, with no increase in present tax rates, and with some surplus for the gradual reduction of our national debt.

To assure such a balance we shall pursue a four-point program of fiscal responsibility.

First, we shall end the gross waste in Federal expenditures which needlessly raises the budgets of many Government agencies.

The most conspicuous unnecessary item is, of course, the excessive cost of interest on the national debt. Courageous action to end duplication and competition among the armed services will achieve large savings. The cost of the agricultural program can be reduced while at the same time prosperity is being restored to the nation's farmers.

Second, we shall collect the billions in taxes which are owed to the Federal Government but not now collected.

The Internal Revenue Service is still suffering from the cuts inflicted upon its enforcement staff by the Republican Administration and the Republican Congress in 1953.

The Administration's own Commissioner of Internal Revenue has testified that billions of dollars in revenue are lost each year because the Service does not have sufficient agents to follow up on tax evasion.

We will add enforcement personnel, and develop new techniques of enforcement, to collect tax revenue which is now being lost through evasion.

Third, we shall close the loopholes in the tax laws by which certain privileged groups legally escape their fair share of taxation.

Among the more conspicuous loopholes are depletion allowances which are inequitable, special consideration for recipients of dividend income, and deductions for extravagant "business expenses" which have reached scandalous proportions.

Tax reform can raise additional revenue and at the same time increase legitimate incentives for growth, and make it possible to ease the burden on the general taxpayer who now pays an unfair share of taxes because of special favors to the few.

Fourth, we shall bring in added Federal tax revenues by expanding the economy itself. Each dollar of additional production puts an additional 18 cents in tax revenue in the national treasury. A 5% growth rate, therefore, will mean that at the end of four years the Federal Government will have had a total of nearly $50 billion in additional tax revenues above those presently received.

By these four methods we can sharply increase the Government funds available for needed services, for correction of tax inequities, and for debt or tax reduction.

Much of the challenge of the 1960s, however, remains unforeseen and unforeseeable.

If, therefore, the unfolding demands of the new decade at home or abroad should impose clear national responsibilities that cannot be fulfilled without higher taxes, we will not allow political disadvantage to deter us from doing what is required.

As we proceed with the urgent task of restoring America's productivity, confidence, and power, we will never forget that our national interest is more than the sum total of all the group interests in America.

When group interests conflict with the national interest, it will be the national interest which we serve.

On its values and goals the quality of American life depends. Here above all our national interest and our devotion to the Rights of Man coincide.

Democratic Administrations under Wilson, Roosevelt, and Truman led the way in pressing for economic justice for all Americans.

But man does not live by bread alone. A new Democratic Administration, like its predecessors, will once again look beyond material goals to the spiritual meaning of American society.

We have drifted into a national mood that accepts payola and quiz scandals, tax evasion and false expense accounts, soaring crime rates, influence peddling in high Government circles, and the exploitation of sadistic violence as popular entertainment.

For eight long critical years our present national leadership has made no effective effort to reverse this mood.

The new Democratic Administration will help create a sense of national purpose and higher standards of public behavior.

CIVIL RIGHTS

We shall also seek to create an affirmative new atmosphere in which to deal with racial divisions and inequalities which threaten both the integrity of our democratic faith and the proposition on which our nation was founded — that all men are created equal. It is our faith in human dignity that distinguishes our open free society from the closed totalitarian society of the Communists.

The Constitution of the United States rejects the notion that the Rights of Man means the rights of some men only. We reject it too.

The right to vote is the first principle of self-government. The Constitution also guarantees to all Americans the equal protection of the laws.

It is the duty of the Congress to enact the laws necessary and proper to protect and promote these constitutional rights. The Supreme Court has the power to interpret these rights and the laws thus enacted.

It is the duty of the President to see that these rights are respected and that the Constitution and laws as interpreted by the Supreme Court are faithfully executed.

What is now required is effective moral and political leadership by the whole Executive branch of our Government to make equal opportunity a living reality for all Americans.

As the party of Jefferson, we shall provide that leadership.

In every city and state in greater or lesser degree there is discrimination based on color, race, religion, or national origin.

If discrimination in voting, education, the administration of justice or segregated lunch counters are the issues in one area, discrimination in housing and employment may be pressing questions elsewhere.

The peaceful demonstrations for first-class citizenship which have recently taken place in many parts of this country are a signal to all of us to make good at long last the guarantees of our Constitution.

The time has come to assure equal access for all Americans to all areas of community life, including voting booths, schoolrooms, jobs, housing, and public facilities.

The Democratic Administration which takes office next January will therefore use the full powers provided in the Civil Rights Acts of 1957 and 1960 to secure for all Americans the right to vote.

If these powers, vigorously invoked by a new Attorney General and backed by a strong and imaginative Democratic President, prove inadequate, further powers will be sought.

We will support whatever action is necessary to eliminate literacy tests and the payment of poll taxes as requirements for voting.

A new Democratic Administration will also use its full powers — legal and moral — to ensure the beginning of good-faith compliance with the Constitutional requirement that racial discrimination be ended in public education.

We believe that every school district affected by the Supreme Court's school desegregation decision should submit a plan providing for at least first-step compliance by 1963, the 100th anniversary of the Emancipation Proclamation.

To facilitate compliance, technical and financial assistance should be given to school districts facing special problems of transition.

For this and for the protection of all other Constitutional rights of Americans, the Attorney General should be empowered and directed to file civil injunction suits in Federal courts to prevent the denial of any civil right on grounds of race, creed, or color.

The new Democratic Administration will support Federal legislation establishing a Fair Employment Practices Commission to secure effectively for everyone the right to equal opportunity for employment.

In 1949 the President's Committee on Civil Rights recommended a permanent Commission on Civil Rights. The new Democratic Adminstration will broaden the scope and strengthen the powers of the present commission and make it permanent.

Its functions will be to provide assistance to communities, industries, or individuals in the implementation of Constitutional rights in education, housing, employment, transportation, and the administration of justice.

In addition, the Democratic Administration will use its full executive powers to assure equal employment opportunities and to terminate racial segregation throughout Federal services and institutions, and on all Government contracts. The successful desegregation of the armed services took place through such decisive executive action under President Truman.

Similarly the new Democratic Administration will take action to end discrimination in Federal housing programs, including Federally assisted housing.

To accomplish these goals will require executive orders, legal actions brought by the Attorney General, legislation, and improved Congressional procedures to safeguard majority rule.

Above all, it will require the strong, active, persuasive, and inventive leadership of the President of the United States.

The Democratic President who takes office next January will face unprecedented challenges. His Administration will present a new face to the world.

It will be a bold, confident, affirmative face. We will draw new strength from the universal truths which the founder of our Party asserted in the Declaration of Independence to be "self-evident."

Emerson once spoke of an unending contest in human affairs, a contest between the Party of Hope and the Party of Memory.

For 7½ years America, governed by the Party of Memory, has taken a holiday from history.

As the Party of Hope it is our responsibility and opportunity to call forth the greatness of the American people.

In this spirit, we hereby rededicate ourselves to the continuing service of the Rights of Man — everywhere in America and everywhere else on God's earth.

Prohibition Platform 1960

PREAMBLE

We, the representatives of the Prohibition Party, assembled in the National Convention at Winona Lake, Indiana, September 1, 2, and 3, 1959, recognizing Almighty God as the source of all just government, and with faith in the teachings of the Lord Jesus Christ, do solemnly promise that, if our party is chosen to administer the affairs of the

nation, we will, with earnest dedication to the principles of righteousness, seek to serve the needs and to preserve the rights, the prerogatives and the basic freedoms, of the people of the United States. For the realization of these ends we propose the following programs of government:

CONSTITUTIONAL GOVERNMENT

First of all, we affirm our sincere loyalty to the Constitution of the United States, and express our deep confidence in that document as the basic law of our land. We deplore all attempts to violate it, whether by legislation, by means of evasion, or through judicial interpretation. We believe in the principles of liberty and justice enunciated in the Declaration of Independence and in the Preamble and Bill of Rights of our Constitution. We declare ourselves in hearty support of our system of representative government, with its plan of checks and balances, and express our firm intent to serve the people of our nation with a constructive, forward-looking program of good government, dedicated to the welfare of our citizenry.

COMMUNISM-TOTALITARIANISM

We are positively, aggressively and unalterably, opposed to Communism as a way of life or as a governmental system. We believe that the program of Communism, with its intent to infiltrate and to overthrow our present form of government, must be pitilessly exposed. We challenge all loyal citizens to become fully aware of this menace to civilization, to exert every effort to defeat these "masters of deceit," and to help preserve our American way of life.

We also declare ourselves opposed to any other form of totalitarian philosophy or form of government. We endorse the efforts of those agencies which have been honestly and earnestly exposing subversive activities and groups.

GOVERNMENTAL ECONOMY AND TAXATION

We live in an era of extravagance and wasteful spending. This spirit has invaded government at all levels, demanding an ever-increasing tax load upon our people. The constant increase in taxation, requiring nearly one-third of the total income of our citizens to pay the expenses of government, is approaching the point of confiscation, leading to economic bankruptcy. We believe that good government ought not to attempt to do for people what they can do for themselves. With proper economy, governmental costs can be lowered, the tax load can be lightened, and the public debt can be reduced. We promise to devote ourselves to such an end, even though it involves the reorganization and/or abolition of certain departments, bureaus and vested interests.

Money and Finance

A sound financial program and a dependable monetary policy are fundamental to a stable economy. Our Constitution gives to Congress the power to "coin money" and to "regulate the value thereof." We believe that Congress, working with the executive department of our government, should take immediate steps to establish a financial program that will block inflationary trends, insure a sound currency, stabilize price levels and provide for systematic retirement of the national debt. We urge that careful consideration be given to a return to the gold standard, suggesting that such a step would help stabilize our economy, would promote confidence in our monetary system and would underwrite a continuing program of sound finance and expanding industrial progress.

The Federal Budget

Good government and a sound economy demand a balanced federal budget. The inflationary effects and the disturbing influences of unbalanced budgets must be eliminated. We cannot, with impunity, continue to increase the mortgage on our future and the interest load of the present. As the level of taxation is already excessive, there must be either a decided reduction in governmental services and federal spending or a substantial improvement in efficiency, with consequent elimination of waste in both personnel and materials. Actually, both areas need careful exploration with a view not only to maintaining a balanced budget, but also to reduction of the national debt.

Foreign Aid

Many billions of dollars of our taxpayers' money have been and are still being given to foreign countries. Unfortunately, substantial portions have been used to support governments and programs considerably at variance with American ideals and concepts. It is frankly recognized that complex and baffling problems are involved in this area of international relations, but it is likewise believed that the practice needs most careful scrutiny and review.

Free Enterprise

We deplore the current trend toward development of a socialistic state. We are strongly opposed to governmental restraints on our free enterprise system, to detailed regulation of our economic life and to federal interference with individual initiative. We declare ourselves for freedom of opportunity, for private industry financed within the structure of our present anti-trust laws and for a sound economic system based upon recognized business practice. To this end, we propose that our government withdraw, with reasonable promptness, from the field of business activity and sell to private industry those business enterprises now owned and operated by the federal government.

Labor and Industry

In the area of labor and industrial relations we believe that the public welfare must be given paramount consideration. Both management and labor must be held responsible for their economic and their social behavior. Neither should be permitted to dominate at the expense of the other or of the common good. Rather, the anti-trust laws must be applied equally to all monopolies, whether of business or labor. Whenever the public welfare is seriously endangered because of disputes affecting quasi-public businesses and utilities we favor the compulsory arbitration of labor-management disputes.

Employee-Employer Rights

Every individual has certain basic and fundamental rights. A person's right to join or not to join a labor union without affecting his employment and his right to work for an employer willing to hire him must be protected. Likewise, employees and employers must be free to bargain and to contract as they wish. Mass picketing, rioting, terrorism, and all other forms of violence and coercion, secondary boycotts and industry-wide bargaining should be prohibited.

INDIVIDUAL AND STATES' RIGHTS

Our founding fathers recognized the importance of both individual and states' rights, and determined to preserve them by making the Bill of Rights an integral part of our Constitution. During recent years there has been an increasing tendency toward an undesirable concentration of power and authority in the federal government. We pledge ourselves to action that will preserve all legitimate individual rights and will maintain among the several states their constitutional place in our system of government. We maintain that all American citizens, regardless of race, religion or national origin, are equal before the law and are entitled to equality of treatment under the laws of our land. We deplore the use of violence, from whatever source, as a means of trying to resolve tensions and divergencies of opinion among our citizenry.

PUBLIC MORALITY AND LAW ENFORCEMENT

Moral and spiritual considerations must be primary factors in determining both state and national policies. We deplore the gross neglect of such matters by the dominant political parties, culminating in the shocking revelations of crime and of political and economic corruption which have characterized recent years. We charge these parties with basic responsibility for the rapid decline in moral standards which followed repeal of the Eighteenth Amendment. We believe that the program of nullification of law through non-enforcement which led to repeal contributed greatly to the disintegration of public morals, to a general deterioration of standards and to a lowering of values among our people.

We pledge ourselves to break the unholy alliance which has made these things possible. We propose to strengthen and to enforce laws against gambling, narcotics, and commercialized vice, to emphasize the basic importance of spiritual and moral values to the development and growth of an enduring nation, and to maintain the integrity of our democracy by careful enforcement of law and loyal support of our Constitution.

WORLD PEACE

We live in an age of atomic and hydrogen bombs, in an era of missiles and jet propulsion, in a world filled with animosities and cruel hatreds. Instruments for the destruction of civilization have been developed. Under these conditions, we pledge ourselves to search for peaceful solutions to international conflict, by seeking to deal creatively and constructively with the underlying causes of international tension, and, to strive for world peace and order based upon the teachings and practices of the Prince of Peace.

UNIVERSAL MILITARY TRAINING

Although we seek for world peace and order, we declare our firm belief, under existing world conditions, in a sound program of national preparedness. At the same time, we seriously question the desirability of the existing program of peacetime compulsory military training. We doubt that it represents a genuine safeguard to world peace. Rather, we believe it to be contrary, in principle, to our American way of life, to place an unnecessary burden upon our peacetime economy, to threaten us with possible military dictatorship, and, as currently conducted, to permit and very often to promote the moral and spiritual deterioration of our Youth. Therefore, we declare our opposition to any program of peacetime compulsory military training and urge a complete evaluation and reorientation of our entire program of national preparedness.

NUCLEAR BOMB TESTS

Many scientists throughout the world have warned us that radioactive fallout, resulting from the testing of nuclear weapons, endangers the health of human beings throughout the world, and will increase the number of seriously defective children who will be born to future generations. It is unjust that the people of the world, and especially those of nations not engaged in nuclear testing, should be exposed to this peril without their consent. The danger and the injustice will become progressively greater with each additional test. In addition, there is the added danger that continuation of the armaments race will lead to an atomic war of annihilation.

We, therefore, urge that, as a step toward world disarmament, all testing of nuclear weapons be indefinitely suspended on a multilateral basis and that our government seek with renewed vigor and persistence an agreement among all nuclear powers for the permanent and complete cessation of nuclear tests for military purposes.

RELIGIOUS LIBERTY

We believe in religious liberty. Freedom of the individual to worship, to fellowship with others of similar faith, to evangelize, to educate and to establish religious institutions, must be preserved. When religious liberty is lost political liberty will perish with it. We believe, also, that our government should take a firm, positive position against religious intolerance and persecution anywhere in the world.

MARRIAGE AND DIVORCE

Ordained of God, the home is a sacred institution. Its sanctity must be protected and preserved. We favor the enactment of uniform marriage and divorce laws in the various states as an aid to building strong and enduring homes throughout our nation.

OLD AGE INSURANCE

We endorse the general principle of an actuarially sound social security program which includes all employed groups. We question the soundness of the existing program. We deplore the widespread current abuse of the privileges involved; we condemn the maladministration of its provisions for political ends; we pledge ourselves to correct these evils.

BALLOT LAW REFORM

True democracy requires that the needs and interests of minority groups be given fair, honest and appropriate consideration. Instead, in many of our states, ballot laws have been enacted which are designed to make a two-party system into a bipartisan political monopoly, keeping minor parties off the ballot. We demand the repeal of all laws which deny to independent voters and to loyal minority groups the fundamental right of free political expression.

SEPARATION OF CHURCH AND STATE

We affirm our continuing loyalty to the constitutional principle of separation of Church and State. We will expose, and resist vigorously, any attempt from whatever source to weaken or subvert this fundamental principle. In the area of government, we endorse encouragement of non-profit educational and religious institutions on a tax-exempt basis, but we declare strong opposition to all efforts, direct or indirect, to secure appropriations of public money for private religious or sectarian purposes.

EDUCATION

It is altogether appropriate that our federal government should be interested in and concerned about matters pertaining to all areas of educational growth and development. However, under the Tenth Amendment, public education is clearly a matter of state concern. We approve of the work of the Office of Education in collecting and disseminating essential educational information, but we are opposed to any sort of direct federal aid to education, believing that each state should both support and control its own educational program.

AGRICULTURE

The production and distribution of agricultural products is of vital importance to the economy of any people. We believe that those engaged in agricultural pursuits, like other American citizens, should be free from authoritarian control and coercion. Hence we declare ourselves opposed to regimentation of farms and farmers and urge a sensible and orderly return to a free market program.

PUBLIC HEALTH

The health of our people is a matter of high importance. We are deeply concerned with this problem in its numerous aspects. In particular, we insist that genuine caution be taken when dealing with mental health cases lest there be unjust and prejudiced incarcerations. Also we deplore those programs of mass medication which many maintain are in violation of the rights of individuals under our Constitution.

SERVICE, NOT SPOILS

In spite of our "civil service" system, first sponsored by the Prohibition Party, the dominant political parties are positively committed to the "spoils" system and, when in office, have prostituted governmental power to serve their own selfish party interests instead of the whole people. This has led to excessive expenditures, higher taxes and, in some situations, to an unfortunate alliance of crime with politics. We pledge ourselves to an honest, efficient and economical administration.

THE ALCOHOL PROBLEM

The widespread and increasing use of alcoholic beverages has now become a national tragedy and must be recognized as a major cause of poverty, broken homes, juvenile delinquency, vice, crime, political corruption, wasted manpower and highway accidents. Of all the unfortunate mistakes of our government and people, none has been worse than the legalization of the liquor traffic. It can be legitimately said that no political issue confronting the citizens of our land compares in magnitude with the need for suppressing the beverage alcohol industry.

The sponsors of this national curse are not only highly capitalized and strongly organized, but are also socially irresponsible. Out of enormous profits the liquor industry spends huge sums to promote sales, to create habitual use of its products by both youth and adults and to encourage a weakening of moral resistance to its program of social and economic exploitation. It is linked with and supports a nationwide network of organized gambling, vice and crime. Through its advertising it has corrupted large segments of the nation's press, and it is endeavoring to extend its control increasingly to both radio and television.

Unfortunately, the liquor traffic has been able to extend its power until, in all too many instances, it dominates our political life and controls our governmental officials. Both of our major political parties are dominated by it, and neither dares to take a stand against it. And so long as they continue to be yoked by party membership with the liquor traffic and the underworld, just so long will they be unable to make moral principles prevail.

The beverage alcohol problem is a matter of national concern. It has reached proportions which demand immediate action looking to a solution. First of all, scientific facts about beverage alcohol must be widely publicized. People must come to know and to understand the demon which we harbor. Secondly, a program of publicity, education, legislation and administration, leading to the elimination of the beverage alcohol industry, must be developed. People must come to know that there is no satisfactory solution to the problem except through political action which supresses it and a political administration which destroys it.

Accordingly the Prohibition Party demands the repeal of all laws which legalize the liquor traffic and the enactment and rigorous enforcement of new laws which prohibit the manufacture, distribution and sale of alcoholic beverages. You are urged to elect an administration pledged to the above program. Such is essential to the permanent solution of this devastating problem.

CONCLUSION

The need today in the United States of America is a re-alignment of voters and the union of all good citizens in a political party that is dedicated to a constructive program of clean, honest, and humane government. The Prohibition Party is that kind of political organization. Therefore, we challenge the citizens of our land to elect the candidates of the Prohibition Party; to put into office persons of unquestioned integrity, who will set an example of public and private morality, and who will marshal the resources of government — executive, legislative and judicial — to right the wrong and to preserve for our nation a government "of the people, by the people and for the people," under God.

Republican Platform 1960

PREAMBLE

The United States is living in an age of profoundest revolution. The lives of men and of nations are undergoing such transformations as history has rarely recorded. The birth of new nations, the impact of new machines, the threat of new weapons, the stirring of new ideas, the ascent into a new dimension of the universe — everywhere the accent falls on the new.

At such a time of world upheaval, great perils match great opportunities — and hopes, as well as fears, rise in all areas of human life. Such a force as nuclear power symbolizes the greatness of the choice before the United States and mankind. The energy of the atom could bring devastation to humanity. Or it could be made to serve men's hopes for peace and progress — to make for all peoples a more healthy and secure and prosperous life than man has ever known.

One fact darkens the reasonable hopes of free men: the growing vigor and thrust of Communist imperialism. Everywhere across the earth, this force challenges us to prove our strength and wisdom, our capacity for sacrifice, our faith in ourselves and in our institutions.

Free men look to us for leadership and support, which we dedicate ourselves to give out of the abundance of our national strength.

The fate of the world will be deeply affected, perhaps determined, by the quality of American leadership. American leadership means both how we govern ourselves and how we help to influence others. We deliberate the choice of national leadership and policy, mindful that in some measure our proposals involve the fate of mankind.

The leadership of the United States must be responsible and mature; its promises must be rational and practical, soberly pledged and faithfully undertaken. Its purposes and its aspirations must ascend to that high ground of right and freedom upon which mankind may dwell and progress in decent security.

We are impressed, but not dismayed, by the revolutionary turbulence that is wracking the world. In the midst of violence and change, we draw strength and confidence from the changeless principles of our free Constitution. Free men are invincible when the power and courage, the patience and the fortitude latent in them are drawn forth by reasonable appeal.

In this Republican Platform we offer to the United States our program — our call to service, our pledge of leadership, our proposal of measures in the public interest. We call upon God, in whose hand is every blessing, to favor our deliberations with wisdom, our nation with endurance, and troubled mankind everywhere with a righteous peace.

FOREIGN POLICY

The Republican Party asserts that the sovereign purpose of our foreign policy is to secure the free institutions of our nation against every peril, to hearten and fortify the love of freedom everywhere in the world, and to achieve a just peace for all of anxious humanity.

The pre-eminence of this Republic requires of us a vigorous, resolute foreign policy — inflexible against every tyrannical encroachment, and mighty in its advance toward our own affirmative goals.

The Government of the United States, under the administration of President Eisenhower and Vice President Nixon, has demonstrated that firmness in the face of threatened aggression is the most dependable safeguard of peace. We now reaffirm our determination to defend the security and the freedom of our country, to honor our commitments to our allies at whatever cost or sacrifice, and never to submit to force or threats. Our determination to stand fast has forestalled aggression before Berlin, in the Formosa Straits, and in Lebanon. Since 1954 no free nation has fallen victim behind the Iron Curtain. We mean to adhere to the policy of firmness that has served us so well.

We are unalterably committed to maintaining the security, freedom and solidarity of the Western Hemisphere. We support President Eisenhower's reaffirmation of the Monroe Doctrine in all its vitality. Faithful to our treaty commitments, we shall join the Republics of the Americas against any intervention in our hemisphere, and in refusing to tolerate the establishment in this hemisphere of any government dominated by the foreign rule of communism.

In the Middle East, we shall continue to support the integrity and independence of all the states of that area including Israel and the Arab States.

With specific reference to Israel and the Arab Nations we urge them to undertake negotiations for a mutually acceptable settlement of the causes of tension between them. We pledge continued efforts:

To eliminate the obstacles to a lasting peace in the area, including the human problem of the Arab refugees.

To seek an end to transit and trade restrictions, blockades and boycotts.

To secure freedom of navigation in international waterways, the cessation of discrimination against Americans on the basis of religious beliefs, and an end to the wasteful and dangerous arms race and to the threat of an arms imbalance in the area.

Recognition of Communist China and its admission to the United Nations have been firmly opposed by the Republican Administration. We will continue in this opposition because of compelling evidence that to do otherwise would weaken the cause of freedom and endanger the future of the free peoples of Asia and the world. The brutal suppression of the human rights and the religious traditions of the Tibetan people is an unhappy evidence of the need to persist in our policy.

The countries of the free world have been benefited, reinforced and drawn closer together by the vigor of American support of the United Nations, and by our participation in such regional organizations as NATO, SEATO, CENTO, the Organization of American States and other collective security alliances. We assert our intention steadfastly to uphold the action and principles of these bodies.

We believe military assistance to our allies under the mutual security program should be continued with all the vigor and funds needed to maintain the strength of our alliances at levels essential to our common safety.

The firm diplomacy of the Eisenhower-Nixon Administration has been supported by a military power superior to any in the history of our nation or in the world. As long as world tensions menace us with war, we are resolved to maintain an armed power exceeded by no other.

Under Republican administration, the Government has developed original and constructive programs in many fields — open skies, atoms for peace, cultural and technical exchanges, the peaceful uses of outer space and Antarctica — to make known to men everywhere our desire to advance the cause of peace. We mean, as a Party, to continue in the same course.

We recognize and freely acknowledge the support given to these principles and policies by all Americans, irrespective of party. Standing as they do above partisan challenge, such principles and policies will, we earnestly hope, continue to have bipartisan support.

We established a new independent agency, the United States Information Agency, fully recognizing the tremendous importance of the struggle for men's minds. Today, our information program throughout the world is a greatly improved medium for explaining our policies and actions to audiences overseas, answering Communist propaganda, and projecting a true image of American life.

This is the Republican record. We rededicate ourselves to the principles that have animated it; and we pledge ourselves to persist in those principles, and to apply them to the problems, the occasions, and the opportunities to be faced by the new Administration.

We confront today the global offensive of Communism, increasingly aggressive and violent in its enterprises. The agency of that offensive is Soviet policy, aimed at the subversion of the world.

Recently we have noted Soviet Union pretexts to intervene in the affairs of newly independent countries, accompanied by threats of the use of nuclear weapons. Such interventions constitute a form of subversion against the sovereignty of these new nations and a direct challenge to the United Nations.

The immediate strategy of the Soviet imperialists is to destroy the world's confidence in America's desire for peace, to threaten with violence our mutual security arrangements, and to sever the bonds of amity and respect among the free nations. To nullify the Soviet conspiracy is our greatest task. The United States faces this challenge and resolves to meet it with courage and confidence.

To this end we will continue to support and strengthen the United Nations as an instrument for peace, for international cooperation, and for the advancement of the fundamental freedoms and humane interests of mankind.

Under the United Nations we will work for the peaceful settlement of international disputes and the extension of the rule of law in the world.

And, in furtherance of President Eisenhower's proposals for the peaceful use of space, we suggest that the United Nations take the initiative to develop a body of law applicable thereto.

Through all the calculated shifts of Soviet tactics and mood, the Eisenhower-Nixon Administration has demonstrated its willingness to negotiate in earnest with the Soviet Union to arrive at just settlements for the reduction of world tensions. We pledge the new Administration to continue in the same course.

We are similarly ready to negotiate and to institute realistic methods and safeguards for disarmament, and for the suspension of nuclear tests. We advocate an early agreement by all nations to forego nuclear tests in the atmosphere, and the suspension of other tests as verification techniques permit. We support the President in any decision he may make to re-evaluate the question of re-sumption of underground nuclear explosions test-ing, if the Geneva Conference fails to produce a satisfactory agreement. We have deep concern about the mounting nuclear arms race. This con-cern leads us to seek disarmament and nuclear agreements. And an equal concern to protect all peoples from nuclear danger, leads us to insist that such agreements have adequate safeguards.

We recognize that firm political and military policies, while imperative for our security, cannot in themselves build peace in the world.

In Latin America, Asia, Africa and the Middle East, peoples of ancient and recent independence, have shown their determination to improve their standards of living, and to enjoy an equality with the rest of mankind in the enjoyment of the fruits of civilization. This determination has become a primary fact of their political life. We declare our-selves to be in sympathy with their aspirations.

We have already created unprecedented dimen-sions of diplomacy for these purposes. We recog-nize that upon our support of well-conceived pro-grams of economic cooperation among nations rest the best hopes of hundreds of millions of friendly people for a decent future for themselves and their children. Our mutual security program of economic help and technical assistance; the De-velopment Loan Fund, the Inter-American Bank, the International Development Association and the Food for Peace Program, which create the condi-tions for progress in less-developed countries; our leadership in international efforts to help children, eliminate pestilence and disease and aid refugees — these are programs wise in concept and gener-ous in purpose. We mean to continue in support of them.

Now we propose to further evolution of our pro-grams for assistance to and cooperation with other nations, suitable to the emerging needs of the future.

We will encourage the countries of Latin Amer-ica, Africa, the Middle East and Asia, to initiate appropriate regional groupings to work out plans for economic and educational development. We anticipate that the United Nations Special Fund would be of assistance in developing such plans. The United States would offer its cooperation in planning, and the provision of technical personnel for this purpose. Agreeable to the developing na-tions, we would join with them in inviting countries with advanced economies to share with us a pro-portionate part of the capital and technical aid required. We would emphasize the increasing use of private capital and government loans, rather than outright grants, as a means of fostering inde-pendence and mutual respect. The President's recent initiative of a joint partnership program for Latin America opens the way to this approach.

We would propose that such groupings adopt means to attain viable economies following such examples as the European Common Market. And if from these institutions, there should follow stronger economic and political unions, we would welcome them with our support.

Despite the counterdrive of international Com-munism, relentless against individual freedom and subversive of the sovereignty of nations, a power-ful drive for freedom has swept the world since World War II and many heroic episodes in the Communist countries have demonstrated anew that freedom will not die.

The Republican Party reaffirms its determina-tion to use every peaceful means to help the cap-tive nations toward their independence, and thus their freedom to live and worship according to conscience. We do not condone the subjugation of the peoples of Hungary, Poland, East Germany, Czechoslovakia, Rumania, Albania, Bulgaria, Lat-via, Lithuania, Estonia, and other once-free na-tions. We are not shaken in our hope and belief that once again they will rule themselves.

Our time surges with change and challenge, peril and great opportunities. It calls us to great tasks and efforts — for free men can hope to guard freedom only if they prove capable of historic acts of wisdom and courage.

Dwight David Eisenhower stands today through-out the world as the greatest champion of peace and justice and good.

The Republican Party brings to the days ahead trained, experienced, mature and courageous lead-ership.

Our Party was born for freedom's sake. It is still the Party of full freedom in our country. As in Lincoln's time, our Party and its leaders will meet the challenges and opportunities of our time and keep our country the best and enduring hope of freedom for the world.

NATIONAL DEFENSE

The future of freedom depends heavily upon America's military might and that of her allies. Under the Eisenhower-Nixon Administration, our military might has been forged into a power second to none. This strength, tailored to serve the needs of national policy, has deterred and must continue to deter aggression and encourage the growth of freedom in the world. This is the only sure way to a world at peace.

We have checked aggression. We ended the war in Korea. We have joined with free nations in creating strong defenses. Swift technological change and the warning signs of Soviet aggressiveness make clear that intensified and courageous efforts are necessary, for the new problems of the 1960's will of course demand new efforts on the part of our entire nation. The Republican Party is pledged to making certain that our arms, and our will to use them, remain superior to all threats. We have, and will continue to have, the defenses we need to protect our freedom.

The strategic imperatives of our national defense policy are these:

A second-strike capability, that is, a nuclear retaliatory power that can survive surprise attack, strike back, and destroy any possible enemy.

Highly mobile and versatile forces, including forces deployed, to deter or check local aggressions and "brush fire wars" which might bring on all-out nuclear war.

National determination to employ all necessary military capabilities so as to render any level of aggression unprofitable. Deterrence of war since Korea, specifically, has been the result of our firm statement that we will never again permit a potential aggressor to set the ground rules for his aggression; that we will respond to aggression with the full means and weapons best suited to the situation.

Maintenance of these imperatives requires these actions:

Unremitting modernization of our retaliatory forces, continued development of the manned bomber well into the missile age, with necessary numbers of these bombers protected through dispersal and airborne alert.

Development and production of new strategic weapons, such as the Polaris submarine and ballistic missile. Never again will they be neglected, as intercontinental missile development was neglected between the end of World War II and 1953.

Accelerate as necessary, development of hardening, mobility, dispersal, and production programs for long-range missiles and the speedy perfection of new and advanced generations of missiles and anti-missile missiles.

Intensified development of active civil defense to enable our people to protect themselves against the deadly hazards of atomic attack, particularly fallout; and to develop a new program to build a reserve of storable food, adequate to the needs of the population after an atomic attack.

Constant intelligence operations regarding Communist military preparations to prevent another Pearl Harbor.

A military establishment organized in accord with a national strategy which enables the unified commands in Europe, the Pacific, and this continent to continue to respond promptly to any kind of aggression.

Strengthening of the military might of the free-world nations in such ways as to encourage them to assume increasing responsibility for regional security.

Continuation of the "long pull" preparedness policies which, as inaugurated under the Eisenhower-Nixon Administration, have avoided the perilous peaks and slumps of defense spending and planning which marked earlier administrations.

There is no price ceiling on America's security. The United States can and must provide whatever is necessary to insure its own security and that of the free world and to provide any necessary increased expenditures to meet new situations, to guarantee the opportunity to fulfill the hopes of men of good will everywhere. To provide more would be wasteful. To provide less would be catastrophic. Our defense posture must remain steadfast, confident, and superior to all potential foes.

ECONOMIC GROWTH AND BUSINESS

To provide the means to a better life for individual Americans and to strengthen the forces of freedom in the world, we count on the proved productivity of our free economy.

Despite the lamentations of the opposition in viewing the economic scene today, the plain fact is that our 500 billion dollar economy finds more

Americans at work, earning more, spending more, saving more, investing more, building more than ever before in history. The well-being of our people, by virtually every yardstick, has greatly advanced under this Republican Administration.

But we can and must do better. We must raise employment to even higher levels and utilize even more fully our expanding, overall capacity to produce. We must quicken the pace of our economic growth to prove the power of American free enterprise to meet growing and urgent demands: to sustain our military posture, to provide jobs for a growing labor force in a time of rapid technological change, to improve living standards, to serve all the needs of an expanding population.

We therefore accord high priority to vigorous economic growth and recognize that its mainspring lies in the private sector of the economy. We must continue to foster a healthy climate in that sector. We reject the concept of artificial growth forced by massive new federal spending and loose money policies. The only effective way to accelerate economic growth is to increase the traditional strengths of our free economy — initiative and investment, productivity and efficiency. To that end we favor:

Broadly-based tax reform to foster job-making and growth-making investment for modernization and expansion, including realistic incentive depreciation schedules.

Use of the full powers of government to prevent the scourges of depression and inflation.

Elimination of featherbedding practices by labor and business.

Maintenance of a stable dollar as an indispensable means to progress.

Relating wage and other payments in production to productivity — except when necessary to correct inequities — in order to help us stay competitive at home and abroad.

Spurring the economy by advancing the successful Eisenhower-Nixon program fostering new and small business, by continued active enforcement of the anti-trust laws, by protecting consumers and investors against the hazard and economic waste of fraudulent and criminal practices in the market place, and by keeping the federal government from unjustly competing with private enterprise upon which Americans mainly depend for their livelihood.

Continued improvement of our vital transportation network, carrying forward rapidly the vast Eisenhower-Nixon national highway program and promoting safe, efficient, competitive and integrated transport by air, road, rail and water under equitable, impartial and minimal regulation directed to those ends.

Carrying forward, under the Trade Agreements Act, the policy of gradual selective — and truly reciprocal — reduction of unjustifiable barriers to trade among free nations. We advocate effective administration of the Act's escape clause and peril point provisions to safeguard American jobs and domestic industries against serious injury. In support of our national trade policy we should continue the Eisenhower-Nixon program of using this government's negotiating powers to open markets abroad and to eliminate remaining discrimination against our goods. We should also encourage the development of fair labor standards in exporting countries in the interest of fair competition in international trade. We should, too, expand the Administration's export drive, encourage tourists to come from abroad, and protect U.S. investors against arbitrary confiscations and expropriations by foreign governments. Through these and other constructive policies, we will better our international balance of payments.

Discharge by government of responsibility for those activities which the private sector cannot do or cannot so well do, such as constructive federal-local action to aid areas of chronic high unemployment, a sensible farm policy, development and wise use of natural resources, suitable support of education and research, and equality of job opportunity for all Americans.

Action on these fronts, designed to release the strongest productive force in human affairs — the spirit of individual enterprise — can contribute greatly to our goal of a steady, strongly growing economy.

LABOR

America's growth cannot be compartmentalized. Labor and management cannot prosper without each other. They cannot ignore their mutual public obligation.

Industrial harmony, expressing these mutual interests, can best be achieved in a climate of free collective bargaining, with minimal government intervention except by mediation and conciliation.

Even in dealing with emergency situations imperiling the national safety, ways of solution must be found to enhance and not impede the processes of free collective bargaining — carefully considered ways that are in keeping with the policies of national labor relations legislation and with the need to strengthen the hand of the President in dealing with such emergencies.

In the same spirit, Republican leadership will continue to encourage discussions, away from the bargaining table, between labor and management to consider the mutual interest of all Americans in maintaining industrial peace.

Republican policy firmly supports the right of employers and unions freely to enter into agreements providing for the union shop and other forms of union security as authorized by the Labor-Management Relations Act of 1947 (the Taft-Hartley Act).

Republican-sponsored legislation has supported the right of union members to full participation in the affairs of their union and their right to freedom from racketeering and gangster interference whether by labor or management in labor-management relations.

Republican action has given to millions of American working men and women new or expanded protection and benefits, such as:

Increased federal minimum wage;

Extended coverage of unemployment insurance and the payment of additional temporary benefits provided in 1958-59;

Improvement of veterans' re-employment rights;

Extension of federal workman's compensation coverage and increase of benefits;

Legislative assurance of safety standards for longshore and harbor workers and for the transportation of migratory workers;

An increase of railroad workers' retirement and disability benefits.

Seven past years of accomplishments, however, are but a base to build upon in fostering, promoting and improving the welfare of America's working men and women, both organized and unorganized. We pledge, therefore, action on these constructive lines:

Diligent administration of the amended Labor-Management Relations Act of 1947 (Taft-Hartley Act) and the Labor-Management Reporting and Disclosure Act of 1959 (Landrum-Griffin Act) with recommendations for improvements which experience shows are needed to make them more effective or remove any inequities.

Correction of defects in the Welfare and Pension Plans Disclosure Act to protect employees' and beneficiaries' interests.

Upward revision in amount and extended coverage of the minimum wage to several million more workers.

Strengthening the unemployment insurance system and extension of its benefits.

Improvement of the eight-hour laws relating to hours and overtime compensation on federal and federally-assisted construction, and continued vigorous enforcement and improvement of minimum wage laws for federal supply and construction contracts.

Continued improvement of manpower skills and training to meet a new era of challenges, including action programs to aid older workers, women, youth, and the physically handicapped.

Encouragement of training programs by labor, industry and government to aid in finding new jobs for persons dislocated by automation or other economic changes.

Improvement of job opportunities and working conditions of migratory farm workers.

Assurance of equal pay for equal work regardless of sex; encouragement of programs to insure on-the-job safety, and encouragement of the States to improve their labor standards legislation, and to improve veterans' employment rights and benefits.

Encouragement abroad of free democratic institutions, higher living standards and higher wages through such agencies as the International Labor Organization, and cooperation with the free trade union movement in strengthening free labor throughout the world.

Agriculture

Americans are the best-fed and the best-clothed people in the world. Our challenge fortunately is one of dealing with abundance, not overcoming shortage. The fullness of our fields, forests and grazing lands is an important advantage in our struggle against worldwide tyranny and our crusade against poverty. Our farmers have provided us with a powerful weapon in the ideological and economic struggle in which we are now engaged.

Yet, far too many of our farm families, the source of this strength, have not received a fair return for their labors. For too long, Democratic-controlled Congresses have stalemated progress by clinging to obsolete programs conceived for different times and different problems.

Promises of specific levels of price support or a single type of program for all agriculture are cruel deceptions based upon the pessimistic pretense that only with rigid controls can farm familes be aided. The Republican Party will provide within the framework of individual freedom a greater bargaining power to assure an equitable return for the work and capital supplied by farmers.

The Republican Party pledges itself to develop new programs to improve and stabilize farm family income. It recognizes two main challenges: the immediate one of utilizing income-depressing surpluses, and the long-range one of steady balanced growth and development with a minimum of federal interference and control.

To utilize immediately surpluses in an orderly manner, with a minimum impact on domestic and foreign markets, we pledge:

Intensification of the Food for Peace program, including new cooperative efforts among food-surplus nations to assist the hungry peoples in less favored areas of the world.

Payment-in-kind, out of existing surpluses, as part of our land retirement program.

Creation of a Strategic Food Reserve properly dispersed in forms which can be preserved for long periods against the contingency of grave national emergency.

Strengthened efforts to distribute surpluses to schools and low-income and needy citizens of our own country.

A reorganization of Commodity Credit Corporation's inventory management operations to reduce competition with the marketings of farmers.

To assure steady balanced growth and agricultural progress, we pledge:

A crash research program to develop industrial and other uses of farm products.

Use of price supports at levels best fitted to specific commodities, in order to widen markets, ease production controls, and help achieve increased farm family income.

Acceleration of production adjustments, including a large scale land conservation reserve program on a voluntary and equitable rental basis, with full consideration of the impact on local communities.

Continued progress in the wise use and conservation of water and soil resources.

Use of marketing agreements and orders, and other marketing devices, when approved by producers, to assist in the orderly marketing of crops, thus enabling farmers to strengthen their bargaining power.

Stepped-up research to reduce production costs and to cut distribution costs.

Strengthening of the educational programs of the U.S. Department of Agriculture and the Land-Grant institutions.

Improvement of credit facilities for financing the capital needs of modern farming.

Encouragement of farmer owned and operated cooperatives including rural electric and telephone facilities.

Expansion of the Rural Development Program to help low-income farm families not only through better farming methods, but also through opportunities for vocational training, more effective employment services, and creation of job opportunities through encouragement of local industrialization.

Continuation and further improvement of the Great Plains Program.

Legislative action for programs now scheduled to expire for the school milk program, wool, and sugar, including increased sugar acreage to domestic areas.

Free movement in interstate commerce of agricultural commodities meeting federal health standards.

To prevent dumping of agricultural imports upon domestic markets.

To assure the American farmer a more direct voice in his own destiny, we pledge:

To select an official committee of farmers and ranchers, on a regional basis, broadly representative of American agriculture, whose function will be to recommend to the President guidelines for improving the operation of government farm programs.

NATURAL RESOURCES

A strong and growing economy requires vigorous and persistent attention to wise conservation and sound development of all our resources. Teamwork between federal, state and private entities is essential and should be continued. It has resulted in sustained conservation and resource development programs on a scale unmatched in our history.

The past seven years of Republican leadership have seen the development of more power capacity, flood control, irrigation, fish and wildlife projects, recreational facilities, and associated multi-purpose benefits than during any previous administration in history. The proof is visible in the forests and waters of the land and in Republican initiation of and support for the Upper Watershed Program and the Small Reclamation Projects Act. It is clear, also, in the results of continuing administration-encouraged forest management practices which have brought, for the first time, a favorable balance between the growth and cutting of America's trees.

Our objective is for further growth, greater strength, and increased utilization in each great area of resource use and development.

We pledge:

Use of the community watershed as the basic natural unit through which water resource, soil, and forest management programs may best be developed, with interstate compacts encouraged to handle regional aspects without federal domination.

Development of new water resource projects throughout the nation.

Support of the historic policy of Congress in preserving the integrity of the several States to govern water rights.

Continued federal support for Republican-initiated research and demonstration projects which will supply fresh water from salt and brackish water sources.

Necessary measures for preservation of our domestic fisheries.

Continued forestry conservation with appropriate sustained yield harvesting, thus increasing jobs for people and increasing revenue.

To observe the "preference clause" in marketing federal power.

Support of the basic principles of reclamation.

Recognition of urban and industrial demands by making available to states and local governments, federal lands not needed for national programs.

Full use and preservation of our great outdoors are pledged in:

Completion of the "Mission 66" for the improvement of National Park areas as well as sponsorship of a new "Mission 76" program to encourage establishment and rehabilitation of local, state, and regional parks, to provide adequate recreational facilities for our expanding population.

Continued support of the effort to keep our great out-of-doors beautiful, green, and clean.

Establishment of a citizens board of conservation, resource and land management experts to inventory those federal lands now set aside for a particular purpose; to study the future needs of the nation for parks, seashores, and wildlife and other recreational areas; and to study the possibility of restoring lands not needed for a federal program.

Minerals, metals, fuels, also call for carefully considered actions in view of the repeated failure of Democratic-controlled Congresses to enact any long-range minerals legislation. Republicans, therefore, pledge:

Long-range minerals and fuels planning and programming, including increased coal research.

Assistance to mining industries in bridging the gap between peak defense demands and anticipated peacetime demands.

Continued support for federal financial assistance and incentives under our tax laws to encourage exploration for domestic sources of minerals and metals, with reasonable depletion allowances.

To preserve our fish and wildlife heritage, we pledge:

Legislation to authorize exchange of lands between state and federal governments to adapt programs to changing uses and habits.

Vigorous implementation of long-range programs for fish and wildlife.

GOVERNMENT FINANCE

To build a better America with broad national purposes such as high employment, vigorous and steady economic growth, and a dependable currency, responsible management of our federal finances is essential. Even more important, a sound economy is vital to national security. While leading Democrats charge us with a "budget balancing" mentality, their taunts really reflect their frustration over the people's recognition that as a nation we must live within our means. Government that is careless with the money of its citizens is careless with their future.

Because we are concerned about the well-being of people, we are concerned about protecting the value of their money. To this end, we Republicans believe that:

Every government expenditure must be tested by its contribution to the general welfare, not to any narrow interest group.

Except in times of war or economic adversity, expenditures should be covered by revenues.

We must work persistently to reduce, not to increase, the national debt, which imposes a heavy economic burden on every citizen.

Our tax structure should be improved to provide greater incentives to economic progress, to make it fair and equitable, and to maintain and deserve public acceptance.

We must resist assaults upon the independence of the Federal Reserve System; we must strengthen, not weaken, the ability of the Federal Reserve System and the Treasury Department to exercise effective control over money and credit in order better to combat both deflation and inflation that retard economic growth and shrink people's savings and earnings.

In order of priority, federal revenues should be used: first, to meet the needs of national security; second, to fulfill the legitimate and urgent needs of the nation that cannot be met by the States, local governments or private action; third, to pay down on the national debt in good times; finally, to improve our tax structure.

National security and other essential needs will continue to make enormous demands upon public revenues. It is therefore imperative that we weigh carefully each demand for a new federal expenditure. The federal government should undertake not the most things nor the least things, but the right things.

Achieving this vital purpose demands:

That Congress, in acting on new spending bills, have figures before it showing the cumulative effect of its actions on the total budget.

That spending commitments for future years be clearly listed in each budget, so that the effect of built-in expenditure programs may be recognized and evaluated.

That the President be empowered to veto individual items in authorization and appropriation bills.

That increasing efforts be made to extend business-like methods to government operations, particularly in purchasing and supply activities, and in personnel.

GOVERNMENT ADMINISTRATION

The challenges of our time test the very organization of democracy. They put on trial the capacity of free government to act quickly, wisely, resolutely. To meet these challenges:

The President must continue to be able to reorganize and streamline executive operations to keep the executive branch capable of responding effectively to rapidly changing conditions in both foreign and domestic fields. The Eisenhower-Nixon Administration did so by creating a new Department of Health, Education and Welfare, by establishing the National Aeronautics and Space Agency and the Federal Aviation Agency, and by reorganizations of the Defense Department.

Two top positions should be established to assist the President in, (1) the entire field of National Security and International Affairs, and, (2) Governmental Planning and Management, particularly in domestic affairs.

We must undertake further reorganization of the Defense Department to achieve the most effective unification of defense planning and command.

Improved conflict-of-interest laws should be enacted for vigilant protection of the public interest and to remove deterrents to governmental service by our most able citizens.

The federal government must constantly strengthen its career service and must be truly progressive as an employer. Government employment must be a vocation deserving of high public respect. Common sense demands continued improvements in employment, training and promotion practices based on merit, effective procedures for dealing with employment grievances, and salaries which are comparable to those offered by private employers.

As already practiced by the Republican membership, responsible Policy Committees should be elected by each party in each house of Congress. This would provide a mechanism for meetings of party Congressional leaders with the President when circumstances demand.

Needed federal judgeships, appointed on the basis of the highest qualifications and without limitation to a single political party, should be created to expedite administration of justice in federal courts.

The remarkable growth of the Post Office since 1952 to serve an additional 9 million urban and 1½ million farm families must be continued. The Post Office must be continually improved and placed on a self-sustaining basis. Progressive Republican policies of the past seven years have resulted in reduced costs, decentralization of postal operations, liberal pay, fringe benefits, improved working conditions, streamlined management, and improved service.

Vigorous state and local governments are a vital part of our federal union. The federal government should leave to state and local governments those programs and problems which they can best handle and tax sources adequate to finance them. We must continue to improve liaison between federal, state and local governments. We believe that the federal government, when appropriate, should render significant assistance in dealing with our urgent problems of urban growth and change. No vast new bureaucracy is needed to achieve this objective.

We favor a change in the Electoral College system to give every voter a fair voice in presidential elections.

We condemn bigotry, smear and other unfair tactics in political campaigns. We favor realistic and effective safeguards against diverting non-political funds to partisan political purposes.

Republicans will continue to work for Congressional representation and self-government for the District of Columbia and also support the constitutional amendment granting suffrage in national elections.

We support the right of the Puerto Rican people to achieve statehood, whenever they freely so determine. We support the right of the people of the Virgin Islands to an elected Governor, national representation and suffrage, looking toward eventual statehood, when qualified. We also support the right of the people of Guam to an elected Governor and national representation. These pledges

are meaningful from the Republican leadership under which Alaska and Hawaii have newly entered the Union.

Congress should submit a constitutional amendment providing equal rights for women.

EDUCATION

The rapid pace of international developments serves to re-emphasize dramatically the challenge which generations of Americans will face in the years ahead. We are reminded daily of the crucial importance of strengthening our system of education to prepare our youth for understanding and shaping the powerful emerging forces of the modern world and to permit the fullest possible development of individual capacities and potentialities.

We express our gratefulness and we praise the countless thousands of teachers who have devoted themselves in an inspired way towards the development of our greatest heritage — our own children — the youth of the country.

Education is not a luxury, nor a gift to be bestowed upon ourselves and our children. Education is an investment; our schools cannot become second best. Each person possesses the right to education — it is his birthright in a free Republic.

Primary responsibility for education must remain with the local community and state. The federal government should assist selectively in strengthening education without interfering with full local control of schools. One objective of such federal assistance should be to help equalize educational opportunities. Under the Eisenhower-Nixon Administration, the federal government will spend more than a billion dollars in 1960 to strengthen American education.

We commend the objective of the Republican Administration in sponsoring the National Defense Education Act to stimulate improvement of study and teaching in selected fields at the local level.

Toward the goal of fullest possible educational opportunity for every American, we pledge these actions:

Federal support to the primary and secondary schools by a program of federal aid for school construction — pacing it to the real needs of individual school districts in states and territories, and requiring state approval and participation.

Stimulation of actions designed to update and strengthen vocational education for both youth and adults.

Support of efforts to make adequate library facilities available to all our citizens.

Continued support of programs to strengthen basic research in education; to discover the best methods for helping handicapped, retarded, and gifted children to realize their highest potential.

The federal government can also play a part in stimulating higher education. Constructive action would include:

The federal program to assist in construction of college housing.

Extension of the federal student loan program and graduate fellowship program.

Consideration of means through tax laws to help offset tuition costs.

Continued support of the East-West Center for cultural and technical interchange in Hawaii for the purpose of strengthening our relationship with the peoples of the Pacific world.

Federal matching grants to help states finance the cost of state surveys and inventories of the status and needs of their school systems.

Provision should be made for continuous attention to education at all levels by the creation of a permanent, top-level commission to advise the President and the Secretary of Health, Education and Welfare, constantly striving to focus the interest of each citizen on the quality of our education at every level, from primary through postgraduate, and for every age group from children to adults.

We are aware of the fact that there is a temporary shortage of classrooms for our elementary and secondary schools in a limited number of states. But this shortage, due to the vigilant action of state legislatures and local school boards, is not increasing, but is decreasing.

We shall use our full efforts in all the states of the Union to have these legislatures and school boards augment their present efforts to the end that this temporary shortage may be eliminated and that every child in this country shall have the opportunity to obtain a good education. The respective states as a permanent program can shoulder this long-standing and cherished responsibility easier than can the federal government with its heavy indebtedness.

We believe moreover that any large plan of federal aid to education, such as direct contributions to or grants for teachers salaries can only lead ultimately to federal domination and control of our schools to which we are unalterably opposed.

In the words of President Eisenhower, "Education best fulfills its high purpose when responsibility for education is kept close to the people it serves — when it is rooted in the homes, nurtured in the community and sustained by a rich variety of public, private and individual resources. The bond linking home and school and community — the responsiveness of each to the needs of the others—is a precious asset of American education."

SCIENCE AND TECHNOLOGY

Much of America's future depends upon the inquisitive mind, freely searching nature for ways to conquer disease, poverty and grinding physical demands, and for knowledge of space and the atom.

We Republicans express our profound gratitude to the great scientists and engineers of our country, both in and out of government, for the remarkable progress they have made. Reliable evidence indicates, all areas of scientific knowledge considered, that our country has been, is, and under our system of free inquiry, will continue to be the greatest arsenal and reservoir of effective scientific knowledge in the world.

We pledge our continued leadership in every field of science and technology, earthbound as well as spacial, to assure a citadel of liberty from which the fruits of freedom may be carried to all people.

Our continuing and great national need is for basic research — a wellspring of knowledge and progress. Government must continue to take a responsible role in science to assure that worthwhile endeavors of national significance are not retarded by practical limitations of private and local support. This demands from all Americans the intellectual leadership and understanding so necessary for these creative endeavors and an equal understanding by our scientists and technicians of the needs and hopes of mankind.

We believe the federal roles in research to be in the area of (1) basic research which industry cannot be reasonably expected to pursue, and (2) applied research in fields of prime national concern such as national defense, exploration and use of space, public health, and better common use of all natural resources, both human and physical. We endorse the contracting by government agencies for research and urge allowance for reasonable charges for overhead and management in connection therewith.

The vigor of American science and technology may best be inspired by:

An environment of freedom and public understanding in which intellectual achievement and scientific research may flourish.

A decentralization of research into as many centers of creativity as possible.

The encouragement of colleges and universities, private enterprise, and foundations as a growing source of new ideas and new applications.

Opportunity for scientists and engineers, in and out of government, to pursue their search with utmost aggressiveness.

Continuation of the advisory committee to represent the views of the scientific community to the President and of the Federal Council for Science and Technology to foster coordination in planning and execution.

Continued expansion of the Eisenhower-Nixon Atoms-for-Peace program and a constant striving, backed by scientific advice, for international agreement for peaceful and cooperative exploration and use of space.

HUMAN NEEDS

The ultimate objective of our free society and of an ever-growing economy is to enable the individual to pursue a life of dignity and to develop his own capacities to his maximum potential.

Government's primary role is to help provide the environment within which the individual can seek his own goals. In some areas this requires federal action to supplement individual, local and state initiative. The Republican Party has acted and will act decisively, compassionately, and with deep human understanding in approaching such problems as those of the aged, the infirm, the mentally ill, and the needy.

This is demonstrated by the significant increase in social security coverage and benefits as a result of recommendations made by the Eisenhower-Nixon Administration. As a result of these recommendations and normal growth, 14 million persons

are receiving benefits today compared to five million in 1952, and benefit payments total $10.3 billion as compared to $2.5 billion in 1952. In addition, there have been increases in payments to those on public assistance, both for their basic needs and for their health and medical care; and a broad expansion in our federal-state program for restoring disabled persons to useful lives — an expansion which has accomplished the rehabilitation of over half a million persons during this Administration.

New needs, however, are constantly arising in our highly complex, interdependent, and urbanized society.

Older Citizens

To meet the needs of the aging, we pledge:

Expansion of coverage, and liberalization of selected social security benefits on a basis which would maintain the fiscal integrity of the system.

Support of federal-state grant programs to improve health, welfare and rehabilitation services for the handicapped older persons and to improve standards of nursing home care and care and treatment facilities for the chronically and mentally ill.

Federal leadership to encourage policies that will make retirement at a fixed age voluntary and not compulsory.

Support of programs that will persuade and encourage the nation to utilize fully the skills, wisdom and experience of older citizens.

Prompt consideration of recommendations by the White House Conference on Aging called by the President for January, 1961.

Health Aid

Development of a health program that will provide the aged needing it, on a sound fiscal basis and through a contributory system, protection against burdensome costs of health care. Such a program should:

Provide the beneficiaries with the option of purchasing private health insurance — a vital distinction between our approach and Democratic proposals in that it would encourage commercial carriers and voluntary insurance organizations to continue their efforts to develop sound coverage plans for the senior population.

Protect the personal relationship of patient and physician.

Include state participation.

For the needs which individuals of all age groups cannot meet by themselves, we propose:

Removing the arbitrary 50-year age requirement under the disability insurance program while amending the law also to provide incentives for rehabilitated persons to return to useful work.

A single, federal assistance grant to each state for aid to needy persons rather than dividing such grants into specific categories.

A strengthened federal-state program to rehabilitate the estimated 200,000 persons who annually could become independent after proper medical services and occupational training.

A new federal-state program, for handicapped persons completely dependent on others, to help them meet their needs for personal care.

Juvenile Delinquency

The Federal Government can and should help state and local communities combat juvenile delinquency by inaugurating a grant program for research, demonstration, and training projects and by placing greater emphasis on strengthening family life in all welfare programs for which it shares responsibility.

Veterans

We believe that military service in the defense of our Republic against aggressors who have sought to destroy the freedom and dignity of man imposes upon the nation a special responsibility to those who have served. To meet this responsibility, we pledge:

Continuance of the Veterans Administration as an independent agency.

The highest possible standard of medical care with increasing emphasis on rehabilitation.

Indian Affairs

As recently as 1953, thirty per cent of Indian school-age children were unable to obtain an education. Through Republican efforts, this fall, for the first time in history, every eligible Indian child will be able to attend an elementary school. Having accomplished this, we will now accelerate our efforts to open up both secondary and higher education opportunities for every qualified Indian youth.

As a result of a stepped-up health program there has been a marked decrease in death rates from tuberculosis and in the infant mortality rate. Also substantial progress has been made in the modernization of health facilities. We pledge continued progress in this area.

We are opposed to precipitous termination of the federal Indian trusteeship responsibility, and pledge not to support any termination plan for any tribe which has not approved such action.

Housing

Despite noteworthy accomplishments, stubborn and deep-seated problems stand in the way of achieving the national objective of a decent home in a suitable environment for every American. Recognizing that the federal government must help provide the economic climate and incentives which make this objective obtainable, the Republican Party will vigorously support the following steps, all designed to supplement and not supplant private initiative.

Continued effort to clear slums, and promote rebuilding, rehabilitation, and conservation of our cities.

New programs to stimulate development of specialized types of housing, such as those for the elderly and for nursing homes.

A program of research and demonstration aimed at finding ways to reduce housing costs, including support of efforts to modernize and improve local building codes.

Adequate authority for the federal housing agencies to assist the flow of mortgage credit into private housing, with emphasis on homes for middle- and lower-income families and including assistance in urban residential areas.

A stepped-up program to assist in urban planning, designed to assure far-sighted and wise use of land and to coordinate mass transportation and other vital facilities in our metropolitan areas.

Health

There has been a five-fold increase in government-assisted medical research during the last six years. We pledge:

Continued federal support for a sound research program aimed at both the prevention and cure of diseases, and intensified efforts to secure prompt and effective application of the results of research. This will include emphasis on mental illness.

Support of international health research programs.

We face serious personnel shortages in the health and medical fields. We pledge:

Federal help in new programs to build schools of medicine, dentistry, and public health and nursing, and financial aid to students in those fields.

We are confronted with major problems in the field of environmental health. We pledge:

Strengthened federal enforcement powers in combatting water pollution and additional resources for research and demonstration projects. Federal grants for the construction of waste disposal plants should be made only when they make an identifiable contribution to clearing up polluted streams.

Federal authority to identify, after appropriate hearings, air pollution problems and to recommend proposed solutions.

Additional resources for research and training in the field of radiological medicine.

Protection of Consumers

In safeguarding the health of the nation the Eisenhower-Nixon Administration's initiative has resulted in doubling the resources of the Food and Drug Administration and in giving it new legal weapons. More progress has been made during this period in protecting consumers against harmful food, drugs, and cosmetics than in any other time in our history. We will continue to give strong support to this consumer-protection program.

CIVIL RIGHTS

This nation was created to give expression, validity and purpose to our spiritual heritage — the supreme worth of the individual. In such a nation — a nation dedicated to the proposition that all men are created equal — racial discrimination has no place. It can hardly be reconciled with a Constitution that guarantees equal protection under law to all persons. In a deeper sense, too, it is immoral and unjust. As to those matters within reach of political action and leadership, we pledge ourselves unreservedly to its eradication.

Equality under law promises more than the equal right to vote and transcends mere relief

from discrimination by government. It becomes a reality only when all persons have equal opportunity, without distinction of race, religion, color or national origin, to acquire the essentials of life — housing, education and employment. The Republican Party — the party of Abraham Lincoln — from its very beginning has striven to make this promise a reality. It is today, as it was then, unequivocally dedicated to making the greatest amount of progress toward the objective.

We recognize that discrimination is not a problem localized in one area of the country, but rather a problem that must be faced by North and South alike. Nor is discrimination confined to the discrimination against Negroes. Discrimination in many, if not all, areas of the country on the basis of creed or national origin is equally insidious. Further we recognize that in many communities in which a century of custom and tradition must be overcome heartening and commendable progress has been made.

The Republican Party is proud of the civil rights record of the Eisenhower Administration. More progress has been made during the past eight years than in the preceding 80 years. We acted promptly to end discrimination in our nation's capital. Vigorous executive action was taken to complete swiftly the desegregation of the armed forces, veterans' hospitals, navy yards, and other federal establishments.

We supported the position of the Negro school children before the Supreme Court. We believe the Supreme Court school decision should be carried out in accordance with the mandate of the Court.

Although the Democratic-controlled Congress watered them down, the Republican Administration's recommendations resulted in significant and effective civil rights legislation in both 1957 and 1960 — the first civil rights statutes to be passed in more than 80 years.

Hundreds of Negroes have already been registered to vote as a result of Department of Justice action, some in counties where Negroes did not vote before. The new law will soon make it possible for thousands and thousands of Negroes previously disenfranchised to vote.

By executive order, a committee for the elimination of discrimination in government employment has been reestablished with broadened authority. Today, nearly one-fourth of all federal employees are Negro.

The President's Committee on Government Contracts, under the chairmanship of Vice President Nixon, has become an impressive force for the elimination of discriminatory employment practices of private companies that do business with the government.

Other important achievements include initial steps toward the elimination of segregation in federally-aided housing; the establishment of the Civil Rights Division of the Department of Justice, which enforces federal civil rights laws; and the appointment of the bi-partisan Civil Rights Commission, which has prepared a significant report that lays the groundwork for further legislative action and progress.

The Republican record is a record of progress — not merely promises. Nevertheless, we recognize that much remains to be done.

Each of the following pledges is practical and within realistic reach of accomplishment. They are serious — not cynical — pledges made to result in maximum progress.

1. *Voting.* We pledge:

Continued vigorous enforcement of the civil rights laws to guarantee the right to vote to all citizens in all areas of the country.

Legislation to provide that the completion of six primary grades in a state accredited school is conclusive evidence of literacy for voting purposes.

2. *Public Schools.* We pledge:

The Department of Justice will continue its vigorous support of court orders for school desegregation. Desegregation suits now pending involve at least 39 school districts. Those suits and others already concluded will affect most major cities in which school segregation is being practiced.

It will use the new authority provided by the Civil Rights Act of 1960 to prevent obstruction of court orders.

We will propose legislation to authorize the Attorney General to bring actions for school desegregation in the name of the United States in appropriate cases, as when economic coercion or threat of physical harm is used to deter persons from going to court to establish their rights.

Our continuing support of the President's proposal, to extend federal aid and technical assistance to schools which in good faith attempted to desegregate.

We oppose the pretense of fixing a target date 3 years from now for the mere submission of plans for school desegregation. Slow-moving school districts would construe it as a three-year moratorium during which progress would cease, postponing until 1963 the legal process to enforce compliance. We believe that each of the pending court actions should proceed as the Supreme Court has directed and that in no district should there be any such delay.

3. *Employment.* We pledge:

Continued support for legislation to establish a Commission on Equal Job Opportunity to make permanent and to expand with legislative backing the excellent work being performed by the President's Committee on Government Contracts.

Appropriate legislation to end the discriminatory membership practices of some labor union locals, unless such practices are eradicated promptly by the labor unions themselves.

Use of the full-scale review of existing state laws, and of prior proposals for federal legislation, to eliminate discrimination in employment now being conducted by the Civil Rights Commission, for guidance in our objective of developing a Federal-State program in the employment area.

Special consideration of training programs aimed at developing the skills of those now working in marginal agricultural employment so that they can obtain employment in industry, notably in the new industries moving into the South.

4. *Housing.* We pledge:

Action to prohibit discrimination in housing constructed with the aid of federal subsidies.

5. *Public Facilities and Services.* We pledge:

Removal of any vestige of discrimination in the operation of federal facilities or procedures which may at any time be found.

Opposition to the use of federal funds for the construction of segregated community facilities.

Action to ensure that public transportation and other government authorized services shall be free from segregation.

6. *Legislative Procedure.* We pledge:

Our best efforts to change present Rule 22 of the Senate and other appropriate Congressional procedures that often make unattainable proper legislative implementation of constitutional guarantees.

We reaffirm the constitutional right to peaceable assembly to protest discrimination in private business establishments. We applaud the action of the businessmen who have abandoned discriminatory practices in retail establishments, and we urge others to follow their example.

Finally we recognize that civil rights is a responsibility not only of states and localities; it is a national problem and a national responsibility. The federal government should take the initiative in promoting inter-group conferences among those who, in their communities, are earnestly seeking solutions of the complex problems of desegregation — to the end that closed channels of communication may be opened, tensions eased, and a cooperative solution of local problems may be sought.

In summary, we pledge the full use of the power, resources and leadership of the federal government to eliminate discrimination based on race, color, religion or national origin and to encourage understanding and good will among all races and creeds.

IMMIGRATION

Immigration has historically been a great factor in the growth of the United States, not only in numbers but in the enrichment of ideas that immigrants have brought with them. This Republican Administration has given refuge to over 32,000 victims of Communist tyranny from Hungary, ended needless delay in processing applications for naturalization, and has urged other enlightened legislation to liberalize existing restrictions.

Immigration has been reduced to the point where it does not provide the stimulus to growth that it should, nor are we fulfilling our obligation as a haven for the oppressed. Republican conscience and Republican policy require that:

The annual number of immigrants we accept be at least doubled.

Obsolete immigration laws be amended by abandoning the outdated 1920 census data as a base and substituting the 1960 census.

The guidelines of our immigration policy be based upon judgment of the individual merit of each applicant for admission and citizenship.

CONCLUSION

We have set forth the program of the Republican Party for the government of the United States. We have written a Party document, as is our duty, but we have tried to refrain from writing a merely partisan document. We have no wish to exaggerate differences between ourselves and the Democratic Party; nor can we, in conscience, obscure the differences that do exist. We believe that the Republican program is based upon a sounder understanding of the action and scope of government. There are many things a free government cannot do for its people as well as they can do them for themselves. There are some things no government should promise or attempt to do. The functions of government are so great as to bear no needless enlargement. We limit our proposals and our pledges to those areas for which the government of a great republic can reasonably be made responsible. To the best of our ability we have avoided advocating measures that would go against the grain of a free people.

The history and composition of the Republican Party make it the natural instrument for eradicating the injustice and discrimination in this country. We Republicans are fortunate in being able to contend against these evils, without having to contend against each other for the principle.

We believe that we see, so far as men can see through the obscurity of time and trouble, the prudent course for the nation in its hour of trial. The Soviet Union has created another of the new situations of peril which has been the Communist record from the beginning and will continue to be until our strategy for victory has succeeded. The speed of technological change makes it imperative that we measure the new situations by their special requirements and accelerate as appropriate our efforts in every direction, economic and military and political to deal with them.

As rapidly as we perfect the new generations of weapons we must arm ourselves effectively and without delay. In this respect the nation stands now at one of the new points of departure. We must never allow our technology, particularly in nuclear and propulsion fields, to lag for any reason until such time as we have dependable and honest safeguards of inspection and control. We must take steps at once to secure our position in this regard and at the same time we must intensify our efforts to develop better safeguards in the field of disarmament.

The free nations of the world must ever be rallied to the cause and be encouraged to join together in more effective alliances and unions strong enough to meet all challenges and sustain the common effort. It is urgent that we innovate to keep the initiative for our free cause.

We offer toil and sweat, to ward off blood and tears. We advocate an immovable resistance against every Communist aggression. We argue for a military might commensurate with our universal tasks. We end by declaring our faith in the Republic and in its people, and in the deathless principles of right from which it draws its moral force.

Socialist Platform 1960

INTRODUCTION

The Dilemma of Modern Man

Never have Americans talked more about the importance of the private citizen; never has he felt more powerless in the face of events.

We possess the tools to build a world of peace and prosperity, and use them instead to engage in a deadly arms race. We possess the power to abolish poverty, yet unemployment continues. We possess the time to devote ourselves to great causes, but can find nothing to believe in.

From earliest schooldays to the age of retirement, on the job and at home and in our use of leisure time, when we buy and when we vote, we are subjected to a barrage of commercial, political, and social hucksterism. Our lives are shaped by public and private bureaucracies, self-perpetuating and outside our immediate control. Leaders in every field, who should be our servants, see us not as people but as *things* to be lied to, prodded, and manipulated into acquiescence. We live in a rigged society, in that the whole economy depends upon the manufacture of consent, *our* consent — to planned obsolescence, to tailfins instead of schools, to cold war and the armaments race. We live frustrated lives, because we are allowed to express our yearnings only through commercially-successful channels. We live trammelled lives, because dissent is stifled. We live cheap lives, because we are taught to value ourselves cheaply.

If we are to be free, we must discover new patterns for our lives. And then we must live according to those patterns, in the midst of a hostile society, until we have created nothing less than a new social order, a society in which the commanding value is the infinite preciousness of the human spirit and of every single man, woman, and child.

For man must master society instead of being mastered by it. This is the most fundamental statement of the socialist goal.

The Role of the Socialist Party

There are many ways in which free men can live free lives within a rigged society; but if their lives are to have social meaning beyond an immediate circle of friends, they need to join together and work for change in a way that is politically meaningful. It is this need which the Socialist Party is designed to meet. For the SP-SDF seeks to bring together, and give political expression to, the entire spectrum of democratic dissent in America. It gives unity, coherence, and practical purpose to what would otherwise be inchoate strivings.

Since the 1930's the two old parties have produced virtually no progressive social legislation. As productivity has grown, so have slums; as medical research has advanced, the ability of ordinary people to pay for medical care has regressed; as our standard of living has risen, fifty million Americans have continued to dwell in poverty. The weapons of a new warfare threaten our very lives, and we are offered only the insane satisfaction of knowing that two minutes after we die, so will our enemies. We stand condemned before the world and in our own hearts for our inability to achieve the racial justice that most of us so much desire. Our society is deadlocked and frustration is our predominant feeling in every area of life; and the primary source of our political frustration is a party alignment that cannot reflect the will of the people. A coalition of Northern Republicans and Southern Democrats thwarts the wishes of the majority, and will continue to do so until there is a political realignment in this country.

The potential for political change exists. It is found in the millions of trade unionists, farmers, Negroes, liberals, lovers of peace, who together form the bulk of the populace. And the prospect for change moves closer, for there are stirrings in the land: the reunited labor movement, the civil rights movement, the growing protest against nuclear weapons. It is to our fellow-citizens engaged with us in these activities that we especially direct this platform, for we share their aspirations and believe that they share ours. We offer them a vision of a new society, a vision that gives depth and meaning to the things that we and they are doing now.

The Socialist Vision

Our goal is a new and truly democratic society in the United States, a society in which human rights come before property rights. We are pledged to building and maintaining this new society by democratic means: For just as there can be no meaningful and enduring freedom without socialism, so there can be no true socialism without freedom.

Socialists call for social ownership and democratic control of the commanding heights of industry, not as an end in itself, but as a step in the creation of a truly human society in which all economic and class barriers to individual freedom have been removed. For the enduring ethical values which now are falteringly applied to our political institutions are absent most conspicuously in our economic institutions, and this absence affects the whole quality of our lives. If we are to lead full lives a prerequisite is that production be democratically planned for the benefit of all.

We do *not* propose totalitarian nationalization as under Communism. We oppose it because in theory it is oriented toward the welfare of posterity, at the expense of the welfare and even the human dignity of the present generation; and because in practice it means that the economy is run for the benefit of the bureaucratic class that controls the state. Neither do we propose simply nationalization with political democracy; for under such a system the people participate only at election time in the decisions that control their lives. We propose rather a society of free, continuing, and democratic *participation* — through political parties in the determination of basic economic and social and political policy for the nation; through shop councils, consumer cooperatives, neighborhood associations, and all the other organs of community in the decisions of daily life; through decentralized agencies for the management of each industry by those most affected by it; through encouragement of the maximum expression of individual creativity.

We propose a society in which democratic participation in economic and political life will set us free to attack and conquer war, racial antagonism, hunger, disease, poverty, and oppression. We propose a nation which can take its place in a World Federation of Cooperative Commonwealths, to the end that all men may lead lives that are rich and free. We propose a world in which man is the measure of all things.

FOREIGN POLICY

The end of the old colonialisms, the rise of new nations, the explosion of populations without birth control, the drive of dictatorial Communism — these are taking place in our anarchic world of absolute national states grossly unequal in wealth and power. In this situation men by their own scientific and technological genius have made war, immemorially the grim arbiter of their disputes, unusable for any purpose but annihilation of their civilization if not of their race. If there are to be survivors of a war inevitably to be fought with chemical, bacteriological, and nuclear weapons, liberty will not be among them. The supreme task of our time is the avoidance of war in the settlement of national conflict.

This would be our supreme task even if there had not been a Communist imperialist drive for power. All the more so, then, when this drive against the politically democratic but capitalist nations of the West has resulted in the Cold War and the arms race — clearly the outstanding fact affecting American foreign policy.

The present conflict has often been presented as ideological. To the Western nations, it is the struggle of democracy against totalitarianism; to the Communists, it is a contest between "socialism" and "capitalism." Yet beneath these descriptions exists a more sordid reality of two rival alliances each seeking economic, social, and political power. In the Soviet Union, the military bureaucracy and, doubtless, other elements, have acquired a stake in the continuation of a cold war which brings them prestige and power. Likewise in the United States the military, the great corporations, and many scientists have acquired a vital material interest in the arms race. For this reason the economics of disarmament must be a major concern of socialist planning.

No political solution can be achieved by opposing Communist imperialism with free-enterprise capitalism. Democracy is debased when Soviet satellites are called "People's Democracies"; freedom is debased when the word "free" is applied to any despot allied to the West, when it is used to cover up the search for areas of exploitation. Saudi Arabia and Spain are cases in point. As this platform is written, Cuba is going through a social revolution which the Communists are trying to exploit, though they were not part of the revolutionary movement itself; South Korea and Turkey have overthrown native dictators, only yesterday supported by the United States, and the movements which accomplished this were hardly Communist.

The situation cries out for political, economic, and moral support by the United States of *all* struggles for self-determination, of *all* efforts of people everywhere to free themselves from exploitation. If we wish the friendship of those who seek freedom, we must cease making alliances of expediency with tyrannous regimes; we must cease our dogmatic espousal of a "capitalism" which other nations cannot understand, could not use, and do not want. We must learn to support the demand of underdeveloped countries for independence, and we must support them *on their terms*. We must make their new independence meaningful by underwriting democratic paths to industrialization. Our answer to Mao's dictatorship cannot be Chiang's dictatorship; rather, it must be a commitment to aid in the creation of democratic, modern societies throughout the ex-colonial world.

A socialist foreign policy is wholly inconsistent with indefinite continuation of the Cold War and the arms race. In that race neither national security nor human freedom can be achieved. At most balance of terror can give only a little time for precarious peace behind the so-called shield of deterrence. Sooner or later this poor protection will be shattered by accident, by the mistakes of fallible men, or by the passions of men and nations mad for power. And while the arms race goes on the nations waging it will inevitably be caught in the toils of a garrison state, whose assumed needs will increasingly dictate their economy and override their supposedly inalienable rights as private citizens.

Prevention of war obviously requires the nations to dispossess themselves of the terrible weapons which they now frantically seek to make more terrible. We can no more trust ourselves with H-bombs, missiles, chemical and bacteriological weapons, than we can trust kindergarten children with rifles and bayonets. Disarmament is a necessity. But not mere disarmament without a conscious provision of law as an alternative to war and conscious dedication to the universal conquest of bitter poverty, a dedication which in our generation must be the moral equivalent of war. Recognition of these facts not only in words but in action must lie — as it does not today — at the basis of our foreign policy.

The life-line to peace must then be braided of four strands —

Disarmament

Universal disarmament down to a police level for maintaining order within nations and between nations. Such disarmament may be achieved by stages; but to be genuine and enduring, it must rapidly become universal and total. It must be begun by a treaty for ending tests of atomic weapons above or below ground. The fact that as yet all conceivable underground tests cannot be detected does not justify failure to reach an agreement now nearly arrived at. No risk is as great as a continuance of tests adding inevitably to the hazards of atomic fallout and inviting nation after nation to join the nuclear club, thereby tremendously increasing the danger of war by accident or design.

If no agreement should be reached at Geneva, the Socialist Party will call for the immediate unilateral cessation of nuclear weapons production and testing by this government. We will propose that U.N. teams be invited to establish monitoring stations on our territory for the purpose of proving to the world the reality of our action. We would then be in a sound position to call upon the Soviet Union to take similar action. Present U.S. nuclear power is such that the unilateral action we outline would not impair our security but would, on the contrary, break the present stalemate and create a new possibility — of turning the arms race into a disarmament race.

Successful progress in disarmament requires supranational authority not only for verification and inspection but for progressively assuring peace by substituting law for war. Hence our second essential:

Strengthening the United Nations

The strengthening of the United Nations and the creation or strengthening of regional federations. Such regional federations are peculiarly necessary to the healthy economy of the emerging nations of Africa. Our present imperfect U.N. has proved its value, but cannot adequately serve the great cause of peace without some revision of its charter and some provision for an international police force subject only to it, adequate to deal with brushfire wars before they kindle the great conflagration. The appeal to law instead of war must be strengthened by repeal of the Connolly reservations under which the United States is the judge of the cases involving it that it will allow to go to the World Court.

Disengagement

Progressive disengagement from imperfectly understood but probably binding commitments which cannot be fulfilled without war. But with this must go friendly cooperation for peace. This means, among other things, the progressive but rapid termination of agreements providing for American military bases on foreign soil; a principle which should be urged on every nation.

Progress toward either disarmament or disengagement requires them to go hand in hand. Disarmament is not possible without disengagement, nor disengagement without disarmament. This principle requires special and immediate application —

In pressing our ally, France, for negotiated peace fully recognizing the principle of self-determination in Algeria.

In giving moral and economic support to peoples emerging from colonialism or domestic tyranny and in giving moral and political support to struggles of still-subject peoples for liberty and self-determination in the "free world" as well as in the Communist world. This means an end of all aid to Franco, Trujillo, or any other despot. It means opposing racism and apartheid in South Africa, in particular by ending any possible subsidy to that government through unrestricted purchase of its gold. It means that our proposals for European disengagement must have as one of their objectives the self-determination of the Russian-dominated countries in Eastern Europe.

In beginning at once negotiation looking to recognition of the effective government of China, the most populous nation on earth. It is admitted by our nation's leaders that the absolutely essential ending of tests of nuclear weapons must require Communist China's adherence to any agreement. Yet we contemplate a situation in which we will say, "We don't recognize you, but sign on the dotted line." Sooner or later, we shall either get the real China into the U.N. or fight her. We Americans, under both Democratic and Republican governments, compounded our folly in dealing with China by insisting that Chiang, ingloriously driven out of China to an island in which he has not dared commit his rule to popular election, represents the whole nation. He represents only the American Seventh Fleet. We are obligated not to throw Chiang and the people of Taiwan into the arms of the vengeful Communist government. But they must be protected under an agreement which provides self-determination for the people of Taiwan.

In extending the Austrian principle of demilitarization into Central Europe by phased withdrawal of military forces on both sides. In a disarmed Central Europe, West Berlin can be guaranteed against imposed Communist rule and the Germans left to work out their own reunification. The SP-SDF is unalterably opposed to the rearmament of a united or divided Germany.

In seeking to get Soviet agreement to support U.N. action looking toward disarmament in the Middle East and a guarantee of any and all nations in it against military aggression or any attempt to change boundaries by force. The U.S. should be a party to a solution of the Arab refugee problem with the cooperation of the U.N., Israel, and the Arab nations.

War Against Poverty

Cooperative struggle against the bitter poverty in which 70 per cent of the world's people live — this at a time when all the nations, poor and rich, spend together $100 billion annually on the arms race. Less than one-third that amount, properly spent, might conquer world poverty in one or two generations.

Loans and grants to industrial and agricultural projects should be administered by the U.N. or its agencies. The SP-SDF heartily support the suggestion of the Socialist International, to which it belongs, that each nation pay at least 1 per cent of its national income into a general fund out of which grants be made according to need. So long as any such aid must be given on a bilateral basis the Socialist Party insists that it be genuinely economic, not military.

Implementation of the principles we have set forth, in a world where the United States has neither the power nor the wisdom to play Almighty God, will necessarily depend somewhat on the stream of events and the opinions and actions of other nations. But the purpose and the general direction outlined in this statement must be the fixed policy of the United States in its leadership for peace with freedom and justice.

DOMESTIC AFFAIRS

THE ECONOMY

American capitalism today is far different from what it was even a generation ago. It has moved in the direction of a welfare state. It has acquired a subsidized sector, mainly devoted to war spending, which affects a major portion of the gross national product. It is characterized by a growing concentration of corporate wealth, by intervention of the state in many areas of economic life, by private, public, and military bureaucracies which are increasingly powerful and all-pervasive.

Some of these changes are the result of popular demands for reforms which Socialists pioneered: social security, minimum wage laws, unemployment insurance, child labor laws, and so on.

Some of these changes are part of the drift toward a bureaucratized, centralized capitalism, more impersonal and powerful than ever before.

Some of these changes have been brought about by the Cold War. They point toward a garrison state, in which personal liberties are increasingly stifled and the nation is increasingly mobilized around one overriding purpose, the need to be prepared at all times for total war.

Contrary to popular myth, Socialists do not favor "big government." However, where the Federal government is the only institution capable of fairly and efficiently administering a social pro-gram, we do not dogmatically shy away from using it. But we oppose all unnecessary government bureaucracy, and seek always to find alternative ways of doing things, ways based on direct participation by the citizenry. We believe bureaucracy is the result less of carefully-considered planning, than of hasty and improvised methods of meeting emergencies which arise precisely because of lack of planning. Wherever possible we advocate a maximum of decentralized control under national standards.

It is undeniable that American capitalism has proved resourceful beyond the expectation of Socialists in the past. But the theory that this society has conquered all the fundamental problems of the old capitalism is patently false.

Thus, the enormous growth of American productivity has meant more money to go around and has concealed glaring inequality in the *division* of wealth. Yet it is a fact that the lower half of our population receives a smaller percentage of the total money income now than it did in 1910.

Thus, we are seriously told that America has banished economic want and insecurity — when one family in ten receives an annual income of less than $1,000 a year, and more than two families in ten have less than $2,000. According to the most recent statistics of the Joint Economic Committee of Congress, well over twenty million Americans live below the most minimal standard of life; if the definition of adequacy is the one proposed by the AFL-CIO, this figure rises to over fifty million, and includes semi-skilled workers, the aged, residents of economically-depressed areas, members of minority groups, poor farmers and farm workers.

The American economy in the post-war period has been periodically wracked by crises of "overproduction" — that is, in a nation and a world that desperately needs goods, there is a glut of those items which are most profitable. In 1949, 1954, and 1958, millions of American workers were thrown out of work. Each "recovery" has seen the definition of "normal" unemployment increase, until now America accepts four million jobless as consonant with prosperity.

These glaring inequities can be corrected only by a society which allocates its resources on the basis of need rather than of profit. That is basic to the socialist program.

In the absence of such a society, here and now socialists join with trade unionists and liberals in demanding immediate action —

For a higher minimum wage, from which farm labor must not be excluded;

For an integrated national campaign against poverty, with massive Federal aid to housing, community services, and education;

For a program of public investment as an anti-recession measure;

For an Area Redevelopment Bill to provide aid for distressed sections of the nation — a Point Four for our own underdeveloped regions;

For a national resources policy which will extend the program which proved itself in the Tennessee Valley Authority to other areas of the country, such as the Columbia River Valley and the Missouri River Valley;

For socialization of the oil industry on terms that give due regard to the needs and interests of a world peculiarly dependent upon oil. Today this industry is a power unto itself influencing domestic and foreign policy. Socialization of the oil industry must include social ownership of the oil fields.

For socialization of basic means of transportation. We deplore and oppose the tendency to subsidize railroad passenger traffic while allowing private operators to reap the profits from freight traffic.

For overhauling our confused system of taxation, imposing withholding taxes on dividends, ending favoritism to the oil industry, regulating exemptions on expense accounts, and imposing a tax for the recovery of socially-created rental values of land. We oppose general sales taxes, which hit low-income families the hardest.

In making these demands, we note that the one piece of important social legislation passed since World War II, the Employment Act of 1946, is hardly more than a general statement of good intentions. In the post-war recessions, that Act failed to commit the Executive to any specific action, and the battle for meaningful remedies had to be fought anew each time in Congress. Therefore, we stand for a new law which will automatically require Executive action whenever unemployment rises: Federal spending for worthwhile social purposes, progressive tax relief for the broad mass of consumers, a government banking and finance policy to stimulate maximum investment, and so on.

We note further that these are no more than the things which need to be done *first* and that their effect will be nullified unless they are followed by further legislation in the same direction, a direction which we believe must lead to a democratic socialist society. In the following sections, therefore, we spell out in detail some of the further changes we feel are most necessary in the immediate future.

SOCIAL WELFARE

The ranks of the chronically poor are swelled constantly by those who are rendered penniless by sickness, sudden unemployment, and other forms of personal disaster. Whether poverty is individual or general, in a country as wealthy as ours it is unnecessary, and therefore a reproach to all of us. We propose Federal action to guarantee to every family (1) a decent minimum standard of living and (2) maximum protection against economic mischance. As immediate steps toward this goal, we offer the following proposals:

Unemployment

Unemployment compensation must be made available to all citizens who cannot find work, for as long as they remain unemployed. It should amount to two-thirds of normal income. The Federal government must supplement compensation payments (1) by creating jobs, where unemployment is general; (2) by introducing new industry into depressed areas, or relocating the unemployed where this cannot be done; (3) by retraining those displaced by technological change.

Disability

Disabled persons must be trained so far as possible to perform useful work, with benefits ranging up to two-thirds of normal income for the totally disabled. A special no-interest loan fund must be made available to disabled persons who wish to build new lives as small businessmen. Persons handicapped from childhood must be given scholarships or job training so far as it can benfit them, and should receive pensions on the basis of need to whatever degree is necessary for a decent standard of living. All payments must be pegged to the cost-of-living index.

Social Security

Social Security should not be, as it is today, merely a palliative measure designed to supplement the savings of retired citizens. It must be extended to become a true national pension plan, designed to supply the full economic security necessary for a dignified and fruitful old age. Payments must be much higher than they are now, must be pegged to the cost-of-living index, and must be available to all persons of appropriate age regardless of their prior contributions in taxes. Women should receive benefits at age 60; maternal and child services must be greatly expanded; family allowances must be made for children of low-income families. Orphan beneficiaries, for whom payments now lapse when they reach age 18, must have access to a special fund for college scholarships or for training for a trade.

Medical Care

We support, as a step in the right direction, current efforts to give medical benefits to old people, although we deplore the inadequacy of this approach to a proper program of socialized medicine. At very least, the programs now being considered should provide coverage for medical, dental, psychiatric, and out-of-hospital care, as well as surgical fees and hospitalization; coverage should not be limited as to time.

We propose a National Health Service for the United States which will provide every man, woman, and child in this country with the best available medical care. We regard it as a scandal that health care in America is still run on the antiquated, nineteenth-century basis of cash and carry. Nations whose resources are much less than those of America have proved that socialized medicine is the way to safeguard national health while retaining a maximum of individual freedom in the doctor-patient relationship. The American people should not be denied the benefits which the citizens of Britain, Scandinavia, and other countries enjoy.

Under a program of socialized medicine, the individual is free to choose the doctor and the type of medical care he desires. Medical cooperatives should be encouraged through tax incentives and other measures; these are the plans in which a group of consumers build a clinic and hire physicians on a salary basis to give them complete medical care. Fee-for-service medicine would continue so long as the people in a given community wanted it, with the health service paying the cost.

Administration of the medical program would be local and democratically responsible to the public, with the Federal government's role limited to maintaining standards and underwriting costs.

We have socialized the protection of the citizenry from crime and fire. Now we must socialize the protection of life itself.

We favor drastic government action in support of the costs of medical education. It must be made possible for any qualified person to become a doctor so long as there is a shortage of doctors, and to live a decent life during the many years of medical and specialist training. We favor subsidy of the costs of training nurses and medical technologists. We favor a decent wage scale for lower-echelon hospital employees, and endorse their right to form unions. We support, and favor extension of, present government hospital-building programs; every community should possess a medical center with emergency-ward and nursing-home facilities.

Prescribed drugs should be available to all citizens without cost. Pharmaceutical companies should have their profits held down to a reasonable level, and an independent government corporation should enter and become a major competitive entity in the pharmaceutical industry. At the same time the drug companies should continue to receive financial incentives for genuine pharmaceutical research. The government itself should engage much more heavily in pharmaceutical and medical research.

Other Reforms

Our social services must be expanded and strengthened to provide for more adequate treatment and rehabilitation of the victims of alcoholism and narcotic addiction. They should be strengthened to deal more adequately with mental illness and the ravages of community and family deterioration.

It cannot be expected that our competitive and segregated society will effectively prevent juvenile delinquency. However, we urge the immediate provision of ample Federal financial aid for carefully-prepared projects for preventing and treating juvenile delinquency.

We urge the institution of a full-scale program for rehabilitation of criminals as well as for eradication of the societal and environmental causes of criminal behavior. We are opposed to the punitive rather than the rehabilitative approach to criminal jurisprudence, and consequently we regard capital punishment as a grim and uncivilized vestige of the past. We pledge ourselves to work for its eradication.

Administration of Social Services

Social services are not charity, but a right of all members of the human family. They must be administered with courtesy and dignity, and in a manner that permits recipients to retain their self-respect.

LABOR

As Socialists, we support the labor movement and view it as the greatest single mass basis for democratic change in America. Its efforts to raise the living standards of working people, and enlarge their role in society, are a basic contribution to our freedom.

In recent years sectors of the American labor movement have become bureaucratic and have lost much of the social idealism that sparked labor's great advances in the past. We believe the solution to this problem must come from within the labor movement itself. Therefore we join with all those unionists who fight corruption and undemocratic bureaucracy within their unions. The fundamental solution to the problems of the labor movement will come only with a revival of social and political consciousness on all levels within the trade unions.

We opposed the Taft-Hartley law in the past; we oppose the Landrum-Griffin law today. The latter is a hastily-assembled jumble of reform measures and reactionary attacks upon America's organized workers. Both were aimed at weakening the power of organized labor; whereas Socialists seek to strengthen and extend unionism in America.

We believe that legislation has a positive role to play in helping the democratic forces within the American labor movement. The impact of the law should be in the direction of encouraging voluntary union creation of democratic structures, with government intervention confined to the minority of crooked and undemocratic unions. Therefore we propose a "reserved powers" approach. Where an international union is found to have voluntarily established adequate guarantees for rights designated in a national labor policy, it should be free of any legal obligations which might be applied to unions refusing to take such steps on their own. In the absence of appropriate action by the union, the law should require dsclosure of union funds (and of labor relations expenditures by management); it should set limits upon trusteeship; it should provide for the right of appeal to the courts where the union appeals process is inordinately prolonged; it should guarantee free elections within the unions.

We particularly hail the United Automobile Workers for its institution of a Public Review Board providing an impartial system of appeal for union members. We believe that the review-board principle, if adopted by the rest of the labor movement, can be a major aid in strengthening democratic unionism and an unanswerable argument to those reactionaries who use union abuses as a cover for labor-wrecking laws.

We advocate the repeal of "right-to-work" laws.

We uphold the right of government employees to organize into unions and to strike.

Unionists have long opposed speed-up, stretch-out, and other inhuman techniques which management uses to increase its profits. Socialists support, of course, all union measures taken to *defend* the worker against the inhumanity of the machine and management. But we also propose that the labor movement consider a positive program on this issue. We suggest that unionists begin to raise questions of machine design in collective bargaining, and that the power of organized workers be turned toward fostering the human factor in industrial engineering. Other useful proposals include the rotation of work, the "self-pacing" of the work process in the shop, and so on; and we consider it vital that the union movement make the character of the work process an important factor in its thinking and actions.

CIVIL RIGHTS AND CIVIL LIBERTIES

Negro Struggle for Freedom

The most dynamic single social struggle in the United States today is the magnificent movement of America's Negroes and their white allies for civil rights. Socialists have always been wholeheartedly part of this struggle.

The Negro in America is doubly the victim of oppression. As a member of a racial minority, he suffers the special indignity of segregation. And as a worker, he is hired last and fired first, given the dirtiest and lowest-paid jobs, is herded into the most miserable of slums. Yet in this fact of double oppression lies a great hope: the natural alliance of the Negroes, in their struggle for civil rights, and the labor movement in its battle against exploitation.

In May 1954 the great legal struggle of the National Association for the Advancement of Colored People brought about the historic decision on school desegregation. Since then the racists have responded with a variety of tactics: token integration, the threat of a "century of litigation," outright refusal to comply with the Court's decision, economic pressure, and direct violence.

The legal battle remains important, but now the civil rights movement has entered a new stage. The generalties of the May 1954 decision can only be made meaningful through a mobilization of millions of Negroes and whites for political and direct, nonviolent action.

The very necessities of this political struggle point toward political realignment. It was a coalition of Northern Republicans and reactionary Southern Democrats who made the Civil Rights Acts of 1957 and 1960 into pitiful documents. This same coalition united to fight against medical care for the aged, against a program to relieve distressed areas, and for anti-labor legislation. Its power rests, to a considerable extent, upon the fact that the racist Democrats of the South gain important committe chairmanships in Congress because of their alliance with the Northern labor and liberal forces and through the workings of the seniority system. A vote for a Northern liberal Democrat *is* a vote to make Eastland chairman of the Senate Judiciary Committee under our present party alignment. If there is to be civil rights — if there is to be any real social progress on any major issue — the power of this coalition must be shattered. In practical terms, this means that the progressive forces, the Negroes, the labor movement, the farmers, the liberals, must take the road of independent political action. To achieve civil rights, there must be a real second party in the United States.

The immediate political fight focuses upon the attainment of a meaningful Civil Rights Act. It must include —

Adequate guarantees of the right of Negroes to vote, with the power of action, once a pattern of discrimination is found, vested in the Executive;

Legislation requiring the Federal government to initiate legal action on behalf of school integration, voting rights, or any other civil right;

Adoption of the principle that only integrated institutions shall qualify for Federal funds;

Implementation of Section 2 of the Fourteenth Amendment, depriving states of representation in Congress in proportion to the number of citizens they deprive of the right to vote on account of race, color, or previous servitude.

Another vital aspect of the struggle for civil rights is the fight against discrimination in housing, education, and employment, particularly in the North. Much attention, and rightfully so, has been given to the fight against separate public-school facilities for Negroes in the South. However, the *de facto* segregation that exists in Northern schools must be opposed also, for the damage it does is just as great in terms of inferior education resulting from overcrowding, inadequate facilities, and inequitable distribution of teaching personnel.

We support legislation and board-of-education policies designed to foster integration in school districting, in the building of schools, in the assignment of teachers.

Ghetto patterns buttress *de facto* segregation in Northern public schools. We oppose the use of government funds, whether Federal or local, in the financing of segregated housing. We support all efforts directed toward ending housing discrimination, public and private, such as open-occupancy legislation and the dispersal of public housing in such a manner as to foster integration.

Discrimination in employment has been and continues to be of major concern to Negroes and other minority groups. The average annual wage today for the white worker is almost twice as much as that of the Negro worker. Employment barriers, particularly in the white-collar and technical fields, still exist for Negroes. We urge the enactment of FEPC legislation with adequate enforcement provisions on a Federal level, and in cities and states where nonexistent.

Finally, there must be a gigantic, nonviolent mobilization of Negroes and whites for a direct challenge to Jim Crow wherever it exists. The

Montgomery Bus Boycott and the Sit-In Campaign of the Negro students point the path of this development. We gladly pledge our energies and resources to the support of nonviolent mass action for civil rights. We believe that this, along with legal action and the fight for political realignment, is the essence of the battle for civil rights today.

Other Minorities

Mexican-Americans, Puerto Ricans, and other minority groups are also the victims of discrimination. We support the democratic movement of all these minorities as part of the united struggle for the principle of equality for all.

We are opposed to the current effort to deprive American Indians of their remaining community lands and resources. Premature and enforced assimilation of Indians into the dominant culture is no answer to their special problems. No major programs affecting Indians should be launched without the free consent of the tribes or bands involved. As a first step to alleviate sufferings and amend ancient wrongs, we endorse the proposal of the National Congress of American Indians, for a "Point Four" program for Indians.

McCarthyism

We urge a campaign to root the institutions of McCarthyism out of our life: repeal of the Smith Act and pardon for all its victims; abolition of the Attorney General's "subversive" list; repeal of the loyalty-oath provision of the National Defense Education Act; abolition of the House Un-American Activities Committee and the Senate Internal Security Committee.

Ballot Access

We advocate a Constitutional amendment guaranteeing the right of ready ballot access in all states to minority political parties.

Conscription

Hostility to peacetime conscription in the Old World was one of the great forces motivating immigration to this country, and Americans have traditionally regarded it as alien and a threat to freedom. Under the conditions of modern military technology it cannot even be justified on grounds of need. It serves only to maintain the power of military bureaucracy and to subject a portion of the populace each year to military conditioning.

We demand its immediate abolition. We also condemn compulsory ROTC as military conditioning which has no place in our educational system.

AGRICULTURE

In the post-war period mechanization has rapidly increased productivity per worker in agriculture as in other fields. Our government has so far utterly failed to cope with the problems this has created. It has failed to assume responsibility for helping displaced farmers and farm workers find productive employment; and has, indeed, adopted farm policies which have made their problems much more acute. Corporate farms with absentee ownership have more and more tended to dominate American agriculture; these huge managerial units are the prime beneficiaries of the Federal subsidy program. The family farm, long regarded as an important institution of our democracy, is almost completely forgotten in our agricultural policy. Hundreds of thousands of people are forced to flee the land and start from scratch in the unfamiliar, frustrating environment of the big city.

The farm worker, and particularly the migratory laborer, is victimized by the most cruel exploitation. Unorganized, unprotected by the laws which cover industrial workers, the men and women who toil in the factories of the field live under the miserable conditions which predated the rise of the mass union movement and the emergence of the welfare state.

Our basic principle in confronting this situation is that occupancy and use should be the only rightful title to farmland. Where conditions favor family farming, the security of such farmers should be strengthened through cooperative credit purchasing and marketing, aided by government financing. Where modern techniques and specialization require large-scale farm ownership, we call for social ownership and cooperative operation to replace the corporation farm.

More immediately, we strongly oppose all those programs which seek to foster scarcity as a means to agricultural equity. Our nation contains millions of families who desperately need assistance to maintain a decent diet. Consequently, we seek the enlargement of the school lunch program and other public-welfare food programs. We also favor a domestic food-allotment program for low-income families.

Internationally, food "surpluses" can play an important role in the fight against world poverty. Specifically, we favor the international administration of a U.N. food program to alleviate starvation, to promote economic development, and to encourage price stability.

We wholeheartedly support the labor movement in its effort to bring the benefits of trade unionism to America's farm workers. We believe that the American labor movement must give top priority to this effort, with more financial assistance than is now provided for. Jurisdictional disputes should in no way be allowed to block development of the organization of farm workers.

We favor extension to farm workers of all the safeguards now protecting industrial workers: minimum wage, safety and sanitary legislation, and so on.

We see an immediate need for Federal aid to farmers' cooperatives and a strengthening of the rural electrification program.

We demand a major attack on rural slums.

In short, the family farmer and the farm worker cannot be our forgotten citizens. A vigorous, immediate program to protect them, and to limit the power of the corporate farm, must be a basic goal of all those who favor social change in the United States today.

URBAN PROBLEMS

Planning for People

The old-party politicians have concocted plans without vision and projects without plans. Proposals for urban renewal are not arrived at through democratic participation of the people involved; they are not designed as part of a comprehensive and rational scheme to rebuild cities around the human needs of the people who live in them.

Highways are given priority over communities; largesse is distributed to real-estate speculators in the name of slum-clearance. Neighborhoods and communities are destroyed; neighborliness is made more difficult; ordinary natural contact between people is frustrated. "Old" slums are spreading as the nation falls well behind the rate of housing obsolescence; "new" slums are created by our haphazard and inadequate public housing. Too much public housing is built in the form of high-rise human rabbit-warrens, income ghettoes. Our government has not created housing for human beings; it has not planned communities.

One conspicuous example of bad planning is the half-billion dollar Federal highway program, which puts a misplaced emphasis on private modes of vehicular transport at a time when our congested cities urgently require a revamping of the means of mass transportation. The new highways continue the process of disrupting communities in the interests of automobiles. Moreover, they must meet design requirements for the moving of military equipment through, as well as between, cities. The Socialist Party believes that cities are for people, not for cars — and most emphatically, not for atomic missiles.

We advocate reestablishment of the National Resources Planning Board for properly coordinating the use of resources and their distribution from area to area. We urge the creation by the Federal government of regional planning agencies in cooperation with state and local governments, to supervise overall planning for all Federal expenditures in public improvement. These agencies should help each region to help itself. They should play a major role in handling such problems as massive population displacement.

In the long run what is needed is democratic planning to make possible a tremendous decentralization of living, a nation of home-owners and communities. This clearly cannot be accomplished by private industry, nor even by the Federal government acting as it now does. It requires a human concept of the economy and of the problem of the city; a determination to build on the basis of need rather than of profit.

The City

As immediate steps to meet the problems of our cities, we advocate —

A Department of Urban Development, with a cabinet-rank Secretary in the Federal government;

National sponsorship of satellite cities to reduce urban congestion and to provide a decent environment for the rearing of children and the enjoyment of life;

Permanent and automatic reapportionment of all state legislatures subject to review by the courts, so as to end minority domination of state governments, and so that city governments will no longer find it necessary to bypass the state and look for aid solely to the Federal government;

Federal matching funds for metropolitan planning, sewer control, water-works expansion, and mass transportation;

Public ownership and nonprofit operation of power and transportation utilities.

Housing

The Socialist Party calls for planning a human housing environment in a vastly-expanded program of public housing. There should be as much decentralization and local autonomy as possible in the handling of Federal housing funds. Public housing must be planned as part of a community — with architecture related to the needs of people; with integration of races, income groups, and types of housing in genuine neighborhoods. Above all, public housing must avoid the tendency to create huge impersonal ghettoes. We do not need modern poor-farms; we need new communities.

Here and now, we call for a housing program that incorporates —

Arrangements for the relocation of persons displaced by renewal projects protecting not only their right to sanitary housing, but also their investment in their community. Relocation must be designed to prevent the disruption of societal ties as is now so brutally prevalent.

Application of the principle that the rental value of land is a social creation and should be appropriated by taxation for social purposes. All housing projects should insure a continuous return to the local government of increases in values created by public investment.

Sanctions against the creation of income or racial ghettoes. Grants-in-aid should be withheld where discrimination of any kind exists.

Approaches that will foster the idea of community, and encourage democratic participation of citizens in community decisions. Rochdale-type cooperatives should receive high priority.

Aid for lower and middle income home-owners who are able to refurbish existing homes as part of the program of community renewal.

Special programs for the housing of the aged, the economically-displaced, and the socially backward.

EDUCATION

A democratic society requires an educational system which gives to each child opportunity for maximum development of all his potentialities. We reject the demand, made popular by Russia's launching of the Sputniks, for gearing our educational system to the needs of a war machine, or for imitating the narrow objectives of education in the Soviet Union and other totalitarian states. We believe in education for the whole man, education geared to the aptitude of each student and designed to produce well-informed citizens capable of thinking for themselves and participating responsibly in the rights and duties of citizenship.

We favor Federal aid for school construction, for higher teacher salaries, and for guidance services. We favor a Federal college scholarship plan. We oppose giving Federal aid to communities which refuse to integrate their school system as required by the May 1954 decision of the Supreme Court. We favor the extension of unionism among teachers. We oppose loyalty oaths in schools and colleges, for either teachers or students, because their only effect is to create a climate of suspicion incongruous to education in a free society.

RESOLUTIONS

This platform was adopted at a national convention of the SP-SDF held May 28-30, 1960, in Washington, D.C. The same convention also adopted a number of resolutions; of which it directed that the following three be printed with the platform because they serve to expand on special topics of outstanding importance, which could not appropriately be treated within the editorial confines of the platform itself.

RESOLUTION ON FOREIGN AID

It is imperative that the United States, with nearly 50 per cent of the total world income and only 7 per cent of its population, do its utmost to aid the rapidest possible development of the underdeveloped two-thirds of the world. For the peoples of the underdeveloped countries, economic aid is essential not only for their standard of living, but also for the future of their democracy.

So far United States aid has been insufficient, and has too often been unacceptable because of the political and military considerations which have largely inspired it. We therefore urge that the U.S. foreign aid program be given a general reorientation —

The United States should propose, and push in the United Nations for, a world-wide crusade against low productivity, poverty, and misery. As a first step, we should give full backing to the suggested Special United Nations Fund for Economic Development (SUNFED). We should also move to expand greatly the facilities of such U.N. subsidiaries as the International Finance Corporation and the International Development Association.

Pending establishment of a world-wide U.N. program, the United States should greatly increase its own program of aid to the underdeveloped nations. Special attention should be given to the pressing needs of the Republic of India.

All United States aid should be extended in a spirit of cooperation, with the intention of bringing mutual advantages to the underdeveloped nations and to this country. Our present attitude must be abandoned; for now we offer aid in the spirit of the charity of a profit-hungry banker. The SP-SDF especially opposes those policies which force underdeveloped nations to turn their petroleum industries over to exploitation by U.S. firms, and which force recipient nations to accept stringent austerity programs as the price of getting even inadequate help from this country.

Finally, the United States must take the lead in working out arrangements for stabilizing at equitable levels the prices of the raw material and foodstuff exports on which underdeveloped nations depend for their foreign-exchange income. Without such stabilization, even very large intergovernmental grant and loan programs may be completely negated by sudden declines in world prices.

RESOLUTION ON LATIN AMERICA

At no time in the past thirty years has U.S. prestige in Latin America been at a lower ebb. Our government has only itself to blame for this situation. It results from the U.S. policy of supporting dictatorial regimes, and from U.S. failure to give adequate support to the economic development efforts of the peoples of Latin America.

The bankruptcy and harm that this policy has done to U.S.-Latin American relations is being dramatically demonstrated by the anti-U.S. attitude of the revolutionary government of Cuba, and the response this attitude has evoked elsewhere in Latin America. The Socialist Party salutes the Cuban people and expresses its full support of the revolutionary overthrow of the criminal Batista regime. We are in full sympathy with the objectives of the Cuban revolution, and are emphatically opposed to any attempt on the part of the U.S. government to intervene either directly or indirectly against the Castro regime.

We believe that the U.S. must show by deeds, not words, that it does not support dictatorial regimes. It should make clear its disgust with the Trujillo dictatorship in the Dominican Republic and protest the frequent meddling of that regime in the internal affairs of the United States and other American republics. It should name as ambassadors to the Dominican Republic — and to Nicaragua, Paraguay, and Haiti — men who will clearly act as representatives of a democracy and not as apologists for the dictatorship to which they are accredited. The U.S. should also strongly support the new Inter American Commission on Human Rights established in 1959 by the Foreign Ministers Conference in Santiago, Chile.

The United States must abandon forthwith all programs of military aid to regimes that use the equipment thus acquired to oppress their own people. It should encourage and promote the idea advocated by the government of Chile for general disarmament by the Latin American nations, and for application of the funds so saved to education, health, and other social purposes. It should itself contribute technical and financial assistance to these and similar projects.

The slow pace of economic growth in Latin America is leading many to conclude that development is only possible if political democracy is sacrificed. The U.S. has ignored this tendency, and indeed has stimulated it by giving aid that is insufficient and bound by too-orthodox banking conditions. U.S. aid must be enormously expanded; our country must seek to assist materially toward raising the standard of living of the Latin American peoples by helping to lay the foundations for industrialization and future economic growth. To this end —

The U.S. must cooperate in programs for stabilizing the prices of the principal exports on which the Latin American countries depend for their foreign-exchange income; and

The U.S., through the Organization of American States, must propose to the other republics of this hemisphere a general cooperative program for economic development. In such a program, each of the Latin American countries should draw up a plan for overcoming all the principal bottlenecks hampering its development, and should estimate what portion of the cost of that plan can be met from its own resources, by cooperative endeavor with other Latin American countries, and from extrahemispheric resources. The United States should then be prepared to supply however much additional aid may be required.

RESOLUTION ON MEXICAN FARM LABORERS

During the domestic farm labor shortage of World War II, the emergency program of importing Mexican workers reached a peak of 63,000 in 1944. Today there is no longer a domestic farm labor shortage — yet nearly 450,000 Mexican workers are being imported annually.

For hungry workers from the poor rural regions of northern Mexico, this program means the relative wealth of wages ranging from 50 cents an hour in Texas to nearly 90 cents in northern California. But it also means working under conditions which, in the words of Father Vizzard of the National Catholic Rural Life Association, are "an ill-disguised substitute for slavery." For some two million American farm workers, and the 500,000 among them who migrate with their families in search of work, the Mexican program means continued poverty and oppression, since these workers are displaced by the Mexicans and are forced to work for 30 cents an hour in Texas and 40 cents an hour in Arkansas.

For the big factory farms and growers associations of California and the Southwest, the Mexicans provide an abundance of cheap labor. It was these growers who fostered the mass ingress of illegal workers or "wetbacks," an influx which reached an estimated one million a year at its height. It was these growers whose persistent pressure brought about enactment of Public Law 78 in 1951, which legalized and made "moral" an illegal and immoral system. It is these growers who dominate the employment and farm placement

services and have made a dead letter of the law giving preference to domestic workers. It is these growers who have nurtured corruption throughout the Mexican placement system, corruption evidenced last year by the limited removal of public officials in California. It is the selfishness and arrogance of these growers, and their great influence within the Eisenhower administration, which has made impossible any real solution to the general problem of migratory labor.

Therefore, in addition to our other proposals concerning migratory labor (see under "Agriculture," page 630), the SP-SDF urges —

That Public Law 78 be allowed to terminate on its expiration date of June, 1961; and

That Congress prepare for its termination by authorizing a program of economic and technical aid designed to provide a stable means of livelihood in those areas of Mexico from which the Mexican workforce of 450,000 is drawn.

Socialist Labor Platform 1960

The overriding issue of the 1960 campaign is SOCIALISM and SURVIVAL v. CAPITALISM and CATASTROPHE.

This conclusion is based on a sober and realistic appraisal of a situation that actually exists and from which no one can hide. The whole human race is poised on the razor edge of nuclear catastrophe. As each day ends with the missiles resting on their launching pads, the danger is so much greater that the next will witness the outbreak, by accident or design, of a suicidal nuclear war.

The political heads of the great Powers solemnly declare that all-out thermonuclear war is unthinkable. We are told that there is an atomic stalemate — a balance of terror that deters both sides from starting World War III. But, for two reasons, this confidence is unjustified.

The first reason is that behind the fateful arms race there is a fierce international struggle between capitalist imperialism and Soviet imperialism for the markets and raw materials of the world. For the capitalist masters of the Western bloc and the bureaucratic masters of the Soviet bloc — the ones who really determine their nations' policies regardless of which politicians or bureaucrats hold office — the markets of the world are indispensable. In the case of U.S. capitalism, lack of these overseas outlets for the surplus products that result from the exploitation of American labor causes commodities to pile up and threatens the economy with mass unemployment, stagnation and final collapse.

Reason and experience tell us that ruling classes faced with the breakdown of their system, and blinded by the threatened loss of their property and privileges, become desperate. Desperate men do desperate things. It is cause for the most sober reflection that today a few hundred top capitalists and their military and political pawns — or their Soviet imperialist adversaries — can, when they feel compelled by their material interests, set in motion fateful forces that could destroy the world.

The second reason our fears are not allayed by the assurances of statesmen is the danger that an unauthorized or accidental nuclear explosion may trigger an all-out nuclear war. The grim but simple facts are these: First, each side now has ready for instant use nuclear weapons of unimaginable power. Second, these weapons are in charge of militarists who, being human, are prone to err. As one deeply perturbed Congressman described our peril:

"If you place six champanzees in a small room with a couple of baskets of live hand grenades, a minor catastrophe is inevitable. If you place error-prone human beings in proximity to thousands of nuclear weapons, a major catastrophe is inevitable and the triggering of an all-out massive exchange is probable."

The Socialist Labor Party urges every person to face this grim truth: We survive from day to day as hostages of a criminal, outmoded social system careening to its doom.

Nor does the danger to our survival stem from war alone. As a result of the capitalists' insatiable profit hunger we are all exposed to a host of mortal dangers — unsuspected chemical poisons in our food, chemical and radioactive pollutants in our water, noxious gases in the air we breathe. Capitalism's irresponsible hunger to exploit for private profit the advances of science is illustrated by the fact that there are now 65 million gallons of high-level, boiling-hot, radioactive waste stored in tanks that are estimated to last from 10 to 50 years. This is enough radioactive material to pollute all the land and water area of the United States, and it will remain deadly to man for centuries. By 1980 there will be another 65 million gallons. Neither the Atomic Energy Commission nor anyone else knows how to dispose of this poisonous atomic waste.

The Socialist Labor Party declares that the alternative to capitalist catastrophe is Socialism. Socialism, which will eliminate competitive production for the profit of a handful of capitalist parasites, and which will create the economic conditions for peace and cooperation, is the only hope of humanity. Socialism has nothing in common with the bureaucratic despotism that masquerades as "Socialism" in Soviet Russia. Socialism, as its founder, Karl Marx, conceived it, as Daniel De-Leon, the great American Marxist and social scientist, developed it, and as advocated by the Socialist Labor Party, is a society of industrial democracy —

in which the factories, mills, mines, railroads, land, etc., are owned collectively by all the people;

in which production is carried on for use and not for the profit of a handful of capitalists;

and in which the industries are administered democratically by the workers themselves through an integrated industrial union.

In the United States the capitalist class is master. In Soviet Russia the master is a bureaucratic hierarchy. But the Socialist Industrial Union government proposed by the Socialist Labor Party eliminates both capitalist masters and bureaucratic masters. It is the only conceivable form of social and industrial administration that gives the workers collectively a democratic mastery of their tools and products.

Socialism is the answer to all our grave and pressing social problems.

It is the cure for recurring war because it replaces the international struggle for markets and other forms of economic competition with economic cooperation, thus creating a foundation for durable peace.

It is the cure for recurring economic depression because it replaces capitalist production for private profit with production for human needs, thus freeing social production from the anarchy, waste and restrictions of private ownership and an unpredictable market.

It is the answer to the problem of poverty in the midst of plenty, for it ends the exploitation of class by class and assures that every worker will receive the full social value of his labor.

It is the answer to the threat of unemployment — a threat underscored by the rapid spread of automation — because democratic control of industry empowers the workers to utilize new machinery to reduce working hours rather than to eliminate jobs.

It is the cure for race prejudice because it cleanses society of the sordid material interests that foment racism and because it creates the economic foundation and cooperative climate for universal human brotherhood.

Socialism is also the answer to crime and juvenile delinquency, to the alarming spread of mental illness, alcoholism, dope addiction, and other manifestations of capitalist decadence, for it will replace irrational, inhuman relationships with rational, human ones.

To bring to birth this same society of peace, abundance and freedom, the Socialist Labor Party appeals to the working class of America, and to all social-minded citizens, to support its principles at the polls by voting for the candidates of the Socialist Labor Party. It appeals to all voters to repudiate the Republican and Democratic parties, the political Siamese twins of capitalism. It appeals to them also to reject the self-styled "radicals" and "liberals" whose platforms consist of reform demands, every one of which is a concealed measure of reaction.

Finally, the Socialist Labor Party appeals to the working class to repudiate the present procapitalist unions. All of them accept capitalism as a finality, and they are under the domination and control of leaders who are in effect "labor lieutenants" of the capitalist class. The Socialist Labor Party calls on the workers to build a new union, one which denies the false claim that there is a brotherhood between exploiting capital and exploited labor — a union which has Socialism as its goal. It calls on them to build the all-embracing integral Socialist Industrial Union as the only power capable of enforcing a majority vote for Socialism and of taking over the administration of social production.

Supported at the polls by the working-class majority, the elected candidates of the Socialist Labor Party will take over the political State, not to administer it, but to disband it. The reins of government will simultaneously be passed to the integrally organized Socialist Industrial Union.

This is the peaceful and civilized way to accomplish the Socialist revolution in America so imperatively demanded in this greatest crisis in human history.

We repeat: The issue in this campaign is *Socialism and survival versus capitalism and catastrophe.*

Unite with us to save humanity from destruction — and to set an example in free industrial self-government for all mankind! Unite with us to establish the Socialist Commonwealth of Peace, Plenty and International Brotherhood!

Socialist Workers Platform 1960

Humanity today faces three key problems: (1) How can the world be freed from the threat of nuclear destruction? (2) How can hunger and poverty be wiped out? (3) How can equality and democracy be won and maintained?

These are also the three key issues in the 1960 elections. What can America contribute toward a world of enduring peace, abundance and freedom?

THE STRUGGLE FOR PEACE

At one time America was regarded as the hope of the oppressed everywhere. This is no longer true. The majority of the human race have turned toward the Soviet Union and China as representing the road of progress. Whether we like it or not, this happens to be today's outstanding fact. It is high time to ask ourselves, why has America become so feared and hated?

One of the main reasons is that people in other countries have become convinced that America bears chief responsibility for the frightening drift toward a third world war. They note that our military experts have repeatedly admitted that the Soviet Union does not need war, does not want war, and is not planning an attack. Yet the Pentagon continues to spend approximately $40 billion a year for armaments; continues to stockpile nuclear weapons; continues to tighten a vast ring of military bases around the Soviet bloc countries; and continues such aggressive actions as spy-plane invasions deep into Soviet territory. The public abroad noted the State Department insistence on the "need" to renew nuclear tests and the Soviet initiative in giving them up. The contrast in attitudes is explainable only if America is actively preparing for nuclear war while the Soviet bloc seeks to avoid such a catastrophe.

It is common knowledge in other lands that the basic causes of war are economic. America's drive toward nuclear disaster is therefore seen as the end result of the need of its capitalist economy for cheap labor, cheap raw materials and lucrative markets, not to mention the profits in armament and a war boom. The Soviet avoidance of war, on the other hand, is seen to follow from the antagonism of planned economy to private profits and its need for peace to run in a smooth, co-ordinated way.

This is the basic explanation for the fact that more and more people in the world today feel that they must oppose America's belligerent foreign aims and support the Soviet bloc. They see it as an elemental question of survival.

The Struggle for Economic Security

Out of every eleven persons on this earth, it has been estimated that seven go to bed hungry every night. Few of these unfortunates believe any longer that this fate is beyond remedy. The sputniks orbiting overhead are daily reminders of what a daring, energetic and forward-looking people can accomplish through revolution and a planned economy.

Two roads offer economic security — the American and the Soviet. During World War II and for a few years after, the American road appeared more attractive to the colonial peoples. But they ran into bitter experiences. They found in practice that America blocked them from achieving freedom and independence.

The U.S. poured some $2 billion in arms and economic aid into the effort to keep dictator Chiang Kai-shek in power. The U.S. plunged into full-scale war in Korea to prevent the country from uniting and ousting dictator Syngman Rhee. In Indochina, the U.S. backed emperor Bao Dai and the French invaders; in Indonesia, the Dutch imperialists; in Japan, the Mikado; in Cuba, the bloody Batista. The State Department still backs butcher Franco and the unspeakable Trujillo. When a civil war broke out in Iraq, the U.S. landed marines in Lebanon. This year the State Department shoved a war pact down the throats of the Japanese people despite protest demonstrations involving hundreds of thousands of student youth and millions of organized workers. Ten years after the Chinese Revolution, both Democrats and Republicans still refuse to recognize the new government.

To the underprivileged of the earth, America appears as a frighteningly malevolent country. With $9 billion worth of grain in storage, prominent Americans answer pleas for bread with stony advice to cut down the colored birth rate; and to emphasize the advice, Democrats and Republicans have withdrawn millions of acres of the most fertile American soil from production. A spectacular instance of this inhuman foreign policy was the refusal to help Egypt build the Aswan dam. Today the bipartisan Republican and Democratic coalition is bringing increasing pressure against tiny Cuba's efforts to win a decent standard of living.

Hungry people, scorned by America, are inclined to turn in the Soviet direction. Sympathetic help from this source becomes quite dramatic, for the Soviet people are not yet well to do. More important, the Soviet Union appears as a living example of how to achieve industrialization without waiting for aid that may never arrive from the cruel North American power.

As a result, hundreds of millions of the poverty-stricken, from China to Africa, from the Middle East to the Caribbean, have felt forced, however reluctantly, to take the road of revolution in defiance to advice, threats and reprisals from Wall Street, Congress, the White House and the Pentagon. The starved and the ragged see planned economy as the shortest way from feudal stagnation to the benefits of modern civilization.

Two big lessons can be learned from this: (1) We cannot afford to leave our fate in the hands of self-seeking corporations and money-mad monopolists bent on blocking world progress for the sake of private profit. Instead, we should listen to the agonized cries to help make this globe a livable place. (2) The demonstrated successes of planned economy in underdeveloped countries show what tremendous benefits it could bring to America. In less than forty years planned economy brought Russia from one of the weakest of powers to one of the mightiest; and that despite gross bureaucracy, bad government, mismanagement, dire poverty, a heritage of backwardness and the most terrible war in history. There is not the least doubt that a planned economy in the United States, with our skilled labor, our rich resources, tremendous industrial plant and highly developed science, could quickly end poverty on this continent and assure everyone a life of abundance, opportunity and deeply satisfying achievement.

THE STRUGGLE FOR DEMOCRACY AND FULL EQUALITY

Both Republicans and Democrats proclaim that America stands for a "free" world of democracy and equality whereas the Soviet Union and the countries allied with it stand for totalitarianism. It is obvious that these lands suffer from bureaucratic police regimes that stifle freedom of thought and expression not only in politics but in many other spheres. We have the right and the duty to express our opinions about such evils but we have neither the right nor the duty to meddle in the internal affairs of other countries. The Russian people, the Chinese, the East Europeans will most certainly rectify matters themselves in due time by installing democratic workers and farmers governments. Their tendency to do this has already been amply demonstrated in the uprisings in East Germany, Poland and Hungary.

Our first concern must be with the shape of things at home. Here we confront a sorry spectacle. Forty-three years after entering the first global conflict to "Make the World Safe for Democracy," America has yet to make its lunch counters safe for Negroes in the South. Negro children are still barred from equal educational facilities. Job opportunities are still restricted by skin color, sex, age and religious belief. In the fields of government, industry, education and even entertainment, political inquisitors decide according to secret blacklist who shall work and who shall not.

In the South a totalitarian one-party system prevails, while in the country as a whole a bipartisan coalition of agents of big business monopolize politics. Labor does not have a single spokesman of its own in Congress. Minority parties are systematically excluded from the ballot and denied equal access to TV, radio and the public press.

The ranks of the armed forces of the country have no democratic rights whatever and a monstrous military caste, built on the notorious Prussian model, is spreading like a cancer throughout all our institutions.

How far America has slipped toward dictatorial rule is demonstrated by a single outstanding fact — the people have lost the right to decide the most fateful of all questions, war or peace. Congress has abdicated its war powers, leaving these to whatever figure big business puts in the White House. And the White House, in turn, has placed an obscure general in charge of the row of nuclear push buttons.

The erosion of democracy in America is evident in every sector, including the unions where a reactionary bureaucracy, hostile to the least manifestations of militancy or assertion of democratic rights by the rank and file, guards its special privileges by any means.

This land of Jim Crow and antilabor laws, of political witch-hunting and lying commercials, of multitudinous mechanical gadgets and crushing conformity of spirit, is boasted as a model of freedom and morality. The fact is that falsehood, cynicism and worship of the dollar have become entrenched from the White House down to the TV quiz.

FOR A SOCIALIST AMERICA

We urge every thinking American to consider the socialist alternative. We mean the socialist alternative first brought to nationwide attention by Albert Parsons, Daniel DeLeon, William D. Haywood and Eugene V. Debs. We mean the international economic order, based on scientific planning, advocated by Karl Marx and Frederick Engels. We mean a democracy, such as V. I. Lenin and Leon Trotsky fought for, that will give the working people control over their economy and government, free the arts and sciences, and eventually reduce government to scientific management of industry.

The Socialist Workers party urges an immediate end to the insane preparations for nuclear suicide. The Socialist Workers party urges that we turn our industrial plant away from war and toward an economy of abundance. The Socialist Workers party urges that we revive the democratic outlook and the democratic practices that were once the pride of America. Instead of resisting the course taken by the majority of mankind, the United States, we think, should help lead in winning the benefits of socialism for the entire world.

We realize that the road to a rational economy is not an easy one and that many partial steps must be taken before success is finally achieved. As a beginning, we propose the following planks for your consideration in 1960:

(1) For a peaceful foreign policy.

Let Congress and the White House pledge to the world that America will never resort to war under any circumstances. As proof of our desire for peace, let us withdraw all troops from foreign soil, give up all foreign military bases, put a permanent halt to nuclear-weapon tests, and dismantle the stockpile of A-bombs and H-bombs.

Support all colonial struggles against imperialism and the right of all peoples to a government of their own choice.

Recognize the government of the People's Republic of China. Support the Cuban revolution.

(2) Against capitalist militarism.

Turn the armaments budget into a peace budget for homes, schools, hospitals, medical research, nurseries, playgrounds, highways, transportation and public parks. End capitalist conscription and the Prussian-type military training practiced in the armed forces and ROTC which poison the minds of the youth against the labor movement at home, struggles for freedom and independence abroad and the movement for international socialism. Grant full democratic rights to the ranks of the armed forces, including free speech, free assembly, election of officers and collective bargaining.

(3) End economic insecurity.

For the 30-hour week at 40 hours pay. Extend unemployment insurance to every worker, and at the full union scale for the full period of waiting for a job. Let the government take over all facilities made idle by cutbacks, automation, mergers, decentralization, run-aways, or depression and operate them under charge of committees elected by the workers. Place control of production rates and speeds in the hands of the unions.

Equal pay for equal work regardless of sex or age. Full job and seniority rights and maternity care for women.

A government-guaranteed college education for all youth. Federally financed nurseries and summer camps for children.

For America's "Forgotten Generation," our thirteen million aged people, let's provide full disability benefits, free medical care and hospitalization, and adequate pensions. As an immediate measure, pass the Forand bill.

(4) Restore and expand democratic rights.

End restrictions on the right to organize, strike and picket. No government interference in internal union affairs. Repeal the oppressive Kennedy-Landrum-Griffin, Taft-Hartley, and Humphrey-Butler Acts, the misnamed "right to work" laws and other federal, state and city antilabor laws and ordinances.

Abolish the "subversive" list. Repeal the McCarran Internal Security and Immigration laws. Halt all deportations. Repeal the Smith Act and grant amnesty to all remaining victims of this thought-control law. Abolish "loyalty" oaths and "loyalty" purges. Repeal the law abridging the Fifth Amendment. Uphold the First Amendment. Abolish the House Un-American Activities Committee and the Senate Internal Security Subcommittee. Halt all political prosecutions for "contempt" and "perjury" based on the testimony of stool pigeons.

Liberalize the election laws. Lower the voting age to 18. Give minority parties equal time on TV and radio and in the columns of the public press.

(5) Guarantee minority rights.

Full economic, social and political equality to the Negro people and to all other minority groups. Solidarity with mass actions aimed at securing these rights as exemplified in the sit-in movement of the Negro students and their allies.

For immediate enforcement of the Supreme Court decision to desegregate the schools.

Enact and enforce federal legislation against lynch murder and police brutality. Abolish the poll tax.

For a federal agency fully empowered to combat all forms of racist discrimination and segregation in employment, politics and public and private services.

End the barbaric death penalty. Reform our antiquated prison system.

(6) For adequate government aid to the farmers.

Under a federal program set up and administered by elected representatives of the working farmers, let the government underwrite the full cost of production on all farm commodities. No limitation on crops so long as people suffer from hunger anywhere in the world. Government food subsidies for families in America living on a substandard diet.

Moratoriums on repayment of distress loans as long as debtors need them.

Abolish sharecropping and landlordism — crops to those who grow them; land to those who work it.

(7) For an emergency government housing and public works program.

As a starter on ending the scandalous national housing crisis, let the government build twenty million low-rent housing units on an emergency schedule. Put rigid rent controls on all private housing; elect tenants committees to supervise enforcement.

For a full-scale federal program on flood control, water supply, irrigation, cheap electricity and conservation of natural resources.

(8) Repeal taxes on low incomes.

Abolish all payroll and sales taxes and hidden forms of taxes passed on to the consumer. No taxes on incomes under $7,500 a year. A 100% tax on incomes above $25,000 a year. Confiscate all profits on war goods. Open the tax returns of the rich to public scrutiny.

(9) For government ownership of industry.

Nationalize the banks, basic industries, food trusts, medical monopolies and all natural resources, including nuclear power. Elect committees of workers and technicians to manage these facilities in the interests of the producers and consumers. Institute a planned system of economy.

(10) For independent political action.

End the Democratic-Republican monopoly of politics. Break all ties with the capitalist political machines. Organize an independent labor party, basing it on the unions and including the Negro people and working farmers. Put a Workers and Farmers government in office to reorganize America on a socialist basis.

In the election that concluded the 1964 campaign, the Democratic Party, lead by President Lyndon B. Johnson, polled 61.4 per cent of the more than 68,000,000 ballots cast and amassed the largest popular vote plurality in American history. The Republican Party was victorious in six southern states, Alabama, Georgia, Louisiana, Mississippi, South Carolina, and Arizona, the home state of its presidential candidate, Senator Barry Goldwater.

As was the case in 1960, the Prohibition Party (on the ballot in ten states), the Socialist Labor Party (in seventeen states), and the Socialist Workers Party (in eleven states) offered candidates and drafted platforms. The platforms of these permanent minor parties are included here; not included are the platforms of several small parties such as the National States Rights Party (on the ballot only in Arkansas, Kentucky, and Montana), or the Universal Party in California, or the Constitution Party which appeared in Texas. Nor does this compilation contain the statements of principles of groups such as the American Party, the Poor Man's Party, or the Theocratic Party that urged voters to write in the names of their candidates.

Minor parties received fewer than 150,000 votes in 1964.

Democratic Platform 1964

ONE NATION, ONE PEOPLE

America is *One Nation, One People*. The welfare, progress, security and survival of each of us reside in the common good—the sharing of responsibilities as well as benefits by all our people.

Democracy in America rests on the confidence that people can be trusted with freedom. It comes from the conviction that we will find in freedom a unity of purpose stronger than all our differences.

We have drawn upon that unity when the forces of ignorance, hate, and fear fired an assassin's bullet at the nation's heart, incited violence in our land, and attacked the outposts of freedom around the world.

Because of this unity, those who traffic in fear, hate, falsehood, and violence have failed to undermine our people's deep love of truth and quiet faith in freedom.

Our program for the future is to make the national purpose—the human purpose of us all—fulfill our individual needs.

Accordingly, we offer this platform as a covenant of unity.

We invite all to join us who believe that narrow partisanship takes too small account of the size of our task, the penalties for failure and the boundless rewards to all our people for success.

We offer as the goal of this covenant peace for all nations and freedom for all peoples.

PEACE

Peace should be the first concern of all governments as it is the prayer of all men.

At the start of the third decade of the nuclear age, the preservation of peace requires the strength to wage war and the wisdom to avoid it. The search for peace requires the utmost intelligence, the clearest vision, and a strong sense of reality.

Because for four years our nation has patiently demonstrated these qualities and persistently used them, the world is closer to peace today than it was in 1960.

In 1960, freedom was on the defensive. The Communists—doubting both our strength and our will to use it—pressed forward in Southeast Asia, Latin America, Central Africa and Berlin.

President Kennedy and Vice President Johnson set out to remove any question of our power or our will. In the Cuban crisis of 1962 the Communist offensive shattered on the rock of President Kennedy's determination—and our ability—to defend the peace.

Two years later, President Johnson responded to another Communist challenge, this time in the Gulf of Tonkin. Once again power exercised with restraint repulsed Communist aggression and strengthened the cause of freedom.

Responsible leadership, unafraid but refusing to take needless risk, has turned the tide in freedom's favor. No nation, old or new, has joined the Communist bloc since Cuba during the preceding Republican Administration. Battered by economic failures, challenged by recent American achievements in space, torn by the Chinese-Russian rift, and faced with American strength and courage—international Communism has lost its unity and momentum.

NATIONAL DEFENSE

By the end of 1960, military strategy was being shaped by the dictates of arbitrary budget ceilings instead of the real needs of national security. There were, for example, too few ground and air forces to fight limited war, although such wars were a means to continued Communist expansion.

Since then, and at the lowest possible cost, we have created a balanced, versatile, powerful defense establishment, capable of countering agression across the entire spectrum of conflict, from nuclear confrontation to guerrilla subversion.

We have increased our intercontinental ballistic missiles and Polaris missiles from fewer than 100 to more than 1,000, more than four times the force of the Soviet Union. We have increased the number of combat ready divisions from 11 to 16.

Until such time as there can be an enforceable treaty providing for inspected and verified disarmament, we must, and we will, maintain our military strength, as the sword and shield of freedom and the guarantor of peace.

Specifically, we must and we will:

Continue the overwhelming supremacy of our Strategic Nuclear Forces.

Strengthen further our forces for discouraging limited wars and fighting subversion.

Maintain the world's largest research and development effort, which has initiated more than 200 new programs since 1961, to ensure continued American leadership in weapons systems and equipment.

Continue the nationwide Civil Defense program as an important part of our national security.

Pursue our examination of the Selective Service program to make certain that it is continued only as long as it is necessary and that we meet our military manpower needs without social or economic injustice.

Attract to the military services the highest caliber of career men and women and make certain they are adequately paid and adequately housed.

Maintain our Cost Reduction Program, to ensure a dollar's worth of defense for every dollar spent, and minimize the disruptive effects of changes in defense spending.

BUILDING THE PEACE

As citizens of the United States, we are determined that it be the most powerful nation on earth.

As citizens of the world, we insist that this power be exercised with the utmost responsibility.

Control of the use of nuclear weapons must remain solely with the highest elected official in the country—the President of the United States.

Through our policy of never negotiating from

fear but never fearing to negotiate, we are slowly but surely approaching the point where effective international agreements providing for inspection and control can begin to lift the crushing burden of armaments off the backs of the people of the world.

In the Nuclear Test Ban Treaty, signed now by over 100 nations, we have written our commitment to limitations on the arms race, consistent with our security. Reduced production of nuclear materials for weapons purposes has been announced and nuclear weapons have been barred from outer space.

Already the air we and our children breathe is freer of nuclear contamination.

We are determined to continue all-out efforts through fully-enforceable measures to halt and reverse the arms race and bring to an end the era of nuclear terror.

We will maintain our solemn commitment to the United Nations, with its constituent agencies, working to strengthen it as a more effective instrument for peace, for preventing or resolving international disputes, and for building free nations through economic, technical, and cultural development. We continue to oppose the admission of Red China to the United Nations.

We believe in increased partnership with our friends and associates in the community which spans the North Atlantic. In every possible way we will work to strengthen our ties and increase our cooperation, building always more firmly on the sure foundation of the NATO treaty.

We pledge unflagging devotion to our commitments to freedom from Berlin to South Vietnam.

We will:

Help the people of developing nations in Asia, Africa and Latin America raise their standards of living and create conditions in which freedom and independence can flourish.

Place increased priority on private enterprise and development loans as we continue to improve our mutual assistance programs.

Work for the attainment of peace in the Near East as an urgent goal, using our best efforts to prevent a military unbalance, to encourage arms reductions and the use of national resources for internal development and to encourage the resettlement of Arab refugees in lands where there is room and opportunity. The problems of political adjustment between Israel and the Arab countries can and must be peacefully resolved and the territorial integrity of every nation respected.

Support the partnership of free American Republics in the Alliance for Progress.

Move actively to carry out the Resolution of the Organization of American States to further isolate Castroism and speed the restoration of freedom and responsibility in Cuba.

Support our friends in and around the rim of the Pacific, and encourage a growing understanding among peoples, expansion of cultural exchanges, and strengthening of ties.

Oppose aggression and the use of force or the threat of force against any nation.

Encourage by all peaceful means the growing independence of the captive peoples living under Communism and hasten the day that Albania, Bulgaria, Czechoslovakia, East Germany, Estonia, Hungary, Latavia, Lithuania, Poland, Rumania and the other captive nations will achieve full freedom and self-determination. We deplore Communist oppression of Jews and other minorities.

Encourage expansion of our economic ties with other nations of the world and eliminate unjustifiable tariff and non-tariff barriers, under authority of the Trade Expansion Act of 1962.

Expand the Peace Corps.

Use even more of our Food for Peace.

THE CONQUEST OF SPACE

In four vigorous years we have moved to the forefront of space exploration. The United States must never again settle for second place in the race for tomorrow's frontiers.

We will continue the rapid development of space technology for peaceful uses.

We will encourage private industry to increase its efforts in space research.

We will continue to ensure that any race in space is won for freedom and for peace.

THE LEADERSHIP WE OFFER

The complications and dangers in our restless, constantly changing world require of us consummate understanding and experience. One rash act, one thoughtless decision, one unchecked reaction —and cities could become smouldering ruins and farms parched wasteland.

The leadership we offer has already been tested

in the crucible of crisis and challenge. To this Nation and to all the world we reaffirm President Johnson's resolve to ". . . use every resource at the command of the Government . . . and the people . . . to find the road to peace."

We offer this platform as a guide for that journey.

FREEDOM AND WELL BEING

There can be full freedom only when all of our people have opportunity for education to the full extent of their ability to learn, followed by the opportunity to employ their learning in the creation of something of value to themselves and to the nation.

The Individual

Our task is to make the national purpose serve the human purpose: that every person shall have the opportunity to become all that he or she is capable of becoming.

We believe that knowledge is essential to individual freedom and to the conduct of a free society. We believe that education is the surest and most profitable investment a nation can make.

Regardless of family financial status, therefore, education should be open to every boy or girl in America up to the highest level which he or she is able to master.

In an economy which will offer fewer and fewer places for the unskilled, there must be a wide variety of educational opportunities so that every young American, on leaving school, will have acquired the training to take a useful and rewarding place in our society.

It is increasingly clear that more of our educational resources must be directed to pre-school training as well as to junior college, college and post-graduate study.

The demands on the already inadequate sources of state and local revenues place a serious limitation on education. New methods of financial aid must be explored, including the channeling of federally collected revenues to all levels of education, and, to the extent permitted by the Constitution, to all schools. Only in this way can our educational programs achieve excellence throughout the nation, a goal that must be achieved without interfering with local control and direction of education.

In order to insure that all students who can meet the requirements for college entrance can continue their education, we propose an expanded program of public scholarships, guaranteed loans, and work-study grants.

We shall develop the potential of the Armed Forces for training young men who might otherwise be rejected for military service because their work skills are underdeveloped.

The health of the people is important to the strength and purpose of our country and is a proper part of our common concern.

In a nation that lacks neither compassion nor resources, the needless suffering of people who cannot afford adequate medical care is intolerable:

We will continue to fight until we have succeeded in including hospital care for older Americans in the Social Security program, and have insured adequate assistance to those elderly people suffering from mental illness and mental retardation.

We will go forward with research into the causes and cures of disease, accidents, mental illness and mental retardation.

We will further expand our health facilities, especially medical schools, hospitals, and research laboratories.

America's veterans who served their Nation so well must, in turn, be served fairly by a grateful Nation. First-rate hospitals and medical care must be provided veterans with service-connected injuries and disabilities, and their compensation rates must insure an adequate standard of living. The National Service Life Insurance program should be reopened for those who have lost their insurance coverage, and an equitable and just pension system must help meet the need of those disabled veterans and their survivors who require financial assistance.

Democracy of Opportunity

The variety of our people is the source of our strength and ought not to be a cause of disunity or discord. The rights of all our citizens must be protected and all the laws of our land obeyed if America is to be safe for democracy.

The Civil Rights Act of 1964 deserves and requires full observance by every American and fair, effective enforcement if there is any default.

Resting upon a national consensus expressed by the overwhelming support of both parties, this new law impairs the rights of no American; it affirms the rights of all Americans. Its purpose is not to divide, but to end division; not to curtail the opportunities of any, but to increase opportunities for all; not to punish, but to promote further our commitment to freedom, the pursuit of justice, and a deeper respect for human dignity.

We reaffirm our belief that lawless disregard for the rights of others is wrong—whether used to deny equal rights or to obtain equal rights.

We cannot and will not tolerate lawlessness. We can and will seek to eliminate its economic and social causes.

True democracy of opportunity will not be served by establishing quotas based on the same false distinctions we seek to erase, nor can the effects of prejudice be neutralized by the expedient of preferential practices.

The immigration laws must be revised to permit families to be reunited, to welcome the persecuted and oppressed, and to eliminate the discriminatory provisions which base admission upon national origins.

We will support legislation to carry forward the progress already made toward full equality of opportunity for women as well as men.

We will strive to eliminate discrimination against older Americans, especially in their employment.

Ending discrimination based on race, age, sex, or national origin demands not only equal opportunity but the opportunity to be equal. We are concerned not only with people's right to be free, but also with their ability to use their freedom.

We will:

Carry the War on Poverty forward as a total war against the causes of human want.

Move forward with programs to restore those areas, such as Appalachia, which the Nation's progress has by-passed.

Help the physically handicapped and mentally disadvantaged develop to the full limit of their capabilities.

Enhance the security of older Americans by encouraging private retirement and welfare programs, offering opportunities like those provided for the young under the Economic Opportunities Act of 1964, and expanding decent housing which older citizens can afford.

Assist our Indian people to improve their stand-ard of living and attain self-sufficiency, the privileges of equal citizenship, and full participation in American life.

The Social Security program, initiated and developed under the National leadership of the Democratic Party and in the face of ceaseless partisan opposition, contributes greatly to the strength of the Nation. We must insure that those who have contributed to the system shall share in the steady increase in our standard of living by adjusting benefit levels.

We hold firmly to the conviction, long embraced by Democratic Administrations, that the advancing years of life should bring not fear and loneliness, but security, meaning, and satisfaction.

We will encourage further support for the arts, giving people a better chance to use increased leisure and recognizing that the achievements of art are an index of the greatness of a civilization.

We will encourage the advance of science and technology—for its material rewards, and for its contribution to an understanding of the universe and ourselves.

The Economy

The American free enterprise system is one of the great achievements of the human mind and spirit. It has developed by a combination of the energetic efforts of working men and women, bold private initiative, the profit motive and wise public policy, until it is now the productive marvel of mankind.

In spite of this, at the outset of 1961, America was in the depths of the fourth postwar recession.

Since then, in 42 months of uninterrupted expansion under Presidents Kennedy and Johnson, we have achieved the longest and strongest peacetime prosperity in modern history:

Almost four million jobs have been added to the economy—almost 1½ million since last December.

Workers' earnings and corporate profits are at the highest level in history.

Prices have been more stable than in any other industrial nation in the free world.

This did not just happen. It has come about because we have wisely and prudently used our increasing understanding of how the economy works.

It is the national purpose, and our commitment, to continue this expansion of the American economy toward its potential, without a recession, with continued stability, and with an extension of the benefits of this growth and prosperity to those who have not fully shared in them.

This will require continuation of flexible and innovative fiscal, monetary, and debt management policies, recognizing the importance of low interest rates.

We will seek further tax reduction—and in the process we need to remove inequities in our present tax laws. In particular we should carefully review all our excise taxes and eliminate those that are obsolete. Consideration should be given to the development of fiscal policies which would provide revenue sources to hard-pressed state and local governments to assist them with their responsibilities.

Every penny of Federal spending must be accounted for in terms of the strictest economy, efficiency and integrity. We pledge to continue a frugal government, getting a dollar's value for a dollar spent, and a government worthy of the citizen's confidence.

Our goal is a balanced budget in a balanced economy.

Our enviable record of price stability must be maintained—through sound fiscal and monetary policies and the encouragement of responsible private wage and price policies. Stability is essential to protect our citizens—particularly the retired and handicapped—from the ravages of inflation. It is also essential to maintain confidence in the American dollar; this confidence has been restored in the past four years through sound policies.

Radical changes in technology and automation contribute to increased productivity and a higher standard of living. They must not penalize the few while benefiting the many. We maintain that any man or woman displaced by a machine or by technological change should have the opportunity, without penalty, to another job. Our common responsibility is to see that this right is fulfilled.

Full employment is an end in itself and must be insisted upon as a priority objective.

It is the national purpose, and our commitment, that every man or woman who is willing and able to work is entitled to a job and to a fair wage for doing it.

The coverage of the Fair Labor Standards Act must be extended to all workers employed in industries affecting interstate commerce, and the minimum wage level and coverage increased to assure those at the bottom of the economic scale a fairer share in the benefits of an ever-rising standard of American living.

Overtime payment requirements must be increased to assure maximum employment consistent with business efficiency. The matter of the length of work periods should be given continuing consideration.

The unemployment insurance program must be basically revised to meet the needs of the unemployed and of the economy, and to assure that this program meets the standards the nation's experience dictates.

Agricultural and migratory workers must be given legal protection and economic encouragement.

We must develop fully our most precious resource—our manpower. Training and retraining programs must be expanded. A broad-gauge manpower program must be developed which will not only satisfy the needs of the economy but will also give work its maximum meaning in the pattern of human life.

We will stimulate as well as protect small business, the seedbed of free enterprise and a major source of employment in our economy.

The antitrust laws must be vigorously enforced.

Our population, which is growing rapidly and becoming increasingly mobile, and our expanding economy are placing greater demands upon our transportation system than ever before. We must have fast, safe, and economic modes of transportation. Each mode should be encouraged to develop in accordance with its maximum utility, available at the lowest cost under the principles of fair competition. A strong and efficient American Flag merchant marine is essential to peacetime commerce and defense emergencies.

The industrial democracy of free, private collective bargaining and the security of American trade unions must be strengthened by repealing Section 14(b) of the Taft-Hartley Act. The present inequitable restrictions on the right to organize and to strike and picket peaceably must also be eliminated.

In order to protect the hard earned dollars of American consumers, as well as promote their basic consumer rights, we will make full use of existing authority, and continue to promote efforts on behalf of consumers by industry, voluntary organizations, and state and local governments. Where protection is essential, we will enact legislation to protect the safety of consumers and to provide them with essential information. We will continue to insist that our drugs and medicines are safe and effective, that our food and cosmetics are free from harm, that merchandise is labeled and packaged honestly and that the true cost of credit is disclosed.

It is the national purpose, and our commitment to increase the freedom and effectiveness of the essential private forces and processes in the economy.

RURAL AMERICA

The roots of our economy and our life as a people lie deep in the soil of America's farm land.

Our policies and programs must continue to recognize the significant role of agricultural and rural life.

To achieve the goals of higher incomes to the farm and ranch, particularly the family-sized farm, lower prices for the consumer, and lower costs to the government, we will continue to carry forward this three-dimensional program.

1. Commodity Programs to strengthen the farm income structure and reach the goal of parity of income in every aspect of American agriculture. We will continue to explore and develop new domestic and foreign markets for the products of our farms and ranches.

2. Consumer Programs including expansion of the Food Stamp Program and the school lunch and other surplus food programs, and acceleration of research into new industrial uses of farm products, in order to assure maximum use of and abundance of wholesome foods at fair prices here and abroad. We will also study new low-cost methods and techniques of food distribution for the benefit of our housewives to better feed their families.

3. Community Programs and agricultural cooperatives to assure rural America decent housing, economic security and full partnership in the building of the great society. We pledge our continued support of the rural telephone program and the Rural Electrification Administration, which are among the great contributions of the Democratic Party to the well-being and comfort of rural America.

THE NATION'S NATURAL RESOURCES

America's bountiful supply of natural resources has been one of the major factors in achieving our position of world leadership, in developing the greatest industrial machine in the world's history, and in providing a richer and more complete life for every American. But these resources are not inexhaustible. With our vastly expanding population—an estimated 325 million people by the end of the century—there is an ever-increasing responsibility to use and conserve our resources wisely and prudently if we are to fulfill our obligation to the trust we hold for future generations. Building on the unsurpassed conservation record of the past four years, we shall:

Continue the quickened pace of comprehensive development of river basins in every section of the country, employing multi-purpose projects such as flood control, irrigation and reclamation, power generation, navigation, municipal water supply, fish and wildlife enhancement and recreation, where appropriate to realize the fullest possible benefits.

Provide the people of this nation a balanced outdoor recreation program to add to their health and well-being, including the addition or improved management of national parks, forests, lake shores, seashores and recreation areas.

Preserve for us and our posterity through the means provided by the Wilderness Act of 1964 millions of acres of primitive and wilderness areas, including countless beautiful lakes and streams.

Increase our stock of wildlife and fish.

Continue and strengthen the dynamic program inaugurated to assure fair treatment for American fishermen and the preservation of fishing rights.

Continue to support balanced land and forest development through intensive forest management on a multiple-use and sustained yield basis, reforestation of burned land, providing public access roads, range improvement, watershed management, concern for small business operations and recreational uses.

Unlock the resources of the sea through a strong oceanography program.

Continue the attack we have launched on the polluted air that envelops our cities and on eliminating the pollution of our rivers and streams.

Intensify our efforts to solve the critical water

problems of many sections of this country by de-salinization.

Sustain and promote strong, vigorous domestic minerals, metals, petroleum and fuels industries.

Increase the efficient use of electrical power through regional inter-ties and more extensive use of high voltage transmission.

Continue to promote the development of new and improved methods of generating electric power, such as the recent important gains in the field of atomic energy and the Passamaquoddy tidal power project.

Preserve the T.V.A., which has played such an instrumental role in the revitalization of the area it serves and which has been the inspiration for regional development programs throughout the world.

The City

The vitality of our cities is essential to the healthy growth of American civilization. In the next 40 years urban populations will double, the area of city land will double and we will have to construct houses, highways and facilities equal to all those built since this country was first settled.

Now is the time to redouble our efforts, with full cooperation among local, state and federal governments, for these objectives:

The goal of our housing program must be a decent home for every American family.

Special effort must be made in our cities to provide wholesome living for our young people. We must press the fight against narcotics and, through the war against poverty, increase educational and employment opportunities, turning juvenile delinquents into good citizens and tax-users into tax payers.

We will continue to assist broad community and regional development, urban renewal, mass transit, open space and other programs for our metropolitan areas. We will offer such aid without impairing local Administration through unnecessary Federal interference.

Because our cities and suburbs are so important to the welfare of all our people, we believe a department devoted to urban affairs should be added to the President's cabinet.

The Government

We, the people, are the government.

The Democratic Party believes, as Thomas Jefferson first stated that "the care of human life and happiness is the first and only legitimate object of good government:"

The government's business is the people's business. Information about public affairs must continue to be freely available to the Congress and to the public.

Every person who participates in the government must be held to a standard of ethics which permits no compromise with the principles of absolute honesty and the maintenance of undivided loyalty to the public interest.

The Congress of the United States should revise its rules and procedures to assure majority rule after reasonable debate and to guarantee that major legislative proposals of the President can be brought to a vote after reasonable consideration in committee.

We support home rule for the District of Columbia. The seat of our government shall be a workshop for democracy, a pilot-plant for freedom, and a place of incomparable beauty.

We also support a constitutional amendment giving the District voting representation in Congress and, pending such action, the enactment of legislation providing for a non-voting delegate from District of Columbia to the House of Representatives.

We support the right of the people of the Virgin Islands to the fullest measure of self-government, including the right to elect their Governor.

The people of Puerto Rico and the people of the United States enjoy a unique relationship that has contributed greatly to the remarkable economic and political development of Puerto Rico. We look forward to the report on that relationship by a commission composed of members from Puerto Rico and the United States, and we are confident that it will contribute to the further enhancement of Puerto Rico and the benefit that flows from the principles of self-determination.

The Democratic Party holds to the belief that government in the United States—local, state and federal—was created in order to serve the people. Each level of government has appropriate powers and each has specific responsibilities. The first responsibility of government at every level is to protect the basic freedoms of the people. No government at any level can properly complain of violation of its power, if it fails to meet its responsibilities.

The federal government exists not to grow larger, but to enlarge the individual potential and achievement of the people.

The federal government exists not to subordinate the states, but to support them.

All of us are Americans. All of us are free men. Ultimately there can be no effective restraint on the powers of government at any level save as Americans exercising their duties as citizens insist upon and maintain free, democratic processes of our constitutional system.

ONE NATION, ONE PEOPLE

On November 22, 1963, John Fitzgerald Kennedy was shot down in our land.

We honor his memory best—and as he would wish—by devoting ourselves anew to the larger purposes for which he lived.

Of first priority is our renewed commitments to the values and ideals of democracy.

We are firmly pledged to continue the Nation's march towards the goals of equal opportunity and equal treatment for all Americans regardless of race, creed, color or national origin.

We cannot tolerate violence anywhere in our land—north, south, east or west. Resort to lawlessness is anarchy and must be opposed by the Government and all thoughtful citizens.

We must expose, wherever it exists, the advocacy of hatred which creates the clear and present danger of violence.

We condemn extremism, whether from the Right or Left, including the extreme tactics of such organizations as the Communist Party, the Ku Klux Klan and the John Birch Society.

We know what violence and hate can do. We have seen the tragic consequences of misguided zeal and twisted logic.

The time has come now for all of us to understand and respect one another, and to seek the unity of spirit and purpose from which our future greatness will grow—for only as we work together with the object of liberty and justice for all will the peace and freedom of each of us be secured.

These are the principles which command our cause and strengthen our effort as we cross the new frontier and enter upon the great society.

AN ACCOUNTING OF STEWARDSHIP, 1961—1964

One hundred and twenty-four years ago, in 1840, the Democratic National Convention meeting in Baltimore adopted the first platform in the history of a national political party. The principles stated in that platform are as valid as ever:

"Resolved, That the liberal principles embodied by Jefferson in the Declaration of Independence, and sanctioned in the Constitution, which makes ours the land of liberty, and the asylum of the oppressed of every nation, have ever been cardinal principles in the democratic faith."

One hundred and twenty years later, in 1960, our nation had grown from 26 to 50 states, our people from 17 million to 179 million.

That year, in Los Angeles, the Democratic National Convention adopted a platform which reflected, in its attention to 38 specific subjects, the volume of unfinished business of the American people which had piled up to the point of national crisis.

The platform declared that as a Party we would put the people's business first, and stated in plain terms how we proposed to get on with it.

Four year have passed, and the time has come for the people to measure our performance against our pledges.

We welcome the comparison; we seek it.

For the record is one of four years of unrelenting effort, and unprecedented achievement—not by a political party, but by a people.

THE RECORD

NATIONAL DEFENSE

In 1960, we proposed to—

"Recast our military capacity in order to provide forces and weapons of a diversity, balance, and mobility sufficient in quantity and quality to deter both limited and general aggression."

Since January 1961, we have achieved:

A 150% increase in the number of nuclear warheads and a 200% increase in total megatonnage available in the Strategic Alert Forces.

A 60% increase in the tactical nuclear strength in Western Europe.

A 45% increase in the number of combat-ready Army divisions.

A 15,000 man increase in the strength of the Marine Corps.

A 75% increase in airlift capability.

A 100% increase in ship construction to modernize our fleet.

A 44% increase in the number of tactical fighter squadrons.

An 800% increase in the special forces trained to deal with counter-insurgency threats.

In 1960, we proposed to create—

"Deterrent military power such that the Soviet and Chinese leaders will have no doubt that an attack on the United States would surely be followed by their own destruction."

Since 1961, we have increased the intercontinental ballistic missiles and Polaris missiles in our arsenal from fewer than 100 to more than 1,000.

Our Strategic Alert Forces now have about 1,100 bombers, including 550 on 15-minute alert, many of which are equipped with decoy missiles and other penetration aids to assure that they will reach their targets.

In 1960, we proposed—

"Continuous modernization of our forces through intensified research and development, including essential programs slowed down, terminated, suspended, or neglected for lack of budgetary support."

Since 1961, we have—

Increased funds for research and development by 50% over the 1957-60 level.

Added 208 major new research and development projects including 77 weapons programs with costs exceeding $10 million each, among which are the SR-71 long-range, manned, supersonic strategic military reconnaissance aircraft, the NIKE-X anti-ballistic missile system, the A7A navy attack aircraft, and the F-111 fighter-bomber and a new main battle tank.

Increased, by more than 1,000%, the funds for the development of counter-insurgency weapons and equipment, from less than $10 million to over $103 million per year.

In 1960, we proposed—

"Balanced conventional military forces which will permit a response graded to the intensity of any threats of aggressive force."

Since 1961, we have—

Increased the regular strength of the Army by 100,000 men, and the numbers of combat-ready Army divisions from 11 to 16.

Increased the number of tactical fighter squadrons from 55 to 79 and have substantially increased the procurement of tactical fighters.

Trained over 100,000 officers in counter-insurgency skills necessary to fight guerilla and anti-guerilla warfare, and increased our special forces trained to deal with counter-insurgency by 800%.

Acquired balanced stocks of combat consumables for all our forces so that they can engage in combat for sustained periods of time.

In reconstructing the nation's defense establishment, the Administration has insisted that the services be guided by these three precepts:

Buy only what we need.

Buy only at the lowest sound price.

Reduce operating costs through standardization, consolidation, and termination of unnecessary operations.

As a result, our expanded and reconstituted defense force has cost billions of dollars less than it would have cost under previous inefficient and unbusinesslike methods of procurement and operation. These savings amounted to more than $1 billion in the fiscal year 1963, and to $2.5 billion in the fiscal year just completed. Furthermore, under the cost reduction program we have established, we will be saving $4.6 billion each year, every year, by Fiscal Year 1968.

We have successfully met the challenges of Berlin and Cuba, and attacks upon our Naval forces on the high seas, thus decreasing the prospect of further such challenges and brightening the outlook for peace.

Arms Control

In 1960, we proposed—

"A national peace agency for disarmament planning and research to muster the scientific ingenuity, coordination, continuity, and seriousness of purpose which are now lacking in our arms control efforts."

In 1961, the United States became the first nation in the world to establish an "agency for peace"—the Arms Control and Disarmament Agency.

This agency is charged by law with the development of a realistic arms control and disarmament policy to promote national security and provide an impetus towards a world free from the threat of war. Working closely with the senior military leaders of the Department of Defense, the Arms Control and Disarmament Agency has enabled the United States to lead the world in a new, continuous, hard-headed and purposeful discussion, negotiation and planning of disarmament.

In 1960, we proposed—

"To develop responsible proposals that will help break the deadlock on arms control."

In the aftermath of the Cuban crisis the United States pressed its advantage to seek a new breakthrough for peace. On June 10, 1963, at American University, President Kennedy called on the Soviet leadership to join in concrete steps to abate the nuclear arms race. After careful negotiations experienced American negotiators reached agreement with the Russians on a Nuclear Test Ban Treaty—an event that will be marked forever in the history of mankind as a first step on the difficult road of arms control.

One hundred and six nations signed or acceded to the treaty.

In the United States it was supported by the Joint Chiefs of Staff, and ratified in the Senate by an 80-20 vote.

To insure the effectiveness of our nuclear development program in accord with the momentous Test Ban Treaty, the Joint Chiefs of Staff recommended, and the Administration has undertaken:

A comprehensive program of underground testing of nuclear explosives.

Maintenance of modern nuclear laboratory facilities.

Preparations to test in the atmosphere if essential to national security, or if the treaty is violated by the Soviet Union.

Continuous improvement of our means for detecting violations and other nuclear activities elsewhere in the world.

In 1960, we proposed—

"To the extent we can secure the adoption of effective arms control agreeemnts, vast resources will be freed for peaceful use."

In January and April 1964, President Johnson announced cutbacks in the production of nuclear materials: twenty percent in plutonium production and forty percent in enriched uranium. When the USSR followed this United States initiative with a similar announcement, the President welcomed the response as giving hope "that the world may yet, one day, live without the fear of war."

INSTRUMENTS OF FOREIGN POLICY

In 1960, we proposed that—

"American foreign policy in all its aspects must be attuned to our world of change.

"We will recruit officials whose experience, humanity and dedication fit them for the task of effectively representing America abroad.

"We will provide a more sensitive and creative direction to our overseas information program."

Since 1961, the Department of State has had its self-respect restored, and has been vitalized by more vigorous recruitment and more intensive training of foreign service officers representing all elements of the American people.

Forty days after taking office President Kennedy established the Peace Corps. The world did not change overnight. Neither will it ever be quite the same again. The foreign minister of one large Asian nation has called the Peace Corps "the most powerful idea in recent times."

One hundred thousand Americans have volunteered for the Peace Corps. Nine thousand have served in a total of 45 countries.

Nearly every country to which volunteers have been sent has asked for more. Two dozen new countries are on the waiting list.

Volunteer organizations on the Peace Corps model are already operating in 12 countries and there has been a great expansion of volunteer service in many others.

An International Secretariat for Volunteer Service is working in 32 economically advanced and developing nations.

The United States Information Agency has been transformed into a powerful, effective and respected weapon of the free world. The new nations of the world have come to know an America that is not afraid to tell the truth about itself—and so can be believed when it tells the truth about Communist imperialism.

WORLD TRADE

In 1960, we said—

". . . We shall expand world trade in every responsible way.

"Since all Americans share the benefits of this policy, its costs should not be the burden of a few. We shall support practical measures to ease the necessary adjustments of industries and communities which may be unavoidably hurt by increases in imports.

"Our government should press for reduction of foreign barriers on the sale of the products of American industry and agriculture."

This pledge was fulfilled in the Trade Expansion Act of 1962.

The Trade Expansion Act of 1962, gives the President power to negotiate a 50 percent across-the-board cut in tariff barriers to take place over a five-year period.

Exports have expanded over 10 percent—by over $2 billion—since 1961.

Foreign trade now provides jobs for more than 4 million workers.

Negotiations now underway will permit American businessmen and farmers to take advantage of the greatest trading opportunity in history—the rapidly expanding European market.

The Trade Expansion Act provides for worker training and moving allowances, and for loans, tax rebates and technical assistance for businesses if increased imports resulting from concessions granted in trade agreements result in unemployment or loss of business.

Where American agriculture or industrial products have been unfairly treated in order to favor domestic products, prompt and forceful action has been taken to break down such barriers. These efforts have opened new United States export opportunities for fruits and vegetables, and numerous other agricultural and manufactured products to Europe and Japan.

The Long Term Cotton Textile Agreement of 1962 protects the textile and garment industry against disruptive competition from imports of cotton textiles. The Cotton Act of 1964 enables American manufacturers to buy cotton at the world market price, so they can compete in selling their products at home and abroad.

IMMIGRATION

In 1960, we proposed to—

"Adjust our immigration, nationality and refugee policies to eliminate discrimination and to enable members of scattered families abroad to be united with relatives already in our midst.

"The national-origins quota system of limiting immigration contradicts the founding principles of this nation. It is inconsistent with our belief in the rights of men."

The immigration law amendments proposed by the Administration, and now before Congress, by abolishing the national-origin quota system, will eliminate discrimination based upon race and place of birth and will facilitate the reunion of families.

The Cuban Refugee Program begun in 1961 has resettled over 81,000 refugees, who are now self-supporting members of 1,800 American communities. The Chinese Refugee Program, begun in 1962, provides for the admission to the United States of 12,000 Hong Kong refugees from Red China.

THE UNDERDEVELOPED WORLD

In 1960, we pledged—

"To the non-Communist nations of Asia, Africa, and Latin America: We shall create with you working partnerships based on mutual respect and understanding" and "will revamp and refocus the objectives, emphasis and allocation of our foreign assistance programs."

In 1961, the administration created the Agency for International Development, combining the three separate agencies that had handled foreign assistance activities into an orderly and efficient instrument of national policy.

Since 1961, foreign aid has been conducted on a spartan, cost conscious basis, with emphasis on self-help, reform and performance as conditions of American help.

These new policies are showing significant returns.

Since the beginning of the Marshall Plan in 1948, U. S. economic assistance has been begun and ended in 17 countries. In 14 other countries in Asia, Africa and Latin America, the transition to economic self-support is well under way, and U. S. assistance is now phasing out. In the 1965 AID program, 90 percent of economic assistance will go to just 25 countries.

In 1960, only 41 percent of aid-financed commodities were purchased in America. In 1964, under AID, 85 percent of all aid-financed commodities were U. S. supplied.

The foreign aid appropriation of $3.5 billion for fiscal year 1965 represents the smallest burden on U. S. resources that has been proposed since foreign aid began after World War II.

Since 1961, the United States has insisted that our allies in Europe and Japan must share responsibility in the field of foreign assistance, particularly to their former colonies. They have responded with major programs. Several nations now contribute a larger share of their gross national production to foreign assistance than does the United States.

The Alliance for Progress, launched at the Conference of Punta del Este in Uraguay in 1961, has emerged as the greatest undertaking of social reform and international cooperation in the history of the Western Hemisphere.

The American republics agreed to work together "To make the benefits of economic progress available to all citizens of all economic and social groups through a more equitable distribution of national income, raising more rapidly the income and standard of living of the needier sectors of the population, at the same time that a higher proportion of the national product is devoted to investment."

The results so far:

Major tax reform legislation has been adopted in eight countries.

Agrarian reform legislation has been introduced in twelve countries, and agricultural credit, technical assistance and resettlement projects are going forward in sixteen countries.

Fifteen countries have self-help housing programs, and savings and loan legislation has been adopted by nine countries.

Private or public development banks have been established or are being established in eight countries, providing new sources of capital for the small businessman.

Education budgets have risen by almost 13 percent a year, and five million more children are going to school. U. S. aid has helped build 23,000 schoolrooms.

A Latin American school lunch program is feeding 10 million children at least one good meal every day, and the program will reach 12 million by the end of the year.

The Alliance for Progress has immeasurably strengthened the collective will of the nations of the Western Hemisphere to resist the massive efforts of Communist subversion that conquered Cuba in 1959 and then headed for the mainland.

In 1960, we urged—

". . . Continued economic assistance to Israel and the Arab peoples to help them raise their living standards.

"We pledge our best efforts for peace in the Middle East by seeking to prevent an arms race while guarding against the dangers of a military imbalance resulting from Soviet arms shipments."

In the period since that pledge was made the New East has come closer to peace and stability than at any time since World War II.

Economic and technical assistance to Israel and Arab nations continues at a high level, although with more and more emphasis on loans as against grants. The United States 's determined to help bring the revolution in the technology of desalinization to the aid of the desert regions of this area.

The Atlantic Community

In 1960, we said—

"To our friends and associates in the Atlantic Community: We propose a broader partnership that goes beyond our common fears to recognize the depth and sweep of our common political, economic, and cultural interests."

In 1961, the United States ratified the conventions creating the Organization for Economic Cooperation and Development, a body made up of ourselves, Canada and 18 European States which carries forward on a permanent basis the detailed cooperation and mutual assistance that began with the Marshall Plan.

Since 1961, we have progressed in the building of mutual confidence, unity, and strength. NATO has frequently been used for consultation on foreign policy issues. Strong Atlantic unity emerged in response to Soviet threats in Berlin and in Cuba. Current trade negotiations reflect the value of the Trade Expansion Act and the utility of arrangements for economic cooperation. NATO military forces are stronger in both nuclear and conventional weapons.

The United States has actively supported the proposal to create a multilateral, mix-manned, seaborne nuclear missile force which could give all NATO countries a direct share in NATO's nuclear deterrent without proliferating the number of independent, national nuclear forces.

The Communist World

In 1960, we said—

"To the rulers of the Communist World: We confidently accept your challenge to competition in every field of human effort.

"We believe your Communist ideology to be sterile, unsound, and doomed to failure . . .

". . . We are prepared to negotiate with you whenever and wherever there is a realistic possibility of progress without sacrifice of principle.

"But we will use all the will, power, resources, and energy at our command to resist the further encroachment of Communism on freedom—whether at Berlin, Formosa or new points of pressure as yet undisclosed."

Following the launching of Sputnik in 1957, the Soviet Union began a world-wide offensive. Russian achievements in space were hailed as the forerunners of triumph on earth.

Now, seven years later, the Communist influence has failed in its efforts to win Africa. Of the 31 African nations formed since World War II, not one has chosen Communism.

Khrushchev had to back down on his threat to sign a peace treaty with East Germany. Access to West Berlin remains free.

In Latin America, the Alliance for Progress has begun to reduce the poverty and distress on which Communism breeds.

In Japan, where anti-American riots in 1960 prevented a visit from the President, relations with the United States have been markedly improved.

In the United Nations the integrity of the office of Secretary General was preserved despite the Soviet attack on it through the Troika proposal.

When Red China attacked India, the U. S. promptly came to India's aid with modern infantry supplies and equipment.

On the battlefield of the Cold War one engagement after another has been fought and won.

Frustrated in its plans to nibble away at country after country, the Soviet Union conceived a bold stroke designed to reverse the trend against it. With extreme stealth Soviet intermediate range and medium range offensive missiles were brought into Cuba in 1962.

Shortly after the missiles arrived in Cuba, and before any of them became operational, they were discovered and photographed by U. S. reconnaissance flights.

The U. S. response was carefully planned and prepared, and calmly, deliberately, but effectively executed. On October 22, President Kennedy called on the Soviet Union to dismantle and remove the weapons from Cuba. He ordered a strict quarantine on Cuba enforced by the U. S. Navy.

The Organization of American States acted swiftly and decisively by a unanimous vote of 20 to 0 to authorize strong measures, including the use of force, to ensure that the missiles were withdrawn from Cuba and not re-introduced.

At the end of a tense week Khrushchev caved in before this demonstration of Western power and determination. Soviet ships, closely observed by U. S. pilots, loaded all the missiles and headed back to Russia. U. S. firmness also compelled withdrawal of the IL-28 bombers.

A turning point of the Cold War had been reached.

The record of world events in the past year reflects the vigor and successes of U. S. policy:

Berlin, October-November 1963. Communist efforts to interfere with free Western access to Berlin were successfully rebuffed.

Venezuela, March 1964. Despite the threats and terror tactics of Castro-inspired agitators, over 90 percent of the people voted in the election that chose President Leoni to succeed Romulo Betancourt—the first democratic succession in that office in Venezuela's history.

Panama, 1964. Patient negotiation achieved a resumption of diplomatic relations, which had been severed after the riots in January; President Johnson achieved a dignified and an honorable solution of the crisis.

Vietnam, August 1964. Faced with sudden unprovoked attacks by Communist PT boats on American destroyers on the high sea, President Johnson ordered a sharp immediate retaliation on the hostile vessels and their supporting facilities.

Speaking on that occasion, the President said:

"Aggression—deliberate, willful and systematic aggression has unmasked its face to the world. The world remembers—the world must never forget—that aggression unchallenged is aggression unleashed.

"We of the United States have not forgotten.

"That is why we have answered this aggression with action."

Cuba, 1961-1964. Cuba and Castro have been virtually isolated in the Hemisphere.

Only 2 out of 20 OAS countries maintain diplomatic relations with Cuba.

Cuban trade with the Free World has dropped sharply from the 1958 level.

Free world shipping to Cuba has fallen sharply. Isolation of Cuba by air has tightened greatly.

Hundreds of thousands of Cubans have left the island or have indicated their desire to come to the United States.

The Castro regime has been suspended from participation in the OAS.

The Cuban economy is deteriorating: the standard of living is 20 percent below pre-Castro levels, with many items rationed; industrial output is stagnant; sugar production is at the lowest level since the 1940's.

The United Nations

In 1960, we pledged—

"To our fellow members of the United Nations: we shall strengthen our commitments in this, our great continuing institution for conciliation and the growth of a world community."

Over the past four years the Administration has fulfilled this pledge as one of the central purposes of foreign policy.

During that time the United States has supported—and frequently led—efforts within the United Nations.

—to strengthen its capacity as peacekeeper and peacemaker—with the result that the UN remained on guard on armistice lines in Korea, Kashmir and the Middle East; preserved peace in the Congo, West New Guinea and Cyprus; provided a forum for the U. S. during crises in the Caribbean and the Gulf of Tonkin; began to develop a flexible call-up system for emergency peace-keeping forces; and moved toward a revival of the Security Council as the primary organ for peace and security without loss of the residual powers of the General Assembly.

—to discover and exploit areas of common interest for the reduction of world dangers and world tensions—with the result that the orbiting of weapons of mass destruction has been banned and legal principles adopted for the use of outer space; projects of scientific cooperation in meteorology, oceanography, Antarctic exploration and peaceful uses of atomic energy, have been promoted; and the search for further moves toward arms control have been pursued to supplement the limited test ban treaty.

—to further the work of the United Nations in improving the lot of mankind—with the result that the Decade of Development has been launched; the World Food Program undertaken; aid to children extended; projects to promote economic and social progress in the developing world have been expanded; and the impact of technology and world trade upon development has been explored.

—to maintain the integrity of the organization —its Charter and its Secretariat—with the result that the Troika proposal was defeated; the functions of the Secretary-General have been kept intact; the authority of the General Assembly to levy assessments for peacekeeping has been sustained despite attempted financial vetoes by Communist and other members.

In fulfilling its pledge to the United Nations, the Administration has helped to strengthen peace, to promote progress, and to find areas of international agreement and cooperation.

Economic Growth

In 1960, we said—

"The new Democratic Administration will confidently proceed to unshackle American enterprise and to free American labor, industrial leadership, and capital, to create an abundance that will outstrip any other system.

"We Democrats believe that our economy can and must grow at an average rate of 5 percent annually, almost twice as fast as our average annual rate since 1953. We pledge ourselves to policies that will achieve this goal without inflation."

In January 1961, the nation was at the bottom of the fourth recession of the postwar period—the third in the eight-year period, 1953-60. More men and women were out of work than at any time since the Great Depression of the 1930's. In February 1961, the unemployment rate was 6.8 percent, with a total of 5,705,000 unemployed.

Today we are in the midst of the longest peacetime expansion in our history, during the past 42 months of unbroken economic expansion:

Our economic growth rate has risen now to over 5 percent—twice the average rate for the 1953-60 period.

3,900,000 jobs have been added to the economy, and the unemployment rate was down in July 1964 to 4.9 percent.

The Gross National Product has risen by $120 billion in less than four years! No nation in peacetime history has ever added so much to its wealth in so short a time.

The average manufacturing worker's weekly earnings rose from $89 in January 1961, to $103 in July 1964—an increase of over 15 percent.

Industrial production has increased 28 percent; average operating rates in manufacturing have risen from 78 percent of capacity to 87 percent.

Profits after taxes have increased 62 percent—from an annual rate of $19.2 billion in early 1961 to an estimated $31.2 billion in early 1964.

Total private investment has increased by 43 percent—from an annual rate of $61 billion in early 1961 to $87 billion in the spring of 1964.

There are a million and a half more Americans at work today than there were a year ago.

Our present prosperity was brought about by the enterprise of American business, the skills of the American work force, and by wise public policies.

The provision in the Revenue Act of 1962 for a credit for new investment in machinery and equipment, and the liberalization of depreciation allowance by administrative ruling, resulted in a reduction of $2.5 billion in business taxes.

The Revenue Act of 1964 cut individual income taxes by more than $9 billion, increasing consumer purchasing power by that amount; and corporate taxes were cut another $2.5 billion, with the effect of increasing investment incentives. Overall individual Federal income taxes were cut an average of 19 percent; taxpayers earning $3,000 or less received an average 40 percent cut.

The Temporary Extended Unemployment Compensation Act of 1961 provided $800 million to 2.8 million jobless workers who had exhausted their benefits.

The Area Redevelopment Act of 1961 has meant a $227 million Federal investment in economically hard-hit areas, creating 110,000 new jobs in private enterprise.

The Accelerated Public Works Act of 1962 added $900 million for urgently needed State and local government construction projects.

An End to Tight Money

In 1960, we proposed—

"As the first step in speeding economic growth, a Democratic president will put an end to the present high interest, tight money policy.

"This policy has failed in its stated purpose—to keep prices down. It has given us two recessions within five years, bankrupted many of our farmers, produced a record number of business failures, and added billions of dollars in unnecessary higher interest charges to government budgets and the cost of living."

Since 1961, we have maintained the free flow of credit so vital to industry, home buyers, and State and local governments.

Immediately, in February 1961, the Federal Housing Agency interest rate was cut from 5¾ percent to 5½ percent. It is now down to 5¼ percent.

Today's home buyer will pay about $1,700 less for FHA-insured financing of a 30-year $15,000 home mortgage than he would have had he taken the mortgage in 1960.

Today after 42 months of expansion, conventional home mortgage rates are lower than they were in January 1961, in the midst of a recession. So are borrowing costs for our States and municipalities, and for long-term corporate issues.

Short-term interest rates have been brought into reasonable balance with interest rates abroad, reducing or eliminating incentives to place short-term funds abroad and thus reducing gold outflow.

We have prudently lengthened the average maturity of the Federal debt, in contrast to the steady shortening that characterized the 1950's.

Control of Inflation

In 1960, we asserted—

"The American consumer has a right to fair prices. We are determined to secure that right.

"A fair share of the gains from increasing productivity in many industries should be passed on to the consumer through price reductions."

Today, after 42 months of economic expansion, wholesale prices are lower than they were in January 1961, in the midst of a recession! The Wholesale Price Index was 101.0 in January 1961; in July 1964, it is 100.4.

The Consumer Price Index, which measures the price of goods and services families purchase, has been brought back to stability, averaging now less than 1.3% increase per year—as compared, for example, with an increase rate about three times this large in the European common market countries.

Since January 1961, the increase in average after-tax family income has been twice the increase in prices.

The Administration has established guideposts

for price and wage movements alike, based primarily on productivity developments, and designed to protect the economy against inflation.

In the single year, 1960, the overall balance of payments deficit reached $3.9 billion, and we lost $1.7 billion in gold. Now for 1964, the prospective balance of payments deficit has been cut to $2 billion, and the gold outflow has ceased.

FULL EMPLOYMENT

In 1960, we reaffirmed our—

"support of full employment as a paramount objective of national policy."

In July 1964, total employment in the United States rose to the historic peak of 72,400,000 jobs. This represents an increase of 3,900,000 jobs in 42 months.

In the past twelve months, total civilian employment has increased by 1,600,000 jobs, and nonfarm employment by 1,700,000. Most of this job expansion has occurred in the past eight months.

In July 1964, the jobless total was one-half million below a year ago, and was at its lowest July level since 1959.

In July, 1964, the overall unemployment rate was 4.9%—compared with 6.5% in January 1961; and the jobless rate for men who are heads of families was down to 2.7%.

There have been more than a million full-time jobs added to the private profit sector of the economy in the past 12 months. This is the largest increase in any one-year period in the past decade.

We have brought ourselves now within reach of the full employment objective.

AID TO DEPRESSED AREAS

In 1960, we recognized that—

"General economic measures will not alone solve the problems of localities which suffer some special disadvantage. To bring prosperity to these depressed areas and to enable them to make their full contribution to the national welfare, specially directed action is needed."

The Area Redevelopment Administration was created in 1961 to help depressed areas organize their human and material resources for economic growth. Since its establishment, the ARA has:

Approved 512 financial assistance projects involving a Federal investment of $243.5 million.

Created, in partnership with local government, private workers and other investors, 118,-000 new jobs in private enterprise.

Provided retraining programs, with tuition and subsistence, for 37,327 jobless workers, equipping them with new skills to fill available jobs in their areas.

In 1961, Congress authorized $900 million for the Accelerated Public Works Program to speed construction of urgently needed public facilities and increase employment in areas which had failed to recover from previous recessions.

Between October 1962, when the first appropriations were made available, and April 1, 1964, 7,762 projects, involving an estimated 2,500,000 man-months of employment, were approved.

In early 1961, there were 101 major areas in the United States in which unemployment was 6 percent or more, discounting seasonal or temporary factors. By July 1964, this number had been cut two-thirds, to a total of 35.

The concept of "depressed areas" has been broadened in these 3½ years to include clear recognition of the inequity and waste of poverty wherever it exists, and in the Economic Opportunity Act of 1964 the nation has declared, in historic terms, a War on Poverty.

Title I of the Economic Opportunity Act creates the Job Corps, Work-Training programs, and Work-Study programs to provide useful work for about 400,000 young men and women. Job Corps volunteers will receive work and vocational training, part of which will involve conservation work in rural areas. The Work-Training, or Neighborhood Youth Corps program, is open to young persons living at home, including those who need jobs in order to remain in school. The Work-Study programs will enable youth from poor families to earn enough income to enable them to attend college.

Title II of the Act authorized $340 million for the Community Action programs to stimulate urban and rural communities to mobilize their resources to combat poverty through programs designed especially to meet local needs.

Title III provides for special programs to combat poverty in rural areas, including loans up to $1,500 for low income farmers, and loans up to $2,500 for families, to finance non-agricultural enterprises which will enable such families to supplement their incomes. This section of the law provides funds for housing, sanitation education, and day care of children of migrant farm workers.

Title IV of the Act provides for loans up to $25,000 for small businesses to create jobs for the long-term unemployed.

Title V of the Act provides constructive work experience and other needed training to persons who are unable to support or care for themselves or their families.

The Report of the President's Appalachian Regional Commission, submitted to President Johnson in April 1964, proposed a wide-ranging development program. The Appalachian Redevelopment Act, now before Congress, provides for more than $1.1 billion investment in needed basic facilities in the area, together with a regional organization to help generate the full development potential of the human and material resources of this mountain area.

Registration and regulation of migrant labor crew chiefs has been provided to require that crew chiefs or labor brokers, who act on behalf of domestic migrant labor and operate across state lines, shall be registered, show financial responsibility, and meet certain requirements as to moral character and honest dealing with their clients.

DISCRIMINATION IN EMPLOYMENT

In 1960, we insisted that—

"The right to a job requires action to break down artificial and arbitrary barriers to employment based on age, race, sex, religion, or national origin."

The great Civil Rights Act of 1964 is the strongest and most important law against discrimination in employment in the history of the United States.

It states unequivocally that "It shall be an unlawful employment practice for an employer . . . an employment agency . . . or a labor organization" to discriminate against any person because of his or her "race, color, religion, sex, or national origin."

On March 6, 1961, President Kennedy issued an Executive Order establishing the President's Committee on Equal Employment Opportunity to combat racial discrimination in the employment policies of Government agencies and private firms holding Government contracts. Then–Vice President Johnson, in his capacity as Chairman of the new Committee, assumed personal direction of this program.

As a consequence of the enforcement of the Executive Order, not only has discrimination been eliminated in the Federal Government, but strong affirmative measures have been taken to extend meaningful equality of opportunity to compete for Federal employment to all citizens.

The private employers of 8,076,422 men and women, and trade unions with 12,500,000 members, have signed public agreements establishing non-discriminatory practices.

The Equal Pay Act of 1963 guarantees equal pay to women doing the same work as men, by requiring employers who are covered by the Fair Labor Standards Act to pay equal wages for equal work, regardless of the sex of their workers.

Executive Order 11141, issued by President Johnson on February 12, 1964, establishes for the first time in history a public policy that "contractors and subcontractors engaged in the performance of Federal contracts shall not, in connection with the employment, advancement, or discharge of their employees, or in connection with the terms, conditions, or privileges of their employment, discriminate against persons because of their age . . ."

COLLECTIVE BARGAINING

In 1960, we pledged—

"an affirmative labor policy which will encourage free collective bargaining through the growth and development of free and responsible unions."

These have been good years for labor-management relations. Time lost from strikes is at the lowest point in history.

The President's Advisory Committee on Labor-Management Policy, made up of distinguished leaders of business and trade unions, has spoken out consistently in favor of creative and constructive solutions to common problems.

Executive Order 10988, issued by President Kennedy on January 17, 1962, extended the rights of union recognition to Federal employees—a goal which some employee organizations had been trying to reach for three quarters of a century.

In the spring of 1964, under President Johnson's personal leadership, the five-year-old railroad dispute that would have resulted in a critical nationwide strike, was at last ended—by free collective bargaining. A cause many thought lost was won; industrial self-government was saved from a disastrous setback.

Planning for Automation

In 1960, we proposed to—

"provide the government leadership necessary to insure that the blessings of automation do not become burdens of widespread unemployment. For the young and the technologically displaced workers, we will provide the opportunity for training and retraining that equips them for jobs to be filled."

The Manpower Development and Training Act of 1962 provides for the training or retraining of unemployed or underemployed people, particularly those threatened or displaced by technological advances. The 1963 amendments to the Act emphasize the problem of youth employment.

In the two years of the administration of this program, training projects for 240,471 persons have been approved, and more than 54,000 persons have completed their training.

Under the Manpower Development and Training Act an active manpower policy is being developed to keep the nation ahead of the problems of automation.

Congress has now enacted, in August 1964, legislation creating a National Commission on Technology, Automation and Economic Progress to undertake a searching inquiry into the problems created by automation, and means by which they can be prevented or solved.

In its own activities, the Federal Government has taken full account of human considerations in instituting technological developments.

Minimum Wages

In 1960, we pledged—

"To raise the minimum wage to $1.25 an hour and to extend coverage to several million workers not now covered."

The Fair Labor Standards Act Amendments of 1961 raised the minimum wage to $1.25 over a three-year period, and extended the coverage of the Act to 3.6 million additional workers.

The Administration has proposed further amendments to the Fair Labor Standards Act, which are now before the Congress, and which would extend minimum wage coverage to near three quarters of a million workers in laundry, and dry cleaning establishments. Overtime coverage would be extended to an additional 2.6 million workers.

It has proposed a Fringe Benefit amendment to the Bacon-Davis law to provide that the cost of fringe benefits should be included in the definition of "prevailing wage" under the Bacon-Davis law, so that wage rates required in government construction contracts will be in accord with prevailing practice.

Agriculture

In 1960, we said—

"In every way we will seek to help the men, women, and children whose livelihood comes from the soil to achieve better housing, education, and decent earnings and working conditions."

This is the record:

Total net farm income in 1961-63 averaged nearly a billion dollars a year higher than in 1960.

Total net income per farm was 18 percent higher in 1963 than in 1960.

Farm purchasing power, or gross farm income, rose from $37.9 billion in 1960 to nearly $42 billion in 1963.

Percent of family income spent for food today has declined. In 1960, 20 percent of disposable family income was spent for food. This has now been reduced to less than 19 percent.

Grain surpluses have been brought down to manageable levels; wheat surpluses this year will be the lowest since 1958, and feed grains have been reduced from 80 to 70 million tons.

Reduction of wheat and feed grain surpluses from their 1960 levels to present levels has resulted in an accumulated savings of about a quarter of a billion dollars in storage, transportation, interest and other costs.

Total farm exports have increased 35 percent in 4 years, and have reached a record high in fiscal 1964 of $6.1 billion.

Credit resources administered by the Farmers Home Administration are up 141 percent over 1960, and are averaging now $687 million a year.

Commodity programs to strengthen the farm income structure and reach the goal of parity of income in every aspect of American agriculture. We also cite the parity program providing American cotton to American factories and processes at the same price at which they are exported.

The Rural Areas Development program has

helped create an estimated 125,000 new jobs, and more than 12,000 projects in the process of approval will provide new employment for as many as 200,000 persons.

Participation in the Agricultural Conservation Program has increased 20 percent since 1960.

More than 20,000 farmers have received technical help to develop recreation as an income-making "crop" on land which had been producing surpluses.

Over 600 rural Communities have been aided in providing modern water services.

During the winter of 1964, a special lunch program was instituted for 315 schools and 12,000 children in rural areas where families have extremely low incomes.

Since January 1, 1961, $1.1 billion in electric loans has been made by the Rural Electrification Administration, to rural electric cooperatives, or some $350 million more than in the previous 3½ years. Improved service, as a result, has meant customer savings of $7.5 million a year.

American farmers, in 1964, have protected crop investments totaling $500.5 million with Federal All-Risk Crop Insurance—more than double the amount of insurance in force three years ago, and an all-time record.

Soil and water conservation activities in the past 3½ years have shown a constant upward trend in their contributions to the physical, social and economic welfare of rural areas.

289 new small upstream watershed projects were authorized.

3,000 local soil and water conservation districts have updated their long-range programs to reflect the broadened concepts of economic development.

The Great Plains Conservation Program has been extended for 10 years and 36 counties have been added to the program.

In June 1964, Congress authorized the creation of a National Commission on Food Marketing to investigate the operation of the food industry from producer to consumer.

On January 24, 1961, President Kennedy established by executive order, the Food for Peace program to utilize America's agricultural abundance "to promote the interests of peace . . . and to play an important role in helping to provide a more adequate diet for peoples all around the world."

In the last 3½ years, over $5 billion worth of surplus farm commodities went overseas under Public Law 480 programs. This is one and one-half billion dollars more than during the previous 3½ years.

SMALL BUSINESS

In 1960, we pledged—

"Action to aid small business in obtaining credit and equity capital at reasonable rates.

"Protection of the public against the growth of monopoly.

"A more equitable share of government contracts to small and independent business."

Through liberalizing amendments to the Small Business Investment Act in 1961 and 1964, and special tax considerations, the investment of equity capital and long term loan funds in small businesses has been greatly accelerated by privately owned and operated small business investment companies licensed under that Act. Moreover, since January 1961, over 21,000 small businesses have obtained SBA business loans, totalling over $1.14 billion, as a result of liberalized and simplified procedures.

The Federal Trade Commission has stepped up its activities to promote free and fair competition in business, and to safeguard the consuming public against both monopolistic and deceptive practices.

The reorganized Antitrust Division of the Department of Justice has directed special emphasis to price fixing, particularly on consumer products, by large companies who distribute through small companies. These include eye glasses, salad oil, flour, cosmetics, swimsuits, bread, milk, and even sneakers.

Since January 1961, some 166,000 government contracts, worth $6.2 billion have been set aside for small business. In the preceding 3½ years there were 77,838 contracts set aside, with a worth of $2.9 billion.

HOUSING

In 1960 we proposed—

"To make possible the building of 2,000,000 homes a year in wholesome neighborhoods, the home building industry should be aided by special mortgage assistance, with low interest rates, long-term mortgage periods and reduced down payments.

"There will still be need for a substantial low-rent public housing program authorizing as many units as local communities require and are prepared to build."

The Housing Act of 1961 provides many of the necessary new and improved tools for providing housing for low and moderate income families, and for housing for the elderly.

For the 3½ year period ending June 30, 1964, some 5.3 million new units of public and private housing have been built at a cost of approximately $65 billion. The construction rate has risen above 1.5 million units a year, with an annual output of over $20 billion, and we are moving close now to the goal of 2 million a year.

Since January 1961, nearly 400 local housing authorities have been formed to provide housing for low income families. More than 100,000 new units have been approved for construction, at an annual rate about three times that of 1960.

The annual rate of grant assistance for Urban Renewal has risen from $262 million per year (1956 through 1961) to a rate of better than $630 million during the past 12 months.

In the past 3½ years, more than 750 new urban renewal transactions have been approved, equal to nearly 90 percent of the number approved for the entire period from 1949 to 1960.

Cities with community urban renewal programs jumped from a cumulative total of seven in December 1960 to 118 by mid-1964.

To house families whose income is not quite low enough to qualify for public housing, a new rental housing program providing a "below market" interest rate (currently 3⅞%) insured by FHA, has been made available. Mortgage purchase funds have been allocated for about 78,000 such rental units.

Reflecting the fuller recognition of the special equities and needs of older people:

FHA mortgage insurance written on housing projects for the elderly since 1961 has provided more than 3 times as many units as were being provided prior to that time.

Low rent public housing under Federal assistance is being provided senior citizens at an annual rate more than twice that for 1960.

Direct loan authorizations for housing for the elderly increased from $50 million in 1961 to $275 million in 1963.

Maximum loan amounts have been increased to 100% of development cost.

The Housing Act of 1961 expanded and strengthened the Federal program in this area.

The Senior Citizens Housing Act of 1962 moved us another long step forward.

Applications for the provision of nursing homes increased from 30 in January 1961 to more than 580 by the middle of 1964, involving more than 50,000 beds for community nursing homes.

Assistance has been given for more than 1,000 college housing projects including housing for more than 290,000 students and faculty, plus dining halls and other school facilities.

The 1963 Executive Order on Equal Opportunity in Housing assures that the benefits of Federal housing programs and assistance are available without discrimination as to race, color, creed or national origin.

HEALTH

In 1960, we proposed to—

"Provide medical care benefits for the aged as part of the time-tested social security system.

"Step up medical research on the major killers and crippling diseases.

"Expand and improve the Hill-Burton hospital construction program.

"Federal aid for construction, expanding and modernizing schools of medicine, dentistry, nursing and public health.

"Greatly increased federal support for psychiatric research and training and community mental health programs."

More health legislation has been enacted during the past 3½ years than during any other period in American history.

The Community Health Services and Facilities Act of 1961 has made possible 149 projects for testing and demonstrating new or improved services in nursing homes, home care services, central information and referral centers; and providing additional personnel to serve the chronically ill and aged. It has also provided additional federal funds for the construction of nursing homes.

The Hill-Burton Amendments of 1964, extend the program of Federal grants for construction of hospitals, public health centers, long-term facilities, rehabilitation facilities and diagnostic or treatment centers for five additional years. For the first time provision is made for the modernization and renovation of hospitals and health facilities. Funds for the construction of nursing homes and other long-term care facilities are substantially increased.

The Mental Retardation Facilities and Community Mental Health Construction Act of 1963, authorized grants of $150,000,000 to States for constructing community Mental Health Centers, which emphasize the new approach to the care of the mentally ill, centered on care and treatment in the patients' home communities. Thirty-six States have already budgeted more than 75% of their share of Federal funds for planning these new systems.

The Maternal and Child Health and Mental Retardation Planning Amendments of 1963, along with the Mental Retardation Facilities and Community Mental Health Construction Act of 1963, authorized a broad program to prevent, treat, and ameliorate mental retardation. The program provides States and communities needed research, manpower developments, and facilities for health, education rehabilitation, and vocational services to the retarded.

As part of the Federal Government's program to employ the mentally retarded in suitable Federal jobs, the State rehabilitation agencies are certifying persons as qualified for specific suitable Federal jobs. A rising number of placements already made in Federal installations over the country constitutes an encouraging start.

The current need for another 200,000 qualified teachers for the estimated 6 million handicapped children of school age, has been recognized in legislation authorizing grants in aid for the training of professional personnel.

Other legislation provides funds for training teachers of the deaf.

A 1962 amendment to the Public Health Act authorizes a new program of project grants to help meet critical health needs of domestic migratory workers and their families through establishment of family health service clinics.

Forty-nine projects in 24 States have received grants to assist an estimated 300,000 migrant workers.

One out of every ten migrant laborers is estimated to have received some health services through these projects.

The National Institute of Child Health and Human Development, authorized in 1962, is now supporting research and training in eight major areas.

The National Institute of General Medical Sciences, also authorized in 1962, gives recognition to the significance of research training in the sciences basic to medicine. Two thousand research projects are currently being supported.

A $2 million Radiological Health Grant Program was established in 1962 to provide matching grants to assist States in assuming responsibility for adequate radiation control and protection. During Fiscal Year 1964, forty-nine States and Puerto Rico and the Virgin Islands participated.

After two years of scientific evaluation of research and findings, the Report of the Surgeon General's Advisory Committee on Smoking and Health was released in January 1964, calling attention to the health hazards of smoking. An information clearinghouse and a public education program directed toward preventing young people from acquiring the smoking habit are being developed.

A PROGRAM FOR THE AGING

In 1960, we proposed to—

"End the neglect of our older citizens. They deserve lives of usefulness, dignity, independence, and participation. We shall assure them not only health care, but employment for those who want to work, decent housing, and recreation."

The Social Security Act Amendments of 1961 broadened benefits to 5.3 million persons, increased minimum benefits for retired workers from $33 to $40 per month, permitted men as well as women to begin collecting reduced benefits at age 62.

The Social Security program now provides $1.3 billion in benefits each month to 19.5 million persons. One out of every ten Americans receives a Social Security check every month.

The Welfare and Pension Plans Disclosure Act Amendments of 1962 put "enforcement teeth" into this measure, protecting workers' assets in pension programs.

The Housing Act of 1961 increased the scope of Federal housing aids for the elderly by raising from $50 million to $125 million the authorization for low-interest-rate direct loans. In 1962, this was raised further to $225 million and in 1963 to $275 million.

Insurance written by the Federal Housing Administration for mortgage insurance for the elderly since 1961 provides three times as many units as during the preceding Administration.

Low rent public housing under Federal assistance has been provided senior citizens at an annual rate more than twice that for 1960.

The Community Health Services and Facilities Act of 1961 raised the ceiling on appropriations for the construction of nursing homes under the Hill-Burton legislation from $10 million to $20 million; and authorized $10 million per year for a 5-year program of special project grants for the development of new or improved methods of providing health services outside the hospital for the chronically ill or aged.

Executive Order 11114, issued by President Johnson on February 12, 1964, establishes for the first time the policy of non-discrimination in employment based on age by Federal contractors.

WELFARE

In 1960, we proposed to—

"Permit workers who are totally and permanently disabled to retire at any age, removing the arbitrary requirement that the worker be 50 years of age.

"Amend the law so that after six months of total disability, a worker will be eligible for disability benefits, with restorative services to enable the worker to return to work.

"Continued support of legislation for the rehabilitation of physically handicapped persons and improvement of employment opportunities for them.

"Persons in need who are inadequately protected by social insurance are cared for by the states and local communities under public assistance programs. The Federal Government, which now shares the cost of aid to some of these, should share in all, and benefits should be made available without regard to residence.

"Uniform minimum standards throughout the nation for coverage, duration, and amount of unemployment insurance benefits.

"Legislation which will guarantee to women equality of rights under the law, including equal pay for equal work.

"The Child Welfare Program and other services already established under the Social Security Act should be expanded. Federal leadership is required in the nationwide campaign to prevent and control juvenile delinquency.

"A federal bureau of inter-group relations to help solve problems of discrimination in housing, education, employment and community opportunities in general. The bureau would assist in the solution of problems arising from the resettlement of immigrants and migrants within our own country, and in resolving religious, social and other tensions where they arise."

The 1961 Public Assistance Amendments, extended aid for the first time to families with dependent children in which the parent is unemployed. Currently, 18 States have adopted this program. Aid is being provided to about 75,000 families with nearly 280,000 children.

The food stamp program is providing improved purchasing powers and a better diet for families and persons receiving general assistance.

The 1962 Public Welfare amendments provide the authority and financial resources for a new approach to the problems of prolonged dependency and some of the special needs of children.

Under these enactments and related provisions:

49 States have now qualified for increased Federal financial aid to provide help to families with economic and social problems, and to assist families dependent on public assistance back to economic independence.

9 pilot projects have been initiated to help children stay in school.

41 demonstration projects have been designed to improve public assistance operations and to find ways of helping low-income families and individuals to become independent.

18,000 unemployed fathers in needy families are currently on community work and training projects.

Three million children are now covered by the program of aid to families with dependent children; and under the 1962 amendments these children receive, in addition to financial assistance, other needed help toward normal growth and development.

46 States now have approved plans for day care services.

Grants for research and demonstrations in child welfare were first awarded in 1962, and 62 projects have since been approved.

Starting for the first time in 1963, grants for training child welfare workers have been made to 58 institutions of higher learning.

Approximately 453,000 older persons received medical assistance under the Kerr-Mills program in fiscal year 1964.

The Temporary Extended Unemployment Compensation Act of 1961 provided 13 additional weeks of benefits to the long-term unemployed. 2.8 million jobless workers received $800 million in assistance.

The Juvenile Delinquency and Youth Offenses Control Act of 1961 made possible the establishment of training centers at 12 universities. By the end of fiscal year 1964, the program will have reached 12,500 trainees for work in delinquency prevention and control.

The Equal Pay Act of 1963 and the work of the President's Commission on the Status of Women, which reported to the President that same year, were events of historic importance in the struggle for equal opportunity and full partnership for women. The inclusion of women in the employment provisions of the Civil Rights Act of 1964 makes equality in employment at long last the law of the land.

Title X of the Civil Rights Act of 1964 establishes a Community Relations Service "to provide assistance to communities and persons therein in resolving disputes, disagreements, or difficulties relating to discriminatory practices based on race, color, or national origin. . ."

EDUCATION

In 1960, we pledged—

"We believe that America can meet its educational obligations only with generous federal financial support, within the traditional framework of local control. The assistance will take the form of federal grants to States for educational purposes they deem most pressing, including classroom construction and teachers' salaries. It will include aid for the construction of academic facilities as well as dormitories at colleges and universities.

"We pledge further federal support for all phases of vocational education for youth and adults; for libraries and adult education; for realizing the potential of educational television; and for exchange of students and teachers with other nations.

"As part of a broader concern for young people we recommend establishment of a Youth Conservation Corps, to give underprivileged young people a rewarding experience in a healthful environment."

The Higher Education Facilities Act of 1963 provides $1.2 billion for college construction over a three-year period. Over 2,000 institutions are eligible to benefit from its provisions in helping them meet current enrollment increases of 350,000 students each year.

The Health Professions Educational Assistance Act of 1963 will increase the number of professional health personnel through construction grants for health teaching facilities, and through low-interest student loans to assist up to 10,000 students of medicine, dentistry, or osteopathy to pay for their high-cost education.

The Vocational Education Act of 1963 authorizes a $956 million increase in Federal support for vocational education over the next five fiscal years —1964 through 1968. It is estimated that 7,000,000 students will be enrolled in vocational education in 1968, an increase of about 3,000,000 over present annual enrollment.

Legislation approved in 1963, which increased authorization for loans to needy students for college education, will mean that in the coming school year approximately 280,000 students will be borrowing about $142 million from the loan funds to help pay for their higher education, as compared with 115,450 students borrowing $50,152,000 in 1960.

In the last three fiscal years, there have been grants of $153.1 million in Federal funds to the States for purchases of equipment and materials, and remodeling classrooms to strengthen instruction in science, mathematics, and modern foreign languages.

A $32 million program of grants to help establish non-commercial educational television stations was approved in 1962. Thirty-seven grants have been approved, totaling $6.1 million—18 for new stations and 19 for expansion.

The Library Services and Construction Act of 1964 broadened Federal aid to cover urban as well as rural areas, and to provide construction grants in addition to other library services. The new legislation increased the authorization for Federal aid to develop libraries from $7.5 million to the present level of $25 million and included a new program of assistance for public library construction, with an appropriation for Fiscal Year 1965 of $30 million.

The Youth Conservation Corps envisioned by the 1960 proposal is provided for under Title I of the Economic Opportunity Act of 1964.

NATURAL RESOURCES

In 1960, we said—

"A thin layer of earth, a few inches of rain, and a blanket of air makes human life possible on our planet."

"Sound public policy must assure that these essential resources will be available to provide the good life for our children and future generations."

After the 1960 election President Kennedy and President Johnson implemented this platform by a whole series of new conservation policies and programs, some of which emanated from the first White House Conference on Conservation called by any President since the 1908 conference called by President Theodore Roosevelt.

During this Administration two historic conservation measures were enacted. These were:

The Wilderness Bill and the Land and Water Conservation Fund Bill which will together do more to help conserve outdoor America than any legislation passed in a generation.

In addition to this landmark legislation new emphasis has been placed on science as the modern midwife of conservation, and new impetus has been given across the board in the conservation of natural resources.

In the field of water conservation

Twenty-one new major water resources projects have been authorized or started in the West;

A highwater mark has been achieved in the annual level of national investment in water resource projects;

The saline water conversion effort has been quadrupled, and should achieve a dramatic cost-breakthrough during the next Administration.

In electric power

Ending 16 years of argument, a bold plan was developed under President Johnson's personal leadership to interconnect the electric power systems of the Pacific Northwest and the Southwest, thus providing benefits for power users in 11 Western States; under this plan, construction will soon begin on the first direct current long-distance lines in the United States, stretching all the way from the Columbia River to Los Angeles—and a

new era of public and private power cooperation will commence.

Federal hydroelectric generating capacity has been increased by 2,600,000 kilowatts, and 5,150,000 kilowatts of non-Federal capacity has been licensed by the Federal Power Commission.

3,350 miles of vital transmission lines have been added to Federal systems and about 25,000 miles of new transmission lines have also been built by non-Federal power systems.

The FPC has conducted a National Power Survey to encourage both public and private power companies to join in power pools which are bringing lower cost electricity to consumers throughout the nation.

The world's largest atomic electric power plant (at Hanford, Washington) was funded and will soon be generating as much power as two Bonneville dams.

Federal REA loans have made it possible to open up the lignite coal fields of the Dakotas, and to exploit the coal fields of Western Colorado.

In addition, the Congress authorized the Delaware Basin Compact to permit the multi-purpose development of that river, and the Senate ratified the Columbia River Treaty which enables the joint U.S.-Canadian development of the full potential of that great river to begin later this year.

In outdoor recreation

The Congress created three superb new national seashores at Cape Cod (Massachusetts), Padre Island (Texas) and Point Reyes (California).

Pioneering a new park concept, Ozark Rivers National Riverway (Missouri) was established as the first river preservation national park in the Nation, and 12 other major new additions to the Park System were recommended for action by future Congresses.

A Bureau of Outdoor Recreation was created. As a vital part of the war on poverty, during the next year, 20 thousand young Americans will set to work in conservation camps across the land tackling the big backlog of work in the land and water areas owned by all of the people.

In the conservation and development of mineral resources

Research helped coal production surge upward, and there were initiated a series of action steps (including activation of the huge Rifle, Colorado, research center) which will lead to the orderly development of the vast oil shale resources of the Colorado plateau.

For wildlife

Enactment of the Wetlands Bill of 1961 made it possible to create more new Waterfowl Refuges (27) than during any previous four-year period in our history.

The Clean Air Act of 1963 is already providing the first full-scale attack on the air pollution problems that blight living conditions in so many of our cities.

Enactment of the Federal Water Pollution Control Act of 1961 launched the first massive attack on this conservation problem which has already resulted in 1,300 municipal waste treatment plans and the approval of projects that have improved the water quality in 18,000 miles of streams that provide water for 22 million people.

CITIES AND THEIR SUBURBS

In 1960, we declared—

"A new Democratic administration will expand Federal programs to aid urban communities to clear their slums, dispose of their sewage, educate their children, transport suburban commuters to and from their jobs, and combat juvenile delinquency."

The Housing Act of 1961 marked the beginning of a new era of Federal commitment to the problems of a nation in which three-fourths of the population has come to live in urban areas.

Under that Act, funds available for urban planning grants were increased by $55 million and a new $50 million Federal grant program to assist localities in the acquisition of permanent open space land to be used as parks and playgrounds was established.

The Housing Act of 1961 and the Area Redevelopment Act of 1961 authorized public facilities loans of $600 million.

The Juvenile Delinquency and Youth Offenses Control Act of 1961 launched a broad attack on youth problems by financing demonstration projects, training personnel in delinquency work, and providing technical assistance for community youth programs.

In 1960, we pledged—

"Federal aid for comprehensive metropolitan transportation programs, including bus and rail mass transit, commuter railroads as well as highway programs and construction of civil airports."

The Housing Act of 1961 launched the first efforts to help metropolitan and other urban areas solve their mass transportation problems; 75 million in loans and demonstration grants were provided to States and localities to construct and improve mass transportation systems.

The Urban Mass Transportation Act of 1964 establishes a new long-range program for this purpose and authorizes $375 million in Federal grants, over 3 years, for capital construction and improvement which local transit systems cannot otherwise finance.

TRANSPORTATION

In 1960, we observed—

"Over the past seven years we have watched the steady weakening of the Nation's transportation system, and we noted the need for 'a national transportation policy.' "

The National Transportation policy was enunciated in the first Presidential message ever to be sent to the Congress dealing solely with transportation.

The Highway Act of 1961 resolved the lagging problem of financing the 41,000 mile interstate highway program, and the finished construction rate has almost doubled.

The Federal Maritime Commission has been established as an independent agency to guard against prejudice or discrimination harmful to the growth of U. S. World Trade.

The Maritime Administration, U. S. Department of Commerce, was set up to give its full attention to promoting a vigorous policy of strengthening and modernizing our merchant fleet. Seventy big modern cargo and cargo-passenger ships have been added to the U. S. merchant fleet. The Savannah, the world's first nuclear-powered merchant ship, is now on her first foreign voyage.

The far-reaching decision has been made that the United States will design and build a supersonic air transport plane—and thereby maintain our leadership position in international aviation. Congress has provided $60 million for the development of detailed designs. Twenty airlines already have placed orders.

On August 13, President Johnson signed a new highway bill to provide better primary and secondary highways on a 50/50 basis with the states. In addition, it will support needed efforts to improve forest highways, public land roads and national park roads.

SCIENCE

In 1960, we declared—

"We will recognize the special role of our Federal Government in support of basic and applied research," mentioning in particular Space, Atomic Energy, and Oceanography.

Space

Since 1961, the United States has pressed vigorously forward with a 10-year, $35-billion national space program for clear leadership in space exploration, space use, and all important aspects of space science and technology.

Already this program has enabled the United States to challenge the early Soviet challenge in space booster power and to effectively counter the Soviet bid for recognition as the world's leading nation in science and technology.

In the years 1961-1964, the United States has

Successfully flown the Saturn I rocket, putting into orbit the heaviest payloads of the space age to date.

Moved rapidly forward with much more powerful launch vehicles, the Saturn IB and the Saturn V. The Saturn IB, scheduled to fly in 1966, will be able to orbit a payload of 16 tons; and Saturn V, scheduled to fly in 1967 or 1968, will be able to orbit 120 tons or send 45 tons to the moon or 35 tons to Mars or Venus.

Mastered the difficult technology of using liquid hydrogen as a space rocket fuel in the Centaur upper stage rocket and the Saturn I second stage —assuring American leadership in space science and manned space flight in this decade.

Successfully completed six manned space flights in Project Mercury, acquiring 54 hours of space flight experience.

Successfully flight-tested the two-man Gemini spacecraft and Titan II space rocket so that manned Gemini flights can begin late in 1964 or early in 1965.

Developed the three-man Apollo spacecraft which will be able to spend up to two months in earth orbit, operate out to a quarter of a million miles from earth, and land our first astronaut-explorers on the moon.

Taken all actions to conduct a series of manned space flights in the Gemini and Apollo programs which will give the United States some 5,000 man-hours of flight experience in earth orbit, develop U. S. capabilities for rendezvous and joining of spacecraft in orbit, and prove out man's ability to perform valuable missions during long stays in space.

Made man's first close-up observations of another planet during the highly successful Mariner II fly-by of Venus.

Obtained the first close-up pictures of the moon, taken and relayed to earth by Ranger VII.

Initiated an ambitious long-range program for scientific investigations in space utilizing large, versatile spacecraft called Orbiting Observatories for geophysical, solar and stellar studies.

Operated the world's first weather satellites (Tiros).

Set up, under the Communications Satellite Act of 1962, the Communications Satellite Corporation, which is well on the way to establishing a global satellite communications system to provide reliable, low-cost telephone, telegraph, and television services to all parts of the world.

In short, the United States has matched rapid progress in manned space flight with a balanced program for scientific investigations in space, practical uses of space, and advanced research and technological pioneering to assure that the new challenges of space in the next decade can also be met, and U. S. leadership maintained.

Atomic Energy

The number of civilian nuclear power plants has increased from 3 to 14 since January 1961; and now the advent of economic nuclear power provides utilities a wider choice of competitive power sources in many sections of the country.

The world's largest nuclear power reactor, the Atomic Energy Commission's Production Reactor near Richland, Washington, achieved a controlled, self-sustained nuclear reaction on December 31, 1963.

The first deep-sea anchored, automatic weather station powered by nuclear energy has gone into unattended operation in the Gulf of Mexico, and the first lighthouse powered by nuclear energy flashes now in Chesapeake Bay.

Nuclear energy was extended to space for the first time in 1961. Compact nuclear generators supplied part of the power for instruments in two satellites, and in 1963 provided all of the power needs of two other satellites.

Vigorous support has been given to basic research in atomic energy. The world's highest energy accelerator, the AGS, has come into productive operation.

Oceanography

For the first time in history the United States is building a fleet expressly designed for oceanographic research. Since 1961, 29 ships have been completed or are currently under construction. Shoreside facilities and training programs have been established as part of a major government-wide effort, begun in 1961, to capture the enormous potential rewards of research in this area which until now have been almost as remote and inaccessible as space itself.

GOVERNMENT OPERATIONS

"We shall reform the processes of government in all branches—executive, legislative, and judicial. We will clean out corruption and conflicts of interest, and improve government services."

This Administration has brought the personnel, morale, ethics, and performance of the Federal service to a point of high excellence. To accomplish this transformation it made improvements in a broad range of activities affecting the operation of the government.

The conflict of interest laws were strengthened by the first major revision in a century. The comprehensive new law eliminates ambiguities and inconsistencies in existing laws, and increases the range of government matters in which conflict of interest is prohibited. In addition, President Kennedy issued an Executive Order which established more rigid standards of conduct for Federal officials and employees.

The regulatory agencies were made more effective by reorganization programs and by the appointment of highly-qualified officials, dedicated to protecting the public interest.

The Department of Justice has cracked down effectively on organized crime under new anti-racketeering statutes, has uncovered and prosecuted important foreign spies, and has made progress toward more effective procedures for protecting the rights of poor defendants to bail and counsel.

Federal Employee Organizations, many of which have existed for over half a century, were at last extended formal recognition under Executive Order 10988, issued by President Kennedy.

The Federal Pay Raise Act of 1964 updated the pay structure for Federal employees on a basis of equal salary rates for comparable levels of work in private industry. Completing the reforms initiated in the Act of 1962, it provided for long-needed increases in salary for top level Government administrators upon whom major responsibility for program results must rest. In President Johnson's words, this law established a basis for a standard of "brilliance" and "excellence" in the Federal Government.

CONGRESSIONAL PROCEDURES

In 1960, we urged action—

"To improve Congressional procedures so that majority rule prevails."

In 1961, the House Rules Committee was enlarged from 12 to 15 members, making it more representative of the views of the majority, and thereby enabling much important legislation to be reported to the floor for a vote by the entire House membership.

In 1964, for the first time in history, the Senate voted to limit debate on a civil rights measure, thus permitting the Civil Rights Act to come to a vote, and thereby to be enacted.

CONSUMERS

In 1960, we proposed—

"Effective Government representation and protection" for consumers.

In 1962, President Kennedy became the first Chief Executive to send a message to Congress on consumer matters.

This Executive action was closely followed by the creation of a Consumer Advisory Council.

In 1964, President Johnson appointed the first Special Assistant to the President for Consumer Affairs, and created a new President's Committee on Consumer Interests.

The Kefauver-Harris Drug Amendments of 1962 were the most far-reaching improvements in the Food, Drug and Cosmetics Act since 1938. Under these amendments:

Effective legal tools were provided to insure greater safety in connection with the manufacture, distribution and use of drugs.

Vital safeguards were added for drug research and manufacture.

Interstate distribution of new drugs for testing was barred until an adequate plan of investigation was made available to the Food and Drug Administration.

Domestic drug manufacturing establishments will now be required to register annually and be inspected by the FDA at least once a year.

The Administration has vigorously supported Truth-in-Lending, Truth-in-Packaging, and Truth-in-Securities bills.

The titles of these bills explain their objectives. Together, they form a triple armor of protection: for buyers of packaged goods, from prevailing deceptive practices; for borrowers of money, from hidden and unscrupulous interest and carrying charges; and for investors in securities from unfair practices threatening to vital savings. The first two bills are still awaiting Congressional action; the third is now a law.

The upward spiral in the price of natural gas which took place in the decade of the 1950's has been halted by vigorous regulatory action of the Federal Power Commission and the nation's 36 million consumers of natural gas have benefited from rate reductions and refunds in excess of $600 million. Natural gas moving largely in interstate pipelines now supplies almost a third of the nation's energy requirements. Regulation to insure its availability in ample supply and at reasonable prices is an important consumer protection function which is now being effectively discharged.

VETERANS AFFAIRS

In 1960, we proposed—

"Adequate compensation for those with service-connected disabilities," and "pensions adequate for a full and dignified life for disabled and distressed veterans and for needy survivors of deceased veterans."

Since 1961, we have achieved:

Increased disability payments for veterans with service-connected disabilities. In the first year alone, this increase provided veterans with additional payments of about $98 million.

An increase of about 10 percent a month in the compensation for widows, children, and parents of veterans who died of service-connected disabilities.

An increase from $112 to $150 a month in the dependency and indemnity compensation payable to widows of veterans who died of service-connected disabilities.

Increased compensation benefits to veterans disabled by blindness, deafness, and kidney disorders, and increased benefits to widows and orphans of veterans whose deaths were service-connected.

In 1960, we endorsed—

"Expanded programs of vocational rehabilitation for disabled veterans, and education for orphans of servicemen."

Since 1961, vocational rehabilitation and training has enabled thousands of GI's to choose occupations and acquire valuable training. For the first time, veterans with peacetime service-connected disabilities have been afforded vocational rehabilitation training. In addition, vocational rehabilitation was extended to blinded World War II and Korean conflict veterans, and war orphans' educational assistance was extended in behalf of certain reservists called to active duty.

In 1960, we stated—

"The quality of medical care furnished to the disabled veterans has deteriorated. . . . We shall work for an increased availability of facilities for all veterans in need and we shall move with particular urgency to fulfill the need for expanded domiciliary and nursing-home facilities."

Since 1961, we have—

Approved the construction of new, modern hospitals, a number of which are being built near medical schools to improve veterans' care and research.

Added more full-time doctors to the VA staff, bringing it to an all-time high of nearly 5,000.

Provided hospital and medical care, including out-patient treatment, to peacetime ex-servicemen for service-connected disabilities on the same basis furnished war veterans.

Stepped up medical research programs, which have made outstanding contributions to American medicine.

In 1960, we pledged—

"We shall continue the veterans home loan guarantee and direct loan programs and education benefits patterned after the GI Bill of Rights."

Since 1961, legislation has extended veterans home loans for both World War II and Korean conflict veterans. The GI Bill of Rights for Korean veterans was also extended for the benefit of certain reservists called to active duty.

Despite this considerably increased activity, the Veterans Administration has reduced its operating costs.

AMERICAN INDIANS

In 1960, we pledged—

"Prompt adoption of a program to assist Indian tribes in the full development of their human and natural resources and to advance the health, education and economic well-being of Indian citizens while preserving their cultural heritage."

In these 3½ years:

New classrooms have been provided for more than 7,000 Indian children; summer educational programs have been expanded tenfold so they now serve more than 20,000 students; and a special institute to train artistically gifted Indian youth has been established.

Indian enrollment in vocational training programs has been doubled.

For the first time in history, Federal low-rent housing programs have been launched on Indian reservations, and more than 3,100 new housing units have now been authorized.

Industrial plants offering employment opportunities for thousands of Indians are being opened on Indian reservations.

Accelerated Public Works projects on 89 reservations in 21 States have provided nearly 30,000 man-months of employment.

The Vocational Education Act and the Adult Indian Vocational Training Act have been amended to provide improved training for Indians.

THE ARTS

In 1960, we observed—

"The arts flourish where there is freedom and where individual initiative and imagination are encouraged."

No single quality of the new Administration was more immediately evident to the Nation and the world than the recognition it gave to American artists.

President Kennedy early created an advisory commission to assist in the growth and development of the arts, and the Administration secured amendments to the Educational and Cultural Exchange Act to improve the quality and effectiveness of the international educational and cultural exchange programs. This past year, the John F. Kennedy Center for the Performing Arts was established to stimulate widespread interest in the arts.

On Washington's Birthday 1963, President Kennedy, by Executive Order, created a new Presidential Medal of Freedom as the highest civil honor conferred by the President in peace time upon persons who have made distinctive contributions to the security and national interest of the United States, to world peace, or to cultural activities. Henceforth, those men and women selected by the President for the Medal will be announced annually on the Fourth of July and will be presented with medals at an appropriate White House ceremony.

In his address to the University of Michigan in May 1964, President Johnson proposed that we begin to build the Great Society first of all in the cities of America, restoring the beauty and dignity which urban centers have lost.

That same month the President's Council on Pennsylvania Avenue presented to him a sweeping proposal for the reconstruction of the center of the City of Washington. The proposal has been hailed as "a blueprint for glory . . . a realistic and far-seeing redevelopment scheme that may be Washington's last chance to save its 'Avenue of Presidents.' "

CIVIL LIBERTIES

In 1960, we reaffirmed—

"Our dedication to the Bill of Rights. Freedom and civil liberties, far from being incompatible with security, are vital to our national strength."

The era of fear and suspicion brought on by accusations, true and false, of subversive activities and security risks has passed. The good sense of the American people, and the overwhelming loyalty of our citizenry have combined to restore balance and calm to security activities, without in any way diminishing the scope or effectiveness of those activities.

The Administration has jealously guarded the right of each American to protect his good name. Except in those instances where the national security is overriding, confrontation of the accuser is now required in all loyalty hearings. Individuals whose loyalty is being questioned must also be notified of the charges in sufficient time for them to prepare their defense.

The Criminal Justice Act of 1964, now before the President for signature, will for the first time in history ensure that poor defendants in criminal cases will have competent legal counsel in defending themselves in Federal courts.

FISCAL RESPONSIBILITY

In 1960, we promised—

"We shall end the gross waste in Federal expenditures which needlessly raises the budgets of many Government agencies."

Since 1961, we have moved boldly and directly to eliminate waste and duplication wherever it occurs.

For example, the Department of Defense has embarked on a far-reaching program to realize savings through improvements in its efficiency and management. This program has already produced savings of more than $1 billion in Fiscal Year 1963 and $2.5 billion in the Fiscal Year just completed. By 1964, it is expected that the program will produce yearly savings of over $4 billion.

At the close of the past Fiscal Year Federal employment had been reduced by 22,000 over the total one year earlier. The 1965 budget calls for lower expenditures than in the preceding year— only the second time such a feat has been accomplished in the past 10 years.

In 1960, we pledged—

"We shall collect the billions in taxes which are owed to the Federal Government but are not now collected."

To handle additional work in income tax collection, 3,971 new employees were added to the Internal Revenue Service by the Congress in fiscal 1961; 2,817 new positions were added in fiscal 1963; and about 1,000 more in fiscal 1964. The additional revenue which these employees will produce will far exceed the cost of their employment.

In 1960, we pledged—

"We shall close the loopholes in the tax laws by which certain privileged groups legally escape their fair share of taxation."

The Revenue Acts of 1962 and 1964 eliminated more loopholes than all the revenue legislation from 1941 to 1962 combined. They raised $1.7 billion annually in new revenue, nine times the sum raised in this manner during the 1953-60 period. These bills sharply limited expense account abuses, special preferences to U. S. firms and individuals operating abroad, escapes from taxation through personal holding companies and many other unjustified advantages.

CIVIL RIGHTS

In 1960, we pledged—

"We shall . . . seek to create an affirmative new atmosphere in which to deal with racial divisions and inequalities which threaten both the integrity of our democratic faith and the proposition on which our Nation was founded—that all men are created equal."

That pledge was made from the deepest moral conviction.

It was carried out on the same basis.

From the establishment of the President's Committee on Equal Employment Opportunity, under the chairmanship of the then Vice President Lyndon B. Johnson, on March 6, 1961 to this moment, the efforts of the Administration to provide full and equal civil rights for all Americans have never relaxed.

The high point of achievement in this effort was reached with the passage of the Civil Rights Act of 1964, the greatest civil rights measure in the history of the American people.

This landmark of our Democracy bars discrimination in the use of public accommodations, in employment, and in the administering of Federally-assisted programs. It makes available effective procedures for assuring the right to vote in Federal elections, directs Federal technical and financial assistance to local public school systems in desegregation, and strengthens the Civil Rights Commission. This comprehensive legislation resolves many of the festering conflicts which had been a source of irritating uncertainty, and smooths the way for favorable resolution of these problems.

We have also insisted upon non-discrimination in apprenticeship, and have made free, unsegregated access a condition for Federal financial assistance to public libraries, programs for training of teachers of the handicapped, counseling, guidance and foreign language institutes, adult civil defense classes, and manpower development and training programs.

In supporting construction of Hill-Burton hospitals, mental retardation and community health facilities, we have required non-discrimination in admission and provision of services and granting of staff privileges.

We have been equally firm in opposing any policy of quotas or "discrimination in reverse," and all other arbitrary or irrelevant distinctions in American life.

This, then, is the accounting of our stewardship.

The 1960 platform was not directed to any one sector or group of Americans with particular interests.

It proclaimed, rather, the Rights of Man.

The platform asserted the essential fact of that moment in our history—that the next administration to take office would face as never before the "responsibility and opportunity to call forth the greatness of the American people."

That responsibility was met; that opportunity was seized. The years since have been times of towering achievement.

We are proud to have been a part of this history. The task of leadership is to lead, and that has been our purpose. But the achievements of the nation over this period outreach the contribution of any party: they are the work of the American people.

In the 1,000 days of John F. Kennedy, in the eventful and culminating months of Lyndon B. Johnson, there has been born a new American greatness.

Let us continue.

Prohibition Platform 1964

PREAMBLE

We, the representatives of the Prohibition Party, assembled in the National Convention at St. Louis, Mo., August 29-30, 1963, recognizing Almighty God as the source of all just government, and with faith in the teachings of the Lord Jesus Christ, do solemnly promise that, if our party is chosen to administer the affairs of the nation, we will, with earnest dedication to the principles of righteousness, seek to serve the needs and to preserve the rights, the prerogatives and the basic freedoms, of the people of the United States. For the realization of these ends we propose the following program of government:

CONSTITUTIONAL GOVERNMENT

We affirm our sincere loyalty to the Constitution of the United States, and express our deep confidence in that document as the basic law of our land. We deplore all attempts to violate it, whether by legislation, by means of evasion, or through judicial interpretation. We believe in the principles of liberty and justice enunciated in the Declaration of Independence and in the Preamble and Bill of Rights of our Constitution. We declare ourselves in hearty support of our system of representative government, with its plan of checks and balances, and express our firm intent to serve the people of our nation with a constructive, forward-looking program of good government, dedicated to the general welfare.

COMMUNISM-TOTALITARIANISM

We are positively, aggressively and unalterably, opposed to Communism as a way of life or as a governmental system. We believe that the program of Communism, with its intent to infiltrate and to overthrow our present form of government, must be pitilessly exposed. We challenge all loyal citizens to become fully aware of this menace to civilization, to exert every effort to defeat these "masters of deceit," and to help preserve our American way of life.

We also declare ourselves opposed to any other form of totalitarian philosophy or form of government. We endorse the efforts of those agencies which have been honestly and earnestly exposing subversive activities and groups.

GOVERNMENTAL ECONOMY AND TAXATION

We live in an era of extravagance and wasteful spending. This spirit has invaded government at all levels, demanding an ever-increasing tax load upon our people. The constant increase in taxation, requiring nearly one-third of the total income of our citizens to pay the expenses of government, is approaching the point of confiscation, leading to economic bankruptcy. We believe that good government ought not to attempt to do for people what they can do for themselves. With proper economy, governmental costs can be lowered, the tax load can be lightened, and the public debt can be reduced. We promise to devote ourselves to such an end, even though it involves the reorganization and/or abolition of certain departments, bureaus and vested interests.

MONEY AND FINANCE

A sound financial program and a dependable monetary policy are fundamental to a stable economy. Our Constitution gives to Congress the power to "coin money" and to "regulate the value thereof." We believe that Congress, working with the executive department of our government, should take immediate steps to establish a financial program that will block inflationary trends, insure a sound currency, stabilize price levels and provide for systematic retirement of the national debt. We urge that careful consideration be given to a return to the gold standard, suggesting that such a step would help stabilize our economy, would promote confidence in our monetary system and would underwrite a continuing program of sound finance and expanding industrial progress.

THE FEDERAL BUDGET

Good government and a sound economy demand a balanced federal budget. The inflationary effects and the disturbing influences of unbalanced budgets must be eliminated. We cannot, with impunity, continue to increase the mortgage on our future and the interest load of the present. As the level of taxation is already excessive, there must be either a decided reduction in governmental services and federal spending or a substantial improvement in efficiency, with consequent elimination of waste in both personnel and materials. Actually, both areas need careful exploration with a view not only to maintaining a balanced budget, but also to reduction of the national debt.

FOREIGN AID

Many billions of dollars of our taxpayers' money have been and are still being given to foreign countries. Unfortunately, substantial portions have been used to support governments and programs considerably at variance with American ideals and concepts. It is frankly recognized that complex and baffling problems are involved in this area of international relations, but it is likewise believed that the practice needs most careful scrutiny and review.

FREE ENTERPRISE

We are strongly opposed to governmental restraints on our free enterprise system, to detailed regulation of our economic life and to federal interference with individual initiative. We believe that free enterprise is threatened in three ways: (1) by excessive governmental regulation, (2) by growth of public and/or private monopoly, and (3) by unethical practices of unscrupulous groups.

It will be the policy of our administration to encourage independent, non-monopolistic business enterprises which serve genuine consumer needs and are operated with a sense of responsibility to the public. We will take necessary steps to prevent the evils both of monopoly, and of excessive regulation by government and to protect adequately the consuming public from irresponsible or deceptive practices contrary to public welfare.

We propose that our government withdraw, with reasonable promptness, from the field of business activity and sell to private industry, at proper investment prices, those business enterprises now owned and operated by the federal government.

LABOR AND INDUSTRY

In the area of labor and industrial relations we believe that the public welfare must be given paramount consideration. Both management and labor must be held responsible for their economic and their social behavior. Neither should be permitted to dominate at the expense of the other or of the common good. Rather, the anti-trust laws must be applied equally to all monopolies, whether of business or labor. Whenever the public welfare is seriously endangered because of disputes affecting quasi-public businesses and utilities we favor the compulsory arbitration of labor-management disputes.

EMPLOYEE-EMPLOYER RIGHTS

Every individual has certain basic and fundamental rights. A person's right to join or not to join a labor union without affecting his employment and his right to work for an employer willing to hire him must be protected. Likewise, employees and employers must be free to bargain and to contract as they wish. Mass picketing, rioting, terrorism, and all other forms of violence and coercion, secondary boycotts and industry-wide bargaining should be prohibited.

INDIVIDUALS AND STATES' RIGHTS

Our founding fathers recognized the importance of both individual and states' rights, and determined to preserve them by making the Bill of Rights an integral part of our Constitution. During recent years there has been an increasing tendency toward an undesirable concentration of power and authority in the federal government.

This tendency has two principal causes: (1) the ever-growing power and influence of the "military-industrial complex," and (2) a widespread tendency of groups of citizens to look to the federal government for the protection of rights and the satisfaction of needs which they feel are not adequately cared for by state and local governments or by private enterprise.

To deal with the first of these causes, we pledge the utmost vigilance in resisting the growth of militarism and to maintain the constitutional principle of civilian supremacy over the military.

To deal with over-centralization we urge more vigorous action by state and local governments for the protection of the rights and the promotion of the welfare of their people, greater resort to the solution of local community problems through the voluntary action of existing or new civic and other non-governmental associations, where this is feasible, and the increasing pursuit by private business concerns of policies which promote the public interest.

We pledge ourselves to action that will preserve all legitimate individual rights and will maintain among the several states their constitutional place in our system of government.

CIVIL RIGHTS

We maintain that all American citizens, regardless of race, religion, or National origin, are entitled to equality of treatment under the provisions of our Constitution and under the laws of our land. No person or group of persons shall be subjected to ostracism, humiliation, or embarrassment because of color or national background. At the same time we must deplore the use of violence and/or arbitrary pressure tactics, from whatever source, as a means of seeking to resolve tensions and divergencies of opinion among our citizens.

We are opposed to those proposals which would destroy our neighborhood school systems through a program of artificial integration or convey special privileges to any minority group.

PUBLIC MORALITY AND LAW ENFORCEMENT

Moral and spiritual considerations must be primary factors in determining both state and national policies. We deplore the gross neglect of such matters by the dominant political parties, culminating in the shocking revelations of crime and of political and economic corruption which have characterized recent years. We charge these parties with basic responsibility for the rapid decline in moral standards which followed repeal of the Eighteenth Amendment. We believe that the program of nullification of law through non-enforcement which led to repeal contributed greatly to the disintegration of public morals, to a general deterioration of standards and to a lowering of values among our people.

We pledge ourselves to break the unholy alliance which has made these things possible. We propose to strengthen and to enforce laws against gambling, narcotics, and commercialized vice, to emphasize the basic importance of spiritual and moral values to the development and growth of an enduring nation, and to maintain the integrity of our democracy by careful enforcement of law and loyal support of our Constitution.

WORLD PEACE

We live in an age of atomic and hydrogen bombs, in an era of missiles and jet propulsion, in a world filled with animosities and cruel hatreds. Instruments for the destruction of civilization have been developed. Under these conditions, we pledge ourselves to search for peaceful solutions to international conflict, by seeking to deal creatively and constructively with the underlying causes of international tension, and to strive for world peace and order based upon the teachings and practices of the Prince of Peace.

NATIONAL SOVEREIGNTY

We declare our belief in national sovereignty and oppose surrender of this sovereignty to any international group.

MILITARY TRAINING

Although we seek for world peace and order, we declare our firm belief, under existing world conditions, in a sound program of national preparedness. At the same time, we seriously question the desirability of the existing program of peacetime compulsory military training. We doubt that it represents a genuine safeguard to world peace. Rather, we believe it to be contrary, in principle, to our American way of life, to place an unnecessary burden upon our peacetime economy, to threaten us with possible military dictatorship, and, as currently conducted, to permit and very often to promote the moral and spiritual deterioration of our Youth. Therefore, we declare our opposition to any program of peacetime compulsory military training and urge a complete evaluation and re-orientation of our entire program of national preparedness.

Nuclear Weapons Testing

Many of the leading scientists of our day have warned that radioactive fallout, resulting from testing of nuclear weapons, endangers the health of human beings throughout the world, and, if continued, will increase the number of seriously defective children who will be born to future generations. It is unjust that the people of the world, and especially those of nations not engaged in the development of nuclear weapons, should be exposed to such peril. The danger and the injustice will become progressively greater with any additional testing. In addition, there is the danger that continuation of the armaments race will lead to an atomic war of annihilation.

In our 1960 platform we urged that, "as a step toward world disarmament, all testing of nuclear weapons be indefinitely suspended on a multilateral basis and that our government seek with renewed vigor and persistence an agreement among all nuclear power for the permanent and complete cessation of nuclear tests for military purposes." It appears that some progress has been made toward realization of this goal. We insist that continual attention must be given to this problem.

Religious Liberty

We believe in religious liberty. Freedom of the individual to worship, to fellowship with others of similar faith, to evangelize, to educate and to establish religious institutions, must be preserved. When religious liberty is lost political liberty will perish with it. We believe, also, that our government should take a firm, positive position against religious intolerance and persecution anywhere in the world.

Marriage and Divorce

Ordained of God, the home is a sacred institution. Its sanctity must be protected and preserved. We favor the enactment of uniform marriage and divorce laws in the various states as an aid to building strong and enduring homes throughout our nation.

Old Age Insurance

We endorse the general principle of an actuarially sound voluntary social security program which includes all employed groups. We question the soundness of the existing program. We deplore the wide-spread current abuse of the privileges involved; we condemn the maladministration of its provisions for political ends; we pledge ourselves to correct these evils.

Ballot Law Reform

True democracy requires that the needs and interests of minority groups be given fair, honest and appropriate consideration. Instead, in many of our states, ballot laws have been enacted which are designed to make a two-party system into a bipartisan political monopoly, keeping minor parties off the ballot. We demand the repeal of all laws which deny to independent voters and to loyal minority groups the fundamental right of free political expression.

Separation of Church and State

We affirm our continuing loyalty to the constitutional principle of separation of Church and State. We will expose, and resist vigorously, any attempt from whatever source to weaken or subvert this fundamental principle.

We declare our belief that the Bible is not a sectarian book, but is a volume of universal appeal and application which is woven into our history, our laws, and our culture. We deplore any interpretation which would limit its use in any area of our national life.

In the area of government, we endorse encouragement of non-profit educational and religious institutions on a tax-exempt basis, but we declare strong opposition to all efforts, direct or indirect, to secure appropriations of public money for private religious or sectarian purposes.

Education

It is altogether appropriate that our federal

government should be interested in and concerned about matters pertaining to all areas of educational growth and development. However, under the Tenth Amendment, public education is clearly a matter of state concern. We approve of the work of the Office of Education in collecting and disseminating essential educational information, but we are opposed to any sort of direct federal aid to education, believing that each state should both support and control its own educational program.

AGRICULTURE

The production and distribution of agricultural products is of vital importance to the economy of any people. We believe that those engaged in agricultural pursuits, like other American citizens, should be free from authoritarian control and coercion. Hence we declare ourselves opposed to regimentation of farms and farmers and urge a sensible and orderly return to a free market program.

PUBLIC HEALTH

The health of our people is a matter of high importance. We are deeply concerned with this problem in its numerous aspects. In particular, we insist that genuine caution be taken when dealing with mental health cases lest there be unjust and prejudiced incarcerations. Also we deplore those programs of mass medication which many maintain are in violation of the rights of individuals under our Constitution.

SERVICE, NOT SPOILS

In spite of our "civil service" system, first sponsored by the Prohibition Party, the dominant political parties are positively committed to the "spoils" system and, when in office, have prostituted governmental power to serve their own selfish party interests instead of the whole people. This has led to excessive expenditures, higher taxes and, in some situations, to an unfortunate alliance of crime with politics. We pledge ourselves to an honest, efficient and economical administration.

THE ALCOHOL PROBLEM

The widespread and increasing use of alcoholic beverages has now become a national tragedy and must be recognized as a major cause of poverty,

broken homes, juvenile delinquency, vice, crime, political corruption, wasted manpower, and highway accidents. Of all the unfortunate mistakes of our government and people, none has been worse than the legalization of the liquor traffic. It can be legitimately said that no political issue confronting the citizens of our land compares in magnitude with the need for suppressing the beverage alcohol industry.

The sponsors of this national curse are not only highly capitalized and strongly organized, but are also socially irresponsible. Out of enormous profits the liquor industry spends huge sums to promote sales, to create habitual use of its products by both youth and adults and to encourage a weakening of moral resistance to its program of social and economic exploitation. It is linked with and supports a nationwide network of organized gambling, vice and crime. Through its advertising it has corrupted large segments of the nation's press, and it is endeavoring to extend its control increasingly to both radio and television.

Unfortunately, the liquor traffic has been able to extend its power until, in all too many instances, it dominates our political life and controls our governmental officials. Both of our major political parties are dominated by it, and neither dares to take a stand against it. And so long as they continue to be yoked by party membership with the liquor traffic and the underworld, just so long will they be unable to make moral principles prevail.

The beverage alcohol problem is a matter of national concern. It has reached proportions which demand immediate action looking to a solution. First of all, scientific facts about beverage alcohol must be widely publicized. People must come to know and to understand the demon which we harbor. Secondly, a program of publicity, education, legislation and administration, leading to the elimination of the beverage alcohol industry, must be developed. People must come to know that there is no satisfactory solution to the problem except through political action which suppresses it and a political administration which destroys it.

Accordingly the Prohibition Party demands the repeal of all laws which legalize the liquor traffic and the enactment and rigorous enforcement of new laws which prohibit the manufacture, distribution and sale of alcoholic beverages. You are urged to elect an administration pledged to the above program. Such is essential to the permanent solution of this devastating problem.

Republican Platform 1964

"FOR THE PEOPLE"

SECTION ONE

For a Free People

Humanity is tormented once again by an age-old issue—is man to live in dignity and freedom under God or be enslaved—are men in government to serve, or are they to master, their fellow men?

It befalls us now to resolve this issue anew—perhaps this time for centuries to come. Nor can we evade the issue here at home. Even in this Constitutional Republic, for two centuries the beacon of liberty the world over, individual freedom retreats under the mounting assault of expanding centralized power. Fiscal and economic excesses, too long indulged, already have eroded and threatened the greatest experiment in self-government mankind has known.

We Republicans claim no monopoly of love of freedom. But we challenge as unwise the course the Democrats have charted; we challenge as dangerous the steps they plan along the way; and we deplore as self-defeating and harmful many of the moves already taken.

Dominant in their council are leaders whose words extol human liberty, but whose deeds have persistently delimited the scope of liberty and sapped its vitality. Year after year, in the name of benevolence, these leaders have sought the enlargement of Federal power. Year after year, in the guise of concern for others, they have lavishly expended the resources of their fellow citizens. And year after year freedom, diversity and individual, local and state responsibility have given way to regimentation, conformity and subservience to central power.

We Republicans hold that a leadership so misguided weakens liberty in America and the world. We hold that the glittering enticements so invitingly proffered the people, at their own expense, will inevitably bring disillusionment and crue disappointment in place of promised happiness.

Such leaders are Federal extremists—impulsive in the use of national power, improvident in the management of public funds, thoughtless as to the long-term effects of their acts on individual freedom and creative, competitive enterprise. Men so recklessly disposed cannot be safely entrusted with authority over their fellow citizens.

To Republicans, liberty is still today man's most precious possession. For every citizen, and for the generations to come, we Republicans vow that it shall be preserved.

In substantiation of this belief the Republican Party submits this platform. To the American people it is our solemn bond.

To Stay Free

The shape of the future is our paramount concern. Much of today's moral decline and drift—much of the prevailing preoccupation with physical and material comforts of life—much of today's crass political appeals to the appetites of the citizenry—can be traced to a leadership grown demagogic and materialistic through indifference to national ideals founded in devoutly held religious faith. The Republican Party seeks not to renounce this heritage of faith and high purpose; rather, we are determined to reaffirm and reapply it. So doing, these will be our guides:

1. Every person has the right to govern himself, to fix his own goals, and to make his own way with a minimum of governmental interference.

2. It is for government to foster and maintain an environment of freedom encouraging every individual to develop to the fullest his God-given powers of mind, heart and body; and, beyond this, government should undertake only needful things, rightly of public concern, which the citizen cannot himself accomplish.

We Republicans hold that these two principles must regain their primacy in our government's relations, not only with the American people, but also with nations and peoples everywhere in the world.

3. Within our Republic the Federal Government should act only in areas where it has Constitutional authority to act, and then only in respect to proven needs where individuals and local or state governments will not or cannot adequately perform. Great power, whether governmental or private, political or economic, must be so checked, balanced and restrained and, where necessary, so

dispersed as to prevent it from becoming a threat to freedom any place in the land.

4. It is a high mission of government to help assure equal opportunity for all, affording every citizen an equal chance at the starting line but never determining who is to win or lose. But government must also reflect the nation's compassionate concern for those who are unable, through no fault of their own, to provide adequately for themselves.

5. Government must be restrained in its demands upon and its use of the resources of the people, remembering that it is not the creator but the steward of the wealth it uses; that its goals must ever discipline its means; and that service to all the people, never to selfish or partisan ends, must be the abiding purpose of men entrusted with public power.

Deeds Not Words

The future we pledge, then, for freedom, by faithful adherence to these guides. Let the people compare these guides with those of the Democratic Party, then test, not the words of the two Parties, but their performance during the past four years of Democratic control.

Let the people ask:

Is the Republic stronger today or wiser than when the present Administration took office four years ago?

Is its guardianship of freedom more respected at home and throughout the world?

For these four years the leaders of the Democratic Party have been entrusted with the nation's executive power and overwhelmingly in control of the Congress. The question must be asked: Have these leaders successfully advanced the purposes of this mightiest nation mankind has known?

Tragically, in each instance, the answer must be "no."

Let the Democratic Party stand accused.

SECTION TWO

Failures of Foreign Policy

This Democratic Administration has been, from its beginning, not the master but the prisoner of major events. The will and dependability of its leadership, even for the defense of the free world, have come to be questioned in every area of the globe.

DISREGARD OF ALLIES

This Administration has neglected to consult with America's allies on critical matters at critical times, leading to lack of confidence, lack of respect and disintegrating alliances.

It has permitted an erosion of NATO force and unity, alienating most of its member nations by negotiating with the common foe behind their backs. It has offered concessions to the Communists while according our allies little understanding, patience, or cooperation.

This Administration has created discord and distrust by failing to develop a nuclear policy for NATO.

It has provoked crises of confidence with our oldest friends, including England and France, by bungling such major projects as Skybolt and NATO's nuclear needs.

It has allowed other great alliances—SEATO and CENTO—also to deteriorate, by failing to provide the leadership required for their revitalization and by neglecting their cooperation in keeping the peace.

WEAKNESS BEFORE COMMUNISM

This Administration has sought accommodations with Communism without adequate safeguards and compensating gains for freedom. It has alienated proven allies by opening a "hot line" first with a sworn enemy rather than with a proven friend, and in general pursued a risky path such as began at Munich a quarter century ago.

It has misled the American people and forfeited a priceless opportunity to win concessions for freedom by mishandling sales of farm commodities to Communists. At first it disavowed any intent to subsidize prices or use credit; later it demanded such authority and forced the Democrats in Congress to acquiesce. At first it hinted at concessions for freedom in return for wheat sold to Russia; later it obtained no concessions at all. At first it pledged not to breach restraints on trade with Communist countries in other parts of the world; later it stimulated such trade itself, and thus it encouraged trade with Cuba by America's oldest friends.

This Administration has collaborated with Indonesian imperialism by helping it to acquire territory belonging to the Netherlands and control over the Papuan people.

It has abetted further Communist takeover in

Laos, weakly accepted Communist violations of the Geneva Agreement, which the present Administration perpetrated, and increased Soviet influence in Southeast Asia.

It has encouraged an increase of aggression in South Vietnam by appearing to set limits on America's willingness to act—and then, in the deepening struggle, it has sacrificed the lives of American and allied fighting men by denial of modern equipment.

This Administration has permitted the shooting down of American pilots, the mistreatment of American citizens, and the destruction of American property to become hallmarks of Communist arrogance.

It has stood by as a wire barricade in Berlin became a wall of shame, defacing that great city, humiliating every American, and disgracing free men everywhere.

It has turned its back on the captive peoples of Eastern Europe, abandoning their cause in the United Nations and in the official utterances of our government.

This Administration has forever blackened our nation's honor at the Bay of Pigs, bungling the invasion plan and leaving brave men on Cuban beaches to be shot down. Later the forsaken survivors were ransomed, and Communism was allowed to march deeper into Latin America.

It has turned a deaf ear to pleas from throughout the Western Hemisphere for decisive American leadership to seal off subversion from the Soviet base just off our shore.

It has increased the long-term troubles for America by retreating from its pledge to obtain on-the-spot proof of the withdrawal of Soviet offensive weapons from Cuba.

It left vacant for many critical months the high posts of ambassador in Panama and with the Organization of American States, and thus it failed to anticipate and forestall the anti-American violence that burst forth in Panama.

UNDERMINING THE UNITED NATIONS

This Administration has failed to provide forceful, effective leadership in the United Nations.

It has weakened the power and influence of this world organization by failing to demand basic improvements in its procedures to guard against its becoming merely a forum of anti-Western insult and abuse.

It has refused to insist upon enforcement of the United Nations' rules governing financial support though such enforcement is supported by an advisory opinion of the International Court of Justice.

It has shouldered virtually the full costs of the United Nations' occupation of the Congo, only to have the ousted leadership asked back when United Nations forces had withdrawn.

FORSAKING AMERICA'S INTERESTS

This Administration has subsidized various forms of socialism throughout the world, to the jeopardy of individual freedom and private enterprise.

It has proved itself inept and weak in international trade negotiations, allowing the loss of opportunities historically open to American enterprise and bargaining away markets indispensable to prosperity of American farms.

Failure of National Security Planning

LOSING A CRITICAL LEAD

This Administration has delayed research and development in advanced weapons systems and thus confronted the American people with a fearsome possibility that Soviet advances, in the decade of the 1970's, may surpass America's present lead. Its misuse of "cost effectiveness" has stifled the creativity of the nation's military, scientific and industrial communities.

It has failed to originate a single new major strategic weapons system after inheriting from a Republican Administration the most powerful military force of all time. It has concealed a lack of qualitative advance for the 1970's by speaking of a quantitative strength which by then will be obsolete. It has not demonstrated the foresight necessary to prepare a strategic strength which in future years will deter war.

It has endangered security by downgrading efforts to prepare defenses against enemy ballistic missiles. It has retarded our own military development for near and outer space, while the enemy's development moves on.

INVITATIONS TO DISASTER

This Administration has adopted policies which will lead to a potentially fatal parity of power with Communism instead of continued military superiority for the United States.

It has permitted disarmament negotiations to

proceed without adequate consideration of military judgment—a procedure which tends to bring about, in effect, a unilateral curtailment of American arms rendered the more dangerous by the Administration's discounting known Soviet advances in nuclear weaponry.

It has failed to take minimum safeguards against possible consequences of the limited nuclear test ban treaty, including advanced underground tests where permissible and full readiness to test elsewhere should the need arise.

DISTORTIONS AND BLACKOUTS

This Administration has adopted the policies of news management and unjustifiable secrecy, in the guise of guarding the nation's security; it has shown a contempt of the right of the people to know the truth.

This Administration, while claiming major defense savings, has in fact raised defense spending by billions of dollars a year, and yet has shortchanged critical areas.

UNDERMINING MORALE

This Administration has weakened the bonds of confidence and understanding between civilian leaders and the nation's top military professionals. It has bypassed seasoned military judgment in vital national security policy decisions.

It has permitted non-military considerations, political as well as spurious economic arguments, to reverse professional judgment on major weapons and equipment such as the controversial TFX, the X-22, and the nuclear carrier.

In sum, both in military and foreign affairs, the Democratic record all the world around is one of disappointment and reverses for freedom.

And this record is no better at home.

Failures at Home

INABILITY TO CREATE JOBS

This Administration has failed to honor its pledges to assure good jobs, full prosperity and a rapidly growing economy for all the American people:

—failing to reduce unemployment to four percent, falling far short of its announced goal every single month of its tenure in office; and

—despite glowing promises, allowing a disheartening increase in long-term and youth unemployment.

This Administration has failed to apply Republican-initiated retraining programs where most needed particularly where they could afford new economic opportunities to Negro citizens. It has preferred, instead, divisive political proposals.

It has demonstrated its inability to measure up to the challenge of automation which, wisely guided, will enrich the lives of all people. Administration approaches have been negative and unproductive, as for example the proposed penalties upon the use of overtime. Such penalties would serve only to spread existing unemployment and injure those who create jobs.

It has failed to perform its responsibility under Republican amendments to the Manpower Training Act. It has neglected, for example, the basic requirement of developing a dictionary of labor skills which are locally, regionally and nationally in short supply, even though many thousands of jobs are unfilled today for lack of qualified applicants.

FAILING THE POOR

This Administration has refused to take practical free enterprise measures to help the poor. Under the last Republican Administration, the percentage of poor in the country dropped encouragingly from 28% to 21%. By contrast, the present Administration, despite a massive increase in the Federal bureaucracy, has managed a mere two percentage point reduction.

This Administration has proposed a so-called war on poverty which characteristically overlaps, and often contradicts, the 42 existing Federal poverty programs. It would dangerously centralize Federal controls and bypass effective state, local and private programs.

It has demonstrated little concern for the acute problems created for the poor by inflation. Consumer prices have increased in the past three and a half years by almost 5%, amounting in effect to a 5% national sales tax on the purchases of a family living on fixed income.

Under housing and urban renewal programs, notably in the Nation's Capital, it has created new slums by forcing the poor from their homes to make room for luxury apartments, while neglecting the vital need for adequate relocation assistance.

RETARDING ENTERPRISES

This Administration has violently thrust Federal power into the free market in such areas as steel prices, thus establishing precedents which in future years could critically wound free enterprise in the United States.

It has so discouraged private enterprise that the annual increase in the number of businesses has plummeted from the Republican level of 70,000 a year to 47,000 a year.

It has allowed the rate of business failures to rise higher under its leadership than in any period since depression days.

It has aggravated the problems of small business by multiplying Federal record-keeping requirements and has hurt thousands of small businessmen by forcing up their costs.

This Administration has curtailed, through such agencies as the National Labor Relations Board, the simple, basic right of Americans voluntarily to go into or to go out of business.

It has failed to stimulate new housing and attract more private capital into the field. In the past three years it has fallen short by 1,500,000 units of meeting its pledge of 2,000,000 new homes each year.

It has sought to weaken the patent system which is so largely responsible for America's progress in technology, medicine and science.

It has required private electric power companies to submit to unreasonable Federal controls as a condition to the utilization of rights-of-way over public lands. It has sought to advance, without Congressional authorization, a vastly expensive nationwide electrical transmission grid.

BETRAYAL OF THE FARMER

This Administration has refused, incredibly, to honor the clear mandate of American wheat farmers, in the largest farm referendum ever held, to free them of rigid Federal controls and to restore their birthright to make their own management decisions.

It has strangled the Republican rural development program with red tape and neglected its most essential ingredient, local initiative.

It has broken its major promises to farm people, dropping the parity ratio to its lowest level since 1939. It has dumped surplus stocks so as to lower farm income and increase the vicious cost-price squeeze on the farmer.

It has evidenced hostility toward American livestock producers by proposals to establish mandatory marketing quotas on all livestock, to fine and imprison dairy farmers failing to maintain Federally-acceptable records, and to establish a subsidized grazing cropland conversion program. It has allowed imports of beef and other meat products to rise to an all-time high during a slump in cattle prices which was aggravated by government grain sales.

NEGLECT OF NATURAL RESOURCES

This Administration has delayed the expeditious handling of oil shale patent applications and the early development of a domestic oil shale industry.

It has allowed the deterioration of the domestic mining and petroleum industries including displacement of domestic markets by foreign imports.

It has failed to protect the American fishing industry and has retreated from policies providing equitable sharing of international fishing grounds.

FISCAL IRRESPONSIBILITY

This Administration has misled the American people by such budget manipulations as crowding spending into the previous fiscal year, presenting a proposal to sell off $2.3 billion in government assets as a cut in spending, and using bookkeeping devices to make expenditures seem smaller than they actually are.

It has, despite pledges of economy, burdened this nation with four unbalanced budgets in a row, creating deficits totaling $26 billion, with still more debt to come, reflecting a rate of sustained deficit spending unmatched in peacetime.

It has failed to establish sensible priorities for Federal funds. In consequence, it has undertaken needlessly expensive crash programs, as for example accelerating a trip to the moon, to the neglect of other critical needs such as research into health and the increasingly serious problems of air and water pollution and urban crowding.

This Administration has continued to endanger retirement under Social Security for millions of citizens; it has attempted to overload the System with costly, unrelated programs which ignore the dangers of overly regressive taxation and the unfairness of forcing the poor to finance such programs for the rich.

It has demanded the elimination of a substantial portion of personal income tax deductions for charitable and church contributions, for real property taxes paid by home owners, and for interest payments. The elimination of these deductions would impose great hardship upon millions of our citizens and discourage the growth of some of the finest organizations in America.

This Administration has impeded investigations of suspected wrongdoing which might implicate public officials in the highest offices in the land. It has thus aroused justifiable resentment against those who use the high road of public service as the low road to illicitly acquired wealth.

It has permitted the quality and morale of the postal system to deteriorate and drastically restricted its services. It has made the Post Office almost inaccessible to millions of working people, reduced the once admired Parcel Post System to a national laughing stock—and yet it is intimated that Americans may soon have to pay 8¢ for a first-class postage stamp.

It has resisted personal income tax credits for education, always preferring the route leading to Federal control over our schools. Some leading Democrats have even campaigned politically in favor of such tax credits while voting against them in Congress.

Contrary to the intent of the Manpower Training Act, it has sought to extend Department of Labor influence over vocational education.

DISCORD AND DISCONTENT

This Administration has exploited interracial tensions by extravagant campaign promises, without fulfillment, playing on the just aspirations of the minority groups, encouraging disorderly and lawless elements, and ineffectually administering the laws.

It has subjected career civil servants and part-time Federal employees, including employees of the Agriculture Department, to political pressures harmful to the integrity of the entire Federal service. It has weakened veterans' preference in Federal jobs.

It has made Federal intervention, even on the Presidential level, a standard operating practice in labor disputes, thus menacing the entire system of free collective bargaining.

It has resorted to police state tactics, using the great power of Federal Departments and agencies, to compel compliance with Administration desires, notably in the steel price dispute. The Department

of Justice, in particular, has been used improperly to achieve partisan political, economic, and legislative goals. This abuse of power should be the subject of a Congressional investigation.

WEAKENING RESPONSIBILITY

This Administration has moved, through such undertakings as its so-called war on poverty, accelerated public works and the New Communities Program in the 1964 housing proposal, to establish new Federal offices duplicating existing agencies, bypassing the state capitals, thrusting aside local government, and siphoning off to Washington the administration of private citizen and community affairs.

It has undermined the Federally-assisted, State-operated medical and hospital assistance program, while using—and abusing—Federal authority to force a compulsory hospital program upon the people and the Congress.

This enumeration is necessarily incomplete. It does not exhaust the catalog of misdeeds and failures of the present Administration. And let the nation realize that the full impact of these many ill-conceived and ill-fated activities of the Democratic Administration is yet to come.

SECTION THREE
The Republican Alternative

We Republicans are not content to record Democratic misdeeds and failures. We now offer policies and programs new in conception and dynamic in operation. These we urge to recapture initiative for freedom at home and abroad and to rebuild our strength at home.

Nor is this a new role. Republican Presidents from Abraham Lincoln to Dwight D. Eisenhower stand as witness that Republican leadership is steadfast in principle, clear in purpose and committed to progress. The many achievements of the Eisenhower Administration in strengthening peace abroad and the well-being of all at home have been unmatched in recent times. A new Republican Administration will stand proudly on this record.

We do not submit, in this platform, extravagant promises to be cynically cast aside after election day. Rather, we offer examples of Republican initiatives in areas of overriding concern to the whole nation—North, South, East and West—which befit a truly national party. In the interest of brevity, we do not repeat the commitments of the 1960 Republican Platform, "Building a Better America," and the 1962 "Declaration of Republican Principle and Policy." We incorporate into this Platform as pledges renewed those commitments which are relevant to the problems of 1964.

These, then, will be our guides, and these our additional pledges, in meeting the nation's needs.

Faith in the Individual

1. We Republicans shall first rely on the individual's right and capacity to advance his own economic well-being, to control the fruits of his efforts and to plan his own and his family's future; and, where government is rightly involved, we shall assist the individual in surmounting urgent problems beyond his own power and responsibility to control. For instance, we pledge:

—enlargement of employment opportunities for urban and rural citizens, with emphasis on training programs to equip them with needed skills; improved job information and placement services; and research and extension services channeled toward helping rural people improve their opportunities;

—tax credits and other methods of assistance to help needy senior citizens meet the costs of medical and hospital insurance;

—a strong, sound system of Social Security, with improved benefits to our people;

—continued Federal support for a sound research program aimed at both the prevention and cure of diseases, and intensified efforts to secure prompt and effective application of the results of research. This will include emphasis on mental illness, drug addiction, alcoholism, cancer, heart disease and other diseases of increasing incidence;

—revision of the Social Security laws to allow higher earnings, without loss of benefits, by our elderly people;

—full coverage of all medical and hospital costs for the needy elderly people, financed by general revenues through broader implementation of Federal-State plans, rather than the compulsory Democratic scheme covering only a small percentage of such costs, for everyone regardless of need;

—adoption and implementation of a fair and adequate program for providing necessary supplemental farm labor for producing and harvesting agricultural commodities;

—tax credits for those burdened by the expenses of college education;

—vocational rehabilitation, through cooperation between government—Federal and State—and industry, for the mentally and physically handicapped, the chronically unemployed and the poverty-stricken;

—incentives for employers to hire teenagers, including broadening of temporary exemptions under the minimum wage law;

—to repeal the Administration's wheat certificate "bread-tax" on consumers, so burdensome to low-income families and overwhelmingly rejected by farmers;

—revision of present non-service-connected pension programs to provide increased benefits for low income pensioners, with emphasis on rehabilitation, nursing homes and World War I veterans;

—re-evaluation of the armed forces' manpower procurement programs with the goal of replacing involuntary inductions as soon as possible by an efficient voluntary system, offering real career incentives;

—enactment of legislation, despite Democratic opposition, to curb the flow through the mails of obscene materials which has flourished into a multimillion dollar obscenity racket;

—support of a Constitutional amendment permitting those individuals and groups who choose to do so to exercise their religion freely in public places, provided religious exercises are not prepared or prescribed by the state or political subdivision thereof and no person's participation therein is coerced, thus preserving the traditional separation of church and state;

—full implementation and faithful execution of the Civil Rights Act of 1964, and all other civil rights statutes, to assure equal rights and opportunities guaranteed by the Constitution to every citizen;

—improvements of civil rights statutes adequate to changing needs of our times;

—such additional administrative or legislative actions as may be required to end the denial, for whatever unlawful reason, of the right to vote;

—immigration legislation seeking to re-unite families and continuation of the "Fair Share" Refugee Program;

—continued opposition to discrimination based on race, creed, national origin or sex. We recognize that the elimination of any such discrimination is a matter of heart, conscience, and education, as well as of equal rights under law.

In all such programs, where Federal initiative is properly involved to relieve or prevent misfortune or meet overpowering need, it will be the Republican way to move promptly and energetically, and wherever possible to provide assistance of a kind enabling the individual to gain or regain the capability to make his own way and to have a fair chance to achieve his own goals. In all matters relating to human rights it will be the Republican way fully to implement all applicable laws and never to lose sight of the intense need for advancing peaceful progress in human relations in our land. The Party of Abraham Lincoln will proudly and faithfully live up to its heritage of equal rights and equal opportunities for all.

In furtherance of our faith in the individual, we also pledge prudent, responsible management of the government's fiscal affairs to protect the individual against the evils of spendthrift government —protecting most of all the needy and fixed-income families against the cruelest tax, inflation —and protecting every citizen against the high taxes forced by excessive spending, in order that each individual may keep more of his earnings for his own and his family's use. For instance, we pledge:

—a reduction of not less than five billion dollars in the present level of Federal spending;

—an end to chronic deficit financing, proudly reaffirming our belief in a balanced budget;

—further reduction in individual and corporate tax rates as fiscal discipline is restored;

—repayments on the public debt;

—maintenance of an administrative, legislative and regulatory climate encouraging job-building enterprise to help assure every individual a real chance for a good job;

—wise, firm and responsible conduct of the nation's foreign affairs, backed by military forces kept modern, strong and ready, thereby assuring every individual of a future promising peace.

In all such matters it will be the Republican way so to conduct the affairs of government as to give the individual citizen the maximum assurance of a peaceful and prosperous future, freed of the discouragement and hardship produced by wasteful and ineffectual government.

In furtherance of our faith in the individual, we also pledge the maximum restraint of Federal intrusions into matters more productively left to the individual. For instance, we pledge:

—to continue Republican sponsorship of practical Federal-State-local programs which will effectively treat the needs of the poor, while resisting direct Federal handouts that erode away individual self-reliance and self-respect and perpetuate dependency;

—to continue the advancement of education on all levels, through such programs as selective aid to higher education, strengthened State and local tax resources, including tax credits for college education, while resisting the Democratic efforts which endanger local control of schools;

—to help assure equal opportunity and a good education for all, while opposing Federally-sponsored "inverse discrimination," whether by the shifting of jobs, or the abandonment of neighborhood schools, for reasons of race;

—to provide our farmers, who have contributed so much to the strength of our nation, with the maximum opportunity to exercise their own management decisions on their own farms, while resisting all efforts to impose upon them further Federal controls;

—to establish realistic priorities for the concentration of Federal spending in the most productive and creative areas, such as education, job training, vocational rehabilitation, educational research, oceanography, and the wise development and use of natural resources in the water as well as on land, while resisting Democratic efforts to spend wastefully and indiscriminately;

—to open avenues of peaceful progress in solving racial controversies while discouraging lawlessness and violence.

In all such matters, it will be the Republican way to assure the individual of maximum freedom as government meets its proper responsibilities, while resisting the Democratic obsession to impose from above, uniform and rigid schemes for meeting varied and complex human problems.

Faith in the Competitive System

2. We Republicans shall vigorously protect the dynamo of economic growth—free, competitive enterprise—that has made America the envy of the world. For instance, we pledge:

—removal of the wartime Federal excise taxes, favored by the Democratic Administration, on pens, pencils, jewelry, cosmetics, luggage, handbags, wallets and toiletries;

—assistance to small business by simplifying

Federal and State tax and regulatory requirements, fostering the availability of longer term credit at fair terms and equity capital for small firms, encouraging strong State programs to foster small business, establishing more effective measures to assure a sharing by small business in Federal procurement, and promoting wider export opportunities;

—an end to power-grabbing regulatory actions, such as the reach by the Federal Trade Commission for injunctive powers and the ceaseless pressing by the White House, the Food and Drug Administration and Federal Trade Commission to dominate consumer decisions in the market place;

—returning the consumer to the driver's seat as the chief regulator and chief beneficiary of a free economy, by resisting excessive concentration of power, whether public or private;

—a drastic reduction in burdensome Federal paperwork and overlapping regulations, which weigh heavily on small businessmen struggling to compete and to provide jobs;

—a determined drive, through tough, realistic negotiations, to remove the many discriminatory and restrictive trade practices of foreign nations;

—greater emphasis on overseas sales of surplus farm commodities to friendly countries through long-term credits repayable in dollars under the Republican Food for Peace program;

—dedication to freedom of expression for all news media, to the right of access by such media to public proceedings, and to the independence of radio, television and other news-gathering media from excessive government control;

—improvement, and full and fair enforcement, of the anti-trust statutes, coupled with long-overdue clarification of Federal policies and interpretations relating thereto in order to strengthen competition and protect the consumer and small business;

—constant opposition to any form of unregulated monopoly, whether business or labor;

—meaningful safeguards against irreparable injuries to any domestic industries by disruptive surges of imports, such as in the case of beef and other meat products, textiles, oil, glass, coal, lumber and steel;

—enactment of law, such as the Democratic Administration vetoed in the 88th Congress, requiring that labels of imported items clearly disclose their foreign origin;

—completely reorganize the National Labor Relations Board to assure impartial protection of the rights of the public, employees and employers, ending the defiance of Congress by the present Board;

—the redevelopment of an atmosphere of confidence throughout the government and across the nation, in which vigorous competition can flourish.

In all such matters it will be the Republican way to support, not harass—to encourage, not restrain—to build confidence, not threaten—to provide stability, not unrest—to speed genuine growth, not conjure up statistical fantasies and to assure that all actions of government apply fairly to every element of the nation's economy.

In furtherance of our faith in the competitive system, we also pledge:

—a continual re-examination and reduction of government competition with private business, consistent with the recommendations of the second Hoover Commission;

—elimination of excessive bureaucracy;

—full protection of the integrity of the career governmental services, military and civilian, coupled with adequate pay scales;

—maximum reliance upon subordinate levels of government and individual citizens to meet the nation's needs, in place of establishing even more Federal agencies to burden the people.

In all such matters relating to Federal administration it will be the Republican way to provide maximum service for each tax dollar expended, watchfully superintend the size and scope of Federal activities, and assure an administration always fair, efficient and cooperatively disposed toward every element of our competitive system.

Faith in Limited Government

3. We Republicans shall insist that the Federal Government have effective but limited powers, that it be frugal and efficient, and that it fully meet its Constitutional responsibilities to all the American people. For instance, we pledge:

—restoration of collective bargaining responsibility to labor and management, minimizing third-party intervention and preventing any agency of government from becoming an advocate for any private economic interest;

—development of truly voluntary commodity programs for commercial agriculture, including payments in kind out of government-owned surpluses, diversion of unneeded land to conservation uses, price supports free of political manipulation in order to stimulate and attain fair market prices, together with adequate credit facilities and continued support of farm-owned and operated cooperatives including rural electric and telephone facilities, while resisting all efforts to make the farmer dependent, for his economic survival, upon either compensatory payments by the Federal Government or upon the whim of the Secretary of Agriculture;

—full cooperation of all governmental levels and private enterprise in advancing the balanced use of the nation's natural resources to provide for man's multiple needs;

—continuing review of public-land laws and policies to assure maximum opportunity for all beneficial uses of the public lands; including the development of mineral resources;

—comprehensive water-resource planning and development, including projects for our growing cities, expanded research in desalinization of water, and continued support of multi-purpose reclamation projects;

—support of sustained yield management of our forests and expanded research for control of forest insects, disease, and forest fires;

—protection of traditional domestic fishing grounds and other actions, including tax incentives, to encourage modernization of fishing vessels, and improve processing and marketing practices;

—continued tax support to encourage exploration and development of domestic sources of minerals and metals, with reasonable depletion allowances;

—stabilization of present oil programs, private development of atomic power, increased coal research and expansion of coal exports;

—a replanning of the present space program to provide for a more orderly, yet aggressively pursued, step-by-step development, remaining alert to the danger of overdiversion of skilled personnel in critical shortage from other vital areas such as health, industry, education and science.

In furtherance of our faith in limited, frugal and efficient government we also pledge:

—credit against Federal taxes for specified State and local taxes paid, and a transfer to the States of excise and other Federal tax sources, to reinforce the fiscal strength of State and local govern-

ments so that they may better meet rising school costs and other pressing urban and suburban problems such as transportation, housing, water systems and juvenile delinquency;

—emphasis upon channeling more private capital into sound urban development projects and private housing;

—critical re-examination and major overhaul of all Federal grant-in-aid programs with a view to channeling such programs through the States, discontinuing those no longer required and adjusting others in a determined effort to restore the unique balance and creative energy of the traditional American system of government;

—revitalization of municipal and county governments throughout America by encouraging them, and private citizens as well, to develop new solutions of their major concerns through a streamlining and modernizing of state and local processes of government, and by a renewed consciousness of their ability to reach these solutions, not through Federal action, but through their own capabilities;

—support of a Constitutional amendment, as well as legislation, enabling States having bicameral legislatures to apportion one House on bases of their choosing, including factors other than population;

—complete reform of the tax structure, to include simplification as well as lower rates to strengthen individual and business incentives;

—effective budgetary reform, improved Congressional appropriation procedures, and full implementation of the anti-deficiency statute;

—a wide-ranging reform of other Congressional procedures, including the provision of adequate professional staff assistance for the minority membership on Congressional Committees, to insure that the power and prestige of Congress remain adequate to the needs of the times;

—high priority for the solution of the nation's balance of payment difficulties to assure unquestioned confidence in the dollar, maintenance of the competitiveness of American products in domestic and foreign markets, expansion of exports, stimulation of foreign tourism in the United States, greater foreign sharing of mutual security burdens abroad, a drastic reorganization and redirection of the entire foreign aid effort, gradual reductions in overseas U. S. forces as manpower can be replaced by increased firepower; and strengthening of the international monetary system without sacrifice of our freedom of policy making.

In all such matters it will be the Republican way to achieve not feigned but genuine savings, allowing a reduction of the public debt and additional tax reductions while meeting the proper responsibilities of government. We pledge an especially determined effort to help strengthen the ability of State and local governments to meet the broad range of needs facing the nation's urban and suburban communities.

SECTION FOUR

Freedom Abroad

The Republican commitment to individual freedom applies no less abroad.

America must advance freedom throughout the world as a vital condition of orderly human progress, universal justice, and the security of the American people.

The supreme challenge to this policy is an atheistic imperialism-Communism.

Our nation's leadership must be judged by—indeed, American independence and even survival are dependent upon—the stand it takes toward Communism.

That stand must be: victory for freedom. There can be no peace, there can be no security, until this goal is won.

As long as Communist leaders remain ideologically fixed upon ruling the world, there can be no lesser goal. This is the supreme test of America's foreign policy. It must not be defaulted. In the balance is human liberty everyplace on earth.

Reducing the Risks of War

A dynamic strategy aimed at victory pressing always for initiatives for freedom, rejecting always appeasement and withdrawal—reduces the risk of nuclear war. It is a nation's vacillation, not firmness, that tempts an aggressor into war. It is accommodation, not opposition, that encourages a hostile nation to remain hostile and to remain aggressive.

The road to peace is a road not of fawning amiability but of strength and respect. Republicans judge foreign policy by its success in advancing freedom and justice, not by its effect on international prestige polls.

In making foreign policy, these will be our guidelines:

Trusting Ourselves and Our Friends

1. Secrecy in foreign policy must be at a minimum, public understanding at a maximum. Our own citizens, rather than those of other nations, should be accorded primary trust.

2. Consultation with our allies should take precedence over direct negotiations with Communist powers. The bypassing of our allies has contributed greatly to the shattering of free world unity and to the loss of free world continuity in opposing Communism.

Communism's Course

3. We reject the notion that Communism has abandoned its goal of world domination, or that fat and well-fed Communists are less dangerous than lean and hungry ones. We also reject the notion that the United States should take sides in the Sino-Soviet rift.

Republican foreign policy starts with the assumption that Communism is the enemy of this nation in every sense until it can prove that its enmity has been abandoned.

4. We hold that trade with Communist countries should not be directed toward the enhancement of their power and influence but could only be justified if it would serve to diminish their power.

5. We are opposed to the recognition of Red China. We oppose its admission into the United Nations. We steadfastly support free China.

6. In negotiations with Communists, Republicans will probe tirelessly for reasonable, practicable and trustworthy agreements. However, we will never abandon insistence on advantages for the free world.

7. Republicans will continue to work for the realization of the Open Skies policy proposed in 1955 by President Eisenhower. Only open societies offer real hope of confidence among nations.

Communism's Captives

8. Republicans reaffirm their long-standing commitment to a course leading to eventual liberation of the Communist-dominated nations of Eastern Europe, Asia and Latin America, including the peoples of Hungary, Poland, East Germany, Czechoslovakia, Rumania, Albania, Bulgaria, Latvia, Lithuania, Estonia, Armenia, Ukraine, Yugoslavia, and its Serbian, Croatian and Slovene peoples, Cuba, mainland China, and many others.

We condemn the persecution of minorities, such as the Jews, within Communist borders.

The United Nations

9. Republicans support the United Nations. However, we will never rest in our efforts to revitalize its original purpose.

We will press for a change in the method of voting in the General Assembly and in the specialized agencies that will reflect population disparities among the member states and recognize differing abilities and willingness to meet the obligations of the Charter. We will insist upon General Assembly acceptance of the International Court of Justice advisory opinion, upholding denial of the votes of member nations which refuse to meet properly levied assessments, so that the United Nations will more accurately reflect the power realities of the world. Further to assure the carrying out of these recommendations and to correct the above abuses, we urge the calling of an amending convention of the United Nations by the year 1967.

Republicans will never surrender to any international group the responsibility of the United States for its sovereignty, its own security, and the leadership of the free world.

NATO: The Great Shield

10. Republicans regard NATO as indispensable for the prevention of war and the protection of freedom. NATO's unity and vitality have alarmingly deteriorated under the present Administration. It is a keystone of Republican foreign policy to revitalize the Alliance.

To hasten its restoration, Republican leadership will move immediately to establish an international commission, comprised of individuals of high competence in NATO affairs, whether in or out of government, to explore and recommend effective new ways to strengthen alliance participation and fulfillment.

Freedom's Further Demands

11. To our nation's associates in SEATO and CENTO, Republicans pledge reciprocal dedication of purpose and revitalized interest. These great alliances, with NATO, must be returned to the forefront of foreign policy planning. A strengthened alliance system is equally necessary in the Western Hemisphere.

This will remain our constant purpose: Republicans will labor tirelessly with free men everywhere and in every circumstance toward the defeat of Communism and victory for freedom.

The Geography of Freedom

12. In diverse regions of the world, Republicans will make clear to any hostile nation that the United States will increase the costs and risks of aggression to make them outweigh hopes for gain. It was just such a communication and determination by the Eisenhower Republican Administration that produced the 1953 Korean Armistice. The same strategy can win victory for freedom and stop further aggression in Southeast Asia.

We will move decisively to assure victory in South Vietnam. While confining the conflict as closely as possible, America must move to end the fighting in a reasonable time and provide guarantees against further aggression. We must make it clear to the Communist world that, when conflict is forced with America, it will end only in victory for freedom.

We will demand that the Berlin Wall be taken down prior to the resumption of any negotiations with the Soviet Union on the status of forces in, or treaties affecting, Germany.

We will reassure our German friends that the United States will not accept any plan for the future of Germany which lacks firm assurance of a free election on reunification.

We will urge the immediate implementation of the Caracas Declaration of Solidarity against international Communist intervention endorsed in 1954 by the Organization of American States during the Eisenhower Administration, which Declaration, in accordance with the historic Monroe Doctrine, our nation's official policy since 1823, opposes domination of any of our neighbor-nations by any power outside this Hemisphere.

We will vigorously press our OAS partners to join the United States in restoring a free and independent government in Cuba, stopping the spread of Sino-Soviet subversion, forcing the withdrawal of the foreign military presence now in Latin America, and preventing future intrusions. We Republicans will recognize a Cuban government in exile; we will support its efforts to regain the independence of its homeland; we will assist Cuban freedom fighters in carrying on guerrilla warfare against the Communist regime; we will work for an economic boycott by all nations of the free world in trade with Cuba; and we will encourage free elections in Cuba after liberty and stability are restored.

We will consider raising the economic participation of the Republic of Panama in the operation of the Panama Canal and assure the safety of Americans in the area. We will reaffirm this nation's treaty rights and study the feasibility of a substitute, sea-level canal at an appropriate location including the feasibility of nuclear excavation.

Republicans will make clear to all Communists now supporting or planning to support guerrilla and subversive activities, that henceforth there will be no privileged sanctuaries to protect those who disrupt the peace of the world. We will make clear that blockade, interception of logistical support, and diplomatic and economic pressure are appropriate United States counters to deliberate breaches of the peace.

We will make clear to all Communist leaders everywhere that aggressive actions, including those in the German air corridors, will be grounds for re-evaluation of any and all trade or diplomatic relations currently to Communism's advantage.

We will take the cold war offensive on all fronts, including, for example, a reinvigorated USIA. It will broadcast not our weaknesses but our strengths. It will mount a psychological warfare attack on behalf of freedom and against Communist doctrine and imperialism.

Republicans will recast foreign aid programs. We will see that all will serve the cause of freedom. We will see that none bolster and sustain anti-American regimes; we will increase the use of private capital on a partnership basis with foreign nationals, as a means of fostering independence and mutual respect but we assert that property of American Nationals must not be expropriated by any foreign government without prompt and adequate compensation as contemplated by international law.

Respecting the Middle East, and in addition to our reaffirmed pledges of 1960 concerning this area, we will so direct our economic and military assistance as to help maintain stability in this region and prevent an imbalance of arms.

Finally, we will improve the efficiency and coordination of the foreign service, and provide adequate allowance for foreign service personnel.

The Development of Freedom

13. Freedom's wealth must never support freedom's decline, always its growth. America's tax revenues derived from free enterprise sources must never be employed in support of socialism. America must assist young and underdeveloped nations. In the process, however, we must not sacrifice the trust of old friends.

Our assistance, also, must be conditional upon self-help and progress toward the development of free institutions. We favor the establishment in underdeveloped nations of an economic and political climate that will encourage the investment of local capital and attract the investment of foreign capital.

Freedom's Shield—and Sword

Finally, Republicans pledge to keep the nation's sword sharp, ready, and dependable.

We will maintain a superior, not merely equal, military capability as long as the Communist drive for world domination continues. It will be a capability of balanced force, superior in all its arms, maintaining flexibility for effective performance in the rapidly changing science of war.

Republicans will never unilaterally disarm America.

We will demand that any arms reduction plan worthy of consideration guarantee reliable inspection. We will demand that any such plan assure this nation of sufficient strength, step by step, to forestall and defend against possible violations.

We will take every step necessary to carry forward the vital military research and development programs. We will pursue these programs as absolutely necessary to assure our nation of superior strength in the 1970's.

We will revitalize research and development programs needed to enable the nation to develop advanced new weapons systems, strategic as well as tactical.

We will include the fields of anti-submarine warfare, astronautics and aeronautics, special guerrilla forces, and such other defense systems required to keep America ready for any threat.

We will fully implement such safeguards as our security requires under the limited nuclear test ban treaty. We will conduct advanced tests in permissible areas, maintain facilities to test elsewhere in case of violations, and develop to the fullest our ability to detect Communist transgressions. Additionally, we will regularly review the status of nuclear weaponry under the limited nuclear test ban to assure this nation's protection. We shall also provide sensible, continuing reviews of the treaty itself.

We will end "second-best" weapons policies. We will end the false economies which place price ahead of the performance upon which American lives may depend. Republicans will bring an end once again to the "peak and valley" defense planning, so costly in morale and strength as well as in dollars. We will prepare a practical civil defense program.

We will restore the morale of our armed forces by upgrading military professionalism, and we will allow professional dissent while insuring that strong and sound civilian authority controls objective decision-making.

We will return the Joint Chiefs of Staff to their lawful status as the President's principal military advisors. We will insure that an effective planning and operations staff is restored to the National Security Council.

We will reconsecrate this nation to human liberty, assuring the freedom of our people, and rallying mankind to a new crusade for freedom all around the world.

We Republicans, with the help of Almighty God, will keep those who would bury America aware that this nation has the strength and also the will to defend its every interest. Those interests, we shall make clear, include the preservation and expansion of freedom—and ultimately its victory—everyplace on earth.

We do not offer the easy way. We offer dedication and perseverance, leading to victory. This is our Platform. This is the Republican way.

Socialist Labor Platform 1964

The Socialist Labor Party of America, in National Convention assembled on the 3rd day of May, 1964, reaffirms its previous platform pronouncements and declares:

Humanity stands today on the threshold of a new social order. The old order—capitalism—is doomed; it is an outmoded system charged with fatal contradictions.

On the one hand, since World War II, there

have come into being productive industrial and scientific forces which no former epoch in human history ever experienced. On the other hand, there exist unmistakable symptoms of social anarchy, dissolution and decay. "Everything seems pregnant with its contrary." Automated machinery, gifted with the wonderful power of freeing mankind from want and arduous toil, becomes a menace, intensifying the insecurity of the workers.

It is a grim and portentous fact that for the mass of mankind, that is, for the wage workers who perform the mental and manual labors of society, the future never loomed more threateningly. At the very time when, because of the great upsurge in population, youths are pouring into the labor market in unprecedented numbers, automation is wiping out jobs at the rate of more than 2,000,000 a year. And there is every evidence that this rate will rise as new automation techniques and systems, already completed and tested, spread through America's offices and factories.

President Johnson has attested that by 1970 "this country, because of increased productivity, will be able to match the output of the 1960s with 20 million fewer workers."

Phony Antipoverty Wars

Against this bleak background, the antipoverty "wars" recently declared by the politicians of both major parties—to the accompaniment of much self-glorification—are exposed as hypocritical exercises in utter futility.

The forces under capitalism that breed poverty and that make the lives of workers more insecure, are in the ascendant. Therefore, reform attempts at lessening poverty must inevitably fail.

In opposition to the capitalist politicians with their phony antipoverty "wars", the Socialist Labor Party proposes a plan, not for lessening poverty, but for its total abolition. We present a summary of the plan here and earnestly urge the serious consideration of it by all thoughtful voters.

In all previous epochs of human history poverty for the mass of the people was inescapable. There was simply not enough to go around. It was unavoidable that some should suffer deprivation in order that others might have the freedom from want and the leisure in which to develop science and culture.

Capitalism's Best-Kept Secret

Not so today. The most luminous fact of our age is this: *There is no longer any excuse whatever for the involuntary poverty of a single member of society.* Material conditions have changed so radically that, far from insufficiency, there is today the material possibility of abundance for everyone, and the promise of leisure in which to enjoy it.

Accordingly, today—right now—the material foundations exist for a world of general affluence, cooperation and social harmony, which is to say, for a Socialist world. In this world, all the means of production, distribution and social services will be socially owned and democratically controlled and administered in the interest of all society. The insane contradiction of poverty in the midst of plenty will be completely eliminated. Private profit, as the objective of human endeavor, will be abolished. Instead, every decision will be determined by human needs and human desires. The ugly, unsanitary workshops of capitalism will be turned into pleasant, sanitary production laboratories. Factories will be designed and constructed to insure the greatest possible measure of safety, health and efficiency.

Work itself will cease to be an ordeal in tedium, a spiritless repetition of motions for someone else's profits. Wherever possible tasks that are hazardous or strenuous will be mechanized. Where this is not possible, special dispensations will be made, such as shorter hours of work for those performing these tasks. Meanwhile, in this Socialist world, the working day, week and year for everyone will be cut to a fraction of what it is today.

The whole concept of work will undergo drastic change. Education, emancipated from the anti-intellectual conditions and restrictions of capitalism, will be greatly expanded and revolutionized. Every youth will have the widest possible opportunity to develop all his potentialities for living fully, cooperatively and constructively.

In this Socialist world all who perform useful work will receive, directly and indirectly, all that they produce. And this will be the equivalent of several times the average income of workers today.

In our Socialist world, democracy will be a vibrant, meaningful reality, not the mask for economic despotism that it is today. There will be no such ridiculous thing as a political government based, as today, on wholly arbitrary and artificial demarcations. (Some of our state boundaries were determined by a king's grant two and a half centuries ago; they are meaningless in the industrial age!) To administer social production in the interests of the people we need an *industrial democracy,* a government based on industrial constituencies.

In this society there will be no capitalist masters and no political or bureaucratic masters either. We will vote where we work, electing our representatives to administrative and planning bodies on an ascending scale. But note this: The people whom we elect to administrative posts will have the privilege to serve, never the power to rule. For the same rank and file that elects them will have the power to recall and replace them at will.

Government's Duties Under Socialism

Unlike the politicians of capitalism, who spend their time pulling the wool over the eyes of the workers, the democratically elected administrators and planners of Socialism will be concerned with such practical things as what and how much to produce to insure an uninterrupted flow of the good things of life in abundance; the number of working hours required in the various industries; the erection of plants of production and of educational, health and recreational facilities; the development of new technology; the disposition of machinery; the erection of new housing in the proper places; the de-pollution of streams and lakes; the conservation of resources and the restoration of the natural environment and its preservation in perpetuity.

All that stands in the way of this heaven on earth, a world in which all may enjoy good housing, abundant and nourishing food, the finest clothing, and the best of cultural, educational and recreational advantages, is the outmoded capitalist system.

This is no exaggeration. Nor merely a beautiful dream. It is based on the solid foundation of present facts. Automation, the supreme triumph of technology, has brought this heaven on earth within our reach. Yet, privately owned, as are all productive instruments under capitalism, automation is a blessing only to the capitalist owner; for workers—white collar and blue collar alike—it is a curse, a job-killer, which adds terrifying dimensions to their insecurity and suffering.

THE NUMBER ONE QUESTION

Thus the question we face comes down to this: In the words of Supreme Court Justice William O. Douglas: *"When the machine displaces man and does most of the work, who will own the machines and receive the rich dividends?"*

The American Constitution, in effect, legalizes revolution. The right to alter or abolish the social system and form of government is implicit in Article V, the Constitution's amendment clause. The Socialist Labor Party proposes to the American workers that we use our huge majorities at the polls to outlaw capitalist ownership and to make the means of social production the property of all the people collectively.

The Socialist Labor Party proposes further that we workers consolidate our economic forces on the industrial field in one integral Socialist Industrial Union to back up the peaceful Socialist ballot with an irresistible and invincible might capable of taking and holding the industries, locking out the outvoted capitalist class, if it defies the victory at the ballot box, and continuing social production without interruption.

The Scottish essayist and historian, Thomas Carlyle, is credited with the following statement: "We must some day, at last and forever, cross the line between Nonsense and Common Sense. And on that day we shall pass from Class Paternalism . . . to Human Brotherhood . . . ; from Political Government to Industrial Administration; from Competition in Individualism to Individuality in Cooperation; from War and Despotism, in any form, to Peace and Liberty."

We must cross that line some day—why not now? Repudiate the Republican and Democratic parties, the political Siamese twins of capitalism—and reject also the self-styled "radicals" and "liberals" whose platforms consist of measures to reform and patch up the poverty-breeding capitalist system, which is past reforming and patching. Study the Socialist Labor Party's Socialist Industrial Union program. Support the Socialist Labor Party's entire ticket at the polls. Unite with us to save humanity from catastrophe—and to set an example in free industrial self-government for all mankind, in affluence and enduring peace!

Socialist Workers Platform 1964

In his State of the Union message President Johnson spoke of "one-fifth of all American families with income too small to even meet their basic needs." It is to these underprivileged millions, and to all whose lives are blighted under capitalism, that the Socialist Workers Party addresses itself. We advance a socialist program for a real and lasting solution of the grave problems afflicting our society today, and they are many.

Technological change and speed-up, designed to cut labor costs and hike corporation profits, displace workers from their jobs at an increasing rate. Meanwhile, the rate at which new jobs are created is slowing down, causing a built-in rise in chronic unemployment. Hardest hit are the unskilled and older workers, youth, Negroes and other minorities; and to an increasing degree whole local areas are becoming depression pockets of hunger and poverty.

At the best, jobless benefits fall short of take-home pay and force a cut in living standards, and in no case is compensation guaranteed for the full period of unemployment. Some categories of workers get no jobless benefits at all. Older people retired from their jobs get pitifully small pensions, sometimes none whatever. People forced to ask for public relief get a stingy dole; they are subjected to a humiliating "poverty" test; children are pressured to take financial responsibility for their parents; and those on relief are slandered as "shiftless and immoral" by venal politicians anxious to curry favor with the wealthy tax dodgers.

People able to earn their own income are gouged by stiff taxes in open and concealed forms. Employed and unemployed alike face steadily rising prices. To try to get ahead, and often even to get by, families must resort more and more to installment buying, mortgaging tomorrow's earnings to meet today's needs.

Decent housing becomes ever scarcer and rents more outrageous. Public transportation systems break down almost as fast as fares go up. Classrooms in decaying school buildings are overcrowded with students and understaffed by underpaid teachers. There are not enough hospitals, not enough nurses or doctors, and the cost of medical care under the profit system is a crime against humanity.

BLEAK FUTURE

Millions of the nation's youth face a bleak future. Those lucky enough to get a fairly good education have no assurance they will find a decent, permanent job with good prospects for advancement, on which they could begin to build a secure and rewarding life. Young men have far greater assurance of being drafted into military service, maybe to die in some far away land, made to fight for something they don't really understand. When jobless in civilian life, youth generally are treated more as a police problem of "juvenile delinquency" than as economically-displaced humans who deserve a better break from society.

For Negroes, Mexicans, Puerto Ricans and other minorities the problems are the most severe. Those employed usually draw the dirtiest, hardest, lowest-paid jobs. They are largely restricted to ghetto life in slum areas where they must pay high rent for squalid quarters. Their neighborhood schools are the poorest, most overcrowded, least well staffed. Such social services as are extended to them are at the lowest level. Police brutality is an unending part of their everyday existence, and most everywhere they go they face open or thinly-veiled discrimination that violates their human dignity and blights their lives.

Under capitalism today only one thing is shared by all. Men and women, old and young, the well-off and the poverty stricken, white and colored—all face the danger of nuclear war. Fear of a nuclear cataclysm haunts the lives of every adult, every child of knowing age, and there is no place to hide. The pretense of setting up bomb shelters is simply a cruel hoax.

The Socialist Workers Party contends that these social evils stem directly from the capitalist system under which the country is ruled by big banks and giant corporations. The few who control the monopolies put their private interests ahead of the needs of the many who do the work. These privileged few enjoy lavish and growing prosperity, but their greed remains insatiable. Not content with today's peak profits, they clamor and scheme to get more.

In their quest for greater wealth the monopolists resort to the imperialist practice of exploiting peoples in other lands for private profit. But in country after country, right up to Cuba, 90 miles off our shores, the working people are revolting against such exploitation. They demand use of the national wealth, not to fatten profiteers, but to meet the needs of those who produce the wealth. Dire necessity steadily pushes them away from capitalism and impels them toward nationalized production and a planned economy, as they take the first steps to reorganize society on a socialist basis.

Use Pretext

The American banks and corporations plot to crush these revolts abroad. Using as a pretext the violations of workers' democracy in the Soviet-bloc, they even hope to restore capitalism in countries where it has been abolished, including China and the Soviet Union. Cloaking their aims with hate propaganda against a so-called "communist conspiracy," they resort to increasingly brutal and unscrupulous methods. The revolutionary Cuban workers and farmers are branded enemies, while the fascist dictator Franco is embraced as an ally. Military interventions in other people's affairs become harsher and more brazen, even going to the brink of all-out nuclear war. No wonder America is feared and hated throughout the world.

Bluntly stating the monopolist creed in a recent speech at the University of Chicago, Henry Ford II said, "The target of private business is private profit." He argued for bigger profits on the ground that business could then invest more to create new jobs, implying that all social problems could thus be solved. His kind want the tax money to be used for military measures to maintain a "free world" open to their exploitation for private profit. They will brook no nonsense about government spending to correct the social evils inflicted by "free-enterprise" profiteering here at home; and the monopolists of Ford's class carry more weight in Washington than all the working people in the country.

Apologists for the Democrats claim it is only the Republicans who act as political flunkies for the monopolists, but the facts don't bear them out. In basic foreign policy, Democratic and Republican outlook is consistently bipartisan; so much so that one party can take over the White House from the other without a moment's pause in military interventions abroad. On the bread-and-butter issues in domestic policy the two parties act as one in the services of the banks and corporations. The Democrats, masquerading as a "people's" party, are simply a shade more hypocritical about it than the Republicans, and they are notorious for the accommodations to the Dixiecrats.

Through bipartisan endeavor, military alliances

have been forged with other capitalist governments. A far-flung network of American military bases rings the world. Deadly nuclear weapons, able to "over-kill" all humanity, stand ready for use in missile silos and U.S. submarines. Since 1948 universal military service has been imposed to conscript American youth into the armed forces, in which there is no democracy, and send them overseas as occupation troops to prop up puppet regimes. And the government has repeatedly been caught lying here at home about what it is doing abroad.

Our tax money is used to arm and train counter-revolutionary gangs who try to suppress revolts against poverty and overturn anti-capitalist governments in other lands. The bipartisans refuse to recognize the chosen government of 700 million Chinese, but they back to the hilt military overlords in South Vietnam. Eisenhower's administration first sent U.S. troops into Vietnam as "advisers," and the Kennedy and Johnson administrations continued and intensified the policy at the cost of mounting American casualties.

Troops commanded by a Democratic President shoot down unarmed Panamanians demonstrating against U.S. exploitation of their country and the Republicans back him up. The bipartisans maintain an economic blockade against Cuba and try to discipline allied countries who disagree with their policy. The criminal Bay of Pigs invasion in 1961 was planned under the Republicans and set into motion under the Democrats. Washington's anti-Cuba policy was carried to the very brink of general nuclear war in the 1962 missile crisis. The brutal tensions of that crisis made clear that under today's capitalist rule the question of war or peace can hinge on the decision of one man, the President. America's millions have no voice whatever.

Washington claims to know all about everything going on in Cuba, but its CIA-FBI gang can't find the bombers who murdered four little Negro girls in a Birmingham, Alabama, church. The bipartisans are too busy sabotaging and trying to overthrow the Castro regime that established genuine equality for racial minorities in Cuba.

TOKEN RIGHTS BILL

With great fanfare a token civil-rights bill is introduced into Congress where capitalist politicians will cynically play preelection politics with it. Negro freedom fighters peacefully demonstrating for their civil rights are subjected to brutal police attacks. Freedom fighters who defend themselves against white supremacist violence are framed up, as were four people recently convicted on fake "kidnap" charges in Monroe, North Carolina, and sentenced to long prison terms.

Those who would maintain racial oppression have, as a current NAACP report correctly states, "resisted the Constitution and court rulings by force, by deceit, by tokenism, by stalling litigation and by such legislative maneuvers as the filibuster."

As in the case of civil rights, tokenism and repression typify bipartisan policy on all questions of general social need. What little they do under mass pressure follows the "trickle-down" theory of the banks and corporations. The new tax cut does far more for the tax-dodging monopolies than it does for the tax-gouged working people. For economically-depressed areas like Appalachia plans are afoot to make low-interest federal loans to local capitalists who would use the money to turn a handsome profit for themselves. As a sop to the unemployed a vague promise is made of future government pressure to cut down on overtime hours and spread the work a little.

President Johnson was quick to reaffirm the long-standing White House opposition to union demands for a reduction in hours with no cut in take-home pay and to warn labor against "inflationary" wage demands. On these matters the bipartisans mean business. They demonstrated as much last year by rushing a bill through Congress which legalized compulsory arbitration and in effect outlawed a railroad strike.

On the minimum wage, jobless benefits, public relief, housing, health, education and other social problems, the Democratic administration makes token promises of slow improvement. For his much-publicized "war on poverty" which President Johnson calls "unconditional," about $1 billion, only one-third of it new money, is promised for the next fiscal year. In the same budget 54 times as much is allocated to the Pentagon for its military crackdown on poverty-stricken people in other countries who are in revolt against capitalist exploitation.

To conceal the truth about events elsewhere in the world the Democrats and Republicans join in imposing unconstitutional restrictions on the right to travel. Inside the country they resort to thought-control measures designed to suppress criticism and enforce conformity. Advocates of social change are branded "subversive." Critics of Washington's policies are harassed by the FBI on their jobs and in their neighborhoods. The despised stoolpigeon is glorified as a patriot. Mail is tampered with. Electronic eavesdropping devices are used to invade people's privacy. And the military brass is penetrating all civilian institutions.

CONGRESSIONAL INQUISITIONS

Congressional committees hold public inquisitions over TV in which people are cruelly pilloried before the whole nation. The victims are bombarded with loaded questions that violate their democratic rights and invade their personal lives. Those who invoke their constitutional right not to answer the inquisitors are publicly smeared as suspicious characters who "have something to hide." Victims of the Congressional inquisitors have been framed up on "contempt" or "perjury" charges.

Abuse of youth's inherent right to challenge the status quo is vividly illustrated in the case of three University of Indiana students. They had criticized Washington's Cuba policy; they had invited a Negro youth to address a student meeting on the right of self-defense against white-supremacist violence; and they had expressed the view that the American people would fare better in a socialist society. For that, and nothing more, a politically-ambitious prosecutor secured indictments against them under an Indiana thought-control law on the ridiculous charge of conspiring to advocate the overthrow of the government. The trial judge held the law unconstitutional and quashed the indictments. In an effort to overturn the ruling the prosecutor has appealed to a higher court where the case is now pending.

Minority political parties trying to exercise their democratic right to contend for votes run up against repressive election laws rigged to maintain a two-party monopoly of the ballot. Bipartisan schemes are hatched to deny minority parties equal free time with the Democrats and Republicans over TV and radio. Manipulating the two major parties like a pair of loaded dice, the banks and corporations use them against all non-capitalist organizations.

Legislative enactments, executive orders and court rulings steadily encroach on labor's freedom. The right to strike becomes more restricted; whether openly or through trickery, public officials side with the bosses in collective bargaining; and the bosses' government intrudes more and more into internal union affairs. The capitalists are equally quick to use police measures against the civil-rights movement. Whenever pious promises and token concessions fail to keep dissatisfied people in line, repression is the inevitable weapon to which the political custodians of capitalism resort. At all hazards they uphold the sacred capitalist principle that sets private profit above human need.

Fed up with a century of tokenism, the Negro people are demanding *freedom now,* and they are fighting for it. Their mood was symbolized by the big Southern demonstrations last year, called to protest discrimination and segregation and to demand the right to vote. Wave after wave of Negro freedom fighters went up against police dogs and fire hoses; undaunted by mass arrests, they came out of jail determined to continue the battle for human dignity and elementary rights.

In the giant March on Washington, sparked by the Southern demonstrations, Negroes came from all over the land to voice their demands for jobs and freedom. The big turnout reflected a rise in Northern militancy under the impetus of the Southern struggle. Rent strikes soon began in Northern cities where minorities are segregated in rat-infested slums. School boycotts followed in opposition to segregation of Negro and Puerto Rican children in the educational system. Negroes, and Puerto Ricans inspired by the Negro example, are demanding their democratic rights in the unions and pressing for union support of their right to full equality in employment.

Confronted with a lack of response from conservative union officials, they are taking action on their own. Construction sites, hotels and other places are picketed to protest discrimination in hiring and to demand equal rights on the job. Demands are pressed for higher minimum-wage laws covering all workers and for a shorter workweek to provide more jobs. Protest demonstrations are conducted against police brutality and there is growing sentiment to exercise the constitutional right of self-defense against extra-legal hooligan attacks on civil-rights demonstrators.

NEGRO AND WHITE YOUTH

Stimulated by the heroism of the Negro freedom fighters and sensing a basic kinship with them, white student youth are coming to their support in increasing numbers. A goodly number participated in the Freedom Rides and there has since been a widening involvement of white students in the overall struggle. Negro and white youth face a common plight in many aspects of modern life under capitalism. Together they are confronted with militarism, economic insecurity, witch hunting and other problems. As a result, to quote uneasy liberals on the subject, "They are asking deep and complicated questions."

Slower to respond to the fighting example set by Negroes are the unions which suffer paralysis under a conservative and dictatorial leadership. Strikes are made official only under extreme provocation from the bosses. No real support is given the civil-rights movement, even though most Negroes are workers. Little effort is made to fuse Negro and white labor in united efforts to defend their common interests as wage earners. Instead, the general run of union officials resist Negro demands for union equality.

The union officialdom calls for reliance on the Democrats to solve labor's problems. Most Negro leaders take a similar view of Democrats outside the South as allies in the civil-rights fight. But in neither case have these capitalist politicians fulfilled the hopes placed in them. What to do then? "Elect more liberals," the Negro freedom fighters and union members are told. Rejuvenate the government with "true friends" of labor and civil rights.

The record shows, however, that liberals, Democrats and Republicans alike, are simply masters of the pious promise and token concession. In the name of peace they consistently support a warlike foreign policy. In dealing with the nation's grave social problems they prove to be nothing more than glib bipartisans who talk a lot but do nothing that would cut across the sanctity of private profit. As do all capitalist politicians, they take reprisals against people who refuse to accept gradualism in social reform.

Consider the example of the newly-enacted "Stop-and-Frisk" and "No-Knock" laws in New York. Governor Rockefeller, a liberal Republican, rammed them through the state legislature over strong protests from civil-rights groups. Negroes and Puerto Ricans are concerned because the laws empower the police to search people on the streets and to barge into private quarters without even knocking. Harlem residents know very well that Rockefeller's new laws will be freely invoked against them by New York City cops under the command of Mayor Wagner, a liberal Democrat, who urged swift passage of these repressive measures.

John Lewis, chairman of the Student Nonviolent Coordinating Committee, stated a truth which describes all capitalist politicians, Democratic or Republican, liberal or conservative. In the prepared text of a speech he was prevented from delivering at the March on Washington, he said, "This nation is still a place of cheap political leaders who build their careers on immoral compromises and ally themselves with open forms of political, economic and social exploitation." Then he put the question, "Where is *our* party?"

Echoing John Lewis' question, a group of prominent Negroes distributed a manifesto at the March on Washington calling for independent Negro political action. "One hundred years of waiting for Democratic and Republican politicians to correct our grievances is too long," they said. "We have to *take* our freedom; no one will hand it to us. That is why . . . we call upon all who believe in true emancipation to join us in forming the Freedom Now Party."

Although addressed directly to Negroes, this summons to independent political action describes an even larger need. It points the way for the whole working class, for all victims of capitalist misrule. Their problems can't be solved through the twin parties of war, racism, unemployment and witch hunts. Progress can be made only by breaking completely with both the Democrats and Republicans.

A FREEDOM NOW PARTY

For these reasons the Socialist Workers Party supports independent Negro political action of the type manifested in the call for a Freedom Now Party. We urge the formation of an independent labor party based on the unions. We advocate an anti-capitalist political alliance of all who suffer discrimination and exploitation, black and white, in industry and on the land, in blue collars and white. As a means to register a desire for such political change, we ask those whose thinking runs along similar lines to support the SWP candidates in the November elections.

To solve the nation's many problems fully, we contend that capitalism must be abolished and a socialist society created. A society with jobs for all. One in which those who produce would democratically organize and plan production to serve everybody's needs on a fair basis. A society free from discrimination and segregation wherein all would have equal opportunity to prosper. A society in which all individuals could freely develop their creative powers, artistic talents and human potentialities. An America that would lend a helping hand to people in other lands instead of mobilizing and arming to make war on them.

As concrete steps toward the creation of a society of peace, prosperity, freedom and equality, the Socialist Workers Party submits the following planks:

1) *For a peaceful foreign policy*

Stop the "dirty war" in Vietnam. Pull out of Guantanamo. Lift the economic blockade and restore friendly relations with Cuba. Recognize Panamanian sovereignty over the Panama Canal. Give up all military alliances and foreign military bases. Withdraw all troops from foreign soil. Halt all nuclear-weapon tests and scrap the stockpile of A and H-bombs.

Recognize the Peking government and establish trade relations with China. Support the right of all peoples to a government of their own choice.

No secret diplomacy or propaganda lies. Tell the whole truth. Let the people vote on all issues of war and peace.

2) *Against capitalist militarism*

Turn the arms budget into a peace budget devoted to the nation's social needs. End capitalist conscription, ROTC and Prussian-type rule over the military establishment. Grant full democratic rights to the ranks of the armed forces, including free speech and assembly, election of officers and collective bargaining.

3) *FREEDOM NOW for all minorities*

Full economic, social and political equality for the Negro people and for all other minority groups. Solidarity with mass actions aimed at securing these rights as exemplified in the rent strikes, school boycotts, picketing of construction sites, public demonstrations and sit-ins. Uphold the right of self-defense against white-supremacist violence.

Full use of the federal power to enforce all laws and court orders against discrimination and segregation. Enforce existing laws against lynch murder and police brutality and enact new ones. End the barbaric death penalty and reform the antiquated prison system.

Establish an FEPC with teeth and compensate minorities for the disadvantages they have suffered. Create a federal agency fully empowered and equipped to enforce minority rights in all spheres of national life. Federal action to guarantee and protect the right to vote in all national, state, county and city elections. Abolish all existing poll taxes.

Teach Negro and African history in the nation's schools. Combat all forms of anti-Semitism.

4) *Restore and expand democratic rights*

Repeal all federal, state and local laws restricting labor's right to organize, strike and picket. No government interference in internal union affairs.

Abolish the "subversive" list, "loyalty" oaths and "loyalty" purges. No political tampering with social-security benefits. End FBI harassment of political dissidents. Abolish the House Un-American Activities Committee, the Senate Internal Security Sub-committee and their counterparts in state legislatures.

Repeal all legislative enactments, executive decrees and court orders violating the Bill of Rights. Stop the thought-control frame-ups and political prosecutions for "contempt" and "perjury." Rescind all deportation orders and lift all restrictions on the right to travel. Amnesty all victims of the witch hunt.

Liberalize the election laws. Lower the voting age to 18. Give minority parties equal time on TV and radio and in all public media.

5) *End economic insecurity*

For the 30-hour week at 40 hours' pay and further reductions in hours without cuts in pay when needed to secure full employment. Jobless benefits to every worker at the full union scale for the entire period of unemployment. Let the government take over all idle production facilities and operate them under charge of committees elected by the workers. Union control of production speeds by majority vote of the workers involved.

Equal pay for equal work regardless of race, sex

or age. Full job and seniority rights and maternity care for women. Federally financed nurseries and summer camps for children. A government guaranteed college education for all youth.

Provide the millions of aged people with full disability benefits, free medical care and hospitalization, and adequate pensions. Nationalize the entire medical system. As an immediate measure pass the King-Anderson Medicare Bill now bottled up in Congress.

6) *For adequate government aid to the farmers*

A federal program, set up and administered by elected representatives of working farmers, to guarantee them the full cost of production on all farm commodities. No limitation on crops so long as people suffer from hunger anywhere in the world. Government food subsidies for families in America living on a substandard diet.

Moratoriums on repayment of distress loans made to working farmers as long as debtors need them. Abolish share-cropping and landlordism—crops to those who grow them; land to those who work it.

7) *For an emergency housing and public works program*

Immediate government construction of 20 million low-rent housing units. Rigid rent controls on all private housing, enforced by elected representatives of the tenants. A large-scale federal program to build schools, hospitals and other public facilities. Government action on flood control, improved water supply, irrigation, cheap electricity and conservation of natural resources. All programs to be financed with funds now spent for armaments.

8) *Repeal taxes on low incomes*

Abolish all payroll and sales taxes, all hidden taxes passed on to the consumer. No taxes on incomes under $7,500 a year. A 100 per cent tax on incomes above $25,000 a year. Confiscate all profits on war goods. Open the tax returns of the rich to public scrutiny.

9) *For government ownership of industry*

Nationalize the banks, basic industries, food trusts and all natural resources, including nuclear power. Elect committees of workers and technicians to manage these facilities in the interests of the producers and consumers. Institute a planned system of economy.

10) *For independent political action*

End the Democratic-Republican monopoly of politics. Break all ties with the capitalist political machines. For an independent labor party based on the unions. For an independent Negro party running its own candidates. For an anti-capitalist political alliance of all who suffer discrimination and exploitation.

Bring to power a Workers' and Farmers' government, with full representation for minorities, to reorganize America on a socialist basis.

☒ CAMPAIGN OF 1968

In 1968 voters of America divided their loyalties among three national parties and more than a dozen contenders representing smaller parties. At least one minor party candidate appeared on the ballot in twenty-five states, although not all of the aspirants were constitutionally eligible for the Presidency.

The contest between the two principal candidates was exceedingly close. Republican Richard M. Nixon was elected President with 43.41 per cent of the 73,175,000 popular votes cast (302 electoral votes) over Democrat Hubert H. Humphrey, who obtained 42.72 per cent (191 electoral votes). George C. Wallace, running on the American Independent party ticket, received more than nine million votes—13.52 per cent of the total—and won the electoral votes of five southern states. His percentage of the popular vote was the highest for a third-party candidate since Progressive Robert LaFollette polled 16.6 per cent of the ballots in 1924.

Although more than 73 million people, the largest number in American history, went to the polls, this turnout represented only 60 per cent of the eligible voters—the lowest percentage in twelve years. Minor parties, other than the American Independent party, received less than one-third of 1 per cent of the votes.

As in the previous editions of this collection, the platforms of the permanent, organized, minor parties have been included in the volume; those of the many parties that appeared for the first time this year or those that received only a few scattered votes, together with those that named candidates ineligible for the Presidency, have been omitted. Thus, in 1968 statements of principles from the New party, the Best party, the Peace and Freedom party, the Universal party, the Constitution party, the Freedom and Peace party, and the revived Communist party have not been included. The Socialist party, as in recent elections, published a platform that is not included here because the party nominated no candidate for President.

American Independent Platform 1968

PREAMBLE

A sense of destiny pervades the creation and adoption of this first Platform of the American Independent Party, a Platform personifying the ideals, hopes, aspirations and proposals for action of the Party and its candidates for the Presidency and Vice Presidency of the United States, George C. Wallace and Curtis E. LeMay.

As this great nation searched vainly for leadership while beset by riots, minority group rebellions, domestic disorders, student protests, spiraling living costs, soaring interest rates, a frightening increase in the crime rate, war abroad and loss of personal liberty at home; while our national political parties and their leaders paid homage to the legions of dissent and disorder and worshipped at the shrine of political expediency, only this Party, the American Independent Party, and its candidates, George C. Wallace and Curtis E. LeMay, possessed the courage and fortitude to openly propose and advocate to the nation those actions which are necessary to return this country to its accustomed and deserved position of leadership among the community of nations and to offer hope to our people of some relief from the continued turmoil, frustration and confusion brought about through the fearful and inept leadership of our national political parties.

It is to this end and for this purpose that this Platform is designed. Herein will be set forth the policies, attitude, proposals and position of this Party and its candidates, with matters of deepest concern to the average American, his home, his family, his property, his employment, his right to safety and security in the pursuit of the activities of his daily life, his right to freedom from interference and harassment from and by the government at all levels and, lastly, his pride in himself and this nation and all that it has stood for.

We feel that this American has an intense devotion to his country, glorifies in its accomplishments and is saddened by its failures and shortcomings; that he is tolerant of the mistakes of political leaders if he senses their actions to be in good faith and directed to the best interest of the country, but he is confused and dismayed when these leaders desert the principle of government for the people and dedicate themselves to minority appeasement as the country burns and decays.

This document treats both foreign and domestic policy and is basically designed to present the proposals and action programs of this Party and its candidates in the area of:

1. Peace abroad and domestic tranquility at home.

2. An enlightened and advancing educational program, assisted but not controlled by the federal government.

3. Job training and opportunity for all Americans willing and able to seek and hold gainful employment.

4. An alliance and partnership with the private sector of our economy seeking an end to poverty among our people.

5. Efficiency and prudence in governmental spending leading to a helpful and stable economy free from the need for ever continuing taxation.

6. Inclusion of the farmer in our program of prosperity through his own efforts rather than total reliance on government subsidy.

7. Reestablishment of the authority and responsibility of local government by returning to the states, counties and cities those matters properly falling within their jurisdiction and responsibility.

8. Ending the inflationary spiral of the past decade through fiscal responsibility and efficiency in all echelons of government.

9. The orderly and economical utilization of the natural resources of this nation coupled with a sensible program of conservation of these resources.

10. An insistence that the laboring man and woman be given his fair share of responsibility and reward for the development of the mighty potential of this nation.

11. A re-dedication of this country to the love of God and country and the creation of a judiciary mindful of the attitudes of the people in this regard.

With these cardinal principles in mind, we herein set forth the precepts of our Party and Candidates in the following areas of concern:

DOMESTIC POLICY

Clearly, our citizens are deeply concerned over the domestic plight of this nation. Its cities are in decay and turmoil; its local schools and other institutions stand stripped of their rightful authority; law enforcement agencies and officers are hampered by arbitrary and unreasonable restrictions imposed by a beguiled judiciary; crime runs rampant through the nation; our farmers exist only through unrealistic government subsidies; welfare rolls and costs soar to astronomical heights; our great American institutions of learning are in chaos; living costs rise ever higher as do taxes; interest rates are reaching new heights; disciples of dissent and disorder are rewarded for their disruptive actions at the expense of our law-abiding, God fearing, hard working citizenry. America is alarmed that these conditions have come to exist and that our national leadership takes no corrective action. We feel that the programs and policies of our Party offer this leadership and provide constructive proposals of action for the elimination of the conditions now existing. This we would do in the following manner:

LOCAL GOVERNMENT

The Founding Fathers of our country, when they had won their freedom from King George III in the American Revolution, and were engaged in setting up our Federal Government, in their infinite wisdom, visualized the tyranny and despotism which would inevitably result from an omnipotent central government; and, they sought to avoid that peril by delegating to that central or federal government only those powers which could best be administered by a central or federal government, such as the laying and collecting of taxes to pay the national debt, providing for the common defense, regulating commerce between the states, declaring and waging war, coining money and establishing and maintaining a postal system. And then they provided, in Article X of the Bill of Rights, the Tenth Amendment to the Constitution of the United States, that:

"The powers, not delegated to the United States by the Constitution, nor prohibited by it to the states, are reserved to the states respectively, or to the people."

The Federal Government, in derogation and flagrant violation of this Article of the Bill of Rights, has in the past three decades seized and usurped many powers not delegated to it, such as, among others: the operation and control of the public school system of the several states; the power to prescribe the eligibility and qualifications of those who would vote in our state and local elections; the power to intrude upon and control the farmer in the operation of his farm; the power to tell the property owner to whom he can and cannot sell or rent his property; and, many other rights and privileges of the individual citizen, which are properly subject to state or local control, as distinguished from federal control. The Federal Government has forced the states to reapportion their legislatures, a prerogative of the states alone. The Federal Government has attempted to take over and control the seniority and apprenticeship lists of the labor unions; the Federal Government has adopted so-called "Civil Rights Acts," particularly the one adopted in 1964, which have set race against race and class against class, all of which we condemn.

It shall be our purpose to take such steps and pursue such courses as may be necessary and required to restore to the states the powers and authority which rightfully belong to the state and local governments, so that each state shall govern and control its internal affairs without interference or domination of the Federal Government. We feel that the people of a given state are in better position to operate its internal affairs, such as its public schools, than is the Federal Government in Washington; and, we pledge our best efforts to restore to state governments those powers which rightfully belong to the respective states, and which have been illegally and unlawfully seized by the Federal Government, in direct violation of Article X of the Bill of Rights.

THE FEDERAL JUDICIARY

Our forebears, in building our government, wisely provided and established, in the Constitution of the United States, that the Federal Government should consist of three branches, the Legislative, represented by the Congress, whose duty and responsibility it is to enact the laws; the Executive, represented by the President, whose duty it is to enforce the laws enacted by the Congress; and, the Judicial, whose duty and responsibility it is to interpret and construe those laws, not to enact them.

The Constitution of the United States provides that the judicial power of the United States shall be vested in a Supreme Court and in such inferior courts as the Congress shall from time to time ordain and establish; and, further, that the judges of the Federal courts shall hold their offices for life, during good behavior.

In the period of the past three decades, we have seen the Federal judiciary, primarily the Supreme Court, transgress repeatedly upon the prerogatives of the Congress and exceed its authority by enacting judicial legislation, in the form of decisions based upon political and sociological considerations, which would never have been enacted by the Congress. We have seen them, in their solicitude for the criminal and lawless element of our society, shackle the police and other law enforcement agencies; and, as a result, they have made it increasingly difficult to protect the law-abiding citizen from crime and criminals. This is one of the principal reasons for the turmoil and the near revolutionary conditions which prevail in our country today, and particularly in our national capitol. The members of the Federal judiciary, feeling secure in their knowledge that their appointment is for life, have far exceeded their constitutional authority, which is limited to interpreting or construing the law.

It shall be our policy and our purpose, at the earliest possible time, to propose and advocate and urge the adoption of an amendment to the United States Constitution whereby members of the Federal judiciary at District level be required to face the electorate on his record at periodical intervals; and, in the event he receives a negative vote upon such election, his office shall thereupon become vacant, and a successor shall be appointed to succeed him.

With respect to the Supreme Court and the Courts of Appeals I would propose that this amendment require re-confirmations of the office holder by the United States Senate at reasonable intervals.

PRIVATE PROPERTY

We hold that the ownership of private property is the right and privilege of every American citizen and is one of the foundation stones upon which this nation and its free enterprise system has been built and has prospered. We feel that private property rights and human rights are inseparable and indivisible. Only in those nations that guarantee the right of ownership of private property as basic and sacred under their law is there any recognition of human rights.

We feel that the American system of private property ownership, coupled with its system of free enterprise, upon the basis of which our country has grown and prospered for more than two hundred years, is sacred; and, we repudiate and condemn those who propose to transform our nation into a socialist state; and, we propose to furnish and provide a national leadership that is dedicated to the preservation and perpetuation of the great American system of private enterprise and private ownership of property.

We repudiate and condemn any federal action regulating or controlling the sale or rental of private property as a socialistic assault upon not only the system of private ownership of property, but upon the right of each American citizen to manage his private affairs without regulation from an all-powerful central government.

There is no provision in the Federal Constitution which gives Congress the power to regulate the sale or rental of private property. Such legislation strikes at the very heart of the American system and if followed to its logical conclusion will inevitably lead to a system alien to our concept of free government, where citizens are no longer able to make decisions for themselves or manage their personal affairs. We pledge to take the Federal Government out of the business of controlling private property and return to the people the right to manage their lives and property in a democratic manner.

CRIME AND DISORDER

Lawlessness has become commonplace in our present society. The permissive attitude of the executive and judiciary at national level sets the tone for this moral decay. The criminal and anarchist who preys on the decent law-abiding citizen is rewarded for his misconduct through never ending justification and platitudes from those in high places who seem to have lost their concern for that vast segment of America that so strongly believes in law and order.

We hear much of the "root causes" for the depredations committed in our streets and in our towns and cities. We hold that these are to be found in the apparent absence of respect for the law on the part of the perpetrators of these offenses, and the unexplainable compassion for the criminal evidenced by our executive and judicial officers and officials. We advocate and seek a society and a government in which there is an attitude of respect for the law and for those who seek its enforcement and an insistence on the part of our citizens that the judiciary be ever mindful of their primary duty and function of punishing the guilty and protecting the innocent.

We urge full support for law enforcement agencies and officers at every level of government and a situation in which their actions will not be unreasonably fettered by arbitrary judicial decrees.

We will insist on fair and equal treatment for all persons before the bar of justice.

We will provide every assistance to the continued training and improvement of our law enforcement facilities at federal and local level, providing and encouraging mutual cooperation between each in his own sphere of responsibility.

We will support needed legislation and action to seek out and bring to justice the criminal organizations of national scope operating in our country.

We will appoint as Attorney General a person interested in the enforcement rather than the disruption of legal processes and restore that office to the dignity and stature it deserves and requires.

We will provide leadership and action in a national effort against the usage of drugs and drug addiction, attacking this problem at every level and every source in a full-scale campaign to drive this evil from our society.

We will provide increased emphasis in the area of juvenile delinquency and juvenile offenses in order to deter and rehabilitate young offenders.

We will not accept violence as the answer to any problem be it social, economic, or self-developed. Anarchists and law violators will be treated as such and subjected to prompt arrest and prosecution.

We will oppose federal legislation to enforce the registration of guns by our citizens, feeling that this measure would do little or nothing to deter criminal activity, but, rather, would prove restrictive to our decent, law-abiding citizens, and could well encourage further activity by the criminal. We will preserve to the states their rights to take such reasonable measures as they deem appropriate in this area.

CITIES AND SUBURBS

The urban areas of our nation are in a state of social and economic unrest, largely brought about through unfilled promises hastily and carelessly made and the failure of ill-conceived programs enacted under duress and compulsion. For this, we must hold responsible the national leadership of the other two parties, for they were joint partners in this disastrous course of action resulting in the situation now existing in our cities.

We object to a federal policy which has poured billions of dollars into our cities over the past decades but which has not been able to prevent their stagnation and decay and has resulted in the flight of millions to the suburbs. We reject the notion that the solution is untold additional billions to be poured into the cities in the same manner, whether such huge sums are to be raised from taxes on the middle class in general, or by unwelcome taxes on those who live in the suburbs of the individual cities. We submit that no government can buy contentment for those living in the cities, suburbs, or rural areas. We advocate the formulation of a mutually arrived at, joint federal, state and local policy which will make it economically and socially attractive and physically safe for people to live again in all sections of all of our cities. We submit that the science and technology, which made possible the development and growth of these cities, is the instrument whereby this can be brought about.

Specifically, there must be a restoration and maintenance of law and order before any program, no matter how well conceived, will succeed. We pledge ourselves to this accomplishment and will exert forceful leadership at local level to such effort.

Those totally unfitted by training, background and environment for urban living who have been lured to the metropolitan areas by the wholly false promises and commitments of self-seeking political leaders must be afforded an opportunity for training or, in the alternative, an opportunity to return to gainful employment in the less urbanized area from whence they came. This we propose to accomplish in conjunction with private industry through a program of diversification and decentralization of expanding industry into areas away from metropolitan centers, thereby providing relief for many of the problems of the area while providing productive life for those afforded the opportunity to depart these overcrowded areas.

We advocate assistance, but not control, to

local governmental units from the federal level to enable them to cope with their multiplicity of problems, feeling they are better prepared to offer solution than those more removed therefrom.

We advocate and will sponsor a partnership with the private sector of our economy in the restoration of job opportunity and a healthy living environment to our cities through programs made economically attractive to industry.

We will support programs designed to provide means by which home-ownership can become a reality to our city dwellers, thereby instilling a greater feeling of dignity, stability and responsibility in those benefiting from such a program.

Above all, there must be a restoration of order in our cities as a prelude to any program of assistance, for without order neither government nor private industry will meet with success. Herein lies the cause of much failure in the past.

JOB OPPORTUNITY AND THE POOR

We feel that the matter of our citizens in need and the existence of job opportunies are so closely related as to warrant concurrent consideration.

We are convinced that the average American believes in the inherent dignity of gainful employment, preferring this method of attaining a livelihood to any welfare grant or benefit not earned through his own efforts. For this reason we consider the solution to the problem of our needy citizens, capable of gainful employment to be the provision of job opportunity. This will be the goal of our Party and our administration.

Our first consideration will be the inclusion of private industry in this program and effort. We believe that the private sector of our economy has the will and capability of providing a solution to the problem of poverty much more promptly and efficiently than any or all governmental programs of indiscriminate welfare contributions. Based on this premise, we will work in partnership with private industry in a program mutually beneficial to each to provide these job opportunities. We propose to make this program economically attractive to industry through tax incentives and other means of economic benefit, believing fully that the answer to this problem lies in the vigor and capability of our tremendous free enterprise system.

We would propose that the federal government aid and assist in a well-designed program of job training or retraining for those in need thereof. This will be at the vocational school and lower level, depending on the needs of the trainees. We will encourage and assist the states in programs of job training or retraining through realistic productive efforts in this respect, including assistance to the establishment and maintenance of vocational trade schools and other like institutions designed to provide skilled and semi-skilled personnel for industrial employment, as well as means whereby 'in-training" programs can be carried out by private industry in cooperation with government.

In the event a public works program becomes necessary to provide employment for all employable Americans, we will provide such a program assuring, however, that these programs be needful and productive and that the participants engage in labor beneficial to the nation and its economy rather than becoming wards of the government and the recipients of gratuitous handouts.

For those unemployable by reason of age, infirmity, disability or otherwise, provision will be made for their adequate care through programs of social services based on the requirements and needs of these persons. We hold that all Americans are deserving of and will have the care, compassion and benefits of the fullness of life.

HEALTH AND WELFARE: OUR SENIOR CITIZENS

Social Security is basically an old age, survivors and disability Insurance Plan. It provides for citizens to pay into the Trust Fund during their working years and is designed to replace part of the earning capacity of the participant, or his family, lost due to retirement, death or disability. During past administrations, the Social Security Trust Fund has been depleted and current payments are being made from current revenues. Social Security cannot be financed from current revenues or from the Federal Treasury without raising taxes or jeopardizing other essential programs of government. Such a policy is irresponsible.

We pledge to restore the Social Security Trust Fund to a sound financial basis and by responsible fiscal policies to insure the following:

1. An immediate increase in Social Security payments with a goal of a 60% increase in benefits.

2. An increase in the minimum payment to $100, with annual cost of living increases.

3. Restoration of the 100% income tax deduction for drugs and medical expenses paid out by people 65 and over.

4. Removal of the earnings limitation of people 65 and over in order that they may earn any amount of additional income.

Our goal is to make every senior citizen a first-class citizen; to restore their dignity, prestige, self-respect, independence and their security, without intrusion into their private lives by federal bureaucrats and guideline writers.

Health Care

It is the obligation of a responsible government to help people who are unable to help themselves. There should be adequate medical assistance available to the aged and those unable to afford treatment. This can best be achieved through a partnership between federal and state governments and private enterprise. Medicare should be improved. It should be strengthened in conjunction with medical care provided at state and local governmental levels and by private insurance. Through sound fiscal management we set as a goal the following improvements in Medicare:

1. Relief to persons unable to pay deductible charges under Medicare.

2. Relief to persons unable to have deducted from their Social Security checks the monthly fee for physician service coverage under Medicare.

3. Providing for uninterrupted nursing home care for those with chronic illness who require such care.

4. We will encourage low-cost insurance programs for the elderly and will assist the states and local communities in building hospitals, nursing homes, clinics as well as medical and nursing schools.

In this land of plenty, no one should be denied adequate medical care because of his financial condition.

We are particularly disturbed about the doctor-patient, and the hospital-patient relationship. We stand solidly for freedom of choice in this rela-tionship. It is our intent that medical care programs be carried out without subjecting our professional people and our hospital administrators and personnel to the harassment which has been their lot since the implementation of the Medicare program. We believe that those assisted by the Medicare program should have some degree of selection in the medical and hospital services furnished to them, and that simplification in the administration of this program would prove of benefit to government, patient and the professional practitioner alike.

American medical and dental practice is the admitted marvel of the world. Its traditional freedom is one of the chief reasons why this is so. The American Independent Party pledges continuous study and effort to maintain that freedom both for doctor and for patient.

Other Social Services

The people of this land are the fiber of our nation. Their well-being is essential to a strong America. Unfortunately, many of our citizens are unable to earn an adequate living, due to no fault of their own. Our aged, our blind, and our disabled who are unemployed are the concern of us all.

In every area of social welfare, rehabilitation should be of paramount concern. This includes physical restoration where possible, training to develop new skills, adult education in many instances, and broad cooperative endeavors between government and private industry to develop jobs that the less skilled can fill. We believe that every American prefers independence and a wage earned. For those whose infirmities, age, or other problems prevent such independence, welfare services should be adequate to provide a living with dignity and honor.

Dependent children become the responsibility of government when they lack the care and support of parents or guardians. Every effort should be made to provide support by responsible persons rather than the government, where possible. However, when children are separated permanently, by death or other cause from their families, all facilities of government should safeguard, protect, serve and care for them.

In every area possible, federal grants should be administered through existing state and local governmental agencies, thus eliminating additional federal offices and agencies which merely duplicate efforts of existing state and local agencies.

We will review and examine the administration of these programs with a view to the elimination of waste and duplication and thereby better serve the purposes and people designed to be assisted. We subscribe to the principle of block grants, administered by state agencies as a possible solution to these problems.

National Economy

The national economy must be restored to and maintained in a healthy, viable posture under conditions assuring to each individual American the opportunity to participate in and enjoy the benefits arising from a real prosperity, as distinguished from the false, inflationary conditions presently existing. As a first step the nation's business, industry and other agencies and organizations of production must be freed from the ever-increasing intrusions of government into the affairs of these institutions and organizations. This nation achieved its economic greatness under a system of free enterprise, coupled with human effort and ingenuity, and thus it must remain. This will be the attitude and objective of this Party.

There must be an end to inflation and the ever-increasing cost of living. This is of vital concern to the laborer, the housewife, the farmer and the small business man, as well as the millions of Americans dependent upon their weekly or monthly income for sustenance. It wrecks the planned lives and retirement of our elderly who must survive on pensions or savings gauged by the standards of another day.

We will take immediate, affirmative steps to bring these conditions to an end through selective decreases in the lavish expenditures of our federal government and through the institution of efficiency into the operation of the machinery of government, so badly plagued with duplication, overlapping and excesses in employment and programs. Bureaucracy will cease to exist solely for bureaucracy's own sake, and the institutions and functions of government will be judged by their efficiency of operation and their contribution to the lives and welfare of our citizens.

We will support and assist business and industry in those areas needful and desirable, such as in the area of small business.

We will enforce those laws designed to protect the consumer and wage earner, but will eliminate those programs and agencies serving only to harass and intimidate our business community.

We will review and propose revisions to our present tax structure so as to ease the load of the small income citizen and to place upon all their rightful share of the tax burden.

We will work toward a reduction in the tax burden for all our citizens, using as our tools efficiency and economy in the operation of government, the elimination of unnecessary and wasteful programs and reduction in government expenditures at home and abroad.

We will eliminate the favorable treatment now accorded the giant, non-tax-paying foundations and institutions and require these organizations to assume their rightful responsibility as to the operation of our government.

To achieve these goals and objectives, we would use government for the strengthening of the free enterprise system rather than the replacement of the free enterprise system by government. We believe that strength and confidence in the American political and economic system will tend to encourage domestic private investment and prosperity in our economy.

We would propose that effective use be made during our administration of economic advisors dedicated to the preservation and strengthening of our economic freedoms in the areas of enterprise, labor and marketing that have contributed so much to the strength of the American system.

Our administration will be dedicated to the maintenance of prosperity and price stability in our economy. We will institute a strong anti-inflationary fiscal, monetary and debt management policy in our nation as the first requirement to solving international problems.

We propose to rely heavily upon a competitive market structure rather than upon prices administered or fixed by bureaucratic procedures.

We do not propose to use periodic, intermittent tax adjustments or surcharges as a tool of economic policy under the guise of stabilizing the inflationary spiral we are experiencing.

We feel little is done to curb inflationary trends in the nation's economy merely by taking from the taxpayer in order to enrich the spending programs of big government. We propose, rather, a stabilized and equitable tax base affording fair treatment to those of small income and designed to cause all persons, organizations and foundations to assume their rightful financial responsibility for government coupled with selective and prudent reductions in the wasteful expenditures of government.

AGRICULTURE

America's agriculture, and especially the small farmer, is on the brink of disaster. Under both Democratic and Republican administrations, the income of our farmers has steadily declined. Farm prices have been ranging at a parity level the lowest since the dark days of the great depression. Individual producers are unable to regulate the output or price of their products and stringent government controls have been forced upon farmers. Revolutionary methods of production have resulted in increased yield from less acreage and requiring less manpower. The farmer is hampered by a faulty system of distribution, and his costs have continued to increase at an astronomical rate. Yet, all America's farmers have received from either of the other two parties have been broken promises.

The following is the pledge of the American Independent Party to our nation's farmers:

1. We pledge ourselves to the protection and preservation of the family farm, which is the backbone of American Agriculture.

2. We pledge that the new Secretary of Agriculture will immediately begin to support prices at 90% of parity which is the highest level provided under present law.

3. Congress will be urged to increase the maximum support to 100% of parity.

4. Legislation will be sought to permit farmers to exercise their freedom of choice to vote whether or not to come under self-imposed controls.

5. We propose the creation of a National Feed Grain Authority, authorized to make long-term loans for development of farmer-owned and controlled warehouses, to be strategically located, permitting farmers to store large quantities of grain and to sell direct to the trade through their own local organizations.

6. We propose that no portion of the nation's emergency reserves of food, feed or fiber be sold for less than 115% of the prevailing farm price support of that commodity.

7. A limit to subsidy payments should be set in order to prevent an unfair advantage being built up by giant corporate farm structures over our small farmer or family farms.

8. We propose to impose reasonable limitations on the import of foreign farm and meat products into this country.

9. It is our belief that continued support of the REA and other cooperative programs designed to improve marketing methods and conditions throughout the nation is vital to our farming interests.

10. It is our belief that federal support for farm research is important, and that Agriculture Colleges and Extension Services should be more effectively utilized.

11. Governmental agencies similar to the Farm Home Administration have been beneficial to farmers and should be improved and continued.

12. We propose that the State Department and the Agriculture Department work together in a joint effort to develop new foreign markets for our farm products and develop a vigorous export program.

13. We support a good soil conservation program and pledge the continuation and improvement of such program.

14. It is our policy to assist in improving farm production reporting in order that farmers obtain more accurate production forecasts for planning purposes.

15. It is our intention to simplify the administration of all farm programs, and to eliminate wasteful duplication and red tape within the Department of Agriculture.

16. We will work toward gradual relaxation and elimination of farm regulation and control with a concurrent reduction in required subsidization as farm income increases, the eventual goal being the elimination of both controls and the need for subsidy, such program being contingent upon the increase in farm income to a level making subsidy unnecessary.

17. We will require that programs for disease and insect control be continued and expanded where needed if it is indicated that state and local bodies need and desire assistance from the federal level. Such program would, among other things, provide for necessary steps to eradicate the imported fire ants. This pest is now prevalent

throughout a major portion of the southern region but will eventually affect three-fourths of the land area of the United States if eradication is not accomplished promptly.

The farmers of this nation are entitled to a fair, just and equitable profit on their investment, just as citizens in other fields of endeavor. It is our belief that a major step toward solving our problems in agriculture would be to insure a substantial increase in farm income. It is time for a new Secretary of Agriculture who represents the views and interests of the farmer and the rancher, and who will work ceaselessly and tirelessly to improve the income and the lives of America's farm families. We pledge to you such a Secretary and such a program.

LABOR

America achieved its greatness through the combined energy and efforts of the working men and women of this country. Retention of its greatness rests in their hands.

Through the means of their great trade organizations, these men and women have exerted tremendous influence on the economic and social life of the nation and have attained a standard of living known to no other nation. In the meantime, American labor has become a bulwark against the intrusion of foreign ideology into our free society. America must be eternally grateful to its working men and women.

The concern of this Party is that the gains which labor struggled so long to obtain not be lost to them either through inaction or subservience to illogical domestic policies of our other national parties.

We propose and pledge:

To guarantee and protect labor in its right of collective bargaining;

To assert leadership at the federal level toward assuring labor its rightful reward for its contribution to the productivity of America;

To propose and support programs designed to improve living and employment conditions of our working men and women;

To prohibit intrusion by the federal government into the internal affairs of labor organizations, seeking to direct and control actions as to seniority and apprentice lists and other prerogatives;

To provide for and protect the working men

and women in the exercise of democratic processes and principles in the conduct of the affairs of their organizations, free from threats, coercion, or reprisals from within or without such organization;

To support programs and legislation designed to afford an equitable minimum wage, desirable working hours and conditions of employment, and protection in the event of adversity or unemployment;

To add efficiency and dispatch to the actions and activities of the National Labor Relations Board, resulting in more prompt decisions by this agency;

To pledge and assure that labor will be adequately represented in all deliberations of this Party and its administration of the affairs of government;

To cause all agents of government to refrain from any coercive action in strike settlements, serving in the role of counselor and advisor only, believing that good faith bargaining between the parties concerned is the best solution to any settlement.

EDUCATION

Without question education offers the answer to many of the nation's social and economic problems. It is tragic that during the past two decades, while governed alternately by the Republican and Democratic parties, we have witnessed the deterioration of our public school systems into a state of disruption wherein the maintenance of order is the major problem and quality education is a forgotten objective. Our educational leaders and administrators are discouraged and dismayed by the continuing attacks upon, and erosion of, their duties and authority by agents of the federal bureaucracy and members of the federal judiciary.

Local educational officials have been stripped of their authority to administer the affairs of their school systems. Harassing directives and requirements of an unreasonable and unrealistic nature are constantly being imposed upon them. Parents, students and educators alike are dismayed, confused and at a loss as to where to turn for relief. Many of our institutions of higher learning have been completely disrupted by a small band of revolutionaries, encouraged by the permissive attitude of executive and judicial officials of government and the activities of other anarchists throughout the nation.

Many of our primary and secondary school systems have become centers for social experimentation rather than centers of learning, serving merely as pawns for the whims and caprices of some member of the federal judiciary or some agent of the federal bureaucracy.

These conditions must come to an end. Our educational systems and institutions must once again be given the opportunity to resume their rightful duty of preparing the youth of America for entry into our highly competitive society.

As a first and immediate step we must absolutely prohibit the agencies and agents of the federal government from intruding into and seeking to control the affairs of the local school systems of the states, counties and cities of the nation. Control of these schools must be returned to the local officials, representatives of the people, who have the rightful duty and authority to administer such school.

Once returned to proper control, order must be restored and education of our children again become the primary matter of concern in these schools. Sociological experiments must cease. The people of the several states, counties, cities and communities must be given the right to administer the affairs of their schools as they see fit without fear or threat or reprisal, economic or punitive, from the federal government.

We must cooperate with the administrators of our institutions of higher learning now in the hands of revolutionaries. We must support these officials in the restoration of order on their campuses and we must assure that no assistance, financial or otherwise, from the federal level be given to those seeking to disrupt and destroy these great institutions.

America is a nation "Under God" and we must see that it remain such a nation. We will support with all the power of the Executive action to restore to our educational institutions and the children they serve the right and freedom of prayer and devotions to God.

We must assure that the federal government assist in all phases of the educational processes of the nation without attempting to control these processes.

With these thoughts in mind:

We advocate a greater role of the states in administering federal aid and in determining national policy;

We advocate the return of our school systems to the states and to local, county and city officials;

We advocate support for administrators of our educational institutions in their efforts to restore order to these institutions;

We advocate fewer federal guidelines, regulations, and administrative procedures and greater simplification and consolidation of programs and procedures;

We advocate less categorical aid and more general aid to states with funding provided for well in advance;

We advocate educational opportunity for all people regardless of race, creed, color, economic or social status.

The complexities of education are many. State and local officials are faced with tremendous pressures to provide early childhood education, increased teacher salaries, provide vocational technical education, improved elementary and secondary education, provide adult education, continuing education, and urban and rural education, provide for higher education, graduate and professional education.

The goals of the American Independent Party are to improve the educational opportunity for all our citizens from early childhood through the graduate level. We believe that the improvement of educational opportunity can best be accomplished at the state and local level with adequate support from the federal level.

SCIENCE AND TECHNOLOGY

The scientific and technological skills and accomplishments of America are the marvel of modern civilization. Our potential in this area is unlimited. Our development of this potential must be commensurate with our capability. We live in a fiercely competitive world in the area of science and technology. For social, economic and security reasons we must not lag behind.

We would propose, encourage and provide from the federal level assistance to those of our youth showing demonstrated capacity in these areas of endeavor. Federal grants based on ability and aptitude will be provided to assure development of skills in this field.

Federal assistance will be made available for research in various fields of science for in research lies the key to tomorrow. Such assistance will be directed both to individuals and to institutions.

We propose that this research, development and scientific knowledge so acquired be directed to human problems as well as national security. In the fields of housing, transportation, education, industry and related activities, these skills and the knowledge so acquired can make for a better life for all Americans.

Emphasis on the further exploration and utilization of space must be renewed. This, again, is a highly competitive area between nations, but not for this reason alone, but for the welfare and security of this nation, we must not be lacking in our effort in this field.

We fully support renewed and expanded efforts in our space program with the objective of acquiring knowledge and experience of benefit to the peaceful pursuits of mankind as well as that essential to the military security of this nation.

TRANSPORTATION

The expansion of America's industry, commerce and its economy depends upon its transportation system. America cannot maintain its position as world leader in industry and commerce unless all modes of transportation are able to meet the demanding challenges of the future. To solve America's transportation problems requires ingenuity and planning.

Airport congestion around most major cities is not only a growing problem, but an ever-increasing danger. We face a major railroad crisis and citizens in many urban areas are unable to travel short distances without delays due to congested highway traffic. Our merchant marine fleet has dwindled and our shipbuilding industry suffers today. This not only affects our economy, but is a serious handicap to America's military might.

We therefore favor:

1. The development of a modern, low-cost domestic mass transportation system within our congested urban areas;

2. Development of high-speed passenger trains between urban areas;

3. An emergency program carried out cooperatively by the federal government and the airline industry to develop adequate methods of controlling air congestion, and for financing and improving airport facilities;

4. Developing a program of assistance to modernize and stimulate our merchant marine fleet and our shipbuilding industry.

The Interstate Highway System is one of America's wisest investments. Every effort must be made to speed up construction on existing plans, and farsighted planning of additional facilities must be accomplished. The Interstate Highway System must be expanded, adding new routes between population centers, and extra attention should be given to constructing additional freeways in and around congested urban areas. Not only is this necessary for the expansion of commerce and the economy, but highway safety demands it.

Thousands of Americans lose their lives each year on the nation's highways. Most of these deaths are unnecessary. With proper highway planning, stricter enforcement of highway laws, and intensified driver education, along with proper safety devices provided on automobiles, we will be able to cut these needless and tragic fatalities to a small fraction.

Public safety and convenience demand that we engage in a vast program to improve and four-lane many of the local road and highway networks. Highway construction is financed by those persons using the highways and is one of the few federal programs that is self-financed which amounts to a capital investment of public funds, and this we greatly favor.

We will encourage the development within the transportation industry of organizations who are specialists in the movement of passenger and cargo from point to point, using all modes and means of transportation, and we will encourage healthy competition between such agencies and organizations.

NATURAL RESOURCES AND CONSERVATION

The preservation of our natural resources and the quality of our natural environment has greatly been ignored during the past decade. We are vitally concerned about the future well-being of our citizens and fully realize that positive action programs must be undertaken, in a cooperative effort between the federal government and the states, to assure adequate outdoor recreational facilities and to assure necessary health safeguards for generations to come. To these ends we make the following pledge to the American people:

1. We will promote an aggressive campaign at all levels of government to combat the serious air and water pollution problem.

2. Full support will be given to the establishment of adequate water quality standards to protect the present high quality waters, to abate pollution, and to improve the status of waters not now considered of high quality.

3. We will work in close cooperation with private industry and governmental agencies toward engineering designs to abate the mounting air pollution problems.

4. We will actively support research to control pests through biological means and chemical means which are more selective and less persistent than those now used.

5. Legislation and an active program are necessary to protect our endangered wildlife species. This problem is of serious concern and will receive our immediate attention and action.

6. We will work for protection of our waterfowl wetlands and nesting areas.

7. Our estuarine areas must be protected as vital to the production of fish, shellfish, furbearers, waterfowl and other aquatic creatures.

8. All federal assistance programs to the states in the areas of game and fish and for outdoor recreation will be streamlined to gain the maximum benefit from each dollar invested.

9. Our increasing population demands improved and additional outdoor recreational areas. To this end we will support active programs at all levels of government for the development of existing parks and proper outdoor recreational programs. Public lands must be utilized for multiple uses to benefit all of our people.

10. The preservation of our forest and timber resources is of utmost concern to the nation. We pledge federal cooperation with efforts of state and local governments and with private industry for a sound and economically regulated basis to avoid depletion of this vital natural resource. Government and industry will be encouraged to participate in planned reforestation programs, and programs for protection of our forests from the ravages of fire and other destructive causes.

America is blessed with an abundance of natural resources, with beautiful scenery and bountiful waters. This land of ours should not be marred and its resources wasted. We recognize that progress invites construction and industrial

development and we recognize its necessity, but we must assure that the intangible values of our parks, forests and estuarine areas will be protected, promoted and developed and that America shall retain its scenic beauty for centuries to come.

We will place particular emphasis on the problems of air and water pollution and will initiate joint cooperative programs with private industry to attack and solve these problems, as their correction is in the interest of all segments of our national life, the people, the government and the nation's industry.

Veterans

America owes no other group of citizens so much as it does our veterans. To that group of self-sacrificing and patriotic individuals who have risked their lives for our nation and its principles in past wars and conflicts, and to our brave men and women returning from service in Vietnam, we pledge the support of the American Independent Party. We pledge to you and your dependents our assurance of active and vigorous assistance in seeking out job opportunities, job training, further educational opportunities and business opportunities. We likewise support a program to provide educational benefits to children of deceased veterans in order that they may receive a quality education and participate in America's competitive society of the future.

We pledge to our veterans, their families and dependents the cooperation and active assistance of their government in providing adequate medical treatment and hospital care. Veterans' benefits and disability benefits will be updated and revised periodically in order to meet the increased cost of living. The Veterans Administration and its hospitals will remain as an independent agency of the government, and its one objective will be to serve our veterans and their families.

Indian Affairs

For over 100 years the other two parties have been making promises to our fellow citizens, the American Indians and Eskimos. For over 100 years the promises of those parties have not been kept. Our Party offers to these independent and hard-working people a new hope. We promise that all of the programs of the federal government which have so lavishly bestowed benefits upon minority groups of this country will be made equally applicable to the American Indians and Eskimos. There will be no discrimination with respect to these two ancient and noble races.

We also promise that the federal government will cooperate fully to insure that job opportunity, job training, full educational opportunity, and equal application of all health and housing programs are afforded to these, our native citizens, in order that they may enjoy the same benefits and privileges enjoyed by every American. We will foster and support measures through which the beauties and accomplishments of their native culture will be preserved and enhanced.

FOREIGN POLICY

One of the greatest needs of our country at this moment in history is a strong, realistic, well-defined policy to guide our relationship with the other nations of the world. The policy developed to govern our actions in foreign affairs must be one well stated and well understood, first by our own people and, equally as important, by friends and foes alike throughout the world. The absence of any such well-defined and consistent policy throughout the past two decades has contributed immeasurably to the chaotic world conditions now existing.

Our foreign policy will be one designed to secure a just and lasting peace. We feel that such a situation can best come to exist when nations deal with one another on a basis of mutual trust and understanding. If this be lacking, as is so often the case in today's world, the only alternative is complete frankness and determination to adhere to stated objectives and courses of action. If a nation, as is the case with an individual, will only say what it means and mean what it says, it will gain the respect, if not always the admiration, of its sister nations. It is in this regard that we have failed, so often equivocating in such a manner as to cause friendly, as well as unfriendly, nations to have grave doubt as to our stability, determination and reliability of purpose.

We feel that the road to peace lies through international cooperation and understanding. We will pursue this goal to the limits consistent with our own national interest. We will become participants in international programs of aid and development from which all member nations, including our own, derive benefit.

We will not abandon the United Nations Organization unless it first abandons us. It should be given fair opportunity at resolving international disputes; however, we will not subordinate the interest of our nation to the interest of any international organization. We feel that in this organization, as in any other, participating members should bear proportionate shares of the cost of operation and we will insist on financial responsibility on the part of the member nations. We also feel that the officers and officials of such organization must conduct themselves with an abstract air of objectivity and impartiality, and we will so insist. We will give this organization every opportunity to succeed in its purpose but should it fail, we will reappraise our relationship with it.

Foreign Aid

Foreign aid and assistance, both of an economic and military nature, will be granted on a basis of what is in the best interest of our own nation as well as the receiving nation.

We will deny aid and assistance to those nations who oppose us militarily in Vietnam and elsewhere, as well as those who seek our economic and military destruction by giving aid and comfort to our avowed enemies. This must be so in order to protect the economic welfare and national security of this country.

We will continue aid to those countries who need, deserve and have earned the right to our help. This will be done freely and willingly with every effort directed to elimination of waste and dishonesty from such programs.

Foreign aid must become an instrument of foreign policy and be used in such manner as to further the interest of this nation.

Export-Import

We believe strongly in the free enterprise system for America, internally as well as in its trade relations with other nations. However, should the increasing inflow of imports from low-wage nations endanger employment or marketing by American industry, we will approve reasonable quantitative limits on these imports. We feel that our home industry is entitled to a fair share of the present market and of future growth. Before seeking additional legislation in the import field all efforts will be exerted toward securing negotiated agreements that would fully protect American industry.

We will insist on equitable tax treatment for any industry adversely affected by foreign imports, in the area of depreciation allowances for plants and equipment and in like measure.

We will cause the Department of State and other interested agencies of government to work toward the lowering of trade barriers against American goods in a manner consistent with the policy of our administration on controlling imports into the American market.

In the event certain segments of our industrial economy are adversely affected by foreign imports to such an extent as to cause economic harm, we will sponsor and develop programs of re-training and re-employment for those so affected.

Balance of Payments

A serious situation now exists in our balance of payments and this must be ended.

We feel that the adoption of the programs and proposals set out in this Platform will result in a more favorable balance of payments situation. Specifically, we feel that the relief we so badly need in this respect may be achieved through reductions in spending for foreign aid, more efficiency in the use of funds for international programs, and more reliance on our allies in meeting heavy military expenditures abroad.

We have earlier proposed that foreign aid be granted on a basis of need and in a manner consistent with the best interest of this country and that it be denied those who aggressively seek our destruction. We strongly advocate efficiency in operation and the elimination of waste and corruption from expenditures under international programs and we will insist that our allies assume their proportionate and rightful share of the burden of defenses in those areas in which we have mutual interest.

Our export-import situation remains in reasonable balance but our disastrous situation as to balance of payments is caused by excesses in our foreign aid program and other international gratuitous expenditures.

We will work to reduce our military expenditures overseas, not by lessening our military strength and preparedness, but by causing our allies to assume and bear their proportionate share of the burden.

Middle East

The Middle East remains a source of high potential danger to world peace. In the interest of securing a stable peace in this part of the world, we will take the initiative in seeking mutual cooperation between the adversaries in this area in reaching agreement in their age-old dispute. We will encourage the initiation of multilateral discussions to arrive at the best possible terms of settlement. This will mean resolving and stabilizing boundaries and the free use of water and land routes throughout this area. Binding non-aggression agreements must be developed and we must seek the mutual respect of both Israel and the Arab nations.

First and foremost is the need for sincere negotiations between these two parties. Until this is accomplished we must assure that no imbalance of force comes to exist in this area. Nothing could more endanger the peace.

Should arms continue to be introduced into this area by foreign powers to such an extent as to endanger the peace in this part of the world, we must take steps to assure that a balance of force is brought to exist. We will join with other nations of the free world in providing the means whereby this balance of force will continue and the threat of aggression of one nation against another is made less likely. More importantly, this nation will strive in every way to merit and receive the friendship of all parties to this dispute and to earn the respect and good will of Israel and the Arab nations alike. The road to peace in the Middle East lies in this direction rather than in the continued use of military might.

Europe

We continue to regard Western Europe as an area of vital importance to America. In our concern with the interminable conflict in Southeast Asia we must not lose sight of the strategic importance of our relationship with our European allies. We must retain a posture of strength in this area and must work with and for our allies to assure that they remain economically and militarily strong.

We will continue to support the North Atlantic Treaty Organization and seek to strengthen it through the cooperative efforts of all member nations. We will retain the necessary troop strength in this vital area and will insist that our allies and member nations do likewise.

We will deal patiently but firmly with the present French Government feeling that in due time its actions will, of necessity, be directed toward increased cooperation with its Western allies of long standing.

We will remain concerned for the captive satellite nations of Eastern Europe and share with them their hopes and aspirations for their eventual and inevitable return to the family of free nations.

Latin America

The interests of the nations of Latin America are closely related to those of this country, economically, geographically, security-wise, socially and politically.

We must and will provide aid and assistance to these nations to enable them to achieve political and economic stability and to better prepare them to resist the threat of communist infiltration and subversion from the Red satellite, Cuba.

We will develop a program of assistance to these countries designed to relieve the conditions of economic and social poverty existing in some segments of these nations and to provide for their less fortunate citizens a better condition of life.

We will assist in the development of the agricultural and industrial potential of these nations and the development and proper utilization of their tremendous natural resources rather than the exploitation thereof, to the end that the nations of this hemisphere may live in peace, prosperity and harmony with one another and that the principles of the Monroe Doctrine may once again become a cornerstone of our national policy.

We will work with and support the Organization of American States.

Cuba

As for Cuba, we will continue and strengthen the economic pressures on the Castro tyranny. In order to do this, we must secure a greater degree of cooperation from nations of the free world than we have had in the past. Trade with Cuba by our allies must be effectively minimized, if not completely curtailed.

To frustrate Castro's attempt to export subversion, we must increase the quality and effectiveness of our military aid and assistance to Latin American allies with a primary objective of developing realistic indigenous counterinsurgency capabilities within those countries. Economic aid, more carefully planned and scrupulously administered, will be continued through the Alliance for Progress Program, or an improved version thereof.

Africa and Asia

The emerging nations of Africa and Asia desiring assistance and demonstrating a capability of reasonably assimilating such help and assistance will be aided. We will not aid in the replacing of one form of despotism with another, nor will we become concerned with the internal quarrelings of dissident groups and factions.

We disagree with present economic sanctions and pressures applied to Rhodesia and the Union of South Africa and will seek to have these removed and eliminated. We consider these to be nations friendly to this country and they will be respected and treated as such.

General

We will conduct the foreign affairs of this country on a basis of aiding, assisting and cooperating with our friends and recognizing and treating our enemies and adversaries as such. We feel that foreign affairs can be conducted effectively only when there is respect for our nation and this respect is best engendered by attaining a position of strength and adopting an attitude of firmness and fairness. This we will do.

We feel that when this nation again becomes a strong and determined nation, dedicated to a fixed national and international policy, many of our existing difficulties throughout the world will become resolved and new difficulties are less likely to arise.

We will oppose aggression and subversion, Communist or otherwise, whenever it infringes upon the national interest of this country or its friendly allies through means appropriate to the situation.

We do not propose, nor does this or any other nation have the capability, to police the entire world. We will avoid unilateral entanglement in situations not vital to our national interest and will seek the cooperation of our allies at every opportunity.

Vietnam

The current situation in Southeast Asia, and particularly in Vietnam, is one of the most critical which has ever faced this nation. The American people are angry, frustrated and bewildered as they seek for leadership which apparently fails to exist. There is no parallel in American history of such a situation as now exists, not even our engagement in Korea, where there were at least vaguely defined objectives.

It is too late to engage in debate as to why we are so deeply involved and committed in Vietnam. The fact is that we are so involved. No one can retrace the steps of the last ten years and correct and adjust all that has gone wrong. We presently have more than one-half million Americans committed to this conflict and they must be supported with the full resources of this nation. The question now is what does America do to maintain its honor, its respect and its position in this most strategic part of the world, Southeast Asia?

The prime consideration at this time is the honorable conclusion of hostilities in Vietnam. This must be accomplished at the earliest possible moment.

We earnestly desire that the conflict be terminated through peaceful negotiations and we will lend all aid, support, effort, sincerity and prayer to the efforts of our negotiators. Negotiation will be given every reasonable and logical chance for success and we will be patient to an extreme in seeking an end to the war through this means. If it becomes evident that the enemy does not desire to negotiate in good faith, that our hopes of termination of hostilities are not being realized and that the lives and safety of our committed troops are being further endangered, we must seek a military conclusion.

Hopefully such a situation will never arise, but should it come to pass, I would then seek the advice and good judgment of my joint Chiefs of Staff as to ways and means of reaching a military conclusion to this conflict with the least loss of life to our American servicemen and our South Vietnamese allies, stressing the fact that this is to be accomplished through the use of conventional weapons.

Military force has always been recognized as an instrument of national policy and its use to obtain national objectives has always been accepted. However, once national policy is established by the civilian government and military force has been selected as one of the means of attaining national objectives, the tactical employment of this force should be left to the military so long as this employment is consistent with national policy, and the mission of the military should be to attain these national objectives—nothing less.

I would retain full control, as a civilian Commander-in-Chief, of final decision, but I would pay heed to and consider to the fullest extent the advice and judgment of my military advisors.

Unfortunately, there is no clearly defined national policy with respect to the conflict in Vietnam. If there were, much of the doubt, debate and despair of the American people would be eased. There is a total absence of clearly announced and understood national objectives with respect to Vietnam. We are told that it is not victory over the enemy we seek but something else—what we do not know. In battle, and certainly this is battle, there can be but one objective—that is victory. Anything worth dying for is worth winning.

As a first step we must develop a clearly defined national policy as to Vietnam. This policy will be made known to the people of this country and will be based on our own national interest. The essence of this policy will be a timely and successful termination of the conflict, either through negotiation or by victory over the enemy. We will not allow this conflict to drag on indefinitely with its great drain on our national resources and manpower.

As President, we will designate a Secretary of Defense who holds the confidence and trust of the people, the Congress and the military establishments and one with the capability and desire of working in harmony with each. He will be required to reduce the excessive manpower of the Pentagon and rid the Department of Defense of those who have fostered the "no-win" policy.

We will then require the establishment of firm objectives in Vietnam. Should negotiations fail, and we pray that they will not fail, these objectives must provide for a military conclusion to the war. This would require the military defeat of the Vietcong in the South and the destruction of the will to fight or resist on the part of the government of North Vietnam, which is equipping and supporting the enemy troops in the South. We feel that the prompt and effective application of military force could achieve this objective with minimized loss of life, and the tactical employment of this force will be left in the hands of the military commanders, so long as they act pursuant to defined national policy.

We will require the military to plan and conduct military operations once policies and objectives are established and we will not, nor will we permit civilian subordinates, to usurp these functions and assume the role of "commander" or "tactician." This must be a team effort with officials and leaders of civil government performing their required functions and the military establishment being allowed to perform in the manner and for the purpose for which it is trained.

Once hostilities have ceased, efforts must be undertaken to stabilize the government and economy of Vietnam. This must be through programs of self-help and not through completely meaningless "give away" programs. We are dealing with a proud people of ancient culture. They are not, and never will be, adapted to all the facets of western civilization, nor should they be. We must help them to become secure in their government, their lands, their economy and in their homes, as their friends and allies and not as sanctimonious intruders. In this manner, we will gain a lasting ally.

National Defense

Nothing is of greater importance to the American people at this time than the state of our National Defense, and, sadly, there is no area of our national structure so fraught with misrepresentations and inconsistencies. As we near the end of the era of "computerized defense" and "cost effectiveness" rather than military reliability, it is difficult, if not impossible, for the nation to ascertain the true state of its defenses.

We are aware of basic fallacies in the doctrines and logic of those who have been charged with the responsibility of our national security.

We have been told that strength is weakness and weakness is strength—This is not true.

We have been told that parity rather than superiority in weapons and munitions is sufficient

to assure the keeping of the peace and the protection of this country—This is not true.

We have been told a "deterrent" capability is preferable to an offensive capability in maintaining peace and assuring freedom from attack—This is not true.

We have been told that commitment of our military forces need not always be followed by a quest for victory—This is not true.

We have been led to believe in the proven invulnerability of our "second strike" capability—This is not true.

We have been told that the complete disruption of the structure of our Reserve Components resulted in a more readily responsive Reserve—This is not true.

We have been told that our research and development program, especially in the area of space research and development, is not lagging—This is not true,—And so on.

We propose an intensive and immediate review of the policies, practices and capabilities of the Department of Defense with a view to reestablishing sound principles of logic and reasoning to the decisions and directives of that agency and to eliminating from its ranks all of those who have been party to the dissemination and promulgation of the false doctrines of security and the coercion, intimidation and punishment of all who would oppose or disagree with them.

We are in accord with civilian control of our defense establishment but will insist that the civilian authorities work in partnership and harmony with the splendid military force with which this country is blessed. We propose to restore to their proper duties, functions and authority the leaders of our military services so that the nation may once again profit from their wisdom and experience.

We will require our civilian and military leaders of defense to establish a reasonable relationship between defensive and offensive capabilities and provide our services with the proper arms, munitions and equipment to afford a proper mix of both type weapons and munitions.

We will place increased emphasis on research and development in the area of space, weaponry and mobility, as well as other areas vital to our national security.

We support the installation of an anti-ballistic missile defense for the protection of our nation and its citizens. We will expedite this program.

We will assure to our services the best attainable weapons, equipment, machines and munitions without resort to devious distinctions of cost effectiveness and the substitution of arbitrary, unsound judgment for that of the professional military.

We will guarantee to the services and to the nation that American troops will never be committed with less than full support of available resources.

We will seek efficiency in the collection and evaluation of vital intelligence throughout the services.

We will never permit a static situation to develop wherein America stands still while her potential enemies continue to advance in all areas of development.

We will hasten the reconstitution of an adequate and efficiently organized reserve force throughout the several states of the nation. We will accept these reserve component forces into full partnership with the regular military establishment and will assure stability to their organizational structure and operation.

We will take all steps necessary to return our Merchant Marine fleet to its rightful place among the maritime nations of the world. This is not only vital to our national security but to the economic progress and viability of the nation. Maritime shipping has been, and will once again become, a vital part of the nation's economy and trade activity.

We will take steps to make military service more attractive to the enlistee, the inductee and the career personnel at all levels. We will support programs for better pay; better housing and living conditions, both on and off post; more realistic programs of promotion potential so that merit and performance may be rewarded; equitable sharing of hardship assignments; an increase and more uniform retirement benefit to correct serious inequities now existing; a pay scale commensurate with that of private employment, with provisions for periodic increases measured by the cost of living index; improved and expanded medical and hospital benefits for dependents, and a restoration of the dignity and prestige rightfully due those engaged in the defense of our nation.

With military services becoming more attrac-

tive the requirement for involuntary inductions through the Selective Service System is reduced. However, we favor retention of such system for so long as there is a need for manpower being acquired by this means. We would approve any changes to such system designed to eliminate inequities in the selection of inductees, and quite likely some do exist.

We would feel that eventually manpower requirements may be met on a voluntary basis. In such event, a fair and equitable system of civilian induction will be kept in existence, on standby basis, for use in the event of national emergency.

CONCLUSION

This Platform represents the attitude, policy, position, judgment and determination of this Party with respect to the major problems confronting America.

We believe that our analysis of the nature of these problems is in keeping with the feelings of the great majority of our people. We further feel that our approach to solution of these matters is sound, logical, practical and attainable and in keeping with the basic, inherent good judgment of the American people.

Among other proposals:

We offer opportunity for early peace to a nation at war.

We offer order and domestic tranquility to a nation sorely beset by disorder.

We offer a program of job opportunity for the jobless.

We offer a return to respect for the law and an opportunity for every citizen to pursue his daily activities in safety and security.

We offer to relieve our citizens, their businesses and institutions, from harassment and intimidation by agents of the federal bureaucracy.

We offer to return to the offiicals of local government those matters rightly and properly falling within their scope of responsibility.

We offer the laboring man and woman an opportunity to provide for himself and his family a better and fuller life and a greater democratic freedom in the management of the affairs of his organizations, free from intrusion by the federal government.

We offer to the farmer an opportunity to regain a place of prominence in the economy of this nation, a fair price for the products of his labor and less dependence on federal subsidation.

We offer to restore the dignity, strength and prestige of this nation to a level commensurate with its position as acknowledged leader of the nations of the free world.

We offer a national defense designed to assure the security of this nation and its citizens.

And, above all, we offer to each individual citizen a system of government recognizing his inherent dignity and importance as an individual and affording him an opportunity to take a direct hand in the shaping of his own destiny and the destiny of this nation. Under such a system, we are convinced, America will reach new heights of greatness.

Democratic Platform 1968

THE TERMS OF OUR DUTY

America belongs to the people who inhabit it. The source of the nation's strength is the people's freedom to be the source of the laws governing them. To uphold this truth, when Thomas Jefferson and James Madison brought the Democratic Party to birth 175 years ago, they bound it to serve the people and their government as a united whole.

Today, in our 175th anniversary year, the Democratic Party in national convention assembled, again renews the covenant of our birth. We affirm the binding force of our inherited duty to serve the people and their government. We here, therefore, account for what we have done in the Democratic years since 1961. We here state what we will do when our party is again called to lead the nation.

In America and in the world over, strong forces for change are on the move. Systems of thought have been jarred, ways of life have been uprooted, institutions are under siege. The governed challenge those who govern.

We are summoned, therefore, to a fateful task —to ensure that the turmoil of change will prove to be the turmoil of birth instead of decay. We cannot stand still until we are overtaken by events. We dare not entrust our lives to the blind play of accident and force. By reflection and choice, we must make the impulse for change the agent of orderly progress.

There is no alternative.

In the world around us, people have patiently lived with hopes long deferred, with grievances long endured. They are now impatient with patience. Their demands for change must not only be heard, they must be answered.

This is the reality the world as a whole faces.

In America itself, now, and not later, is the right time to strengthen the fabric of our society by making justice and equity the cornerstones of order. Now, and not later, is the right time to uphold the rule of law by securing to all the people the natural rights that belong to them by virtue of their being human. Now, and not later, is the right time to unfurl again the flag of human patriotism and rededicate ourselves under it, to the cause of peace among nations. Now, and not later, is the right time to reclaim the strength spent in quarrels over the past and to apply that strength to America's future. Now is the right time to proceed with the work of orderly progress that will make the future become what we want it to be.

It has always been the object of the Democratic Party to march at the head of events instead of waiting for them to happen. It is our resolve to do that in the years ahead—just as we did in the Democratic years since 1961 when the nation was led by two Democratic Presidents and four Democratic Congresses.

THIS WE HAVE DONE

Our pride in the achievements of these Democratic years in no way blinds us to the large and unfinished tasks which still lie ahead. Just as we know where we have succeeded, we know where our efforts still fall short of our own and the nation's hopes. And we candidly recognize that the cost of trying the untried, of ploughing new ground, is bound to be occasional error. In the future, as in the past, we will confront and correct such errors as we carry our program forward.

In this, we are persuaded that the Almighty judges in a different scale those who err in warmly striving to promote the common good, and those who are free from error because they risked nothing at all and were icily indifferent to good and evil alike. We are also persuaded of something else. What we have achieved with the means at hand—the social inventions we have made since 1961 in all areas of our internal life, and the initiatives we have pressed along a broad front in the world arena—gives us a clear title of right to claim that we know how to move the nation forward toward the attainment of its highest goals in a world of change.

THE ECONOMY

In presenting first the record of what we have achieved in the economic life of the American people, we do not view the economy as being just dollar signs divorced from the flesh and blood concerns of the people. Economics, like politics, involves people and it means people. It means for them the difference between what they don't want and what they do want. It means the difference between justice or injustice, health or sickness, better education or ignorance, a good place to live or a rat infested hovel, a good job or corrosive worry.

In the Democratic years since 1961, under the leadership of Presidents Kennedy and Johnson, we managed the national economy in ways that kept the best aspirations of people in clear view, and brought them closer to fulfillment.

The case was different in the 1950's, when the Republicans held the trust of national leadership. In those years, the American economy creaked and groaned from recurrent recessions. One wasteful recession came in 1954, another in 1958, and a third in 1960. The loss in national production from all three recessions and from a sluggish rate of growth—a loss that can fairly be called the GOP-gap—was a staggering $175 billion, computed in today's prices.

The Democratic Party, seeing the Republican inertia and the dangers it led to, promised to get America moving again. President Kennedy first made that promise for us, and we kept it. We brought an end to recurring recessions, each one of which had followed closer on the heels of the last. Full cooperation between our government officials and all sectors of American life led to new public policies which unlocked the creative power of America's free enterprise system. The magnificent response of all the people comprising that system made the world stand in awe of the results.

Since 1961, we have seen:

A 90-month period of recession-free prosperity, the longest and strongest period of sustained economic growth in American history;

A slash in the unemployment rate from 7 to under 4 percent;

An increase of nearly 40 percent in real wages and salaries and nearly one-third in the average person's real income;

And, on the eight year average, a reduction in the rate levels of the individual income tax.

America's private enterprise system flourished as never before in these years of Democratic leadership. Compared with the preceding eight Republican years, private enterprise in the Democratic 1960's grew twice as fast, profits increased twice as rapidly, four times as many jobs were created, and thirteen million Americans—or one-third of those in poverty in 1960—have today escaped its bondage.

Democrats, however, were not satisfied. We saw—and were the first to see—that even sustained prosperity does not eliminate hardcore unemployment. We were the first to see that millions of Americans would never share in America's abundance unless the people as a whole, through their government, acted to supplement what the free enterprise could do.

So, under the leadership of President Johnson, this nation declared war on poverty—a war in which the government is again working in close cooperation with leaders of the free enterprise system.

It would compromise the integrity of words to claim that the war on poverty and for equal opportunity has been won. Democrats are the first to insist that it has only begun—while 82 percent of the House Republicans and 69 percent of the Senate Republicans voted against even beginning it at all. Democrats know that much more remains to be done. What we have done thus far is to test a series of pilot projects before making them bigger, and we have found that they DO work.

Thus:

The new pre-school program known as Head Start has proven its effectiveness in widening the horizons of over two million poor children and their parents.

The new programs known as the Job Corps and the Neighborhood Youth Corps, entailing close cooperation between the government and private enterprise, have helped nearly two million unskilled boys and girls—most of them drop-outs from school—get work in the community and in industry.

The new program known as Upward Bound has helped thousands of poor but talented young men and women prepare themselves for college.

The new structure of neighborhood centers brings modern community services directly to the people who need them most.

THE PEOPLE

We emphasize that the coldly stated statistics of gains made in the war on poverty must be translated to mean people, in all their yearnings for personal fulfillment. That is true as well of all other things in the great outpouring of constructive legislation that surpassed even the landmark years of the early New Deal.

Education is one example. From the beginning of our Party history, Democrats argued that liberty and learning must find in each other the surest ground for mutual support. The inherited conviction provided the motive force behind the educational legislation of the 1960's that we enacted:

Because of the Elementary and Secondary Education Act of 1965, local education has been enriched to the benefit of over 13 million young Americans;

Because of the Higher Education Act of 1965, new college classrooms, laboratories and libraries have been built to assure that higher education will not be the monopoly of the few but the right of the many;

Because of federal assistance to students, the doors to college have been opened for over a million young men and women coming from families with modest means—so that about one out of every five college students is now pursuing his higher education with some kind of federal help;

Because Democrats are convinced that the best of all investments is in the human resources represented by the youth of America, we brought about a four-fold increase in the federal investment in education since 1960. The level now approaches $12 billion annually.

As it promoted better education, so did Democratic leadership promote better health for all.

The program of mercy and justice known as health care for the aged, which President Truman originally proposed and Presidents Kennedy and Johnson fought for, finally became law in the summer of 1965. Because of it, more than seven million older citizens each year are now receiving modern medical care in dignity—no longer forced to depend on charity, no longer a burden on relatives, no longer in physical pain because they cannot afford to pay for the healing power of modern medicine. Virtually all older Americans, the well and the sick alike, are now protected, their lives more secure, their afflictions eased.

To deal with other aspects of the nation's health needs, measures were enacted in the Democratic years representing an almost four-fold increase in the government's investment in health. Programs were enacted to cope with the killing diseases of heart, cancer and stroke; to combat mental retardation and mental illness; to increase the manpower supply of trained medical technicians; to speed the construction of new hospitals.

Democrats in the Presidency and in the Congress have led the fight to erase the stain of racial discrimination that tarnished America's proudly announced proposition that all men are created equal.

We knew that racial discrimination was present in every section of the country. We knew that the enforcement of civil rights and general laws is indivisible. In this conviction, Democrats took the initiative to guarantee the right to safety and security of the person, the right to all the privileges of citizenship, the right to equality of opportunity in employment, and the right to public services and accommodations and housing. For example:

Because of the Civil Rights Act of 1964, all men born equal in the eyes of their Creator are by law declared to be equal when they apply for a job, or seek a night's lodging or a good meal;

Because of the Voting Rights Act of 1965, the right to the ballot box—the right on which all other rights depend—has been reinforced by law;

Because of the Civil Rights Act of 1968, all families will have an equal right to live where they wish.

THE NATION

The frontier on which most Americans live is the vertical frontier of the city. It is a frontier whose urgent needs hold a place of very high priority on the national agenda—and on the agenda of the Democratic Party.

Democrats recognize that the race to save our cities is a race against the absolute of time itself. The blight that threatens their future takes many forms. It is the physical decay of homes and neighborhoods. It is poverty and unemployment. It is broken homes and social disintegration. It is crime. It is congestion and pollution. The Democratic program attacked all of these forms of blight—and all at once.

Since we know that the cities can be saved only by the people who live there, Democrats have invigorated local effort through federal leadership and assistance. In almost every city, a community action agency has mounted a many-sided assault on poverty. Through varied neighborhood organizations, the poor themselves are tackling their own problems and devising their own programs of self-help. Under Model Cities legislation, enacted in 1966, seventy-five cities are now launching the most comprehensive programs of economic, physical, and social development ever undertaken—and the number of participating cities will be doubled soon. In this effort, the residents of the areas selected to become the model neighborhoods are participating fully in planning their future and deciding what it will be.

In a series of housing acts beginning in 1961, Democrats have found ways to encourage private enterprise to provide modern, decent housing for low-income and moderate-income families. The Housing and Urban Development Act of 1968 is the most far-reaching housing legislation in America's history. Under its terms, the genius of American business will combine with the productivity of American labor to meet a 10-year goal of 26 million new housing units—6 million of them for the poor. The objective is to enable the poor to own their own homes, to rebuild entire neighborhoods, to spur the pace of urban renewal, and to deal more humanely with the problems of displaced people.

To give our cities a spokesman of Cabinet rank, Democrats in 1965 took the lead in creating a Department of Housing and Urban Development.

Democratic Presidents and Congresses have moved with equal vigor to help the people of America's vast hinterland outside the metropolitan centers to join the march of economic progress. Of the 101 major areas classified as "depressed areas" when the Democrats assumed office in 1961, 90 have now solved their problems of excessive unemployment and the others are on their way. The Area Redevelopment Act, the expansion of resource development programs, and the massive effort to restore Appalachia and other lagging regions to economic health assisted the people of these areas in their remarkable progress.

In these legislative undertakings of primary concern to people—American people—it is to the credit of some Republicans that they joined the Democratic majority in a common effort. Unfortunately, however, most Republicans sat passively by while Democrats wrote the legislation the nation's needs demanded. Worse, and more often, Republicans did what they could to obstruct and defeat the measures that were approved by Democrats in defiance of hostile Republican votes. Thus:

In the case of the Elementary and Secondary Education Act, 73 percent of the Republicans in the House voted to kill it.

In the case of medical care for the aged, 93 percent of the Republicans in the House and 64 percent in the Senate voted to kill it.

In the case of the Model Cities program, 88 percent of the Republicans in the House voted to kill it.

In the case of the program to help Appalachia, 81 percent of House Republicans and 58 percent of Senate Republicans voted to kill it, and 75 percent of House Republicans voted to kill corresponding programs of aid for other depressed regions of the country.

The same negative attitude was present among Republicans in the 1950's, and one of the results was a crisis in the farm sector of the economy—which the Democrats inherited in the 1960's. In the late Republican 1950's, the glut of farm surpluses amounted to over $8 billion, and the taxpayers were forced to pay $1 billion every year in interest and storage charges alone. Democrats, however, set out resolutely to reverse the picture. Democratic farm programs supported farm income, expanded farm exports and domestic consumption, helped farmers adjust their production to the size of the expanded markets, and reduced farm surpluses and storage costs to the lowest level since 1952.

Democrats have also acted vigorously to assure that American science and technology shall continue to lead the world.

In atomic energy, in space exploration, in communications, in medicine, in oceanology, in fundamental and applied research in many fields, we have provided leadership and financial aid to the nation's scientists and engineers. Their genius has, in turn, powered our national economic growth.

Other measures affected all Americans everywhere.

Under our constitutional system of federalism, the primary responsibility for law enforcement rests with selected local officials and with governors, but the federal government can and should play a constructive role in support of state and local authorities.

In this conviction, Democratic leadership secured the enactment of a law which extended financial assistance to modernize local police departments, to train law enforcement personnel, and to develop modern police technology. The effect of these provisions is already visible in an improved quality of law enforcement throughout the land.

Under Democratic leadership, furthermore, the Juvenile Delinquence Prevention and Control Act was passed to aid states and communities to plan and carry out comprehensive programs to prevent and combat youth crime. We have added more personnel to strengthen the Federal Bureau of Investigation and the enforcement of narcotics laws, and have intensified the campaign against organized crime. The federal government has come swiftly to the aid of cities needing help to bring major disturbances under control, and Democratic leadership secured the enactment of a new gun control law as a step toward putting the weapons of wanton violence beyond the reach of criminal and irresponsible hands.

To purify the air we breathe and the water we drink, Democrats led the way to the enactment of landmark anti-pollution legislation.

To bring order into the administration of transportation programs and to coordinate transportation policy, Democrats in 1966 established a new Cabinet-level Department of Transportation.

For the consumer, new standards of protec-

tion were enacted—truth-in-lending and truth-in-packaging, the Child Safety Act, the Pipeline Safety Act, the Wholesome Meat and Wholesome Poultry Acts.

For America's 100 million automobile drivers, auto and highway safety legislation provided protection not previously known.

For every American family, unparalleled achievements in conservation meant the development of balanced outdoor recreation programs—involving magnificent new national parks, seashores, and lakeshores—all within an afternoon's drive of 110 million Americans. For the first time, we are beating the bulldozer to the nation's remaining open spaces.

For the sake of all living Americans and for their posterity, the Wilderness Preservation Act of 1964 placed in perpetual trust millions of acres of primitive and wilderness areas.

For America's sons who manned the nation's defenses, a new G.I. bill with greatly enlarged equitable benefits was enacted gratefully and proudly.

America's senior citizens enjoyed the large t increase in social security since the system was inaugurated during the Democratic Presidency of Franklin D. Roosevelt.

For the hungry, our food distribution programs were expanded to provide more than $1 billion worth of food a year for domestic use, giving millions of children, for the first time, enough to eat.

A new minimum wage law raised paychecks and standards of living for millions, while a new network of training programs enabled more than a million Americans to learn new skills and become productive workers in the labor force.

A new Immigration Act removed the harsh injustice of the national origins quota system and opened our shores without discrimination to those who can contribute to the growth and strength of America.

Many more measures enacted under Democratic leadership could be added to this recital of achievements in our internal life since 1961. But what we could list shares the character of what we have listed. All the measures alike are a witness to our desire to serve the people as a united whole, to chart the way for their orderly progress, to possess their confidence—by striving through our conduct to deserve to possess it.

THE WORLD

The conscience of the entire world has been shocked by the brutal and unprovoked Soviet aggression against Czechoslovakia. By this act, Moscow has confessed that it is still the prisoner of its fear of freedom. And the Czechoslovakian people have shown that the love of freedom, in their land and throughout Eastern Europe, can never be crushed.

This severe blow to freedom and self-determination reinforces our commitment to the unending quest for peace and security in the world. These dark days should not obscure the solid achievements of the past eight years. Nuclear war has been avoided. West Berlin and Western Europe are still free.

The blend of American power and restraint, so dramatically demonstrated in the Cuban missile crisis, earned the respect of the world and prepared the way for a series of arms control agreements with the Soviet Union. Long and patient negotiation by Presidents Kennedy and Johnson resulted in the Nuclear Test Ban, Nuclear Non-Proliferation, and Space treaties and the "hot line." These hard-won agreements provide the base for pursuing other measures to reduce the risk of nuclear war.

The unprecedented expansion of the American economy has invigorated the whole free world. Many once skeptical nations, including some communist states, now regard American economic techniques and institutions as a model.

In Asia the tragic Vietnam war has often blinded us to the quiet and constructive developments which affect directly the lives of over a billion people and the prospects for peace everywhere.

An economically strong and democratic Japan has assumed a more active role in the development of the region. Indonesia has a nationalist, non-communist government seeking to live at peace with its neighbors. Thailand, Taiwan, Singapore, Malaysia, and the Republic of Korea have more stable governments and steadily growing economies. They have been aided by American economic assistance and by the American military presence in the Pacific. They have also been encouraged by a confidence reflecting successive Presidential decisions to assist nations to live in peace and freedom.

Elsewhere in the developing world, there has been hopeful political and economic progress. Though Castro's Cuba is still a source of subversion, the other Latin American states are moving ahead under the Alliance for Progress. In Africa, many of the new states have chosen moderate leaders committed to peaceful nation-building. They are beginning to cooperate with their neighbors in regional agencies of their own design. And like developing countries on other continents, they are for the first time giving serious attention to agricultural development. This new emphasis on food will buy time to launch effective programs of population control.

* * *

In all these constructive changes America, under Democratic leadership, has played a significant role. But we Democrats do not believe in resting on past achievements. We view any success as a down payment on the hard tasks that lie ahead. There is still much to be done at home and abroad and we accept with confidence the challenge of the future.

THIS WE WILL DO

TOWARD A PEACEFUL WORLD

In the pursuit of our national objectives and in the exercise of American power in the world, we assert that the United States should:

Continue to accept its world responsibilities—not turn inward and isolate ourselves from the cares and aspirations of mankind;

Seek a world of diversity and peaceful change, where men can choose their own governments and where each nation can determine its own destiny without external interference;

Resist the temptation to try to mold the world, or any part of it, in our own image, or to become the self-appointed policeman of the world;

Call on other nations, great and small, to contribute a fair share of effort and resources to world peace and development;

Honor our treaty obligations to our allies;

Seek always to strengthen and improve the United Nations and other international peace-keeping arrangements and meet breaches or threatened breaches of the peace according to our carefully assessed interests and resources;

In pursuing these objectives, we will insure that our policies will be subject to constant review so they reflect our true national interests in a changing world.

National Defense

The tragic events in Czechoslovakia are a shocking reminder that we live in a dangerous and unpredictable world. The Soviet attack on and invasion of a small country that only yesterday was Moscow's peaceful ally, is an ominous reversal of the slow trend toward greater freedom and independence in Eastern Europe. The reimposition of Soviet tyranny raises the spectre of the darkest days of the Stalin era and increases the risk of war in Central Europe, a war that could become a nuclear holocaust.

Against this somber backdrop, whose full portent cannot now be seen, other recent Soviet military moves take on even greater significance. Though we have a significant lead in military strength and in all vital areas of military technology, Moscow has steadily increased its strategic nuclear arsenal, its missile-firing nuclear submarine fleet, and its anti-missile defenses. Communist China is providing political and military support for so-called wars of national liberation. A growing nuclear power, Peking has disdained all arms control efforts.

We must and will maintain a strong and balanced defense establishment adequate to the task of security and peace. There must be no doubt about our strategic nuclear capability, our capacity to meet limited challenges, and our willingness to act when our vital interests are threatened.

To this end, we pledge a vigorous research and development effort. We will also continue to pursue the highly successful efforts initiated by Democratic administrations to save tax dollars by eliminating waste and duplication.

We face difficult and trying times in Asia and in Europe. We have responsibilities and commitments we cannot escape with honor. But we are not alone. We have friends and allies around the world. We will consult with them and ask them to accept a fair share of the burdens of peace and security.

North Atlantic Community

The North Atlantic Community is strong and free. We must further strengthen our ties and be constantly alert to new challenges and opportunities. We support a substantially larger European contribution to NATO.

Soviet troops have never stepped across the border of a NATO country. By harassment and threat the Kremlin has repeatedly attempted to push the West out of Berlin. But West Berlin is still free. Western Europe is still free. This is a living tribute to the strength and validity of the NATO alliance.

The political differences we have had with some of our allies from time to time should not divert us from our common task of building a secure and prosperous Atlantic community based on the principles of mutual respect and mutual dependence. The NATO alliance has demonstrated that free nations can build a common shield without sacrificing their identity and independence.

Arms Control

We must recognize that vigilance calls for the twin disciplines of defense and arms control. Defense measures and arms control measures must go hand in hand, each serving national security and the larger interests of peace.

We must also recognize that the Soviet Union and the United States still have a common interest in avoiding nuclear war and preventing the spread of nuclear weapons. We also share a common interest in reducing the cost of national defense. We must continue to work together. We will press for further arms control agreements, insisting on effective safeguards against violations.

For almost a quarter of a century America's pre-eminent military strength, combined with our political restraint, has deterred nuclear war. This great accomplishment has confounded the prophets of doom.

Eight years ago the Democratic Party pledged new efforts to control nuclear weapons. We have fulfilled that pledge. The new Arms Control and Disarmament Agency has undertaken and coordinated important research. The sustained initiatives of President Kennedy and President Johnson have resulted in the "hot line" between the White House and the Kremlin, the limited Nuclear Test Ban Treaty, the Non-Proliferation Treaty, and the treaty barring the orbiting of weapons of mass destruction.

Even in the present tense atmosphere, we

strongly support President Johnson's effort to secure an agreement with the Soviet Union under which both states would refrain from deploying anti-missile systems. Such a treaty would result in the saving of billions of dollars and would create a climate for further arms control measures. We support concurrent efforts to freeze the present level of strategic weapons and delivery systems, and to achieve a balanced and verified reduction of all nuclear and conventional arms.

The Middle East

The Middle East remains a powder keg. We must do all in our power to prevent a recurrence of war in this area. A large Soviet fleet has been deployed to the Mediterranean. Preferring short-term political advantage to long-range stability and peace, the Soviet Union has rushed arms to certain Arab states to replace those lost in the Arab-Israeli War of 1967. As long as Israel is threatened by hostile and well-armed neighbors, we will assist her with essential military equipment needed for her defense, including the most advanced types of combat aircraft.

Lasting peace in the Middle East depends upon agreed and secured frontiers, respect for the territorial integrity of all states, the guaranteed right of innocent passage through all international waterways, a humane resettlement of the Arab refugees, and the establishment of a non-provocative military balance. To achieve these objectives, we support negotiations among the concerned parties. We strongly support efforts to achieve an agreement among states in the area and those states supplying arms to limit the flow of military equipment to the Middle East.

We support efforts to raise the living standards throughout the area, including desalinization and regional irrigation projects which cut across state frontiers.

Vietnam and Asia

Our most urgent task in Southeast Asia is to end the war in Vietnam by an honorable and lasting settlement which respects the rights of all the people of Vietnam. In our pursuit of peace and stability in the vital area of Southeast Asia we have borne a heavy burden in helping South Vietnam to counter aggression and subversion from the North.

We reject as unacceptable a unilateral withdrawal of our forces which would allow that aggression and subversion to succeed. We have never demanded, and do not now demand, unconditional surrender by the communists.

We strongly support the Paris talks and applaud the initiative of President Johnson which brought North Vietnam to the peace table. We hope that Hanoi will respond positively to this act of statesmanship.

In the quest for peace no solutions are free of risk. But calculated risks are consistent with the responsibility of a great nation to seek a peace of reconciliation.

Recognizing that events in Vietnam and the negotiations in Paris may affect the timing and the actions we recommend, we would support our Government in the following steps:

Bombing: Stop all bombing of North Vietnam when this action would not endanger the lives of our troops in the field; this action should take into account the response from Hanoi.

Troop Withdrawal: Negotiate with Hanoi an immediate end or limitation of hostilities and the withdrawal from South Vietnam of all foreign forces—both United States and allied forces, and forces infiltrated from North Vietnam.

Election of Postwar Government: Encourage all parties and interests to agree that the choice of the postwar government of South Vietnam should be determined by fair and safeguarded elections, open to all major political factions and parties prepared to accept peaceful political processes. We would favor an effective international presence to facilitate the transition from war to peace and to assure the protection of minorities against reprisal.

Interim Defense and Development Measures: Until the fighting stops, accelerate our efforts to train and equip the South Vietnamese army so that it can defend its own country and carry out cutbacks of U.S. military involvement as the South Vietnamese forces are able to take over their larger responsibilities. We should simultaneously do all in our power to support and encourage further economic, political and social development and reform in South Vietnam, including an extensive land reform program. We support President Johnson's repeated offer to provide a substantial U.S. contribution to the postwar reconstruction of South Vietnam as well as to the economic development of the entire region, including North Vietnam. Japan and the European industrial states should be urged to join in this postwar effort.

For the future, we will make it clear that U.S. military and economic assistance in Asia will be selective. In addition to considerations of our vital interests and our resources, we will take into account the determination of the nations that request our help to help themselves and their willingness to help each other through regional and multilateral cooperation.

We want no bases in South Vietnam; no continued military presence and no political role in Vietnamese affairs. If and when the communists understand our basic commitment and limited goals and are willing to take their chances, as we are, on letting the choice of the post-war government of South Vietnam be determined freely and peacefully by all of the South Vietnamese people, then the bloodshed and the tragedy can stop.

Japan, India, Indonesia, and most of the smaller Asian nations are understandably apprehensive about Red China because of its nuclear weapons, its support of subversive efforts abroad, and its militant rhetoric. They have been appalled by the barbaric behavior of the Red Guards toward the Chinese people, their callous disregard for human life and their mistreatment of foreign diplomats.

The immediate prospect that China will emerge from its self-imposed isolation is dim. But both Asians and Americans will have to coexist with the 750 million Chinese on the mainland. We shall continue to make it clear that we are prepared to cooperate with China whenever it is ready to become a responsible member of the international community. We would actively encourage economic, social and cultural exchange with mainland China as a means of freeing that nation and her people from their narrow isolation.

We support continued assistance to help maintain the independence and peaceful development of India and Pakistan.

Recognizing the growing importance of Asia and the Pacific, we will encourage increased cultural and educational efforts, such as those undertaken in multi-racial Hawaii, to facilitate a better understanding of the problems and opportunities of this vast area.

The Developing World

The American people share the aspirations for a better life in the developing world. But we are committed to peaceful change. We believe basic political rights in most states can be more effectively achieved and maintained by peaceful action than by violence.

In their struggle for political and economic development, most Asian, African, and Latin American states are confronted by grinding poverty, illiteracy and a stubborn resistance to constructive change. The aspirations and frustrations of the people are frequently exploited by self-serving revolutionaries who employ illegal and violent means.

Since World War II, America's unprecedented program of foreign economic assistance for reconstruction and development has made a profound contribution to peace, security, and a better life for millions of people everywhere. Many nations formerly dependent upon American aid are now viable and stable as a result of this aid.

We support strengthened U.S. and U.N. development aid programs that are responsive to changing circumstances and based on the recognition, as President Johnson put it, that "self-help is the lifeblood of economic development." Grant aid and government loans for long-term projects are part of a larger transfer of resources between the developed and underdeveloped states, which includes international trade and private capital investment as important components.

Like the burden of keeping the peace, the responsibility for assisting the developing world must be shared by Japan and the Western European states, once recipients of U.S. aid and now donor states.

Development aid should be coordinated among both donors and recipients. The World Bank and other international and regional agencies for investment and development should be fully utilized. We should encourage regional cooperation by the recipients for the most efficient use of resources and markets.

We should press for additional international agreements that will stimulate mutually beneficial trade and encourage a growing volume of private investment in the developing states. World-wide commodity agreements that stabilize prices for particular products and other devices to stabilize export earnings will also spur development.

We believe priority attention should be given to agricultural production and population control. Technical assistance which emphasizes manpower training is also of paramount importance. We support the Peace Corps which has sent thousands of ambassadors of good will to three continents.

Cultural and historic ties and a common quest for peace with freedom and justice have made Latin America an area of special concern and interest to the United States. We support a vigorous Alliance for Progress program based upon the Charter of Punta del Este which affirms that "free men working through the institutions for representative democracy can best satisfy man's aspirations."

We support the objective of Latin American economic integration endorsed by the presidents of the American Republics in April 1967 and urge further efforts in the areas of tax reform, land reform, educational reform, and economic development to fulfill the promise of Punta del Este.

United Nations

Since the birth of the United Nations, the United States has pursued the quest for peace, security and human dignity through United Nations channels more vigorously than any other member state. Our dedication to its purpose and its work remains undiminished.

The United Nations contributed to dampening the fires of conflict in Kashmir, the Middle East, Cyprus and the Congo. The agencies of the United Nations have made a significant contribution to health, education and economic well-being in Asia, Africa and Latin America. These efforts deserve continued and expanded support. We pledge that support.

Since we recognize that the United Nations can be only as effective as the support of its members, we call upon other states to join with us in a renewed commitment to use its facilities in the great tasks of economic development, the non-military use of atomic energy, arms control and peace-keeping. It is only with member nations working together that the organization can make its full contribution to the growth of a world community of peace under law, rather than by threat or use of military force.

We are profoundly concerned about the continued repression of Jews and other minorities in the Soviet Union and elsewhere, and look forward to the day when the full light of liberty and freedom shall be extended to all countries and all peoples.

Foreign Trade and Financial Policy

World trade is essential to economic stability. The growing interdependence of nations, particularly in economic affairs, is an established fact of contemporary life. It also spells an opportunity for constructive international cooperation that will bring greater well-being for all and improve the prospects for international peace and security.

We shall build upon the Trade Expansion Act of 1962 and the Kennedy round of trade negotiations, in order to achieve greater trade cooperation and progress toward freer international trade. In future negotiations, which will require careful preparation, we shall: 1) seek continued reciprocal reduction and elimination of tariff barriers, based on the most favored nation principle; 2) negotiate the reciprocal removal of non-tariff barriers to international trade on all products, including agriculture; 3) give special attention to the needs of the developing countries for increased export earnings; and 4) develop and improve the rules governing fair international competition affecting both foreign commerce and investment.

To lessen the hardships suffered by industries and workers as the result of trade liberalization, we support improvements in the adjustment assistance provisions of present law. Provision of law to remedy unfair and destructive import competition should be reviewed and strengthened, and negotiated international agreements to achieve this purpose should be employed where appropriate.

The United States has experienced balance-of-payments deficits for over a decade, mainly because of our security obligations in the free world. Faced with these deficits, we have behaved responsibly by avoiding both economic deflation at home and severe unilateral restrictive measures on international transactions, which would have weakened the international economy and international cooperation.

We shall continue to take the path of constructive measures by relying on steps to increase our exports and by the development of further cooperative arrangements with the other countries. We intend, as soon as possible, to dismantle the restrictions placed on foreign investment and finance, so that American free enterprise can play its full part as the agent of economic development. We will continue to encourage persons from other lands to visit America.

Steps of historical importance have already been taken to improve the functioning of the international monetary system, most notably the new special drawing rights under the international monetary fund. We shall continue to work for the further improvement of the international monetary system so as to reduce its vulnerability to monetary crises.

Economic Growth and Stability

The Democratic policies that more than doubled the nation's rate of economic expansion in the past eight years can double and redouble our national income by the end of this century. Such a rate of economic growth will enable us to win total victory in our wars on ignorance, poverty, and the misery of the ghettos.

But victory will not come automatically. To realize our full economic potential will require effective, businesslike planning and cooperation between government and all elements of private economy. The Democratic Party pledges itself to achieve that purpose in many ways.

Fiscal and Monetary Policy

Taxes were lowered in 1962, 1964, and 1965 to encourage more private spending and reach full employment; they were raised in 1966 and 1968 to help prevent inflation, but with a net reduction in the eight Democratic years. We will continue to use tax policy to maintain steady economic growth by helping through tax reduction to stimulate the economy when it is sluggish and through temporary tax increases to restrain inflation. To promote this objective, methods must be devised to permit prompt, temporary changes in tax rates within prescribed limits with full participation of the Congress in the decisions.

The goals of our national tax policy must be to distribute the burden of government equitably among our citizens and to promote economic efficiency and stability. We have placed major reliance on progressive taxes, which are based on the democratic principle of ability to pay. We pledge ourselves to continue to rely on such taxes, and to continue to improve the way they are levied and collected so that every American contributes to government in proportion to his ability to pay.

A thorough revamping of our federal taxes has been long overdue to make them more equitable as between rich and poor and as among people with the same income and family responsibilities. All corporation and individual preferences that do not serve the national interest should be removed. Tax preferences, like expenditures, must be rigorously evaluated to assure that the benefit to the nation is worth the cost.

We support a proposal for a minimum income tax for persons of high income based on an individual's total income regardless of source in order that wealthy persons will be required to make some kind of income tax contribution, no matter how many tax shelters they use to protect their incomes. We also support a reduction of the tax burden on the poor by lowering the income tax rates at the bottom of the tax scale and increasing the minimum standard deduction. No person or family below the poverty level should be required to pay federal income taxes.

Our goal is a balanced budget in a balanced economy. We favor distinguishing current operating expenditures from long term capital outlays and repayable loans, which should be amortized consistent with sound accounting principles. All government expenditures should be subject to firm tests of efficiency and essentiality.

An effective policy for growth and stability requires careful coordination of fiscal and monetary policies. Changes in taxes, budgets, interest rates, and money supply must be carefully blended and flexibly adjusted to assure:

Adaptation to changing economic conditions;

Adequate supplies of money and credit for the expansion of industry, commerce, and housing;

Maintenance of the lowest possible interest rates;

Avoidance of needless hardships on groups that depend heavily on credit.

Cooperation between fiscal and monetary authorities was greatly strengthened in the past eight years, and we pledge ourselves to continue to perfect this cooperation.

Price Stability with Growth

Price stability continues to be an essential goal of expansive economic policy. Price inflation hurts most of the weak among us and could interfere with the continued social gains we are determined to achieve in the immediate years ahead.

The answer to rising prices will never be sought, under Democratic administrations, in unemployment and idle plant facilities. We are firmly committed to the twin objectives of full employment and price stability.

To promote price stability in a dynamic and growing economy, we will:

Pursue flexible fiscal and monetary policies designed to keep total private and public demand in line with the economy's rising productive capacity.

Work effectively with business, labor, and the public in formulating principles for price and wage policies that are equitable and sound for consumers as well as for workers and investors.

Strictly enforce antitrust and trade practice laws to combat administered pricing, supply limitations and other restrictive practices.

Strengthen competition by keeping the doors of world trade open and resisting the protectionism of captive markets.

Stimulate plant modernization, upgrade labor skills, and speed technological advance to step up productivity.

Agriculture

Twice in this century the Republican Party has brought disaster to the American farmer—in the thirties and in the fifties. Each time, the American farmer was rescued by the Democratic Party, but his prosperity has not yet been fully restored.

Farmers must continue to be heard in the councils of government where decisions affecting agriculture are taken. The productivity of our farmers—already the world's most productive—must continue to rise, making American agricul-

ture more competitive abroad and more prosperous at home.

A strong agriculture requires fair income to farmers for an expanding output. Family farmers must be protected from the squeeze between rising production costs and low prices for their products. Farm income should grow with productivity just as industrial wages rise with productivity. At the same time, market prices should continue to reflect supply and demand conditions and American farm products must continue to compete effectively in world markets. In this way, markets at home and abroad will continue to expand beyond the record high levels of recent years.

To these ends, we shall:

Take positive action to raise farm income to full parity level in order to preserve the efficient, full-time family farm. This can be done through present farm programs when these programs are properly funded, but these programs will be constantly scrutinized with a view to improvement.

Actively seek out and develop foreign commercial markets, since international trade in agricultural products is a major favorable factor in the nation's balance of payments. In expanding our trade, we shall strive to ensure that farmers get adequate compensation for their production going into export.

Expand our food assistance programs to America's poor and our Food for Peace program to help feed the world's hungry.

Establish a Strategic Food and Feed Reserve Plan whereby essential commodities such as wheat, corn and other feed grains, soybeans, storable meat and other products will be stockpiled as a safeguard against crop failures, to assist our nation and other nations in time of famine or disaster, and to ensure adequate supplies for export markets, as well as to protect our own farm industry. This reserve should be insulated from the market.

Support the right of farmers to bargain collectively in the market place on a commodity by commodity basis. Labor and industry have long enjoyed this right to bargain collectively under existing legislation. Protective legislation for bargaining should be extended to agriculture.

Continue to support and encourage agricultural co-operatives by expanded and liberal credit, and to protect them from punitive taxation.

Support private or public credit on reasonable terms to young farmers to enable them to purchase farms on long term, low interest loans.

Support the federal crop insurance program.

Reaffirm our support of the rural electrification program, recognizing that rural America cannot be revitalized without adequate low-cost electric power. We pledge continued support of programs to assure supplemental financing to meet the growing generating and distributing power needs of rural areas. We support the rural telephone program.

Support a thorough study of the effect of unlimited payments to farmers. If necessary, we suggest graduated open-end limitations of payments to extremely large corporate farms that participate in government programs.

Take a positive approach to the public interest in the issue of health and tobacco at all levels of the tobacco economy. We recommend a cooperative effort in health and tobacco research by government, industry and qualified scientific bodies, to ascertain relationships between human health and tobacco growth, curing, storage and manufacturing techniques, as well as specific medical aspects of tobacco smoke constituents.

Small Business

Small business plays a vital role in a dynamic, competitive economy; it helps maintain a strong social fabric in communities across the land; it builds concerned community leadership deriving from ownership of small enterprises; and it maintains the challenge and competition essential to a free enterprise system.

To assure a continuing healthy environment for small business, the Democratic Party pledges to:

Assure adequate credit at reasonable costs;

Assure small business a fair share of government contracts and procurement;

Encourage investment in research and development of special benefit to small enterprise;

Assist small business in taking advantage of technological innovations;

Provide centers of information on government procurement needs and foreign sales opportunities.

The Democratic Party is pledged to develop programs that will enable members of minority groups to obtain the financing and technical management assistance needed to succeed in launching and operating new enterprises.

Labor-Management Relations

Private collective bargaining and a strong and independent labor movement are essential to our system of free enterprise and economic democracy. Their development has been fostered under each Democratic administration in this century.

We will thoroughly review and update the National Labor Relations Act to assure an effective opportunity to all workers to exercise the right to organize and to bargain collectively, including such amendments as:

Repeal of the provision permitting states to enact compulsory open shop laws;

Extension of the Act's protection to farm workers, employees of private non-profit organizations, and other employees not now covered;

Removal of unreasonable restrictions upon the right of peaceful picketing, including situs picketing;

Speedier decisions in unfair labor practice cases and representation proceedings;

Greater equality between the remedies available under the Act to labor and those available to management;

Effective opportunities for unions as well as employers to communicate with employees, without coercion by either side or by anyone acting in their behalf.

The Federal Government will continue to set an example as an employer to private business and to state and local governments. The Government will not do business with firms that repeatedly violate Federal statutes prohibiting discrimination against employees who are union members or refuse to bargain with duly authorized union representatives.

By all these means, we will sustain the right of workers to organize in unions of their own choosing and will foster truly effective collective bargaining to provide the maximum opportunity for just and fair agreements between management and labor.

Consumer Protection

Rising incomes have brought new vigor to the market place. But the march of technology which has brought unparalleled abundance and opportunity to the consumer has also exposed him to new hazards and new complexities. In providing economic justice for consumers, we shall strengthen business and industry and improve the quality of life for all 200 million Americans.

We commend the Democratic Congress for passing the landmark legislation of the past several years which has ushered in a new era of consumer protection—truth-in-lending, truth-in-packaging, wholesome meat and poultry, auto and highway safety, child safety, and protection against interstate land swindles.

We shall take steps, including necessary legislation, to minimize the likelihood of massive electric power failures, to improve the safety of medical devices and drugs, to penalize deceptive sales practices, and to provide consumer access to product information now being compiled in the Federal Government.

We will help the states to establish consumer fraud and information bureaus, and to update consumer credit laws.

A major objective of all consumer programs, at all levels, must be the education of the buying public, particularly the poor who are the special targets of unscrupulous and high-pressure salesmanship.

We will make the consumer's voice increasingly heard in the councils of government. We will strengthen consumer education and enforcement programs by consolidation of functions now dispersed among various agencies, through the establishment of an Office of Consumer Affairs to represent consumer interests within the government and before courts and regulatory agencies.

Housing

For the first time in history, a nation is able to rebuild or replace all of its substandard housing, even while providing housing for millions of new families.

This means rebuilding or replacing 4.5 million dwelling units in our urban areas and 3.9 million in rural areas, most in conditions of such dilapidation that they are too often dens of despair for millions of Americans.

Yet this performance is possible in the next decade because of goals and programs fashioned by Democratic Presidents and Democratic Congresses in close partnership with private business.

The goal is clear and pressing—"a decent home and a suitable living environment for every American family," as set forth in the 1949 Housing Act by a Democratic Congress and Administration.

To achieve this goal in the next ten years:

We will assist private enterprise to double its volume of homebuilding, to an annual rate of 2.6 million units a year—a ten year total of 26 million units. This is the specific target of the history-making Housing and Urban Development Act of 1968.

We will give the highest priority to Federally-assisted home-building for low income families, with special attention given to ghetto dwellers, the elderly, the physically handicapped, and families in neglected areas of rural America, Indian reservations, territories of the United States, and migratory worker camps. All federal subsidy programs—whether in the form of public housing, interest rates at 1%, rent supplements, or direct loans—will be administered to favor these disadvantaged families, with full participation by the neighborhood residents themselves.

We will cooperate with private home builders to experiment boldly with new production technology, with financial institutions to marshal capital for housing where it is most needed, and with unions to expand the labor force needed for a doubling of production.

Above all, we will work toward the greatest possible freedom of choice—the opportunity for every family, regardless of race, color, religion, or income, to choose home ownership or rental, high-rise or low-rise, cooperatives or condominiums, detached or town house, and city, suburban or country living.

We urge local governments to shape their own zoning laws and building codes to favor consumers and hold down costs.

Rigid enforcement of State and local health and building codes is imperative to alleviate conditions of squalor and despair in deteriorating neighborhoods.

Democrats are proud of their housing record. But we are also painfully aware of how much more needs to be done to reach the final goal of decent shelter for all Americans and we pledge a steadfast pursuit of that goal.

Transportation

America is a nation on the move. To meet the challenge of transportation, we propose a dynamic partnership between industry and government at all levels.

Of utmost urgency is the need to solve congestion in air traffic, especially in airports and between major metropolitan centers. We pledge intensified efforts to devise equitable methods of financing new and improved airport and airway facilities.

Urban and inter-urban transportation facilities are heavily overburdened. We support expanded programs of assistance to mass transit in order to avoid unnecessary congestion in air traffic, especially at air-link residential and work areas.

Despite the tremendous progress of our interstate highway program, still more super-highways are needed for safe and rapid motor transport. We need to establish local road networks to meet regional requirements.

The efficiency of our railroads has improved greatly but there is need for further strengthening of the nation's railroads so that they can contribute more fully to the nation's transport requirements. In particular, we will press forward with the effort to develop high-speed passenger trains to serve major urban areas.

To assume our proper place as a leading maritime nation, we must launch an aggressive and balanced program to replace and augment our obsolete merchant ships with modern vessels built in American shipyards. We will assist U.S. flag operators to overcome the competitive disparity between American and foreign costs.

We will continue to foster development of harbors, ports, and inland waterways, particularly regional waterways systems, and the St. Lawrence Seaway, to accommodate our expanded water-borne commerce. We support modernization of the Panama Canal.

We pledge a greater investment in transportation research and development to enhance safety and increase speed and economy; to implement the acts that have been passed to control noxious vehicle exhausts; and to reduce aircraft noise.

The expansion of our transportation must not be carried out at the expense of the environment through which it moves. We applaud the leadership provided by the First Lady to enhance the highway environment and initiate a national beautification program.

Communications

America has the most efficient and comprehensive communications system in the world. But a healthy society depends more on the quality of what is communicated than on either the volume or form of communication.

Public broadcasting has already proven that it can be a valuable supplement to formal education and a direct medium for non-formal education. We pledge our continuing support for the prompt enactment of a long-range financing plan that will help ensure the vigor and independence of this potentially vital but still underdeveloped new force in American life.

We deplore the all too frequent exploitation of violence as entertainment in all media.

In 1962 the Democratic Party sensed the great potential of space communication and quickly translated this awareness into the Communications Satellite Act. In a creative partnership between government and business, this revolutionary idea soon became a reality. Six years later we helped establish a consortium of 61 nations devoted to the development of a global satellite network.

We will continue to develop new technology and utilize communications to promote worldwide understanding as an essential pre-condition of world peace. But, in view of rapidly changing technology, the entire federal regulatory system dealing with telecommunication should be thoroughly reappraised.

Science and Technology

We lead the world in science and technology. This has produced a dramatic effect on the daily lives of all of us. To maintain our undisputed national leadership in science and further its manifold applications for the betterment of mankind, the Federal Government has a clear obligation to foster and support creative men and women in the research community, both public and private.

Our pioneering space program has helped mankind on earth in countless ways. The benefits from improved weather forecasting which can soon be available thanks to satellite observations and communications will by themselves make the space efforts worthwhile.

Observation by satellite of crops and other major earth resources will for the first time enable man to see all that is available to him on earth, and therefore to take maximum advantage of it. High endurance metals developed for spacecraft help make commercial planes safer; similarly, micro-electronics are now found in consumer appliances. Novel space food-preservation techniques are employed in the tropical climates of underdeveloped countries. We will move ahead in aerospace research and development for their unimagined promise for man on earth as well as their vital importance to national defense.

We shall continue to work for our goal of leadership in space. To this end we will maximize the effectiveness and efficiency of our space programs through utilization of the best program, planning and budgeting systems.

To maintain our leadership in the application of energy, we will push forward with research and development to assure a balanced program for the supply of energy for electric power, both public and private. This effort should go hand in hand with development of "breeder" reactors and large-scale nuclear desalting plants that can provide pure water economically from the sea for domestic use and agricultural and industrial development in arid regions, and with broadened medical and biological applications of atomic energy.

In addition to the physical sciences, the social sciences will be encouraged and assisted to identify and deal with the problem areas of society.

OPPORTUNITY FOR ALL

We of the Democratic Party believe that a nation wealthy beyond the dreams of most of mankind—a nation with a twentieth of the world's population, possessing half the world's manufactured goods—has the capacity and the duty to assure to all its citizens the opportunity to enjoy the full measure of the blessings of American life.

For the first time in the history of the world, it is within the power of a nation to eradicate from within its borders the age-old curse of poverty.

Our generation of Americans has now made those commitments. It remains to implement and adequately fund the host of practical measures that demonstrate their effectiveness and to continue to devise new approaches.

We are guided by the recommendations of the National Advisory Commission on Civil Disorders concerning jobs, housing, urban renewal, and education on a scale commensurate with the needs of the urban ghettos. We are guided by the report of the Commission on Rural Poverty in tackling the equally compelling problems of the rural slums.

Economic growth is our first antipoverty program. The best avenue to an independent, confident citizenry is a dynamic, full-employment economy. Beyond that lie the measures necessary to assure that every American, of every race, in every region, truly shares in the benefits of economic progress.

Those measures include rehabilitation of the victims of poverty, elimination of the urban and rural slums where poverty is bred, and changes throughout the system of institutions that affect the lives of the poor.

In this endeavor, the resources of private enterprise—not only its economic power but its leadership and ingenuity—must be mobilized. We must marshal the power that comes from people working together in communities—the neighborhood communities of the poor and the larger communities of the city, the town, the village, the region.

We support community action agencies and their programs, such as Head Start, that will prevent the children of the poor from becoming the poor of the next generation. We support the extension of neighborhood centers. We are committed to the principle of meaningful participation of the poor in policy-making and administration of community action and related programs.

Since organizations of many kinds are joined in the war on poverty, problems of coordination inevitably arise. We pledge ourselves to review current antipoverty efforts to assess how responsibility should be distributed among levels of government, among private and public agencies, and between the permanent agencies of the federal government and an independent antipoverty agency.

Toward a Single Society

We acknowledge with concern the findings of the report of the bi-partisan National Advisory

Commission on Civil Disorders and we commit ourselves to implement its recommendations and to wipe out, once and for all, the stain of racial and other discrimination from our national life.

"The major goal," the Commission wrote, "is the creation of a true union—a single society and a single American identity." A single society, however, does not mean social or cultural uniformity. We are a nation of many social, ethnic and national groups. Each has brought richness and strength to America.

The Civil Rights Act of 1964 and 1968 and the Voting Rights Act of 1965, all adopted under the vigorous leadership of President Johnson, are basic to America's long march toward full equality under the law.

We will not permit these great gains to be chipped away by opponents or eroded by administrative neglect. We pledge effective and impartial enforcement of these laws. If they prove inadequate, or if their compliance provisions fail to serve their purposes, we will propose new laws. In particular, the enforcement provisions of the legislation prohibiting discrimination in employment should be strengthened. This will be done as a matter of first priority.

We have also come to recognize that freedom and equality require more than the ending of repression and prejudice. The victims of past discrimination must be encouraged and assisted to take full advantage of opportunities that are now opening to them.

We must recognize that for too long we have neglected the abilities and aspirations of Spanish speaking Americans to participate fully in American life. We promise to fund and implement the Bilingual Education Act and expand recruitment and training of bilingual federal and state employees.

The American Indian has the oldest claim on our national conscience. We must continue and increase federal help in the Indian's battle against poverty, unemployment, illiteracy, ill health and poor housing. To this end, we pledge a new and equal federal-Indian partnership that will enable Indian communities to provide for themselves many services now furnished by the federal government and federal sponsorship of industrial development programs owned, managed, and run by Indians. We support a quick and fair settlement of land claims of Indians, Eskimo and Aleut citizens of Alaska.

The Inner City

In the decaying slums of our larger cities, where so many of our poor are concentrated, the attack on poverty must embrace many inter-related aspects of development—economic development, the rehabilitation or replacement of dilapidated and unsafe housing, job training and placement, and the improvement of education, health, recreation, crime control, welfare, and other public services.

As the framework of such an effort, we will continue to support the Model Cities program under which communities themselves are planning and carrying out the most comprehensive plans ever put together for converting their worst slum areas into model neighborhoods—with full participation and leadership by the neighborhood residents themselves. The Model Cities program will be steadily extended to more cities and more neighborhoods and adequately financed.

The resources and leadership of private enterprise must be marshaled in the attack on slums and poverty, and such incentives as may be essential for that purpose we will develop and enact.

Some of the most urgent jobs in the revival of the inner city remain undone because the hazards are too great and the rewards too limited to attract sufficient private capital. To meet this problem, we will charter a new federal banking structure to provide capital and investment guaranties for urban projects planned and implemented through local initiative—neighborhood development corporations, minority programs for self-employment, housing development corporations, and other urban construction and planning operations. We will also enact legislation providing tax incentives for new business and industrial enterprises in the inner city. Our experience with aid to small business demonstrates the importance of increased local ownership of business enterprises in the inner city.

We shall aid the universities to concentrate their resources more fully upon the problems of the cities and facilitate their cooperation with municipal agencies and local organizations in finding solutions to urban problems.

Rural Development

Balanced growth is essential for America. To achieve that balanced growth, we must greatly increase the growth of the rural non-farm economy. One-third of our people live in rural areas, but only one rural family in ten derives its principal income from farming. Almost thirty percent of the nation's poor are non-farm people in rural areas.

The problem of rural poverty and the problem of migration of poor people from rural areas to urban ghettos are mainly non-farm problems. The creation of productive jobs in small cities and towns can be the best and least costly solution of these problems.

To revitalize rural and small-town America and assure equal opportunity for all Americans wherever they live, we pledge to:

Create jobs by offering inducements to new enterprises—using tax and other incentives—to locate in small towns and rural areas;

Administer existing federal programs and design new programs where necessary to overcome the disparity between rural and urban areas in opportunities for education, for health services, for low income housing, for employment and job training, and for public services of all kinds;

Encourage the development of new towns and new growth centers;

Encourage the creation of comprehensive planning and development agencies to provide additional leadership in non-metropolitan areas, and assist them financially.

The experience of the Appalachian and other regional commissions indicates that municipalities, counties, and state and federal agencies can work together in a common development effort.

Jobs and Training

Every American in need of work should have opportunity not only for meaningful employment, but also for the education, training, counselling, and other services that enable him to take advantage of available jobs.

To the maximum possible extent, our national goal of full employment should be realized through creation of jobs in the private economy, where six of every seven Americans now work. We will continue the Job Opportunities in the Business Sector (JOBS) program, which for the first time has mobilized the energies of business and industry on a nationwide scale to provide training and employment to the hardcore unemployed. We will develop whatever additional incentives may be necessary to maximize the opportunities in the private sector for hardcore unemployed.

We will continue also to finance the operation by local communities of a wide range of training programs for youth and retraining for older workers whose skills have become obsolete, coupled with related services necessary to enable people to undertake training and accept jobs—including improved recruitment and placement services, day-care centers, and transportation between work and home.

For those who can work but cannot find jobs, we pledge to expand public job and job-training programs, including the Neighborhood Youth Corps, to provide meaningful employment by state and local government and nonprofit institutions.

For those who cannot obtain other employment, the federal government will be the employer of last resort, either through federal assistance to state and local projects or through federally sponsored projects.

Employment Standards

American workers are entitled to more than the right to a job. They have the right to fair and safe working conditions and to adequate protection in periods of unemployment or disability.

In the last thirty years Democratic administrations and Congresses have enacted, extended and improved a series of measures to provide safeguards against exploitation and distress. We pledge to continue these efforts.

The minimum standards covering terms and conditions of employment must be improved:

By increasing the minimum wage guarantee to assure those at the bottom of the economic scale a fairer share in rising living standards;

By extending the minimum wage and overtime provision of the Fair Labor Standards Act to all workers;

By enacting occupational health and safety legislation to assure the material reduction of the present occupational death rate of 14,500 men and women each year, and the disabling accident rate of over 2 million per year;

By assuring that the "green card" worker does not depress wages and conditions of employment for American workers;

By updating of the benefit provisions of the Longshoremen and Harbor Workers Act.

The unemployment compensation program should be modernized by national minimum standards for level and duration of benefits, eligibility, and universal coverage.

Older Citizens

A lifetime of work and effort deserves a secure and satisfying retirement.

Benefits, especially minimum benefits, under Old Age, Survivors, and Disability Insurance should be raised to overcome present inadequacies and thereafter should be adjusted automatically to reflect increases in living costs.

Medical care for the aged should be expanded to include the costs of prescription drugs.

The minimum age for public assistance should be lowered to correspond to the requirements for social security.

America's self-employed citizens should be encouraged by tax incentive legislation to supplement social security benefits for themselves and their employees to the same extent that employees of corporations are encouraged.

In addition to improving social security, we must develop in each community a wide variety of activities to enrich the lives of our older citizens, to enable them to continue to contribute to our society, and to permit them to live in dignity. The aged must have access to better housing, opportunites for regular or part-time employment and community volunteer services, and cultural and recreational activities.

People in Need

Every American family whose income is not sufficient to enable its members to live in decency should receive assistance free of the indignities and uncertainties that still too often mar our present programs. To support family incomes of the working poor a number of new program proposals have recently been developed. A thorough evaluation of the relative advantages of such proposals deserves the highest priority attention

by the next Administration. This we pledge to do.

Income payments and eligibility standards for the aged, the blind, the disabled and dependent children should be determined and financed on a federal basis—in place of the present inequitable, under-financed hodge podge state plans. This would, among other things, assure the eligibility in all states of needy children of unemployed parents who are now denied assistance in more than half the states as long as the father remains in the home.

Assistance payments should not only be brought to adequate levels but they should be kept adequate by providing for automatic adjustment to reflect increases in living costs.

Congress has temporarily suspended the restrictive amendment of 1967 that placed an arbitrary limit on the number of dependent children who can be aided in each state. We favor permanent repeal of that restriction and of the provision requiring mothers of young children to work.

The new federal-state program we propose should provide for financial incentives and needed services to enable and encourage adults on welfare to seek employment to the extent they are able to do so.

The time has come when we should make a national commitment that no American should have to go hungry or undernourished. The Democratic Party here and now does make that commitment. We will move rapidly to implement it through continued improvement and expansion of our food programs.

The Democratic Congress this year has already enacted legislation to expand and improve the school lunch and commodity distribution programs, and shortly will complete action on legislation now pending to expand the food stamp program. We will enact further legislation and appropriations to assure on a permanent basis that the school lunch program provides free and reduced price meals to all needy school children.

Health

The best of modern medical care should be made available to every American. We support efforts to overcome the remaining barriers of distance, poverty, ignorance, and discrimination that separate persons from adequate medical services.

During the last eight years of Democratic administrations, this nation has taken giant steps forward in assuring life and health for its citizens. In the years ahead, we Democrats are determined to take those final steps that are necessary to make certain that every American, regardless of economic status, shall live out his years without fear of the high costs of sickness.

Through a partnership of government and private enterprise we must develop new coordinated approaches to stem the rise in medical and drug costs without lowering the quality or availability of medical care. Out-of-hospital care, comprehensive group practice arrangements, increased availability of neighborhood health centers, and the greater use of sub-professional aides can all contribute to the lowering of medical costs.

We will raise the level of research in all fields of health, with special programs for development of the artificial heart and the heart transplant technique, development of drugs to treat and prevent the recurrence of heart diseases, expansion of current task forces in cancer research and the creation of new ones including cancer of the lung, determination of the factors in mental retardation and reduction of infant mortality, development of drugs to reduce the incidence of suicide, and construction of health research facilities and hospitals.

We must build new medical, dental and medical service schools, and increase the capacity of existing ones, to train more doctors, dentists, nurses, and medical technicians.

Medical care should be extended to disabled beneficiaries under the Old Age, Survivors and Disability Insurance Act to the same extent and under the same system that such care is available to the aged.

Thousands of children die, or are handicapped for life, because their mothers did not receive proper pre-natal medical attention or because the infants were unattended in the critical first days of life. Maternal and child health centers, located and designed to serve the needs of the poor, and voluntary family planning information centers should be established throughout the country. Medicaid programs administered by the states should have uniform standards so that no mother or child is denied necessary health services. Finally, we urge consideration of a program comparable to Medicare to finance pre-natal care for mothers and post-natal care for children during the first year of life.

Veterans

American veterans deserve our enduring gratitude for their distinguished service to the nation.

In 1968 some 750,000 returning servicemen will continue their education with increased benefits under the new G.I. Bill passed by an education-minded Democratic Congress. Two million disabled veterans and survivors of those killed in action are receiving larger pensions and higher disability payments.

Guided by the report of the Veterans Advisory Commission, established by the Democratic administration, we will:

Continue a strong one-stop agency vested with sole responsibility for all veterans programs;

Sustain and upgrade veteran medical services and expand medical training in VA hospitals;

Maintain compensation for disabled veterans and for widows and dependents of veterans who die of service-connected causes, in line with the rise in earnings and living standards;

Assure every veteran the right of burial in a national cemetery;

Provide incentives for veterans to aid their communities by serving in police, fire departments, educational systems and other public endeavors;

Make veterans and their widows eligible for pension benefits at the same age at which Social Security beneficiaries may receive old age benefits.

We recommend the establishment of a standing Committee on Veterans Affairs in the Senate.

Education

Education is the chief instrument for making good the American promise. It is indispensable to every man's chance to achieve his full potential. We will seek to open education to all Americans.

We will assure equal opportunity to education and equal access to high-quality education. Our aim is to maintain state-local control over the nation's educational system, with federal financial assistance and help in stimulating changes through demonstration and technical assistance. New concepts of education and training employing new communications technology must be developed to educate children and adults.

Every citizen has a basic right to as much education and training as he desires and can master—from preschool through graduate studies —even if his family cannot pay for this education.

We will marshal our national resources to help develop and finance new and effective methods of dealing with the educationally disadvantaged —including expanded preschool programs to prepare all young children for full participation in formal education, improved teacher recruitment and training programs for inner city and rural schools, the Teacher Corps, assistance to community controlled schools to encourage pursuit of innovative practices, university participation in research and operation of school programs, a vocational education system that will provide imaginative new ties between school and the world of work, and improved and more widespread adult education programs.

We will fully fund Title I of the Elementary and Secondary Education Act of 1965, which provides federal funds for improving education in schools serving large numbers of students from low income families.

The financial burden of education continues to grow as enrollments spiral and costs increase. The home owner's property tax burden must be eased by increased levels of financial aid by both the states and the Federal government.

Our rapidly expanding educational frontiers require a redoubling of efforts to insure the vitality of a diverse higher education system— public and private, large and small, community and junior colleges, vocational and technical schools, and great universities. We also pledge support for high quality graduate and medical education.

We will enlarge the federal scholarship program to remove the remaining financial barriers to post-secondary education for low income youths, and increase assistance to students in the form of repayable loans out of future income.

We will encourage support for the arts and the humanities, through the national foundations established by a Democratic Congress, to provide incentives for those endowed with extraordinary talent, enhance the quality of our life, and make productive leisure available to all our people.

We recommend greater stress on the arts and humanities in elementary and secondary curricula to ensure a proper educational balance.

Youth

For generations, the Democratic Party has renewed its vitality with young people and new ideas. Today, young people are bringing new vigor and a deep concern for social justice into the political process, yet many feel excluded from full participation.

We of the Democratic Party welcome the bold thinking and exciting ideas of youth. We recognize, with deep satisfaction, that their healthy desire for participation in the democratic system must lead to a series of reforms in the direction of a greater democracy and a more open America.

The Democratic Party takes pride in the fact that so many of today's youth have channeled their interests and energies into our Party. To them, and to all young Americans we pledge the fullest opportunity to participate in the affairs of our Party at the local, state, and national levels. We call for special efforts to recruit young people as candidates for public office.

We will support a Constitutional amendment lowering the voting age to 18.

We favor an increase in youth representation on state delegations in future Democratic conventions.

Steps should be taken to include youth advisers on all government studies, commissions, and hearings which are relevant to their lives.

We will establish a youth commission involving young people between the ages of 18 and 26.

Every young person should have an opportunity to contribute to the social health of his community or to humanitarian service abroad. The extraordinary experience of the Teacher Corps, VISTA, and the Peace Corps points the way for broadening the opportunities for such voluntary service. Hundreds of thousands of America's youth have sought to enlist in these programs, but only tens of thousands have been able to serve. We will expand these opportunities.

The lives of millions of young men are deeply affected by the requirement for military service. The present system leaves them in uncertainty through much of their early manhood. Until our manpower needs can be fully met by voluntary enlistment, the Democratic Party will insist upon the most equitable and just selection system that can be devised. We support a random system of selection which will reduce the period of eligibility to one year, guarantee fair selection, and remove uncertainty.

We urge review of draft board memberships to make them more representative of the communities they serve.

ENVIRONMENT, CONSERVATION AND NATURAL RESOURCES

These United States have undergone 200 years of continuous change and dramatic development resulting in the most technologically advanced nation in the world. But with rapid industrialization, the nation's air and water resources have been degraded, the public health and welfare endangered, the landscape scarred and littered, and the very quality of our national life jeopardized.

We must assure the availability of a decent environment for living, working and relaxation.

To this end, we pledge our efforts:

To accelerate programs for the enhancement of the quality of the nation's waters for the protection of all legitimate water uses, with special emphasis on public water supplies, recreation, fish and wildlife;

To extend the national emission control program to all moving sources of air pollution;

To work for programs for the effective disposal of wastes of our modern industrial society;

To support the efforts on national, state, and local levels to preserve the historic monuments and sites of our heritage;

To assist in planning energy production and transportation to fit into the landscape, to assure safety, and to avoid interference with more desirable uses of land for recreation and other public purposes;

To continue to work toward abating the visual pollution that plagues our land;

To focus on the outdoor recreation needs of those who live in congested metropolitan areas;

To continue to work toward strong measures for the reclamation of mined and depleted lands and the conservation of soil.

Public Domain

We pledge continued support of the Public Land Law Review Commission, which is reviewing public land laws and policies to assure maximum opportunity for all beneficial uses of the public lands, including lands under the sea, and to develop a comprehensive land use policy.

We support sustained yield management of our forests, and expanded research for control of forest insects, disease, and fires.

We plan to examine the productivity of the public lands in goods, services, and local community prosperity, with a view to increasing such productivity.

We shall enforce existing federal statutes governing federal timber.

We support the orderly use and development of mineral resources on federal lands.

Recreation

We will continue the vigorous expansion of the public recreational domain to meet tomorrow's increasing needs. We will add national parks, recreation areas and seashores, and create national systems of scenic and wild rivers and of trails and scenic roads. We will support a growing wilderness preservation system, preservation of our redwood forests, and conservation of marshland and estuarine areas.

Recognizing that the bulk of the task of acquisition and development must be accomplished at the state and local levels we shall foster federal assistance to encourage such action, as well as recreational expansion by the private sector. To this end, we shall build upon the landmark Land and Water Conservation Fund Act, which has assured a foundation of a recreational heritage for future generations. We will assist communities to rehabilitate and expand inadequate and deteriorating urban park systems, and develop open space, waterways, and waterfront renovation facilities.

Resources of the Oceans

In and beneath the seas are resources of untold dimension for the benefit of mankind. Recognizing and protecting the paramount public interest in the seas, Congress under Democratic leadership enacted the Sea Grant College Act of 1965 and the Marine Resources and Engineering

Development Act of 1966, which established for the first time a comprehensive long-range policy and program for the marine sciences. We pledge to pursue vigorously the goals of that Act. Specifically, we will:

Foster marine application of new technology —spacecraft, buoys, data networks, and advanced navigation systems—and develop an engineering capability to work on and under the sea at any depth;

Encourage development of underseas resources by intensified research and better weather forecasting, with recognition to the coastal, insular and other littoral states of their unique interest and responsibility;

Foster an extensive program of oceanologic research and development, financed by a portion of the mineral-royalty receipts from the outer continental shelf;

Accelerate public and private programs for the development of food and other marine resources to meet world-wide malnutrition, to create new industries, and to utilize under-employed manpower living near the waterfront;

Promote our fisheries by providing incentives for private investment, enforcing our 12-mile fishing zone, and discouraging other nations from excessive territorial and fishery claims;

Conclude an appropriate Ocean Space treaty to secure rules and agreements that will facilitate public and private investment, guarantee security of investment and encourage efficient and orderly development of the sea's resources.

THE GOVERNMENT

In the coming four years, the Democratic President and Democratic Congress will give priority to simplifying and streamlining the processes of government, particularly in the management of the great innovative programs enacted in the 1960's.

The Executive branch of the federal government is the largest and most complicated enterprise in the world, with programs distributed among 150 separate departments, agencies, bureaus, and boards. This massive operation contributes to and often results in duplication, administrative confusion, and delay.

We will seek to streamline this machinery by improving coordination and management of federal programs.

We realize that government must develop the capacity to anticipate problems. We support a thorough study of agency operations to determine priorities for governmental action and spending, for examination of the structure of these agencies, and for establishing more systematic means of attacking our nation's problems.

We recognize that citizen participation in government is most meaningful at the levels of government closest to the people. For that reason, we recognize the necessity of developing a true partnership between state, local, and Federal governments, with each carrying its share of the financial and administrative load. We acknowledge the tremendous strides made by President Johnson in strengthening federal-state relations through open communication with the governors and local officials, and we pledge to cont:nue and expand on this significant effort.

The complexities of federal-state local relationships must be simplified, so that states and local communities receiving federal aid will have maximum freedom to initiate and carry out programs suited to their own particular needs. To give states and communities greater flexibility in their programs, we will combine individual grant programs into broader categories.

As the economy grows, it is the federal revenue system that responds most quickly, yet it may be the states and local governments whose responsibilities mount most rapidly. To help states and cities meet their fiscal challenges, we must seek new methods for states and local governments to share in federal revenues while retaining responsibility for establishing their own priorities and for operating their own programs. To this end, we will seek out new and innovative approaches to government to assure that our Federal system does, in fact, deliver to the people the services for which they are paying.

Public Employees

The Democratic administration has moved vigorously in the past eight years—particularly with regard to pay scales—to improve the conditions of public service.

We support:

A federal service that rewards new ideas and leadership;

Continued emphasis on education and training

programs for public employees, before and during their service;

Parity of government salaries with private industry;

A proper respect for the privacy and independence of federal employees;

Equal opportunities for career advancement;

Continued application of the principles of collective bargaining to federal employment;

Encouragement to state and local governments to continue to upgrade their personnel systems in terms of pay scales and training;

Interchange of employees between federal and state government.

Elections

We are alarmed at the growing costs of political participation in our country and the consequent reliance of political parties and candidates on large contributors, and we want to assure full public information on campaign expenditures. To encourage citizen participation we urge that limited campaign contributions be made deductible as a credit from the federal income tax.

We fully recognize the principle of one man, one vote in all elections. We urge that due consideration be given to the question of presidential primaries throughout the nation. We urge reform of the electoral college and election procedures to assure that the votes of the people are fully reflected.

We urge all levels of our Party to assume leadership in removing all remaining barriers to voter registration.

We will also seek to eliminate disenfranchisement of voters who change residence during an election year.

The District of Columbia

With the reorganization of the government of the District of Columbia, the nation's capital has for the first time in nearly a century the strong leadership provided by a mayor-council form of government. This, however, is no substitute for an independent and fiscally autonomous District government. We support a federally funded charter commission—controlled by District residents—to determine the most appropriate form of government for the District, and the prompt implementation of the Commission's recommendations.

The Democratic Party supports full citizenship for residents of the District of Columbia and a Constitutional amendment to grant such citizenship through voting representation in Congress. Until this can be done, we propose non-voting representation.

Puerto Rico

In accordance with the democratic principle of self-determination the people of Puerto Rico have expressed their will to continue in permanent union with the United States through commonwealth status. We pledge our continued support to the growth of the commonwealth status which the people of Puerto Rico overwhelmingly approved last year.

Virgin Islands and Guam

We favor an elected governor and a non-voting delegate in the House of Representatives for the Virgin Islands and Guam, and will consider methods by which American citizens residing in American territories can participate in presidential elections.

JUSTICE AND LAW

We are firm in our commitment that equal justice under law shall be denied to no one. The duty of government at every level is the safety and security of its people. Yet the fact and fear of crime are uppermost in the minds of Americans today. The entire nation is united in its concern over crime, in all forms and wherever it occurs. America must move aggressively to reduce crime and its causes.

Democratic Presidents, governors and local officials are dedicated to the principle that equal justice under law shall remain the American creed. Those who take the law into their own hands undermine that creed. Anyone who breaks the law must be held accountable. Organized crime cannot be accepted as a way of life, nor can individual crime or acts of violence be permitted.

As stated in the report of the National Advisory Commission on Civil Disorders, the two fundamental questions confronting the American people are:

"How can we as a people end the resort to violence while we build a better society?

"How can the nation realize the promise of

a single society—one nation indivisible—which yet remains unfulfilled?"

This platform commits the Democratic Party to seek resolution of these questions.

We pledge a vigorous and sustained campaign against lawlessness in all its forms—organized crime, white collar crime, rioting, and other violations of the rights and liberties of others. We will further this campaign by attack on the root causes of crime and disorder.

Under the recent enactments of a Democratic Congress we will continue and increase federal financial support and technical assistance to the states and their local governments to:

Increase the numbers, raise the pay, and improve the training of local police officers;

Reduce delays and congestion in our criminal courts;

Rehabilitate and supervise convicted offenders, to return offenders to useful, decent lives, and to protect the public against habitual criminals;

Develop and deploy the most advanced and effective techniques and equipment for the public safety;

Assure the availabil'ty in every metropolitan area of quick, balanced, coordinated control forces, with ample manpower, thoroughly trained and properly equipped, to suppress rioting;

Encourage responsible and competent civic associations and business and labor groups to cooperate with the law enforcement agencies in new efforts to combat organized crime, build community support for police work, and assist in rehabilitating convicted offenders—and for the attainment of these ends, encourage our police to cooperate with any such groups and to establish links of communication with every element of the public they serve, building confidence and respect;

Establish and maintain open and responsive channels of communication between the public and the police through creative police-community relations programs;

Develop innovative programs to reduce the incidence of juvenile delinquency;

Promote the passage and enforcement of effective federal, state and local gun control legislation.

In all these efforts, our aim is to strengthen state and local law enforcement agencies so that they can do their jobs. In addition, the federal government has a clear responsibility for national action. We have accepted that responsibility and will continue to accept it with these specific objectives:

Prompt and effective federal support, upon request of appropriate authorities, to suppress rioting: improvement of the capabilities of all agencies of law enforcement and justice—the police, the military, the courts—to handle more effectively problems attending riots;

A concentrated campaign by the Federal government to wipe out organized crime: by employment of additional Federal investigators and prosecutors; by computerizing the present system of collecting information; by enlarging the program of technical assistance teams to work with the states and local governments that request assistance in this fight; by launching a nationwide program for the country's business and labor leaders to alert them to the problems of organized crime;

Intensified enforcement, research, and education to protect the public from narcotics and other damaging drugs: by review of federal narcotics laws for loopholes and difficulties of enforcement; by increased surveillance of the entire drug traffic; through negotiations with those foreign nations which grow and manufacture the bulk of drug derivatives;

Vigorous federal leadership to assist and coordinate state and local enforcement efforts, and to ensure that all communities benefit from the resources and knowledge essential to the fight on crime;

Further implementation of the recommendations of the President's crime commission;

Creation in the District of Columbia of a model system of criminal justice;

Federal research and development to bring to the problems of law enforcement and the administration of justice the full potential of the scientific revolution.

In fighting crime we must not foster injustice. Lawlessness cannot be ended by curtailing the hard-won liberties of all Americans. The right of privacy must be safeguarded. Court procedures must be expedited. Justice delayed is justice denied.

A respect for civil peace requires also a proper respect for the legitimate means of expressing dissent. A democratic society welcomes criticism within the limits of the law. Freedom of speech, press, assembly and association, together with free exercise of the franchise, are among the legitimate means to achieve change in a democratic society. But when the dissenter resorts to violence he erodes the institutions and values which are the underpinnings of our democratic society. We must not and will not tolerate violence.

As President Johnson has stated, "Our test is to rise above the debate between the rights of the individual and the rights of society by securing the rights of both."

. . .

We freely admit that the years we live in are years of turbulence. But the wisdom of history has something hopeful to say about times like these. It tells us that the giant American nation, on the move with giant strides, has never moved —and can never move—in silence.

We are an acting, doing, feeling people. We are a people whose deepest emotions are the source of the creative noise we make—precisely because of our ardent desire for unity, our wish for peace, our longing for concord, our demand for justice, our hope for material well being, our impulse to move always toward a more perfect union.

In that never-ending quest, we are all partners together—the industrialist and the banker, the workman and the storekeeper, the farmer and the scientist, the clerk and the engineer, the teacher and the student, the clergyman and the writer, the men of all colors and of all the different generations.

The American dream is not the exclusive property of any political party. But we submit that the Democratic Party has been the chief instrument of orderly progress in our time. As heirs to the longest tradition of any political party on earth, we Democrats have been trained over the generations to be a party of builders. And that experience has taught us that America builds best when it is called upon to build greatly.

We sound that call anew. With the active consent of the American people, we will prove anew that freedom is best secured by a government that is responsive and compassionate and committed to justice and the rule of law.

Prohibition Platform 1968

PREAMBLE

We, the representatives of the Prohibition Party, assembled in National Convention at Detroit, Michigan, June 28 and 29, 1967, recognizing Almighty God as the source of all just government, and with faith in the teachings of the Lord Jesus Christ, do solemnly promise that, if our party is chosen to administer the affairs of the nation, we will, with earnest dedication to the principles of righteousness, seek to serve the needs and to preserve the rights, the prerogatives and the basic freedoms, of the people of the United States of America. For the realization of these ends we propose the following program of government.

CONSTITUTIONAL GOVERNMENT

We affirm our sincere loyalty to the Constitution of the United States, and express our deep confidence in that document as the basic law of the land. We will resist all attempts to violate it, whether by legislation, by means of evasion, or through judicial interpretation. We believe in the principles of liberty and justice enunciated in the Declaration of Independence and in the Preamble and Bill of Rights of our Constitution. We declare ourselves in hearty support of our system of representative government, with its plan of checks and balances, and express our firm intent to serve the people of our nation with a constructive, forward-looking program of good government, dedicated to the general welfare.

COMMUNISM-TOTALITARIANISM

Recognizing that Communism is aggressively and unalterably opposed to our Constitutional government, we declare our opposition to it both as a way of life and as a governmental system. We believe that the program of Communism, with its intent to infiltrate and to overthrow our present form of government, must be pitilessly exposed. We challenge all loyal citizens to become fully aware of this menace to civilization, to exert every effort to defeat these "masters of deceit," and to help preserve our American way of life.

We also declare ourselves opposed to any other form of totalitarian philosophy or form of government. We endorse the efforts of those agencies which have been honestly and earnestly exposing subversive activities and groups.

GOVERNMENTAL ECONOMY AND TAXATION

We view with alarm the extravagance and wasteful spending which have invaded government at all levels, demanding an ever-increasing tax load upon our people. The constant increase in taxation, requiring approximately one third of the total income of our citizens to pay the expenses of government, is approaching the point of confiscation, leading to economic chaos. We believe that good government does not attempt to do for people what they can do for themselves. With proper economy, governmental costs can be lowered, the tax load lightened, and the public debt can be reduced. We promise to devote ourselves to such an end, even though it involves either the reorganization or abolition of certain departments, bureaus and vested interests.

MONEY AND FINANCE

A sound financial program and dependable monetary policy are fundamental to a stable economy. Our Constitution gives to Congress the power to "coin money" and "to regulate the value thereof." We believe that Congress, working with the executive branch of government, should take immediate steps to establish a financial program that will block inflationary trends, insure a sound currency, stabilize price levels and provide for systematic retirement of the national debt. We urge that careful consideration be given to a return to the gold standard, believing that such a step would help stabilize our economy, would promote confidence in our monetary system and would underwrite a continuing program of sound finance and expanding industrial progress.

TAX SHARING

Recognizing that local and state governments are having real difficulty in meeting their basic financial needs, we advocate a division of the revenue received from the federal income tax, with appropriate amounts of the tax collected in each state being distributed to each of the state governments before becoming the property of the federal government.

THE FEDERAL BUDGET

Good government and a sound economy require a balanced budget. The inflationary effects and the disturbing influences of unbalanced budgets must be eliminated. We cannot, with impunity, continue to increase the mortgage on our future and the interest load of the present. As the level of taxation is already excessive, there must be either a decided reduction in governmental services and federal spending or a substantial improvement in efficiency, with consequent elimination of waste in both personnel and materials. Actually, both areas need careful exploration with a view not only to maintaining a balanced budget, but also to reduction of the national debt.

THE INCOME TAX

A federal income tax was first proposed by the Prohibition Party in 1896. However, the graduated tax and confiscatory rates of the present day were not contemplated. We seriously question the appropriateness of the present system and demand a thorough review of the basic fiscal policies of our government.

FOREIGN AID

Many billions of dollars of our taxpayers' money have been and are still being given to foreign countries. Unfortunately, substantial portions have been used to support governments and programs considerably at variance with American ideals and concepts. It is frankly recognized that complex and baffling problems are involved in this area of international relations, but we insist that foreign governments have no inherent right to financial gifts at the expense of American taxpayers. Such aid does not purchase friendship, so should usually be in the form of repayable loans which will enable the beneficiaries to maintain their dignity and self-respect.

A FREE ECONOMY

We are strongly opposed to burdensome restraints on our free enterprise system, to detailed regulation of our economic life and to federal interference with individual initiative. We believe that free enterprise is threatened in three ways: (1) by excessive governmental regulation, (2) by growth of public or private monopoly, and (3) by unethical practices of unscrupulous groups.

It will be the policy of our administration

to encourage independent, non-monopolistic business enterprises which serve genuine consumer needs and are operated with a sense of responsibility to the public. We will take necessary steps to prevent the evils both of monopoly and of excessive regulation by government, and to protect adequately the consuming public from irresponsible or deceptive practices contrary to the general welfare.

We propose that our government withdraw, with reasonable promptness, from the fields of business activity and sell to private industry, at proper investment prices, those business enterprises now owned and operated by the federal government.

LABOR AND INDUSTRY

In the area of labor and industrial relations we believe that the public welfare must be given paramount consideration. Both management and labor must be held responsible for their economic and their social behavior. Neither should be permitted to dominate at the expense of the other or of the common good. Rather, the anti-trust laws must be applied equally to all monopolies, whether of business or labor. Whenever the public welfare is seriously endangered because of disputes affecting quasi-public businesses and utilities we favor the compulsory arbitration of labor-management disputes.

EMPLOYEE-EMPLOYER RIGHTS

Every individual has certain basic and fundamental rights. A person's right to join or not to join a labor union without affecting his employment and his right to work for an employer willing to hire him must be protected. Likewise, employees and employers must be free to bargain and to contract as they wish. Violence or coercion, whether on the part of management or labor, should be prohibited.

STATES RIGHTS

Our founding fathers recognized the importance of both individual and states rights, and determined to preserve them by making the Bill of Rights an integral part of our Constitution. During recent years there has been an increasing tendency toward an undesirable concentration of power and authority in the federal government. This tendency has two principal causes:

(1) the ever-growing power and influence of the "military-industrial complex," and (2) a widespread tendency of groups of citizens to look to the federal government for the protection of rights and the satisfaction of needs which they feel are not adequately cared for by state and local governments or by private enterprise.

To deal with the first of these causes, we pledge the utmost vigilance in resisting the growth of militarism and in maintaining the constitutional principle of civilian supremacy over the military. To deal with overcentralization we urge more vigorous action by the state and local governments for the protection of the rights and the promotion of the welfare of their people, greater resort to the solution of local community problems through the voluntary action of existing or new civic and other non-governmental associations, where this is feasible, and the increasing pursuit by private business concerns of policies which promote the public interest.

We pledge ourselves to action that will preserve all legitimate rights and will maintain among the several states their constitutional place in our system of government.

HUMAN RIGHTS

All American citizens, regardless of race, religion, or national origin are entitled to equality of treatment under the provisions of our constitution and under the laws of our land. No person or group of persons should be subjected to ostracism, humiliation, or embarrassment because of color or national background. At the same time, we must deplore the use of either violence or arbitrary pressure tactics, from whatever source, as a means of seeking to resolve tensions and divergencies of opinion among our citizens.

We are opposed to those proposals which would destroy our neighborhood school systems through a program of artificial integration or convey special privileges to any minority group.

PUBLIC MORALITY

Moral and spiritual considerations must be primary factors in determining both state and national policies. We deplore the gross neglect of such matters by the dominant political parties, culminating in the shocking revelations of crime and of political and economic corruption which have characterized recent years. We charge these parties with basic responsibility for the rapid decline in moral standards which followed repeal of the Eighteenth Amendment. We believe that the program of nullification of law through non-enforcement which led to repeal contributed greatly to the disintegration of public morals, to a general deterioration of standards and to a lowering of values among our people.

We pledge ourselves to break the unholy alliance which has made these things possible. We propose to strengthen and to enforce laws against gambling, narcotics, and commercialized vice, to emphasize the basic importance of spiritual and moral values to the development and growth of an enduring nation, and to maintain the integrity of our democracy by careful enforcement of law and loyal support of our Constitution.

World Peace

We pledge ourselves to search for peaceful solutions to international conflict by seeking to deal creatively and constructively with the underlying causes of international tension before they explode into hostilities, and to strive for world peace and order based upon the teachings and practices of the Prince of Peace.

National Sovereignty

We declare our belief in national sovereignty and oppose surrender of this sovereignty to any international group.

National Preparedness

Believing that "eternal vigilance is the price of liberty," we declare for a sound program of national military preparedness. While praying for peace we cannot place our freedom in peril by ignoring the potential threat to our nation.

However, we believe that the present program of compulsory peacetime military training does not represent a genuine safeguard to world peace. We rather believe it to be contrary, in principle, to our American way of life. This system places an unnecessary burden upon our peacetime economy, threatens us with possible military dictatorship, and often permits and promotes the moral and spiritual deterioration of our youth.

We urge that our peacetime defense be entrusted to professionally trained volunteers.

Nuclear Weapons Testing

Radioactive fallout, resulting from testing of nuclear weapons, endangers the health of human beings throughout the world, and if testing is engaged in, will increase the number of seriously defective children who will be born to future generations. The danger may become progressively greater with any additional testing. Also, there is the danger that continuation of the armaments race will lead to an atomic war of annihilation. We urge that all testing of nuclear weapons be indefinitely suspended on a multilateral basis with proper inspection safeguards, and that our government seek with renewed vigor and persistence an agreement among all nuclear powers for the permanent and complete cessation of nuclear tests for military purposes.

Religious Liberty

We believe in religious liberty. Freedom of the individual to worship, to fellowship with others of similar faith, to evangelize, to educate and to establish religious institutions, must be preserved. When religious liberty is lost political liberty will perish with it. We deplore ever increasing efforts to restrict freedom of religious broadcasting and the establishment of new churches. We caution the Internal Revenue Service against using the power to control tax exemptions to discriminate against evangelical Christianity.

We believe, also, that our government should take a firm, positive position against religious intolerance and persecution anywhere in the world.

Marriage and Divorce

Ordained of God, the home is a sacred institution. Its sanctity must be protected and preserved. We favor the enactment of uniform marriage and divorce laws in the various states as an aid to building strong and enduring homes throughout our nation.

Social Security

We endorse the general principle of an actuarially sound social security insurance program which includes all employed groups. We question the soundness of the existing program, and the recent trend toward a welfare emphasis. We deplore the widespread current abuse of the privileges involved; we condemn the maladministration of its provisions for political ends; we pledge ourselves to correct these evils.

BALLOT LAW REFORM

True democracy requires that the needs and interests of minority groups be given fair, honest and appropriate consideration. Instead, in many of our states, ballot laws have been enacted which are designed to make a two party system into a bipartisan political monopoly, keeping minor parties off the ballot. We demand the repeal of all laws which deny to independent voters and all loyal minority groups the fundamental right of free political expression.

CHURCH AND STATE

We affirm our continuing loyalty to the constitutional principle of separation of Church and State. We will expose, and resist vigorously, any attempt from whatever source to weaken or subvert this fundamental principle.

We declare our belief that the Bible is not a sectarian book, but is a volume of universal appeal and application which is woven into our history, our laws, and our culture. We deplore any interpretation which would limit its use in any area of our national life.

In the area of government, we endorse encouragement of non-profit educational and religious institutions on a tax-exempt basis, but we declare strong opposition to all efforts, direct or indirect, to secure appropriations of public money for private religious or sectarian purposes.

EDUCATION

It is altogether appropriate that our federal government should be interested in and concerned about matters pertaining to all areas of educational growth and development. However, under the Tenth Amendment, public education is clearly to be under the control of the states. We are opposed to direct federal aid to education, believing that each state should both support and control its own educational program.

AGRICULTURE

The production and distribution of agricultural products is of vital importance to the economy of any people. We believe that those engaged in agricultural pursuits, like other American citizens, should be free from authoritarian control and coercion. Hence we declare ourselves opposed to regimentation of farms and farmers and urge a sensible and orderly return to a free market program.

PUBLIC HEALTH

The health of our people is a matter of fundamental importance. We are deeply concerned with this matter in its many aspects. We are disturbed by the increasing use of narcotic and psychedelic drugs. Recognizing that the use of tobacco products constitutes a health hazard, we are opposed to promotional advertising of such products and to subsidization of tobacco growing. We insist that caution must be taken in dealing with mental health cases, lest there be unjust and prejudiced incarcerations. We deplore those programs of mass medication which violate the rights of individuals. We insist on the right of everyone to a pure water supply and to an unpolluted atmosphere, and hold that each of our states must insure these.

We pledge enforcement of existing laws regulating these health concerns, the enactment of additional needed legislation and cooperation with state efforts to deal with the problems.

SERVICE, NOT SPOILS

The Prohibition Party first sponsored our civil service system. On the other hand, the dominant political parties are positively committed to the "spoils" system and, when in office, have prostituted governmental power to serve their own selfish party interests instead of the whole people. This has led to excessive expenditures, higher taxes and, in some situations, to an unfortunate alliance of crime with politics. We pledge ourselves to an honest, efficient and economical administration.

THE ALCOHOL PROBLEM

Beverage alcohol must today be recognized as the chief cause of poverty, broken homes, juvenile delinquency, vice, crime, political corruption, wasted manpower and highway accidents. By the most conservative estimates, more than 6,000,000 alcoholics and 6,000,000 problem drinkers are currently victims of alcohol.

No greater mistake has ever been made by the American people and their government than the Repeal of Prohibition. Contrary to the promises made by the advocates of repeal, bootlegging has increased to the point where the liquor industry itself claims that one-third of all alcohol consumed today in America is illicit; drinking among our young people has reached epidemic proportions; liquor taxes pay only a small fraction of the traffic's cost to the taxpayers and the "open saloon" which was to be "banished forever" is back in a newer form and more numerous than ever.

The liquor traffic is linked with and supports a nationwide network of gambling, vice and crime. It also dominates both major political parties and, thru them, much of the governmental and political life of our nation. As long as the two dominant parties are largely controlled by the liquor traffic, just so long will they be unable to make moral principles prevail.

The Prohibition Party alone offers a program to deal with this greatest of social ills. We pledge ourselves to a program of publicity, education, legislation and administration, leading to the elimination of beverage alcohol industry. We will repeal all laws which legalize the liquor traffic and enact and rigorously enforce new laws which prohibit the manufacture, distribution and sale of alcoholic beverages.

We urge all Americans who favor sobriety and righteousness to join with us in electing an administration pledged to the above program.

Republican Platform 1968

PREAMBLE, PURPOSES AND PLEDGES

Twice before, our Party gave the people of America leadership at a time of crisis—leadership which won us peace in place of war, unity in place of discord, compassion in place of bitterness.

A century ago, Abraham Lincoln gave that leadership. From it came one nation, consecrated to liberty and justice for all.

Fifteen years ago, Dwight D. Eisenhower gave that leadership. It brought the end of a war, eight years of peace, enhanced respect in the world, orderly progress at home, and trust of our people in their leaders and in themselves.

Today, we are in turmoil.

Tens of thousands of young men have died or been wounded in Vietnam.

Many young people are losing faith in our society.

Our inner cities have become centers of despair.

Millions of Americans are caught in the cycle of poverty—poor education, unemployment or serious under-employment, and the inability to afford decent housing.

Inflation has eroded confidence in the dollar at home and abroad. It has severely cut into the incomes of all families, the jobless, the farmers, the retired and those living on fixed incomes and pensions.

Today's Americans are uncertain about the future, and frustrated about the recent past.

America urgently needs new leadership—leadership courageous and understanding—leadership that will recapture control of events, mastering them rather than permitting them to master us, thus restoring our confidence in ourselves and in our future.

Our need is new leadership which will develop imaginative new approaches assuring full opportunity to all our citizens—leadership which will face and resolve the basic problems of our country.

Our Convention in 1968 can spark a "Republican Resurgence" under men and women willing to face the realities of the world in which we live.

We must urgently dedicate our efforts toward restoration of peace both at home and abroad.

We must bring about a national commitment to rebuild our urban and rural slum areas.

We must enable family farm enterprise to participate fully in the nation's prosperity.

We must bring about quality education for all.

We must assure every individual an opportunity for satisfying and rewarding employment.

We must attack the root causes of poverty and eradicate racism, hatred and violence.

We must give all citizens the opportunity to influence and shape the events of our time.

We must give increasing attention to the views of the young and recognize their key role in our present as well as the future.

We must mobilize the resources, talents and energy of public and private sectors to reach these goals, utilizing the unique strength and initiative of state and local governments.

We must re-establish fiscal responsibility and put an end to increases in the cost of living.

We must reaffirm our commitment to Lincoln's challenge of one hundred six years ago. To Congress he wrote: "The dogmas of the quiet past are inadequate to the stormy present. The occasion is piled high with difficulty and we must rise with the occasion. As our case is new, so we must think anew and act anew. We must disenthrall ourselves and then we shall save our country."

In this, our stormy present, let us rededicate ourselves to Lincoln's thesis. Let the people know our commitment to provide the dynamic leadership which they rightly expect of this Party—the Party not of empty promises, but of performance—the Party not of wastefulness, but of responsibility—the Party not of war, but the Party whose Administrations have been characterized by peace—the Republican Party.

To these ends, we solemnly pledge to every American that we shall think anew and act anew.

DOMESTIC POLICY

A peaceful, reunified America, with opportunity and orderly progress for all—these are our overriding domestic goals.

Clearly we must think anew about the relationship of man and his government, of man and his fellow-man. We must act anew to enlarge the opportunity and autonomy of the individual and the range of his choice.

Republican leadership welcomes challenge.

We eagerly anticipate new achievement.

A new, vital partnership of government at all levels will be a prime Republican objective. We will broaden the base of decision-making. We will create a new mix of private responsibility and public participation in the solution of social problems.

There is so much which urgently needs to be done.

In many areas poverty and its attendant ills afflict large numbers of Americans. Distrust and fear plague us all. Our inner cities teem with poor, crowded in slums. Many rural areas are run down and barren of challenge or opportunity. Minorities among us—particularly the black community, the Mexican-American, the American Indian—suffer disproportionately.

Americans critically need—and are eager for—new and dynamic leadership. We offer that leadership—a leadership to eradicate bitterness and discrimination—responsible, compassionate leadership that will keep its word—leadership every citizen can count on to move this nation forward again, confident, reunited, and sure of purpose.

Crisis of the Cities

For today and tomorrow, there must be—and we pledge—a vigorous effort, nation-wide, to transform the blighted areas of cities into centers of opportunity and progress, culture and talent.

For tomorrow, new cities must be developed—and smaller cities with room to grow, expanded—to house and serve another 100 million Americans by the turn of the century.

The need is critical. Millions of our people are suffering cruelly from expanding metropolitan blight—congestion, crime, polluted air and water, poor housing, inadequate educational, economic and recreational opportunities. This continuing decay of urban centers—the deepening misery and limited opportunity of citizens living there—is intolerable in America. We promise effective, sustainable action enlisting new energies by the private sector and by governments at all levels. We pledge:

Presidential leadership which will buttress state and local government;

Vigorous federal support to innovative state programs, using new policy techniques such as urban development corporations, to help rebuild our cities;

Energetic, positive leadership to enforce statutory and constitutional protections to eliminate discrimination;

Concern for the unique problems of citizens long disadvantaged in our total society by race, color, national origin, creed, or sex;

A greater involvement of vast private enterprise resources in the improvement of urban life, induced by tax and other incentives;

New technological and administrative approaches through flexible federal programs enabling and encouraging communities to solve their own problems;

A complete overhaul and restructuring of the competing and overlapping jumble of federal programs to enable state and local governments to focus on priority objectives.

These principles as urgently apply to rural poverty and decay. There must be a marked improvement of economic and educational opportunities to relieve widespread distress. Success with urban problems in fact requires acceleration of rural development in order to stem the flow of people from the countryside to the city.

Air and water pollution, already acute in many areas, require vigorous state and federal action, regional planning, and maximum cooperation among neighboring cities, counties and states. We will encourage this planning and cooperation and also spur industrial participation by means of economic incentives.

Skyrocketing building costs and interest rates have crippled home building and threaten a housing crisis in the nation, endangering the prospect of a decent home and a suitable living environment for every family. We will vigorously implement the Republican-conceived home-ownership program for lower income families and also the Republican-sponsored rent certificate program. Economic incentives will be developed to attract private industry and capital to the low-cost housing market. By reducing interest rates through responsible fiscal and monetary policy we will lower the costs of homeownership, and new technologies and programs will be developed to stimulate low-cost methods of housing rehabilitation. Local communities will be encouraged to adopt uniform, modern building codes, research in cost-cutting technology through private enterprise will be accelerated, and innovative state and local programs will be supported. We will also stimulate the investment of "sweat equity" by home owners.

Our metropolitan transportation systems—the lifelines of our cities—have become tangled webs of congestion which not only create vast citizen inconvenience, discontent and economic inefficiency, but also tend to barricade inner city people against job opportunities in suburban areas. We will encourage priority attention by private enterprise and all levels of government to sound planning and the rapid development of improved mass transportation systems. Additionally, in the location of federal buildings and installations and the awarding of federal contracts,

account will be taken of such factors as traffic congestion, housing, and the effect on community development.

Americans are acutely aware that none of these objectives can be achieved unless order through law and justice is maintained in our cities. Fire and looting, causing millions of dollars of property damage, have brought great suffering to home owners and small businessmen, particularly in black communities least able to absorb catastrophic losses. The Republican Party strongly advocates measures to alleviate and remove the frustrations that contribute to riots. We simultaneously support decisive action to quell civil disorder, relying primarily on state and local governments to deal with these conditions.

America has adequate peaceful and lawful means for achieving even fundamental social change if the people wish it. We will not tolerate violence!

Crime

Lawlessness is crumbling the foundations of American society.

Republicans believe that respect for the law is the cornerstone of a free and well-ordered society. We pledge vigorous and even-handed administration of justice and enforcement of the law. We must re-establish the principle that men are accountable for what they do, that criminals are responsible for their crimes, that while the youth's environment may help to explain the man's crime, it does not excuse that crime.

We call on public officials at the federal, state and local levels to enforce our laws with firmness and fairness. We recognize that respect for law and order flows naturally from a just society; while demanding protection of the public peace and safety, we pledge a relentless attack on economic and social injustice in every form.

The present Administration has:

Ignored the danger signals of our rising crime rates until very recently and even now has proposed only narrow measures hopelessly inadequate to the need;

Failed to implement most of the recommendations of the President's own Crime Commission;

Opposed legislative measures that would assist law enforcement officials in bringing law-breakers to justice;

Refused to sanction the use of either the court-supervised wiretapping authority to combat organized crime or the revised rules of evidence, both made available by Congress;

Failed to deal effectively with threats to the nation's internal security by not prosecuting identified subversives.

By contrast, Republican leadership in Congress has:

Provided funds for programs administered by state and local governments to control juvenile delinquency and crime;

Created a National Institute of Law Enforcement and Criminal Justice to conduct crime research and facilitate the expansion of police training programs;

Secured enactment of laws enabling law enforcement officials to obtain and use evidence needed to prosecute criminals, while at the same time protecting the rights and privacy of all citizens;

Secured new laws aimed at "loan-sharking," the intimidation of witnesses, and obstruction of investigations;

Established disability as well as survivorship benefits for local police officers wounded or killed in pursuit of federal lawbreakers.

For the future, we pledge an all-out, federal-state-local crusade against crime, including:

Leadership by an Attorney General who will restore stature and respect to that office;

Continued support of legislation to strengthen state and local law enforcement and preserve the primacy of state responsibility in this area;

Full support of the F.B.I. and all law enforcement agencies of the federal government;

Improved federal cooperation with state and local law enforcement agencies;

Better coordination of the federal law enforcement, crime control, and criminal justice systems;

A vigorous nation-wide drive against trafficking in narcotics and dangerous drugs, including special emphasis on the first steps toward addiction—the use of marijuana and such drugs as LSD;

Total commitment to a federal program to deter, apprehend, prosecute, convict and punish the overlords of organized crime in America, including full implementation of the Congressional mandate that court-supervised wiretapping and

electronic surveillance tools be used against the mobsters and racketeers;

Increased public protection against racketeer infiltration into legitimate business;

Increased research into the causes and prevention of crime, juvenile delinquency, and drug addiction;

Creation of a Federal Corrections Service to consolidate the fragmented and overlapping federal efforts and to assist state and local corrections systems;

A new approach to the problem of chronic offenders, including adequate staffing of the corrections system and improvement of rehabilitative techniques;

Modernization of the federal judicial system to promote swift, sure justice;

Enactment of legislation to control indiscriminate availability of firearms, safeguarding the right of responsible citizens to collect, own and use firearms for legitimate purposes, retaining primary responsibility at the state level, with such federal laws as necessary to better enable the states to meet their responsibilities.

Youth

More than any other nation, America reflects the strength and creative energy of youth. In every productive enterprise, the vigor, imagination and skills of our young people have contributed immeasurably to progress.

Our youth today are endowed with greater knowledge and maturity than any such generation of the past. Their political restlessness reflects their urgent hope to achieve a meaningful participation in public affairs commensurate with their contributions as responsible citizens.

In recognition of the abilities of these younger citizens, their desire to participate, and their service in the nation's defense, we believe that lower age groups should be accorded the right to vote. We believe that states which have not yet acted should reevaluate their positions with respect to 18-year-old voting, and that each such state should decide this matter for itself. We urge the states to act now.

For greater equity we will further revise Selective Service policies and reduce the number of years during which a young man can be considered for the draft, thereby providing some certainty to those liable for military service. When military manpower needs can be appreciably reduced, we will place the Selective Service System on standby and substitute a voluntary force obtained through adequate pay and career incentives.

We encourage responsible young men and women to join actively in the political process to help shape the future of the nation. We invite them to join our Republican effort to assure the new direction and the new leadership which this nation so urgently needs and rightfully expects.

Education

The birthplace of American opportunity has been in the classrooms of our schools and colleges. From early childhood through the college years, American schools must offer programs of education sufficiently flexible to meet the needs of all Americans—the advantaged, the average, the disadvantaged and the handicapped alike. To help our educators meet this need we will establish a National Commission to Study the Quality and Relevance of American Education.

To treat the special problems of children from impoverished families, we advocate expanded, better programs for pre-school children. We will encourage state, local or private programs of teacher training. The development and increased use of better teaching methods and modern instruction techniques such as educational television and voluntary bilingual education will continue to have our support.

To help assure excellence and equality of educational opportunity, we will urge the states to present plans for federal assistance which would include state distribution of such aid to non-public school children and include non-public school representatives in the planning process. Where state conditions prevent use of funds for non-public school children, a public agency should be designated to administer federal funds.

Greater vocational education in high school and post-high school years is required for a new technological and service-oriented economy. Young people need expansion of post-high school technical institutes to enable them to acquire satisfactory skills for meaningful employment. For youths unable to obtain such training, we propose an industry youth program, coupled with a flexible approach to minimum wage laws for young entry-level workers during their training periods.

The rapidly mounting enrollments and costs of colleges and universities deprive many qualified young people of the opportunity to obtain a quality college education. To help colleges and universities provide this opportunity, we favor grant and loan programs for expansion of their facilities. We will also support a flexible student aid program of grants, loans and work opportunities, provided by federal and state governments and private organizations. We continue to favor tax credits for those burdened with the costs of higher education, and also tax deductions to encourage savings for this purpose. No young American should be denied a quality education because he cannot afford it or find work to meet its costs.

HUMAN DEVELOPMENT

The inability of the poor to cope meaningfully with their environment is compounded by problems which blunt opportunity—inadequate income, inferior education, inadequate health care, slum housing, limited job opportunities, discrimination, and crime.

Full opportunity requires a coordinated attack on the total problem through community human development programs. Federal revenue sharing would help provide the resources to develop such coordinated programs.

Jobs

The nation must look to an expanding free enterprise system to provide jobs. Republican policies and programs will encourage this expansion.

To qualify for jobs with permanence and promise, many disadvantaged citizens need special assistance and job training. We will enact the Republican-proposed Human Investment Act, offering tax credits to employers, to encourage such training and upgrading.

A complete overhaul of the nation's job programs is urgent. There are some 70 federally funded job training programs, with some cities having as many as 30 operating side by side. Some of these programs are ineffective and should be eliminated. We will simplify the federal effort and also encourage states and localities to establish single-headed manpower systems, to correlate all such federal activities and gear them to local conditions and needs. Local business advisory boards will assist in the design of such programs to fit training to employment needs. To help the unemployed find work we will also inaugurate a national Job Opportunity Data Bank to report the number, nature and location of unfilled jobs and to match the individuals with the jobs.

The Poor

Welfare and poverty programs will be drastically revised to liberate the poor from the debilitating dependence which erodes self-respect and discourages family unity and responsibility. We will modify the rigid welfare requirements that stifle work motivation and support locally operated children's day-care centers to free the parents to accept work.

Burdensome administrative procedures will be simplified, and existing programs will be revised so that they will encourage and protect strong family units.

This nation must not blink the harsh fact—or the special demands it places upon us—that the incidence of poverty is consistently greater among Negroes, Mexican-Americans, Indians and other minority groupings than in the population generally.

An essential element of economic betterment is the opportunity for self-determination—to develop or acquire and manage one's own business enterprise. This opportunity is bleak for most residents of impoverished areas. We endorse the concept of state and community development corporations. These will provide capital, technical assistance and insurance for the establishment and renewal of businesses in depressed urban and rural areas. We favor efforts to enable residents of such areas to become owners and managers of businesses and, through such agencies as a Domestic Development Bank, to exercise economic leadership in their communities.

Additionally, we support action by states, with federal re-insurance, to help provide insurance coverage for homes and small businesses against damage and fire caused by riots.

We favor maximum reliance on community leaders utilizing the regular channels of government to provide needed public services. One approach is the Republican-sponsored Community Service Corps which would augment cooperation and communication between community residents and the police.

In programs for the socially and economically disadvantaged we favor participation by representatives of those to be served. The failure so to encourage creative and responsible participation from among the poor has been the greatest among the host of failures of the War on Poverty.

Recent studies indicate that many Americans suffer from malnutrition despite six separate federal food distribution programs. Here again, fragmentation of federal effort hinders accomplishment. We pledge a unified federal food distribution program, as well as active cooperation with the states and innovative private enterprise, to help provide the hungry poor sufficient food for a balanced diet.

A new Republican Administration will strive for fairness for all consumers, including additional information and protection programs as necessary, state and local consumer education, vigorous enforcement of the numerous protection laws already enacted, and active encouragement of the many consumer-protection initiatives and organizations of private enterprise.

Health

The inflation produced by the Johnson-Humphrey Administration has struck hardest in the area of health care. Hospital costs are rising 16 percent a year—four times the national average of price increases.

We pledge to encourage the broadening of private health insurance plans, many of which cover hospital care only, and to review the operation of government hospital care programs in order to encourage more patients to utilize non-hospital facilities. Expansion of the number of doctors, nurses, and supporting staff to relieve shortages and spread the availability of health care services will have our support. We will foster the construction of additional hospitals and encourage regional hospital and health planning for the maximum development of facilities for medical and nursing care. We will also press for enactment of Republican-sponsored programs for financing of hospital modernization. New diagnostic methods and also preventive care to assure early detection of physical impairments, thus fostering good health and avoiding illnesses requiring hospitalization, will have our support.

Additionally, we will work with states and local communities to help assure improved services to the mentally ill within a community setting and will intensify research to develop better treatment methods. We will encourage extension of private health insurance to cover mental illness.

While believing no American should be denied adequate medical treatment, we will be diligent in protecting the traditional patient-doctor relationship and the integrity of the medical practitioner.

We are especially concerned with the difficult circumstances of thousands of handicapped citizens who daily encounter architectural barriers which they are physically unable to surmount. We will support programs to reduce and where possible to eliminate such barriers in the construction of federal buildings.

The Elderly

Elderly Americans desire and deserve independence, dignity, and the opportunity for continued useful participation. We will strengthen the Social Security system and provide automatic cost of living adjustments under Social Security and the Railroad Retirement Act. An increase in earnings permitted to Social Security recipients without loss of benefits, provision for post-age 65 contributions to Social Security with deferment of benefits, and an increase in benefits to widows will also be provided. The age for universal Social Security coverage will be gradually reduced from 72 to 65 and the former 100 percent income tax deduction will be restored for medical and drug expenses for people over 65. Additionally, we will take steps to help improve and extend private pension plans.

Veterans

The Republican Party pledges vigorous efforts to assure jobs for returning Vietnam war veterans, as well as other assistance to enable them and their families to establish living conditions befitting their brave service. We pledge a rehabilitation allowance for paraplegics to afford them the means to live outside a hospital environment. Adequate medical and hospital care will be maintained for all veterans with service-connected disabilities and veterans in need, and timely revisions of compensation programs will be enacted for service-connected death and disability to help assure an adequate standard of living for all disabled veterans and their survivors. We will see that every veteran is accorded the right to be interred in a national cemetery as near as possible to his home, and we pledge to maintain all veterans' programs in an independent Veterans Administration.

Indian Affairs

The plight of American Indians and Eskimos is a national disgrace. Contradictory government policies have led to intolerable deprivation for these citizens. We dedicate ourselves to the promotion of policies responsive to their needs and desires and will seek the full participation of these people and their leaders in the formulation of such policies.

Inequality of jobs, of education, of housing and of health blight their lives today. We believe the Indian and Eskimo must have an equal opportunity to participate fully in American society. Moreover, the uniqueness and beauty of these native cultures must be recognized and allowed to flourish.

THE INDIVIDUAL AND GOVERNMENT

In recent years an increasingly impersonal national government has tended to submerge the individual. An entrenched, burgeoning bureaucracy has increasingly usurped powers, unauthorized by Congress. Decentralization of power, as well as strict Congressional oversight of administrative and regulatory agency compliance with the letter and spirit of the law, are urgently needed to preserve personal liberty, improve efficiency, and provide a swifter response to human problems.

Many states and localities are eager to revitalize their own administrative machinery, procedures, and personnel practices. Moreover, there is growing inter-state cooperation in such fields as education, elimination of air and water pollution, utilization of airports, highways and mass transportation. We pledge full federal cooperation with these efforts, including revision of the system of providing federal funds and reestablishment of the authority of state governments in coordinating and administering the federal programs. Additionally, we propose the sharing of federal revenues with state governments. We are particularly determined to revise the grant-in-aid system and substitute bloc grants wherever possible. It is also important that state and local governments retain the historic right to raise funds by issuing tax-exempt securities.

The strengthening of citizen influence on government requires a number of improvements in political areas. For instance, we propose to reform the electoral college system, establish a nation-wide, uniform voting period for Presidential elections, and recommend that the states remove unreasonable requirements, residence and otherwise, for voting in Presidential elections. We specifically favor representation in Congress for the District of Columbia. We will work to establish a system of self-government for the District of Columbia which will take into account the interests of the private citizens thereof, and those of the federal government.

We will support the efforts of the Puerto Rican people to achieve statehood when they freely request such status by a general election, and we share the hopes and aspirations of the people of the Virgin Islands who will be closely consulted on proposed gubernatorial appointments.

We favor a new Election Reform Act that will apply clear, reasonable restraints to political spending and fund-raising, whether by business, labor or individuals, ensure timely publication of the financial facts in campaigns, and provide a tax deduction for small contributions.

We will prevent the solicitation of federal workers for political contributions and assure comparability of federal salaries with private enterprise pay. The increasing government intrusion into the privacy of its employees and of citizens in general is intolerable. All such snooping, meddling, and pressure by the federal government on its employees and other citizens will be stopped and such employees, whether or not union members, will be provided a prompt and fair method of settling their grievances. Further, we pledge to protect federal employees in the exercise of their right freely and without fear of penalty or reprisal to form, join or assist any employee organization or to refrain from any such activities.

Congress itself must be reorganized and modernized in order to function efficiently as a co-equal branch of government. Democrats in control of Congress have opposed Republican efforts for Congressional reform and killed legislation embodying the recommendations of a special bipartisan committee. We will again press for enactment of this measure.

We are particularly concerned over the huge and mounting postal deficit and the evidence, recently stressed by the President's Commission on Postal Organization, of costly and inefficient practices in the postal establishment. We pledge full consideration of the Commission's recommendations for improvements in the nation's postal service. We believe the Post Office Department must attract and retain the best qualified and most capable employees and offer them improved opportunities for advancement and better working conditions and incentives. We favor extension of the merit principle to postmasters and rural carriers.

Public confidence in an independent judiciary is absolutely essential to the maintenance of law and order. We advocate application of the highest standards in making appointments to the courts, and we pledge a determined effort to rebuild and enhance public respect for the Supreme Court and all other courts in the United States.

A HEALTHY ECONOMY

The dynamism of our economy is produced by millions of individuals who have the incentive to participate in decision-making that advances themselves and society as a whole. Government can reinforce these incentives, but its overinvolvement in individual decisions distorts the system and intrudes inefficiency and waste.

Under the Johnson-Humphrey Administration we have had economic mismanagement of the highest order. Inflation robs our pay checks at a present rate of 4½ percent per year. In the past three years the real purchasing power of the average wage and salary worker has actually declined. Crippling interest rates, some the highest in a century, prevent millions of Americans from buying homes and small businessmen, farmers and other citizens from obtaining the loans they need. Americans must work longer today than ever before to pay their taxes.

New Republican leadership can and will restore fiscal integrity and sound monetary policies, encourage sustained economic vitality, and avoid such economic distortions as wage and price controls. We favor strengthened Congressional control over federal expenditures by scheduled Congressional reviews of, or reasonable time limits on, unobligated appropriations. By responsibly applying federal expenditure controls to priority needs, we can in time live both within our means and up to our aspirations. Such funds as become available with the termination of the Vietnam war and upon recovery from its impact on our national defense will be applied in a balanced way to critical domestic needs and to reduce the heavy tax burden. Our objective is not an endless expansion of federal programs and expenditures financed by heavier taxation. The imperative need for tax reform and simplification will have our priority attention. We will also improve the management of the national debt, reduce its heavy interest burden, and seek amendment of the law to make reasonable price stability an explicit objective of government policy.

The Executive Branch needs urgently to be made a more efficient and economical instrument of public policy. Low priority activities must be eliminated and conflicting missions and functions simplified. We pledge to establish a new Efficiency Commission to root out the unnecessary and overlapping, as well as a Presidential Office of Executive Management to assure a vigorous follow-through.

A new Republican Administration will undertake an intensive program to aid small business, including economic incentives and technical assistance, with increased emphasis in rural and urban poverty areas.

In addition to vigorous enforcement of the antitrust statutes, we pledge a thorough analysis of the structure and operation of these laws at home and abroad in the light of changes in the economy, in order to update our antitrust policy and enable it to serve us well in the future.

We are determined to eliminate and prevent improper federal competition with private enterprise.

Labor

Organized labor has contributed greatly to the economic strength of our country and the well-being of its members. The Republican Party vigorously endorses its key role in our national life.

We support an equitable minimum wage for American workers—one providing fair wages without unduly increasing unemployment among those on the lowest rung of the economic ladder—and will improve the Fair Labor Standards Act, with its important protections for employees.

The forty-hour week adopted 30 years ago needs re-examination to determine whether or not a shorter work week, without loss of wages, would produce more jobs, increase productivity and stabilize prices.

We strongly believe that the protection of individual liberty is the cornerstone of sound labor policy. Today, basic rights of some workers, guaranteed by law, are inadequately guarded against abuse. We will assure these rights through vigorous enforcement of present laws, including the Taft-Hartley Act and the Landrum-Griffin Act, and the addition of new protections where needed. We will be vigilant to prevent any administrative agency entrusted with labor-law enforcement from defying the letter and spirit of these laws.

Healthy private enterprise demands responsibility—by government, management and labor—to avoid the imposition of excessive costs or prices and to share with the consumer the benefits of increased productivity. It also demands responsibility in free collective bargaining, not only by labor and management, but also by those in government concerned with these sensitive relationships.

We will bar government-coerced strike settlements that cynically disregard the public interest and accelerate inflation. We will again reduce government intervention in labor-management disputes to a minimum, keep government participation in channels defined by the Congress, and prevent back-door intervention in the administration of labor laws.

Repeated Administration promises to recommend legislation dealing with crippling economic strikes have never been honored. Instead, settlements forced or influenced by government and overriding the interests of the parties and the public have shattered the Administration's own wage and price guidelines and contributed to inflation.

Effective methods for dealing with labor disputes involving the national interest must be developed. Permanent, long-range solutions of the problems of national emergency disputes, public employee strikes and crippling work stoppages are imperative. These solutions cannot be wisely formulated in the heat of emergency. We pledge an intensive effort to develop practical, acceptable solutions that conform fully to the public interest.

Transportation

Healthy economic growth demands a balanced, competitive transportation system in which each mode of transportation—train, truck, barge, bus and aircraft—is efficiently utilized. The Administration's failure to evolve a coordinated transportation policy now results in outrageous delays at major airports and in glacial progress in developing high-speed train transportation linking our major population centers.

The nation's air transport system performs excellently, but under increasingly adverse conditions. Airways and airport congestion has become acute. New and additional equipment, modern facilities including the use of computers, and additional personnel must be provided without further delay. We pledge expert evaluation of these matters in developing a national air transportation system.

We will make the Department of Transportation the agency Congress intended it to be—effective in promoting coordination and preserving competition among carriers. We promise equitable treatment of all modes of transportation in order to assure the public better service, greater safety, and the most modern facilities. We will also explore a trust fund approach to transportation, similar to the fund developed for the Eisenhower interstate highway system, and perhaps in this way speed the development of modern mass transportation systems and additional airports.

RESOURCES AND SCIENCE

Agriculture

During seven and a half years of Democrat Administrations and Democrat Congresses the farmer has been the forgotten man in our nation's economy. The cost-price squeeze has steadily worsened, driving more than four and a half million people from the farms, many to already congested urban areas. Over eight hundred thousand individual farm units have gone out of existence.

During the eight years of the Eisenhower Administration, the farm parity ratio averaged 85. Under Democratic rule, the parity ratio has consistently been under 80 and averaged only 74 for all of 1967. It has now fallen to 73. Actions by the Administration, in line with its apparent cheap food policy, have held down prices received by farmers. Government payments to farmers, from taxes paid by consumers, have far from offset this loss.

Inflationary policies of the Administration and its Congress have contributed greatly to increased costs of production. Using 1958 as a base year with an index of 100, prices paid by farmers in 1967 had risen to a weighted index of 117, whereas the prices they received were at a weighted index of only 104. From the 1958 index of 100, interest was up to 259, taxes 178, labor costs 146, and farm machinery 130.

The cost-price squeeze has been accompanied by a dangerous increase in farm debt—up nearly $24 billion in the last seven years. In 1967 alone, net debt per farm increased $1,337 while net income per farm went down $605. While net farm equity has increased, it is due mainly to inflated land values. Without adequate net income to pay off indebtedness, the farm owner has no choice but to liquidate some of his equity or go out of business. Farm tenants are even worse off, since they have no comparable investment for inflation to increase in value as their indebtedness increases.

The Republican Party is committed to the concept that a sound agricultural economy is imperative to the national interest. Prosperity, opportunity, abundance, and efficiency in agriculture benefit every American. To promote the development of American agriculture, we pledge:

Farm policies and programs which will enable producers to receive fair prices in relation to the prices they must pay for other products;

Sympathetic consideration of proposals to encourage farmers, especially small producers, to develop their bargaining position;

Sound economic policies which will brake inflation and reduce the high interest rates;

A truly two-way export-import policy which

protects American agriculture from unfair foreign competition while increasing our overseas commodity dollar sales to the rapidly expanding world population;

Reorganization of the management of the Commodity Credit Corporation's inventory operations so that the Corporation will no longer compete with the marketings of farmers;

Improved programs for distribution of food and milk to schools and low-income citizens;

A strengthened program to export our food and farm technology in keeping with the Republican-initiated Food for Peace program;

Assistance to farm cooperatives including rural electric and telephone cooperatives, consistent with prudent development of our nation's resources and rural needs;

Greater emphasis on research for industrial uses of agricultural products, new markets, and new methods for cost-cutting in production and marketing techniques;

Revitalization of rural America through programs emphasizing vocational training, economic incentives for industrial development, and the development of human resources;

Improvement of credit programs to help finance the heavy capital needs of modern farming, recognizing the severe credit problems of young farm families seeking to enter into successful farming;

A more direct voice for the American farmer in shaping his own destiny.

Natural Resources

In the tradition of Theodore Roosevelt, the Republican Party promises sound conservation and development of natural resources in cooperative government and private programs.

An expanding population and increasing material wealth require new public concern for the quality of our environment. Our nation must pursue its activities in harmony with the environment. As we develop our natural resources we must be mindful of our priceless heritage of natural beauty.

A national minerals and fuels policy is essential to maintain production needed for our nation's economy and security. Present economic incentives, including depletion allowances, to encourage the discovery and development of vital minerals and fuels must be continued. We must recognize the increasing demand for minerals and fuels by our economy, help ensure an economically stable industry, maintain a favorable balance of trade and balance of payments, and encourage research to promote the wise use of these resources.

Federal laws applicable to public lands and related resources will be updated and a public land-use policy formulated. We will manage such lands to ensure their multiple use as economic resources and recreational areas. Additionally, we will work in cooperation with cities and states in acquiring and developing green space—convenient outdoor recreation and conservation areas. We support the creation of additional national parks, wilderness areas, monuments and outdoor recreation areas at appropriate sites, as well as their continuing improvement, to make them of maximum utility and enjoyment to the public.

Improved forestry practices, including protection and improvement of watershed lands, will have our vigorous support. We will also improve water resource information, including an acceleration of river basin commission inventory studies. The reclaiming of land by irrigation and the development of flood control programs will have high priority in these studies. We will support additional multi-purpose water projects for reclamation, flood control, and recreation based on accurate cost-benefit estimates.

We also support efforts to increase our total fresh water supply by further research in weather modification, and in better methods of desalinization of salt and brackish waters.

The United States has dropped to sixth among the fishing nations of the world. We pledge a reversal of present policies and the adoption of a progressive national fisheries policy, which will make it possible for the first time to utilize fully the vast ocean reservoir of protein. We pledge a more energetic control of pollution, encouragement of an increase in fishery resources, and will also press for international agreements assuring multi-national conservation.

We pledge a far more vigorous and systematic program to expand knowledge about the unexplored storehouses of the sea and polar regions. We must undertake a comprehensive polar plan and an oceanographic program to develop these abundant resources for the continued strength of the United States and the betterment of all mankind.

Science

In science and technology the nation must maintain leadership against increasingly challenging competition from abroad. Crucial to this leadership is growth in the supply of gifted, skilled scientists and engineers. Government encouragement in this critical area should be stable and related to a more rational and selective scheme of priorities.

Vigorous effort must be directed toward increasing the application of science and technology, including the social sciences, to the solution of such pressing human problems as housing, transportation, education, environmental pollution, law enforcement, and job training. We support a strong program of research in the sciences, with protection for the independence and integrity of participating individuals and institutions. An increase in the number of centers of scientific creativity and excellence, geographically dispersed, and active cooperation with other nations in meaningful scientific undertakings will also have our support.

We regret that the Administration's budgetary mismanagement has forced sharp reductions in the space program. The Republican Party shares the sense of urgency manifested by the scientific community concerning the exploration of outer space. We recognize that the peaceful applications of space probes in communications, health, weather, and technological advances have been beneficial to every citizen. We regard the ability to launch and deploy advanced spacecraft as a military necessity. We deplore the failure of the Johnson-Humphrey Administration to emphasize the military uses of space for America's defense.

FOREIGN POLICY

Our nation urgently needs a foreign policy that realistically leads toward peace. This policy can come only from resolute, new leadership—a leadership that can and will think anew and act anew—a leadership not bound by mistakes of the past.

Our best hope for enduring peace lies in comprehensive international cooperation. We will consult with nations that share our purposes. We will press for their greater participation in man's common concerns and encourage regional approaches to defense, economic development, and peaceful adjustment of disputes.

We will seek to develop law among nations and strengthen agencies to effectuate that law and cooperatively solve common problems. We will assist the United Nations to become the keystone of such agencies, and its members will be pressed to honor all charter obligations, including specifically its financial provisions. Worldwide resort to the International Court of Justice as a final arbiter of legal disputes among nations will have our vigorous encouragement, subject to limitations imposed by the U.S. Senate in accepting the Court's jurisdiction.

The world abounds with problems susceptible of cooperative solution—poverty, hunger, denial of human rights, economic development, scientific and technological backwardness. The worldwide population explosion in particular, with its attendant grave problems, looms as a menace to all mankind and will have our priority attention. In all such areas we pledge to expand and strengthen international cooperation.

A more selective use of our economic strength has become imperative. We believe foreign aid is a necessary ingredient in the betterment of less developed countries. Our aid, however, must be positioned realistically in our national priorities. Only those nations which urgently require America's help and clearly evince a desire to help themselves will receive such assistance as can be diverted from our pressing needs. In providing aid, more emphasis will be given to technical assistance. We will encourage multilateral agencies so that other nations will help share the burden. The administration of all aid programs will be revised and improved to prevent waste, inefficiency and corruption. We will vigorously encourage maximum participation by private enterprise.

No longer will foreign aid activities range free of our foreign policy. Nations hostile to this country will receive no assistance from the United States. We will not provide aid of any kind to countries which aid and abet the war efforts of North Vietnam.

Only when Communist nations prove by actual deeds that they genuinely seek world peace and will live in harmony with the rest of the world, will we support expansion of East-West trade.

We will strictly administer the Export Control Act, taking special care to deny export licenses for strategic goods.

In the development and execution of the nation's foreign policy, our career Foreign Service officers play a critical role. We strongly support the Foreign Service and will strengthen it by improving its efficiency and administration and providing adequate allowances for its personnel.

The principles of the 1965 Immigration Act —non-discrimination against national origins, re-unification of families, and selective support for the American labor market—have our unreserved backing. We will refine this new law to make our immigration policy still more equitable and non-discriminatory.

The Republican Party abhors the activities of those who have violated passport regulations contrary to the best interests of our nation and also the present policy of re-issuing passports to such violators. We pledge to tighten passport administration so as to bar such violators from passport privileges.

The balance of payments crisis must be ended, and the international position of the dollar strengthened. We propose to do this, not by peremptory efforts to limit American travel abroad or by self-defeating restraints on overseas investments, but by restraint in Federal spending and realistic monetary policies, by adjusting overseas commitments, by stimulating exports, by encouraging more foreign travel to the United States and, as specific conditions require, by extending tax treatment to our own exports and imports comparable to such treatment applied by foreign countries. Ending inflation is the first step toward solving the payments crisis.

It remains the policy of the Republican Party to work toward freer trade among all nations of the free world. But artificial obstacles to such trade are a serious concern. We promise hard-headed bargaining to lower the non-tariff barriers against American exports and to develop a code of fair competition, including international fair labor standards, between the United States and its principal trading partners.

A sudden influx of imports can endanger many industries. These problems, differing in each industry, must be considered case by case. Our guideline will be fairness for both producers and workers, without foreclosing imports.

Thousands of jobs have been lost to foreign producers because of discriminatory and unfair trade practices.

The State Department must give closest attention to the development of agreements with exporting nations to bring about fair competition. Imports should not be permitted to capture excessive portions of the American market but should, through international agreements, be able to participate in the growth of consumption.

Should such efforts fail, specific counter-measures will have to be applied until fair competition is re-established. Tax reforms will also be required to preserve the competitiveness of American goods.

The basis for determining the value of imports and exports must be modified to reflect true dollar value.

Not the least important aspect of this problem is the relative obsolescence of machinery in this country. An equitable tax write-off is necessary to strengthen our industrial competitiveness in the world.

We also favor the broadening of governmental assistance to industries, producers and workers seriously affected by imports—assistance denied by the Johnson-Humphrey Administration's excessively stringent application of the Trade Expansion Act of 1962.

Ties of history and geography link us closely to Latin America. Closer economic and cultural cooperation of the United States and the Latin American countries is imperative in a broad attack on the chronic problems of poverty, inadequate economic growth and consequent poor education throughout the hemisphere. We will encourage in Latin America the progress of economic integration to improve opportunity for industrialization and economic diversification.

The principles of the Monroe Doctrine, affirmed at Caracas 14 years ago by all the independent nations of this hemisphere, have been discarded by Democrat Administrations. We hold that they should be reaffirmed and should guide the collective policy of the Americas. Nor have we forgotten in this context, the Cuban people who still cruelly suffer under Communist tyranny.

In cooperation with other nations, we will encourage the less developed nations of Asia and Africa peacefully to improve their standards of living, working with stronger regional organizations where indicated and desired.

In the tinderbox of the Middle East, we will pursue a stable peace through recognition by all nations of each other's right to assured boundaries, freedom of navigation through international waters, and independent existence free from the threat of aggression. We will seek an end to the arms race through international agreement and the stationing of peace-keeping forces of the United Nations in areas of severe tension, as we encourage peace-table talks among adversaries.

Nevertheless, the Soviets persist in building an imbalance of military forces in this region. The fact of a growing menace to Israel is undeniable. Her forces must be kept at a commensurate strength both for her protection and to help keep the peace of the area. The United States, therefore, will provide countervailing help to Israel, such as supersonic fighters, as necessary for these purposes. To replace the ancient rivalries of this region with new hope and opportunity, we vigorously support a well-conceived plan of regional development, including the bold nuclear desalinization and irrigation proposal of former President Eisenhower.

Our relations with Western Europe, so critical to our own progress and security, have been needlessly and dangerously impaired. They must be restored, and NATO revitalized and strengthened. We continue to pursue the goal of a Germany reunified in freedom.

The peoples of the captive nations of Eastern Europe will one day regain their freedom and independence. We will strive to speed this day by encouraging the greater political freedom actively sought by several of these nations. On occasions when a liberalization of trade in nonstrategic goods with the captive nations can have this effect, it will have our support.

We do not intend to conduct foreign policy in such manner as to make the United States a world policeman. However, we will not condone aggression, or so-called "wars of national liberation," or naïvely discount the continuing threats of Moscow and Peking. Nor can we fail to condemn the Soviet Union for its continuing anti-Semitic actions, its efforts to eradicate all religions, and its oppression of minorities generally. Improved relations with Communist nations can come only when they cease to endanger other states by force or threat. Under existing conditions, we cannot favor recognition of Communist China or its admission to the United Nations.

We encourage international limitations of armaments, provided all major powers are proportionately restrained and trustworthy guarantees are provided against violations.

VIETNAM

The Administration's Vietnam policy has failed —militarily, politically, diplomatically, and with relation to our own people.

We condemn the Administration's breach of faith with the American people respecting our heavy involvement in Vietnam. Every citizen bitterly recalls the Democrat campaign oratory of 1964: "We are not about to send American boys 9-10,000 miles away from home to do what Asian boys ought to be doing for themselves." The Administration's failure to honor its own words has led millions of Americans to question its credibility.

The entire nation has been profoundly concerned by hastily extemporized, undeclared land wars which embroil massive U.S. armed forces thousands of miles from our shores. It is time to realize that not every international conflict is susceptible of solution by American ground forces.

Militarily, the Administration's piecemeal commitment of men and material has wasted our massive military superiority and frittered away our options. The result has been a prolonged war of attrition. Throughout this period the Administration has been slow in training and equipping South Vietnamese units both for fighting the war and for defending their country after the war is over.

Politically, the Administration has failed to recognize the entirely novel aspects of this war. The overemphasis on its old-style, conventional aspects has blinded the Administration to the fact that the issue is not control of territory but the security and loyalty of the population. The enemy's primary emphasis has been to disrupt orderly government.

The Administration has paid inadequate attention to the political framework on which a successful outcome ultimately depends. Not only has the Administration failed to encourage assumption of responsibility by the Vietnamese, but their sense of responsibility has been in fact undermined by our approach to pacification. An added factor has been a lack of security for the civilian population.

At home, the Administration has failed to share with the people the full implication of our challenge and of our commitments.

To resolve our Vietnam dilemma, America obviously requires new leadership—one capable of thinking and acting anew, not one hostage to the many mistakes of the past. The Republican Party offers such leadership.

We pledge to adopt a strategy relevant to the real problems of the war, concentrating on the security of the population, on developing a greater sense of nation-hood, and on strengthening the local forces. It will be a strategy permitting a progressive de-Americanization of the war, both military and civilian.

We will see to it that our gallant American servicemen are fully supported with the highest quality equipment, and will avoid actions that unnecessarily jeopardize their lives.

We will pursue a course that will enable and induce the South Vietnamese to assume increasing responsibility.

The war has been conducted without a coherent program for peace.

We pledge a program for peace in Vietnam—neither peace at any price nor a camouflaged surrender of legitimate United States or allied interests—but a positive program that will offer a fair and equitable settlement to all, based on the principle of self-determination, our national interests and the cause of long-range world peace.

We will sincerely and vigorously pursue peace negotiations as long as they offer any reasonable prospect for a just peace. We pledge to develop a clear and purposeful negotiating position.

We will return to one of the cardinal principles of the last Republican Administration: that American interests are best served by cooperative multilateral action with our allies rather than by unilateral U.S. action.

Our pride in the nation's armed forces in Southeast Asia and elsewhere in the world is beyond expression.

In all our history none have fought more bravely or more devotedly than our sons in this unwanted war in Vietnam.

They deserve—and they and their loved ones have—our total support, our encouragement, and our prayers.

NATIONAL DEFENSE

Grave errors, many now irretrievable, have characterized the direction of our nation's defense.

A singular notion—that salvation for America lies in standing still—has pervaded the entire effort. Not retention of American superiority but parity with the Soviet Union has been made the controlling doctrine in many critical areas. We have frittered away superior military capabilities, enabling the Soviets to narrow their defense gap, in some areas to outstrip us, and to move to cancel our lead entirely by the early Seventies. In a host of areas, advanced military research and development have been inhibited and stagnated by inexpert, cost-oriented administrators imbued with a euphoric concept of Soviet designs. A strange Administration preference for such second-best weaponry as the costly Navy F111-B(TFX) has deprived our armed forces of more advanced weapons systems. Improvements in our submarines have been long delayed as the Soviets have proceeded apace with their own. Our anti-submarine warfare capabilities have been left seriously inadequate, new fighter planes held up, and new strategic weaponry left on the drawing boards.

This mismanagement has dangerously weakened the ability of the United States to meet future crises with great power and decisiveness. All the world was respectful of America's decisive strategic advantage over the Soviets achieved during the Eisenhower Administration. This superiority proved its worth in the Cuban missile crisis six years ago. But now we have had an augury of things to come—a shameful, humiliating episode, the seizure of the USS *Pueblo* and its crew, with devastating injury to America's prestige everywhere in the world.

We pledge to include the following in a comprehensive program to restore the pre-eminence of U.S. military strength:

Improve our deterrent capability through an ocean strategy which extends the Polaris-Poseidon concept and accelerates submarine technology;

Redirect and stimulate military strength to encourage major innovations rather than merely respond belatedly to Communist advances;

Strengthen intelligence gathering and evaluation by the various military services;

Use the defense dollar more effectively through simplification of the cumbersome, overcentralized administration of the Defense Department, expanded competitive bidding on defense contracts, and improved safeguards against excessive profits;

Reinvigorate the nation's most important security planning organization—the National Security Council—to prevent future haphazard diplomatic and military ventures, integrate the nation's foreign and military policies and programs, and enable our nation once again to anticipate and prevent crises rather than hastily contriving counter-measures after they arise.

Our merchant marine, too, has been allowed to deteriorate. Now there are grave doubts that it is capable of adequate response of emergency security needs.

The United States has drifted from first place to sixth place in the world in the size of its merchant fleet. By contrast, the Russian fleet has been rapidly expanding and will attain a dominant position by 1970. Deliveries of new ships are now eight to one in Russia's favor.

For reasons of security, as well as of economics, the decline of our merchant marine must be reversed. We therefore pledge a vigorous and realistic ship replacement program to meet the changing pattern of our foreign commerce. We will also expand industry-government maritime research and development, emphasizing nuclear propulsion, and simplify and revise construction and operating subsidy procedures.

Finally, we pledge to assemble the nation's best diplomatic, military and scientific minds for an exhaustive reassessment of America's worldwide commitments and military preparedness. We are determined to assure our nation of the strength required in future years to deter war and to prevail should it occur.

CONCLUSION

We believe that the principles and programs we have here presented will find acceptance with the American people. We believe they will command the victory.

There are points of emphasis which we deem important.

The accent is on freedom. Our Party historically has been the Party of freedom. We are the only barricade against those who, through excessive government power, would overwhelm and destroy man's liberty. If liberty fails, all else is dross.

Beyond freedom we emphasize trust and credibility. We have pledged only what we honestly believe we can perform. In a world where broken promises become a way of life, we submit that a nation progresses not on promises broken but on pledges kept.

We have also accented the moral nature of the crisis which confronts us. At the core of that crisis is the life, the liberty, and the happiness of man. If life can be taken with impunity, if liberty is subtly leeched away, if the pursuit of happiness becomes empty and futile, then indeed are the moral foundations in danger.

We have placed high store on our basic theme. The dogmas of the quiet past simply will not do for the restless present. The case is new. We must most urgently think anew and act anew. This is an era of rapid, indeed violent change. Clearly we must disenthrall ourselves. Only then can we save this great Republic.

We rededicate ourselves to this Republic—this one nation, under God, indivisible, with liberty and justice for all.

Socialist Labor Platform 1968

"There is in the land a certain restlessness, a questioning."

The words were uttered by President Johnson in his January 17, 1968, State of the Union Message. They understated the case.

The American people in 1968 are assailed by foreboding and bitterness, frustration and fear, bewilderment and doubt. It is not the Socialist Labor Party alone that makes this severe assessment. Late in 1967, the National Committee for an Effective Congress issued a report in which it declared:

"At all levels of American life, people share similar fears, insecurities and gnawing doubts to such an intense degree that the country may in fact be suffering from a kind of national nervous breakdown."

Why? The Socialist Labor Party declares that when a sickness of this scope and intensity grips a nation it signifies that something very extraordinary is taking place, something far greater in a historical sense than division and dissent over a criminal and unconstitutional war, greater even than the crisis in race relations with its dire prospect of urban insurrection and, worse, of genocide.

The Socialist Labor Party declares that what this mortal national—really universal—sickness signifies is a vague and undefined, but mounting distrust in the ability of society *as presently organized* to cope with the problems that have arisen under it.

It is a serious error to imagine, as most people do, that revolutions occur when the mass of the people are starving and otherwise suffering intense deprivation. On the contrary, experience shows that revolutions occur when expectations of a better, more secure and more happy life are rising—and when these expectations are prevented from being fulfilled by outmoded laws and institutions. "Evils which are patiently endured when they seem inevitable," wrote de Tocqueville, "become intolerable when once the idea of escape from them is suggested."

Material justifications for rising expectations abound today on every hand. Since World War II industrial and scientific advances have been phenomenal. Output of the nation's industries is now more than twice as great as it was in 1950. In the past 10 years it has swollen an incredible 60 percent.

Failure of Reforms

Why, then, in the face of such material progress, do massive poverty and insecurity persist? What explains the dismal failure of President Johnson's "Great Society" reforms and the "war on poverty" on which billions of dollars have been spent without even beginning to solve a single problem?

The conspicuous failure of reforms, which raised the hopes of many so high when enacted, is not the least contributing reason for the despair, frustration and doubt that pervade this nation.

The Socialist Labor Party declares and proves that the maladies afflicting our society—maladies ranging from the monetary inflation that erodes the living standards of all workers, combined with fierce capitalist resistance to increase wages to offset it, to the frightening surge of crime

and violence, from deadly pollution of the natural environment to a crisis in race relations—have, not many causes, but *one* cause. This one cause is a social system—capitalism—that is outmoded, destructively competitive and profit-motivated. The Socialist Labor Party warns that if we keep this outmoded form of society, in which wealth is produced for the private profit of a few, not for the welfare and benefit of the people, catastrophic consequences, of which today's fears are a portent, are sure to follow.

Socialist Alternative

The alternative to the rapidly disintegrating capitalist world is a world organized on a sane foundation of social ownership and democratic administration of the industries and services, and production to satisfy human needs instead of for sale and private profit. The alternative to contradiction-ridden capitalism is a Socialist world of cooperation and human brotherhood.

In this hour of deadly peril when the whole world seems to be trembling on the very brink of chaos and cataclysmic disaster, the Socialist Labor Party appeals to all workers of all races, and to socially minded people generally, to reflect on the logic and downright common sense of a fundamental Socialist reconstruction of society.

Once society—which means all of us, collectively—gains control of the nation's productive facilities, once social production is planned and decisions respecting production are determined by human needs and human desires, poverty will be speedily eliminated. The nation's immensely productive resources will be mobilized, not to wage criminal and brutalizing wars, not to enable a small class of capitalist parasites to accumulate mountains of wealth, but constructively to replace slum areas with parks and habitations fit for humans to live in, to purify our polluted rivers, lakes and air—in short, to repossess America from the vandal capitalist class and make of it the heaven on earth it can be and ought to be.

In our Socialist world, democracy will be a vibrant, meaningful reality, not the mask for economic despotism that it is today. There will be no such ridiculous thing as a political government based, as today, on wholly arbitrary and artificial geographical demarcations. (Some of our state boundaries were determined by a king's grant two and a half centuries ago; they are meaningless in the industrial age!) To administer social production in the interests of the people, we need an *industrial democracy*, a government based on industrial constituencies.

In Socialist society there will be neither masters nor slaves. We will vote where we work, electing our representatives to administrative and planning bodies on an ascending scale. But note this: The people whom we elect to administrative posts will have the privilege to serve, never the power to rule. For the same rank and file that elects them will have the power to recall and replace them at will.

ADMINISTRATION OF THINGS

The democratically elected administrators and planners of Socialism will concern themselves with such practical things as what and how much to produce to insure an uninterrupted flow of the good things of life in abundance; the number of working hours required in the various industries; the erection of plants of production and educational, health and recreational facilities; the development of new technology; the planning and rebuilding of cities; the conservation of resources and the restoration of the natural environment and its preservation for all time.

All that stands in the way of this heaven on earth, a world in which all may enjoy good housing, abundant and nourishing food, the finest clothing, and the best of cultural, educational and recreational advantages, is the outmoded capitalist system.

This is no exaggeration. Nor merely a beautiful dream. It is based on the solid foundation of material facts. Automation, the supreme triumph of technology, has brought this heaven on earth within our reach. Yet, privately owned, as are all productive instruments under capitalism, automation is a blessing only to the capitalist owners; for workers it is a curse, a job-killer, which adds terrifying dimensions to worker insecurity.

THE BASIC SOCIAL QUESTION

Thus the question we face comes down to this: *"When the machine displaces man and does most of the work, who will own the machines and receive the rich dividends?"* (Supreme Court Justice William O. Douglas.)

The United States Constitution, in effect, legalizes revolution. The right to alter or abolish the social system and form of government is implicit in Article V, the Constitution's amendment clause. The Socialist Labor Party proposes to the American workers—and by "workers" we mean all who perform useful labor, teachers, technicians, stenographers and musicians, as well as machinists, assembly-line workers, longshoremen and miners—that we use our huge majorities at the polls to outlaw capitalist ownership and to make the means of social production the property of all the people collectively.

The Socialist Labor Party proposes further that we workers consolidate our economic forces on the industrial field in one integral Socialist Industrial Union to back up the Socialist ballot with an irresistible and invincible power capable of taking and holding the industries, locking out the outvoted capitalist class, and continuing social production without interruption.

THE LINE BETWEEN NONSENSE
AND COMMON SENSE

Thomas Carlyle is credited with saying: "We must some day, at last and forever, cross the line between nonsense and common sense. And on that day we shall pass from class paternalism . . . to human brotherhood . . . ; from political government to industrial administration; from competition in individualism to individuality in cooperation; from war and despotism, in any form, to peace and liberty."

We *must* cross that line some day—why not now? Repudiate the Republican and Democratic parties, the political Siamese twins of capitalism —and reject also the self-styled "radicals," the so-called New Left and "liberals" whose platforms consist of measures to reform and patch up the poverty-breeding capitalist system, which is past reforming and patching. Study the Socialist Labor Party's Socialist Industrial Union program. Support the Socialist Labor Party's entire ticket at the polls. Unite with us to save humanity from catastrophe—and to set an example in free nonpolitical self-government for all mankind, in affluence and enduring peace.

Socialist Workers Platform 1968

The bipartisan policies of the Democrats and Republicans are leading the people of the United States toward disaster.

Despite negotiations the war in Vietnam continues to escalate—more bombing, more troops, more death and destruction for the Vietnamese and more American casualties. And further escalation increases the danger of a nuclear war, a war which would leave the world's cities—our own included—heaps of radioactive rubble.

While U.S. troops are in Vietnam attempting to crush a popular revolution, police, national guard and army units are used to viciously smash the uprisings of black people in our own cities.

In spite of big promises and small concessions, black people remain subject to discrimination and oppression in housing, in jobs, in education and every other area of economic, political and social life. Police brutality, slumlord rent-hogs and price-gouging merchants are daily facts of life for Afro-Americans. Unemployment and low wages hit black people the hardest.

Tens of millions of Americans, black and white, live in poverty. One third of the nation lives below the "poverty line," by admission of the government itself. These Americans have not shared in the "prosperity" based on war production and exploitation of the colonial world.

The workers as a whole are feeling the squeeze of the war economy. Rising taxes and inflated prices have cut into pay checks, actually lowering real wages since the escalation of the war in Vietnam. And while they wallow in super profits, the corporations do everything they can to keep wages down and encroach upon union control over working conditions.

The bosses turn more and more to the government for aid in their crusade against the workers, and the Democrats and Republicans have proven more than willing servants of their class. The move by Congress forcing compulsory slave-labor arbitration on the railroad workers is only the latest in a long list of anti-labor laws and actions by the government.

Democratic rights, too, are being eroded. The response of the government—federal, state and local—to the black revolt has been the harassment and hounding of the most authoritative spokesmen of the movement for black power. This is creating the atmosphere in which all dissenting views will be liable to witchhunt attack.

Moral and cultural values are twisted and mangled in this war-breeding, racist system. The big lie has become standard operating procedure in everything from advertising swindles to White House ballyhoo on Vietnam.

The basic policies pursued by the Democratic and Republican politicians are not the accidental results of arbitrary decisions. They flow from the needs of the capitalist system and the outlook of the ruling capitalist class.

The Vietnam war is a prime example. It is now crystal clear that the U.S. ruling class is not fighting in Vietnam for "freedom" or "democracy." Their war aim is to prevent the workers and peasants of Vietnam from taking control of their own country. The Democrats and Republicans are sending our young men to die in Vietnam as part of a reckless global strategy of preserving and extending the capitalist system and capitalist profits.

Racism is also part and parcel of American capitalist society. Racism serves to keep white workers from realizing that their interests lie with the black masses, and not with the white capitalist rulers. Racism is a source of profit for the ruling class, providing a ready-made pool of cheap and available labor. Racism is utilized in the U.S. imperialist drive to subjugate and enslave the colored people around the world, as in Vietnam.

War, racism, poverty, the attack on labor, the erosion of the Bill of Rights—all these are bitter fruits of the capitalist system or of the measures taken by the capitalist rulers to uphold their system and increase their profits.

To fight against these evils, it is necessary to expose their roots in the system which produced them. We have to uproot this vicious system and fight for a new and better one.

That's why the Socialist Workers Party stands for a complete break with every form of capitalist politics. When black people, and workers as a whole, cease supporting the capitalist Democratic and Republican parties and organize parties of their own, a gigantic step forward will have been taken in the struggle against the system.

In 1968, a clear-cut opposition and radical alternative to the war-making and racist Democrats and Republicans will be presented by the SWP candidates for President and Vice President, Fred Halstead and Paul Boutelle.

Halstead and Boutelle are campaigning for the following program:

Stop the war in Vietnam—bring our men home now! Support the right of GIs to discuss the war and freely express their opposition to it. Abolish the draft—no draftees for Washington's imperialist war machine. Organize a national referendum to give the people the right to vote to withdraw all U.S. troops from Vietnam.

Hands off Cuba and China. Support the struggles of the Asian, Latin American, African and Arab peoples for national independence and social liberation.

Support the right of self-determination of all oppressed national minorities (Afro-Americans, Puerto Ricans, Mexican-Americans, Indians, etc.) inside the U.S.

Support the black people's fight for freedom, justice, and equality through black power. Black people have the unconditional right to control their own communities. The black communities should have control over their schools, and city, state and federal funds should be made available to them in whatever amount needed to overcome years of deprivation in education.

Appropriate what funds are necessary to provide jobs for every unemployed Afro-American, with preferential hiring and upgrading to equalize opportunities in apprenticeship programs, skilled trades, and higher paying technical and supervisory occupations.

In place of price-gouging merchants and landlords preying on the black community, black nonprofit cooperative shops and housing projects should be set up with federal financial aid. Price committees elected by the community should police prices.

It is the right of Afro-Americans to keep arms and organize themselves for self-defense from all attacks.

Keep the troops and racist cops out of the black community, and replace them with deputized, elected representatives of the community. As an immediate step, organize genuine review boards, elected by the black community, to control the cops.

For an independent black political party to organize and lead the struggle for black power on all fronts and by any means necessary.

Support labor's fight against inflation and government control. No freeze on wages. For union escalator clauses to offset rises in the cost of living. The trade unions should take the lead in setting up general committees of consumers to regulate prices.

Repeal all anti-labor laws. Defense of the unconditional right to strike. Complete union independence from government control and interference. Rank and file control over all union affairs.

A reduced work week with no cut in pay, and unemployment compensation at the union wage scale for all jobless persons 18 and over, whether or not they have been previously employed.

Equal rights in the union and on the job for black workers and for members of other minorities, and full union support to the Afro-American struggle for equality.

For an independent labor party based on the trade unions, to defend the rights of all working people against the parties of the bosses, and to fight for a workers government.

For a crash program of public housing and other public works. Take the billions spent on war and use them to build decent, low-rent homes for the working millions who need them, and to build schools and hospitals instead of bombs.

Support the demands of America's youth.

The right to vote at 18.

Free public education through the university level, with adequate pay for all students who need it. Student participation in all university decisions and functioning.

Support to young people's rejection of the sterile cultural values of our decaying capitalist order.

For a planned, democratic socialist America. Nationalize the major corporations and banks under the control of democratically elected workers committees. Plan the economy democratically for the benefit of all instead of for the profit of the few.

A socialist America will be an America of peace and prosperity, without poverty or slums or unemployment, and without wars like that in Vietnam. It will put an end to racism and, for the first time after over 400 years of oppression, guarantee unconditionally, the right of self-determination for the black Americans. It will signal an unparalleled growth in culture, freedom and in the development of the individual.

Republican President Richard Nixon, running for reelection in 1972, received 47,042,923 votes compared to 29,071,629 for the Democratic candidate, Senator George McGovern. This margin of 17,971,294 votes was the largest in American history, but the President's 60.73 per cent of the total vote fell short of the record 61.1 per cent of the vote cast for Lyndon Johnson in 1964. Mr. Nixon captured 520 electoral votes to 17 for Mr. McGovern. One Republican elector in Virginia voted for the candidate of the Libertarian party.

The 77,460,056 persons who went to the polls also represented the greatest number of voters ever to participate in a presidential election, but because of the many newly enfranchised voters in 1972, they represented less than 55 per cent of the eligible vote, and this was the lowest turnout in twenty-four years.

Representative John G. Schmitz, running on the American party ticket, received 1,080,541 votes for third place. Dr. Benjamin Spock, the candidate of the People's party, was fourth with 78,801. The Socialist Workers party polled 65,290 votes, and the Socialist Labor party received 53,614. The Communist party candidate polled 25,222, and the Prohibitionists received 13,444.

The platforms of these major and minor parties are presented here; there were thirty-five other minor presidential candidates, who received a total of 28,592 votes scattered in individual states. For the reasons stated in the preface to this volume, the statements of principles or platforms of these candidates have been omitted.

American Platform 1972

PREAMBLE

The American Party of the United States of America gratefully acknowledges the Lord God as the Creator, Preserver, and Ruler of the Universe and of the Nation, hereby appeals to Him for aid, comfort, and continuing guidance in its efforts to preserve this nation as a government of the people, by the people, and for the people in this time of peril.

The American Party speaks for the majority of Americans, the hard-working, productive taxpaying citizens who constitute the strength of America.

No other party today speaks for the average American or expresses his concepts, hopes, and goals.

The average man today does not think of himself in ideological terms, such as liberal and conservative. Rather, the average man thinks in terms of the basic problems which confront him. He is concerned with the opportunity for gainful employment, educational opportunity for his children, the safety of his wife and child on the streets of his community, an equity in taxation which makes him neither the victim of those who by refusing to work have no income to tax, or the multi-millionaires who use tax loopholes to avoid the payment of any taxes. He is concerned about the never-ending use of his sons for gunfodder in futile international involvements.

The platform of the American Party is a response to his desires, a voice which speaks for him as no other political party in America today so speaks.

No nation can survive if it fails to meet the problems which concern the average citizen. The American Party confronts these problems with the conviction that the little people of America are right and will be heard in a free Nation committed to Government of, by, and for the people. The people will ultimately have their way.

To these, the great American people, we offer this platform.

II. DOMESTIC POLICY

Local Government

The average man in America today believes in local, voter controlled institutions of government.

The American Party is totally committed to the governmental framework embodied in the Constitution of the United States with its emphasis on a maximum of individual freedom and local autonomy. We are unalterably opposed to Federal domination of local institutions, particularly our public schools.

Individual Rights

The American Party speaks for individual freedom; the right of each citizen to the ownership of property and the control of his own property, the right to engage in business or participate in his labor union without governmental interference.

We shall steadfastly oppose Federal legislation permitting the Federal bureaucracy to tell a business man who he must hire or fire, tamper with Union seniority lists and apprenticeship programs or invade the individual's right of privacy.

We call for the elimination of government competition with free and competitive institutions.

Federal Judiciary

The greatest obstacle to the achievement by the average man of his goals and desires for America is the unrepresentative, unresponsive, dictatorial, federal judiciary.

The American Party would end judicial usurpation of the constitutional process by requiring federal judges at the district court level to be directly elected by the people, by requiring federal judges at the appellate level, including Supreme Court Justices, to be reconfirmed in their appointments every four years, and by limiting the appellate jurisdiction of the federal courts in state constitutional cases.

Protection from Crime and Violence

The law-abiding citizen of the United States has a right to be protected from crime, violence and lawlessness.

The American Party pledges full support to local law enforcement in their crusade to control crime; reforms in our judicial system to provide a speedy and just determination in criminal cases; and retention of the historic constitutional right of each state and the federal government, to impose capital punishment for aggravated criminal offenses.

We support maximum penalties for the crime of skyjacking and political assassinations.

We support local control and financing of our local police forces and will oppose all attempts to establish federal control over them.

Drug Abuse

The American Party asserts that drugs are a serious problem in our nation, particularly among our youth, threatening the physical and mental health and even the life of users and leading to many crimes, accidents and other misfortunes.

We oppose legalization of marijuana. We favor strong local and state laws making it a criminal offense with a mandatory jail sentence for anyone convicted of selling or supplying drugs, excepting for prescribed medical purposes.

The ultimate source of most hard drugs in the United States is the poppy fields of Red China. We deplore President Nixon's failure to take any meaningful action to stop the flow of hard drugs from Red China to the United States and pledge our full support to stop this assault on our American youth.

Respect for Life

A companion to the rise of crime in America has been the growing lack of respect for life and the institutions of home, marriage and family.

The American Party recognizes that the first and most important role of government at any level is the protection of the right to life. The American Party opposes all attempts to liberalize any anti-abortion laws which laws, by their very nature, protect the lives of those innocents least able to defend themselves.

We are opposed to euthanasia, the so-called "Mercy killing" of the aged, ailing or infirm, by the administration of drugs or the withholding of medication essential to the patient's comfort or possible recovery.

We fully support laws providing criminal penalties for the unsolicited presentation or exhibition of obscenity, including any public display of homosexuality.

Gun Control

The American Party supports the right of all citizens to be fully protected in their homes, persons and property.

The Constitution of the United States affords to every citizen the right to keep and bear arms.

The lawless always acquire weapons and the result of disarming our citizens, coupled with judicial emasculation of local police protection, would be to leave the average citizen without protection from the lawless. We support a mandatory jail sentence for anyone using a firearm in the commission of a felony.

The American Party opposes laws which would deny the right of our citizens to own firearms.

Welfare

The American Party is sensitive to the needs of America's aged, blind and disabled citizens and fully supports state and local programs to enable these citizens to live in dignity and economic security.

We are unalterably opposed to tax supported subsidies to able bodied persons who refuse to work, engage in welfare fraud, or utilize their reproductive capacities for the purpose of securing even larger welfare payments.

We support all necessary statutory and administrative amendments necessary to achieve the complete elimination of rampant fraud in public assistance programs.

We oppose all federal funding in public assistance programs.

Social Security

The American Party fully appreciates the rightful aspiration of the aged to live in dignity and economic security.

The aged have been the principal victims of an irresponsible government fostered inflation. We support legislation to require the Federal government to protect Social Security Funds as a special trust, using those funds solely for the purpose of providing benefits to the beneficiaries. We support the removal of the earnings limitation of 62 and over in order that they may earn any amount of additional income.

We support the right of those entering the labor market to elect to participate in approved private retirement plans as an alternative to the Federal Social Security Program. Current studies establish that, at present rates, the same funds paid into social security over the average worker's productive life would produce, if paid into a private investment trust fund, a principal sum sufficient to provide the worker a retirement income at least several times larger than present social security benefits.

Health Care

The average man today is threatened in his economic security by the high cost of medical care. We believe that the advantages of our scientific achievements in the medical field should be available to every citizen, through the free enterprise system.

We support cooperative efforts between private insurance carriers and private charitable institutions to provide low-cost medical insurance for the average citizen. We oppose any form of government controlled insurance.

We fully support the freedom of the citizen to choose his own physician.

We are particularly sensitive to the special needs of the handicapped and support state administered programs which offer these citizens the educational and employment opportunities to lead productive lives.

Inflation

The average family in America is today the victim of government created inflation which robs the working man of the advantage achieved by high wage standards.

Government created the problem of inflation by deficit spending and Government must be curbed in such further activity.

The American Party supports all steps necessary to halt the inflationary spiral, including putting the Federal Government on a pay-as-you-go basis and restoring a sound monetary standard by permitting the individual citizen to own and exchange gold, and the American Party advocates the abolition of the Federal Reserve System (a private corporation), and together with such abolition, the American Party advocates a return to the gold standard.

We object strongly to the policy of present and past administrations in blaming either the working man or the business man for the problem of inflation.

The imposition of wage and price controls, ostensibly established to curb inflation, is a fraud upon every citizen of America. We call for the removal of such fraud upon every citizen of America. We call for the removal of such fraudulent wage and price controls.

Taxation

Through ever-increasing tax rates the average man in America carries the full burden of the cost of a reckless and wasteful Federal government. The able-bodied who refuse to work produce no income, pay no taxes, and draw lavish welfare subsidies. The ultra-rich acquire vast sums, but use tax loopholes and tax-exempt foundations to evade the payment of taxes.

The American Party supports immediate tax relief for the lower and middle-income citizens of America, a closing of the tax loopholes for the ultra-rich, and taxation of the presently exempt foundations unless their purposes are narrowly limited to charitable pursuits.

We believe that the American Party should encourage the full consideration of a constitutional amendment reflecting long-standing and never refuted studies establishing that if the federal government is restricted to its constitutional functions, the present income, estate and gift tax programs can be eliminated at a proven profit of approximately 20% to the average American wage earner.

Employment

The creation of job opportunities for our citizens is an essential requirement of today's economy.

The American Party would eliminate governmental red tape and restrictions which discourage the development and expansion of business enterprises which create job opportunities.

This is in the tradition of a free America which, without government restriction, has created the greatest abundance the world has ever known.

Consumer Protection

The American Party supports reasonable programs to provide protection for consumers and wage earners against hazards to their health and safety.

Believing in free competitive enterprise, we are unrelenting in our opposition to government maintained monopolies which stifle competition. Where these monopolies exist, they must be strictly regulated to protect the public from unfair and arbitrary rate increases.

We are opposed to the use by those monopolies, such as the telephone company, of its consumer derived revenues for political purposes for the direct or indirect influencing of elections.

Agriculture

The American Party supports honest value to the farmer for the crop he produces.

We support the phased complete withdrawal of government controls, restrictions, and subsidies from agriculture within a period of three to five years, as we withdraw similar subsidies from other areas of American economic life.

To protect the American farmer from unjust

foreign competition, we protest foreign imports from slave nations.

Labor

The American Party fully supports the advances made by the working people of America. We shall continue to support the right of workers to organize, bargain collectively, and control the internal affairs of their union organizations without Federal government interference. We oppose compulsory federally enforced arbitration on local unions.

The American Party recognizes that all retirement and pension programs are a deferred part of every workers' wage or salary. As such, all participation in retirement and pension programs should remain the property of every participating employee regardless of wherever he may be employed. We strongly support legislation, union agreements, or professional organization efforts to guarantee that interest. Every working man, union or non-union, waged or salaried, should be allowed to take his pension benefits with him to wherever he might be employed, from his first job to his last.

We support the right of rank and file union members to control the destiny of their own local unions through democratic processes.

There is no "acceptable" level of unemployment as is implied by the current philosophies of the Democrat and Republican Parties. The unalterable position of the American Party is that there is opportunity for full employment through the free enterprise system.

Education

The American Party fully supports the concept of quality education for every American child. We believe that education is a local responsibility and we are unalterably committed to the preservation of the neighborhood school without Federal control or interference. We believe that the educational dollar should be spent for improved classroom instruction, not for unproductive busing of pupils for purposes of social experimentation or racial balance. We strongly reaffirm our opposition to such busing and to the transfer of teachers for such purposes.

We also support all necessary legislation to encourage the development of systems of private education including tax setoffs for parents who choose to place their children in private schools.

We support the concept of voluntary non-denominational prayer in the public schools. We would protect the right of an individual not to participate, but do not believe the minority has the right to bar participation by the majority in desired religious exercises. We will resist any and all attempts by governmental agencies such as H.E.W. and the National Institute On Mental Health, et al, to use our educational systems to experiment with, or capture the minds and lives of our children through such programs as "National Child Advocacy System," sex-education, sensitivity training, and drug experimentation.

We favor placing our schools under the jurisdiction of parents and their local school boards, and school financing by state and local taxation.

Natural Resources and Protection of the Environment

The American Party is deeply concerned with the protection of our environment and the conservation of our natural resources.

We support all reasonable efforts to solve the problems of air and water pollution, and America's other environmental maladies.

We do not believe that the solution to pollution can be found in destroying the private capital investment system, but rather by urging the enforcement of the common and statutory laws affecting these matters by the states and local enforcement agencies, and by the inventive genius of a free people in a competitive economic system.

Elections

The development of the American Party is dependent upon an opportunity to fully participate in the election process in the several states. We shall work for the elimination of discriminatory state laws which make it difficult or impossible for new parties to participate in the election process. We shall support judicial or legislative action wherever necessary to achieve this objective, including legislation enabling the name "American Party" to be used in every state.

We support full disclosure of campaign contributions and expenditures.

The American Party welcomes America's young voters and invites them to participate in the only political party which offers real solutions to the problems encountered by young Americans. We encourage our newly enfranchised young voters to play an active part in the leadership and development of the American Party.

Secrecy in Government

The American Party believes that government must be conducted in the full light of public scrutiny. Secrecy is the tool of dictatorship, not of government of, by and for the people. We pledge our full support to all necessary legislation to assure full disclosure to the people of the activities of their government, excepting for matters clearly in the interests of national security.

Regional Government

The American Party is unalterably opposed to the creation of regional government entities which exercise tax and police powers without direct responsibility to the voters and the taxpayers which such agencies are alleged to serve. Too often, the objective of those seeking to create such regional bodies is the destruction or usurpation of the authority of local or state governments.

In connection with necessary vigilance on the subject of regional government, we encourage a re-examination of the concept of zoning laws, which frequently are a thinly veiled transfer of power from private property owners to local collectivist planners.

Internal Subversion

The American Party expresses its undying opposition to the criminal Communist conspiracy and, in that regard, urges the enforcement of the Constitution and laws of the United States.

Women's Liberation

Although "Equal Rights" for women may seem a desirable objective, in practice it means great loss—not gain. This deceit is planned to "liberate" women from their families, homes and property, and as in Communist countries, they would share hard labor alongside men. Women of the American Party say "NO" to this insidious socialistic plan to destroy the home, make women slaves of the government, and their children wards of the state. We urge the people to notify their state legislators to resist adoption of the so-called "Equal Rights Amendment" commonly known as "Women's Lib."

Public Housing

We oppose public, subsidized and scatter site housing in any neighborhood or community unless first approved by a majority of the voters in the precinct and in the municipality concerned.

III. FOREIGN POLICY

National Sovereignty

The United States is a free and sovereign republic which desires to live in friendship with all free nations, without interfering in their internal affairs, and without permitting their interference in ours. We are, therefore, unalterably opposed to entangling alliances, via treaties or any other form of commitment, which compromise our national sovereignty. To this end, we shall:
—Steadfastly oppose American participation in any form of world government organization;
—Call upon the President and Congress to terminate United States membership in the United Nations and its subsidiary organizations; and
—Propose that the Constitution be amended to prohibit the United States Government from entering any treaty or other agreement which makes any commitment of American military forces or tax money, compromises the sovereignty of the United States, or accomplishes a purpose properly the subject of domestic law.

Pacts and Agreements

Since World War II, the United States has increasingly played the undesirable role of an international policeman. Through our involvements abroad, our country is being changed from a republic to a world empire in which our freedoms are being sacrificed on an altar of international involvement. The United States is now committed by treaty to defend 42 foreign nations in all parts of the world, and by agreements other than treaties to defend at least 19 more. Therefore, we:
—Call upon the President and the Congress to immediately commence a systematic withdrawal from any such treaties and agreements, unless such withdrawal would threaten the immediate national security of the United States; and
—Reaffirm our support of the Monroe Doctrine under which the United States has clearly stated its perpetual interest in the independence from foreign domination of the several

republics of the Western Hemisphere, so that all expansionist powers will be forewarned of our commitment to the freedom of the Western Hemisphere from foreign domination.

Vietnam

The Executive Branch of our government, with the tacit approval of Congress, has involved us in an unconstitutional war in Vietnam which is contrary to the best interest of this nation. Through unbelievable mismanagement, or conscious design, the war has been prolonged, any goal of traditional military victory abandoned, and the enemy has been given privileged sanctuaries while over 50,000 American boys have been slaughtered on the battlefield.

Despite the fact that our nation became involved illegally in the Indo-China war there are, none the less, hundreds of valiant American service men now languishing in the prison camps of North Vietnam. America owes a duty and responsibility to these brave men and their families to force the Communist government of North Vietnam to release these American prisoners of war. America must not turn its back upon these brave men and abandon them to living deaths in Communist captivity, as has been the case with so many other American nationals held prisoner by Communist Russia and Red China.

The American Party further demands that never again shall U.S. troops be employed on any foreign field of battle without a declaration of war by Congress as required by the U.S. Constitution; that Congress refuse to fund unconstitutional, undeclared wars pursuant to Presidential whim or international obligations under which American sovereignty has been transferred to multinational agencies; and that such statutes be adopted as may be required to achieve these objectives. We further recognize that most of the wars to which America has been a party throughout our history as a nation, not excepting Vietnam, have resulted from the machinations of international finance in their centuries old drive toward world government. Let us never again help them build the traps with which they would ensnare us.

We are unalterably opposed to any American aid to *North* Vietnam upon termination of our participation in Southeast Asian hostilities.

We oppose unequivocally any amnesty for military deserters and draft dodgers.

Relations with Communist Nations

The American Party is deeply concerned by the President's recent accord with Communist China during the very hour when American boys are being killed by the Communist enemy in Vietnam. Instead of consorting with Communist governments, we believe that the United States should terminate all trade with, and aid to, Communist countries. It has been estimated that the entirety of the Communist empire would collapse within six months if absolutely without aid and trade from the free world. It is in this fashion that the freedom-loving patriots of the Communist empire, including Nationalist China, Vietnam, Laos, and Cambodia, will regain their freedom. We should provide moral encouragement to the peoples of captive nations whose homelands are presently oppressed by the Communist tyranny. We specifically urge the United States to reiterate its friendship for Nationalist China. We are unalterably opposed to any recognition of the Castro Communist government in Cuba. In addition, we pledge the repudiation of the Kennedy-Khrushchev Pact which guarantees the communist enslavement of the Cuban people. We pledge the enforcement of the Monroe Doctrine which keeps foreign powers out of the Western Hemisphere, including the stationing of Soviet soldiers, sailors and airmen in Cuba and Chile.

We pledge not to interfere with Cuban exiles in their legitimate goals and aims of freeing their country from Communist tyranny.

We pledge to release all Cuban exiles held in United States jails for past activities connected with the liberation of their homeland.

Middle East

The American Party is unalterably opposed to American involvement in the Middle East conflict between Israel and Arab States. The United States has no interest in the Middle East which justifies the sacrifice of our sons on a desert battlefield nor is our country properly cast as a merchant of death in the Middle East arms race.

At a time when all of our attention should be focused on termination of our involvement in the Indo-China war, it is shocking to find both the Republican administration and the Democratic presidential candidate openly thrusting us toward war on another foreign battlefield. We are not prepared to endorse an exchange of the slaughter of our sons in the jungle for the slaughter of our sons on the desert.

We therefore propose that:

—America declare its neutrality in the Middle East; and

—Repudiate any commitment expressed or implied to send U.S. troops to participate in the Middle East conflict.

South Africa and Rhodesia

As it is not the prerogative of foreign nations to determine the internal policies of the United States, so it is not our prerogative to dictate the internal policies of foreign countries. We should, therefore, declare our friendship with all nations who genuinely desire friendship with us. Consequently, we:

—Call upon our government to cease its acts of hostility toward South Africa and Rhodesia, and, indeed, all other non-Communist countries who have by word and deed demonstrated their friendship for the United States;

—Commend the Congress for its action in ending American participation in U.N. sanctions against Rhodesia as they apply to chromite and certain other strategic minerals; and

—Pledge to end the present administration's anti-Rhodesian sanctions policy and extend to Rhodesia the full diplomatic recognition to which that nation is clearly entitled.

Foreign Aid

Since World War II, the United States has been engaged in the greatest international giveaway program ever conceived by man, and is now spending over $32,000,000,000 a year to aid foreign nations. These expenditures have won us no friends and constitute a major drain on the resources of our taxpayers. Therefore, we demand that:

—No further funds be appropriated for any kind of foreign aid programs;

—United States participation in international lending institutions, such as the World Bank and the International Monetary Fund, be ended;

—All government subsidies and investment guarantees to encourage U.S. businesses to invest in foreign lands be immediately terminated; and

—All debts owed to the United States by foreign countries from previous wars be collected, by confiscation of property, if necessary.

Tariffs and Trade

The American Party urges that:

—Congress take all necessary action to protect American workers, farmers, and businesses threatened by slave labor foreign competition;

—The United States cease participation in international tariff cutting organizations such as the General Agreement on Tariffs and Trade (GATT);

—The United States Government establish a firm policy that U.S. businesses investing abroad do so at their own risk and that there is no obligation by our Government to protect those investments with the lives of our sons, or the taxes of our citizens.

It is believed that the libertarian ideal of totally tariff free international trade is not realistic at this time in world history.

We support restoration of America's place as a major sea power with a far ranging merchant fleet.

Immigration

Liberalization of American immigration laws is upsetting the labor balance in our country, and having an adverse effect on our economy. The mass importation of peoples with low standards of living threatens the wage structure of the American working man and, frequently, the political subversion of our American institutions. Therefore, we recommend that:

—United States immigration laws be re-written to limit immigration to modest quotas of immigrants from European and Western hemisphere countries and other people who share our general cultural traditions and background;

—All other immigration be prohibited except in hardship cases or other special circumstances; and that

—All immigrants be carefully screened to guarantee the loyalty to the United States of all persons entering this country.

State Department

The State Department for almost 40 years has been actively engaged in the promotion of internationalism contrary to the best interests of the United States. Therefore, we recommend that:

—All necessary legislative and administrative action be taken to assure that every person serving in the State Department adheres to the objectives set forth in this platform; all persons found to be security risks be summarily discharged, defining sexual deviates and subversives as "security risks per se";

—Expenditures by the Department be reduced sufficiently to limit its activities to the purposes embodied in this platform;

—All non-conforming functions, such as the Peace Corps, USIA, etc., be eliminated; and that

—Our Government be prohibited from conducting secret negotiations or entering into secret treaties or agreements in any way binding on the United States.

In addition we recognize the Council on Foreign Relations as the principal organization controlling our State Department, and indeed, the general foreign policy of the United States, in the Council's drive to make America a part of a one-world socialist government.

We pledge full exposure of this conspiratorial apparatus.

Defense Policies

The defense of the United States is a primary responsibility of the Federal Government.

The American Party supports all necessary measures to provide full protection of the United States from any threat.

We recognize that it is impossible to restore fiscal responsibility to Government without a complete reappraisal of defense expenditures. We insist that all so called defense programs not directly related to the protection of our national security be eliminated; that every item of expenditure be carefully reviewed to eliminate waste, fraud, theft, inefficiency and excess profits from all defense contracts and military expenditures.

We are opposed to compulsory military training but support a well trained and highly organized volunteer state home militia. Since World War II, the domestic prosperity of the United States has been built upon a hot and cold war economy. In this context, war has become an integral part of the domestic economic policy of both the Democrat and Republican administrations. Therefore we urge that:

—The United States Government take immediate steps to encourage the reorientation of the economy to provide domestic prosperity without the artificial and inflationary stimulus of war and threats of war;

—The United States Government continue to recognize the contribution of our servicemen to the national welfare by the extension of appropriate benefits to all veterans;

—In any war in which our country engages, sufficient taxes be imposed to take the profit out of war, and to equalize the sacrifices of those at home with those called upon to fight on the battlefield abroad.

Disarmament

The principle of universal disarmament is a desirable goal. It can be achieved, however, only if all nations conform equally to disarmament agreements. There is no current evidence of a sincere desire by major world powers to disarm. Therefore, we recommend that:

—Public Law 87-297, otherwise known as the Arms Control and Disarmament Act be repealed;

—No further disarmament treaties be adopted in the absence of full evidence of good faith by all concerned powers, including the right of inspection and true equality of arms reductions;

—No disarmament treaty be adopted involving the implied or expressed obligation of the United States to go to war to enforce arms limitations, or to protect foreign nations jeopardized by powers violating disarmament agreements; and that

—No disarmament treaty be adopted granting to the United Nations the power to establish an international police force to enforce the provision of such treaty.

World Government by the Back Door

Just as we are opposed to World Government by direct action, so we are opposed to World Government by the back door by bestowal of statehood on remote and sparsely populated insular territories. The present American territories should, upon qualification, be granted Commonwealth status—not statehood.

Fishing Rights

The American Party hereby records its opposition to the unlawful commercial invasion of its maritime seas by foreign governments which, in violation of heretofore recognized international law and custom, seize our fishing ships, destroy our gear, lobster pots and nets. This invasion of American rights cannot be tolerated, and a redefinition of the limits of our maritime waters should be established to secure American rights in our commercial fishing waters.

Communist Platform 1972

PREAMBLE

The United States of America is a deeply troubled nation—more troubled than ever before. Corruption and deceit are rampant. For solutions, the old-line politicians offer more deceit, false promises, bigotry and fear. While a heinous, immoral war is being waged and the profits of giant corporate interests soar, the quality of life for the overwhelming majority of America's people is steadily deteriorating. Unemployment mounts, our cities decay, drug addiction has reached epidemic proportions, and the very air we breathe is dangerously polluted.

The United States is not threatened from abroad. Yet, since the end of World War II, more than a trillion dollars has been spent on armaments and the military establishment. Almost $120 billion has been used for militarism and the war is Indochina. The total expenditure will exceed $350 billion. The Vietnamese did not invade our country: U.S. military forces invaded theirs. Tax money for tanks, planes, missiles; money for death and destruction is readily available. Why is there no money for urgently needed homes, schools and hospitals or mass transit?

The Nixon mis-administration has instituted a wage freeze. Demands for increased productivity are accompanied by increased pressure on the workers to work harder and faster in order to get the country out of a disastrous economic slump. It is the workers who are being blamed for the miserable failure of the Nixon economic policies. These policies will not create more jobs. They will put more workers out of work, thereby deepening the crises. The Nixon mis-administration speaks of price controls, but prices (and profits) continue to rise. Only wages are frozen: how convenient for business! The great wealth of this country, produced by generations of workers, has been usurped by giant corporations. This is the root cause of our social decay.

The history of U.S. capitalism is one of shameful oppression of minority peoples. Vicious racism is instigated and perpetuated by the capitalist ruling class in order to divide the people one from another. This racism serves to increase capitalist profits by preventing the unification of the people, thereby keeping them vulnerable to exploitation. In fostering racism, the capitalist ruling class seeks to obscure and divert attention from the fact that it alone is the real enemy of the people.

To reap even greater profits, the giant corporations invest their surplus capital abroad. These multinational corporations spread their tentacles throughout the world, oppressing, robbing, and exploiting people everywhere. As a result of the use and exploitation of overseas labor, millions of American workers are laid off.

Even as the ruling class robs foreign lands and hurls bombs and napalm on peoples fighting for their national liberation in Indochina, so does it also seek to destroy hard-won constitutional liberties and the living standards of the people at home—particularly of those fighting for peace, liberation of minority peoples, and the needs of labor. We have seen increased repression and police state measures, more frequent frameups (as in the Angela Davis and Berrigan cases), and a variety of measures designed to cancel the Bill of Rights and the rights of labor to organize and strike. There is a grave danger of a military-racist-fascist type of state, under which the survival of even limited capitalist democracy is threatened.

Both major parties represent big business. There is no real distinction between the Republican Nixon Administration and one under a Democratic president. Both serve as the voice and agent of the huge corporate monopolies that are the real rulers of this country.

A revolutionary change in the social system is the only real answer to the crises that confront our people. Capitalism has proved itself unable to provide the well-being, freedom, peace and security which are the "inalienable rights" of every human being. Only Socialism, wherein the working people own and control the country's wealth can achieve those humanistic ends. Only a united people, first of all the working class, convinced in the course of mass struggle, can achieve Socialism, the one real answer to the fundamental need for true democracy.

The platform of the Communist Party is geared to win what must be fought for today and in the immediate years ahead. In this election campaign, the Communist Party calls upon the people to unite their ranks and to organize a powerful movement that will challenge the might of the monopoly corporations and ultimately win power for the people. Toward this end, we urge the unity of all anti-racist, anti-fascist, and pro-labor forces in the country: unite to defeat the most reactionary, pro-war, racist, and anti-labor candidates.

We call for the largest possible vote for Gus Hall and Jarvis Tyner, the Communist Party presidential and vice-presidential candidates. This will be the most meaningful and forceful electoral protest against the reactionary policies and rule of monopoly capitalism. This will be the most affirmative and effective vote for peace, jobs, freedom and socialism. Only a determined people, united in struggle, can win a society that truly provides for their needs. The following platform points the way.

An End to War, Militarism, and Imperialist Intrigue

End the war in Indochina by a complete, unconditional withdrawal of all men, arms and supplies. Dismantle all military bases. End all support to the corrupt Thieu regime. The people of Indochina must have the right to determine their own form of government and social system without outside interference. Reparations must be paid to the peoples of Vietnam for the massive destruction caused by U.S. aggression. Establish peaceful relations with the Democratic Republic of Vietnam.

End all military expenditures and padlock the Pentagon. Shut down all foreign U.S. military bases.

End all economic, military and political intrigue against Chile. End all military and economic intervention against democratic people's movements in Latin America, Asia, Africa and Europe, particularly in Angola, Rhodesia, South Africa and Greece. Recognize the sovereign right of all nations to regain ownership of foreign properties on their soil. Provide interest-free loans and credits for upbuilding underdeveloped countries without strings attached.

Recognize and establish full diplomatic and trade relations with People's Republic of China, Cuba, the German Democratic Republic, the Democratic People's Republic of Korea, Albania, and the People's Republic of Bangla Desh. End

all barriers to full trade relations with all socialist countries.

Immediate unconditional independence for Puerto Rico.

End all complicity with British imperialism in its suppression of the Irish freedom struggle.

End the alliance of U.S. imperialism and Israeli expansionism and aggression against the peoples of the Arab countries and Africa. Total Israeli withdrawal from all occupied Arab lands in accord with the November, 1967 U.N. resolution as a prerequisite to a political settlement. Guarantee the rights of the Palestinian peoples and the continued existence of Israel.

An End to Poverty; Raising of Living Standards; Defense of Labor's Right to Organize and Strike

End all government intervention against labor in contract negotiations. End the wage freeze. Abolish the Pay Board.

End all restrictions on the right to strike and defeat all attempts at compulsory arbitration. Repeal the Taft-Hartley, Landrum-Griffin and the so-called state "right to work" laws. Outlaw strike-breaking.

Outlaw all discrimination in employment or union membership based on race, color, age, sex, religion, or political beliefs. Black, Puerto Rican, Chicano, Indian and Asian workers, women and youth must have full equality within all unions at all levels.

Provide decent jobs or adequate income for all families and persons. Raise welfare benefits to provide decent living standards (at this time, $6,500 per family of four). Raise Social Security to adequate income levels and provide full retirement benefits at age 55.

Establish uniform and universal unemployment compensation for full period of unemployment at full take-home pay wages. Provide unemployment compensation for all strikers and for first-time job seekers.

Increase minimum wages to $5 an hour for all workers in all states and occupations, including agriculture, and regardless of age, sex or race. Reduce, by Federal law, the work week to 30 hours at 40 hours pay, with time-and-a-half after 30 hours and double pay after 40 hours.

Launch a massive public housing construction program of millions of low-rent quality housing units annually to end slums; hiring without discrimination to give first jobs to those unemployed in the community at union pay and conditions. Build urban and inter-urban mass transit systems to provide free transportation.

Establish a national health care program providing to every man, woman and child the best medical, dental, hospital and other health care as a public service free of charge. Prosecute the profiteers and pushers of drugs—not the victims. Rehabilitate the drug addicts.

Develop a people's farm program. Use government subsidies to protect small family farms by guaranteeing adequate income, thus encouraging production and reducing prices to the consumer. Support the organization of agricultural workers into unions.

Prohibit employers from introducing new machinery or other devices that speed up workers, create unemployment, and endanger health and safety of workers. Introduction of new machines must have prior consent of union committee on the job. Strengthen existing accident and safety laws and enforcement procedures. Guarantee fair compensation to victims of industrial accidents.

Nationalize major industries, plants, and factories under democratic controls. This shall be done wherever necessary to protect the jobs of workers, their safety, health and union conditions and to provide essential services to meet the needs of the people. Monopoly corporations, major stockholders and financial overlords who have profited from government subsidies, tax swindles and the exploitation of workers shall not be further compensated. The needs of the workers and the people shall be the only guidelines in nationalization with a committee of representatives from workers, and people's organizations to formulate proposals for immediate nationalization of certain industries and to plan for further steps.

AN END TO RACISM, FREEDOM FOR BLACK, CHICANO, PUERTO RICAN, ASIAN AND INDIAN PEOPLES

Full equality for all, regardless of race, nationality, religion or sex, in employment, housing, education, culture, and in all aspects of economic, political and social life. Rebalance the scale of hundreds of years of slavery and repression by massive compensatory measures.

Spend $120 billion per year—equal to current spending for war and related purposes—for the needs of the poor, the Black people and other oppressed nationalities and the impoverished white workers. Priority spending for housing, education, transportation, health care, child care, and other services to the oppressed peoples.

Make racism, anti-Semitism, or any form of racial, national or religious bigotry, a federal crime. Racists and religious bigots should be removed from all positions of authority in the armed forces, in the educational system, and in all public services. Declare as felonies all racist propaganda and actions, punishable by severe terms of imprisonment as well as by fines. Officials responsible for enforcement of anti-racist laws shall be removed from office, and made liable to criminal action, if they fail to enforce these laws.

The rights of all racial and national minorities must be respected. Political subdivisions should be restructured to give oppressed minorities maximum rights to local self-government and to fullest representation on all levels. The people living in ghettos and barrios shall have the right to control the schools, police, welfare bodies and all other institutions of their communities. Institute proportional representation on all governmental bodies and school boards and end all political gerrymandering. Remove all language barriers and protect voters from racist harassment at the polls and registration places.

The centuries-old Indian and Mexican treaties must be honored to guarantee the rights of Indian and Chicano peoples to their lands (including restoration of lands and natural resources taken from them), culture, language and other features of life.

·End the brutality, terror, and repression directed against the Black, Chicano, Puerto Rican, Asian and Indian peoples and their militant leaders. Police must live in the communities they serve. Police departments must be under strict community control. Support the right of Black and other oppressed peoples to armed self-defense to protect themselves from racist violence.

Demand freedom for Angela Davis and all imprisoned victims of racism. Black, Chicano, Puerto Rican and other minority peoples accused of crime must be charged and tried by juries of their peers. Where language is a barrier, all court proceedings shall be conducted in both English and the mother tongue of the defendant.

End racism in the armed forces. Halt harassment and persecution of minority servicemen. Prosecute officers guilty of racist practices.

Taxing the Rich—Taxing the Monopolies

Institute a sharply graduated tax on corporation profits and on assessed valuation of all corporation properties. End all tax give-aways to big business for depreciation and depletion allowances. Corporation advertising, executive expense allowances and other devices shall no longer be deductible. Close all tax loop-holes with stiff penalties for violations. Open all corporation books to public inspection to overcome tax evasion.

Abolish all income taxes on family earnings of $15,000 a year or less. Abolish property taxes on homes assessed at $25,000 or less. Establish sharply graduated personal income taxes on incomes above $15,000.

End tax exemption for trust funds and private foundations. End tax exemptions to institutions making profit on slum housing or income from investments. Update and enforce inheritance tax laws.

Return the bulk of federal tax money to the communities to be distributed according to the people's needs and population size and with guarantees against racial, religious, political, or ethnic discrimination.

Extension of Democracy; An End to Police-State Methods

Curb the excessive powers of the presidency. End the illegal Presidential use of war-making powers.

Abolish the FBI and end political frame-ups, eavesdropping and wiretapping. Abolish the Subversive Activities Control Board, the House and Senate Internal Security Committees, and repeal all repressive laws.

End police brutality. Disarm all police. Forbid use of police, National Guard or the army to suppress labor and people's struggles. Repeal all stop and frisk, preventive detention and political conspiracy laws.

Remove all restrictive election laws aimed against minority and new parties. Remove all bars to the right of the Communist Party to ballot status in all states. End discrimination against Communists in employment, education and political life.

End the system of congressional seniority which perpetuates racist and reactionary control over congressional committees.

Demand a judicial and penal system that is not biased against working people and oppressed nationalities. The government must pay all court costs in trial cases, including the cost of the defense. The defense shall be entitled to its own choice of legal counsel. Persons charged with a crime shall be given release on bail in accord with their ability to pay or on personal word pending trial. All persons imprisoned today shall have their cases reviewed by Citizens Courts composed of their peers. Prisoners shall have the right to organize and all other rights under the Constitution and its Bill of Rights.

Free Angela Davis, the Harrisburg 7 and all other political prisoners. Remove all charges against draft resisters and military deserters.

Democratize the armed forces. All servicemen shall have the right to free speech, press, and assembly and to belong to organizations of their own choosing, including servicemen's unions. Servicemen under charges shall be tried only by a jury of their peers, not by military brass. Servicemen shall have the right to prefer charges against superior officers and to remove them from rank.

A National Youth Act—Administered by Youth for the Needs of Youth

End the militarization of the youth. Bring all military forces home from all parts of the world. End the draft. Reduce domestic armed forces to minimum peace time needs. Provide civilian jobs at union conditions and wages for all vets and G.I.'s. Provide job-training and skilled-work opportunities.

Provide jobs for all youth who need them, at union pay and conditions. Create a massive job-training program to meet the full economic and social needs of the youth. Give special attention and priority to the Black, Puerto Rican, Chicano and Indian youth who are victims of racism. Provide full unemployment compensation to first job seekers from day of job application to day of employment.

Make available free public quality education from grade school through the university and graduate schools. Provide government subsidies to meet living expenses of students in college and higher education. Offer special programs, including open enrollment, to guarantee full opportunity for working class, Black and other minority youth. Achieve total integration of the schools through busing, redistricting, and school site selection and any other means necessary. Eliminate military and corporate controls and influence from the education process. Establish meaningful student-faculty participation in all administrative bodies. Establish a National Student Bill of Rights to be formulated and adopted by student referendum.

Organize a massive, peace-oriented cultural, recreational, athletic and health project for youth with young people having decisive positions in all policy-making bodies. Finance such a project with Federal funds now used for military forces and facilities of the Pentagon. Convert the Pentagon's properties to peaceful uses. Launch international, cultural and student exchanges, athletic events and conferences to strengthen international understanding and relationships. Organize similar domestic and national events to develop the struggle against racism.

Strengthen youth participation in all levels of political life, including election to public office at the age of 18 and insure full exercise of their right to vote.

Women's Equality and Working Class Unity

Pass a Labor Bill of Rights for Women that would guarantee the rights of working class women on the job and would be inclusive of all workers where applicable. Such a bill would include the following: End discrimination against women on the job. End all wage differentials on the basis of sex. Guarantee equal pay for equal work. End the practice of giving the lowest paid and menial jobs to Black, Puerto Rican and Chicano women. Establish a system of skilled job training and upgrading of all women workers. Prosecute the employer who discriminates by use of separate male and female seniority lists and other devices.

Guarantee full enforcement of laws protecting the health and safety of women workers, particularly in those areas where women's biological and reproductive capacities are endangered. Provide maternity leaves at full pay for six months and abortion leaves on a similar basis. Both types of leave to be in addition to regular sick leave.

Pass a comprehensive Child Development Act. Guarantee equality for all women by freeing them of the major responsibility for child care and education and placing it on society as a whole. Provide nation-wide, 24 hour child care facilities on or near work places and in the communities. Such facilities shall be financed by the employers but controlled by the trade unions and the workers whose children attend these centers. Guarantee access to child care facilities to all women, regardless of age, or whether they are full-time housewives or employed outside the home.

Abolish the degrading, inhuman features of the present welfare system and the Nixon starvation-and-forced-labor program. Support the guaranteed family income program of the National Welfare Rights Organization for $6,500 per year, decent living standard for a family of four.

Guarantee full participation by women in all levels of political organization. Ensure active participation and leadership of women on all levels of government: local, state and federal, administrative and judicial.

Democratic Platform 1972

New Directions: 1972–76

Skepticism and cynicism are widespread in America. The people are *skeptical* of platforms filled with political platitudes—of promises made by opportunistic politicians.

The people are *cynical* about the idea that a rosy future is just around the corner.

And is it any wonder that the people are skeptical and cynical of the whole political process?

Our traditions, our history, our Constitution, our laws, all say that America belongs to its people.

But the people no longer believe it.

They feel that the government is run for the privileged few rather than for the many—and they are right.

No political party, no President, no government can by itself restore a lost sense of faith. No Administration can provide solutions to all our problems. What we can do is to recognize the doubts of Americans, to speak to those doubts, and to act to begin turning those doubts into hopes.

As Democrats, we know that we share responsibility for that loss of confidence. But we also know, as Democrats, that at decisive moments of choice in our past, our party has offered leadership that has tapped the best within our country.

Our party—standing by its ideals of domestic progress and enlightened internationalism—has served America well. We have nominated or elected men of the high calibre of Woodrow Wilson, Franklin Delano Roosevelt, Harry S. Truman, Adlai E. Stevenson, John Fitzgerald Kennedy, Lyndon Baines Johnson—and in the last election Hubert Humphrey and Edmund S. Muskie. In that proud tradition we are now prepared to move forward.

We know that our nation cannot tolerate any longer a government that shows no regard for the people's basic needs and no respect for our right to the truth from those who lead us.

What do the people want?

They want three things:

They want a personal life that makes us all feel that life is worth living;

They want a social environment whose institutions promote the good of all; and

They want a physical environment whose resources are used for the good of all.

They want an opportunity to achieve their aspirations and their dreams for themselves and their children.

We believe in the rights of citizens to achieve to the limit of their talents and energies. We are determined to remove barriers that limit citizens because they are black, brown, young or women; because they never had the chance to gain an education; because there was no possibility of being anything but what they were.

We believe in hard work as a fair measure of our own willingness to achieve. We are determined that millions should not stand idle while work demands to be done. We are determined that the dole should not become a permanent way of life for any. And we are determined that government no longer tax· the product of hard work more rigorously than it taxes inherited wealth, or money that is gained simply by having money in the first place.

We believe that the law must apply equally to all, and that it must be an instrument of justice. We are determined that the citizen must be protected in his home and on his streets. We are determined also that the ordinary citizen should not be imprisoned for a crime before we know whether he is guilty or not while those with the right friends and the right connections can break the law without ever facing the consequences of their actions.

We believe that war is a waste of human life. We are determined to end forthwith a war which has cost 50,000 American lives, $150 billion of our resources, that has divided us from each other,

drained our national will and inflicted incalculable damage to countless people. We will end that war by a simple plan that need not be kept secret: The immediate total withdrawal of all Americans from Southeast Asia.

We believe in the right of an individual to speak, think, read, write, worship, and live free of official intrusion. We are determined that our government must no longer tap the phones of law-abiding citizens nor spy on those who have broken no law. We are determined that never again shall government seek to censor the newspapers and television. We are determined that the government shall no longer mock the supreme law of the land, while it stands helpless in the face of crime which makes our neighborhoods and communities less and less safe.

Perhaps most fundamentally, we believe that government is the servant, not the master, of the people. We are determined that government should not mean a force so huge, so impersonal, that the complaint of an ordinary citizen goes unheard.

That is not the kind of government America was created to build. Our ancestors did not fight a revolution and sacrifice their lives against tyrants from abroad to leave us a government that does not know how to listen to its own people.

The Democratic Party is proud of its past; but we are honest enough to admit that we are part of the past and share in its mistakes. We want in 1972 to begin the long and difficult task of reviewing existing programs, revising them to make them work and finding new techniques to serve the public need. We want to speak for, and with, the citizens of our country. Our pledge is to be truthful to the people and to ourselves, to tell you when we succeed, but also when we fail or when we are not sure. In 1976, when this nation celebrates its 200th anniversary, we want to tell you simply that we have done our best to give the government to those who formed it—the people of America.

Every election is a choice: In 1972, Americans must decide whether they want their country back again.

II. Jobs, Prices and Taxes

"I went to school here and I had some training for truck driver school and I go to different places and put in applications for truck driving but they say, 'We can't hire you without the experience.'

Now, I don't have the experience. I don't get the experience without the job first. I have four kids, you know, and I'm on unemployment. And when my unemployment runs out, I'll probably be on relief, like a lot of other people. But, being that I have so many kids, relief is just not going to be enough money. I'm looking for maybe the next year or two, if I don't get a job, they'll probably find me down at the county jail, because I have to do something."—Robert Coleman, Pittsburgh Hearing, June 2, 1972.

The Nixon Administration has deliberately driven people out of work in a heartless and ineffective effort to deal with inflation. Ending the Nixon policy of creating unemployment is the first task of the Democratic Party.

The Nixon "game plan" called for *more* unemployment. Tens of millions of families have suffered joblessness or work cutbacks in the last four years in the name of fighting inflation . . . and for nothing.

Prices rose faster in early 1972 than at any time from 1960 to 1968.

Today there are 5.5 million unemployed. The nation will have suffered $175 billion in lost production during the Nixon Administration by election day. Twenty per cent of our people have suffered a period without a job each year in the last three.

Business has lost more in profits than it has gained from this Administration's business-oriented tax cuts.

In pockets of cities, up to 40 per cent of our young people are jobless.

Farmers have seen the lowest parity ratios since the Great Depression.

For the first time in 30 years, there is substantial unemployment among aerospace technicians, teachers and other white-collar workers.

The economic projections have been manipulated for public relations purposes.

The current Nixon game plan includes a control structure which keeps workers' wages down while executive salaries soar, discourages productivity and distributes income away from those who need it and has produced no significant dent in inflation, as prices for food, clothes, rent and basic necessities soar.

These losses were unnecessary. They are the price of a Republican Administration which has no consistent economic philosophy, no adequate regard for the human costs of its economic decisions and no vision of what a full employment economy could mean for all Americans.

Jobs, Income and Dignity

Full employment—a guaranteed job for all—is the primary economic objective of the Democratic Party. The Democratic Party is committed to a job for every American who seeks work. Only through full employment can we reduce the burden on working people. We are determined to make economic security a matter of right. This means a job with decent pay and good working conditions for everyone willing and able to work and an adequate income for those unable to work. It means abolition of the present welfare system.

To assure jobs and economic security for all, the next Democratic Administration should support:

A full employment economy, making full use of fiscal and monetary policy to stimulate employment;

Tax reform directed toward equitable distribution of income and wealth and fair sharing of the cost of government;

Full enforcement of all equal employment opportunity laws, including federal contract compliance and federally-regulated industries and giving the Equal Employment Opportunity Commission adequate staff and resources and power to issue cease and desist orders promptly;

Vastly increased efforts to open education at all levels and in all fields to minorities, women and other under-represented groups;

An effective nation-wide job placement system to enhance worker mobility;

Opposition to arbitrarily high standards for entry to jobs;

Overhaul of current manpower programs to assure training—without sex, race or language discrimination—for jobs that really exist with continuous skill improvement and the chance for advancement;

Economic development programs to ensure the growth of communities and industry in lagging parts of the nation and the economy;

Use of federal depository funds to reward banks and other financial institutions which invest in socially productive endeavors;

Improved adjustment assistance and job creation for workers and employers hurt by foreign competition, reconversion of defense-oriented companies, rapid technological change and environmental protection activities;

Closing tax loopholes that encourage the export of American jobs by American-controlled multi-national corporations;

Assurance that the needs of society are considered when a decision to close or move an industrial plant is to be made and that income loss to workers and revenue loss to communities does not occur when plants are closed;

Assurance that, whatever else is done in the income security area, the social security system provides a decent income for the elderly, the blind and the disabled and their dependents, with escalators so that benefits keep pace with rising prices and living standards;

Reform of social security and government employment security programs to remove all forms of discrimination by sex; and

Adequate federal income assistance for those who do not benefit sufficiently from the above measures.

The last is not least, but it is last for good reason. The present welfare system has failed because it has been required to make up for too many other failures. Millions of Americans are forced into public assistance because public policy too often creates no other choice.

The heart of a program of economic security based on earned income must be creating jobs and training people to fill them. Millions of jobs —real jobs, not make-work—need to be provided. Public service employment must be greatly expanded in order to make the government the employer of last resort and guarantee a job for all. Large sections of our cities resemble bombed-out Europe after World War II. Children in Appalachia cannot go to school when the dirt road is a sea of mud. Homes, schools and clinics, roads and mass transit systems need to be built.

Cleaning up our air and water will take skills and people in large numbers. In the school, the police department, the welfare agency or the recreation program, there are new careers to be developed to help ensure that social services reach the people for whom they are intended.

It may cost more, at least initially, to create decent jobs than to perpetuate the hand-out system of present welfare. But the return—in new public facilities and services, in the dignity of bringing a paycheck home and in the taxes that will come back in—far outweigh the cost of the investment.

The next Democratic Administration must end the present welfare system and replace it with an income security program which places cash assistance in an appropriate context with all of the measures outlined above, adding up to an earned income approach to ensure each family an income substantially more than the poverty level ensuring standards of decency and health, as officially defined in the area. Federal income assistance will supplement the income of working poor people and assure an adequate income for those unable to work. With full employment and simpler, fair administration, total costs will go down, and with federal financing the burden on local and state budgets will be eased. The program will protect current benefit goals during the transitional period.

The system of income protection which replaces welfare must be a part of the full employment policy which assures every American a job at a fair wage under conditions which make use of his ability and provide an opportunity for advancement.

H.R. 1, and its various amendments, is not humane and does not meet the social and economic objectives that we believe in, and it should be defeated. It perpetuates the coercion of forced work requirements.

Economic Management

Every American family knows how its grocery bill has gone up under Nixon. Every American family has felt the bite of higher and higher prices for food and housing and clothing. The Administration attempts to stop price rises have been dismal failures—for which the working people have paid in lost jobs, missed raises and higher prices.

This nation achieved its economic greatness under a system of free enterprise, coupled with human effort and ingenuity, and thus it must remain. This will be the attitude and objective of the Party.

There must be an end to inflation and the ever-increasing cost of living. This is of vital concern to the laborer, the housewife, the farmer and the small businessman, as well as the millions of

Americans dependent upon their weekly or monthly income for sustenance. It wrecks the retirement plans and lives of our elderly who must survive on pensions or savings gauged by the standards of another day.

Through greater efficiency in the operation of the machinery of government, so badly plagued with duplication, overlapping and excesses in programs, we will ensure that bureaucracy will cease to exist solely for bureaucracy's own sake. The institutions and functions of government will be judged by their efficiency of operation and their contribution to the lives and welfare of our citizens.

A first priority of a Democratic Administration must be eliminating the unfair, bureaucratic Nixon wage and price controls.

When price rises threaten to or do get out of control—as they are now—strong, fair action must be taken to protect family income and savings. The theme of that action should be swift, tough measures to break the wage-price spiral and restore the economy. In that kind of economic emergency, America's working people will support a truly fair stabilization program which affects profits, investment earnings, executive salaries and prices, as well as wages. The Nixon controls do not meet that standard. They have forced the American worker, who suffers most from inflation, to pay the price of trying to end it.

In addition to stabilizing the economy, we propose:

To develop automatic instruments protecting the livelihood of Americans who depend on fixed incomes, such as savings bonds with purchasing power guarantees and cost-of-living escalators in government social security and income support payments;

To create a system of "recession insurance" for states and localities to replace lost local revenues with federal funds in economic downturns, thereby avoiding reduction in public employment or public services;

To establish longer-term budget and fiscal planning; and

To create new mechanisms to stop unwarranted price increases in concentrated industries.

Toward Economic Justice

The Democratic Party deplores the increasing concentration of economic power in fewer and fewer hands. Five per cent of the American people control 90 per cent of our productive national wealth. Less than one per cent of all manufacturers have 88 per cent of the profits. Less than two per cent of the population now owns approximately 80 per cent of the nation's personally-held corporate stock, 90 per cent of the personally-held corporate bonds and nearly 100 per cent of the personally-held municipal bonds. The rest of the population—including all working men and women —pay too much for essential products and services because of national policy and market distortions.

The Democratic Administration should pledge itself to combat factors which tend to concentrate wealth and stimulate higher prices.

To this end, the federal government should:

Develop programs to spread economic growth among the workers, farmers and businessmen;

Help make parts of the economy more efficient —such as medical care—where wasteful and inefficient practices now increase prices;

Step up anti-trust action to help competition, with particular regard to laws and enforcement curbing conglomerate mergers which swallow up efficient small business and feed the power of corporate giants;

Strengthen the anti-trust laws so that the divestiture remedy will be used vigorously to break up large conglomerates found to violate the anti-trust laws;

Abolish the oil import quota that raises prices for consumers;

Deconcentrate shared monopolies such as auto, steel and tire industries which administer prices, create unemployment through restricted output and stifle technological innovation;

Assure the right of the citizen to recover costs and attorneys fees in all successful suits including class actions involving Constitutionally-guaranteed rights, or rights secured by federal statutes;

Adjust rate-making and regulatory activities, with particular attention to regulations which increase prices for food, transportation and other necessities;

Remove artificial constraints in the job market by better job manpower training and strictly enforcing equal employment opportunity;

Stiffen the civil and criminal statutes to make corporate officers responsible for their actions; and

Establish a temporary national economic commission to study federal chartering of large multinational and international corporations, concentrated ownership and control in the nation's economy.

Tax Reform

The last ten years have seen a massive shift in the tax burden from the rich to the working people of America. This is due to cuts in federal income taxes simultaneous with big increases in taxes which bear heavily on lower incomes—state and local sales and property taxes and the payroll tax. The federal tax system is still grossly unfair and over-complicated. The wealthy and corporations get special tax favors; major reform of the nation's tax structure is required to achieve a more equitable distribution of income and to raise the funds needed by government. The American people neither should nor will accept anything less from the next Administration.

The Nixon Administration, which fought serious reform in 1969, has no program, only promises, for tax reform. Its clumsy administrative favoring of the well-off has meant quick action on corporate tax giveaways like accelerated depreciation, while over-withholding from workers' paychecks goes on and on while the Administration tries to decide what to do.

In recent years, the federal tax system has moved precipitously in the wrong direction. Corporate taxes have dropped from 30 per cent of federal revenues in 1954 to 16 per cent in 1973, but payroll taxes for Social Security—regressive because the burden falls more heavily on the worker than on the wealthy—have gone from ten per cent to 29 per cent over the same period. If legislation now pending in Congress passes, payroll taxes will have increased over 500 per cent between 1960 and 1970—from $144 to $755—for the average wage earner. Most people earning under $10,000 now pay more in regressive payroll tax than in income tax.

Now the Nixon Administration—which gave corporations the largest tax cut in American history—is considering a hidden national sales tax (Value Added Tax) which would further shift the burden to the average wage earner and raise prices of virtually everything ordinary people buy. It is cruel and unnecessary to pretend to relieve one bad tax, the property tax, by a new tax which is just as bad. We oppose this price-raising unfair tax in any form.

Federal income tax. The Democratic Party believes that all unfair corporate and individual tax preferences should be removed. The tax law is clogged with complicated provisions and special interests, such as percentage oil depletion and other favors for the oil industry, special rates and rules for capital gains, fast depreciation unrelated to useful life, easy-to-abuse "expense-account" deductions and the ineffective minimum tax. These hidden expenditures in the federal budget are nothing more than billions of "tax welfare" aid for the wealthy, the privileged and the corporations.

We, therefore, endorse as a minimum step the Mills-Mansfield Tax Policy Review Act of 1972, which would repeal virtually all tax preferences in the existing law over the period 1974–1976, as a means of compelling a systematic review of their value to the nation. We acknowledge that the original reasons for some of these tax preferences may remain valid, but believe that none should escape close scrutiny and full public exposure. The most unjustified of the tax loopholes should, however, be closed immediately, without waiting for a review of the whole system.

After the implementation of the minimum provisions of the Mills-Mansfield Act, the Democratic Party, to combat the economically-depressing effect of a regressive income tax scheme, proposes further revision of the tax law to ensure economic equality of opportunity to ordinary Americans.

We hold that the federal tax structure should reflect the following principles:

The cost of government must be distributed more fairly among income classes. We reaffirm the long-established principle of progressive taxation —allocating the burden according to ability to pay —which is all but a dead letter in the present tax code.

The cost of government must be distributed fairly among citizens in similar economic circumstances:

Direct expenditures by the federal government which can be budgeted are better than tax preferences as the means for achieving public objectives. The lost income of those tax preferences which are deemed desirable should be stated in the annual budget.

When relief for hardship is provided through federal tax policy, as for blindness, old age or poverty, benefits should be provided equally by credit rather than deductions which favor recipients with more income, with special provisions for those whose credits would exceed the tax they owe.

Provisions which discriminate against working women and single people should be corrected. In addition to greater fairness and efficiency, these principles would mean a major redistribution of personal tax burdens and permit considerable simplification of the tax code and tax forms.

Social security tax. The Democratic Party commits itself to make the Social Security tax progressive by raising substantially the ceiling on earned income. To permit needed increases in Social Security benefits, we will use general revenues as necessary to supplement payroll tax receipts. In this way, we will support continued movement toward general revenue financing for social security.

Property tax. Greater fairness in taxation at the federal level will have little meaning for the vast majority of American households if the burden of inequitable local taxation is not reduced. To reduce the local property tax for all American families, we support equalization of school spending and substantial increases in the federal share of education costs and general revenue sharing.

New forms of federal financial assistance to states and localities should be made contingent upon property tax reforms, including equal treatment and full publication of assessment ratios.

Tax policy should not provide incentives that encourage overinvestment in developed countries by American business, and mechanisms should be instituted to limit undesirable capital exports that exploit labor abroad and damage the American worker at home.

Labor-Management Relations

Free private collective bargaining between management and independent labor unions has been, and must remain, the cornerstone of our free enterprise system. America achieved its greatness through the combined energy and efforts of the working men and women of this country. Retention of its greatness rests in their hands. Through their great trade union organizations, these men and women have exerted tremendous influence on the economic and social life of the nation and have attained a standard of living known to no other nation. The concern of the Party is that the gains which labor struggled so long to obtain not be lost to them, whether through inaction or subservience to illogical Republican domestic policies.

We pledge continued support for our system of free collective bargaining and denounce any attempt to substitute compulsory arbitration for it. We, therefore, oppose the Nixon Administration's effort to impose arbitration in transportation disputes through its last-offer-selection bill.

The National Labor Relations Act should be updated to ensure:

Extension of protection to employees of non-profit institutions;

Remedies which adequately reflect the losses caused by violations of the Act;

Repeal of section 14(b), which allows states to legislate the open shop and remove the ban on common-sites picketing; and

Effective opportunities for unions, as well as employers, to communicate with employees, without coercion by either side or by anyone acting on their behalf.

The Railway Labor Act should be updated to ensure:

That strikes on a single carrier or group of carriers cannot be transformed into nation-wide strikes or lockouts;

Incentives for bargaining which would enable both management and labor to resolve their differences without referring to government intervention; and

Partial operation of struck railroads to ensure continued movement of essential commodities.

New legislation is needed to ensure:

Collective bargaining rights for government employees;

Universal coverage and longer duration of the Unemployment Insurance and Workmen's Compensation programs and to establish minimum federal standards, including the establishment of equitable wage-loss ratios in those programs, including a built-in escalator clause that fairly reflects increases in average wage rates; and

That workers covered under private pension plans actually receive the personal and other fringe benefits to which their services for their employer entitle them. This requires that the fixed right to benefits starts early in employment, that reserves move with the worker from job to job and that re-insurance protection be given pension plans.

Labor Standards

American workers are entitled to job safety at a living wage. Most of the basic protections needed have been recognized in legislation already enacted by Congress.

The Fair Labor Standards Act should be updated, however, to:

Move to a minimum wage of $2.50 per hour, which allows a wage earner to earn more than a poverty level income for 40 hours a week, with no subminimums for special groups or age differentials;

Expand coverage to include the 16 million workers not presently covered, including domestic workers, service workers, agricultural employees and employees of governmental and nonprofit agencies; and

Set overtime premiums which give an incentive to hire new employees rather than to use regular employees for extended periods of overtime.

The Longshoremen and Harbor Workers' Compensation Act should be updated to provide adequate protection for injured workers and federal standards for workmen's compensation should be set by Congress.

The Equal Pay Act of 1963 should be extended to be fully effective, and to cover professional, executive and administrative workers.

Maternity benefits should be made available to all working women. Temporary disability benefits should cover pregnancy, childbirth, miscarriage and recovery.

Occupational Health and Safety

Each year over 14,000 American workers are killed on their jobs, and nine million injured. Unknown millions more are exposed to long-term danger and disease from exposure to dangerous substances. Federal and state laws are supposed to protect workers; but these laws are not being enforced. This Administration has hired only a handful of inspectors and proposes to turn enforcement over to the same state bureaucracies that have proven inadequate in the past. Where violations are detected, only token penalties have been assessed.

We pledge to fully and rigorously enforce the laws which protect the safety and health of workers on their jobs and to extend those laws to all jobs, regardless of number of employees. This must include standards that truly protect against all health hazards, adequate federal enforcement machinery backed up by rigorous penalties and an opportunity for workers themselves to participate

in the laws' enforcement by sharing responsibility for plant inspection.

We endorse federal research and development of effective approaches to combat the dehumanizing debilitating effects of monotonous work.

Farm Labor

The Sixties and Seventies have seen the struggle for unionization by the poorest of the poor in our country—America's migrant farm workers.

Under the leadership of Cesar Chavez, the United Farm Workers have accomplished in the non-violent tradition what was thought impossible only a short time ago. Through hard work and much sacrifice, they are the one group that is successfully organizing farm workers.

Their movement has caught the imagination of millions of Americans who have not eaten grapes so that agribusiness employers will recognize their workers as equals and sit down with them in meaningful collective bargaining.

We now call upon all friends and supporters of this movement to refrain from buying or eating non-union lettuce.

Furthermore, we support the farm workers' movement and the use of boycotts as a non-violent and potent weapon for gaining collective bargaining recognition and contracts for agricultural workers. We oppose the Nixon Administration's effort to enjoin the use of the boycott.

We also affirm the right of farm workers to organize free of repressive anti-labor legislation, both state and federal.

III. RIGHTS, POWER AND SOCIAL JUSTICE

"We're just asking, and we don't ask for much. Just to give us opportunity to live as human beings as other people have lived."—Dorothy Bolden, Atlanta Hearing, June 9, 1972.

"All your platform has to say is that the rights, opportunities and political power of citizenship will be extended to the lowest level, to neighborhoods and individuals. If your party can live up to that simple pledge, my faith will be restored." —Bobby Westbrooks, St. Louis Hearing, June 17, 1972.

"We therefore urge the Democratic Party to adopt the principle that America has a responsibility to offer every American family the best in health care, whenever they need it, regardless of income or any other factor. We must devise a system which will assure that . . . every American receives comprehensive health services from the day he is born to the day he dies, with an emphasis on preventive care to keep him healthy."— Joint Statement of Senator Edward M. Kennedy and Representative Wilbur Mills, St. Louis Hearing, June 17, 1972.

The Democratic Party commits itself to be responsive to the millions of hard working, lower- and middle-income Americans who are traditionally courted by politicians at election time, get bilked at tax-paying time, and are too often forgotten the balance of the time.

This is an era of great change. The world is fast moving into a future for which the past has not prepared us well; a future where to survive, to find answers to the problems which threaten us as a people, we must create qualitatively new solutions. We can no longer rely on old systems of thought, the results of which were partially successful programs that were heralded as important social reforms in the past. It is time *now* to rethink and reorder the institutions of this country so that everyone—women, blacks, Spanish-speaking, Puerto Ricans, Indians, the young and the old —can participate in the decision-making process inherent in the democratic heritage to which we aspire. We must restructure the social, political and economic relationships throughout the entire society in order to ensure the equitable distribution of wealth and power.

The Democratic Party in 1972 is committed to resuming the march toward equality; to enforcing the laws supporting court decisions and enacting new legal rights as necessary, to assuring every American true opportunity, to bringing about a more equal distribution of power, income and wealth and equal and uniform enforcement in all states and territories of civil rights statutes and acts.

In the 1970's, this commitment requires the fulfillment—through laws and policies, through appropriations and directives; through leadership and exhortation—of a wide variety of rights:

The right to full participation in government and the political process;

The rights of free speech and free political expression, of freedom from official intimidation, harassment and invasion of privacy, as guaranteed by the letter and the spirit of the Constitution;

The right to a decent job and an adequate income, with dignity;

The right to quality, accessibility and sufficient quantity in tax-supported services and amenities —including educational opportunity, health care, housing and transportation;

The right to quality, safety and the lowest possible cost on goods and services purchased in the market place;

The right to be different, to maintain a cultural or ethnic heritage or lifestyle, without being forced into a compelled homogeneity;

The rights of people who lack rights: Children, the mentally retarded, mentally ill and prisoners, to name some; and

The right to legal services, both civil and criminal, necessary to enforce secured rights.

Free Expression and Privacy

The new Democratic Administration should bring an end to the pattern of political persecution and investigation, the use of high office as a pulpit for unfair attack and intimidation and the blatant efforts to control the poor and to keep them from acquiring additional economic security or political power.

The epidemic of wiretapping and electronic surveillance engaged in by the Nixon Administration and the use of grand juries for purposes of political intimidation must be ended. The rule of law and the supremacy of the Constitution, as these concepts have traditionally been understood, must be restored.

We strongly object to secret computer data banks on individuals. Citizens should have access to their own files that are maintained by private commercial firms and the right to insert corrective material. Except in limited cases, the same should apply to government files. Collection and maintenance by federal agencies of dossiers on law-abiding citizens, because of their political views and statements, must be stopped, and files which never should have been opened should be destroyed. We firmly reject the idea of a National Computer Data Bank.

The Nixon policy of intimidation of the media and Administration efforts to use government power to block access to media by dissenters must end, if free speech is to be preserved. A Democratic Administration must be an open one, with the fullest possible disclosure of information, with an end to abuses of security classifications and executive privilege, and with regular top-level press conferences.

The Right to Be Different

The new Democratic Administration can help lead America to celebrate the magnificence of the diversity within its population, the racial, national, linguistic and religious groups which have contributed so much to the vitality and richness of our national life. As things are, official policy too often forces people into a mold of artificial homogeneity.

Recognition and support of the cultural identity and pride of black people are generations overdue. The American Indians, the Spanish-speaking, the Asian Americans—the cultural and linguistic heritage of these groups is too often ignored in schools and communities. So, too, are the backgrounds, traditions and contributions of white national, ethnic, religious and regional communities ignored. All official discrimination on the basis of sex, age, race, language, political belief, religion, region or national origin must end. No American should be subject to discrimination in employment or restriction in business because of ethnic background or religious practice. Americans should be free to make their own choice of lifestyles and private habits without being subject to discrimination or prosecution. We believe official policy can encourage diversity while continuing to place full emphasis on equal opportunity and integration.

We urge full funding of the Ethnic Studies bill to provide funds for development of curriculum to preserve America's ethnic mosaic.

Rights of Children

One measure of a nation's greatness is the care it manifests for all of its children. The Nixon Administration has demonstrated a callous attitude toward children repeatedly through veto and administrative decisions. We, therefore, call for a reordering of priorities at all levels of American society so that children, our most precious resource, and families come first.

To that end, we call for:

The federal government to fund comprehensive development child care programs that will be family centered, locally controlled and universally available. These programs should provide for active participation of all family members in the development and implementation of the program. Health, social service and early childhood education should be part of these programs, as well as a variety of options most appropriate to their needs. Child care is a supplement, not a substitute, for the family;

The establishment of a strong child advocacy program, financed by the federal government and other sources, with full ethnic, cultural, racial and sexual representation;

First priority for the needs of children, as we move toward a National Health Insurance Program;

The first step should be immediate implementation of the federal law passed in the 1967 Social Security Amendments providing for "early and periodic screening, diagnosis and treatment" of children's health problems;

Legislation and administrative decisions to drastically reduce childhood injuries—prenatal, traffic, poisoning, burns, malnutrition, rat bites and to provide health and safety education.

Full funding of legislation designed to meet the needs of children with special needs: The retarded, the physically and mentally handicapped, and those whose environment produces abuse and neglect and directs the child to anti-social conduct;

Reaffirmation of the rights of bilingual, handicapped or slow-learning children to education in the public schools, instead of being wrongly classified as retarded or uneducable and dismissed;

Revision of the juvenile court system; dependency and neglect cases must be removed from the corrections system, and clear distinctions must be drawn between petty childhood offenses and the more serious crimes;

Allocation of funds to the states to provide counsel to children in juvenile proceedings, legal or administrative; and

Creation by Congress of permanent standing committees on Children and Youth.

Rights of Women

Women historically have been denied a full voice in the evolution of the political and social institutions of this country and are therefore allied with all under-represented groups in a common desire to form a more humane and compassionate society. The Democratic Party pledges the following:

A priority effort to ratify the Equal Rights Amendment;

Elimination of discrimination against women in public accommodations and public facilities, public education and in all federally-assisted programs and federally-contracted employment:

Extension of the jurisdiction of the Civil Rights Commission to include denial of civil rights on the basis of sex;

Full enforcement of all federal statutes and executive laws barring job discrimination on the basis of sex, giving the Equal Employment Opportunities Commission adequate staff and resources and power to issue cease-and-desist orders promptly;

Elimination of discriminatory features of criminal laws and administration;

Increased efforts to open educational opportunities at all levels, eliminating discrimination against women in access to education, tenure, promotion and salary;

Guarantee that all training programs are made more equitable, both in terms of the numbers of women involved and the job opportunities provided; jobs must be available on the basis of skill, not sex;

Availability of maternity benefits to all working women; temporary disability benefits should cover pregnancy, childbirth, miscarriage and recovery;

Elimination of all tax inequities that affect women and children, such as higher taxes for single women;

Amendment of the Social Security Act to provide equitable retirement benefits for families with working wives, widows, women heads of households and their children;

Amendment of the Internal Revenue Code to permit working families to deduct from gross income as a business expense, housekeeping and child care costs;

Equality for women on credit, mortgage, insurance, property, rental and financial contracts;

Extension of the Equal Pay Act to all workers, with amendment to read "equal pay for comparable work;"

Appointment of women to positions of top responsibility in all branches of the federal government to achieve an equitable ratio of women and men. Such positions include Cabinet members, agency and division heads and Supreme Court Justices; inclusion of women advisors in equitable ratios on all government studies, commissions and hearings; and

Laws authorizing federal grants on a matching basis for financing State Commissions of the Status of Women.

Rights of Youth

In order to ensure, maintain and secure the proper role and functions of youth in American government, politics and society, the Democratic Party will endeavor to:

Lower the age of legal majority and consent to 18;

Actively encourage and assist in the election of youth to federal, state and local offices;

Develop special programs for employment of youth, utilizing governmental resources to guarantee development, training and job placement; and

Secure the electoral reforms called for under "People and the Government."

Rights of Poor People

Poor people, like all Americans, should be represented at all levels of the Democratic Party in reasonable proportion of their numbers in the general population. Affirmative action must be taken to ensure their representation at every level. The Democratic Party guidelines guaranteeing proportional representation to "previously discriminated against groups" (enumerated as "women, young people and minorities") must be extended to specifically include poor people.

Political parties, candidates and government institutions at all levels must be committed to working with and supporting poor people's organizations and ending the tokenism and co-optation that has characterized past dealings.

Welfare rights organizations must be recognized as representative of welfare recipients and be given access to regulations, policies and decision-making processes, as well as being allowed to represent clients at all governmental levels.

The federal government must protect the right of tenants to organize tenant organizations and negotiate collective bargaining agreements with private landlords and encourage the participation of the tenants in the management and control of all subsidized housing.

Rights of American Indians

We support rights of American Indians to full rights of citizenship. The federal government should commit all necessary funds to improve the lives of Indians, with no division between reservation and non-reservation Indians. We strongly oppose the policy of termination, and we urge the government to provide unequivocal advocacy for the protection of the remaining Indian land and water resources. All land rights due American Indians, and Americans of Spanish and Mexican descent, on the basis of treaties with the federal government will be protected by the federal government. In addition we support allocation of Federal surplus lands to American Indians on a first priority basis.

American Indians should be given the right to receive bilingual medical services from hospitals and physicians of their choice.

Rights of the Physically Disabled

The physically disabled have the right to pursue meaningful employment and education, outside a hospital environment, free from unnecessary discrimination, living in adequate housing, with access to public mass transportation and regular medical care. Equal opportunity employment practices should be used by the government in considering their application for federal jobs and equal access to education from pre-school to the college level guaranteed. The physically disabled like all disadvantaged peoples, should be represented in any group making decisions affecting their lives.

Rights of the Mentally Retarded

The mentally retarded must be given employment and educational opportunities that promote their dignity as individuals and ensure their civil rights. Educational treatment facilities must guarantee that these rights always will be recognized and protected. In addition, to assure these citizens a more meaningful life, emphasis must be placed on programs of treatment that respect their right to life in a non-institutional environment.

Rights of the Elderly

Growing old in America for too many means neglect, sickness, despair and, all too often, poverty. We have failed to discharge the basic obligation of a civilized people—to respect and assure the security of our senior citizens. The Democratic Party pledges, as a final step to economic security for all, to end poverty—as measured by official standards—among the retired, the blind and the disabled. Our general program of economic and social justice will benefit the elderly

directly. In addition, a Democratic Administration should:

Increase social security to bring benefits in line with changes on the national standard of living;

Provide automatic adjustments to assure that benefits keep pace with inflation;

Support legislation which allows beneficiaries to earn more income, without reduction of social security payments;

Protect individual's pension rights by pension re-insurance and early vesting;

Lower retirement eligibility age to 60 in all government pension programs;

Expand housing assistance for the elderly;

Encourage development of local programs by which senior citizens can serve their community in providing education, recreation, counseling and other services to the rest of the population;

Establish federal standards and inspection of nursing homes and full federal support for qualified nursing homes;

Take the needs of the elderly and the handicapped into account in all federal programs, including construction of federal buildings, housing and transportation planning;

Pending a full national health security system, expand Medicare by supplementing trust funds with general revenues in order to provide a complete range of care and services; eliminate the Nixon Administration cutbacks in Medicare and Medicaid; eliminate the part B premium under Medicare and include under Medicare and Medicaid the costs of eyeglasses, dentures, hearing aids, and all prescription drugs and establish uniform national standards for Medicaid to bring to an end the present situation which makes it worse to be poor in one state than in another.

The Democratic Party pledges itself to adopt rules to give those over 60 years old representation on all Party committees and agencies as nearly as possible in proportion to their percentage in the total population.

Rights of Veterans

It is time that the nation did far more to recognize the service of our 28 million living veterans and to serve them in return. The veterans of Vietnam must get special attention, for no end of the war is truly honorable which does not provide these men the opportunities to meet their needs.

The Democratic Party is committed to extending and improving the benefits available to American veterans and society, to ending the neglect shown by the Nixon Administration to these problems and to the human needs of our ex-servicemen.

Medical care.—The federal government must guarantee quality medical care to ex-servicemen, and to all disabled veterans, expanding and improving Veterans Administration facilities and manpower and preserving the independence and integrity of the VA hospital program. Staff-patient ratios in these hospitals should be made comparable to ratios in community hospitals. Meanwhile, there should be an increase in the VA's ability to deliver out-patient care and home health services, wherever possible treating veterans as part of a family unit.

We support future coordination of health care for veterans with the national health care insurance program, with no reduction in scale or quality of existing veterans care and with recognition of the special health needs of veterans.

The VA separate personnel system should be expanded to take in all types of health personnel, and especially physician's assistants; and VA hospitals should be used to develop medical schools and area health education centers.

The VA should also assume responsibility for the care of wives and children of veterans who are either permanently disabled or who have died from service-connected causes. Distinction should no longer be made between veterans who have seen "wartime," as opposed to "peacetime," service.

Education.—Educational benefits should be provided for Vietnam-era veterans under the GI Bill at levels comparable to those of the original Bill after World War II, supplemented by special veteran's education loans. The VA should greatly expand and improve programs for poor or educationally disadvantaged veterans. In addition, there should be a program under which servicemen and women can receive high school, college or job training while on active duty. GI Bill trainees should be used more extensively to reach out to other veterans who would otherwise miss these educational opportunities.

Drug addiction.—The Veterans Administration should provide either directly or through community facilities, a comprehensive, individually tailored treatment and rehabilitation program for all drug- and alcohol-addicted veterans, on a voluntary and confidential basis, and regardless of the nature of their discharge or the way in which they acquired their condition.

Unemployment.—There should be an increase in unemployment compensation provided to veterans, and much greater emphasis on the Veterans Employment Service of the Department of Labor, expanding its activities in every state. There should be a greatly enlarged effort by the federal government to employ Vietnam-era veterans and other veterans with service-connected disabilities. In addition, veterans' preferences in hiring should be written into every federal contract or subcontract and for public service employment.

Rights of Servicemen and Servicewomen

Military discipline must be maintained, but unjustifiable restriction on the Constitutional rights of members of the armed services must cease.

We support means to ensure the protection of GI rights to express political opinion and engage in off-base political activity.

We should explore new procedures for providing review of discharges other than honorable, in cases involving political activity.

We oppose deferential advancement, punishment assignment or any other treatment on the basis of race, and support affirmative action to end discrimination.

We support rights of women in the armed forces to be free from unfair discrimination.

We support an amendment of the Uniform Code of Military Justice to provide for fair and uniform sentencing procedures.

Rights of Consumers

Consumers need to be assured of a renewed commitment to basic rights and freedoms. They must have the mechanisms available to allow self-protection against the abuses that the Kennedy and Johnson programs were designed to eliminate. We propose a new consumer program:

In the Executive Branch. The executive branch must use its power to expand consumer information and protection:

Ensure that every policy-making level of government concerned with economic or procurement decisions should have a consumer input either through a consumer advisory committee or through consumer members on policy advisory committees;

Support the development of an independent

consumer agency providing a focal point on consumer matters with the right to intervene on behalf of the consumer before all agencies and regulatory bodies; and

Expand all economic policy-making mechanisms to include an assessment of social as well as economic indicators of human well-being.

In the Legislative Branch.—We support legislation which will expand the ability of consumers to defend themselves:

Ensure an extensive campaign to get food, drugs and all other consumer products to carry complete informative labeling about safety, quality and cost. Such labeling is the first step in ensuring the economic and physical health of the consumer. In the food area, it should include nutritional unit pricing, full ingredients by percentage, grade, quality and drained weight information. For drugs, it should include safety, quality, price and operation data, either on the label or in an enclosed manual;

Support a national program to encourage the development of consumer cooperatives, patterned after the rural electric cooperatives in areas where they might help eliminate inflation and restore consumer rights; and

Support federal initiatives and federal standards to reform automobile insurance and assure coverage on a first-party, no-fault basis.

In the Judicial Branch.—The Courts should become an effective forum to hear well-founded consumer grievances.

Consumer class action: Consumers should be given access to the federal courts in a way that allows them to initiate group action against fraudulent, deceitful, or misleading or dangerous business practices.

Small Claims Court: A national program should be undertaken to improve the workings of small claims courts and spread their use so that consumers injured in economically small, though individually significant amounts (e.g. $500), can bring their complaints to the attention of a court and collect their damages without self-defeating legal fees.

The Quality and Quantity of Social Service

The new Democratic Administration can begin a fundamental re-examination of all federal domestic social programs and the patterns of service delivery they support. Simply advocating the expenditure of more funds is not enough, although

funds are needed, for billions already have been poured into federal government programs—programs like urban renewal, current welfare and aid to education, with meager results. The control, structure and effectiveness of every institution and government grant system must be fully examined and these institutions must be made accountable to those they are supposed to serve.

We will, therefore, pursue the development of new rights of two kinds: Rights to the service itself and rights to participate in the delivery process.

Health Care

Good health is the least this society should promise its citizens. The state of health services in this country indicates the failure of government to respond to this fundamental need. Costs skyrocket while the availability of services for all but the rich steadily declines.

We endorse the principle that good health is a right of all Americans.

America has a responsibility to offer to every American family the best in health care whenever they need it, regardless of income or where they live or any other factor.

To achieve this goal the next Democratic Administration should:

Establish a system of universal National Health Insurance which covers all Americans with a comprehensive set of benefits including preventive medicine, mental and emotional disorders, and complete protection against catastrophic costs, and in which the rule of free choice for both provider and consumer is protected. The program should be federally-financed and federally-administered. Every American must know he can afford the cost of health care whether given in a hospital or a doctor's office;

Incorporate in the National Health Insurance System incentives and controls to curb inflation in health care costs and to assure efficient delivery of all services;

Continue and evaluate Health Maintenance Organizations;

Set up incentives to bring health service personnel back to inner-cities and rural areas;

Continue to expand community health centers and availability of early screening diagnosis and treatment;

Provide federal funds to train added health

manpower including doctors, nurses, technicians and para-medical workers;

Secure greater consumer participation and control over health care institutions;

Expand federal support for medical research including research in heart disease, hypertension, stroke, cancer, sickle cell anemia, occupational and childhood diseases which threaten millions and in preventive health care;

Eventual replacement of all federal programs of health care by a comprehensive National Health Insurance System;

Take legal and other action to curb soaring prices for vital drugs using anti-trust laws as applicable and amending patent laws to end price-raising abuses, and require generic-name labeling of equal-effective drugs; and

Expand federal research and support for drug abuse treatment and education, especially development of non-addictive treatment methods.

Family Planning

Family planning services, including the education, comprehensive medical and social services necessary to permit individuals freely to determine and achieve the number and spacing of their children, should be available to all, regardless of sex, age, marital status, economic group or ethnic origin, and should be administered in a non-coercive and non-discriminatory manner.

Puerto Rico

The Democratic Party respects and supports the frequently-expressed desire of the people of Puerto Rico to freely associate in permanent union with the United States, as an autonomous commonwealth. We are committed to Puerto Rico's right to enjoy full self-determination and a relationship that can evolve in ways that will most benefit both parties.

To this end, we support equal treatment for Puerto Rico in the distribution of all federal grants-in-aid, amendment of federal laws that restrict aid to Puerto Rico; and we pledge no further restrictions in future laws. Only in this way can the people of Puerto Rico come to participate more fully in the many areas of social progress made possible by Democratic efforts, on behalf of all the people.

Finally, the Democratic Party pledges to end all Naval shelling and bombardment of the tiny,

inhabited island of Culebra and its neighboring keys, not later than June 1, 1975. With this action, and others, we will demonstrate the concern of the Democratic Party to develop and maintain a productive relationship between the Commonwealth and the United States.

Virgin Islands, Guam, American Samoa and the Trust Territories of the Pacific

We pledge to include all of these areas in federal grant-in-aid programs on a full and equitable basis.

We praise the Democratic Congress for providing a non-voting delegate to the House of Representatives from Guam and the Virgin Islands and urge that these elected delegates be accorded the full vote in the committees to which they are assigned.

We support the right of American Samoans to elect their Governor, and will consider methods by which American citizens residing in American territories can participate in Presidential elections.

IV. Cities, Communities, Counties and the Environment

"When the Democratic Platform is written and acted on in Miami, let it be a blueprint for the life and survival of our cities and our people."

—Mayor Kenneth A. Gibson
U.S. Conference of Mayors
New Orleans
June 19, 1972

Introduction

Always the vital center of our civilization, the American city since World War II has been suffering growing pains, caused partly by the change of the core city into a metropolitan city and partly by the movement of people from towns and rural areas into the cities.

The burgeoning of the suburbs—thrust outward with too little concern for social, economic and environmental consequences—has both broadened the city's limits and deepened human and neighborhood needs.

The Nixon Administration has failed to meet most of these needs. It has met the problem of urban decay with tired, decaying "solutions" that are unworthy of the name. It could act to revitalize our urban areas; instead, we see only rising crime, fear and flight, racial and economic polarization, loss of confidence and depletion of community resources.

This Administration has ignored the cities and suburbs, permitting taxes to rise and services to decline; housing to deteriorate faster than it can be replaced, and morale to suffer. It actually has impounded funds appropriated by a Democratic Congress to help cities in crisis.

The Administration has ignored the needs of city and suburban residents for public services, for property tax relief and for the planning and coordination that alone can assure that housing, jobs, schools and transportation are built and maintained in suitable locations and in needed numbers and quality.

Meanwhile, the Nixon Administration has forgotten small-town America, too, refusing to provide facilities that would make it an attractive alternative to city living.

This has become the American crisis of the 1970's. Today, our highest national priority is clear and precise: To deal effectively—and *now* with the massive, complex and urgent needs of our cities, suburbs and towns.

The federal government cannot solve all the problems of these communities. Too often, federal bureaucracy has failed to deliver the services and keep the promises that are made. But only the federal government can be the catalyst to focus attention and resources on the needs of every neighborhood in America.

Under the Nixon Administration, piecemeal measures, poorly funded and haphazardly applied, have proved almost totally inadequate. Words have not halted the decline of neighborhoods. Words have not relieved the plight of tenants in poorly managed, shoddy housing. Our scarce urban dollars have been wasted, and even the Republican Secretary of Housing and Urban Development has admitted it.

The Democratic Party pledges to stop the rot in our cities, suburbs and towns, and stop it now. We pledge commitment, coordination, planning and funds:

Commitment to make our communities places where we are proud to raise our children;

Coordination and planning to help all levels of government achieve the same goals, to ensure that physical facilities meet human needs and to ensure that land—a scarce resource—is used in ways that meet the needs of the entire nation; and

Funds to reduce the burden of the inequitable property tax and to help local government meet legitimate and growing demands for public facilities and services.

The nation's urban areas must and can be habitable. They are not only centers of commerce and trade, but also repositories of history and culture, expressing the richness and variety of their region and of the larger society. They are worthy of the best American can offer. They are America.

Partnership among Governments

The federal government must assist local communities to plan for their orderly growth and development, to improve conditions and opportunities for all their citizens and to build the public facilities they need.

Effective planning must be done on a regional basis. New means of planning are needed that are practical and realistic, but that go beyond the limits of jurisdictional lines. If local government is to be responsive to citizen needs, public services and programs must efficiently be coordinated and evolved through comprehensive regional planning and decision-making. Government activities should take account of the future as well as the present.

In aiding the reform of state and local government, federal authority must insist that local decisions take into account the views and needs of all citizens, white and black, haves and have-nots, young and old, Spanish and other non-English-speaking, urban, suburban and rural.

Americans ask more and more of their local governments, but the regressive property tax structure makes it impossible for cities and counties to deliver. The Democratic Party is committed to ensure that state and local governments have the funds and the capacity to achieve community service and development goals—goals that are nationally recognized. To this end:

We fully support general revenue sharing and the principle that the federal income tax should be used to raise more revenues for local use;

We pledge adequate federal funds to halt property tax increases and to begin to roll them back. Turning over federal funds to local governments will permit salaries of underpaid state and local government employees to climb to acceptable levels; and it will reduce tax pressures on the aged, the poor, Spanish and other non-English-speaking Americans and young couples starting out in life;

We further commit ourselves to reorganize categorical grant programs. They should be consolidated, expanded and simplified. Funding should be adequate, dependable, sustained, long-term and related to state and local fiscal time-tables and priorities. There should be full funding of all programs, without the impounding of funds by the Executive Branch to thwart the will of Congress. And there should be performance standards governing the distribution of all federal funds to state and local governments; and

We support efforts to eliminate gaps and costly overlaps in services delivered by different levels of government.

Urban Growth Policy

The Nixon Administration has neither developed an effective urban growth policy designed to meet critical problems, nor concerned itself with the needed re-creation of the quality of life in our cities, large and small. Instead, it has severely over-administered and underfunded existing federal aid programs. Through word and deed, the Administration has widened the gulf between city and suburb, between core and fringe, between haves and have-nots.

The nation's urban growth policies are seen most clearly in the legitimate complaints of suburban householders over rising taxes and center-city families over houses that are falling apart and services that are often non-existent. And it is here, in the center city, that the failure of Nixon Administration policies is most clear to all who live there.

The Democratic Party pledges:

A national urban growth policy to promote a balance of population among cities, suburbs, small towns and rural areas, while providing social and economic opportunities for everyone. America needs a logical urban growth policy, instead of today's inadvertent, chaotic and haphazard one that doesn't work. An urban growth policy that truly deals with our tax and mortgage insurance and highway policies will require the use of federal policies as leverage on private investment;

A policy on housing—including low- and middle-income housing—that will concentrate effort in areas where there are jobs, transportation, schools, health care and commercial facilities. Problems of over-growth are not caused so much by land

scarcity, as by the wrong distribution of people and the inadequate servicing of their needs; and

A policy to experiment with alternative strategies to reserve land for future development—land banks—and a policy to recoup publicly created land values for public benefit.

The Cities

Many of the worst problems in America are centered in our cities. Countless problems contribute to their plight: decay in housing, the drain of welfare, crime and violence, racism, failing schools, joblessness and poor mass transit, lack of planning for land use and services.

The Democratic Party pledges itself to change the disastrous policies of the Nixon Administration toward the cities and to reverse the steady process of decay and dissolution. We will renew the battle begun under the Kennedy and Johnson Administrations to improve the quality of life in our cities. In addition to pledging the resources critically needed, we commit ourselves to these actions:

Help localities to develop their own solutions to their most pressing problems—the federal government should not stifle or usurp local initiative;

Carry out programs developed elsewhere in this Platform to assure every American decent shelter, freedom from hunger, good health care, the opportunity to work, adequate income and a decent education;

Provide sufficient management and planning funds for cities, to let them increase staff capacity and improve means of allocating resources;

Distribute funds according to standards that will provide center cities with enough resources to revitalize old neighborhoods and build new ones, to expand and improve community services and to help local governments better to plan and deliver these services; and

Create and fund a housing strategy that will recognize that housing is neighborhood and community as well as shelter—a strategy that will serve all the nation's urban areas and all the American people.

Housing and Community Development

The 1949 Housing Act pledged "a decent home and suitable living environment for every American family." Twenty-three years later, this goal is still far away. Under this Administration, there simply has been no progress in meeting our housing needs, despite the Democratic Housing Act of 1968. We must build 2.6 million homes a year, including two-thirds of a million units of federally-subsidized low- and middle-income housing. These targets are not being met. And the lack of housing is particularly critical for people with low and middle incomes.

In the cities, widespread deterioration and abandonment are destroying once sound homes and apartments, and often entire neighborhoods, faster than new homes are built.

Federal housing policy creates walled compounds of poor, elderly and ethnic minorities, isolating them in the center city.

These harmful policies include the Administration's approach to urban renewal, discrimination against the center city by the Federal Housing Administration, highway policies that destroy neighborhoods and create ghettoes and other practices that work against housing for low- and middle-income families.

Millions of lower—and middle-class Americans—each year the income level is higher—are priced out of housing because of sharply rising costs.

Under Republican leadership, the Federal Housing Administration (FHA) has become the biggest slumlord in the country. Some unsophisticated home buyers have purchased homes with FHA mortgage insurance or subsidies. These consumers, relying on FHA appraisals to protect them, often have been exploited by dishonest real estate speculators. Unable to repair or maintain these houses, the buyers often have no choice but to abandon them. As a result, the FHA will acquire a quarter million of these abandoned houses at a cost to the taxpayers of billions of dollars.

Under the Republican Administration, the emphasis has been on housing subsidies for the people who build and sell houses rather than for those people who need and live in them. In many cases, the only decent shelter provided is a tax shelter.

To correct this inequity the Democratic Party pledges:

To overhaul completely the FHA to make it a consumer-oriented agency;

To use the full faith and credit of the Treasury to provide direct; low-interest loans to finance the construction and purchase of decent housing for the American people; and

To insist on building practices, inspection standards and management that will assure quality housing.

The next Administration must build and conserve housing that not only meets the basic need for shelter, but also provides a wider choice of quality housing and living environments. To meet this challenge, the Democratic Party commits itself to a housing approach that:

Prevents the decay and abandonment of homes and neighborhoods. Major rehabilitation programs to conserve and rehabilitate housing are needed. Consumers should be aided in purchasing homes, and low-income housing foreclosed by the FHA should be provided to poor families at minimal cost as an urban land grant. These houses should be rehabilitated and lived in, not left to rot;

Provides federal funds for preservation of existing neighborhoods. Local communities should decide whether they want renewal or preservation. Choosing preservation should not mean steady deterioration and inadequate facilities;

Provides for improved housing quality for all families through strict enforcement of housing quality standards and full compliance with state and local health and safety laws;

Provides effective incentives to reduce housing costs—to the benefit of poor and middle-income families alike—through effective use of unused, undeveloped land, reform of building practices and the use of new building techniques, including factory-made and modular construction;

Assures that residents have a strong voice in determining the destiny of their own neighborhoods;

Promotes free choice in housing—the right of all families, regardless of race, color, religion or income, to choose among a wide range of homes and neighborhoods in urban, suburban and rural areas—through the greater use of grants to individuals for housing, the development of new communities offering diversified housing and neighborhood options and the enforcement of fair housing laws; and

Assures fair and equitable relationships between landlords and tenants.

New Towns

New towns meet the direct housing and community needs of only a small part of our populations. To do more, new towns must be developed in concert with massive efforts to revitalize central cities and enhance the quality of life in still growing suburban areas.

The Democratic Party pledges:

To strengthen the administration of the New Towns program; to reduce onerous review requirements that delay the start of New Towns and thus thwart Congressional mandates; to release already appropriated monies and provide new planning and development funds needed to assure the quality of life in New Towns; and

To assure coordination between development of New Towns and renewed efforts to improve the quality of life in established urban and suburban areas. We also promise to use effectively the development of New Towns to increase housing choices for people now living in central and suburban areas.

Transportation

Urban problems cannot be separated from transportation problems. Whether tying communities together, connecting one community to another or linking our cities and towns to rural areas, good transportation is essential to the social and economic life of any community. It joins workers to jobs; makes commercial activity both possible and profitable and provides the means for expanding personal horizons and promoting community cultural life.

Today, however, the automobile is the principal form of transportation in urban areas. The private automobile has made a major contribution to economic growth and prosperity in this century. But now we must have better balanced transportation—more of it public. Today, 15 times as much federal aid goes to highways as to mass transit; tomorrow this must change. At the same time, it is important to preserve and improve transportation in America's rural areas, to end the crisis in rural mobility.

The Democratic Party pledges:

To create a single Transportation Trust Fund, to replace the Highway Trust Fund, with such additional funds as necessary to meet our transportation crisis substantially from federal resources. This fund will allocate monies for capital projects on a regional basis, permitting each region to determine its own needs under guidelines that will ensure a balanced transportation system and adequate funding of mass transit facilities.

Moreover, we will:

Assist local transit systems to meet their capital operating needs;

End the deterioration of rail and rural transportation and promote a flexible rural transportation system based on local, state and regional needs;

Take steps to meet the particular transportation problems of the elderly, the handicapped and others with special needs; and

Assist development of airport terminals, facilities and access to them, with due regard to impact on environment and community.

Environment, Technology and Resources

Every American has the right to live, work and play in a clean, safe and healthy environment. We have the obligation to ourselves and to our children. It is not enough simply to prevent further environmental deterioration and the despoilation of our natural endowment. Rather, we must improve the quality of the world in which we and they will live.

The Nixon Administration's record on the environment is one of big promises and small actions.

Inadequate enforcement, uncertain requirements, reduced funding and a lack of manpower have undercut the effort commenced by a Democratic Administration to clean up the environment.

We must recognize the costs all Americans pay for the environmental destruction with which we all live: Poorer health, lessened recreational opportunities, higher maintenance costs, lower land productivity and diminished beauty in our surroundings. Only then can we proceed wisely, yet vigorously, with a program of environmental protection which recognizes that, although environmental protection will not be cheap, it is worth a far greater price, in effort and money, than we have spent thus far.

Such a program must include adequate federal funding for waste management, recycling and disposal and for purification and conservation of air and water resources.

The next Administration must reconcile any conflicts among the goals of cleaner air and water, inexpensive power and industrial development and jobs in specific places. These difficulties do exist—to deny them would be deceptive and irresponsible. At the same time, we know they can be resolved by an Administration with energy, intelligence and commitment—qualities notably absent from the current Administration's handling of the problem.

We urge additional financial support to the United States Forest Service for planning and management consistent with the environmental ideal stated in this Platform.

Choosing the Right Methods of Environmental Protection

The problem we face is to choose the most efficient, effective and equitable techniques for solving each new environmental problem. We cannot afford to waste resources while doing the job, any more than we can afford to leave the job undone.

We must enforce the strict emission requirements on all pollution sources set under the 1970 Clean Air Act.

We must support the establishment of a policy of no harmful discharge into our waters by 1985.

We must have adequate staffing and funding of all regulatory and enforcement agencies and departments to implement laws, programs and regulations protecting the environment, vigorous prosecution of violators and a Justice Department committed to enforcement of environmental law.

We must fully support laws to assure citizens' standing in federal environmental court suits.

Strict interstate environmental standards must be formulated and enforced to prevent pollution from high-density population areas being dumped into low-density population areas for the purpose of evasion of strict pollution enforcement.

The National Environmental Policy Act should be broadened to include major private as well as public projects, and a genuine commitment must be made to making the Act work.

Our environment is most threatened when the natural balance of an area's ecology is drastically altered for the sole purpose of profits. Such practices as "clear cut" logging, strip mining, the indiscriminate destruction of whole species, creation of select ocean crops at the expense of other species and the unregulated use of persistent pesticides cannot be justified when they threaten our ability to maintain a stable environment.

Where appropriate, taxes need to be levied on pollution, to provide industry with an incentive to clean up.

We also need to develop new public agencies that can act to abate pollution—act on a scale commensurate with the size of the problem and the technology of pollution control.

Expanded federal funding is required to assist local governments with both the capital and operating expenses of water pollution control and solid waste management.

Jobs and the Environment

The United States should not be condemned to the choice between the development of resources and economic security *or* preservation of those resources.

A decent job for every American is a goal that need not, and must not, be sacrificed to our commitment to a clean environment. Far from slowing economic growth, spending for environmental protection can create new job opportunities for many Americans. Nevertheless, some older and less efficient plants might find themselves in a worse competitive position due to environmental protection requirements. Closely monitored adjustment assistance should be made available to those plants willing to modernize and institute environmental protection measures.

Science and Technology

For years, the United States was the world's undisputed leader in science and technology. Now that leadership is being challenged, in part because of the success of efforts in other countries, and in part because of the Nixon Administration's neglect of our basic human and material resources in this field.

As Democrats, we understand the enormous investment made by the nation in educating and training hundreds of thousands of highly skilled Americans in science and technology. Many of these people are now unemployed, as aerospace and defense programs are slowly cut back and as the Administration's economic policies deprive these Americans, as well as others, of their livelihood.

So far, however, the Nixon Administration has paid scant attention to these problems. By contrast, the Democratic Party seeks both to increase efforts by the federal government and to stimulate research in private industry.

In addition, the Democratic Party is committed to increasing the overall level of scientific research in the United States, which has been allowed to fall under the Nixon Administration. And we are eager to take management methods and techniques devised for the space and defense programs, as well as our technical resources, and apply them to the city, the environment, education, energy, transportation, health care and other urgent domestic needs. We propose also to work out a more effective relationship between government and industry in this area, to stimulate the latter to a greater research and development effort, thus helping buoy up the economy and create more jobs.

Finally, we will promote the search for new approaches in science and technology, so that the benefits of progress may be had without further endangering the environment—indeed, so that the environment may be better preserved. We must create a systematic way to decide which new technologies will contribute to the nation's development, and which will cause more problems than they solve. We are committed to a role for government in helping to bring the growth of technology into a harmonious relationship with our lives.

Energy Resources

The earth's natural resources, once in abundant and seemingly unlimited supply, can no longer be taken for granted. In particular, the United States is facing major changes in the pattern of energy supply that will force us to reassess traditional policies. By 1980, we may well have to depend on imports from the Eastern Hemisphere for as much as 30 to 50 per cent of our oil supplies. At the same time, new forms of energy supply—such as nuclear, solar or geothermal power—lag far behind in research and development.

In view of these concerns, it is shocking that the Nixon Administration still steadfastly refuses to develop a national energy policy.

The Democratic Party would remedy that glaring oversight. To begin with, we should:

Promote greater research and development, both by government and by private industry, of unconventional energy sources, such as solar power, geothermal power, energy from water and a variety of nuclear power possibilities to design clean breeder fission and fusion techniques. Public funding in this area needs to be expanded, while retaining the principle of public administration of public funds;

Re-examine our traditional view of national security requirements in energy to reconcile them with our need for long-term abundant supplies of clean energy at reasonable cost;

Expand research on coal technology to minimize pollution, while making it possible to expand the efficiency of coal in meeting our energy needs;

Establish a national power plant siting procedure to examine and protect environmental values;

Reconcile the demand for energy with the demand to protect the environment;

Redistribute the cost of power among consumers, so that all, especially the poor, may be guaranteed adequate power at reasonable costs;

Develop a national power grid to improve the reliability and efficiency of our electricity system;

End the practice of allowing promotional utility advertising as an expense when rates are set; and

Find new techniques to encourage the conservation of energy. We must also require full disclosure of the energy needs of consumer products and home heating to enable consumers to make informed decisions on their use of energy.

The Oceans

As with the supply of energy, no longer can we take for granted the precious resources we derive from the oceans. Here, too, we need comprehensive national and international policies to use and protect the vast potential contained in the sea. In particular we must:

Agree with other nations on stopping pollution of the seas, if they are not one day to become one large sewer, or be filled with dangerous poisons that will deprive us of vital food resources;

Agree with other nations on the conservation of food resources in the seas and promote the use of management techniques that will end the decline of the world's fish catch on the continental shelf through international cooperation for fishing gear regulations and species quota and preserve endangered species;

Agree on an international accord for the seas, so resources can be shared equitably among the world's nations. We must be prepared to act constructively at next year's Conference on the Law of the Seas;

Begin to reconcile competing interests in the future of the seas, including our national security objectives, to protect ocean resources in cooperation with other nations; and

Support strongly the protection of ocean mammals (seal, whale, walrus) from indiscriminate destruction by both foreign and tuna fishing industries, but specifically exempting those native Americans whose subsistence depends completely on their total use of the ocean's resources.

Ninety percent of all salt water fish species live on our continental shelves, where plant life is plentiful. For this reason, we support monitoring and strict enforcement of all safety regulations on all offshore drilling equipment and on environmentally-safe construction of all tankers transporting oil.

Public Lands

For generations, Americans have been concerned with preserving the natural treasures of our country: Our lakes and rivers, our forests and mountains. Enlightened Americans of the past decided that the federal government should take a major role in protecting these treasures, on behalf of everyone. Today, however, neglect on the part of the Nixon Administration is threatening this most valued heritage—and that of our children. Never before in modern history have our public lands been so neglected and the responsible agencies so starved of funds.

The Democratic Party is concerned about preserving our public lands, and promoting policies of land management in keeping with the broad public interest. In particular, it is imperative to restore lost funds for land, park and forest management. It is imperative that decisions about the future use of our public lands be opened up to all the people for widespread public debate and discussion. Only through such an open process can we set ground rules that appropriately limit the influence of special interests and allow for cohesive guidelines for national land-use planning.

We are particularly aware of the potential conflicts among the use of land, rivers, lakes and the seashore for economic development, large-scale recreation and for preservation as unspoiled wilderness. We recognize that there are competing goals, and shall develop means for resolving these conflicts in a way that reflects the federal government's particular responsibilities as custodian for the public. We need more National Seashores and expansion of the National Park system. Major steps must be taken to follow up on Congressional commitment to scenic riverways.

Recreation areas must be made available to people where they live. This includes the extension of our national wilderness preserves to include de facto wilderness areas and their preservation free of commercialization. In this way, we will help to preserve and improve the quality of life for millions of our people.

With regard to the development of the vast natural resources on our public lands, we pledge a renewed commitment to proceed in the interests of all our citizens.

V. Education

"The American people want overwhelmingly to give to our children and adults equitable educational opportunities of the highest possible quality, *not* predicated on race, *not* predicated on past social accomplishment or wealth, except in a compensatory way to those who have been deprived in the past."—Governor Jimmy Carter, Atlanta Hearing, June 9, 1972.

Our schools are failing our children. Never, more than now, have we needed the schools to play their traditional role—to create a sense of national unity and to reconcile ethnic, religious and racial conflicts. Yet the Nixon Administration—by ignoring the plight of the nation's schools, by twice vetoing funds for education—has contributed to this failure.

America in the 1970's requires something the world has never seen: Masses of educated people —educated to feel and to act, as well as to think. The children who enter school next fall still will be in the labor force in the year 2030; we cannot even imagine what American society will be like then, let alone what specific jobs they may hold. For them, education must be done by teaching them how to learn, how to apply man's wisdom to new problems as they arise and how to recognize new problems as they arise. Education must prepare students not just to earn a living but to live a life—a creative, humane and sensitive life.

School Finance

Achieving educational excellence requires adequate financial support. But today local property taxes—which do not keep pace with inflation—can no longer support educational needs. Continued reliance on this revenue source imposes needless hardship on the American family without supplying the means for good schools. At the same time, the Nixon recession has sapped the resources of state government, and the Administration's insensitivity to school children has meant inadequate federal expenditures in education.

The next Democratic Administration should:

Support equalization in spending among school districts. We support Court decisions holding unconstitutional the disparities in school expenditures produced by dependence on local property taxes. We pledge equality of spending as a way to improve schools and to assure equality of access to good education for all children;

Increase federal financial aid for elementary and secondary education to enhance achievement of quality education anywhere, and by fully funding the programs passed by the Congress and by fully funding ESEA Title I;

Step up efforts to meet the special needs and costs of educationally disadvantaged children handicapped by poverty, disability or non-English-speaking family background;

Channel financial aid by a Constitutional formula to children in non-public schools;

Support suburban-urban cooperation in education to share resources and expenses;

Develop and implement the retraining of displaced black and other minority teachers affected by desegregation; and

Continue with full federal funding the breakfast and lunch programs for all children and the development of other programs to combat hunger.

Early Childhood Education

Our youngest children are most ignored by national policy and most harshly treated by the Nixon Administration. President Nixon's cruel, irresponsible veto of the Comprehensive Child Development Act of 1971 indicates dramatically the real values of the present Administration.

That legislation struck down by President Nixon remains the best program to bring support to family units threatened by economic and social pressures; to eliminate educational handicaps which leave disadvantaged children unable to compete in school; to prevent early childhood disease before it results in adult disability; to interrupt the painful, destructive cycle of welfare dependence, and, most important, to allow all children happy lives as children and the opportunity to develop their full potential.

We support legislation for positive and preventive approaches to early childhood education.

These approaches should be designed to help eliminate educational handicaps before they require remedial treatment. A Democratic President will support and sign a program for universal comprehensive child development.

We should give reality to the right of mentally retarded children to adequate health care and educational opportunities through such measures as including necessary care under national health insurance and federal aid to assure an opportunity for education for all retarded persons.

Equal Access to Quality Education

The Supreme Court of the United States in Brown v Board of Education established the Constitutional principle that states may not discriminate between school children on the basis of their race and that separate but equal has no place in our public education system. Eighteen years later the provision of integration is not a reality.

We support the goal of desegregation as a means to achieve equal access to quality education for all our children. There are many ways to desegregate schools: School attendance lines may be redrawn; schools may be paired; larger physical facilities may be built to serve larger, more diverse enrollments; magnet schools or educational parks may be used. Transportation of students is another tool to accomplish desegregation. It must continue to be available according to Supreme Court decisions to eliminate legally imposed segregation and improve the quality of education for all children.

Bilingual Education

Ten per cent of school children in the United States speak a language other than English in their homes and communities. The largest of the linguistic and cultural groups—Spanish-speaking and American Indians—are also among the poorest people in the United States. Increasing evidence indicates an almost total failure of public education to educate these children.

The drop-out rates of Spanish-speaking and Indian children are the worst of any children in the country. The injury is compounded when such children are placed in special "compensatory" programs or programs for the "dumb" or the "retarded" on the basis of tests and evaluations conducted in English.

The passage of the Bilingual Education Act

of 1967 began a commitment by the nation to do something about the injustices committed against the bilingual child. But for 1972–73, Congress appropriated $35 million—enough to serve only two per cent of the children who need help.

The next Democratic Administration should:

Increase federal support for bilingual, bicultural educational programs, pre-school through secondary school, including funding of bilingual Adult Basic Education;

Ensure sufficient teacher training and curriculum development for such schools;

Implement an affirmative action program to train and to hire bilingual-bicultural Spanish-speaking persons at all levels in the educational system;

Provide inventories for state and local districts to initiate bilingual-bicultural education programs;

Require testing of bilingual-bicultural children in their own languages; and

Prohibit discrimination against bilingual-bicultural children in school.

Career Education

Academic accomplishment is not the only way to financial success, job satisfaction or rewarding life in America. Many young Americans think that college is the only viable route when for some a vocational-technical career offers as much promise of a full life. Moreover, the country desperately needs skilled workers, technicians, men and women who understand and can handle the tools and equipment that mean growth and jobs. By 1975 the need for skilled craftsmen will increase 18 per cent while the need for college-trained persons will remain stable.

Young people should be permitted to make a career choice consistent with their interests, aptitudes and aspirations. We must create an atmosphere where the dignity of work is respected, where diversity of talent and taste is encouraged and where continuing opportunity exists to keep pace with change and gives a saleable skill.

To aid this, the next Democratic Administration can:

Give vocational-technical education the same priority in funds and emphasis previously given academic education;

Support full appropriations for the recently-passed Occupational Education Act;

Strengthen the career counseling programs in elementary, secondary and post-secondary education so that young people are made aware of all of the opportunities open to them and provide special kinds of vocational-technical education and experience to meet specific area needs;

Develop and promote a climate conducive to free, rational choice by young people, dispelling the current prejudices that influence career decisions for most young people almost from birth;

Establish a lifetime system of continuing education to enhance career mobility, both vertically and laterally, so that the career choice made at 18 or 20 years of age does not have to be the only or the final choice; and

Grant equal representation to minorities and women in vocational-technical education.

Higher Education

We support universal access to opportunities to post-secondary education. The American education system has always been an important path toward social and economic advancement. Federal education policy should ensure that our colleges and universities continue as an open system. It must also stimulate the creative development and expansion of higher education to meet the new social, economic and environmental problems confronting society. To achieve the goals of equal opportunity in education, to meet the growing financial crisis in higher education and to stimulate reform of educational techniques, the next Democratic Administration should:

Support guaranteed access for all students to loan funds with long-term repayment based on future earnings. Not only the poor, but families with moderate incomes must be provided relief from the cost of a college and professional education;

Grant supplements and contingent loans to institutions, based on enrollment of federally-aided students;

Provide research funds to stimulate a partnership between post-secondary, secondary and primary education, in an effort to find new patterns for learning and to provide training and retraining of teachers, especially in urban areas;

Develop broad opportunities for lifelong learning including encouragement for post-secondary education throughout adult years and permit "stopping-off" during higher education;

Develop affirmative programs in universities

and colleges for recruitment of minorities and women for administrative and teaching positions and as students; and

Create incentives for non-traditional education which recognize the contribution of experience to an individual's educational status.

Arts and Humanities

Support for the arts and humanities is one of the benchmarks of a civilized society. Yet, the continued existence of many of America's great symphonies, theatres and museums, our film institutes, dance companies and other art forms, is now threatened by rising costs, and the public contribution, far less than in most advanced industrial societies, is a fraction of the need.

We should expand support of the arts and humanities by direct grants through the National Foundation for the Arts and Humanities, whose policy should be to stimulate the widest variety of artistic and scholarly expression.

We should support long-range financing for public broadcasting, insulated from political pressures. We deplore the Nixon Administration's crude efforts to starve and muzzle public broadcasting, which has become a vital supplement to commercial television.

VI. CRIME, LAW AND JUSTICE

"I think we can reduce crime. Society has no more important challenge because crime is human conduct and more than any other activity of people it reflects the moral character of a nation." —Ramsey Clark, Washington Hearing, June 23, 1972.

We advocate and seek a society and a government in which there is an attitude of respect for the law and for those who seek its enforcement and an insistence on the part of our citizens that the judiciary be ever mindful of their primary duty and function of punishing the guilty and protecting the innocent. We will insist on prompt, fair and equal treatment for all persons before the bar of justice.

The problem of crime in America is real, immediate and fundamental; its costs to the nation are staggering; nearly three-quarters of a million victims of violent crime in one year alone; more than 15,000 murders, billions of dollars of property loss.

The indirect, intangible costs are even more ominous. A frightened nation is not a free nation. Its citizens are prisoners, suspicious of the people they meet, restricted in when they go out and when they return, threatened even in their own homes. Unless government at all levels can restore a sense of confidence and security to its people, there is the ever-present danger that alarm will turn to panic, triggering short-cut remedies that jeopardize hard-won liberties.

When law enforcement breaks down, not only the victims of street violence suffer; the worker's health and safety is imperiled by unsafe, illegal conditions on the job; the society is defenseless against fraud and pollution; most tragically of all, parents and communities are ravaged by traffic in dangerous drugs.

The Nixon Administration campaigned on a pledge to reduce crime—to strengthen the "peace forces" against the "criminal forces." Despite claims to the contrary, that pledge has been broken:

Violent crime has increased by one-third, to the highest levels in our history;

Fueled by the immense profits of narcotics traffic, organized crime has thrust its corruption farther and farther, into law enforcement agencies and the halls of justice;

The Department of Justice has become the handmaiden of the White House political apparatus, offering favors to those special interests which buy their "law" in Washington.

The Justice Department has failed to enforce laws protecting key legal rights, such as the Voting Rights Act of 1965;

Nixon and Mitchell use federal crime control funds for political purposes, squandering $1.5 billion.

To reverse this course, through equal enforcement of the law, and to rebuild justice the Democratic Party believes:

The impact of crime in America cuts across racial, geographic and economic lines;

Hard-line rhetoric, pandering to emotion, is both futile and destructive;

We can protect all people without undermining fundamental liberties by ceasing to use "law and order" as justification for repression and political persecution, and by ceasing to use stop-gap measures as preventive detention, "no-knock" entry, surveillance, promiscuous and unauthorized use of wire taps, harassment, and secret dossiers; and

The problems of crime and drug abuse cannot be isolated from the social and economic conditions that give rise to them.

Preventing Crime

Effective law enforcement requires tough planning and action. This Administration has given us nothing but tough words. Together with unequal law enforcement by police, prosecutors and judges, the result is a "turnstile" system of injustice, where most of those who commit crime are not arrested, most of those arrested are not prosecuted, and many of those prosecuted are not convicted. Under this Administration, the conviction rate for federal prosecutions has declined to one-half its former level. Tens of thousands of offenders simply never appear in court and are heard from again only when they commit another crime. This system does not deter crime. It invites it. It will be changed only when all levels of government act to return firmness and fairness to every part of the criminal justice system.

Fear of crime, and firm action against it, is not racism. Indeed the greatest victims of crime today—whether of business fraud or of the narcotics plague—are the people of the ghetto, black and brown. Fear now stalks their streets far more than it does the suburbs.

So that Americans can again live without fear of each other the Democratic Party believes:

There must be equally stringent law enforcement for rich and poor, corporate and individual offenders;

Citizens must be actively involved with the police in a joint effort;

Police forces must be upgraded, and recruiting of highly qualified and motivated policemen must be made easier through federally-assisted pay commensurate with the difficulty and importance of their job, and improved training with comprehensive scholarship and financial support for anyone who is serving or will contract to serve for an appropriate period of police service;

The complex job of policing requires a sensitivity to the changing social demands of the communities in which police operate;

We must provide the police with increased technological facilities and support more efficient use of police resources, both human and material;

When a person is arrested, both justice and effective deterrence of crime require that he be speedily tried, convicted or acquitted, and if convicted, promptly sentenced. To this end we support financial assistance to local courts, prosecutors, and independent defense counsel for expansion, streamlining, and upgrading, with trial in 60 days as the goal;

To train local and state police officers, a Police Academy on a par with the other service academies should be established as well as an Academy of Judicial Administration;

We will provide every assistance to our law enforcement agencies at federal and local levels in the training of personnel and the improvement of techniques and will encourage mutual cooperation between each in its own sphere of responsibility;

We will support needed legislation and action to seek out and bring to justice the criminal organization of national scope operating in our country;

We will provide leadership and action in a national effort against the usage of drugs and drug addiction, attacking this problem at every level and every source in a full scale campaign to drive this evil from our society. We recognize drug addiction as a health problem and pledge that emphasis will be put on rehabilitation of addicts;

We will provide increased emphasis in the area of juvenile delinquency and juvenile offenses in order to deter and rehabilitate young offenders;

There must be laws to control the improper use of hand guns. Four years ago a candidate for the presidency was slain by a handgun. Two months ago, another candidate for that office was gravely wounded. Three out of four police officers killed in the line of duty are slain with hand guns. Effective legislation must include a ban on sale of hand guns known as Saturday night specials which are unsuitable for sporting purposes;

A comprehensive fully-funded program is needed to improve juvenile justice, to ensure minimum standards, to expand research into rehabilitation techniques, including alternatives to reform schools and coordinate existing programs for treating juvenile delinquency; and

The block-grant system of the Law Enforcement Assistance Administration which has produced ineffectiveness, waste and corruption should be eliminated. Funds should go directly to operating agencies that are committed to change and improvement in local law enforcement, including agencies concerned with research, rehabilitation, training and treatment.

Narcotic Drugs

Drug addiction and alcoholism are health problems. Drugs prey on children, destroy lives and communities, force crimes to satisfy addicts, corrupt police and government and finance the expansion of organized crime. A massive national effort, equal to the scale and complexity of the problem, is essential.

The next Democratic Administration should support:

A massive law enforcement effort, supported by increased funds and personnel, against the suppliers and distributors of heroin and other dangerous drugs, with increased penalties for major narcotics traffickers;

Full use of all existing resources to halt the illegal entry of narcotics into the United States, including suspension of economic and military assistance to any country that fails to take appropriate steps to prevent narcotic drugs produced or processed in that country from entering the United States illegally, and increases in customs personnel fighting smuggling of hard drugs;

An all-out investigative and prosecutory effort against corruption in government and law enforcement. Where corruption exists it is a major factor in permitting criminal activity, especially large-scale narcotic distribution, to flourish. It also destroys respect for the law in all who are conscious of its operation. We are determined that our children—whether in the ghetto or in a suburban high school—shall no longer be able to see a pusher protected from prosecution, openly plying his trade;

Strict regulation and vigorous enforcement of existing quotas regulating production and distribution of dangerous drugs, including amphetamines and barbiturates, to prevent diversion into illegal markets, with legislation for strong *criminal* penalties against drug manufacturers engaging in illegal overproduction, distribution and importation;

Expanded research into dangerous drugs and their abuse, focusing especially on heroin addiction among the young and development of effective, non-addictive heroin treatment methods;

Concentration of law enforcement efforts on major suppliers and distributors, with most individual users diverted into treatment before prosecution;

Immediate placement in medical or psychiatric treatment, available to any individual drug abuser without fear of disclosure or harassment. Work opportunities should be provided for addicts in treatment by supported work and other programs; and

Drug education in schools based on fact, not scare tactics to teach young people the dangers of different drugs, and full treatment opportunities for youthful drug abusers. Hard drug trafficking in schools must be met with the strongest possible law enforcement.

Organized and Professional Crime

We are determined to exert the maximum power and authority of the federal government to protect the many victims who cannot help themselves against great criminal combinations.

Against the organized criminal syndicates, we pledge an expanded federal enforcement effort; one not restricted to criminals of any particular ethnic group, but which recognizes that organized crime in the United States cuts across all boundaries of race, national origin and class.

Against white-collar crime, we pledge to enforce the maximum penalties provided by law. Justice cannot survive when, as too often is the case, a boy who steals a television set is sentenced to a long jail term, while a stock manipulator who steals millions is only commanded to sin no more.

At least where life or personal injury are at stake, we pledge to seek expanded criminal penalties for the violation of federal laws. Employers who violate the worker safety and health laws, or manufacturers who knowingly sell unsafe products or drugs profit from death and injury as knowingly as the common mugger. They deserve equally severe punishment.

Rehabilitation of Offenders

Few institutions in America are as uniformly condemned and as consistently ignored as our existing prison system. Many prisons that are supposed to rehabilitate and separate, in fact train their inmates for nothing but brutality and a life of further crime. Only when public understanding recognizes that our existing "corrections" system *contributes* to escalating crime, will we get the massive effort necessary for fundamental restructuring.

Therefore, the Democratic Party commits itself to:

Restoration, after release, of rights to obtain drivers licenses and to public and private employment, and, after completion of sentence and conditions of parole, restoration of civil rights to vote and hold public office;

Revision of sentencing procedures and greater use of community-based rehabilitation facilities, especially for juveniles;

Recognition of the constitutional and human rights of prisoners; realistic therapeutic, vocational, wage-earning, education, alcoholism and drug treatment programs;

Making correctional personnel an integral part of the rehabilitative process;

Emergency, educational and work-release furlough programs as an available technique, support for "self-help" programs; and

Restoration of civil rights to ex-convicts after completion of their sentences, including the right to vote, to hold public office, to obtain drivers' licenses and to public and private employment.

The Quality of Justice

Justice is not merely effective law enforcement —though that is an essential part of it. Justice, rather, expresses the moral character of a nation and its commitment to the rule of law, to equality of all people before the law.

The Democratic Party believes that nothing must abridge the faith of the American citizens in their system of law and justice.

We believe that the quality of justice will be enhanced by:

Equal treatment for all citizens in the court without fear or favor—corporations as well as individual offenders;

Swift trials for accused persons;

Equitable pre-trial release systems and the elimination of plea bargaining abuses;

Ending subversion of the legal system for political gain in court appointments, in antitrust cases and in administration of law enforcement programs;

Administering the laws and funding enacted by the Congress;

Respecting and abiding by Constitutional protections of due process; and

Abolishing capital punishment, recognized as an ineffective deterrent to crime, unequally applied and cruel and excessive punishment.

VII. Farming and Rural Life

"A blight hangs over the land caused by misguided farm policies."—Tony Dechant, Sioux City hearing, June 16, 1972.

For many decades, American agriculture has been the envy of the world; and American farmers and American ranchers have made possible a level of nutrition and abundance for our people that is unrivaled in history, while feeding millions of people abroad.

The basis for this success—and its promise for the future—lies with the family-type farm. It can and must be preserved, in the best interests of all Americans and the nation's welfare.

Today, as dwindling income forces thousands of family farmers into bankruptcy each year, the family-type farm is threatened with extinction. American farming is passing to corporate control.

These trends will benefit few of our people, while hurting many. The dominance of American food production by the large corporation would destroy individual enterprise and links that millions of our people have with the land; and it would lead to higher prices and higher food costs for everyone.

Major efforts must be made to prevent this disaster for the fabric of rural life, for the American farmer, rancher, farm worker and for the consumer and other rural people throughout our nation;

Farm income must be improved to enable farmers, ranchers and farm workers to produce a steady and dependable supply of food and fiber products in return for full parity; and

We must recognize and fulfill the social contract that exists between the family-farm producers of food and the non-farm consumer.

The Democratic Party understands these urgent needs; the Nixon Administration does not and has failed the American farmer. Its record today is consistent with the Republican record of the past: Low prices, farm surpluses that depress the market and callous disregard for the people in rural America.

This Administration has sold out agriculture to interests bent on eliminating family-type farmers and bent on delivering agriculture to conglomerates, agribusiness giants and rich investors seeking to avoid taxes.

Its policies have driven farm income as low as 67 per cent of parity, unequalled since the Depression. Between 50,000 and 75,000 farm families are driven off the land each year. Hundreds of thousands of demoralized people are being forced into overcrowded cities, emptying the countryside and bankrupting small business in rural towns and cities.

The Nixon Administration tries to hide its failures by misleading the people, juggling the parity formula to make prices look higher, distorting reports to make corporate farming look insignificant and trying to break up the U.S. Department of Agriculture and still the farmer's voice.

The Democratic Party will reverse these disastrous policies, and begin to recreate a rural society of widespread family farming, individual opportunity and private and cooperative enterprises, where honest work will bring a decent income.

We repudiate the Administration's set-aside program, which pushes up the cost of farm programs while building huge surpluses that depress prices.

We repudiate the Report of the USDA Young Executives Committee which would eliminate the family-type farm by ending price support, loan and purchasing programs on all farm commodities and which would put farm people on the welfare rolls.

We repudiate a Presidential commission report recommending that future federal investment in many small towns and cities should make their decline merely more bearable rather than reverse it.

In place of these negative and harmful policies, the Democratic Party pledges itself to take positive and decisive action:

We will replace the 1970 Farm Act, when it expires next year, with a permanent law to provide fair prices to family-type farm and ranch operators. This law will include loans and payments to farmers and effective supply management to raise family farm income to 100 percent of parity, based on the 1910–14 ratios:

We will resist a price ceiling on agriculture products until farm prices reach 110 per cent of parity, based on the 1910–14 ratios, and we will conduct a consumer education program to inform all Americans of the relationship between the prices of raw commodities and retail prices;

We will end farm program benefits to farm units larger than family-size; and

We will work for production adjustment that will assure adequate food and fiber for all our people, including low-income families and individuals whose purchasing power is supplemented with food stamps and that can provide enough commodities for export and for the Food for Peace Program.

Exporting Our Abundance

For many years, farm exports have made a major contribution to our balances of trade and payments. But this benefit for the entire nation must not be purchased with depressed prices for the producer.

The Democratic Party will ensure that:

Prices for commodities sent abroad as exports or aid return the cost of production plus a profit for the American farmer;

We will negotiate international commodity agreements to include prices that guarantee prices to producers based on cost of production plus a reasonable profit;

We will require U.S. corporations producing commodities outside the country for consumption here to pay duties high enough to prevent unfair competition for domestic producers;

We will assure that the same rigid standards for inspection of domestic dairy products and meat will be applied to imports; and

We will create a strategic reserve of storable commodities, insulated from the market, rotated regularly to maintain quality and stored to the extent possible on farms.

Strengthening the Family Farm

These policies and actions will not be enough on their own to strengthen the family farm. The Democratic Party also recognizes that farmers and ranchers must be able to gain economic strength in the marketplace by organizing and bargaining collectively for the sale of their products. And they need to be free of unfair competition from monopoly and other restrictive corporate practices. We therefore pledge:

To remove all obstacles to farm bargaining for the sale of products;

To extend authority for marketing orders to all farm commodities including those used for processing;

To prohibit farming, or the gaining of monopolistic control of production, on the part of corporations whose resources and income derive primarily from non-farm sources;

To investigate violations and enforce anti-trust laws in corporation-agriculture-agribusiness interlocks;

To prohibit corporations and individuals from setting up tax shelters or otherwise engaging in agriculture primarily for the purpose of tax avoidance or tax loss;

To encourage and support the use of cooperatives and membership associations in all areas of the country, which we pledge to protect from interference, punitive taxation or other hindrances; and

To assist small rural cooperatives to promote projects in housing, health, social services, marketing, farming, employment and transportation for rural areas with such things as technical assistance and credit.

Guaranteeing Farm People a Voice

None of these policies can begin to work unless farmers, ranchers, farm workers and other rural people have full rights of participation in our democratic institutions of government. The Democratic Party is committed to seeing that family-type farmers and ranchers will be heard and that they will have ample opportunity to help shape policies affecting agriculture and rural America. To this end:

We support the appointment of a farmer or rancher as Secretary of Agriculture;

We oppose all efforts to abolish or dismantle the U.S. Department of Agriculture;

We will require that decisions relating to dams and other public land-use projects in rural areas involving federal funds be considered at well-publicized public hearings. Government is not now giving adequate protection to individual rights in condemnation procedures. It must set new and better procedures and requirements to assure individual rights;

We supported the United Farm Workers in their non-violent efforts to gain collective bargaining recognition and contracts. We also support unemployment insurance compensation benefits, workman's compensation benefits and delivery of health services for farm workers; and

We support the removal of sugar workers from the custody of the U.S. Department of Agriculture.

Revitalizing Rural America

Sound rural development must start with improved farm income, which also promotes the prosperity of the small businesses that serve all rural people. But there must be other efforts, as well, to ensure equity for farm and rural people in the American economy. The Democratic Party pledges:

To support the rural cooperative electrification and telephone programs and to implement rural transportation programs as explained in the section Cities, Communities, Counties and the Environment of this Platform. We will extend the agricultural exemption in the Motor Carriers Act to products and supplies and ensure rural areas an equitable share of Highway Trust Funds;

To apply general revenue sharing in ways that will permit state and local taxation of family farm lands on the basis of value for farm use rather than value for land speculation;

To guarantee equal treatment of rural and urban areas in the provision of federal funds for schools, poverty programs, health facilities, housing, highways, air services, pollution control, senior citizen programs and employment opportunities and manpower and training programs;

To provide loans to aid young farm families and small businesses to get established in rural areas; and

To ensure agricultural research toward an examination of the social and economic consequences of technology.

The prime goal of land grant colleges and research should be to help family farms and rural people.

VIII. FOREIGN POLICY

"The Administration is continuing a war—continuing the killing of Americans and Vietnamese—when our national security is not at stake.

"It is our duty as the opposition party to point out the Administration's errors and to offer a responsible alternative."—W. Averell Harriman, New York Hearing, June 22, 1972.

Strength in defense and wisdom in foreign affairs are essential to prosperity and tranquility. In the modern world, there can be no isolationism in reality or policy. But the measure of our nation's rank in the world must be our success in achieving a just and peaceful society at home.

For the Nixon Administration, foreign policy results have fallen short of the attention and the slogans:

After four years of "Vietnamization," the war in Southeast Asia continues and Nixon's plan is still a secret;

Vital foreign policy decisions are made without consultation with Congress or our allies; and

Executive secrecy runs wild with unparalleled efforts to intimidate the media and suppress those who seek to put a different view before the American people.

The next Democratic Administration should:

End American participation in the war in Southeast Asia;

Re-establish control over military activities and reduce military spending, where consistent with national security;

Defend America's real interests and maintain our alliances, neither playing world policeman nor abandoning old and good friends;

Not neglect America's relations with small third-world nations in placing reliance in great power relationships;

Return to Congress, and to the people, a meaningful role in decisions on peace and war; and

Make information public, except where real national defense interests are involved.

Vietnam

Nothing better describes the need for a new American foreign policy than the fact that now, as for the past seven years, it begins with the war in Vietnam.

The task now is still to end the war, not to decide who is to blame for it. The Democratic Party must share the responsibility for this tragic war. But, elected with a secret plan to end this war, Nixon's plan is still secret, and we—and the Vietnamese—have had four more years of fighting and death.

It is true that our involvement on the ground has been reduced. Troops are coming home. But the war has been extended in Laos and Cambodia; the bombing of North Vietnam has been expanded to levels of destruction undreamed of four years ago; North Vietnam has been blockaded; the number of refugees increases each day, and the Secretary of Defense warns us of still further escalation.

All this has accomplished nothing except to prolong the war.

The hollowness of "Vietnamization"—a delusive slogan seeming to offer cheap victory—has been exposed by the recent offensive. The Saigon Government, despite massive U.S. support, is still not viable. It is militarily ineffective, politically corrupt and economically near collapse. Yet it is for this regime that Americans still die, and American prisoners still rot in Indo-China camps.

The plight of these American prisoners justly arouses the concern of all Americans. We must insist that any resolution of the war include the return of all prisoners held by North Vietnam and other adversary forces and the fullest possible accounting for the missing. With increasing lack of credibility, the Nixon Administration has sought to use the prisoners of war as an excuse for its policies. It has refused to make the simple offer of a definite and final end to U.S. participation in the war, in conjunction with return of all U.S. prisoners.

The majority of the Democratic Senators have called for full U.S. withdrawal by October 1, 1972. We support that position. If the war is not ended before the next Democratic Administration takes office, we pledge, as the first order of business, an immediate and complete withdrawal of all U.S. forces in Indo-China. All U.S. military action in Southeast Asia will cease. After the end of U.S. direct combat participation, military aid to the Saigon Government, and elsewhere in Indo-China, will be terminated.

The U.S. will no longer seek to determine the political future of the nations of Indo-China. The issue is not whether we will depose the present South Vietnamese Government, rather when we will cease insisting that it must be the core of any political settlement. We will do what we can to foster an agreement on an acceptable political solution—but we recognize that there are sharp limits to our ability to influence this process, and to the importance of the outcome to our interest.

Disengagement from this terrible war will not be a "defeat" for America. It will not imply any weakness in America's will or ability to protect its vital interests from attack. On the contrary, disengagement will enable us to heal domestic diversions and to end the distortion of our international priorities which the war has caused.

A Democratic Administration will act to ease the hard transitions which will come with the end of this war. We pledge to offer to the people of Vietnam humanitarian assistance to help them repair the ravages of 30 years of war to the economy and to the people of that devastated land.

To our own people, we pledge a true effort to extend the hand of reconciliation and assistance to those most affected by the war.

To those who have served in this war, we pledge a full G.I. Bill of Rights, with benefits sufficient to pay for an education of the veteran's choice, job training programs and the guarantee of employment and the best medical care this country can provide, including a full program of rehabilitation for those who have returned addicted to dangerous drugs. To those who for reasons of conscience refused to serve in this war and were prosecuted or sought refuge abroad, we state our firm intention to declare an amnesty, on an appropriate basis, when the fighting has ceased and our troops and prisoners of war have returned.

Military Policy

We propose a program of national defense which is both prudent and responsible, which will retain the confidence of our allies and which will be a deterrent to potential aggressors.

Military strength remains an essential element of a responsible international policy. America must have the strength required for effective deterrence.

But military defense cannot be treated in isolation from other vital national concerns. Spending for military purposes is greater by far than federal spending for education, housing, environmental protection, unemployment insurance or welfare. Unneeded dollars for the military at once add to the tax burden and pre-empt funds from programs of direct and immediate benefit to our people. Moreover, too much that is now spent on defense not only adds nothing to our strength but makes us less secure by stimulating other countries to respond.

Under the Nixon stewardship of our defense policy, lack of sound management controls over defense projects threatens to price us out of an adequate defense. The reaction of the Defense Department to exposure of cost overruns has been to strike back at the critics instead of acting to stop the waste.

Needless projects continue and grow, despite evidence of waste, military ineffectiveness and even affirmative danger to real security. The "development" budget starts pressures for larger procurement budgets in a few years. Morale and

military effectiveness deteriorate as drugs, desertion and racial hatreds plague the armed forces, especially in Vietnam.

The Democratic Party pledges itself to maintain adequate military forces for deterrence and effective support of our international position. But we will also insist on the firm control of specific costs and projects that are essential to ensure that each defense dollar makes a real contribution to national security. Specifically, a Democratic Administration should:

Plan military budgets on the basis of our present needs and commitments, not past practices or force levels;

Stress simplicity and effectiveness in new weapons and stop goldplating and duplication which threatens to spawn a new succession of costly military white elephants; avoid commitment to new weapons unless and until it becomes clear that they are needed;

Reject calls to use the SALT agreement as an excuse for wasteful and dangerous acceleration of our military spending;

Reduce overseas bases and forces; and

Rebuild the morale and military tradition of our armed forces through creative programs to combat drug abuse, racial tensions and eroded pride in service. We will support reforms of the conditions of military life to restore military service as an attractive career for men and women from all segments of our society.

By these reforms and this new approach to budgeting, coupled with a prompt end to U.S. involvement in the war in Indo-China, the military budget can be reduced substantially with no weakening of our national security. Indeed a leaner, better-run system will mean added strength, efficiency and morale for our military forces.

Workers and industries now dependent on defense spending should not be made to pay the price of altering our priorities. Therefore, we pledge reconversion policies and government resources to assure jobs and new industrial opportunities for all those adversely affected by curtailed defense spending.

Draft

We urge abolition of the draft.

Disarmament and Arms Control

The Democratic Party stands for keeping America strong; we reject the concept of unilateral reductions below levels needed for adequate military defense. But effective international arms control and disarmament do not threaten American security; they enhance it.

The last Democratic Administration took the lead in pressing for U.S.-Soviet agreement on strategic arms limitation. The recent SALT agreement is an important and useful first step.

The SALT agreement should be quickly ratified and taken as a starting point for new agreements. It must not be used as an excuse for new "bargaining chip" military programs or the new round of the arms race.

The next Democratic Administration should:

Carry on negotiations to expand the initial SALT agreement to other areas, especially to seek limits to the qualitative arms race and to begin reducing force levels on each side;

Seek a comprehensive ban on all nuclear testing, verified, as SALT will be, by national means;

Press for wide adherence to the Non-Proliferation Treaty, signed in 1968, and for extension of the concept of nuclear-free regions;

Seek ratification of the Protocol on Chemical Warfare without reservations;

In concert with our allies, pursue with the U.S.S.R. mutual force reductions in Europe; and

Widen the range of arms control discussions to include new subjects, such as mutual budget cuts, control of arms transfer to developing countries, restrictions on naval force deployments and other measures to limit conventional forces.

U.S. and the World Community

A new foreign policy must be adequate for a rapidly changing world. We welcome the opportunity this brings for improved relations with the U.S.S.R. and China. But we value even more America's relations with our friends and allies in the Hemisphere, in Western Europe, Japan and other industrialized countries, Israel and the Middle East, and in the developing nations of Asia and Africa. With them, our relations must be conducted on a basis of mutual trust and consultation, seeking to strengthen our ties and to resolve differences on a basis of mutual advantage. Throughout the world, the focus of our policy should be a commitment to peace, self-determination, development, liberty and international cooperation, without distortion in favor of military points of view.

Europe.—Europe's increasing economic and political strength and the growing cooperation and self-confidence of its people have made the Atlantic Alliance a partnership of equals. If we face the challenge of this new relationship, our historic partnership can endure.

The next Democratic Administration should:

Reduce U.S. troop levels in Europe in close consultation with our allies, as part of a program to adjust NATO to changed conditions. What is essential in our relations with the other NATO nations is not a particular troop level, but our continued commitment to collective defense;

Pledge to work in greater cooperation with the European economic communities to ensure that integration in Europe does not serve as a formula for discrimination against American goods and enterprises;

Cease American support for the repressive Greek military government; and

Make the voice of the United States heard in Northern Ireland against violence and terror and against the discrimination, repression and deprivation which brought about that awful civil strife.

We welcome every improvement in relations between the United States and the Soviet Union and every step taken toward reaching vital agreements on trade and other subjects. However, in our pursuit of improved relations, America cannot afford to be blind to the continued existence of serious differences between us. In particular, the United States should, by diplomatic contacts, seek to mobilize world opinion to express concern at the denial to the oppressed peoples of Eastern Europe and the minorities of the Soviet Union, including the Soviet Jews, of the right to practice their religion and culture and to leave their respective countries.

Middle East.—The United States must be unequivocally committed to support of Israel's right to exist within secure and defensible boundaries. Progress toward a negotiated political settlement in the Middle East will permit Israel and her Arab neighbors to live at peace with each other, and to turn their energies to internal development. It will also free the world from the threat of the explosion of Mid-East tensions into world war. In working toward a settlement, our continuing pledge to the security and freedom of Israel must be both clear and consistent.

The next Democratic Administration should:

Make and carry out a firm, long-term public

commitment to provide Israel with aircraft and other military equipment in the quantity and sophistication she needs to preserve her deterrent strength in the face of Soviet arsenaling of Arab threats of renewed war;

Seek to bring the parties into direct negotiations toward a permanent political solution based on the necessity of agreement on secure and defensible national boundaries;

Maintain a political commitment and a military force in Europe and at sea in the Mediterranean ample to deter the Soviet Union from putting unbearable pressure on Israel.

Recognize and support the established status of Jerusalem as the capital of Israel, with free access to all its holy places provided to all faiths. As a symbol of this stand, the U.S. Embassy should be moved from Tel Aviv to Jerusalem; and

Recognize the responsibility of the world community for a just solution to the problems of the Arab and Jewish refugees.

Africa.—The central feature of African politics today is the struggle against racism and colonialism in Southern Africa. There should be no mistake about which side we are on. We stand for full political, civil and economic rights for black and other nonwhite peoples in Southern Africa. We are against white-minority rule. We should not underwrite a return to the interventionism of the past. But we can end United States complicity with such governments.

The focus of America's concern with Africa must be on economic and social development. Economic aid to Africa, without political conditions, should be expanded, and African states assured an adequate share of the aid dollar. Military aid and aid given for military purposes should be sharply reduced.

All military aid to Portugal should be stopped and the Nixon $435 million deal for unneeded Azores bases should be canceled.

U.N. sanctions against the illegal racist regime in Southern Rhodesia should be supported vigorously, especially as they apply to chrome imports.

The U.S. should give full support to U.N. assertion of its control over Namibia (South West Africa), in accordance with the World Court's ruling.

The U.S. should make clear its opposition to the radical totalitarianism of South Africa. The U.S. government should act firmly to press U.S. businesses in South Africa to take measures for the fullest possible justice for their black employees. Blacks should be assigned at all levels to U.S. offices in South Africa, and throughout Africa. The South African sugar quota should be withdrawn.

No U.S. company or its subsidiary should be given U.S. tax credit for taxes paid to white-minority-ruled countries of Africa.

Japan.—Our relations with Japan have been severely strained by a series of "Nixon shocks." We must restore our friendship with Japan, the leading industrial nation of Asia and a growing world power. There are genuine issues between us and Japan in the economic area, but accommodation of trade problems will be greatly eased by an end to the Nixon Administration's calculated insensitivity to Japan and her interests, marked by repeated failures to afford advance warnings, much consultation over sudden shifts in U.S. diplomatic and economic policy that affect Japan.

India, Pakistan and Bangla Desh.—A Democratic Administration should work to restore the damage done to America's friendship with India as a result of the Administration's folly in "tilting" in favor of Pakistan and against Bangla Desh. The alienation by the Nixon Administration of India, the world's largest democracy, and the continued suspension of economic aid to India have seriously damaged the status of the United States in Asia. We pledge generous support for the essential work of reconstruction and reconciliation in Bangla Desh. At the same time, we will maintain friendship and developmental assistance to the "new" Pakistan which has emerged from these sad events.

China.—The beginnings of a new U.S.-China relationship are welcome and important. However, so far, little of substance has changed, and the exaggerated secrecy and rhetoric of the Nixon Administration have produced unnecessary complications in our relationship with our allies and friends in Asia and with the U.S.S.R.

What is needed now is serious negotiation on trade, travel exchanges and progress on more basic issues. The U.S. should take the steps necessary to establish regular diplomatic relations with China.

Other Asian Countries.—The future of Asia will be determined by its people, not by the United States. We should support accommodation and cooperation among all Asian countries and continue to assist in economic development.

Canada.—A Democratic Administration should restore close U.S.-Canadian cooperation and communication, respecting Canada's nationhood and pride. In settling economic issues, we should not compromise our interests; but seek mutually advantageous and equitable solutions. In areas such as environmental protection and social policies, the Americans and Canadians share common problems and we must act together.

Latin America.—The Good Neighbor policy of Franklin Roosevelt and the Alliance for Progress of John Kennedy set still-living goals—insulation from external political conflicts, mutual non-interference in internal affairs, and support for political liberty, social justice and economic progress. The Nixon Administration has lost sight of these goals, and the result is hostility and suspicion of the U.S. unmatched in generations.

The next Democratic Administration should:

Re-establish an inter-American alliance of equal sovereign nations working cooperatively for development;

Sharply reduce military assistance throughout the area;

Strive to deepen the exchange of people and ideas within the Hemisphere;

Take account of the special claims of democratically-elected governments on our resources and sympathy;

Pursue a policy of non-intervention by military means in domestic affairs of Latin American nations;

Recognize that, while Cuba must not be permitted to become a foreign military base, after 13 years of boycott, crisis and hostility, the time has come to re-examine our relations with Cuba and to seek a way to resolve this cold war confrontation on mutually acceptable terms; and

Re-establish a U.S.-Mexico border commission, with Mexican-American representatives, to develop a comprehensive program to desalinate and eradicate pollution of the Colorado River and other waterways flowing into Mexico, and conduct substantial programs to raise the economic level on both sides of the border. This should remove the economic reasons which contribute to illegal immigration and discourage run-away industries. In addition, language requirements for citizenship should be removed.

The United Nations. The U.N. cannot solve all the great political problems of our time, but in an increasingly interdependent world, a world body is essential and its potential must be increasingly relied upon.

The next Democratic Administration should:

Re-establish the U.N. as a key forum for international activity, and assign representatives with the highest qualification for diplomacy;

Give strong executive branch leadership for U.S. acceptance of its obligations for U.N. financing, while renegotiating arrangement for sharing U.N. costs;

Abide by the binding U.N. Security Council decision on Rhodesia sanctions, and support U.N. peace-keeping efforts;

Work for development of enforceable world law as a basis for peace, and endorse repeal of the Connally Reservation on U.S. acceptance of World Court jurisdiction; and

Work to involve the U.N. increasingly on the complex technical and social problems such as pollution, health, communication, technology and population policy, which are worldwide in scope and demand a worldwide approach, and help provide the means for these U.N. efforts and for U.N. economic development functions.

International Economic Policy

In a prosperous economy, foreign trade has benefits for virtually everyone. For the consumer, it means lower prices and a wider choice of goods. For the worker and the businessman, it means new jobs and new markets. For nations, it means greater efficiency and growth.

But in a weak economy—with over five million men and women out of work—foreign imports bring hardships to many Americans. The automobile or electrical worker, the electronics technician, the small businessman—for them, and millions of others, foreign competition coinciding with a slack economy has spelled financial distress. Our national commitment to liberal trade policies takes its toll when times are bad, but yields its benefits when the economy is fully employed.

The Democratic Party proposes no retreat from this commitment. Our international economic policy should have these goals: To expand jobs and business opportunities in this country and to establish two-way trade relations with other nations. To do this, we support the following policies:

End the high-unemployment policy of the Nixon Administration. When a job is available for everyone who wants to work, imports will no longer be a threat. Full employment is a realistic goal, it is a goal which has been attained under Democratic Administrations, and it is a goal we intend to achieve again;

Adopt broad programs to ease dislocations and relieve the hardship of workers injured by foreign competition;

Seek higher labor standards in the advanced nations where productivity far outstrips wage rates, thus providing unfair competition to American workers and seek to limit harmful flows of American capital which exploit both foreign and American workers;

Adhere to liberal trade policies, but we should oppose actions and policies which harm American workers through unfair exploitation of labor abroad and the encouragement of American capital to run after very low wage opportunities for quick profits that will damage the economy of the United States and further weaken the dollar;

Negotiate orderly and reciprocal reductions of trade barriers to American products. Foreign nations with access to our markets should no longer be permitted to fence us out of theirs;

Support reform of the international monetary system. Increased international reserves, provision for large margins in foreign exchange fluctuations and strengthened institutions for the coordination of national economic policies can free our government and others to achieve full employment;

Support efforts to promote exports of American farm products; and

Develop ground rules for pollution controls with our industrialized trading partners so that no country gains competitive advantage at the expense of the environment.

Developing Nations

Poverty at home or abroad is part of a common problem. Great and growing income gaps among nations are no more tenable than such gaps among groups in our own country. We should remain committed to U.S. support for economic and social development of countries in need. Old ways of providing aid must be revised—to reduce U.S. involvement in administration; to encourage other nations to contribute jointly with us. But funding must be adequate to help poor countries achieve accelerated rates of growth.

Specifically, the next Democratic Administration should support:

Provision of more assistance through international organizations, along with measures to strengthen the development agencies of the U.N.;

A curtailment of military aid;

Improved access to the markets of industrial nations for the products of the developing countries;

A greater role in international monetary affairs for poor countries; in particular distributing the new Special Drawing Rights in support of the poor countries; and

A fair share for poor countries in the resources of the seabeds.

The Methods and Structures of U.S. Foreign and Military Policy

The needed fundamental reordering of U.S. foreign and military policy calls for changes in the structure of decision-making, as well as in particular policies. This means:

Greater sharing with Congress of real decisions on issues of war and peace, and providing Congress with the information and resources needed for a more responsible role;

More honest information policies, beginning with a fundamental reform of the document classification system and including regular press conferences by the President, his cabinet and senior advisors;

Ending the present drastic overbalance in favor of military opinion by redefining the range of agencies and points of view with a proper claim to be heard on foreign and military policies;

Subjecting the military budget to effective civilian control and supervision;

Establishing effective executive control and legislative oversight of the intelligence agencies;

Ending political domination of USIA's reporting and Peace Corps dedication and, in general, making it clear that the White House understands the crucial distinction between dissent and disloyalty; and

Urging the appointment of minority Americans to top positions of ambassadors and diplomats, to let the world know that America is a multi-racial nation and proud of it.

IX. THE PEOPLE AND THE GOVERNMENT

"Our people are dispirited because there seems to be no way by which they can call to office a government which will cut the ties to the past, meeting the challenge of leadership and begin a new era of bold action.

"Bold action by innovative government—responsive to the people's needs and desires—is essential to the achievement of our national hopes." —Leonard Woodcock, President, United Auto Workers, New York Hearing, June 22, 1972.

Representative democracy fails when citizens cannot know:

When public officials ignore or work against the principles of due process;

How their public officials conduct the public's business;

Whether public officials have personal financial stakes in the very matters they are legislating, administering or enforcing; and

What special interest pressures are being exerted on public officials by lobbyists.

Today, it is imperative that the Democratic Party again take the lead in reforming those practices that limit the responsiveness of government and remove it from the control of the people.

Seniority

The seniority system is one of the principal reasons that party platforms—and parties themselves—have lost meaning and importance in our political life. Seniority has weakened Congress as an effective and responsive institution in a changing society. It has crippled effective Congressional leadership and made it impossible to present and enact a coherent legislative program. It has permitted the power of the Democratic majority to be misused and abused. It has stifled initiative and wasted the talents of many members by making length of service the *only* criterion for selection to the vital positions of Congressional power and leadership.

We, therefore, call on the Democratic Members of the Congress to use the powers inherent in their House and Senate caucuses to implement the policies and programs of the National Democratic Party. It is specifically not intended that Democratic members be directed how to vote on issues on the floor. But, in order that they be responsive to broad party policies and programs, we nonetheless call upon Members of Congress to:

Choose committee chairmen as provided in existing caucus rules and procedures, but by separate open ballot; chair-people should be chosen who will carry out party policies and programs which come within the jurisdiction of their committees;

Assure that Democratic programs and policies receive full and fair consideration and are brought to a vote in each house;

Discipline committee members, including chairpeople, who refuse to comply with caucus instructions regarding the reporting of legislation from their committees; and

Withhold any seniority benefits from a Member of Congress who fails to overtly identify with the Democratic organization in his state which is recognized by the National Democratic Party.

Secrecy

Public business should be transacted publicly, except when national security might be jeopardized.

To combat secrecy in government, we call on the Democratic Members of Congress and state legislatures to:

Enact "open meetings" legislation, barring the practice of conducting the public business behind closed doors. This should include so-called mark-up sessions by legislative committees, but should allow for exceptions involving national security and invasions of privacy. To the extent possible, the same principle should apply to the Executive Branch;

Assure that all committee and floor votes are taken in open session, recorded individually for each legislator; record caucus votes, and make all of these available to the public;

Urge reservation of executive privilege for the President alone;

Urge that the judgment in the U.S. Senate in a contested election case be rendered in open Senate session;

Immediately strengthen the Federal Freedom of Information Act. Congress should improve its oversight of Executive secrecy by requiring federal agencies to report annually on every refusal to grant information requested under the Act. Citizens should have full recourse to the courts to deal with violation or circumvention of the Act. It should be amended to allow courts to review the reasonableness of a claim of executive privilege; and

Administer the security system so as to limit the number of officials who can make a document secret, and provide for frequent declassification of documents. Congress should be given the means to obtain documents necessary to fulfill its responsibilities.

We also call on the Democratic Members of

the House of Representatives to take action through their caucus to end the "closed rule," which is used to prevent amendments and votes on vital tax matters and other important issues, and we call on the Democratic Members of the Senate to liberalize the cloture rule, which is used to prevent votes in that body, so that after full and extensive debate majority rule can prevail.

Administrative Agencies

There is, among more and more citizens, a growing revolt against large, remote and impersonal government agencies that are not responsive to human needs. We pledge to build a representative process into the Executive Branch, so that individuals affected by agency programs can be involved in formulating, implementing and revising them. This requires a basic restructuring of procedures—public hearings before guidelines and regulations are handed down, the processing of citizen complaints, the granting of citizen standing and the recovery of litigation fees for those who win suits against the government.

We recommend these specific changes in the rule making and adjudication process of the federal government:

There should be no non-written communication between an agency and outside parties about pending decisions. All written communications should promptly be made a part of the public record;

All communications between government employees and outside parties about possible future action should be made a part of the public record;

All government employees involved in rule-making and adjudication should be subject to conflict of interest laws;

The Justice Department should make available to the public any consent decree 90 days prior to its submission to court, to allow any interested party to comment on it to the Court; and

The Justice Department should report to Congress each year, to explain its action on major suits.

In addition, we must more effectively protect consumer rights before the government. The consumer must be made an integral part of any relationship between government and institutions (public or private) at every level of proceedings whether formal or informal.

A Democratic Administration would instruct all federal agencies to identify American Indians, Asian Americans and Spanish-speaking Americans in separate categories in all statistical data that note racial or ethnic heritage. Only in this way can these Americans be assured their rights under federal programs.

Finally, in appropriate geographical areas, agencies of the federal government should be equipped to conduct business in such a fashion that Spanish-speaking citizens should not be hampered by language difficulties.

Conflict of Interest

The public interest must not be sacrificed to personal gain. Therefore, we call for legislation requiring full disclosure of the financial interests of Members of Congress and their staffs and high officials of the Executive Branch and independent agencies. Disclosure should include business directorships held and associations with individuals or firms lobbying or doing business with the government.

Further, Congress should forbid its members to engage in the practice of law or to retain association with a law firm while in office. Legislators serving on a committee whose jurisdiction includes matters in which they have a financial interest should divest themselves of the interest or resign from the committee.

Campaign Finance

A total overhaul of the present system of financing elections is a national necessity. Candidates should not be dependent on large contributors who seek preferential treatment. We call for Congressional action to provide for public financing of more election costs by 1974. We recommend a statutory ceiling on political gifts at a reasonable limit. Publicly owned communications facilities such as television, radio and the postal service should be made available, but on a limited basis, to candidates for federal office.

Regulation of Lobbyists

We also call upon Congress to enact rigorous lobbying disclosure legislation, to replace the present shockingly ineffective law. There should be full disclosure of all organized lobbying—including names of lobbyists, identity of the source of funds, total receipts and expenditures, the nature of the lobbying operation and specific target issues or bills. Reports should be filed at least quarterly, with criminal penalties for late filing. Lobbying regulations should cover attempts to influence both legislative and Executive Branch decisions. The legislation should specifically cover lobbying appeals in subscription publications.

As a safeguard, we urge the availability of subpoena and cease-and-desist powers to enforce these conflict of interest, campaign financing and lobby disclosure laws. We also affirm the citizens' right to seek enforcement through the courts, should public officials fail in enforcement.

Taking Part in the Political Process

The Presidential primary system today is an unacceptable patchwork. The Democratic Party supports federal laws that will embody the following principles:

Protect the opportunity for less-known candidates to build support;

Establish uniform ground rules;

Reduce the cost of primary campaigns;

Promote maximum voter turnout;

Ensure that issues are clarified;

Foster the selection of nominees with broad popular support to assure the continued viability of the two party system;

Ensure every citizen the ability to take part in the Presidential nomination process; and

Equalize the ability of people from all income levels to participate in the political decision-making processes of the Democratic Party, by providing financial assistance through party funds for delegates, alternates and standing committee members to state and national conventions.

We also call for full and uniform enforcement of the Voting Rights Act of 1965. But further steps are needed to end all barriers to participation in the political process:

Universal voter registration by post card;

Bilingual means of registration and voting;

Bilingual voter education programs;

Liberalized absentee voting;

Lower minimum age requirements for service in the Senate and House of Representatives;

Minimum residency requirements of 30 days for all elections, including primaries;

Student voting where they attend schools;

Study and review of the Hatch Act, to see what can be done to encourage good citizenship and reasonable participation by government employees;

Full home rule for the District of Columbia, including an elected mayor-city council government, broad legislative power, control over appointments, automatic federal payment and voting representation in both Houses of Congress;

No discriminatory districting;

We favor a Constitutional change to abolish the Electoral College and to give every voter a direct and equal voice in Presidential elections. The amendment should provide for a run-off election, if no candidate received more than 40 percent of the popular vote;

Early ratification of the equal rights amendment to the Constitution;

Appointment of women to positions of top responsibilities in all branches of the federal government, to achieve an equitable ratio of women and men;

Inclusion of women advisors in equitable ratios on all government studies, commissions and hearings; and

Laws authorizing federal grants on a matching basis for financing state commissions of the status of women.

These changes in themselves will not solve the problems of government for all time. As our society changes, so must the ways we use to make government more responsive to the people. Our challenge, today, as always, is to ensure that politics and institutions belong in spirit and in practice to all the people of our nation. In 1972, Americans are deciding that they want their country back again.

People's Platform 1972

PREAMBLE

Though a leader in the world in wealth and technology and possessed of vast resources sufficient to give—right now—an abundant life to all our people, our nation is in crisis. Our Black, Spanish-speaking and Indian citizens are victims of institutionalized discrimination and oppression. Our workers, small home owners, small business people and family farmers are squeezed by inflation and unequal taxation. Our women, gay people, young people and old people are still denied their full rights. In short, our institutions have become perverted, our natural resources have been raped and polluted because private profit for the few has been given priority over the fulfillment of the basic needs of the people. And, because of this profit motive which underlies all of our policies, we have become increasingly the object of fear and distrust among the people of the world.

We recognize that the fulfillment of the basic needs common to all of us is frustrated by the big-finance, big-corporation, big-military establishment which maintains its control through its servants in the Demo-publican Party and which constantly tightens its stranglehold over our foreign and domestic policies and our very lives. This hold can only be broken if we the people, in our neighborhoods, in our schools, in our workplace, begin to organize our power to take back control of the institutions which affect the nature of our lives and the future of our nation.

Since we believe that the present political parties of the United States neither represent or reflect the political, economic and social hopes of a large segment of people in this country, we shall unite into a new party for positive change which will ensure a creative future of our people.

This new party, born out of the experience in struggle of the growing peoples' movement will be called the People's Party. Now in its formative period, the party seeks to unite all people in the various aspects of the people's movement—red, yellow, black, brown and white, regardless of age and sexual persuasion—into one mass party on the left. We shall organize, not merely for political electoral activity, but for the on-going struggle for the radical changes needed to assure the beneficial and creative rather than destructive use of our tremendous resources—natural, technological and human.

We advocate a complete program of action which will ensure for all people the full measure of political, social and economic justice which has been our nation's promise unfulfilled for two centuries. We must establish for ourselves a position of honor and harmony with all of humanity.

(The following platform was written and adopted by the over 200 delegates who attended the July 27–30, 1972 National Convention of the People's Party in St. Louis. The same convention nominated Dr. Benjamin Spock and Julius Hobson to be the party's Presidential and Vice-Presidential candidates.)

AGEISM

Ageism is an attitude institutionalized in our society which discriminates against individuals solely on the basis of age. Under the present system, young people and senior citizens are denied their basic rights and opportunities and often are treated more like property than like human beings. The People's Party believes that peoples' rights and potentials should never be determined on the basis of one's age. Therefore, we support the following demands:

For Young People—

1) The right to vote and the right to hold electoral office, beginning at whatever age an individual decides to accept those responsibilities.

2) The right to be independent of one's parents if one so desires.

3) the full rights and responsibilities of citizenship.

4) The right to control those institutions that control their lives. Especially we support the right of young people to have an equal say with parents, teachers and administrators in their education.

5) The right to equal treatment under the law in the courts of the land. Young people must be treated with respect rather than as property.

6) The right to determine their own life style as full citizens.

For Senior Citizens—

1) The right to work productively, if they so desire. An end to mandatory retirement.

2) The right to guaranteed annual income, providing supplementary income, if necessary.

3) The right to make decisions about how one will spend the remaining years of one's life without interference from doting children or the law.

4) The right to control those institutions which control their lives.

5) The right to decent housing, without the burden of property tax, and the right to good transportation, without the burden of high costs.

CULTURE AND THE ARTS

A Department of Culture and the Arts is as relevant to our society as is a Department of Agriculture. In peace or at war, in prosperity or depression, all the arts must be a part of the fabric of our society. All people should have the opportunity to participate in art, especially in light of the increasing leisure time for such activities. Our music, dance, poetry, fiction, visual and plastic arts, horticulture, craft, drama—all reflect, interpret or shape our political and social system. Our artists interpret and give form to the spirit of our society. The society, in turn, draws its moral and ethical sustenance from the expressions of its artists and inventors.

The United States, far from leading the world in the arts that are essential to the survival and well-being of the spirit of the people, lags far behind many other countries. This neglect is visible in the unrelieved barrenness of most public buildings, a significant factor contributing to the psychic breakdown in many of our urban and suburban areas. Israel, though living under the siege mentality perpetuated by its ruling class, manages to spend $1.35 per capita per year for the arts, Canada $1.40, Sweden and Austria $2.00 and Holland $3.69. The United States, the richest country in the world, spends only seven cents per capita.

Another factor contributing to the low state of our arts is the notion of professionalism as defined by the ruling economic powers which maintain strict control over our culture and continually create an elitist division between the paid and unpaid, producers and consumers.

The People's Party, therefore, proposes that:

1) We begin to recognize the achievements of our creative artists, as well as to stress the importance of art as an area of activity for all people and to encourage them by providing opportunities for their meaningful contributions to the society.

2) We establish a Department of Culture and the Arts, headed by a secretary at the cabinet level, which would be responsible for the creation of vastly increased opportunities for artists to do work without competition, censorship or discrimination in subject matter.

3) The department should encourage and fund local culture groups in all the arts.

4) The department commission works commemorating people-designated occasions.

5) The department provide a clearing house of artists available to offer skills to communities.

We want to de-professionalize the arts in order to encourage the creative potential in every individual, to stimulate creativity in everyday life by eliminating traditions and restraints placed so artificially upon the arts, to get away from com-

mercialism in art and to "bring art into the streets." Our long-range goal is to make America beautiful once again and to provide a visually healthy environment for present and future generations.

Ecology and Environment

Life on earth is a delicate and complex interaction among all living things and the materials of the earth. Technology, by reordering these natural relationships, interferes with the life-supporting processes of the earth. A small technology, one which is carefully controlled, can draw upon the environment while preserving the balance of natural systems which support life, including human life. Our technology, however, is neither small or controlled; it has grown to the point of affecting vital processes over the entire planet. We have seized the immediate benefits of technology without accepting the responsibility for maintaining a well-balanced ecosystem favorable to human life. This now poses the serious and imminent threat that the ecological system will break down, triggering catastrophes of human suffering and social collapse.

The issue is one of such importance that we must begin now to change the attitude of our society toward the question of consumption. Great consumption is negative; it results in the gross exploitation of nature and lack of regard for the land and human life. Produce less, consume less and there will be less demand, less production. Education of the public is our immediate concern.

The United States has to a great extent created and controlled modern technology; it also bears a responsibility for the misuse of this technology, from air pollution to depletion of non-renewable resources. It is incumbent upon the United States, therefore, to take the lead in regulating technology and assuring the ecological balance upon which we depend. This most difficult and urgent job will require immediate and forceful action, including a change in our value system, a shift from exploitative goals and considerable rearrangement of our social structures (e.g., government agencies) and our daily lives (e.g., transportation).

The People's Party believes that technology can serve without destroying precious human life-support systems; that, if controlled and harmonized with nature's uncompromising demands, it can well be expected to transform the conditions of human life with an increasing quality; that, without intelligent management, it may well destroy human life.

The following steps, as a minimum, must be taken to achieve favorable balances in ecological relationships:

1) Control over natural resources must shift from profit-centered organizations to community-centered motivation. Policy decisions must place community well-being above the profits of corporations. Quality of life must be redefined and based on the right of all living things to eat, breathe and live in health with the assurance that they are not being poisoned. We must maximize human potential to the fullest.

2) New national policies must eliminate the widespread misuse of our resources. Renewable resources (plant and animal life, rivers, atmosphere, etc.) must be conserved and guarded from misuse. Non-renewable resources (mineral, fuel, etc.) must be extracted without destroying or upsetting the natural ecological balance in the area and must be used under strict controls reflecting the real needs of the community. We demand the immediate abolition of strip-mining and the reclamation of all stripped lands. This reclamation must be paid for by the corporations which through their greed have "eaten up" the land.

3) A center for Ecological Research and Action must be established and charged with the three-fold task of:

a. Researching areas, such as solar energy; air, water, noise and land pollution; subsoil, mineral and water rights; collecting data on pollution-related health, deaths and illnesses.

b. Utilizing computer simulation techniques of decision analysis, such as now used in war, business management and other complex systems guidance and control processes. Thus, it will be possible to analyze trends in the earth's ecosystem and to prescribe sensible and appropriate remedial action.

c. Preparation and dissemination of the necessary materials to provide the people with continuing education in ecological matters. And development and implementation of the necessary technological bases for improving and maintaining the environment.

4) Our energy policy must change. Presently, it assumes that the need for more and more energy to run an enlarged and exploitive technology is inexhaustible. Such thinking lies behind many unsound decisions, like increasing our min-

ing and consumption of coal and oil, damming more rivers for electrical power and building nuclear reactors and other energy systems that may well prove to be unsafe. Instead, we must assume the need for sound ecological practices. This means adjusting fuel consumption, halting construction of fission reactors and other energy systems until satisfactory systems are developed in terms of safety; stopping dam construction where undesirable ecological damage would result and sponsoring research to find better means of generating and using power. It will be necessary to reorder our society to get along on the energy which serves real community needs instead of building excessive weaponry, lighting unnecessary neon signs and running over-powered cars. We can make do with far less energy and at the same time preserve a favorable ecological balance and achieve an increasingly better quality of living. We call for an urban rapid transit system to be constructed and operated free to riders in order to encourage the drastic reduction of automobile use. Community advisory committees should help plan the routes to avoid unnecessary disruption of communities.

5) Though we do not accept the contention that population growth is responsible for ecological imbalance, a program aimed at a reasonable quality of life must be undertaken, including steps to voluntary control of U.S. population growth and steps to aid and encourage other countries in this respect. To this end, we propose the following:

a. Community education programs on sex and reproduction.

b. Publicity about contraceptives devices and instruction in their use. Contraceptives should be available at no cost to those unable to afford them.

c. Funding should be made immediately available for research into safer and more efficient methods of birth control.

d. All laws prohibiting safe abortions on request should be eliminated. Abortions should be provided free to anyone requesting them, also sterilization. However, we wish to make clear that we condone no efforts to force a person into an abortion or a sterilization as a requirement for receiving welfare assistance.

e. Under U.N., not U.S., control, we should develop a system of population control as a model for all countries. The population growth analysis of world problems is a smokescreen used to blame human fertility for the disasters being created by a capitalist elite. Population is not the problem; but congestion (i.e., population density created in certain places by capitalistic policies) leads to ecological problems. Population control policies, such as "zero population growth," are invariably aimed at lower class and Third World Peoples. The unstated racist assumption behind population growth analysis is that the average white nuclear family is the model for growth stability.

If the emphasis is that population is a key problem leading to ecological disaster (i.e., Paul Ehrlich and company), then the logical conclusion is not voluntary birth control but involuntary control—again aimed at "the most irresponsibly fertile" sector (meaning the lower classes and the Third World, at home and abroad). The People's Party categorically denies this emphasis on population as the problem.

When a society develops in such a way that it satisfies the physical, social, economic and psycho-cultural needs of the populace, population growth invariably stabilizes itself. It is poverty and oppression, not sexuality, that are the environmental stimuli to population growth. Therefore, population growth must be dealt with not by genocidal control policies, but through the destruction of poverty and oppression.

6) We must restructure the economy to meet requirements for a balanced ecosystem:

a. Non-biodegradable, toxic or radioactive chemicals released into the environment must be kept within strict tolerance limits until such time as it is possible to limit or prohibit their release completely. This means an immediate crackdown on enforcement of such laws as the Clean Water Act of 1899. The crackdown should begin with the largest industries first, right down to the smallest.

b. All reusable materials must be recycled on a sound ecological and economical basis. All containers should be reusable or recyclable. In recycling, most companies will save money on not using and developing raw materials. Some of this money should be passed on to the people recycling (collecting, transporting, etc.) the material so that recycling efforts will not have to rely solely on volunteer help and will, thus, encourage a more effective job. This will decrease waste and pollution and slow down our consumption of raw materials.

c. New products and drugs must satisfy improved health and safety standards before being cleared for sale. This places community safety before community profits. Also, steps must be taken to prevent the marketing and sale of products which are inadequately tested.

7) Government environmental agencies must serve the community:

a. The U.S. Atomic Energy Commission should be reconstructed as the U.S. Energy Commission. The responsibilities of such an agency would be to deal solely with the development and use of energy.

b. The development and enforcement of safety and ecological standards should be the responsibility of the Environmental Protection Agency.

c. All government construction (including the Army Corps of Engineers' projects) must receive community approval in the place projected for the construction.

d. Information gathered by government regulatory agencies must be made freely available to the public. The public must also have access to information on ecological and health consequences of any product and in decision-making with respect to policies of government agencies.

Economics

Despite the fact that we have developed the productive capacity to put people on the moon, and despite the fact that the output per person hour of American workers has grown more than 7.5 per cent in the last five years, the economic condition of the American people is degenerating.

Our cities are in decay. Twenty-five per cent of our population lives below the poverty level. Unemployment is running rampant. For every person unemployed there are ten who are underemployed. Even those who are fully employed are forced to accept dehumanizing conditions on the job and inadequate wages because of the constant threat of unemployment. Our wages are under "voluntary" control while prices are spiraling.

Third World people and women especially suffer from political, social and economic oppression, and our Third World communities are forced to bear the brunt of an economic system in decline.

The ownership of our economy has fallen into a few hands (i.e., 1.7 per cent of the adult population owns more than 82 per cent of the publicly held shares in American corporations), which, in pursuit of personal profits, have resorted more and more to planned obsolescence and the production of useless goods. This wastes our resources, poisons our environment and produces a sense of frustration on the part of working people who can no longer take pride in their work.

Although the U.S. government has spent a trillion dollars on armaments since 1945, the nation is more insecure than ever as a result of the proliferation of nuclear weapons and the threat of nuclear destruction.

By defending and encouraging growing investments abroad by U.S. corporations (which grew by $32.4 billion in 1970), the U.S. ruling elite is responsible for the impoverishment of other peoples, turning the people of the Third World against the U.S. We have been drawn by that same lying elite into foreign wars which support dictatorships and oligarchies which represent only a tiny percentage of the world's population.

The People's Party sees the mounting problems and the growing personal alienation that afflicts our country as a manifestation of the conflicts of interests between the people and the power and profit interests of the handful who control our entire economy.

Long Range Program:

We, therefore, put forward as our long range program the transformation of the economic system to let people control the institutions that affect their lives. The decision-making power for the nature and amount of things produced must pass from the owners of the large corporations to the workers and the communities affected by their production. And, the economy must be organized to improve the standard of living and the quality of human life to the highest level technologically possible. Wealth and production must be redistributed and adverse conditions that have been produced abroad by American corporate capitalism must be alleviated. The economy must be not only just humane, but also must conform to the ecological constraints dictated by the biological and physical order of this planet. To this end we propose the following long range program:

1) The major economy of this country should become the property of the people collectively, exercising their ownership through democratic institutions with adequate safeguards for local autonomy, the exact details of said institutions should be determined by a new constitutional convention.

2) Corporations should be reconstituted as public trusts with their day to day operations controlled by the worker, with governing bodies composed of workers and representatives responsible to the people.

3) Public funds should subsidize companies to produce goods needed by the community, yet which need external financial support, such as public transportation, medical services, education, non-commercial television, radio and newspapers, local housing, etc.

4) Welfare programs for the rich in the form of federal crop subsidies for wealthy farmers and special tax breaks for the big corporations must be eliminated, along with the present dehumanizing welfare system with its racist and piecemeal approach. All persons must have a reasonable base income. A maximum annual personal wealth should also be established to protect against excessive concentrations of wealth.

5) We must reorder our priorities to provide an adequate supply of all the necessities of life—health care, shelter, food, clothing and education —should be immediately made available to all. The cost should come out of the commonwealth of the people (represented by an appropriate tax system) which represents the wealth of the people held in common as the people's heritage.

6) Concerning the federal tax system:

All taxes should be levied in a simple and direct manner, understandable to all, and without manipulation, special privileges, or fraud.

The federal and state taxes shall no longer be taken involuntarily out of pay checks.

The establishment of a minimum income ($6,500 per year for a family of four) and a maximum wealth ($50,000 per year) and a steeply progressive income and wealth tax should apply in order to help break down the existing concentration of economic power. Property and inheritance should be assessed as wealth. These should be the only forms of taxes by all levels of government.

To equitably meet the social needs of all the people, tax revenues should be distributed to the different levels of the community on a per capita basis.

7) On the subject of large-scale coordination of a populist economic system, we propose that there should be a people's national planning and review board, directly elected by and subject to recall by the people, which would provide broad economic parameters within which regional and local development would take place, using an efficient and responsible allocation of resources, consistent with ecological balance.

Emergency Program:

The people must be mobilized immediately to head off the developing crisis and to fight for immediate aims under the present system. Only in this way can we defeat the enemies of the people and develop the institutions and attitudes necessary for popular control. Therefore, we seek to mobilize people around the following emergency program:

1) An end to the wage freeze; replacement of the phony price freeze by energetic government action combined with a general offensive of labor and consumers to roll back the inflated prices fixed by the multi-national corporations and to raise the wages of labor to a level that can support a standard of living worthy of a nation that can put people on the moon.

2) Tax reform to lift the burden of taxation from the backs of the poor and people of ordinary means and to increase the taxation of the super-rich and the greedy corporations. In particular, we oppose the sales taxes. And we uphold such proposals as:

   a. Plugging the tax loopholes by which the super-rich escape taxation (i.e., tax incentives for U.S. companies investing overseas).

   b. A progressive tax on wealth.

   c. An excess profits tax.

   d. As a transitional step to a one-tax system, tax relief up to $30,000 real value on owner's first residence. A proportionate tax reduction for renters should also be developed.

   e. Abolish tax allowances such as the oil depletion allowance.

   f. Abolish capital gains taxes and tax capital gains as income.

3) A federal job administration should assure a socially useful job at decent pay to every inhabitant of our country who wishes to work. This can be achieved through federal spending on the scale of total war, spending directed instead for a coordinated program of inexpensive housing, mass transportation, health facilities, pollution control, etc.

4) An end to further investment abroad by U.S. corporations (over 17 per cent of whose investments last year were in foreign countries). A tax on income of existing U.S. corporations located in other countries and a tax, at the highest income rate, on all income received by U.S. residents from foreign investments. These private investments not only exploit the workers of other countries, but aggravate international tensions and bring unemployment and economic hardship to workers at home as well. We support, also, the concept that private investments in other countries are the investor's own risk and should be controlled by the people in those countries. We also encourage maximum trade between this country and other countries on an equitable basis.

5) Decent payment and treatment for those who cannot work or cannot find work must be achieved. In particular:

   a. We support the National Welfare Rights Organization's proposal for a $6,500 guaranteed annual income for a family of four.

   b. Welfare should be paid directly through the federal government.

   c. We oppose forced labor at welfare wages.

   d. We support the strengthening and increasing of unemployment insurance coverage.

6) There should be a 30-hour work week for a minimum of 40 hours worth of pay.

7) Transferable, vested retirement rights should be funded by corporations.

8) There should be free mass transportation, child care centers and medical care.

9) The people should participate in making up the federal budget and full publicity concerning that budget should be made available.

10) We support unconditionally all presently existing alternative economic survival programs.

To eradicate the U.S. empire, we demand the nationalization by the people of the means of production, distribution and communication. Specifically, we propose that this nationalization begin with the largest U.S. corporation and continue until people's control is a reality.

We serve warning on the wealthy handful who control our economy that if this very minimal program to head off the present crisis is answered by sabotage and non-cooperation by great corporations, we will not hesitate to give this the rebuff it deserves by encouraging the seizure of property of the corporations by the people.

EDUCATION

The public schools of the United States serve the interests of the ruling class of the nation, the governing class of the rich and the powerful. Our schools perpetuate the myth of an open, free society. In practice, however, the schools are instruments of class, sexual and racial oppression. They also teach misconceptions of the role of the United States in the world. They oppress the working class by reinforcing class differences through elaborate and subtle tracking systems. This system offers the students limited choices in their learning experiences. Each student's choices are determined by that student's race, class and sex. The schools oppress racial minorities by supressing and distorting the true heritage of these students as well as by outright discrimination. They oppress men and women by teaching narrow and sexist role models. And they, like our other social institutions, turn those oppressed by the system against each other. In whatever direction the tracks lead students, there is an attempt to mold them into passive, obedient, interchangeable consumers and workers. The process ignores the individual differences and needs and stifles joyful and creative growth. To create an authentic and relevant education we must reverse this process so that it moves toward educational self-determination for young people. Education should inspire people to *be* more, rather than to have more. A new era in education geared to the above goal will profoundly change the character of our country.

Compulsory Education—

Compulsory education is the strength of the stranglehold of the traditional school over the student, stifling creativity, independent thinking and even learning itself. Compulsory education must be abolished. At the same time, young people must be protected from exploitation and guaranteed their right to an education. Public school must be "disestablished" as the state of education for American youth because the power of law is being used to force young people into institutions whose major purpose is social manipulation. This step must be taken if we wish to establish a funda-

mental dynamic for change in education soon enough to meet the real needs of young people currently in school. Young people must have the right to work and the right to receive money for the work of obtaining an education.

Community Control—

Schools should be subject to community control. Only general school policies affecting the school system as a whole should be set by state or local school boards. Individual schools should be directed by a board of students, parents and staff (one third for each segment), democratically elected by their peers. Teacher qualifications, hiring and firing should be determined by the individual boards. The administration should serve to coordinate the policies of the student-teacher-parent board. Major decisions should be made by these interest groups and the power of administrators should be limited to making recommendations. The board must guarantee the rights reiterated throughout this platform.

If quality education is to be achieved in this country, students, teachers, parents and administrators need to communicate more about the educational process. Each group must have power over the aspects of the process which are relevant to it. The schools should be more fully integrated into the communities and should make facilities available for the use of the groups in the community.

Statement on Bussing—

The People's Party supports bussing to achieve quality education and racial balance. But we recognize bussing as merely a temporary measure, contingent upon equal financing in the school. Our greatest problem with bussing is that it is opposed to the concept of community control. Therefore, we propose that programs of bussing be approved by the affected communities, both black and white. In cases where bussing is approved, we support pairing of districts and bussing of people to the community control board meetings.

Student Rights—

The People's Party supports the following Bill of Rights for Students:

1) An education which meets individual needs and allows a person to grow at her or his own pace. This must be the highest priority. Young people must be free from adult controls so they can adapt in authentic and viable ways to a

rapidly changing reality and through this adaptive process build a civilization that will be more humane.

2) Democratically elected student courts and trials by peers, not administrative hearings. Discipline should not be punitive; rather, it should be viewed in terms of a solution to a problem. If both the jury and the student feel the problem is no longer solvable by them, the case should be referred to the bipartite board—50 per cent students, 50 per cent teachers.

3) Student and parent presence at all hearing procedures, if the student so desires.

4) Student's right to counsel of her or his own choice.

5) An end to corporal punishment.

6) The right to privacy, including a no access or no search policy for individual lockers, as well as an adamant prohibition of electronic surveillance equipment. We call for prohibition of medical tests used as a tool of oppression by school authorities; no test may be performed without the consent of the student and her or his legal guardian.

7) Recognition as equal members of society and protection of students' dignity as individuals.

8) Immunity from prosecution for violation of rules that either the elected bipartite board or an elected student board has not passed or made public.

9) The right to due process of law, to freedom of assembly, to form and join political organizations and unions and the concomitant right to strike. Students must also have a right to free access to information on all aspects of a question. Leafletting on school grounds should never be prohibited.

10) The right of all cultural and ethnic minorities to have their heritage included in the curriculum in an accurate and dignified fashion, including if necessary bilingual and non-standard education as determined by the community.

11) Education should be a universal right, in other words available to those who have been traditionally excluded from public schools due to mental retardation and other handicaps.

12) Students of all grades should have access to all books and materials in the library as well as access to other educational resources (e.g., advanced educational software and electronic hardware resource centers).

The People's Party recognizes that no public school system can be considered independent of the social forces that act upon it. Even if a single school system decided to eliminate all formal tracking, the entrance policies of universities and the hiring policies of industries would impose an informal system of tracking on the schools. Nevertheless, the People's Party must insist that the schools actively resist tracking and keep educational options open to all from kindergarten through life-long education. The specific instruments of tracking, such as grades, advanced classes, achievement and standardized tests, teacher recommendations, etc., must be dropped since they serve only to reproduce class distinctions and raise fallacious notions of "ability" and "failure" which deprive students of the right to explore their own potentials.

The classroom itself should be directed through a lateral transaction of experiences shared by teachers and students reciprocally and not by the administration or school board. We can tolerate no censorship of any form at any level. Opportunities to hear all sides of an issue must be constantly available.

We encourage experimental and innovative teaching methods and expansion of curricula to include any material in which students indicate interest. For example, by developing total environmental and educational communities, students and teachers could explore novel models of theoretical cultures, which could be experienced for an understanding of human and non-human possibilities.

Certification and the Rights of Teachers and Other School Workers—

Teachers and other school workers should be treated as individuals and their individual rights should be respected, especially by school administrators. Teachers, like any other employees, have the inherent right to strike. Teachers should be considered for tenure, but firings for cause should remain within the jurisdiction of the community-controlled board. The board should also be able to require in-service training for teachers regarding issues and concerns deemed important.

Though teachers are important to the educational process, present certification requirements exclude many competent teachers and do not in any way guarantee the quality of those who are certified. A prime concern for the community-controlled board should be to actively seek out teachers who represent a broad spectrum of racial and ethnic backgrounds. Community-controlled boards should be allowed to hire teachers they feel are best qualified to teach.

All school employees have guaranteed to them through the Bill of Rights the right to privacy, to due process, to freedom of assembly, to form and join political organizations and unions, and to strike.

Financing—

1) All levels and aspects of education (books, supplies, resources, transportation, etc.) should be provided free.

2) The People's Party supports an end to non-commercial property taxes and flat rate taxes for financing education. The People's Party proposes financing public education by means of a steeply graduated personal income tax. We call for a vigorous campaign to change the Constitution to allow for such a tax.

3) The People's Party supports a tax on business profits. Provisions should be made to prevent any businesses from passing that tax on to the consumer or to the worker.

4) The People's Party also favors the equalization of school support on a nation-wide basis.

5) As an additional alternative and supplement, the People's Party believes support should be given to alternative educational institutions, though we oppose any schools run for private profit. We feel that these "free schools" should be helped either through a voucher plan or equalizing funds from the government. All non-research and developmental educational funds from the municipal, state and federal levels should be allocated yearly on a per capita basis, for educational use in the form of educational certificates. The individual student should be allowed to spend the certificates at any school he or she chooses, for self-directed study or for apprenticeship.

6) We call for the elimination of all state accreditation requirements at all levels of education.

7) All students shall be automatically registered to vote.

University Community—

Universities should not be involved in any way in military research or military education. This is especially so if such research or education has as its specific intention or result the degradation of human life. It is time to exert all energies toward improving the quality of life and not toward improving methods of death and destruction. Universities should devote an ever-increasing part

of their capabilities to the communities in which they are located. Universities should be open to all seeking to enter them.

FARMER LIBERATION

Our farmers need to be liberated from the cost-price squeeze resulting from the scuttling of the parity formula that makes farmers the main shock absorber of an inflation-ridden economy.

Farmers need to be liberated also from the bipartisan crunch they have been put into by being used to help meet the U.S. balance of payments. They are told that grain prices must be kept low in order to "compete in the world market." Yet the government as the chief grain exporter in the world sets the world market price and sets it low deliberately at $1.05 per bushel for corn, while the price in Europe is over twice that high.

Actually, there is no real "world market" as such, since every surplus grain producing country has been running a subsidized international discount house. The significant thing about the U.S. practice is that the U.S. farmer, not the government, is paying the subsidy in sub-parity prices.

The European Common Market comes nearest to being a "world market" for corn as it buys the largest volume. The extent to which the U.S. farmers are deceived and robbed is indicated by comparing the price supports here and in the Common Market. The national price support figure on corn in the U.S. is $1.05 per bushel. In the Common Market countries it is $2.45 per bushel now and will be $2.82 next year. Yet farmers are told such low price supports are needed here in order to compete with the very much higher figure abroad.

There is no single thing on which the people have been so misled, deceived and brainwashed as on the farm issue. There is no other matter on which so much misinformation, half truths and outright lies have been peddled to confuse voters as on the farm problem and its possible solutions.

There was perhaps one exception to that for a time—the long cold war and the hot wars in Southeast Asia. But, at long last people have become enlightened even on that question.

But the farm story still remains to be told. It is part of the mission of the People's Party to expose the falsifications about the farm problem and to substitute facts for fiction.

Some of the major points that need to be cleared up are:

1) What the farm problem is and what it is not. It is simply a very extended period of sub-parity prices—not a matter of too many farmers and unmanageable surpluses as the anti-farm propagandists would have us believe.

2) Farm legislation. We must have national planning for national goals, for the farm problem is a national problem. The nonsense that all farm programs, especially price supports, have been failures and very costly needs to be replaced with known facts. The earlier programs did work, including 90 per cent of parity price supports. Earlier programs that gave farmers parity cost but a fraction of what the recent programs have cost.

3) The government must be held to its commitment of parity to the farmers. This is not at all an impossible goal. Farmers averaged parity during the Roosevelt years and it was not because of three-and-a-half years of war. If war and military spending were good for farm prices, then corn should be getting $3.00 per bushel now.

4) The question of who is subsidizing whom needs to be cleared up. Leon K. Keyserling published his findings over ten years ago before the farm prices got down to the really low levels of recent years. He said that farmers had been short-changed seven billion dollars over the previous ten-year period. Recently, with farm prices lower, the estimate is ten billion dollars per year that farmers have been subsidizing consumers with cheap food. So the farmers get robbed of ten billion dollars per year, and when the thief—the federal government—gives back two billion in payments, it has the gall to accuse the farmers of an undeserved subsidy. In fact, the federal government has been subsidizing the big food corporations which are forcing up food prices for the consumer.

5) A "market oriented" agriculture is what the aim of the government is now. We hold that sound national policy requires an abundance of food and reserves for emergencies. But in a surplus situation the support price becomes the market price, with the rate being $1.05 per bushel that acts as a ceiling as well as a floor. Given the fact of abundance, a market-oriented agriculture and fair farm prices are incompatible. In fact, a market oriented system is an abomination without a single hope of redemption. If farm price relief is to be made contingent on scarcity, then the farm cause is indeed hopeless.

What Must Be Done—

Short Range Program:

1) Set price supports on storable grains at the maximum rate now permitted, 90 per cent of parity. This should apply immediately to crops.

2) Stop all sales of storable grains at less than parity prices.

3) Stop all sales of Commodity Credit Corp. bins. They will be needed in the near future.

4) Announce that it is the general policy to achieve the equivalent of parity prices for all farm program participants for the next four years and that the "social contract" made by the government commitment to parity will be honored.

5) Assure agricultural workers full rights under the Wagner Act. The People's Party supports the concept of the secondary boycott and the United Farm Workers Organizing Committee (UFWOC) lettuce boycott.

6) Farm workers must be included under the federal wage law.

7) In keeping with the concept of abundance, there shall no longer be payments for not growing food in order to raise prices on farm produced goods. Surplus food shall be used to subsidize hungry areas of the world and shall be held in reserve for emergencies. In other words, if farm production is based on supply and demand, farmers will be forced to produce just enough or not quite enough in order to get the prices they so deserve.

Long Range Program:

There should be instituted a land reform program or land use, residency requirement, the primary criteria for the right to land ownership. The policy must take into consideration conservation practices to conserve the soil for future generations and must also emphasize ecological advantages that family-type farming has over the large farming conglomerates.

With family-type farming and a small herd of cattle, hogs or poultry, and often some of each, the animal wastes are returned to the fields and plowed under to enrich the soil. Big conglomerates have operations where thousands of livestock are fed in one concentrated area and the wastes pollute streams, rivers and even the air.

Animal and grain producing agriculture are being separated. With the present cheap grain policy of the government, the grain farmers are subsidizing the big feeding operations by providing them with cheap corn—at about 40 per cent of parity.

Such a program of family-type farms will vary in size and types of farming and differing farming regions; but acreage limitations and residency requirements will not only assure a wider distribution of ownership and control of productive property, but it will halt the forced farm-to-city migration that merely compounds the problems of the cities while solving no farm problems whatever. In some areas, a back to the land program could well be called for as well as cooperative farms if desired.

But the most important step is a reversal of the low farm policy of the last 20 years, especially with respect to grains and a turnabout to carry out the commitment of the parity prices made in the first Agricultural Adjustment Act of 1933. A repudiation of the low price policy of recent years —about 40 per cent of parity for corn—is most imperative, not only for U.S. farmers but for farmers of the world. For in manipulating prices to as low a level as possible, the U.S. government exploits not only its own farmers but also the farmers of the world; for the U.S. farm production is the main supplier of the various markets and to a certain extent it sets the world price. In fact, some government officials have boasted of setting the world market price for corn.

This policy then constitutes a vicious form of neo-colonialism; and since U.S. farm production is the biggest contributor to the U.S. balance of payments, it is also a contributor to imperialist designs throughout the world; the farmers, therefore, are unwillingly helping to undergird U.S. militarism and to sustain such atrocities as the Vietnam War.

FOREIGN POLICY

Foreign policy is the way a nation relates to other nations. In our world, nations are interdependent. The United States has built a worldwide empire. U.S.-based companies hold $125 billion in assets abroad. Our highly industrialized economy depends on materials imported from other countries (oil from Venezuela, tin from Malaya and Bolivia, etc.) and on the use of cheap labor in countries like Taiwan and Korea. U.S. corporations have chosen to exploit the weakness and poverty of these people rather than to pay for better conditions and higher wages for American workers. Our government gives economic aid to poor nations on the condition that they buy U.S.

products and participate in the system which exploits their people. This is called neo-colonialism.

U.S. enterprises abroad help to maintain wealth in a few hands, while the masses are forced to struggle against overwhelming odds. The Central Intelligence Agency (CIA) and the Agency for International Development (AID) deliberately interfere in the international affairs of other nations, stunting their national development and supporting an elite at the expense of the people.

U.S. military forces protect our assets abroad. This has necessitated maintenance of 2,000 military bases abroad (not including Vietnam) and the allocation of much of the national budget to the burgeoning military system. It provides weapons supporting many unpopular governments (Greece, Pakistan, etc.) and fighting two major wars in Korea and Southeast Asia. On numerous occasions, liberation movements have tried to regain popular control from a corrupt regime and have been defeated with the assistance of the U.S. The actual defense of the U.S., as opposed to maintain an empire, would require only a small, home-based army under the direct control of the people.

Global problems such as ecological imbalance, over-population and the spread of nuclear weapons threaten human survival. To cope with these, we must first transform our foreign policy to affirm our basic humaness and the need for planetary survival through unity. We cannot continue to provide weapons and support for governments that oppress their own people. We must create a new trans-nationalism in which we unite with these around the world who also seek to change oppressive institutions and values.

To this end, the People's Party proposes that:

1) United States foreign policy must respect the right of self-determination of all peoples of the world.

a. U.S. and U.S.-supported troops must be withdrawn from Southeast Asia immediately and unilaterally. All aggressive military and economic intervention must cease.

b. U.S. troops and equipment must be withdrawn from foreign countries and military alliances must cease.

c. Military aid must cease.

d. The U.S. should recognize all governments—whether capitalist, communist or socialist—that draw support from broad masses of their people and do not engage in repression. There should be an end to trade with all governments that do not receive the support of their people.

e. All subversive intelligence and neo-colonial agencies, including the CIA and AID must be abolished.

Ultimately, we must recognize that the survival of all people depends on an end to nationalism and militarism on the part of all countries. The U.S. armed forces must be abolished, and only the Coast Guard and local militia should be retained.

2) Foreign policy should represent the best interests of the American people, not of the American corporations. Our real interests are in human unity and sharing. America, holding a disproportionate share of the world's wealth, must now redefine its aid policies and practices in order to:

a. Provide meaningful assistance to Third World people.

b. Guarantee supervision of all aid, not unilaterally, but through international organizations which truly serve the people of the world, not their own selfish interests.

3) U.S. foreign policy must be changed to reflect two-way cultural exchanges for mutual enrichment.

4) The present U.S. space program has distorted domestic priorities and misdirected the public into viewing space as an arena for jingoistic pride, thus contributing to a neglect of world-wide needs.

a. The present space program must be halted.

b. We must establish an international program of space research, directed at advancing the development of medicine and other world-wide needs. This includes such things as communications and weather forecasting.

c. The fruits of all space research must be shared toward an end of enlarging benefits for all mankind.

5) We propose that the U.S. announce policies to settle all international disputes it has through binding decisions of a World Court when it is the desire of the conflicting states to use that means. This is the first step toward setting up a binding world law for all nations.

6) We propose that further development of and additions to our nuclear strength cease. Furthermore, we urge an international convention of all nations to discuss a means of world-wide nuclear weapons abolition.

7) We call for the freedom of all territories not within the continental United States (i.e., Guam and Puerto Rico).

GOVERNANCE

People function within society both as individuals and as communities. A community comes into being when cultural, social, economic or environmental circumstances create a natural common bond among a group of people.

Governance is how a community makes decisions. When the power to make decisions rests with a group of individuals who are isolated from the needs and ideas of the people, social structures become tools for exploiting the people instead of serving their common interests.

Our social ills have provoked a growing sense of alienation and frustration among many Americans. Some people lapse into apathy, some turn to bombs and guns, some drop out to create new life styles and others withdraw into drugs. Politically, people have voted "no confidence" in the present system by withdrawing their participation in it. Of all adults eligible to vote in the United States, only some 69 per cent usually register to vote. Of these, only 80 per cent or fewer vote in national elections. Turnout for local election runs as low as 20 per cent.

A growing number of Americans feel powerless to influence government. Political institutions that claim to respond to the peoples' will respond instead to the demands of paid lobbyists and big-money interests that help them get elected by buying election through use of the mass media. This powerlessness constitutes a crisis in governance in our country.

If government is to respond to the needs of the people, institutions will have to undergo radical changes to return power of government back to the people. This means decentralizing the power structure, encouraging participation by all the people and bringing decision-making back to a level at which the public has access to it. Decentralization of power makes good the right of people to control the institutions that deal with their social policy, collective interests and general well-being. In all such proposals we must recognize the interrelationships among individual liberty, community control and social planning, and find imaginative ways to deal with these relationships.

Several changes must be made in this area:

1) Bipartisan gerrymandering of anachronistic legislative districts must be ended. Reapportionment of districts should be radically reformed to make meaningful the "one man, one vote" Supreme Court principle. Mandatory guidelines for districting, such as communities of interest, ecological factors, social planning considerations, etc., should be established.

2) Public institutions that serve a community (police, welfare agencies, educational agencies, etc.) should be controlled by that community. Community boards should be established to oversee their operation, including the hiring and firing of personnel.

3) The government should fund independent groups to develop new technical systems of communication between the people and their political institutions. These could include new methods of voting or public opinion polling, new uses of the media in politics, or the use of computer technology to make socio-political information available to the people. We should consider the eventual establishment of a participatory democracy using phone-computer technology to enable each citizen to vote on key issues and policies.

4) The government should encourage the formation of community groups charged with conveying the community's opinions to those in power. These groups should develop methods to measure popular opinion (by referenda, for example), to bring these opinions into the open, and to carry them through into action.

5) Voting procedures should be made fair and simple. Elections should be by direct vote, including direct primaries that are binding on the parties. The electoral college should be abolished. Residency requirements, except for the need to register before an election, should also be eliminated.

6) A Fair Campaign Practices Code should be enacted, including the principle that every political campaign be ensured a basic minimum funding from public monies and be mandatorily limited to a ceiling on expenditures.

7) In order for the people to exercise power, the control of non-governmental institutions such as corporations and the media must change.

Short Range Proposals:

1) The establishment of counter-institutions run by the community to fill community needs that are not fillable by present public institutions.

2) Massive voter registration drives among 18 to 21-year-olds and among members of disenfranchised communities, especially minority communities. Felons and inmates of mental institutions must have the right to vote.

3) The use of initiative, referendum and recall procedures, as provided for in the Constitution, to limit the abuses of corporate and political power under which we presently suffer.

4) We support the demands of the Washington, D.C. Statehood Party for the District to become a state in its own right. We also support the American Indian Nations' struggle to regain their sovereignty and have their treaties with the U.S. honored.

The People's Party feels that no individual can be coerced in any way that conflicts with his/her will. All conscription of men or women for military or military-related duty should be abolished. We call for establishment of a Department of Peace and Priorities with the principal goals of advising the American people, the Congress and the President on the best means of rechanneling funds to life-sustaining activities. This Department could also advise on actual and perceived threats to peace and could serve to mediate such threats. What cannot be resolved in this manner should be referred to the World Court. This Department should be separate from the executive branch and should be headed by a secretary elected by the American people for four-year terms in non-presidential general elections. We are committed to the radical reconstruction of local, state and national government to allow us to take control of our collective lives.

HEALTH

Health care is a right, not a privilege. A high standard of health care must be made equally available to everyone. An effective attack on the problems of health care is impossible without a simultaneous and comprehensive attack on all social and economic conditions which breed poverty and illness. Unless education and living conditions improve at the same time, any improvement in health care will be minimal and temporary. We must translate our present vast health knowledge into effective health care. The allocation of resources for guaranteeing and promoting health and the prevention and treatment of disease should have high priority. It is the right of every community to participate in the planning and governing of its health care program.

Our existing system of health services has utterly failed its responsibility to the people:

1) The medical profession has absolute power over the patient; the community has no control over the delivery of services.

2) The AMA represents the reactionary force maintaining the present intolerable state of health care.

3) Health conditions among the poor and the minorities in the U.S. are statistically no better than those in underdeveloped countries. There are serious diseases which are almost limited in this country to the disadvantaged population groups. This is a form of institutionalized racism and reflects the basic injustice of the system.

4) The medical schools have also perpetrated poor health care. The emphasis of medical education should give priority to the delivery of health care.

5) The number of health professionals is inadequate. We must begin to provide greater numbers and more appropriately trained persons.

6) Too many people make exorbitant profit from the sickness of others. This injustice must stop.

A society which maintains economic and political power in the hands of a few cannot end these frustrations. The People's Party, therefore, supports all efforts by the people to challenge and attain power over those institutions of medicine which affect or oppress them. In essence, we believe in free quality physical, mental and preventive medical care for all our people.

Labor

Working people constitute the great majority in the United States. Realistically, there could be no wealth without the labor of workers. Yet workers are being forced to absorb the economic consequences of an inflation created by the decisions of business and government bosses, decisions which are based on price fixing, excessive profits and the wasteful production of materials for continuing the exploitation of Third World countries such as those in Southeast Asia.

We therefore support the following:

1) Rejection of wage controls as a solution to inflation. We would support an independent move by workers to oppose the Nixon economics, using any means necessary up to and including a general strike. Recovery from inflation will come not from helping business increase profits, but by channeling money directly back to the consumer/ worker through price controls, increased pay and tax rebates.

2) We believe workers have the right to fight to liberate themselves from the grip of nonrepresentative leadership. Workers at even the lowest organizational level must have a democratic say in hiring practices, hours, working conditions, training, retraining and organizing production.

3) The People's Party encourages a rank and file labor movement that would guarantee everyone the right to productive work and make the present apprentice program available to all potential workers. The apprentice program should be under the full control of the union locals.

4) Retraining at no loss of pay for workers whose jobs are phased out and for workers whose jobs are eliminated, full benefits until new jobs can be found for them. Retraining should also be under union control.

5) No discrimination against either of the sexes, ethnic minorities, homosexuals or former convicts in employment and promotions.

6) No restrictions on the right to strike and organize secondary boycotts. Public employees should have the right to bargain collectively and to strike.

7) We support rank and file demands for a 30 hour work week, perhaps in the form of three ten-hour workdays, with no reduction in pay—in other words, 30 hours with 40 hours of pay. This would provide the added benefit of developing full employment.

8) We feel that workers should be provided with a guaranteed insured pension free from corporate control with automatic standard of living increases to allow workers freedom from a specific job or place of work.

9) We wholeheartedly support the current movement of rank and file workers to organize caucuses within the presently unrepresentative unions. Further, we support the unionization of all American workers to protect themselves from the greed of the management and owners.

10) We support the right of the rank and file to organize into and to democratically control unions.

Management has made consumers believe that the worker and his union are to blame for inflation, for lack of jobs, for the decline in the quality of American goods, for all the ills of our economy. It's called blaming the victim for the crime. And this division is false and misleading. For the most part, workers and consumers are the same people, with the same hopes and desires. It is unnatural that workers and consumers should be pitted against each other. It's like a snake biting its own tail rather than defending itself from something afflicting it—in this case the affliction is the power structure. Consumers and workers should come together to determine their needs, establish priorities and develop movements in their communities for full employment and ecological balance. This means taking control of the means of production in the community and working closely with other communities.

LAW AND JUSTICE

Laws provide a system for the resolution of conflicts between individuals. We believe it is not the function of the legal system to either preserve or defend the government of the community or to regulate personal behavior or the individual.

When certain people and institutions have greater access to the legal resources of a society than the masses of people or when the few have greater influence over the decision-making (particularly through the selection of judges), the inequities of the society are legitimized, exacerbated and prolonged; conflicts are not resolved; and freedom is not shared by all.

If a legal system in any way violates these precepts, it is oppressive of the individual. We feel that the following steps must be taken immediately to erase these inequities in the American judicial system:

1) Law enforcement must come from and be controlled by the people in a specific community. A number of plans for community control have been developed. Obviously, the plan must fit the community's needs. The main element of such plans is that the local police force be appointed and reviewed by an elected board of community members. We also believe, with the Constitution, that citizens have the right to bear arms. Over and over we have seen that when people lay down their arms, they lose the power for which they have struggled.

2) Most access to legal institutions is through lawyers. Lawyers come from a specific segment of society, rarely from the poor minorities. Legal education must be made available financially and scholastically as well; and it must be available to anyone who wishes to pursue such a course of study. Lawyers from varied segments of society are more likely to represent the interests of the specific segment from which they come. Furthermore, legal education must provide para-professionals to increase the availability of legal services.

3) People must have access to lawyers. In many respects the working class has least access to lawyers, being ineligible for poverty lawyers and too poor to pay the price for private lawyers. Legal aid and public defender programs must be funded generously and without political strings attached so that people without sufficient funds can have access to legal remedies and protection. In addition, we advocate legal insurance programs that allow groups, such as unions, student bodies, etc., and individuals to hire lawyers on a salary basis and to insure themselves against the high cost of attorneys.

4) Minors must be ensured of all protections as outlined in the Constitution.

5) Individuals must be liable for breaking the law through their business practices. Fines on corporations must not be allowed to be deducted from taxes as a "cost of doing business" expense. The legal and financial responsibility for a corporation's illegalities should be borne by the person who is guilty of handling the illegality.

6) All judges should be elected, even when vacancies occur during a term of office. Community courts should be set up where disputes between citizens can be settled by citizens' judges. This would effectively remove some of the burden from present courts and give a wider range of legal knowledge to a greater number of people.

The parameters of acceptable behavior are set by criminal law. Criminal law is, by nature, repressive. It sets limits beyond which one should not go. While it is necessary to repress some destructive behavior, the extent of repression in our present society and the manner of dealing with unacceptable behavior is cruel and unusual. The majority of laws today are based on protection of the power structure's property. And the resulting repression today affects great proportions of society; and the so-called prison solution is counterproductive and merely trains criminals rather than rehabilitating them. We, therefore, call for these additional changes:

1) Both community members and police will deal with each other as human beings if they are both made answerable to the community for their actions. Law enforcement must come from and be controlled by the people.

2) Society must not legislate individual morality. We propose, therefore, the abolition of crimes without victims. The defendant also has the right to present his/her own defense with free legal advice and further, should have the choice of his/her own defense.

3) We propose the elimination of preventive detention and no-knock legislation, domestic spying, undercover agents, wiretapping, and other such unconstitutional methods of law enforcement.

4) Grand juries have become tools of government prosecutors, rather than the objective investigative bodies they are in theory. We would return the grand jury to its intended function; that is, a jury of peers determining whether a case against an individual is sufficient to warrant a trial. Witnesses before a grand jury must be protected by Constitutional guarantees. Prosecutors who introduce false, misleading, or illegally gathered evidence to a grand jury are guilty of a serious criminal offense against the accused and should be treated before the law as such.

5) Trial juries must include true representation by one's peers. Services should be made available to jurors (e.g., child care) to ensure that all can serve.

6) Most criminal defendants should be released on their own personal recognizance without having to post bail. If bail is required, it must relate to the person's ability to pay. Speedy trial must be given specific statutory recognition, and this right must be personally waived only by the defendant.

7) The present penal system should be abolished. We call for the establishment of community-controlled re-education centers, adequate for comfortable human living, where the emphasis is directed at training which will enable the inmates to function as individuals in society. These centers should be staffed by psychiatrists, psychologists, sociologists, instructors, and vocational counselors, rather than prison guards and wardens. Vocational and academic educational opportunities should be available to the inmates. The staff of each center should have authority to release a person in their care when, in their opinion, the person is ready for release. This would mean that judges would no longer be able to establish minimum sentences.

8) We support the United Prisoners' Union and its demand for a Bill of Rights for prisoners, parolees, probationers and ex-convicts, including payment at union wages (no less than minimum wage) for work, an end to abuse of the indeterminate sentences, access to law books, the right to receive, send and possess any letters and publications and the abolition of capital punishment.

9) We support 24-hour communication programs between the inmates of correctional institutions and the outside community via the news media and other methods of communication in order that the abuses of inmates will stop and will receive immediate attention if it does happen.

10) We propose the following changes in the approach to drug users:

a. Abolition of laws dealing with the criminality of use, sale and possession of psycho-active drugs.

b. Creation of public clinics to educate and treat drug users and provide them with such (psycho-active) drugs at a nominal cost upon demand. There should be no charge to the indigent.

c. All such services will be performed by qualified educational and medical personnel.

It is to be understood that the People's Party takes no moral stand in favor of the use of psycho-active drugs. We realize that current trends in drug usage are a direct result of social forces which make chemical intoxication seem appealing in contrast to the tension of "normal" social interaction. The community's solution to any resulting insanity must be solved with the highest regard for human dignity. Drug addiction is recognized as a personal, not a criminal, problem. Therefore, we call for the decriminalization of all drug use. This means that there should be no arrests or convictions for use, though individuals must be held responsible for their behavior while using drugs.

11) We support the immediate abolition of laws making the possession, sale or use of marijuana a crime.

12) The People's Party demands that the U.S. government make reparations to foreign and domestic peoples who have been the victims of military, economic and other oppression.

13) We support the repatriation of all people

who have been imprisoned or who have fled the country because of their opposition to the Vietnam war.

14) The Universal Code of Military Justice must be abolished, and military personnel must be subject to civilian codes of law.

RACISM

Racism is the concept or ideology that holds that one race or group of people is superior to another. In the U.S., this has taken the form of white people feeling and acting superior to non-white people. The People's Party totally rejects this concept.

The Native Americans, depicted as inferior and savage, were subjected to genocide and in the course of expansion, their lands, culture, heritage, and pride as a race were lost.

Black people were brought in chains from their African homeland, robbed of their culture and language and forced into chattel slavery for nearly two centuries. This bloody past has left an all-encompassing and codified system which perpetuates the concept of racial superiority.

Spaniards, who previously conquered the Native Americans and blended with them to form the people of Mexico, were conquered in turn in a war of annexation in which a major part of Mexico was taken from them by the U.S. They were thereby forced into the U.S. and were also treated as an inferior and conquered people.

The waves of foreign born that came to the U.S. in succeeding generations were looked upon as a source of cheap labor, were victims of greed, and were subjected to the indignities of ghetto life.

The foreign born white population has generally been assimilated into the broad scheme of American life, but the non-whites today continue to be the racist victims of a special oppression.

Thus, the racial question manifests itself in the separation of people by physical characteristics. This separation is maintained by those in power through a policy of divide and conquer among the people, by institutionalizing racism, which reveals itself in patterns of discrimination, segregation, increased police repression, population control programs (genocide), and the denial of dignity. The result is the psychological destruction of the self, the sociological destruction of the individual family, and the destruction of the culture.

The fight against racism is essentially the fight for full social, political, and economic equality. The fight for equality cannot be tokenism, but a massive onslaught against the whole concept of racism whenever and wherever it manifests itself.

White Americans must now resurrect, respect, fulfill, and honor the principles and articles of the Declaration of Independence and the Constitution and their solemn treaties with all nations and especially those with Native Americans.

The fight for equality is a class struggle as well as a radical one. Because the majority of the non-white peoples are members of the working class, the capitalist class employs the strategy of pitting the white workers against the non-white workers in order to increase profits. The white workers generally comply, and these racist actions are rewarded by token economic and social privileges granted to them by the capitalist class.

The fight for equality is also a national issue in that it is a struggle by the non-white peoples to maintain their existence and identities as peoples and nations. Recognizing this as a national issue means that we affirm and reaffirm to the non-white peoples their right of self-determination.

We realize that the future direction of the quest for self-determination will depend upon the past and present conditions and struggles of the various non-white peoples.

We know that this question can best be solved with a complete change of the economic and political systems, but until that change is made we are concerned with the fight for equality *now*.

Therefore, we support and will participate in movements for:

1) Elimination of institutionalized racism (discrimination) against non-white people in the choice of jobs, education, and housing.

2) Immediate release from prison of all political prisoners, those jailed because of their opposition as Third World people against the oppression of a racist system.

3) Democratic representation of Third World people in all institutions and processes that affect people's lives, including ethnic reapportionment of all electoral districts.

4) Community control of police. The People's Party upholds the principle of a Third World individual's or a group's right to defend itself with any means against unprovoked and unjustified police attacks.

5) Community control of all educational and social institutions and processes. We oppose regionalism where the purpose is to dilute the power or strength of minority groups, such as city planning.

6) Realization of the demands, aspirations, and visions of the Native Americans, African-Americans, and Chicanos in their liberation struggle:

a. Enforcement of treaties for their benefit.

b. Protection of traditional lands.

c. National autonomy (i.e., Independent Hopi Nation, Northern New Mexico Alianza Movement, Republic of New Africa). Bicultural urban areas which would have separate city status for bi-national and bilingual government and schools.

d. Autonomous nations would be independent of U.S. laws; yet they would retain the right to vote in state and U.S. elections.

e. We support the traditional right of Chicanos to move freely across the U.S. border.

7) The People's Party supports the following anti-racism bill:

a. 1) No federal troops shall be sent to ghettos to suppress demonstrations or rebellions against racist treatment.

2) Any local, state, or federal policeman or other local, state, or federal government official who murders any person, especially a Black, Latin, Asian, or Native American person, shall be deemed to have committed a federal offense punishable by life imprisonment.

3) Any local, state, or federal policeman or other local, state, or federal government official who assaults any person, especially minority persons, except in provable self-defense, shall be deemed to have committed a federal offense punishable by not less than ten years imprisonment, depending upon the severity of the offense.

4) Anyone on trial for any offense shall have his or her choice of a lawyer, particularly Third World people.

b. 1) Rescind the Talmadge Amendment, which would force people on welfare, especially Third World people, to work at less than minimum wages.

2) There shall be a guaranteed annual income of $6500 for a family of four, available to anyone with no legal exceptions. This would be important for Third World people who are often kept deliberately below the poverty level.

3) Children shall not be taken forcibly from mothers and fathers on welfare, a procedure now being recommended for many Third World people by welfare bureaucrats.

c. 1) Repeal the racist immigration codes.

2) People born in other countries and residing in the U.S. shall not be deported or harassed. This is often done to Third World non-citizens in the U.S.

d. No college or university, public or private school, which employs officials who commit acts of racism against students, faculty or other employees, or which uses texts that propagate the view that Black or other minority people are culturally or genetically inferior shall receive any federal aid.

e. 1) Medical researchers who experiment on minors, especially Third World minors, shall be deemed to have committed a federal offense punishable by not less than ten years imprisonment and with a maximum of life imprisonment.

2) Medical researchers who experiment on any people, especially Third World people, without their full consent, shall be deemed to have committed a federal offense punishable by not less than ten years imprisonment and with a maximum of life imprisonment.

3) Anyone who practices forced sterilization or lobotomies on people, especially Third World people, shall be deemed to have committed a federal offense punishable by life imprisonment.

4) Captive populations such as prisoners, particularly Asian, African, Hispanic, and Native Americans, shall never be experimented on or medically abused. Anyone who commits this crime shall be deemed to have committed a federal offense punishable by not less than ten years imprisonment depending on the severity of the offense.

8) The People's Party recognizes the special repression coming down on Black people in the South, and it pledges its full support of those fighting that oppression.

9) We demand that the Small Business Administration help to solve the special problems of Black business people due to generations of discrimination. This agency should give special consideration to Black business people in granting

loans and shall not use these loans as a partisan tool.

10) All government agencies providing emergency services in hurricanes, floods, earthquakes and other disasters shall alert and advise all qualified recipients of their right to aid. Members of minority groups shall not be intimidated or denied assistance because of their minority status.

SEXISM

Sexism means ascribing, or withholding, certain rights, opportunities, attitudes, and potentials to individuals on the basis of their sex. To eliminate this form of discrimination, both sexes must be liberated from stereotyped men-women role-playing and provided with equal opportunities in work and life-style. This will mean changing our laws, social organization, and beliefs about homosexuality and about male and female competence.

The traditional value system places the woman in the home, supported by her husband. Today, however, women make up 37 per cent of all workers and are the sole parent in 10 per cent of the families in the nation. Yet the structure of our society continues to reflect the traditional system and holds women to the lowest economic positions, while denying them fair representation in decision-making structures.

Of all male workers, 48 per cent hold jobs as proprietors, managers, professionals, or craftsmen; only 20 per cent of all women workers are so employed. Only one engineer, three lawyers, and seven doctors out of one hundred are women. At the other end of the scale, however, women swell the ranks of clerical, sales, service, and household workers. Over 64 per cent of all women workers hold this type of job, as opposed to 20 per cent of all the male workers. The highest economic positions in the country exclude women almost totally; a recent survey of the 60 largest corporations in California showed that, of the 1,009 directors, only six were women and, of these, only two were unrelated to other directors. At all levels of full-time employment, women receive approximately $3,000 less per year than their male counterparts.

Women also lack representation in the governing bodies that control the society. The U.S. Senate includes one woman senator out of a hundred. Of the 435 members of the House of Representatives, 12 are women. There are no woman governors, and of the 50 largest U.S. cities, only two have women mayors. Thus, while women constitute 51 per cent of the population, they have been selectively excluded from the higher levels of decision-making, and relegated unfairly to the lowest positions in the society.

The word "gay" refers to types of non-heterosexual expression, including that of female and male homosexuals, bisexuals, transsexuals, and transvestites. The People's Party recognizes and affirms that the goals and aims of Gay Liberation are an essential part of the general struggle against oppression. The state has no right to regulate the sex lives of its citizens either directly through punitive legislation or indirectly through selective employment practices.

Women's liberation is people liberation. The exploitation of women by our present legal, social and economic system is accompanied by a corresponding exploitation of men. Economically, women are discriminated against in hiring and paying practices. Men are economically unable to choose home and child care as their employment. Both situations are unfair. Socially, women are expected to be dependent upon and subservient to men, who, in turn, are expected to be independent and aggressive. Both expectations are narrow and unrealistic. Legally, women are considered the property of their husbands and men are responsible for their support. This is unfair to both because it keeps the women from a fulfilling life and men tied down with unjust responsibilities. We must do away with all legal, social and economic discrimination of men and women, straights and gays.

The People's Party therefore proposes that:

1) Legal discrimination against women must be eliminated. Specifically:

a. The U.S. Congress should pass and the states should ratify an Equal Rights amendment to the Constitution giving women specific guarantees of equal rights under the law.

b. Certain states maintain discriminatory laws concerning women, regarding jury service, property rights, use of birth name, alimony, rights to make binding contracts, severity of punishment for crimes, identification as heads of households, and sexual relations. We oppose these laws.

c. Protective legislation, initially written to

lessen hardships on female workers, now serves to justify sex discrimination. These laws must be eliminated or extended to cover all workers.

d. Vice laws must be rewritten to end the prosecution of prostitutes (male and female) and the regulation of sexual behavior between consenting individuals over the age of 13.

e. Federal and state legislation must ensure the right of women to be educated equally with men. All discrimination and segregation by sex, written or unwritten, must be eliminated at all levels of education, including college, graduate and professional school, loans and fellowships, and federal and state training programs such as Job Corps, and on-the-job training.

f. The "man in the household" welfare laws that preclude child support payment if a man lives in the house must be abolished.

g. Women in prisons should obtain work furloughs and conjugal visits to the same extent that men prisoners do. The understaffing of female prisons must be corrected.

h. Although the People's Party is opposed to the U.S. military draft, it is the right of women in the military to be trained, promoted and assigned on an equal basis with men. We do not ask that women be drafted. On the contrary, we consider the drafting of men an oppression rather than a privilege denied women.

i. Laws discriminating against unmarried persons, such as higher tax rates, unequal treatment by welfare departments, Social Security benefits, refusal to allow single people to adopt children, etc., must be abolished, whether applied to persons living singly or cohabiting.

j. The government has no business interfering in the private relationships of individuals. All laws relating to marriage and divorce must be abolished. Provisions must be made for equal rights for children and full protection under laws which would assure sufficient food, clothing, shelter and medical care, etc.

2) We must rearrange our social organization to give women an equal position in society. And there can be no equality as long as women do not receive, as a right, financial aid from the government to help them solve their special problems in an economic system organized to meet the needs of men. A federal stipend for women in pregnancy, in childbirth and in the care and education of their children is the minimum economic basis

which would move them toward winning their freedom.

a. Society should not control women's reproductive functions. We must abolish laws that limit access to birth control information and devices, or that govern abortions. The government should support birth control and abortion clinics staffed by qualified personnel. We oppose forced abortions and sterilizations.

b. We oppose forced maternity leave. Women should be paid maternity leave as a form of social security and/or employee benefit or accumulated sick leave. Legislation must protect the right of women to return to their jobs within a reasonable time after childbirth without loss of seniority or other accrued benefits.

c. The responsibility of caring for children should not rest entirely on women, but should be assumed by both parents and/or by the wider society. The standard work day should vary in length, with workers choosing the amount of time spent at work and the amount spent with the family. This would let both parents contribute to the care of their children. Fully-equipped 24-hour child care centers for children pre-school through adolescence should be provided as a public service. On-the-job child care facilities should be provided for nursing mothers. Methods of financing would include:

—government-financed child care centers for all public employees and civil servants located at places of work;

—government-financed neighborhood child care centers situated throughout the community;

—company-financed, parent-controlled child care centers located at the place of work;

—initiation of a government agency to take action in enforcing the above.

All of the above should be adopted to assure equal rights and full protection to men and women alike.

3) Homosexuals, both male and female, suffer from discrimination in employment, education, government, the military, and the society at large. The fundamental right of consenting individuals to engage in sexual practices of their own choosing must be recognized. The state has no right to regulate the sexual behavior of consenting citizens.

a. We must eliminate all laws that limit the right of self-determination of all people in the free expression of their true sexual natures. This includes laws that legislate sexual behavior in the private lives of any consenting individuals, as well as all educational, occupational, governmental, military and social legislation that discriminates against gays.

b. We must abolish all laws, institutions and practices of the government, both federal and state, that discriminate against persons because of actions expressive of their sexual natures.

c. Rights guaranteed by the Declaration of Independence and the Constitution, including the Bill of Rights, should not be denied or abridged because of sexual preference.

d. All "sex education" schooling should accord the same validity to homosexual and other forms of expression as to heterosexual forms.

e. We oppose laws which discriminate against the parental rights of gays.

f. There must be immediate release, restoration to full participation in society, and full reparation to all persons incarcerated in prisons and in mental institutions on charges of non-victim sexual crimes.

4) Widespread beliefs about female competence and decision-making ability have inhibited women from full participation in the society. Stereotypes of "real man" and "real woman" must be systematically eliminated.

a. The media—radio, television and newspapers—cater to these beliefs, facilitating further discrimination against women. We must eliminate the stereotyped, negative portrayal of women often depicted in advertisements. Stereotypes that portray men as aggressive and dominant and women as passive and supportive should be balanced in the public media by occasionally showing human beings as they really are.

b. Education does not expose female children to the full range of available occupations, but mostly teaches them about "female" occupations. Male children also fail to receive information about traditionally "female" occupations, such as child care and homemaking. All children should receive information and training and guidance for all types of occupations, without regard to sex.

c. Legislation must eliminate references in school textbooks to male supremacy, unique male competencies, and female ineptness. Textbooks must present the full range of occupations as occupied by both men and women workers, including portraying men occupied at domestic tasks. History texts should include women's history and gay history.

d. Institutions such as churches, the medical and psychiatric professions, schools, and the media perpetuate beliefs about appropriate sex role behaviors and practices which are oppressive. These beliefs must be eliminated.

Women must become inculturated. In many cases they have accepted as normal their status as second class citizens in a male-dominated society. As a result of the oppression with which they are forced to deal from birth, if women were to achieve their rightful place as equals in a society today, there would still be many who would self-impose oppression because of the process of inculturation. Some women will find it difficult to cope when they have spent their lives learning to play out a pre-determined role in society. Thus, the People's Party supports all consciousness-raising alternatives and supports the institution of many new alternatives.

Prohibition Platform 1972

PREAMBLE

We, the representatives of the Prohibition Party, assembled in National Convention at Wichita, Kansas, June 24 and 25, 1971, recognizing Almighty God as the source of all just government, and with faith in the teachings of the Lord Jesus Christ, do solemnly promise that, if our party is chosen to administer the affairs of the nation, we will, with earnest dedication to the principles of righteousness, seek to serve the needs and to preserve the rights, the prerogatives, and the basic freedoms of the people of the United States of America. For the realization of these ends we propose the following program of government:

CONSTITUTIONAL GOVERNMENT

We affirm our sincere loyalty to the Constitution of the United States, and express our deep confidence in that document as the basic law of the land. We will resist all attempts to violate it, whether by legislation, by means of evasion, or through judicial interpretation. We believe in the Declaration of Independence and in the Preamble and Bill of Rights of our Constitution. We declare ourselves in hearty support of our system of representative government, with its plan of checks and balances, and express our firm intent to serve the people of our nation with a constructive, forward looking program of good government, dedicated to the general welfare.

COMMUNISM–TOTALITARIANISM

Recognizing that Communism is aggressively and unalterably opposed to our Constitutional government, we declare our opposition to it both as a way of life and as a governmental system. We believe that the program of Communism, with its intent to infiltrate and to overthrow our present form of government, must be pitilessly exposed. We challenge all loyal citizens to become fully aware of this menace to civilization, to exert every effort to defeat the Marxist program and to help preserve our American way of life.

We also declare ourselves opposed to any other form of totalitarian philosophy or form of government. We endorse the efforts of those agencies which have been honestly and earnestly exposing subversive activities and groups.

GOVERNMENTAL ECONOMY AND TAXATION

We view with alarm the extravagance and wasteful spending which have invaded government at all levels, demanding an ever increasing tax load upon our people. The constant increase in taxation, requiring approximately one third of the total income of our citizens to pay the expenses of government, is approaching the point of confiscation, leading to economic chaos. We believe that good government does not attempt to do for people what they can do for themselves. With proper economy, governmental costs can be lowered, the tax load lightened, and the public debt can be reduced. We promise to devote ourselves to such an end, even though it involves either the reorganization or abolition of certain departments, bureaus, and vested interests.

THE FEDERAL BUDGET

Good government and a sound economy require a balanced budget. The inflationary effects and the disturbing influences of unbalanced budgets must be eliminated. We cannot, with impunity, continue to increase the mortgage on our future

and the interest load of the present. As the level of taxation is already excessive, there must be either a decided reduction in governmental services and federal spending or a substantial improvement in efficiency, with consequent elimination of waste in both personnel and materials. Actually, both areas need careful exploration with a view not only to maintaining a balanced budget, but also to reduction of the national debt.

MONEY AND FINANCE

A sound financial program and dependable monetary policy are fundamental to a stable economy. Our Constitution gives to Congress the power to "coin money" and to "regulate the value thereof." We believe that Congress, working with the executive branch of government, should take immediate steps to establish a financial program that will block inflationary trends, insure a sound currency, stabilize price levels, and provide for systematic retirement of the national debt. We urge that careful consideration be given to a constructive program of monetary policy involving a favorable balance of payments in international exchange, believing that such a step would help stabilize our economy, would promote confidence in our monetary system and would underwrite a continuing program of sound finance and expanding industrial progress.

THE INCOME TAX

A federal income tax was first proposed by the Prohibition Party in 1896. However, the graduated tax and confiscatory rates of the present day were not contemplated. We question the exemption from taxation of certain types of bonds issued by government bodies. We seriously doubt the wisdom of the present system of taxation and demand a thorough review of the basic fiscal policies of our government.

REVENUE SHARING

Recognizing that local and state governments are having real difficulty in meeting their basic financial needs, we advocate a division of the revenue received from the federal income tax, with appropriate amounts of the tax collected in each state being distributed to each of the state governments before becoming the property of the federal government.

INFLATION

For a period of years our people have been confronted with the problem of increasing prices and lowered purchasing power. There is both a need and a desire for appropriate stability in this area. We propose that immediate steps be developed to stabilize wages and prices, to secure more efficient production, and to maintain a proper relationship between the rates of growth of our monetary supply and of the gross national product.

ENVIRONMENTAL AWARENESS

An awareness of the various problems related to the area of ecology is essential. We believe that all men have a right to a wholesome environment. Accordingly, government must establish standards and enforce a program which will insure a satisfactory stewardship of land, water and air throughout the nation. In particular, we insist on the right of everyone to a pure water supply and to an unpolluted atmosphere. We urge increased emphasis on tertiary treatment of sewage, on the development of fission type reactors and, as soon as technologically feasible, atomic fusion as a substitute for fossil fuels in electric power generation, and on the substitution of relatively non-polluting sources of power in motor vehicles.

FOREIGN AFFAIRS

It has been charged that our government lacks a consistent, positive foreign policy. This is an area which involves both complex and baffling problems. There are no easy solutions.

We pledge ourselves to search for peaceful solutions to the problems of international relations and to deal with conflicts among nations by seeking to react creatively and constructively to the underlying causes of international tension and frustration before they explode into hostilities, and to strive for world peace and order based upon the teachings of the Prince of Peace.

We insist that no foreign government has an inherent right to financial aid at the expense of American taxpayers. In fact such aid does not usually purchase friendship. Often it seems to generate exactly the opposite. In order to maintain our national solvency and to sustain our ability to meet genuine need, great caution is essential. Most aid should be in the form of repayable loans which will enable the beneficiaries to maintain their dignity and self respect. Direct aid should be limited to disaster relief and to under-developed countries of good will. It must be honestly used for internal development and must be denied to corrupt governments and to aggressor nations.

A FREE ECONOMY

We are strongly opposed to burdensome restraints on our free enterprise system, to detailed regulation of our economic life and to federal interference with individual initiative. We believe that free enterprise is threatened in three ways: (1) by excessive governmental regulation, (2) by growth of public or private monopoly, and (3) by unethical practices of unscrupulous groups.

It will be the policy of our administration to encourage independent, non-monopolistic business enterprises which serve genuine consumer needs and are operated with a sense of responsibility to the public. We will take necessary steps to prevent the evils both of monopoly and of excessive regulation by government, and to protect adequately the consuming public from irresponsible or deceptive practices contrary to the general welfare.

We propose that our government withdraw, with reasonable promptness, from the fields of business activity and sell to private industry, at proper investment prices, those business enterprises now owned and operated by the federal government.

LABOR AND INDUSTRY

In the area of labor and industrial relations we believe that the public welfare must be given paramount consideration. Both management and labor must be held responsible for their economic and their social behavior. Neither should be permitted to dominate at the expense of the other or of the common good. Rather, the antitrust laws must be applied equally to all monopolies, whether of business or of labor. Whenever the public welfare is seriously endangered because of disputes affecting quasi-public businesses and utilities we favor the compulsory arbitration of labor-management disputes, particularly in the area of public transportation. We would, in contrast to preceding administrations, enforce stringently the laws forbidding strikes by federal government employees.

EMPLOYEE–EMPLOYER RIGHTS

Every individual has certain basic and fundamental rights. A person's right to join or not to join a labor union without affecting his employment and his right to work for an employer willing to hire him must be protected. Likewise, employees and employers must be free to bargain and to contract as they wish. Violence or coercion, whether on the part of management or of labor, should be prohibited.

STATES RIGHTS

Our founding fathers recognized the importance of both individual and states rights, and determined to preserve them by making the Bill of Rights an integral part of our Constitution. During recent years there has been an increasing tendency toward an undesirable concentration of power and authority in the federal government.

To deal with overcentralization we urge more vigorous action by the state and local governments for the protection of the rights and the promotion of the welfare of their people, greater resort to the solution of local community problems through the voluntary action of existing or new civic and other non-governmental associations, where this is feasible, and the increasing pursuit by private business concerns of policies which promote the public interest.

We pledge ourselves to action that will preserve all legitimate rights and will maintain among the several states their constitutional place in our system of government.

HUMAN RIGHTS

All American citizens, regardless of race, sex, religion, or national origin are entitled to equality of treatment under the provisions of our constitutions and under the laws of our land. No person or group of persons should be subjected to ostracism, humiliation, or embarrassment because of color or national background. We deplore the use of violent, anarchistic, or arbitrary pressure tactics, from whatever source, as a means of seeking to resolve tensions and divergences of opinion among our citizens.

We are opposed to those proposals which would destroy our neighborhood school systems through a program of artificial integration or convey special privileges to any minority group.

PUBLIC MORALITY

Moral and spiritual considerations must be primary factors in determining both state and national policies. We deplore the gross neglect of such matters by the dominant political parties, culminating in the shocking revelations of crime and of political and economic corruption which have characterized recent years. We charge these parties with basic responsibility for the rapid decline in moral standards which followed the repeal of the Eighteenth Amendment. We believe that the program of nullification of law through non-enforcement which led to repeal contributed greatly to the disintegration of public morals, to a general deterioration of standards, and to a lowering of values among our people.

We pledge ourselves to break the unholy alliance which has made these things possible. We propose to strengthen and to enforce laws against gambling, narcotics, and commercialized vice, to emphasize the basic importance of spiritual and moral values to the development and growth of an enduring nation, and to maintain the integrity of our democracy by careful enforcement of law and loyal support of our Constitution.

It is our judgment that the emphasis in certain quarters upon civil disobedience represents a most unfortunate and a most distressing development of our era.

NATIONAL PREPAREDNESS

Believing that "eternal vigilance is the price of liberty" we declare for a sound program of national military preparedness. While praying for peace we cannot place our freedom in peril by ignoring potential threats to our nation.

However, we believe that the present program of compulsory peacetime military training does not represent a genuine safeguard to world peace. We, rather, believe it is to be contrary, in principle, to our American way of life. This system places an unnecessary burden upon our peacetime economy, threatens us with possible military dictatorship, and often permits and promotes the moral and spiritual deterioration of our youth.

We urge that our peacetime defense be entrusted to professionally trained volunteers.

NATIONAL SOVEREIGNTY

We declare our belief in national sovereignty

and oppose surrender of this sovereignty to any international group.

CIVIL SERVICE

The Prohibition Party first sponsored our civil service system. On the other hand, the dominant political parties are positively committed to the "spoils" system and, when in office, have prostituted governmental power to serve their own selfish party interests instead of the whole people. This has led to excessive expenditures, higher taxes and, in some situations, to an unfortunate alliance of crime with politics. We pledge ourselves to an honest, efficient, and economical administration. Veteran preference in civil service must be limited as to time, and favoritism toward certain institutions in government appointments must be curbed.

TIME STANDARDIZATION

We take exception to the twice yearly changes of our time. We believe that these changes add to our lives unnecessary confusion and avoidable frustration and are costly and unjust to those who need standardized time. We advocate the stabilization of our timekeeping by establishing Daylight Savings Time year round.

THE NEWS MEDIA

We believe in the importance of freedom of the press and of other news media. There must be no suppression of this freedom when properly exercised. On the other hand, we deplore the role of the media in sensationalizing a growing moral permissiveness. We believe that this creates the impression that the media are acting as approving and applauding onlookers. We deplore the decline of investigative reporting, and demand that the media once again become responsible informants of the public.

WELFARE

The present welfare programs of our state and national governments are a disgraceful shambles. As presently administered in many areas the chief outcome is to create a dependent economic and social sub-stratum. All too many welfare officials and employees seem determined to help increase the number on our welfare rolls at a rate many times that of our general population increase.

The Prohibition Party, which has always pioneered in social reform, insists that the handicapped, the aged, the chronically ill and those families without a breadwinner or one who is capable of working should be helped. The tragedy is that many who are truly deserving today are receiving insufficient aid. A large proportion of our welfare dollars is being siphoned off by those who are capable of working.

If the mushrooming welfare costs are not reduced and those undeserving of assistance are not removed from the welfare rolls, a taxpayers' revolt may one day kill the entire welfare program. The Prohibition Party believes that a complete overhaul of our welfare system is needed.

We specifically reject the concept of a guaranteed annual income. Such a concept will accelerate rather than retard the growth of the number of people on welfare rolls and will tend to destroy initiative among those whose earnings would be only slightly above such a guaranteed minimum income.

RELIGIOUS LIBERTY

We believe in religious liberty. Freedom of the individual to worship, to fellowship, with others of similar faith, to evangelize, to educate, and to establish religious institutions, must be preserved. When religious liberty is lost, political liberty will perish with it. We deplore ever increasing efforts to restrict freedom of religious broadcasting and the establishment of new churches. We caution the Internal Revenue Service against using the power to control tax exemptions to discriminate against evangelical Christianity.

We believe, also, that our government should take a firm positive position against religious intolerance and persecution anywhere in the world.

MARRIAGE AND DIVORCE

Ordained of God, the home is a sacred institution. Its sanctity must be protected and preserved. We favor the enactment of uniform marriage and divorce laws in the various states as an aid to building strong and enduring homes throughout our nation.

SOCIAL SECURITY

We endorse the general principle of an actuarially sound social security insurance program which includes all employed groups. We question the recent trend toward a welfare emphasis. We condemn the maladministration of its provisions for political ends; we pledge ourselves to correct these evils, particularly, the denial of benefits to persons who have earned them and who are qualified for them, but who choose to continue in productive service.

BALLOT LAW REFORM

True democracy requires that the needs and interests of minority groups be given fair, honest, and appropriate consideration. Instead, in many of our states, ballot laws have been enacted which are designed to make a two party system into a bipartisan political monopoly, keeping minor parties off the ballot. We demand passage of laws which protect independent voters and which guarantee to minority groups access to the ballot and the fundamental right of free political expression.

CHURCH AND STATE

We affirm our continuing loyalty to the constitutional principle of separation of Church and State. We will expose, and resist vigorously, any attempt from whatever source to weaken or subvert this fundamental principle.

We declare our belief that the Bible is not a sectarian book, but is a volume of universal appeal and application which is woven into our history, our laws, and our culture. We deplore any interpretation which would limit its use in any area of our national life.

In the area of government, we endorse encouragement of nonprofit educational and religious institutions on a tax exempt basis, but we declare strong opposition to all efforts, direct or indirect, to secure appropriations of public money for private religious or sectarian purposes. We are opposed, however, to tax exemption on income received by religious organizations engaged in competition with commercial business enterprises, except for specific religious services, such as church publishing houses.

EDUCATION

It is altogether appropriate that our federal government should be interested in and concerned about matters pertaining to all areas of educa-

tional growth and development. However, under the Tenth Amendment, public education is clearly to be under the control of the states. We are opposed to direct federal aid to education, believing that each state should both support and control its own educational program.

AGRICULTURE

The production and distribution of agricultural products is of vital importance to the economy of any people. We believe that those engaged in agricultural pursuits, like other American citizens, should be free from authoritarian control and coercion. Hence we declare ourselves opposed to regimentation of farms and farmers and urge a sensible and orderly return to a free market program.

PUBLIC HEALTH

The health of our people is a matter of fundamental importance. We are deeply concerned with this matter in its many aspects. We are disturbed by the increasing use of narcotic and psychedelic drugs. Recognizing that the use of tobacco products constitutes a health hazard, we are opposed to promotional advertising of such products and to subsidization of tobacco growing. We insist that caution must be taken in dealing with mental health cases, lest there be unjust and prejudiced incarcerations. We deplore those programs of mass medication which violate the rights of individuals. We pledge enforcement of existing laws regulating these health concerns, the enactment of additional needed legislation, and cooperation with state efforts to deal with the problems.

THE ALCOHOL PROBLEM

Beverage alcohol must today be recognized as the chief cause of poverty, broken homes, juvenile delinquency, vice, crime, political corruption, wasted manpower and highway accidents. By the most conservative estimates, more than 8,000,000 alcoholics and 8,000,000 problem drinkers are currently victims of alcohol.

No greater mistake has ever been made by the American people and their government than the Repeal of Prohibition. Contrary to the promises made by the advocates of repeal, bootlegging has increased to the point where the liquor industry itself claims that one-third of all alcohol consumed today in America is illicit; drinking among our young people has reached epidemic proportions; liquor taxes pay only a small fraction of the traffic's cost to the taxpayers and the "open saloon" which was to be "banished forever" is back in a newer form and more numerous than ever.

The liquor traffic is linked with and supports a nationwide network of gambling, vice and crime. It also dominates both major political parties and, through them, much of the governmental and political life of our nation. As long as the two dominant parties are largely controlled by the liquor traffic, just so long will they be unable to make moral principles prevail.

The Prohibition Party alone offers a program to deal with this greatest of social ills. We pledge ourselves to a program of publicity, education, legislation and administration, leading to the elimination of beverage alcohol industry. We will repeal all laws which legalize the liquor traffic and enact and rigorously enforce new laws which prohibit the manufacture, distribution and sale of alcoholic beverages.

We urge all Americans who favor sobriety and righteousness to join with us in electing an administration pledged to the above program.

Republican Platform 1972

PREAMBLE

This year our Republican Party has greater reason than ever before for pride in its stewardship.

When our accomplishments are weighed—when our opponents' philosophy, programs and candidates are assessed—we believe the American people will rally eagerly to the leadership which since January 1969 has brought them a better life in a better land in a safer world.

This political contest of 1972 is a singular one. No Americans before have had a clearer option. The choice is between going forward from dramatic achievements to predictable new achievements, or turning back toward a nightmarish time in which the torch of free America was virtually snuffed out in a storm of violence and protest.

It is so easy to forget how frightful it was.

There was Vietnam—so bloody, so costly, so bitterly divisive—a war in which more than a half-million of America's sons had been committed to battle—a war, it seemed, neither to be won nor lost, but only to be endlessly fought—a war emotionally so tormenting as almost to obliterate America's other worldly concerns.

And yet, as our eyes were fixed on the carnage in Asia, in Europe our alliance had weakened. The Western will was dividing and ebbing. The isolation of the People's Republic of China with one-fourth of the world's population, went endlessly on.

At home our horrified people watched our cities burn, crime burgeon, campuses dissolve into chaos. A mishmash of social experimentalism, producing such fiscal extravaganzas as the abortive war on poverty, combined with war pressures to drive up taxes and balloon the cost of living. Working men and women found their living standards fixed or falling, the victim of inflation. Nationwide, welfare skyrocketed out of control.

The history of our country may record other crises more costly in material goods, but none so demoralizing to the American people. To millions of Americans it seemed we had lost our way.

So it was when our Republican Party came to power.

Now, four years later, a new leadership with new policies and new programs has restored reason and order and hope. No longer buffeted by internal violence and division, we are on course in calmer seas with a sure, steady hand at the helm. A new spirit, buoyant and confident, is on the rise in our land, nourished by the changes we have made. In the past four years:

We have turned toward concord among all Americans;

We have turned toward reason and order;

We have turned toward government responding sensitively to the people's hopes and needs;

We have turned toward innovative solutions to the nation's most pressing problems;

We have turned toward new paths for social progress—from welfare rolls to payrolls; from wanton pollution to vigorous environmental protection;

We have moved far toward peace: withdrawal of our fighting men from Vietnam, constructive new relationships with the Soviet Union and the People's Republic of China, the nuclear arms race checked, the Mid-East crisis dampened, our alliances revitalized.

So once again the foreign policy of the United States is on a realistic footing, promising us a nation secure in a full generation of peace, promising the end of conscription, promising a further allocation of resources to domestic needs.

It is a saga of exhilarating progress.

We have come far in so short a time. Yet, much remains to be done.

Discontents, frustrations and concerns still stir in the minds and hearts of many of our people, especially the young. As long as America falls short of being truly peaceful, truly prosperous, truly secure, truly just for all, her task is not done.

Our encouragement is in the fact that things as they are, are far better than things that recently were. Our resolve is that things to come can be, and will be, better still.

Looking to tomorrow, to President Nixon's second term and on into the third century of this Republic, we of the Republican Party see a quarter-billion Americans peaceful and prospering as never before, humane as never before, their nation strong and just as never before.

It is toward this bright tomorrow that we are determined to move, in concert with millions of discerning Democrats and concerned Independents who will not, and cannot, take part in the convulsive leftward lurch of the national Democratic Party.

The election of 1972 requires of the voters a momentous decision—one that will determine the kind of nation that is to be on its 200th birthday four years hence. In this year we must choose between strength and weakness for our country in the years to come. This year we must choose between negotiating and begging with adversary nations. This year we must choose between an expanding economy in which workers will prosper and a hand-out economy in which the idle live at ease. This year we must choose between running our own lives and letting others in a distant bureaucracy run them. This year we must choose between responsible fiscal policy and fiscal folly.

This year the choice is between moderate goals historically sought by both major parties and far-out goals of the far left. The contest is not between the two great parties Americans have known in previous years. For in this year 1972 the national Democratic Party has been seized by a radical clique which scorns our nation's past and would blight her future.

We invite our troubled friends of other political affiliations to join with us in a new coalition for progress. Together let us reject the New Left prescription for folly and build surely on the solid achievements of President Nixon's first term.

Four years ago we said, in Abraham Lincoln's words, that Americans must think anew and act anew. This we have done, under gifted leadership. The many advances already made, the shining prospects so clearly ahead, are presented in this Platform for 1972 and beyond.

May every American measure our deeds and words thoughtfully and objectively, and may our opponents' claims be equally appraised. Once this is done and judgment rendered on election day, we will confidently carry forward the task of doing for America what her people need and want and deserve.

Toward a Full Generation of Peace

Foreign Policy

When Richard Nixon became President, our country was still clinging to foreign policies fashioned for the era immediately following World War II. The world has changed dramatically in the 1960's, but our foreign policies had not.

America was hopelessly enmeshed in Vietnam. In all parts of the globe our alliances were frayed. With the principal Communist powers our relations showed little prospect of improvement. Trade and monetary problems were grave. Periodic crises had become the way of international economic life.

The nation's frustrations had fostered a dangerous spirit of isolationism among our people. America's influence in the world had waned.

In only four years we have fashioned foreign policies based on a new spirit of effective negotiation with our adversaries, and a new sense of real partnership with our allies. Clearly, the prospects for lasting peace are greater today than at any time since World War II.

New Era of Diplomacy

Not all consequences of our new foreign policy are yet visible, precisely because one of its great purposes is to anticipate crises and avoid them rather than merely respond. Its full impact will be realized over many years, but already there are vivid manifestations of its success:

Before this Administration, a Presidential visit

to Peking would have been unthinkable. Yet our President has gone there to open a candid airing of differences so that they will not lead some day to war. All over the world tensions have eased as, after a generation of hostility, the strongest of nations and the most populous of nations have started discoursing again.

During the 1960's, Presidential visits to Moscow were twice arranged and twice cancelled. Now our President has conferred, in the Soviet Union, with Soviet leaders, and has hammered out agreements to make this world a much safer place. Our President's quest for peace has taken him to 20 other countries, including precedent-shattering visits to Rumania, Yugoslavia and Poland.

Around the globe America's alliances have been renewed and strengthened. A new spirit of partnership shows results in our NATO partners' expenditures for the common defense—up by some $2 billion in two years.

Historians may well regard these years as a golden age of American diplomacy. Never before has our country negotiated with so many nations on so wide a range of subjects—and never with greater success. In the last four years we have concluded agreements:

To limit nuclear weapons.

To ban nuclear weapons from the world's sea-beds.

To reduce the risk of an accidental nuclear war.

To end the threat of biological and toxin war-fare.

To terminate American responsibility for the administration of Okinawa.

To end the recurrent crises over Berlin.

To provide for U.S.-Soviet cooperation in health and space research.

To reduce the possibility of dangerous incidents at sea.

To improve emergency communications between the White House and the Kremlin.

To exercise restraint in situations threatening conflict.

To realign the world's currencies.

To reduce barriers to American exports.

To combat the international drug traffic.

To protect the international environment.

To expand cultural relations with peoples of Eastern Europe.

To settle boundary disputes with Mexico.

To restore the water quality of the Great Lakes in cooperation with Canada.

In Vietnam, too, our new policies have been dramatically effective.

In the 1960's, our nation was plunged into another major war—for the fourth time in this century, the third time in a single generation.

More than a half-million Americans were fighting in Vietnam in January 1969. Fatalities reached 562 in a single week. There was no plan for bringing Americans home; no hope for an end of the war.

In four years, we have marched toward peace and away from war. Our forces in Vietnam have been cut by 93 per cent. No longer do we have a single ground combat unit there. Casualties are down by 95 per cent. Our young draftees are no longer sent there without their consent.

Through it all, we have not abandoned an ally to aggression, not turned our back on their brave defense against brutal invasion, not consigned them to the bloodbath that would follow Communist conquest. By helping South Vietnam build a capability to withstand aggression, we have laid the foundation for a just peace and a durable peace in Southeast Asia.

From one sector of the globe to another, a sure and strong America, in partnership with other nations, has once again resumed her historic mission—the building of lasting peace.

The Nixon Doctrine

When President Nixon came into office, America's foremost problem was the bloody, costly, divisive involvement in Vietnam. But there was an even more profound task—to redefine the international role of the United States in light of new realities around the globe and new attitudes at home. Precisely and clearly, the President stated a new concept of a positive American role. This —the Nixon Doctrine—is monumentally important to every American and to all other people in the world.

The theme of this Doctrine is that America will remain fully involved in world affairs, and yet do this in ways that will elicit greater effort by other nations and the sustaining support of our people.

For decades, our nation's leaders regarded virtually every problem of local defense or economic development anyplace in the world as an exclusive American responsibility. The Nixon Doctrine recognizes that continuing defense and development are impossible unless the concerned nations shoulder the principal burden.

Yet, strong economic and military assistance programs remain essential. Without these, we are denied a middle course—the course between abruptly leaving allies to struggle alone against economic stagnation or aggression, or intervening massively ourselves. We cannot move from the overinvolvement of the Sixties to the selective involvement of the Seventies if we do not assist our friends to make the transition with us.

In the Nixon Doctrine, therefore, we define our interests and commitments realistically and clearly; we offer, not an abdication of leadership, but more rational and responsible leadership.

We pledge that, under Republican leadership, the United States will remain a leader in international affairs. We will continue to shape our involvement abroad to national objectives and realities in order to sustain a strong, effective American role in the world.

Over time we hope this role will eventually lead the peace-loving nations to undertake an exhaustive, coordinated analysis of the root causes of war and the most promising paths of peace, so that those causes may in time be removed and the prospects for enduring peace strengthened year by year.

Peace in the 1970's

We stand with our President for his strategy for Peace—a strategy of national strength, a new sense of international partnership, a willingness to negotiate international differences.

We will strengthen our relationships with our allies, recognizing them as full-fledged partners in securing the peace and promoting the common well-being.

With our adversaries, we will continue to negotiate in order to improve our security, reduce tension, and extend the realm of cooperation. Especially important is continued negotiation to maintain the momentum established by the Strategic Arms Limitation agreements to limit offensive and defensive nuclear weapons systems and further to reduce the danger of nuclear conflict. In addition, we will encourage increased trade for the benefit of our consumers, businessmen, workers, and farmers.

Along with NATO allies, we will seek agreement with the Warsaw Pact nations on a mutual and balanced reduction of military forces in Europe.

We will press for expansion of contacts with the people of Eastern Europe and the People's Republic of China, so long isolated from most of the world.

We will continue to seek a settlement of the Vietnam war which will permit the people of Southeast Asia to live in peace under political arrangements of their own choosing. We take specific note of the remaining major obstacle to settlement—Hanoi's demand that the United States overthrow the Saigon government and impose a Communist-dominated government on the South Vietnamese. We stand unequivocally at the side of the President in his effort to negotiate honorable terms, and in his refusal to accept terms which would dishonor this country.

We commend his refusal to perform this act of betrayal—and we most emphatically say the President of the United States should not go begging to Hanoi. We believe that the President's proposal to withdraw remaining American forces from Vietnam four months after an internationally supervised ceasefire has gone into effect throughout Indochina and all prisoners have been returned is as generous an offer as can be made by anyone—by anyone, that is, who is not bemused with surrender—by anyone who seeks, not a fleeting peace at whatever cost, but a real peace that will be both just and lasting.

We will keep faith with American prisoners of war held by the enemy, and we will keep faith, too, with their families here at home who have demonstrated remarkable courage and fortitude over long periods of uncertainty. We will never agree to leave the fate of our men unclear, dependent upon a cruel enemy's whim. On the contrary—we insist that, before all American forces are withdrawn from Vietnam, American prisoners must be returned and a full accounting made of the missing in action and of those who have died in enemy hands.

We pledge that upon repatriation our returned prisoners will be received in a manner befitting their valor and sacrifice.

We applaud the Administration's program to assure each returned prisoner the finest medical care, personal counseling, social services and career orientation. This around-the-clock personal service will ease their reintegration into American life.

North Vietnam's violation of the Geneva Convention in its treatment of our prisoners of war has called forth condemnation from leaders around the world—but not by our political opposition at home. We denounce the enemy's flagrant breach of international law and common decency. We will continue to demand full implementation of the rights of the prisoners.

If North Vietnam continues obdurately to reject peace by negotiation, we shall nevertheless achieve peace for our country through the successful program of Vietnamization, phasing out our involvement as our ally strengthens his defense against aggression.

In the Middle East, we initiated arrangements leading to a cease-fire which has prevailed for two years. We pledge every effort to transform the cease-fire into lasting peace.

Since World War II, our country has played the major role in the international effort to assist the developing countries of the world. Reform of our foreign assistance program, to induce a greater international sharing of the aid effort, is long overdue. The reforms proposed by the President have been approved only in part. We call for further reforms to make our aid more effective and protect the taxpayer's interests.

We stand for an equitable, non-discriminatory immigration policy, reaffirming our support of the principles of the 1965 Immigration Act—non-discrimination against national origins, reunification of families, and the selective admission of the specially talented. The immigration process must be just and orderly, and we will increase our efforts to halt the illegal entry of aliens into the United States.

We also pledge to strengthen the agencies of international cooperation. We will help multilateral organizations focus on international issues affecting the quality of life—for example the peaceful uses of nuclear energy and the protection of man's cultural heritage and freedom of communication, as well as drug abuse, pollution, overpopulation, exploitation of the oceans and seabeds, aircraft hijacking and international crime. We will seek to improve the performance of the United Nations, including more objective leadership. We support a more equitable sharing of the costs of international organizations and have serious concerns over the delinquency of many UN members in meeting their financial obligations.

Our country, which from its beginnings has proclaimed that all men are endowed with certain rights, cannot be indifferent to the denial of human rights anywhere in the world. We deplore oppression and persecution, the inevitable hallmarks of despotic systems of rule. We will continue to strive to bring them to an end, both to reestablish the right of self-determination and to encourage where and when possible the political freedom of subjugated peoples everywhere in the world.

We firmly support the right of all persons to emigrate from any country, and we have consistently upheld that doctrine. We are fully aware of and share the concern of many citizens for the plight of Soviet Jews with regard to their freedoms and emigration. This view, together with our commitment to the principles of the Universal Declaration of Human Rights of the United Nations, was made known to Soviet leaders during the President's discussions in Moscow.

The Middle East

We support the right of Israel and its courageous people to survive and prosper in peace. We have sought a stable peace for the Middle East and helped to obtain a cease-fire which contained the tragic conflict. We will help in any way possible to bring Israel and the Arab states to the conference table, where they may negotiate a lasting peace. We will continue to act to prevent the development of a military imbalance which would imperil peace in the region and elsewhere by providing Israel with support essential for her security, including aircraft, training and modern and sophisticated military equipment, and also by helping friendly Arab governments and peoples, including support for their efforts to diminish their dependence on outside powers. We support programs of economic assistance to Israel pursued by President Nixon that have helped her achieve a nine-per cent annual economic growth rate. This and the special refugee assistance ordered by the President have also helped to provide resettlement for the thousands of immigrants seeking refuge in Israel.

We will maintain our technical forces in Europe and the Mediterranean area at adequate strength and high levels of efficiency. The irresponsible proposals of our political opposition to slash the defense forces of the United States—specifically, by cutting the strength of our fleet, by reducing our aircraft carriers from 16 to six and by unilateral withdrawals from Europe—would increase the threat of war in the Middle East and gravely menace Israel. We flatly reject these dangerous proposals.

With a settlement fair to all nations of the Middle East, there would be an opportunity for their peoples to look ahead to shared opportunities rather than backward to rancorous animosities. In a new environment of cooperation, Israel will be able to contribute much to economic renaissance in the Mid-East crossroads of the world.

The Atlantic Community

We place high priority on the strengthening of the North Atlantic Alliance. One of the President's first initiatives was to visit Western European capitals to reinvigorate the NATO alliance and indicate its importance in U.S. foreign policy.

Right now, with plaintive cries of "come home America" echoing a new isolationism, the Republican Party states its firm belief that no nation can be an island or a fortress unto itself. Now, more than ever, there is need for interdependence among proven friends and old allies.

The North Atlantic Alliance remains the strongest most successful peacetime association ever formed among a group of free nations. The continued strengthening of the Alliance will remain an important element in the foreign policies of the second Nixon Administration.

Japan

During the 1960's a number of economic and political issues developed in our country's relations with Japan, our major ally in Asia. To resolve these, President Nixon terminated our responsibility for the administration of Okinawa and initiated action to reduce our trade deficit with Japan. We are consulting closely to harmonize our two countries' separate efforts to normalize relations with Peking. In these ways we have shifted our vital alliance with Japan to a more sustainable basis for the long term, recognizing that the maintenance of United States-Japanese friendship advances the interests of both countries.

The Soviet Union

Over many years our relations with the Soviet Nation have oscillated between superficial improvements and new crises. False hopes have been repeatedly followed by disillusioned confrontation. In the closing months of 1968, our relations with the Soviet Union deteriorated steadily, forcing the cancellation of a scheduled Presidential visit to Moscow and immobilizing projected negotiations on strategic arms limitation.

President Nixon immediately began the difficult task of building a new relationship—one based on a realistic acceptance of the profound differences in the values and systems of our two nations. He moved decisively on key issues—such as the Berlin problem and strategic arms limitation—so that progress in one area would add momentum to progress in other areas. The success of these efforts was demonstrated at the summit in Moscow. Agreements were reached on new areas of cooperation—public health, environmental control, space exploration and trade. The first historic agreements limiting strategic arms were signed last May 26 in Moscow, and the Soviet Union subscribed to a broad declaration of principles governing our relations.

We pledge to build upon these promising beginnings in reorienting relations between the world's strongest nuclear powers to establish a truly lasting peace.

China

In the 1960's it seemed beyond possibility that the United States could dispel the ingrained hostility and confrontation with the China mainland. President Nixon's visit to the People's Republic of China was, therefore, an historic milestone in his effort to transform our era from one of confrontation to one of negotiation. While profound differences remain between the United States and China, at least a generation of hostility has been replaced by frank discussions. In February 1972 rules of international conduct were agreed upon which should make the Pacific region a more peaceful area now and in the future. Both the People's Republic and the United States affirmed the usefulness of promoting trade and cultural exchanges as ways of improving understanding between our two peoples.

All this is being done without affecting our mutual defense treaty or our continued diplomatic relations with our valued friend and ally on Taiwan, the Republic of China.

Latin America

Our common long-range interests, as well as history and geography, give the relations among nations of the Western Hemisphere a special importance. We will foster a more mature partnership among the nations of this hemisphere, with a wider sharing of ideas and responsibility, a broader understanding of diversities, and firm commitment to the common pursuit of economic progress and social justice.

We believe the continuing campaign by Cuba to foment violence and support subversion in other countries makes it ineligible for readmission to the community of American states. We look forward to the day when changes in Cuba's policies will justify its re-entry into the American community—and to the day when the Cuban people achieve again their freedom and their true independence.

Africa

Our ties with Africa are rooted in the heritage of many Americans and in our historic commitment to self-determination. We respect the hard-earned sovereignty of Africa's new states and will continue to do our utmost to make a meaningful contribution to their development. We have no illusions that the United States can single-handedly solve the seemingly intractable problems of apartheid and minority rule, but we can and will encourage non-violent, evolutionary change by supporting international efforts peacefully to resolve the problems of southern Africa and by maintaining our contacts with all races on the Continent.

Defense

We believe in keeping America strong.

In times past, both major parties shared that belief. Today this view is under attack by militants newly in control of the Democratic Party. To the alarm of free nations everywhere, the New Democratic Left now would undercut our defenses and have America retreat into virtual isolation, leaving us weak in a world still not free of aggression and threats of aggression. We categorically reject this slash-now, beg-later, approach to defense policy.

Only a strong America can safely negotiate with adversaries. Only a strong America can fashion partnerships for peace.

President Nixon has given the American people their best opportunity in this century to achieve lasting peace. The foundations are well laid. By adhering to a defense policy based on strength at home, partnership abroad and a willingness to negotiate everywhere, we hold that lasting peace is now achievable.

We will surely fail if we go crawling to the conference table. Military weakness is not the path to peace; it is invitation to war.

A Modern, Well-Equipped Force

We believe that the first prerequisite of national security is a modern, well-equipped armed force.

From 1965 to 1969 the Vietnam war so absorbed the resources of the Defense Department that maintenance, modernization, and research and development fell into neglect. In the late 1960's the Soviet Union outspent the United States by billions of dollars for force modernization, facing the United States with the dangerous prospect that its forces would soon be qualitatively inferior. Our Reserve Forces and the National Guard had become a dumping ground for cast-off arms and equipment. The military posture of our country became seriously undermined.

To assure our strength and counter the mounting Soviet threat, President Nixon directed:

The most significant ship construction and modernization program since World War II;

The development of new types of tactical aircraft such as the F-155, a lightweight fighter, and a fighter plane for close support of ground troops;

Improvements in our strategic bomber force and development of the new B-1 strategic bomber;

Development of a new Trident submarine and undersea missile system;

Greatly increasing the capability of existing strategic missiles through multiple warheads;

Strengthening of strategic defenses, including initial deployment of an anti-ballistic missile system;

The largest research and development budget in history to insure continued technological superiority;

Equipping of the National Guard and Reserves with the most modern and sophisticated weapons;

Improved command and control communications systems.

We draw a sharp distinction between prudent reductions in defense spending and the meat-ax slashes with which some Americans are now beguiled by the political opposition. Specifically, we oppose plans to stop the Minuteman III and Poseidon programs, reduce the strategic bomber force by some 60 per cent, cancel the B-1 bomber, reduce aircraft carriers from 16 to 6, reduce tactical air wings by a third, and unilaterally reduce U.S. forces in Europe by half.

These slashes are worse than misguided; they are dangerous.

They would torpedo negotiations on arms and troop reductions, create a crisis of confidence with our allies, damage our own industrial and technological capacity, destabilize Europe and the Middle East, and directly endanger the nation's security.

A New Partnership

The Nixon Doctrine has led to a new military strategy of realistic deterrence. Its essence is the sharing of the responsibilities and the burdens of defense. The strategy is based on the efficient utilization of the total force available—our own and our allies', and our civilian reserve elements as well as our regular forces.

For years our country shouldered the responsibility for the defense of other nations. There were fears that we were attempting to be the policeman of the world. Our country found it necessary to maintain a military force of 3.5 million persons, more than a million overseas at 2,270 installations.

A new partnership is emerging between the United States and other nations of the free world. Other countries are assuming a much greater responsibility for the common defense. Twice in the last two years our European allies have agreed to substantial increases in their support for NATO forces. In Asia we have been heartened by the efforts of the Koreans, Vietnamese, Thais, Nationalist Chinese, Australians, New Zealanders and others who have sought improvements in their own forces.

We have been able to reduce our military forces by more than one million men and women. We have cut by half the number deployed overseas, reduced overseas installations by more than 10 per cent, and sharply reduced the economic burden of defense spending from the Vietnam high. All this has been done by virtue of our new security posture, without impairing our own or our allies' security.

We pledge to press on toward a lasting peace. To that end we declare ourselves unalterably opposed to a unilateral slash of our military power, and we reject a whimpering "come back America" retreat into isolationism.

An All-Volunteer Armed Force

We wholeheartedly support an all-volunteer armed force and are proud to our historic initiatives to bring it to pass.

Four years ago, the President pledged to work toward an early end of the draft. That promise has been kept. Today we approach a zero draft that will enlarge the personal freedom of millions of young Americans.

Prior to 1969, annual draft calls exceeded 300,000. The Selective Service System was inequitable in operation, and its rules caused prolonged uncertainty for young men awaiting call.

Since 1969, the Selective Service System has been thoroughly reorganized, and local draft boards are more representative than ever before. Today draftees are called by random selection of the youngest first, so that the maximum length of vulnerability is no longer seven years but one year only. Youth advisory committees are in operation all across the country.

Of critical importance, we are nearing the elimination of draft calls altogether. In every year since 1968, draft calls have been reduced. Monthly draft calls are now down to a few thousand, and no draftees are sent involuntarily to Vietnam. We expect to achieve our goal by July 1973. Then, for the first time in a quarter-century, we hope and expect that young Americans of all ages will be free from conscription.

Our political opponents have talked for years of their concern for young people. It is our Republican Administration that has taken the strong, effective action required to end the draft, with its many hardships and uncertainties for the youth of America.

Improvements in Service Life

We believe that the men and women in the uniformed services deserve the gratitude and respect of all Americans and are entitled to better treatment than received in the past.

For years most servicemen have been underpaid, harassed with restrictions, and afforded few opportunities for self-development. Construction of military housing was allowed to fall badly behind.

Since 1968 improvements in service life have been many and major:

The largest pay raises in military history have been enacted. While increases have been in all grades, the largest have gone to new recruits whose base pay will have risen more than 300 per cent by the end of this year.

Construction of new housing for military personnel and their families has increased sixfold since January 1969.

Without sacrificing discipline, needlessly harsh, irksome and demeaning practices of the past have been abandoned.

An effective program against dangerous drugs has been initiated.

Educational and training opportunities have been expanded.

Major strides have been made toward wiping out the last vestiges of racial discrimination.

We regard these tasks as never completed, but we are well on the way and pledge ourselves to press forward assuring all men and women in the armed forces rewarding careers.

Better Defense Management

In the 1960's, the Department of Defense became administratively top-heavy and inefficient. The acquisition of new weapons systems was handled with inadequate attention to cost or performance, and there was little recognition of the human dimensions of the Department. Morale was low.

Our improvements have been many and substantial. Healthy decentralization has taken place. The methods of acquiring new weapons systems have been reformed by such procedures as "fly before you buy," the use of prototypes and the elimination of frills. Service personnel and civilian employees are now treated as the most important asset of the Department.

We have sharply reduced defense spending. In 1968, 45 per cent of the Federal budget was spent for defense and 32 per cent for human resources. In the 1973 budget the proportions were reversed —45 per cent for human resources, 32 per cent for defense. The 1973 defense budget imposes the smallest economic burden on the country of any defense budget in more than 20 years, consuming only 6.4 per cent of the estimated Gross National Product.

Arms Limitation

We believe in limiting arms—not unilaterally, but by mutual agreement and with adequate safeguards.

When the Nixon Administration began, the Soviet Union was rapidly building its strategic armaments, and any effort to negotiate limitations on such weapons seemed hopeless. The Soviet build-up threatened the efficacy of our strategic deterrent.

The Nixon years have achieved a great breakthrough in the long-term effort to curb major armaments by international agreement and given new momentum to arms limitations generally. Of greatest importance were agreements with the Soviet leaders to limit offensive and defensive nuclear weapons. The SALT accords established mutually agreed restraints between the United States and the Soviet Union and reduced tensions throughout the world.

With approval of the SALT agreements by the Congress, negotiations will be resumed to place further restrictions on nuclear weapons, and talks will begin on mutual, balanced force reductions in Europe.

We believe it is imperative that these negotiations go forward under President Nixon's continuing leadership. We pledge him our full support.

For the Future

We will continue the sound military policies laid down by the President—policies which guard our interests but do not dissipate our resources in vain efforts to police the world. As stated by the President:

We will maintain a nuclear deterrent adequate to meet any threat to the security of the United States or of our allies.

We will help other nations develop the capability of defending themselves.

We will faithfully honor all of our treaty commitments.

We will act to defend our interests whenever and wherever they are threatened.

But where our vital interests or treaty commitments are not involved our role will be limited.

We are proud of the men and women who wear our country's uniform, especially of those who have borne the burden of fighting a difficult and unpopular war. Here and now we reject all proposals to grant amnesty to those who have broken the law by evading military service. We reject the claim that those who fled are more deserving, or obeyed a higher morality, than those next in line who served in their places.

In carrying out our defense policies, we pledge to maintain at all times the level of military strength required to deter conflict, to honor our commitments to our allies, and to protect our people and vital interests against all foreign threats. We will not let America become a second-class power, dependent for survival on the good will of adversaries.

We will continue to pursue arms control agreements—but we recognize that this can be successful only if we maintain sufficient strength and will fail if we allow ourselves to slip into inferiority.

A New Prosperity

Jobs, Inflation and the Economy

The goal of our Party is prosperity, widely shared, sustainable in peace.

We stand for full employment—a job for everyone willing and able to work in an economy freed of inflation, its vigor not dependent upon war or massive military spending.

Under the President's leadership our country is once again moving toward these peacetime goals. We have checked the inflation which had started to skyrocket when our Administration took office, making the difficult transition from inflation toward price stability and from war toward peace. We have brought about a rapid rise in both employment and in real income, and laid the basis for a continuing decline in the rate of unemployment.

All Americans painfully recall the grave economic troubles we faced in January 1969. The Federal budget in fiscal 1968 had a deficit of more than $25 billion even though the economy was operating at capacity. Predictably, consumer prices soared by an annual rate of 6.6 per cent in the first quarter of 1969. "Jawboning" of labor and business had utterly failed. The inevitable tax increase had come too late. The kaleidoscope of "Great Society" programs added to the inflationary fires. Our international competitive position slumped from a trade surplus of $7 billion in 1964

to $800 million in 1968. Foreign confidence in the value of the dollar plummeted.

Strategies and Achievements

Our Administration took these problems head on, accepting the unpopular tasks of holding down the budget, extending the temporary tax surcharge, and checking inflation. We welcomed the challenge of reorienting the economy from war to peace, as the more than two and one-half million Americans serving the military or working in defense-related industries had to be assimilated into the peacetime work force.

At the same time, we kept the inflation fight and defense employment cuts from triggering a recession.

The struggle to restore the health of our nation's economy required a variety of measures. Most important, the Administration developed and applied sound economic and monetary policies which provided the fundamental thrust against inflation.

To supplement these basic policies, Inflation Alerts were published; a new National Commission on Productivity enlisted labor, business and public leaders against inflation and in raising real incomes through increased output per worker; proposed price increases in lumber, petroleum, steel and other commodities were modified. A new Construction Industry Stabilization Committee, with the cooperation of unions and management, braked the dangerously skyrocketing costs in the construction industry.

Positive results from these efforts were swift and substantial. The rate of inflation, more than 6 per cent in early 1969, declined to less than 4 per cent in early 1971.

Even so, the economic damage inflicted by past excesses had cut so deeply as to make a timely recovery impossible, forcing the temporary use of wage and price controls.

These controls were extraordinary measures, not needed in a healthy free economy, but needed temporarily to recapture lost stability.

Our mix of policies has worked. The nation's economic growth is once again strong and steady.

The rate of increase of consumer prices is now down to 2.7 per cent.

On the employment front, expenditures for manpower programs were increased from $2.3 billion to a planned $5.1 billion; new enrollees receiving training or employment under these programs were increased by more than half a million; computerized job banks were established in all cities; more than a million young people received jobs this summer through Federal programs, 50 per cent more than last year; engineers, scientists and technicians displaced by defense reductions were given assistance under the nation-wide Technology Mobilization and Reemployment program; 13 additional weeks of unemployment compensation were authorized; and a Special Revenue Sharing Program for Manpower was proposed to train more people for more jobs—a program still shelved by the opposition Congress.

Civilian employment increased at an annual rate of about 2.4 million from August 1971 to July 1972. Almost four and one-half million new civilian jobs have been added since President Nixon took office, and total employment is at its highest level in history.

The total productive output of this country increased at an annual rate of 9.4 per cent in the second quarter of 1972, the highest in many years.

Workers' real weekly take-home pay—the real value left after taxes and inflation—is increasing at an annual rate of 4.5 per cent, compared to less than one per cent from 1960 to 1970. For the first time in six years real spendable income is going up, while the rate of inflation has been cut in half.

Time lost from strikes is at the lowest level in many years.

The rate of unemployment has been reduced from 6.1 per cent to 5.5 per cent, lower than the average from 1961 through 1964 before the Vietnam buildup began, and is being steadily driven down.

In negotiation with other countries we have revalued the dollar relative to other currencies, helping to increase sales at home and abroad and increasing the number of jobs. We have initiated a reform of the international monetary and trading system and made clear our determination that this reform must lead to a strong United States position in the balance of trade and payments.

The Road Ahead

We will continue to pursue sound economic policies that will eliminate inflation, further cut unemployment, raise real incomes, and strengthen our international economic position.

We will fight for responsible Federal budgets to help assure steady expansion of the economy without inflation.

We will support the independent Federal Reserve Board in a policy of non-inflationary monetary expansion.

We have already removed some temporary controls on wages and prices and will remove them all once the economic distortions spawned in the late 1960's are repaired. We are determined to return to an unfettered economy at the earliest possible moment.

We reaffirm our support for the basic principles of capitalism which underlie the private enterprise system of the United States. At a time when a small but dominant faction of the opposition Party is pressing for radical economic schemes which so often have failed around the world, we hold that nothing has done more to help the American people achieve their unmatched standard of living than the free-enterprise system.

It is our conviction that government of itself cannot produce the benefits to individuals that flow from our unique combination of labor, management and capital.

We will continue to promote steady expansion of the whole economy as the best route to a long-term solution of unemployment.

We will devote every effort to raising productivity, primarily to raise living standards but also to hold down costs and prices and to increase the ability of American producers and workers to compete in world markets.

In economic policy decisions, including tax revisions, we will emphasize incentives to work, innovate and invest; and research and development will have our full support.

We are determined to improve Federal manpower programs to reduce unemployment and increase productivity by providing better information on job openings and more relevant job training. Additionally, we reaffirm our commitment to removing barriers to a full life for the mentally and physically handicapped, especially the barriers to rewarding employment. We commit ourselves to the full educational opportunities and the humane care, treatment and rehabilitation services necessary for the handicapped to become fully integrated into the social and economic mainstream.

We will press on for greater competition in our economy. The energetic antitrust program of the past four years demonstrates our commitment to free competition as our basic policy. The Antitrust Division has moved decisively to invalidate those "conglomerate" mergers which stifle competition and discourage economic concentration. The 87 antitrust cases filed in fiscal year 1972 broke the previous one-year record of more than a decade ago, during another Republican Administration.

We will pursue the start we have made for reform of the international monetary and trading system, insisting on fair and equal treatment.

Since the 1930's it has been illegal for United States citizens to own gold. We believe it is time to reconsider that policy. The right of American citizens to buy, hold, or sell gold should be reestablished as soon as this is feasible. Review of the present policy should, of course, take account of our basic objective of achieving a strengthened world monetary system.

Taxes and Government Spending

We pledge to spread the tax burden equitably, to spend the Federal revenues prudently, to guard against waste in spending, to eliminate unnecessary programs, and to make sure that each dollar spent for essential government services buys a dollar's worth of value.

Federal deficit spending beyond the balance of the full employment budget is one sure way to refuel inflation, and the prime source of such spending is the United States Congress. Because of its present procedures and particularly because of its present political leadership, Congress is not handling Federal fiscal policies in a responsible manner. The Congress now permits its legislative committees—instead of its fiscal committees—to decide, independently of each other, how much should be devoted to individual programs. Total Federal spending is thus haphazard and uncontrolled. We pledge vigorous efforts to reform the Congressional budgeting process.

As an immediate first step, we believe the Nation needs a rigid spending ceiling on Federal outlays each fiscal year—a ceiling controlling both the executive branch and the Congress—as President Nixon strongly recommended when he submitted his fiscal 1973 budget. Should the total of all appropriations exceed the ceiling, some or all of them would be reduced by Executive action to bring the total within the ceiling.

Our tax system needs continual, timely reform. Early in this Administration we achieved the first comprehensive tax reform since 1954. The record shows that as a result of the Tax Reform Act of 1969 and the Revenue Act of 1971:

9.5 million low-income Americans are removed from the Federal income tax rolls.

Persons in the lowest income tax bracket will pay 82 per cent less this year than they would have paid, had the 1969 and 1971 tax reforms not been enacted; those in the $10,000 to $15,000 income range will pay 13 per cent less, and those with incomes above $100,000 will pay about 7 per cent more.

This year the tax reduction for a family of four earning $7,500 a year will be $270.

In this fiscal year individual taxpayers will pay $22 billion less in Federal income taxes than they would have paid if the old tax rates and structures were still in force.

The tax disadvantage of single taxpayers is sharply reduced and we urge further changes to assure full equality.

Working parents can now deduct more of their costs for the care of their children during working hours.

The seven per cent automobile excise tax is repealed, saving the new-car buyer an average of $200 and creating more jobs in that part of the economy.

This is sound tax reform, the kind that more equitably spreads the tax burden and avoids incentive-destroying tax levels which would cripple the economy and put people out of work.

We reject the deceitful tax "reform" cynically represented as one that would soak the rich, but in fact one that would sharply raise the taxes of millions of families in middle-income brackets as well. We reject as well the lavish spending promised by the opposition Party which would more than double the present budget of the United States Government. This, too, would cause runaway inflation or force heavy increases in personal taxes.

Taxes and government spending are inseparable. Only if the taxpayers' money is prudently managed can taxes be kept at reasonable levels.

When our Administration took office, Federal spending had been mounting at an average annual rate of 17 per cent—a rate we have cut almost in half. We urge the Congress to serve all Americans by cooperating with the President in his efforts to curb increases in Federal spending—increases which will ordain more taxes or more inflation.

Since 1969 we have eliminated over $5 billion

of spending on unneeded domestic and defense programs. This large saving would have been larger still, had Congress passed the Federal Economy Act of 1970 which would have discontinued other programs. We pledge to continue our efforts to purge the Government of these wasteful activities.

Tax reform must continue. During the next session of Congress we pledge:

To pursue such policies as Revenue Sharing that will allow property tax relief;

Further tax reform to ensure that the tax burden is fairly shared;

A simplified tax system to make it easier for all of us to pay no more and no less than we rightly owe;

Prudent fiscal management, including the elimination of unnecessary or obsolete programs, to keep the tax burden to a minimum.

International Economic Policy

In tandem with our foreign policy innovations, we have transformed our international economic policy into a dynamic instrument to advance the interests of farmers, workers, businessmen and consumers. These efforts are designed to make the products of American workers and farmers more competitive in the world. Within the last year we achieved the Smithsonian Agreements which revalued our currency, making our exports more competitive with those of our major trading partners, and we pledge continuing negotiations further to reform the international monetary system. We also established negotiations to expand foreign market access for products produced by United States workers, with further comprehensive negotiations committed for 1973.

As part of our effort to begin a new era of negotiations, we are expanding trade opportunities and the jobs related to them for American workers and businessmen. The President's Summit negotiations, for example, yielded an agreement for the Soviet purchase, over a three-year period, of a minimum of $750 million in United States grains —the largest long-term commercial trade purchase agreement ever made between two nations. This amounts to a 17-per cent increase in grain exports by United States farmers. A U.S.-Soviet Commercial Commission has been established, and negotiations are now underway as both countries seek a general expansion of trade.

As we create a more open world market for American exports, we are not unmindful of dangers to American workers and industries from severe and rapid dislocation by changing patterns of trade. We have several agreements to protect these workers and industries—for example, for steel, beef, textiles and shoes. These actions, highly important to key American industries, were taken in ways that avoided retaliation by our trading partners and the resultant loss of American jobs.

As part of this adjustment process, we pledge improvement of the assistance offered by government to facilitate readjustment on the part of workers, businessmen and affected communities.

In making the world trading system a fairer one, we have vigorously enforced anti-dumping and countervailing duty laws to make them meaningful deterrents to foreign producers who would compete unfairly.

The growth of multinational corporations poses both new problems and new opportunities in trade and investment areas. We pledge to ensure that international investment problems are dealt with fairly and effectively—including consideration of effects on jobs, expropriation and treatment of investors, as well as equitable principles of taxation.

At the same time that we seek a better environment for American exports, we must improve our productivity and competitiveness. We must have a strong domestic economy with increased investment in new plants and equipment and an advancing technology.

We pledge increased efforts to promote export opportunities, including coordination of tax policy and improved export financing techniques—designed to make America more competitive in exporting. Of critical importance will be new legislative proposals to equip American negotiators with the tools for constructing an open and fair world trading system.

We deplore the practice of locating plants in foreign countries solely to take advantage of low wage rates in order to produce goods primarily for sale in the United States. We will take action to discourage such unfair and disruptive practices that result in the loss of American jobs.

Small Business

Small business, so vital to our economic system, is free enterprise in its purest sense. It holds forth opportunity to the individual, regardless of race or color, to fulfill the American dream. The seedbed of innovation and invention, it is the starting point of many of the country's large businesses, and today its roll in our increasingly technological economy is crucial. We pledge to sustain and expand that role.

We have translated this philosophy into many beneficial actions. Primarily through the Small Business Administration, we have delivered financial assistance to small business at a dramatically increasing rate. Today small business is receiving double the SBA funds it was receiving when our Administration took office. During the 1970–72 fiscal years the Agency loaned small business $3.3 billion—40 per cent of the total amount loaned in the entire 19-year history of the Small Business Administration.

Financial help to minorities has been more than tripled, and now more than 17 per cent of the SBA dollar goes to minority businesses. Procurement of Federal contracts for small business has surged above $12 billion.

In his first year in office, the President established a Task Force to discover ways in which the prospects of the small businessman could be improved.

The findings, reported to Congress, were followed by legislative proposals to give small business tax and interest advantages, to provide incentives for more participation on small business, to make venture capital and long-term credit easier to obtain, and to open the doors for disadvantaged minorities to go into business for themselves. Some of these measures have been signed into law. Others are still in the hands of the indifferent opposition in control of Congress.

The results of our efforts have been significant. Today small business is once again gaining ground. Incorporations are at a record level and the number of business failures is dropping. The current new growth of small businesses is about 100,000 units a year. For tomorrow, the challenges are many. We will:

Continue to fill the capital gap in the small business community by increasing SBA financing to upwards of $3 billion next year.

Provide more incentives for the private sector to join the SBA in direct action programs, such as lease guarantees, revolving lines of credit, and other sophisticated financial techniques, such as factoring and mortgage financing.

Increase SBA's Community Development program so that growth-minded communities can help themselves by building industrial parks and shopping centers.

Continue the rejuvenation of the Small Business Investment Company (SBIC) program, leading to greater availability of venture capital for new business enterprises.

See that a fair share of all Federal dollars spent on goods and services goes to small business.

Create established secondary financial markets for SBA loans, affording ready liquidity for financial institutions and opening up more financial resources to small firms.

Through tax incentives, encourage the start-up of more new businesses, and work for a tax system that more fairly applies to small business.

Establish special programs that will permit small firms to comply with consumer, environmental, and other new government regulations without undue financial burden.

IMPROVING THE QUALITY OF LIFE

Health Care

Our goal is to enable every American to secure quality health care at reasonable cost. We pledge a balanced approach—one that takes into account the problems of providing sufficient medical personnel and facilities.

Last year President Nixon proposed one of the most all-inclusive health programs in our history. But the opposition Congress has dragged its feet and most of this program has yet to be enacted into law.

To increase the supply of medical services, we will continue to support programs to help our schools graduate more physicians, dentists, nurses, and allied health personnel, with special emphasis on family practitioners and others who deliver primary medical care.

We will also encourage the use of such allied personnel as doctors' assistants, foster new area health education centers, channel more services into geographic areas which now are medically deprived, and improve the availability of emergency medical care.

We note with pride that the President has already signed the most comprehensive health manpower legislation ever enacted.

To improve efficiency in providing health and medical care, we have developed and will continue to encourage a pluralistic approach to the delivery of quality health care, including innovative experiments such as health maintenance organizations. We also support efforts to develop ambulatory medical care services to reduce hospitalization and keep costs down.

To reduce the cost of health care, we stress our efforts to curb inflation in the economy; we will also expand the supply of medical services and encourage greater cost consciousness in hospitalization and medical care. In doing this we realize the importance of the doctor-patient relationship and the necessity of insuring that individuals have freedom of choice of health providers.

To assure access to basic medical care for all our people, we support a program financed by employers, employees and the Federal Government to provide comprehensive health insurance coverage, including insurance against the cost of long-term and catastrophic illnesses and accidents and renal failure which necessitates dialysis, at a cost which all Americans can afford. The National Health Insurance Partnership plan and the Family Health Insurance Plan proposed by the President meet these specifications. They would build on existing private health insurance systems, not destroy them.

We oppose nationalized compulsory health insurance. This approach would at least triple in taxes the amount the average citizen now pays for health and would deny families the right to choose the kind of care they prefer. Ultimately it would lower the overall quality of health care for all Americans.

We believe that the most effective way of improving health in the long run is by emphasis on preventive measures.

The serious physical fitness problem in our country requires urgent attention. The President recently reorganized the Council on Physical Fitness and Sports to increase the leadership of representatives of medicine, physical education, sports associations and school administrations. The Republican Party urges intensification of these efforts, particularly in the Nation's school systems, to encourage widespread participation in effective physical fitness programs.

We have initiated this Nation's first all-out assault against cancer. Led by the new National Cancer Institute, the drive to eliminate this cruel killer will involve Federal spending of nearly $430 million in fiscal year 1973, almost twice the funding of just two years ago.

We have also launched a major new attack on sickle cell anemia, a serious blood disorder afflicting many black Americans, and developed a comprehensive program to deal with the menace of lead-based paint poisoning, including the screening of approximately 1,500,000 Americans.

We support expanded medical research to find cures for the major diseases of the heart, blood vessels, lungs and kidneys—diseases which now account for over half the deaths in the United States.

We have significantly advanced efforts to combat mental retardation and established a national goal to cut its incidence in half by the year 2000.

We continue to support the concept of comprehensive community mental health centers. In this fiscal year $135 million—almost three times the 1970 level—will be devoted to the staffing of 422 community mental health centers serving a population of 56 million people. We have intensified research on methods of treating mental problems, increasing our outlays from $76 million in 1969 to approximately $96 million for 1973. We continue to urge extension of private health insurance to cover mental illness.

We have also improved consumer protection, health education and accident prevention programs. And in Moscow this year, President Nixon reached an agreement with the Soviet Union on health research which may yield substantial benefits in many fields in the years ahead.

Education

We take pride in our leadership these last four years in lifting both quality and equality in American education—from pre-school to graduate school —working toward higher standards than ever before.

Our two most pressing needs in the 1970's are the provision of quality education for all children, an equitable financing of steadily rising costs. We pledge our best efforts to deal effectively with both.

Months ago President Nixon sent Congress a two-part comprehensive proposal on school busing. The first is the Student Transportation Moratorium Act of 1972—legislation to halt immediately all further court-ordered busing and give Congress time to devise permanent new arrangements for assuring desegregated, quality education.

The details of such arrangements are spelled

out in a companion bill, the Equal Educational Opportunities Act. This measure would:

Provide $2.5 billion in Federal aid funds to help promote quality education while preserving neighborhood schools;

Accord equal educational opportunities to all children;

Include an educational bill of rights for Spanish-speaking people, American Indians, and others who face special language problems in schools;

Offer, for the first time, a real chance for good schooling for the hundreds of thousands of children who live in urban centers;

Assure that the people's elected representatives in Congress play their proper role in developing specific methods for protecting the rights guaranteed by the 14th amendment, rather than leaving this task to judges appointed for life.

We are committed to guaranteeing equality of educational opportunity and to completing the process of ending de jure school segregation.

At the same time, we are irrevocably opposed to busing for racial balance. Such busing fails its stated objective—improved learning opportunities —while it achieves results no one wants—division within communities and hostility between classes and races. We regard it as unnecessary, counterproductive and wrong.

We favor better education for all children, not more transportation for some children. We favor the neighborhood school concept. We favor the decisive actions the President has proposed to support these ends. If it is necessary to accomplish these purposes, we would favor consideration of an appropriate amendment to the Constitution.

In the field of school finance, we favor a coordinated effort among all levels of government to break the pattern of excessive reliance on local property taxes to pay educational costs.

Our nation's intellectual resources are remarkable for their strength and public availability. American intellectuals have at least two important historical roles of which we are deeply conscious. One is to inform the public, the other is to assist government by thoughtful criticism and consultation. We affirm our confidence in these functions and especially in the free play of ideas and discourse which they imply.

We cherish the nation's universities as centers of learning, as conservers of our culture, and as analysts of our society and its institutions. We will continue to strive to assure their economic well-being. The financial aid we have given and will continue to give in the form of funds for scholarships, research, building programs and new teaching methods must never be used as a device for imposing political controls on our schools.

We believe that universities should be centers of excellence—that they should recruit faculty on the basis of ability to teach and admit students on the basis of ability to learn. Yet, excellence can be too narrowly confined—abilities overlooked, and social conformity mistaken for educational preparation.

We pledge continued support of collegiate and university efforts to insure that no group in our society—racial, economic, sexual or regional—is denied access to the opportunities of higher education.

Our efforts to remedy ancient neglect of disadvantaged groups will continue in universities as well as in society at large, but we distinguish between such efforts and quotas. We believe the imposition of arbitrary quotas in the hiring of faculties or the enrollment of students has no place in our universities; we believe quotas strike at the excellence of the university.

We recognize that the public should have access to the most rational and most effective kinds of education. Vocational training should be available to both young and old. We emphasize the importance of continuing education, of trades and technologies, and of all the honorable vocations which provide the society with its basic necessities. Such training must complement our more traditional forms of education; it will relieve the pressures on our universities and help us adapt to the rapid pace of technological change. Perhaps most important, it will help to restore a public sense of importance to these essential jobs and trades.

Moreover, we believe our educational system should not instruct in a vacuum, unmindful that the students ultimately will engage in a career. Our institutions of learning, from earliest years to graduate schools, can perform a vital function by coupling an awareness of the world of work to the delivery of fundamental education. We believe this kind of career education, blended into our school curricula, can help to prevent the aimlessness and frustration now experienced by large numbers of young people who leave the education system unable to cope with today's complex society.

In recognizing the fundamental necessity for quality education of all children, including the exceptional child, we recommend research and assistance in programs directed to the problems of dyslectic and hyperkinetic children who represent an estimated ten per cent of the school population.

By every measure, our record in the field of education is exceptionally strong. The United States Office of Education is operating this year under its highest budget ever—$5.1 billion. Federal aid to elementary and secondary education has increased 60 per cent over the past four years. Federal aid for college students has more than tripled.

We are proud of these accomplishments. We pledge to carry them forward in a manner consistent with our conviction that the Federal Government should assist but never control the educational process. But we also believe that the output of results, not the input of dollars, is the best yardstick of effectiveness in education. When this Administration took office in 1969, it found American schools deficient at many points. Our reform initiatives have included:

An Office of Child Development to coordinate all Federal programs targeted on the first five years of life and to make the Head Start Program work better;

A Right to Read Program, aimed at massive gains in reading ability among Americans of all ages;

A Career Education curriculum which will help to prepare students for the world of work;

A National Institute of Education to be a center for research on the learning process; and

A proposed National Foundation for Higher Education.

We have also proposed grant and loan programs to support a national commitment that no qualified student should be barred from college by lack of money. The Education Amendment of 1972 embodied substantial portions of that proposal and marked the Nation's most far-reaching commitment to make higher education available to all.

Our non-public schools, both church-oriented and nonsectarian, have been our special concern. The President has emphasized the indispensable role these schools play in our educational system —from the standpoints of the large numbers of pupils they serve, the competition and diversity they help to maintain in American education, and the values they help to teach—and he has stated his determination to help halt the accelerating trend of nonpublic school closures.

We believe that means which are consistent with the Constitution can be devised for channeling public financial aid to support the education of all children in schools of their parents' choice, nonpublic as well as public. One way to provide such aid appears to be through the granting of income tax credits.

For the future, we also pledge Special Revenue Sharing for Education, continued work to develop and implement the Career Education concept, and continued efforts to establish a student financial aid system to bring together higher education within the reach of any qualified person.

Welfare Reform

The Nation's welfare system is a mess. It simply must be reformed.

This system, essentially unchanged since the 1930's has turned into a human and fiscal nightmare. It penalizes the poor. It provides discriminatory benefits. It kills any incentives its victims might have to work their way out of the morass.

Among its victims are the taxpayers. Since 1961 the Federal cost of welfare has skyrocketed over 10 times—from slightly over $1 billion then to more than $11 billion now. State and local costs add to this gigantic expenditure. And here are things we are paying for:

The present system drains work incentive from the employed poor, as they see welfare families making as much or more on the dole.

Its discriminatory benefits continue to ensnare the needy, aged, blind and disabled in a web of inefficient rules and economic contradictions.

It continues to break up poor families, since a father's presence makes his family ineligible for benefits in many States. Its dehumanizing lifestyle thus threatens to envelop yet another "welfare generation."

Its injustices and costs threaten to alienate taxpayer support for welfare programs of any kind.

Perhaps nowhere else is there a greater contrast in policy and philosophy than between the Administration's remedy for the welfare ills and the financial orgy proposed by our political opposition.

President Nixon proposed to change our welfare system "to provide each person with a means of escape from welfare into dignity." His goals were these:

A decent level of payment to genuinely needy welfare recipients regardless of where they live.

Incentives not to loaf, but to work.

Requiring all adults who apply for welfare to register for work and job training and to accept work or training. The only exceptions would be the aged, blind and disabled and mothers of pre-school children.

Expanding job training and child care facilities so that recipients can accept employment.

Temporary supplements to the incomes of the working poor to enable them to support their families while continuing to work.

Uniform Federal payment standards for all welfare recipients.

In companion actions, our efforts to improve the nutrition of poor people resulted in basic reforms in the Food Stamp Program. The number of recipients increased from some three million to 13 million, and now 8.4 million needy children participate in the School Lunch Program, almost three times the number that participated in 1968.

Now, nearly 10,000 nutrition aides work in low-income communities. In 1968 there were none.

Since 1969, we have increased the Federal support for family planning threefold. We will continue to support expanded family planning programs and will foster research in this area so that more parents will be better able to plan the number and spacing of their children should they wish to do so. Under no circumstances will we allow any of these programs to become compulsory or infringe upon the religious conviction or personal freedom of any individual.

We all feel compassion for those who through no fault of their own cannot adequately care for themselves. We all want to help these men, women and children achieve a decent standard of living and become self-supporting.

We continue to insist, however, that there are too many people on this country's welfare rolls who should not be there. With effective cooperation from the Congress, we pledge to stop these abuses.

We flatly oppose programs or policies which embrace the principle of a government-guaranteed income. We reject as unconscionable the idea that all citizens have the right to be supported by the government, regardless of their ability or desire to support themselves and their families.

We pledge to continue to push strongly for sound welfare reform until meaningful and helpful change is enacted into law by the Congress.

LAW ENFORCEMENT

We have solid evidence that our unrelenting war on crime is being won. The American people know that once again the thrust of justice in our society will be to protect the law-abiding citizenry against the criminal, rather than absolve the criminal of the consequences of his own desperate acts.

Serious crimes rose only one per cent during the first quarter of this year—down from six per cent last year and 13 per cent the year before. From 1960 to 1968 major crime went up 122 per cent.

The fact is, in the first quarter of 1972, 80 of our 155 largest cities had an actual decline in reported crime.

In our Nation's Capitol, our anti-crime programs have been fully implemented. Through such measures as increased police, street lighting, a Narcotics Treatment Administration, court reform and special prosecuting units for major offenders, we have steadily dropped the crime rate since November 1969. By the first quarter of this year, the serious crime rate was down to half its all-time high.

When our Administration took office, a mood of lawlessness was spreading rapidly, undermining the legal and moral foundations of our society. We moved at once to stop violence in America. We have:

Greatly increased Federal aid to State and local law enforcement agencies across the country, with more than $1.5 billion spent on 50,000 crime-fighting projects.

Augmented Justice Department funding four-fold and provided more marshals, more judges, more narcotics agents, more Assistant United States Attorneys in the field.

Raised the Law Enforcement Assistance Administration budget ten-fold, earmarking $575 million of the $850 million for 1973 to upgrade State and local police and courts through revenue sharing.

Added 600 new Special Agents to the FBI.

Raised Federal spending on juvenile delinquency from $15 million to more than $180 million and proposed legislation to launch a series of model youth services.

Appointed Attorneys General with a keen sense of the rights of both defendants and victims, and determination to enforce the laws.

Appointed judges whose respect for the rights of the accused is balanced by an appreciation of the legitimate needs of law enforcement.

Added to the Supreme Court distinguished lawyers of firm judicial temperament and fidelity to the Constitution.

Even more fundamentally, we have established a renewed climate of respect for law and law enforcement. Now those responsible for enforcing the law know they have the full backing of their Government.

We recognize that programs involving work release, study release and half-way houses have contributed substantially to the rehabilitation of offenders and we support these programs. We further support training programs for the staffs in our correctional institutions and will continue to see that minority group staff members are recruited to work in these institutions.

The Fight against Organized Crime

To most of us, organized criminal activity seems remote and unreal—yet syndicates supply the narcotics pushed on our youth, corrupt local officials, terrify legitimate businesses and fence goods stolen from our homes. This Administration strongly supported the Organized Crime Control Act of 1970, and under our Strike Force concept we have combined Federal enforcement agencies to wage a concerted assault on organized crime. We have expanded the number of these strike forces and set a high priority for a new campaign against the syndicates.

Last year we obtained indictments against more than 2,600 members or associates of organized crime syndicates—more than triple the number indicted in 1968.

At last we have the lawless elements in our society on the run.

The Republican Party intends to keep them running.

Rehabilitation of Offenders

We have given the rehabilitation of criminal offenders more constructive, top-level attention than it has received at any time in our Nation's history. In November 1969, the President ordered a ten-year improvement program in prison facilities, correctional systems and rehabilitation methods and procedures.

We believe the correctional system not only should punish, but also should educate and rehabilitate. We are determined to press ahead with reform of the system to make it more effective against crime.

Almost a decade of inadequate Federal support of law enforcement has left deep scars in our society, but now a new mood pervades the country. Civil disorders and campus violence are no longer considered inevitable. Today, we see a new respect for law and order.

Our goal is justice—for everyone.

We pledge a tireless campaign against crime—to restore safety to our streets, and security to law-abiding citizens who have a right to enjoy their homes and communities free from fear.

We pledge to:

Continue our vigorous support of local police and law enforcement agancies, as well as Federal law enforcement agencies.

Seek comprehensive procedural and substantive reform of the Federal Criminal Code.

Accelerate the drive against organized crime.

Increase the funding of the Federal judiciary to help clear away the logjam in the courts which obstructs the administration of justice.

Push forward in prison reform and the rehabilitation of offenders.

Intensify efforts to prevent criminal access to all weapons, including special emphasis on cheap, readily-obtainable handguns, retaining primary responsibility at the State level, with such Federal law as necessary to enable the States to meet their responsibilities.

Safeguard the right of responsible citizens to collect, own and use firearms for legitimate purposes, including hunting, target shooting and self-defense. We will strongly support efforts of all law enforcement agencies to apprehend and prosecute to the limit of the law all those who use firearms in the commission of crimes.

Drug Abuse

The permissiveness of the 1960's left no legacy more insidious than drug abuse. In that decade narcotics became widely available, most tragically among our young people. The use of drugs became endowed with a sheen of false glamour identified with social protest.

By the time our Nation awakened to this cancerous social ill, it found no major combat weapons available.

Soon after we took office, our research disclosed there were perhaps hundreds of thousands of heroin users in the United States. Their cravings multiplied violence and crime. We found many more were abusing other drugs, such as amphetamines and barbiturates. Marijuana had become commonplace. All this was spurred by criminals using modern methods of mass distribution against outnumbered authorities lacking adequate countermeasures.

We quickly launched a massive assault against drug abuse.

We intercepted the supply of dangerous drugs at points of entry and impeded their internal distribution. The budget for international narcotics control was raised from $5 million to over $50 million. Narcotics control coordinators were appointed in 59 United States embassies overseas to work directly with foreign governments in stopping drug traffic. We have narcotics action agreements with over 20 countries. Turkey has announced a total ban on opium production and, with our cooperation, France has seized major heroin laboratories and drugs.

To inhibit the distribution of heroin in our own country, we increased the law enforcement budget for drug control more than 10 times—from $20 million to $244 million.

We are disrupting major narcotics distribution in wholesale networks through the combined efforts of the Bureau of Narcotics and Dangerous Drugs, Customs operations at our borders, and a specially credited unit of over 400 Internal Revenue agents who conduct systematic tax investigations of targeted middle and upper echelon traffickers, smugglers, and financiers. Last January we established the Office of Drug Abuse Law Enforcement to disrupt street and mid-level heroin traffickers.

We established the "Heroin Hot Line"—a nationwide toll free phone number (800/368–5363) —to give the public a single number for reporting information on heroin pushers.

Last year we added 2,000 more Federal narcotics agents, and the Bureau of Narcotics and Dangerous Drugs has trained over 170,000 State and local personnel.

And we are getting results. This past year four times as much heroin was seized as in the year this Administration took office. Since 1969, the number of drug-related arrests has nearly doubled.

For drug abuse prevention and treatment we increased the budget from $46 million to over $485 million.

The demand for illicit drugs is being reduced through a massive effort directed by a newly created office in the White House. Federally funded drug treatment and rehabilitation programs were more than doubled last fiscal year, and Federal programs now have the capacity to treat more than 60,000 drug abusers a year.

To alert the public, particularly the youth, to the dangers of drugs, we established a National Clearinghouse for Drug Abuse Information in 1970 as well as a $3.5 million Drug Education and Training Program.

We realize that the problem of drug abuse cannot be quickly solved, but we have launched a massive effort where practically none existed before. Nor will we relax this campaign:

We pledge to seek further international agreements to restrict the production and movement of dangerous drugs.

We pledge to expand our programs of education, rehabilitation, training and treatment. We will do more than ever before to conduct research into the complex psychological regions of disappointment and alienation which have led many young people to turn desperately toward drugs.

We firmly oppose efforts to make drugs easily available. We equally oppose the legalization of marijuana. We intend to solve problems, not create bigger ones by legalizing drugs of unknown physical impact.

We pledge the most intensive law enforcement war ever waged. We are determined to drive the pushers of dangerous drugs from the streets, schools and neighborhoods of America.

Agriculture and Rural Life

Our agriculture has become the economic marvel of the world. Our American farmers and ranchers have tripled per worker production in the last 20 years, while non-farm industries have increased theirs a little over half.

Yet when we took office three and a half years

ago, the farm community was being shockingly shortchanged for its remarkable achievements.

Inflation was driving up both the cost of farming and the cost of living—indeed, driving up all prices except the prices of products the farmers were taking to market. Overall farm income was down. Farm exports were low. Bureaucratic planting regulations were oppressive. All across the country family farms were failing.

Our moves to deal with these problems have been numerous and effective.

The rate of inflation has been curbed without forcing down prices for commodities, even as we have stepped up our drive against rising food costs in the cities.

Net farm income has soared to a record high of more than $18 billion. During these Republican years average net farm income has been over $2 billion a year higher than during the last two Administrations. For the same period average income per farm is up more than 40 percent.

And farm exports now stand at a record $8 billion, sharply up from the $5.7 billion when we took office.

Operating loans to help young farmers have reached the highest levels in history. Administration-backed legislation has given farmers much greater freedom to plant what they choose, and we have given assistance to cooperatives to strengthen the farmers' bargaining positions.

Rural development has been energetically carried forward, and small towns and rural areas have been helped to adjust and grow. The loan programs of the Farmers Home Administration for farm and rural people have been dramatically increased. Electric and telephone service in rural areas has been substantially expanded, a Rural Telephone Bank has been enacted, and the Farm Credit Administration has been streamlined. The total national investment in rural development has almost tripled. Heading the Department of Agriculture have been leaders who understand and forcefully speak out for the farming people of America.

Farmers are benefiting markedly from our successful efforts to expand exports—notably a $750 million sale of United States grains to the Soviet Union, with prospects of much more. Last year we negotiated a similar sale amounting to $135 million.

For the future, we pledge to intensify our efforts to:

Achieve a $10 billion annual export market by opening new foreign markets, while continuing to fight for fair treatment for American farm products in our traditional markets;

Follow sound economic policies to brake inflation and reduce interest rates;

Expand activities to assist farmers in bargaining for fair prices and reasonable terms in a rapidly changing marketing system;

Keep farm prices in the private sector, not subject to price controls;

Support family farms as the preferred method of organizing agricultural production, and protect them from the unfair competition of farming by tax-loss corporations and non-farm enterprises;

Reform Federal estate tax laws, which often force the precipitate sale of family farms to help pay the tax, in such ways as to help support the continuance of family farms as institutions of great importance to the American way of life;

Provide greater credit, technical assistance, soil and water conservation aid, environmental enhancement, economic stimulus and sympathetic leadership to America's rural areas and communities;

Concentrate research on new uses of agricultural products;

Continue assistance to farm cooperatives, including rural electric and telephone cooperatives, in their efforts to improve their members;

Develop land and water policy that takes account of the many uses to which these resources may be put;

Establish realistic environmental standards which safeguard wise resource use, while avoiding undue burdens on farmers;

Use forums of national leaders to create a better understanding by all citizens, those in the cities and suburbs as well as those in small towns, of the difficult problems confronting farm and ranch families in a modern agriculture.

We will not relax our efforts to increase net farm income, to narrow the spread between farm and non-farm income levels, and to pursue commodity programs that will enable farmers and ranchers to receive fair prices for what they produce.

Community Development

For more than a quarter century the Federal Government has sought to assist in the conservation and rebuilding of our urban centers. Yet, after the spending of billions of dollars and the commitment of billions more to future years, we now know that many existing programs are unsuited to the complex problems of the 1970's. Programs cast in the mold of the "big government" philosophy of the 1930's are simply incapable of meeting the challenge of today.

Our Party stands, therefore, for major reform of Federal community development programs and the development of a new philosophy to cope with urban ills.

Republican urban strategy rejects throwing good money after bad money. Instead, through fundamental fiscal, management and program reforms, we have created a new Federal partnership through which State, county and municipal governments can best cope with specific problems such as education, crime, drug abuse, transportation, pollution and housing.

We believe the urban problems of today fall into these categories:

The fiscal crises of State, county and municipal governments;

The need for a better quality and greater availability of urban services;

The continual requirement of physical development;

The need for better locally designed, locally implemented, locally controlled solutions to the problems of individual urban areas.

In the last category—the importance of grass roots planning and participation—our Republican Party has made its most important contribution to solving urban problems.

We hold the government planners should be guided by the people through their locally elected representatives. We believe that real solutions require the full participation of the private sector.

To help ease the fiscal crises of State, county and municipal governments, we pledge increased Federal assistance—assistance we have more than doubled in the past four years. And, as stressed elsewhere in this Platform, we remain committed to General Revenue Sharing, which could reduce the oppressive property tax.

Our proposals for Special Revenue Sharing for Urban Development, transportation, manpower and law enforcement—all still bottled up by the opposition Congress—are designed to make our towns and cities places where Americans can once again live and work without physical or environ-

mental hazard. Urban areas are already benefiting from major funding increases which we fought for in the Law Enforcement Assistance Administration programs and in our $10 billion mass transit program.

Urban areas are also benefiting from our new Legacy of Parks program, which is bringing recreation opportunities closer to where people live.

We are committed also to the physical development of urban areas. We have quadrupled subsidized housing starts for low and moderate income families since 1969, and effected substantial increases for construction of municipal waste treatment facilities.

We strongly oppose the use of housing or community development programs to impose arbitrary housing patterns on unwilling communities. Neither do we favor dispersing large numbers of people away from their homes and neighborhoods against their will. We do believe in providing communities, with their full consent, guidance and cooperation with the means and incentives to increase the quantity and quality of housing in conjunction with providing increased access to jobs for their low-income citizens.

We also pledge to carry forward our policy on encouraging the development of new towns in order to afford all Americans a wider range of residential choices. Additionally, our Special Revenue Sharing for Urban and Rural Community Development, together with General Revenue Sharing and nationwide welfare reform, are basic building blocks for a balanced policy of national growth, leading to better lives for all Americans, whether they dwell in cities, suburbs or rural areas.

Our Party recognizes counties as viable units of regional government with a major role in modernizing and restructuring local services, eliminating duplication and increasing local cooperation. We urge Federal and State governments, in implementing national goals and programs, to utilize the valuable resources of counties as area-wide, general-purpose governments.

Housing

Our Republican Administration has made more and better housing available to more of our citizens than ever before.

We are building two-and-a-third million new homes a year—65 per cent more than the average in the eight years of the two previous Administrations. Progress has not been in numbers alone; housing quality has also risen to an all-time high—far above that of any other country.

We will maintain and increase this pattern of growth. We are determined to attain the goal of a decent home for every American.

Significant numbers of Americans still lack the means for decent housing, and in such cases—where special need exists—we will continue to apply public resources to help people acquire better apartments and homes.

We further pledge:

Continued housing production for low and moderate income families, which has sharply increased since President Nixon took office;

Improvement of housing subsidy programs and expansion of mortgage credit activities of Federal housing agencies as necessary to keep Americans the best-housed people in the world;

Continued development of technological and management innovations to lower housing costs—a program begun by Operation Breakthrough, which is assisting in the development of new methods for more economical production of low-cost, high-quality homes.

We urge prompt action by State, county and municipal governments to seek solutions to the serious problems caused by abandoned buildings in urban areas.

Transportation

When President Nixon took office a crisis in transportation was imminent, as indicated by declining mass transportation service, mounting highway deaths, congested urban streets, long delays at airports and airport terminals, deterioration of passenger train service, and a dwindling Merchant Marine. Within two years the President had proposed and signed into law:

A $10 billion, 12-year program—the Urban Mass Transportation Act of 1970—to infuse new life into mass transportation systems and help relieve urban congestion;

A major 10-year program involving $280 million annually for airport development projects as well as an additional $250 million annually to expand airways systems and facilities;

The Rail Passenger Service Act of 1970 to streamline and improve the Nation's passenger train service;

New research and development projects, including automatic people movers, improved Metroliner and Turbo-trains, quieter aircraft jet engines, air pollution reduction for mass transportation vehicles, and experimental safety automobiles. We strongly support these research and development initiatives of the Department of Transportation.

Four years ago we called attention to the decline of our Merchant Marine due to previous neglect and apathy. We promised a vigorous ship replacement program to meet the changing pattern of our foreign commerce. We also pledged to expand maritime research and development and the simplification and revision of construction and operating subsidy procedures.

By the enactment of the Merchant Marine Act of 1970, we have reversed the long decline of our Merchant Marine. We reaffirm our goals set forth in 1968 and anticipate the future development of a merchant fleet that will give us defensive mobility in time of emergency as well as economic strength in time of peace.

To reduce traffic and highway deaths, the National Highway Traffic Safety Administration has been reorganized and expanded, with dramatic results. In 1971, the number of traffic deaths per hundred million miles driven was the lowest in history.

To help restore decision-making to the people, we have proposed a new Single Urban Fund providing almost $2 billion a year by 1975 to State and metropolitan areas to assist local authorities in solving their own transportation problems in their own way.

Our proposal for Special Revenue Sharing for Transportation would also help governments close to the people meet local needs and provide greater freedom to achieve a proper balance among the Nation's major transportation modes.

To revitalize the surface freight transportation industry, we have recommended measures to modernize railway equipment and operations and to update regulatory practices. These measures, on which Congress still dawdles, would help curb inflation by saving the public billions of dollars a year in freight costs. Their enactment would also expand employment and improve our balance of trade.

The Nation's transportation needs are expected to double in the next 20 years. Our Party will continue to pursue policies and programs that will meet these needs and keep the country well ahead of rapidly changing transportation demands.

Environment

In January 1969, we found the Federal Government woefully unprepared to deal with the rapidly advancing environmental crisis. Our response was swift and substantial.

First, new decision-making organizations were set in place—the first Council on Environmental Quality, the Environmental Protection Agency, the National Oceanic and Atmospheric Administration. We also proposed a new Department of Natural Resources, but Congress has failed to act. We also created a National Industrial Pollution Control Council to enlist the private sector more actively against environmental decay, and Presidential Federal Property Review Board was appointed to ferret out Federal property for transfer to local park and recreational uses.

Second, we gave top priority in the Federal Budget to environmental improvements. This fiscal year approximately $2.4 billion will be expended for major environmental programs—three times more than was being spent when President Nixon took office.

Third, sweeping environment messages were sent to Congress in 1970, 1971 and 1972 covering air quality, water quality, toxic waste substances, ocean dumping, noise, solid waste management, land use, parklands and many other environmental concerns. Almost all of these proposals still languish in the opposition Congress.

Although the President cannot move until and unless Congress passes laws in many of these areas, he nevertheless can act—and has acted—forcefully on many fronts:

He has directed the Federal Government to practice ecological leadership by using low-lead gasoline and recycled paper. He has cracked down on flagrant polluters, greatly increasing prosecutions and making the first use of Federal authority to shut down major industries during an air pollution crisis. The fragile and unique Everglades were saved from a jetport. Pesticide abuses were curtailed.

Strict new clean-air standards were set, and in many urban centers the air is improving. Regulations were issued to make one grade of lead-free and phosphorous-free gasoline available throughout the Nation by July 1, 1974, and a phased reduction was required in the lead content of regular and premium gasolines. Auto makers were required to design air pollution control systems to assure that vehicles comply with Federal emission standards throughout their usual life.

Additionally, the President launched the Legacy of Parks program to convert underutilized Federal properties to park and recreational use, with special emphasis on new parks in or near urban areas. More than 140 areas have already been made available to States, counties and municipalities for such use, including priceless stretches of ocean beach. Moreover, nearly two million acres of land have been purchased by Federal, State and local governments for recreation and for historical and natural preservation purposes.

A system of recreational trails for hiking, bicycling and horseback riding will help meet the pressing recreational needs of our increasingly urbanized society. Many State, county and municipal governments are developing bicycle, hiking, and horseback trails with our active assistance through various Federal programs. We pledge our continued commitment to seeking out practical ways for more and safer bicycling opportunities within our cities and metropolitan areas.

We have also provided effective leadership in international environmental activity. The President has negotiated the Great Lakes Water Quality Agreement with Canada and a Cooperative Agreement on Environmental Protection with the Soviet Union.

The United Nations Conference on the Human Environment in Stockholm adopted our government's initiatives for the creation of an international fund for the environment, a continuing United Nations agency for environmental problems, and the control of ocean dumping. Our President has led the effort for a ten-year moratorium on commercial whaling everywhere in the world.

We call upon the Congress to act promptly on the President's environmental proposals still stalled there—more than 20 in all. These include:

Legislation to control, and in some cases prohibit, the dumping of wastes into the oceans, estuaries and the Great Lakes;

A Federal Noise Control Act to reduce and regulate unwanted sound from aircraft, construction and transportation equipment;

Authority to control hundreds of chemical substances newly marketed each year;

Legislation to encourage the States to step up

to pressing decisions on how best to use land. Both environmentally critical areas such as wetlands and growth-inducing developments such as airports would have particular scrutiny;

A proposal to provide for early identification and protection of endangered wildlife species. This would, for the first time, make the taking of endangered species a Federal offense;

Establishment of recreational areas near metropolitan centers such as the Gateway National Recreational Area in New York and New Jersey and the Golden Gate National Recreation Area in and around San Francisco Bay.

The nostalgic notion of turning the clock back to a simpler time may be appealing but is neither practical nor desirable. We are not going to abandon the automobile, but we are going to have a clean-burning engine.

We are not going to give up electric lighting and modern industry, but we do expect cleanly-produced electric power to run them.

We are not going to be able to do without containers for our foods and materials, but we can improve them and make them reusable or biodegradable.

We pledge a workable balance between a growing economy and environmental protection. We will resolve the conflicts sensibly within that framework.

We commit ourselves to comprehensive pollution control laws, vigorous implementation of those laws and rigorous research into the technological problems of pollution control. The beginnings we have made in these first years of the 1970's are evidence of our determination to follow through.

We intend to leave the children of America a legacy of clean air, clean water, vast open spaces and easily accessible parks.

Natural Resources and Energy

Wilderness areas, forests, fish and wildlife are precious natural resources. We have proposed 36 new wilderness areas, adding another 3.6 million acres to the National Wilderness Preservation System. We have made tough new proposals to protect endangered species of wildlife.

Public lands provide us with natural beauty, wilderness and great recreational opportunities as well as minerals, timber, food and fiber. We pledge to develop and manage these lands in a balanced way, both to protect the irreplaceable environment and to maximize the benefits of their use to our society. We will continue these conservation efforts in the years ahead.

We recognize and commend the humane societies and the animal welfare societies in their work to protect animals.

Water supplies are not a boundless resource. The Republican Party is committed to developing additional water supplies by desalinization, the discovery of new groundwater stocks, recycling and wiser and more efficient use of the waters we have.

We will continue the development of flood control, navigation improvement and reclamation projects based on valid cost-benefit estimates, including full consideration of environmental concerns.

No modern nation can thrive without meeting its energy needs, and our needs are vast and growing. Last year we proposed a broad range of actions to facilitate research and development for clean energy, provide energy resources on Federal lands, assure a timely supply of nuclear fuels, use energy more efficiently, balance environmental and energy needs and better organize Federal efforts.

The National Minerals Policy Act of 1970 encourages development of domestic resources by private enterprise. A program to tap our vast shale resources has been initiated consistent with the National Environmental Policy Act of 1969.

We need a Department of Natural Resources to continue to develop a national, integrated energy policy and to administer and implement that policy as the United States approaches the 21st Century. Energy sources so vitally important to the welfare of our Nation are becoming increasingly interchangeable. There is nothing inherently incompatible between an adequate energy supply and a healthy environment.

Indeed, vast quantities of energy are needed to do the work necessary to clean up our air and streams. Without sufficient supplies of power we will not be able to attain our goals of reducing unemployment and poverty and enhancing the American standard of living.

Responsible government must consider both the short-term and the long-term aspects of our energy supplies. Avoidance of brown-outs and power disruptions now and in the future call for sound policies supporting incentives that will encourage the exploration for, and development of, our fossil fuels. Such policies will buy us time to develop the sophisticated and complex technologies needed to utilize the exotic energy sources of the future.

National security and the importance of a favorable balance of trade and balance of payments dictate that we must not permit our Nation to become overly dependent on foreign sources of energy. Since more than half our Nation's domestic fossil resources now lie under Federal lands, high priority must be given to the governmental steps necessary to the development of these resources by private industry.

A liquid metal fast breeder reactor demonstration plant will be built with the financial support of the Atomic Energy Commission, the electric power industry and the Tennessee Valley Authority.

We will accelerate research on harnessing thermo-nuclear energy and continue to provide leadership in the production of energy from the sun and geothermal steam. We recognize the serious problem of assuring adequate electric generating capacity in the Nation, and pledge to meet this need without doing violence to our environment.

Oceans

The oceans are a vast, largely untapped reservoir of resources, a source of food, minerals, recreation and pleasure, with great potential for economic development. For their maintenance we must:

Encourage the development of coastal zone management systems by the States, in cooperation with the Federal Government, to preserve the coastal environment while allowing for its prudent social and economic development;

Protect the oceans from pollution through the creation of binding domestic and international legal and institutional arrangements;

Foster arrangements to develop the untapped mineral resources of the seas in an equitable and environmentally sound manner;

Establish domestic and international institutions for the management of the ocean fisheries. Fishing in international waters, a way of life for many Americans, must be maintained without harassment on the high seas or unreasonable restrictions;

Protect and conserve marine mammals and other marine species to ensure their abundance and especially to protect species whose survival is endangered;

Maintain a national capability in ocean science and technology and, through the United Nations Conference on the Law of the Sea, work to codify an international legal framework for the peaceful conduct of ocean activities.

Science and Technology

Basic and applied scientific research and development are indispensable to our national security, our international competitive position, and virtually every aspect of the domestic economy. We have initiated a new research-and-development strategy which emphasizes a public-private partnership in searching out new ideas and technologies to create new jobs, new internationally competitive industries and new solutions for complex domestic problems.

In support of this strategy we have increased Federal efforts in civilian research and development by 65 per cent—from $3.3 billion to $5.4 billion—and expanded research in drug abuse, law enforcement, health care, home building, motor vehicle safety, energy and child development as well as many other fields.

We will place special emphasis on these areas in which breakthroughs are urgently needed:

Abundant, clean energy sources;

Safe, fast and pollution-free transportation;

Improved emergency health care;

Reduction of loss of life, health and property in natural disasters;

Rehabilitation of alcoholics and addicts to dangerous drugs.

Additionally, we urge the fair and energetic enforcement of all fire-prevention laws and applaud the work of the National Commission on Fire Prevention and Control. We encourage accelerated research on methods of fire prevention and suppression, including studies on flammable fabrics, hazardous materials, fire equipment and training procedures.

The space program is yielding impressive dividends in earth-oriented applications of space technology—advances in medicine, industrial techniques and consumer products that would still be unknown had we not developed the technology to reach the moon. We will press ahead with the space shuttle program to replace today's expendable launch vehicles and provide low-cost access to space for a wide variety of missions, including those related to earth resources. We pledge to continue to extend our knowledge of the most distant frontiers in space.

We will also extend our exploration of the sea-bed and the sea. We will seek food for the hungry, power for future technologies, new medicines for the sick and new treatments of water for arid regions of the world.

The quantities of metals and minerals needed to maintain our economic health and living standards are so huge as to require the re-use of all recoverable commodities from solid waste materials. We pledge a vigorous program of research and development in order to seek out more economical methods to recover and recycle such commodities, including the processing of municipal solid wastes.

We pledge to extend the communications frontier, and to foster the development of orbiting satellite systems that will make possible wholly new, world-wide educational and entertainment programs.

We recognize that the productivity of our Nation's research and development efforts can be enhanced through cooperative international projects. The signing of the Moscow agreements for cooperation in space, environment, health and science and technology has opened a new era in international relations. A similar agreement between the United States and Polish Governments will permit expansion of programs such as the jointly-funded Copernicus Astronomical Center and Krakow Children's Hospital.

Finally, we pledge expanded efforts to aid unemployed scientists and engineers. We are determined to see that such on-going efforts as the Technology Mobilization and Reemployment Program are effective.

The Individual and Government

Even though many urgently-needed Administration proposals have been long delayed or stopped by the opposition Congress, we have kept our 1968 promise to make government more accountable and more responsive to the citizen. One such proposal is General Revenue Sharing with State and local governments—a means of returning to the people powers which for 40 years have grown increasingly centralized in the remote Washington bureaucracy. Another is consolidation of scores of categorical grant programs into six Special Rev-

enue Sharing programs which would make available some $12 billion annually in broad policy fields for States and localities to apply in their own ways to their own needs. Yet another is our proposal to modernize the Executive Branch of the Federal Government by combining six Cabinet departments and several independent agencies into four new departments. So far, the opposition controlled Congress has blocked or ignored all of these proposals.

In addition, we have:

Improved domestic policy formulation and implementation by the new Domestic Council and Office of Management and Budget within the Executive Office of the President;

Established stronger liaison between the Federal Government and the States, counties and municipalities by a new Office of Intergovernmental Relations, headed by the Vice President;

Overhauled the fragmented and poorly coordinated Federal agencies concerned with drug abuse and the environment;

Utilized voluntary citizen effort through the formation of the ACTION agency in government and the National Center for Voluntary Action outside of government;

Proposed reorganization of the Federal regulatory agencies and appointed distinguished people to those agencies;

Assured more open government, ending abuse of document classification and providing fuller information to the public.

We pledge continuing reform and revitalization of government to assure a better response to individual needs.

We express deep concern for the flood victims of tropical Storm Agnes, the worst natural disaster in terms of property damage in our Nation's history. Past laws were totally inadequate to meet this crisis, and we commend the President's leadership in urgently recommending the newly-enacted $1.8 billion flood relief measure, greatly expanding and enlarging the present program. We pledge to reevaluate and enlarge the national flood disaster insurance program so that it will be adequate for future emergencies.

We will continue to press for the enactment of General and Special Revenue Sharing and to pursue further initiatives both to decentralize governmental activities and to transfer more such activities to the private sector.

We will continue to defend the citizen's right

to privacy in our increasingly interdependent society. We oppose computerized national data banks and all other "Big Brother" schemes which endanger individual rights.

We reaffirm our view that voluntary prayer should be freely permitted in public places—particularly, by school children while attending public schools—providing that such prayers are not prepared or prescribed by the state or any of its political subdivisions and that no person's participation is coerced, thus preserving the traditional separation of church and state.

We remain committed to a comprehensive program of human rights, social betterment and political participation for the people of the District of Columbia. We will build on our strong record in this area—a record which includes cutting the District of Columbia crime rate in half, aggressive support for a balanced transportation system in metropolitan Washington, initiation of a Bicentennial program and celebration in the national capital region, and support for the first Congressional Delegate in nearly a century. We support voting representation for the District of Columbia in the United States Congress and will work for a system of self-government for the city which takes fair account of the needs and interests of both the Federal Government and the citizens of the District of Columbia.

The Republican Party adheres to the principle of self-determination for Puerto Rico. We will welcome and support statehood for Puerto Rico if that status should be the free choice of its people in a referendum vote.

Additionally, we will pursue negotiations with the Congress of Micronesia on the future political status of the Trust Territories of the Pacific Islands to meet the mutual interests of both parties. We favor extending the right of electing the territorial Governor to the people of American Samoa, and will take complementary steps to increase local self-government in American Samoa. We vigorously support such action as is necessary to permit American citizens resident in Guam, Puerto Rico and the Virgin Islands to vote for President and Vice President in national elections. We support full voting rights in committees for the Delegates to Congress from Guam and the Virgin Islands.

In our territorial policy we seek a maximum degree of local self-sufficiency and self-government, while encouraging greater inclusion in Federal services and programs and greater participation in national decision-making.

Volunteerism

In our free system, the people are not only the source of our social problems but also the main source of solutions Volunteerism, therefore, an indispensable national resource, is basic to our Republican philosophy. We applaud the Administration's efforts to encourage volunteerism by all Americans and commend the millions of volunteers who are working in communities and states across the country on myriad projects. We favor further implementation of voluntary action programs throughout the fifty States to assist public and private agencies in working to assure quality life for all human beings.

Arts and Humanities

The United States is experiencing a cultural renaissance of inspiring dimension. Scores of millions of our people are now supporting and participating in the arts and humanities in quest of a richer life of the mind and the spirit. Our national culture, no longer the preserve of the elite, is becoming a people's heritage of importance to the whole world.

We believe, with the President, that "the Federal Government has a vital role as catalyst, innovator, and supporter of public and private efforts for cultural development."

We have supported a three-year extension of the National Foundation on the Arts and the Humanities, and increased the funding of its two endowments by more than four times the level of three years ago. The State Arts Councils, which operate in all 50 States and the five special jurisdictions, have also been strengthened.

The Arts Endowment has raised its support for the Nation's museums, orchestras, theatre, dance, opera companies and film centers and encouraged the creativity of individual artists and writers. In addition, the new Federal Expansion Arts Program has been sharply increased.

We have encouraged Federal agencies to use the arts in their programs, sponsored an annual Design Assembly for Federal administrators, requested the National Endowment for the Arts to recommend a program for upgrading the design of Federal buildings, and moved to set new standards of excellence in all design endeavors of the Federal Government.

Moreover, the National Endowment for the Humanities, now greatly enlarged, is fostering improved teaching and scholarship in history, literature, philosophy and ethics. The Endowment also supports programs to raise levels of scholarship and teaching in Afro-American, American Indian and Mexican-American studies, has broadened its fellowship programs to include junior college teachers, and stresses adult or continuing education, including educational television and film series. We have also expanded the funding of public broadcasting.

For the future, we pledge continuance of our vigorous support of the arts and humanities.

A Better Future for All

Children

We believe, with the President, that the first five years of life are crucial to a child's development, and further, that every child should have the opportunity to reach his full potential as an individual.

We have, therefore, established the Office of Child Development, which has taken a comprehensive approach to the development of young children, combining programs dealing with their physical, social and educational needs and development.

We have undertaken a wide variety of demonstration programs to assure our children, particularly poor children, a good start in life—for example, the Parent and Child Center program for infant care, Home Start to strengthen the environment of the preschool child, and Health Start to explore new delivery systems of health care for young children.

We have redirected Head Start to perform valuable full-day child care and early education services, and more than 380,000 preschool children are now in the program. We have doubled funds for early childhood demonstration programs which will develop new tools and new teaching techniques to serve children who suffer from deafness, blindness and other handicaps.

So that no child will be denied the opportunity for a productive life because of inability to read effectively, we have established the Right to Read Program.

To add impetus to the entire educational effort,

our newly-created National Institute of Education ensures that broad research and experimentation will develop the best educational opportunities for all children. Additionally, we have taken steps to help ensure that children receive proper care while their parents are at work.

Moreover, as stated elsewhere in this Platform, we have broadened nutritional assistance to poor children by nearly tripling participation in the Food Stamp Program, more than doubling the number of needy children in the school lunch program, operating a summer feeding program for three million young people, increasing the breakfast program fivefold, and doubling Federal support for child nutritional programs. We are improving medical care for poor children through more vigorous treatment procedures under Medicaid and more effectively targeting maternal and child health services to low-income mothers. We will continue to seek out new means to reach and teach children in their crucial early years.

Youth

We believe that what our youth most want and need is not special treatment as a group apart, but just the opposite—the opportunity for full participation by exercising the rights and responsibilities of adults.

In 1970 the President approved legislation which gave the vote to more than 11 million 18-to-20 year olds. The 26th Amendment, which places this important new right in the Constitution, has our enthusiastic backing.

Our Administration has already made the draft a far less arbitrary factor in young men's lives. Now we near the point where we can end conscription altogether and achieve our goal of an all-volunteer armed force.

Our total war on drug abuse has had special benefits for youth, hardest hit by this menace. Last year we held the first White House Conference ever held by and for young people themselves. The Administration gave the Conference's more than 300 recommendations a searching review, and last spring the President returned a detailed response and action report to the conferees.

The anarchy which swept major campuses in the late 1960's penalized no one more severely than the young people themselves. The recent calm on campus is, we believe, in part the result of the President's leadership in winding down the war in Vietnam, reducing the draft, and taking a strong stand against lawlessness, but our view is that colleges themselves are responsible for maintaining a campus climate that will preserve academic freedom.

We have proposed legislation to ensure that no qualified student is denied a higher education by lack of funds, and have also moved to meet the often-overlooked concerns of the two-thirds of the college-age young not in school. We have developed a new job-oriented, career-education concept, expanded Federal manpower programs and provided a record number of summer job opportunities for young men and women.

To engage youthful idealism and energies more effectively, we have created the new ACTION volunteer service agency, bringing together the Peace Corps, VISTA, and other volunteer programs; and we encouraged the establishment of the independent National Center for Voluntary Action.

We stand for lowering the legal age of majority in all jurisdictions to 18; and we will seek to broaden the involvement of young people in every phase of the political process—as voters, party workers and leaders, candidates and elected officials, and participants in government at municipal, State and Federal levels.

We will continue to build on these solid achievements in keeping with our conviction that these young people should have the opportunity to participate fully in the affairs of our society.

Equal Rights for Women

The Republican Party recognizes the great contributions women have made to our society as homemakers and mothers, as contributors to the community through volunteer work, and as members of the labor force in careers outside the home. We fully endorse the principle of equal rights, equal opportunities and equal responsibilities for women, and believe that progress in these areas is needed to achieve the full realization of the potentials of American women both in the home and outside the home.

We reaffirm the President's pledge earlier this year: "The Administration will . . . continue its strong efforts to open equal opportunities for women, recognizing clearly that women are often denied such opportunities today. While every woman may not want a career outside the home, every woman should have the freedom to choose whatever career she wishes—and an equal chance to pursue it."

This Administration has done more than any before it to help women of America achieve equality of opportunity.

Because of its efforts, more top-level and middle-management positions in the Federal Government are held by women than ever before. The President has appointed a woman as his special assistant in the White House, specifically charged with the recruitment of women for policy-making jobs in the United States Government. Women have also been named to high positions in the Civil Service Commission and the Department of Labor to ensure equal opportunities for employment and advancement at all levels of the Federal service.

In addition we have:

Significantly increased resources devoted to enforcement of the Fair Labor Standards Act, providing equal pay for equal work;

Required all firms doing business with the Government to have affirmative action plans for the hiring and promotion of women;

Requested Congress to expand the jurisdiction of the Commission on Civil Rights to cover sex discrimination;

Recommended and supported passage of Title IX of the Higher Education Act opposing discrimination against women in educational institutions;

Supported the Equal Employment Opportunity Act of 1972 giving the Equal Employment Opportunity Commission enforcement power in sex discrimination cases;

Continued our support of the Equal Rights Amendment to the Constitution, our Party being the first national party to back this Amendment.

Other factors beyond outright employer discrimination—the lack of child care facilities, for example—can limit job opportunities for women. For lower and middle income families, the President supported and signed into law a new tax provision which makes many child care expenses deductible for working parents. Part of the President's recent welfare reform proposal would provide comprehensive day care services so that women on welfare can work.

We believe the primary responsibility for a child's care and upbringing lies with the family. However, we recognize that for economic and many other reasons many parents require assistance in the care of their children.

To help meet this need, we favor the development of publicly or privately run, voluntary, comprehensive, quality day care services, locally controlled but federally assisted, with the requirement that the recipients of these services will pay their fair share of the costs according to their ability.

We oppose ill-considered proposals, incapable of being administered effectively, which would heavily engage the Federal Government in this area.

To continue progress for women's rights, we will work toward:

Ratification of the Equal Rights Amendment;

Appointment of women to highest level positions in the Federal Government, including the Cabinet and Supreme Court;

Equal pay for equal work;

Elimination of discrimination against women at all levels in Federal Government;

Elimination of discrimination against women in the criminal justice system, in sentencing, rehabilitation and prison facilities;

Increased opportunities for the part-time employment of women, and expanded training programs for women who want to reenter the labor force;

Elimination of economic discrimination against women in credit, mortgage, insurance, property, rental and finance contracts.

We pledge vigorous enforcement of all Federal statutes and executive orders barring job discrimination on the basis of sex.

We are proud of the contributions made by women to better government. We regard the active involvement of women at all levels of the political process, from precinct to national status, as of great importance to our country. The Republican Party welcomes and encourages their maximum participation.

Older Americans

We believe our Nation must develop a new awareness of the attitudes and needs of our older citizens. Elderly Americans are far too often forgotten Americans, relegated to lives of idleness and isolation by a society bemused with the concerns of other groups. We are distressed by the tendency of many Americans to ignore the heartbreak and hardship resulting from the generation gap which separates so many of our people from those who have reached the age of retirement. We deplore what is tantamount to cruel discrimination—age discrimination in employment, and the discrimination of neglect and indifference, perhaps the cruelest of all.

We commit ourselves to helping older Americans achieve greater self-reliance and greater opportunities for direct participation in the activities of our society. We believe that the later years should be, not isolated years, not years of dependency, but years of fulfillment and dignity. We believe our older people are not to be regarded as a burden but rather should be valuable participants in our society. We believe their judgment, their experience, and their talents are immensely valuable to our country.

Because we so believe, we are seeking and have sought in many ways to help older Americans— for example:

Federal programs of direct benefit to older Americans have increased more than $16 billion these past four years;

As part of this, social security benefits are more than 50 per cent higher than they were four years ago, the largest increase in the history of social security;

Social security benefits have become inflation proof by making them rise automatically to match cost-of-living increases, a protection long advocated by the Republican Party;

We have upgraded nursing homes.

Expenditures under the Older Americans Act have gone up 800 per cent since President Nixon took office, with a strong emphasis on programs enabling older Americans to live dignified, independent lives in their own homes.

The valuable counsel of older people has been sought directly through the White House Conference on Aging. The President has appointed high-level advisers on the problems of the aging to his personal staff.

We have urged upon the opposition Congress— again, typically to no avail—numerous additional programs of benefit to the elderly. We will continue pressing for these new initiatives:

Increase the amount of money a person can earn without losing social security benefits;

Increase widow, widower, and delayed retirement benefits;

Improve the effectiveness of Medicare, including elimination of the monthly premium required under Part B of Medicare—the equivalent of more than a three per cent social security increase;

Strengthen private pension plans through tax deductions to encourage their expansion, improved vesting, and protection of the investments in these funds;

Reform our tax system so that persons 65 or over will receive increased tax-free income;

Encourage volunteer service activities for older Americans, such as the Retired Senior Volunteer Program and the Foster Grandparents Program;

Give special attention to bringing full government services within the reach of the elderly in rural areas who are often unable to share fully in their deserved benefits because of geographic inaccessibility;

Upgrade other Federal activities important to the elderly including programs for nutrition, housing and nursing homes, transportation, consumer protection, and elimination of age discrimination in government and private employment.

We encourage constructive efforts which will help older citizens to be better informed about existing programs and services designed to meet their needs, and we pledge to cut away excessive Federal redtape to make it easier for older Americans to receive the benefits to which they are entitled.

Working Men and Women

The skill, industry and productivity of American workers are the driving force of our free economy. The Nation's labor unions, comprised of millions of working people, have advanced the well-being not only of their members but also of our entire free-enterprise system. We of the Republican Party reaffirm our strong endorsement of Organized Labor's key role in our national life.

We salute the statesmanship of the labor union movement. Time and time again, at crucial moments, it has voiced its outspoken support for a firm and effective foreign policy and for keeping the Armed Forces of the United States modern and strong.

The American labor movement and the Republican Party have always worked against the spread of totalitarian forms of government. Together we can continue to preserve in America the best system of government ever devised for human happiness and fulfillment.

We are for the right of American workers and their families to enjoy and to retain to the greatest possible extent the rewards of their own labor.

We regard collective bargaining as the cornerstone of the Nation's labor relations policy. The government's role is not to encroach upon this process but rather to aid the differing parties to make collective bargaining more effective both for themselves and for the public. In furtherance of that concept, we will continue to develop procedures whereby the imagination, ingenuity and knowledge of labor and management can more effectively seek solutions for such problems as structural adjustment and productivity.

In the construction industry, for example, we will build on a new joint effort between government and all parts of the industry to solve such problems as seasonality and varying peaks of demand to ensure a stable growth in the number of skilled craftsmen.

We call upon management and labor to devote their best efforts to finding better ways to conduct labor-management relations so the good of all the people can be advanced without strikes or lockouts.

We will continue to search for realistic and fair solutions to emergency labor disputes, guided by two basic principles; first, that the health and safety of the people of the United States should always be paramount; and second, that collective bargaining should be kept as free as possible from government interference.

For mine health and safety, we have implemented the most comprehensive legislation in the Nation's history, resulting in a major reduction in mine-related accidents. We pledge continued advancement of the health and safety of workers.

We will continue to press for improved pension vesting and other statutory protections to assure that Americans will not lose their hard-earned retirement income.

We pledge further modernization of the Federal Civil Service System, including emphasis on executive development. We rededicate ourselves to promotion on merit, equal opportunity, and the setting of clear incentives for higher productivity. We will give continuing close attention to the evolving labor-management relationship in the Federal service.

We pledge realistic programs of education and training so that all Americans able to do so can make their own way, on their own ability, receiving an equal and fair chance to advance themselves. We flatly oppose the notion that the hard-earned tax dollars of American workers should be used to support those who can work but choose not to, and who believe that the world owes them a living free from any responsibility or care.

We are proud of our many other solid achievements on behalf of America's working people—for example:

Nearly five million additional workers brought under the coverage of the unemployment insurance system, and eligibility deadlines twice extended;

Funding for more than 166,000 jobs under the Emergency Employment Act;

Expansion of vocational education and manpower training programs;

Use of the long-neglected Trade Expansion Act to help workers who lose their jobs because of imports. We strongly favor vigorous competition by American business in the world market but in ways that do not displace American jobs;

Negotiation of long-needed limitations on imports of man-made fibers, textiles and other products, thus protecting American jobs.

We share the desire of all Americans for continued prosperity in peacetime. We will work closely with labor and management toward our mutual goal of assuring a job for every man and woman seeking the dignity of work.

Ending Discrimination

From its beginning, our Party has led the way for equal rights and equal opportunity. This great tradition has been carried forward by the Nixon Administration.

Through our efforts de jure segregation is virtually ended. We pledge continuation of these efforts until no American schoolchild suffers educational deprivation because of the color of his skin or the language he speaks and all school children are receiving high quality education. In pursuit of this goal, we have proposed $2.5 billion of Federal aid to school districts to improve educational opportunities and build facilities for disadvantaged children. Further to assure minority progress, we have provided more support to predominantly black colleges than ever before—twice the amount being spent when President Nixon took office.

Additionally, we have strengthened Federal enforcement of equal opportunity laws. Spending for civil rights enforcement has been increased from $75 million to $602 million—concrete evidence of our commitment to equal justice for all. The President also supported and signed into law the Equal Employment Opportunity Act of 1972, which makes the Equal Employment Opportunity Commission a much more powerful body.

Working closely with leaders of construction unions, we have initiated 50 "home-town" plans which call for more than 35,000 additional minority hirings in the building trades during the next four years. We will continue to search out new employment opportunities for minorities in other fields as well. We believe such new jobs can and should be created without displacing those already at work. We will give special consideration to minority Americans who live and make their way in the rural regions of our Country—Americans too often bypassed in the advances of the general society.

We have made unprecedented progress in strengthening minority participation in American business. We created the Office of Minority Business Enterprise in March 1969 to coordinate the Federal programs assisting members of minority groups who seek to establish or expand businesses. We have more than tripled Federal loans, guarantees and grants to minority-owned businesses. More minority Americans are now in our Nation's economic mainstream than at any other time in our history, and we pledge every effort to expand these gains.

Minority businesses now receive 16 per cent of the Small Business Administration dollar—more than double the proportion in 1968. Many Minority Enterprise Small Business Investment Companies have been licensed since 1969 to provide venture capital for minority enterprises. More than $200 million is now available through this program, and we have requested additional funding.

In late 1970, we initiated a combined Government-private program to increase minority bank deposits. This year our goal of $100 million has been reached four times over.

We pledge to carry forward our efforts to place minority citizens in responsible positions—efforts we feel are already well under way. During the last four years the percentage of minority Federal employees has risen to a record high of almost 20 per cent and, perhaps more important, the quality of jobs for minority Americans has improved. We have recruited more minority citizens for top managerial posts in Civil Service than ever before. We will see that our progress in this area will continue and grow.

In 1970 President Nixon approved strong new amendments to the Voting Rights Act of 1965, and we pledge continued vigilance to ensure that the rights affirmed by this act are upheld.

The cultural diversity of America's heritage groups has always been a source of strength for our society and our Party. We reaffirm our commitment to the basic American values which have made this Nation the land of opportunity for these groups, originating from all sectors of the world, from Asia to Africa to Europe to Latin America. We will continue our Party's open-door policy and work to assure all minorities full opportunity for participation in the political process. We pledge vigorous support of the Bilingual Act and the Ethnic Studies Heritage Act.

Spanish-Speaking Americans

In recognition of the significant contributions to our country by our proud and independent Spanish-speaking citizens, we have developed a comprehensive program to help achieve equal opportunity.

During the last four years Spanish-speaking Americans have achieved a greater role in national affairs. More than thirty have been appointed to high federal positions.

To provide the same learning opportunities enjoyed by other American children, we have increased bilingual education programs almost sixfold since 1969. We initiated a 16-point employment program to help Spanish-speaking workers, created the National Economic Development Association to promote Spanish-speaking business development and expanded economic development opportunities in Spanish-speaking communities.

We will work for the use of bilingual staffs in localities where this language capability is desirable for effective health care.

Indians, Alaska Natives, and Hawaiians

President Nixon has evolved a totally new Indian policy which we fully support. The opposition Congress, by inaction on most of the President's proposals, has thwarted Indian rights and opportunities.

We commend the Department of the Interior for its stalwart defense of Indian land and water rights, and we urge the Congress to join in support of that effort. We further request Congress to permit Indian tribal governments to assume control over the programs of the Departments of Interior and Health, Education and Welfare in their homelands, to assure Indians a role in determining how funds can best be used for their children's schools, to expand Indian economic development opportunity, to triple the funds for Indian credit and create a new Assistant Secretary of the Interior for Indian and Territorial Affairs.

These reforms, all urged by the President, have been ignored by the Congress. We—with the Indian people—are impatiently waiting.

Knowing the Indians' love for their land and recognizing the many wrongs committed in years past, the President has restored Blue Lake in New Mexico to the Taos Pueblo and the Mt. Adams area in Washington to the Yakima Nation. We are seeking to protect Indian water rights in Pyramid Lake by bringing suit in the Supreme Court.

We are fully aware of the severe problems facing the Menominee Indians in seeking to have Federal recognition restored to their tribe and promise a complete and sympathetic examination of their pleas.

We have increased the Bureau of Indian Affairs' budget by 214 per cent, nearly doubled funds for Indian health, and are arranging with tribal leaders for the allocation of Bureau funds in accordance with priorities set by the tribal governments themselves.

We pledge continued attention to the needs of off-reservation Indians and have launched demonstration projects at Indian centers in nine major cities. We are determined that the first Americans will not be the forgotten Americans, and that their rights will be respected.

We will continue the policy of Indian preference in hiring and promotion and apply it to all levels, including management and supervisory positions in those agencies with programs affecting Indian peoples.

The standard of living of Indian Americans is still far below that of any of the peoples of the United States. This intolerable level of existence should be alleviated by the enactment of new legislation designed to further Indian self-determination without termination and to close this economic gap and raise the Indian standard of life to that of the rest of America. We favor the development of such legislation in the 93d Congress.

At the President's recommendation, the Congress voted an Alaska Native Claims Settlement which confirms the titles of the Eskimos, Indians and Aleuts to 40 million acres and compensates them with a generous cash settlement.

We will also preserve and continue to protect the Hawaiian Homes Commission Act which provides land already set aside for Hawaiians for homes and the opportunity to preserve their culture.

Our achievements for human dignity and opportunity are specific and real, not idle promises. They have brought tremendous progress to many thousands of minority citizens and made our society more just for all.

We will press on with our fight against social injustice and discrimination, building upon the achievements already made. Knowing that none of us can reap the fullest blessings of liberty until all of us can, we reaffirm our commitment to the upward struggle for universal freedom led by Abraham Lincoln a century ago.

Consumers

The American consumer has a right to product safety; clearly specified qualities and values, honest descriptions and guarantees, fair credit procedures, and due recourse for fraud and deception. We are addressing these concerns forcefully, with executive action and legislative and legal initiatives.

The issues involved in this accelerating awareness on the part of consumers lie close to the heart of the dynamic American market: Good products at fair prices made it great; the same things will keep it great.

Enlightened business management is as interested in consumer protection and consumer education as are consumers themselves. In a marketplace as competitive and diverse as ours, a company's future depends on the reputation of its products. One safety error can wipe out an established firm overnight.

Unavoidably, the remoteness of business management from the retail counter tends to hamper consumers in resolving quality and performance questions. Technical innovations make it harder for the consumer to evaluate new products. Legal complexities often deny efficient remedies for deception or product failure.

To assist consumers and business, President Nixon established the first Office of Consumer Affairs in the White House and made its Director a member of his personal staff and of the Cost of Living Council. We have also proposed a Buyer's Bill of Rights, including:

Federal authority for the regulation of hazardous consumer products;

Requirement of full disclosure of the terms of warranties and guarantees in language all can understand.

We support the establishment of an independent Consumer Protection Agency to present the consumer's case in proceedings before Federal agencies and also a consumer product safety agency in the Department of Health, Education and Welfare. We oppose punitive proposals which are more anti-business than pro-consumer.

We pledge vigorous enforcement of all consumer protection laws and to foster more consumer education as a vital necessity in a marketplace ever increasing in variety and complexity.

Veterans

We regard our Nation's veterans precisely as our President does:

"Americans have long known that those who defended the great values of our Nation in wartime are of great value to the Nation when the war is over. It is traditional that the American veteran has been helped by his Nation so that he can create his own 'peace story', a story of prosperity, independence and dignity.

"Veterans benefit programs have therefore become more than a recognition for services performed in the past; they have become an investment in the future of the veteran and of his country."

Under Republican leadership, far more for our veterans is being done than ever before:

G.I. Bill education benefits have been increased more than 35 per cent. Vietnam-era veterans have the highest assistance levels in history to help them pursue educational opportunities.

Major cost-of-living adjustments have been made in compensation and pension payments.

Medical services are the best in the history of the Veterans Administration and now include a strong new drug treatment and rehabilitation program.

Disability benefits have been increased.

G.I. home loan benefits have been expanded and improved.

The total Administration commitment is massive—$12.4 billion for this fiscal year. This is the largest Veterans Administration budget in history, and the third largest of all Federal agencies and departments.

We are giving the highest priority to the employment problems of Vietnam veterans. In 1971 we initiated a comprehensive program which recently placed more than one million Vietnam-era veterans in jobs, training and education programs.

For the future, we pledge:

Continuation of the Veterans Administration as a strong, independent agency;

Continuation of an independent system of Veterans Administration health care facilities to provide America's veterans with the best medical care available, including appropriate attention to the problems of the ex-serviceman afflicted with drug and alcohol problems;

Continuing attention to the needs of the Vietnam-era veteran, with special emphasis on employment opportunities, education and housing.

Continuation of our efforts to raise GI Bill education benefits to a level commensurate with post-World War II benefits in adjusted dollars;

Continued effort for a better coordinated national policy on cemeteries and burial benefits for veterans.

We will not fail our obligation to the Nation's 29 million veterans and will stand ever watchful of their needs and rights.

CONCLUSION

The record is clear.

More than any President, Richard Nixon has achieved major changes in policy and direction in our government. He has restored faith—faith that our system will indeed reflect the will of the people —faith that there will be a new era of peace and human progress at home and around the world.

To be sure there is unfinished business on the agenda of our ever-restless Nation. We have great concern for those who have not participated more fully in the general prosperity. The twin evils of crime and drug abuse are still to be conquered. Peace in the world is not yet won.

But Republican leadership has restored stability and sanity to our land once again. We have vigorously attacked every major problem.

Once again our direction is peace; once again our determination is national strength; once again we are prospering; once again, on a host of fronts, we are making progress.

Now we look to tomorrow.

We pledge ourselves to go forward at an accelerated pace—with a determination and zeal unmatched before.

In four years we mark the 200th anniversary of the freest, most productive, most benevolent Nation of all human history. In four years we celebrate one of man's highest achievements—two hundred years as a constitutional republic founded on the noble concept that every person is a sovereign being, possessed of dignity and inalienable rights.

Almost two centuries ago, the Founding Fathers envisioned a Nation of free people, at peace with themselves and the world—each with equal opportunity to pursue happiness in his own way. Much of that dream has come true; much is still to be fulfilled.

We, the Republican Party, pledge ourselves to go forward, hand-in-hand with every citizen, to solve those problems that yet stand in the way of realizing that more perfect union, the dream of the Founding Fathers—a dream enhanced by the free and generous gift of people working together, not in shifting alliances of separated minorities, but in unison of spirit and purpose. We cannot favor, nor can we respect, the notion of group isolation in our United States of America. We must not divide and weaken ourselves by attitudes or policies which would segregate our citizens into separate racial, ethnic, economic, religious or social groups. It is the striving of all of us—our striving together as Americans—that will move our Nation continually onward to our Founders' dream.

Building on the foundations of peace in the world, and reason and prosperity at home, our Republican Party pledges a new era of progress for man—progress toward more freedom, toward greater protection of individual rights, toward more security from want and fear, toward greater fulfillment and happiness for all.

We pledge to the American people that the 200th anniversary of this Nation in 1976 will be more than a celebration of two centuries of unequaled success; we pledge it also to be the beginning of the third and greatest century for all of our countrymen and, we pray, for all people in the world.

Socialist Labor Platform 1972

During the three centuries since it emerged from the expiring feudal order, capitalism has profoundly transformed the world.

It has revolutionized the mode and scale of production.

It has revolutionized transportation and communication.

It has gathered the scattered continents into an interdependent global economy.

It has created the industrial means of abundance for all mankind.

But in accomplishing this tremendous historic task, capitalism has exacted a terrible price.

It has wantonly squandered the planet's natural wealth and polluted its lands, skies and waters.

It has repeatedly pitted nations against nations in devastating, decimating wars.

It has inexcusably perpetuated poverty and insecurity, thereby fomenting racial and ethnic strife.

It has engendered a social climate that breeds corruption, crime, drug abuse and mental illness.

Social systems are mortal.

Like the human beings who compose them, they are born, mature, decline, and eventually die.

The history of capitalist society shows it is no exception. It too has moved from birth through maturity to decline, and is now approaching death.

Capitalism is dying because of a serious malfunction. This malfunction is not just a disorder of the system's old age. It first appeared in capitalism's lusty youth and has been revealing itself ever since through the periodic business crises that have punctuated capitalism's life.

In these crises, society has again and again faced an absurd catastrophe: an epidemic of "overproduction," with millions of workers deprived of their livelihoods because they were producing too much.

Not one of these catastrophes has ever resulted from an overproduction of society's needs. On the contrary, each time immense social wants were left unsatisfied as industry shut down.

Every business crisis has thus demonstrated anew that capitalist industry does not operate primarily to satisfy social wants. It produces to sell at a profit. And whenever more goods and services are being produced than can be profitably sold,

capitalist industry naturally cuts back its operations.

WHY CAPITALISM "OVERPRODUCES"

The recurrent crises have been inevitable because capitalism is basically geared to overproduce its market. The greatest part of that market consists of worker consumers. As producers, however, the workers are paid only a small part of the value of their products. That explains how capitalist profits are realized. But that also explains why the workers' purchasing power is nowhere near sufficient to absorb the full national output.

The ten-year-long crisis of the thirties marked the beginning of capitalism's end. It was the first in which drying up the oversupply of goods by holding down production failed to bring economic recovery. It was the first in which the capitalist State had to intervene and attempt a massive stimulation of demand.

The principal stimulant used was government deficit spending, the Keynesian prescription inspired by a frank recognition of capitalism's inherent malfunction. In the doses administered, the prescription proved to be inadequate.

Meanwhile, the struggle to win foreign markets for products that could not be sold at home embroiled the capitalist powers in an escalating commercial warfare which culminated in military conflict. Once World War II broke out, the problem of "overproduction" was temporarily overcome.

The problem remained dormant for a brief period after peace returned. As soon, though, as capitalist industry had satisfied the deferred demand of the war years, plus the orders arising from the rehabilitation of war-torn countries, "overproduction" reappeared. And again war stepped in to relieve it—the Korean War and the Cold War.

STIMULANTS HAVE SIDE EFFECTS

Since then, the prolonged war in Vietnam and huge deficit spending in other directions have served to further postpone capitalism's final, total collapse. But these stimulants cannot go on doing so forever because they are having dangerous side effects that must ultimately ensure the system's collapse.

The most dangerous is inflation. Almost 40 years of government deficit spending has inordinately inflated the national money supply and thus depreciated the dollar to a fraction of its former value. As the dollar's value has fallen, prices have risen correspondingly, causing a serious erosion of domestic purchasing power.

Moreover, an acceleration of inflation in recent years pushed prices so high that American products found themselves being undersold by foreign products here at home as well as abroad. And to make bad enough worse, the long-standing international monetary arrangements based on the dollar were finally shattered by its steepening depreciation.

So, capitalism is plainly damned if it feeds inflation . . . but equally damned if it doesn't. For, when President Nixon opted in 1969 to cease deficit spending, his decision brought on a business slump. And despite the fact that he subsequently reversed himself and began outspending his predecessors, the downturn stubbornly refused to become an upturn. The only thing that headed upward again was inflation—and, consequently, prices.

Emergency Economic Controls

By mid-1971, the situation had grown so grave that President Nixon, responding to capitalist forebodings of a complete breakdown, acted to halt inflation by imposing economic controls. Experience with Phases One and Two indicates that the controls are merely aggravating capitalism's basic plight because, while they are necessarily and conspicuously failing to curb inflation and prices, they are curbing wages and therefore making still smaller the part of the national output that the workers can buy.

A similar result is being produced by technology, which capitalism compulsively continues to revolutionize. Each improvement in the methods or tools of production that increases the workers' productivity also increases the already large difference between the value represented by their wages and that embodied in their products.

Accordingly, the inherent malfunction that engulfed capitalism in a great crisis of "overproduction" at the outset of the thirties is unmistakably driving it towards a far greater one in the not distant future. When that far greater crisis arrives, the enormously swollen public debt and recklessly depreciated currency with which the system has bought a longer lease on life will provide two big nails for its coffin. The vast industrial capacity built to meet the demands of war will provide a third.

Workers Have Historic Task

And capitalism has prepared its gravediggers. They are the very workers whom the system has brought together and trained to carry on production. A total economic collapse is going to blast any remaining illusions workers may have that comfortable, secure lives are possible for them within capitalist society. They will be at last compelled to recognize that their well-being and aspirations require the construction of a new form of social organization.

Once the workers have reached a revolutionary frame of mind, they will quickly discover a number of important truths: They will discover that they are endowed with an irresistible power for social change by virtue of their industrial role. They will discover that capitalist industrialization has laid the foundation and erected the framework of a new society that can ensure their prosperity and security. They will discover that they have an inalienable right to reconstruct society and the possibility of democratically affirming this right via the ballot.

The workers will most certainly discover these truths because the Socialist Labor Party has for many, many years been exerting itself to make them known and will keep on so exerting itself throughout the approaching national campaign and in the days that follow.

Furthermore, when the revolutionary moment comes, the workers will have available a simple, workable program with which they can consummate the needed social reconstruction—the program of Socialist Industrial Unionism.

That program aims to unite the workers politically as well as industrially. Political unity is necessary because it will enable the worker majority to deliver a democratic mandate for social ownership of industry and production for social use. While industrial unity will supply the indispensable power with which to enforce and execute that mandate.

Through their Socialist Industrial Unions, the workers themselves can take peaceful possession of the nation's economy in the name of all society. Then on the basis of their Industrial Unions, they can set up a democratic administration of production for the benefit of all society. This administration will be composed of representatives elected from the various industries by the workers voting in their respective industries. It will be an industrial self-government, an economic democracy, the highest, fullest freedom the human race has ever known.

Socialist Workers Platform 1972

The Democratic and Republican parties bear joint responsibility for the situation facing the people of the United States.

The Republican Nixon has carried on the military intervention in Indochina initiated by the Democrats Kennedy and Johnson. The White House continues to order murderous air raids on the people and countryside of Indochina. Despite Nixon's election promise to end the war, Vietnamese, Cambodians, Laotians, and Americans are still dying.

At home, continued war spending gives added impetus to the inflationary spiral. Working people are being forced to pay the astronomical costs of the war. While prices and taxes keep going up, wage controls imposed by the government prevent working people from gaining fair wage adjustments to offset the soaring cost of living. Skyrocketing prices make the continued high unemployment even more painful.

These economic hardships inflicted upon the American people result from the needs of the very wealthy—a tiny minority who run this country—to improve their competitive position on the world market. In line with this, the bosses are determined to hold real wages down and to squeeze more out of the workers by intensifying speedups and layoffs.

The Black community is confronted with savage police assaults and political frame-ups of activists such as Angela Davis, the Soledad Brothers, and others. Afro-Americans face racial discrimination in housing, education, job opportunities, and every other area of economic, social, and political life. Similar problems confront Chicanos, Puerto Ricans, Native Americans, and other oppressed nationalities.

Responsibility for the erosion of civil liberties in the United States lies squarely with the Republicans and Democrats. The twin parties of big business have failed to offer any meaningful programs to meet the needs of women; they have turned a deaf ear to the demands of American youth; and they have refused to deal effectively with the ecological disaster that faces the country. Virtually an entire generation of young people feels increasingly alienated because of the sterility and decay marking the culture of American capitalism.

THE CAPITALIST SYSTEM

The basic policies pursued by the Democrats and Republicans are not accidental, nor merely the results of decisions made by individual politicians. The policies of the capitalist parties flow from the needs of the capitalist system itself and from the outlook of the ruling capitalist class.

The Vietnam war is a prime example. The objectives of the U.S. government have nothing to do with "democracy" or "freedom" in Indochina. The war is part of a global strategy of counterrevolution designed to maintain world capitalism and to preserve the position of U.S. imperialism on an international scale.

This same policy has led to U.S. military interventions in the Dominican Republic, Cuba, the Congo, Korea, Lebanon, and many other countries—under both Democratic and Republican administrations. The capitalist politicians consider it part of the "game plan" to send young men to die all over the world to maintain and extend the capitalist system and capitalist profits.

Racism is also woven into the fabric of American capitalism. Racial oppression pays off in profits for the capitalist class, providing a pool of cheap labor to be drawn upon in periods of expansion. Racism is also used to justify imperialist domination of the colonial world by perpetuating the myth that it is "natural" for rich nations to exploit poor nations. Racism also serves to keep white workers from realizing that their interests lie with the Black and Brown masses, and not with the white capitalist rulers.

The imposition of wage controls shows once again how the capitalist government stands on the side of the rich and against the poor. Wage controls pare down the standard of living of the working people. They benefit only the bosses, who are already hauling in superprofits.

The government of the United States is not a neutral defender of the interests of the "public," as it claims to be. It is the instrument through which the profit-hungry capitalist class runs society in accordance with its own interests.

The passing differences that crop up among

politicians of the two capitalist parties reflect tactical differences over how best to maintain capitalist rule or factional squabbles over control of the pork barrel of government patronage. There is no fundamental difference between the Democrats and Republicans—they are both committed to preserving capitalist exploitation.

Regardless of how "sincere" or "honest" or even "militant" the politicians of the Democratic and Republican parties make themselves out to be, no real improvement in the conditions of working people can come about through supporting them. There is no "lesser evil" among the candidates of the capitalist parties.

Social progress has never been achieved except when masses of people have organized themselves and fought for it. That is how the capitalist system itself, along with all its evils, will be uprooted.

More and more people are coming to the conclusion that from the point of view of satisfying human needs, this system is totally irrational.

Millions of Americans, not to mention those in other countries, are underfed, while the government pays farmers not to produce. Why? Because producing abundant, inexpensive food isn't *profitable*.

In the richest of all countries, the crisis in housing in our cities has reached the proportions of a national disaster. Yet there is virtually no low-cost housing construction. Why? Because building low-cost housing is not *profitable*.

Today's technology makes possible substantial improvements in the quality of life for all Americans, yet this technological capacity is not used to make adequate medical care available to working people; it is not used in any effective way to stop pollution; it is not used to protect consumers against shoddy, worthless, or dangerous products. Why? Because none of this is as *profitable* as war spending or defrauding the consumer.

Billions of dollars are spent on instruments of mass destruction to be used in nuclear, chemical, and biological warfare; other billions are put into gadgets to be rocketed into outer space. Yet the government refuses with utmost callousness to make possible a decent life for millions of older citizens who live in poverty on paltry pensions or Social Security benefits. Funds are denied to schools, libraries, and hospitals. Child-care centers are not built. Why? Because under this system the private profit of the few comes first.

WHAT SOCIALISTS WANT

The Socialist Workers Party is campaigning in 1972 for the following program to meet the crisis facing the American people:

Bring All the Troops Home Now! Stop the Bombing of Indochina!

Nixon talks about "winding down the war" to confuse the majority of Americans into thinking that he is heeding their demand for peace. Yet the killing goes on and Nixon escalates the air war. Many politicians talk about "setting a date" for withdrawal—sometime in the future. But what the Vietnamese people want, and what the majority of Americans want, is the withdrawal of all U.S. troops and war matériel right now!

Abolish the draft! No more draftees for Washington's war machine. Support the right of GIs to freely express their views on any issues of concern to them, including racism in the military and the need to end the war in Indochina. Organize a national referendum to give the people the right to vote on whether to continue the war or end it at once. Unconditional amnesty for all those in jail or in exile who have been accused of evading the draft or deserting.

Dismantle all U.S. bases around the world. End all U.S. interference in the internal affairs of other countries.

Support the struggles of the Asian, Latin American, African, and Arab peoples for national independence and social liberation. Support national liberation struggles such as those in Ireland, Palestine, Bangladesh, Québec, and Puerto Rico.

For a Program to Meet the Needs of Working People

To fight the government's assault upon the rights and wages of the working people, the Socialist Workers Party calls for a united mobilization of the entire labor movement. We propose the convocation of a national conference of the labor movement, with delegates democratically elected by rank-and-file workers, to map out a campaign of struggle on all fronts against wage controls, inflation, and unemployment.

The Socialist Workers Party proposes the following program for an effective, united challenge to the government's antilabor policies:

Opposition to all wage controls.

End the war and war spending, the most important cause of inflation.

Cost-of living escalator clauses in all contracts to protect workers against inflation. Include cost-of-living increases in all pensions and social security payments, and in welfare and unemployment benefits.

Organize committees of the unions and consumer groups with the power to regulate prices.

To combat unemployment, shorten the workweek—with no reduction in pay—to whatever extent necessary to spread the available work to all those who need a job. As an immediate step, reduce the workweek to 30 hours.

Launch a crash program of public works to provide jobs for the unemployed.

Guaranteed unemployment compensation at union wages for all those out of work, whether or not they have worked before.

While the corporations rake in superprofits, they turn more and more to the government for aid in their crusade against the standard of living and democratic rights of working people. The right to strike is an unconditional right. Repeal all laws restricting the right to strike, and all laws undermining union independence from the government, such as the Taft-Hartley Act. For an end to "special" antistrike legislation, such as was threatened in the West Coast longshoremen's strike.

For rank-and-file control over all union affairs.

For equal rights in the unions and on the job for Black and Raza workers and for women, and for full union support to their struggles. Preferential hiring for women and for workers of the oppressed nationalities.

For an independent labor party based on the trade unions to defend the rights and standard of living of working people against the parties of the bosses, and to fight for a workers government.

End the Burden on Low-Income Families

Today, one of every 10 U.S. families is living in poverty. Yet, while welfare rolls continue to rise, welfare spending is cut back.

To help alleviate the problems faced by working people and the unemployed, we propose:

Abolish all taxes on incomes under $10,000 a year. Confiscate all profits on war goods. A 100-per cent tax on incomes above $25,000 per year.

Roll back all rents on apartments to a maximum of 10 per cent of family income.

Free quality medical and dental care for all, through socialization of medicine.

For a food and drug administration controlled by workers and consumers, not the food and drug corporations.

For a nationally coordinated program to build safe, efficient, comfortable mass public transit systems. All mass transit to be free.

For the Democratic Right of Black People to Control Their Own Communities

Slumlords and price-gouging merchants are a permanent part of life in the Black communities. Inequality of wages is being perpetuated by wage controls imposed by the Democrats and Republicans in office. Black youth continue to be drafted and killed in disproportionate numbers in the war in Indochina.

Black people should have control over schools, police, housing programs, hospitals, and other institutions in the Black community. Launch a crash program with federal, state, and city funds to build new housing, decent schools, and other projects in the Black communities to overcome years of deprivation and discrimination. The funds should be administered by the Black community.

Support busing in cases where Black people see that it can help obtain better education for their children. All decisions about busing should be made by the Black community.

Appropriate whatever funds are necessary to provide jobs for all Afro-Americans who need them, with preferential hiring and upgrading as needed to equalize opportunities.

It is the right of Afro-Americans to keep arms and organize themselves for self-defense against all attacks.

Black people are hampered in their struggle because they are denied equal political representation and lack political power. To fight effectively for control of the Black community and to help win the struggle for justice and equality, a mass Black political party is needed, a party independent of the Democrats and Republicans. The Gary, Ind., national Black political conference of nearly 8,000 Blacks showed the growing sentiment for Black political action and was an indication of the potential support such a party can have.

A mass Black political party, to be effective, would do much more than participate in elections.

Gearing its demands around actions, it would seek to mobilize all the forces of the Black people in the struggle to win Black community demands.

Chicano Liberation

The massive Chicano Moratorium marches against the war have dramatized Chicano opposition to the slaughter in Indochina. Yet La Raza still suffers disproportionately from the draft and war casualties. Chicanos are denied the use of the Spanish language—in school, on the job, in the courtroom, and in prison. Discrimination in housing, education, and jobs confronts Chicanos at every turn.

Chicano and Mexican workers are continually harassed by U.S. government immigration agents. Attempts to organize agricultural workers are met with violence and other strikebreaking tactics by the growers.

The true history of the Chicano people is not taught, and racist stereotypes continue to appear in textbooks and advertising.

Chicanos have begun to organize themselves independently of the capitalist parties through La Raza Unida parties. The fight for Chicano control of the Chicano communities will be advanced by building these parties into mass parties on a national as well as a local scale.

End the Oppression of Women

Laws restricting abortions deny women the right to choose whether to bear children. The Socialist Workers Party calls for repeal of all anti-abortion laws and removal of all restrictions on contraceptive information and devices. End forced sterilization.

For a massive government-funded program to develop safe and effective birth-control devices. Abortion and contraceptives to be free on demand.

Equal pay for equal work. For ratification of the Equal Rights Amendment, and enforcement of Title VII of the 1964 Civil Rights Act, which prohibits discrimination on the basis of sex. Protective legislation beneficial to women should be extended to cover men as well.

End discrimination against women in education. For open admissions to all institutions of higher learning.

For free, quality 24-hour child-care facilities, available to all children.

Halt the Destruction of the Environment

The rape of the environment by the big corporations continues unchecked by government control. Legislation without teeth allows polluters to continue practices that threaten the entire continent with ruin.

For a 100 per cent tax on every cent in profits made by the polluters. All corporations to be compelled, under threat of confiscation, to install pollution-control equipment and to meet standards set and enforced by committees of workers and consumers.

Support the Demands of America's Youth

Students and young working people face unique problems in this society. Students are told to "stay in school," but even college diplomas no longer guarantee a decent job. What is taught in school is increasingly irrelevant to today's problems and needs.

Cutbacks in funds for education and soaring college tuition costs keep many young people out of school. We call for free education through the university level, with government stipends for those students who need it. For guaranteed jobs when students leave school.

For *student-faculty* control of education. School facilities should be made available to the antiwar movement, the women's liberation movement, the labor movement, the oppressed nationalities, and others fighting for social progress.

Abolish all laws that discriminate against youth. Full constitutional rights for all students. For the right of young people to serve on juries, to register and vote where they go to school, and to run for public office.

End Inhuman Treatment of Prisoners

Prisoners under capitalism are instruments of oppression against the most exploited sections of the population. They will have no place in a socialist society. As immediate steps toward establishing basic civil and human rights, we demand: An end to censorship and restrictions on mail, books, and newspapers. All labor to be paid at union wages. Humane treatment and conditions for all prisoners.

For Democratic Election Laws

The lack of equality under the law is shown by the fact that independent candidates and parties other than the Democrats and Republicans face a labyrinth of discriminatory and onerous election laws that make it difficult, often impossible, for any but the capitalist parties to get on the ballot. These laws have the intent and effect of legislating a permanent electoral monopoly for the capitalist parties.

Full Civil and Human Rights for Gay People

For an end to all laws that discriminate against homosexuals. For legislation and executive orders to prohibit harassment and discrimination against gay people.

Protect and Extend Civil Liberties

The government is resorting more and more to political trials of activists in its attempts to silence opposition to its policies and intimidate those who are fighting for social change. We are faced with increasing government use of police-state practices such as infiltration of agents-provocateurs, wiretaps, harassment of activists by FBI and U.S. Treasury agents, illegal surveillance of citizens, and continued use of the unconstitutional Attorney General's list of so-called "subversive" organizations.

For Government Ownership of Industry

Expropriate the major corporations and banks and operate them under the control of democratically elected workers committees. Plan the economy democratically for the benefit of all instead of for the profit of the few.

For a Socialist America

Bring to power a workers government, with full recognition of the right of self-determination to the oppressed nationalities, to reorganize America on a socialist basis.

Support the Socialist Campaign

Support the demonstrations of the antiwar movement. Support mass actions against the oppression of Blacks, Chicanos, and women.

For an independent labor party! For an independent Black party and an independent Chicano party!

The Socialist Workers Party campaign is the only national campaign in 1972 that presents this perspective of political action independent of capitalist politics.

The candidates of the Socialist Workers Party are dedicated to ending the capitalist system of war and inequality—a system that degrades human life, warps cultural values, and prevents the masses of people from controlling the institutions that affect their lives.

The Socialist Workers Party is fighting to build a society without war, poverty, or unemployment and to put an end to racism, sexism, and the exploitation of the working class. We want to open the way for the unparalleled growth in culture, freedom and development of every individual that will be possible when the vast resources available to us are used to serve human needs instead of serving private profits.

Such a society, a socialist society, is worth fighting to achieve. Join us!

Support the socialist campaign!